AF889355

All in One®

Recommended by Teachers Trusted by Toppers

APPLIED MATHEMATICS

Class 11

EVERYTHING YOU NEED TO SCORE

- Simplified Theory
- Topic & Chapter Exercises
- CBQs; MCQs, A-R, Case Based
- Sample Question Papers

CBSE Exams 2026

Authors
Laxman Prasad
Brijesh Dwevedi

arihant
SUCCESS AND NOTHING LESS

arihant
SUCCESS AND NOTHING LESS

ARIHANT PRAKASHAN
(School Division Series)

卐 ADMINISTRATIVE & PRODUCTION OFFICES
Regd. Office
'Ramchhaya' 4577/15, Agarwal Road, Darya Ganj, New Delhi -110002
Tele: 011- 47630600, 43518550; Fax: 011- 23280316
卐 *Head Office*
Kalindi, TP Nagar, Meerut (UP) - 250002, Tel: 0121-7156203, 7156204

卐 SALES & SUPPORT OFFICES
Agra, Ahmedabad, Bengaluru, Bareilly, Chennai, Delhi, Guwahati, Hyderabad, Jaipur, Jhansi, Kolkata, Lucknow, Nagpur & Pune.

PO No : TXT-XX-XXXXXXX-X-XX

Published By Arihant Publications (India) Ltd.

For further information about the books published by Arihant, log on to www.arihantbooks.com or e-mail at info@arihantbooks.com

Follow us on

卐 PRICE ₹ 500.00

PRODUCTION TEAM

Publishing Managers	Cover Designer	Inner Designer
Mahendra Singh Rawat & Keshav Mohan	Salman Shaikh	Ankit Tyagi
Project Head	**Page Layouting**	**Proof Reader**
Ashwani	Mayank Saini	Rekha Singh, Mukul Kaushik

Index *cum* Study Planner

One Book- Endless Features

to Help you Succeed

In this Chapter

At the start of each chapter, all the chapter topics have been listed , so that students may know what they are going to study.

CHAPTER 03

Logarithms

In this Chapter...

- Logarithm
- Common and Natural Logarithm

Topic Practice 1

1 Express each of the following in the logarithmic form.
(i) $3^6 = 729$ (ii) $(81)^{3/4} = 27$ (iii) $8^{-1} = 0.125$
(iv) $5^3 = 125$ (v) $25^{1/2} = 5$

2 Prove that
(i) $\log_{10} 0.001 = -3$ (ii) $\log_5 125 = 3$
(iii) $\log_a 1 = 0$ (iv) $\log_{10} 100 = 2$
(v) $\log_{10}(0.0001) = -4$

3 Solve for x of each of the following.
(i) $\log_{10} x = -4$ (ii) $\log_{\sqrt{5}}(x-1) = 2$
(iii) $\log_{\sqrt{3}} x = 6$

4 Find the logarithm of each of the following.
(i) 256 to the base 4 (ii) 8 to the base 2
(iii) $\frac{1}{125}$ to the base 5 (iv) 625 to the base 25
(v) $\frac{1}{256}$ to the base 16

5 Solve each of the following.
(i) $\log_{125} 625$ (ii) $\log_{1/8} \frac{1}{256}$ (iii) $\log_{12} 1728$

16 If $x = \log 0.6$, $y = \log 1.25$ and $z = \log 3 - 2\log 2$, then find $5^{(x+y-z)}$.

17 Given that $x = 1 + \log 2 - \log 5$, $y = 2\log 3$ and $z = \log a - \log 5$. If $x + y = 2z$, then find the value of a.

18 If $\log 27 = 1.431$, then evaluate $\log 9$.

19 If $\log_{10} x = m + n$ and $y = 10^{2m-n}$, then evaluate $\log_{10} x^3 y^4$ in terms of m and n.

20 Find the value of x, if
(i) $5^{\log x} + 3^{\log x} = 3^{\log x + 1} - 5^{\log x - 1}$
(ii) $\log(3x+2) + \log(3x-2) = 5\log 2$
(iii) $\log_x 49 - \log_x 7 + \log_x \frac{1}{343} + 2 = 0$
(iv) $\log(x+2) + \log(x-2) = \log 3 + 3\log 4$
(v) $\log_3(3+x) + \log_3(8-x) - \log_3(9x-8) = 2 - \log_3 9$

21 Show that $\frac{\log\sqrt{27} + \log\sqrt{8} - \log\sqrt{125}}{\log 6 - \log 5} = \frac{3}{2}$.

22 If $a^{3-x} \cdot b^{5x} = a^{x+5} \cdot b^{3x}$, then show that $x \log \frac{b}{a} = \log a$.

Logarithm

If a is any positive real number ($a \neq 1$) and m is any rational number and n be any real number such that $a^m = n$, then $m = \log_a n$, where m is called logarithm of n to the base a.

Thus, $a^m = n$ is called the **exponential form** and $m = \log_a n$ is called the **logarithmic form.**

Simplified Theory

It contains the necessary study material well supported by Definitions, Facts, Figures, Flow Charts, etc.

Topical Exercises

To make students understand the chapter in a smooth part-by-part manner, Topical Exercises have been given in each chapter. These Exercises help students to assess the understanding of related concepts at regular interval.

One Book- Endless Features

to Help you Succeed

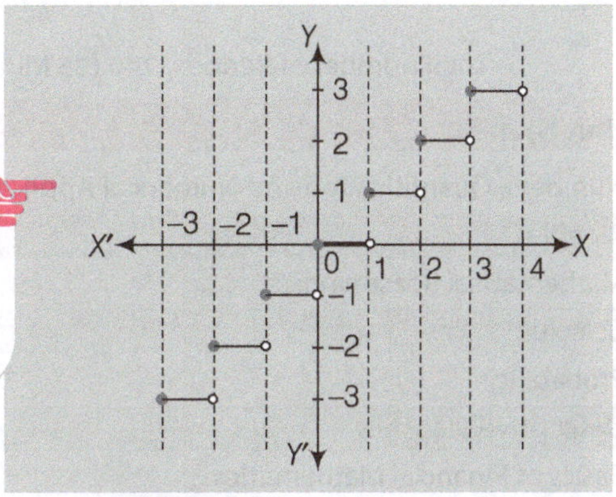

Illustrative Figures

At the start of each chapter, all the chapter topics have been listed , so that students may know what they are going to study.

Exam Pattern Exercise

To make students completely prepared for examination, this Exercise contains Exam Pattern Questions. This exercise covers all types of questions, like; MCQs, Case Based Questions, Assertion-Reason, VSA, SA & LA Type Questions.

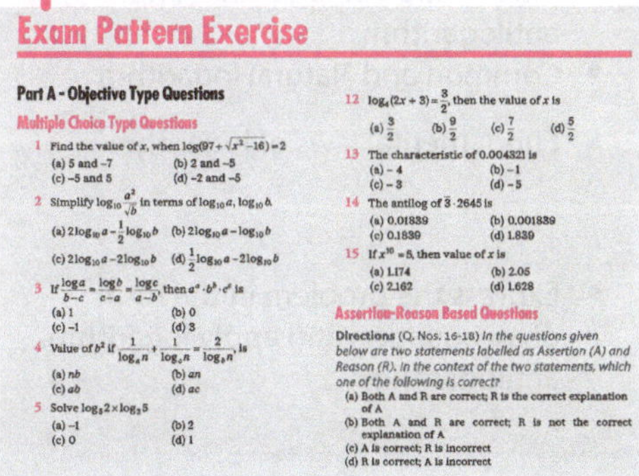

Exam Pattern Exercise

Part A - Objective Type Questions

Multiple Choice Type Questions

1 Find the value of x, when $\log(97+\sqrt{x^2-16})=2$

(a) 5 and –7 (b) 2 and –5
(c) –5 and 5 (d) –2 and –5

2 Simplify $\log_{10}\frac{a^2}{\sqrt{b}}$ in terms of $\log_{10}a$, $\log_{10}b$.

(a) $2\log_{10}a-\frac{1}{2}\log_{10}b$ (b) $2\log_{10}a-\log_{10}b$
(c) $2\log_{10}a-2\log_{10}b$ (d) $\frac{1}{2}\log_{10}a-2\log_{10}b$

3 If $\frac{\log a}{b-c}=\frac{\log b}{c-a}=\frac{\log c}{a-b}$, then $a^a\cdot b^b\cdot c^c$ is

(a) 1 (b) 0
(c) –1 (d) 3

4 Value of b^2 if $\frac{1}{\log_a n}+\frac{1}{\log_c n}=\frac{2}{\log_b n}$, is

(a) nb (b) an
(c) ab (d) ac

5 Solve $\log_3 2\times\log_2 5$

(a) –1 (b) 2
(c) 0 (d) 1

12 $\log_4(2x+3)=\frac{3}{2}$, then the value of x is

(a) $\frac{3}{2}$ (b) $\frac{9}{2}$ (c) $\frac{7}{2}$ (d) $\frac{5}{2}$

13 The characteristic of 0.004321 is

(a) – 4 (b) –1
(c) – 3 (d) – 5

14 The antilog of $\bar{3}\cdot 2645$ is

(a) 0.01839 (b) 0.001839
(c) 0.1839 (d) 1.839

15 If $x^{10}=5$, then value of x is

(a) 1.174 (b) 2.05
(c) 2.162 (d) 1.628

Assertion-Reason Based Questions

Directions (Q. Nos. 16-18) *In the questions given below are two statements labelled as Assertion (A) and Reason (R). In the context of the two statements, which one of the following is correct?*

(a) Both A and R are correct; R is the correct explanation of A
(b) Both A and R are correct; R is not the correct explanation of A
(c) A is correct; R is incorrect
(d) R is correct; A is incorrect

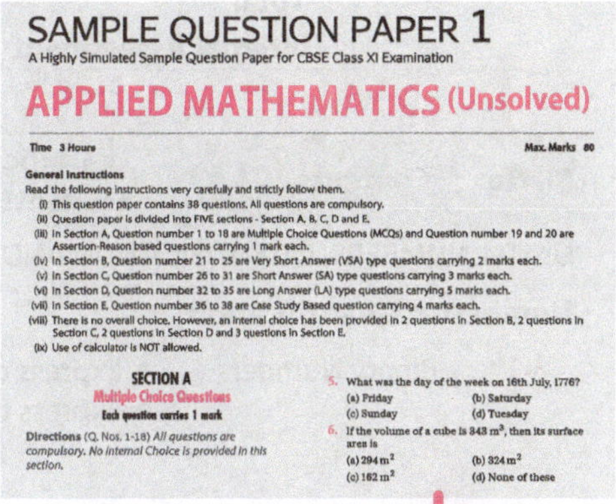

SAMPLE QUESTION PAPER 1

A Highly Simulated Sample Question Paper for CBSE Class XI Examination

APPLIED MATHEMATICS (Unsolved)

Time 3 Hours **Max. Marks 80**

General Instructions

Read the following instructions very carefully and strictly follow them.

(i) This question paper contains 38 questions. All questions are compulsory.
(ii) Question paper is divided into FIVE sections - Section A, B, C, D and E.
(iii) In Section A, Question number 1 to 18 are Multiple Choice Questions (MCQs) and Question number 19 and 20 are Assertion-Reason based questions carrying 1 mark each.
(iv) In Section B, Question number 21 to 25 are Very Short Answer (VSA) type questions carrying 2 marks each.
(v) In Section C, Question number 26 to 31 are Short Answer (SA) type questions carrying 3 marks each.
(vi) In Section D, Question number 32 to 35 are Long Answer (LA) type questions carrying 5 marks each.
(vii) In Section E, Question number 36 to 38 are Case Study Based question carrying 4 marks each.
(viii) There is no overall choice. However, an internal choice has been provided in 2 questions in Section B, 2 questions in Section C, 2 questions in Section D and 3 questions in Section E.
(ix) Use of calculator is NOT allowed.

SECTION A

Multiple Choice Questions

Each question carries 1 mark

Directions (Q. Nos. 1-18) *All questions are compulsory. No internal Choice is provided in this section.*

5. What was the day of the week on 16th July, 1776?

(a) Friday (b) Saturday
(c) Sunday (d) Tuesday

6. If the volume of a cube is 343 m^3, then its surface area is

(a) 294 m^2 (b) 324 m^2
(c) 162 m^2 (d) None of these

Sample Question Papers

To make students practice of examination in real sense, there are 3 Sample Question Papers at the end. All these Sample Questions Papers are exactly prepared on the latest syllabus & pattern of examination.

Latest Course *Structure*

Time: 3 Hours | Total number of Periods: 240 (35 Minutes Each) | Max Marks: 80

Unit	Unit Name	No. of Periods	Marks
I	Numbers, Quantification and Numerical Applications	25	09
II	Algebra	45	15
III	Mathematical Reasoning	15	06
IV	Calculus	35	10
V	Probability	25	08
VI	Descriptive Statistics	35	12
VII	Basics of Financial Mathematics	45	15
VIII	Coordinate Geometry	15	05
	Total	**240**	**80**
	Internal Assessment		**20**

Sl. No.	Contents	Learning Outcomes: Students will be able to	Notes / Explanation
UNIT-1 NUMBERS, QUANTIFICATION AND NUMERICAL APPLICATIONS			
Numbers & Quantification			
1.1	Binary Numbers	• Express decimal numbers in binary system • Express binary numbers in decimal system	• Definition of number system (decimal and binary) • Conversion from decimal to binary system and vice - versa
1.2	Indices, Logarithm and Antilogarithm	• Relate indices and logarithm / antilogarithm • Find logarithm and antilogarithms of given number	• Applications of rules of indices • Introduction of logarithm and antilogarithm • Common and Natural logarithm
1.3	Laws and properties of logarithms	• Enlist the laws and properties of logarithms • Apply laws of logarithm	• Fundamental laws of logarithm
1.4	Simple applications of logarithm and antilogarithm	• Use logarithm in different applications	• Express the problem in the form of an equation and apply logarithm/ antilogarithm

Numerical Applications			
1.5	Clock	• Evaluate the angular value of a minute • Calculate the angle formed between two hands of clock at given time • Calculate the time for which hands of clock meet	• Number of rotations of minute hand / hour hand of a clock in a day • Number of times minute hand and hour hand coincides in a day
1.6	Calendar	• Determine Odd days in a month/ year/ century • Decode the day for the given date	• Definition of odd days • Odd days in a year/ century. • Day corresponding to a given date
1.7	Time, Work and Distance	• Establish the relationship between work and time • Compare the work done by the individual / group *w.r.t.* time • Calculate the time taken/ distance covered / Work done from the given data	• Basic concept of time and work • Problems on time taken / distance covered / work done
1.8	Seating arrangement	• Create suitable seating plan/ draft as per given conditions (Linear/circular) • Locate the position of a person in a seating arrangement	• Linear and circular seating arrangement • Position of a person in a seating arrangement
UNIT-2 ALGEBRA			
Sets			
2.1	Introduction to sets-definition	• Define set as well-defined collection of objects	• Definition of a Set • Examples and Non-examples of Set
2.2	Representation of sets	• Represent a set in Roster form and Set builder form	• Write elements of a set in Set Builder form and Roster Form • Convert a set given in Roster form into Set builder form and vice-versa
2.3	Types of sets and their notations	• Identify different types of sets on the basis of number of elements in the set • Differentiate between equal set and equivalence set	• Types of Sets: Finite Set, Infinite Set, Empty Set, Singleton Set

2.4	Subsets	• Enlist all subsets of a set • Find number of subsets of a given set • Find number of elements of a power set	• Subset of a given set • Familiarity with terms like Superset, Improper subset, Universal set, Power set
2.5	Intervals	• Express subset of real numbers as intervals	• Open interval, closed interval, semi open interval and semi closed interval
2.6	Venn diagrams	• Apply the concept of Venn diagram to understand the relationship between sets • Solve problems using Venn diagram	• Venn diagrams as the pictorial representation of relationship between sets • Practical Problems based on Venn Diagrams
2.7	Operations on sets	• Perform operations on sets to solve practical problems	• Operations on sets include (i) Union of sets (ii) Intersection of sets (iii) Difference of sets (iv) Complement of a set (v) De Morgan' Laws
Relations			
2.8	Ordered Pairs, Cartesian product of two sets	• Explain the significance of specific arrangement of elements in a pair • Write Cartesian product of two sets Find the number of elements in a cartesian product of two sets	• Ordered pair, order of elements in an ordered pair and equality of ordered pairs • Cartesian product of two non-empty sets
2.9	Relations	• Express relation as a subset of Cartesian product • Find domain and range of a relation	• Definition of Relation, examples pertaining to relations in the real number system
Sequences and Series			
2.10	Sequence and Series	• Differentiate between sequence and series	• Sequence: $a_1, a_2, a_3, \dots, a_n$ • Series: $a_1 + a_2 + a_3 + \dots + a_n$
2.11	Arithmetic Progression	• Identify Arithmetic Progression (AP) • Establish the formulae of finding *n*th term and sum of *n* terms • Solve application problems based on AP • Find arithmetic mean (AM) of two positive numbers	• General term of AP: $t_n = a + (n - 1)\,d$ • Sum of n terms of AP : $S_n = n/2\,[2a + (n - 1)d]$ • AM of a and b = $(a + b)/2$

2.12	Geometric Progression	• Identify Geometric Progression (GP) • Derive the *n*th term and sum of n terms of a given GP • Solve problems based on applications of GP • Find geometric mean (GM) of two positive numbers • Solve problems based on relation between AM and GM	• General term of GP: $t_n = ar^{n-1}$ • Sum of n terms of a GP: $S_n = \frac{a(r^n - 1)}{r - 1}$ • Sum of infinite term of GP = $\frac{a}{r-1}$ where $-1 < r < 1$ • Geometric mean of *a* and *b* = ab • For two positive numbers *a* and *b*, AM ≥ GM i.e. $\frac{a+b}{2} \geq \sqrt{ab}$
2.13	Applications of AP and GP	• Apply appropriate formulas of AP and GP to solve application problems	Applications based on • Economy Stimulation • The Virus spread etc.
Permutations and Combinations			
2.14	Factorial	• Define factorial of a number • Calculate factorial of a number	• Definition of factorial: $n! = n(n-1)(n-2)...3.2.1$ Usage of factorial in counting principles
2.15	Fundamental Principle of Counting	• Appreciate how to count without counting	• Fundamental Principle of Addition • Fundamental Principle of Multiplication
2.16	Permutations	• Define permutation • Apply the concept of permutation to solve simple problems	• Permutation as arrangement of objects in a definite order taken some or all at a time • Theorems under different conditions resulting in ${}^nP_r = \frac{n!}{(n-r)!}$ or n^r Or $\frac{n!}{n_1!n_2!...n_k!}$ arrangements
2.17	Combinations	• Define combination • Differentiate between permutation and combination • Apply the formula of combination to solve the related problems	The number of combinations of *n* different objects taken *r* at a time is given by ${}^nC_r = \frac{n!}{r!(n-r)!}$ Some results on combinations: • ${}^nC_0 = 1 = {}^nC_n$ • ${}^nC_a = {}^nC_b \Rightarrow a = b$ or $a + b = n$ • ${}^nC_r = {}^nC_{n-r}$ • ${}^nC_r + {}^nC_{r-1} = {}^{n+1}C_r$

UNIT-3 MATHEMATICAL REASONING			
3.1	Logical reasoning	• Solve logical problems involving odd man out, syllogism, blood relation and coding decoding	• Odd man out • Syllogism • Blood relations • Coding Decoding
UNIT-4 CALCULUS			
4.1	Functions	• Identify dependent and independent variables • Define a function using dependent and independent variable	• Dependent variable and independent variable • Function as a rule or law that defines a relationship between one variable (the independent variable) and another variable (the dependent variable)
4.2	Domain and Range of a function	• Define domain, range and co-domain of a given function	• Domain as a set of all values of independent variable • Co-domain as a set of all values of dependent variable Range of a function as set of all possible resulting values of dependent variable
4.3	Types of functions and their graphical representation	• Define various types of functions • Identify domain, co-domain and range of the function • Representation of function graphically	• Following types of functions with definitions and characteristics and their graphs Constant function, Identity function, Polynomial function, Rational function, Composite function, Logarithm function, Exponential function, Modulus function, Algebraic function

4.4	Concepts of limits and continuity of a function	• Define limit of a function • Solve problems based on the algebra of limits • Define continuity of a function	• Left hand limit, Right hand limit, Limit of a function, Continuity of a function
4.5	Instantaneous rate of change	• Define instantaneous rate of change	• The ratio $\frac{\Delta y}{\Delta x} = \frac{f(x+\Delta x)-(x)\Delta y}{\Delta x}$ as instantaneous rate of change, where Δy is change in y and Δx is change in x at any instant
4.6	Differentiation as a process of finding derivative	• Find the derivative of the functions	• Derivatives of functions (non-trigonometric only)
4.7	Derivatives of algebraic functions using Chain Rule	• Find the derivative of function of a function	• If $y = f(u)$ where $u = g(x)$ then differential coefficient of y w.r.t x is $dy/dx = dy/du \times du/dx$
UNIT-5 PROBABILITY			
5.1	Introduction	• Appreciate the use of probability in daily life situations	• Probability as quantitative measure of uncertainty • Use of probability in determining the insurance premium, weather forecasts etc.
5.2	Random experiment and sample space	• Define random experiment and sample space with suitable examples	• Sample space as set of all possible outcomes
5.3	Event	• Define an event Recognize and differentiate different types of events and find their probabilities	• Types of Event: Impossible and sure event, Independent and dependent event mutually exclusive and exhaustive event
5.4	Conditional Probability	• Define the concept of conditional probability • Apply reasoning skills to solve problems based on conditional probability	• Conditional Probability of event E given that F has occurred is: $P(E/F) = \frac{P \cap F}{P(F)}$ $P(F) \neq 0$

UNIT-6 DESCRIPTIVE STATISTICS			
6.1	Data Interpretation		
	Measure of Dispersion	• Understand meaning of dispersion in a data set • Differentiate between range, quartile deviation mean deviation and standard deviation • Calculate range, quartile deviation, mean deviation and standard deviation for ungrouped and grouped data set • Choose appropriate measure of dispersion to calculate spread of data	• Mean deviation around mean and median • Standard deviation and variance • Examples of different kinds of data helping students to choose and compare different measures of dispersion
6.2	Percentile rank	• Define Percentile rank • Calculate and interpret Percentile rank of scores in a given ungrouped data set	• Emphasis on visualizing, analysing and interpreting percentile rank scores
6.3	Correlation	• Define correlation in values of two data sets • Calculate Spearman's rank correlation • Interpret the coefficient of correlation	• Emphasis on application, analysis and interpreting the results of coefficient of correlation using practical examples
UNIT-7 FINANCIAL MATHEMATICS			
7.1	Interest and Interest Rates	• Define the concept of Interest Rates • Compare the difference between Nominal Interest Rate, Effective Rate and Real Interest Rate • Solve Practical applications of interest rate	• Impact of high interest rates and low interest rates on the business

7.2	Accumulation with simple and compound interest	• Interpret the concept of simple and compound interest • Calculate Simple Interest and Compound Interest	• Meaning and significance of simple and compound interest • Compound interest rates applications on various financial products
7.3	Simple and compound interest rates with equivalency	• Explain the meaning, nature and concept of equivalency • Analyze various examples for understanding annual equivalency rate	• Concept of Equivalency • Annual Equivalency Rate
7.4	Effective rate of interest	• Define with examples the concept of effective rate of interest	• Effective Annual Interest Rate $= (1 + i/n)^n - 1$ where: i = Nominal Interest Rate n = Number of Periods
7.5	Annuities, Calculating value of Regular Annuity	• Explain the concept of Immediate Annuity, Annuity due and Deferred Annuity • Calculate General Annuity	• Definition, Formulae and Examples
7.6	Simple applications of regular annuities (upto 3 period)	• Calculate the future value of regular annuity, annuity due • Apply the concept of Annuity in real life situations	• Examples of regular annuity: Mortgage Payment, Car Loan Payments, Leases, Rent Payment, Insurance payouts etc.
7.7	Tax, calculation of tax, simple applications of tax calculation in Goods and service tax, Income Tax	• Explain fundamentals of taxation • Differentiate between Direct and Indirect tax Define and explain GST • Calculate GST • Explain rules under State • Goods and Services Tax (SGST) Central Goods and Services Tax (CGST) and Union Territory Goods and Services Tax (UTGST)	• Computation of income tax, Add Income from Salary, house property, business or profession, capital gain, other sources, etc. Less deductions PF, PPF, LIC, Housing loan, FD, NSC etc. • Assess the Individuals under Income Tax Act • Formula for GST Different Tax heads under GST

7.8	Bills, tariff rates, fixed charge, surcharge, service charge	• Describe the meaning of bills and its various types • Analyze the meaning and rules determining tariff rates • Explain the concept of fixed charge	• Tariff rates- its basis of determination Concept of fixed charge service charge and their applications in various sectors of Indian economy
7.9	Calculation and interpretation of electricity bill, water supply bill and other supply bills	• To interpret and analyze electricity bills, water bills and other supply bills • Evaluate how to calculate units consumed under electricity bills/water bill	• Components of electricity bill/water supply and other supply bills: (i) overcharging of electricity (ii) Units consumed in water supply bills (iii) units consumed in electricity bills
UNIT-8 COORDINATE GEOMETRY			
8.1	Straight line	• Find the slope and equation of line in various form • Find angle between the two lines • Find the perpendicular from a given point on a line • Find the distance between two parallel lines	• Gradient of a line • Equation of line: Parallel to axes, point-slope form, two-points form, slope intercept form, intercept form • Application of the straight line in demand curve related to economics problems
8.2	Circle	• Define a circle • Find different form of equations of a circle • Solve problems based on applications of circle	• Circle as a locus of a point in a plane • Equation of a circle in standard form, central form, diameter form and general form
8.3	Parabola	• Define parabola and related terms	• Parabola as a locus of a point in a plane. • Equation of a parabola in standard form:

CHAPTER 01

Binary Numbers

In this Chapter...

- Number System
- Number System Conversions

In digital system, all the data are represented by equivalent strings of symbols where each symbol called a **bit** (binary digit), either 0 or 1.

The two main categories of the data used in digital computers are

(i) Numbers

(ii) Alphanumeric characters

Numbers are represented by number system and alphanumeric characters are represented by character encoding in the computer system.

Number System

A set of values used to represent different quantities is known as number system. When we enter data into the computer, it translates them in binary numbers (i.e. 0 and 1) as computer can understand only 0 or 1.

A computer can understand **positional number system** where only a few symbols, called **digits,** represent different values depending on the position, they occupy in the number.

A value of each digit in a number can be determined using

- The digit.
- The position of the digit in the number.
- The base or radix of the number systems (where base or radix is defined as the number of distinct digits available in the number system).

1. Decimal Number System

The number system that we use in our day-to-day life is the decimal number system. It has base 10 as it uses 10 digits from 0 to 9 (i.e. 0, 1, 2, 3, 4, 5, 6, 7, 8 and 9). Any decimal number is a string of any combination of these digits.

A decimal number showing its base would be written as

$$(257)_{10} \quad \text{or} \quad (257)_d$$

where, '10' and the small letter 'd' designate that it is a decimal number.

Digits Weighting in Decimal Number

The value of each digit of a decimal number depends on its relative position in the number. As it is a positional value system, where each decimal digit has its own weight expressed as a power of 10.

In left (before decimal point), this power increases in positive and in right (after decimal point), it increases in negative.

The number $(967514.40032)_{10}$ has been represented in the following figure

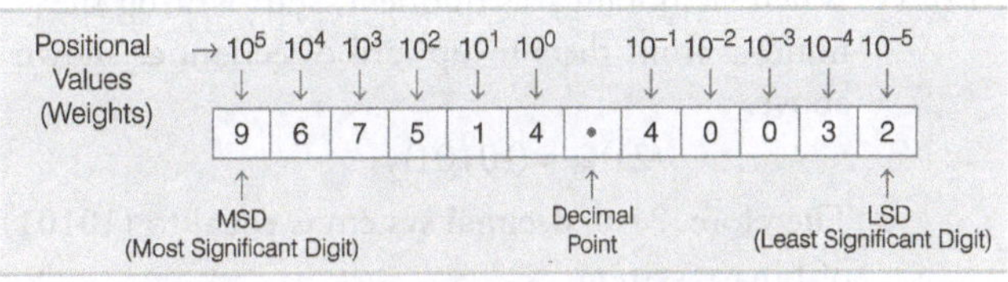

Positional values (weights) in decimal number

2. Binary Number System

Computers use binary number system for counting and arithmetic operations. This number system has base 2 as it uses 2 digits 0 and 1. A string which have any combination of these two digits is called binary number. A binary number showing its base would be written as $(11001)_2$.

Bits Weighting in Binary Number

Binary numbers are written as sequence of bits. Each bit in a binary number carry a special weight.

The number $(101101.10110)_2$ has been represented in the following figure

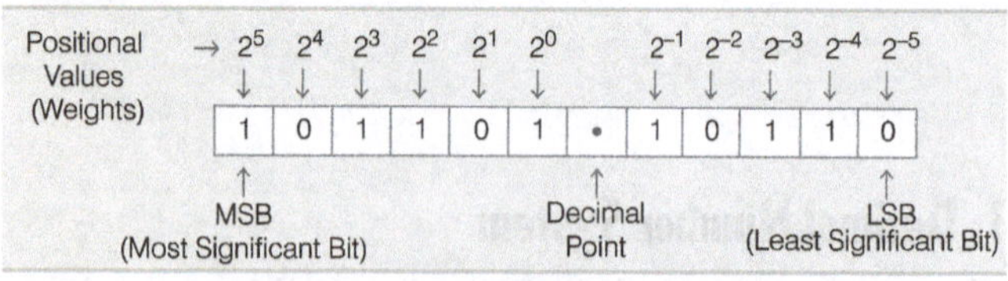

Positional values (weights) in binary number

Decimal to Binary Conversion

1. Conversion of Integral Decimal Numbers

Step I Take the LCM of the given decimal number taking only 2 as divisor (as the base or radix of binary number is 2).

Step II Write the remainder at each step in bracket as shown in the given example.

Step III Repeat this process until we obtain quotient less than the divisor.

e.g. Write $(21)_{10}$ into binary number system.

2	21	
2	10	1
2	5	0
2	2	1
	1	0

Step IV When we obtain 1 as quotient, start writing the number from there to upward direction, as shown above.

$\therefore \quad (21)_{10} = (10101)_2$

Therefore, 21 of decimal system is equal to (10101) of binary system.

EXAMPLE 1. Convert $(175)_{10}$ to the binary form.

Sol.

2	175	
2	87	1
2	43	1
2	21	1
2	10	1
2	5	0
2	2	1
	1	0

$\therefore \quad (175)_{10} = (10101111)_2$

2. Conversion of Fractional Decimal Numbers

Fractional numbers can be converted to binary form by successive multiplication by 2. In each step, the digit before the decimal point is being transfered to the binary record and the process is repeated with the remaining fractional number.

The last step is reached, if the fractional part is zero or it is terminated, when the desired accuracy is attained. The first bit obtained is the most significant and the last is the least significant.

EXAMPLE 2. Convert the following decimal fraction to the binary fraction.

(i) 0.2 (ii) 0.638

Sol. (i) As base of binary is 2. So,

	Integer Part	Fraction
$0.2 \times 2 = 0.4$	0	0.4
$0.4 \times 2 = 0.8$	0	0.8
$0.8 \times 2 = 1.6$	1	0.6
$0.6 \times 2 = 1.2$	1	0.2

(repetition start so stop)

$\therefore \ (0.2)_{10} = (0.0011)_2$

(ii)

	Binary
$0.638 \times 2 = 1.276$	1
$0.276 \times 2 = 0.552$	0
$0.552 \times 2 = 1.104$	1
$0.104 \times 2 = 0.208$	0
$0.208 \times 2 = 0.416$	0
$0.416 \times 2 = 0.832$	0
$0.832 \times 2 = 1.664$	1
$0.664 \times 2 = 1.328$	1
$0.328 \times 2 = 0.656$	0
$0.656 \times 2 = 1.312$	1

Rounding off after 10 bits, the binary result is

$(0.638)_{10} = (0.1010001101)_2$

EXAMPLE 3. Convert $(17.35)_{10}$ to binary form.

Sol. First, convert the integer part by remainder method

2	17	Remainder	
2	8	1	LSB
2	4	0	↑
2	2	0	↑
2	1	0	↑
	0	1	MSB

$$(17)_{10} = (10001)_2$$

Second, convert the fractional part

	Integer Part	Fraction
$0.35 \times 2 = 0.70$	0	0.70
$0.70 \times 2 = 1.40$	1	0.40
$0.4 \times 2 = 0.80$	0	0.80
$0.8 \times 2 = 1.6$	1	0.60
$0.6 \times 2 = 1.2$	1	0.20
$0.2 \times 2 = 0.4$	0 ↓	0.40

$$(0.35)_{10} = (0.010110)_2$$

$$\therefore \quad (17.35)_{10} = (10001.010110)_2$$

Binary to Decimal Conversion

1. Conversion of Integral Binary Numbers

For converting integral binary number to decimal number, we start from the least significant bit, i.e. from right, by multiplying them with the powers of 2 in increasing order, i.e. with 2^0, 2^1, 2^2 and so on.

This process is repeated until the most significant bit, i.e. left bit has been processed. Adding all of them, we get the required decimal number.

EXAMPLE 4. Convert $(1101)_2$ to decimal form.

Sol.

Weight →	2^3	2^2	2^1	2^0
	↓	↓	↓	↓
	1	1	0	1
Position →	3	2	1	0

Now, multiply each binary digit with its respective weight and then add the products.

$$\therefore (1101)_2 = (1 \times 2^3) + (1 \times 2^2) + (0 \times 2^1) + (1 \times 2^0)$$

$$= 8 + 4 + 0 + 1$$

$$= (13)_{10}$$

2. Conversion of Fractional Binary Numbers

For converting fractional binary number to decimal number, we start from left by multiplying them with the powers of 2 in decreasing order, i.e. 2^{-1}, 2^{-2}, 2^{-3} and so on.

After multiplying, add all the terms to get the decimal number.

EXAMPLE 5. Convert $(0.1101)_2$ to decimal form.

Sol.

Weight →			2^{-1}	2^{-2}	2^{-3}	2^{-4}
			↓	↓	↓	↓
	0	•	1	1	0	1
		↑ Decimal Point	−1	−2	−3	−4 ← Position

$$\therefore \quad (01101)_2 = (1 \times 2^{-1}) + (1 \times 2^{-2}) + (0 \times 2^{-3}) + (1 \times 2^{-4})$$

$$= \frac{1}{2} + \frac{1}{4} + 0 + \frac{1}{16}$$

$$= \frac{8+4+1}{16} = \frac{13}{16}$$

$$(0.1101)_2 = (0.8125)_{10}$$

EXAMPLE 6. Convert $(1011.10001)_2$ to decimal form.

Sol. First, we take the integer part

Integer part = 1011

$$= 1 \times 2^3 + 0 \times 2^2 + 1 \times 2^1 + 1 \times 2^0$$

$$= 8 + 0 + 2 + 1 = 11$$

Now, take the fraction part

Fraction part = 010001

$$= 1 \times 2^{-1} + 0 \times 2^{-2} + 0 \times 2^{-3} + 0 \times 2^{-4} + 1 \times 2^{-5}$$

$$= \frac{1}{2} + 0 + 0 + 0 + \frac{1}{32}$$

$$= \frac{16+1}{32} = \frac{17}{32}$$

$$= 0.53125$$

$$\therefore (1011.10001)_2 = (11.53125)_{10}$$

Exam Pattern Exercise

Part A - Objective Type Questions

Multiple Choice Questions

1 The decimal number equivalent to $(0.011)_2$

(a) $(0.215)_{10}$ (b) $(0.0215)_{10}$

(c) $(0.375)_{10}$ (d) $(0.0375)_{10}$

2 $(101)_{10}$ is equivalent to

(a) $(1100001)_2$ (b) $(1100101)_2$

(c) $(1001100)_2$ (d) $(100000)_2$

3 Decimal equivalent of $(11.11)_2$

(a) $(4.15)_{10}$ (b) $(3.45)_{10}$

(c) $(4.265)_{10}$ (d) $(3.75)_{10}$

Assertion-Reason Based Questions

4 **Assertion (A)** If $(6503)_{10} = 6\times10^3 + 5\times10^{k_1} + 3\times10^{k_2}$, then $(k_1 + k_2)$ is 2.

Reason (R) Decimal number system have base 8.

(a) Both A and R are correct; R is the correct explanation of A

(b) Both A and R are correct; R is not the correct explanation of A

(c) A is correct; R is incorrect

(d) R is correct; A is incorrect

Part B - Descriptive Questions

5 Convert binary to decimal.

(i) $(1011)_2$ (ii) $(1001)_2$

(iii) $(11101011)_2$ (iv) $(10010)_2$

(v) $(11101.001)_2$ (vi) $(111000.0101)_2$

(vii) $(0.1101)_2$

6 Convert the following decimal to binary numbers.

(i) $(182)_{10}$ (ii) $(251)_{10}$

(iii) $(259)_{10}$ (iv) $(387)_{10}$

(v) $(0.3125)_{10}$ (vi) $(13.0625)_{10}$

(vii) $(127.25)_{10}$ (viii) $(57.375)_{10}$

(ix) $(18.5625)_{10}$

Case Study Based Questions

7 To convert value of a binary number to its decimal equivalent, we multiply every digit by its place value and then add all the values of digits, so calculated.

(i) 11.011 is equivalent to

(a) $1\times2^1 + 1\times2^0 + 1\times2^{-2} + 1\times2^{-3}$

(b) $1\times2^1 + 1\times2^0 + 1\times2^{-1} + 1\times2^{-2}$

(c) $1\times2^2 + 1\times2^1 + 1\times2^{-1} + 1\times2^{-2}$

(d) None of the above

(ii) $(110010)_2$ is equal to

(a) 40

(b) 50

(c) 30

(d) 45

(iii) $(1100.1101)_2$ is

(a) 12.8125

(b) 0.9230

(c) 0.7014

(d) 0.652

(iv) $(1011011)_2$ is

(a) 75 (b) 81

(c) 87 (d) 91

Hints & Solutions

1. (c) *2.* (b) *3.* (d) *4.* (c)

5. (i) $(11)_{10}$ (ii) $(9)_{10}$ (iii) $(235)_{10}$ (iv) $(18)_{10}$ (v) $(29.125)_{10}$ (vi) $(56.3125)_{10}$ (vii) $(0.8125)_{10}$

6. (i) $(10110110)_2$ (ii) $(11111011)_2$ (iii) $(100000011)_2$ (iv) $(110000011)_2$ (v) $(0.0101)_2$ (vi) $(1101.001)_2$ (vii) $(1111111.01)_2$ (viii) $(111001.011)_2$ (ix) $(10010.1001)_2$

7. **Hint**

(i) (a) $(11.011)_2 = 1\times2^1 + 1\times2^0 + 0\times2^{-1} + 1\times2^{-2} + 1\times2^{-3}$

(ii) (b) $(110010)_2 = 1\times2^5 + 1\times2^4 + 1\times2^1$

(iii) (a) $1\times2^3 + 1\times2^2 + 1\times2^{-1} + 1\times2^{-2} + 1\times2^{-4}$

(iv) (d) $1\times2^6 + 1\times2^4 + 1\times2^3 + 1\times2^1 + 1\times2^0$

CHAPTER 02

Indices/Exponents

In this Chapter...

- Laws of Integral Exponents
- Laws of Rational Exponents

If a is any real number and n is any natural number, then $a \times a \times a \times a \times \ldots$ upto n times can be expressed as a^n. Here, a is called the **base**, n is called the **exponent** or **index** and a^n is called the **exponential form** of a.

e.g. $9765625 = 5 \times 5 \times 5 \times 5 \times \ldots$ upto 10 times $= 5^{10}$.

Handling Positive, Fractional, Negative and Zero Indices

1. **Indices with Positive Integer** If a is any non-zero real numbers and n is a positive integer, then $a^n = a \times a \times a \times \ldots\ldots$ up to n times

   e.g. $2^3 = 2 \times 2 \times 2 = 8$ etc.

2. **Indices with Fractional/Rational Number** If a is any non-zero real number and m, n are fractional/rational numbers. Then,

   $$a^{m/n} = (a^m)^{1/n} = \sqrt[n]{a^m}$$

   e.g. $(2)^{5/3} = [(2)^5]^{1/3} = (32)^{1/3}$

   $= \sqrt[3]{32} = \sqrt[3]{(4)^2 \times 2} = 2\sqrt[3]{4} = 2(4)^{1/3}$

   and $(-7)^{2/5} = [(-7)^2]^{1/5} = (49)^{1/5} = \sqrt[5]{49}$ etc.

   Note The symbol '$\sqrt{\ }$' is known as the radical sign.

3. **Indices with Negative Integer** If a is any non-zero real number and n is any positive integer, then

   $$a^{-n} = \frac{1}{a^n}$$

   e.g. $4^{-3} = \frac{1}{4^3} = \frac{1}{4 \times 4 \times 4} = \frac{1}{64}$

4. **Indices with Zero** For any non-zero number raised to the power zero, is always equal to 1

   i.e. $a^0 = 1$

   e.g. $(-289)^0 = 1$

   and $(7^5)^0 = 1$ etc.

Laws of Integral Exponents

1. Product Law

If a is any real number and m, n are integers, then $a^m \times a^n = a^{m+n}$

EXAMPLE 1. Evaluate

(i) $3^4 \times 3^5$ (ii) $\left(\frac{1}{3}\right)^5 \times \left(\frac{1}{3}\right)^2$

Sol. (i) We have, $3^4 \times 3^5 = 3^{4+5}$ $[\because a^m \times a^n = a^{m+n}]$

$= 3^9$

$= 19683$

(ii) We have, $\left(\frac{1}{3}\right)^5 \times \left(\frac{1}{3}\right)^2 = \left(\frac{1}{3}\right)^{5+2}$ $[\because a^m \times a^n = a^{m+n}]$

$= \left(\frac{1}{3}\right)^7 = \frac{1}{2187}$

2. Division Law

If a is any non-zero real number and m, n are integers, then $\frac{a^m}{a^n} = a^{m-n}$ or $a^m \div a^n = a^{m-n}$, whether $m > n$ or $m = n$ or $m < n$.

EXAMPLE 2. Evaluate

(i) $3^7 \div 3^5$ (ii) $\left(\frac{1}{3}\right)^5 \div \left(\frac{1}{3}\right)^2$

Sol. (i) We have, $3^7 \div 3^5 = 3^{7-5} = 3^2 = 9$ $\left[\because \frac{a^m}{a^n} = a^{m-n}\right]$

(ii) We have, $\left(\frac{1}{3}\right)^5 \div \left(\frac{1}{3}\right)^2 = \left(\frac{1}{3}\right)^{5-2} = \left(\frac{1}{3}\right)^3 = \frac{1}{27}$

$\left[\because \frac{a^m}{a^n} = a^{m-n}\right]$

3. Power Law

If a and b are real numbers and m is a positive integers, then

(i) $(ab)^m = a^m \cdot b^m$ (ii) $\left(\frac{a}{b}\right)^m = \frac{a^m}{b^m}$

Note (i) $(-a)^m = a^m$, if m is even number.

(ii) $(-a)^m = -a^m$, if m is odd number.

EXAMPLE 3. Solve (i) 6^4 (ii) $(2/3)^4$

Sol. (i) We have, $6^4 = (2 \times 3)^4 = 2^4 \times 3^4$ $[\because (ab)^m = a^m \cdot b^m]$

$= 16 \times 81$

$= 1296$

(ii) We have, $\left(\frac{2}{3}\right)^4 = \frac{2^4}{3^4} = \frac{16}{81}$ $\left[\because \left(\frac{a}{b}\right)^m = \frac{a^m}{b^m}\right]$

4. Power-to-Power Law

If a is any real number and m, n are positive integers, then $(a^m)^n = a^{mn}$.

EXAMPLE 4. Evaluate (i) $(4^2)^3$ (ii) $\left\{\left(\frac{1}{2}\right)^4\right\}^3$

Sol. (i) We have, $(4^2)^3 = 4^{2\times 3} = 4^6$ $[\because (a^m)^n = a^{mn}]$

(ii) We have, $\left\{\left(\frac{1}{2}\right)^4\right\}^3 = \left(\frac{1}{2}\right)^{4\times 3} = \left(\frac{1}{2}\right)^{12}$ $[\because (a^m)^n = a^{mn}]$

$= \frac{1}{4096}$

Laws of Rational Exponents

1. Product Law

If a is any non-zero real number and m, n are rational numbers, then $a^m \times a^n = a^{m+n}$.

EXAMPLE 5. Evaluate

(i) $a^{-7/2} \times a^{1/2} \times a^{7/2}$ (ii) $5^{2/3} \times 5^{4/3}$

Sol. (i) We have, $a^{-\frac{7}{2}} \times a^{\frac{1}{2}} \times a^{\frac{7}{2}}$

$= a^{-\frac{7}{2}+\frac{1}{2}+\frac{7}{2}}$ $[\because a^m \times a^n = a^{m+n}]$

$= a^{\frac{1}{2}} = \sqrt{a}$

(ii) We have, $5^{2/3} \times 5^{4/3} = 5^{2/3+4/3}$ $[\because a^m \times a^n = a^{m+n}]$

$= 5^{\frac{2+4}{3}} = 5^{\frac{6}{3}} = 5^2 = 25$

2. Division Law

If a is any non-zero real number and m, n are rational numbers, then $\frac{a^m}{a^n} = a^{m-n}$ or $a^m \div a^n = a^{m-n}$.

Note (i) Why $a^0 = 1$?

Reason We know that $\frac{a^m}{a^n} = a^{m-n}$.

If $m = n$, then $\frac{a^m}{a^m} = a^{m-m} \Rightarrow 1 = a^0$

(ii) $\frac{1}{a^n} = \frac{a^0}{a^n} = a^{0-n} = a^{-n}$. Thus, $a^{-n} = \frac{1}{a^n}$

or $\frac{1}{a^{-n}} = a^n$, for any rational number n.

EXAMPLE 6. Solve

(i) $3^{7/2} \div 3^{5/2}$ (ii) $\left(\frac{2}{3}\right)^{7/2} \div \left(\frac{2}{3}\right)^{3/2}$

Sol. (i) We have, $3^{7/2} \div 3^{5/2} = 3^{7/2-5/2} = 3^{2/2} = 3$

$\left[\because \frac{a^m}{a^n} = a^{m-n}\right]$

(ii) We have, $\left(\frac{2}{3}\right)^{7/2} \div \left(\frac{2}{3}\right)^{3/2} = \left(\frac{2}{3}\right)^{7/2-3/2}$

$\left[\because \frac{a^m}{a^n} = a^{m-n}\right]$

$= \left(\frac{2}{3}\right)^{\frac{7-3}{2}} = \left(\frac{2}{3}\right)^{4/2} = \left(\frac{2}{3}\right)^2 = \frac{4}{9}$

3. Power Law

If a and b are non-zero real numbers and m is a rational number, then

(i) $(ab)^m = a^m \cdot b^m$ (ii) $\left(\frac{a}{b}\right)^m = \frac{a^m}{b^m}$

Note (i) $(-a)^m = a^m$, if m is even number.
(ii) $(-a)^m = -a^m$, if m is odd number.

EXAMPLE 7. Evaluate (i) $(4/9)^{1/2}$ (ii) $(3136)^{1/2}$

Sol. (i) We have, $\left(\frac{4}{9}\right)^{\frac{1}{2}} = \frac{(4)^{\frac{1}{2}}}{(9)^{\frac{1}{2}}}$ $\left[\because \left(\frac{a}{b}\right)^m = \frac{a^m}{b^m}\right]$

$= \frac{2}{3}$

(ii) We have, $(3136)^{\frac{1}{2}} = (49 \times 64)^{\frac{1}{2}}$

$= (49)^{\frac{1}{2}} \times (64)^{\frac{1}{2}}$ $[\because (ab)^m = a^m \cdot b^m]$

$= \sqrt{49} \times \sqrt{64}$

$= 7 \times 8 = 56$

4. Power-to-Power Law

If a is any non-zero real number and m, n are rational numbers, then $(a^m)^n = a^{mn}$.

Note $a^{m/n} = (a^m)^{1/n} = (a^{1/n})^m$ or $\sqrt[n]{a^m} = (\sqrt[n]{a})^m$, where $n > 0$.

EXAMPLE 8. Evaluate

(i) $(4^{2/3})^{3/2}$ (ii) $\left[\left(\frac{2}{3}\right)^{5/2}\right]^{6/5}$

Sol. (i) We have, $\left(4^{\frac{2}{3}}\right)^{\frac{3}{2}} = 4^{\frac{2}{3} \times \frac{3}{2}} = 4$ $[\because (a^m)^n = a^{mn}]$

(ii) We have, $\left[\left(\frac{2}{3}\right)^{5/2}\right]^{6/5} = \left(\frac{2}{3}\right)^{\frac{5}{2} \times \frac{6}{5}} = \left(\frac{2}{3}\right)^3$

$[\because (a^m)^n = a^{mn}]$

$= \frac{8}{27}$

EXAMPLE 9. Evaluate

(i) $(4)^{3/2}$ (ii) $(27)^{4/3}$

(iii) $\frac{1}{(27)^{-2/3}}$ (iv) $\left[\left((1296)^{-\frac{1}{2}}\right)^{-\frac{1}{4}}\right]^2$

Sol. (i) We have, $4^{3/2} = (4^{1/2})^3$ $[\because (a^{m/n}) = (a^{1/n})^m]$

$= (2)^3 = 8$

(ii) We have, $(27)^{4/3} = (27^{1/3})^4$ $[\because a^{m/n} = (a^{1/n})^m]$

$= [(3^3)^{1/3}]^4 = (3^{3 \times (1/3)})^4$ $[\because (a^m)^n = a^{mn}]$

$= 3^4 = 81$

(iii) We have, $\frac{1}{(27)^{-2/3}} = (27)^{2/3}$ $\left[\because \frac{1}{a^{-n}} = a^n\right]$

$= (3 \times 3 \times 3)^{2/3} = (3^3)^{2/3}$

$= 3^{3 \times (2/3)} = 3^2$

$= 3 \times 3 = 9$ $[\because (a^m)^n = a^{m \times n}]$

(iv) We have, $\left[\left((1296)^{-\frac{1}{2}}\right)^{-\frac{1}{4}}\right]^2 = (1296)^{\frac{1}{8} \times 2}$

$= (1296)^{\frac{1}{4}} = (6^4)^{\frac{1}{4}}$

$= (6)^{4 \times \frac{1}{4}}$ $[\because (a^m)^n = a^{m \times n}]$

$= 6^1 = 6$

EXAMPLE 10. Find the value of $3^3 \times (243)^{-2/3} \times 9^{1/3}$.

Sol. We have, $3^3 \times (243)^{-2/3} \times 9^{1/3}$

$= 3^3 \times (3 \times 3 \times 3 \times 3 \times 3)^{-2/3} \times (3 \times 3)^{1/3}$

$= 3^3 \times (3^5)^{-2/3} \times (3^2)^{1/3}$

$= 3^3 \times 3^{5 \times (-2/3)} \times 3^{2 \times 1/3}$ $[\because (a^m)^n = a^{m \times n}]$

$= 3^3 \times 3^{-10/3} \times 3^{2/3}$

$= 3^{3 - \frac{10}{3} + \frac{2}{3}}$ $[\because a^l \times a^m \times a^n = a^{l+m+n}]$

$= 3^{\frac{9-10+2}{3}} = 3^{\frac{11-10}{3}} = 3^{1/3}$

EXAMPLE 11. If $x^3 = \sqrt[3]{8} + \sqrt[3]{27} + \sqrt[3]{64} + \sqrt[3]{125} + \sqrt[3]{216} + \sqrt[3]{343}$, then find the value of x^2.

Sol. We have, $x^3 = \sqrt[3]{8} + \sqrt[3]{27} + \sqrt[3]{64} + \sqrt[3]{125} + \sqrt[3]{216} + \sqrt[3]{343}$

$\Rightarrow x^3 = (2^3)^{\frac{1}{3}} + (3^3)^{\frac{1}{3}} + (4^3)^{\frac{1}{3}} + (5^3)^{\frac{1}{3}} + (6^3)^{\frac{1}{3}} + (7^3)^{\frac{1}{3}}$

$\Rightarrow x^3 = (2)^{3 \times \frac{1}{3}} + (3)^{3 \times \frac{1}{3}} + (4)^{3 \times \frac{1}{3}} + (5)^{3 \times \frac{1}{3}} + (6)^{3 \times \frac{1}{3}} + (7)^{3 \times \frac{1}{3}}$

$[\because (a^m)^n = a^{m \times n}]$

$\Rightarrow x^3 = 2 + 3 + 4 + 5 + 6 + 7$

$\Rightarrow x^3 = 27 \Rightarrow x = 3$

Hence, $x^2 = 3^2 = 9$

5. Reciprocal Law

If a and b are non-zero real numbers and n is any rational number, then $\left(\frac{a}{b}\right)^n = \left(\frac{b}{a}\right)^{-n}$.

EXAMPLE 12. Find the value of x, when $\sqrt{\frac{2}{3}} = \left(\frac{3}{2}\right)^{1-2x}$.

Sol. We have, $\sqrt{\frac{2}{3}} = \left(\frac{3}{2}\right)^{1-2x}$

We know that $\frac{a}{b} = \left(\frac{b}{a}\right)^{-1}$ [reciprocal law]

$$\therefore \quad \sqrt{\frac{2}{3}} = \left[\left(\frac{2}{3}\right)^{-1}\right]^{1-2x}$$

$$\Rightarrow \quad \left(\frac{2}{3}\right)^{1/2} = \left(\frac{2}{3}\right)^{-1(1-2x)} \quad [\because (a^m)^n = a^{m \times n}]$$

$$\Rightarrow \quad \left(\frac{2}{3}\right)^{1/2} = \left(\frac{2}{3}\right)^{2x-1}$$

On comparing the exponents of 2/3 from both sides, we get

$$2x - 1 = \frac{1}{2}$$

$$\Rightarrow \quad 2x = 1 + \frac{1}{2} = \frac{3}{2} \Rightarrow x = \frac{3}{4}$$

EXAMPLE 13. Evaluate $\left(\frac{81}{16}\right)^{-\frac{3}{4}} \times \left[\left(\frac{25}{9}\right)^{-\frac{3}{2}} \div \left(\frac{5}{2}\right)^{-3}\right]$

Sol. We have, $\left(\frac{81}{16}\right)^{-\frac{3}{4}} \times \left[\left(\frac{25}{9}\right)^{-\frac{3}{2}} \div \left(\frac{5}{2}\right)^{-3}\right]$

$$= \left(\left(\frac{3}{2}\right)^4\right)^{-\frac{3}{4}} \times \left[\left(\left(\frac{5}{3}\right)^2\right)^{-\frac{3}{2}} \div \left(\frac{5}{2}\right)^{-3}\right]$$

$$= \left(\frac{3}{2}\right)^{4 \times \left(-\frac{3}{4}\right)} \times \left[\left(\frac{5}{3}\right)^{2 \times \left(-\frac{3}{2}\right)} \div \left(\frac{5}{2}\right)^{-3}\right] \quad [\because (a^m)^n = a^{mn}]$$

$$= \left(\frac{3}{2}\right)^{-3} \times \left[\left(\frac{5}{3}\right)^{-3} \div \left(\frac{5}{2}\right)^{-3}\right]$$

$$= \left(\frac{2}{3}\right)^3 \times \left[\left(\frac{3}{5}\right)^3 \div \left(\frac{2}{5}\right)^3\right] \quad \left[\because \left(\frac{a}{b}\right)^{-m} = \left(\frac{b}{a}\right)^m\right]$$

$$= \frac{2^3}{3^3} \times \left[\frac{3^3}{5^3} \times \frac{5^3}{2^3}\right] = 1$$

Miscellaneous Examples

EXAMPLE 14. If $\frac{16^n \times 4^2 \times 4^n - 64^n}{4^{3m} \times 15} = \frac{1}{64}$, then show that $m - n = 1$.

Sol. We have, $\frac{16^n \times 4^2 \times 4^n - 64^n}{4^{3m} \times 15} = \frac{1}{64}$

$$\Rightarrow \quad \frac{(4^2)^n \times 4^2 \times 4^n - (4^3)^n}{4^{3m} \times 15} = \frac{1}{64}$$

$$\Rightarrow \quad \frac{4^{2n} \times 4^2 \times 4^n - 4^{3n}}{4^{3m} \times 15} = \frac{1}{64} \quad [\because (a^m)^n = a^{mn}]$$

$$\Rightarrow \quad \frac{4^{2n+2+n} - 4^{3n}}{4^{3m} \times 15} = \frac{1}{4^3}$$

$$\Rightarrow \quad \frac{4^{3n+2} - 4^{3n}}{4^{3m} \times 15} = \frac{1}{4^3}$$

$$\Rightarrow \quad \frac{4^{3n} \times 4^2 - 4^{3n}}{4^{3m} \times 15} = \frac{1}{4^3}$$

$$[\because a^m \times a^n = a^{m+n}]$$

$$\Rightarrow \quad \frac{4^{3n}(4^2 - 1)}{4^{3m} \times 15} = \frac{1}{4^3}$$

$$\Rightarrow \quad \frac{4^{3n} \times 15}{4^{3m} \times 15} = \frac{1}{4^3}$$

$$\Rightarrow \quad 4^{3n-3m} = 4^{-3}$$

$$\left[\because \frac{a^m}{a^n} = a^{m-n}, a^{-m} = \frac{1}{a^m}\right]$$

On comparing exponents, we get

$$3n - 3m = -3$$

$$\Rightarrow \quad n - m = -1$$

Hence, $m - n = 1$

EXAMPLE 15. Prove that $\frac{1}{1 + x^{m-n} + x^{l-n}} + \frac{1}{1 + x^{n-l} + x^{m-l}} + \frac{1}{1 + x^{l-m} + x^{n-m}} = 1.$

Sol. Consider, LHS $= \frac{1}{1 + x^{m-n} + x^{l-n}} + \frac{1}{1 + x^{n-l} + x^{m-l}} + \frac{1}{1 + x^{l-m} + x^{n-m}}$

$$= \frac{1}{1 + \frac{x^m}{x^n} + \frac{x^l}{x^n}} + \frac{1}{1 + \frac{x^n}{x^l} + \frac{x^m}{x^l}} + \frac{1}{1 + \frac{x^l}{x^m} + \frac{x^n}{x^m}}$$

$$\left[\because a^{m-n} = \frac{a^m}{a^n}\right]$$

$$= \frac{1}{\dfrac{x^n + x^m + x^l}{x^n}} + \frac{1}{\dfrac{x^l + x^n + x^m}{x^l}} + \frac{1}{\dfrac{x^m + x^l + x^n}{x^m}}$$

$$= \frac{x^n}{x^l + x^m + x^n} + \frac{x^l}{x^l + x^m + x^n} + \frac{x^m}{x^l + x^m + x^n}$$

$$= \frac{x^l + x^m + x^n}{x^l + x^m + x^n} = 1 = \text{RHS}$$

Hence proved.

EXAMPLE 16. Simplify $\dfrac{5\cdot(25)^{m+1} - 25\cdot(5)^{2m}}{5\cdot(5)^{2m+3} - (25)^{m+1}}$.

Sol. We have, $\dfrac{5\cdot(25)^{m+1} - 25\cdot(5)^{2m}}{5\cdot(5)^{2m+3} - (25)^{m+1}} = \dfrac{5\times(5^2)^{m+1} - 5^2\times 5^{2m}}{5\times 5^{2m+3} - (5^2)^{m+1}}$

$$= \frac{5\times 5^{2(m+1)} - 5^2\times 5^{2m}}{5\times 5^{2m+3} - 5^{2(m+1)}} \qquad [\because (a^m)^n = a^{m\times n}]$$

$$= \frac{5^1\times 5^{2m+2} - 5^2\times 5^{2m}}{5^1\times 5^{2m+3} - 5^{2m+2}}$$

$$= \frac{5^{2m+2+1} - 5^{2+2m}}{5^{2m+3+1} - 5^{2m+2}} \qquad [\because a^m\cdot a^n = a^{m+n}]$$

$$= \frac{5^{2m+3} - 5^{2m+2}}{5^{2m+4} - 5^{2m+2}} = \frac{5^{2m+2}(5-1)}{5^{2m+2}(5^2-1)}$$

[taking 5^{2m+2} common from both numerator and denominator]

$$= \frac{4}{(25-1)} = \frac{4}{24} = \frac{1}{6}$$

EXAMPLE 17. Simplify $\left(\dfrac{x^m}{x^n}\right)^{m+n}\left(\dfrac{x^n}{x^l}\right)^{n+l}\left(\dfrac{x^l}{x^m}\right)^{l+m}$.

Sol. We have, $\left(\dfrac{x^m}{x^n}\right)^{m+n}\left(\dfrac{x^n}{x^l}\right)^{n+l}\left(\dfrac{x^l}{x^m}\right)^{l+m}$

$$= (x^{m-n})^{m+n}\cdot(x^{n-l})^{n+l}\cdot(x^{l-m})^{l+m}$$

$$= x^{m^2-n^2}\cdot x^{n^2-l^2}\cdot x^{l^2-m^2}$$

$$[\because (a-b)(a+b) = a^2 - b^2]$$

$$= x^{m^2-n^2+n^2-l^2+l^2-m^2}$$

$$[\because x^m\cdot x^n = x^{m+n}]$$

$$= x^0$$

$$= 1$$

Exam Pattern Exercise

Part A - Objective Type Questions

Multiple Choice Type Questions

1 Value of $\sqrt[5]{\sqrt[3]{9^2}}$ is

(a) $(9)^{1/5}$ (b) $3^{6/5}$ (c) $3^{4/15}$ (d) $9^{4/5}$

2 $[\{(-1)\times(-1)\}^2]^3-(1)^{(-2)}$

(a) 1 (b) 0 (c) 2 (d) 3

3 $\{(2^0)^3\}^{-1/5}$

(a) 32 (b) $\frac{1}{32}$ (c) 1 (d) $2^{-3/5}$

4 Which one is the value of x, if $\sqrt{\frac{p}{q}}=\left(\frac{q}{p}\right)^{1-3x}$.

(a) $-\frac{3}{4}$ (b) $-\frac{4}{3}$ (c) $\frac{4}{3}$ (d) $\frac{1}{2}$

5 Value of x, $(13)^{\sqrt{x}}=4^4-3^4-6$

(a) 4 (b) 3 (c) 2 (d) 2

6 $(1296)^{0.006}\times(1296)^{0.161}$ is equal to

(a) $6^{\frac{1}{3}}$ (b) $6^{\frac{2}{3}}$ (c) 6 (d) 6^2

7 The product of $\sqrt[3]{3}$, $\sqrt[4]{3}$ and $\sqrt[12]{243}$ is equal to

(a) 3 (b) 9 (c) $\sqrt{3}$ (d) $(3)^{\frac{3}{2}}$

8 Which of the following option results in a?

(a) $a^{\frac{12}{7}}-a^{\frac{5}{7}}$ (b) $\sqrt[12]{(a^4)^{\frac{1}{3}}}$

(c) $(\sqrt{a^3})^{\frac{2}{3}}$ (d) $a^{\frac{12}{7}}\times a^{\frac{7}{12}}$

9 If $4^{x-3}\times 3^{2x-8}=144$, then the value of x is

(a) 4 (b) 5 (c) 3 (d) 6

10 For what value of x the equation $3^{2x}=\frac{1}{243}$ is true?

(a) $-\frac{5}{2}$ (b) $\frac{5}{2}$ (c) $-\frac{3}{2}$ (d) $\frac{7}{2}$

Assertion-Reason Based Questions

Directions (Q. Nos. 11-13) *In the questions given below are two statements labelled as Assertion (A) and Reason (R). In the context of the two statements, which one of the following is correct?*

(a) Both A and R are correct; R is the correct explanation of A

(b) Both A and R are correct; R is not the correct explanation of A

(c) A is correct; R is incorrect

(d) R is correct; A is incorrect

11 **Assertion (A)** $(2^2)^5$ is equal to $a^{5-2}=a^3$.

Reason (R) The Power-to-Power Law states that $(a^m)^n=a^{mn}$.

12 **Assertion (A)** $(a^{-1}+b^{-1})\div(a^{-2}-b^{-2})$ is equal to $\frac{ab}{a+b}$.

Reason (R) If a is any non-zero real number and n is any positive integer, then $a^{-n}=\frac{1}{a^n}$.

13 **Assertion (A)** $\frac{7x^4y^3}{42x^3y^5}=\frac{x}{6y^2}$

Reason (R) Division Law states that if a is any non-zero real number and m, n are rational numbers, then $\frac{a^m}{a^n}=a^{m-n}$.

Part B - Descriptive Questions

Very Short Answer Type Questions

14 Evaluate $\frac{(4\times10^8)(6\times10^{-6})}{8\times10^{11}}$

15 If $5^{3x}=125$ and $10^y=0.001$, then find $5x+y$.

16 Find the value of $\sqrt[4]{625\times81}$.

17 What is the value of $(256)^{-(4^{-3/2})}$.

18 Solve $\sqrt[4]{28}\div\sqrt[3]{7}$.

Short Answer Type Questions

19 Simplify $\frac{5}{(125)^{-\frac{2}{3}}}+\frac{3}{(2401)^{-\frac{3}{4}}}+\frac{2}{(1024)^{-\frac{1}{5}}}$

20 Evaluate $\frac{3\times27^{n+1}+9\times3^{3n-1}}{8\times3^{3n}-5\times27^n}$.

21 If $3^x=9\times3^y$ and $8\times2^y=4^x$, then find the value of $3x+2y$.

22 Solve for y, if $(\sqrt[3]{4})^{2y+\frac{1}{2}}=(\sqrt[3]{8})^5$.

23 Show that $\left[\left\{\frac{x^{l(l-m)}}{x^{l(l+m)}}\right\}\div\left\{\frac{x^{m(m-l)}}{x^{m(m+l)}}\right\}\right]^{a+b}=1$

24 Simplify $(x^{1/3}-x^{-1/3})(x^{2/3}+1+x^{-2/3})$

25 If $x = 2^{1/3} + 2^{2/3}$, then find the value of $x^3 - 6x$.

26 Solve for x, $3(2^x + 1) - 2^{x+2} + 5 = 0$.

27 Simplify each of the following

(i) $\left(\dfrac{27^{-3}}{9^{-3}}\right)^{1/5}$ (ii) $(32)^{-2/5} \div (125)^{-2/3}$

Long Answer Type Questions

28 Simplify $\left(\dfrac{64}{125}\right)^{-2/3} \div \dfrac{1}{\left(\dfrac{256}{625}\right)^{1/4}} + \left(\dfrac{\sqrt{25}}{3}\right)^0$.

29 Prove that $\dfrac{\sqrt{2} \times \sqrt[3]{3} \times \sqrt[4]{4}}{(10)^{-1/5} \times (5)^{3/5}} \div \dfrac{(3)^{4/3} \times (5)^{-7/5}}{(4)^{-3/5} \times 6} = 10$

30 If $5^{2x-1} = 25^{x-1} + 100$, then find the value of 4^{3+x}.

31 If $\dfrac{9^y \times 3^2 \times (3^{-y/2})^{-2} \div (27)^x}{3^{3x} \times 3^2} = \dfrac{1}{27}$, then show that $2x - y = 1$.

32 Solve for x and y such that $27^{x+1} = 81^{y+2}$ and $\left(\dfrac{1}{3}\right)^{3+x} = \left(\dfrac{1}{9}\right)^{3y}$.

33 Solve for x and y such that $(\sqrt{32})^x \div 2^{y+1} = 1$ and $8^y \div 16^{4-\frac{x}{2}} = 1$.

34 If $a^x = b, b^y = c$ and $c^z = a$, then prove that $xyz = 1$.

35 Prove that $\dfrac{x^{-1}}{x^{-1} + y^{-1}} + \dfrac{x^{-1}}{x^{-1} - y^{-1}} = \dfrac{2y^2}{y^2 - x^2}$.

36 If $x = -3$ and $y = 2$, then find the value of $x^x + y^y + x^y + y^x$.

37 If $a = x^{m+n} \cdot y^l, b = x^{n+l} \cdot y^m$ and $c = x^{l+m} \cdot y^n$, then show that $a^{m-n} \cdot b^{n-l} \cdot c^{l-m} = 1$.

38 If $a\sqrt[3]{x^2} + b\sqrt[3]{x} + c = 0$, then show that $a^3x^2 + b^3x + c^3 = 3abcx$

39 If $1176 = 2^p \cdot 3^q \cdot 7^r$, then find the value of $2^p \cdot 3^q \cdot 7^{-r}$ as a fraction.

40 If $\dfrac{9^{n+1}(3^{-n/2})^{-2} - 27^n}{(2 \times 3^m)^3} = \dfrac{1}{729}$, then prove that $m - n = 2$.

Case Study Based Questions

41 On Monday, Sahil invited 3 friends on a party. On Tuesday, each of these friends invited 3 other friends. This pattern continued till Friday.

Based on above information, answer the following questions.

(i) If there are 3^{15-2x} friends in the party on Friday, then find the value of x.

(ii) If total of $2^a \times b \times c$ friends were invited till Thursday, then find the value of $a \times b^{-1}$.

(iii) How many people were invited in all? Write the answer in exponent form.

42 An expression $x^m \times x^n \times x^{-p}$ can be represented as $\dfrac{x^m \times x^n}{x^p}$.

(i) Find the value of $11^2 \times 11^{-4} \times 11^8$.

(ii) Solve $\left(\dfrac{1}{3}\right)^{-4} \times \left(\dfrac{1}{3}\right)^{-8} \times \left(\dfrac{1}{3}\right)^2 + \left(\dfrac{1}{9}\right)^2 \times \left(\dfrac{1}{9}\right)^{-6} \times \left(\dfrac{1}{9}\right)^2$

(iii) Solve $7^{3x-3} = 7^2 \times (\sqrt{7})^3 \times 7$ for x.

Hints & Solutions

1. (c) *2.* (b) *3.* (c) *4.* (d)

5. (a) *6.* (b) *7.* (a) *8.* (c)

9. (b) *10.* (a) *11.* (d) *12.* (d)

13. (a)

14. **Hint** $\dfrac{(4 \times 10^8)(6 \times 10^{-6})}{8 \times 10^{11}} = \dfrac{4 \times 6 \times 10^{8-6}}{8 \times 10^{11}}$ $[\because a^m \times a^n = a^{m+n}]$

$= 3 \times 10^{2-11}$ $\left[\because \dfrac{a^m}{a^n} = a^{m-n}\right]$

Ans. 3×10^{-9}

15. **Hint** We have, $5^{3x} = 5^3$ and $10^y = 10^{-3}$ **Ans.** 2

16. **Hint** $\sqrt[4]{625 \times 81} = \sqrt[4]{5 \times 5 \times 5 \times 5 \times 3 \times 3 \times 3 \times 3}$

Ans. 15

17. **Hint** Here, $(256)^{-(4^{-3/2})} = (256)^{-[(2^2)^{-3/2}]}$

$= (256)^{-[2^{2 \times (-3/2)}]}$ $[\because (a^m)^n = a^{mn}]$

$= (256)^{-(2^{-3})} = (2^8)^{(-1/8)}$

$= 2^{8 \times (-1/8)}$ $[\because (a^m)^n = a^{mn}]$

Ans. $\dfrac{1}{2}$

18. **Hint** Here, $\sqrt[4]{28} \div \sqrt[3]{7} = (28)^{1/4} \div (7)^{1/3} = (4 \times 7)^{1/4} \times \frac{1}{7^{1/3}}$

$$= (4)^{1/4} \times 7^{1/4} \times \frac{1}{7^{1/3}} \quad [\because (ab)^m = a^m b^m]$$

Ans. $\sqrt[12]{\frac{64}{7}}$

19. **Hint** $5(125)^{\frac{2}{3}} + 3(2401)^{\frac{3}{4}} + 2(1024)^{\frac{1}{5}}$

$$= 5(5^3)^{\frac{2}{3}} + 3(7^4)^{\frac{3}{4}} + 2(4^5)^{\frac{1}{5}}$$

Now, apply Power-to-Power Law and solve further.

Ans. 1162

20. 28

21. **Hint** We have, $3^x = 9 \times 3^y$ and $8 \times 2^y = 4^x$

$\Rightarrow \quad 3^x = 3^2 \times 3^y$ and $2^3 \times 2^y = (2^2)^x$

$\Rightarrow \quad 3^x = 3^{y+2}$ and $2^{y+3} = 2^{2x}$

$[\because a^m \cdot a^n = a^{m+n}$ and $(a^m)^n = a^{mn}]$

Now, comparing the exponents of 3 and 2, we get

$x = y + 2$ ...(i)

and $y + 3 = 2x$ ...(ii)

On solving Eqs. (i) and (ii), we get $x = 1$ and $y = -1$

Ans. 1

22. **Hint** $(\sqrt[3]{4})^{2y+\frac{1}{2}} = (\sqrt[3]{8})^5 \Rightarrow (2^{2/3})^{2y+\frac{1}{2}} = 2^5$

On comparing the power of 2, we get

$$\frac{2}{3}\left(2y + \frac{1}{2}\right) = 5 \quad \textbf{Ans. } 3\frac{1}{2}$$

23. **Hint** LHS $= \left[\left\{\frac{x^{l^2-lm}}{x^{l^2+lm}}\right\} \div \left\{\frac{x^{m^2-ml}}{x^{m^2+ml}}\right\}\right]^{a+b}$

$$= [x^{l^2-lm-l^2-lm} \div x^{m^2-ml-m^2-ml}]^{a+b}$$
$$= [x^{-2lm} \div x^{-2lm}]^{a+b}$$
$$= [x^{-2lm-(-2lm)}]^{a+b}$$

24. **Hint** We have, $(x^{1/3} - x^{-1/3})(x^{2/3} + 1 + x^{-2/3})$

$$= \left(x^{1/3} - \frac{1}{x^{1/3}}\right)\left(x^{2/3} + 1 + \frac{1}{x^{2/3}}\right)\left[\because a^{-m} = \frac{1}{a^m}\right]$$
$$= (x^{1/3})^3 - \left(\frac{1}{x^{1/3}}\right)^3$$
$$[\because (a-b)(a^2 + b^2 + ab) = a^3 - b^3]$$

Ans. $x - \frac{1}{x}$

25. **Hint** We have, $x = 2^{1/3} + 2^{2/3}$

$\Rightarrow x^3 = (2^{1/3} + 2^{2/3})^3$

$$= (2^{1/3})^3 + (2^{2/3})^3 + 3 \cdot 2^{1/3} \cdot 2^{2/3}(2^{1/3} + 2^{2/3})$$
$$[\because (a+b)^3 = a^3 + b^3 + 3ab(a+b)]$$

Ans. 6

26. **Hint** We have, $3 \cdot 2^x + 3 - 2^x \cdot 2^2 + 5 = 0$

$\Rightarrow \quad 3 \cdot 2^x - 4 \cdot 2^x + 8 = 0$

$\Rightarrow \quad -2^x + 8 = 0$ **Ans.** $x = 3$

27. (i) **Hint** Here, $\left(\frac{27^{-3}}{9^{-3}}\right)^{1/5} = \left(\frac{27}{9}\right)^{-3/5}$ **Ans.** $(3)^{-3/5}$

(ii) **Hint** $\frac{(32)^{-2/5}}{(125)^{-2/3}} = \frac{(2^5)^{-2/5}}{(5^3)^{-2/3}}$ **Ans.** $6\frac{1}{4}$

28. **Hint** $\left(\left(\frac{4}{5}\right)^3\right)^{-2/3} \div \frac{1}{\left(\left(\frac{4}{5}\right)^4\right)^{1/4}} + \left(\frac{\sqrt{25}}{3}\right)^0$

Use the law $(a^m)^n = a^{mn}$ and $a^0 = 1$ **Ans.** $\frac{9}{4}$

29. **Hint** LHS $= \frac{2^{1/2} \cdot 3^{1/3} \cdot 2^{1/2}}{2^{-1/5} \cdot 5^{-1/5} \cdot 5^{3/5}} \times \frac{2^{-6/5} \times 2 \times 3}{3^{4/3} \times 5^{-7/5}}$

$$= 2^{\frac{1}{2}+\frac{1}{2}+\frac{1}{5}-\frac{6}{5}+1} \cdot 3^{\frac{1}{3}+1-\frac{4}{3}} \cdot 5^{\frac{1}{5}-\frac{3}{5}+\frac{7}{5}}$$

30. **Hint** We have, $5^{2x-1} = 25^{x-1} + 100$

$\Rightarrow \quad 5^{2x-1} = 5^{2\times(x-1)} + 100 \quad [\because (a^m)^n = a^{mn}]$

$\Rightarrow \quad 5^{2x-1} - 5^{2x-2} = 100 \Rightarrow 5^{2x-2}[5-1] = 100$

$\Rightarrow \quad 5^{2x-2} \times 4 = 100 \Rightarrow 5^{2x-2} = 25 = 5^2$

Now, equating exponents of 5 on both sides, we get

$2x - 2 = 2 \Rightarrow x = 2$ **Ans.** 1024

31. **Hint** We have, $\frac{9^y \times 3^2 \times (3^{-y/2})^{-2} \div (27)^x}{3^{3x} \times 3^2} = \frac{1}{27}$

$\Rightarrow \quad \frac{3^{2y} \times 3^2 \times 3^y \div 3^{3x}}{3^{3x} \times 3^2} = \frac{1}{3^3} \quad [\because (a^m)^n = a^{mn}]$

$\Rightarrow \quad \frac{3^{2y+2+y-3x}}{3^{3x+2}} = \frac{1}{3^3} \quad [\because a^m \times a^n = a^{m+n}]$

$\Rightarrow \quad 3^{3y-3x+2-3x-2} = 3^{-3} \quad \left[\because \frac{1}{a^n} = a^{-n}\right]$

$\Rightarrow \quad 3^{3y-6x} = 3^{-3}$

Now, equating exponents of 3 on both sides, we get

$3y - 6x = -3$

32. **Hint** We have, $(27)^{x+1} = (81)^{y+2}$

and $\left(\frac{1}{3}\right)^{3+x} = \left(\frac{1}{9}\right)^{3y} \Rightarrow 3^{3x+3} = 3^{4y+8}$

and $\left(\frac{1}{3}\right)^{3+x} = \left(\frac{1}{3}\right)^{6y}$

On equating exponent from both sides, we get

$3x + 3 = 4y + 8$ and $3 + x = 6y$

or $3x - 4y = 5$ and $x - 6y = -3$

On solving the above equations, we get the required result. **Ans.** $x = 3$ and $y = 1$

33. **Hint** We have, $(\sqrt{32})^x \div 2^{y+1} = 1 \Rightarrow [(2^5)^{1/2}]^x \div 2^{y+1} = 1$

$$\Rightarrow \quad 2^{\frac{5x}{2}-(y+1)} = 2^0$$

$[\because (a^m)^n = a^{mn} \text{ and } a^0 = 1]$

On comparing the exponents from 2 both sides, we get

$$5x - 2y - 2 = 0 \quad ...(i)$$

and $8^y \div 16^{4-x/2} = 1$

$$\Rightarrow 2^{3y} \div 2^{4(4-x/2)} = 2^0 \Rightarrow 2^{3y-16+2x} = 2^0$$

$$\Rightarrow 2x + 3y - 16 = 0 \quad ...(ii)$$

On solving Eqs. (i) and (ii), we get the required result.

Ans. $x = 2$ and $y = 4$

34. **Hint** Given, $a^x = b, b^y = c$ and $c^z = a$

Now, $a^x = b \Rightarrow (c^z)^x = b \Rightarrow c^{xz} = b$

$\Rightarrow (b^y)^{xz} = b \Rightarrow b^{xyz} = b^1$

35. LHS $= \dfrac{x^{-1}}{x^{-1}+y^{-1}} + \dfrac{x^{-1}}{x^{-1}-y^{-1}}$

$$= \frac{\frac{1}{x}}{\frac{1}{x}+\frac{1}{y}} + \frac{\frac{1}{x}}{\frac{1}{x}-\frac{1}{y}} \quad \left[\because a^{-n} = \frac{1}{a^n}\right]$$

$$= \frac{\frac{1}{x}}{\frac{y+x}{xy}} + \frac{\frac{1}{x}}{\frac{y-x}{xy}}$$

$$= \frac{xy}{(x+y)x} + \frac{xy}{(y-x)x} \quad \left[\because \frac{a}{b} \div \frac{c}{d} = \frac{ad}{bc}\right]$$

$$= \frac{y}{x+y} + \frac{y}{y-x} = \frac{y(y-x)+y(x+y)}{(y+x)(y-x)}$$

$$= \frac{y^2 - xy + xy + y^2}{y^2 - x^2} \quad [\because (a+b)(a-b) = a^2 - b^2]$$

$$= \frac{2y^2}{y^2 - x^2} = \text{RHS}$$

Hence proved.

36. We have,

$x^x + y^y + x^y + y^x = (-3)^{-3} + (2)^2 + (-3)^2 + (2)^{-3}$

[given, $x = -3$ and $y = 2$]

$$= \frac{1}{(-3)^3} + 4 + 9 + \frac{1}{2^3} \quad \left[\because a^{-n} = \frac{1}{a^n}\right]$$

Ans. 13.09

37. **Hint** Consider, LHS $= a^{m-n} \cdot b^{n-l} \cdot c^{l-m}$

$= (x^{m+n} \cdot y^l)^{m-n} \cdot (x^{n+l} \cdot y^m)^{n-l} \cdot (x^{l+m} \cdot y^n)^{l-m}$

$= [x^{(m+n)(m-n)} \cdot y^{l(m-n)} \cdot x^{(n+l)(n-l)} \cdot y^{m(n-l)} \cdot x^{(l+m)(l-m)} \cdot y^{n(l-m)}]$ $[\because (a^m)^n = a^{mn}]$

$= [x^{m^2-n^2} y^{l(m-n)} \cdot x^{n^2-l^2} \cdot y^{m(n-l)} x^{l^2-m^2} \cdot y^{n(l-m)}]$

$[\because (a+b)(a-b) = a^2 - b^2]$

$= x^{m^2-n^2+n^2-l^2+l^2-m^2} \cdot y^{lm-nl+mn-lm+nl-mn}$

38. **Hint** We have, $ax^{2/3} + bx^{1/3} = -c \quad ...(i)$

$\Rightarrow (ax^{2/3} + bx^{1/3})^3 = (-c)^3$ [cubing both sides]

$\Rightarrow a^3x^2 + b^3x + 3ax^{2/3} \cdot bx^{1/3}(ax^{2/3} + bx^{1/3}) = -c^3$

$[\because (A+B)^3 = A^3 + B^3 + 3AB(A+B)]$

$\Rightarrow a^3x^2 + b^3x + 3abx(-c) = -c^3$ [from Eq. (i)]

39. **Hint** First, we find $p = 3, q = 1$ and $r = 2$.

Then, we get $2^p 3^q 7^{-r} = \dfrac{24}{49}$. **Ans.** $\dfrac{24}{49}$

40. **Hint** $\dfrac{9^{n+1}(3^{-n/2})^{-2} - 27^n}{(2 \times 3^m)^3} = \dfrac{1}{729}$

$$\Rightarrow \frac{(3^2)^{n+1}\left(3^{\left(-\frac{n}{2}\right)(-2)}\right) - (3^3)^n}{2^3 \times 3^{m \times 3}} = \frac{1}{729}$$

$$\Rightarrow \frac{3^{2n+2} \times 3^n - 3^{3n}}{2^3 \times 3^{3m}} = \frac{1}{3^6}$$

$$\Rightarrow \frac{3^{3n+2} - 3^{3n}}{2^3 \times 3^{3m}} = \frac{1}{3^6} \Rightarrow \left(\frac{9-1}{2^3}\right)\left[\frac{1}{3^{3m-3n}}\right] = \frac{1}{3^6}$$

41. (i) Monday : 3 friends

Tuesday : 9 friends

Wednesday : 27 friends

Thursday : 81 friends

Friday : 243 friends

Given that there are 3^{15-2x} friends on Friday.

So, $3^{15-2x} = 243 \Rightarrow 3^{15-2x} = 3^5$

Now, equating components of 3 on both sides, we get

$$15 - 2x = 5 \Rightarrow 2x = 10 \Rightarrow x = 5$$

(ii) Number of friends till Thursday $= 3 + 9 + 27 + 81 = 120$

So, $2^a \times b \times c = 120 \Rightarrow 2^a \times b \times c = 2^3 \times 3 \times 5$

Hence, $a \times b^{-1} = 3 \times \dfrac{1}{3} = 1$

(iii) Total people invited till Friday

$$= 3 + 9 + 27 + 81 + 243 = 363 = 3 \times 11^2$$

42. (i) $11^2 \times 11^{-4} \times 11^8 = \dfrac{11^2 \times 11^8}{11^4} = \dfrac{11^{10}}{11^4} = 11^{10-4} = 11^6$

(ii) $\left(\dfrac{1}{3}\right)^{-4} \times \left(\dfrac{1}{3}\right)^{-8} \times \left(\dfrac{1}{3}\right)^{2} + \left(\dfrac{1}{9}\right)^{+2} \times \left(\dfrac{1}{9}\right)^{-6} \times \left(\dfrac{1}{9}\right)^{2}$

$$= \frac{\left(\frac{1}{3}\right)^2}{\left(\frac{1}{3}\right)^{12}} + \frac{\left(\frac{1}{9}\right)^4}{\left(\frac{1}{9}\right)^6} = \left(\frac{1}{3}\right)^{-10} + \left(\frac{1}{9}\right)^{-2}$$

$$= 3^{10} + (3^2)^2 = 3^{10} + 3^4$$

(iii) $7^{3x-3} = 7^2 \times (\sqrt{7})^3 \times 7 \Rightarrow 7^{3x-3} = 7^3 \times (7)^{\frac{3}{2}}$

$$\Rightarrow 7^{3x-3} = 7^{3+\frac{3}{2}} \Rightarrow 7^{3x-3} = 7^{\frac{9}{2}}$$

Ans. $x = \dfrac{5}{2}$

CHAPTER 03

Logarithms

In this Chapter...

- Logarithm
- Common and Natural Logarithm

Logarithm

If a is any positive real number ($a \neq 1$) and m is any rational number and n be any real number such that $a^m = n$, then $m = \log_a n$, where m is called logarithm of n to the base a.

Thus, $a^m = n$ is called the **exponential form** and $m = \log_a n$ is called the **logarithmic form.**

Interchanging (Logarithmic form vis-a-vis expontential form)

Exponential form	Logarithmic form
$2^4 = 16$	$4 = \log_2 16$
$5^0 = 1$	$0 = \log_5 1$
$3^{-4} = \frac{1}{3^4} = \frac{1}{81}$	$-4 = \log_3 \frac{1}{81}$
$(10)^{-4} = \frac{1}{(10)^4} = \frac{1}{10000}$	$-4 = \log_{10} \frac{1}{10000}$

Properties of Logarithms

1. $a^0 = 1 \Rightarrow \log_a 1 = 0, a \neq 1,$
2. $a^1 = a \Rightarrow \log_a a = 1,$
3. If $x = a^m$ and $y = a^m$, then $x = y$.

   Hence, $\log_a x = \log_a y \Rightarrow x = y$.
4. If the base of logarithms is not given, then we always take 10 as a base. Logarithms to the base 10 are called common logarithms.
   e.g. $\log 50 = \log_{10} 50$

EXAMPLE 1. Write each of the following in the logaritmic form.

(i) $7^3 = 343$ (ii) $2^{-10} = \frac{1}{1024}$ (iii) $4^{3/2} = 8$

(iv) $(0.2)^3 = 0.008$

Sol. (i) We have, $7^3 = 343$

$\Rightarrow \quad 3 = \log_7 343 \quad [\because a^m = n \Rightarrow m = \log_a n]$

(ii) We have, $2^{-10} = \frac{1}{1024}$

$\Rightarrow \quad -10 = \log_2 \frac{1}{1024} \quad [\because a^m = n \Rightarrow m = \log_a n]$

(iii) We have, $4^{3/2} = 8$

$\Rightarrow \quad \frac{3}{2} = \log_4 8 \quad [\because a^m = n \Rightarrow m = \log_a n]$

(iv) We have, $(0.2)^3 = 0.008$

$\Rightarrow \quad 3 = \log_{0.2}(0.008) [\because a^m = n \Rightarrow m = \log_a n]$

EXAMPLE 2. Convert the following to exponential form.

(i) $\log_3 81 = 4$ (ii) $\log_{10}(0.1) = -1$

Sol. (i) $\log_3 81 = 4$

$3^4 = 81 \quad [\because \log_a n = m \Rightarrow a^m = n]$

(ii) $\log_{10}(0.1) = -1$

$10^{-1} = 0.1 \quad [\because \log_a n = m \Rightarrow a^m = n]$

EXAMPLE 3. Find the values of x in each of the following.

(i) $\log_3 x = 3$ (ii) $\log_4 x = 3/2$

(iii) $\log_{10} x = -3$ (iv) $\log_x 16 = 2$

(v) $\log_9 27 = 2x + 3$

Sol. (i) We have, $\log_3 x = 3$

$\Rightarrow \quad x = (3)^3 = 27 [\because \log_a n = m \Rightarrow a^m = n]$

(ii) We have, $\log_4 x = \frac{3}{2}$

$\Rightarrow \quad x = (4)^{3/2} = 8 \quad [\because \log_a n = m \Rightarrow a^m = n]$

(iii) We have, $\log_{10} x = -3$

$\Rightarrow \quad x = (10)^{-3} \quad [\because \log_a n = m \Rightarrow a^m = n]$

$\therefore \quad x = \frac{1}{10^3} = \frac{1}{1000} \quad \left[\because a^{-m} = \frac{1}{a^m}\right]$

(iv) We have, $\log_x 16 = 2$

$\Rightarrow \quad x^2 = 16 \quad [\because \log_a n = m \Rightarrow a^m = n]$

$\Rightarrow \quad x = 4$

(v) We have, $\log_9 27 = 2x + 3$

$\Rightarrow \quad (9)^{2x+3} = 27 \quad [\because \log_a n = m \Rightarrow a^m = n]$

$\Rightarrow \quad 3^{4x+6} = 3^3$

$\therefore \quad x = -\frac{3}{4}$

EXAMPLE 4. Find the logarithm in each of the following.

(i) 64 to the base 4 (ii) 0.008 to the base 5

Sol. (i) Let $\log_4 64 = x$, then $64 = 4^x$

$[\because \log_a n = m \Rightarrow a^m = n]$

$\Rightarrow \quad 4^x = 4 \times 4 \times 4 \Rightarrow 4^x = 4^3$

On comparing the exponents of 4 both sides, we get

$x = 3$

Hence, $\log_4 64 = 3$

(ii) Let $\log_5 0.008 = x$, then

$0.008 = 5^x \quad [\because \log_a n = m \Rightarrow a^m = n]$

$\Rightarrow \quad \frac{8}{1000} = 5^x \Rightarrow \frac{1}{125} = 5^x$

$\Rightarrow \quad (5)^{-3} = (5)^x \quad \left[\because \frac{1}{a^n} = a^{-n}\right]$

On comparing the exponents of 5 both sides, we get

$x = -3$

Hence, $\log_5 0.008 = -3$

Laws of Logarithms

(i) **Product Law** $\log_a m \cdot n = \log_a m + \log_a n$

e.g. $\log(10) = \log(2 \times 5) = \log 2 + \log 5$

(ii) **Quotient Law** $\log_a \left(\frac{m}{n}\right) = \log_a m - \log_a n$

e.g. $\log \frac{10}{3} = \log 10 - \log 3$

(iii) **Power Law** $\log_a (m)^n = n \log_a m$

e.g. $\log (10)^3 = 3 \log 10$

(iv) $\log_n m = \frac{\log_a m}{\log_a n}$ e.g. $\log_2 3 = \frac{\log_{10} 3}{\log_{10} 2}$

(v) $a^{\log_a m} = m$ e.g. $4^{\log_4 64} = 64$

(vi) $x^{\log_a y} = y^{\log_a x}$ e.g. $3^{\log_{10} 4} = 4^{\log_{10} 3}$

(vii) **Reciprocal Law** $\log_a b = \frac{1}{\log_b a}$

EXAMPLE 5. Evaluate the following.

(i) $\frac{\log 8 \log 9}{\log 27}$ (ii) $3 + \frac{1}{2}\log_{10} 9 - 2\log_{10} 5$

(iii) $4 + \log_{10}(0.001)$

Sol. (i) We have, $\frac{\log 8 \log 9}{\log 27} = \frac{\log(2)^3 \times \log(3)^2}{\log(3)^3}$

$= \frac{3\log 2 \times 2\log 3}{3\log 3} = 2\log 2$

(ii) We have, $3 + \frac{1}{2}\log_{10} 9 - 2\log_{10} 5$

$= 3 \times 1 + \frac{1}{2}\log_{10}(3 \times 3) - 2\log_{10} 5$

$= 3\log_{10} 10 + \frac{1}{2}\log_{10} 3^2 - 2\log_{10} 5$

$[\because 1 = \log_{10} 10]$

$= \log_{10} 10^3 + \log_{10} 3^{2 \times \frac{1}{2}} - \log_{10}(5)^2$

$[\because n\log m = \log m^n]$

$= \log_{10} 1000 + \log_{10} 3 - \log_{10} 25$

$= \log_{10}(1000 \times 3) - \log_{10} 25$

$[\because \log m + \log n = \log mn]$

$= \log_{10} \frac{3000}{25} \quad \left[\because \log m - \log n = \log \frac{m}{n}\right]$

$= \log_{10} 120$

(iii) $4 + \log_{10}(0.001) = 4 + \log_{10}(10)^{-3}$

$= 4 - 3\log_{10} 10 \quad [\because \log m^n = n\log m]$

$= 4 - 3 \times 1 \quad [\because \log_{10} 10 = 1]$

$= 1$

EXAMPLE 6. If $\log_{10} 2 = m$ and $\log_{10} 3 = n$, then express each of the following in terms of m and n.

(i) $\log_{10} 90$ (ii) $\log_{10} 0.54$

Sol. Given, $\log_{10} 2 = m$ and $\log_{10} 3 = n$

(i) We have,

$\log_{10} 90 = \log_{10}(10 \times 9)$

$= \log_{10} 10 + \log_{10} 3^2 \quad [\because \log mn = \log m + \log n]$

$= 1 + 2\log_{10} 3 \quad [\because \log m^n = n\log m]$

$= 2\log_{10} 3 + 1 = 1 + 2n \quad [\because \log_a a = 1]$

(ii) We have,

$$\log_{10} 0.54 = \log_{10} \frac{54}{100} = \log_{10} \frac{27 \times 2}{100}$$

$$= \log_{10} 27 \times 2 - \log_{10} 100 \quad \left[\because \log \frac{m}{n} = \log m - \log n\right]$$

$$= \log_{10} 27 + \log_{10} 2 - \log_{10} 100 \quad [\because \log mn = \log m + \log n]$$

$$= \log_{10} 3^3 + \log_{10} 2 - \log_{10} 10^2$$

$$= 3\log_{10} 3 + \log_{10} 2 - 2\log_{10} 10 \quad [\because \log m^n = n \log m]$$

$$= 3n + m - 2 \quad [\because \log_{10} 10 = 1]$$

$$= m + 3n - 2$$

EXAMPLE 7. Determine the logarithmic expansion of $y = \dfrac{5^p 7^q}{3^r}$.

Sol. Given, $y = \dfrac{5^p 7^q}{3^r}$

On taking log both sides, we get

$$\log y = \log \frac{5^p\, 7^q}{3^r}$$

$$\Rightarrow \log y = \log 5^p 7^q - \log 3^r \quad \left[\because \log \frac{m}{n} = \log m - \log n\right]$$

$$\Rightarrow \log y = \log 5^p + \log 7^q - \log 3^r \quad [\because \log mn = \log m + \log n]$$

$$\Rightarrow \log y = p \log 5 + q \log 7 - r \log 3 \quad [\because n \log m = \log m^n]$$

Hence, $\log y = p \log 5 + q \log 7 - r \log 3$ is the logarithmic expansion of $y = \dfrac{5^p 7^q}{3^r}$.

EXAMPLE 8. If $\log 7 - \log 2 + \log 16 - 2 \log 3 - \log \dfrac{7}{45} = 1 + \log x$, then find x.

Sol. We have,

$$\log 7 - \log 2 + \log 16 - 2\log 3 - \log \frac{7}{45} = 1 + \log x$$

$$\Rightarrow \log 7 - \log 2 + \log 16 - \log 3^2 - \log \frac{7}{45} = 1 + \log x \quad [\because n \log m = \log m^n]$$

$$\Rightarrow \log 7 - \log 2 + \log 16 - \log 9 - (\log 7 - \log 45) = 1 + \log x \quad \left[\because \log \frac{m}{n} = \log m - \log n\right]$$

$$\Rightarrow \log 7 - \log 2 + \log 16 - \log 9 - \log 7 + \log 45 = 1 + \log x$$

$$\Rightarrow (\log 16 + \log 45) - (\log 2 + \log 9) = 1 + \log x$$

$$\Rightarrow \log(16 \times 45) - \log(2 \times 9) = 1 + \log x \quad [\because \log m + \log n = \log mn]$$

$$\Rightarrow \log \frac{16 \times 45}{2 \times 9} = 1 + \log x \quad \left[\because \log m - \log n = \log \frac{m}{n}\right]$$

$$\Rightarrow \log 40 = 1 + \log x = \log 10 + \log x \quad [\because 1 = \log 10]$$

$$\Rightarrow \log 40 = \log 10x \Rightarrow 10x = 40$$

$$\therefore x = 4$$

EXAMPLE 9. Solve for x, if $\log_{10} (x^2 - 21) = 2$.

Sol. We have, $\log_{10} (x^2 - 21) = 2$

$$\Rightarrow x^2 - 21 = (10)^2 \quad [\because \log_a n = m \Rightarrow a^m = n]$$

$$\Rightarrow x^2 - 21 = 100$$

$$\Rightarrow x^2 = 100 + 21 = 121$$

$$\therefore x^2 = (11)^2$$

$$\Rightarrow x = \pm 11 \quad \text{[taking square root]}$$

EXAMPLE 10. Solve for x, if $(\log_{10} x)^2 - (\log_{10} x) - 2 = 0$.

Sol. We have, $(\log_{10} x)^2 - (\log_{10} x) - 2 = 0$

Let $\log_{10} x = t$, then the given expression reduces to $t^2 - t - 2 = 0$

Now, factorise by splitting the middle term, we get

$$t^2 - 2t + t - 2 = 0$$

$$\Rightarrow t(t - 2) + 1(t - 2) = 0$$

$$\Rightarrow (t - 2)(t + 1) = 0$$

$$\Rightarrow t - 2 = 0 \text{ or } t + 1 = 0$$

$$\Rightarrow t = 2 \text{ or } t = -1$$

On putting the value of t, we get

$$\log_{10} x = -1 \text{ or } \log_{10} x = 2$$

$$\Rightarrow x = (10)^{-1} \text{ or } x = (10)^2 \quad [\because \log_a n = m \Rightarrow a^m = n]$$

Hence, $x = \dfrac{1}{10}$ and 100

EXAMPLE 11. Simplify $\dfrac{\log_3 8}{\log_9 16 \log_4 10}$.

Sol. We have, $\dfrac{\log_3 8}{\log_9 16 \log_4 10}$

$$= \frac{\dfrac{\log_{10} 8}{\log_{10} 3}}{\dfrac{\log_{10} 16}{\log_{10} 9} \times \dfrac{\log_{10} 10}{\log_{10} 4}} \quad \left[\because \log_n m = \frac{\log_{10} m}{\log_{10} n}\right]$$

$$= \frac{\log_{10} 8 \times \log_{10} 9 \times \log_{10} 4}{\log_{10} 16 \times \log_{10} 3 \times \log_{10} 10} \quad \left[\because \frac{a/b}{c/d} = \frac{ad}{bc}\right]$$

$$= \frac{\log_{10} 2^3 \times \log_{10} 3^2 \times \log_{10} 2^2}{\log_{10} 2^4 \times \log_{10} 3 \times 1} \quad [\because \log_{10} 10 = 1]$$

$$= \frac{3\log_{10} 2 \times 2\log_{10} 3 \times 2\log_{10} 2}{4 \log_{10} 2 \times \log_{10} 3}$$

$$= 3\log_{10} 2$$

EXAMPLE 12. If $p = \log_x yz, q = \log_y zx$ and $r = \log_z xy$, then prove that $\dfrac{1}{1+p} + \dfrac{1}{1+q} + \dfrac{1}{1+r} = 1$.

Sol. Given, $\frac{1}{1+p} = \frac{1}{1+\log_x yz} = \frac{1}{\log_x x + \log_x yz}$ $[\because 1 = \log_x x]$

$= \frac{1}{\log_x xyz}$ $[\because \log m + \log n = \log mn]$

$= \log_{xyz} x$ $\left[\because \frac{1}{\log_b a} = \log_a b\right]$

Similarly, $\frac{1}{1+q} = \log_{xyz} y$ and $\frac{1}{1+r} = \log_{xyz} z$

$\therefore$ LHS $= \frac{1}{1+p} + \frac{1}{1+q} + \frac{1}{1+r}$

$= \log_{xyz} x + \log_{xyz} y + \log_{xyz} z$

$= \log_{xyz} xyz = 1$ $[\because \log m + \log n = \log mn]$

$=$ RHS **Hence proved.**

EXAMPLE 13. Prove that $\log_{3^4} 4^3 = \frac{3}{4}\log_3 4.$

Sol. Let $\log_{3^4} 4^3 = x$

$\Rightarrow (3^4)^x = 4^3$ $[\because a^m = n \Rightarrow \log_a n = m]$

$\Rightarrow 3^{4x} = 4^3$

Taking log with base 3 both sides, we get

$\log_3 3^{4x} = \log_3 4^3$

$\Rightarrow 4x = \log_3 4^3$ $[\because \log_a a = 1]$

$\Rightarrow 4x = 3\log_3 4$

$\Rightarrow x = \frac{3}{4}\log_3 4$

$\therefore$ LHS = RHS **Hence proved.**

EXAMPLE 14. Solve the equations for x

$$\log_x 2 \times \log_{x/16} 2 = \log_{x/64} 2$$

Sol. Given, $\log_x 2 \times \log_{x/16} 2 = \log_{x/64} 2$

$\Rightarrow \frac{1}{\log_2 x} \times \frac{1}{\log_2\left(\frac{x}{16}\right)} = \frac{1}{\log_2\left(\frac{x}{64}\right)}$ $\left[\because \log_a b = \frac{1}{\log_b a}\right]$

By cross multiplication, we get

$\Rightarrow \log_2(x/64) = \log_2 x \times \log_2(x/16)$

$\Rightarrow \log_2 x - \log_2 64 = \log_2 x(\log_2 x - \log_2 16)$ $\left[\because \log_a \frac{m}{n} = \log_a m - \log_a n\right]$

$\Rightarrow \log_2 x - \log_2 2^6 = \log_2 x(\log_2 x - \log_2 2^4)$

$\Rightarrow \log_2 x - 6\log_2 2 = \log_2 x(\log_2 x - 4\log_2 2)$ $[\because \log_a m^n = n\log_a m]$

$\Rightarrow \log_2 x - 6\times 1 = \log_2 x(\log_2 x - 4\times 1)$ $[\because \log_a a = 1]$

$\Rightarrow (\log_2 x)^2 - 5\log_2 x + 6 = 0$

Let $y = \log_2 x$

$\Rightarrow y^2 - 5y + 6 = 0$ ...(i)

$\Rightarrow y^2 - 3y - 2y + 6 = 0$

$\Rightarrow y(y-3) - 2(y-3) = 0$

$\Rightarrow (y-3)(y-2) = 0$

$\Rightarrow y = 3$ or $y = 2$

Putting the values of y in Eq. (i),

$\Rightarrow \log_2 x = 3$ or $\log_2 x = 2$

$\Rightarrow x = 2^3$ or $x = 2^2$

$\Rightarrow x = 8$ or $x = 4$

Hence, the solutions of the given equation are 8, 4.

EXAMPLE 15. Evaluate the following expression of log.

(i) $(81)^{1/\log_5 3} + (27)^{\log_9 36} + (3)^{(4/\log_7 9)}$

(ii) $\log_9 27 - \log_{27} 9$

(iii) $3^{2-\log_3 4}$

(iv) $8^{1/3 + \log_2 (121)^{1/3}}$

Sol. (i) $(81)^{1/\log_5 3} + (27)^{\log_9 36} + (3)^{4/\log_7 9}$

$= (81)^{\log_3 5} + (27)^{\log_9 36} + (3)^{4\log_9 7}$ $\left[\because \log_m n = \frac{1}{\log_n m}\right]$

$= (3)^{4\log_3 5} + (3)^{3\log_{3^2} 6^2} + 3^{4\log_{3^2} 7}$

$= (3)^{\log_3 5^4} + (3)^{\log_3 6^3} + (3)^{\log_3 7^2}$

$= 5^4 + 6^3 + 7^2$

$= 890$ $[\because (a)^{\log_a n} = n]$

(ii) $\log_9(27) - \log_{27} 9$

$= \log_{3^2} 3^3 - \log_{3^3}(3)^2$

$= \frac{3}{2}\log_3 3 - \frac{2}{3}\log_3 3$ $[\because \log_{a^q} n^p = \frac{p}{q}\log_a n]$

$= \frac{3}{2} - \frac{2}{3} = \frac{5}{6}$

(iii) $3^{2-\log_3 4} = (3)^2(3)^{-\log_3 4}$

$= 9 \times 3^{\log_3 4^{-1}}$ $[\because n\log m = \log m^n]$

$= 9 \times 4^{-1} = \frac{9}{4}$ $[\because m^{\log_m x} = x]$

(iv) $8^{1/3 + \log_2 (121)^{1/3}}$

$= 8^{1/3} \times 8^{\log_2 (121)^{1/3}}$ $[\because x^{n+m} = x^n \cdot x^m]$

$= 2 \times 8^{1/3 \log_2 121}$ $[\because \log_a x^n = n\log_a x]$

$= 2 \times 2^{\log_2 121}$

$= 2 \times 121$ $[\because a^{\log_a n} = n]$

$= 242$

Topic Practice 1

1 Express each of the following in the logarithmic form.

(i) $3^6 = 729$ (ii) $(81)^{3/4} = 27$ (iii) $8^{-1} = 0.125$

(iv) $5^3 = 125$ (v) $25^{1/2} = 5$

2 Prove that

(i) $\log_{10} 0.001 = -3$ (ii) $\log_5 125 = 3$

(iii) $\log_a 1 = 0$ (iv) $\log_{10} 100 = 2$

(v) $\log_{10}(0.0001) = -4$

3 Solve for x of each of the following.

(i) $\log_{10} x = -4$ (ii) $\log_{\sqrt{5}}(x-1) = 2$

(iii) $\log_{\sqrt{3}} x = 6$

4 Find the logarithm of each of the following.

(i) 256 to the base 4 (ii) 8 to the base 2

(iii) $\frac{1}{125}$ to the base 5 (iv) 625 to the base 25

(v) $\frac{1}{256}$ to the base 16

5 Solve each of the following.

(i) $\log_{125} 625$ (ii) $\log_{1/8} \frac{1}{256}$ (iii) $\log_{12} 1728$

6 Evaluate $\log_{2\sqrt{3}} 1728$.

7 Express $\log \frac{27}{4} + \log \frac{4}{32}$ in terms of log 2 and log 3.

8 If $\log v = 2\log 2 - \log 3 + \log \pi + 3\log r$, then find v.

9 Simplify $\log_{10} 8 + \log_{10} 25 + 2\log_{10} 3 - \log_{10} 18$.

10 If $\log_{10} m = n$, then evaluate 10^{2n-3} in terms of m.

11 If $\log_{10} 2 = m$ and $\log_{10} 3 = n$, then express $\log_{10} 120$ in terms of m and n.

12 Solve for x, if

(i) $\log_{10}(x^2 - 24) = 3$

(ii) $\log(x+4) - \log(x+5) = 1$

(iii) $(\log_{10} x)^2 + 5(\log_{10} x) + 6 = 0$

13 Prove that

(i) $2\log \frac{15}{18} - \log \frac{25}{162} + \log \frac{4}{9} = \log 2$

(ii) $\log \frac{70}{33} + \log \frac{22}{135} - \log \frac{7}{18} = 3\log 2 - 2\log 3$

14 If $x^2 + y^2 = 9xy$, then prove that

$$2\log(x+y) = \log x + \log y + 2\log 3.$$

15 If $\frac{3}{2}\log m + \frac{2}{3}\log n - 1 = 0$, then evaluate $m^9 n^4$.

16 If $x = \log 0.6$, $y = \log 1.25$ and $z = \log 3 - 2\log 2$, then find $5^{(x+y-z)}$.

17 Given that $x = 1 + \log 2 - \log 5$, $y = 2\log 3$ and $z = \log a - \log 5$. If $x + y = 2z$, then find the value of a.

18 If $\log 27 = 1.431$, then evaluate log 9.

19 If $\log_{10} x = m + n$ and $y = 10^{2m-n}$, then evaluate $\log_{10} x^3 y^4$ in terms of m and n.

20 Find the value of x, if

(i) $5^{\log x} + 3^{\log x} = 3^{\log x + 1} - 5^{\log x - 1}$

(ii) $\log(3x+2) + \log(3x-2) = 5\log 2$

(iii) $\log_x 49 - \log_x 7 + \log_x \frac{1}{343} + 2 = 0$

(iv) $\log(x+2) + \log(x-2) = \log 3 + 3\log 4$

(v) $\log_3(3+x) + \log_3(8-x) - \log_3(9x-8) = 2 - \log_3 9$

21 Show that $\frac{\log\sqrt{27} + \log\sqrt{8} - \log\sqrt{125}}{\log 6 - \log 5} = \frac{3}{2}$.

22 If $a^{3-x} \cdot b^{5x} = a^{x+5} \cdot b^{3x}$, then show that $x \log \frac{b}{a} = \log a$.

23 If $a^{2x-3} \cdot b^{2x} = a^{6-x} \cdot b^{5x}$, then prove that $3\log a = x \log \frac{a}{b}$.

24 If $\log 2 = 0.3010$ and $\log 3 = 0.4771$, then find the value of $\log 3 + \log 8 - \log\sqrt{6}$.

25 Solve for x and y, if

(i) $\log xy = 2$ and $\log \frac{x}{y} + 2\log 2 = 2$

(ii) $\frac{\log_{10} x}{\log_{10} y} = \frac{3}{2}$ and $\log_{10} xy = 5$

(iii) $\log_{10} x^3 y^4 = 7$ and $\log_{10} \frac{x^2}{y} = 1$

(iv) $\frac{\log(x+y)}{\log 2} = \frac{\log(x-y)}{\log 5} = \frac{\log 4}{\log(0.5)}$

26 Evaluate $\log_3\sqrt{6} + \log_3\sqrt{\frac{2}{3}} - \log_3(\log_3 9)$.

27 If $x^2 + y^2 = 23xy$, then prove that

$$\log\left(\frac{x+y}{5}\right) = \frac{1}{2}(\log x + \log y).$$

28 If $2x - \log 48 + 3\log 2 = \frac{1}{3}\log 125 - \log 3$, then find $(100)^x$.

29 Solve for a and b :

$$\log_{10}(ab) = 2, \log_{10}\left(\frac{a}{b}\right) + 2\log_{10} 2 = 2$$

Hints & Solutions

1. Do same as Example 1.

Ans. (i) $6=\log_3 729$ (ii) $\log_{81} 27 = 3/4$

(iii) $-1=\log_8 0.125$ (iv) $3=\log_5 125$ (v) $\frac{1}{2}=\log_{25} 5$

2. Hint Apply $\log_a n = m \Rightarrow a^m = n$

Ans. (i) $(10)^{-3}=0.001$ (ii) $5^3=125$

(iii) $a^0=1$ (iv) $10^2=100$ (v) $10^{-4}=0.0001$

3. Do same as Example 3.

Ans. (i) $x=\frac{1}{10000}=0.0001$ (ii) $x=6$ (iii) $x=27$

4. Do same as Example 4.

Ans. (i) 4 (ii) 3 (iii) −3 (iv) 2 (v) − 2

5. Hint Apply power law

$\log_a(m)^n = n\log_a m$ and $\log_{a^n} m = \frac{1}{n}\log_a m$

Ans. (i) $\frac{4}{3}$ (ii) $\frac{8}{3}$ (iii) 3

6. Hint $\log_{2\sqrt{3}} 1728 = \log_{(12)^{1/2}}(12)^3$ **Ans.** 6

7. Do same as Example 6. **Ans.** $3\log 3 - 5\log 2$

8. Hint $\log v = \log\frac{4\pi r^3}{3}$. **Ans.** $v=\frac{4\pi r^3}{3}$

9. Hint $3\log_{10}2+2\log_{10}5+2\log_{10}3-\log_{10}9-\log_{10}2$

Ans. 2

10. Hint $\because \log_{10} m = n \Rightarrow m = 10^n$

Now, $10^{2n-3}=(10^n)^2\cdot 10^{-3}=\frac{m^2}{10^3}$ **Ans.** $\frac{m^2}{1000}$

11. Do same as Example 7. **Ans.** $2m+n+1$

12. (i) Do same as Example 11. **Ans.** $x=\pm 32$

(ii) Do same as Example 12. **Ans.** $\frac{-46}{9}$

(iii) Do same as Example 13. **Ans.** $x=\frac{1}{1000},\frac{1}{100}$

13. (i) **Hint** Use the formulae, $\log m - \log n = \log\frac{m}{n}$,

$n\log m = \log m^n$ and $\log m + \log n = \log mn$.

(ii) **Hint** Let LHS $= \log 70 - \log 33 + \log 22 - \log 135$

$- \log 7 + \log 18$

$= (\log 2 + \log 5 + \log 7) - (\log 11 + \log 3)$

$+ (\log 11 + \log 2) - (3\log 3 + \log 5)$

$- \log 7 + (\log 2 + 2\log 3)$

14. Hint $(x+y)^2 = 9xy$

Taking log on both sides, we get

$2\log(x+y)=\log x+\log y+2\log 3$

15. Hint $\because \log m^{\frac{3}{2}}\cdot n^{\frac{2}{3}} = \log 10$

$\Rightarrow m^{\frac{3}{2}}\cdot n^{\frac{2}{3}}=10 \Rightarrow m^{\frac{3}{2}\times 6}\cdot n^{\frac{2}{3}\times 6}=10^6$ **Ans.** 10^6

16. Hint $x+y-z=\log 0.6+\log 1.25-(\log 3-2\log 2)$

$=\log(0.6\times 1.25\times 4)-\log 3$

$=\log\frac{0.6\times 1.25\times 4}{3}=\log\frac{6}{10}\times\frac{125}{100}\times\frac{4}{3}$

$=\log 1 = 0$

$\therefore \quad 5^{x+y-z}=5^0$ **Ans.** 1

17. Hint Given, $x+y=2z$

$\Rightarrow 1+\log 2-\log 5+2\log 3 = 2(\log a - \log 5)$

$\Rightarrow \quad \log 900 = \log a^2$ **Ans.** $a=\pm 30$

18. Hint $\log 3^3 = 1.431$

$\Rightarrow \quad 3\log 3 = 1.431$ $[\because \log m^n = n\log m]$

Now, $\log 9 = \log 3^2 = 2\log 3$

$=2\times\frac{1.431}{3}$ [substituting the value of log 3]

Ans. 0.954

19. Hint $\log_{10}x^3y^4=\log_{10}x^3+\log_{10}y^4$

$=3\log_{10}x+4\log_{10}y$ **Ans.** $11m-n$

20. (i) **Hint** $5^{\log x}+5^{\log x-1}=3^{\log x+1}-3^{\log x}$

$\Rightarrow \quad 5^{\log x}\left[1+\frac{1}{5}\right]=3^{\log x}[3-1]\Rightarrow\left(\frac{5}{3}\right)^{\log x}=\left(\frac{5}{3}\right)^1$

Ans. $x=10$

(ii) **Hint** $\log(3x+2)(3x-2)=\log 2^5$

$\Rightarrow \quad 9x^2-4=32$ **Ans.** $x=2$

(iii) **Hint** We have, $\log_x 49-\log_x 7+\log_x\frac{1}{343}+2=0$

$\Rightarrow \quad 2\log_x 7-\log_x 7-3\log_x 7+2=0$

Ans. $x=7$

(iv) **Hint** $\log(x+2)(x-2)=\log 3\cdot 4^3$

Ans. $x=\pm 14$

(v) **Hint** $\log_3\left[\frac{(3+x)(8-x)}{(9x-8)}\right]=0$ **Ans.** $x=4$

21. Hint Let LHS $=\frac{\log(3)^{3/2}+\log(2)^{3/2}-\log(5)^{3/2}}{\log 6-\log 5}$

$=\frac{\frac{3}{2}[\log 6-\log 5]}{\log 6-\log 5}$

22. Hint $\frac{b^{2x}}{a^{2x+2}}=1\Rightarrow\left(\frac{b}{a}\right)^{2x}=a^2$

Taking log on both sides, we get

$x\log\left(\frac{b}{a}\right)=\log a$

23. Do same as Q. 22.

24. **Hint** $\log 3 + 3\log 2 - \frac{1}{2}(\log 2 + \log 3)$

Ans. 0.99105

25. (i) **Hint** $\log x + \log y = 2$ and $\log x - \log y = 2 - 2\log 2$

Ans. $x = \pm 50,\ y = \pm 2$

(ii) **Hint** $\frac{\log_{10} x}{\log_{10} y} = \frac{3}{2} \Rightarrow \log_{10} x^2 = \log_{10} y^3$

$\Rightarrow x^2 = y^3$

$\Rightarrow x = y^{3/2}$ ...(i)

$\Rightarrow y \cdot y^{3/2} = 10^5$ $[\because xy = 10^5]$

$\Rightarrow y^{1/2} = 10$

$\Rightarrow y = 100$

$\Rightarrow 100x = 10^5$ $[\because xy = 10^5]$

Ans. $x = 1000,\ y = 100$

(iii) **Hint** We have, $\log_{10} x^3 \cdot y^4 = 7$

$\Rightarrow 3\log_{10} x + 4\log_{10} y = 7$ ...(i)

and $\log_{10} \frac{x^2}{y} = 1$

$\Rightarrow 2\log_{10} x - \log_{10} y = 1$ ...(ii)

$\Rightarrow \log_{10} x = 1$ and $\log_{10} y = 1$

$[\because \log_a n = m \Rightarrow a^m = n]$

$\Rightarrow x = (10)^1$ and $y = (10)^1$

Ans. $x = 10$ and $y = 10$

(iv) **Hint** $\frac{\log(x+y)}{\log 2} = \frac{\log 4}{\log(0.5)} \Rightarrow x + y = \frac{1}{4}$ ...(i)

and $\frac{\log(x-y)}{\log 5} = \frac{\log 4}{\log(0.5)} \Rightarrow x - y = \frac{1}{25}$ ...(ii)

On solving Eqs. (i) and (ii), we get the required result.

Ans. $x = \frac{29}{200}$ and $y = \frac{21}{200}$

26. **Hint** $\log_3 \sqrt{6} \times \sqrt{\frac{2}{3}} - \log_3 2 = \log_3 2 - \log_3 2$ **Ans.** 0

27. **Hint** We have, $x^2 + y^2 = 23xy \Rightarrow (x+y)^2 = 25xy$

$\Rightarrow \left(\frac{x+y}{5}\right)^2 = xy$

Taking log on both sides, we get the required result.

28. **Hint** $2x + \log\frac{1}{6} = \log 5 - \log 3$

$\Rightarrow 2x - \log 2 - \log 5 = 0 \Rightarrow 2x = \log 10$

Ans. 10

29. **Hint** $ab = (10)^2 = 100$ and $\log_{10} \frac{a}{b} = 2 - 2\log_{10} 2$

$= 2\log_{10} 10 - 2\log_{10} 2$

$\therefore \log_{10} \frac{a}{b} = 2\log_{10} \frac{10}{2} = 2\log_{10} 5 = \log_{10} 25$

$\therefore \frac{a}{b} = 25$ so, $ab \cdot \frac{a}{b} = 100 \times 25$

Ans. $a = 50,\ b = 2,\ a = -50,\ b = -2$

Common and Natural Logarithm

Common Logarithm

The common logarithm is a logarithm with base10. This system is also called Brigg's system. If no base is given, then the base is always taken as 10.

e.g. $\log 58$ means $\log_{10} 58$

$\therefore \log 100 = \log_{10} 100 = \log_{10} 10^2 = 2\log_{10} 10 = 2$

Natural Logarithm

The natural logarithm is a logarithm with base e. The irrational number e is approximately 2.71828 and e is defined as an irrational number given by

$$e = 1 + \frac{1}{1!} + \frac{1}{2!} + \frac{1}{3!} + \frac{1}{4!} + \dots$$

Natural logarithm of x is represented as $\log_e x$ or $\ln x$.

Decimal Number System

In decimal number system, exponents of 10 start from a maximum value and go on decreasing till 0.

e.g. 46562 can also be written as

$$4 \times 10000 + 6 \times 1000 + 5 \times 100 + 6 \times 10 + 2 \times 1$$

or $4 \times 10^4 + 6 \times 10^3 + 5 \times 10^2 + 6 \times 10^1 + 2 \times 10^0$

It is also called **expanded form** of a number.

EXAMPLE 1. Write expanded form of the following numbers.

(i) 2638 (ii) 69170 (iii) 56439

Sol. (i) $2638 = 2 \times 1000 + 6 \times 100 + 3 \times 10 + 8 \times 1$
$= 2 \times 10^3 + 6 \times 10^2 + 3 \times 10^1 + 8 \times 10^0$

(ii) $69170 = 6 \times 10000 + 9 \times 1000 + 1 \times 100 + 7 \times 10 + 0 \times 1$
$= 6 \times 10^4 + 9 \times 10^3 + 1 \times 10^2 + 7 \times 10^1 + 0 \times 10^0$

(iii) $56439 = 5 \times 10000 + 6 \times 1000 + 4 \times 100 + 3 \times 10 + 9 \times 1$
$= 5 \times 10^4 + 6 \times 10^3 + 4 \times 10^2 + 3 \times 10^1 + 9 \times 10^0$

EXAMPLE 2. Find the number from following expanded forms.

(i) $2\times10^5+5\times10^3+6\times10^2+2\times10^0$

(ii) $3\times10^6+4\times10^4+6\times10^2+4\times10^1$

Sol. (i) We have, $2\times10^5+5\times10^3+6\times10^2+2\times10^0$

$$= 2\times100000+5\times1000+6\times100+2\times1$$
$$= 205602$$

(ii) We have, $3\times10^6+4\times10^4+6\times10^2+4\times10^1$

$$= 3\times1000000+4\times10000+6\times100+4\times10$$
$$= 3040640$$

Expressing Large Numbers in the Standard Form

A number is said to be in the **standard form** when it is written as $k\times10^n$, where $1\le k<10$ and n is an integer.

Standard form is also called **scientific notation.**

To write very small or very large numbers in standard form. There are two cases arise

Case I

When decimal moved to right i.e. very small number

EXAMPLE 3. Express 0.00000532 in standard form.

Sol. To express 0.00000532 in standard form.

Firstly, count the number of decimal places you need to move.

Here, we need to move the decimal point by 6 places.

1 2 3 4 5 6
0.00000532

Decimal is moved 6 places to the right.

We would write it as 5.32

i.e. $1<5.32<10$

Now, determine the power of 10 required. Decimal is moved to 6 places right which means that we need to multiply by 10^{-6}.

So, in standard form 0.00000532 can be expressed as 5.32×10^{-6}.

Case II

When decimal moved to left i.e. very large number

EXAMPLE 4. Express 5329800000 in standard form.

Sol. To express 5329800000 in standard form.

First, count the number of decimal place.

9 8 7 6 5 4 3 2 1
5 329800000

Write it as $1<5.3298<10$.

Secondly, decimal is moved to 9 places left which means that we need to multiply by 10^9.

So, the standard form will be 5.3298×10^9.

EXAMPLE 5. Express the following numbers in usual form.

(i) 6.671×10^5 (ii) 5.332×10^{-6}

Sol. (i) We have, $6.671\times10^5=6.671\times100000$

$$=667100$$

(ii) We have, $5.332\times10^{-6}=\frac{5.332}{10^6}=\frac{5.332}{1000000}$

$$=0.000005332$$

Characteristics and Mantissa of a Logarithm

Let n be a positive real number and let the standard form of n be $m\times10^P$, where P is an integer and m is a real number lying in the interval $[1, 10)$ i.e. $1\le m<10$

Then, $n=m\times10^P$

$$\Rightarrow \log n=\log(m\times10^P)=\log m+\log10^P$$
$$=\log m+P\log10$$
$$=P+\log m \qquad [\because \log 10=1]$$

$\because \quad 1\le m<10$

$\Rightarrow \log1\le\log m<\log10 \Rightarrow 0\le\log m<1$

Thus, the logarithm of a positive real number n consists of two parts.

(i) Integral part P which is called characteristics and it may be negative, zero or positive.

(ii) $\log m$, the decimal part which is called mantissa and which is zero or a positive number less than 1.

$\therefore$ **log n = Characteristics + Mantissa**

Characteristics (Integer Part of a Number)

(i) If the given number is greater than or equal to 1, then characteristics = (number of digits to the left of decimal point) − 1

(ii) If the given number is less than 1, then characteristics = − (number of zeroes just after the decimal + 1)

Mantissa (Fractional Number Part of a Number)

The logarithm table is used to find the mantissa of logarithms of numbers. It consists of 90 rows and 20 columns.Every row begins with a two-digit number 10, 11, 12, ..., 99 and every column is headed by a one-digit number 0, 1, 2, ..., 9. On the right of the table, we have a big column which is divided into 9 sub-columns headed by the digits 1, 2, 3, ... 9. This column is called the column of mean differences.

How to Determine Mantissa

For finding the mantissa and position of the decimal point in a number, there are following steps are used.

Step I For mantissa, take a number formed by first four digits by using log table.

Step II Read logarithmic table in a horizontal line lead by the first two figures and in the vertical column headed by the third figure. Note down the number written at this place, then read in the same horizontal line, the number written in the mean difference column headed by the fourth figure and add it to the previous number. Sum of these two gives the required mantissa.

Step III If the given number has only one digit, we replace it by a two-digit number obtained by adjoining zero to the right of the number. Thus, 5 is to be replaced by 50, for finding the mantissa.

Step IV If there are more than four significant figures,we shall consider only first four and approximate the fourth with the help of the fifth.

EXAMPLE 6. Find the value of $\log 25.795$.

Sol. $\because 25.795 > 1$ and there are two digits to the left of the decimal point.

So, characteristics of $\log 25.795$ is $2 - 1$ i.e. 1.

Now for mantissa, take the number formed by first four digits. The number formed by the first four digits is 2579. Now in the row starting with 25 look at the number in the column headed by 7. The number is 4099.

Now, read across the same row 25 and down the column 9 of mean difference, we get 15. On adding 4099 and 15, we get 4114. This is the required mantissa.

$\therefore \quad \log 25.795 = 1.4114$

EXAMPLE 7. Find the value of $\log 8.39$.

Sol. The number 8.39 can be written as 8.390

$\because 8.390 > 1$ and there is one digit to the left of the decimal point. So, characteristics of $\log 8390$ is $1 - 1$ i.e. 0.

Now, for mantissa, take the number formed by first four digits. The number is 8.390.

Now, in the row starting with 83 look at the number in the column headed by 9, we get 9238.

$\therefore \quad \log 8.39 = 0.9238$

EXAMPLE 8. Find the value of $\log 0.00003568$.

Sol. $\because 0.00003568 < 1$, so characteristics of $\log 0.00003568$ is $-(4+1)$ i.e. -5

Now for mantissa, take the number 3568. Now in the row starting with 35 look at the number in the column headed by 6, we get 5514.

Now, read across the same row 35 and down the column 8 of mean difference, we get 10.

On adding 5514 and 10, we get 5524

$\therefore \quad \log 0.00003568 = -5 + 5524 = \bar{5}.5524$

Antilogarithm

Consider, $y = \log x$

Here, x is called antilogarithm of y and it is written as $x = \text{antilog } y$.

To find the antilog of a given number, we use the antilogarithm table in which left most column consists of numbers from 0.00 to 0.99, which is followed by 10 columns in which numbers 0, 1, 2, 3, 4, 5, 6, 7, 8, 9 are written at the top.

These 10 columns are further followed by 9 more columns of mean difference in which numbers 1, 2, 3, 4, 5, 6, 7, 8, 9 are written at the top.

How to Determine Antilogarithms

To find antilogarithms of y i.e. x, when $\log x$ is given, we use only the mantissa part. The characteristic is used only in determining the number of digits in the integral part or the number of zeroes on the right side of the decimal point in the required number.

How to Find Antilogarithm of a Given Number

Step I Write the given numbers.

Step II If the decimal part of the given number is negative, then make it positive by adding 1 to the decimal part and subtracting 1 from the integral part.

e.g. In -2.5983, the decimal part -0.5983 is negative, now we have to make it positive in the following way.

$$-2.5983 = -2 - 0.5983 = -2 - 1 + 1 - 0.5983$$
$$= -3 + 0.4017$$
$$= \bar{3}.4017$$

Step III Now look into the row containing the first two digits in the decimal part of the given number.

Step IV Now in the same row, look at the number in the column headed by the third digit in the decimal part.

Step V Now again in the same row, move in the column mean differences and look at the number in the column headed by the fourth digit in the decimal part. Add this number to the number obtained in step 4.

Step VI Now if the integral part (characteristic) of the given number is positive and is equal to x, then insert a decimal point after $(n+1)$ digits in the number obtained in step 5.

If $n > 4$, then write zeroes on the right side to get $(n+1)$ digits and if the characteristic is negative and is equal to $-n$ or $\bar{n}$, then on the right side of decimal point, write $(n-1)$ consecutive zeros and then write the number obtained in step 5.

EXAMPLE 9. Find antilog 2.1647.

Sol. The decimal part of 2.1647 is positive and is equal to 0.1647.

In antilog table, look into the row starting with 0.16. In this row, look at the number in the column headed by 4. The number is 1459.

Now, read across the same row 0.16 and down the column 7 of mean difference, we get 2.

On adding 1459 and 2, we get 1461.

$\because$ The integral part is 2 which is positive. So, the decimal point is put after 2 + 1 i.e. 3 digits from the left of 1461.

$\therefore$ antilog 2.1647 = 146.1

EXAMPLE 10. If $\log x = \bar{3}.4856$, then find x.

Sol. Given, $\log x = \bar{3}.4856 \Rightarrow x = \text{antilog } \bar{3}.4856$

The decimal part of $\bar{3}.4856$ is positive and is equal to 0.4856

In antilog table, look into the row starting with 0.48. In this row, look at the number in the column headed by 5. The number is 3055.

Now, read across the same row 0.48 and down the column 6 of mean difference, we get 4.

On adding 3055 and 4, we get 3059.

$\because$ The integral is $\bar{3}$ i.e. – 3, which is negative.

So, write 3 – 1 i.e. 2 zeros on the right side of the decimal point.

$\therefore x = \text{antilog } \bar{3}.4856 = 0.003059$

EXAMPLE 11. Find antilog (– 2.4325).

Sol. The decimal part of – 2.4325 is negative. So, we first make it positive as follows

$$-2.4325 = -2 - 0.4325 = -2 - 1 + 1 - 0.4325$$
$$= -3 + 0.5675 = \bar{3}.5675$$

Now, the decimal part of $\bar{3}.5675$ is positive and is equal to 0.5675.

In antilog table, look into the row starting with 0.56. In this row, look at the number in the column headed by 7. The number is 3690.

Now, read across the same row 0.56 and down the column 5 of mean difference, we get 4.

On adding 3690 and 4, we get 3694.

$\because$ The interest part is $\bar{3}$ i.e. – 3, which is negative.

So, write 3 – 1 i.e. 2 zeros on the right side of the decimal point.

$\therefore$ antilog (– 2.4325) = 0.003694

Application of Logarithms

log tables can be used to evaluate numerical expressions.

EXAMPLE 12. Using log table, evaluate $3.423 \times 27.74 \times 9.32$

Sol. Let $x = 3.423 \times 27.74 \times 9.32$

Now, taking log of both sides, we get

$$\log x = \log(3.423 \times 27.74 \times 9.32)$$
$$\Rightarrow \log x = \log 3.423 + \log 27.74 + \log 9.32$$
$$\Rightarrow \log x = 0.5344 + 1.4431 + 0.9694 = 2.9469$$
$$\Rightarrow x = \text{antilog } (2.9469) \Rightarrow x = 884.9$$

Hence, $3.423 \times 27.74 \times 9.32 = 884.9$.

EXAMPLE 13. Using log table, evaluate $(0.009)^{1/3}$.

Sol. Let $x = (0.009)^{1/3}$

Now, taking log of both sides, we get

$$\log x = \log(0.009)^{1/3}$$
$$= \frac{1}{3}\log(0.009) = \frac{1}{3}(\bar{3}.9542)$$
$$\log x = \frac{-3 + 0.9542}{3}$$
$$= -1 + 0.3187 = \bar{1}.3187$$
$$\Rightarrow x = \text{antilog } (\bar{1}.3187) = 0.2083$$

Hence, $(0.009)^{1/3} = 0.2083$

EXAMPLE 14. Using log table, evaluate $\sqrt[3]{\dfrac{(45.4)^2}{(3.2)^2 \times (5.6)^3}}$.

Sol. Let $x = \sqrt[3]{\dfrac{(45.4)^2}{(3.2)^2 \times (5.6)^3}}$

Now, taking log of both sides, we get

$$\log x = \log \sqrt[3]{\frac{(45.4)^2}{(3.2)^2 \times (5.6)^3}} = \log \left\{\frac{(45.4)^2}{(3.2)^2 \times (5.6)^3}\right\}^{1/3}$$
$$\Rightarrow \log x = \frac{1}{3}\log \left\{\frac{(45.4)^2}{(3.2)^2 \times (5.6)^3}\right\}$$
$$= \frac{1}{3}[\log(45.4)^2 - \log\{(3.2)^2 \times (5.6)^3\}]$$
$$\Rightarrow \log x = \frac{1}{3}[2\log(45.4) - \log(3.2)^2 - \log(5.6)^3]$$
$$= \frac{1}{3}[2 \times 1.6571 - 2\log 3.2 - 3\log 5.6]$$

$\Rightarrow \log x = \frac{1}{3}[3.3142 - 2 \times 0.5051 - 3 \times 0.7482]$

$\Rightarrow \log x = \frac{1}{3}[3.3142 - 1.0102 - 2.2446]$

$= \frac{1}{3}(0.0594)$

$= 0.0198$

$\Rightarrow \quad x = \text{antilog}\,(0.0198) = 1.047$

Hence, $\sqrt[3]{\frac{(45.4)^2}{(3.2)^2 \times (5.6)^3}} = 1.047$

EXAMPLE 15. The present population of a country is 9261000. If it has been increasing at the rate of 3% annually, what was its population 3 years ago?

Sol. Let P_0 be the population 3 years ago.

Here, $P = 9261000$, $r = 3$ and $n = 3$

We know that $P = P_0\left(1 + \frac{r}{100}\right)^n$

$\Rightarrow \quad 9261000 = P_0\left(1 + \frac{3}{100}\right)^3$

$\Rightarrow \quad 9261000 = P_0\left(\frac{103}{100}\right)^3$

$\Rightarrow \quad P_0 = \frac{9261000 \times (100)^3}{(103)^3}$

$= \frac{9261 \times 10^9}{(103)^3}$

$\Rightarrow \quad \log P_0 = \log\left\{\frac{9261 \times 10^9}{(103)^3}\right\}$

$= \log 9261 + 9 \log 10 - 3 \log 103$

$\Rightarrow \quad \log P_0 = 3.9667 + 9 - 3(2.0128)$

$= 12.9667 - 6.0384 = 6.9283$

$\Rightarrow \quad P_0 = \text{Antilog}\,(6.9283)0$

$= 8476000$

Hence, its population was 8476000.

EXAMPLE 16. The value of a xerox machine depreciates by 11% annually. If its present value is 38440, then find its value 3 years ago.

Sol. Let V_0 be the value of xerox machine 3 years ago.

We know that $V = V_0\left(1 - \frac{r}{100}\right)^n$

Then, $\quad 38440 = V_0\left(1 - \frac{11}{100}\right)^3$

$\Rightarrow \quad 38440 = V_0\left(\frac{89}{100}\right)^3$

$\Rightarrow \quad \log 38440 = \log V_0 + 3(\log 89 - \log 100)$

$\Rightarrow \quad 4.5848 = \log V_0 + 3(1.9494 - 2)$

$\Rightarrow \quad \log V_0 = 4.5848 - 3(1.9494 - 2)$

$\Rightarrow \quad \log V_0 = 4.433$

$\Rightarrow \quad V_0 = \text{antilog}\,(4.433)$

$= 27102$

Hence, the value of the machine 3 years ago was ₹ 27102.

Topic Practice 2

1 Express each of the following number in the standard form of decimal.

(i) 35.7 (ii) 0.0029
(iii) 31230.5 (iv) 328.59
(v) 17.143

2 Evaluate the following.

(i) $\log 2$ (ii) $\log 7.89$
(iii) $\log 2.5795$ (iv) $\log 5.3498$
(v) $\log 12.70$ (vi) $\log 0.000425$
(vii) $\log 0.0074$ (viii) $\log 0.005$ (ix) $\log(0.053498)$
(x) $\log 0.3582$

3 Find x in each of the following.

(i) $\log x = 2.7523$ (ii) $\log x = 2.7671$
(iii) $\log x = \bar{3}.7523$ (iv) $\log x = \bar{2}.7523$
(v) $\log x = -1.2084$

4 Using log tables evaluate the following.

(i) $\frac{(42.87)^{1/2} \times 84.9}{0.234}$ (ii) 0.0064×1.507

(iii) $\sqrt{\frac{31.67 \times 42.36}{9.25}}$ (iv) $\sqrt[4]{0.6789}$

(v) $\sqrt[3]{\frac{31.42 \times 7.192}{(0.236)^2}}$

5 The population of a town at the beginning of the year 2019 was 265000. If the rate of increase be 52 per thousand of the population, then find the population at the beginning of the year 2024.

6 The value of a machine depreciates 10% annually. Its present value is ₹ 45540. Find its value 5 years ago.

Hints & Solutions

1. (i) **Hint** Shift the decimal point 1 place to the left.
Ans. 3.57×10^1

(ii) **Hint** Shift the decimal point 3 place to the right.
Ans. 2.9×10^{-3}

(iii) **Hint** Shift the decimal point 4 place to the left.
Ans. 3.12305×10^4

(iv) **Hint** Shift the decimal point 2 place to the left.
Ans. 3.2859×10^2

(v) **Hint** Shift the decimal point 1 place to the left.
Ans. 1.7143×10^1

2. (i) **Hint** 2 can be written as 2.000
Characteristics of log 2.000 is 0 and required mantissa is 3010. **Ans.** 0.3010

(ii) **Hint** $7.98 > 1$
Characteristics of log7.98 is 0 and required mantissa is 8971. **Ans.** 0.8971

(iii) **Hint** $2.5795 > 1$
Characteristics of log 2.5795 is 0 and required mantissa is 4114. **Ans.** 0.4114

(iv) **Hint** Characteristics of log5.3498 is 0 and required mantissa is 7283. **Ans.** 0.7283

(v) **Hint** Characteristics of log12.70 is 1 and required mantissa is 1038. **Ans.** 1.1038

(vi) **Hint** $0.000425 < 1$
Characteristics of log0.0000425 is -4 and required mantissa is 6284. **Ans.** $\bar{4}.6284$

(vii) **Hint** $0.000425 < 1$
Characteristics of log0.0074 is -3 and required mantissa is 8692. **Ans.** $\bar{3}.8692$

(viii) **Hint** Characteristics of log0.005 is -3 and required mantissa is 6990. **Ans.** $\bar{3}.6990$

(ix) **Hint** Characteristics of log(0.053498) is -2 and required mantissa is 7283. **Ans.** $\bar{2}.7283$

(x) **Hint** Characteristics of log0.3582 is -1 and required mantissa is 5541. **Ans.** $\bar{1}.5541$

3. (i) **Hint** $x = \text{antilog}\,(2.7523)$
The decimal part of 2.7523 is 0.7523
Now, look into the row starting with 0.75
The decimal point is put after $2+1$ i.e. 3 digits from the left of number obtained. **Ans.** 565.3

(ii) **Hint** $x = \text{antilog}\,(2.7671)$
The decimal part of 2.7671 is 0.7671
Now, look into the row starting with 0.76
The decimal point is put after $2+1$ i.e. 3 digits from the left of number obtained.
Ans. 584.9

(iii) **Hint** $x = \text{antilog}\,(\bar{3}.7523)$
The decimal part of $\bar{3}.7523$ is 0.7523
Now, look into the row starting with 0.75
The integral part is $\bar{3}$ i.e. -3, so write $3-1$ i.e. 2 zeroes on the right side of the decimal point. **Ans.** 0.005653

(iv) **Hint** $x = \text{antilog}\,(\bar{2}.7523)$
The decimal part of $\bar{2}.7523$ is 0.7523
Now, look into the row starting with 0.75
The integral part is $\bar{2}$ i.e. -2, so write $2-1$ i.e. 1 zero on the right side of the decimal point. **Ans.** 0.05653

(v) **Hint** First make the decimal part of -1.2084 positive as follows

$$-1.2084 = -1 - 0.2084 = -1 - 1 + 1 - 0.2084$$
$$= -2 + 0.7916 = \bar{2}.7916$$

Now, the decimal part of $\bar{2}.7916$ in 0.7916, look into the row starting with 0.79.
The integral part is $\bar{2}$ i.e. -2, so write $2-1$ i.e. 1 zero on the right side of the decimal point.
Ans. 0.06189

4. (i) **Hint** Let $x = \dfrac{(42.87)^{1/2} \times 84.9}{0.234}$

$$\Rightarrow \quad \log = \frac{1}{2}\log(42.87) + \log(84.9) - \log(0.234)$$

Ans. 3.3748

(ii) **Hint** Let $x = 0.0064 \times 1.507$

$\Rightarrow \quad \log x = \log(0.0064) + \log(1.507)$ **Ans.** 0.009645

(iii) **Hint** Let $x = \sqrt{\dfrac{31.67 \times 42.36}{9.25}}$

$$\Rightarrow \quad \log x = \frac{1}{2}[\log 31.67 + \log 42.36 - \log 9.25]$$

Ans. 12.04

(iv) **Hint** Let $x = \sqrt[4]{0.6789} \Rightarrow \log x = \dfrac{1}{4}\log(0.6789)$

Ans. 0.9076

(v) **Hint** Let $x = \sqrt[3]{\dfrac{31.42 \times 7.192}{(0.236)^2}}$

$$\log x = \frac{1}{3}[\log 31.42 + \log 7.192 - 2\log 0.236]$$

Ans. 15.95

5. **Hint** r = Rate of increase $= \left(\dfrac{52}{1000} \times 100\right) = 5.2\%$,
$n = 5$, $P_0 = 265000$
Let the population at the beginning of 2024 be P.
Then, use the formula, $P = P_0\left(1 + \dfrac{r}{100}\right)^n$ **Ans.** 341400

6. Solve as Example 26. **Ans.** ₹ 77001.64 ≈ ₹ 77002

Exam Pattern Exercise

Part A - Objective Type Questions

Multiple Choice Type Questions

1 Find the value of x, when $\log(97+\sqrt{x^2-16})=2$

(a) 5 and –7 (b) 2 and –5
(c) –5 and 5 (d) –2 and –5

2 Simplify $\log_{10}\frac{a^2}{\sqrt{b}}$ in terms of $\log_{10}a$, $\log_{10}b$.

(a) $2\log_{10}a-\frac{1}{2}\log_{10}b$ (b) $2\log_{10}a-\log_{10}b$
(c) $2\log_{10}a-2\log_{10}b$ (d) $\frac{1}{2}\log_{10}a-2\log_{10}b$

3 If $\frac{\log a}{b-c}=\frac{\log b}{c-a}=\frac{\log c}{a-b}$, then $a^a\cdot b^b\cdot c^c$ is

(a) 1 (b) 0
(c) –1 (d) 3

4 Value of b^2 if $\frac{1}{\log_a n}+\frac{1}{\log_c n}=\frac{2}{\log_b n}$, is

(a) nb (b) an
(c) ab (d) ac

5 Solve $\log_5 2\times\log_2 5$

(a) –1 (b) 2
(c) 0 (d) 1

6 The value of $\log_{\sqrt{2}}4$ is

(a) 4 (b) 3
(c) 5 (d) 6

7 If $\log_9 x=2.5$, then value of x is

(a) 343 (b) 400
(c) 243 (d) 441

8 $\log_2 7$ is a/an

(a) rational number (b) irrational number
(c) imaginary number (d) whole number

9 If $\log 3=0.4771$, then value of $\log 9+\log 81$ is

(a) 1.9272 (b) 3.4145
(c) 2.8627 (d) 3.6284

10 $4\log_{10}5+2\log_{10}4$ is

(a) 5 (b) 4
(c) 6 (d) 3

11 If $y^2=xz$ and $a^x=b^y=c^z$, then

(a) $\log a=\log b$ (b) $\log_a b=\log_b c$
(c) $\log_b a=\log_c b$ (d) $\log(ab)=\log(bc)$

12 $\log_4(2x+3)=\frac{3}{2}$, then the value of x is

(a) $\frac{3}{2}$ (b) $\frac{9}{2}$ (c) $\frac{7}{2}$ (d) $\frac{5}{2}$

13 The characteristic of 0.004321 is

(a) – 4 (b) –1
(c) – 3 (d) – 5

14 The antilog of $\bar{3}\cdot 2645$ is

(a) 0.01839 (b) 0.001839
(c) 0.1839 (d) 1.839

15 If $x^{10}=5$, then value of x is

(a) 1.174 (b) 2.05
(c) 2.162 (d) 1.628

Assertion-Reason Based Questions

Directions (Q. Nos. 16-18) *In the questions given below are two statements labelled as Assertion (A) and Reason (R). In the context of the two statements, which one of the following is correct?*

(a) Both A and R are correct; R is the correct explanation of A
(b) Both A and R are correct; R is not the correct explanation of A
(c) A is correct; R is incorrect
(d) R is correct; A is incorrect

16 **Assertion (A)** If $\log_4 64=5x+7$, then value of x is $-\frac{4}{5}$.

Reason (R) $\log x=\log y \Rightarrow x=y$

17 **Assertion (A)** If $1563(1+x)^8=1624$, then $x=0.12$.

Reason (R) $\log_a\sqrt{x}=\frac{1}{2}\log_a x$

18 **Assertion (A)** $\log_8 x+\log_8(x+6)=\log_8(5x+12)$.
Then, $x=-4, 3$

Reason (R) The value of $49^{(1-\log_7 2)}+5^{-\log_5 4}$.

Part B - Descriptive Questions

Very Short Answer Type Questions

19 If $\log_{0.5}64=x$, then find the value of x.

20 Write the standard form of 0.0001359.

21 Write the characteristic of $\log 0.0003798$.

Short Answer Type Questions

22 Simplify $\left(\frac{81}{16}\right)^{\frac{-3}{4}} \times \left[\left(\frac{25}{9}\right)^{\frac{-3}{2}} \div \left(\frac{5}{2}\right)^{-3}\right]$.

23 Find the value of $\frac{4}{(216)^{-\frac{2}{3}}} + \frac{1}{(256)^{-\frac{3}{4}}} + \frac{2}{(243)^{-\frac{1}{3}}}$.

24 Find the value of x, in each of the following

(i) $\log_2 x = 5$ (ii) $\log_4 x = 2.5$

(iii) $\log_{64} x = \frac{2}{3}$

25 Solve for x, $\log_2 x + \log_4 x + \log_{16} x = \frac{21}{4}$.

26 Using log table, evaluate $\frac{76.03 \times 9.08}{101.2 \times 63.17}$.

Long Answer Type Questions

27 Simplify the following

(i) $(3x^4y^3)(18x^3y^5)$ (ii) $\frac{3x^4y^3}{18x^3y^5}$

(iii) $\left(-\frac{2x^2}{y^3}\right)^3$ (iv) $\sqrt[3]{27^{-2}}$

(v) $\left[\{(625)^{-\frac{1}{2}}\}^{-\frac{1}{4}}\right]^2$

28 Evaluate the following

(i) $\left(5\frac{1}{16}\right)^{-\frac{3}{4}}$ (ii) $\sqrt[4]{\sqrt[3]{2^2}}$

(iii) $\sqrt[3]{2} \cdot \sqrt[4]{2} \cdot \sqrt[12]{32}$ (iv) $\sqrt[4]{(81)^{-2}}$

(v) $(256)^{0.16} \times (256)^{0.09}$

29 Find the value of the following (by converting to exponential form)

(i) $\log_2 16$ (ii) $\log_{16} 2$

(iii) $\log_3 \frac{1}{3}$ (iv) $\log_{\sqrt{2}} 8$

(v) $\log_5(0.008)$

30 Using log table, evaluate the following

(i) $\log 6$ (ii) $\log 30$

(iii) $\log 76$ (iv) $\log 0.0007$

(v) $\log 0.05812$

31 Using log table, evaluate

(i) $\frac{(5.364)^3 \times (49.76)^{1/2}}{(83.45)^{1/3}}$ (ii) $(57.8)^{1/2} \times (0.0027)^{1/3}$

32 Simplify $\frac{\log\sqrt{27} + \log 64 + \log\sqrt{1000}}{\log 480}$.

33 If $x = (100)^a$, $y = (10000)^b$ and $z = (10)^c$, then express $\log\left(\frac{10\sqrt{y}}{x^2z^3}\right)$ in terms of a, b and c.

Case Study Based Questions

34 If a is any positive real number $(a \neq 1)$ and m is any rational number and n be any real number such that $a^m = n$, then $m = \log_a n$, where m is called logarithm of n to the base a

Three standard laws of logarithm are

I. Product law

$$\log_a(m \cdot n \cdot p....) = \log_a m + \log_a n + \log_a p + ...$$

II. Quotient Law

$$\log_a \frac{m}{n} = \log_a m - \log_a n$$

III. Power law

$$\log_a m^n = n \log_a m$$

Based on the above information, answer the following questions.

(i) Express $\log_{10} \frac{a^2c}{\sqrt{b}}$ in terms of $\log_{10} a$, $\log_{10} b$, $\log_{10} c$.

(ii) Evaluate $3 + \log_{10}(10)^{-2}$.

(iii) Evaluate $\frac{\log 125}{\log\sqrt{5}}$.

Or

Evaluate $\log_6 72 - \log_6 2$.

35 Logarithm of a positive real number n has two parts

I. **Characteristics** It is an integral part of $\log n$ which may be negative, zero or positive.

If n is greater than or equal to 1, then

Characteristics = Number of digits to the left of decimal − 1

If n is less than 1, then

Characteristics = − (Number of 0 's just after the decimal + 1)

II. **Mantissa** It is positive fractional part of $\log n$. It is same for same significant figures in the same order and does not depend on the position of the decimal point.

Based on the above information, answer the following questions.

(i) If $\log 2.378 = 0.3762$, then find $\log 237.8$.

(ii) If $\log 0.0004598 = \bar{4}.6626$, then find $\log 45.98$.

(iii) If $\log 6832 = 3.8345$, then find $\log 0.06832$.

Or

If $\log 712.5 = 2.8528$ and $\log x = \bar{3}.8528$, then find the value of x.

Hints & Solutions

1. (c)	2. (a)	3. (a)	4. (d)
5. (d)	6. (a)	7. (c)	8. (b)
9. (c)	10. (b)	11. (c)	12. (d)
13. (c)	14. (b)	15. (a)	16. (b)
17. (c)	18. (b)		

19. -6

20. 1.359×10^{-4}

21. $\bar{4}$

22. **Hint** $\left\{\left(\frac{3}{2}\right)^4\right\}^{\frac{-3}{4}} \times \left[\left\{\left(\frac{5}{3}\right)^2\right\}^{\frac{-3}{2}} \div \left(\frac{5}{2}\right)^{-3}\right]$

$$= \left(\frac{3}{2}\right)^{-3} \times \left(\frac{5}{3}\right)^{-3} \times \left(\frac{2}{5}\right)^{-3}$$

Ans. 1

23. **Hint** $4 \times (216)^{\frac{2}{3}} + (256)^{\frac{3}{4}} + 2 \times (243)^{\frac{1}{5}}$

Ans. 214

24. (i) 32 (ii) 32 (iii) 16

25. 8

26. 0.2163

27. (i) $54x^7y^8$ (ii) $\frac{x}{6y^2}$ (iii) $-\frac{8x^6}{y^9}$
(iv) $\frac{1}{9}$ (v) 5

28. (i) $\frac{8}{27}$ (ii) $2^{1/6}$ (iii) 2
(iv) $\frac{1}{9}$ (v) 4

29. (i) **Hint** Let us consider $\log_2 16 = x$

$$2^x = 16$$

Ans. 4

(ii) Do same as part (i). **Ans.** $\frac{1}{4}$

(iii) Do same as part (i). **Ans.** -1

(iv) Do same as part (i). **Ans.** 6

(v) Do same as part (i). **Ans.** -3

30. (i) 0.7782 (ii) 1.4771 (iii) 1.8808
(iv) $\bar{4}.8451$ (v) $\bar{2}.7643$

31. (i) 249.1 (ii) 1.059

32. **Hint** $\dfrac{\frac{3}{2}\log 3 + 6\log 2 + \frac{3}{2}[\log 2 + \log 5]}{5\log 2 + \log 15}$

Ans. $\frac{3}{2}$

33. **Hint** $\log\dfrac{10\sqrt{y}}{x^2z^3} = \log 10 + \frac{1}{2}\log y - 2\log x - 3\log z$

$$= 1 + \frac{1}{2}\log(10000)^b - 2\log(100)^a - 3\log(10)$$

Ans. $-4a + 2b - 3c + 1$

34. (i) $2\log_{10} a + \log_{10} c - \frac{1}{2}\log_{10} b$
(ii) 1 (iii) 6 *Or* 2

35. (i) 2.3762 (ii) 1.6626 (iii) 2.8345 *Or* 0.007125

CHAPTER 04

Clock and Calendar

In this Chapter...

- Clock
- Calendar

Clock

A clock is an instrument which displays time divided into hours, minutes and seconds.

A clock mainly consists of four components.

Dial

A clock is a circular dial. The periphery of the dial is numbered 1 to 12 indicating the hours in a 12 h cycle. The circumference of a dial is divided into 60 equal spaces called minute spaces and 12 equal spaces called hour spaces. Every clock has mainly two hands, one is smaller and other is bigger. The smaller hand is slower and the bigger hand is faster.

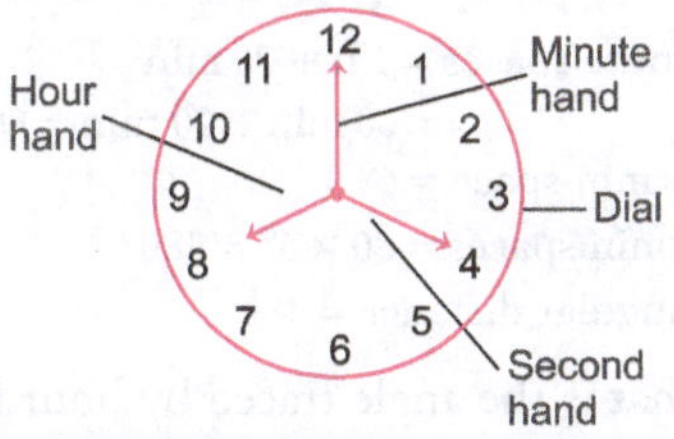

Hour Hand

The smaller or slower hand of a clock is called the hour hand. It makes two revolutions in a day.

Minute Hand

The bigger or faster hand of a clock is called the minute hand. It makes one revolution in every hour.

Second Hand

Second hand indicates seconds on a circular dial. It makes one revolution per minute.

Note In 1 h, minute hand covers 60 min spaces whereas the hour hand covers 5 min spaces.
Therefore, minute hand gains (60 – 5) = 55 min in 1 h.

Important Points Related to Clock

1. In 1 h, both hands coincide once (i.e. 0° apart)

   e.g. Between 3 and 4 O' clock, hands are together as shown in adjacent figure.

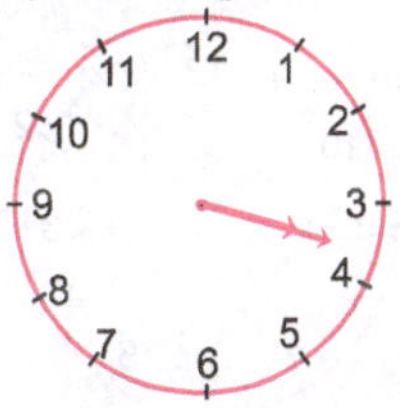

2. In 12 h, both hands coincide 11 times (between 11 and 1 O' clock they coincide once) and in a day both hands coincide 22 times.

   e.g. Between 11 and 1 O' clock, hands are together as shown in adjacent figure.

3. If two hands are at 90°, they are 15 min spaces apart. This happens twice in 1 h. In a period of 12 h, the hands are at right angle 22 times (2 common positions) and in a day both hands are at right angle 44 times.

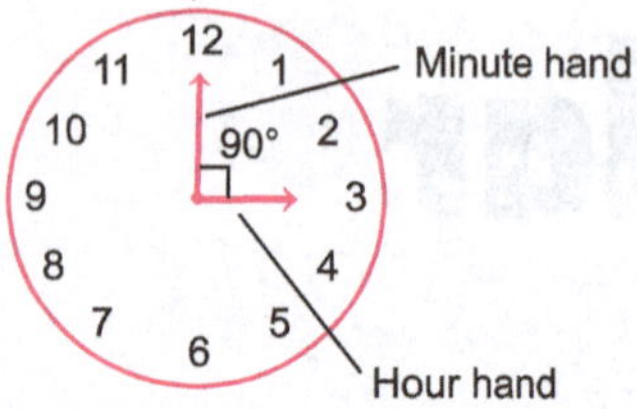

4. If two hands are in opposite direction. (i.e. 180° apart), then they are 30 min spaces apart. This happens once in 1 h. In a period of 12 h both hands are in opposite direction 11 times and in a day both hands are in opposite direction 22 times.

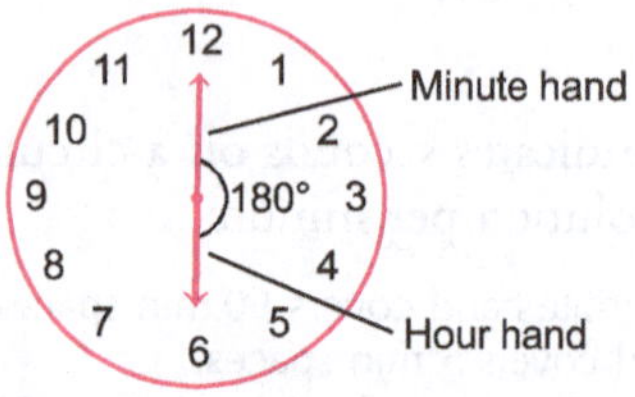

5. Angle covered by minute hand in 1 min

$$= \frac{\text{Total angle}}{\text{Number of spaces}}$$

$$= \frac{360°}{60} = 6° \text{ in } 1 \text{ min}$$

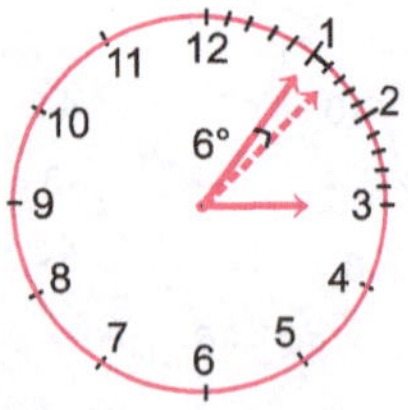

6. Angle covered by hour hand in 1 min.
As hour hand covers 360° in 12 h. Hence, hour hand covers $\left(\frac{360°}{12}\right) = 30°$ in 1 h

Hence, hour hand covers $\left(\frac{30°}{60}\right) = \frac{1°}{2}$ in 1 min

7. From point 5 and 6, we can say that the minute hand goes ahead by $5\frac{1°}{2}$ in comparison to hour hand.

Slow or Fast Clocks

If a watch/clock indicates 9 : 15, when the correct time is 9, then it is said to be 15 min fast. On the other hand, if the watch/clock indicates 6 : 45, when the correct time is 7, then it is said to be 15 min slow.

EXAMPLE 1. What will be angle between the two hands of a clock at 9:50?

Sol. $\because$ Angle traced by the hour hand in 12 h = 360°

$\therefore$ Angle traced by the hour hand in 1 h = $\frac{360°}{12}$

and angle traced by the hour hand in 9 h 50 min

i.e. $\frac{59}{6}$ h $= \frac{360°}{12} \times \frac{59}{6} = 295°$

Similarly,

$\because$ Angle traced by the minute hand in 60 min = 360°

$\therefore$ Angle traced by minute hand in 50 min $= \frac{360°}{60} \times 50$

$= 300°$

$\therefore$ Required angle = 300° − 295° = 5°

EXAMPLE 2. A clock gains 10 s in every 3 h. If the clock was set right at 4:00 am on Monday morning, then what time it will indicate on Tuesday evening at 7:00 pm?

Sol. Difference of time between 4:00 am on Monday to 7:00 pm Tuesday = 24 + 12 + 3 = 39 h

Now, time gained by clock in 3 h = 10 s

Time gained by clock in 1 h = $\frac{10}{3}$ s

and time gained by clock in 39 h = $\frac{10 \times 39}{3} = 130$ s

The clock will show 7 : 02 : 10 pm.

EXAMPLE 3. When the minute hand covers a distance of 1h 20 min, then what is the angular distance covered by it?

Sol. Total minute spaces = 1 h + 20 min

= 60 min + 20 min = 80 min

$\because$ 1 min space = 6°

$\therefore$ 80 min spaces = 80 × 6° = 480°

Hence, angular distance = 480°

EXAMPLE 4. What is the angle traced by hour hand in 15 min?

Sol. $\because$ Angle traced by hour hand in 1 min $= \left(\frac{1}{2}\right)^{\circ}$

$\therefore$ Angle traced by hour hand in 15 min $= 15 \times \frac{1°}{2} = 7.5°$

EXAMPLE 5. At what time between 4 O'clock and 5 O'clock, will the hands of a clock be together?

Sol. At 4 O'clock, the hour hand is at 4 and the minute hand is at 12. It means that they are 20 min spaces apart.

To be together, the minute hand must gain 20 min over the hour hand. As we know,
55 min is gained by minute hand in 60 min.

$\therefore$ 20 min will be gained in $\left(\frac{60}{55} \times 20\right)$ min

$$= \frac{60 \times 4}{11} = \frac{240}{11} = 21\frac{9}{11} \text{ min}$$

Hence, the hands will coincide at $21\frac{9}{11}$ min past 4.

EXAMPLE 6. At what time between 7 O'clock and 8 O'clock in the morning, will the both hands of a clock be at right angle?

Sol. At 7 O'clock the minute hand will be 35 min spaces behind the hour hand. Now, when the two hands are at right angle, they are 15 min spaces apart. So, they are at right angles in the following cases.

***Case* I** When minute hand is 15 min spaces behind the hour hand.

In this case, minute hand will have to gain (35 – 15) min spaces

= 20 min spaces

55 min spaces are gained by it in 60 min.

20 min spaces will be gained by it in $\left(\frac{60}{55} \times 20\right)$ min

$$= \frac{240}{11} = 21\frac{9}{11} \text{ min}$$

Hence, they are at right angle at $21\frac{9}{11}$ min past 7.

***Case* II** When the minute hand is 15 min spaces ahead of the hour hand.

To be in this position, the minute hand will have to gain (35 + 15) min spaces = 50 min spaces.

55 min spaces are gained in 60 min.

50 min spaces are gained in $\left(\frac{60}{55} \times 50\right)$ min

$$= \left(\frac{60}{11} \times 10\right) = 54\frac{6}{11} \text{ min}$$

Hence, they are at right angle at $54\frac{6}{11}$ min past 7.

EXAMPLE 7. At what time between 7 O'clock and 8 O'clock, will the hands of a clock be in the same straight line but not together?

Sol. At 7 O'clock, the hour hand is at 7 and the minute hand is at 12. It means that the two hands are 25 min spaces apart.

To be in the same straight line (but not together), they will be 30 min spaces apart.

$\therefore$ The minute hand will have to gain (30 – 25) min spaces = 5 min spaces over the hour hand

As we know, 55 min spaces are gained in 60 min.

$\therefore$ 5 min will be gained in $\left(\frac{60}{55} \times 5\right)$ min $= 5\frac{5}{11}$ min

Hence, the hands will be in the same straight line but not together at $5\frac{5}{11}$ min past 7.

EXAMPLE 8. At what time between 3 O'clock and 4 O'clock, will the hands of a clock be in opposite directions?

Sol. At 3 O'clock, the hour hand is at 3 and the minute hand is at 12. It means that the two hands are 15 min spaces apart. But to be in opposite directions, the hands must be 30 min spaces apart.

Therefore, the minute hand will have to gain (30 + 15) min spaces = 45 min spaces over the hour hand.

$\because$ 55 min spaces are gained in 60 min.

$\therefore$ 45 min spaces are gained in $\left(\frac{60}{55} \times 45\right)$ min

$$= \frac{60 \times 9}{11} = \frac{540}{11} = 49\frac{1}{11} \text{ min}$$

Hence, required time is $49\frac{1}{11}$ past 3.

EXAMPLE 9. At what time between 3 O'clock and 4 O'clock, will the hands of a clock be 4 min apart?

Sol. At 3 O'clock, the minute hand is 15 min spaces behind the hour hand.

***Case* I** When the minute hand is 4 min spaces behind the hour hand.

In such case, the minute hand has to gain (15 – 4) min spaces = 11 min spaces

$\because$ 55 min are gained in 60 min.

$\therefore$ 11 min are gained in $\left(\frac{60 \times 11}{55}\right)$ min $= \frac{12 \times 11}{11} = 12$ min

The hands will be 4 min apart at 12 min past 3.

***Case* II** When the minute hand is 4 min spaces ahead of the hour hand.

In such case, the minute hand has to gain (15 + 4) min spaces = 19 min spaces

$\because$ 55 min are gained in 60 min.

$\therefore$ 19 min are gained in $\left(\frac{60}{55} \times 19\right)$ min

$$= \left(\frac{12 \times 19}{11}\right) = 20\frac{8}{11} \text{ min}$$

Hence, the hands will be 4 min apart at $20\frac{8}{11}$ min past 3.

EXAMPLE 10. The minute hand of a clock overtakes the hour hand at intervals of 63 min of the correct time. How much does a clock gain or loss in a day?

Sol. As we know that in a correct clock, the min hand gains 55 min spaces over the hour hand in 60 min.
To be together again, the minute hand must gain 60 min over the hour hand.

$\because$ 55 min are gained in $\left(\frac{60}{55} \times 60\right)$ min $= 65\frac{5}{11}$ min

But they are together after 63 min.

$\therefore$ Gain in 63 min $= \left(65\frac{5}{11} - 63\right) = 2\frac{5}{11} = \frac{27}{11}$min

$\therefore$ Gain in 24 h (one day) $= \left(\frac{27}{11} \times \frac{60 \times 24}{63}\right)$ min

$= \frac{4320}{77}$

$= 56\frac{8}{77}$ min

As the result is positive, therefore the clock gains $56\frac{8}{77}$ min.

Topic Practice 1

1. If in a clock, the hour hand rotates 18°, then how much angle the second hand will rotate in the same clock?
2. How much angular distance will be covered by the minute hand of a correct clock in a period of 2 h 20 min?
3. Find the angle between the minute hand and the hour hand of a clock, when the time is 4 : 20.
4. What will be the angle between the hands of clock at 9 : 30?
5. Find the angle traced by hour hand of a correct clock between 8 O'clock and 2 O'clock.
6. At what time between 5 O'clock and 6 O'clock are the hands of a clock coincide?
7. At what time between 6 O'clock and 7 O'clock will the hands of a clock be at right angle?
8. At what time between 4 O'clock and 5 O'clock will the hands of a watch point in opposite directions?
9. The minute hand of a clock overtakes the hour hand at intervals of 62 min of the correct time. How much does a clock gain or lose in a day?
10. Two clocks are set correctly at 10 am on Sunday. One clock loses 3 min in an hour while the other gains 2 min in an hour. By how many minutes do the two clocks differ at 4 pm on the same day?
11. A clock is set right at 5 am. The clock loses 16 min in 24 h. What will be the right time when the clock indicates 10 pm on the 3rd day?
12. A watch, which gains uniformly is 2 min slow at noon on Monday and is 4 min 48s fast at 2 pm on the following Monday. At what time it was correct?
13. A clock becomes 12 s fast in every 3 h. If it is made correct at 3 O'clock in the afternoon of Sunday, then what time will it show at 10 O'clock Tuesday morning?
14. At present a wall clock is showing 07 : 40 : 06. If it loses 4 s in each hour, then after $6\frac{1}{2}$ h, what time it will be showing?
15. Aseem leaves his house at 20 min to 7 in the morning, reaching Kaushal's house in 25 min, they finish their breakfast in another 5 min and leave for their office which takes another 35 min. At what time do they leave Kaushal's house to reach their office?
16. Reaching the place of meeting 20 min before 8 : 50 h, Sujay found himself 30 min earlier than the person who came 40 min late. What was the scheduled time of meeting?
17. The first period of a class start at 10:30 am and fourth ends at 13 : 45 pm. If periods are of equal duratioin and after each period a break of 5 min is given to the students, then find the exact duration of each period.
18. In the noon, a man observes that his watch is 5 min slow and showing 11:55 am instead of the correct time i.e. 12:00 pm. In the evening, he observes that his watch is 9 min fast and showing 7:09 pm instead of the correct time i.e. 7:00 pm. Find the time, when the watch would be showing the correct time.
19. A watch is one minute slow at 1 : 00 pm on Tuesday and 2 min fast at 1 : 00 pm on Thursday. When did it show the correct time?
20. At what time, in between 6 O'clock and 7 O'clock, will the minute hand of a clock be ahead of hour hand by 3 min?

Hints & Solutions

1. **Hint** In 1 min, hour hand rotates $\left(\frac{1}{2}\right)^\circ$.

   Then, to rotate 18°, it will take $\frac{1}{\left(\frac{1}{2}\right)} \times 18$ min $= 36$ min

   In 36 min, the second hand will rotate $= 36 \times 6 = 216^\circ$

2. **Hint** Angle traced by minute hand per minute $= 6^\circ$

   $\therefore$ Angle traced by minute hand in 2 h 20 min
   $= [(2 \times 60) + 20] \times 6^\circ = 840^\circ$

3. Do same as Example 1. **Ans.** 10°

4. Do same as Example 1. **Ans.** 105°

5. **Hint** $\because$ Angle traced by hour hand per minute $= \left(\frac{1}{2}\right)^\circ$

8 O'clock

2 O'clock

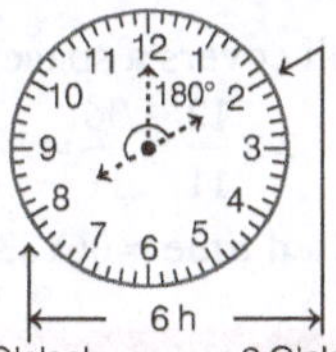

8 O'clock 2 O'clock

   $\therefore$ Angle traced by hour hand in 1 h $= \frac{1^\circ}{2} \times 60$
   $= 30^\circ$

   Time period between 8 O'clock to 2 O' clock = 6 h

   $\therefore$ Angle traced by hour hand in 6h $= 30^\circ \times 6$
   $= 180^\circ$

6. From the figure, we find that min hand is 25 min spaces behind the hour hand.

   In order to coincide, it has to gain 25 min spaces.

   Now, 55 min are gained by minute hand in 60 min.

   $\therefore$ 25 min will be gained in $\frac{60}{55} \times 25 = 27\frac{3}{11}$ min

   So, the hands will coincide at $27\frac{3}{11}$ min past 5.

7. Do same as Example 6.

   Ans. Hands will be at right angle at $49\frac{1}{11}$ min past 6.

8. Do same as Example 8.

   Ans. The hands of the clock will be in opposite direction at $54\frac{6}{11}$ min past 4.

9. Do same as Example 10.

   Ans. $80\frac{80}{341}$ min gain [gain as sign is positive]

10. According to the question,

    One clock loses = 3 min/h

    Other clock gains = 2 min/h

    So, the difference in minutes between these two clocks in one hour $= 2 - (-3) = 5$ min loss

    [$\because$ loss in minutes = negative sign]

    Total time from 10 am to 4 pm on Sunday =6h

    Therefore, the difference in minutes between these two clocks from 10 am to 4 pm on Sunday
    $= (5 \times 6) = 30$ min

11. Time from 5 am of a particular day to 10 pm on the 3rd day is 89 h. Now, the clock loses 16 min in 24 h or in other words, we can say that 23 h 44 min of this clock is equal to 24 h of the correct clock.

    $\left(23 + \frac{44}{60}\right) = \frac{356}{15}$ h of this clock
    = 24h of the correct clock

    $\therefore$ 89 h of this clock $= \left(\frac{24 \times 15}{356} \times 89\right)$ h of the correct clock
    = 90 h of the correct clock

    or 89 h of this clock = 90 h of the correct clock.

    Therefore, it is clear that in 90 h this clock loses 1 h.

    Hence, the correct time is 11 pm when this clock shows 10 pm.

12. Time from Monday noon (12 O'clock) to 2 pm the following Monday = 7 days 2 h = 170 h

    Now, the watch gains $\left(2 + 4\frac{4}{5}\right)$ min from Monday (12 pm) to 2 pm, the following Monday.

    In other words, the watch gains $\frac{34}{5}$ min in 170 h.

    Therefore, it will gain 2 min in $\left(\frac{170 \times 5}{34} \times 2\right) = 50$ h
    = 2 days 2 h

    Therefore, the watch is correct after 2 days 2 h from Monday noon or at 2 pm on Wednesday.

13. Total time from 3 O' clock Sunday afternoon to 10 O' clock Tuesday morning = 43 h

    Total increased time $= \frac{12}{3} \times 43 = 172$ s = 2 min 52 s

    $\therefore$ Time at 10 O' clock Tuesday morning
    = 2 min 52 s past 10

14. In each hour, the wall clock is losing 4s.

Then, in $6\frac{1}{2}$ h it will be losing $= 4 \times 6\frac{1}{2} = 2 \times 13 = 26$ s

Hence, time after $6\frac{1}{2}$ h = 07:40:06 + (6:30:00 – 00:00:26)

= 07:40:06 + 6:29:34 = 14:09:40

15. Aseem leaves his house at 20 min to 7, i.e. at 6 : 40 am.
He reaches Kaushal's house at 6 : 40 + 0 : 25 = 7 : 05 am
They finish their breakfast at 7 : 05 + 0 : 05 = 7 : 10 am
Then, both leave for office at 7 : 10 + 0 : 35 = 7 : 45 am

16. Time of Sujay's reaching the place = (8 : 50 – 0 : 20)h
= 8 : 30 h

It is clear that the person who was 40 min late would reach the place at 9 : 00 h.

∴ Scheduled time of meeting = (9 : 00 – 0 : 40) h
= 8 : 20 h

17. Time interval between the first period and fourth period
= 13 : 45 pm – 10 : 30 am
= 3 h 15 min

∴ Total break $= 3 \times 5 = 15$ min

∴ Time period of classes $= (3 \times 60) + 15 - 15$
$= 180$ min

∴ Exact duration of each period $= \frac{180}{4} = 45$ min

18. According to the question, at 12 O'clock, the watch was 5 min slow and at 7 O'clock, it is 9 min fast.

So, in this time duration, the watch becomes $9 + 5 = 14$ min ahead.

From 12 O'clock to 7 O'clock there is 7 h.

So per hour, the clock becomes fast $= \frac{14}{7} = 2$ min

Because at the initial time, it was 5 min too slow, so it will show the correct time when it becomes 5 min fast.

19. As it is given that on Tuesday at 1 : 00 pm the watch is one minute slow and on Thursday at 1 : 00 pm, it is 2 min fast, it means that the clock has gained 3 min in 48 h from Tuesday to Thursday.

Now, to show the correct time, the clock needs to gain only 1 min starting from 1 : 00 pm on Tuesday.

As, 3 min are gained in 48 h,

1 min is gained in $\frac{48}{3}$ h = 16 h

So,the clock showed the correct time at 5 : 00 am on Wednesday i.e. 16 h later to 1:00 pm on Tuesday.

20. In between 6 O'clock and 7 O'clock, 06:33 will be the time at which the minute hand will be ahead of hour hand.

As we know that the minute hand covers a space of 1 min in $\frac{12}{11}$ min.

∴ In 3 min, it will covers a space of

$$3 \times \frac{12}{11} = \frac{36}{11} = 3\frac{3}{11} \text{ min} \approx 3 \text{ min}$$

Hence, the required time = 06 : 33 + 00:03 = 06:36 h

Calendar

A calendar is chart or series of pages showing the days, weeks and months of a particular year. A calendar consist of 365 or 366 days divided into 12 months.

Ordinary Year

A year having 365 days is called an ordinary year i.e. 52 complete weeks + 1 extra day = 365 days

Leap Year

A leap year has 366 days (the extra day is 29th of February)

i.e. 52 complete weeks + 2 extra days = 366 days

A leap year is divisible by 4 except for a century.

For a century to be a leap year it must be divisible by 400.

e.g.

- Years like 1988, 2008 are leap year (divisible by 4).
- Centuries like 2000, 2400 are leap year (divisible by 400).
- Years like 1999, 2003 are not leap year (not divisible by 4).
- Centuries like 1700, 1800 are not leap year (not divisible by 400).
- In a century, there is 76 ordinary year and 24 leap years.

Odd Days

Extra days, apart from the complete weeks in a given period are called odd days. An ordinary year has 1 odd day, while a leap year has 2 odd days.

Months	Odd days
January	3
February	0/1 (ordinary/leap)
March	3
April	2
May	3
June	2
July	3
August	3
September	2
October	3
November	2
December	3

To find the numbers of odd days

- Number of days in an ordinary year = 365
  $= (52 \times 7) + 1$
  $= 52$ weeks + 1 odd day

  ∴ An ordinary year has 1 odd day.
- Number of days in a leap year $= 366 = (52 \times 7) + 2$
  $= 52$ weeks + 2 days

  ∴ A leap year has 2 odd days.
- Number of days in a century (100 yr)
  = 76 ordinary years + 24 leap years
  $= (76 \times 1 + 24 \times 2)$
  $= 124 = 17 \times 7 + 5$
  = 17 weeks + 5 odd days

  ∴ 100 yr has 5 odd days.
- Number of odd days in 200 yr $= 5 \times 2 = 10$ days
  = 1 week + 3 days
  = 3 odd days
- Number of odd days in 300 yr $= 5 \times 3 = 15$ days
  = 2 weeks + 1 day
  = 1 odd day
- Number of odd days in 400 yr $= (5 \times 4 + 1)$
  = 21 days = 3 weeks = 0 odd days

As 400th is a leap year, therefore 1 more day has been taken.

Similarly, each one of 800 yr, 1200 yr, 1600 yr, 2000 yr, 2400 yr etc. has no odd days.

- In an ordinary year, February has no odd days, but in a leap year, February has one odd day.
- The 1st day of a century must be Tuesday, Thursday or Saturday.
- The last day of a century cannot be Tuesday, Thursday or Saturday.

EXAMPLE 1. Find the number of odd days in 1985 years.

Sol. $1985 = 400 \times 4 + 300 + 21$ (leap years) + 64 (ordinary years)

∴ Number of odd days in

$1985 = (0 + 1 + 21 \times 2 + 64 \times 1)$ odd days
= 107 odd days
= 15 weeks +2 days = 2 odd days

Day Gain/Loss

For Ordinary Year (± 1 day)

- When we proceed forward by 1 yr, then 1 day is gained.

  e.g. 9th August, 2013 is Friday, then 9th August, 2014 has to be Friday + 1 = Saturday.
- When we move backward by 1 yr, then 1 day is lost.

  e.g. 24th December, 2013 is Tuesday, then 24th December, 2012 has to be Tuesday − 1 = Monday

For Leap Year (± 2 days)

- When we proceed forward by 1 leap year, then 2 days are gained.

  e.g. If it is Wednesday on 25th December, 2011, then it would be Friday on 25th December, 2012 (Wednesday + 2) because 2012 is a leap year.
- When we move backward by 1 leap year, then 2 days are lost.

  e.g. If it is Wednesday on 18th December, 2012 then it would be Monday on 18th December, 2011. (Wednesday − 2) because 2012 is a leapyear.

Important Concepts Regarding Days

(i) Day after yesterday = Today
(ii) Day before yesterday = Today − 2 days
(iii) Day after tomorrow = Today + 2 days
(iv) Day before tomorrow = Today
(v) Day after the day before yesterday
= (Yesterday − 1 day) + 1 day
= Yesterday
= Today − 1 day

(vi) Day before the day after tomorrow
= (Tomorrow + 1 day) – 1 day
= Tomorrow
= Today + 1 day

(vii) Day before the day after yesterday
= (Yesterday + 1 day) – 1 day
= Yesterday
= Today – 1 day

(viii) Day after the day before tomorrow
= (Tomorrow – 1 day) + 1 day
= Tomorrow
= Today + 1 day

Exception

- The day must have crossed 29th February for adding 2 days otherwise 1 day should be added.
  e.g. If 26th January, 2011 is Wednesday, 26th January, 2012 would be Wednesday + 1 = Thursday (even if 2012 is leap year, we have added + 1 day because 29 February is not crossed).
  If 23rd March, 2011 is Wednesday, then 23rd March, 2012 would be Wednesday + 2 = Friday (+ 2 days 29th February of leap year is crossed).

To Find a Particular Day on the Basis of Given Day and Date

Following steps are taken into consideration to solve such questions

Step I Firstly, you have to find the number of odd days between the given date and the date for which the day is to be determined.

Step II The day (for a particular date) to be determined, will be that day of the week which is equal to the total number of odd days and this number is counted forward from the given day, in case the given day comes before the day to be determined. But, if the given day comes after the day to be determined, then the same counting is done backward from the given day.

EXAMPLE 2. If 5th January, 1991 was Saturday, what day of the week was it on 4th March, 1992?

Sol. Number of days between 5th January, 1991 and 4th March, 1992
= (365 – 5) days of year 1991 + 31 days of January 1992
+ 29 days of February 1992 + 4 days of March 1992
[as 1992 is completely divisible by 4, hence it is a leap year and that's why February has 29 days]
= 360 + 31 + 29 + 4 = 424 = 60 weeks + 4 days
∴ Number of odd days = 4
∴ 4th March, 1992 will be 4th day after Saturday.
∴ The required day will be Wednesday.

EXAMPLE 3. What day of the week was it on 5th November, 1987 if it was Monday on 4th April, 1988?

Sol. Number of days between 5th November, 1987 and 4th April, 1988
= (30 – 5) days of November 1987
+ 31 days of December 1987 + 31 days of January 1988
+ 29 days of February 1988 + 31 days of March 1988
+ 4 days of April 1988
[1988 is a leap year, so February has 29 days]
= 25 + 31 + 31 + 29 + 31 + 4
= 151 days
= 21 weeks + 4 days
∴ Number of odd days = 4
∴ 5th November, 1987 will be 4 days before Monday.
∴ Required day is Thursday.

EXAMPLE 4. Find the day of the week on 26th January, 1950.

Sol. Number of odd days upto 26th January, 1950
= Odd days for 1600 yr + Odd days for 300 yr
+ Odd days for 49 yr
+ Odd days of 26 days of January, 1950
$= 0 + 1 + (12 \times 2 + 37) + 5$
$= 0 + 1 + 61 + 5 = 67$ days
= 9 weeks + 4 days
= 4 odd days
∴ It was Thursday on 26th January 1950.

Note 49 yr has 12 leap year and 37 ordinary year

To Find a Particular Day without Given Date and Day

Following steps are taken into consideration to solve such questions

Step I Firstly, you have to find the number of odd days upto the date for which the day is to be determined.

Step II Your required day will be according to the following conditions

(i) If the number of odd days = 0, then required day is Sunday.
(ii) If the number of odd days = 1, then required day is Monday.
(iii) If the number of odd days = 2, then required day is Tuesday.
(iv) If the number of odd days = 3, then required day is Wednesday.
(v) If the number of odd days = 4, then required day is Thursday.
(vi) If the number of odd days = 5, then required day is Friday.
(vii) If the number of odd days = 6, then required day is Saturday.

EXAMPLE 5. Prove that the calendar for the year 2007 will be same for the year 2018.

Sol. Count the number of odd days from year 2007 and onwards to get the sum equal to odd days.

Years	Odd days
2007	1
2008	2
2009	1
2010	1
2011	1
2012	2
2013	1
2014	1
2015	1
2016	2
2017	1

Sum = 14 odd days = 0 odd day

∴ Calendar for the year 2018 will be same as for the year 2007.

Miscellaneous Examples

EXAMPLE 6. If today is Sunday, then what day of the week will be 3 days after tomorrow?

Sol. Today = Sunday

Tomorrow = Sunday + 1 = Monday

3 days after tomorrow = Monday + 3 odd days

= Thursday

EXAMPLE 7. If the day before yesterday was Wednesday, when will Sunday be?

Sol. If the day before yesterday was Wednesday, then yesterday = Wednesday + 1 = Thursday and today will be Friday and the day after tomorrow will be Sunday.

i.e.

Wednesday	Thursday	Friday	Saturday	Sunday
↓	↓	↓	↓	↓
Day before yesterday	Yesterday	Today	Tomorrow	The day after tomorrow

Thus, the day after tomorrow will be Sunday.

EXAMPLE 8. If the day before yesterday was Saturday, then what day of the week will it be after tomorrow?

Sol. Day before yesterday = Saturday

Today = Saturday + 2 = Monday

∴ Tomorrow = Monday + 1 = Tuesday

∴ Day after Tomorrow = Tuesday + 1

= Wednesday

∴ Required day = Wednesday

EXAMPLE 9. Adam's birthday is on Friday 18th June. On what day of the week will be Eve's birthday in the same year if Eve's was born on 20th September?

Sol. Total days from 18th June to 20th September in the same year = (30 – 18) in June + 31 (July)

+ 31 (August) + 20 September

= 12 + 31 + 31 + 20 = 94 days

∵ Number of odd days

$$7\overline{)94}(13$$

$$\underline{7}$$

$$24$$

$$\underline{21}$$

3 odd days

∴ Required day i.e. Eve's birthday = Friday + 3

= Monday

EXAMPLE 10. Find the number of days from 26th January, 2011 to 23rd September, 2011 (both days are included).

Sol. According to the question,

26th January to 31st January = 6 days

February = 28 days

March = 31 days

April = 30 days

May = 31 days

June = 30 days

July = 31 days

August = 31 days

1st September to 23rd September = 23 days

Total days = 241

∴ Required days = 241

EXAMPLE 11. If the National day of a country was celebrated on the 4th Saturday of a month, then find the date of celebration, when the first day of that month is Tuesday.

Sol. According to the question,

National day = 4 th Saturday

∵ 1st day = Tuesday

∴ 1st Saturday = Tuesday + 4 = 1 + 4 = 5 th day

2nd Saturday = 5 + 7 = 12 th day

3rd Saturday = 12 + 7 = 19 th day

4th Saturday = 19 + 7 = 26 th day

So, National day was celebrated on 26th of that month.

EXAMPLE 12. If Republic day was celebrated in 1996 on Friday, then on which day in 2000 Independence day was celebrated?

Sol. Number of days in 1996 (366-26) = 340

Number of days in 1997 = 365

Number of days in 1998 =365

Number of days in 1999 =365

Number of days from January 2000 to July 2000

$= 31+29+31+30+31+30+31$

$= 213$

Number of days from 1st to 15th August, 2000 = 15

$\therefore$ Total days $= 340+365+365+365+213+15$

$= 1663$

$1663 \div 7 \Rightarrow$

$$7)\,1663\,(237$$
$$\begin{array}{r} 14 \\ \hline 26 \\ 21 \\ \hline 53 \\ 49 \\ \hline 4 \end{array}$$

$\because$ 1663 days = $(237 \times 7 + 4)$ days

= 237 weeks + 4 odd days

$\therefore$ Number of odd days = 4

$\therefore$ Day on 15th August, 2000 = Friday + 4 odd days

= Tuesday

EXAMPLE 13. If the date 7 of a month is on three days before Friday, then find the date 19 of the same month.

Sol. The day falls on date 7 of the month = Friday − 3

= Tuesday

$\therefore$ Tuesday on that month will fall on = 7, 14, 21 and 28

The date 19 will fall on Tuesday − 2 days = Sunday

$\therefore$ Required day = Sunday

EXAMPLE 14. On what dates of August, 1980 did Monday fall?

Sol. First of all, we have to find the day on 1st August, 1980.

1st August, 1980 means (1979 yr, 7 months and 1 day)

Now, 1900 yr have 1 odd day

79 yr have 19 leap years and 60 ordinary years, which have $(19 \times 2 + 60 \times 1) = 98$ odd days = 0 odd day

7 months and 1 day

Months	Number of days
January	31
February	29
March	31
April	30
May	31
June	30
July	31
August	1 (required)

= 214 days = 4 odd days

Total number of odd days = (1 + 4) = 5

So, it was Friday on 1st August, 1980 and 1st Monday of the month was on 4th and subsequent Monday of the month were on 4th, 11th, 18th and 25th.

EXAMPLE 15. In a particular month of some year, there are three Monday which have even dates. On which day of the week does the 15th of that month fall?

Sol. Three Monday on even dates in a month are only possible when 1st Monday is on 2nd day of the month.

So, Date 2 $\Rightarrow$ Monday

Date 9 $\Rightarrow$ Monday

Date 16 $\Rightarrow$ Monday

Date 23 $\Rightarrow$ Monday

Date 30 $\Rightarrow$ Monday

$\therefore$ 16th date of the month falls on Monday.

$\therefore$ 15th is on Sunday.

EXAMPLE 16. If Monday falls on the first of October which day will fall three days after the 20th in that month?

Sol. Here, 1st October is Monday.

Three days after 20th of that month is 23rd October.

Number of days between 1st October and 23rd October

= 22 days

Number of odd days $= \frac{22}{7} = 1$ odd day

$\therefore$ Required day = Monday + 1 odd day = Tuesday

Topic Practice 2

1. How many odd days are in 2119 years?
2. If there was Monday on 5th January, 2012, then what will be the day on 31st March, 2013?
3. If there was Thursday on 25th September in a year, then what day was on 25th October in the same year?
4. If 27th March, 1995 was Monday, then what day of the week was 1st November, 1994?
5. If 1st January, 2007 was Monday, then what day of the week lies on 1st January, 2008?
6. What was the day on 1st January, 1901?
7. If 1st January is a Friday, then what is the first day of the month of March in a leap year?
8. If 15th June falls on 3 days after tomorrow which is Friday, then what day of week will fall on last date of month?

9 If the third day of a month is Monday, then which of the following will be the fifth day from 21st of that month?

10 Sudha went to watch movie 9 days ago. She goes to watch movies only on Thursday. What is the day of the week today?

11 If there was Monday on 17th April in a year, then what was on 17th May in the same year?

12 On which day of the week does 4th July, 1776 fall?

13 What was the day of the week on 15th August, 1947?

14 The day on 18th September, 1977 was Sunday. A couple was married on this date. How many marriage anniversaries would fall on Sunday in the next 15 yr?

15 On what dates in April, 2001, did Wednesday fall?

16 A girl was born on 6th September, 1970 which happened to be a Sunday. When would her birthday have fallen again on Sunday?

17 The Republic day of India in 1980 falls on Saturday, X was born on 3rd March, 1980 and Y is older to X by four days. When would Y's birthday have fallen?

18 Anil reaches at a certain place on Friday and found, he reaches the place 3 days before. If he had reached the place on coming Sunday, then how many days before or after he would have reached the place?

19 2 days before yesterday was Friday, then what day of the week will be day after tomorrow?

20 If Thursday falls 2 days after tomorrow, then what day of the week was it on three days before yesterday?

21 If day before yesterday was Thursday, then when will be the Monday?

22 If day after tomorrow is Sunday, then what day of the week was it on day before yesterday?

23 What is the year next to 1990 which have the same calendar as that of the year 1990?

24 In a month of 31 days, third Thursday falls on 16th, then what will be the last day of the month?

Hints & Solutions

1. Do same as Example 1. **Ans.** 0 odd days
2. Do same as Example 2. **Ans.** Thursday
3. Do same as Example 2. **Ans.** Saturday
4. Do same as Example 3. **Ans.** Tuesday
5. $\because$ 2007 is an ordinary year.
   $\therefore$ 1st January = 31 st December
   As, 1st January = Monday
   $\therefore$ 31st December = Monday
   $\therefore$ 1st January, 2008 = Monday + 1 odd day = Tuesday
6. Do same as Example 4. **Ans.** Tuesday
7. **Hint** Total number of days from 1st January to 1st March
   $= 30 + 29 + 1 = 60$ days
   [February in a leap years = 29 days]
   $\therefore$ $60 \div 7 = 8$ weeks and 4 odd days
   So, the fourth day from Friday = Tuesday
8. Tomorrow = Friday
   3 days after tomorrow = 15th June
   = Friday + 3 odd days = Monday
   Days from 15th to 30th June = 15
   $$15 \div 7 \Rightarrow 7\overline{)15}(2$$
   $$\underline{14}$$
   1 odd day
   30th June = Monday + 1 odd day = Tuesday
9. Fifth day from 21st will be 26th and Monday lies on 3rd, 10th, 17th, 24th.
   So, the day on 26th will be Wednesday.
10. Day 9 days ago = Thursday
    $\therefore$ Today = Thursday + 9 = Thursday + 7 + 2
    = Thursday + 2
    = Saturday
    $\therefore$ Required day = Saturday
11. Do same as Example 9. **Ans.** Wednesday
12. 1776 yr = (1600 + 100 + 75) yr
    Number of odd days in 1600 yr = 0
    Number of odd days in 100 yr = 5
    Number of odd days in 75 yr
    $= 18 \times 2 + 57 \times 1 = 93$ days
    [$\because$ in 76 yr, there are 18 leap years and 57 ordinary years]
    = 13 weeks and 2 odd days
    = 2 odd days
    and odd days from 1st January, 1776 to 4th July, 1776
    = odd days in
    $(31 + 29 + 31 + 30 + 31 + 30 + 4)$ days
    = odd days in 186 days
    $\because$ 186 days = 26 weeks and 4 odd days
    $\therefore$ Odd days = 4 days
    Total number of odd days
    $= 0 + 5 + 2 + 4$
    = 4 odd days
    There are 4 odd days, so the required day = Thursday

13. Odd days in 1600 yr = 0

Odd days in 300 yr = 1

Odd days in 46 yr = (11 leap year + 35 ordinary year)

$= (11 \times 2 + 35 \times 1) = 1$ odd day

$\therefore$ Odd days in 1946 yr = (0+1+1) = 2

Month	Odd days
January	3
February	0 (ordinary year)
March	3
April	2
May	3
June	2
July	3
August	1 (15 ÷ 7)
Total	17

$17 \div 7 \Rightarrow 7)17(2$

$\underline{14}$

3 odd days

Total odd days = 2 + 3 = 5

$\therefore$ Required day = Friday

14. 1977 is an ordinary year. We know that the calendar of an ordinary year repeats after 6 yr or 11 yr. Let us check for the number of odd days in 6th and 11th yr.

Years	Number of odd days
1978	1
1979	1
1980	2
1981	1
1982	1
1983	1
1984	2

Years	1985	1986	1987	1988
Number of odd days	1	1	1	2

From the above table,

Number of odd days from 18th September, 1977 to 18th September, 1983 = 7, i.e. 0 odd day

It means that in 1983, 18th September would fall on Sunday.

From the above table, number of odd days from 18th September, 1977 to 18th September, 1988 = 14, i.e. 0 odd day.

Now, it is clear that 2 marriage anniversaries would fall on Sunday in the next 15 yr.

15. First of all, we have to find the day on 1st April, 2001.

Now, 2000 yr have 0 odd day.

Number of odd days in 3 months and 1 day

$$= \frac{31 + 28 + 31 + 1}{7}$$

$$= \frac{91}{7} = 0 \text{ odd day}$$

$\because$ Total number of odd days = (0 + 0) = 0 odd day

Hence, it was Sunday on 1st April, 2001 and it was Wednesday on 4th April, 2001.

Subsequently, Wednesday of the month were on 4th, 11th, 18th and 25th.

16. 1970 is an ordinary year. We know that the calendar of an ordinary year repeats after 6 yr or 11 yr.

6 yr after 1970 is 1976.

17. Republic day in 1980 i.e. 26th January, 1980 = Saturday

Number of odd days till 3rd March, 1980

January February March

↓ ↓ ↓

5 29 3 → 37 odd days

or $\frac{37}{7} = 2$ odd days

So, 3rd March is Monday and Y is 4 days older to X. So, his birthday must be four days ahead of X i.e. on Friday.

18. The correct day on which Anil has to reach the place

= Friday + 3 = Monday

Therefore, if Anil reaches on Sunday, then he reaches there on the day which is (Monday – 1) or 1 day before the correct day.

19. Do same as Example 8. **Ans.** Wednesday

20. Two days after tomorrow = Thursday

Tomorrow = Thursday – 2 = Tuesday

Today = Tuesday – 1 = Monday

Yesterday = Monday – 1 = Sunday

$\therefore$ 3 days before yesterday = Sunday – 3 = Thursday

$\therefore$ Required day = Thursday

21. Do same as Example 7. **Ans.** Day after tomorrow

22. Day after tomorrow = Sunday

Tomorrow = Sunday – 1 = Saturday

Today = Saturday – 1 = Friday

Yesterday = Friday – 1 = Thursday

$\therefore$ Day before yesterday = Thursday – 1 = Wednesday

$\therefore$ Required day = Wednesday

23. The year 1990 has 365 days i.e. 1 odd day, year 1991 has 365 days i.e. 1 odd day, year 1992 has 366 days i.e. 2 odd days. Likewise years 1993, 1994, 1995 have 1 odd day each.

The sum of odd days, so calculated from years 1990 to 1995 = 1 + 1 + 2 + 1 + 1 + 1 = 7 odd days = 0 odd day

Hence, the year 1996 will have the same calendar as that of the year 1990.

24. Number of days left in the month after 16th

= 31 – 16 = 15 days

Number of odd days $= \frac{15}{7} = 2$ weeks + 1 odd day

$\therefore$ Required day = Thursday + 1 odd day = Friday

As, 16th of the month is third Thursday,the day which is two weeks after this day is fifth Thursday.

So, one day after 5th Thursday is 5th Friday.

Exam Pattern Exercise

Part A - Objective Type Questions

Multiple Choice Type Questions

1 The minute hand of a clock overtakes the hour hand at intervals of 70 min of the correct time. How much in a day does the clock gain or loss?
(a) $\frac{7200}{77}$ loss (b) $\frac{7200}{75}$ profit
(c) $\frac{7200}{77}$ profit (d) $\frac{7200}{75}$ loss

2 At what time between 3 O'clock and 4 O'clock, will the hands of a clock be together?
(a) $16\frac{3}{11}$ past 5 (b) $16\frac{4}{11}$ past 4
(c) $16\frac{3}{11}$ past 3 (d) $16\frac{4}{11}$ past 3

3 Which angle will be traced by the hands of a clock at 12 : 55?
(a) $87\frac{1}{2}^\circ$ (b) $67\frac{1}{2}^\circ$ (c) $57\frac{1}{2}^\circ$ (d) $27\frac{1}{2}^\circ$

4 How many times, the hand of a clock are at right angle in a day?
(a) 24 (b) 48
(c) 22 (d) 44

5 By which of the following, a leap year must be divisible?
(a) 9 (b) 6
(c) 5 (d) 4

6 Which of the following is a leap year?
(a) 2007 (b) 2016
(c) 2001 (d) 1997

7 If 5th March, 1999 was Friday, what day of the week was it on 9th March 2000?
(a) Wednesday (b) Friday
(c) Thursday (d) Tuesday

8 On 6th March, 2005, Monday falls. What was the day of the week on 7th March, 2004?
(a) Monday (b) Sunday
(c) Tuesday (d) Saturday

9 On which day of week does 18th September, 1991 fall?
(a) Wednesday (b) Tuesday
(c) Friday (d) Saturday

10 Mansi's birthday is on Monday 19th June. On what day of the week will be Riya's birthday in the same year, if Riya was born on 17th November?
(a) Saturday (b) Wednesday
(c) Friday (d) Sunday

Assertion-Reason Based Questions

Directions (Q. Nos. 11-13) *In the questions given below are two statements labelled as Assertion (A) and Reason (R). In the context of the two statements, which one of the following is correct?*
(a) Both A and R are correct; R is the correct explanation of A
(b) Both A and R are correct; R is not the correct explanation of A
(c) A is correct; R is incorrect
(d) R is correct; A is incorrect

11 **Assertion (A)** The angle traced by hour hand in 15 min is $7\frac{1}{2}^\circ$.
Reason (R) Hour hand traces an angle of 6° in one minute.

12 **Assertion (A)** 2009 has the same calander as that of 2015.
Reason (R) The calendar of ordinary years repeat after 6 years or 11 years.

13 **Assertion (A)** In 100 years, there are 75 ordinary years and 25 leap years.
Reason (R) A leap year is a year which is exactly divisible by 4.

Part B - Descriptive Questions

Very Short Answer Type Questions

14 Find the number of hours and minutes from 6 : 14 am to 8 : 02 pm on the same days.

15 Find the angle between the hour hand and the minute hand of a clock when the time is 4 : 10.

16 A clock is set right at 6 am. The clock losses 16 min in 24 h. What will be true time, if the clock indicates 11 pm on 4th day?

17 3rd January, 2007 was Wednesday. What day of the week fell on 3rd January, 2008?

18 3rd January, 2008 was Friday. What day of the week fell on 3rd January, 2009?

19 How many Monday are there in a particular month of a particular year, if the month ends on Wednesday?

Short Answer Type Questions

20 At what time between 9 O'clock and 10 O'clock, will the hands of a clock be in the same straight line but not together?

21 At what point of time after 3 O' clock, hour hand and the minute hand are at right angles for the first time?

22 A clock is set right at 9 am. The clock gains 10 min in 24 h. What will be true time, when the clock indicates 2 pm on the following day?

23 A watch which gains uniformly, is 5 min slow at 7 O'clock in the morning on Sunday and it is 5 min 48 s fast at 7 pm on following Sunday. Which day was it correct?

24 Prove that calendar for the year 2008 will be the same for the year 2019.

25 Prove that the last day of century cannot be Tuesday, Thursday or Saturday.

26 What was the day of the week on 2nd Jan, 2010 if it was Sunday on 1st Jan, 2006?

27 4th April, 1988 was Monday. What day of the week was it on 6th November 1987?

Long Answer Type Questions

28 At what time between 5 O'clock and 6 O'clock in the morning, will both hands of a clock be at right angle?

29 At what time between 2 O'clock and 3 O'clock, will the hands of a clock point in opposite directions?

30 How much does a watch gain per day, if its hands coincide every 64 min?

31 What was the day of the week on 5th June, 2002?

32 What was the day of the week on 17th July, 1776?

33 What was the day of the week on 17th August, 2010?

34 On what dates of March, 2005 did Saturday fall?

Case Study Based Questions

35 A clock has two hands, the longer hand is called the minute hand and the shorter hand is called hour hand. The minute hand trace an angle of 6° in one minute and hour hand trace an angle of $\left(\frac{1}{2}\right)^\circ$ in one minute.

Based on the above information, answer the following questions.

(i) How much angular distance will be covered by the minute hand of a correct clock in a period of 2 hr 20 min?

(ii) What is the angle traced by hour hand in 30 minutes?

(iii) What will be the angle between the two hands of a clock, when the time is 8 : 50?

Or

At half past 5 in the evening, find the smaller angle between the hour and minute hands of a clock.

36 In a given period, the number of days more than the complete weeks are called odd days. In order to find the number of odd days in a given period, divide the number by 7 and get the remainder. The remainder is number of odd days.

Number of odd days in week Sunday, Monday, Tuesday, Wednesday, Thursday, Friday and Saturday have 0, 1, 2, 3, 4, 5, 6 respectively. The number of odd days in 100 yr, 200 yr, 300 yr and 400 yr are 5, 3, 1 and 0 respectively.

Based on the above information, answer the following questions.

(i) Find the number of odd days in 1985 year.

(ii) How many odd days are in 2119 year?

(iii) What was the day of week on 26th January 1950?

Or

Monday fell on which dates of June 2003?

Hints & Solutions

1. (a)	*2.* (d)	*3.* (c)	*4.* (d)
5. (d)	*6.* (b)	*7.* (c)	*8.* (a)
9. (a)	*10.* (c)	*11.* (c)	*12.* (a)

13. (d)

14. Total hours from 6 : 14 am morning to evening 6:14 pm = 12 h

and total hours from 6 : 14 pm evening to 8 : 02 pm evening

$= 8:02 - 6:14$

$= 1:48$ h

i.e. 1 h and 48 min

$\therefore$ Total hours and minutes = 12 h + 1 h 48 min

= 13 h and 48 min

15. 65°

16. Time from 6 am on a day to 11 pm on 4th day = 89 h

Now, 23 h 44 min of this clock = 24 h of correct clock

$$89 \text{ h of this clock} = \left(24 \times \frac{15}{356} \times 89\right) \text{ h of correct clock}$$

$$= 90 \text{ h of correct clock}$$

∴ Correct time will be 12 O'clock (mid-night).

17. The year 2007 is an ordinary year, so it has 1 odd day.

3rd day of the year 2007 was Wednesday.

∴ 3rd day of the year 2008 will be one day after the Wednesday.

Hence, it will be Thursday.

18. The year 2008 is a leap year, so it has 2 odd days,

3rd day of the year 2008 was Friday.

∴ 3rd day of the year 2009 will be 2 days after the Friday.

Hence, the required answer is Sunday.

19. There are months of 30, 31 and 28 days and last day of month is Wednesday.

So, using 28 and 30 days, there are 4 Monday.

Using 31 days, there are 5 Monday.

It cannot be specified.

20. $16\frac{4}{11}$ min past 9

21. At 3 O'clock, the minute hand will be 15 min spaces behind the hour hand.

When the two hands are at right angle, they are 15 min spaces.

So, they are at right angles at (15 + 15) min spaces

= 30 min spaces

∴ 55 min spaces are gained in 60 min.

$$30 \text{ min spaces are gained in } \left(\frac{60}{55} \times 30\right) \text{ min}$$

$$= 32\frac{8}{11} \text{ min past 3}$$

22. Time from 9 am in a day to 2 pm on the following day

= 29 h

24 h 10 min of this clock = 24 h of the correct clock

or $\frac{145}{6}$ h of this clock = 24 h of the correct clock

$$29 \text{ h of this clock} = \left(24 \times \frac{6}{145} \times 29\right) \text{ h of the correct clock}$$

$$= 28 \text{ h } 48 \text{ min of correct clock}$$

∴ The correct time is 28 h 48 min after 9 am.

This will be 48 min past 1.

23. Time from 7 am on Sunday to 7 pm on following Sunday

= 7 days 12 h = 180 h

∴ Watch gains $\left(5 + 5\frac{4}{5}\right)$ min or $\frac{54}{5}$ min in 180 h.

Now, $\frac{54}{5}$ min are gained in 180 h.

$$\therefore \text{ 5 min are gained in } \left(180 \times \frac{5}{54} \times 5\right) \text{ h}$$

= 83 h 20 min = 3 days 11 h and 20 min

∴ Watch is correct after 3 days 11 h and 20 min after 7 am of Sunday.

∴ It will be correct at 20 min past 6 pm on Wednesday.

24. Count the number of odd days from the year 2008 onwards to get the sum equal to 0 odd day.

Let us see

2008	2009	2010	2011	2012	2013
2	1	1	1	2	1

2014	2015	2016	2017	2018
1	1	2	1	1

Sum = 2 + 1 + 1 + 1 + 2 + 1 + 1 + 1 + 2 + 1 + 1

= 14 days = 2 weeks = 0 odd days

∴ Calendar for the year 2019 will be the same as for the year 2008.

25. ∵ 100 yr have 5 odd days.

∴ Last day of 1st century is Friday.

200 yr have (5 × 2) = 1 week + 3 odd days

= 3 odd days

∴ Last day of 2nd century is Wednesday,

300 yr have (5 × 3) = 2 week + 1 odd day

= 1 odd day

∴ Last day of 3rd century is Monday.

400 yr have 0 odd day.

∴ Last day of 4th century is Sunday.

This cycle is repeated.

∴ Last day of a century cannot be Tuesday or Thursday or Saturday.

26. Saturday

27. Friday

28. $43\frac{7}{11}$ min past 5 and $10\frac{10}{11}$ min past 5

29. $\frac{480}{11}$ min past 2

30. We know that in a correct clock, the minute hand gains 55 min.

Spaces over the hour hand in 60 min.

To be together again, the minute hand must gain 60 min over the hour hand.

$$\therefore \text{ 55 min are gained in } \left(\frac{60}{55} \times 60\right) \text{ min} = 65\frac{5}{11} \text{ min}$$

$$\therefore \text{ Gain in 64 min} = \left(65\frac{5}{11} - 64\right) = 1\frac{5}{11} = \frac{16}{11} \text{ min}$$

$$\therefore \text{ Gain in 24 hours} = \frac{16}{11} \times \frac{24 \times 60}{64} = 32\frac{8}{11} \text{ min}$$

31. Period upto 5th June, 2002

= (2001 yr + Period from 1st January, 2002 to 5th June, 2002)

$\therefore$ Odd days in 1600 yr = 0

Odd days in 400 yr = 0

Odd days in 1 ordinary year = 1

i.e. odd days in 2001 year = (0 + 0 + 1) = 1

Number of days from 1st January, 2002 to 5th June, 2002

(January + February + March + April + May + June)

= 31 + 28 + 31 + 30 + 31 + 5

= 156 days

= 22 weeks + 2 days = 2 odd days

$\therefore$ Total number of odd days

= (1 + 2) = 3 odd days

$\therefore$ The required day is Wednesday.

32. Wednesday

33. Tuesday

34. First, we find out the day on 1st March, 2005.

Period upto 1st March, 2005

= (2004 yr + period from 1st January, 2005 to 1st March, 2005)

$\therefore$ Odd day in 1600 yr = 0

Odd day in 400 yr = 0

4 yr = (1 leap year + 3 ordinary years)

$= (1 \times 2 + 3 \times 1)$

= 5 odd days

Number of days between 1st January, 2005 to 1st March, 2005

(January + February + March)

= 31 + 28 + 1

= 60 days = (8 weeks + 4 days)

= 4 odd days

Total number of odd days

= (0 + 0 + 5 + 4) = 9

= 1 week + 2 odd days

= 2 odd days

$\therefore$ 1st March 2005 was Tuesday.

So, Saturday will fall on 5th March, 2005.

Hence, Saturday falls on 5th, 12th, 19th, and 26th of March, 2005.

35. (i) Angle traced by minute hand per minute = 6°

$\therefore$ Angle traced by minute hand in 2 h 20 min

$= (2 \times 60 + 20) \times 6°$

$= (120 + 20) \times 6°$

$= 840°$

(ii) Angle traced by hour hand in 1 min $= \left(\frac{1}{2}\right)^\circ$

$\therefore$ Angle traced by hour hand in 30 min $= 30 \times \frac{1}{2}^\circ = 15°$

(iii) Angle traced by the hour hand in 12 h = 360°

So, angle traced by the hour hand in 8 h 50 min

i.e. $\frac{53}{6}$ h $= \left(\frac{53}{6} \times \frac{360}{12}\right)^\circ = 265°$

$\therefore$ Angle traced by minute hand in 60 min = 360°

$\therefore$ Angle traced by minute hand in 50 min

$= \left(\frac{360}{60} \times 50\right)^\circ = 300°$

$\therefore$ Required angle = (300°–265°) = 35°

Or

At 5:30 pm, hour hand is behind minute hand.

$\therefore$ Angle traced by the hour hand in

5 h 30 min $= \left(5 \times 60 \times \frac{1}{2} + 30 \times \frac{1}{2}\right)^\circ = 165°$

Angle traced by minute hand in 30 min

$= (30 \times 6)° = 180°$

Angle between both the hand is

$(180° - 165°) = 15°$

36. (i) $1985 = 400 \times 4 + 300 + 21$ (leap years) + 64 (ordinary years)

Number of odd days in 1985

$= (0 + 1 + 21 \times 2 + 64 \times 1)$ odd days

= 107 odd days

When 107 divide by 7, remainder is 2.

$\therefore$ Number of odd days = 2

(ii) $2119 = 400 \times 5 + 100 + 4$ (leap years) + 15 (ordinary years)

Number of odd days $= 0 + 5 + 4 \times 2 + 15 \times 1$

$= 5 + 8 + 15 = 28$

28 is divisible by 7.

$\therefore$ Number of odd days = 0

(iii) Period of 26 January 1950 = (1949 years + 26 days)

26 January 1950 $= 400 \times 4 + 300 + 12$ (leap years) + 37 (ordinary years) + 26 days

Number of odd days upto 26 January 1950

$= 0 + 1 + 12 \times 2 + 37 \times 1 + 26$

$= 1 + 24 + 37 + 26 = 88$ odd days

$88 = 12 \times 7 + 4$

$\therefore$ 4 odd days

$\therefore$ Fourth odd day = Thursday

Or

$2002 = 400 \times 5 + 2$ (ordinary years)

Number of odd days in 2002 = 0 + 2 = 2 odd days

From Ist January 2003 to Ist June 2003,

Number of odd days $= 31 + 28 + 31 + 30 + 31 + 1$

= 152 days

$= 21 \times 7 + 5 = 5$ odd days

$\therefore$ Total number of odd days = 2 + 5 = 7 odd days

$\therefore$ 1st June 2003 is Sunday.

2nd June 2003 is Monday.

So, Monday fell on date 2, 9, 16, 23, 30 of June 2003.

CHAPTER 05

Time and Work

In this Chapter...

- Basic Rules Related to Work and Time
- Pipe and Cisterns

In this chapter, we will study techniques to solve problems based on work and its completion time as well as number of persons required to finish the given work in stipulated time.

Suppose that you are a contractor and you got a contract to construct a flyover in a certain time. For this, you need to calculate the number of men required to finish the work according to their work efficiency.

Some Important Relations

- One day's work $= \dfrac{1}{\text{Number of days to complete the work}}$
- Number of days to complete a work $= \dfrac{1}{\text{One day's work}}$
- Time required to do a certain work $= \dfrac{\text{Work to be done}}{\text{One day's work}}$

Basic Rules Related to Work and Time

Rule 1

(i) If A can do a piece of work in x days and B can do the same work in y days, then $(A+B)$'s 1 day's work

$$= \frac{1}{x} + \frac{1}{y} = \frac{x+y}{xy}$$

Time taken by $(A+B)$ to complete the work

$$= \frac{xy}{x+y} \text{ days}$$

(ii) If A can do a piece of work in x days, B can do the same work in y days and C can do the same work in z days, then

Time taken by $(A+B+C)$ to complete the work

$$= \frac{xyz}{xy+yz+zx} \text{ days}$$

For n persons, their 1 day's work

$$= \frac{1}{x_1} + \frac{1}{x_2} + \frac{1}{x_3} + \ldots + \frac{1}{x_n}$$

where, $x_1, x_2, x_3, \ldots, x_n$ represent numbers of days taken by them to complete a work.

EXAMPLE 1. A can do a piece of work in 10 days and B can do the same work in 12 days. How long will they take to finish the work, if both work together?

Sol. A's 1 day's work $= \dfrac{1}{10}$ and B's 1 day's work $= \dfrac{1}{12}$

$(A+B)$'s 1 day's work $= \dfrac{1}{10} + \dfrac{1}{12} = \dfrac{6+5}{60} = \dfrac{11}{60}$

$\therefore$ $(A+B)$ complete the whole work in $\dfrac{60}{11}$ days

$= 5\dfrac{5}{11}$ days

EXAMPLE 2. A and B together can do a piece of work in 12 days and A alone can do it in 18 days. In how many days can B alone do it?

Sol. $(A+B)$'s 1 day's work $= \dfrac{1}{12}$

and A's 1 day's work $= \dfrac{1}{18}$

$\therefore$ B's 1 day's work = $(A+B)$'s 1 day's work − A's 1 day's work

$$= \frac{1}{12} - \frac{1}{18} = \frac{3-2}{36} = \frac{1}{36}$$

$\therefore$ Time taken by B to complete the work alone = 36 days

EXAMPLE 3. A and B can do a piece of work in 40 days and 50 days, respectively. Both begin together but after a certain time, A leaves off. In this case B finishes the remaining work in 20 days. After how many days did A leave?

Sol. B's 20 day's work $= \frac{20}{50} = \frac{2}{5}$;

Remaining work $= 1 - \frac{2}{5} = \frac{3}{5}$

$(A+B)$'s 1 day's work $= \frac{1}{40} + \frac{1}{50} = \frac{5+4}{200} = \frac{9}{200}$

$(A+B)$ do $\frac{9}{200}$ work in 1 day.

$\therefore$ $(A+B)$ will do $\frac{3}{5}$ work in $= \frac{3}{5} \times \frac{200}{9}$

$$= \frac{40}{3} = 13\frac{1}{3} \text{ days}$$

Rule 2

If a person is n times efficient than the second person, then work done by

First person : Second person = n : 1

and time taken to complete a work by

First person : Second person = 1 : n

EXAMPLE 4. P can do a work 3 times faster than Q and therefore takes 40 days less than Q. Find the time in which P and Q can complete the work individually.

Sol. We know that if a person is n times efficient than the second person, then time taken to complete a work by

First person : Second person = 1 : n

$\therefore$ Time taken to complete the work by $P : Q = K : 3K$

According to the question,

Time taken by Q − Time taken by $P = 40$

$\Rightarrow$ $3K - K = 40$

$\Rightarrow$ $2K = 40$

$\Rightarrow$ $K = 20$

$\therefore$ Number of days required by $P = 20$

and number of days required by $Q = 60$

EXAMPLE 5. Kamal can do a work in 15 days and Vimal is 50% more expert than Kamal to complete the same work, then find total time taken to complete the work by Vimal.

Sol. Work done by Kamal : Vimal $= 1 : 1 \times \frac{150}{100} = 1 : \frac{3}{2}$

$\therefore$ Time taken to complete the work by Kamal : Vimal

$$= \frac{3}{2} : 1$$

$\therefore \frac{3}{2} \rightarrow 15$ days

$\therefore 1 \rightarrow \frac{15 \times 2}{3} = 10$ days

$\therefore$ Time taken by Vimal in 10 days.

Rule 3

If ratio of numbers of men required to complete a work is $m : n$, then the ratio of time taken by them will be $n : m$.

EXAMPLE 6. 10 men can make 20 toys in 12 days working 12 h a day. Then, in how many days can 24 men make 32 toys working 16 h a day?

Sol. 10 men can make 20 toys working 12 h per day $= 12$ days

$\therefore$ 1 man can make 20 toys working 12 h per day $= 10 \times 12$ days

$\therefore$ 1 man can make 1 toy working 12 h per day $= \frac{10 \times 12}{20}$ days

$\therefore$ 1 man can make 1 toy working 1 h per day $= \frac{10 \times 12 \times 12}{20}$ days

$\therefore$ 24 men can make 32 toys working 16 h per day

$$= \frac{10 \times 12 \times 12 \times 32}{20 \times 24 \times 16}$$

$= 6$ days

EXAMPLE 7. If 6 men or 8 women can reap a field in 86 days, how long will 14 men and 10 women take to reap it?

Sol. Given, 6 men = 8 women

$\therefore$ 1 man $= \frac{8}{6} = \frac{4}{3}$ women

$\therefore$ 14 men $= \frac{56}{3}$ women

14 men + 10 women $= \frac{56}{3} + 10$

$= \frac{86}{3}$ women

Now, 8 women can reap a field in 86 days.

$\therefore$ 1 woman can reap a field in 86×8 days.

$\therefore \frac{86}{3}$ women can reap a field in $\frac{86 \times 8 \times 3}{86} = 24$ days

EXAMPLE 8. If 5 men can do a work in 2 days and 3 boys can do the same work in 5 days, then find the time taken to complete same work by 10 men and 3 boys.

Sol. $\because$ Work done by 5 men in 2 days = 1

Work done by 1 man in one day $= \frac{1}{5 \times 2} = \frac{1}{10}$

$\therefore$ Work done by 10 men in 1 day $= \frac{10}{10} = 1$

and work done by 3 boys in 5 days = 1

Work done by 1 boy in 1 day $= \frac{1}{3 \times 5} = \frac{1}{15}$

Work done by 3 boys in 1 day $= \frac{3}{15} = \frac{1}{5}$

$\therefore$ Work done by 10 men and 3 boys in 1 day $= 1 + \frac{1}{5}$

$= \frac{6}{5}$

Hence, time taken to complete a work by 10 men and 3 boys $= \frac{5}{6}$ days

Pipe and Cisterns

Inlet pipe It fills a tank/cistern/reservoir.

Outlet pipe It empties a tank/cistern/reservoir.

Important Facts Related to Pipes and Cisterns

(i) If a pipe can fill/empty a tank in 'm' h, then the part of tank filled/emptied in 1 h $= \frac{1}{m}$.

e.g. If a pipe can fill the tank in 7 h, then the volume of tank filled in 1 h $= \frac{1}{7}$.

(ii) If a pipe can fill/empty '$1/m$' part of a tank in 1 h, then it can fill/empty the whole tank in 'm' h.

e.g. If a pipe can fill 1/5 part of a tank in 1 h, then it can fill the whole tank in 5 h.

(iii) If a pipe fills a tank in m h and another pipe can empty the tank in n h.

Then, part filled by both pipes in 1 h $= \frac{1}{m} - \frac{1}{n}$

(if $m < n$)

EXAMPLE 9. If a pipe can fill a tank in 2 h and another pipe can fill the same tank in 6 h, then what part of a tank will be filled by both the pipes in 1 h, if they are opened simultaneously?

Sol. In 1 h, part filled by 1st pipe $= \frac{1}{m} = \frac{1}{2}$

In 1 h, part filled by 2nd pipe $= \frac{1}{n} = \frac{1}{6}$

$\therefore$ In 1 h, part filled by both the pipes together

$= \left(\frac{1}{m} + \frac{1}{n}\right) = \left(\frac{1}{2} + \frac{1}{6}\right) = \frac{3+1}{6} = \frac{4}{6} = \frac{2}{3}$

EXAMPLE 10. A tap can fill a tank in 36 min. While another tap can empty it in $1\frac{1}{2}$ h. If both the taps are opened at 11 : 20 am, when will the tank be filled?

Sol. Part filled by first tap in 1 min $= \frac{1}{36}$

Part empty by second tap in 1 min $= \frac{1}{90}$

$\left[\because 1\frac{1}{2} \text{h} = 90 \text{ min}\right]$

Part filled by both tap in 1 min $= \frac{1}{36} - \frac{1}{90}$

$= \frac{5-2}{180} = \frac{1}{60}$

$\therefore$ Time taken to filled a tank $= \frac{1}{\frac{1}{60}}$ min = 60 min = 1 h

$\therefore$ Tank filled at = 11: 20 am + 1 h = 12 : 20 pm

EXAMPLE 11. Tap A can fill a tank 3 times faster than tap B and takes 28 min less than tap B to fill the tank. If both the taps are opened simultaneously, then find the time taken to fill the tank.

Sol. Let the time taken by tap A to fill the tank be x min.

Then, time taken by tap B to fill the tank be $3x$ min.

Then, according to the question,

$3x - x = 28 \Rightarrow 2x = 28$

$\Rightarrow \quad x = \frac{28}{2} = 14$ min

$\therefore$ Time taken by tap $A = 14$ min;

Part filled by tap A in 1 min $= \frac{1}{14}$

Time taken by tap $B = 3 \times 14 = 42$ min

Part filled by tap B in 1 min $= \frac{1}{42}$

$\therefore$ Part filled by both taps in 1 min $= \frac{1}{14} + \frac{1}{42} = \frac{3+1}{42}$

$= \frac{4}{42} = \frac{2}{21}$

So, time taken by both taps to fill the tank working together $= \frac{21}{2}$ min

Exam Pattern Exercise

Part A - Objective Type Questions

Multiple Choice Type Questions

1 A alone can complete a work in 12 days and B alone can complete the same work in 24 days. In how many days can A and B together complete the same work?
(a) 6 days (b) 4 days
(c) 8 days (d) 10 days

2 A can complete a piece of work in 18 days and B can complete the same work in half time taken by A. Then, working together, what part of the same work they can complete in a day?
(a) 6 days (b) 4 days
(c) 8 days (d) 9 days

3 X can complete a job in 12 days. If X and Y work together, they can complete the job in $6\frac{2}{3}$ days. Y alone can complete the job in
(a) 10 days (b) 12 days
(c) 15 days (d) 18 days

4 A is thrice as good a workman as B and therefore is able to finish a job in 30 days less than B. How many days will they take to finish the job working together?
(a) $10\frac{1}{4}$ days (b) $11\frac{3}{4}$ days
(c) $11\frac{1}{4}$ days (d) $11\frac{1}{3}$ days

5 X can do a work in 16 days. In how many days will the work be completed by Y, if the efficiency of Y is 60% more than that of X?
(a) 10 days (b) 12 days
(c) 25 days (d) 30 days

6 A can do a piece of work in 10 days and B in 20 days. They begin together but A leaves 2 days before the completion of the work. The whole work will be done in
(a) 8 days (b) 6 days
(c) 7 days (d) 9 days

7 20 men can cut 30 trees in 4 h. If 4 men leave the job, how many trees will be cut in 12 h?
(a) 72 (b) 80
(c) 68 (d) 79

8 20 workers working for 5 h per day complete a work in 10 days. If 25 workers are employed to work 10 h per day, what is the time required to complete the work?
(a) 1 day (b) 2 days
(c) 3 days (d) 4 days

9 15 men complete a work in 16 days. If 24 men are employed, then the time required to complete that work will be
(a) 10 days (b) 15 days
(c) 20 days (d) 5 days

10 There are two tanks A and B to fill up a water tank. The tank can be filled in 40 min, if both taps are on. The same tank can be filled in 60 min, if tap A alone is on. How much time will tap B alone take to fill up the same tank?
(a) 64 min (b) 80 min
(c) 96 min (d) 120 min

11 Through an inlet, a tank takes 8 h to get filled up. Due to a leak in the bottom, it takes 2 h more to get it filled completely. If the tank is full, then how much time will the leak take to empty it?
(a) 16 h (b) 20 h (c) 32 h (d) 40 h

Assertion-Reason Based Questions

Directions (Q. Nos. 12-14) *In the questions given below are two statements labelled as Assertion (A) and Reason (R). In the context of the two statements, which one of the following is correct?*

(a) Both A and R are correct; R is the correct explanation of A
(b) Both A and R are correct; R is not the correct explanation of A
(c) A is correct; R is incorrect
(d) R is correct; A is incorrect

12 **Assertion (A)** P can do a piece of work in 30 days, while Q can do it in 40 days. Both P and Q together can do the work in $17\frac{1}{7}$ days.

Reason (R) A is twice as good a workman as B and together they finish a piece of work in 18 days. A alone can finish the work in 27 days.

13 **Assertion (A)** *A* and *B* working separately can do a piece of work in 9 and 12 days, respectively. If they work for 10 days alternately, then the number of days taken by *A* to finish the remaining work in 15 days.

Reason (R) *P* can do $\frac{1}{3}$ of the work in 5 days and *Q* can do $\frac{2}{5}$ of the work in 10 days, then the number of days taken by both *P* and *Q* together can do the work are $9\frac{3}{8}$ days.

14 **Assertion (A)** If 3 men or 5 boys take 40 h to do a certain piece of work, then number of hours will be taken by 6 men and 10 boys together to complete the work is 20 h.

Reason (R) 6 men can cut 12 trees in 8 days working 4 h a day. Then, number of days taken by 12 men cut 48 trees working 8 h a day is 8 days.

Part B - Descriptive Questions

Very Short Answer Type Questions

15 *A* and *B* can do a piece of work in 6 and 12 days, respectively. They (both) will complete the work in how many days?

16 *A* and *B* together can do a piece of work in 12 days, while *B* alone can finish it in 30 days. *A* alone can finish the work in how many days?

17 *A*, *B* and *C* can complete a work in 2 h. If *A* does the job alone in 6 h and *B* in 5 h, how long will it take for *C* to finish the job alone?

18 *A* and *B* can do a job together in 12 days. *A* is 2 times as efficient as *B*. In how many days can *B* alone complete the work?

19 90 men are engaged to do a piece of work in 40 days but it is found that in 25 days, 2/3 work is completed. How many men should be allowed to go off, so that the work may be finished in time?

20 *A*, *B* and *C* can do a piece of work in 18, 24 and 36 days, respectively. They work alternately, first day *C*, second day *B*, third day *A*, fourth day *C* and so on. How many days will be needed to complete the work like this way?

21 *A* does 20% less work than *B*. If *A* can complete a piece of work in 7½h, then *B* can do it in how many hours?

22 If one man or two women or three boys can finish a work in 88 days, then how many days will one man, one woman and one boy together take to finish the same work?

23 *A* and *B* together can complete a work in 3 days. They started together but after 2 days, *B* left the work. If the work is completed after 2 more days, *B* alone could do the work in how many days?

24 If 3 men and 4 boys can do a piece of work in 8 days, then 6 men and 8 boys can do the same work in how many days?

25 A tank can be filled by pipe *X* in 2 h and pipe *Y* in 6 h. At 10 am, pipe *X* was opened. At what time will the tank be filled, if pipe *Y* is opened at 11 am?

26 A tank (of capacity 160 L) has one inlet, *A* and one outlet, *B*. Inlet *A*, alone can fill the empty tank in 6 h and outlet *B* alone can empty the full tank in 24 h. In how many hours will inlet *A* fill 16 L water in the tank when outlet *B* is also open?

27 15 taps are fitted in a tank in which some are inlet taps and some are outlet taps. Each inlet tap can fill the tank in 30 h and each outlet tap can empty the tank in 60 h. Find the number of inlet taps if the whole tank is filled in 4 h when all the 15 taps are open.

Short Answer Type Questions

28 *A* can complete a work in 20 days and *B* in 30 days. *A* worked alone for 4 days and then *B* completed the remaining work along with *C* in 18 days. In how many days can *C* working alone complete the work?

29 *A* and *B* can do a piece of work in 10 h. *B* and *C* can do it in 15 h, while *A* and *C* take 12 h to complete the work. *B* independently can complete the work in how many hours?

30 *A* and *B* can do a piece of work in 9 days and 18 days, respectively. As they were ill, they could do 90% and 72% of their efficiency, respectively. How many days will they take to complete the work together?

31 40 men can build a wall 200 m long in 12 days, working 8 h a day. What will be the number of days that 30 men will take to build a similar wall 300 m long, working 6 h per day?

32 3 men can do a piece of work in 6 days. 5 women can do the same work in 18 days. If 4 men and 10 women work together, then how long will it take to finish the work?

33 It is given that 16 men working 18 h a day can build a wall 36 m long, 4 m broad and 24 m high in 20 days. How many men will be required to build a wall 64 m long, 6 m broad and 18 m high working 12 h a day in 16 days?

Long Answer Type Questions

34 A, B and C can do a piece of work individually in 8, 12 and 15 days, respectively. A and B start working but A quits after working for 2 days. After this, C joins B till the completion of work. In how many days will the work be completed?

35 A takes twice the time taken by B and thrice the time taken by C to do a particular piece of work. Working together, they can complete the work in 2 days. Find the number of days taken by A, B and C respectively to complete the work alone.

36 Rashmi can do a piece of work in 16 days. Ravina can do the same work in $12\frac{4}{5}$ days, while Gitika can do it in 32 days. All of them started to work together but Rashmi leaves after 4 days. Ravina leaves the job 3 days before the completion of the work. How long would the work last?

37 A can build up a structure in 8 days and B can break it in 3 days. A has worked for 4 days and then B joined to work with A for another 2 days only. In how many days will A alone build up the remaining part of the structure ?

38 A contract is to be completed in 92 days and 234 men were set to work, each working 16 h a day. After 66 days, 4/7 of the work is completed. How many additional men may be employed, so that the work may be completed in time, each man now working 18 h a day?

39 A certain number of men can do a piece of work in 80 days. If there were 10 men less, it could be finished in 20 days more. How many men are there in the starting?

40 Pipe A is 4 times faster than pipe B and takes 30 min less than the pipe B to fill the tank. When will the cistern be full, if both pipes are opened together?

41 There are 7 pipes attached with a tank out of which some are inlets and some are outlets. Every inlet can fill the tank in 10 h and every outlet can empty the tank in 15 h. When all the pipes are opened simultaneously, the tank is filled up in $2\frac{8}{11}$h. Find the number of inlets and outlets.

42 Three pipes A, B and C can fill a tank in 30 min, 20 min and 10 min, respectively. When the tank is empty, all the three pipes are opened. If A, B and C discharge chemical solutions P, Q and R respectively, then find the part of solution R in the liquid in the tank after 3 min.

Case Study Based Questions

43 A takes twice as much time as B and thrice as much time as C to finish a piece of work, working together they can finish the work in 3 days.

(i) The time will take to finish the work by A is

(a) 20 days (b) 15 days
(c) 18 days (d) 14 days

(ii) The time will take to finish the work by B is

(a) 9 days (b) 10 days
(c) 7 days (d) 12 days

(iii) The time will take to finish the work by C is

(a) 5 days (b) 6 days
(c) 8 days (d) 7 days

44 A can do a piece of work in 90 days, B in 40 days and C in 12 days. They work for a day each in turn i.e. first day A does it alone, B does if the second day and C the third day. After that A does it for another day, and so on. After finishing the work they get ₹ 2400. If the wages are divided in proportion to the work done by them.

(i) The whole work is completed in

(a) $26\frac{1}{10}$ days (b) $30\frac{1}{3}$ days
(c) $24\frac{5}{7}$ days (d) $32\frac{1}{12}$ days

(ii) A's share is

(a) ₹ 300 (b) ₹ 360
(c) ₹ 240 (d) ₹ 280

(iii) B's share is

(a) ₹ 540 (b) ₹ 600 (c) ₹ 440 (d) ₹ 610

(iv) C's share is

(a) ₹ 1580 (b) ₹ 1690 (c) ₹ 1590 (d) ₹ 1620

Hints & Solutions

1. (c) 2. (a) 3. (c) 4. (c)
5. (a) 6. (a) 7. (a) 8. (d)
9. (a) 10. (d) 11. (d) 12. (b)
13. (d) 14. (b)

15. 4 days

16. 20 days

17. **Hint** Let C alone can finish the job in x h.
According to the question,
Work done by A, B and C in 1 h $= \frac{1}{2}$
$\Rightarrow \frac{1}{6}+\frac{1}{5}+\frac{1}{x}=\frac{1}{2}$ **Ans.** $7\frac{1}{2}$ h

18. **Hint** Time taken by A to complete a work $= x$ days
$\therefore$ Time taken by B to complete the same work $= 2x$ days
According to the question,
$$\frac{1}{x}+\frac{1}{2x}=\frac{1}{12} \quad \textbf{Ans. } 36 \text{ days}$$

19. 15

20. Work done in first 3 days $= \frac{1}{18}+\frac{1}{24}+\frac{1}{36}$
$$= \frac{4+3+2}{72}=\frac{1}{8}$$
$\because$ Time taken to complete $\frac{1}{8}$ part of work $= 3$ days
$\therefore$ Time taken to complete the whole work $= 3 \times 8$
$= 24$ days

21. 6 h

22. 48 days

23. $(A+B)$'s 2 day's work $= 2 \times \frac{1}{3}=\frac{2}{3}$
$\therefore$ Remaining work $= 1-\frac{2}{3}=\frac{1}{3}$
A will complete $\frac{1}{3}$ work in 2 days.
A will complete 1 work in 6 days.
A's 1 day's work $= \frac{1}{6}$
B's 1 day's work $= \frac{1}{3}-\frac{1}{6}=\frac{1}{6}$
$\therefore$ B will take 6 days to complete the work alone.

24. Let the men do the work in a days and the boys in b days.
$$\therefore \quad \frac{3}{a}+\frac{4}{b}=\frac{1}{8} \quad \text{...(i)}$$
Now, $\frac{6}{a}+\frac{8}{b}=2\left(\frac{3}{a}+\frac{4}{b}\right)=2\times\frac{1}{8}=\frac{1}{4}$ [from Eq. (i)]
So, 6 men and 8 boys can do the same work in 4 days.

25. 11 : 45 am

26. $\frac{4}{5}$ h

27. **Hint** Number of taps in the tank = 15
Let the number of inlet taps $= x$
and the number of outlet taps $= 15-x$
According to the question,
$$\frac{x}{30}-\frac{(15-x)}{60}=\frac{1}{4} \quad \textbf{Ans. } 10$$

28. **Hint** Work done by A in 4 days $= \frac{4}{20}=\frac{1}{5}$
$\therefore$ Remaining work $= 1-\frac{1}{5}=\frac{4}{5}$
Let C can working alone complete the work in x days.
According to the question,
$$\frac{18}{30}+\frac{18}{x}=\frac{4}{5} \quad \textbf{Ans. } 90 \text{ days}$$

29. A's and B's 1 h work $= \frac{1}{10}$
B's and C's 1 h work $= \frac{1}{15}$
and A's and C's 1 h work $= \frac{1}{12}$
$\therefore$ A's, B's and C's 1 h work $= \frac{1}{2}\left(\frac{1}{10}+\frac{1}{15}+\frac{1}{12}\right)$
$$= \frac{1}{2}\times\frac{1}{4}=\frac{1}{8}$$
Hence, B's work in 1 h $= \frac{1}{8}-\frac{1}{12}=\frac{1}{24}$
$\therefore$ B independently can complete the work in 24 h.

30. **Hint** Because of illness,
A's 1 day's work $= 90\%$ of $\frac{1}{9}=\frac{1}{10}$
B's 1 day's work $= 72\%$ of $\frac{1}{18}=\frac{1}{25}$
$\therefore$ $(A+B)$'s 1 day's work $= \frac{1}{10}+\frac{1}{25}=\frac{5+2}{50}=\frac{7}{50}$
Ans. $7\frac{1}{7}$ days

31. 32 days

32. 3 days

33. 60

34. $5\frac{8}{9}$ days

35. **Hint** Let A, B and C take x, $\frac{x}{2}$ and $\frac{x}{3}$ days, respectively to complete the work.

$(A+B+C)$'s 1 day's work $= \frac{1}{x}+\frac{2}{x}+\frac{3}{x}=\frac{6}{x}$

According to the question, $\frac{6}{x}=\frac{1}{2}$

$\left[\text{as, } (A+B+C)\text{'s 1 day's work} = \frac{1}{2}\right]$

$\Rightarrow \quad x = 12$ **Ans.** 12, 6, 4

36. **Hint** Let the work lasted for x days.
Then, Rashmi's 4 day's work + Ravina's $(x-3)$ day's work + Gitika's x day's work = 1
According to the question,

$$\frac{4}{16}+\frac{x-3}{12\frac{4}{5}}+\frac{x}{32}=1$$ **Ans.** 9 days

37. A's 1 day's work $= \frac{1}{8}$

B's 1 day's work in breaking the building $= \frac{1}{3}$

Now, according to the question,

A's 4 day's work $= 4\times\frac{1}{8}=\frac{1}{2}$

Now, A's and B's 2 day's work $= 2\left(\frac{1}{8}-\frac{1}{3}\right)=\frac{-10}{24}$

Total work done in 6 days $= \frac{1}{2}+\left(\frac{-10}{24}\right)=\frac{1}{12}$

Remaining work $= 1-\frac{1}{12}=\frac{11}{12}$

Now, A has to complete the work, so A can complete in x days.

$$\frac{1}{8}\times x=\frac{11}{12}$$ **Ans.** $7\frac{1}{3}$ days

38. **Hint** Remaining work $= \left(1-\frac{4}{7}\right)=\frac{3}{7}$
Remaining period = (92 − 66) = 26 days
Let the number of additional men = x
Ans. 162

39. **Hint** Let original number of men = x
Time taken by x = 80 days
Now, $(x-10)$ men can finish the work in (80 + 20) = 100 days
Ans. 50

40. 8 min

41. **Hint** Let the number of outlets be x.
$\therefore$ Number of inlets $= (7-x)$
Time taken to fill the tank, when all the pipes are opened $= \frac{30}{11}$ h
Part of tank filled in 1 h, when all the pipes are opened $= \frac{11}{30}$ h

According to the question,

$$\frac{7-x}{10}-\frac{x}{15}=\frac{11}{30} \Rightarrow x=2$$ **Ans.** 5, 2

42. Total quantity of solutions P, Q and R from A, B and C respectively, after 3 min $= \frac{3}{30}+\frac{3}{20}+\frac{3}{10}=3\left(\frac{2+3+6}{60}\right)$

$$=\frac{3\times 11}{60}=\frac{11}{20}$$

Quantity of solution R in liquid in 3 min $= \frac{3}{10}$

$\therefore$ Part of solution $R = \frac{3/10}{11/20}=\frac{3\times 20}{10\times 11}=\frac{6}{11}$

43. **Hint** Let A takes x days to finish a work, then B would take $\frac{x}{2}$ days and C would take $\frac{x}{3}$ days to finish the same work

$\therefore (A+B+C)$'s efficiency per day $= \left(\frac{1}{x}+\frac{2}{x}+\frac{3}{x}\right)$ work

$= \left(\frac{6}{x}\right)$ work

They all will complete one work, working together in $\left(\frac{x}{6}\right)$ days.

$\therefore \quad \frac{x}{6}=3 \Rightarrow x=18$ days

(i) (c) (ii) (a) (iii) (b)

44. **Hint** One day work of A, B and C is

$$\frac{1}{90}+\frac{1}{40}+\frac{1}{12}=\frac{4+9+30}{360}=\frac{43}{360}$$

So, A, B and C together can finish the work in $\frac{360}{43}$ days or $8\frac{16}{43}$ days, each must work for 8 days to complete

$$8\left(\frac{1}{90}+\frac{1}{40}+\frac{1}{12}\right)=8\left(\frac{43}{360}\right)=\frac{344}{360}$$

$\therefore$ Remaining work $= 1-\frac{344}{360}=\frac{360-344}{360}=\frac{16}{360}=\frac{4}{90}$

So, A, B and C one after the other complete $\frac{344}{360}$ part of the work in $8\times 3 = 24$ days

Work done by A on 25th day $= \frac{1}{90}$

Remaining work $= \frac{4}{90}-\frac{1}{90}=\frac{3}{90}=\frac{1}{30}$

Work done by B on 26th $= \frac{1}{40}$

$\therefore$ Remaining work $= \frac{1}{30}-\frac{1}{40}=\frac{1}{120}$

(i) (a) (ii) (c) (iii) (a) (iv) (d)

CHAPTER 06

Speed, Time and Distance

In this Chapter...

- Speed
- Relative Speed
- Average Speed

Speed

The rate at which a body or an object travels to cover a certain distance is called speed of that body.

Time

The duration in hours, minutes or seconds spent to cover a certain distance is called the time.

Distance

The length of the path travelled by any object or a person between two places is known as distance.

Relation between Speed, Time and Distance

Speed is the distance covered by an object in unit time. It is calculated by dividing the distance travelled by the time taken.

- $\text{Speed} = \frac{\text{Distance}}{\text{Time}}$
- $\text{Time} = \frac{\text{Distance}}{\text{Speed}}$
- $\text{Distance} = \text{Speed} \times \text{Time}$

Important Points

1. When distance is constant, then

$$\text{Speed} \propto \frac{1}{\text{Time}}$$

i.e. $\text{Speed} \times \text{Time} = \text{Constant}$

$$\Rightarrow \quad S_1T_1 = S_2T_2$$

2. When time is constant, then

$$\text{Distance} \propto \text{Speed}$$

i.e. $$\frac{\text{Distance}}{\text{Speed}} = \text{Constant}$$

$$\Rightarrow \quad \frac{D_1}{S_1} = \frac{D_2}{S_2}$$

3. When speed is constant, then

$$\text{Distance} \propto \text{Time}$$

i.e. $$\frac{\text{Distance}}{\text{Time}} = \text{Constant}$$

$$\Rightarrow \quad \frac{D_1}{T_1} = \frac{D_2}{T_2}$$

EXAMPLE 1. A car covers 125 km in 5 h, then find the speed of the car.

Sol. We know that $\text{Speed} = \frac{\text{Distance}}{\text{Time}}$

$\therefore$ Required speed $= \frac{125}{5} = 25$ km/h

EXAMPLE 2. A train covers a distance of 200 km with a speed of 10 km/h. What time is taken by the train to cover this distance?

Sol. Given, speed = 10 km/h and distance = 200 km

$$\text{Time} = \frac{\text{Distance}}{\text{Speed}} \Rightarrow \text{Time} = \frac{200}{10}$$

$\therefore$ Required time = 20 h

EXAMPLE 3. A bike crosses a bridge with a speed of 30 m/s. What will be the length of the bridge, if the bike takes 8 h to cross the bridge?

Sol. $\because 1 \text{ m/s} = \frac{18}{5} \text{ km/h}$

$\therefore 30 \text{ m/s} = \frac{30 \times 18}{5} = 108 \text{ km/h}$

Here, length of the bridge
= Distance travelled by bike in 8 h
= Speed × Time

Given, speed = 108 km/h and time = 8 h

$\therefore$ Length of the bridge = 108 × 8
= 864 km

Note 1. To convert speed in km/h to m/s multiply by $\frac{5}{18}$.

2. To convert speed in m/s to km/h multiply by $\frac{18}{5}$.

EXAMPLE 4. A person covers $20\frac{2}{5}$ km in 3 h. What distance will he cover in 5 h?

Sol. Speed of the person $= \frac{\text{Distance}}{\text{Time}} = \frac{20\frac{2}{5}}{3} = \frac{102}{5 \times 3}$ km/h

$\therefore$ Distance covered in 5 h $= \frac{102 \times 5}{5 \times 3} = 34$ km

EXAMPLE 5. A person covers a distance of 12 km, while walking at a speed of 4 km/h. How much distance he would cover in same time, if he walks at a speed of 6 km/h?

Sol. Time taken by person to cover a distance of 12 km at speed 4km/h $= \frac{\text{Distance}}{\text{Speed}} = \frac{12}{4} = 3$ h

$\therefore$ Distance covers by person in 3 h at speed 6 km/h
= 3 × 6
= 18 km

EXAMPLE 6. A person covers a certain distance with a speed of 18 km/h in 8 min. If he wants to cover the same distance in 6 min, what should be his speed?

Sol. We know that

$$\text{Speed} = \frac{\text{Distance}}{\text{Time}}$$

$$\Rightarrow 18 = \frac{\text{Distance} \times 60}{8} \qquad \left[\because 8 \text{ min} = \frac{8}{60} \text{ h}\right]$$

$$\therefore \text{Distance} = \frac{18 \times 8}{60} = \frac{12}{5} \text{ km}$$

$\therefore$ Speed to cover $\frac{12}{5}$ km in 6 min $= \frac{\text{Distance}}{\text{Time}} = \frac{12/5}{1/10}$ $\left[\because 6 \text{ min} = \frac{1}{10} \text{ h}\right]$

$= \frac{12}{5} \times 10 = 12 \times 2 = 24$ km/h

Relative Speed

When two bodies A and B are moving with speed a km/h and b km/h respectively, then the relative speed of two bodies is

- $(a + b)$ km/h (if they are moving in opposite direction).
- $(a - b)$ km/h (if they are moving in same direction).

EXAMPLE 7. Two persons are moving in the directions opposite to each other. The speeds of the both persons are 5 km/h and 3 km/h, respectively. Find the relative speed of the two persons with respect of each other.

Sol. We know that the two speeds will be added, if the motions of two objects are in opposite directions.

$\therefore$ Required relative speed = 5 + 3 = 8 km/h

EXAMPLE 8. Two trains are running in the same direction. The speeds of two trains are 5 km/h and 15 km/h, respectively. What will be the relative speed of second train with respect to first?

Sol. We know that if two trains are running in same direction, then difference of speeds is the required relative speed.

$\therefore$ Required relative speed = 15 − 5 = 10 km/h

Average Speed

When a body travels with different speeds for different durations, then average speed of that body for the complete journey is defined as the total distance covered by the body divided by the total time taken to cover the distance.

$$\text{Average speed} = \frac{\text{Total distance covered by a body}}{\text{Total time taken by the body}}$$

Note If a body covers a distance D_1 at S_1 km/h, D_2 at S_2 km/h, D_3 at S_3 km/h and so on upto D_n at S_n, then

$$\text{Average speed} = \frac{D_1 + D_2 + D_3 + D_4 + \ldots + D_n}{\frac{D_1}{S_1} + \frac{D_2}{S_2} + \frac{D_3}{S_3} + \frac{D_4}{S_4} + \ldots + \frac{D_n}{S_n}}$$

$$\text{Average speed} \neq \frac{S_1 + S_2 + S_3 + S_4 + \ldots + S_n}{n}$$

EXAMPLE 9. A person covers a distance of 20 km by bus in 35 min. After deboarding the bus, he took rest for 20 min and covers another 10 km by a taxi in 20 min. Find his average speed for the whole journey.

Sol. Total distance covered = 20 + 10 = 30 km

Total time taken = 35 + 20 + 20 = 75 min = $\frac{5}{4}$ h

∴ According to the formula,

$$\text{Average speed} = \frac{\text{Total distance covered}}{\text{Total time taken}} = \frac{30}{\frac{5}{4}} = 24 \text{ km/h}$$

So, the average speed of the person for the whole journey is 24 km/h.

EXAMPLE 10. If a person covers 40 km at a speed of 10 km/h by a cycle, 25 km at 5 km/h on foot and another 100 km at 50 km/h by bus, then find his average speed for the whole journey?

Sol. Here, total distance covered by the person

= 40 + 25 + 100 = 165 km

Time taken to cover 40 km = $\frac{40}{10} = 4$ h

Time taken to cover 25 km = $\frac{25}{5} = 5$ h

Time taken to cover 100 km = $\frac{100}{50} = 2$ h

∴ Total time taken for whole journey = 4 + 5 + 2 h = 11 h

According to the formula,

$$\text{Average speed} = \frac{\text{Total distance covered}}{\text{Total time taken}}$$

$$= \frac{165}{11} = 15 \text{ km/h}$$

EXAMPLE 11. Shantanu covers a certain distance by car driving at 35 km/h and he returns back to the starting point riding on a scooter with a speed of 25 km/h. Find the average speed for the whole journey.

Sol. Let us assume that the distance covered by Shantanu in one direction = D km

∴ Time taken in first case = $\frac{D}{35}$ h

Time taken in second case = $\frac{D}{25}$ h

$$\therefore \text{Average speed} = \frac{\text{Total distance covered}}{\text{Total time taken}}$$

$$= \frac{D + D}{\frac{D}{35} + \frac{D}{25}} = \frac{2D}{D\left(\frac{1}{35} + \frac{1}{25}\right)}$$

$$= \frac{2 \times 35 \times 25}{60} = 29.16 \text{ km/h}$$

EXAMPLE 12. A person covers half of his journey at 30 km/h, one-third at 40 km/h and rest of his journey at 20 km/h. Find his average speed for the whole journey.

Sol. Here, the person cover $\frac{1}{2}$ of his journey at 30 km/h, $\frac{1}{3}$ at 40 km/h and rest $\left(1 - \frac{1}{2} - \frac{1}{3} = \frac{1}{6}\right)$ at 20 km/h

∴ Average speed for whole journey

$$= \frac{1}{\frac{1}{2 \times 30} + \frac{1}{3 \times 40} + \frac{1}{6 \times 20}}$$

$$= \frac{1}{\frac{1}{60} + \frac{1}{120} + \frac{1}{120}} = \frac{1}{\frac{2 + 1 + 1}{120}}$$

$$= \frac{120}{4} = 30 \text{ km/h}$$

EXAMPLE 13. Aashutosh covers a certain distance between his home and college by cycle. Having an average speed of 30 km/h, he is late by 20 min. However, with a speed of 40 km/h, he reaches his college 10 min earlier. Find the distance between his house and college.

Sol. Let the distance = x

Difference between the time taken = 20 + 10

= 30 min = $\frac{30}{60}$ h

According to the question,

$$\frac{x}{30} - \frac{x}{40} = \frac{30}{60} \Rightarrow \frac{x}{30} - \frac{x}{40} = \frac{1}{2}$$

$\Rightarrow \quad 4x - 3x = 60$

$\therefore \quad x = 60$ km

EXAMPLE 14. A boy walking at a speed of 20 km/h reaches his school 30 min late. Next time, he increases his speed by 4 km/h but still he is late by 10 min. Find the distance of the school from his home.

Sol. Let the distance = x

Here, the difference in time = 30 − 10 = 20 min

$= \frac{20}{60}$ h $= \frac{1}{3}$ h

Speed during next journey = (20 + 4) = 24 km/h

According to the question,

$$\frac{x}{20} - \frac{x}{24} = \frac{1}{3}$$

$$\Rightarrow \quad \frac{6x - 5x}{120} = \frac{1}{3} \Rightarrow x = 40 \text{ km}$$

EXAMPLE 15. Sonu and Monu travel from point P to Q, a distance of 42 km, at 6 km/h and 8 km/h, respectively. Monu reaches Q first and returns immediately and meets Sonu at R. Find the distance from points P to R.

Sol. Let $RQ = x$ km, then $PR = (42 - x)$ km

Since, Sonu and Monu meets at R.

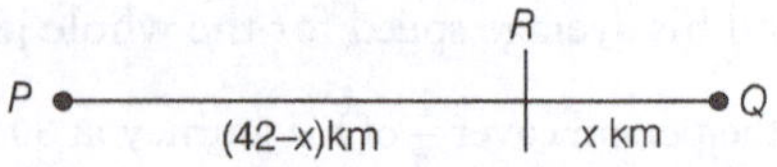

$\therefore$ Distance covered by Sonu $= (42 - x)$ km

and distance covered by Monu $= (42 + x)$ km

$\therefore$ Time taken by Sonu to cover $(42 - x)$ km

= Time taken by Monu to cover $(42 + x)$ km

$$\Rightarrow \frac{(42-x)}{6} = \frac{42+x}{8} \Rightarrow \frac{42-x}{3} = \frac{42+x}{4}$$

$$\Rightarrow 168 - 4x = 126 + 3x \Rightarrow 42 = 7x \Rightarrow x = 6 \text{ km}$$

$\therefore$ Distance travelled by Sonu $= (42 - x) = 36$ km

Some Basic Properties Related to Speed, Time and Distance of Train

- The distance covered by train in passing a pole or a standing man or a signal post or any other object (of negligible length) is equal to the length of the train.
- If a train passes a stationary object (bridge, platform etc.) having some length, then the distance covered by train is equal to the sum of the lengths of train and that particular stationary object which it is passing.
- If two trains of lengths x and y are moving in opposite directions with speeds of u and v respectively, then time taken by the trains to cross each other is equal to $\frac{(x+y)}{(u+v)}$.
- If two trains of lengths x and y are moving in the same direction with speeds of u and v respectively, then time taken by the faster train to cross the slower train is equal to $\left(\frac{x+y}{u-v}\right)$. [here, $u > v$]

EXAMPLE 16. A train covers 85 m in passing a signal post. What is the length of the train?

Sol. We know that the distance covered by a train in passing a pole or a standing man or a signal post or any other object (of negligible length) is equal to the length of the train.

So, in this case, train covers 85 m to pass a signal post.

$\therefore$ Length of the train = 85 m

EXAMPLE 17. A 29 m long train passes a platform which is 100 m long. Find the distance covered by the train in passing the platform.

Sol. We know that when a train passes a stationary object having some length, then the distance covered by train is equal to the sum of the lengths of train and that particular stationary object. In this case, stationary object is 100 m long platform.

$\therefore$ Required distance = Length of train + Length of platform

$= 29 + 100 = 129$ m

EXAMPLE 18. Two trains are moving in opposite directions with speeds of 4 m/s and 8 m/s, respectively. Find their relative speed.

Sol. When two trains are moving in opposite directions, then their relative speed

= Sum of the speeds of both the trains

$\therefore$ Required relative speed $= 4 + 8 = 12$ m/s

EXAMPLE 19. Two trains are moving in the same direction with speeds of 19 km/h and 25 km/h, respectively. What will be the relative speed of the train running at 25 km/h in respect of the train running at 19 km/h?

Sol. We know that when two trains are running in the same direction, then the relative speed is equal to the difference of speeds of both the trains.

$\therefore$ Required relative speed $= 25 - 19 = 6$ km/h

EXAMPLE 20. Two trains of lengths 80 m and 90 m are moving in opposite directions at 10 m/s and 7 m/s, respectively. Find the time taken by the trains to cross each other.

Sol. According to the formula,

$$\text{Required time} = \frac{x+y}{u+v}$$

where, $x = 80$ m, $y = 90$ m, $u = 10$ m/s and $v = 7$ m/s

$$\therefore \text{Required time} = \frac{80+90}{10+7} = \frac{170}{17} = 10 \text{ s}$$

EXAMPLE 21. A train passes a standing man in 6 s and a 210 m long platform in 16 s. Find the length and the speed of the train.

Sol. Let length of the train be L.

As the speed while crossing a standing man and while crossing the platform remains same. Then, According to the question,

$$\frac{L}{6} = \frac{L+210}{16} \qquad \left[\text{Speed} = \frac{\text{Distance}}{\text{Time}}\right]$$

$$\Rightarrow 16L = 6L + 1260 \Rightarrow 10L = 1260$$

$$\Rightarrow L = \frac{1260}{10} = 126 \text{ m}$$

$$\therefore \text{Speed of the train} = \frac{\text{Distance}}{\text{Time}} = \frac{126}{6} = 21 \text{ m/s}$$

Exam Pattern Exercise

Part A - Objective Type Questions

Multiple Choice Type Questions

1 A car covers 400m in 20 s. Find the average speed (in km/h) of the car.
(a) 124 (b) 36 (c) 108 (d) 72

2 A car runs at the speed of 50 km/h when not serviced and runs at 60 km/h when serviced. After servicing, the car covers a certain distance in 6 h. How much time will the car take to cover the same distance when not serviced?
(a) 7.2 h (b) 8.2 h (c) 7.5 h (d) 8.5 h

3 The ratio of the speeds of A and B is 3 : 4. A takes 20 min more than the time taken by B to reach a particular place. Find the time taken by B to reach that place.
(a) 36 min (b) 42 min
(c) 60 min (d) 18 min

4 A man covers half of his journey at 6 km/h and the remaining half at 3 km/h. Find his average speed.
(a) 4.8 km/h (b) 4.5 km/h
(c) 4.2 km/h (d) 4 km/h

5 A bus travels at the rate of 54 km/h without stoppages and it travels at 45 km/h with stoppages. How many minutes does the bus stop on an average per hour?
(a) 10 min (b) 20 min
(c) 5 min (d) 15 min

6 If you travel 39 km at a speed of 26 km/h, another 39 km at a speed of 39 km/h and again 39 km at a speed of 52 km/h, what is your average speed for the entire journey?
(a) 36 km/h (b) 42 km/h
(c) 35 km/h (d) 30 km/h

7 A person goes from one point to another point with a speed of 5 km/h and comes back to starting point with a speed of 3 km/h. Find the average speed for the whole journey.
(a) 0.375 km/h (b) 13.75 km/h
(c) 37.75 km/h (d) 3.75 km/h

8 Two cars A and B start simultaneously from a certain place at the speed of 30 km/h and 45 km/h, respectively. The car B reaches the destination 2 h earlier than A. What is the distance between the starting point and destination?
(a) 160 km (b) 150 km
(c) 180 km (d) 188 km

9 A 250 m long train is running at 100 km/h. In what time will it pass a man running at 10 km/h in the same direction in which the train is going?
(a) 13 s (b) 11 s
(c) 10 s (d) 12 s

10 A 220 m long train is running at 120 km/h. In what time will it pass a man running in the opposite directions to that of the train at 12 km/h?
(a) 6 s
(b) 5 s
(c) 12 s
(d) 10 s

Assertion-Reason Based Questions

Directions (Q. Nos. 11-13) *In the questions given below are two statements labelled as Assertion (A) and Reason (R). In the context of the two statements, which one of the following is correct?*
(a) Both A and R are correct; R is the correct explanation of A
(b) Both A and R are correct; R is not the correct explanation of A
(c) A is correct; R is incorrect
(d) R is correct; A is incorrect

11 **Assertion** (A) Excluding stoppages, the speed of bus is 54 km/h and including stoppages, it is 45 km/h, the bus stop per hour is 10 min.
Reason (R) A train travels 630 km in 8 h and another 410 km in 5 h, then its average speed is 80 km/h.

12 **Assertion** (A) A train 180 m long is running at a speed of 54 km/h. Time taken by train to pass a tunnel 540 m long is 30 s.
Reason (R) If a student walks from his house to school at 5 km/h, he is late by 30 min. However, if he walks at 6 km/h, he is late by 5 min only. The distance of his school from his house is 12.5 km

13 **Assertion** (A) A car covers four successive 3 km stretches at speed of 10 km/h, 20 km/h, 30 km/h and 60 km/h respectively, the average speed of the car for the entire journey is 20 km/h.
Reason (R) On a tour a man travels at the rate of 64 km/h for the first 160 km, then travels the next 160 km at the rate of 80 km/h. The average speed in km per hour for the first 320 km of the train is 60 km/h.

Part B - Descriptive Questions

Very Short Answer Type Questions

14 A man covered a distance of 12 km in 90 min by cycle. How much distance will he cover in 3 h if he rides the cycle at a uniform speed?

15 A person riding a bike crosses a bridge with a speed of 54 km/h. What is the length of the bridge if he takes 4 min to cross the bridge?

16 A train travels at the rate of 50 km/h without stoppages and it travels at 40 km/h with stoppages. How many minutes does the train stop on an average per hour?

17 Sumit drove at the speed of 45 km/h from home to a resort. Returning over the same route, he got stuck in traffic and took an hour longer. Also, he could drive only at the speed of 40 km/h. How many kilometres did he drive each way?

18 *X* and *Y* start walking towards each other at 8 : 00 am at the speeds of 3 km/h and 4 km/h, respectively. They were initially 17.5 km apart. At what time do they meet?

19 Ram and Shyam are moving in the opposite directions to each other. The speeds of both persons are 10 km/h and 6 km/h, respectively. Find the speed of Ram with respect to Shyam.

20 A thief is noticed by a policeman from a distance of 200 m. The thief starts running and the policeman, chases him. The thief and the policeman run at the rate of 10 km/h and 11 km/h, respectively. Find the distance between them after 6 min.

21 A man completes 30 km of a journey at 6 km/h and the remaining 40 km of the journey in 5 h. Find the average speed for the whole journey.

Short Answer Type Questions

22 The ratio of speeds of a train and a car is 16 : 15, respectively and a bus covered a distance of 480 km in 8 h. The speed of the bus is 3/4th of the speed of train. What distance will be covered by car in 6 h?

23 *A* is twice as fast as *B* and *B* is thrice as fast as *C*. The journey covered by *C* in 56 min. In how many minutes will be covered by *A*?

24 A certain distance is covered at a certain speed. If half of this distance is covered in 4 times of the time, then find the ratio of the two speeds.

25 *A* walks at a uniform rate of 2 km/h and 2 h after his start, *B* cycles after him at the uniform rate of 5 km/h. How far from the starting point will *B* catch *A*?

26 *A* and *B* are two stations 1000 km apart. A train starts from *A* and moves towards *B* at 40 km/h. Another train starts from *B* at the same time and moves towards *A* at 60 km/h. How far from *A* will they cross each other?

27 A truck covers a distance of 368 km at a certain speed in 8 h. How much time would a car take at an average speed which is 18 km/h more than that of the speed of the truck to cover a distance which is 16 km more than that travelled by the truck?

28 A car reached Raipur from Somgarh in 35 min with an average speed of 69 km/h. If the average speed is increased by 36 km/h, how much time will it take to cover the same distance?

29 A train of length 250 m, passes a platform of 350 m length in 50 s, what time will this train take to pass the platform of 230 m length?

Long Answer Type Questions

30 A thief is spotted by a policeman from a distance of 200 m. When the policeman starts chasing, the thief also starts running. If the speed of the thief be 16 km/h and that of the policeman be 20 km/h, how far the thief will have run before he is overtaken?

31 A train leaves Manipur at 6:00 am and reaches Dispur at 10:00 am. Another train leaves Dispur at 8:00 am and reaches Manipur at 11 : 30 am. At what time do the two trains cross each other?

32 An express train travelled at an average speed of 100 km/h, stopping for 3 min after every 75 km. A local train travelled at a speed of 50 km/h, stopping for 1 min after every 25 km. If the trains began travelling at the same time, how many kilometres did the local train travel in the time in which the express train travel 600 km?

33 A man covers a certain distance on scooter. Had he moved 3 km/h faster, he would have taken 40 min less. If he had moved 2 km/h slower, he would have taken 40 min more. Find the distance (in km).

34 The ratio between the rates of travelling of *A* and *B* is 2 : 3 and therefore *A* takes 20 min more than time taken by *B* to reach a destination. If *A* had walked at double the speed, how long would he have taken to cover the distance?

35 A train runs for 3 h at the speed of 40 km/h and then for $4\frac{1}{2}$ h at the speed of 60 km/h. Thus, it covers 3/5th part of the whole distance. It wants to cover the remaining distance in 4 h, find the average speed of the train for remaining distance.

Case Study Based Questions

36 A train running at 54 km/h takes 20 s to pass a platform. Next it takes 12 s to pass a man walking at 6 km/h in the same direction in which the train is going.

Based on the above information, answer the following questions.

(i) Relative speed of train with respect to man is

(a) $\frac{44}{5}$ m/s (b) $\frac{40}{3}$ m/s

(c) $\frac{51}{4}$ m/s (d) $\frac{52}{7}$ m/s

(ii) The length of the train is

(a) 180 m (b) 230 m

(c) 140 m (d) 160 m

(iii) The length of the platform is

(a) 140 m (b) 100 m

(c) 120 m (d) 160 m

37 Three friends Rajan, Raghav and Rohan run along a circular park with a speed of 8 km/h, 5 km/h and 3 km/h, respectively. The circumference of the park is 500 m.

Based on the above information, answer the following questions.

(i) They all will meet together for the first time in

(a) 20 min (b) 40 min (c) 30 min (d) 10 min

(ii) They all would meet for the first time at the starting point

(a) 30 min (b) 10 min

(c) 40 min (d) 20 min

Hints & Solutions

1. (d) 2. (a) 3. (c) 4. (d)
5. (a) 6. (a) 7. (d) 8. (c)
9. (c) 10. (a) 11. (b) 12. (d)
13. (c)

14. We know that $\text{Speed} = \frac{\text{Distance}}{\text{Time}} = \frac{12}{\frac{90}{60}} = 8 \text{ km/h}$

$\therefore$ Distance covered in 3 h = Speed × Time
$= 8 \times 3 = 24$ km

15. Solve as Example 3.
Ans. 3600 m

16. Due to stoppages, it covers 10 km less per hour.

Time taken to cover 10 km $= \left(\frac{10}{50} \times 60\right) = 12$ min

Hence, the train stops on an average 12 min/h.

17. Let distance he drove be x.

Since, $\text{Time} = \frac{\text{Distance}}{\text{Speed}}$

From given condition, $\frac{x}{40} - \frac{x}{45} = 1 \Rightarrow x = 360$ km

18. Let they meet after x h.
Then, according to the question,

$$3x + 4x = 17.5$$
$$\Rightarrow 7x = 17.5$$
$$\therefore x = \frac{17.5}{7} = 2.5 \text{ h}$$

So, they meet 2.5 h after 8 : 00 am.
It means, they meet at 10 : 30 am.

19. Solve as Example 7.
Ans. 16 km/h

20. Relative speed of policeman with respect to thief
$= (11 - 10) = 1$ km/h

Now, relative distance covered by policeman in 6 min
$= \text{Speed} \times \text{Time} = 1 \times \frac{6}{60}$
$= \frac{1}{10} \text{ km} = 100 \text{ m}$

21. Solve as Example 10. **Ans.** 7 km/h

22. Let speed of train $= 16x$

Speed of car $= 15x$

Speed of bus $= \frac{480}{8} = 60$ km/h

According to the question,

$$16x = 60 \times \frac{4}{3} = 80$$
$$\Rightarrow x = 5$$

$\therefore$ Speed of car $= 15x = 15 \times 5$
$= 75$ km/h

$\therefore$ Required distance = Speed × Time = 75 × 6 = 450 km

23. Let time taken by $A = y$

Let speed of $C = x$

Then, speed of $B = 3x$

$\therefore$ Speed of $A = 6x$

Now, ratio of speeds of A and C
= Ratio of time taken by C and A

$$\Rightarrow 6x : x = 56 : y$$
$$\Rightarrow \frac{6x}{x} = \frac{56}{y}$$
$$\therefore y = \frac{56}{6} = 9\frac{2}{6} = 9\frac{1}{3} \text{ min}$$

24. Let x km covered in y h. Then, first speed $= \frac{x}{y}$ km/h

Again, $\frac{x}{2}$ km is covered in $4y$ h.

$\therefore$ New speed $= \left(\frac{x}{2} \times \frac{1}{4y}\right) = \left(\frac{x}{8y}\right)$ km/h

Ratio of speeds $= \frac{x}{y} : \frac{x}{8y} = 1 : \frac{1}{8} = 8 : 1$

25. Let B catches A after x h.

Then, distance travelled by A in $(x+2)$ h

= Distance travelled by B in x h

According to the question,

$$2(x+2) = 5x$$
$$\Rightarrow \quad 2x + 4 = 5x$$
$$\Rightarrow \quad 3x = 4$$
$$\therefore \quad x = \frac{4}{3}$$

Distance travelled by B in $\frac{4}{3}$ h $= \frac{4}{3} \times 5 = \frac{20}{3}$

$= 6\frac{2}{3}$ km

26. Let they meet x km from A.

Then, according to the question,

$$\frac{x}{40} = \frac{(1000 - x)}{60}$$
$$\therefore \quad x = \frac{2000}{5} = 400 \text{ km}$$

27. Speed of truck $= \frac{\text{Distance}}{\text{Time}} = \frac{368}{8} = 46$ km / h

Now, speed of car = (speed of truck + 18)

$= (46 + 18) = 64$ km/h

and distance travelled by car $= 368 + 16 = 384$ km

$\therefore$ Time taken by car $= \frac{\text{Distance}}{\text{Speed}} = \frac{384}{64}$ h $= 6$h

28. Distance between Raipur and Somgarh

= Average speed × Time

$= \frac{69 \times 35}{60} = \frac{161}{4}$ km

New speed $= (69 + 36) = 105$ km/h

$\therefore$ Time $= \frac{\text{Distance}}{\text{Speed}} = \frac{161}{4 \times 105}$ h $= \frac{161 \times 60}{4 \times 105}$ min $= 23$ min

29. Length of train = 250 m, length of platform = 350 m

Time taken to cover the distance = 50 s

So, to cross the platform, the train has to cover a distance = Length of train + Length of platform

$= 250 + 350 = 600$ m

$\therefore$ Speed of train $= \frac{\text{Distance covered}}{\text{Time taken}}$

$= \frac{600}{50} = 12$ m/s

Now, the time taken to cross the platform of length 230 m $= \frac{\text{Total distance covered}}{\text{Speed of train}}$

$= \frac{\text{Length of train + Length of platform}}{\text{Speed of train}}$

$= \frac{250 + 230}{12} = \frac{480}{12} = 40$ s

30. Relative speed of policeman $= (20 - 16)$ km/h

$= (20 - 16) \times \frac{5}{18}$ m/s $= \frac{10}{9}$ m/s

To catch the thief, the policeman has to gain 200 m.

Time taken to gain 200 m $= \frac{200 \times 9}{10} = 180$ s

Actual distance covered by policeman in 180 s

$= 180 \times \frac{50}{9} = 1000$ m

$\therefore$ Distance covered by the thief $= 1000 - 200 = 800$ m

31. Let distance between Manipur and Dispur = x km

Average speed of train from Manipur $= \frac{x}{4}$ km/h

Average speed of train from Dispur $= \frac{2x}{7}$ km/h

Let they meet y h after 6 : 00 am.

Then, according to the question,

$$\left(\frac{x}{4} \times y\right) + \frac{2x}{7} \times (y - 2) = x \Rightarrow 15y = 44$$
$$\therefore \quad y = \frac{44}{15} \text{ h} = 2 \text{ h } 56 \text{ min}$$

Clearly, trains meet 2 h 56 min after 6 : 00 am.

It means, the trains meet at 8 : 56 am.

32. Time taken by express train to cover 75 km including stoppage $= \left(\frac{60}{100} \times 75\right)$ min + 3 min = 48 min

Time taken by express train to cover 600 km

= Time taken by it to cover 525 km

+ Time taken by it to cover 75 km

$= \left(\frac{48}{75} \times 525\right)$ min $+ \left(\frac{60}{100} \times 75\right)$ min

$= (336 + 45)$

$= 381$ min

Time taken by local train to cover 25 km including stoppage $= \left(\frac{60}{50} \times 25\right)$ min + 1 min = 31 min

In 31 min, distance covered = 25 km

In (31×12) min, distance covered $= \left(\frac{25}{31} \times 31 \times 12\right)$

$= 300$ km

In last 9 min, distance covered $= \left(\frac{25}{31} \times 9\right) = 7.25$ km

$\therefore$ Required total distance $= 300 + 7.25 = 307.25$ km

33. Let distance and original speed of the man be d km and s km/h. Then,

$$\frac{d}{s} - \frac{d}{s+3} = \frac{2}{3} \Rightarrow 9d = 2s(s+3) \quad \text{...(i)}$$

and $$\frac{d}{s-2} - \frac{d}{s} = \frac{2}{3}$$

$$\Rightarrow \frac{d(s-s+2)}{s(s-2)} = \frac{2}{3}$$

$$\Rightarrow 3d = s(s-2) \quad \text{...(ii)}$$

From Eqs. (i) and (ii), we get

$$3s(s-2) = 2s(s+3)$$

$$\Rightarrow 3s^2 - 6s = 2s^2 + 6s$$

$$\Rightarrow s^2 = 12s \Rightarrow s = 12$$

From Eq. (ii), we get

$$3d = 12(12-2)$$

$$\therefore d = 40 \text{ km}$$

34. We know that speed is inversely proportional to time.

Therefore, time taken by A : Time taken by $B = \frac{1}{2} : \frac{1}{3}$

Let B takes x min. Then, A takes $(x + 20)$ min.

$$\therefore (x+20) : x = \frac{1}{2} : \frac{1}{3} = 3 : 2$$

$$\Rightarrow \frac{x+20}{x} = \frac{3}{2} \Rightarrow 2x + 40 = 3x$$

$$\therefore x = 40$$

$\therefore$ A takes $(x + 20) = (40 + 20) = 60$ min

$\therefore$ At double the speed, A would have covered it in 30 min.

35. Let total distance $= x$

Now, according to the question,

$$40 \times 3 + 60 \times 4.5 = \frac{3x}{5}$$

$$\Rightarrow 120 + 270 = \frac{3x}{5}$$

$$\therefore x = \frac{390 \times 5}{3} = 650 \text{ km}$$

$\therefore$ Remaining distance $= \left(650 - \frac{3 \times 650}{5}\right)$

$= 650 - 390 = 260$ km

$\therefore$ Required average speed $= \frac{260}{4} = 65$ km/h

36. (i) (b) Relative speed of train with respect to man

$= (54 - 6)$ km/h

$= 48 \times \frac{5}{18} = \frac{40}{3}$ m/s

(ii) (d) In crossing a man, the train covers its own length with relative speed.

$\therefore$ Length of train (distance) = Relative speed $\times$ Time

$= \frac{40}{3} \times 12 = 160$ m

(iii) (a) Train crosses a platform with speed of 54 km/h or 15 m/s.

$\therefore$ Let the length of the platform be x m.

$\Rightarrow$ Distance = Speed $\times$ Time

$\Rightarrow$ $(160 + x) = 15 \times 20$

$\Rightarrow$ $160 + x = 300$

$\Rightarrow$ $x = 300 - 160 = 140$ m

37. (i) (c) Relative speed of Rajan with respect to Raghav

$= (8 - 5) = 3$ km/h

$\therefore$ At a relative speed of 3 km/h, Rajan would meet Raghav after every $\frac{500}{3 \times \frac{5}{18}} = 600$ s or 10 min

Relative speed of Rajan with respect to Rohan

$= (8 - 3) = 5$ km/h

$\therefore$ At a relative speed of 5 km/h, Rajan meets Rohan

$= \frac{500}{5 \times \frac{5}{18}} = 360$ s $= 6$ min

$\therefore$ All of three would meet for the first time

= LCM of 10 and 6 = 30 min

(ii) (a) Time taken by Rajan in making one revolution

$= \frac{500}{8 \times \frac{5}{18}} = 225$ s

Time taken by Raghav in making one revolution

$= \frac{500}{5 \times \frac{5}{18}} = 360$ s

and time taken by rohan in making one revolution

$= \frac{500}{3 \times \frac{5}{18}} = 600$ s

$\therefore$ They would meet for the first time at the starting point = LCM of 225, 360 and 600

$= 1800$ s

$= 30$ min

CHAPTER 07

Seating Arrangement

In this Chapter...

- Linear Arrangement
- Circular Arrangement

The process of arranging the persons/objects according to the given sitting conditions, is called **seating arrangement.**

Seating arrangement questions are based on the seating sequence pattern, direction, facing outside or inside etc.

Based on the various patterns of seating arrangement, they can be divided into the following four types.

Linear Arrangement

In linear arrangement, persons/objects are required to be placed in proper order either in one straight line or in two straight lines.

In these questions, the candidate is required to identify the exact position of the objects and their positions with respect to one another based on the information given.

The linear arrangement can further be of two types, based on the number of rows.

One Row Sequence

In such an arrangement, objects/ persons are placed in a single row as shown below

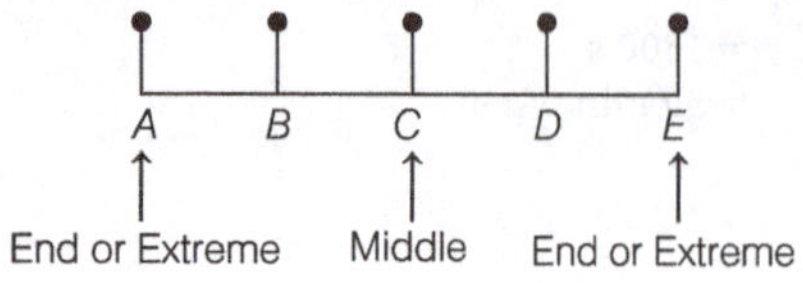

Case I

In the above arrangement, if direction of face is not given, then we should take ourself as a base to determine left and right of the objects/persons.

In other words, we can say that in such cases our left and right are the left and right of the objects/persons. Let us see

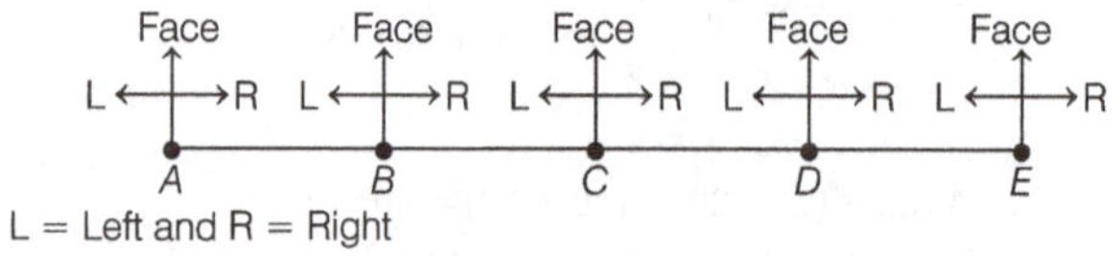

From the above diagram, it is clear that,

(i) *B*, *C*, *D* and *E* are to the right of *A* but only *B* is to the immediate right of *A*.

(ii) *D*, *C*, *B* and *A* are to the left of *E* but only *D* is to the immediate left of *E*.

(iii) *C*, *D* and *E* are to the right of *B* but only *C* is to the immediate right of *B*.

(iv) *C*, *B* and *A* are to the left of *D* but only *C* is to the immediate left of *D*.

(v) *D* and *E* are to the right of *C* but only *D* is to the immediate right of *C*.

(vi) *B* and *A* are to the left of *C* but only *B* is to the immediate left of *C*.

(vii) *A* is to the immediate left of *B* while *E* is to the immediate right of *D*.

EXAMPLE 1. 6 persons are sitting in a row. They are *A, B, C, D, E* and *F*. *D* is sitting on the extreme right end. *B* is between *F* and *D*. *E* is between *A* and *C*. *A* is not sitting beside *F* and *D*.

(i) Write the seating arrangement according to the given conditions.

(ii) Who is at other end of the row ?

(iii) Who is immediate right of *A* ?

(iv) What is the position of *F* with respect to *D* ?

Sol. (i) According to the question,
D is sitting on extreme right.

B is between *F* and *D*

E is between *A* and *C* but *A* is not sitting beside *F*.
So, the final arrangement is

(ii) *A* is at the other end of the row.

(iii) *E* is sitting to the immediate right of *A*.

(iv) *F* is sitting second to the left of *D*.

EXAMPLE 2. There are five houses *P, Q, R, S* and *T*. *P* is right of *Q* and *T* is left of *R* and right of *P*. *Q* is right of *S*. Which house is in the middle?

Sol. According to the question, the houses can be arranged as

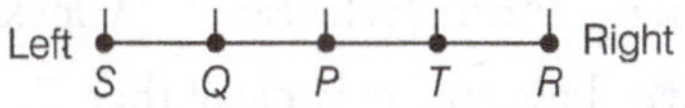

Clearly, the house *P* is in the middle of all the houses.

Case II

If direction of face is given, then left and right is taken according to the given direction of face.

e.g. If 5 students are sitting in a row and their faces are towards you, then in this case, the direction of faces of students is opposite to the direction of your face.

Let us see

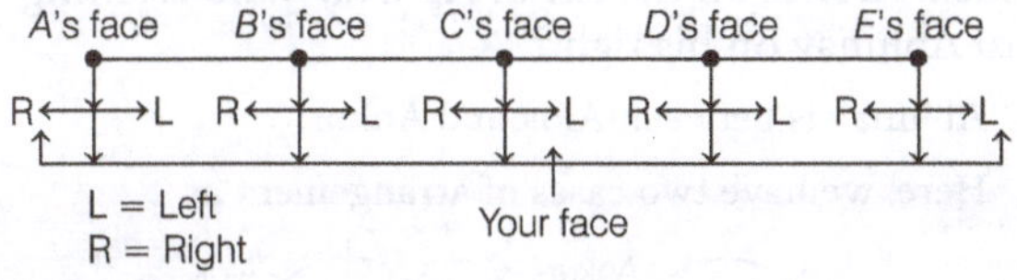

From the above diagram, it is clear that

(i) Left of *A* = *B, C, D* and *E*

(ii) Right of *E* = *D, C, B* and *A*

(iii) B is immediate left of *A, C* is immediate left of *B, D* is immediate left of *C* and *E* is immediate left of *D*.

(iv) *D* is immediate right of *E, C* is immediate right of *D, B* is immediate right of *C* and *A* is immediate right of *B*.

EXAMPLE 3. 5 persons *A, B, C, D* and *E* are sitting in a row facing North such that *D* is on the left of *C* and *B* is on the right of *E*. *A* is on the right of *C* and *B* is on the left of *D*. If *E* occupies a corner position, then who is sitting in the centre?

Sol. Arrangement according to the question is as follows

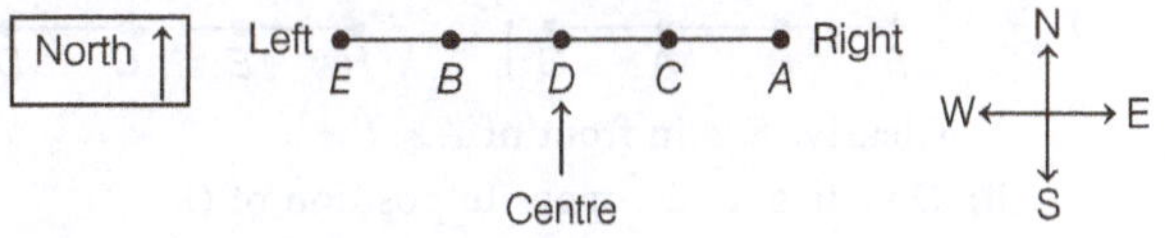

Clearly, *D* is sitting in the centre.

EXAMPLE 4. Five friends are sitting in a row facing the South direction. Among them Mohan is between Balu and Raju, and Raju is to the immediate right of Parveen. In the same way, Amit is to the right of Balu. Who is at the extreme right end?

Sol. According to the question, the sitting arrangement is as follows

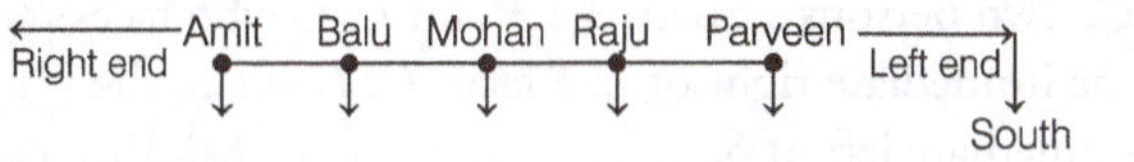

Clearly, Amit is at the extreme right end.

Two Row Sequence

In such arrangement, objects/persons are arranged in two different rows facing each other as follows

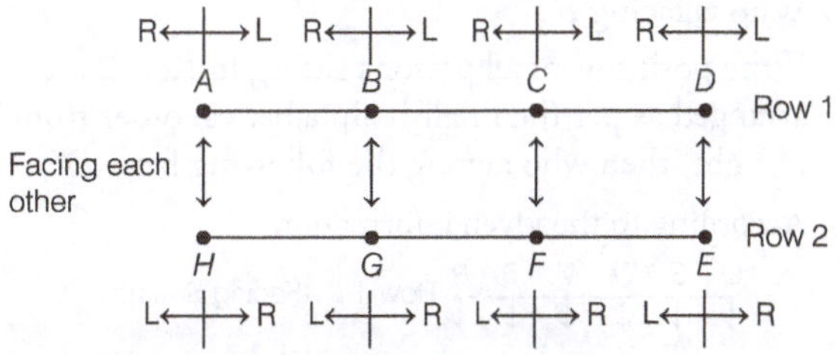

From the above diagram, it is clear that

(i) *A* is sitting opposite to *H*.

(ii) *B* is sitting opposite to *G*.

(iii) *C* is sitting opposite to *F*.

(iv) *D* is sitting opposite to *E*.

(v) *A* and *E* are sitting at diagonally opposite positions.

(vi) *D* and *H* are sitting at diagonally opposite positions.

EXAMPLE 5. 8 persons *A, B, C, D, E, F, G* and *H* are sitting in two rows opposite to each other. Each row has 4 persons. *B* and *C* are sitting in front of each other. *C* is between *D* and *E*. *H* is sitting to the immediate left of *E*. *H* and *F* are diagonally opposite. *G* and *B* are not near to each other.

(i) Who is in front of *A*?

(ii) Who is diagonally opposite position of *G*?

Sol. (i) According to the question, arrangement of persons are as follows

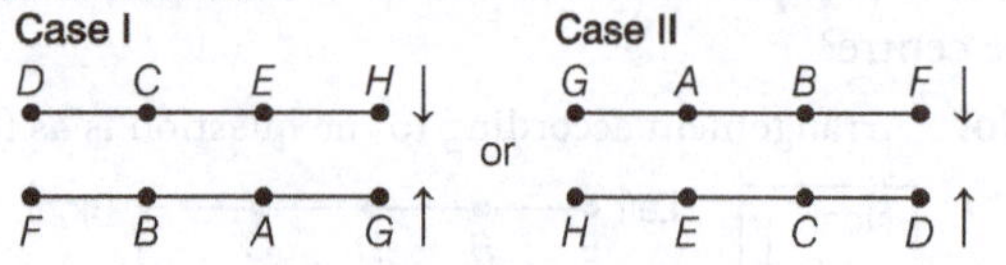

Clearly, *E* is in front of *A*.

(ii) *D* is diagonally opposite position of *G*.

EXAMPLE 6. Twelve persons are sitting in two parallel rows at equal distance facing each other. *Q, R, S, T, U* and *V* are sitting in Row 1 facing South. *B, C, D, E, F* and *G* are sitting in Row 2 facing North (but not necessarily in the same order).

G sits third to the right of *B* and one of them sits at the end of the row. *Q* sits at the right end of the row. Three persons sit between *Q* and *T*. *F* sits to the immediate left of *G*. Two persons sit between *F* and *C*. *C* who faces *R* sits to the immediate right of *E*. *S* faces *D*. *U* sits to the immediate left of *S*.

(i) Which of the following pair sits at the extreme ends of the Row 2?

(ii) Who sits second to the left of the person facing *V*?

(iii) What is the position of *U* with respect to *R*?

(iv) Who is facing *F*?

(v) If the positions of all persons sitting in Row 2 are arranged as per the English alphabetical order from left to right, then who among the following faces *D*?

Sol. According to the given information,

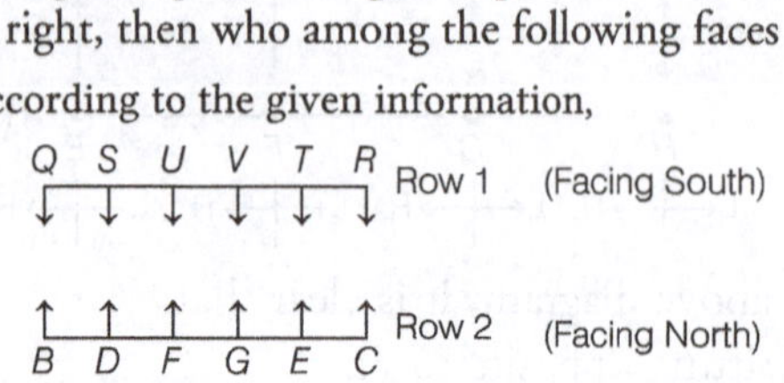

(i) *B* and *C* sit at the extreme ends of Row 2.

(ii) *G* faces *V* and *D* sits second to the left of *G*.

(iii) *U* is third to the right of *R*.

(iv) *U* is facing *F*.

(v) If all the persons sitting in Row 2 are arranged as per the English alphabetical order from left to right, then *U* will face *D*.

Circular Arrangement

In this type of arrangement, objects/persons are placed around a circle either facing the centre or facing the direction opposite to centre. The left and right of each person/object in both the cases can be understood with the help of following diagrams.

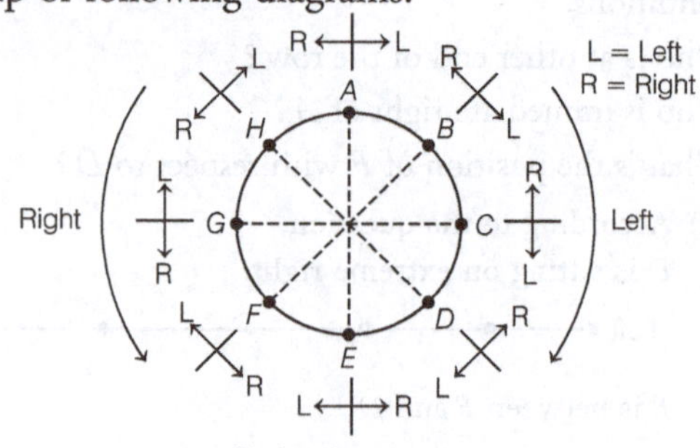

Facing the centre

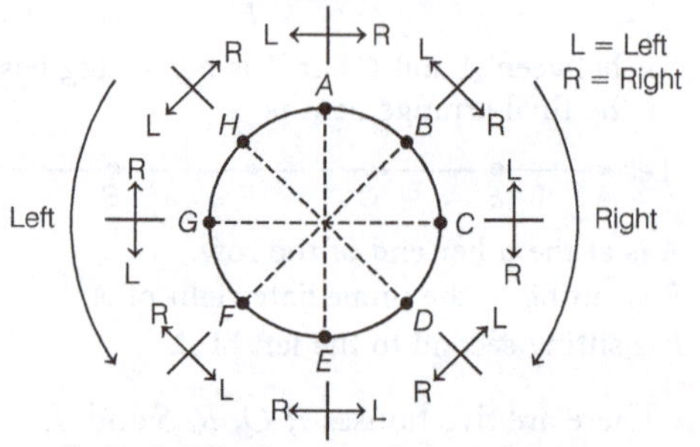

Facing the direction opposite to centre

	Left	Right
Centre facing	Clockwise	Anti-clockwise
Outwards facing	Anti-clockwise	Clockwise

From the above diagram, it is clear that

(i) *A* and *E* are in front of each other.

(ii) *B* and *F* are in front of each other.

(iii) *C* and *G* are in front of each other.

(iv) *D* and *H* are in front of each other.

Now let's discuss the following example to understand how this type of questions are solved.

EXAMPLE 7. Five students are standing in a circle. Abhinav is between Alok and Ankur. Apurva is on the left of Abhishek. Alok is on the left of Apurva. Who is sitting next to Abhinav on his right?

Sol. Abhinav is between Alok and Ankur.

Here, we have two cases of arrangement as

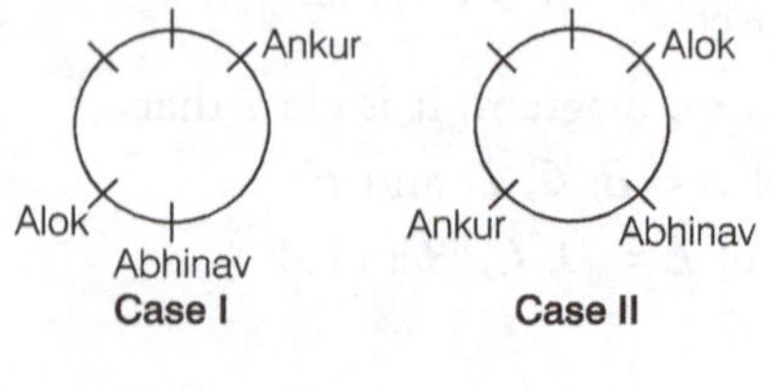

Apurva is on the left of Abhishek.

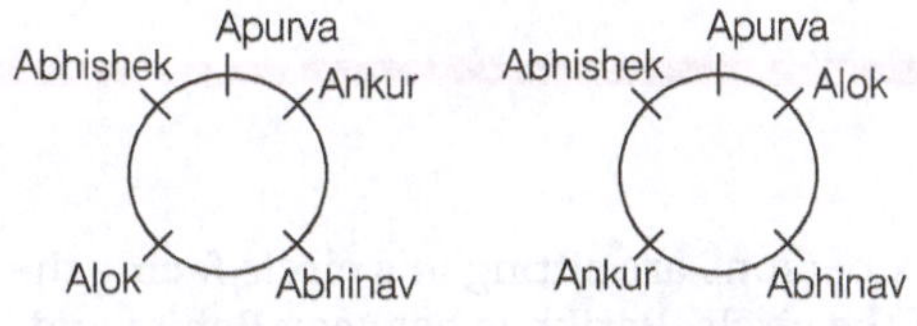

Case I Case II

Alok is on the left of Apurva. Here, Case I is eleminated. So, the final arrangement is

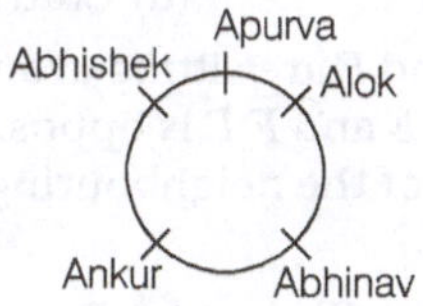

Clearly, Alok is sitting next to Abhinav on his right.

EXAMPLE 8. Study the following information carefully and answer the questions given below. Eight persons are sitting around a circular table facing to the centre but not necessarily in the same order.

Two persons sit between *Q* and *P* (either from left or right). *R* sits immediate to the right of *Q*. One person sits between *R* and *S*, who faces to *T*. *Q* and *T* are not immediate neighbours of each other. *W* sits second to the left of *V*. Three persons sit between *U* and *V*.

(i) Who sits immediate right of *U*?

(ii) Who faces *R*?

(iii) Who sits third to the right of *S*?

Sol. According to the given information,

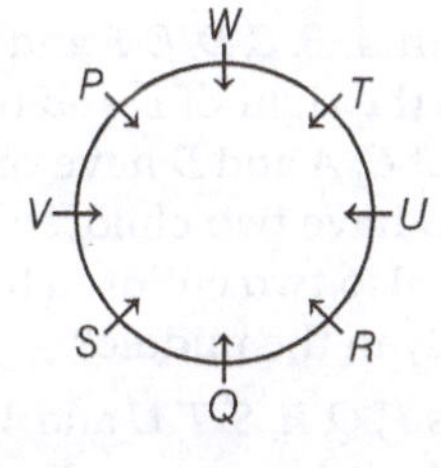

(i) *T* sits immediate right of *U*.

(ii) *P* faces *R*.

(iii) *U* sits third to the right of *S*.

EXAMPLE 9. Study the information carefully and answer the given questions.

L, M, N, O, P, Q, R and *S* are sitting around a circular area at equal distance between each other, but not necessarily in the same order. Some people face towards the centre while some face outside (i.e. in a direction opposite to the centre).

- *O* faces the centre. *S* sits third to the right of *O*. Only one person sits between *S* and *L* (either from left or right).
- *P* sits second to the left of *L*.
- *R* sits second to the right of *N*. *N* is not an immediate neighbour of *S*.
- *Q* sits to the immediate left of *M*. *M* and *L* face the same direction (i.e. *M* faces centre, then *L* also faces the centre and *vice-versa*)
- Immediate neighbours of *Q* face opposite directions (i.e. if one neighbour faces the centre, then the other faces outside and *vice-versa*)
- Immediate neighbours of *O* face opposite directions (i.e. if one neighbour faces the centre, then the other faces outside and *vice-versa*)
- Immediate neighbours of *S* faces the same direction as *S*. (i.e. if *S* faces outside, then both the immediate neighbours of *S* also faces outside and *vice-versa*)

(i) What is *M*'s position with respect to *L*?

(ii) Who amongst the following are immediate neighbours of *O*?

(iii) Four of the following five are alike in a certain way, based on the given seating arrangement and so form a group. Which is the one that does not belong to that group?

(a) *R* (b) *Q* (c) *S* (d) *P* (e) *M*

Sol. According to the given information,

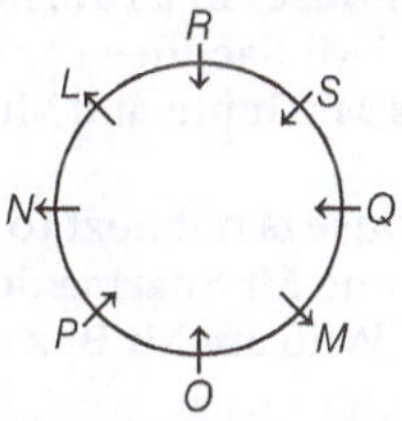

(i) *M* is fourth to the right of *L* or misfourth to the left of *L*.

(ii) *P* and *M* are immediate neighbours of *O*.

(iii) (e) Except *M*, all other faces inside, whereas *M* faces outside.

Exam Pattern Exercise

Part A - Objective Type Questions

Multiple Choice Questions

1 *A*, *B*, *C*, *D*, *E* and *F* are six friends sitting in a long bench. *E* and *F* are at the centre while *A* and *B* are at the two extreme ends. *C* is sitting to the immediate left of *A*. Can you identify who is sitting to the immediate right of *B*?

(a) *C* (b) *D* (c) *F* (d) *E*

2 Six friends *A*, *B*, *C*, *D*, *E* and *F* are sitting in a row facing East. *C* is between *A* and *E*. *B* is just to the right of *E* but left of *D*. *F* is not at the right end. How many persons are to the right of *E*?

(a) 1 (b) 2 (c) 3 (d) 4

3 *A*, *B*, *C*, *D*, *E* and *F* are sitting in a row. *E* and *F* are in the centre and *A* and *B* are at the ends. *C* is sitting on the immediate left of *A*. Then, who is sitting on the fourth right of *B*?

(a) *A* (b) *C*
(c) *E* (d) *F*

4 Five girls are sitting in a row. Kalpita is to the left of Mridula. Megha is to the right of Arpana. Sangeeta is in the middle of Megha and Kalpita. Who among the following is to the right end of the row?

(a) Mridula (b) Arpana
(c) Kalpita (d) Cannot be determined

5 There are six houses in a row. Mr Lal has Mr Bhasin and Mr Sachdeva as neighbours. Mr Bhatia has Mr Gupta and Mr Sharma as neighbours.
Mr Gupta's house is not next to Mr Bhasin or Mr Sachdava and Mr Sharma does not live next to Mr Sachdeva. Who are Mr Bhasin's next door neighbours?

(a) Mr Lal and Mr Bhasin
(b) Mr Lal and Mr Sachdeva
(c) Mr Sharma and Mr Lal
(d) Only Mr Lal

6 In a gathering, seven members are sitting in a row. *C* is sitting left to *B* but on the right of *D*. *A* is sitting right to *B*. *F* is sitting right to *E* but left to *D*. *H* is sitting left to *E*. Find the person sitting in middle.

(a) *C* (b) *D*
(c) *E* (d) *F*

7 Six persons are sitting in a circle facing the centre of the circle. Parikh is between Babita and Narendra. Asha is between Chitra and Pankaj. Chitra is to the immediate left of Babita. Who is immediate right of Babita?

(a) Parikh (b) Pankaj
(c) Narendra (d) Chitra

8 *A*, *B*, *C*, *D*, *E* and *F* are sitting around a round table. *A* is between *E* and *F*. *E* is opposite to *D* and *C* is not in either of the neighbouring seats of *E*. Who is opposite to *B*?

(a) *F* (b) *C* (c) *D* (d) *A*

9 Four friends were playing a game of cards sitting in a circle. Shankar was on the right of Ram and Gopal was on the left of Arvind. Which of the following pairs were partners?

(a) Ram and Shankar (b) Gopal and Shankar
(c) Ram and Arvind (d) Gopal and Ram

10 Thirty six vehicles are packed in a parking lot in a single row. After the first car, there is one scooter. After the second car, there are two scooters. After the third car, there are three scooters and so on. Work out the number of scooters in the second half of the row.

(a) 10 (b) 12 (c) 15 (d) 17

Part B - Descriptive Questions

Very Short Answer Type Questions

11 Seven children *A*, *B*, *C*, *D*, *E*, *F* and *G* are standing in a row. *G* is to the right of *D* and to the left of *B*. *A* is on the right of *C*, *A* and *D* have one child between them. *E* and *B* have two children between them. *D* and *F* have also two children between them. Who is exactly in the middle?

12 Seven friends *P*, *Q*, *R*, *S*, *T*, *U* and *V* are watching hockey match sitting in a stadium. *P* and *U* are sitting at the extreme ends. *S* is sitting second right of *P* and between *T* and *R*. *Q* is sitting between *U* and *V*. *R* is sitting immediate left of *V*. Who is sitting at the middle of all?

13 Six children *A*, *B*, *C*, *D*, *E* and *F* are standing in a row. *B* is between *F* and *D*. *E* is between *A* and *C*. *A* does not stand next to either *F* or *D*. *C* does not stand next to *D*. *F* is between which of the following pairs of children?

14 There are five different houses A to E in a row. A is to the right of B and E is to the left of C and right of A, B is to the right of D. Which of the houses is in the middle?

15 In a college party, 5 girls are sitting in a row. P is to the left of M and to the right of O. R is sitting to the right of N but to the left of O.

(i) Write the sitting arrangement according to the given conditions.

(ii) Who is sitting in the middle?

(iii) Who are at the extreme ends?

16 Six persons M, N, O, P, Q and R are sitting in two rows with three persons in each row. Both the rows are in front of each other. Q is not at the end of any row. P is second to the left of R. O is the neighbour of Q and diagonally opposite to P. N is the neighbour of R. Who is in front of N?

17 Five boys are standing in a row facing East. Pavan is to the left of Tavan, Vipin, Chavan. Tavan, Vipin and Chavan are to the left of Nakul. Chavan is between Tavan and Vipin. If Vipin is fourth from the left, then how far is Tavan from the right?

18 P, A, D, Q, T, M, R and B are sitting around a circle facing at the centre. D is third to the left of T who is fifth to the right of P. A is third to the right of B who is second to the right of D. Q is second to the left of M. Who is second to the right of D?

19 Six friends P, Q, R, S, T and U are sitting at a circular table facing the centre. S is sitting third to the left of T. R is not sitting between T and U. S is not the immediate neighbour of R. Q is seated second to the right of T. Who is sitting between U and Q?

Short Answer Type Questions

20 Read the following information carefully and then answer the questions given below.

Seven boys A, B, C, D, E, F and G are standing in a line.

I. G is between A and E.

II. F and A have one boy between them.

III. E and C have two boys between them.

IV. D is to the immediate right of F.

V. C and B have three boys between them.

(i) Who is second from left?

(ii) C is standing between.

21 Study the following information carefully to answer the questions below.

Five persons are standing in a queue. One of the two persons at the extreme ends is a professor and the other is a businessman. An advocate is standing to the right of a student. An author is to the left of the businessman. The student is between the professor and the advocate.

(i) Counting from the left, the author is at which place?

(ii) Which of the following is in the middle of the queue?

22 Read the following information carefully and answer the questions that follow.

I. Six flats on a floor in two rows facing North and South are allotted to P, Q, R, S, T and U.

II. Q gets a North facing flat and is not next to S.

III. S and U get diagonally opposite flats.

IV. R next to U, gets a South facing flat and T gets a North facing flat.

(i) Whose flat is between Q and S?

(ii) The flats of which of the pair, other than SU, are diagonally opposite to each other?

23 Study the following information carefully and answer the questions given below.

Ten students $A, B, C, D, E, F, G, H, I$ and J are sitting in a row facing West.

I. B and F are not sitting on either of the edges.

II. G is sitting to the left of D and H is sitting to the right of J.

III. There are four persons between E and A.

IV. I is to the North of B and F is to the South of D.

V. J is in between A and D and G is in between E and F.

VI. There are two persons between H and C.

(i) Who is sitting at the seventh place counting from left?

(ii) Who among the following is definitely sitting at one of the ends?

(a) G (b) D (c) E (d) H

(iii) Who are immediate right neighbours of I?

(iv) Who is sitting second left of D?

(v) If G and A interchange their positions, then who become the immediate neighbours of E?

24 Read the following information carefully and then answer the questions that follow.

Eight persons P, M, R, T, Q, U, V and W are sitting in front of one another in two rows. Each row has 4 persons. P is between U and V and facing North. Q, who is to the immediate left of M is facing W. R is between T and M and W is to the immediate right of V.

(i) Who is sitting in front of *R*?

(ii) Who is to the immediate right of *R*?

(iii) In which of the persons are sitting in front of each other?

(a) *M*, *V* (b) *R*, *Q* (c) *R*, *M* (d) *T*, *W*

25 Study the following information carefully and answer the questions given below.

Eight persons are sitting around a circular table facing towards the centre of the table. *A* sits second to the left of *B*. Only two persons sit between *A* and *H*. *G* sits third to the right of *H*. *E* sits immediate left of *G*. *D* sits second to the left of *C*. *F* sits third to the right of *C*.

(i) Who among the following sits second to the left of *H*?

(ii) Who among the following faces *D*?

(iii) Four of the following five are alike in a certain way and hence form a group which of the following does not belong to the group?

(a) *G* and *F* (b) *C* and *H*

(c) *A* and *G* (d) *F* and *H*

(iv) How many persons sit between *H* and *E* when counted from right of *H*?

26 Read the following information carefully to answer the questions given below.

Five friends Ram, Shyam, Atul, Dev and Raj are sitting on a round table and all are facing outside. Atul is sitting third left to Ram and Shyam is sitting immediate left of Raj and immediate right of Atul.

(i) Who is sitting immediate right to Dev?

(ii) Who is sitting between Ram and Shyam?

(iii) Who is second left of Raj?

Long Answer Type Questions

27 Study the following information carefully and answer the questions given below.

Ten persons are sitting in two parallel rows containing five persons in each row such a way that there is an equal distance between adjacent persons.

In the first row, *A*, *B*, *C*, *D* and *E* are seated and all of them all of them are facing North. In the second row, *P*, *Q*, *R*, *S* and *T* are seated and all of them are facing South. Therefore, in the given seating arrangement, each member seated in a row faces another member of the other row.

E sits second from one of the extreme end of the row. *P* faces the one who sits second to the right of *E*. *D* sits second and all of them to the left of *B*, who does not sit at the extreme end. Two persons sit between *S* and *Q*. *R* sits immediate left of *S*. *C* sits next to *B*.

(i) Who among the above faces *Q*?

(ii) Who among the above sits at the extreme end of the row?

(a) *E* (b) *S* (c) *T* (d) *P*

(iii) Four of the following five are alike in a certain way and hence they form a group. Which one of the following does not belong to that group?

(a) *T* (b) *P* (c) *Q*

(d) *D* (e) *A*

(iv) Who among the above sits second to the right of *P*?

(v) What is the position of *A* with respect to *E*?

28 Read the following information carefully and answer the questions given below.

In a party, *A*, *B*, *C*, *D* and *E* are sitting in a circle. The group comprises a professor, an industrialist and a businessman.

The businessman is sitting in between the industrialist and his wife *D*. *A*, the professor is married to *E*, who is the sister of *B*. The industrialist is seated to the right of *C*. Both the ladies are unemployed.

(i) What is the relation of *A* to *B*?

(ii) Who is sitting the right of *C*?

(iii) Who is industrialist?

(iv) Who is unmarried in the group?

(v) Who among them must be graduate?

29 Study the following information carefully and answer the questions given below.

P, *Q*, *R*, *S*, *T*, *V*, *W*, *Z* are sitting around a circle facing at the centre. *R* is fourth to the left to *P*, who is second to the right of *S*. *V* is fourth to right of *S*. *Q* is fourth to the left of *W*, who is not an immediate neighbour of *P* or *S*. *Z* is not an immediate neighbour of *R*.

(i) Who is to the immediate right of *V*?

(ii) Who is the immediate right of *R*?

(iii) Who is the third to the right of *R*?

(iv) Who is the second to the left of *Z*?

30 Study the following information carefully to answer the given questions.

Seven boxes *S, P, L, Q, R, M* and *I* are places one above the other in any particular order. Box number 1 is at the bottom and box number 7 is at the top. Three boxes are placed between *I* and *M*. *M* is placed on the place just above *S*, which did not place on an odd numbered place. *P* is neither placed on odd number place nor on topmost place. I did not place on bottom place. Two boxes are placed between *R* and *S*. *Q* is placed neither on the bottom nor on the fourth place. Box *M* is not placed on top place.

(i) Which box is placed on just above *M*?

(ii) How many boxes are there between *L* and *P*?

(iii) Which of the above pairs of boxes is placed on bottom most and the topmost place, respectively?

(iv) Which of the above box is placed on the topmost place?

Hints & Solutions

1. (b) According to the given information

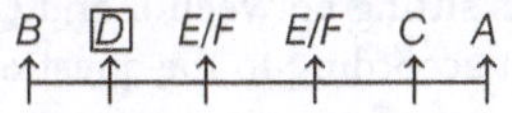

∴ Clearly, *D* is sitting to the immediate right of *B*.

2. (b) According to the given information, following sitting arrangement is formed.

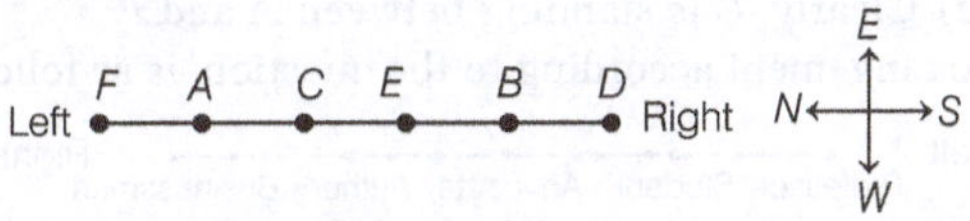

Clearly, 2 persons (*i.e.* B and D) are to the right of *E*.

3. (b) Arrangement according to the question is as follows

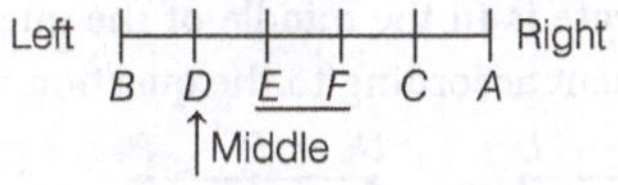

Clearly, *D* is to the right of *B*. Hence, option (b) is the correct answer.

4. (a) Arrangement according to the questions, is as follows

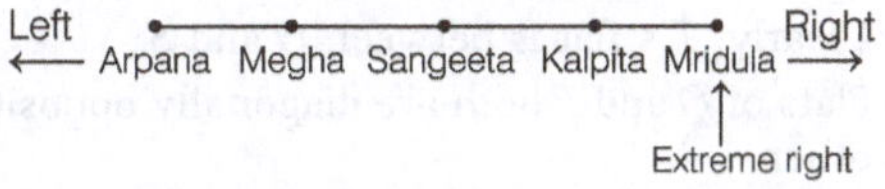

Clearly, Mridula is to the extreme right of the row.

5. (c) According to the question, the arrangement is as follow

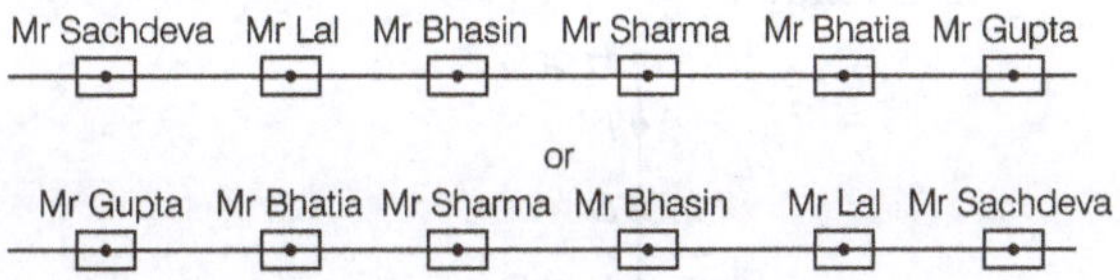

Clearly, Mr Bhasin's next door neighbours are Mr Lal and Mr Sharma both.

6. (b) According to the question, arranging the seven members in a row.

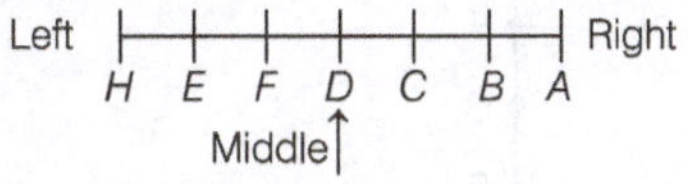

Here, *D* is sitting in middle.

7. (a) Following sitting arrangement is formed using the given information.

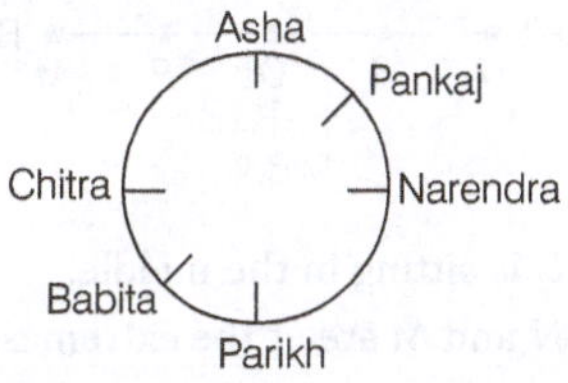

Clearly Parikh is immediate right of Babita.

8. (a) According to information,

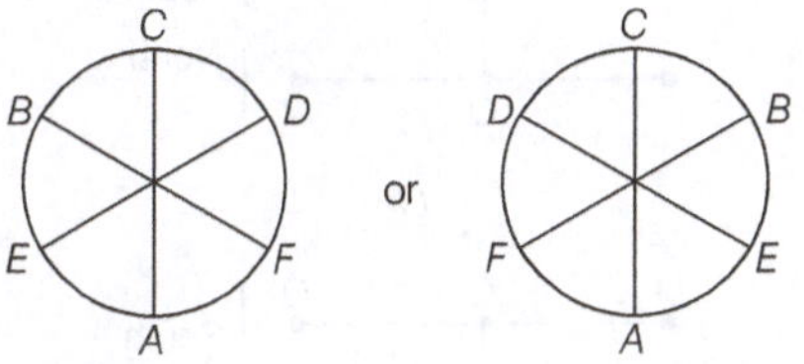

Clearly, *F* is opposite to *B*.

9. (d) According to information,

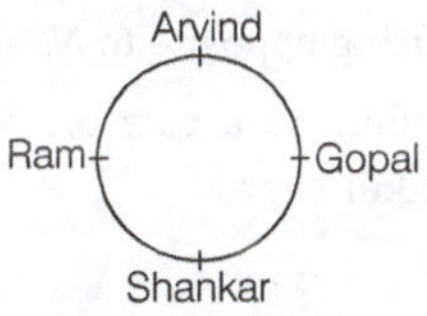

Clearly, two partners are Gopal and Ram, since partners are the friends who are sitting opposite to each other.

10. (c) In the second half of the row, there are 18 vehicles. Thus, the number of scooters is 15.

11. (c) The sequence of children in the row is as follows,

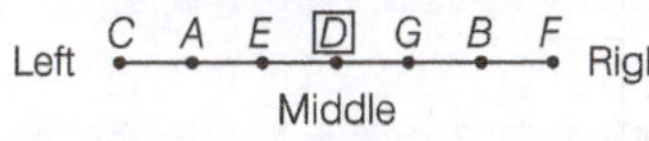

Clearly, *D* is exactly in the middle.

12. (c) From the given information,

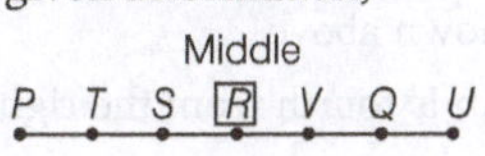

Clearly, *R* sits in the middle of all.

13. According to the given information, the arrangement in which children are standing in the row is as follows

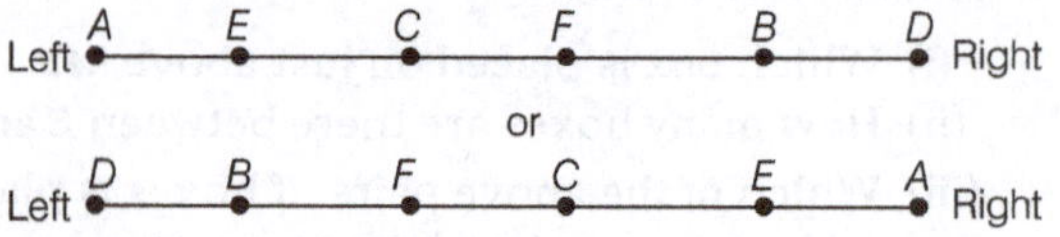

Clearly, *F* is standing between *B* and *C*.

14. According to the given information, houses in the row are arranged as follows

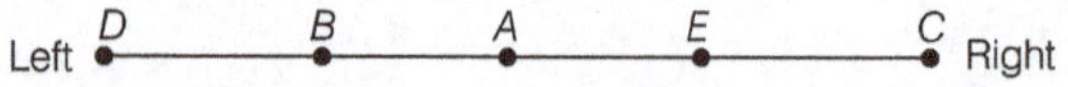

Clearly, the house in the middle is *A*.

15. (i) Arrangement according to the question is as follows

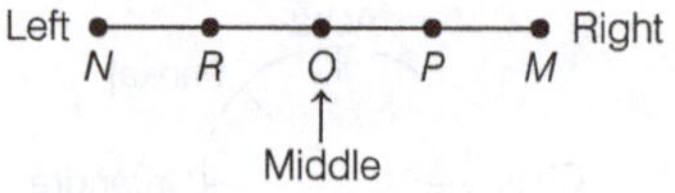

(ii) Clearly, *O* is sitting in the middle.

(iii) Clearly, *N* and *M* are at the extremes.

16. Arrangement according to the question is as follows

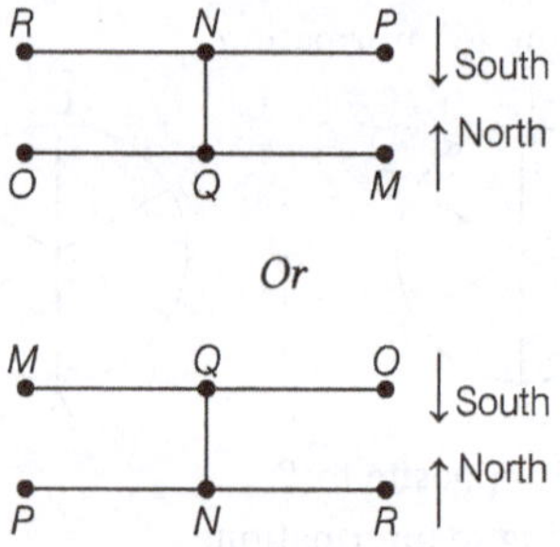

Clearly, *Q* is sitting opposite to *N*.

17. Five boys standing in a row are Pavan, Tavan, Vipin, Chavan and Nakul

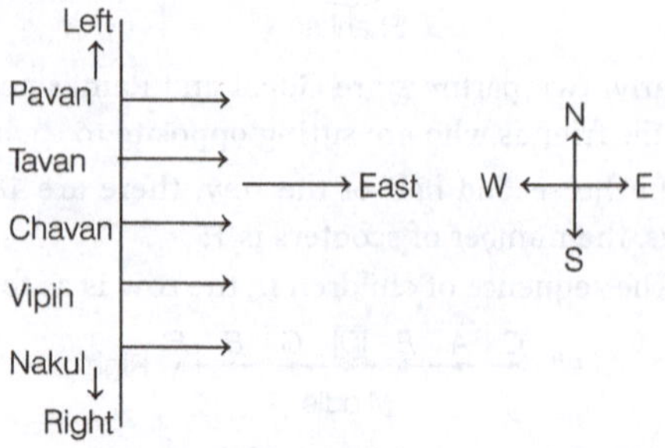

From the given information, the five boys are standing in the row as shown above.

Clearly, Tavan is fourth from the right end.

18. (d) From given information, arrangement is as follows

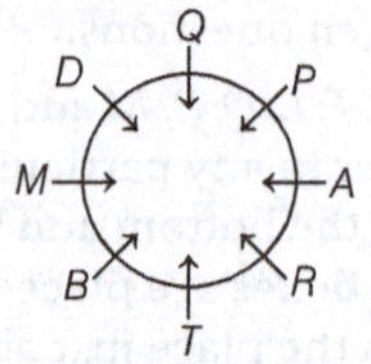

It is clear from above that *B* is second to the right of *D*.

19. (a) According to the given information,

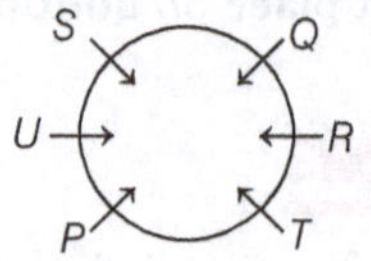

∴ Clearly, *S* is sitting between *U* and *Q*.

20. Arrangement according to the questions is as follows

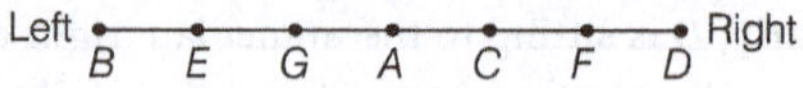

(i) Clearly, *E* is second from left.

(ii) Clearly, *C* is standing between *A* and *F*.

21. Arrangement according to the question, is as follows

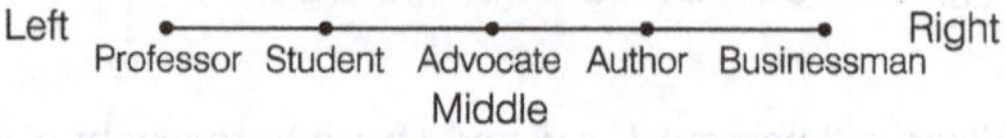

(i) Clearly, author is fourth from the left.

(ii) Advocate is in the middle of the queue.

22. Arrangement according to the question, is as follows.

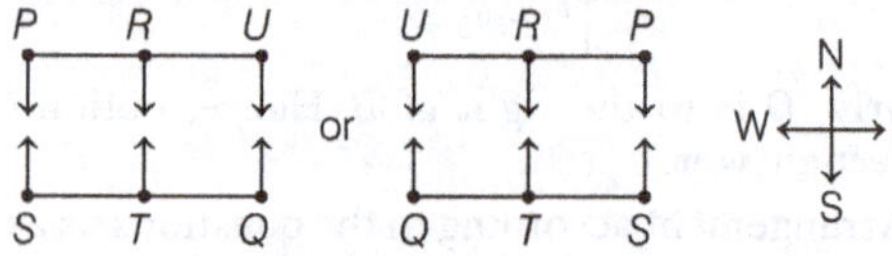

(i) Clearly, *T*'s flat is between *Q* and *S*.

(ii) Flats of *Q* and *P* both are diagonally opposite to each other.

23. On the basis of the given information exact positions of *C* and *H* cannot be determined. However, they will occupy the first and the fourth positions. Now, the arrangement is as follows

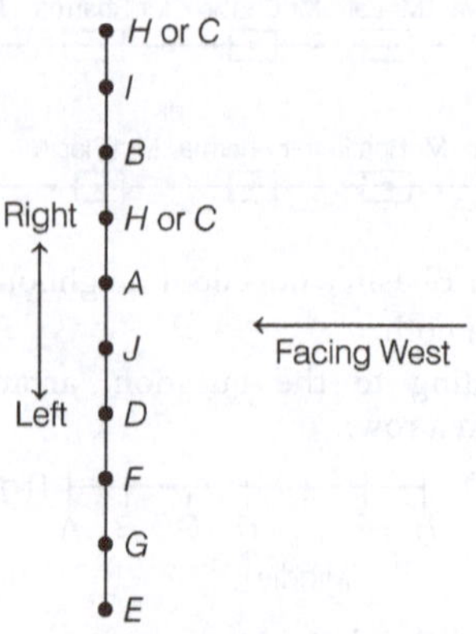

(i) Either *H* or *C* will occupy seventh position from the left.

(ii) (c) Clearly, *E* is definitely sitting at one of the ends.

(iii) The immediate right neighbours of *I* cannot be determined because the position of *H* and *C* are not fixed.

(iv) *G* is sitting to the second left of *D*.

(v). *A* will become the immediate neighbour of *E* after interchanging position.

24. Arrangement according to the question is as follows

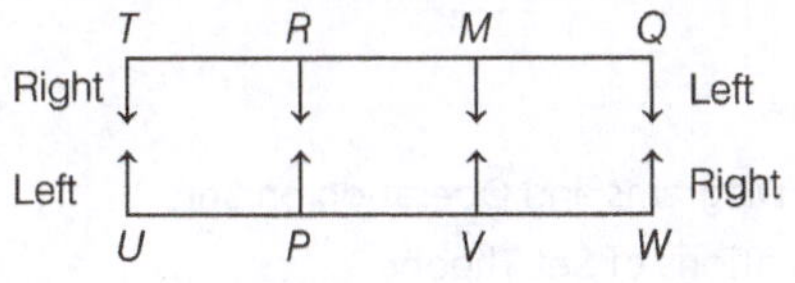

(i) Clearly, *P* is sitting in front of *R*.

(ii) Clearly, *T* is to the immediate right of *R*.

(iii) (a) Clearly, *M* and *V* are sitting in front of each other.

25. According to the given information,

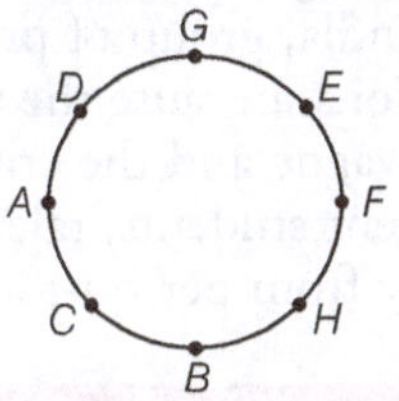

(i) *C* sits second to the left of *H*.

(ii) *H* Faces *D*.

(iii) (d) Except '*F-H*', in all other pairs one person sits between first person and second person.

(iv) One person (*F*) sit between *H* and *E*, when counted from right of *H*.

26. Following sitting arrangement is formed from the given information,

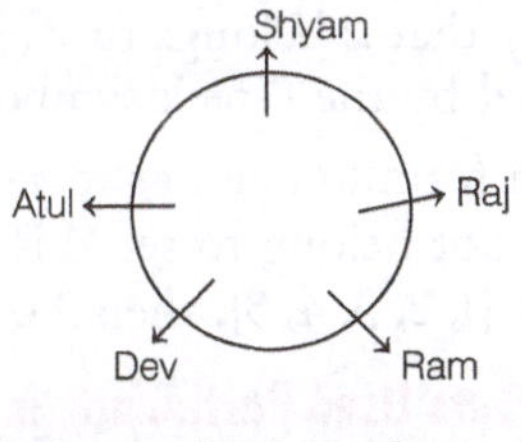

(i) Atul is sitting to the immediate right of Dev

(ii) Raj is sitting between Ram and Shyam.

(iii) Atul is second left of Raj.

27. According to the given information, arrangement is as follows

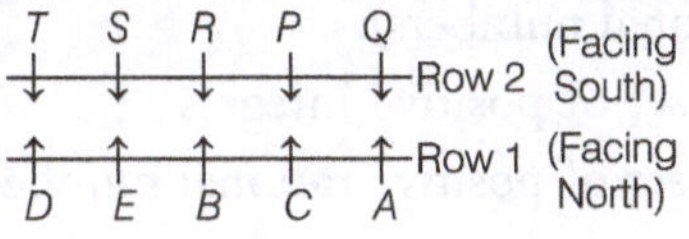

(i) Person *A* sitting in Row 1 faces the person *Q*.

(ii) (c) *T* sits at extreme right end of the Row 2.

(iii) (b) Except *P*, all persons given in the options sit at extreme ends.

(iv) *S* sits second to the right of *P*.

(v) In Row 1, *A* sits third to the right of *E*.

28. Professor *A* is married to *E* and *E* is the sister of *B*. Industrialist is married to *D*. Since, industrialist is seated to the right of *C*. Hence, industrialist cannot be *A* or *C*. Hence, *B* is an industrialist and *C* is businessman.

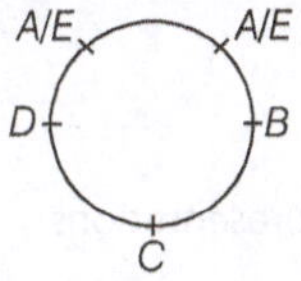

(i) *A* is the husband of *E* and *E* is the sister of *B*. Hence, *A* is brother-in-law of *B*.

(ii) Clearly, right of *C* is *B*.

(iii) *B* is industrialist.

(iv) Businessman is unmarried in the group.

(v) Since, *A* is professor, hence he must be graduate.

29. According to the given information, the sitting arrangement as shown below.

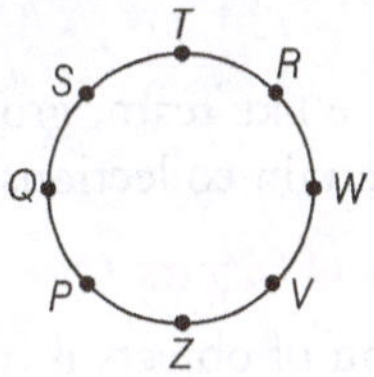

(i) *W* sits to immediate right of *V*.

(ii) *T* is to the immediate right of *R*.

(iii) *Q* is third to the right of *R*.

(iv) *Q* is sitting second to the left of *Z*.

30. According to the given information, arrangement is as follows.

Numbers	Boxes
7	*I*
6	*Q*
5	*R*
4	*P*
3	*M*
2	*S*
1	*L*

(i) Box *P* is placed just above *M*.

(ii) There are two boxes, *M* and *S* between *L* and *P*.

(iii) *L* is placed at the bottom most place and *I* is placed at the top most place.

(iv) Box *I* is placed at topmost place.

CHAPTER 08

Sets

In this Chapter...

- Sets and Their Representations
- Types of Sets
- Subset, Universal Set and Power Set
- Venn Diagrams and Operation on Sets
- Applications of Set Theory

In our daily life, while performing regular work, we often come across a variety of things that occur in groups.
e.g. Team of cricket players, group of tall boys, a pack of cards, etc.

The words used above like team, group, pack, etc. convey the idea of certain collections.

Well-defined Collection of Objects

If any given collection of objects is in such a way that it is possible to tell without any doubt whether a given object belongs to this collection or not, then such a collection of objects is called a **well-defined collection of objects.**
e.g. 'The rivers of India' is a well-defined collection.

Since, we can say that the river Nile does not belong to this collection.
On the other hand, the river Ganga belongs to this collection.

Difference between Not Well-defined and Well-defined Collections

Not well-defined collection	Well-defined collection
A group of intelligent students.	A group of students scoring more than 95% marks of your class.
A group of most talented writers of India.	A group of Indian writers who has published more than 25 books on Geopolitics.
Group of pretty girls.	Group of girls of class XI of your school.

Here, a group of intelligent students, a group of most talented writers of India, group of pretty girls are not well-defined collections, because the term intelligent, talented, pretty are vague and the criterion for determining intelligent students, talented writers and pretty girls may vary from person-to-person.

Sets and Their Representations

Set

A well-defined collection of objects, is called a set. Sets are usually denoted by the capital letters A, B, C, X, Y, Z etc. The elements of a set are represented by small letters a, b, c, x, y, z etc. If a is an element of a set A, then we say that a belongs to A. The word *'belongs to'* denoted by the Greek symbol $\in$ (epsilon).

Thus, in notation form, a belongs to set A is written as $a \in A$ and b does not belong to set A is written as $b \notin A$. e.g. If $A = \{1, 2, 3, 4, 5\}$, then $3 \in A$ and $6 \notin A$.

Some Examples of Sets Used Particularly in Mathematics

- $N \rightarrow$ The set of natural numbers.
- $Z \rightarrow$ The set of all integers.
- $Q \rightarrow$ The set of all rational numbers.
- $R \rightarrow$ The set of real numbers (rational and irrational numbers).
- $Z^+ \rightarrow$ The set of positive integers.
- $Q^+ \rightarrow$ The set of positive rational numbers.
- $R^+ \rightarrow$ The set of positive real numbers (positive rational and irrational numbers).

EXAMPLE 1. Which of the following are sets? Justify your answer. **[NCERT]**

(i) The collection of all the months of a year beginning with the letter J.
(ii) The collection of ten most talented writers of India.
(iii) A collection of novels written by the writer Munshi Premchand.
(iv) A collection of most dangerous animals of the world.

Sol. (i) We are sure that members of this collection are January, June and July.
So, this collection is well-defined.
Hence, it is a set.

(ii) A writer may be most talented for one person and may not be for other. Therefore, we cannot definitely decide which writer will be there in the collection.
So, this collection is not well-defined.
Hence, it is not a set.

(iii) Here, we can definitely decide whether a given novel is written by Munshi Premchand or not.
So, this collection is well-defined.
Hence, it is a set.

(iv) The term most dangerous is vague term. An animal may be most dangerous for one person and may not be for the other.
So, it is not well-defined.
Hence, it is not a set.

EXAMPLE 2. If $A = \{0, 1, 2, 3, 4, 5, 6, 7, 8, 9, 10\}$, then insert appropriate symbol $\in$ or $\notin$ in each of the following blank spaces.

(i) 3 ... A (ii) -2 ... A (iii) 17 ... A
(iv) 9 ... A (v) 0 ... A (vi) -2 ... A

Sol. Given, $A = \{0, 1, 2, 3, 4, 5, 6, 7, 8, 9, 10\}$

(i) Since, 3 is an element of A, therefore $3 \in A$.
(ii) Since, -2 is not an element of A, therefore $-2 \notin A$.
(iii) Since, 17 is not an element of A, therefore $17 \notin A$.
(iv) Since, 9 is an element of A, therefore $9 \in A$.
(v) Since, 0 is an element of A, therefore $0 \in A$.
(vi) Since, -2 is not an element of A, therefore $-2 \notin A$.

Representations of Sets

Sets are generally represented by following two ways

1. Roster Form or Tabular Form or Listing Method
2. Set-Builder Form or Rule Method

Roster form or Tabular Form or Listing Method

In this form, all the elements of a set are listed, the elements are being separated by commas and are enclosed within curly braces { }.

e.g. (i) The set of all natural numbers less than 10 is represented in roster form as $\{1, 2, 3, 4, 5, 6, 7, 8, 9\}$.

(ii) The set of prime numbers is $\{2, 3, 5, 7, \ldots\}$. Here, three dots tell us that the list of prime numbers continues indefinitely.

EXAMPLE 3. Write the set of all vowels in English alphabet which precedes s.

Sol. The vowels which precedes s are a, e, i and o.

So, the required set is $A = \{a, e, i, o\}$.

EXAMPLE 4. Write the set of all natural numbers x such that $4x + 9 < 50$ in roster form.

Sol. We have, $4x + 9 < 50$

$\Rightarrow \quad 4x + 9 - 9 < 50 - 9$ [subtracting 9 from both sides]

$\Rightarrow \quad 4x < 41$

$\Rightarrow \quad x < \dfrac{41}{4}$

$\therefore \quad x < 10.25$

Since, x is a natural number, so x can take values 1, 2, 3, 4, 5, 6, 7, 8, 9, 10.

$\therefore$ Required set $= \{1, 2, 3, 4, 5, 6, 7, 8, 9, 10\}$

Set-builder Form or Rule Method

In this form, all the elements of set possess a single common property $p(x)$, which is not possessed by any other element outside the set.

In such a case, the set is described by $\{x : p(x) \text{ holds}\}$.

e.g. (i) Set of all natural numbers less than 10,

$$A = \{x : x \in N \text{ and } x < 10\}$$

(ii) Set of all real numbers,

$$B = \{x : x \in R\}$$

EXAMPLE 5. Write the set $A = \{14, 21, 28, 35, 42, \ldots, 98\}$ in set-builder form.

Sol. Let x represents the elements of given set.

Given numbers are natural numbers greater than 13, less than 99 and multiples of 7.

Thus, $A = \{x : x$ is a natural number greater than 13, less than 99 and a multiple of 7$\}$, which is the required set-builder form of given set.

This can also be written as

$$A = \{x : x \text{ is a natural number, a multiple of 7 and } 13 < x < 99\}$$

or $\quad A = \{x : x = 7n, n \in N \text{ and } 2 \le n \le 14\}$

EXAMPLE 6. Describe the following set in roster form.
{x : x is positive integer and a divisor of 9}

Sol. Here, x is a positive integer and a divisor of 9.

So, x can take values 1, 3, 9.

$\therefore$ {x : x is a positive integer and a divisor of 9} = {1, 3, 9}

EXAMPLE 7. List the elements of the following sets in roster form.

(i) $\{x : x \in Z \text{ and } |x| \le 2\}$

(ii) $\{x : x = \dfrac{n}{1+n^2} \text{ and } 1 \le n \le 3, \text{ where } n \in N\}$

Sol. (i) Given, $\{x : x \in Z \text{ and } |x| \le 2\}$

Since, $|x| \le 2$

$\therefore \quad -2 \le x \le 2$

Also, as $x \in Z$,

therefore $x = -2, -1, 0, 1, 2$

Hence, $\{x : x \in Z \text{ and } |x| \le 2\} = \{-2, -1, 0, 1, 2\}$

(ii) Given, $\{x : x = \dfrac{n}{1+n^2} \text{ and } 1 \le n \le 3, \text{ where } n \in N\}$

Here, $x = \dfrac{n}{1+n^2}, 1 \le n \le 3, n \in N$

$\Rightarrow \quad x = \dfrac{n}{1+n^2}, n = 1, 2, 3$

$\Rightarrow \quad x = \dfrac{1}{1+1^2}, \dfrac{2}{1+2^2}, \dfrac{3}{1+3^2} = \dfrac{1}{2}, \dfrac{2}{5}, \dfrac{3}{10}$

$\therefore$ Required set is $\left\{\dfrac{1}{2}, \dfrac{2}{5}, \dfrac{3}{10}\right\}$.

EXAMPLE 8. Use listing method to express the following sets.

(i) $A = \{a_n : n \in N, a_{n+1} = 3a_n \text{ and } a_1 = 1\}$

(ii) $B = \{a_n : n \in N, a_{n+2} = a_{n+1} + a_n \text{ and } a_1 = a_2 = 1\}$

Sol. (i) We have, $a_1 = 1$

and $a_{n+1} = 3a_n, \forall\, n \in N$

On putting $n = 1, 2, 3, 4, \ldots$ in $a_{n+1} = 3a_n$, we get

$$a_2 = 3a_1 = 3 \times 1 = 3$$
$$a_3 = 3a_2 = 3 \times 3 = 3^2$$
$$a_4 = 3a_3 = 3 \times 3^2 = 3^3$$
$$a_5 = 3a_4 = 3 \times 3^3 = 3^4$$
$$a_6 = 3a_5 = 3 \times 3^4 = 3^5 \text{ and so on.}$$

$\therefore \quad A = \{1, 3, 3^2, 3^3, 3^4, 3^5, \ldots\}$

(ii) We have, $a_1 = 1, a_2 = 1$

and $a_{n+2} = a_{n+1} + a_n, \forall\, n \in N.$

On putting $n = 1, 2, 3, \ldots$ in $a_{n+2} = a_{n+1} + a_n$, we get

$$a_3 = a_2 + a_1 = 1 + 1 = 2$$
$$a_4 = a_3 + a_2 = 2 + 1 = 3$$
$$a_5 = a_4 + a_3 = 3 + 2 = 5$$
$$a_6 = a_5 + a_4 = 5 + 3 = 8 \text{ and so on.}$$

$\therefore \quad B = \{2, 3, 5, 8, \ldots\}$

EXAMPLE 9. Describe the following set in set-builder form
$B = \{53, 59, 61, 67, 71, 73, 79, 83, 89, 97\}$

Sol. The given set is {53, 59, 61, 67, 71, 73, 79, 83, 89, 97}.

We observe that these numbers are all prime numbers between 50 and 100.

$\therefore B = \{x : x \text{ is a prime number and } 50 < x < 100\}$

EXAMPLE 10. Write the set

$X = \left\{1, \dfrac{1}{4}, \dfrac{1}{9}, \dfrac{1}{16}, \dfrac{1}{25}, \ldots\right\}$ in the set-builder form.

Sol. We observe that the elements of set X are the reciprocals of the squares of all natural numbers.

So, the set X in the set builder form is

$$X = \left\{x : x = \frac{1}{n^2}, n \in N\right\}$$

Topic Practice 1

1 Which of the following are sets?
 (i) The collection of all planets in the solar system.
 (ii) A team of eleven best Cricket batsman of the world.
 (iii) The collection of all boys in your class.
 (iv) The collection of all natural numbers less than 100.
 (v) The collection of five most talented writers of India.
 (vi) The collection of all good athletes of India.

2 Let $A = \{1, 2, 3, 4\}$, $B = \{5, 6, 7\}$ and $C = \{7, 8, 9, 10\}$. Insert the correct symbol $\in$ or $\notin$ in each of the following blanks.
 (i) $2 \dots A$ (ii) $5 \dots C$ (iii) $6 \dots B$
 (iv) $7 \dots A$ (v) $5 \dots B$ (vi) $10 \dots C$

3 Describe the following sets in roster form.
 (i) The set of all letters in the word 'ALGEBRA'.
 (ii) The set of all natural numbers less than 7.
 (iii) The set of squares of integers.
 (iv) The set of all letters in the word "TRIGONOMETRY".
 (v) $\{x : x \text{ is a positive integer and } x^2 = x\}$
 (vi) $\{x : x \text{ is a prime number and } 60 < x < 80\}$
 (vii) $\{x : x \in Z, x^2 < 20\}$
 (viii) $\left\{x : x = \dfrac{n^2 - 1}{n^2 + 1}, n \in N \text{ and } n < 4\right\}$
 (ix) $\{x : x \text{ is a letter of word PROPORTION}\}$
 (x) The set of vowels in the word MATHEMATICS.

4 List all the elements of the following sets:
 (i) $A = \left\{x : x \text{ is an integer}, -\dfrac{1}{2} < x < \dfrac{9}{2}\right\}$
 (ii) $B = \{x : x \in Z \text{ and } x^2 \le 4\}$
 (iii) $C = \left\{x : x = \dfrac{1}{2n - 1}, 1 \le n \le 5\right\}$
 (iv) $D = \{x : x$ is a month of a year not having 31 days$\}$
 (v) $F = \{a_n : n \in N; a_{n+1} = 4a_n \text{ and } a_1 = 1\}$

5 Describe the following sets in set-builder form.
 (i) The set of all letters in the word PROBABILITY.
 (ii) The set of all even natural numbers.
 (iii) $\{5, 25, 125, 625\}$ (iv) $\{10, 11, 12, 13, 14, 15\}$
 (v) $\{1, 4, 9, 16, \dots, 100\}$ (vi) $\left\{1, \dfrac{1}{2}, \dfrac{1}{3}, \dfrac{1}{4}, \dfrac{1}{5}, \dots\right\}$
 (vii) $\left\{\dfrac{1}{2}, \dfrac{2}{5}, \dfrac{3}{10}, \dfrac{4}{17}, \dfrac{5}{26}, \dfrac{6}{37}, \dfrac{7}{50}\right\}$
 (viii) The set of all odd natural numbers.

Hints & Solutions

1. (i), (iii), (iv)

2. (i) $2 \in A$ (ii) $5 \notin C$ (iii) $6 \in B$
 (iv) $7 \notin A$ (v) $5 \in B$ (vi) $10 \in C$

3. (i) {A, L, G, E, B, R} (ii) $\{1, 2, 3, 4, 5, 6\}$
 (iii) $\{0, 1, 4, 9, 16, \dots\}$ (iv) {T, R, I, G, O, N, M, E, Y}
 (v) $\{1\}$ (vi) $\{61, 67, 71, 73, 79\}$
 (vii) **Hint** It can be seen that the square of integers $0, \pm 1, \pm 2, \pm 3, \pm 4$ are less than 20.
 Ans. $A = \{-4, -3, -2, -1, 0, 1, 2, 3, 4\}$
 (viii) $\left\{0, \dfrac{3}{5}, \dfrac{4}{5}\right\}$
 (ix) **Hint** Distinct letters in the word PROPORTION are P, R, O, T, I, N. So, x can be P, R, O, T, I, N.
 Ans. {P, R, O, T, I, N}
 (x) **Hint** The word 'MATHEMATICS' has following vowels. i.e. A, E and I. **Ans.** {A, E, I}

4. Solve as Example 6.
 Ans. (i) $A = \{0, 1, 2, 3, 4\}$ (ii) $B = \{-2, -1, 0, 1, 2\}$
 (iii) $C = \left\{1, \dfrac{1}{3}, \dfrac{1}{5}, \dfrac{1}{7}, \dfrac{1}{9}\right\}$
 (iv) D = {February, April, June, September, November}
 (v) $F = \{1, 4, 4^2, 4^3, 4^4, 4^5, \dots\}$

5. (i) $\{x : x$ is a letter of the word PROBABILITY$\}$
 (ii) $\{x : x = 2n, n \in N\}$ or $\{2n : n \in N\}$
 (iii) $\{x : x = 5^n, n \in N \text{ and } n < 5\}$ or $\{5^n : n \in N \text{ and } n < 5\}$
 (iv) $\{x : x \in N, 9 < x < 16\}$ (v) $\{x^2 : x \in N, 1 \le x \le 10\}$
 (vi) $\left\{x : x = \dfrac{1}{n}, n \in N\right\}$
 (vii) $\left\{x : x = \dfrac{n}{n^2 + 1}, n \in N, n \le 7\right\}$
 (viii) **Hint** An odd natural number can be written in the form $(2n - 1)$. Given set can be described in set builder form.
 Ans. $\{x : x = 2n - 1, n \in N\}$

Types of Sets

In this topic, we will study about different types of sets and cardinal number of a set.

Empty Set

A set which does not contain any element, is called an empty set or null set or void set. It is denoted by ϕ or { }.

e.g. $A = \{x : x$ is a natural number less than $1\}$

We know that there is no natural number less than one. Therefore, set A contains no element and hence it is an empty set.

EXAMPLE 1. Which of the following sets are empty sets?

(i) Set of all even natural numbers divisible by 5.

(ii) Set of all even prime numbers. **[NCERT]**

(iii) $\{x : x^2 - 2 = 0$ and x is rational$\}$

(iv) $\{x : x$ is a point common to any two parallel lines$\}$ **[NCERT]**

Sol. (i) There are infinite even natural numbers which are divisible by 5. e.g. 10, 20, 30, 40, 50, etc.
Therefore, it is not an empty set.

(ii) We know that 2 is only even prime.
Therefore, it is not an empty set.

(iii) Given, $\{x : x^2 - 2 = 0$ and x is rational$\}$

Here, $x^2 - 2 = 0 \Rightarrow x^2 = 2 \Rightarrow x = \pm\sqrt{2} \notin Q$

Therefore, it is an empty set.

(iv) Given,
$\{x : x$ is a point common to any two parallel lines$\}$
We know that no point is common to any two parallel lines. Therefore, it is an empty set.

EXAMPLE 2. Which of the following sets are empty?

(i) $A = \{x : x \in N$ and $x \le 1\}$

(ii) $B = \{x : 3x + 1 = 0,\ x \in N\}$

(iii) $C = \{x : 2 < x < 3,\ x \in N\}$

Sol. (i) We have, $A = \{x : x \in N$ and $x \le 1\} \Rightarrow A = \{1\}$
So, this is not an empty set.

(ii) We have, $B = \{x : 3x + 1 = 0,\ x \in N\}$

Since, $3x + 1 = 0 \Rightarrow x = \dfrac{-1}{3} \notin N$

Thus, set B does not contain any element.
Hence, set B is an empty set.

(iii) We have, $C = \{x : 2 < x < 3,\ x \in N\}$
Since, there is no natural number between 2 and 3.
Hence, set C is an empty set.

Singleton Set

A set containing one element, is called a singleton set.
e.g.

(i) The sets {0}, {5}, {– 7} are singleton sets.

(ii) $A = \{x : x + 8 = 0,\ x \in Z\}$ is a singleton set, because this set contains only one integer, namely – 8.

EXAMPLE 3. Let $T = \left\{x : \dfrac{x+5}{x-7} - 5 = \dfrac{4x-40}{13-x}\right\}$.

Is T a singleton set? Justify your answer.

Sol. We have, $T = \left\{x : \dfrac{x+5}{x-7} - 5 = \dfrac{4x-40}{13-x}\right\}$

$$\because \quad \frac{x+5}{x-7} - 5 = \frac{4x-40}{13-x}$$

$$\Rightarrow \quad \frac{x+5}{x-7} - \frac{5}{1} = \frac{4x-40}{13-x}$$

$$\Rightarrow \quad \frac{x+5-5x+35}{x-7} = \frac{4x-40}{13-x} \Rightarrow \frac{40-4x}{x-7} = \frac{4x-40}{13-x}$$

$$\Rightarrow \quad \frac{-(4x-40)}{x-7} - \frac{4x-40}{13-x} = 0$$

$$\Rightarrow \quad -(4x-40)\left[\frac{1}{(13-x)} + \frac{1}{(x-7)}\right] = 0$$

$$\Rightarrow \quad (4x-40)\left[\frac{6}{(13-x)(x-7)}\right] = 0 \Rightarrow 4x - 40 = 0$$

$$\therefore \quad x = 10$$

Hence, T is a singleton set.

Finite Set

A set which is empty or consists of a definite number of elements, is called a finite set.
e.g.

(i) The set {1, 2, 3, 4} is a finite set, because it contains a definite number of elements, i.e. only 4 elements.

(ii) The set of solutions of $x^2 = 25$ is a finite set, because it contains a definite number of elements, namely 5 and – 5.

Cardinal Number

The number of distinct elements in a finite set A is called **cardinal number** of set A and it is denoted by $n(A)$.

e.g. If $A = \{-3, -1, 8, 10, 13\}$, then $n(A) = 5$.

Infinite Set

A set which consists of infinite number of elements is called an infinite set.

e.g. Set of squares of natural numbers is an infinite set, because such natural numbers are infinite and it can be represented in roster form as {1, 4, 9, 16, 25, ...}.

EXAMPLE 4. Which of the following sets are finite and which are infinite?

(i) Set of concentric circles in a plane.

(ii) The set of lines which are parallel to the X-axis.

(iii) The set of animals living on the Earth. **[NCERT]**

(iv) The set of circles passing through the origin (0, 0).

(v) The set of positive integers greater than 100. **[NCERT]**

(vi) The set of prime numbers less than 99.

(vii) $\{x \in R : 0 < x < 1\}$

(viii) $\{x \in Z : x < 5\}$

Sol. (i) We can draw infinite circles having same centre.
$\therefore$ It is an infinite set.

(ii) We can draw infinite lines parallel to X-axis.
$\therefore$ It is an infinite set.

(iii) There are finite number of animals living on Earth.
$\therefore$ It is a finite set.

(iv) We can draw infinite number of circles, passing through origin.
$\therefore$ It is an infinite set.

(v) It is an infinite set because there are infinite numbers greater than 100, i.e. 101, 102, 103, 104, etc.

(vi) It is a finite set because there are 25 prime numbers less than 99, namely 2, 3, 5, 7, 11, ..., 97.

(vii) Given, $\{x \in R : 0 < x < 1\}$
Here, $0 < x < 1$
We know that between any two real numbers, there are infinite real numbers.
$\therefore$ The set $\{x \in R : 0 < x < 1\}$ is an infinite set.

(viii) Given, $\{x \in Z : x < 5\}$. Here, $x < 5$
We know that there are infinite integers less than 5.
i.e. 4, 3, 2, 1, 0, − 1, ... etc.
$\therefore$ The set $\{x \in Z : x < 5\}$ is an infinite set.

Equivalent Sets

Two sets A and B are said to be equivalent, if their cardinal numbers are same.

i.e. if $n(A) = n(B)$.

e.g. Let $A = \{a, b, c, d\}$ and $B = \{1, 2, 3, 4\}$, then $n(A) = 4$ and $n(B) = 4$.

Therefore, A and B are equivalent sets.

EXAMPLE 5. From the following sets given below, pair the equivalent sets.
$A = \{1, 2, 3\}$, $B = \{t, p, q, r, s\}$, $C = \{\alpha, \beta, \gamma\}$ and $D = \{a, e, i, o, u\}$

Sol. Given, $A = \{1, 2, 3\} \Rightarrow n(A) = 3$
$B = \{t, p, q, r, s\} \Rightarrow n(B) = 5$
$C = \{\alpha, \beta, \gamma\} \Rightarrow n(C) = 3$
$D = \{a, e, i, o, u\} \Rightarrow n(D) = 5$
Here, $n(A) = n(C) = 3$ and $n(B) = n(D) = 5$
$\therefore$ The sets A, C and B, D are equivalent sets.

Equal Sets

Two sets A and B are said to be equal, if they have exactly the same elements and we write it as $A = B$. Otherwise, two sets are said to be **unequal** and we write $A \neq B$.

e.g. Let $A = \{a, b, c, d\}$ and $B = \{c, d, b, a\}$, then $A = B$, because each element of A is in B and *vice-versa.*

Note Two equal sets are always equivalent but two equivalent sets may not be equal.

EXAMPLE 6. From the following sets, select equal sets.
$A = \{2, 4, 6, 8\}$, $B = \{1, 2, 3, 4, 5\}$, $C = \{-2, 4, 6, 8\}$, $D = \{2, 3, 5, 4, 1\}$, $E = \{8, 6, 2, 4\}$

Sol. Since, each element of set A is present in set E and *vice-versa.*
Therefore, A and E are equal sets, i.e. $A = E$.
Also, each element of set B is present in set D and *vice-versa.*
Therefore, B and D are equal sets.

EXAMPLE 7. Are the following pair of sets equal? Give reason. **[NCERT]**

(i) $A = \{2, 3\}$ and $B = \{x : x \text{ is a solution of } x^2 + 5x + 6 = 0\}$

(ii) $A = \{x : x \text{ is a letter of the word "FOLLOW"}\}$ and $B = \{y : y \text{ is a letter of the word "WOLF"}\}$

Sol. (i) Here, $A = \{2, 3\}$
and $B = \{x : x \text{ is a solution of } x^2 + 5x + 6 = 0\}$
Firstly, we find the solution of $x^2 + 5x + 6 = 0$.
By splitting the middle term, we get

$$x^2 + 3x + 2x + 6 = 0$$
$$\Rightarrow \quad x(x + 3) + 2(x + 3) = 0$$
$$\Rightarrow \quad (x + 2)(x + 3) = 0 \Rightarrow x = -2, -3$$
$$\therefore \quad B = \{-2, -3\}$$

Since, the elements of sets A and B are not same. Therefore, $A \neq B$.

(ii) Here, $A = \{x : x \text{ is a letter of the word "FOLLOW"}\}$
$= \{F, O, L, W\}$
and $B = \{y : y \text{ is a letter of the word "WOLF"}\}$
$= \{W, O, L, F\}$
Since, every element of A is in B and every element of B is in A i.e. both have exactly same elements.
$\therefore \quad A = B$

EXAMPLE 8. Which of the following pairs of sets are equal? Justify your answer.

(i) $A = \{x : x$ is a letter of the word "LOYAL"$\}$ and $B = \{x : x$ is a letter of the word "ALLOY"$\}$

(ii) $A = \{x : x \in Z$ and $x^2 \le 8\}$ and $B = \{x : x \in R$ and $x^2 - 4x + 3 = 0\}$

Sol. (i) Given, $A = \{x : x$ is a letter of the word "LOYAL"$\}$
$= \{L, O, Y, A\}$

and $B = \{x : x$ is a letter of the word "ALLOY"$\}$
$= \{A, L, O, Y\}$

Here, we see that both sets have exactly the same elements.

$\therefore \quad A = B$

(ii) Given, $A = \{x : x \in Z$ and $x^2 \le 8\} = \{-2, -1, 0, 1, 2\}$
[$\because$ the squares of integers $0, \pm 1, \pm 2$ are less than 8]

and $B = \{x : x \in R$ and $x^2 - 4x + 3 = 0\} = \{1, 3\}$
[$\because x^2 - 4x + 3 = 0 \Rightarrow (x-1)(x-3) = 0 \Rightarrow x = 1, 3$]

Here, we see that set A has 5 distinct elements and set B has 2 distinct elements.

So, they do not have same elements.

$\therefore \quad A \ne B$

EXAMPLE 9. Identify which of the following set is an empty set, singleton set, infinite set or equal set.

(i) $A = \{x : x$ is a girl living on Jupiter$\}$

(ii) $B = \{x : x$ is a letter in the word "MARS"$\}$

(iii) $C = \{y : y$ is a letter in the word "ARMS"$\}$

(iv) $D = \{x : 3x - 2 = 0, x \in Q\}$

(v) $E = \{x : x \in N$ and x is an odd number$\}$

Sol. (i) $A = \{x : x$ is a girl living on Jupiter$\}$

We know that there is no human being or any girl living on Jupiter.

Therefore, A is an empty set.

(ii) $B = \{x : x$ is a letter in the word "MARS"$\}$

$\Rightarrow \quad B = \{M, A, R, S\}$

(iii) $C = \{y : y$ is a letter in the word "ARMS"$\}$

$\Rightarrow \quad C = \{A, R, M, S\}$

Here, we observe that the elements of sets B and C are exactly same.

Therefore, these sets are equal, i.e. $B = C$.

(iv) $D = \{x : 3x - 2 = 0, x \in Q\}$

$\Rightarrow \quad D = \left\{\frac{2}{3}\right\} \quad \left[\because 3x - 2 = 0 \Rightarrow x = \frac{2}{3} \in Q\right]$

$\therefore D$ is a singleton set.

(v) $E = \{x : x \in N$ and x is an odd number$\}$

Clearly, it is an infinite set because there are infinite natural numbers which are odd.

Topic Practice 2

1 Which of the following sets are empty sets?

(i) $A = \{x : 4 < x < 5, x \in N\}$

(ii) $D = \{x : x^2 = 25$ and x is an odd integer$\}$

(iii) $\{x : x \in N$ and $x^2 = 9\}$

(iv) $\{x : x^2 - 3 = 0, x$ is rational$\}$

(v) $A =$ Set of odd natural numbers divisible by 2.

(vi) $B =$ Set of even prime numbers.

(vii) $A = \{x : x$ is a human being living on Mars$\}$

(viii) $B = \{x : x$ is an even natural number divisible by 3$\}$

(ix) $C = \{x : x$ is a point common to opposite sides of parallelogram$\}$

(x) $D = \{x : x$ is a natural number, $x < 5$ and simultaneously $x > 7\}$

2 State which of the following sets are finite and which are infinite?

(i) $A = \{x : x \in Z$ and $x^2 - 5x + 6 = 0\}$

(ii) $B = \{x : x \in Z$ and x^2 is even$\}$

(iii) $C = \{x : x \in Z$ and $x^2 = 36\}$

(iv) $D = \{x : x \in Z$ and $x > -10\}$

(v) $A = \{x : x \in Z$ and $x^2 - 2x - 3 = 0\}$

(vi) $B =$ Set of lines passing through a point.

3 Which of the following sets are singleton/non-singleton?

(i) $A = \{x : |x| = 7, x \in N\}$

(ii) $B = \{x : x^2 + 2x + 1 = 0, x \in N\}$

(iii) $C = \{x : x^2 = 9, |x| \le 3, x \in N\}$

4 Find the pairs of equal sets, from the following sets, if any, giving reasons.
$A = \{0\}, B = \{x : x > 15$ and $x < 5\}$,
$C = \{x : x - 5 = 0\}, D = \{x : x^2 = 25\}$,
$E = \{x : x$ is an integral positive root of the equation $x^2 - 2x - 15 = 0\}$ [NCERT]

5 Which of the following sets are equal?
$A = \{x : x \in N, x < 3\}, B = \{1, 2\}, C = \{3, 1\}$,
$D = \{x : x \in N, x < 5, x$ is odd$\}, E = \{1, 2, 1, 1\}, F = \{1, 1, 3\}$

6 Show that the set of letters needed to spell "CATARACT" and the set of letters needed to spell "TRACT" are equal.

7 Which of the following pairs of sets are equal?

(i) $A = \{1, 3, 3, 1\}, B = \{1, 4\}$

(ii) $A = \{x : x + 2 = 2\}, B = \{0\}$

(iii) $A = \left\{1, \frac{1}{2}, \frac{1}{3}, \ldots\right\}, B = \left\{\frac{1}{n}, n \in N\right\}$

(iv) $A = \{x : x \in W\}, B = \{x : x \in N\}$

8 From the sets given below, select equal sets and equivalent sets.

$A = \{0, a\}, B = \{1, 2, 3, 4\}, C = \{4, 8, 12\}, D = \{3, 1, 2, 4\}, E = \{1, 0\}, F = \{8, 4, 12\}, G = \{1, 5, 7, 11\}, H = \{a, b\}$

9 From the sets given below, select empty set, singleton set, infinite set and equal sets.

(i) $A = \{x : x < 1 \text{ and } x > 3\}$

(ii) $B = \{x : x^3 - 1 = 0, x \in R\}$

(iii) $C = \{x : x \in N \text{ and } x \text{ is a prime number}\}$

(iv) $D = \{2, 4, 6, 8, 10\}$

$E = \{x : x \text{ is a positive even integer and } x \le 10\}$

Hints & Solutions

1. (i) **Hint** There is no element in this set, so A is empty set.

(ii) **Hint** $D = \{-5, 5\}$, not empty set.

(iii) **Hint** $\{x : x \in N \text{ and } x^2 = 9\} = \{3\}$, so it is not empty set.

(iv) **Hint** $x^2 - 3 = 0 \Rightarrow x = \pm\sqrt{3} \notin Q$ **Ans.** Empty set

(v) **Hint** As no odd natural number is divisible by 2, so set A is empty.

(vi) **Hint** Since, 2 is the only even prime number.

$\therefore \quad B = \{2\}$

So, B is not an empty set.

(vii) **Hint** $A = \{x : x \text{ is a human being living on Mars}\}$

We know that there is no human being living on the Mars. So, this set is an empty set.

(viii) **Hint** $B = \{x : x \text{ is an even natural number divisible by } 3\}$

We know that 6, 12, 18, etc are even numbers divisible by 3. So, this is not an empty set.

(ix) **Hint** $C = \{x : x \text{ is a point common to opposite sides of parallelogram}\}$

We know that there is no common point between opposite sides of the parallelogram. So, this is an empty set.

(x) **Hint** $D = \{x : x \text{ is a natural number, } x < 5 \text{ and simultaneously } x > 7\}$

We know that any natural number cannot be less than 5 and greater than 7, simultaneously.

So, this is an empty set.

2. (i) **Hint** $A = \{2, 3\}$, so A is a finite set.

(ii) **Hint** $B = \{\ldots, -6, -4, -2, 0, 2, 4, 6, \ldots\}$, so B is an infinite set.

(iii) **Hint** $C = \{6, -6\}$, so C is a finite set.

(iv) **Hint** $D = \{-9, -8, -7, \ldots\}$, so D is an infinite set.

(v) **Hint** $A = \{x : x \in Z \text{ and } x^2 - 2x - 3 = 0\} = \{3, -1\}$

Here, A has two elements. So, it is a finite set.

(vi) **Hint** Since, infinite number of lines can pass through a point. So, C is an infinite set.

3. (i) **Hint** We have, $A = \{x : |x| = 7, x \in N\} = \{7\}$,

$[\because |x| = 7 \Rightarrow x = \pm 7, \text{ but } x \in N]$

This set is a singleton set.

(ii) **Hint** We have, $B = \{x : x^2 + 2x + 1 = 0, x \in N\}$

Now, $x^2 + 2x + 1 = 0 \Rightarrow (x+1)^2 = 0 \Rightarrow x = -1$ which is not a natural number.

$\therefore \quad B = \{\} = \phi$

This set is non-singleton set.

(iii) **Hint** We have, $C = \{x : x^2 = 9, |x| \le 3, x \in N\}$

Now, $x^2 = 9 \Rightarrow x = \pm 3$

Now, $|x| \le 3 \Rightarrow x = -3, -2, -1, 0, 1, 2, 3$

Here, $x = -3$ and 3 satisfy $x^2 = 9$ and $|x| \le 3$ both.

But out of -3, 3 only $3 \in N$.

$\therefore \quad C = \{3\}$

This set is a singleton set.

4. **Hint** $A = \{0\}, B = \{\ldots 3, 4 \text{ and } 16, 17, \ldots\}$

$C = \{5\}, D = \{5, -5\}$ and $E = \{5\}$

Since, each element of set C is present in set E and *vice-versa*.

Ans. Sets C and E are equal set.

5. **Hint** $A = B = E, C = D = F$

6. **Hint** Set of letters needed to spell "CATARACT" $= \{C, A, T, R\}$

Set of letters needed to spell "TRACT" = {T, R, A, C}

Both sets are same, so both are equal.

7. (i) **Hint** Given, $A = \{1, 3, 3, 1\} = \{1, 3\}, B = \{1, 4\}$

Since, A and B have different elements. $\therefore A \ne B$

(ii) **Hint** Given, $A = \{x : x + 2 = 2\} = \{0\}$ and $B = \{0\}$

Since, A and B have same elements. $\therefore A = B$

(iii) **Hint** $A = \left\{1, \frac{1}{2}, \frac{1}{3}, \ldots\right\} = \left\{\frac{1}{1}, \frac{1}{2}, \frac{1}{3}, \ldots\right\}$

and $B = \left\{\frac{1}{n} : n \in N\right\} = \left\{\frac{1}{1}, \frac{1}{2}, \frac{1}{3}, \ldots\right\} = \left\{1, \frac{1}{2}, \frac{1}{3}, \ldots\right\}$

Since, A and B have same elements. $\therefore A = B$

(iv) **Hint** Given, $A = \{x : x \in W\}$ and $B = \{x : x \in N\}$

$\Rightarrow A = \{0, 1, 2, 3, \ldots\}$ and $B = \{1, 2, 3, \ldots\}$

Since, A has one element different from B i.e. 0.

$\therefore \quad A \ne B$

8 **Hint** Equal sets : $B = D, C = F$

Equivalent sets : $A, E, H; B, D, G; C, F$

9. (i) **Hint** $A = \{\} = \phi$, so it is empty set.

(ii) **Hint** $B = \{1\}$, so it is singleton set.

(iii) **Hint** $C = \{2, 3, 5, \ldots\}$, so it is infinite set.

(iv) **Hint** $D = \{2, 4, 6, 8, 10\}$

$E = \{2, 4, 6, 8, 10\}$, D and E are equal sets.

Subset, Universal Set and Power Set

Subset

Let A and B be two sets. If every element of A is an element of B, then A is called a subset of B.

If A is a subset of B, then we write $A \subseteq B$, which is read as 'A is a subset of B' or A is contained in B.

In other words, $A \subseteq B$, if whenever $a \in A$, then $a \in B$. It is often convenient to use the symbol '$\Rightarrow$' which means implies.

Using this symbol, we can write the definition of subset as follows

$$A \subseteq B, \text{ if } x \in A \Rightarrow x \in B$$

The above statement is read as

A is subset of B, if x is an element of A, then it implies that x is also an element of B.

If A is not a subset of B, then we write $A \not\subseteq B$.

EXAMPLE 1. If $S = \{1, 3, 5, 7, 9, 11, 13\}$, then which of the following set is a subset of S?

(i) $A = \{3, 5, 7\}$ (ii) $B = \{2, 5, 7\}$

Sol. We have, $S = \{1, 3, 5, 7, 9, 11, 13\}$

(i) Given, $A = \{3, 5, 7\}$

Here, we see that each element of set A lies in set S.

Hence, $A \subseteq S$.

(ii) Given, $B = \{2, 5, 7\}$

Since, element 2 is not belonging to the set S.

$\Rightarrow 2 \notin S$

$\therefore B \not\subseteq S$

Proper Subset

If A is subset of B and $A \neq B$, then A is called a proper subset of B, written as $A \subset B$ and B is called **superset of A.**

e.g. Let $A = \{x : x \text{ is an even natural number}\}$

and $B = \{x : x \text{ is a natural number}\}$

Then, $A = \{2, 4, 6, 8, ...\}$ and $B = \{1, 2, 3, 4, 5, ...\}$

$\therefore A \subset B$

Some Important Results

- Every set is a subset of itself.
- The empty set ϕ is a subset of every set.
- The total number of subsets and proper subsets of a finite set containing n elements is 2^n and $2^n - 1$, respectively.
- If $A \subseteq B$ and $B \subseteq C$, then $A \subseteq C$.
- $A = B$, if and only if $A \subseteq B$ and $B \subseteq A$.

EXAMPLE 2. If $A = \{a, b, c, d\}$ and $B = \{a, b, c, d\}$, then check whether A is a proper subset of B. If it is not, why?

Sol. We have, $A = \{a, b, c, d\}$ and $B = \{a, b, c, d\}$.

Here, we see that all the elements of A exist in B. But there is no element of B, which do not exist in A. Hence, A is a subset of B, but it is not a proper subset.

EXAMPLE 3. Let $A = \{1, 2, \{3, 4\}, 5\}$. Which of the following statements are incorrect and why? **[NCERT]**

(i) $\{3, 4\} \subset A$ (ii) $\{3, 4\} \in A$ (iii) $\{\{3, 4\}\} \subset A$

(iv) $1 \in A$ (v) $1 \subset A$ (vi) $\{1, 2, 5\} \subset A$

(vii) $\{1, 2, 5\} \in A$ (viii) $\phi \subset A$ (ix) $\phi \in A$

(x) $\{\phi\} \subset A$

Sol. We have, $A = \{1, 2, \{3, 4\}, 5\}$

(i) Since, $\{3, 4\}$ is a member of set A.

$\therefore \{3, 4\} \in A$

Hence, $\{3, 4\} \subset A$ is incorrect.

(ii) Since, $\{3, 4\}$ is a member of set A.

$\therefore \{3, 4\} \in A$ is correct.

(iii) Since, $\{3, 4\}$ is a member of set A.

So, $\{\{3, 4\}\}$ is a subset of A.

Hence, $\{\{3, 4\}\} \subset A$ is correct.

(iv) Since, 1 is a member of A.

$\therefore 1 \in A$ is correct.

(v) Since, 1 is a member of set A.

$\therefore 1 \subset A$ is incorrect.

(vi) Since, 1, 2, 5 are members of set A.

So, $\{1, 2, 5\}$ is a subset of set A.

Hence, $\{1, 2, 5\} \subset A$ is correct.

(vii) Since, 1, 2 and 5 are members of set A.

So, $\{1, 2, 5\}$ is a subset of A.

Hence, $\{1, 2, 5\} \in A$ is incorrect.

(viii) Since, ϕ is subset of every set.

$\therefore \phi \subset A$ is correct.

(ix) Since, ϕ is not a member of set A.

$\therefore \phi \in A$ is incorrect.

(x) Since, ϕ is not a member of set A.

$\therefore \{\phi\} \subset A$ is incorrect.

EXAMPLE 4. Insert the correct symbol $\subset$ or $\not\subset$ between each of the following pair of sets.

(i) $\{x : x \text{ is a student of class XI of your school}\}$ ...... $\{x : x \text{ is a student of your school}\}$ **[NCERT]**

(ii) $\{x : x \text{ is a triangle in the plane}\}$ ...... $\{x : x \text{ is a rectangle in the plane}\}$

(iii) $\{x : x$ is an equilateral triangle in the plane$\}$ ...... $\{x : x$ is a triangle in the plane$\}$ [NCERT]

(iv) $\{x : x$ is an even natural number$\}$ ...... $\{x : x$ is an integer$\}$

(v) $\{1, 4, 8\}$ ...... $\{1, 2, 4, 6, 8\}$

Sol. (i) $\{x : x$ is a student of class XI of your school$\}$ $\subset \{x : x$ is a student of your school$\}$

(ii) $\{x : x$ is a triangle in the plane$\}$ $\not\subset \{x : x$ is a rectangle in the plane$\}$

[$\because$ all elements of Ist set are not there in the IInd set]

(iii) $\{x : x$ is an equilateral triangle in the plane$\}$ $\subset \{x : x$ is a triangle in the plane$\}$

[$\because$ elements in the IInd set are triangles, so there will also be equilateral triangle, thus all elements of Ist set are there in the IInd set]

(iv) $\{x : x$ is an even natural number$\}$ $\subset \{x : x$ is an integer$\}$

[$\because$ integers have both even and odd natural numbers, so all elements of Ist set will be there in the IInd set]

(v) $\{1, 4, 8\} \subset \{1, 2, 4, 6, 8\}$

EXAMPLE 5. In each of the following, determine whether the statement is true or false. If it is true, prove it and if it is false, give an example.

(i) If $x \in P$ and $P \in Q$, then $x \in Q$.

(ii) If $P \subset Q$ and $Q \subset R$, then $P \subset R$.

(iii) If $P \subset Q$ and $Q \in R$, then $P \in R$.

(iv) If $P \not\subset Q$ and $Q \not\subset R$, then $P \not\subset R$.

Sol. (i) It is false statement.

e.g. Let $P = \{1\}$, $Q = \{\{1\}, 2\}$

Clearly, $1 \in P$ and $P \in Q$ but $1 \notin Q$.

So, $x \in P$ and $P \in Q$ need not imply that $x \in Q$.

(ii) It is true statement.

Let $x \in P$ be any arbitrary element, then

$P \subset Q \Rightarrow x \in Q$ and $Q \subset R \Rightarrow x \in R$

Thus, $x \in P \Rightarrow x \in R$ for all $x \in P \Rightarrow P \subset R$

Hence, $P \subset Q$ and $Q \subset R \Rightarrow P \subset R$

(iii) It is false statement.

e.g. Let $P = \{1\}$, $Q = \{1, 2\}$ and $R = \{\{1, 2\}, 3\}$, then $P \subset Q$ and $Q \in R$ but $P \notin R$.

Thus, $P \subset Q$ and $Q \in R$ need not imply that $P \in R$.

(iv) It is false statement.

e.g. Let $P = \{1, 2\}$, $Q = \{2, 3\}$ and $R = \{1, 2, 5\}$

Then, $P \not\subset Q$ and $Q \not\subset R$ but $P \subset R$.

Thus, $P \not\subset Q$ and $Q \not\subset R$ need not imply that $P \not\subset R$.

EXAMPLE 6. Two finite sets have m and n elements. The number of subsets of the first set is 112 more than that of the second set. Find the values of m and n. [NCERT Exemplar]

Sol. Let the two sets be A and B such that $n(A) = m$ and $n(B) = n$

Then, number of subsets of set $A = 2^m$

and number of subsets of set $B = 2^n$.

According to the given condition, we have

$$2^m = 112 + 2^n \Rightarrow 2^m - 2^n = 2^7 - 2^4$$

On comparing both sides, we get

$$2^m = 2^7 \text{ and } 2^n = 2^4$$

$$\Rightarrow \quad m = 7 \text{ and } n = 4$$

Subsets of the Set of Real Numbers

We know that every real number is either a **rational** or an **irrational** number and the set of real numbers is denoted by R. There are many important subsets of set of real numbers which are given below

- The set of **natural numbers** is denoted by N.

  Thus, $N = \{1, 2, 3, 4, ...\}$
- The set of **whole numbers** is denoted by W.

  Thus, $W = \{0, 1, 2, 3, ...\}$

  Set of natural numbers is the proper subset of the set of whole numbers.

  i.e. $N \subset W$
- The set of **integers** are denoted by Z.

  Thus, $Z = \{..., -3, -2, -1, 0, 1, 2, 3, ...\}$

  Set of whole numbers is the proper subset of integers.

  i.e. $W \subset Z$
- A number of the form $\frac{p}{q}$, where p and q are integers and $q \neq 0$.

  The set of **rational numbers** is generally denoted by Q.

  Thus, $Q = \left\{\frac{p}{q} : p, q \in Z \text{ and } q \neq 0\right\}$
- A number which cannot be written in the form of $\frac{p}{q}$, where p and q both are integers and $q \neq 0$, is called **irrational number.**

  The set of **irrational numbers** is denoted by Q'.

  Thus, $Q' = \{x : x \in R \text{ and } x \notin Q\}$

Intervals as Subsets of R

Let a, b belong to R and $a < b$. Then, the set of real numbers $\{x : a < x < b\}$ is called an **open interval** and is denoted by (a, b).

All the real numbers between a and b belong to the open interval (a, b) but a and b do not belong to this set (interval).

The interval which contains the end point (a and b) also, is called **closed interval** and it is denoted by $[a, b]$.

Hence, $[a, b] = \{x : a \le x \le b\}$

Semi-closed or Semi-open Interval

Some intervals are closed at one end and open at the other, such intervals are called semi-closed or semi-open interval.

$[a, b) = \{x : a \le x < b\}$ is a semi-open interval from a to b which includes a but excludes b.

$(a, b] = \{x : a < x \le b\}$ is a semi-open interval from a to b which excludes a but includes b.

e.g. (i) (2, 8) is a subset of (−1, 11).

(ii) [4, 6) is a subset of [4, 6].

On real line, we can draw the interval, which is shown by the dark portion on the number line.

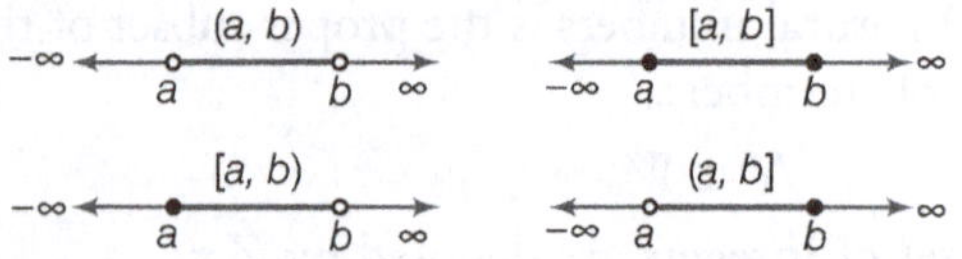

- The set $[0, \infty)$ defines the set of non-negative real numbers.
- The set $(-\infty, 0)$ defines the set of negative real numbers.
- $(-\infty, \infty)$ is the set of real numbers.

Length of an Interval

The number $(b - a)$ is called the length of any of the intervals (a, b), $[a, b]$, $[a, b)$ or $(a, b]$.

EXAMPLE 7. Write the following as intervals and also represent on the number line.

(i) $\{x : x \in R, -5 < x \le 6\}$ (ii) $\{x : x \in R, -11 < x < -9\}$

(iii) $\{x : x \in R, 2 \le x < 8\}$ (iv) $\{x : x \in R, 5 \le x \le 6\}$

Sol. (i) $\{x : x \in R, -5 < x \le 6\}$ is the set that does not contain −5 but contains 6. So, it can be written as a semi-closed interval whose first end point is open and last end point is closed i.e. (−5, 6].

On the real line, (−5, 6] can be graphed as shown in figure given below

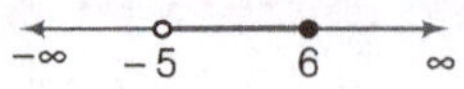

The dark portion on the number line represent (−5, 6].

(ii) $\{x : x \in R, -11 < x < -9\}$ is the set that neither contains −11 nor −9, so it can be represented as open interval i.e. (−11, −9).

On the real line, (−11, −9) can be graphed as shown in figure given below

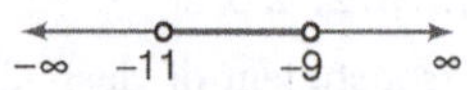

The dark portion on the number line represent (−11, −9).

(iii) $\{x : x \in R, 2 \le x < 8\}$ is the set that contains 2 but does not contain 8. So, it can be represented as a semi-open interval whose first end point is closed and the other end point is open i.e. [2, 8).

On the real line, [2, 8) can be graphed as shown in figure given below

The dark portion on the number line represent [2, 8).

(iv) $\{x : x \in R, 5 \le x \le 6\}$ is the set which contains 5 and 6 both. So, it is equivalent to a closed interval i.e. [5, 6].

On the real line, [5, 6] can be graphed as shown in the figure given below

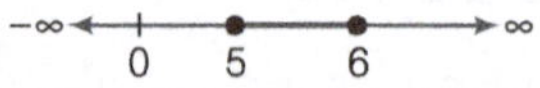

The dark portion on the number line represent [5, 6].

EXAMPLE 8. Write the following intervals in set-builder form.

(i) (−3, 0) (ii) [6, 12] (iii) (6, 12] (iv) [−23, 5)

Also, find the length of each interval.

Sol. We know that closed interval contains end points while open interval does not contain end points.

(i) $(-3, 0) = \{x : x \in R, -3 < x < 0\}$, Length $= 0 - (-3) = 3$

(ii) $[6, 12] = \{x : x \in R, 6 \le x \le 12\}$, Length $= 12 - 6 = 6$

(iii) $(6, 12] = \{x : x \in R, 6 < x \le 12\}$, Length $= 12 - 6 = 6$

(iv) $[-23, 5) = \{x : x \in R, -23 \le x < 5\}$,
Length $= 5 - (-23) = 28$

Universal Set

If there are some sets under consideration, then a set can be chosen arbitrarily which is a **superset** of each one of the given sets. Such a set is known as the universal set and it is denoted by U.

e.g. Let $A = \{2, 4, 6\}$, $B = \{1, 3, 5\}$ and $C = \{0, 7\}$

Then, $U = \{0, 1, 2, 3, 4, 5, 6, 7\}$ is an universal set.

EXAMPLE 9. What universal sets would you propose for each of the following? [NCERT]

(i) The set of right triangles.

(ii) The set of equilateral triangles.

Sol. (i) The universal set for the set of right triangles is set of triangles.

(ii) The universal set for the set of equilateral triangle is set of isosceles triangles or set of triangles.

Power Set

The collection of all subsets of a set, say A, is called the power set of A and it is denoted by $P(A)$. In $P(A)$, every element is a set.

e.g. Let $A = \{3, 4, 5\}$. Then,

$P(A) = \{\phi, \{3\}, \{4\}, \{5\}, \{3, 4\}, \{3, 5\}, \{4, 5\}, \{3, 4, 5\}\}$

Properties of Power Sets

(i) If $A \subseteq B$, then $P(A) \subseteq P(B)$.

(ii) $P(A) \cap P(B) = P(A \cap B)$

(iii) $P(A \cup B) \neq P(A) \cup P(B)$

EXAMPLE 10. If $A = \{1, 2, 3\}$, then find the power set of A.

Sol. All possible subsets of A having single element are $\{1\}, \{2\}, \{3\}$.

All possible subsets of A having two elements at a time are $\{1, 2\}, \{2, 3\}, \{3, 1\}$.

All possible subsets of A having three elements at a time is $\{1, 2, 3\}$.

Thus, the required power set is

$\{\{1\}, \{2\}, \{3\}, \{1, 2\}, \{2, 3\}, \{3, 1\}, \{1, 2, 3\}, \phi\}$.

EXAMPLE 11. Show that $n\{P[P(P(\phi))]\} = 4$.

Sol. We have, $P(\phi) = \{\phi\}$

$\therefore$ $P(P(\phi)) = \{\phi, \{\phi\}\}$

$\Rightarrow$ $P[P(P\ \phi))] = \{\phi, \{\phi\}, \{\{\phi\}\}, \{\phi, \{\phi\}\}\}$

Hence, number of elements in $P[P(P(\phi))]$ is 4.

i.e. $n\{P[P(P(\phi))]\} = 4$ **Hence proved.**

EXAMPLE 12. Let $A = \{1, 2, 3, 4\}$, $B = \{1, 2, 3\}$ and $C = \{2, 4\}$. Find all sets X satisfying each pair of conditions.

(i) $X \subseteq B$ and $X \not\subseteq C$ (ii) $X \subseteq B$, $X \neq B$ and $X \not\subseteq C$

(iii) $X \subset A$, $X \subset B$ and $X \subset C$

Sol. Given, $A = \{1, 2, 3, 4\}$, $B = \{1, 2, 3\}$ and $C = \{2, 4\}$.

Now, $P(A) = \{\phi, \{1\}, \{2\}, \{3\}, \{4\}, \{1, 2\}, \{1, 3\}, \{1, 4\}, \{2, 3\}, \{2, 4\}, \{3, 4\}, \{1, 2, 3\}, \{1, 2, 4\}, \{1, 3, 4\}, \{2, 3, 4\}, \{1, 2, 3, 4\}\}$ ...(i)

$P(B) = \{\phi, \{1\}, \{2\}, \{3\}, \{1, 2\}, \{1, 3\}, \{2, 3\}, \{1, 2, 3\}\}$ ...(ii)

and $P(C) = \{\phi, \{2\}, \{4\}, \{2, 4\}\}$ ...(iii)

(i) Given condition is $X \subseteq B$ and $X \not\subseteq C$.

$\Rightarrow$ $X \in P(B)$ and $X \notin P(C)$

$\therefore$ $X = \{1\}, \{3\}, \{1, 2\}, \{1, 3\}, \{2, 3\}, \{1, 2, 3\}$

[using Eqs. (ii) and (iii)]

(ii) Given condition is $X \subseteq B$, $X \neq B$ and $X \not\subseteq C$.

$\Rightarrow X \in P(B)$, $X \neq B$ and $X \notin P(C)$

$\therefore$ $X = \{1\}, \{3\}, \{1, 2\}, \{1, 3\}, \{2, 3\}$

[using Eqs. (ii) and (iii)]

(iii) Given condition is $X \subset A$, $X \subset B$ and $X \subset C$.

$\Rightarrow X \in P(A)$, $X \in P(B)$, $X \in P(C)$ and $X \neq A, B, C$

$\Rightarrow X$ is proper subset of A, B and $C \Rightarrow X = \phi, \{2\}$

Topic Practice 3

1 Which of the following statements are true? Give reason to support your answer.

(i) For any two sets A and B either $A \subseteq B$ or $B \subseteq A$.

(ii) Every subset of an infinite set is infinite.

(iii) Every subset of a finite set is finite.

(iv) A set can have infinitely many subsets.

2 Prove that $A \subseteq \phi$ implies $A = \phi$.

3 Let $A = \{1, 3, 5\}$ and $B = \{x : x$ is an odd natural number $< 6\}$.

(i) Is $A \subseteq B$? (ii) Is $A = B$?

4 Consider the following sets ϕ, $A = \{2, 5\}$, $B = \{1, 2, 3, 4\}$ and $C = \{1, 2, 3, 4, 5\}$

Insert the correct symbol $\subset$ or $\not\subset$ between each pair of sets

(i) $\phi \ldots B$ (ii) $A \ldots B$ (iii) $A \ldots C$ (iv) $B \ldots C$

5 If $A = \{3, \{4, 5\}, 6\}$, then find which of the following statements are true?

(i) $\{4, 5\} \subset A$ (ii) $\{4, 5\} \in A$

(iii) $\phi \subset A$ (iv) $\{3, 6\} \subset A$

6 Write down the subsets of the following sets.

(i) $\{1, 2, 3\}$ (ii) $\{\phi\}$ [NCERT]

7 Let A, B and C be three sets. If $A \in B$ and $B \subset C$, is it true that $A \subset C$? If not, give an example.

8 Write the following subset of R as interval. Also find the length of interval and represent on number line.

$\{x : x \in R, -12 \le x \le -10\}$

9 Write the following intervals in set-builder form.

(i) $(-6, 0)$ (ii) $[3, 21]$

(iii) $[2, 21]$ (iv) $(-20, 5]$

10 Write the following as intervals and also represent on real line.

(i) $\{x : x \in R, -3 < x \le 7\}$

(ii) $\{x : x \in R, -11 < x < -7\}$

(iii) $\{x : x \in R, 0 \le x < 11\}$

(iv) $\{x : x \in R, 2 \le x \le 9\}$

11 Examine whether the following statements are true or false.

(i) $\{a, b\} \not\subset \{b, c, a\}$

(ii) $\{a, e\} \subset \{x : x$ is a vowel in the English alphabet$\}$

(iii) $\{a\} \in \{a, b, c\}$

(iv) $\{0, 1, 2, 3, 4, 5, 6, 7, 8, 9, 10\}$ is the universal set for the sets $\{1, 3, 5\}$ and $\{2, 4, 6\}$.

12 If $A = \{x : x = n^2, n = 1, 2, 3\}$, then find the number of proper subsets.

13 Determine whether the given statements are true or false.

(i) If $A = \{3, 6, 7\}$ and $B = \{2, 3, 7, 8, 10\}$, then $A \subset B$.

(ii) If $A = \{x : x^2 + 4x - 21 = 0, x \in N\}$ and $B = \{-7, 3\}$, then $A \subseteq B$.

(iii) If $A = \{1, 7, 9\}$, $B = \{2, 4, 6\}$ and $C = \{0, 2, 4\}$, then $U = \{0, 1, 2, 3, 4, 5, 6, 7, 8, 9\}$ is the universal set for all three sets.

(iv) $\{6\} \in \{4, 5, \{6\}, 7\}$

14 Given, the sets $A = \{1, 3, 5\}$, $B = \{2, 4, 6\}$ and $C = \{0, 2, 4, 6, 8\}$. Which of the following may be considered as universal set(s) for all three sets A, B and C? [NCERT]

(i) ϕ

(ii) $\{0, 1, 2, 3, 4, 5, 6, 7, 8, 9, 10\}$

15 In each of the following, determine whether the statement is true or false. If it is true, then prove it. If it is false, then give an example.

(i) If $x \in A$ and $A \in B$, then $x \in B$.

(ii) If $A \subset B$ and $B \in C$, then $A \in C$.

16 If $X = \{4^n - 3n - 1 : n \in N\}$ and $Y = \{9(n-1) : n \in N\}$, then prove that $X \subset Y$.

17 If $X = \{8^n - 7n - 1 : n \in N\}$ and $Y = \{49(n-1) : n \in N\}$, then prove that $X \subseteq Y$.

18 Write down the power set of the following sets.

(i) $B = \{0, 1, 3\}$

(ii) $C = \{1, \{2\}\}$

19 If set $A = \{1, 3, 5\}$, then find the number of elements in $P\{P(A)\}$.

20 For any two sets A and B, prove that $P(A) = P(B)$ implies $A = B$.

Hints & Solutions

1. (i) False;

No, it is not necessary for any two sets A and B to be either $A \subseteq B$ or $B \subseteq A$.

(ii) False;

Here, $A = \{1, 2, 3\}$. It is the finite subset of infinite set N of natural numbers.

(iii) True;

The logically smaller part of something finite can never be infinite.

Therefore, every subset of a finite set is finite.

(iv) False;

Let $A = \{1\}$

Hence, the subsets can be ϕ and $\{1\}$ which are finite.

2. **Hint** Given, $A \subseteq \phi$ ...(i)

But $\phi \subseteq A$ [empty set is a subset of each set] ...(ii)

From Eqs. (i) and (ii), we get $A = \phi$ **Hence proved.**

3. (i) **Hint** Given, $A = \{1, 3, 5\}$

and $B = \{x : x$ is an odd natural number $< 6\}$

$= \{1, 3, 5\}$

So, $A \subseteq B$, because all elements of set A are present in set B. **Ans.** Yes

(ii) **Hint** Here, $B \subseteq A$, because all elements of set B are present in set A.

Hence, $A = B$, because both sets contain equal and same elements. **Ans.** Yes

4. (i) **Hint** ϕ is a proper subset of every set and $\phi \neq B$.

$\therefore \quad \phi \subset B$

(ii) **Hint** $5 \in A$ but $5 \notin B$.

$\therefore \quad A \not\subset B$

(iii) **Hint** Each element of A belongs to C and $A \neq C$.

$\therefore \quad A \subset C$

(iv) **Hint** Each element of B also belongs to C and $B \neq C$

$\therefore \quad B \subset C$

5. (i) **Hint** Since, element of any set is not a subset of any set and here $\{4, 5\}$ is an element of A.

So, statement is false.

(ii) **Hint** $\{4, 5\} \in A$

So, statement is true.

(iii) **Hint** $\phi \subset A$

So, statement is true.

(iv) **Hint** $\{3, 6\}$ makes a set, so it is a subset of A i.e. $\{3, 6\} \subset A$.

So, statement is true.

6. (i) ϕ, {1}, {2}, {3}, {1, 2}, {2, 3}, {1, 3}, {1, 2, 3}
(ii) The subsets are ϕ and {ϕ}.

7. **Hint** Let $A = \{a\}$,
$B = \{\{a\}, b\}$,
$C = \{\{a\}, b, c\}$
Clearly, $A \in B$ and $B \subset C$. But $A \not\subset C$ as $a \in A$ but $a \notin C$
Thus, the given statement is not true.

8. **Hint** $\{x : x \in R, -12 \le x \le -10\}$
Given set can be written in the interval from $[-12, -10]$

Ans. $[-12, -10]$, 2

9. (i) $\{x : x \in R, -6 < x < 0\}$
(ii) $\{x : x \in R, 3 \le x < 21\}$
(iii) $\{x : x \in R, 2 \le x \le 21\}$
(iv) $\{x : x \in R, -20 < x \le 5\}$

10. (i) $(-3, 7]$

(ii) $(-11, -7)$

(iii) $[0, 11)$

(iv) $[2, 9]$

11. (i) **Hint** Since, the elements of the set $\{a, b\}$ are also present in the set $\{b, c, a\}$.
So, $\{a, b\} \subset \{b, c, a\}$
So, statement is false.
(ii) **Hint** Vowels in the English alphabets are a, e, i, o, u.
$\therefore \{a, e\} \subset \{x : x$ is a vowel in English alphabet$\}$
So, statement is true.
(iii) **Hint** Since, $a \in \{a, b, c\}$ and not $\{a\}$.
So, statement is false.
(iv) **Hint** Since, all elements of both sets {1, 3, 5} and {2, 4, 6} are subset of {0, 1, 2, 3, 4, 5, 6, 7, 8, 9, 10}.
Hence, {0, 1, 2, 3, 4, 5, 6, 7, 8, 9, 10} is the universal set for given two sets. So, the statement is true.

12. **Hint** Here, $A = \{1, 4, 9\}$
$\Rightarrow \quad n(A) = 3$
Number of proper subsets $= 2^n - 1 = 7$

13. (i) False (ii) True (iii) True (iv) True

14. **Hint** We know that universal set for sets A, B and C is superset of A, B and C i.e. universal set contains all elements of A, B and C.
(i) ϕ cannot be considered as universal set.
(ii) {0, 1, 2, 3, 4, 5, 6, 7, 8, 9, 10} is the universal set for the given sets.

15. (i) **Hint** Let $A = \{2\}$, $B = \{\{2\}, 3\}$
Clearly, $2 \in A$ and $A \in B$, but $2 \notin B$.
Thus, $x \in A$ and $A \in B$ need not imply that $x \in B$.
So, statement is false.
(ii) **Hint** Let $A = \{2\}$, $B = \{2, 3\}$
and $C = \{\{2, 3\}, 4\}$
Clearly, $A \subset B$ and $B \in C$, but $A \notin C$.
Thus, $A \subset B$ and $B \in C$ need not imply that $A \in C$.
So, statement is false.

16. Let $x_n = 4^n - 3n - 1$, $n \in N$ and $x_1 = 4 - 3 - 1 = 0$ and for any $n \ge 2$, we have

$$x_n = 4^n - 3n - 1 = (1+3)^n - 3n - 1$$
$$= {}^nC_0 + {}^nC_1(3) + {}^nC_2(3)^2 + {}^nC_3(3)^3 + \ldots + {}^nC_n(3)^n - 3n - 1$$
$$= 1 + 3n + {}^nC_2 3^2 + {}^nC_3 3^3 + \ldots + {}^nC_n 3^n - 3n - 1 \quad [\because {}^nC_0 = 1, {}^nC_1 = n]$$
$$= 3^2\{{}^nC_2 + {}^nC_3(3) + {}^nC_4(3)^2 + \ldots + {}^nC_n 3^{n-2}\}$$
$$= 9\{{}^nC_2 + {}^nC_3(3) + {}^nC_4(3)^2 + \ldots + {}^nC_n 3^{n-2}\}$$

$= x_n$ is some positive integral multiple of $9 \forall n \ge 2$.
Thus, X consists of all those positive integral multiples of 9 which are of the form

$$9\{{}^nC_2 + 3 \times {}^nC_3 + 3^2 \times {}^nC_4 + \ldots + 3^{n-2} \times {}^nC_n\}$$

together with 0.
Clearly, $Y = \{9(n-1) : n \in N\}$ consists of all integral multiples of 9 together with 0.
Hence, $X \subset Y$.

17. Solve as Question 16.

18. Solve as Example 10.
Ans.
(i) $P(B) = \{\phi, \{0\}, \{1\}, \{3\}, \{0, 1\}, \{0, 3\}, \{1, 3\}, \{0, 1, 3\}\}$
(ii) $P(C) = \{\phi, \{1\}, \{\{2\}\}, \{1, \{2\}\}\}$

19. **Hint** Given, $A = \{1, 3, 5\}$
$\Rightarrow \quad n(A) = 3$
Number of elements in $P(A) = 2^3 = 8$
$\therefore$ Number of elements in $P(P(A)) = 2^8$
Ans. 256

20. Let $P(A) = P(B)$
Now, as $A \subseteq A$, therefore
$A \in P(A)$
$\Rightarrow \quad A \in P(B) \quad [\because P(A) = P(B)]$
$\Rightarrow \quad A \subseteq B \quad$ ...(i)
Again, $B \subseteq B$
$\Rightarrow \quad B \in P(B)$
$\Rightarrow \quad B \in P(A) \quad [\because P(A) = P(B)]$
$\Rightarrow \quad B \subseteq A \quad$ ...(ii)
From Eqs. (i) and (ii), we get
$A = B$ **Hence proved.**

Venn Diagrams and Operations on Sets

Venn Diagrams

Venn diagrams are named after the English logician, **John Venn** (1834-1883). Venn diagrams represent most of the relationship between sets. These diagrams consist of rectangles and closed curves usually circles.

In Venn diagrams, the universal set is represented by a **rectangular region** and its subset are represented by **circle** or a **closed geometrical figure** inside the universal set. Also, an element of a set is represented by a point within the circle of set. e.g.

(i) If $A = \{1, 2, 3, 5, 9\}$, $B = \{4, 6, 7\}$ and $U = \{1, 2, 3, 4, 5, 6, 7, 8, 9\}$, then

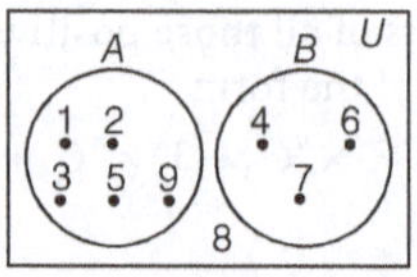

Here, there is no element common in set A and B.

(ii) If $A = \{1, 2, 3, 4, 5\}$ and $B = \{1, 2, 3\}$, then

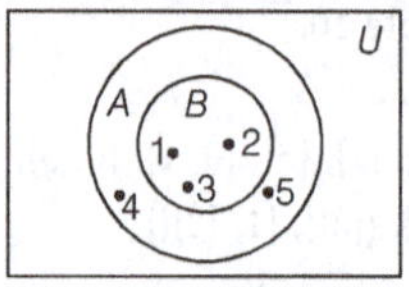

Here, all the elements of B is common in set A.

$\therefore \; B \subset A$

(iii) If $A = \{1,2\}$, $B = \{1,2,3\}$ and $C = \{1,2,3,4,5\}$, then

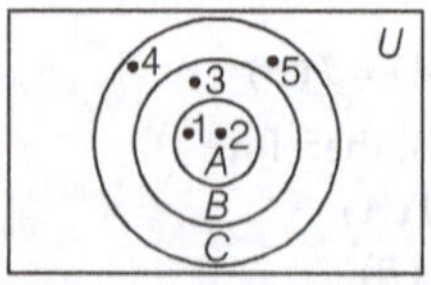

Here, $A \subset B \subset C$

(iv) If $A = \{3, 4, 6, 7\}$ and $B = \{4, 6, 10, 12\}$, then

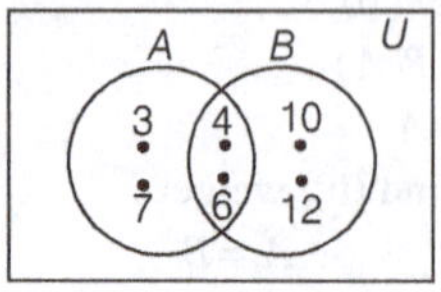

Here, elements 4 and 6 are common in both sets.

EXAMPLE 1. A, B and C are subsets of universal set U. If $A = \{2, 4, 6, 8, 12, 20\}$, $B = \{3, 6, 9, 12, 15\}$, $C = \{5, 10, 15, 20\}$ and U is the set of all whole numbers, draw a Venn diagram showing the relation of U, A, B and C. **[NCERT Exemplar]**

Sol. Given, $A = \{2, 4, 6, 8, 12, 20\}$, $B = \{3, 6, 9, 12, 15\}$,

and $C = \{5, 10, 15, 20\}$

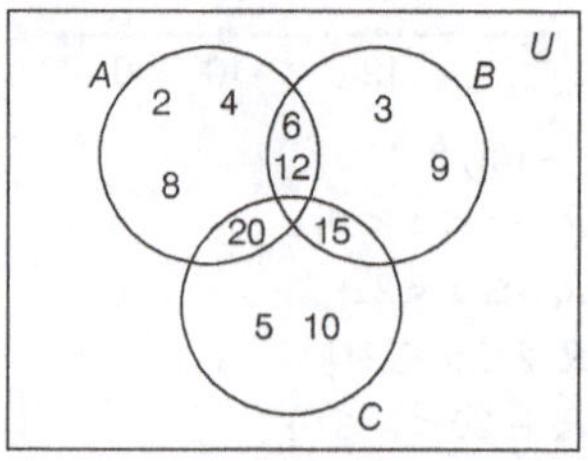

EXAMPLE 2. Draw the Venn diagrams to illustrate the following relationship among sets E, M and U, where E is the set of students studying English in a school, M is the set of students studying Mathematics in the same school and U is the set of all students in that school. **[NCERT Exemplar]**

(i) All the students who study Mathematics also study English, but some students who study English do not study Mathematics.

(ii) Not all students study Mathematics, but every student studying English studies Mathematics.

Sol. Given, E = Set of students studying English

M = Set of students studying Mathematics

U = Set of all students

(i) Since, all of the students who study Mathematics also study English, but some students who study English do not study Mathematics.

$\therefore \quad M \subset E \subset U$

Through Venn diagram, we represent it as

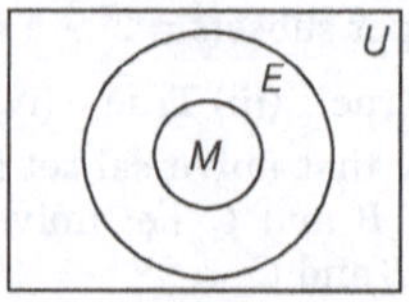

(ii) Since, every student studying English studies Mathematics.

$\therefore \quad E \subset M \subset U$

Through Venn diagram, we represent it as

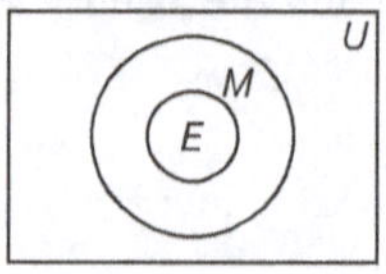

Operations on Sets

There are some operations which when performed on two sets give rise to another set. Here, we will define certain operations on set and examine their properties.

Union of Sets

Let A and B be any two sets. The union of A and B is the set of all those elements which belong to either A or B or both. The symbol '$\cup$' is used to denote the union.

Symbolically, it is denoted by $A \cup B$ and read as **A union B.**

$\therefore \quad A \cup B = \{x : x \in A \text{ or } x \in B\}$

e.g. Let $\quad A = \{2, 3\}$ and $B = \{3, 4, 5\}$

Then, $A \cup B = \{2, 3, 4, 5\}$

The union of sets A and B is represented by the following Venn diagram

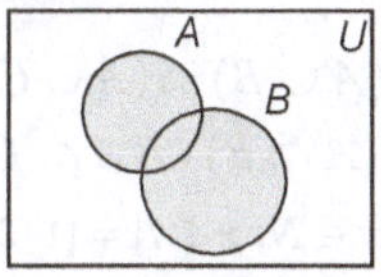

The shaded portion represents $A \cup B$.

Laws of Union of Sets

For any three sets A, B and C, we have

- $A \cup \phi = A$ (Identity law)
- $U \cup A = U$ (Universal law)
- $A \cup A = A$ (Idempotent law)
- $A \cup B = B \cup A$ (Commutative law)
- $(A \cup B) \cup C = A \cup (B \cup C)$ (Associative law)

EXAMPLE 3. Find the union of each of the following pairs of sets.

(i) $A = \{a, e, i, o, u\}$, $B = \{a, c, d\}$

(ii) $A = \{1, 3, 5\}$, $B = \{2, 4, 6\}$

(iii) $A = \{x : x \text{ is a natural number and } 1 < x \le 5\}$ and $B = \{x : x \text{ is a natural number and } 5 < x \le 10\}$

Sol. (i) Given, $A = \{a, e, i, o, u\}$ and $B = \{a, c, d\}$

$A \cup B = \{a, e, i, o, u\} \cup \{a, c, d\}$
$= \{a, c, d, e, i, o, u\}$

(ii) Given, $A = \{1, 3, 5\}$ and $B = \{2, 4, 6\}$

$A \cup B = \{1, 3, 5\} \cup \{2, 4, 6\} = \{1, 2, 3, 4, 5, 6\}$

(iii) Given, $A = \{x : x \text{ is a natural number and } 1 < x \le 5\}$
$= \{2, 3, 4, 5\}$

and $\quad B = \{x : x \text{ is a natural number and } 5 < x \le 10\}$
$= \{6, 7, 8, 9, 10\}$

$\therefore \quad A \cup B = \{2, 3, 4, 5\} \cup \{6, 7, 8, 9, 10\}$
$= \{2, 3, 4, 5, 6, 7, 8, 9, 10\}$

EXAMPLE 4. If $A = \{1, 2, 3, 4\}$, $B = \{3, 4, 5, 6\}$, $C = \{5, 6, 7, 8\}$ and $D = \{7, 8, 9, 10\}$, then find

(i) $A \cup B \cup C$ (ii) $B \cup C \cup D$ **[NCERT]**

Sol. Given, $A = \{1, 2, 3, 4\}$, $B = \{3, 4, 5, 6\}$, $C = \{5, 6, 7, 8\}$ and $D = \{7, 8, 9, 10\}$

(i) $A \cup B \cup C = (A \cup B) \cup C$
$= (\{1, 2, 3, 4\} \cup \{3, 4, 5, 6\}) \cup \{5, 6, 7, 8\}$
$= \{1, 2, 3, 4, 5, 6\} \cup \{5, 6, 7, 8\}$
$= \{1, 2, 3, 4, 5, 6, 7, 8\}$

(ii) $B \cup C \cup D = (B \cup C) \cup D = (\{3, 4, 5, 6\} \cup \{5, 6, 7, 8\}) \cup \{7, 8, 9, 10\}$
$= \{3, 4, 5, 6, 7, 8\} \cup \{7, 8, 9, 10\}$
$= \{3, 4, 5, 6, 7, 8, 9, 10\}$

Intersection of Sets

Let A and B be any two sets. The intersection of A and B is the set of all those elements which belong to both A and B. It is denoted by $A \cap B$ and read as **A intersection B.** The symbol '$\cap$' is used to denote the intersection.

$\therefore \quad A \cap B = \{x : x \in A \text{ and } x \in B\}$

e.g. Let $A = \{2, 3, 4, 5\}$ and $B = \{1, 3, 6, 4\}$

Then, $A \cap B = \{3, 4\}$

The intersection of sets A and B is represented by the following Venn diagram

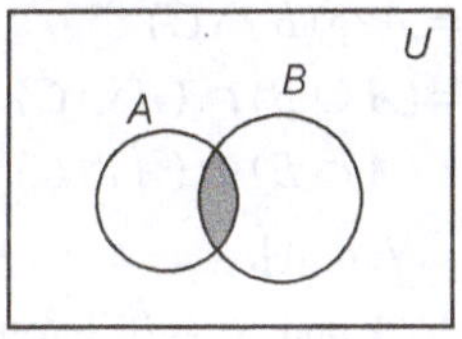

The shaded portion represents $A \cap B$.

Laws of Intersection of Sets

For any three sets, A, B and C, we have

- $A \cap \phi = \phi$ (Identity law)
- $U \cap A = A$ (Universal law)
- $A \cap A = A$ (Idempotent law)
- $A \cap B = B \cap A$ (Commutative law)
- $(A \cap B) \cap C = A \cap (B \cap C)$ (Associative law)
- $A \cap (B \cup C) = (A \cap B) \cup (A \cap C)$ (intersection distributes over union)
- $A \cup (B \cap C) = (A \cup B) \cap (A \cup C)$ (union distributes over intersection)

EXAMPLE 5. Find the intersection of each of the following pairs of sets.

(i) $A = \{1, 3, 5, 7, 9\}$, $B = \{2, 3, 6, 8, 9\}$

(ii) $A = \{e, f, g\}$, $B = \phi$

(iii) $A = \{x : x = 3n, n \in Z\}$, $B = \{x : x = 4n, n \in Z\}$

Sol. (i) Given, $A = \{1, 3, 5, 7, 9\}$ and $B = \{2, 3, 6, 8, 9\}$

$\therefore \quad A \cap B = \{3, 9\}$

[$\because$ 3 and 9 are only elements which are common]

(ii) Given, $A = \{e, f, g\}$ and $B = \phi$

$\therefore \ A \cap B = \phi$ [since, there is no common element]

(iii) Let $x \in A \cap B$

$\Rightarrow \ x \in A$ and $x \in B$

$\Rightarrow$ x is a multiple of 3 and x is a multiple of 4.

$\Rightarrow$ x is a multiple of 3 and 4 both.

$\Rightarrow$ x is a multiple of 12.

$\Rightarrow x = 12n, \ n \in Z$

$\therefore A \cap B = \{x : x = 12n, \ n \in Z\}$

EXAMPLE 6. If $a \in N$ such that $aN = \{an : n \in N\}$, then describe the set $3N \cap 7N$.

Sol. Given, $aN = \{an : n \in N\}$

$\therefore \quad 3N = \{3n : n \in N\}$

$= \{3, 6, 9, 12, 15, 18, 21, 24, 27, ...\}$

and $\quad 7N = \{7n : n \in N\}$

$= \{7, 14, 21, 28, 35, 42, ...\}$

Hence, $3N \cap 7N = \{21, 42, ...\}$

$= \{21n : n \in N\} = 21N$

EXAMPLE 7. If $A = \{4, 5, 7, 8, 10\}$, $B = \{4, 5, 9\}$ and $C = \{1, 4, 6, 9\}$, then verify that

(i) $(A \cap B) \cap C = A \cap (B \cap C)$

(ii) $A \cup (B \cap C) = (A \cup B) \cap (A \cup C)$

(iii) $A \cap (B \cup C) = (A \cap B) \cup (A \cap C)$

Sol. Given, $A = \{4, 5, 7, 8, 10\}$,

$B = \{4, 5, 9\}$ and $C = \{1, 4, 6, 9\}$

(i) Now, $A \cap B = \{4, 5, 7, 8, 10\} \cap \{4, 5, 9\} = \{4, 5\}$

$\therefore \quad$ LHS $= (A \cap B) \cap C$

$= \{4, 5\} \cap \{1, 4, 6, 9\} = \{4\}$ ...(i)

Now, $B \cap C = \{4, 5, 9\} \cap \{1, 4, 6, 9\} = \{4, 9\}$

$\therefore \quad$ RHS $= A \cap (B \cap C)$

$= \{4, 5, 7, 8, 10\} \cap \{4, 9\} = \{4\}$ ...(ii)

From Eqs. (i) and (ii), we get

LHS = RHS = $\{4\}$

Hence, $(A \cap B) \cap C = A \cap (B \cap C)$

(ii) Here, $B \cap C = \{4, 9\}$

$\therefore \quad$ LHS $= A \cup (B \cap C)$

$= \{4, 5, 7, 8, 10\} \cup \{4, 9\}$

$\Rightarrow \quad$ LHS $= \{4, 5, 7, 8, 9, 10\}$ ...(iii)

Now, $A \cup B = \{4, 5, 7, 8, 10\} \cup \{4, 5, 9\}$

$= \{4, 5, 7, 8, 9, 10\}$

and $\ A \cup C = \{4, 5, 7, 8, 10\} \cup \{1, 4, 6, 9\}$

$= \{1, 4, 5, 6, 7, 8, 9, 10\}$

$\therefore \quad$ RHS $= (A \cup B) \cap (A \cup C)$

$= \{4, 5, 7, 8, 9, 10\} \cap \{1, 4, 5, 6, 7, 8, 9, 10\}$

$= \{4, 5, 7, 8, 9, 10\}$ ...(iv)

From Eqs. (iii) and (iv), we get

LHS = RHS = $\{4, 5, 7, 8, 9, 10\}$

Hence, $\ A \cup (B \cap C) = (A \cup B) \cap (A \cup C)$

(iii) Now, $B \cup C = \{4, 5, 9\} \cup \{1, 4, 6, 9\} = \{1, 4, 5, 6, 9\}$

$\therefore$ LHS $= A \cap (B \cup C)$

$= \{4, 5, 7, 8, 10\} \cap \{1, 4, 5, 6, 9\} = \{4, 5\}$ ...(v)

Now, $A \cap B = \{4, 5, 7, 8, 10\} \cap \{4, 5, 9\} = \{4, 5\}$

and $\ A \cap C = \{4, 5, 7, 8, 10\} \cap \{1, 4, 6, 9\} = \{4\}$

$\therefore$ RHS $= (A \cap B) \cup (A \cap C) = \{4, 5\} \cup \{4\} = \{4, 5\}$ ...(vi)

From Eqs. (v) and (vi), we get

LHS = RHS = $\{4, 5\}$

Hence, $A \cap (B \cup C) = (A \cap B) \cup (A \cap C)$

EXAMPLE 8. If $A = \{x : x \in N, x \le 7\}$, $B = \{x : x$ is prime, $x < 8\}$ and $C = \{x : x \in N, x$ is odd and $x < 10\}$, then verify that

(i) $A \cup (B \cap C) = (A \cup B) \cap (A \cup C)$

(ii) $A \cap (B \cup C) = (A \cap B) \cup (A \cap C)$

Sol. Given, $A = \{x : x \in N, x \le 7\} = \{1, 2, 3, 4, 5, 6, 7\}$

$B = \{x : x$ is prime, $x < 8\} = \{2, 3, 5, 7\}$

and $\quad C = \{x : x \in N, x$ is odd and $x < 10\} = \{1, 3, 5, 7, 9\}$

(i) Clearly, $A \cup B = \{1, 2, 3, 4, 5, 6, 7\} = A$,

$A \cup C = \{1, 2, 3, 4, 5, 6, 7, 9\}$,

$B \cap C = \{3, 5, 7\}$

Now, $\quad A \cup (B \cap C) = \{1, 2, 3, 4, 5, 6, 7\} = A$ ...(i)

and $(A \cup B) \cap (A \cup C) = \{1, 2, 3, 4, 5, 6, 7\} = A$ ...(ii)

From Eqs. (i) and (ii), we get

$A \cup (B \cap C) = (A \cup B) \cap (A \cup C)$

(ii) Clearly, $A \cap B = \{2, 3, 5, 7\} = B$

$A \cap C = \{1, 3, 5, 7\}$, $B \cup C = \{1, 2, 3, 5, 7, 9\}$

Now, $\quad A \cap (B \cup C) = \{1, 2, 3, 5, 7\}$ ...(i)

and $\quad (A \cap B) \cup (A \cap C) = \{1, 2, 3, 5, 7\}$ ...(ii)

From Eqs. (i) and (ii), we get

$A \cap (B \cup C) = (A \cap B) \cup (A \cap C)$

Difference of Sets

Let A and B be any two sets. The difference of sets A and B in this order is the set of all those elements of A which do not belong to B.

It is denoted by $A - B$ and read as **A minus B**.

The symbol '–' is used to denote the difference of sets.

$\therefore \quad A - B = \{x : x \in A$ and $x \notin B\}$

Similarly, $B - A = \{x : x \in B$ and $x \notin A\}$

e.g. Let $\quad A = \{1, 2, 3, 4, 5\}$ and $B = \{3, 5, 7, 9\}$

Then, $\quad A - B = \{1, 2, 4\}$ and $B - A = \{7, 9\}$

The difference of two sets A and B can be represented by the following Venn diagram

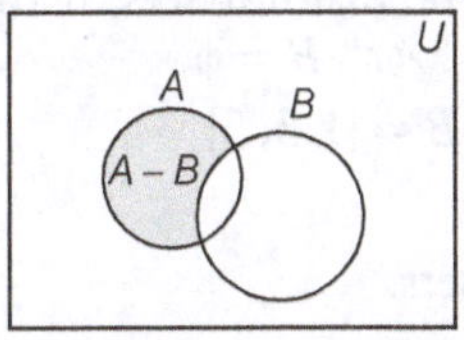

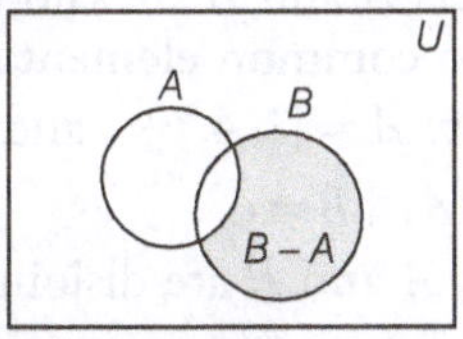

The shaded portion represents the difference of two sets A and B.

Symmetric Difference of Two Sets

Let A and B be any two sets. The symmetric difference of A and B is the set $(A - B) \cup (B - A)$. It is denoted by $A \Delta B$ and read as A **symmetric difference** B.

The symbol 'Δ' is used to denote the symmetric difference.

$\therefore \quad A\Delta B = (A - B) \cup (B - A)$

$\qquad = \{x : x \in A \text{ or } x \in B \text{ but } x \notin A \cap B\}$

e.g. Let $\quad A = \{1, 2, 3, 4\}$ and $B = \{3, 4, 5, 6\}$

Then, $\quad A - B = \{1, 2\}, B - A = \{5, 6\}$

Now, $\quad A\Delta B = (A - B) \cup (B - A) = \{1, 2, 5, 6\}$

The symmetric difference of sets A and B is represented by the following Venn diagram

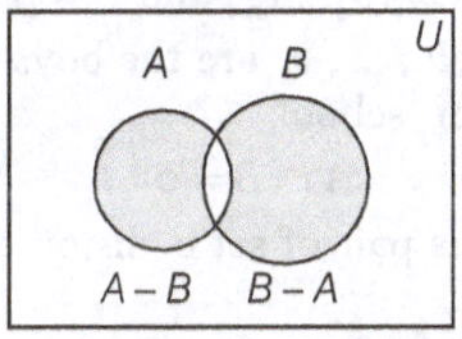

Here, the shaded portion represents the symmetric difference of sets A and B.

Law of Difference of Sets

(i) For any two sets A and B, we have

- $A - B = A \cap B'$ • $B - A = B \cap A'$
- $A - B \subseteq A$ • $B - A \subseteq B$
- $A - B = A \Leftrightarrow A \cap B = \phi$
- $(A - B) \cup B = A \cup B$ • $(A - B) \cap B = \phi$
- $(A - B) \cup (B - A) = (A \cup B) - (A \cap B)$

(ii) If A, B and C are any three sets, then

- $A - (B \cap C) = (A - B) \cup (A - C)$
- $A - (B \cup C) = (A - B) \cap (A - C)$
- $A \cap (B - C) = (A \cap B) - (A \cap C)$
- $A \cap (B \Delta C) = (A \cap B) \Delta (A \cap C)$

where Δ represents symmetric difference and read as 'delta'. $A\Delta B$ is read as 'A delta B' or 'set A symmetric difference set B'.

EXAMPLE 9.

(i) If $X = \{a, b, c, d, e, f\}$ and $Y = \{f, b, d, g, h, k\}$, then find $X - Y$ and $Y - X$.

(ii) If $A = \{1, 2, 3, 4, 5\}$ and $B = \{2, 4, 6\}$, then find $A - B$ and $B - A$.

Also, represent each of these by Venn diagram.

Sol. (i) Given, $X = \{a, b, c, d, e, f\}$ and $Y = \{f, b, d, g, h, k\}$

$\therefore X - Y = \{a, b, c, d, e, f\} - \{f, b, d, g, h, k\} = \{a, c, e\}$

[only those elements of X which do not belong to Y]

and $Y - X = \{f, b, d, g, h, k\} - \{a, b, c, d, e, f\}$

$= \{g, h, k\}$

[only those elements of Y which do not belong to X]

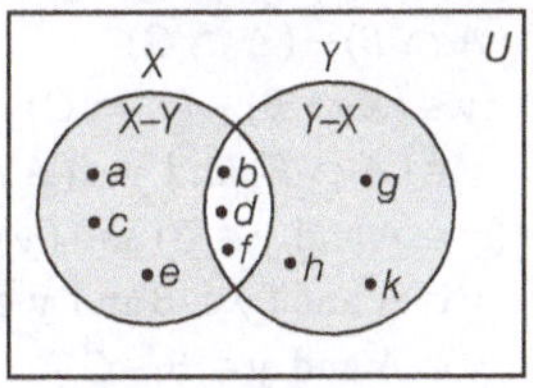

(ii) Given, $\quad A = \{1, 2, 3, 4, 5\}$ and $B = \{2, 4, 6\}$

$\therefore \quad A - B = \{1, 2, 3, 4, 5\} - \{2, 4, 6\}$

$\Rightarrow \quad A - B = \{1, 3, 5\}$

[only those elements of A which do not belong to B]

and $\quad B - A = \{2, 4, 6\} - \{1, 2, 3, 4, 5\} = \{6\}$

[only those elements of B which do not belongs to A]

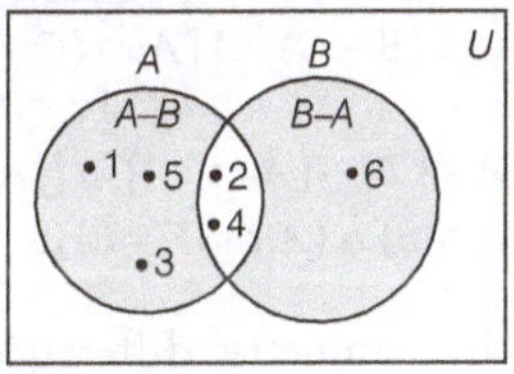

EXAMPLE 10. Prove that

$$A - (B \cap C) = (A - B) \cup (A - C).$$

Sol. To prove, $A - (B \cap C) = (A - B) \cup (A - C)$

Let $\quad x \in A - (B \cap C)$

$\Rightarrow \quad x \in A$ and $x \notin (B \cap C)$

$\Rightarrow \quad x \in A$ and $(x \notin B$ or $x \notin C)$

$\Rightarrow \quad (x \in A$ and $x \notin B)$ or $(x \in A$ and $x \notin C)$

$\Rightarrow \quad x \in (A - B)$ or $x \in (A - C)$

$\Rightarrow \quad x \in (A - B) \cup (A - C)$

$\therefore \quad A - (B \cap C) \subseteq (A - B) \cup (A - C) \quad$ ...(i)

Again, let $y \in (A - B) \cup (A - C)$

$\Rightarrow \quad y \in (A - B)$ or $y \in (A - C)$

$\Rightarrow \quad (y \in A$ and $y \notin B)$ or $(y \in A$ and $y \notin C)$

$\Rightarrow \quad y \in A$ and $(y \notin B$ or $y \notin C)$

$\Rightarrow \quad y \in A$ and $y \notin (B \cap C)$

$\Rightarrow \quad y \in A - (B \cap C)$

$\therefore \quad (A - B) \cup (A - C) \subseteq A - (B \cap C) \quad$ ...(ii)

From Eqs. (i) and (ii), we get

$A - (B \cap C) = (A - B) \cup (A - C)$ **Hence proved.**

EXAMPLE 11. Show that

(i) $A \cap (B - C) = (A \cap B) - (A \cap C)$

(ii) $A \cap (B \Delta C) = (A \cap B) \Delta (A \cap C)$

Sol. (i) Let x be any arbitrary element of $A \cap (B - C)$.

Then, $x \in A \cap (B - C)$

$\Rightarrow x \in A$ and $x \in B - C$

$\Rightarrow x \in A$ and $(x \in B$ and $x \notin C)$

$\Rightarrow (x \in A$ and $x \in B)$ and $(x \in A$ and $x \notin C)$

$\Rightarrow x \in (A \cap B)$ and $x \notin (A \cap C)$

$\Rightarrow x \in (A \cap B) - (A \cap C)$

$\Rightarrow A \cap (B - C) \subseteq (A \cap B) - (A \cap C)$ ...(i)

Now, let y be any arbitrary element of $(A \cap B) - (A \cap C)$

Then, $y \in (A \cap B) - (A \cap C)$

$\Rightarrow y \in (A \cap B)$ and $y \notin (A \cap C)$

$\Rightarrow (y \in A$ and $y \in B)$ and $(y \in A$ and $y \notin C)$

$\Rightarrow y \in A$ and $(y \in B$ and $y \notin C)$

$\Rightarrow y \in A$ and $y \in B - C$

$\Rightarrow y \in A \cap (B - C)$

$\Rightarrow (A \cap B) - (A \cap C) \subseteq A \cap (B - C)$ ...(ii)

From Eqs. (i) and (ii), we get

$A \cap (B - C) = (A \cap B) - (A \cap C)$

(ii) LHS $= A \cap (B \Delta C) = A \cap [(B - C) \cup (C - B)]$

[$\because A \Delta B = (A - B) \cup (B - A)$]

$= [A \cap (B - C)] \cup [A \cap (C - B)]$

[$\because \cap$ distribute over $\cup$]

$= [(A \cap B) - (A \cap C)] \cup [(A \cap C) - (A \cap B)]$

$= (A \cap B) \Delta (A \cap C) =$ RHS **Hence proved.**

EXAMPLE 12. Find the symmetric difference of sets $A = \{1, 3, 5, 6, 7\}$ and $B = \{3, 7, 8, 9\}$.

Sol. Given sets are $A = \{1, 3, 5, 6, 7\}$ and $B = \{3, 7, 8, 9\}$.

Now, $A - B = \{1, 3, 5, 6, 7\} - \{3, 7, 8, 9\} = \{1, 5, 6\}$

[set of those elements of A, which are not present in B]

and $B - A = \{3, 7, 8, 9\} - \{1, 3, 5, 6, 7\} = \{8, 9\}$

[set of those elements of B, which are not present in A]

$\therefore$ Required symmetric difference,

$A \Delta B = (A - B) \cup (B - A) = \{1, 5, 6\} \cup \{8, 9\} = \{1, 5, 6, 8, 9\}$

EXAMPLE 13. Let $A = \{1, 2, 4, 5\}$, $B = \{2, 3, 5, 6\}$, $C = \{4, 5, 6, 7\}$, verify that $A \cap (B \Delta C) = (A \cap B) \Delta (A \cap C)$.

Sol. Given, $A = \{1, 2, 4, 5\}$, $B = \{2, 3, 5, 6\}$ and $C = \{4, 5, 6, 7\}$

Now, $A \cap B = \{2, 5\}$ and $A \cap C = \{4, 5\}$

and $B \Delta C = (B - C) \cup (C - B) = \{2, 3, 4, 7\}$

$\therefore A \cap (B \Delta C) = \{2, 4\}$ ...(i)

and $(A \cap B) \Delta (A \cap C) = \{2, 4\}$ ...(ii)

From Eqs. (i) and (ii), we get

$A \cap (B \Delta C) = (A \cap B) \Delta (A \cap C)$ **Hence proved.**

Disjoint Sets

Two sets A and B are said to be disjoint sets, if they have **no common element** i.e. $A \cap B = \phi$.

e.g. Let $A = \{2, 4, 6\}$ and $B = \{1, 3, 5\}$

Then, $A \cap B = \phi$.

Hence, A and B are disjoint sets.

The disjoint of two sets A and B can be represented by the Venn diagram

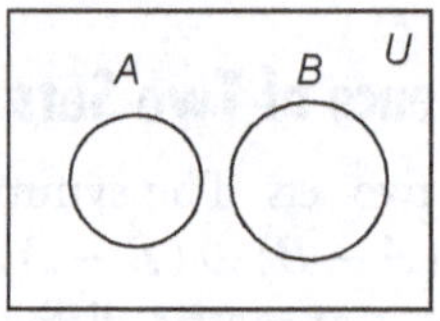

EXAMPLE 14. Which of the following pairs of sets are disjoint?

(i) $A = \{1, 2, 3, 4, 5, 6\}$ and $B = \{x : x$ is a natural number and $4 \le x \le 6\}$

(ii) $A = \{x : x$ is the boy of your school$\}$
$B = \{x : x$ is the girl of your school$\}$

Sol. (i) Given, $A = \{1, 2, 3, 4, 5, 6\}$ and $B = \{4, 5, 6\}$

$\therefore A \cap B = \{1, 2, 3, 4, 5, 6\} \cap \{4, 5, 6\} = \{4, 5, 6\} \ne \phi$

Hence, this pair of set is not disjoint.

(ii) Here, $A = \{b_1, b_2, \dots b_n\}$ and $B = \{g_1, g_2, \dots g_m\}$

where, $b_1, b_2, \dots, b_n$ are the boys and $g_1, g_2, \dots, g_m$ are the girls of school.

Clearly, $A \cap B = \phi$

Hence, this pair of set is disjoint set.

Complement of a Set

Let U be the universal set and A be any subset of U, then complement of A with respect to U is the set of all those elements of U which are not in A. It is denoted by $\overline{A}$ or A' and read as, '**A complement**'.

Thus, $\overline{A} = \{x : x \in U$ and $x \notin A\}$ or $A' = U - A$

e.g. Let $U = \{1, 2, 3, 4, 5, 6\}$ and $A = \{2, 4\}$

Then, $A' = U - A = \{1, 2, 3, 4, 5, 6\} - \{2, 4\} = \{1, 3, 5, 6\}$

The complement of set A is represented by the following Venn diagram

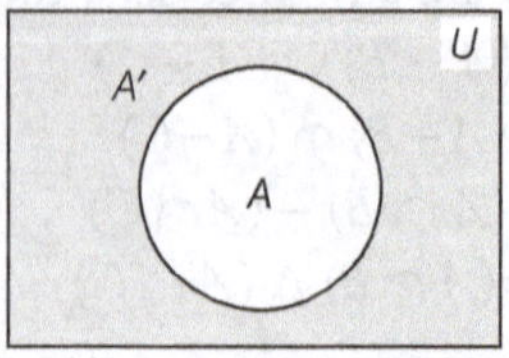

Here, the shaded portion represents the complement of set A.

Some Properties of Complement of Sets

- $(A')' = A = U - A'$ [law of double complementation]
- (a) $A \cup A' = U$ (b) $A \cap A' = \phi$ [complement laws]
- (a) $\phi' = U$ (b) $U' = \phi$ [laws of empty set and universal set]
- $(A \cup B)' = U - (A \cup B)$

EXAMPLE 15. Let $U = \{1, 2, 3, 4, 5, 6, 7, 8, 9\}$, $A = \{1, 2, 3, 4\}$, $B = \{2, 4, 6, 8\}$ and $C = \{3, 4, 5, 6\}$. Find

(i) A' (ii) B' (iii) $(A \cap C)'$
(iv) $(A \cup B)'$ (v) $(A')'$ (vi) $(B - C)'$

Sol. Given, $U = \{1, 2, 3, 4, 5, 6, 7, 8, 9\}$, $A = \{1, 2, 3, 4\}$
$B = \{2, 4, 6, 8\}$ and $C = \{3, 4, 5, 6\}$

(i) $A' = U - A = \{1, 2, 3, 4, 5, 6, 7, 8, 9\} - \{1, 2, 3, 4\}$
$= \{5, 6, 7, 8, 9\}$

(ii) $B' = U - B = \{1, 2, 3, 4, 5, 6, 7, 8, 9\} - \{2, 4, 6, 8\}$
$= \{1, 3, 5, 7, 9\}$

(iii) $A \cap C = \{3, 4\}$
$\therefore (A \cap C)' = U - (A \cap C)$
$= \{1, 2, 3, 4, 5, 6, 7, 8, 9\} - \{3, 4\}$
$= \{1, 2, 5, 6, 7, 8, 9\}$

(iv) $A \cup B = \{1, 2, 3, 4, 6, 8\}$
$(A \cup B)' = U - (A \cup B) = \{1, 2, 3, 4, 5, 6, 7, 8, 9\} - \{1, 2, 3, 4, 6, 8\} = \{5, 7, 9\}$

(v) $(A')' = U - A' = \{1, 2, 3, 4, 5, 6, 7, 8, 9\} - \{5, 6, 7, 8, 9\}$
$= \{1, 2, 3, 4\}$ [using part (i)]

Alternate Method

We know that $(A')' = A$
$\therefore (A')' = \{1, 2, 3, 4\}$

(vi) Now, $B - C = \{2, 8\}$
$(B - C)' = U - (B - C)$
$= \{1, 2, 3, 4, 5, 6, 7, 8, 9\} - \{2, 8\}$
$= \{1, 3, 4, 5, 6, 7, 9\}$

Theorem (De-Morgan's Law)

If A and B are any two sets, then

(i) $(A \cup B)' = A' \cap B'$ (ii) $(A \cap B)' = A' \cup B'$

Proof (i) Let x_1 be any arbitrary element of $(A \cup B)'$.

Then, $x_1 \in (A \cup B)'$
$\Rightarrow x_1 \notin (A \cup B)$
$\Rightarrow x_1 \notin A$ and $x_1 \notin B$
$\Rightarrow x_1 \in A'$ and $x_1 \in B'$
$\Rightarrow x_1 \in A' \cap B'$
$\therefore (A \cup B)' \subseteq A' \cap B'$ [$\because x_1$ is arbitrary]...(i)

Again, let $x_2 \in A' \cap B'$
$\Rightarrow x_2 \in A'$ and $x_2 \in B'$
$\Rightarrow x_2 \notin A$ and $x_2 \notin B$
$\Rightarrow x_2 \notin A \cup B$
$\Rightarrow x_2 \in (A \cup B)'$
$\therefore A' \cap B' \subseteq (A \cup B)'$ [$\because x_2$ is arbitrary] ...(ii)

From Eqs. (i) and (ii), we get
$(A \cup B)' = A' \cap B'$

Similarly, we can prove part (ii).

The Venn diagram of De-Morgan's law is shown below

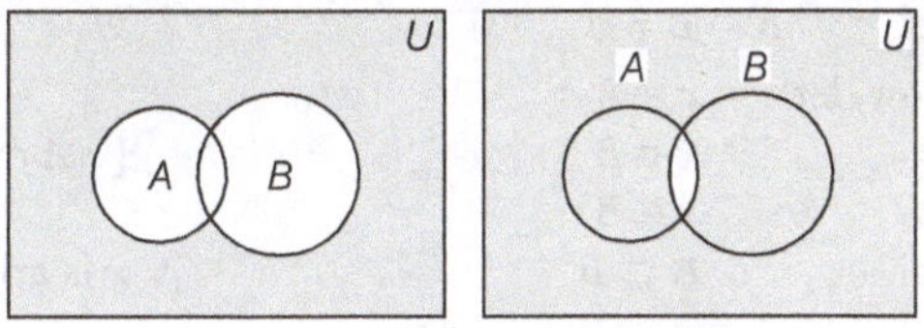

EXAMPLE 16. Let $U = \{1, 2, 3, 4, 5, 6, 7, 8, 9\}$, $A = \{2, 4, 6, 8\}$ and $B = \{2, 3, 5, 7\}$.

Verify that **[NCERT]**

(i) $(A \cup B)' = A' \cap B'$ (ii) $(A \cap B)' = A' \cup B'$

Sol. (i) We have, $U = \{1, 2, 3, 4, 5, 6, 7, 8, 9\}$
$A = \{2, 4, 6, 8\}$ and $B = \{2, 3, 5, 7\}$
$\therefore A \cup B = \{2, 4, 6, 8\} \cup \{2, 3, 5, 7\}$
$= \{2, 3, 4, 5, 6, 7, 8\}$

Now, $(A \cup B)' = U - (A \cup B)$
$= \{1, 2, 3, 4, 5, 6, 7, 8, 9\} - \{2, 3, 4, 5, 6, 7, 8\}$
$= \{1, 9\}$ ...(i)

Now, $A' = U - A$
$= \{1, 2, 3, 4, 5, 6, 7, 8, 9\} - \{2, 4, 6, 8\}$
$= \{1, 3, 5, 7, 9\}$

and $B' = U - B = \{1, 2, 3, 4, 5, 6, 7, 8, 9\} - \{2, 3, 5, 7\}$
$= \{1, 4, 6, 8, 9\}$

$\therefore A' \cap B' = \{1, 3, 5, 7, 9\} \cap \{1, 4, 6, 8, 9\} = \{1, 9\}$ ...(ii)

From Eqs. (i) and (ii), we get
$(A \cup B)' = A' \cap B'$

(ii) Here, $A \cap B = \{2, 4, 6, 8\} \cap \{2, 3, 5, 7\} = \{2\}$
$\therefore (A \cap B)' = U - (A \cap B)$
$= \{1, 2, 3, 4, 5, 6, 7, 8, 9\} - \{2\}$
$\Rightarrow (A \cap B)' = \{1, 3, 4, 5, 6, 7, 8, 9\}$ ...(i)

Now, $A' \cup B' = \{1, 3, 5, 7, 9\} \cup \{1, 4, 6, 8, 9\}$
$= \{1, 3, 4, 5, 6, 7, 8, 9\}$ ...(ii)

From Eqs. (i) and (ii), we get
$(A \cap B)' = A' \cup B'$

EXAMPLE 17. Prove that $(A \cap B')' \cup (B \cap C) = A' \cup B$. **[NCERT Exemplar]**

Sol. LHS $= (A \cap B')' \cup (B \cap C)$

$= \{A' \cup (B')'\} \cup (B \cap C)$ [by De-Morgan's law]

$= (A' \cup B) \cup (B \cap C)$ $[\because (B')' = B]$

$= ((A' \cup B) \cup B) \cap ((A' \cup B) \cup C)$

$= (A' \cup (B \cup B)) \cap (A' \cup B \cup C)$

$= (A' \cup B) \cap (A' \cup B \cup C)$

$= (A' \cup B) =$ RHS **Hence proved.**

EXAMPLE 18. For any two sets A and B, prove that $A \cap B = \phi$ implies $A \subseteq B'$.

Sol. Let $A \cap B = \phi$

Now, let $x \in A$

$\Rightarrow x \notin B$ $[\because A \cap B = \phi]$

$\Rightarrow x \in B'$

$\Rightarrow A \subseteq B'$ $[\because x$ is arbitrary$]$

Thus, $A \cap B = \phi$

$\Rightarrow A \subseteq B'$ **Hence proved.**

EXAMPLE 19. Let A and B be two sets. Prove that $(A - B) \cup B = A$ if and only if $B \subset A$.

Sol. Let $(A - B) \cup B = A$

$\Rightarrow (A \cap B') \cup B = A$ $[\because A - B = A \cap B']$

$\Rightarrow (A \cup B) \cap (B' \cup B) = A$ [by distributive law]

$\Rightarrow (A \cup B) \cap U = A$ $[\because B' \cup B = U]$

$\Rightarrow A \cup B = A$

$\Rightarrow B \subset A$

Conversely, let $B \subset A$

$\therefore (A - B) \cup B = (A \cap B') \cup B$

$= (A \cup B) \cap (B' \cup B)$ [by distributive law]

$= (A \cup B) \cap U$ $[\because B' \cup B = U]$

$= A \cup B = A$ $[\because B \subset A]$ **Hence proved.**

Topic Practice 4

1 Find the union of each of the following pair of sets.

(i) $A = \{a, e, i, o, u\}, B = \{a, b, c\}$

(ii) $A = \{1, 3, 5\}, B = \{1, 2, 3\}$

(iii) $A = \{2, 4, 6, 8\}, B = \{6, 8, 10, 12\}$

2 Find the smallest set A such that $A \cup \{1, 2\} = \{1, 2, 3, 5, 9\}$.

3 If A and B are two sets such that $A \subset B$, then show that $A \cup B = B$. **[NCERT]**

4 Suppose $A_1, A_2, \ldots, A_{30}$ are thirty sets each having 5 elements and $B_1, B_2, \ldots, B_n$ are n sets each with 3 elements, let $\bigcup_{i=1}^{30} A_i = \bigcup_{j=1}^{n} B_j = S$ and each element of S belongs to exactly 10 of the A_i's and exactly 9 of the B_j's. Find 'n'. **[NCERT Exemplar]**

5 Let $A = \{x : x \in N\}, B = \{x : x = 2n, n \in N\}$, $C = \{x : x = 2n - 1, n \in N\}$ and $D = \{x : x$ is a prime natural number$\}$. Find

(i) $A \cap B$ (ii) $A \cap C$

(iii) $B \cap C$ (iv) $B \cap D$

6 For three sets A, B and C, show that $A \cap B = A \cap C$ need not imply $B = C$.

7 For any two sets A and B, prove that

(i) $A \cup (A \cap B) = A$ (ii) $A \cap (A \cup B) = A$

8 Let A and B be two sets. If $A \cap X = B \cap X = \phi$ and $A \cup X = B \cup X$ for some set X, then prove that $A = B$.

9 Let $A = \{3, 6, 12, 15, 18, 21\}, B = \{4, 8, 12, 16, 20\}$, $C = \{2, 4, 6, 8, 10, 12, 14, 16\}$ and $D = \{5, 10, 15, 20\}$. Find

(i) $A - B$

(ii) $A - C$

(iii) $B - C$

(iv) $B - D$

10 If A, B and C are three sets such that $A \subset B$, then prove that $C - B \subset C - A$.

11 Let $A = \{1, 2, 4, 5\}, B = \{2, 3, 5, 6\}, C = \{4, 5, 6, 7\}$. Verify that

(i) $A \cup (B \cap C) = (A \cup B) \cap (A \cup C)$

(ii) $A \cap (B \cup C) = (A \cap B) \cup (A \cap C)$

12 If $A = \{a, b, c, d, e\}, B = \{a, c, e, g\}$ and $C = \{b, e, f, g\}$, then verify that

(i) $A \cap (B - C) = (A \cap B) - (A \cap C)$

(ii) $A - (B \cap C) = (A - B) \cup (A - C)$

13 If A and B are any two sets, then prove that $(A \cap B) \cup (A - B) = A$.

14 Which of the following pairs of sets are disjoint? **[NCERT]**

(i) $\{1, 2, 3, 4\}$ and $\{x : x$ is a natural number and $4 \le x \le 6\}$

(ii) $\{a, e, i, o, u\}$ and $\{c, d, e, f\}$

(iii) $\{x : x$ is an even integer$\}$ and $\{x : x$ is an odd integer$\}$

15 Let $A = \{x : x \in N$ and x is a multiple of 2}
$B = \{x : x \in N$ and x is a multiple of 5}
and $C = \{x : x \in N$ and x is multiple of 10}
Describe the sets
(i) $(A \cap B) \cap C$ (ii) $A \cup (B \cap C)$ (iii) $A \cap (B \cup C)$

16 Give examples of three sets A, B and C such that $A \cap B \neq \phi, B \cap C \neq \phi, A \cap C \neq \phi$ and $A \cap B \cap C = \phi$.

17 Let $A = \{1, 2, 4, 5\}$, $B = \{2, 3, 5, 6\}$ and $C = \{4, 5, 6, 7\}$. Verify the following identities.
(i) $A \cap (B - C) = (A \cap B) - (A \cap C)$
(ii) $A - (B \cup C) = (A - B) \cap (A - C)$
(iii) $A - (B \cap C) = (A - B) \cup (A - C)$

18 Find $A \Delta B$, if
(i) $A = \{1, 3, 4\}$ and $B = \{2, 5, 9, 11\}$.
(ii) $A = \{1, 3, 6, 11, 12\}$ and $B = \{1, 6\}$.

19 Taking the set of a natural numbers as the universal set, write down the complements of the following sets. **[NCERT]**
(i) $\{x : x$ is a natural number divisible by 3 and 5}
(ii) $\{x : x$ is a perfect square}
(iii) $\{x : x$ is a perfect cube}
(iv) $\{x : x + 5 = 8\}$
(v) $\{x : 2x + 5 = 9\}$
(vi) $\{x : x \geq 7\}$
(vii) $\{x : x \in N, 2x + 1 > 10\}$

20 Let $U = \{1, 2, 3, 4, 5, 6, 7, 8, 9, 10\}$, $A = \{1, 2, 3\}$, $B = \{2, 4, 6, 7\}$ and $C = \{2, 3, 4, 8\}$, then find $(B \cup C)'$, $(A \cup B)'$. **[NCERT Exemplar]**

21 Represent the following sets in Venn diagram.
(i) $A' \cap (B \cup C)$ (ii) $A' \cap (C - B)$

22 If $U = \{1, 2, 3, 4, 5, 6, 7, 8, 9, 10\}$, $A = \{1, 3, 4\}$ and $B = \{5, 6\}$, then verify that $A - B = A \cap B' = B' - A'$.

23 If $U = \{1, 2, 3, 4, 5, 6, 7, 8\}$, $A = \{1, 2, 3, 4\}$, $B = \{3, 4, 6\}$ and $C = \{5, 6, 7, 8\}$, then verify that $(A \cap B)' = A' \cup B'$.

24 If $A = \{1, 3, 5, 7, 9, 11, 13, 15, 17\}$, $B = \{2, 4, \ldots, 18\}$ and N, the set of natural numbers is the universal set, then prove that $A' \cup \{(A \cup B) \cap B'\} = N$.

25 Let A and B be two sets. Using properties of set, prove that
(i) $A \cap B' = \phi \Rightarrow A \subseteq B$
(ii) $A' \cup B = U \Rightarrow A \subseteq B$

26 For any natural number a, we define $aN = \{an : n \in N\}$. If $b, c, d \in N$ such that $bN \cap cN = dN$, then prove that d is the LCM of b and c.

Hints & Solutions

1. (i) $A \cup B = \{a, b, c, e, i, o, u\}$
(ii) $A \cup B = \{1, 2, 3, 5\}$
(iii) Given, $A = \{2, 4, 6, 8\}$, $B = \{6, 8, 10, 12\}$,
$A \cup B = \{2, 4, 6, 8, 10, 12\}$

2. $A = \{3, 5, 9\}$

3. **Hint** $A \subset B$ means that, all the elements of set A are in set B and also there are some other elements in B.
We know that $A \cup B$ contains all the elements either in A or in B or in both A and B.
Thus, $A \cup B = B$

4. If elements are not repeated, then number of elements in $A_1 \cup A_2 \cup A_3 \cup \ldots \cup A_{30}$ is 30×5.
But each element is used 10 times, so
$$n(S) = \frac{30 \times 5}{10} = 15$$
If elements in $B_1, B_2, \ldots, B_n$ are not repeated, then total number of elements is $3n$ but each element is repeated 9 times, so $n(S) = \frac{3n}{9} \Rightarrow 15 = \frac{3n}{9} \Rightarrow n = 45$

5. (i) $A \cap B = \{x : x = 2n, n \in N\} = B$
(ii) $A \cap C = \{x : x = 2n - 1, n \in N\} = C$
(iii) $B \cap C = \{\ \} = \phi$
(iv) $B \cap D = \{2\}$

6. **Hint** Let $A = \{1, 2, 3, 4\}$, $B = \{3, 4, 5, 6\}$ and $C = \{3, 4, 7, 8\}$

7. (i) $A \cup (A \cap B) = (A \cup A) \cap (A \cup B)$ [by distributive law]
$= A \cap (A \cup B) = A$ $[\because A \subseteq A \cup B]$
(ii) $A \cap (A \cup B) = (A \cap A) \cup (A \cap B)$ [by distributive law]
$= A \cup (A \cap B) = A$ $[\because A \cap B \subseteq A]$
Hence proved.

8. Given, $A \cup X = B \cup X$
$\Rightarrow A \cap (A \cup X) = A \cap (B \cup X)$
$\Rightarrow A = (A \cap B) \cup (A \cap X)$
$[\because A \subseteq A \cup X, A \cap (A \cup X) = A]$
$\Rightarrow A = (A \cap B) \cup \phi \Rightarrow A = A \cap B$
$\Rightarrow A \subseteq B$ $[\because A \cap B \subseteq B]$ ...(i)
Again, $A \cup X = B \cup X$
$\Rightarrow B \cap (A \cup X) = B \cap (B \cup X)$
$\Rightarrow (B \cap A) \cup (B \cap X) = B$
$[\because B \subseteq B \cup X, B \cap (B \cup X) = B]$
$\Rightarrow (B \cap A) \cup \phi = B$ $[\because B \cap X = \phi$. given]
$\Rightarrow B \cap A = B$
$\Rightarrow B \subseteq A$ $[\because B \cap A \subseteq A]$ ...(ii)
From Eqs. (i) and (ii), we get
$A = B$ **Hence proved.**

9. (i) $\{3, 6, 15, 18, 21\}$ (ii) $\{3, 15, 18, 21\}$
(iii) $\{20\}$ (iv) $\{4, 8, 12, 16\}$

10. Let $x \in C - B \Rightarrow x \in C$ and $x \notin B$
$\Rightarrow$ $x \in C$ and $x \notin A$ $[\because A \subset B]$
$\Rightarrow$ $x \in C - A$
$\therefore$ $C - B \subset C - A$ **Hence proved.**

11. Solve as Example 7.

12. Hint Find LHS and RHS, separately, to verify the result.

13. Hint LHS $= (A \cap B) \cup (A \cap B')$ $[\because A - B = A \cap B']$
Let $A \cap B = X$, then
$\text{LHS} = X \cup (A \cap B') = (X \cup A) \cap (X \cup B')$ ...(i)
$[\because \cup$ distributes over $\cap]$
$\because$ $X = A \cap B$
$\therefore X \cup A = (A \cap B) \cup A = A$ $[\because A \cap B \subseteq A]$
and $X \cup B' = (A \cap B) \cup B' = (A \cup B') \cap (B \cup B')$
$[\because \cup$ distributes over $\cap]$
$= (A \cup B') \cap U$ $[\because B \cup B' = U]$
$= A \cup B'$
Now, substitute the value of $X \cup A$, $X \cup B'$ in Eq. (i), to get result.

14. (i) **Hint** $\{x : x$ is a natural number and $4 \le x \le 6\} = \{4, 5, 6\}$
Now, $\{1, 2, 3, 4\}$ and $\{4, 5, 6\}$ have one element common.
So, these are not disjoint sets.
(ii) **Hint** The sets $\{a, e, i, o, u\}$ and $\{c, d, e, f\}$ have one element 'e' common.
So, these are not disjoint sets.
(iii) **Hint** $E = \{x: x$ is an even integer$\}$
$= \{..., -4, -2, 0, 2, 4, 6, ...\}$
and $O = \{x : x$ is an odd integer$\}$
$= \{..., -5, -3, -1, 1, 3, 5, ...\}$
So, these are disjoint sets.

15. (i) **Hint** Here, $A \cap B = \{2, 4, 6, ...\} \cap \{5, 10, 15, ...\}$
$= \{10, 20, 30 ...\} = C$
$\therefore$ $(A \cap B) \cap C = C \cap C = C = \{10, 20, 30, ...\}$
(ii) **Hint** Here, $B \cap C = \{5, 10, 15, ...\} \cap \{10, 20, 30...\}$
$= \{10, 20, 30, ...\}$
$\therefore$ $A \cup (B \cap C) = \{2, 4, 6, ...\} \cup \{10, 20, 30, ...\} = A$
$= \{2, 4, 6, 8, 10, ...\}$
(iii) **Hint** Here, $B \cup C = \{5, 10, 15, ...\} \cup \{10, 20, 30, ...\}$
$= \{5, 10, 15, 20, 25, ...\}$
$\therefore$ $A \cap (B \cup C) = \{2, 4, 6, ...\} \cap \{5, 10, 15, ...\} = C$
$= \{10, 20, 30, ...\}$

16. Hint Let $A = \{1, 2\}$, $B = \{2, 3, 4\}$ and $C = \{1, 3, 5\}$
Then, $A \cap B = \{1, 2\} \cap \{2, 3, 4\} = \{2\} \ne \phi$
$B \cap C = \{2, 3, 4\} \cap \{1, 3, 5\} = \{3\} \ne \phi$
$A \cap C = \{1, 2\} \cap \{1, 3, 5\} = \{1\} \ne \phi$
and $A \cap B \cap C = \{1, 2\} \cap \{2, 3, 4\} \cap \{1, 3, 5\} = \phi$

17. Hint Find LHS and RHS, separately, to verify the result.

18. (i) **Hint** We have, $A = \{1, 3, 4\}$
and $B = \{2, 5, 9, 11\}$
Now, $(A - B) = \{1, 3, 4\} - \{2, 5, 9, 11\} = \{1, 3, 4\}$
and $(B - A) = \{2, 5, 9, 11\} - \{1, 3, 4\} = \{2, 5, 9, 11\}$
$\therefore$ $A \Delta B = (A - B) \cup (B - A)$
$= \{1, 3, 4\} \cup \{2, 5, 9, 11\} = \{1, 2, 3, 4, 5, 9, 11\}$
(ii) Solve as part (i). **Ans.** $A \Delta B = \{3, 11, 12\}$

19. (i) $\{x : x \in N$ and x is not divisible by $15\}$
(ii) $\{x : x \in N$ and x is not a perfect square$\}$
(iii) $\{x : x \in N$ and x is not a perfect cube$\}$
(iv) $\{x : x \in N$ and $x \ne 3\}$ (v) $\{x : x \in N$ and $x \ne 2\}$
(vi) $\{x : x \in N$ and $x < 7\}$ (vii) $\left\{x : x \in N \text{ and } x \le \frac{9}{2}\right\}$

20. $(B \cup C)' = \{1, 5, 9, 10\}$ and $(A \cup B)' = \{5, 8, 9, 10\}$

21.
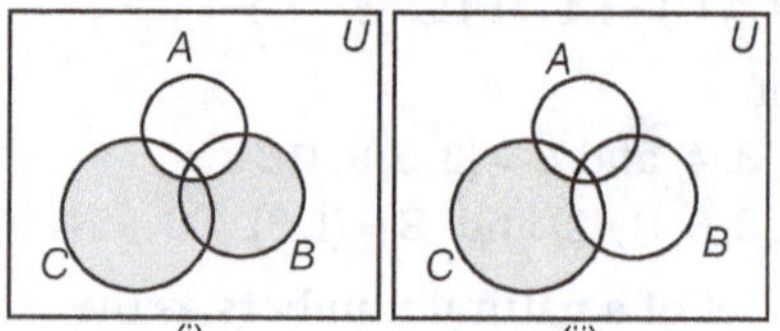

(i) (ii)

22. Hint $A' = \{2, 5, 6, 7, 8, 9, 10\}$, $B' = \{1, 2, 3, 4, 7, 8, 9, 10\}$
$A \cap B' = \{1, 3, 4\}$ and $B' - A' = \{1, 3, 4\}$

23. Hint $A \cap B = \{3, 4\} \Rightarrow (A \cap B)' = \{1, 2, 5, 6, 7, 8\}$
$A' = \{5, 6, 7, 8\}$ and $B' = \{1, 2, 5, 7, 8\}$
$A' \cup B' = \{1, 2, 5, 6, 7, 8\}$
Clearly, $(A \cap B)' = A' \cup B'$

24. Hint $A \cup B = \{1, 2, 3, 4, 5, ..., 16, 17, 18\}$
$A' = \{2, 4, 6, 8, 10, ..., 18, 19, 20\ 21, 22, ...\}$
$B' = \{1, 3, 5, 7, 9, ..., 17, 19, 20, 21, 22, ...\}$
$\therefore$ $(A \cup B) \cap B' = \{1, 3, 5, 7, 9, ...17\}$

25. (i) **Hint** We have, $A = (A \cap U) = A \cap (B \cup B')$
$= (A \cap B) \cup (A \cap B')$
$= (A \cap B) \cup \phi$
$\Rightarrow$ $A = A \cap B \Rightarrow A \subseteq B$
(ii) **Hint** We have, $A' \cup B = U$
$\Rightarrow$ $(A' \cup B)' = U'$
$\Rightarrow$ $(A')' \cap B' = \phi$
$\Rightarrow$ $A \cap B' = \phi$
Now, from part (i), we get
$A \subseteq B$

26. Given, $aN = \{an : n \in N\}$
= Set of positive integral multiples of a
Similarly, $bN = \{bn : n \in N\}$
= Set of positive integral multiples of b
$cN = \{cn : n \in N\}$ = Set of positive integral multiples of c
$\therefore$ $bN \cap cN$ = Set of positive integral multiples of both b and c
$\Rightarrow bN \cap cN = \{\lambda n : n \in N\}$, where λ is LCM of b and c.
Hence, d is the LCM of b and c. **Hence proved.**

Applications of Set Theory

In this topic, we will discuss some word problems related to our daily life, which are based on union and intersection of two sets. Before solving these types of problem, we should know the following formulae.

If A and B are two finite sets, then two cases arise

Case I If A and B are **disjoint sets**, i.e. there is no common element in A and B i.e. $A \cap B = \phi$. Then,

$$n(A \cup B) = n(A) + n(B)$$

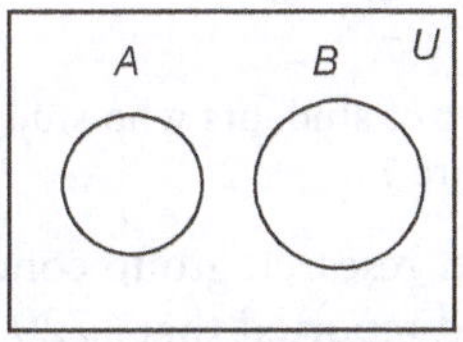

Case II If A and B are **not disjoint sets**, then there are common elements in A and B. Then,

$$n(A \cup B) = n(A) + n(B) - n(A \cap B)$$

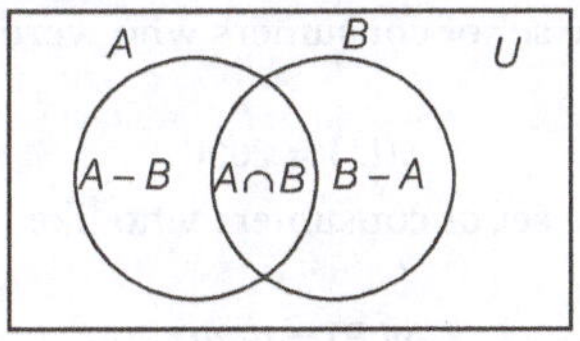

Note Sets $A - B$, $A \cap B$ and $B - A$ are disjoint and their union is $A \cup B$.

Important Results

(i) $n(A \cup B) = n(A - B) + n(B - A) + n(A \cap B)$

(ii) $n(A) = n(A - B) + n(A \cap B)$

(iii) $n(B) = n(B - A) + n(A \cap B)$

(iv) $n(A \Delta B) = n[(A - B) \cup (B - A)]$

$= n(A - B) + n(B - A)$

[since, $(A - B)$ and $(B - A)$ are disjoint sets]

$= n(A) + n(B) - 2n(A \cap B)$

(v) $n(A' \cup B') = n[(A \cap B)'] = n(U) - n(A \cap B)$

(vi) $n(A' \cap B') = n[(A \cup B)'] = n(U) - n(A \cup B)$

(vii) $n(A - B) = n(A \cap B)' = n(A) - n(A \cap B)$

(viii) If A, B and C are finite sets, then

(a) $n(A \cup B \cup C)$

$= n(A) + n(B) + n(C) - n(A \cap B) - n(B \cap C) - n(A \cap C) + n(A \cap B \cap C)$

(b) $n(A \text{ only}) = n(A) - n(A \cap B) - n(A \cap C) + n(A \cap B \cap C)$

(c) $n(\overline{A} \cap \overline{B} \cap \overline{C}) = n(U) - n(A \cup B \cup C)$

Knowledge Plus

Let A, B and C be any three sets, then the meaning of different operations on these sets are given below.

(i) $A' \rightarrow$ Set of those objects which does not belong to A (similar meaning for B' and C').

(ii) $A \cup B \rightarrow$ Set of those objects which lies either in A or in B (similar meaning for $B \cup C$ and $A \cup C$).

(iii) $A \cap B \rightarrow$ Set of those objects which belongs to both the sets A and B (similar meaning for $B \cap C$ and $C \cap A$).

(iv) $A \cap B \cap C \rightarrow$ Set of those objects which belongs to A, B and C.

(v) $A \cup B \cup C \rightarrow$ Set of those objects which belongs to atleast one of the sets A, B and C.

EXAMPLE 1. If X and Y are two sets such that X has 40 elements, $X \cup Y$ has 60 elements and $X \cap Y$ has 10 elements, then how many elements does Y have?

Sol. Given, $n(X) = 40$, $n(X \cup Y) = 60$

and $n(X \cap Y) = 10$

Clearly, $n(X \cup Y) = n(X) + n(Y) - n(X \cap Y)$

$60 = 40 + n(Y) - 10$

$\Rightarrow 60 = 30 + n(Y)$

$\Rightarrow n(Y) = 60 - 30$

$\therefore n(Y) = 30$

Hence, Y have 30 elements.

EXAMPLE 2. If X and Y are two sets such that $n(X) =\quad$, $n(Y) = 23$ and $n(X \cup Y) = 38$, then find $n(X \cap Y)$.

Sol. Given, $n(X) = 17$, $n(Y) = 23$

and $n(X \cup Y) = 38$

Clearly, $n(X \cup Y) = n(X) + n(Y) - n(X \cap Y)$

$\Rightarrow n(X \cap Y) = n(X) + n(Y) - n(X \cup Y)$

$\Rightarrow n(X \cap Y) = 17 + 23 - 38 = 40 - 38 = 2$

EXAMPLE 3. If $n(A) = 4$, $n(B) = 5$, $n(U) = 7$ and $n(A \cap B) = 2$, then find the value of $n(A \cup B)'$.

Sol. Given, $n(A) = 4$, $n(B) = 5$, $n(U) = 7$

and $n(A \cap B) = 2$

$\because n(A \cup B) = n(A) + n(B) - n(A \cap B)$

$\therefore n(A \cup B) = 4 + 5 - 2 = 7$

Now, $n(A \cup B)' = n(U) - n(A \cup B) = 7 - 7 = 0$

EXAMPLE 4. In a class of 60 students, 25 students play Cricket, 20 students play Tennis and 10 students play both the games. Then, find the number of students who play neither games. **[NCERT Exemplar]**

Sol. Let C and T respectively denote the set of students who play Cricket and Tennis, and set U denotes the set of all students in a class.

Then, $n(C) = 25, n(T) = 20, n(C \cap T) = 10$ and $n(U) = 60$

We know that, $n(C \cup T) = n(C) + n(T) - n(C \cap T)$

$\Rightarrow \quad n(C \cup T) = 25 + 20 - 10 = 45 - 10 = 35$

Now, the number of students who play neither game

$n(C' \cap T') = n(C \cup T)$ [by De Morgan's law]

$= n(U) - n(C \cup T) = 60 - 35 = 25$

Hence, 25 students play neither games.

EXAMPLE 5. In a town of 840 persons, 450 persons read Hindi, 300 read English and 200 read both newspapers. Then, find the number of persons who read neither of the newspapers. **[NCERT Exemplar]**

Sol. Let H and E respectively denote the set of persons who read Hindi and English newspapers and let U set of all perseon in a town.

Then, we have $n(U) = 840,$

$n(H) = 450,$

$n(E) = 300$

and $n(H \cap E) = 200$

Clearly, $n(H \cup E) = n(H) + n(E) - n(H \cap E)$

$\therefore \quad n(H \cup E) = 450 + 300 - 200$

$= 750 - 200 = 550$

Now, the number of persons who read neither of the newspaper is given by

$n(H' \cap E') = n(H \cup E)'$ [by De Morgan's law]

$= n(U) - n(H \cup E)$

$= 840 - 550 = 290$

Hence, 290 persons read neither of the newspapers.

EXAMPLE 6. Each student in a class of 40 students study atleast one of the subjects English, Mathematics and Economics. 16 students study English, 22 Economics and 26 Mathematics, 5 study English and Economics, 14 Mathematics and Economics and 2 English, Economics and Mathematics. Find the number of students who study English and Mathematics.

Sol. Let A, B and C denote the set of students who study English, Economics and Mathematics, respectively.

Then, we have,

Total number of students, $n(A \cup B \cup C) = 40$

Number of students who study English, $n(A) = 16$

Number of students who study Economics, $n(B) = 22$

Number of students who study Mathematics, $n(C) = 26$

Number of students who study English and Economics, $n(A \cap B) = 5$

Number of students who study Mathematics and Economics, $n(B \cap C) = 14$

and number of students who study all subjects,

$n(A \cap B \cap C) = 2$

Clearly, $n(A \cup B \cup C) = n(A) + n(B) + n(C) - n(A \cap B) - n(B \cap C) - n(A \cap C) + n(A \cap B \cap C)$

$40 = 16 + 22 + 26 - 5 - 14 - n(C \cap A) + 2$

$\Rightarrow \quad 40 = 66 - 19 - n(C \cap A)$

$\Rightarrow \quad n(C \cap A) = 47 - 40$

$= 7$

Hence, number of students who study English and Mathematics are 7.

EXAMPLE 7. A market research group conducted a survey of 2000 consumers and reported that 1720 consumers liked "Patanjali Ghee" and 1450 consumers liked "Amul Ghee". What is the least number that must have liked both the product?

Sol. Let U be the set of consumers who were participated in the survey.

Then, $n(U) = 2000$

Let P be the set of consumers who liked "Patanjali Ghee".

Then, $n(P) = 1720$

Let A be the set of consumers who liked "Amul Ghee".

Then, $n(A) = 1450$

$\because \quad n(P \cup A) = n(P) + n(A) - n(P \cap A)$

$\therefore \quad n(P \cup A) = 1720 + 1450 - n(P \cap A) = 3170 - n(P \cap A)$

Now, as $n(P \cup A) \le n(U)$

$\therefore \quad 3170 - n(P \cap A) \le 2000$

$\Rightarrow \quad n(P \cap A) \ge 1170$

Hence, the least number of consumers who liked both the product is 1170.

EXAMPLE 8. In a survey of 500 customer in an electronic shop, 400 purchases LG refrigerator and 200 purchases SAMSUNG refrigerator, 50 purchase both refrigerators. Is this data correct?

Sol. Let U be the set of all customers who were participated in the survey. Then, $n(U) = 500$

Let denotes the set of customers who purchased LG refrigerator.

Then, $n(L) = 400$

Let S denotes the set of customers who purchased SAMSUNG refrigerator.

Then $n(S) = 200$

and $n(L \cap S) = 50$

$\because \quad n(L \cup S) = n(L) + n(S) - n(L \cap S)$

$\therefore \quad n(L \cup S) = 400 + 200 - 50$

$\Rightarrow \quad n(L \cup S) = 550$

But $\quad L \cup S \subseteq U \Rightarrow n(L \cup S) \leq n(U)$

$\Rightarrow \quad 550 \leq 500$, which is not true.

This is a contradiction.

So, the given data is incorrect.

EXAMPLE 9. If A and B are two sets containing 3 and 6 elements respectively, what can be the minimum number of elements in $A \cup B$? Also, find the maximum number of elements in $A \cup B$.

Sol Given, $n(A) = 3$ and $n(B) = 6$

We know that

$$n(A \cup B) = n(A) + n(B) - n(A \cap B)$$

Clearly, $n(A \cup B)$ will be maximum when $n(A \cap B)$ is minimum and it will be minimum when $n(A \cap B)$ is maximum. Therefore, two cases arise

***Case* I When $n(A \cap B)$ is minimum**

The minimum value of $n(A \cap B) = 0$

$\therefore \quad n(A \cup B) = n(A) + n(B) = 3 + 6 = 9$

Then, maximum value of $n(A \cup B)$ is 9.

***Case* II When $n(A \cap B)$ is maximum**

$n(A \cap B)$ will be maximum, if $A \subseteq B$

In this case, $n(A \cap B) = 3$

$\therefore \quad n(A \cup B) = 3 + 6 - 3 = 6$

Thus, the minimum number of elements in $A \cup B$ is 6.

EXAMPLE 10. A survey shows that 63% of the Indian like cheese whereas 76% like apples. If x% of the Indian like both cheese and apples, then find the values of x.

Sol. Let the population of India be 100 crore.

Let C denotes the set of Indians who like cheese.

Then, $\quad n(C) = 63$ crore

Again, let A denotes the set of Indians who like apple.

Then, $\quad n(A) = 76$ crore

and $n(C \cap A) = x$ crore

Now, $n(C \cup A) = n(C) + n(A) - n(C \cap A)$

$\Rightarrow \quad n(C \cup A) = 63 + 76 - n(C \cap A)$

$\Rightarrow \quad n(C \cup A) + n(C \cap A) = 139$

$\Rightarrow \quad n(C \cap A) = 139 - n(C \cup A) \quad$ ...(i)

But $n(C \cup A) \leq 100$

$\therefore \quad -n(C \cup A) \geq -100$

$\Rightarrow \quad 139 - n(C \cup A) \geq 139 - 100$

$\Rightarrow \quad 139 - n(C \cup A) \geq 39$

$\Rightarrow \quad n(C \cap A) \geq 39 \quad$ [using Eq. (i)] ...(ii)

Again, $C \cap A \subseteq C$ and $C \cap A \subseteq A$

$\Rightarrow n(C \cap A) \leq n(C)$ and $n(C \cap A) \leq n(A)$

$\Rightarrow n(C \cap A) \leq 63$ and $n(C \cap A) \leq 76$

$\Rightarrow \quad n(C \cap A) \leq 63 \quad$ ...(iii)

From (ii) and (iii), we get

$$39 \leq n(C \cap A) \leq 63$$

$\Rightarrow \quad 39 \leq x \leq 63$

EXAMPLE 11. In a survey of 200 students of a school, it was found that 120 study Mathematics, 90 study Physics and 70 study Chemistry, 40 study Mathematics and Physics, 30 study Physics and Chemistry, 50 study Chemistry and Mathematics and 20 none of these subjects. Find the number of students who study all the three subjects.

[NCERT Exemplar]

Sol. Let M, P and C respectively denote the set of students studying Mathematics, Physics and Chemistry and U denote the set of students who were participated in the survey. Then, we have,

$$n(U) = 200,\ n(M) = 120,\ n(P) = 90,\ n(C) = 70,$$
$$n(M \cap P) = 40,\ n(P \cap C) = 30,\ n(M \cap C) = 50$$

and $\quad n(M' \cap P' \cap C') = n(M \cup P \cup C)' = 20$

Now, $\quad n(M \cup P \cup C)' = n(U) - n(M \cup P \cup C)$

$\therefore \quad 20 = 200 - n(M \cup P \cup C)$

$\Rightarrow \quad n(M \cup P \cup C) = 200 - 20 = 180$

$\because \quad n(M \cup P \cup C) = n(M) + n(P) + n(C) - n(M \cap P) - n(P \cap C) - n(C \cap M) + n(C \cap M \cap P)$

$\therefore \quad 180 = 120 + 90 + 70 - 40 - 30 - 50 + n(C \cap M \cap P)$

$\Rightarrow \quad 180 = 280 - 120 + n(C \cap M \cap P)$

$\Rightarrow \quad 180 + 120 - 280 = n(P \cap C \cap M)$

$\Rightarrow \quad n(P \cap C \cap M) = 300 - 280 = 20$

Hence, 20 students study all the three subjects.

EXAMPLE 12. In a survey of 25 students, it was found that 15 had taken Maths, 12 had taken Physics, 11 had taken Chemistry, 5 had taken Maths and Chemistry, 9 had taken Maths and Physics, 4 had taken Physics and Chemistry and 3 had taken all the three subjects. Find the number of students that had taken

(i) only Chemistry.

(ii) only Maths.

(iii) only Physics.

(iv) Physics and Chemistry but not Maths.

(v) Maths and Physics but not Chemistry.

(vi) only one of the subjects.

(vii) atleast one of the three subjects.

(viii) None of the subjects.

Sol. Let M, P and C respectively denote the set of students who had taken Maths, Physics and Chemistry and denote the set of students who were participated the survey.

Now, let in Venn diagram, a, b, c, d, e, f and g denote the number of students in respective regions.

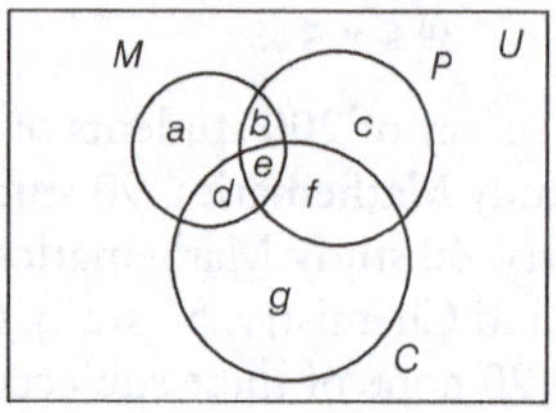

From the Venn diagram, we get

$$n(M) = a + b + d + e,$$
$$n(P) = b + c + e + f,$$
$$n(C) = d + e + f + g,$$
$$n(M \cap P) = b + e,$$
$$n(P \cap C) = e + f,$$
$$n(M \cap C) = d + e \text{ and } n(M \cap P \cap C) = e,$$

Also, we have the followings :

Number of students who had taken all three subjects is 3,

$$n(M \cap P \cap C) = 3 \Rightarrow e = 3$$

Number of students who had taken Maths and Physics is 9, $n(M \cap P) = 9 \Rightarrow b + e = 9$

$\Rightarrow \quad b + 3 = 9 \quad [\because e = 3]$

$\Rightarrow \quad b = 6$

Number of students who had taken Physics and Chemistry is 4

$$n(P \cap C) = 4 \Rightarrow e + f = 4$$

$\Rightarrow \quad 3 + f = 4 \quad [\because e = 3]$

$\Rightarrow \quad f = 1$

Number of students who had taken Maths and Chemistry is 5,

$$n(M \cap C) = 5 \Rightarrow d + e = 5$$

$\Rightarrow \quad d + 3 = 5 \quad [\because e = 3]$

$\Rightarrow \quad d = 2$

Number of students who had taken Maths is 15,

$$n(M) = 15$$

$\Rightarrow \quad a + b + d + e = 15$

$\Rightarrow \quad a + 6 + 2 + 3 = 15 \quad [\because b = 6, d = 2, e = 3]$

$\Rightarrow \quad a = 15 - 11 \Rightarrow a = 4$

Number of students who had taken Physics is 12,

$$n(P) = 12$$

$\Rightarrow \quad b + c + e + f = 12$

$\Rightarrow \quad 6 + c + 3 + 1 = 12 \quad [\because b = 6, e = 3, f = 1]$

$\Rightarrow \quad c = 12 - 10 \Rightarrow c = 2$

Number of students who had taken Chemistry is 11,

$$n(C) = 11 \Rightarrow d + e + f + g = 11$$

$\Rightarrow \quad 2 + 3 + 1 + g = 11 \quad [\because d = 2, e = 3, f = 1]$

$\Rightarrow \quad g = 11 - 6 \Rightarrow g = 5$

Now, the number of students in various cases are as follows

(i) Only Chemistry, $g = 5$ (ii) Only Maths, $a = 4$

(iii) Only Physics, $c = 2$

(iv) Physics and Chemistry but not Maths, $f = 1$

(v) Maths and Physics but not Chemistry, $b = 6$

(vi) Only one of the subjects, $a + c + g = 4 + 2 + 5 = 11$

(vii) Atleast one of the three subjects

$$a + b + c + d + e + f + g = 4 + 6 + 2 + 2 + 3 + 1 + 5 = 23$$

(viii) None of the subjects,

$$25 - (a + b + c + d + e + f + g) = 25 - 23 = 2$$

By Formula

Given, $n(U) = 25, n(M) = 15, n(P) = 12, n(C) = 11,$
$n(M \cap C) = 5, n(M \cap P) = 9, n(P \cap C) = 4,$
$n(M \cap P \cap C) = 3$

(i) Number of students that had taken Chemistry only

$= n(M' \cap P' \cap C) = n((M \cup P)' \cap C)$

$= n(C) - n((M \cup P) \cap C)$

$[\because n(A \cap B') = n(A) - n(A \cap B)]$

$= n(C) - n[(M \cap C) \cup (P \cap C)]$

$= n(C) - [n(M \cap C) + n(P \cap C) - n(M \cap P \cap C)]$

[using, $n(A \cup B) = n(A) + n(B) - n(A \cap B)$

and $n(M \cap C \cap P \cap C) = n\{M \cap P \cap (C \cap C)\}$
$= n(M \cap P \cap C)]$

$= 11 - \{5 + 4 - 3\} = 11 - 6 = 5$

(ii) Number of students that had taken Maths only

$= n(M \cap P' \cap C') = n\{M \cap (P \cup C)'\}$

$= n(M) - n[M \cap (P \cup C)]$

$= n(M) - n[(M \cap P) \cup (M \cap C)]$

$= n(M) - [n(M \cap P) + n(M \cap C) - n(M \cap P \cap C)]$

$= 15 - (9 + 5 - 3) = 15 - 11 = 4$

(iii) Number of students that had taken Physics only

$= n(P \cap M' \cap C') = n(P \cap (M \cup C)')$

$= n(P) - n(P \cap (M \cup C))$

$= n(P) - n[(P \cap M) \cup (P \cap C)]$

$= n(P) - [n(P \cap M) + n(P \cap C) - n(P \cap M \cap C)]$

$= 12 - (9 + 4 - 3) = 12 - 10 = 2$

(iv) Number of students that had taken Physics and Chemistry but not Maths

$= n(P \cap C \cap M')$

$= n(P \cap C) - n(P \cap C \cap M) = 4 - 3 = 1$

(v) Number of students that had taken Maths and Physics but not Chemistry

$= n(M \cap P \cap C')$

$= n(M \cap P) - n(M \cap P \cap C) = 9 - 3 = 6$

(vi) Number of students that had taken only one of the subjects $= n(M) + n(P) + n(C)$

$- 2[n(M \cap P) + n(P \cap C) + n(M \cap C)]$

$+ 3n(P \cap M \cap C)$

$= 15 + 12 + 11 - 2\{9 + 4 + 5\} + 3 \times 3$

$= 38 - 36 + 9$

$= 11$

(vii) Number of students that had taken atleast one of the three subjects $= n(M \cup P \cup C)$

$= n(M) + n(P) + n(C) - n(M \cap P)$

$- n(P \cap C) - n(M \cap C) + n(M \cap P \cap C)$

$= 15 + 12 + 11 - 9 - 4 - 5 + 3 = 23$

(viii) Number of students that had taken none of the subjects $= n(M' \cap P' \cap C')$
$= n(M \cup P \cup C)' = n(U) - n(M \cup P \cup C)$
$= 25 - 23 = 2$

EXAMPLE 13. In a survey of 60 people, it was found that 25 people read newspaper *H*, 26 read newspaper *T*, 26 read newspaper *Z*, 9 read both *H* and *Z*, 11 read both *H* and *T*, 8 read both *T* and *Z* and 3 read all three newspapers. Find

(i) the number of people who read atleast one of the newspaper.

(ii) the number of people who read exactly one newspaper.

Sol. Let *H*, *T* and *Z* respectively denote the set of peoples who read newspapers *H*, *T* and *Z* and *U* denote the set of people who participated in the survey.

Now, let in Venn diagram, *a, b, c, d, e, f* and *g* denote the number of peoples in respective regions.

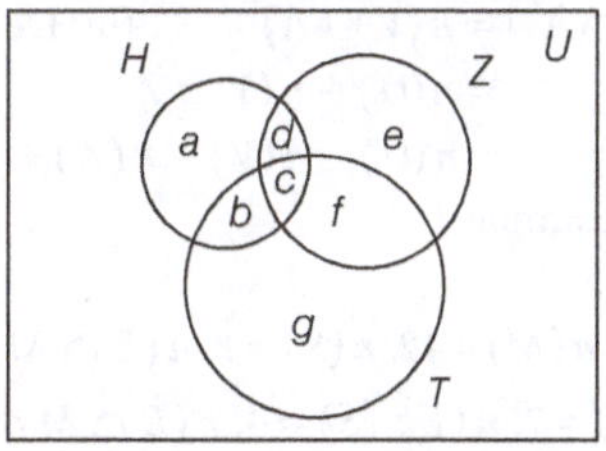

Here, $n(U) = 60$ ...(i)

$n(H) = a + b + c + d = 25$ ...(ii)

$n(T) = b + c + f + g = 26$ ...(iii)

$n(Z) = c + d + e + f = 26$ ...(iv)

$n(H \cap Z) = c + d = 9$ ...(v)

$n(H \cap T) = b + c = 11$ ...(vi)

$n(T \cap Z) = c + f = 8$ ...(vii)

and $n(H \cap T \cap Z) = c = 3$ ...(viii)

On putting the value of *c* in Eq. (vii), we get

$3 + f = 8 \Rightarrow f = 5$

On putting the value of *c* in Eq. (vi), we get

$3 + b = 11 \Rightarrow b = 8$

On putting the value of *c* in Eq. (v), we get

$3 + d = 9 \Rightarrow d = 6$

On putting the values of *c*, *d* and *f* in Eq. (iv), we get

$3 + 6 + e + 5 = 26 \Rightarrow e = 26 - 14 = 12$

On putting the values of *b*, *c* and *f* in Eq. (iii), we get

$8 + 3 + 5 + g = 26 \Rightarrow g = 26 - 16 = 10$

On putting the values of *b*, *c* and *d* in Eq. (ii), we get

$a + 8 + 3 + 6 = 25 \Rightarrow a = 25 - 17 = 8$

Now,

(i) Number of people who read atleast one of the three newspapers

$= n(H \cup T \cup Z)$
$= a + b + c + d + e + f + g$
$= 8 + 8 + 3 + 6 + 12 + 5 + 10$
$= 52$

(ii) Number of people who read exactly one newspaper

$= a + e + g = 8 + 12 + 10$
$= 30$

Topic Practice 5

1 If *A* and *B* are two sets, such that $n(A) = 28, n(B) = 32$ $n(A \cap B) = 10$, then find the value of $n(A \cup B)$.

2 If *X* and *Y* are two sets such that $n(X) = 28, n(Y) = 32$ and $n(X \cup Y) = 45$, then find $n(X \cap Y)$. **[NCERT]**

3 In a group of 400 people, 250 can speak Hindi and 200 can speak English. How many can speak both Hindi and English? **[NCERT]**

4 Let $n(U) = 700, n(A) = 200, n(B) = 300$ and $n(A \cap B) = 100$. Find $n(A' \cap B')$.

5 Let F_1 be the set of parallelograms, F_2 be the set of rectangles, F_3 be the set of rhombus and F_4 be the set of squares. Then, show that F_1 is equal to union of all sets. **[NCERT Exemplar]**

6 In a town with a population of 5000, 3200 people are egg-eaters, 2500 meat-eaters and 1500 eat both egg and meat. How many are pure vegetarians?

7 In a school, there are 20 teachers who teach Maths or Physics. Out of these, 12 teach Maths and 4 teach Physics and Maths. How many teach Physics?

8 In a committee, 50 people speak French, 20 speak Spanish and 10 speak both Spanish and French. How many people speak atleast one of these two languages?

9 The members of a group of 400 people speak either Hindi or English or both. If 270 speak Hindi only and 50 speak both Hindi and English, then how many of them speak English only?

10 In a group of 70 people, 37 like coffee, 52 like tea and each person like atleast one of the two drinks. How many people like both coffee and tea? **[NCERT]**

11. In a survey of 400 movie viewers, 150 were listed as liking 'Veer Zaara', 100 were listed as liking 'Aitraaz' and 75 were listed as both liking 'Aitraaz' as well as 'Veer Zaara'. Find how many people were liking neither 'Aitraaz' nor 'Veer Zaara'?

12 In a survey of 400 students in a school, 100 were listed as taking apple juice, 150 as taking orange juice and 75 were listed as taking both apple as well as orange juice. Find how many sutdents were taking neither apple juice nor orange juice.

13 Out of 100 students, 15 passed in English, 12 passed in Mathematics, 8 in Science, 6 in English and Mathematics, 7 in Mathematics and Science, 4 in English and Science, 4 in all the three. Find how many students passed in

(i) English and Mathematics but not in Science?

(ii) Mathematics and Science but not in English?

14 In a group of 65 people, 40 like Cricket, 10 like both Cricket and Tennis. How many like tennis only and not Cricket? How many like Tennis? [NCERT]

15 There are 200 individuals with a skin disorder, 120 has been exposed to chemical C_1, 50 to chemical C_2 and 30 to both the chemicals C_1 and C_2. Find the number of individuals exposed to

(i) chemical C_1 or chemical C_2.

(ii) chemical C_1 but not chemical C_2.

(iii) chemical C_2 but not chemical C_1.

Hints & Solutions

1. **Hint** $n(A \cup B) = n(A) + n(B) - n(A \cap B) = 28 + 32 - 10$

   Ans. 50

2. **Hint** Use the formula,

   $$n(X \cup Y) = n(X) + n(Y) - n(X \cap Y)$$

   Ans. 15

3. **Hint** $n(H) = 250$, $n(E) = 200$ and $n(H \cup E) = 400$

   $\because n(H \cup E) = n(H) + n(E) - n(H \cap E)$

   Ans. 50

4. **Hint** $n(A' \cap B') = n(U) - n(A \cup B)$ **Ans.** 300

5. All Rectangles, Rhombus and Square are parallelogram because its opposite sides are equal and parallel.

   Therefore, $F_2 \subset F_1$, $F_3 \subset F_1$ and $F_4 \subset F_1$

   $\Rightarrow \quad F_1 = F_2 \cup F_3 \cup F_4$

6. **Hint** Let E be the set of people who are egg-eaters M be set of people who are meat-eaters and U be the set of people in the town.

   Then, number of pure vegetarians

   $= n(U) -$ Number of non- vegetarians

   $= n(U) - n(E \cup M)$

   Ans. 800

7. **Hint** $n(M \cup P) = 20$, $n(M) = 12$, $n(P \cap M) = 4$

   $\because n(M \cup P) = n(M) + n(P) - n(M \cap P)$

   Ans. 12

8. **Hint** $n(F \cup S) = 50 + 20 - 10$

   Ans. 60

9. **Hint** $n(A \cup B) = n(\text{only } A) + n(\text{only } B) + n(A \cap B)$

   $\Rightarrow n(\text{only } B) = 400 - 270 - 50$

   Ans. 80

10. 19

11. The number of people who were liking neither (*A*) 'Aitraaz' nor 'Veer Zaara' (*V*) is given by

    $n(V' \cap A') = n(V \cup A)'$ [by De Morgan's law]

    $= n(U) - n(V \cup A)$

    $= n(U) - n(V) - n(A) + n(V \cap A)$

12. Solve as Example 4.

    Ans. 225

13. $n(E) = 15$, $n(M) = 12$, $n(S) = 8$, $n(E \cap M) = 6$

    $n(M \cap S) = 7$, $n(E \cap S) = 4$, $n(E \cap M \cap S) = 4$

    (i) $n(E \cap m \cap \bar{S}) = n(E \cap M) - n(E \cap M \cap S)$

    $= 6 - 4 = 2$

    (ii) $n(M \cap S \cap \bar{E}) = n(M \cap S) - n(E \cap M \cap S)$

    $= 7 - 4 = 3$

14. **Hint** $n(T \cup C) = n(T) + n(C) - n(T \cap C)$

    $\therefore \quad n(T) = 35$

    Now, $n(T \cap \bar{C}) = n(T) - n(T \cap C) = 35 - 10 = 25$

    Ans. 25, 35

15. **Hint** $n(U) = 200$; $n(C_1) = 120$, $n(C_2) = 50$;

    $n(C_1 \cap C_2) = 30$

    (i) Required number of individuals $= n(C_1 \cup C_2)$

    $= n(C_1) + n(C_2) - n(C_1 \cap C_2)$

    Ans. 140

    (ii) Required number of individuals $= n(C_1 \cap C_2')$

    $= n(C_1) - n(C_1 \cap C_2) = 120 - 30 = 90$

    (iii) Required number of individuals $= n(C_1' \cap C_2)$

    $= n(C_2) - n(C_1 \cap C_2) = 50 - 30 = 20$

Exam Pattern Exercise

Part A - Objective Type Questions

Multiple Choice Questions

1 Let $B = \left\{x : x = \frac{1}{2n-1}, 1 \le n \le 5, \text{ where } n \in N\right\}$, then B equals

(a) $\left\{1, \frac{1}{3}, \frac{1}{5}, \frac{1}{9}, \frac{1}{11}\right\}$ (b) $\left\{1, \frac{1}{3}, \frac{1}{7}, \frac{1}{9}, \frac{1}{11}\right\}$

(c) $\left\{1, \frac{1}{3}, \frac{1}{5}, \frac{1}{7}, \frac{1}{9}\right\}$ (d) None of these

2 The set $(A \cap B')' \cup (B \cap C)$ is equal to **[NCERT Exemplar]**

(a) $A' \cup B \cup C$ (b) $A' \cup B$

(c) $A' \cup C'$ (d) $A' \cap B$

3 If A and B are two sets, then $A \cap (A \cup B)$ equals to **[NCERT Exemplar]**

(a) A (b) B

(c) ϕ (d) $A \cap B$

4 Two finite sets have m and n elements. The number of subsets of the first set is 224 more than of the second. The values of m and n are respectively

(a) 4, 7 (b) 8, 5

(c) 4, 4 (d) 7, 7

5 The intersection of all the intervals having the form $\left[1 + \frac{1}{n}, 6 - \frac{2}{n}\right]$, where n is a positive integer, is

(a) [1, 6] (b) (1, 6)

(c) [2, 4] (d) $\left[\frac{3}{2}, 5\right]$

6 If P and Q are two disjoint sets, then $n(P \cup Q)$ is equal to

(a) $n(P) + n(Q)$

(b) $n(P) + n(Q) - n(P \cap Q)$

(c) $n(P) + n(Q) + n(P \cap Q)$

(d) $n(P)\, n(Q)$

7 If $P = \{x : x \text{ is a multiple of } 3\}$ and $Q = \{x : x \text{ is a multiple of } 5\}$, then $P - Q$ is

(a) $P \cap Q$

(b) $P \cap \overline{Q}$

(c) $\overline{P} \cap \overline{Q}$

(d) $\overline{P \cap Q}$

8 If sets P and Q are defined as

$P = \left\{(x, y) : y = \frac{1}{x}, 0 \ne x \in R\right\}$

$Q = \{(x, y) : y = -x, x \in R\}$, then

(a) $P \cap Q = P$ (b) $P \cap Q = Q$

(c) $P \cap Q = \phi$ (d) $P \cup Q = P$

9 A survey shows that 63% of the people watch a news channel, whereas 76% watch another channel. If x% of the people watch both channel, then

(a) $x = 38$ (b) $x = 63$

(c) $39 \le x \le 63$ (d) $x = 39$

10 In a city 20% of the population travels by car, 50% travels by bus and 10% travels by both car and bus. Then, persons travelling by car or bus is

(a) 60% (b) 40%

(c) 20% (d) 50%

Assertion-Reason Based Questions

Directions (Q. Nos. 11-13) *In the questions given below are two statements labelled as Assertion (A) and Reason (R). In the context of the two statements, which one of the following is correct?*

(a) Both A and R are correct; R is the correct explanation of A

(b) Both A and R are correct; R is not the correct explanation of A

(c) A is correct; R is incorrect

(d) R is correct; A is incorrect

11 **Assertion (A)** If $A = \{1, 3, 5, 7, 9\}$ and $B = \{2, 3, 5, 7, 11\}$. Then, A and B are intersecting sets.

Reason (R) Sets A and B are intersecting if $A \cap B \ne \phi$.

12 **Assertion (A)** If $A = \{x : x \in N, x \text{ is a factor of } 6\}$ and $B = \{x \in N : x \text{ is a factor of } 8\}$, then $A - B$ is $\{4, 6\}$.

Reason (R) For any sets A and B, their difference $(A - B)$ is defined as $(A - B) = \{x : x \in A \text{ and } x \notin B\}$.

13 **Assertion (A)** If $A = \{x : x \in N, x \text{ is a factor of } 12\}$ and $B = \{x : x \in N, x \text{ is a factor of } 18\}$, then $A \cap B$ is $\{1, 3, 4, 6\}$.

Reason (R) If two sets are A and B, then $A \cap B = \{x : x \in A \text{ and } x \in B\}$.

Part B - Descriptive Questions

Very Short Answer Type Questions

14 If $\{x : x \in R, -4 < x \le 6\}$, then find the length of the interval.

15 Find the total number of subsets of a finite set containing 4 elements.

16 What is the difference between a collection and a set? Give reason to support your answer.

17 Match each of the sets on the left described in the roster form with the same set on the right described in the set-builder form.

(i)	{H, R, A, Y, N}	(a)	$\{x : x$ is a natural number and a divisor of 18$\}$
(ii)	{L, I, T, E}	(b)	$\{x : x$ is a letter of the word HARYANA$\}$
(iii)	{1, 2, 3,4, 6, 12}	(c)	$\{x : x$ is a letter of the word LITTLE$\}$
(iv)	{1, 2, 3, 6, 9, 18}	(d)	$\{x : x$ is a natural number and is a divisor of 12$\}$

18 Find the number of subsets of the set $A = \{1, 4, 5\}$.

19 List all the proper subsets of the set $A = \{a, b\}$.

20 When $A = \phi$, then find the number of elements in $P(A)$.

Short Answer Type Questions

21 Which of the following sets are empty set, singleton set and equal set?
$A = \{x : 2x = 10 \text{ and } x^2 - 7x + 10 = 0\}$
$B = \{x : x^2 - 16x + 55 = 0 \text{ and } x^2 = 25\}$
$C = \left\{x : -\frac{1}{2} \le x \le \frac{1}{2}\right\}$, $D = \{x : 0 \le 4x^2 \le 1\}$

22 If $U = \{a, b, c, d, e, f\}$, $A = \{a, b, c\}$, $B = \{c, d, e, f\}$, $C = \{c, d, e\}$ and $D = \{d, e, f\}$, then tabulate the following sets.

(i) $A \cap D$ (ii) $A \cap C$ (iii) $U \cap D$

(iv) $A \cup \phi$ (v) $(U \cap \phi)'$ (vi) $(U \cup A)'$.

23 If $A = \{1, 2, 3, 4, 5\}$, $B = \{1, 3, 5, 8\}$ and $C = \{2, 5, 7, 8\}$, then verify that $A - (B \cup C) = (A - B) \cap (A - C)$.

24 Let A and B be two sets. Then, prove that $A = B \Leftrightarrow A \subseteq B$ and $B \subseteq A$.

25 Express the shaded region of the following Venn diagram in terms of union and difference of sets A, B and C.

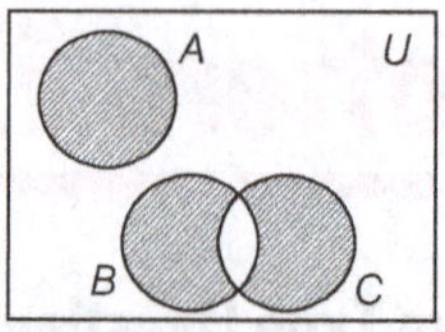

26 If $A = \{4^n - 3n - 1, n \in N\}$ and $B = \{9(n-1) : n \in N\}$, then show that $A \subset B$.

27 From the given venn diagram, determine the following sets.

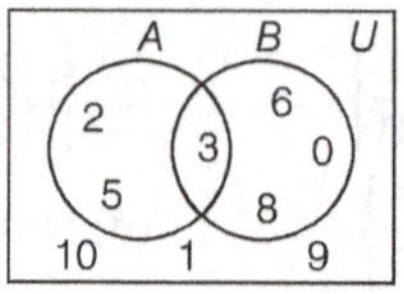

(i) $A \cup B$ (ii) $A \cap B$

(iii) $A - B$ (iv) $(A \cap B)'$

28 Let B be a subset of a set A and let $P(A : B) = \{X \in P(A) : X \supset B\}$.

(i) Show that $P(A : \phi) = P(A)$.

(ii) If $A = \{1, 2, 3, 4\}$ and $B = \{1, 2\}$. List all the members of the set $P(A : B)$.

Long Answer Type Questions

29 State which of the following statements are true and which are false? Justify your answer.

(i) $35 \in \{x : x$ has exactly four positive factors$\}$

(ii) $128 \in \{y :$ the sum of all positive factors of y is $2y\}$

(iii) $3 \notin \{x : x^4 - 5x^3 + 2x^2 - 112x + 6 = 0\}$

(iv) $496 \in \{y :$ the sum of all the positive factors of y is $2y\}$

30 If $X = \{1, 2, 3\}$ and n represents any member of X, write the following sets containing all numbers represented by

(i) $4n$ (ii) $n + 6$ (iii) $\frac{n}{2}$ (iv) $n - 1$

31 Given set $A = \{1, 2, 3, 4, \dots, 100\}$, write the subset

(i) X of A, whose elements are multiple of 7.

(ii) Y of A, whose elements are represented by $x + 3$, where $x \in A$.

32 Each set X, contains 5 elements and each set y, contains 2 elements and $\bigcup_{r=1}^{20} X_r = P = \bigcup_{r=1}^{n} Y_r$. If each element of P belongs to exactly 10 of the X_r^P and to exactly 4 of Y_r^P, then find the value of n.

Case Study Based Questions

33 A class teacher Mamta Sharma of class XI write three sets A, B and C are such that

$A = \{1, 3, 5, 7, 9\}$ $B = \{2, 4, 6, 8\}$ and $C = \{2, 3, 5, 7, 11\}$.

Based on the above information, answer the following questions.

(i) Find $A \cap B$.

(ii) Find $A \cap C$.

(iii) Find $B \cup (A - C)$.

Or Find $A \cap (B \Delta C)$

34. In an university, out of 100 students 15 offered Mathematics only: 12 offered Chemistry only; 8 offered Physics only; 40 offered Physics and Mathematics; 20 offered Physics and Chemistry; 10 offered Mathematics and Chemistry; 65 offered Physics.

Based on the above information, answer the following questions.

(i) Find the number of students who offered Mathematics.

(ii) Find the number of students who offered Chemistry.

(iii) Find the number of students who did not offer any of the above three subjects.

Or Find the number of students who offered all the above three subjects.

Hints & Solutions

1. (c) 2. (b) 3. (a) 4. (b)
5. (c) 6. (a) 7. (b) 8. (c)
9. (c) 10. (a) 11. (a) 12. (d)
13. (d) 14. 10 15. 16

16. Every set is a collection but a collection is not necessarily a set. Only well-defined collection are sets e.g. Collection of most talented writers of India is a collection but it is not a set.

17. (i) → (b); (ii) → (c), (iii) → (d); (iv) → (a)

18. **Hint** Number of subsets of $A = 2^3$ **Ans.** 8

19. ϕ, $\{a\}$, $\{b\}$ 20. 1

21. **Hint** $A = \{x : x = 5 \text{ and } (x-2)(x-5) = 0\} = \{5\}$

$B = \{x : (x-11)(x-5) = 0 \text{ and } x = \pm 5\} = \{5\}$

$C = \left\{x : -\frac{1}{2} \le x \le \frac{1}{2}\right\}$ and $D = \{x : 0 \le 4x^2 \le 1\}$

$= \left\{x : 0 \le x^2 \le \frac{1}{4}\right\} = \left\{x : -\frac{1}{2} \le x \le \frac{1}{2}\right\}$

$\therefore \quad C = D$

Ans. A and B are singleton sets, C and D are equal sets.

22. (i) ϕ (ii) $\{c\}$ (iii) $\{d, e, f\}$
(iv) $\{a, b, c\}$ (v) U (vi) ϕ

23. **Hint** $B \cup C = \{1, 2, 3, 5, 7, 8\}$

$\therefore \quad A - (B \cup C) = \{4\}$

and $(A - B) \cap (A - C) = \{2, 4\} \cap \{1, 3, 4\} = \{4\}$

25. $A \cup (B \Delta C)$ or $A \cup \{(B - C) \cup (C - B)\}$

26. **Hint** Now, $4^n - 3n - 1 = (3+1)^n - 3n - 1$

$= 1 + 3n + \frac{n(n-1)}{2} \cdot (3)^2 + \dots - 3n - 1 = 9\left(\frac{n(n-1)}{2} + \dots\right)$

and $B = \{9(n-1) : n \in N\}$

27. (i) $\{0, 2, 3, 5, 6, 8\}$ (ii) $\{3\}$
(iii) $\{2, 5\}$ (iv) $\{0, 1, 2, 5, 6, 8, 9, 10\}$

28. (ii) $\{\{1, 2\}, \{1, 2, 3\}, \{1, 2, 4\}, \{1, 2, 3, 4\}\}$

29. (i) **Hint** $35 \in \{1, 5, 7, 35\}$ **Ans.** True

(ii) **Hint** $128 \in \{1, 2, 4, 8, 16, 32, 64, 128\}$

Here, $y = \{1, 2, 4, 8, 16, 32, 64, 128\}$

Now, sum of elements of y

$= 1 + 2 + 4 + 8 + 16 + 32 + 64 + 128 = 255 \ne 2y$

Ans. False

(iii) **Hint** We have, $x^4 - 5x^3 + 2x^2 - 112x + 6 = 0$

$\text{LHS} = (3)^4 - 5(3)^3 + 2(3)^2 - 112 \times 3 + 6$

$= 81 - 135 + 18 - 336 + 6 = -366 \ne 0$

Ans. True

(iv) **Hint** $496 \in \{1, 2, 4, 8, 16, 62, 124, 248, 496\}$

Here, $y = \{1, 2, 4, 8, 16, 62, 124, 248, 496\}$

Now, sum of elements of y

$= 1 + 2 + 4 + 8 + 16 + 62 + 124 + 248 + 496 \ne 2y$

Ans. False

30. (i) $\{4, 8, 12\}$ (ii) $\{7, 8, 9\}$ (iii) $\left\{\frac{1}{2}, 1, \frac{3}{2}\right\}$ (iv) $\{0, 1, 2\}$

31. (i) $\{7, 14, 21, 28, 35, 42, 49, 56, 63, 70, 77, 84, 91, 98\}$
(ii) $\{4, 5, 6, \dots, 100\}$

32. 20

33. (i) ϕ (ii) $\{3, 5, 7\}$ (iii) $\{1, 2, 4, 6, 8, 9\}$ *Or* $\{3, 5, 7\}$

34. (i) 62 (ii) 39 (iii) 1 *Or* 3

CHAPTER 09

Relations

In this Chapter...

- Ordered Pairs
- Cartesian Product of Two Sets
- Some Theorems on Cartesian Product of Sets
- Relations
- Domain, Codomain and Range of Relation

In our daily life, we come across many patterns that characterise relations such as brother and sister, father and son, husband and wife. In Mathematics, there is a variety of relations, whose knowledge is crucial. Each relation has its own meaning and significance.

e.g. $\tan\theta = \frac{1}{\cot\theta}$ (relation between $\tan\theta$ and $\cot\theta$)

Ordered Pairs

If a pair of elements written in round bracket and grouped together in a particular order, then such a pair, is called an **ordered pair**. Ordered pair is written by listing two objects in the specific order, separated by **comma** (,) and enclosing the pair in **parentheses.**

e.g. The ordered pair of two elements a and b is denoted by (a, b). a is first element (or first component) and b is second element (or second component).

Graphically, ordered pair (a, b) represents a point in cartesian plane. So, ordered pair (2, 3) implies that **abscissa** $x = 2$ and **ordinate** $y = 3$.

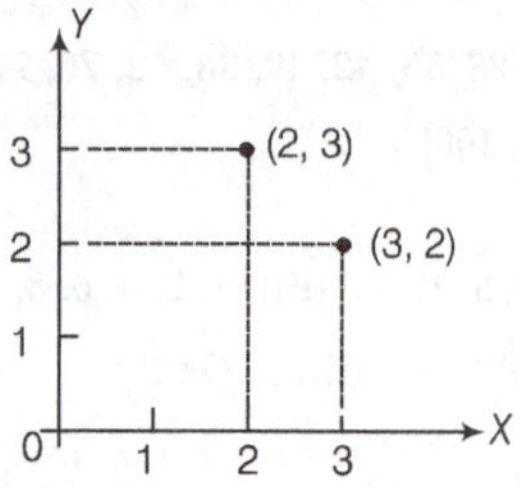

It is clear from the graph that ordered pairs (2, 3) and (3, 2) represent two different points and hence they are not equal.

Equality of Two Ordered Pairs

Two ordered pairs are said to be equal if their corresponding elements are equal.

i.e. $(a, b) = (c, d) \Rightarrow a = c$ and $b = d$

Note $\{a, b\} \neq (a, b)$, because $\{a, b\}$ is a set whereas (a, b) is an ordered pair.

EXAMPLE 1. Find the values of a and b, if

(i) $(2a - 5, 4) = (5, b + 6)$ (ii) $(a - 3, b + 7) = (3, 7)$

Sol. We know that two ordered pairs are said to be equal, if their corresponding elements are equal.

(i) $(2a - 5, 4) = (5, b + 6)$

$\Rightarrow 2a - 5 = 5$ and $4 = b + 6$ [equating corresponding elements]

$\Rightarrow 2a = 5 + 5$ and $4 - 6 = b$

$\Rightarrow 2a = 10$ and $-2 = b \Rightarrow a = 5$ and $b = -2$

(ii) $(a - 3, b + 7) = (3, 7) \Rightarrow a - 3 = 3$ and $b + 7 = 7$ [equating corresponding elements]

$\Rightarrow a = 3 + 3$ and $b = 7 - 7 \Rightarrow a = 6$ and $b = 0$

Cartesian Product of Two Sets

For two non-empty sets A and B, the cartesian product $A \times B$ is the set of all ordered pairs of elements from sets A and B.

In symbolic form, it can be written as

$$A \times B = \{(a, b) : a \in A, b \in B\}$$

EXAMPLE 2. Let $A=\{a,b,c\}$ and $B=\{x: x\in N, x$ is a prime number less than $5\}$. Find $A\times B$ and $B\times A$. Show that $A\times B\neq B\times A$.

Sol. Given sets are $A=\{a,b,c\}$

and $B=\{x: x\in N,\ x$ is a prime number less than $5\}=\{2,3\}$

For element a of set A, all ordered pairs are $(a, 2), (a, 3)$.

For element b of set A, all ordered pairs are $(b, 2), (b, 3)$.

For element c of set A, all ordered pairs are $(c, 2), (c, 3)$.

$\therefore\ A\times B=\{(a, 2), (a, 3), (b, 2), (b, 3), (c, 2), (c, 3)\}$

For element 2 of set B, all ordered pairs are $(2, a), (2, b), (2, c)$.

For element 3 of set B, all ordered pairs are $(3, a), (3, b), (3, c)$.

$\therefore\ B\times A=\{(2, a), (2, b), (2, c), (3, a), (3, b), (3, c)\}$

Since, $(a, 2)\neq(2, a)$

$\therefore\ A\times B\neq B\times A$

EXAMPLE 3. If $A\times B=\{(a, 1), (b, 3), (a, 3), (b, 1), (a, 2), (b, 2)\}$. Then, find A and B.

Sol. Here, first element of each ordered pair of $A\times B$ gives the elements of set A and corresponding second element gives the elements of set B.

$\therefore\ A=\{a, b\}$ and $B=\{1, 3, 2\}$

Number of Elements in Cartesian Product of Two Sets

- If there are p elements in set A and q elements in set B, then there will be pq elements in $A\times B$.
  i.e. if $n(A)=p$ and $n(B)=q$, then
  $$n(A\times B)=pq$$
- If A and B are non-empty sets and either A or B is an infinite set, then $A\times B$ also will be an infinite set.
- If A or B is the null set or an empty set, then $A\times B$ also will be an empty set.
  i.e. $A\times B=\phi$
- If there are p elements in set A and q elements in set B, then the number of subsets of $A\times B$ is 2^{pq}.

EXAMPLE 4. If the set A has 3 elements and set B has 4 elements, then find the number of elements in $A\times B$.

Sol. Given, $n(A)=3$ and $n(B)=4$.

$\therefore$ The number of elements in $A\times B$ is

$$n(A\times B)=n(A)\times n(B)=3\times 4=12$$

EXAMPLE 5. A and B are two sets given in such a way that $A\times B$ contains 6 elements. If three elements of $A\times B$ are $(1, 3)$, $(2, 5)$ and $(3, 3)$, find A, B and remaining elements of $A\times B$.

Sol. It is given that $(1, 3)$, $(2, 5)$ and $(3, 3)$ are in $A\times B$. It follows that 1, 2, 3 are elements of A and 3, 5 are elements of B.

$\therefore\ A=\{1, 2, 3\}$ and $B=\{3, 5\}$

$\therefore\ A\times B=\{1, 2, 3\}\times\{3, 5\}$

$=\{(1, 3), (1, 5), (2, 3), (2, 5), (3, 3), (3, 5)\}$

Hence, the remaining elements of $(A\times B)$ are $(1, 5)$, $(2, 3)$, $(3, 5)$.

EXAMPLE 6. Let $A=\{1,2\}$ and $B=\{3,4\}$. How many subsets will $A\times B$ have? List them.

Sol. Given, $A=\{1, 2\}$ and $B=\{3,4\}$

$\Rightarrow n(A)=2$ and $n(B)=2$

$\therefore$ Total subsets of $A\times B=2^{2\times 2}=2^4=16$

[$\because$ number of subsets $=2^{pq}$]

Subsets of $A\times B$ are

$\{(1, 3)\}, \{(1, 4)\}, \{(2, 3)\}, \{(2, 4)\}, \{(1, 3), (1, 4)\}, \{(1, 3), (2, 3)\}, \{(1, 3), (2, 4)\}, \{(1, 4), (2, 3)\}, \{(1, 4), (2, 4)\}, \{(2, 3), (2, 4)\}, \{(1, 3), (1, 4), (2, 3)\}, \{(1, 3), (1, 4), (2, 4)\}, \{(1, 3), (2, 3), (2, 4)\}, \{(1, 4), (2, 3), (2, 4)\}, \{(1, 3), (1, 4), (2, 3), (2, 4)\}$ and ϕ.

EXAMPLE 7. The cartesian product $P\times P$ has 16 elements among which two are found $(a, 1)$ and $(b, 2)$. Find the set P and the remaining elements of $P\times P$.

Sol. Given, $n(P\times P)=16$

$\Rightarrow\ n(P)\cdot n(P)=16$

$\Rightarrow\ n(P)=4$ ...(i)

Now, as $(a,1)\in P\times P$

$\therefore\ a\in P$ and $1\in P$

Again, $(b, 2)\in P\times P$

$\therefore\ b\in P$ and $2\in P$

Thus, $a, b, 1, 2\in P$

From Eq. (i), it is clear that P has exactly four elements.

$\therefore\ P=\{a, b, 1, 2\}$

Now, $P\times P=\{a, b, 1, 2\}\times\{a, b, 1, 2\}$

$=\{(a, a), (a, b), (a, 1), (a, 2), (b, a), (b, b), (b, 1), (b, 2), (1, a), (1, b), (1, 1), (1, 2), (2, a), (2, b), (2, 1), (2, 2)\}$

Hence, the remaining elements of $P\times P$ are $(a, a), (a, b), (a, 2), (b, a), (b, b), (b, 1), (1, a), (1, b), (1, 1), (1, 2), (2, a), (2, b), (2, 1)$ and $(2, 2)$

Some Theorems on Cartesian Product of Sets

- For any three non-empty sets A, B and C, we have
  (i) $A\times(B\cup C)=(A\times B)\cup(A\times C)$
  (ii) $A\times(B\cap C)=(A\times B)\cap(A\times C)$
- For any three non-empty sets A, B and C, we have
  $$A\times(B-C)=(A\times B)-(A\times C)$$

- If A and B are any two non-empty sets, then
$$A \times B = B \times A \Leftrightarrow A = B$$
- If $A \subseteq B$, then $A \times A \subseteq (A \times B) \cap (B \times A)$
- If $A \subseteq B$, then $A \times C \subseteq B \times C$ for any non-empty set C.
- If $A \subseteq B$ and $C \subseteq D$, then $A \times C \subseteq B \times D$
- For any non-empty sets A, B, C and D, we have
$$(A \times B) \cap (C \times D) = (A \cap C) \times (B \cap D)$$

Corollary

For any non-empty sets A and B,
$$(A \times B) \cap (B \times A) = (A \cap B) \times (B \cap A) = (A \cap B) \times (A \cap B)$$

- For any three sets A, B and C, we have
  (i) $A \times (B' \cup C')' = (A \times B) \cap (A \times C)$
  (ii) $A \times (B' \cap C')' = (A \times B) \cup (A \times C)$
- Let A and B be two non-empty sets having n elements in common, then $A \times B$ and $B \times A$ have n^2 elements in common.
- Let A be a non-empty set such that $A \times B = A \times C$. Then, $B = C$

EXAMPLE 8. If $A = \{1, 4\}$, $B = \{2, 3, 6\}$ and $C = \{2, 3, 7\}$, then verify that

(i) $A \times (B \cup C) = (A \times B) \cup (A \times C)$

(ii) $A \times (B \cap C) = (A \times B) \cap (A \times C)$

Sol. We have, $A = \{1, 4\}$, $B = \{2, 3, 6\}$ and $C = \{2, 3, 7\}$

(i) **To find $A \times (B \cup C)$**

$B \cup C = \{2, 3, 6\} \cup \{2, 3, 7\}$

$\Rightarrow \quad B \cup C = \{2, 3, 6, 7\}$

$\therefore \quad A \times (B \cup C) = \{1, 4\} \times \{2, 3, 6, 7\}$
$= \{(1, 2), (1, 3), (1, 6), (1, 7), (4, 2), (4, 3), (4, 6), (4, 7)\}$ ...(i)

To find $(A \times B) \cup (A \times C)$

$A \times B = \{(1, 2), (1, 3), (1, 6), (4, 2), (4, 3), (4, 6)\}$

and $A \times C = \{(1, 2), (1, 3), (1, 7), (4, 2), (4, 3), (4, 7)\}$

$\therefore \quad (A \times B) \cup (A \times C) = \{(1, 2), (1, 3), (1, 6), (1, 7), (4, 2), (4, 3), (4, 6), (4, 7)\}$ ...(ii)

From Eqs. (i) and (ii), we get
$$A \times (B \cup C) = (A \times B) \cup (A \times C)$$

(ii) **To find $A \times (B \cap C)$**

$B \cap C = \{2, 3\}$

$\therefore \quad A \times (B \cap C) = \{1, 4\} \times \{2, 3\}$
$= \{(1, 2), (1, 3), (4, 2), (4, 3)\}$ ...(iii)

To find $(A \times B) \cap (A \times C)$

$A \times B = \{(1, 2), (1, 3), (1, 6), (4, 2), (4, 3), (4, 6)\}$

$A \times C = \{(1, 2), (1, 3), (1, 7), (4, 2), (4, 3), (4, 7)\}$

$\therefore (A \times B) \cap (A \times C) = \{(1, 2), (1, 3), (4, 2), (4, 3)\}$ ...(iv)

From Eqs. (iii) and (iv), we get
$$A \times (B \cap C) = (A \times B) \cap (A \times C)$$

Topic Practice 1

1 Find x and y, if $(x + 2, 4) = (5, 2x + y)$.

2 If $A = \{a, b, c\}$ and $B = \{r, s\}$, then find
(i) $A \times B$ (ii) $B \times A$

3 If $A \times B = \{(a, x), (a, y), (b, x), (b, y)\}$, then find A and B.

4 If $A = \{1, 3, 5\}$ and $B = \{2, 3\}$ then show that $A \times B \neq B \times A$.

5 The cartesian product $A \times A$ has 9 elements among which are found $(-1, 0)$ and $(0, 1)$. Find the set A and the remaining element of $A \times A$.

6 Let A and B be two sets such that $n(A) = 5$ and $n(B) = 2$. If a, b, c, d, e are distinct and $(a,2), (b,3), (c,2), (d,3), (e,2)$ are elements of $A \times B$, find A and B.

7 If $A = \{x : x^2 - 5x + 6 = 0\}$; $B = \{2, 4\}$, $C = \{4, 5\}$, then find the value of $A \times (B \cap C)$.

8 If $A = \{1, 2, 3\}$, $B = \{3, 4\}$, $C = \{4, 5, 6\}$, then find the value of $(A \times B) \cap (B \times C)$.

9 If $A = \{1,2,3\}$, $B = \{1,2,3,4\}$, $C = \{5,6\}$ and $D = \{5,6,7,8\}$, then verify that $(A \times C) \subset (B \times D)$.

10 If $A = \{1, 2, 3\}$, $B = \{3, 4\}$ and $C = \{4, 5, 6\}$, then find
(i) $A \times (B \cap C)$
(ii) $(A \times B) \cap (A \times C)$

11 If $A = \{a, d\}$, $B = \{b, c, e\}$ and $C = \{b, c, f\}$, then verify that
(i) $A \times (B \cup C) = (A \times B) \cup (A \times C)$
(ii) $A \times (B \cap C) = (A \times B) \cap (A \times C)$

Hints & Solutions

1. Solve as Example 1. **Ans.** $x = 3,\ y = -2$
2. Solve as Example 2.
   (i) $A \times B = \{(a, r), (a, s), (b, r), (b, s), (c, r), (c, s)\}$
   (ii) $B \times A = \{(r, a), (r, b), (r, c), (s, a), (s, b), (s, c)\}$
3. Solve as Example 3. **Ans.** $A = \{a, b\}$, $B = \{x, y\}$
4. Solve as Example 2.
5. Solve as Example 5.
   Ans. $A = \{-1, 0, 1\}$ and remaining elements of $A \times A$ are $(-1, -1), (-1, 1), (0, -1), (0, 0), (1, -1), (1, 0), (1, 1)$.
6. **Hint** $\because$ $(a, 2), (b, 3), (c, 2), (d, 3), (e, 2) \in A \times B$
   $\therefore$ $a, b, c, d, e \in A$ and $2, 3 \in B$
   Also, it is given that $n(A) = 5$, $n(B) = 2$
   $\therefore$ $A = \{a, b, c, d, e\}$, $B = \{2, 3\}$
7. **Hint** $A = \{2, 3\}$, $B \cap C = \{4\}$
   $\therefore$ $A \times (B \cap C) = \{(2, 4), (3, 4)\}$ **Ans.** $\{(2, 4), (3, 4)\}$
8. **Hint** $A \times B = \{(1, 3), (1, 4), (2, 3), (2, 4), (3, 3), (3, 4)\}$
   and $B \times C = \{(3, 4), (3, 5), (3, 6), (4, 4), (4, 5), (4, 6)\}$
   $\therefore (A \times B) \cap (B \times C) = \{(3, 4)\}$
   Ans. $\{(3, 4)\}$
9. **Hint** $A \times C = \{(1, 5), (1, 6), (2, 5), (2, 6), (3, 5), (3, 6)\}$
   $B \times D = \{(1, 5), (1, 6), (1, 7), (1, 8), (2, 5), (2, 6), (2, 7), (2, 8), (3, 5), (3, 6), (3, 7), (3, 8), (4, 5), (4, 6), (4, 7), (4, 8)\}$
   Here, elements $(1, 5), (1, 6), (2, 5), (2, 6), (3, 5), (3, 6) \in A \times C$ are also belongs to $B \times D$, therefore $(A \times C) \subset (B \times D)$.
10. Solve as Example 8.
    Ans. (i) $\{(1, 4), (2, 4), (3, 4)\}$
    (ii) $\{(1, 4), (2, 4), (3, 4)\}$
11. (i) Solve as Example 8 (i).
    (ii) Solve as Example 8 (ii).

Relations

Let A and B be two non-empty sets. Then, a relation R from set A to set B is a subset of cartesian product $A \times B$ i.e. $\boldsymbol{R \subseteq A \times B}$.

If $(a, b) \in R$, then we write it as $a\,R\,b$ and *we say that* **a is related to b by the relation R.**

If $(a, b) \notin R$, then we write it as $a \not{R}\, b$ and *we say that* **a is not related to b by the relation R.**

Now, we discuss the relation between two sets

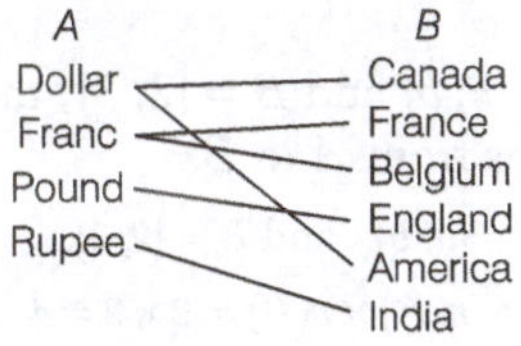

We write this relation as follows

$R = \{(x, y) : x \in A,\ y \in B\ ;\ x$ is a currency of country $y\}$

$= \{$(Dollar, Canada), (Dollar, America), (Franc, France), (Franc, Belgium), (Pound, England), (Rupee, India)$\}$

EXAMPLE 1. If $A = \{1, 2, 3, 4\}$ and $B = \{5, 6, 7, 8\}$, then which of the following are relations from A to B? Give answer.

(i) $R_1 = \{(1, 5), (2, 7), (3, 8)\}$

(ii) $R_2 = \{(6, 2), (3, 7), (4, 7)\}$

Sol. We have, $A = \{1, 2, 3, 4\}$ and $B = \{5, 6, 7, 8\}$

$$A \times B = \{(1, 5), (1, 6), (1, 7), (1, 8), (2, 5), (2, 6), (2, 7), (2, 8), (3, 5), (3, 6), (3, 7), (3, 8), (4, 5), (4, 6), (4, 7), (4, 8)\}$$

(i) Since, $R_1 \subseteq A \times B$,
therefore R_1 is a relation from A to B.

(ii) Since, $(6, 2) \in R_2$ but $(6, 2) \notin A \times B$,
therefore $R_2 \not\subseteq A \times B$.
Thus, R_2 is not a relation from A to B.

Representation of a Relation

A relation can be represented algebraically by roster form or by set-builder form and visually it can be represented by an arrow diagram, which are given below

(i) **Roster form** In this form, we represent the relation by a set of all ordered pairs belongs to R.

e.g. Let R is a relation from set $A = \{-3, -2, -1, 1, 2, 3\}$ to set $B = \{1, 4, 9, 10\}$, defined by

$$aRb \Leftrightarrow a^2 = b$$

Then, $(-3)^2 = 9, (-2)^2 = 4, (-1)^2 = 1, (1)^2 = 1, (2)^2 = 4, (3)^2 = 9$.

Then, in roster form, R can be written as

$$R = \{(-1, 1), (-2, 4), (1, 1), (2, 4), (-3, 9), (3, 9)\}$$

(ii) **Set-builder form** In this form, we represent the relation R from set A to set B as

$R = \{(a, b) : a \in A, b \in B$ and the rule which relates the elements of A and $B\}$

e.g. Let R is a relation from set $A = \{1, 2, 4, 5\}$ to set $B = \left\{1, \frac{1}{2}, \frac{1}{4}, \frac{1}{5}\right\}$ such that

$$R = \left\{(1, 1), \left(2, \frac{1}{2}\right)\left(4, \frac{1}{4}\right)\left(5, \frac{1}{5}\right)\right\}$$

Then, in set-builder form, R can be written as

$$R = \left\{(a, b) : a \in A, b \in B \text{ and } b = \frac{1}{a}\right\}$$

(iii) **Arrow diagram** To represent a relation by an arrow diagram, we draw arrows from first element to second element of all ordered pairs belonging to relation R.

e.g. Let $R = \{(1, 3), (2, 5), (3, 6), (2, 6), (2, 3)\}$ be a relation from set $A = \{1, 2, 3, 4\}$ to set $B = \{3, 4, 5, 6\}$.

Then, by an arrow diagram, it can be represented as

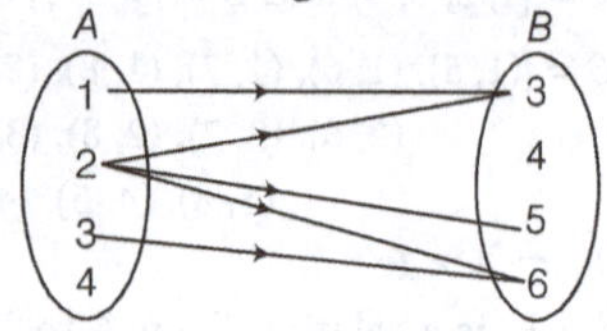

EXAMPLE 2. Express $R = \{(a, b) : 2a + b = 5; a, b \in W\}$ as the set of ordered pairs (in roster form).

Sol. Given, $R = \{(a, b) : 2a + b = 5; a, b \in W\}$

Here, W represent set of whole numbers.

When $a = 0, b = 5$

When $a = 1, b = 3$

When $a = 2, b = 1$

For $a \geq 3$, the value of b given by the above relation are not whole numbers.

$\therefore \quad R = \{(0, 5), (1, 3), (2, 1)\}$

EXAMPLE 3. Write the relation between sets P and Q given by an arrow diagram in

(i) roster form (ii) set-builder form

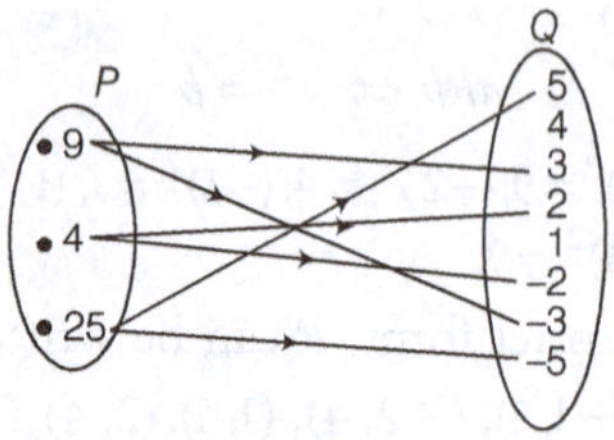

Sol. From arrow diagram, we have

$P = \{9, 4, 25\}$ and $Q = \{5, 4, 3, 2, 1, -2, -3, -5\}$

Here, the relation R is 'x is the square of y', where $x \in P$ and $y \in Q$.

(i) In roster form, it can be written as

$R = \{(9, 3), (9, -3), (4, 2), (4, -2), (25, 5), (25, -5)\}$

(ii) In set-builder form, R can be written as

$R = \{(x, y) : x \in P, y \in Q$ and x is the square of $y\}$

EXAMPLE 4. A relation R is defined, from a set $A = \{2, 3, 4, 5\}$ to a set $B = \{3, 6, 7, 10\}$, as $(x, y) \in R \Leftrightarrow x$ is relatively prime to y. Express R as a set of ordered pairs and depict this relations by arrow diagram.

Sol. Given, $R = \{(x, y) : x \in A, y \in B, x$ is relatively prime to $y\}$

Here, x is relatively prime to y means $\gcd(x, y) = 1$.

$\therefore \quad R = \{(2, 3), (2, 7), (3, 7), (3, 10), (4, 3), (4, 7), (5, 3), (5, 6), (5, 7)\}$

Arrow diagram is shown below:

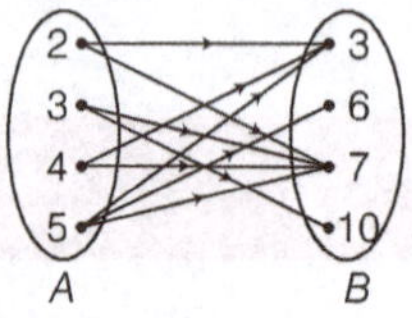

Number of Relations

Let A and B be any two non-empty finite sets containing m and n elements, respectively.

Then, number of ordered pairs in $A \times B$ is mn.

$\therefore$ Total number of subsets of $A \times B$ is 2^{mn}.

Hence, the total number of relations from set A to B is 2^{mn}.

EXAMPLE 5. If $A = \{a, b\}$ and $B = \{2, 3\}$, then find the number of relations from A to B.

Sol. We have, $A = \{a, b\}$ and $B = \{2, 3\}$,

$\therefore \quad n(A \times B) = n(A) \times n(B) = 2 \times 2 = 4$

Now, number of subsets of $A \times B = 2^{n(A \times B)} = 2^4 = 16$

Thus, the number of relations from A to B is 16.

EXAMPLE 6. If $n(A) = 3$ and the number of relations from A to B is 4096, then find $n(B)$.

Sol. Given, $n(A) = 3$

and number of relations from A to $B = 4096$

$$\therefore \quad 2^{n(A) \times n(B)} = 4096$$

$$\Rightarrow \quad 2^{3 \times n(B)} = 2^{12}$$

$$\Rightarrow \quad 3 \times n(B) = 12$$

$$\Rightarrow \quad n(B) = 4$$

Domain, Codomain and Range of Relation

Let us consider the relation R from A to B. Then, the set of first elements of all the ordered pairs present in R is called the **domain** of relation and the set of second elements of all the ordered pairs present in R is called **range** of the relation.

The set B is called the **codomain** of relation R

i.e. $\quad$ **Domain** $(R) = \{a : (a, b) \in R\}$

and $\quad$ **Range** $(R) = \{b : (a, b) \in R\}$

Note that the domain of a relation from set A to B is a subset of set A and range is a subset of set B i.e. range is a subset of codomain.

Range $\subseteq$ Codomain

e.g. Let $R = \{(1, 2), (1, 5), (3, 4), (6, 7)\}$ be a relation from set $A = \{1, 3, 6, 7\}$ to set $B = \{2, 4, 5, 6, 7\}$.

Then, domain $= \{1, 3, 6\}$, range $= \{2, 4, 5, 7\}$

and codomain $=$ set $B = \{2, 4, 5, 6, 7\}$

Clearly, $\quad$ Range $\subseteq$ Codomain

EXAMPLE 7. Determine the domain and range of the relation $R = \{a, b) : a \in N, b = 2a + 3\}$.

Sol. Given, $R = \{a, b) : a \in N, b = 2a + 3\}$

Domain $(R) = \{1, 2, 3, 4, \ldots\} = N$

Range $(R) = \{5, 7, 9, 11, 13, \ldots\} = \{2a + 3 : x \in N\}$

EXAMPLE 8. Determine the domain and range of the relation $R = \{(a, b) : a \in N, a < 5, b = 4\}$

Sol. Given, $\quad R = \{(a, b) : a \in N, a < 5, b = 4\}$

$\Rightarrow \quad R = \{(1, 4), (2, 4), (3, 4), (4, 4)\}$

Domain $(R) = \{a : (a, b) \in R\} = \{1, 2, 3, 4\}$

Range $(R) = \{b : (a, b) \in R\} = \{4\}$

EXAMPLE 9. A relation R is defined from a set $A = \{2, 3, 4, 5\}$ to a set $B = \{3, 6, 7, 10\}$ as follows $(x, y) \in R \Leftrightarrow x$ divides y. Express R as a set of ordered pairs and determine the domain and range of R.

Sol. We have, $A = \{2, 3, 4, 5\}$ and $B = \{3, 6, 7, 10\}$

Relation R is defined as $(x, y) \in R \Leftrightarrow x$ divides y.

$\because$ 2 divides 6, 2 divides 10, 3 divides 3, 3 divides 6, 5 divides 10.

$\therefore \quad R = \{(2, 6) (2, 10) (3, 3) (3, 6) (5, 10)\}$

$\because$ Domain (R) = Set of first elements of the ordered pairs present in R

$\therefore$ Domain of $R = \{2, 3, 5\}$

$\because$ Range (R) = Set of second elements of the ordered pairs present in R

$\therefore$ Range of $R = \{3, 6, 10\}$

EXAMPLE 10. Determine the domain and range of the relation $R = \{(x, y) : x \in N, y \in N$ and $x + y = 10\}$.

Sol. We have, $R = \{(x, y) : x \in N, y \in N$ and $x + y = 10\}$

$\Rightarrow \quad R = \{(1, 9), (2, 8), (3, 7), (4, 6), (5, 5), (6, 4), (7, 3), (8, 2), (9, 1)\}$

$\therefore$ Domain (R) = Set of first elements of the ordered pairs present in R

$= \{1, 2, 3, 4, 5, 6, 7, 8, 9\}$

Range (R) = Set of second elements of the ordered pairs present in $R = \{9, 8, 7, 6, 5, 4, 3, 2, 1\}$

EXAMPLE 11. Let $A = \{1, 2, 3, 4, 5\}$. Define a relation R from A to A by $R = \{(x, y) : y = x - 1, x, y \in A\}$

(i) Depict this relation using an arrow diagram.

(ii) Write down the domain, codomain and range of R.

Sol. (i) Given, $R = \{(x, y) : y = x - 1, x, y \in A\}$

$\therefore \quad R = \{(2, 1), (3, 2), (4, 3), (5, 4)\}$

The corresponding arrow diagram is shown in following figure.

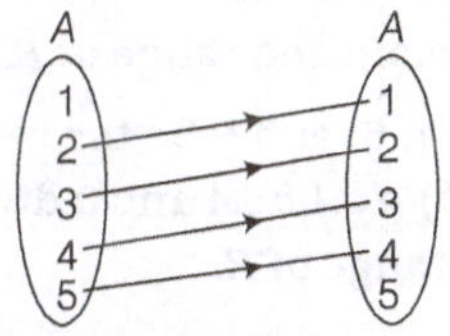

(ii) It is clear from the arrow diagram, that

domain $= \{2, 3, 4, 5\}$,

codomain $= \{1, 2, 3, 4, 5\}$

range $= \{1, 2, 3, 4\}$.

Topic Practice 2

1 Let $A = \{2, 4, 6, 9\}$ and $B = \{4, 6, 18, 27, 54\}$, then find the set of ordered pair (a,b) such that $a \in A$, $b \in B$, a is factor of b, and $a < b$.

2 Let $A = \{1,2,3,5\}$ and $B = \{4,6,9\}$. If a relation R from A to B is defined by $R = \{(x, y)$: the difference between x and y is odd, $x \in A$, $y \in B\}$, then write R in roster form. [NCERT]

3 If $A = \{x, y, z\}$ and $B = \{1, 2\}$, then find the number of relation from A to B. [NCERT]

4 Two finite sets A and B have m and n elements respectively. If the total number of relation from A to B is 64, then find the set of possible values of m and n.

5 The relation on the set $A = \{x : |x| < 3, x \in Z\}$ is defined by $R = \{(x, y) : y = |x|, x \neq -1\}$. Then, find the number of elements in the power set of R.

6 If $n(A) = 5$ and the number of relations A to B is 1024, then find $n(B)$.

7 If a relation R is defined on the set Z of integers as follows $(a, b) \in R \Leftrightarrow a^2 + b^2 = 25$, then find domain (R).

8 Determine the domain and range of the relation R, defined by $R = \{(x, x + 5) : x \in \{0,1,2,3,4,5\}$. [NCERT]

9 If $R = \{(x, y) : x, y \in N, x < 5$ and $y = 3\}$ is a relation, then find domain and range of R.

10 If $A = \{1, 2, 3, 4, 6\}$ and R be the relation defined on A by $R = \{(a,b): a \in A, b \in A$ and a divides $b\}$, then find domain and range of R.

11 Determine the domain and range of the relations R, where $R = \{(x, x^3) : x$ is a prime number less than $10\}$ [NCERT]

12 Determine the domain and range of the relation $R = \{a, b) : a \in N, y = 3x - 1\}$.

13 Determine the domain and range of the relation R, where

(i) $R = \{(-3, 1), (-1, 1), (1, 0), (3, 0)\}$

(ii) $R = \{(x - 2, x^2) : x$ is a prime number less than $15\}$

14 The given figure shows a relationship between the sets P and Q. Write this relation

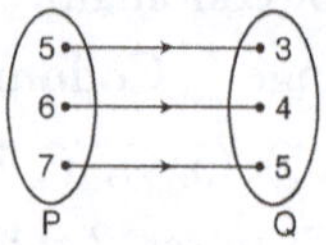

(i) in set- builder form

(ii) in roster form

(iii) What is its domain and range?

15 Let $A = \{1, 2, 3, 4\}$ and $B = \{1, 4, 9, 16, 25\}$ and R be a relation defined from A to B, as $R = \{(x, y): x \in A, y \in B$ and $y = x^2\}$

(i) Depict this relation using arrow diagram

(ii) Find domain of R.

(iii) Find range of R.

(iv) Write codomain of R

16 If $A = \{1, 2, 3, 4, 5, 6\}$, then define a relation R from A to A by $R = \{(x, y) : y = x + 1\}$

(i) Depict this relation using an arrow diagram.

(ii) Write down the domain, co-domain and range of R.

Hints & Solutions

1. **Hint** Here, $A = \{2, 4, 6, 9\}$;

$B = \{4, 6, 18, 27, 54\}$

Let $R = \{(a, b) : a \in A, b \in B, a \text{ is factor of } b \text{ and } a < b\}$

Then,

$R = \{(2, 4), (2, 6), (2, 18), (2, 54), (6, 18), (6, 54), (9, 18), (9, 27), (9, 54)\}$

2. **Hint** $R = \{(x, y)$: the difference between x and y is odd, $x \in A,\ y \in B\}$

In roster form,

$R = \{(1, 4), (1, 6), (2, 9), (3, 4), (3, 6), (5, 4), (5, 6)\}$

3. Solve as Example 5. **Ans.** 64

4. **Hint** Clearly, $n(A \times B) = n(A) \times n(B) = mn$

$\therefore$ Total number of relation from A to $B = 2^{mn}$

Thus, we have $2^{mn} = 64 = 2^6 \Rightarrow mn = 6$

Hence, the set of possible values of m and n is $\{(1, 6), (2, 3), (3, 2), (6, 1)\}$.

5. **Hint** We have, $A = \{x : |x| < 3,\ x \in Z\} = \{-2, -1, 0, 1, 2\}$

and $R = \{(x, y) : y = |x|,\ x \neq -1\}$

$= \{(-2, 2), (0, 0), (1, 1), (2, 2)\}$

$\therefore$ $n(P(R)) = 2^{n(R)} = 2^4 = 16$

6. Solve as Example 6. **Ans.** $n(B) = 2$

7. **Hint** We have, $(a, b) \in R \Leftrightarrow a^2 + b^2 = 25$

$\Rightarrow$ $b = \pm\sqrt{25 - a^2}$

Clearly, $a = 0 \Rightarrow b = \pm 5$

$a = \pm 3 \Rightarrow b = \pm 4$

$a = \pm 4 \Rightarrow b = \pm 3$

and $a = \pm 5 \Rightarrow b = 0$

Hence, domain $(R) = \{0, \pm 3, \pm 4, \pm 5\}$.

8. **Hint** $R = \{(0, 5), (1, 6), (2, 7), (3, 8), (4, 9), (5, 10)\}$

Domain $(R) = \{0, 1, 2, 3, 4, 5\}$;

Range $(R) = \{5, 6, 7, 8, 9, 10\}$

9. **Hint** $R = \{(1, 3), (2, 3), (3, 3), (4, 3)\}$

$\therefore$ Domain $(R) = \{1, 2, 3, 4\}$

and range $(R) = \{3\}$

10. **Hint** Let $R = \{(a, b) : a \in A,\ b \in A, \text{ and } a \text{ divides } b\}$

$R = \{(1, 1), (1, 2), (1, 3), (1, 4), (1, 6), (2, 2), (2, 4), (2, 6), (3, 3), (3, 6), (4, 4), (6, 6)\}$

Domain $= \{1, 2, 3, 4, 6\}$

Range $= \{1, 2, 3, 4, 6\}$

11. **Hint** $R = (x, x^3) : x$ is a prime number less than 10}

$R = \{(2, 8), (3, 27), (5, 125), (7, 343)\}$

[$\because$ 2, 3, 5, 7 are primes less than 10]

Domain $(R) = \{2, 3, 5, 7\}$, Range $(R) = \{8, 27, 125, 343\}$

12. Solve as Example 8.

Ans. Domain $(R) = \{1, 2, 3, 4, \ldots\} = N$,

Range $(R) = \{2, 5, 8, 11, \ldots\} = \{3x - 1 : x \in N\}$

13. (i) **Hint** Given, $R = \{(-3, 1), (-1, 1), (1, 0), (3, 0)\}$

Domain $(R) = \{-3, -1, 1, 3\}$;

Range $(R) = \{1, 0\}$

(ii) **Hint** Given, $R = \{(x - 2, x^2) : x$ is a prime number less than 15}

$\therefore R = \{(0, 4), (1, 9), (3, 25), (5, 49), (9, 121), (11, 169)\}$

Domain $(R) = \{0, 1, 3, 5, 9, 11\}$

Range $(R) = \{4, 9, 25, 49, 121, 169\}$

14. (i) **Hint** $\{(x, y) : x \in P,\ y \in Q,\ x = y + 2\}$

(ii) **Hint** $\{(5, 3), (6, 4), (7, 5)\}$

(iii) **Hint** Domain (R) $= \{5, 6, 7\}$ and Range (R) $= \{3, 4, 5\}$

15. (i) **Hint** The relation $R = \{(1, 1), (2, 4), (3, 9), (4, 16)\}$

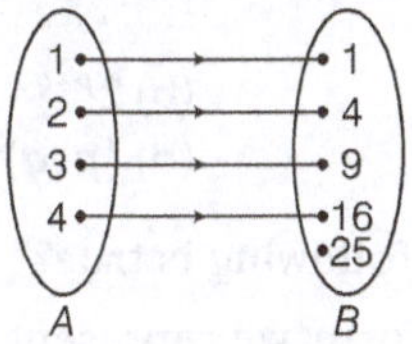

(ii) Domain $(R) = \{1, 2, 3, 4\}$

(iii) Range $(R) = \{1, 4, 9, 16\}$

(iv) Codomain $(R) = \{1, 4, 9, 16, 25\}$

16. **Hint** Given, $A = \{1, 2, 3, 4, 5, 6\}$

$R = \{(x, y) : y = x + 1\} = \{(1, 2), (2, 3), (3, 4), (4, 5), (5, 6)\}$

(i) The arrow diagram is shown below

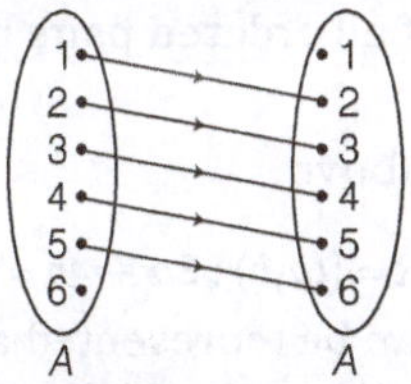

(ii) Clearly, domain $(R) = \{1, 2, 3, 4, 5\}$;

Range $(R) = \{2, 3, 4, 5, 6\}$;

Codomain $= \{1, 2, 3, 4, 5, 6\}$

Exam Pattern Exercise

Part A - Objective Type Questions

Multiple Choice Type Questions

1 If $(3a + 4, 5) = (13, a + 2b)$, then (b,a) is equal to
(a) (2, 3) (b) (3, 2)
(c) (3, 1) (d) (1, 3)

2 If $n(A) = 4$ and $n(B) = 5$, then number of elements in $B \times A$ is
(a) 9 (b) 1
(c) 20 (d) 2^{20}

3 If $n(A) = a$, $n(B) = b$ and $n(A \times B) = 10$, then the value of (a,b) cannot be
(a) (1, 10) (b) (5, 2)
(c) (5, 5) (d) (10, 1)

4 If $n(A) = p$ and $n(B) = q$, then number of subsets of $A \times B$ is
(a) 2^{p+q} (b) $2^{p \cdot q}$
(c) $p \cdot q$ (d) $(p \cdot q)^2$

5 Which of the following is true?
(a) In Roster form, we represent the relation by a set of all ordered pair belongs to relation.
(b) In set-builder form, we represent the relation R from set A to set B as $R = \{(a,b) : a \in A, b \in B$, and the rule which relates the elements of A and $B\}$.
(c) In arrow diagram, we represent the relation by using arrows from first element to second element of all ordered pairs belonging to relation.
(d) All of the above

6 The relation $R = \{(a,b) : 3a + 4b = 20; a, b \in W\}$ in roster form can be represented as
(a) $\{(0, 5), (4, 2)\}$ (b) $\{(5, 0), (2, 4)\}$
(c) $\{(0, 5), (2, 4)\}$ (d) $\{(4, 2), (5, 0)\}$

7 The relation $R = \{(4,8), (9,27), (16,64)\}$ from set $A = \{1, 4, 9, 16, 25\}$ to set $B = \{8, 27, 64, 81\}$ in set-builder form can be represented as
(a) $\{(a,b) : a \in A, b \in B, a^3 = b\}$
(b) $\{(a,b) : a \in A, b \in B, a^2 = b^3\}$
(c) $\{(a,b) : a \in A, b \in B, a^3 = b^2\}$
(d) $\{(a,b) : a \in A, b \in B, a^2 = b^3\}$

8 If $A = \{1, 2, 5, 6\}$ and $B = \{1, 2, 3\}$, then what is $(A \times B) \cap (B \times A)$ equal to?
(a) $\{(1,1), (2,1), (6,1), (3,2)\}$
(b) $\{(1,1), (1,2), (2,1), (2,2)\}$
(c) $\{(1,1), (2,2)\}$
(d) $\{(1,1), (1,2), (2,5), (2,6)\}$

9 Let R be a relation in N defined by
$$R = \{(1 + x, 1 + x^2) : x \le 5, x \in N\}.$$
Which of the following is false?
(a) $R = \{(2,2), (3,5), (4,10), (5,17), (6,25)\}$
(b) Domain of $R = \{2, 3, 4, 5, 6\}$
(c) Range of $R = \{2, 5, 10, 17, 26\}$
(d) None of the above

Assertion-Reason Based Questions

Directions (Q. Nos. 10-13) *In the questions given below are two statements labelled as Assertion (A) and Reason (R). In the context of the two statements, which one of the following is correct?*
(a) Both A and R are correct; R is the correct explanation of A
(b) Both A and R are correct; R is not the correct explanation of A
(c) A is correct; R is incorrect
(d) R is correct; A is incorrect

10 **Assertion (A)** If $(x + y, x - y) = (5, 1)$, then $x = 3$ and $y = 2$.
Reason (R) Two ordered pair are said to be equal, if their corresponding elements are equal.

11 **Assertion (A)** If $A = \{0, 1, 2, 3\}$ and $B = \{1, 3, 5, 7, 9\}$, then number of elements in $A \times B$ is 9.
Reason (R) If $n(A) = p$ and $n(B) = q$, then number of elements in $A \times B$ is $p \cdot q$.

12 **Assertion (A)** If $n(A) = 4$ and $B = \{3, 4, 5, 6, 8, 9\}$, then the number of relations from A to B is 2^{24}.
Reason (R) If A and B be any two non-empty finite sets containing m and n elements respectively, then total number of relations from set A to B is 2^{m+n}.

13 **Assertion (A)** The domain of the relation $R = \{(a, b) : a \in Z, a^2 \le 16, b = 16\}$ is $\{\pm 4, \pm 3, \pm 2, \pm 1, 0\}$.
Reason (R) The range of the relation $R = \{(a, b) : a \in N, a < 10, a + b = 10\}$ is $\{9, 8, 7, 6, 5, 4, 3, 2, 1\}$.

Part B - Descriptive Questions

Very Short Answer Type Questions

14 If $\left(\frac{x}{3}+1, y-\frac{2}{3}\right)=\left(\frac{5}{3}, \frac{1}{3}\right)$, then find the values of x and y.

15 If $A \times B=\{(1,x),(1,y),(1,z),(1,w)\}$, then find A and B.

16 If set $A=\{1,2\}$ and set $B=\{a, b\}$, then find the cartesian product of set A and set B.

17 If the relation R in the set $\{1, 2, 3, 4\}$ given by $R=\{(1,1),(1,2),(1,4),(3,1),(3,2),(4,3),(4,2)\}$, then find the domain of R.

18 If $A=\{a, b\}, B=\{2,3,5,6,7\}$ and $C=\{5,6,7,8,9\}$, then find $A \times(B \cap C)$.

Short Answer Type Questions

19 Let A and B be two sets, such that $A \times B$ consists of 6 elements. If 3 elements of $A \times B$ are (1, 4), (2, 6) and (3, 6), then find $A \times B$ and $B \times A$.

20 If $N=\{1,2,3\}$, then find the relation $R=\{(x, y): x \in N, y \in N$ and $2x+y=10\}$ in $N \times N$. Also, find its domain and range.

21 If $A \times B=\{(1,a),(2,a),(1,b),(2,b)\}$ and $A \times C=\{(1,p),(1,q),(2,p),(2,q)\}$, then find $A \times(B \cup C)$.

22 Determine the domain and range of the relation R, where $R=\{(2x+3, x^{3}): x$ is a prime number less than 10$\}$.

23 If A and B be two sets, such that $n(A)=3$ and $n(B)=2$. If $(x, 1),(y, 2)$ and $(z, 1)$ are in $A \times B$, then find A, B and $A \times B$, where x, y and z are distinct elements.

Long Answer Type Questions

24 If $A=$ $B=$ $C=$ and $D=$, then verify that $(A \times B) \cap(C \times D)=(A \cap C) \times(B \cap D)$.

25 Let $A=$. Define a relation R from A to A by $R=\{$ x, y $x-y=$, where $x, y \in A\}$. Depict this relationship using an arrow diagram. Write down its domain, codomain and range.

26 Find the domain and range of the following relations.

(i) $R=\{(x,y): x,y \in N, y=x^{2}+3$ and $0<x<5\}$

(ii) $R=\{(x,y): x,y \in N, y=\frac{1}{1+x}$ and x is odd natural number$\}$

27 Determine the domain and range of the following relations.

(i) $R_1=\left\{\left(x, \frac{1}{x}\right): 0<x<6, x \in N\right\}$.

(ii) $R_2=\{(x, x^{4}): x$ is a prime number less than 10$\}$.

Case Study Based Questions

28 A general election of Lok Sabha is a gigantic exercise. About 911 million people were eligible to vote and voter turnout was about 67%, the highest ever.

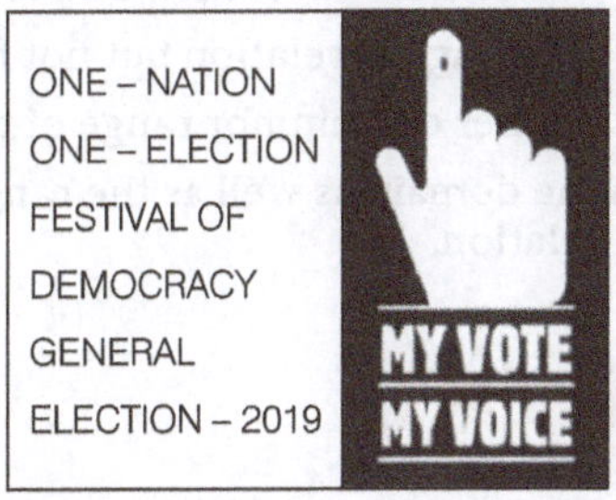

Let I be the set of all citizens of India who were eligible to exercise their voting right in general election held in 2019. A relation 'R' is defined on I as follows

$$R=\{(V_1, V_2): V_1, V_2 \in I$$

and both use their voting right in general election-2019$\}$

Answer the following questions using the above information.

(i) Two neighbors X and $Y \in I$. X exercised his voting right while Y did not cast her vote in general election-2019. Which of the following is true?

(a) $(X, Y) \in R$ (b) $(Y, X) \in R$
(c) $(X, X) \notin R$ (d) $(X, Y) \notin R$

(ii) Mr. 'X' and his wife 'W' both exercised their voting right in general election-2019, Which of the following is true?

(a) both (X, W) and $(W, X) \in R$
(b) $(X, W) \in R$ but $(W, X) \notin R$
(c) both $(X, W) \in R$ and $(W, X) \notin R$
(d) $(W, X) \in R$ but $(X, W) \notin R$

(iii) Three friends F_1, F_2 and F_3 exercised their voting right in general election-2019, then which of the following is true?

(a) $(F_1, F_2) \in R$, $(F_2, F_3) \in R$ and $(F_1, F_3) \in R$
(b) $(F_1, F_2) \in R$, $(F_2, F_3) \in R$ and $(F_1, F_3) \notin R$
(c) $(F_1, F_2) \in R$, $(F_2, F_2) \in R$ but $(F_3, F_3) \notin R$
(d) $(F_1, F_2) \notin R$, $(F_2, F_3) \notin R$ and $(F_1, F_3) \notin R$

(iv) Mr. Shyam exercised his voting right in general election-2019, then Mr. Shyam is related to which of the following?
 (a) All those eligible voters who cast their votes
 (b) Family members of Mr.Shyam
 (c) All citizens of India
 (d) Eligible voters of India

(v) The set of all eligible voters of India who cast their vote in general election-2019 is
 (a) the domain of relation but not the range
 (b) the range of relation but not the domain
 (c) neither domain nor range of the relation
 (d) the domain as well as the range of relation.

29 Class XIth mathematics teacher write a problem on black board to test the preparation about the topic 'Relations'. The problem is describe as following : "Let A be the set of first ten natural numbers and let R be a relation on A defined by

$R = \{(x, y) : x \in A, y \in A \text{ and } x + 2y = 14\}$

Then, answer the following questions which are based on above problem.

(i) Find the relation (R).
(ii) Find the number of ordered pairs in R.
(iii) Which one of the following is correct
 (a) $(2, 6) \in R$ (b) $(2, 6) \notin R$
 (c) $(6, 5) \in R$ (d) $(4, 6) \in R$
(iv) Find Domain(R).
(v) Find Range (R).

Hints & Solutions

1. (d) **2.** (c) **3.** (c) **4.** (b)
5. (d) **6.** (a) **7.** (c) **8.** (b)
9. (d) **10.** (a) **11.** (d) **12.** (c)
13. (b)

14. $x = 2, y = 1$

15. $A = \{1\}, B = \{x, y, z, w\}$

16. $A \times B = \{(1, a), (1, b), (2, a), (2, b)\}$

17. Domain $(R) = \{1, 3, 4\}$

18. $A \times (B \cap C) = \{(a, 5), (a, 6), (a, 7), (b, 5), (b, 6), (b, 7)\}$

19. $A \times B = \{(1, 4), (1, 6), (2, 4), (2, 6), (3, 4), (3, 6)\}$

$B \times A = \{(4, 1), (4, 2), (4, 3), (6, 1), (6, 2), (6, 3)\}$

20. $R = \{(1, 8), (2, 6), (3, 4)\}$

Domain $(R) = \{1, 2, 3\}$
and Range $(R) = \{8, 6, 4\}$

21. $A \times (B \cup C) = \{(1, a), (1, b), (1, p), (1, q), (2, a), (2, b), (2, p), (2, q)\}$

22. Domain $= \{7, 9, 13, 17\}$

Range $= \{8, 27, 125, 343\}$

23. $A = \{x, y, z\}, B = \{1, 2\}$

$A \times B = \{(x, 1), (x, 2), (y, 1), (y, 2), (z, 1), (z, 2)\}$

25.

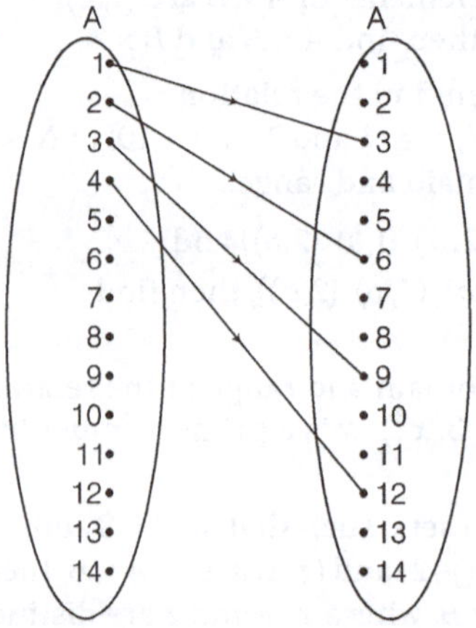

Domain $= \{1, 2, 3, 4\}$, Codomain $= A$,

Range $= \{3, 6, 9, 12\}$

26. (i) Domain $= \{1, 2, 3, 4\}$, Range $= \{4, 7, 12, 19\}$

(ii) Domain $= \{1, 3, 5, \ldots\}$, Range $= \left\{\frac{1}{2}, \frac{1}{4}, \frac{1}{6}, \ldots\right\}$

27. (i) Domain $= \{1, 2, 3, 4, 5\}$, Range $= \left\{1, \frac{1}{2}, \frac{1}{3}, \frac{1}{4}, \frac{1}{5}\right\}$

(ii) Domain $= \{2, 3, 5, 7\}$, Range $= \{16, 81, 625, 2401\}$

28. (i) (d) (ii) (a) (iii) (a) (iv) (a) (v) (d)

29. (i) $\{(2, 6), (4, 5), (6, 4), (8, 3)\}$ (ii) 4 (iii) (a)

(iv) $\{2, 4, 6, 8\}$ (v) $\{6, 5, 4, 3\}$

CHAPTER 10

Sequences and Series

In this Chapter...

- Sequences and Series
- Arithmetic Progression (AP) and Its General Terms
- Sum of n Terms of an AP and Arithmetic Mean (AM)
- Geometric Progression (GP)
- Sum of n Terms of a GP
- Geometric Mean and Its Relation with Arithmetic Mean

Sequence, generally means a **collection**, ordered in such a way that it has an indentified first, second and third members and so on. e.g. Amount of money deposited in bank over a number of years, population of human beings at different times etc. Sequences, following specific patterns are called **progressions.**

Sequences and Series

Sequence

A sequence is an arrangement of numbers according to some rule.

e.g. 1, 4, 9, 16, ... is a sequence as each number follow a rule of n^2, where $n = 1, 2, 3$.

The various numbers occurring in a sequence are called its **terms**. The terms of a sequence are generally denoted by $a_1, a_2, a_3, \ldots, a_n, \ldots$ etc. The number occurring at the nth place of a sequence is called its **nth term** and it is denoted by a_n.

The nth term is also called the **general term** of the sequence.

e.g. 2, 6, 10, 14, ... is a sequence.

Here, $a_1 = 2$, $a_2 = 6$, $a_3 = 10$ and $a_4 = 14$.

Two types of sequence are as follows

1. **Finite Sequence** A sequence containing finite number of terms, is called a finite sequence.

   e.g. 1, 3, 5, 7 is a finite sequence as it contains only 4 terms.

2. **Infinite Sequence** A sequence which is not a finite sequence, is known as infinite sequence. i.e. in an infinite sequence, **number of terms never ends.**

   e.g.

   - 1, 3, 5, 7,... is an infinite sequence, as it contains infinite number of terms.
   - The sequence of successive quotients obtain in the division of 10 by 3 i.e. 3, 3.3, 3.33, 3.333, ...is an infinite sequence.

Representation of a Sequence

A real sequence can be represented by different ways. Some ways of representation are given below

(i) 2, 4, 6, ... is a sequence and rule for writing down other terms is $2n$.

(ii) The sequence 1, 3, 5, 7, ... can be written as $a_n = 2n - 1$.

(iii) The sequence 1, 1, 2, 3, 5, 8, ... has no visible pattern but its recurrence relation is $a_1 = a_2 = 1$ and $a_{n+1} = a_n + a_{n-1}$, $n \geq 2$.

This sequence is called **Fibonacci sequence.**

EXAMPLE 1. Find the 20th term of the sequence, whose nth term is $a_n = \dfrac{n(n-2)}{n+3}$.

Sol. We have, $a_n = \dfrac{n(n-2)}{n+3}$

On putting $n = 20$, we get

$$a_{20} = \frac{20(20-2)}{20+3}$$

$$\Rightarrow \quad a_{20} = \frac{20 \times 18}{23} = \frac{360}{23}$$

EXAMPLE 2. Write first five terms of sequence

(i) $a_n = (-1)^{n-1} 5^{n+1}$ (ii) $a_n = 2n^2 - n + 1$ **[NCERT]**

Sol. (i) We have, $a_n = (-1)^{n-1} 5^{n+1}$

On putting $n = 1$, we get

$$a_1 = (-1)^{1-1} 5^{1+1} = (-1)^0 5^2 = 25$$

On putting $n = 2$, we get

$$a_2 = (-1)^{2-1} 5^{2+1} = (-1)^1 5^3 = -125$$

On putting $n = 3$, we get

$$a_3 = (-1)^{3-1} 5^{3+1} = (-1)^2 5^4 = 625$$

On putting $n = 4$, we get

$$a_4 = (-1)^{4-1} 5^{4+1} = (-1)^3 5^5 = -3125$$

On putting $n = 5$, we get

$$a_5 = (-1)^{5-1} 5^{5+1} = (-1)^4 5^6 = 15625$$

Hence, the first five terms of the given sequence are 25, – 125, 625, – 3125, 15625.

(ii) We have, $a_n = 2n^2 - n + 1$

On putting $n = 1$, we get

$$a_1 = 2(1)^2 - 1 + 1 = 2 - 1 + 1 = 2$$

On putting $n = 2$, we get

$$a_2 = 2(2)^2 - 2 + 1 = 8 - 2 + 1 = 7$$

On putting $n = 3$, we get

$$a_3 = 2(3)^2 - 3 + 1 = 18 - 3 + 1 = 16$$

On putting $n = 4$, we get

$$a_4 = 2(4)^2 - 4 + 1 = 32 - 4 + 1 = 29$$

On putting $n = 5$, we get

$$a_5 = 2(5)^2 - 5 + 1 = 50 - 5 + 1 = 46$$

Hence, the first five terms of the given sequence are 2, 7, 16, 29 and 46.

Series

Let a sequence is $a_1, a_2, a_3, \ldots, a_n, \ldots$. Then, the expression $a_1 + a_2 + a_3 + \ldots + a_n + \ldots$ is called the series associated with the given sequence. A series is **finite** or **infinite**, according as number of terms in the corresponding sequence is finite or infinite.

Series can be represented in compact form, called **sigma notation.** It is denoted by the Greek letter 'Σ' **(sigma).**

e.g. series $a_1 + a_2 + \ldots + a_n + \ldots$ can be represented in compact form as $\sum_{k=1}^{\infty} a_k$.

e.g. (i) $2 + 4 + 6 + 8 + \ldots + 102$ (ii) $1 - \frac{1}{2} - \frac{1}{4} - \frac{1}{8} - \ldots$

EXAMPLE 3. Let the sequence a_n is defined as follows $a_1 = 2, a_n = a_{n-1} + 3$ for $n \geq 2$.

Find first five terms and write corresponding series.

Sol. We have, $a_1 = 2$ and $a_n = a_{n-1} + 3$

On putting $n = 2$, we get

$$a_2 = a_1 + 3 = 2 + 3 = 5$$

On putting $n = 3$, we get

$$a_3 = a_2 + 3 = 5 + 3 = 8$$

On putting $n = 4$, we get

$$a_4 = a_3 + 3 = 8 + 3 = 11$$

On putting $n = 5$, we get

$$a_5 = a_4 + 3 = 11 + 3 = 14$$

Thus, first five terms of given sequence are 2, 5, 8, 11 and 14. Also, the corresponding series is $2 + 5 + 8 + 11 + 14 + \ldots$

EXAMPLE 4. Write the given expression in expanded form.

(i) $\sum_{k=1}^{n} (k^2 + 1)$ (ii) $\sum_{n=1}^{k} (n^2 + 2)$

Sol. (i) Putting $k = 1, 2, 3, 4, \ldots, n$ in $(k^2 + 1)$, we get

$$2, 5, 10, 17, \ldots, n^2 + 1$$

Hence, $\sum_{k=1}^{n} (k^2 + 1) = 2 + 5 + 10 + 17 + \ldots + (n^2 + 1)$

(ii) $\sum_{n=1}^{k} (n^2 + 2)$

Putting $k = 1, 2, 3, 4 \ldots$ in $(n^2 + 2)$, we get

$$3, 6, 11, 18, \ldots, k^2 + 2$$

Hence, $\sum_{n=1}^{k} (n^2 + 2) = 3 + 6 + 11 + 18 + \ldots + k^2 + 2$

Topic Practice 1

1 Find the indicated terms in each of the sequence, whose nth terms are given.

(i) $a_n = 5n - 3;\ a_{12}, a_{15}$

(ii) $b_n = (-1)^n (n^2 - 1);\ b_7, b_{13}$

(iii) $a_n = \frac{n^2}{2^n};\ a_7$

2 Write the first five terms of each of the following sequence whose nth terms are given below.

(i) $a_n = \frac{n}{n+1}$ (ii) $a_n = (-1)^{n+1} 3^{n+2}$

(iii) $b_n = \frac{n(n^2+5)}{4}$ (iv) $a_n = \frac{n^3+1}{2}$

(v) $a_1 = 1, a_n = a_{n-1} + 3$ for $n \geq 2$

3 Write the first five terms of each of the sequence and obtain the corresponding series.

(i) $a_1 = 3, a_n = 3a_{n-1} + 2, \forall\, n > 1$

(ii) $a_1 = a_2 = 2,\ a_n = a_{n-1} - 1, n > 2$

(iii) $a_n = \frac{1}{6}(2n - 3)$

(iv) $a_n = (-1)^{n^2}\left(\frac{2n^2+3}{2}\right)$

(v) $a_1 = -1,\ a_n = \frac{a_{n-1}}{n},\ n \geq 2$

4 The Fibonacci sequence is defined by $1 = a_1 = a_2$ and $a_n = a_{n-1} + a_{n-2}, n > 2$. Find $\frac{a_{n+1}}{a_n}$, for $n = 1, 2, 3, 4, 5$.

Hints & Solutions

1. Solve as Example 1.

Ans.

(i) $a_{12} = 57, a_{15} = 72$

(ii) $b_7 = -48, b_{13} = -168$

(iii) $a_7 = \frac{49}{128}$

2. Solve as Example 2.

Ans.

(i) $\frac{1}{2}, \frac{2}{3}, \frac{3}{4}, \frac{4}{5}$ and $\frac{5}{6}$

(ii) 27, −81, 243, −729, 2187

(iii) $\frac{3}{2}, \frac{9}{2}, \frac{21}{2}, 21, \frac{75}{2}$

(iv) $1, \frac{9}{2}, 14, \frac{65}{2}, 63$

(v) 1, 4, 7, 10, 13

3. Solve as Example 3.

Ans.

(i) Sequence is 3, 11, 35, 107, 323, ...

Series is $3 + 11 + 35 + 107 + 323 + \ldots$

(ii) Sequence is 2, 2, 1, 0, −1, ...

Series is $2 + 2 + 1 + 0 + (-1) + \ldots$

(iii) Sequence is $-\frac{1}{6}, \frac{1}{6}, \frac{1}{2}, \frac{5}{6}, \frac{7}{6}, \ldots$

Series is $-\frac{1}{6} + \frac{1}{6} + \frac{1}{2} + \frac{5}{6} + \frac{7}{6} + \ldots$

(iv) Sequence is $-\frac{5}{2}, \frac{11}{2}, -\frac{21}{2}, \frac{35}{2}, -\frac{53}{2}, \ldots$

Series is $-\frac{5}{2} + \frac{11}{2} - \frac{21}{2} + \frac{35}{2} - \frac{53}{2} + \ldots$

(v) Sequence is $-1, -\frac{1}{2}, -\frac{1}{6}, -\frac{1}{24}, -\frac{1}{120}, \ldots$

Series is $-1 - \frac{1}{2} - \frac{1}{6} - \frac{1}{24} - \frac{1}{120} - \ldots$

4. Given, $1 = a_1 = a_2$ and $a_n = a_{n-1} + a_{n-2}, n > 2$

On putting $n = 3, 4, 5, 6$ respectively, we get

For $n = 3, a_3 = a_{3-1} + a_{3-2} = a_2 + a_1 = 1 + 1 = 2$

For $n = 4, a_4 = a_{4-1} + a_{4-2} = a_3 + a_2 = 2 + 1 = 3$

For $n = 5, a_5 = a_{5-1} + a_{5-2} = a_4 + a_3 = 3 + 2 = 5$

For $n = 6, a_6 = a_{6-1} + a_{6-2} = a_5 + a_4 = 5 + 3 = 8$

Now, $\frac{a_{n+1}}{a_n}$, for $n = 1, 2, 3, 4, 5$.

For $n = 1, \frac{a_2}{a_1} = \frac{1}{1} = 1$; For $n = 2, \frac{a_3}{a_2} = \frac{2}{1} = 2$

For $n = 3, \frac{a_4}{a_3} = \frac{3}{2}$; For $n = 4, \frac{a_5}{a_4} = \frac{5}{3}$

For $n = 5, \frac{a_6}{a_5} = \frac{8}{5}$

Ans. The terms are $1, 2, \frac{3}{2}, \frac{5}{3}$ and $\frac{8}{5}$.

Arithmetic Progression (AP) and Its General Terms

Progression

Those sequence whose terms follow a certain pattern or rule, are called progression.

e.g. 2, 4, 6, 8,..., 100

We observe that each term in above example is formed by adding 2 to the preceding term.

Arithmetic Progression (AP)

A sequence whose terms increases or decreases by a fixed number, is called an arithmetic progression (AP).

In other words, we can say that, a sequence is called an arithmetic progression if the difference of a term and the previous term is always same.

i.e. $a_{n+1} - a_n = \text{constant for all } n.$

This constant or same difference is called the **common difference** of an AP and it is denoted by ***d***.

In an AP, we usually denote the first term by a, common difference by d and the nth term by a_n or T_n and then AP is $a, a+d, a+2d, \ldots$.

e.g. 1, 4, 7, 10, ... is an AP.

Here, first term = 1 and common difference = 4 − 1 = 3.

To check whether a given sequence is an AP or not, we use the following steps

***Step* I** Find nth term a_n.

***Step* II** Replace n by $n+1$ to get $(n+1)$th term i.e. a_{n+1}.

***Step* III** Find difference between a_n and a_{n+1} i.e. calculate $a_{n+1} - a_n$.

***Step* IV** If value obtained in Step III is independent of n i.e. does not contain n, then given sequence is an AP otherwise not.

EXAMPLE 1. The nth term of a sequence is $3n-2$. Is the sequence an AP? If it is an AP, then find its 6th term.

Sol. Given, $a_n = 3n - 2$

Replacing n by $n+1$ in a_n, we get

$$a_{n+1} = 3(n+1) - 2 = 3n + 3 - 2 = 3n + 1$$

Then, common difference, $d = a_{n+1} - a_n$

$$= (3n+1) - (3n-2) = 3n + 1 - 3n + 2 = 3$$

It is independent of n, so given sequence is an AP and its 6th term,

$$a_6 = 3 \times 6 - 2 = 18 - 2 = 16$$

EXAMPLE 2. Write down the next term of the sequence $\frac{1}{6}, \frac{1}{3}, \frac{1}{2}, \ldots$.

Sol. Given sequence is $\frac{1}{6}, \frac{1}{3}, \frac{1}{2}, \ldots$

Here, $a_1 = \frac{1}{6}, a_2 = \frac{1}{3}, a_3 = \frac{1}{2}$

Then $a_2 - a_1 = \frac{1}{3} - \frac{1}{6} = \frac{2-1}{6} = \frac{1}{6}$;

$a_3 - a_2 = \frac{1}{2} - \frac{1}{3} = \frac{3-2}{6} = \frac{1}{6}$

Since, common difference is same, so it is an AP.

Then, $d = \frac{1}{6}$

$\therefore \quad a_4 = a_3 + d = \frac{1}{2} + \frac{1}{6} = \frac{3+1}{6} = \frac{4}{6} = \frac{2}{3}$

Hence, the next term of the given sequence is $\frac{2}{3}$.

General Term of an AP

Let a be the first term and d be the common difference of an AP. Then, its nth term is denoted by a_n or T_n and defined as

$$T_n = a_n = a + (n-1)d$$

Also, $l = a + (n-1)d$,

where l is the last term of the sequence.

EXAMPLE 3. Find the indicated term of given AP .

$$a = 3, d = 2; T_n, T_{10}$$

Sol. Given, $a = 3$ and $d = 2$

$\because \quad T_n = a + (n-1)d$ ...(i)

On putting the values of a and d in Eq. (i), we get

$T_n = 3 + (n-1)2 = 3 + 2n - 2 \Rightarrow T_n = 1 + 2n$

and $T_{10} = a + (10-1)d = a + 9d$ [from Eq. (i)]

$= 3 + 9(2)$ [$\because a = 3, d = 2$]

$= 3 + 18 = 21$

EXAMPLE 4. Is 667 a term of an AP 11, 18, 25,...?

Sol. Given, AP is 11, 18, 25,...

Here, $a = 11$, $d = 18 - 11 = 7$ and $a_n = 667$ (say)

$\because \quad a + (n-1)d = a_n$

$\therefore \quad 11 + (n-1)7 = 667 \Rightarrow 11 + 7n - 7 = 667$

$\Rightarrow \quad 7n + 4 = 667 \Rightarrow 7n = 667 - 4$

$\Rightarrow \quad 7n = 663 \Rightarrow n = \frac{663}{7}$,

which is not a whole number.

Hence, 667 is not a term of an AP.

EXAMPLE 5. How many terms are there in AP 20, 25, 30,..., 100?

Sol. Given AP is 20, 25, 30,..., 100.

Here, $a = 20, d = 25 - 20 = 5$ and $l = 100$

$\because$ Last term, $l = 100$

$\Rightarrow a + (n-1)d = 100$

$\Rightarrow 20 + (n-1)5 = 100$ $[\because a = 20 \text{ and } d = 5]$

$\Rightarrow 20 + 5n - 5 = 100$

$\Rightarrow 15 + 5n = 100$

$\Rightarrow 5n = 100 - 15 = 85$

$\Rightarrow n = 17$

Hence, there are 17 terms in given AP.

EXAMPLE 6. Which term of the sequence 72, 70, 68, 66,... is 40?

Sol. Given seqeunce is 72, 70, 68, 66, ...

Clearly, the successive difference of the terms is same. So, the above sequence forms an AP with first term, $a = 72$, common difference, $d = 70 - 72 = -2$ and $T_n = 40$

$\therefore T_n = a + (n-1)\,d$

$\Rightarrow 40 = 72 + (n-1)(-2)$

$\Rightarrow 40 = 72 - 2n + 2$

$\Rightarrow 2n = 72 - 40 + 2$

$\Rightarrow 2n = 34$

$\Rightarrow n = 17$

Hence, 17th term of the given sequence is 40.

EXAMPLE 7. Which term of the sequence $20, 19\frac{1}{4}, 18\frac{1}{2}, 17\frac{3}{4}, \ldots$ is the first negative term?

Sol. The given sequence is $20, 19\frac{1}{4}, 18\frac{1}{2}, 17\frac{3}{4}, \ldots$

Clearly, the successive difference of the terms is same. So, the above sequence forms an AP with first term, $a = 20$ and common difference, $d = 19\frac{1}{4} - 20 = -\frac{3}{4}$.

Let the nth term of the given AP be the first negative term.

Then, $a_n < 0$

$\Rightarrow a + (n-1)\,d < 0$

$\Rightarrow 20 + (n-1) \times (-3/4) < 0$

$\Rightarrow \frac{83}{4} - \frac{3n}{4} < 0$

$\Rightarrow \frac{3n}{4} > \frac{83}{4}$

$\Rightarrow 3n > 83 \Rightarrow n > 27\frac{2}{3}$

Since, 28 is just greater than $27\frac{2}{3}$.

So, $n = 28$.

Thus, 28th term of the given sequence will be first negative term.

EXAMPLE 8. In the arithmetic progressions, 2, 5, 8, ... upto 50 terms and 3, 5, 7, 9, ... upto 60 terms, find how many terms are identical.

Sol. Given, first AP is 2, 5, 8, ... upto 50 terms,

We have, $a_1 = 2, d_1 = 5 - 2 = 3$

And second AP is 3, 5, 7, 9... upto 60 terms.

We have, $a_2 = 3, d_2 = 5 - 3 = 2$

Let the mth term of the first AP be equal to the nth term of the second AP.

Then, $2 + (m-1) \times 3 = 3 + (n-1) \times 2$

$\Rightarrow 3m - 1 = 2n + 1$

$\Rightarrow 3m = 2n + 2$

$\Rightarrow \frac{m}{2} = \frac{n+1}{3} = k$ (say)

$\Rightarrow m = 2k$ and $n = 3k - 1$

$\Rightarrow 2k \le 50$ and $3k - 1 \le 60$

$[\because m \le 50 \text{ and } n \le 60]$

$\Rightarrow k \le 25$ and $k \le 20\frac{1}{3}$

$\Rightarrow k \le 20$ $[\because k$ is a natural number$]$

$\therefore k = 1, 2, 3, \ldots, 20$

Corresponding to each value of k, we get a pair of identical terms.

Hence, there are 20 identical terms in the two AP's.

EXAMPLE 9. If the mth term of a given AP is n and its nth term is m, then show that its pth term is $(n + m - p)$.

Sol. In the given AP, let the first term = a and the common difference = d.

According to the question,

mth term of a given AP = $n \Rightarrow a_m = n$

and nth term of a given AP = $m \Rightarrow a_n = m$

$\therefore a + (m-1)\,d = n$ ...(i)

and $a + (n-1)\,d = m$ ...(ii)

On subtracting Eq. (ii) from Eq. (i), we get

$(m - n)\,d = (n - m)$

$\Rightarrow d = -1$

On putting $d = -1$ in Eq. (i), we get

$a = (n + m - 1)$

$\therefore$ pth term $= a + (p-1)\,d$

$= (n + m - 1) + (p - 1)(-1)$

$[\because a = (n + m - 1) \text{ and } d = -1]$

$= (n + m - p)$

Hence, the pth term of the given AP is $(n + m - p)$.

EXAMPLE 10. The pth, qth and rth terms of an AP are a, b, c, respectively. Show that

$$(q - r)a + (r - p)b + (p - q)c = 0.$$

Sol. In the given AP, let the first term = A and the common difference = D.

Given, pth term $= A + (p-1)D = a$ ...(i)

qth term $= A + (q-1)D = b$ ...(ii)

rth term $= A + (r-1)D = c$ ...(iii)

Now, we have to prove

$$(q-r)a + (r-p)b + (p-q)c = 0$$

On taking LHS $= (q-r)a + (r-p)b + (p-q)c$ ...(iv)

On putting the values of a, b and c from Eqs. (i), (ii) and (iii) in Eq. (iv), we get

$$\text{LHS} = (q-r)[A+(p-1)D] + (r-p)[A+(q-1)D] + (p-q)[A+(r-1)D]$$
$$= (q-r)A + (q-r)(p-1)D + (r-p)A + (r-p)(q-1)D + (p-q)A + (p-q)(r-1)D$$
$$= A(q-r+r-p+p-q) + D[(q-r)(p-1) + (r-p)(q-1) + (p-q)(r-1)]$$
$$= A(0) + D[qp - q - rp + r + rq - r - pq + p + pr - p - qr + q]$$
$$= 0 + 0 = 0 = \text{RHS}$$

Hence proved.

*m*th Term of an AP from the End

Let a be the first term and d be the common difference of an AP having n terms. Then, mth term from the end is $(n-m+1)$th term from the beginning.

$\therefore$ mth term from the end, a_{n-m+1}

$$= a + (n-m+1-1)d$$
$$= a + (n-m)d, \text{ where } n > m$$

Also, mth term from the end

$$= a_n + (m-1)(-d)$$
$$= a_n - (m-1)d$$

or $\qquad = l - (m-1)d$

where, a_n (or l) is the last term of a sequence.

EXAMPLE 11. Find the 6th term from the end of the sequence 9, 12, 15, ..., 20th term.

Sol. Given sequence is 9, 12, 15, ..., 20th term.

Clearly, the successive difference of the terms is same. So, the above sequence forms an AP with first term, $a = 9$ and common difference, $d = 12 - 9 = 3$.

We know that, if a sequence has n term, then mth term from end is equal to $(n-m+1)$th term from the beginning.

Here, $n = 20$, $m = 6$, $a = 9$ and $d = 3$

Now, 6th term from the end of sequence $= (20-6+1)$

$\therefore$ 15th term from the beginning.

$$T_{15} = 9 + (15-1)3 \qquad [\because T_n = a + (n-1)d]$$
$$= 9 + (14)3$$
$$= 9 + 42$$
$$= 51$$

Hence, the 6th term from the end of the sequence is 51.

EXAMPLE 12. Determine the number of terms in the AP 3, 7, 11, ..., 407. Also, find the 18th term from the end.

Sol. Given AP is 3, 7, 11, ..., 407

Here, first term, $a = 3$ and common difference, $d = 4$ and nth term,

$$T_n = 407$$

Also, $\quad T_n = a + (n-1)d$

$\therefore \quad 407 = 3 + (n-1)4$

$\Rightarrow \quad 407 = 3 + 4n - 4$

$\Rightarrow \quad 4n = 407 - 3 + 4$

$\Rightarrow \quad 4n = 408$

$\Rightarrow \quad n = 102$

Hence, there are 102 terms in the given AP.

Now, 18th term from the end

$= [n - m + 1]$th term from the beginning

$= [102 - 18 + 1]$th term from the beginning

$= 85$th term from the beginning

$= 3 + (85-1)4$

$= 339$

Selection of Terms in an AP

Sometimes, we have to select certain terms in an AP. The convenient ways of selecting terms are given below

Number of terms	Terms	Common difference
3	$a-d, a, a+d$	d
4	$a-3d, a-d, a+d, a+3d$	$2d$
5	$a-2d, a-d, a, a+d, a+2d$	d
6	$a-5d, a-3d, a-d, a+d, a+3d, a+5d$	$2d$

From this table, it is clear that

- If number of terms is odd, then middle term is a and the common difference is d.
- If number of terms is even, then middle terms are $a-d$, $a+d$ and the common difference is $2d$.
- If the terms of an AP are not given, then the terms are chosen as a, $a+d$, $a+2d$, ...

EXAMPLE 13. The sum of three consecutive terms of an AP is 15 and their product is 105. Find the numbers.

Sol. Let three numbers in AP be $a-d$, a and $a+d$.

According to the question,

Sum of three consecutive terms $= 15$

$\therefore \quad (a-d) + a + (a+d) = 15$

$\Rightarrow \quad 3a = 15$

$\Rightarrow \quad a = 5$

and the product of three consecutive terms = 105

$\therefore\ (a-d)(a)(a+d)=105$

$\Rightarrow (5-d)(5)(5+d)=105$ [put $a=5$]

$\Rightarrow (25-d^2)5=105$ [$\because (A-B)(A+B)=A^2-B^2$]

$\Rightarrow 25-d^2=21$ [dividing both sides by 5]

$\Rightarrow d^2=4$

$\therefore d=\pm 2$

When $d=2$, then terms in AP are $5-2$, 5 and $5+2$ i.e. 3, 5, 7.

When $d=-2$, then terms in AP are $5+2$, 5, $5-2$ i.e. 7, 5, 3.

EXAMPLE 14. Divide 20 into four parts which are in AP such that the product of extremes is to the product of mean is 2 : 3.

Sol. Let the four parts be $(a-3d)$, $(a-d)$, $(a+d)$ and $(a+3d)$.

Then, sum of the four parts = 20

$\therefore a-3d+a-d+a+d+a+3d=20 \Rightarrow 4a=20 \Rightarrow a=5$

It is given that the product of extremes is to the product of mean is 2 : 3.

$$\therefore \frac{(a-3d)(a+3d)}{(a-d)(a+d)}=\frac{2}{3}$$

$$\Rightarrow \frac{a^2-9d^2}{a^2-d^2}=\frac{2}{3}$$

$$\Rightarrow \frac{25-9d^2}{25-d^2}=\frac{2}{3}$$

$\Rightarrow 25d^2=25$

$\Rightarrow d^2=1$

$\Rightarrow d=\pm 1$

Thus, the four of 20 parts are 2, 4, 6, 8.

When $a=5$, $d=1$, four parts are 2, 4, 6, 8

When $a=5$, $d=-1$, four parts are 8, 6, 4, 2

Properties of an Arithmetic Progression

- If a **constant is added** to each term of an AP, then the resulting sequence is also an AP with the same common difference.
- If a **constant is subtracted** from each term of an AP, then the resulting sequence is also an AP with the same common difference.
- If each term of an AP is **multiplied by a constant** say k, then the resulting sequence is also an AP with common difference kd, where d is the common difference of the given AP.
- If each term of an AP is **divided by a non-zero constant** say k, then the resulting sequence is also an AP with common difference d/k, where d is the common difference of the given AP.
- In an AP, the sum of terms equidistant from the beginning and end is constant and equal to the sum of first and last term.
  i.e. $a_1+a_n=a_2+a_{n-1}=a_3+a_{n-2}=\dots$
- The resulting sequence formed by adding or subtracting the corresponding terms of two AP's is also an AP.
- A sequence is an AP, iff its nth term is a linear expression in n i.e. $a_n=An+B$, where A and B are constants and coefficient of n is the common difference of the AP.

EXAMPLE 15. If $a\left(\frac{1}{b}+\frac{1}{c}\right), b\left(\frac{1}{c}+\frac{1}{a}\right), c\left(\frac{1}{a}+\frac{1}{b}\right)$ are in AP, prove that a, b, c are in AP.

Sol. Given, $a\left(\frac{1}{b}+\frac{1}{c}\right), b\left(\frac{1}{c}+\frac{1}{a}\right), c\left(\frac{1}{a}+\frac{1}{b}\right)$ are in AP.

$\Rightarrow a\left(\frac{b+c}{bc}\right), b\left(\frac{a+c}{ac}\right), c\left(\frac{b+a}{ab}\right)$ are in AP.

$\Rightarrow \frac{ab+ac}{bc}, \frac{ba+bc}{ac}, \frac{cb+ca}{ab}$ are in AP.

On adding 1 to each term, we get

$\frac{ab+ac}{bc}+1, \frac{ba+bc}{ac}+1, \frac{cb+ca}{ab}+1$ are in AP.

$\Rightarrow \frac{ab+ac+bc}{bc}, \frac{ba+bc+ac}{ac}, \frac{bc+ac+ab}{ab}$ are in AP.

On dividing each term by $ab+bc+ac$, we get

$\frac{1}{bc}, \frac{1}{ac}, \frac{1}{ab}$ are in AP.

On multiplying each term by abc, we get

$\frac{abc}{bc}, \frac{abc}{ac}, \frac{abc}{ab}$ are in AP

$\Rightarrow a, b, c$ are in AP. **Hence proved.**

Topic Practice 2

1 The nth term of a sequence is given by $a_n = 2n + 7$. Show that it is an AP. Also, find its 8th term.

2 Find the indicated terms in each of the following progressions.

(i) 9, 12, 15, 18, ...; T_{16}

(ii) $a = 21, d = -5$; T_n, T_{25}

(iii) 7, 5, 3, 1, ...; T_{23}

(iv) $a = 1, d = 5$; T_{61}

(v) $\sqrt{2}, 3\sqrt{2}, 5\sqrt{2}, 7\sqrt{2}$, ...; T_{10}

3 Find the nth term of the sequence 8, 3, −2, −7,...

4 (i) Is 68 a term of the AP 7, 10, 13,... ?

(ii) Is 302 a term of the AP 3, 8, 13,... ?

5 How many terms are there in the AP $-1, -\frac{5}{6}, -\frac{2}{3}, -\frac{1}{2}, \ldots, \frac{10}{3}$?

6 Which term of the sequence

(i) 5, 8, 11, 14,... is 320. (ii) 84, 80, 76,... , is 0?

7 The first term of an AP is 5, the common difference is 3 and the last term is 80, find the number of terms.

8 If the mth term of an AP be $1/n$ and its nth term be $1/m$, then show that its mnth term is 1.

9 If 9 times the 9th term of an AP is equal to 13 times the 13th term, then find the 22nd term of the AP. **[NCERT Exemplar]**

10 If the 9th term of an AP is 0, prove that its 29th term is double the 19th term.

11 Which term of the progression $19, 18\frac{1}{5}, 17\frac{2}{5}, \ldots$ is negative term?

12 Show that the sum of $(m+n)$th and $(m-n)$th term of an AP is equal to the twice of the mth term.

13 Let a, b, c be respectively the pth, qth, rth terms of an AP. Prove that

$$(a-b)r + (b-c)p + (c-a)q = 0$$ **[NCERT]**

14 Find the number of terms common to the two AP's 3, 7, 11, ... 407 and 2, 9, 16, ... 709.

15 Find the middle terms in the AP 20, 16, 12, ..., −176.

16 Find the 15th term from the end of the AP 3, 5, 7, 9, ..., 201.

17 Three numbers are in AP. If their sum is 27 and the product 648, find the numbers.

18 Find four numbers in AP whose sum is 20 and the sum of whose squares is 120.

19 If a, b, c are in AP, then prove that $(b+c)^2 - a^2, (c+a)^2 - b^2, (a+b)^2 - c^2$ are also in AP.

20 If $a_1, a_2, a_3, \ldots, a_n$ be an AP of non-zero terms, prove that $\frac{1}{a_1a_2} + \frac{1}{a_2a_3} + \ldots + \frac{1}{a_{n-1}a_n} = \frac{n-1}{a_1a_n}$.

21 If $a_1, a_2, a_3, \ldots, a_n$ are in AP, where $a_i > 0$ for all i, show that $\frac{1}{\sqrt{a_1}+\sqrt{a_2}} + \frac{1}{\sqrt{a_2}+\sqrt{a_3}} + \ldots + \frac{1}{a_{n-1}+\sqrt{a_n}}$

$$= \frac{n-1}{\sqrt{a_1}+\sqrt{a_n}}.$$ **[NCERT Exemplar]**

Hints & Solutions

1. Solve as Example 1.
   Ans. 8th term = 23
2. Solve as Example 3.
   Ans. (i) 54 (ii) $26 - 5n, -99$ (iii) −37
   (iv) 301 (v) $19\sqrt{2}$
3. **Hint** nth term = $13 - 5n$
4. Solve as Example 4. **Ans.** (i) No (ii) No
5. Solve as Example 5. **Ans.** 27
6. Solve as Example 6. **Ans.** (i) 106 (ii) 22
7. **Hint** $80 = 5 + (n-1)3$ **Ans.** 26
8. **Hint** In the given AP, let the first term $= a$ and the common difference $= d$.

According to the question,

$$a_m = \frac{1}{n} \text{ and } a_n = \frac{1}{m}$$

$\therefore$ $a + (m-1)d = 1/n$ ...(i)

and $a + (n-1)d = \frac{1}{m}$ ...(ii)

On subtracting Eq. (ii) from Eq. (i), we get

$$(m-n)d = \left(\frac{1}{n} - \frac{1}{m}\right)$$

$$\Rightarrow \quad d = \frac{1}{mn}$$

On putting $d = \frac{1}{mn}$ in Eq. (i), we get

$$a + \frac{(m-1)}{mn} = \frac{1}{n} \Rightarrow a = \frac{1}{n} - \frac{(m-1)}{mn} = \frac{1}{mn}.$$

Now, mnth term $= a + (mn-1)d$

$$= \frac{1}{mn} + \frac{(mn-1)}{mn} = \frac{mn}{mn} = 1$$

Hence, the mnth term of the given AP is 1.

9. **Hint** $9T_9 = 13T_{13}$

$\Rightarrow 9(a+8d) = 13(a+12d)$

$\Rightarrow \quad a = -21d$ **Ans.** 0

10. **Hint** Let a and d be the first term and common difference, respectively of the given AP.

According to the question,

$a_9 = 0 \Rightarrow a + 8d = 0 \Rightarrow a = -8d$ ...(i)

and $a_{29} = a + 28d = a + 28d + 8d - 8d$

$= a + 36d + a$ [from Eq. (i)]

$= 2a + 36d = 2(a + 18d)$

$= 2a_{19}$ **Hence proved.**

11. **Hint** Let $T_n < 0$

$\Rightarrow \left[19 + (n-1)\left(-\frac{4}{5}\right)\right] < 0 \Rightarrow n > 24\frac{3}{4} = 25\text{th term}$

Ans. 25th

12. **Hint** $a_{m+n} = a + (m+n-1)d,\ a_{m-n} = a + (m-n-1)d$

$a_{m+n} + a_{m-n} = 2a + (m+n-1+m-n-1)d$

$= 2a + 2(m-1)d$

$= 2[a + (m-1)]d$

$= 2a_m$ **Hence proved.**

13. Solve as Example 10.

14. **Hint** $407 = 3 + (m-1) \times 4$ and $709 = 2 + (n-1) \times 7$

$\Rightarrow \quad m = 102$ and $n = 102$

Let pth term of first AP = qth term of second AP.

$\Rightarrow \quad 3 + (p-1) \times 4 = 2 + (q-1) \times 7$

$\Rightarrow \quad \frac{p+1}{7} = \frac{q}{4} = k$ (say)

$\Rightarrow \quad p = 7k - 1$ and $q = 4k$

Since, each AP consists of 102 terms.

$\therefore \quad p \le 102$ and $q \le 102$

$\Rightarrow \quad k \le \frac{103}{7}$ and $k \le \frac{102}{4}$

Ans. 14 term

15. **Hint** $-176 = 20 + (n-1)(-4)$

$\Rightarrow \quad n = 50$

Then, middle term $= T_{25}$

Ans. -76

16. Solve as Example 11. **Ans.** 173

17. Solve as Example 13. **Ans.** 6, 9, 12 or 12, 9, 6

18. **Hint** $(a-3d) + (a-d) + (a+d) + (a+3d) = 20$

$\Rightarrow \quad a = 5$

and $(a-3d)^2 + (a-d)^2 + (a+d)^2 + (a+3d)^2 = 120$

$\Rightarrow \quad 4a^2 + 20d^2 = 120$

$\Rightarrow \quad 25 + 5d^2 = 30$

$\Rightarrow \quad d = \pm 1$

Ans. 2, 4, 6, 8 or 8, 6, 4, 2

19. **Hint** $(b+c)^2 - a^2, (c+a)^2 - b^2, (a+b)^2 - c^2$ are in AP.

$\Rightarrow (b+c+a)(b+c-a), (c+a+b)(c+a-b),$
$(a+b+c)(a+b-c)$ are in AP.

$\Rightarrow (b+c-a), (c+a-b), (a+b-c)$ are in AP.

$\Rightarrow (b+c-a)-(a+b+c), (c+a-b)-(a+b+c),$
$(a+b-c)-(a+b+c)$ are in AP.

$\Rightarrow -2a, -2b, -2c$ are in AP.

$\Rightarrow a, b, c$ are in AP, which is true.

20. **Hint** Let $a_2 - a_1 = a_3 - a_2 = \ldots = a_n - a_{n-1} = d$ (say)

Now, $\frac{1}{a_1a_2} + \frac{1}{a_2a_3} + \frac{1}{a_3a_4} + \ldots + \frac{1}{a_{n-1}a_n}$

$$= \frac{1}{d}\left\{\frac{d}{a_1a_2} + \frac{d}{a_2a_3} + \frac{d}{a_3a_4} + \ldots + \frac{d}{a_{n-1}a_n}\right\}$$

$$= \frac{1}{d}\left\{\frac{(a_2-a_1)}{a_1a_2} + \frac{(a_3-a_2)}{a_2a_3} + \frac{(a_4-a_3)}{a_3a_4} + \ldots + \frac{(a_n-a_{n-1})}{a_{n-1}a_n}\right\}$$

$$= \frac{1}{d}\left\{\frac{1}{a_1} - \frac{1}{a_n}\right\} = \frac{1}{d}\left\{\frac{a_n - a_1}{a_1a_n}\right\}$$

$$= \frac{1}{d}\left\{\frac{a_1 + (n-1)d - a_1}{a_1a_n}\right\}$$

$$= \frac{n-1}{a_1a_n}$$

21. **Hint** $a_2 - a_1 = a_3 - a_2 = \ldots = a_n - a_{n-1} = d$ (say)

If $a_2 - a_1 = d$, then $(\sqrt{a_2})^2 - (\sqrt{a_1})^2 = d$

$\Rightarrow \quad (\sqrt{a_2} - \sqrt{a_1})(\sqrt{a_2} + \sqrt{a_1}) = d$

$\Rightarrow \quad \frac{1}{\sqrt{a_1} + \sqrt{a_2}} = \frac{\sqrt{a_2} - \sqrt{a_1}}{d}$

On adding, we get

$$\frac{1}{\sqrt{a_1} + \sqrt{a_2}} + \frac{1}{\sqrt{a_2} + \sqrt{a_3}} + \ldots + \frac{1}{\sqrt{a_{n-1}} + \sqrt{a_n}}$$

$$= \frac{1}{d}[\sqrt{a_2} - \sqrt{a_1} + \sqrt{a_3} - \sqrt{a_2} + \ldots + \sqrt{a_n} - \sqrt{a_{n-1}}]$$

$$= \frac{1}{d}[\sqrt{a_n} - \sqrt{a_1}] \quad \text{...(i)}$$

Also, $a_n - a_1 = (n-1)d$

$\Rightarrow (\sqrt{a_n})^2 - (\sqrt{a_1})^2 = (n-1)d$

$\Rightarrow \quad \sqrt{a_n} - \sqrt{a_1} = \frac{(n-1)d}{\sqrt{a_n} + \sqrt{a_1}}$

Sum of n Terms of an AP and Arithmetic Mean (AM)

Sum of n terms of an AP

If a be the first term, d be the common difference and l be the last term of an AP, then the sum of n terms, S_n of this AP is given by

$$S_n = \frac{n}{2}[2a + (n-1)d] \text{ or } S_n = \frac{n}{2}(a + l)$$

If sum of n terms, S_n of an AP is given, then nth term

$$a_n = S_n - S_{n-1}, \text{ where } a_1 = S_1$$

EXAMPLE 1. Find the sum of the series $45 + 47 + 49 + \ldots + 99$.

Sol. Given series is $45 + 47 + 49 + \ldots + 99$.

Here, $a = 45$ and $d = 47 - 45 = 2$ and $l = a_n = 99$

$\because \quad a_n = 99$

$\Rightarrow \quad a + (n-1)d = 99$

$\Rightarrow \quad 45 + (n-1)2 = 99 \Rightarrow 45 + 2n - 2 = 99$

$\Rightarrow \quad 2n = 56 \Rightarrow n = 28$

$\because \quad S_n = \frac{n}{2}(a + l)$

$\therefore \quad S_{28} = \frac{28}{2}(45 + 99) = 14(144) = 2016$

EXAMPLE 2. Find the sum of indicated number of terms in the following AP.

$x + y, x - y, x - 3y, \ldots$, 22 terms

Sol. Given series is $x + y, x - y, x - 3y, \ldots$, 22 terms.

Here, $a = x + y$

$d = a_2 - a_1 = (x - y) - (x + y) = -2y$ and $n = 22$

$\because \quad S_n = \frac{n}{2}[2a + (n-1)d]$

$\therefore \quad S_{22} = \frac{22}{2}[2 \times (x + y) + (22 - 1)(-2y)]$

$= 11[2x + 2y + (21)(-2y)]$

$= 11[2x + 2y - 42y]$

$= 11[2x - 40y] = 22[x - 20y]$

EXAMPLE 3. If the first term of an AP is a and the sum of the first p terms is zero, then find the sum of its next q terms.

Sol. Let the common difference be d.

Given, sum of first p terms $= 0 \Rightarrow S_p = 0$

$\Rightarrow \quad \frac{p}{2}[2a + (p-1)d] = 0$

[given, a = first term of an AP]

$\Rightarrow \quad 2a + (p-1)d = 0$

$\Rightarrow \quad d = -\frac{2a}{p-1} \quad \ldots(i)$

$\therefore$ Required sum of next q terms

= Sum of first $(p + q)$ terms – Sum of first p terms

$= S_{p+q} - S_p$

$= \frac{p+q}{2}[2a + (p + q - 1)d] - 0 \quad [\because S_p = 0]$

$= \frac{p+q}{2}\left[2a + (p + q - 1)\left(\frac{-2a}{p-1}\right)\right] \quad$ [from Eq. (i)]

$= \frac{p+q}{2} \times 2a\left[\frac{1}{1} - \frac{p+q-1}{p-1}\right]$

$= (p+q)a\left[\frac{p-1-p-q+1}{p-1}\right] = \frac{-a(p+q)q}{p-1}$

EXAMPLE 4. Find the sum of all numbers between 200 and 400 which are divisible by 7.

Sol. The numbers which are divisible by 7 between 200 and 400 are 203, 210, 217,..., 399.

Clearly, they form an AP.

where, $\quad a = 203, d = 7$ and $T_n = 399$

Now, $\quad T_n = a + (n-1)d$

$\Rightarrow \quad 399 = 203 + (n-1)7$

$\Rightarrow \quad (n-1)7 = 399 - 203$

$\Rightarrow \quad (n-1)7 = 196$

$\Rightarrow \quad n - 1 = \frac{196}{7}$

$\Rightarrow \quad n - 1 = 28$

$\Rightarrow \quad n = 29$

Now, $S_n = \frac{n}{2}(a + T_n) \quad [\because T_n = \text{Last term of given AP}]$

$\therefore \quad S_{29} = \frac{29}{2}[203 + 399]$

$= \frac{29}{2} \times 602 = 29 \times 301 = 8729$

EXAMPLE 5. Find the sum to n terms of the AP whose kth term is $5k + 1$.

Sol. The given sequence is an AP whose kth term is $5k + 1$.

$\therefore \quad a_k = 5k + 1$

$\Rightarrow \quad a_1 = 5(1) + 1 = 5 + 1 = 6$

$\Rightarrow \quad a_n = 5n + 1$

Now, sum of n terms of an AP is given by

$$S_n = \frac{n}{2}(a_1 + a_n) = \frac{n}{2}(6 + 5n + 1) = \frac{n}{2}(5n + 7)$$

EXAMPLE 6. If the first term of an AP is 100 and the sum of first six terms is five times the sum of the next six terms, then find the common difference.

Sol. Given, $a = 100$

Let d be the common difference.

According to the question,

$$a_1 + a_2 + ... + a_6 = 5(a_7 + a_8 + ... + a_{12})$$

$\Rightarrow$ $\frac{6}{2}[2a + (6-1)d] = 5[(a+6d) + (a+7d) + ... + (a+11d)]$

$[\because a_7 = a+6d, ..., a_{12} = a+11d]$

$\Rightarrow$ $3[2a+5d] = 5[6a + (6d + 7d + ... + 11d)]$

$\Rightarrow$ $3[2a+5d] = 5\left[6a + \left\{\frac{6}{2}[2\times 6d + (6-1)d]\right\}\right]$

$\left[\because S_n = \frac{n}{2}\{2a+(n-1)d\}\right]$

$\Rightarrow$ $3[2a+5d] = 5[6a + \{3(12d+5d)\}]$

$\Rightarrow$ $3[2a+5d] = 5[6a + 36d + 15d] = 5[6a + 51d]$

$\Rightarrow$ $3(2a+5d) = 5\times 3(2a+17d)$

$\Rightarrow$ $2a + 5d = 10a + 85d$

$\Rightarrow$ $-80d = 8a$

$\Rightarrow$ $-80d = 8(100)$ $[\because a = 100]$

$\Rightarrow$ $d = -10$

EXAMPLE 7. In an AP, if pth term is $\frac{1}{q}$ and qth term is $\frac{1}{p}$, then prove that the sum of first pq terms is $\frac{1}{2}(pq+1)$, where $p \neq q$.

Sol. Let a be the first term and d be the common ratio of the given AP.

Then, $a_p = a + (p-1)d = \frac{1}{q}$ ...(i)

and $a_q = a + (q-1)d = \frac{1}{p}$ ...(ii)

On subtracting Eq. (ii) from Eq. (i), we get

$$(p-q)d = \frac{1}{q} - \frac{1}{p} = \frac{p-q}{pq} \Rightarrow d = \frac{1}{pq}$$

On putting the value of d in Eq. (i), we get

$$a + (p-1)\times\frac{1}{pq} = \frac{1}{q}$$

$\Rightarrow$ $a = \frac{1}{q} - \frac{p-1}{pq} \Rightarrow a = \frac{1}{pq}$

Now, $S_{pq} = \frac{pq}{2}(2a + (pq-1)d)$

$\Rightarrow$ $S_{pq} = \frac{pq}{2}\left(\frac{2}{pq} + \frac{pq-1}{pq}\right)$

$\Rightarrow$ $S_{pq} = \frac{pq}{2}\left(\frac{pq+1}{pq}\right) = \frac{1}{2}(pq+1)$

EXAMPLE 8. How many terms in the AP −9, − 6, − 3, ... must be added together so that the sum may be 66?

Sol. Let 66 be the sum of n terms.

We have, $a = -9$ and $d = -6-(-9) = -6+9 = 3$

$\because$ $S_n = \frac{n}{2}[2a + (n-1)d]$

$\therefore$ $66 = \frac{n}{2}[2(-9) + (n-1)3]$

$\Rightarrow$ $66 = \frac{n}{2}[-18 + 3n - 3]$

$\Rightarrow$ $132 = n[3n - 21]$

$\Rightarrow$ $44 = n[n-7]$ [dividing both sides by 3]

$\Rightarrow$ $n^2 - 7n - 44 = 0$

$\Rightarrow$ $(n-11)(n+4) = 0$

$\Rightarrow$ $n = 11$ or -4

Rejecting $n = -4$ because number of terms cannot be negative.

$\therefore$ $n = 11$

EXAMPLE 9. How many terms of the AP $-6, -\frac{11}{2}, -5$ ..... are needed to give sum − 25?

Sol. Given that the sequence $-6, -\frac{11}{2}, -5, ...$ is in AP.

Here, $a = -6$,

and $d = -\frac{11}{2} - (-6) = -\frac{11}{2} + 6 = \frac{-11+12}{2} = \frac{1}{2}$

Now, $S_n = \frac{n}{2}[2a + (n-1)d]$

$\Rightarrow$ $-25 = \frac{n}{2}\left[2(-6) + (n-1)\frac{1}{2}\right]$

$\Rightarrow$ $-25\times 2 = n\left[\frac{-12}{1} + \frac{(n-1)}{2}\right]$

$\Rightarrow$ $-50 = n\left[\frac{-24+n-1}{2}\right]$

$\Rightarrow$ $-50\times 2 = n(n-25)$

$\Rightarrow$ $-100 = n^2 - 25n$

$\Rightarrow$ $n^2 - 25n + 100 = 0$

$\Rightarrow$ $n^2 - 20n - 5n + 100 = 0$

$\Rightarrow$ $n(n-20) - 5(n-20) = 0$

$\Rightarrow$ $(n-20)(n-5) = 0$

$\Rightarrow$ $n = 5$ or 20

EXAMPLE 10. Solve for x,

$$1 + 4 + 7 + 10 + 13 + ... + x = 590.$$

Sol. The terms of the given series form an AP, whose first term is 1 and common difference = 3.

i.e. $a = 1$, $d = 3$

Let the number of terms in series be n.

$\therefore$ $S_n = 590$

$\Rightarrow$ $\frac{n}{2}(2a + (n-1)d) = 590$

$\Rightarrow$ $\frac{n}{2}(2 + (n-1)3) = 590$

$\Rightarrow \quad n(3n-1)=1180$

$\Rightarrow \quad 3n^2-n-1180=0$

$\Rightarrow \quad (3n+59)(n-20)=0$

$\Rightarrow \quad n=20, \frac{-59}{3}$

Possible value of $n=20$ [$\because n$ cannot be negative]

Now, $x = n$th term

$\therefore \quad x=a+(n-1)d$

$\Rightarrow \quad x=1+(20-1)(3)=1+57$

$\Rightarrow \quad x=58$

EXAMPLE 11. If the sum of n terms of an AP is $3n^2+5n$ and its mth term is 164, then find the value of m.

Sol. Let S_n denotes the sum of n terms and a_n be the nth term of given AP.

Then, $S_n=3n^2+5n$

$\Rightarrow \quad S_m=3m^2+5m$

$\Rightarrow \quad S_1=a_1=3+5=8$

$\therefore \quad S_n=\frac{n}{2}(a_1+a_n)$

$\therefore \quad S_m=\frac{m}{2}(a_1+a_m)$

$\Rightarrow \quad 3m^2+5m=\frac{m}{2}(8+164)$ [$\because a_m=164$]

$\Rightarrow \quad 3m+5=\frac{172}{2}=86$

$\Rightarrow \quad 3m=81$

$\Rightarrow \quad m=\frac{81}{3}=27$

EXAMPLE 12. The sum of the first four terms of an AP is 56. The sum of the last four terms is 112. If its first term is 11, then find the number of terms.

Sol. Let there be n terms in an AP whose first term $a=11$ and common difference is d.

Given sum of first four terms = 56

$\therefore \quad \frac{4}{2}(2a+3d)=56 \Rightarrow 2(2(11)+3d)=56$

$\Rightarrow \quad 22+3d=28 \Rightarrow 3d=6 \Rightarrow d=2$

Also, given sum of last four terms = 112

$\therefore \quad a_n+a_{n-1}+a_{n-2}+a_{n-3}=112$

$\Rightarrow \quad \frac{4}{2}(a_n+a_{n-3})=112$

$\Rightarrow \quad 2(a+(n-1)d+a+(n-4)d)=112$

$\Rightarrow \quad 2a+(2n-5)d=56$

$\Rightarrow \quad 22+(2n-5)2=56$

$\Rightarrow \quad 4n-10=34$

$\Rightarrow \quad 4n=44$

$\Rightarrow \quad n=11$

Hence, there are 11 terms in the AP.

EXAMPLE 13. The first term of an AP is a, the second term is b and the last term is c. Show that the sum of the AP is $\frac{(b+c-2a)(c+a)}{2(b-a)}$.

Sol. Let d be the common difference and n be the number of terms of the AP.

Since, the first term is a and the second term is b.

Therefore, $d=b-a$

Also, last term, $l=c$

$\because \quad l=a+(n-1)d$

$\therefore \quad c=a+(n-1)(b-a)$ [$\because d=b-a$]

$\Rightarrow \quad n-1=\frac{c-a}{b-a}$

$\Rightarrow \quad n=1+\frac{c-a}{b-a}=\frac{b-a+c-a}{b-a}=\frac{b+c-2a}{b-a}$

Therefore, $S_n=\frac{n}{2}(a+l)$

$=\frac{(b+c-2a)}{2(b-a)}(a+c)$

EXAMPLE 14. If the ratio between the sums of n terms of two arithmetic progressions is $(7n+1):(4n+27)$, find the ratio of their 11th terms.

Sol. Let a_1, a_2 be the first terms and d_1, d_2 be the common differences of the first and second arithmetic progressions, respectively.

Then, the sums of n terms of these progressions are given by

$$S_n=\frac{n}{2}\cdot\{2a_1+(n-1)d_1\} \quad \text{...(i)}$$

and

$$S_n'=\frac{n}{2}\cdot\{2a_2+(n-1)d_2\} \quad \text{...(ii)}$$

On dividing Eq. (i) by Eq. (ii), we get

$$\frac{\frac{n}{2}\cdot\{2a_1+(n-1)d_1\}}{\frac{n}{2}\cdot\{2a_2+(n-1)d_2\}}=\frac{S_n}{S_n'}=\frac{7n+1}{4n+27} \quad \text{[given]}$$

$$\Rightarrow \quad \frac{2a_1+(n-1)d_1}{2a_2+(n-1)d_2}=\frac{7n+1}{4n+27} \quad \text{...(iii)}$$

Ratio of 11th terms $=\frac{a_1+10d_1}{a_2+10d_2}=\frac{2a_1+20d_1}{2a_2+20d_2}$

$=\frac{2a_1+(21-1)d_2}{2a_2+(21-1)d_2}$

$=\frac{7\times 21+1}{4\times 21+27}$

$=\frac{148}{111}$ [putting $n=21$ in Eq. (iii)]

Hence, the required ratio is 148 : 111.

EXAMPLE 15. The pth term of an AP is a and qth term is b. Prove that sum of its $(p+q)$th term is $\frac{p+q}{2}\left[a+b+\frac{a-b}{p-q}\right]$.

Sol. Let A be the first term and D be the common difference of the given AP.

Then, $T_p = a \Rightarrow A+(p-1)D = a$ ...(i)

and $T_q = b \Rightarrow A+(q-1)D = b$ ...(ii)

On subtracting Eq. (ii) from Eq. (i), we get

$$(p-q)D = a-b \Rightarrow D = \frac{a-b}{p-q} \quad \text{...(iii)}$$

On adding Eqs. (i) and (ii), we get

$$2A+(p+q-2)D = a+b$$
$$\Rightarrow \quad 2A+pD+qD-2D = a+b$$
$$\Rightarrow \quad 2A+pD+qD-D = a+b+D$$
$$\Rightarrow \quad 2A+(p+q-1)D = a+b+D$$
$$\Rightarrow \quad 2A+(p+q-1)D = a+b+\left(\frac{a-b}{p-q}\right)$$

[from Eq. (iii)] ...(iv)

Now, $S_{p+q} = \frac{p+q}{2}[2A+(p+q-1)D]$

$$= \frac{p+q}{2}\left[a+b+\frac{a-b}{p-q}\right] \quad \text{[from Eq. (iv)]}$$

Hence proved.

EXAMPLE 16. If the sum of m terms of an AP is equal to the sum of either the next n terms or the next p terms; then prove that $(m+n)\left(\frac{1}{m}-\frac{1}{p}\right)=(m+p)\left(\frac{1}{m}-\frac{1}{n}\right)$.

Sol. Let the AP be $a, a+d, a+2d \dots$.

We are given

$$a_1+a_2+\dots+a_m = a_{m+1}+a_{m+2}+\dots+a_{m+n} \quad \text{...(i)}$$

Adding $a_1+a_2+\dots+a_m$ on both sides of Eq. (i), we get

$$2[a_1+a_2+\dots+a_m] = a_1+a_2+\dots+a_m+a_{m+1}+\dots+a_{m+n}$$

$$\Rightarrow \quad 2S_m = S_{m+n}$$

$$\Rightarrow 2\frac{m}{2}\{2a+(m-1)d\} = \frac{m+n}{2}\{2a+(m+n-1)d\}$$

On putting $2a+(m-1)d = x$ in the above equation, we get

$$mx = \frac{m+n}{2}(x+nd)$$
$$\Rightarrow \quad (2m-m-n)x = (m+n)nd$$
$$\Rightarrow \quad (m-n)x = (m+n)nd \quad \text{...(ii)}$$

Similarly,

$$a_1+a_2+\dots+a_m = a_{m+1}+a_{m+2}+\dots+a_{m+p}$$

On adding $a_1+a_2+\dots+a_m$ on both sides, we get

$$2(a_1+a_2+\dots+a_m) = a_1+a_2+\dots+a_{m+1}+\dots+a_{m+p}$$

$$\Rightarrow \quad 2S_m = S_{m+p}$$
$$\Rightarrow 2\left[\frac{m}{2}\{2a+(m-1)d\}\right] = \frac{m+p}{2}\{2a+(m+p-1)d\}$$
$$\Rightarrow \quad mx = \frac{(m+p)}{2}(x+pd)$$
$$\Rightarrow \quad 2mx = mx+mpd+px+p^2d$$
$$\Rightarrow \quad (m-p)x = (m+p)pd \quad \text{...(iii)}$$

On dividing Eq. (ii) by Eq. (iii), we get

$$\frac{(m-n)x}{(m-p)x} = \frac{(m+n)nd}{(m+p)pd}$$
$$\Rightarrow \quad (m-n)(m+p)p = (m-p)(m+n)n$$

On dividing both sides by mnp, we get

$$(m+p)\left(\frac{1}{n}-\frac{1}{m}\right) = (m+n)\left(\frac{1}{p}-\frac{1}{m}\right)$$

or $$(m+n)\left(\frac{1}{m}-\frac{1}{p}\right) = (m+p)\left(\frac{1}{m}-\frac{1}{n}\right)$$

EXAMPLE 17. Prove that the sum of n terms of an AP is of the form An^2+Bn, where A and B are constants.

Sol. Let S_n be the sum of n terms,

a as the first term

and d as the common difference.

$$S_n = \frac{n}{2}\{2a+(n-1)d\}$$
$$= \frac{n}{2}[2a]+\frac{n}{2}\{(n-1)d\}$$
$$= na+\frac{n^2}{2}d-\frac{n}{2}d$$
$$= \left(a-\frac{d}{2}\right)n+\left(\frac{d}{2}\right)n^2 \quad \text{...(i)}$$
$$S_n = An^2+Bn$$

On comparing Eq. (i), we get

$$A = \frac{d}{2},\ B = \left(a-\frac{d}{2}\right)$$

Conversely, the sum of n term of a sequence be of the form (An^2+Bn) is the sequence in AP

$$S_n = An^2+Bn$$
$$S_{n-1} = A(n-1)^2+B(n-1)$$
$$a_n = S_n - S_{n-1}$$
$$a_n = \{An^2+Bn\}-\{A(n-1)^2+B(n-1)\} = \{2An+(B-A)\}$$
$$a_{n+1} = 2A(n+1)+(B-A)$$
$$a_{n+1}-a_n = \{2A(n+1)+B-A\}-2An-(B-A)\} = 2A$$

Clearly, $a_{n+1}-a_n = 2A$ for all $n \in N$.

Remark That a sequence is an AP. If the sum of its n terms is of the form An^2+Bn i.e. a quadratic expression in n and in such a case the common difference is twice the co-efficient of n^2.

Applications of an AP

Sometimes we can solve the some real life problems by using the concept of AP.
Some to them are given below.

EXAMPLE 18. In a potato race, 20 potatoes are placed in a line at intervals of 4 m with the first potato 24 m from the starting point. A contestant is required to put the potatoes back to the starting place on that time. How far would he run in bringing back all the potatoes?

Sol. As per the given information we have the following diagram

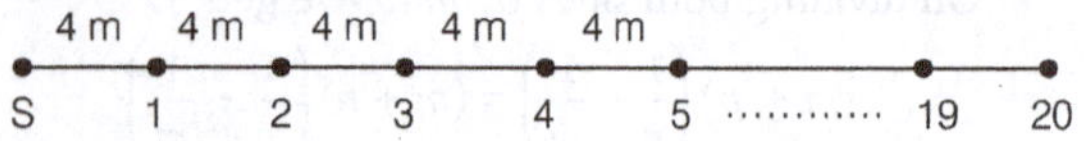

Starting point = S

Distance travelled to bring the first potato
$$= 24 + 24 = 48 \text{ m}$$
Distance travelled to bring the second potato
$$= 2(24 + 4) = 56 \text{ m}$$
Distance travelled to bring the third potato
$$= 2(24 + 4 + 4) = 64 \text{ m}$$
Therefore, the series will be 48, 56, 64, ...

which is clearly an AP in which $a = 48$, $d = 56 - 48 = 8$

We have to find the total distance to bring all the potatoes back, so, $n = 20$

$$\because \quad S_n = \frac{n}{2}[2a + (n-1)d]$$
$$\therefore \quad S_{20} = \frac{20}{2}[2 \times 48 + (20-1)8] = 10[96 + 152]$$
$$= 10 \times 248 = 2480 \text{ m}$$
Hence, the required distance is 2480 m.

EXAMPLE 19. A man arranges to pay-off a debt of ₹ 3600 by 40 annual instalments, which are in AP, when 30 of the instalments are paid, he dies leaving one-third of the debt unpaid. Find the 8th instalment.

Sol. Here, total debt, $S =$ ₹ 3600

and total instalments, $n = 40$

Let a and d be the first instalment and increment in instalment, respectively.

Thus, we get an AP here.

By using sum of n terms, we get
$$3600 = \frac{40}{2}[2a + (40-1)d]$$
$$\Rightarrow \quad 180 = 2a + 39d \quad \text{...(i)}$$
Now, after 30 instalments, one-third of the debt is unpaid.

i.e. $\frac{3600}{3} =$ ₹ 1200 is unpaid and then paid money
$$= 3600 - 1200$$
$$= ₹\ 2400$$

So, again by using sum of n terms, we get
$$S_{30} = 2400 = \frac{30}{2}[2a + (30-1)d]$$
$$\Rightarrow \quad 160 = 2a + 29d \quad \text{...(ii)}$$
On solving Eqs. (i) and (ii), we get
$$a = 51, d = 2$$
We know that, nth term $(T_n) = a + (n-1)d$

$\therefore$ 8th instalment, $T_8 = a + (8-1)d = 51 + 7 \times 2$
$$= 51 + 14 = ₹\ 65$$
Hence, the 8th instalment is ₹ 65.

EXAMPLE 20. The digit of a three-digit number are in AP and their sum is 21. The number obtained by reversing the digit is 396 less than the original number. Find the number.

Sol. Let the hundreds, tens and unit digits be $(a + d)$, a and $(a - d)$ respectively.

Then, $(a + d) + a + (a - d) = 21$
$$\Rightarrow \quad 3a = 21$$
$$\Rightarrow \quad a = 7$$
$\therefore$ Original three-digit number
$$= (7 + d) \times 100 + 7 \times 10 + (7 - d)$$
According to the given condition,
$$(7 + d) \times 100 + 7 \times 10 + (7 - d) - \{(7 - d) \times 100 + 7 \times 10 + (7 + d)\} = 396$$
$$\Rightarrow 777 + 99d - \{777 - 99d\} = 396$$
$$\Rightarrow \quad 198d = 396 \Rightarrow d = 2$$
$\therefore$ Original three-digit number
$$= (7 + 2) \times 100 + 7 \times 10 + (7 - 2)$$
$$= 900 + 70 + 5 = 975$$

EXAMPLE 21. The interior angles of a polygon are in AP. The smallest angle is 120° and the common difference is 5°. Find the number of sides of polygon.

Sol. Let n be the number of sides of the polygon. We know that, sum of interior angles of a polygon of n sides
$$= (2n - 4) \times 90 \quad \text{...(i)}$$
Given, $a = 120°$ and $d = 5°$, $n = n$

$\therefore$ Sum of interior angles of polygon of n sides
$$= \frac{n}{2}[2(120) + (n-1)5] \quad \text{...(ii)}$$
Now, from Eqs. (i) and (ii), we get
$$\frac{n}{2}[2(120) + (n-1)5] = (2n - 4)90$$
$$\Rightarrow \quad n(240 + 5n - 5) = 180(2n - 4)$$
$$\Rightarrow \quad n(235 + 5n) = 360n - 720$$
$$\Rightarrow \quad 5n^2 + 235n = 360n - 720$$
$$\Rightarrow \quad 5n^2 - 125n + 720 = 0$$
$$\Rightarrow \quad n^2 - 25n + 144 = 0 \quad \text{[divide both sides by 5]}$$
$$\Rightarrow \quad (n - 9)(n - 16) = 0$$
$$\therefore \quad n = 9 \text{ or } 16$$

But, if $n = 16$, last (greatest) angle of the polygon
$= 120 + (16 - 1)\,5 = 195°$.

No, interior angle of the polygon can be greater than or equal to 180°.

So, $n \neq 16$.

Therefore, $n = 9$

Hence, the number of sides of polygon is 9.

Arithmetic Mean (AM)

Let a and b be any two numbers and A be a number between them so that a, A, b are in AP, then such a number A is called an **arithmetic mean**.

Thus, a, A, b are in AP.

$$\therefore \quad A - a = b - A \quad \text{[common difference]}$$

$$\Rightarrow \quad 2A = a + b$$

$$\Rightarrow \quad A = \frac{a+b}{2}$$

Thus, Arithmetic mean (or average) between two given numbers is equal to half of their sum

i.e. $$AM = \frac{a+b}{2}$$

EXAMPLE 22. Find AM between 16 and 20.

Sol. $AM = \frac{a+b}{2} = \frac{16+20}{2} = \frac{36}{2} = 18$

Inserting n AM's between Two Positive Numbers

Let a and b be any two positive numbers and $A_1, A_2, A_3, \ldots, A_n$ be the n AM's between a and b.

Then, $a, A_1, A_2, \ldots, A_n, b$ are in AP and total number of terms $= n + 2$.

Here, b is $(n+2)$th term.

i.e. $$b = T_{n+2} = a + (n + 2 - 1)\,d$$

$$\Rightarrow \quad b = a + (n+1)\,d \Rightarrow d = \frac{b-a}{n+1}$$

Thus, the n arithmetic means between a and b are given below

$$A_1 = a + d = a + \frac{b-a}{n+1}$$

$$A_2 = a + 2d = a + \frac{2(b-a)}{n+1}$$

$$A_3 = a + 3d = a + \frac{3(b-a)}{n+1}$$

$$\cdots \quad \cdots \quad \cdots$$

$$\cdots \quad \cdots \quad \cdots$$

$$A_n = a + nd = a + \frac{n(b-a)}{n+1}$$

The sum of n AM's between a and b is equal to n times the single arithmetic mean between a and b

i.e. $$A_1 + A_2 + \ldots + A_n = n\left(\frac{a+b}{2}\right).$$

EXAMPLE 23. Insert 6 arithmetic means between 3 and 24.

Sol. Let A_1, A_2, A_3, A_4, A_5 and A_6 be six arithmetic means between 3 and 24.

Then, $3, A_1, A_2, A_3, A_4, A_5, A_6, 24$ are in AP and number of terms is 8.

$$\therefore \quad a = 3, \text{ and } T_8 = 24$$

$$\Rightarrow \quad a + (8-1)\,d = 24 \qquad [\because T_n = a + (n-1)\,d]$$

$$\Rightarrow \quad a + 7d = 24$$

$$\Rightarrow \quad 3 + 7d = 24 \Rightarrow 7d = 21 \Rightarrow d = 3$$

Now,
$$A_1 = a + d = 3 + 3 = 6$$
$$A_2 = a + 2d = 3 + 2(3) = 9$$
$$A_3 = a + 3d = 3 + 3(3) = 12$$
$$A_4 = a + 4d = 3 + 4(3) = 15$$
$$A_5 = a + 5d = 3 + 5(3) = 18$$
and
$$A_6 = a + 6d = 3 + 6(3) = 21$$

Hence, 6 arithmetic means between 3 and 24 are 6, 9, 12, 15, 18 and 21.

EXAMPLE 24. Prove that the sum of n arithmetic means between two numbers is n times the single AM between them.

Sol. Let $A_1, A_2, \ldots, A_n$ be n arithmetic means between a and b.

Then, $a, A_1, A_2, \ldots, A_n, b$ is an AP with common difference d given by $d = \frac{b-a}{n+1}$.

$$\text{Now, } A_1 + A_2 + \ldots + A_n = \frac{n}{2}(A_1 + A_n) \left[\because S_n = \frac{n}{2}(a+l)\right]$$

$$= \frac{n}{2}(a+b)$$

$$[\because a, A_1, A_2, \ldots, A_n, b \text{ is an AP, so } a + b = A_1 + A_n]$$

$$= n\left(\frac{a+b}{2}\right)$$

$$= n \times (\text{AM between } a \text{ and } b)$$

EXAMPLE 25. If $\frac{a^n + b^n}{a^{n-1} + b^{n-1}}$ is AM between a and b, then find the value of n.

Sol. We know that AM between a and b is $\frac{a+b}{2}$.

$$\therefore \quad \frac{a^n + b^n}{a^{n-1} + b^{n-1}} = \frac{a+b}{2}$$

$$\Rightarrow \quad 2a^n + 2b^n = a^n + ab^{n-1} + ba^{n-1} + b^n$$

$$\Rightarrow \quad 2a^n - a^n + 2b^n - b^n = ab^{n-1} + ba^{n-1}$$

$$\Rightarrow \quad a^n + b^n = ab^{n-1} + ba^{n-1}$$

$$\Rightarrow \quad a^n - ba^{n-1} = ab^{n-1} - b^n$$

$$\Rightarrow \quad a^{n-1}[a-b]=b^{n-1}[a-b]$$

$$\Rightarrow \quad a^{n-1}=b^{n-1} \quad [\because a \neq b]$$

$$\Rightarrow \quad \left(\frac{a}{b}\right)^{n-1}=1=\left(\frac{a}{b}\right)^{0} \quad [\because x^0=1]$$

On comparing the exponential powers, we get

$$n-1=0 \Rightarrow n=1$$

EXAMPLE 26. If x, y, z are in AP and A_1 is the AM of x and y and A_2 is the AM of y and z, then prove that the AM of A_1 and A_2 is y.

Sol. Given, x, y, z are in AP.

$$\therefore \quad 2y=x+z \quad \text{...(i)}$$

Now, A_1 is the AM of x and y.

$$\therefore \quad A_1=\frac{x+y}{2} \quad \text{...(ii)}$$

and A_2 is the AM of y and z.

$$\therefore \quad A_2=\frac{y+z}{2} \quad \text{...(iii)}$$

On adding Eqs. (ii) and (iii), we get

$$A_1+A_2=\frac{x+y}{2}+\frac{y+z}{2}=\frac{x+z+2y}{2}$$

$$\Rightarrow \quad A_1+A_2=\frac{2y+2y}{2} \quad [\because x+z=2y]$$

$$\Rightarrow \quad A_1+A_2=2y$$

$$\Rightarrow \quad y=\frac{A_1+A_2}{2}$$

$\therefore$ y is the AM of A_1 and A_2.

EXAMPLE 27. If m arithmetic means are inserted between 1 and 31 so that the ratio of the 7th and $(m-1)$th mean is 5 : 9. Find the value of m.

Sol. Let $A_1, A_2, A_3, \ldots, A_m$ be m arithmetic means between 1 and 31.

Then, $1, A_1, A_2, A_3, \ldots, A_m, 31$ are AP with $a=1$, $b=31$ and common difference d given by

$$d=\frac{31-1}{m+1}=\frac{30}{m+1} \quad \left[\because d=\frac{b-a}{n+1}\right]$$

Now, $A_7=a+7d=1+\dfrac{7\times 30}{m+1}$

$$=1+\frac{210}{m+1}$$

$$=\frac{m+211}{m+1}$$

and $A_{m-1}=a+(m-1)d$

$$=1+\frac{(m-1)(30)}{m+1}$$

$$=\frac{31m-29}{m+1}$$

Given, $\dfrac{A_7}{A_{m-1}}=\dfrac{5}{9}$

$$\therefore \quad \frac{m+211}{31m-29}=\frac{5}{9}$$

$$\Rightarrow \quad 9m+1899=155m-145$$

$$\Rightarrow \quad 146m=2044$$

$$\Rightarrow \quad m=\frac{2044}{146}=14$$

EXAMPLE 28. Suppose x and y are two real numbers such that the rth mean between x and $2y$ is equal to the rth mean between $2x$ and y when n arithmetic means are inserted between them in both the cases. Show that $\dfrac{n+1}{r}-\dfrac{y}{x}=1$.

Sol. Let $A_1, A_2, \ldots, A_n$ be n arithmetic means between x and $2y$.

Then, $x, A_1, A_2, \ldots, A_n, 2y$ are in AP with common difference d_1 given by $d_1=\dfrac{2y-x}{n+1}$.

$$\therefore \ r\text{th mean}=A_r=x+rd_1=x+r\left(\frac{2y-x}{n+1}\right)$$

$\therefore$ Let $A'_1, A'_2, \ldots, A'_n$ be n arithmetic means between $2x$ and y.

Then, $2x, A_1', A_2', \ldots, A_n', y$ are in AP with common difference d_2 given by $d_2=\left(\dfrac{y-2x}{n+1}\right)$.

$$\therefore \ r\text{th mean}, A_r'=2x+rd_2=2x+r\left(\frac{y-2x}{n+1}\right)$$

It is given that, $A_r=A_r'$

$$\Rightarrow \quad x+r\left(\frac{2y-x}{n+1}\right)=2x+r\left(\frac{y-2x}{n+1}\right)$$

$$\Rightarrow \quad (n+1)x+r(2y-x)=(n+1)2x+r(y-2x)$$

$$\Rightarrow \quad (n+1)x-ry=rx$$

$$\therefore \quad \frac{n+1}{r}-\frac{y}{x}=1$$

Topic Practice 3

1 Find the sum of indicated number of terms in the following AP.

(i) 1, 3, 5, 7, ..., 24 terms

(ii) $6, 5\frac{1}{3}, 4\frac{2}{3}$, ..., 10 terms

(iii) 0.7, 0.71, 0.72, 0.73, ..., 100 terms

(iv) −0.5, −1.0, −1.5, ..., 10 terms

(v) $\sqrt{2}, 2\sqrt{2}, 3\sqrt{2}, 4\sqrt{2}$, ..., 20 terms

2 Determine the sum of first 35 terms of an AP, if its second term is 2 and seventh term is 22.

3 Find the sum of odd integers from 1 to 2001.

4 Solve for x

(i) $1+6+11+16+...+x=148$

(ii) $25+22+19+16+...+x=115$

5 The sum of first 7 terms of an AP is 10 and that of next 7 terms is 17. Find the AP.

6 Find the sum of first 20 terms of an AP, in which 3rd terms is 7 and 7th term is two more than thrice of its 3rd term.

7 Find the sum of all natural numbers between 250 and 1000 which are exactly divisible by 3.

8 Find the sum of all two digit numbers which when divided by 4, yield 1 as remainder.

9 Find the sum of all natural numbers lying between 100 and 1000, which are multiples of 5.

10 The sum of the first five terms of an AP is 50. The sum of the last five terms is 250. If its first term is 5, then find the number of terms.

11 If the sum of n terms of an AP is $(pn+qn^2)$, where p and q are constants, find the common difference.

12 How many terms of the AP 18, 16, 14, 12, ... are needed to give the sum 78? Explain the double answer?

13 The sum of n terms of two arithmetic progressions are in the ratio $(7n-5):(5n+17)$. Show that their 6th terms are equal.

14 If in an AP, $S_n = qn^2$ and $S_m = qm^2$, where S_r denotes the sum of r terms of the AP, then find S_q.

15 Let S_n denote the sum of the first n terms of an AP. If $S_{2n} = 3S_n$, then find $S_{3n} : S_n$.

16 If the sum of first p terms of an AP is equal to the sum of first q terms, then find the sum of first $(p+q)$ terms.

17 Let the sum of n, $2n$, $3n$ terms of an AP be S_1, S_2 and S_3, respectively. Show that $S_3 = 3(S_2 - S_1)$.

18 Sum of the first p, q and r terms of an AP are a, b and c, respectively. Prove that

$$\frac{a}{p}(q-r)+\frac{b}{q}(r-p)+\frac{c}{r}(p-q)=0.$$

19 If the ratio of the sums of m and n terms of an AP be $m^2:n^2$, show that the ratio of mth and nth terms is $(2m-1):(2n-1)$.

20 If $S_1, S_2, S_3, \ldots, S_m$ are the sum of n terms of an AP's whose first terms are 1, 2, 3, ..., m and common difference are 1, 3, 5, ..., $(2m-1)$ respectively. Then, show that $S_1+S_2+S_3+\ldots+S_m=\frac{mn}{2}(mn+1)$.

21 The sum of interior angles of a triangle is 180°. Show that the sum of the interior angles of polygons with 3, 4, 5, 6, ... sides form an arithmetic progression. Find the sum of the interior angles for a 21 sided polygon.

22 A carpenter was hired to build 192 window frames. The first day he made five frames and each day, thereafter he made two more frames than he made the day before. How many days did it take him to finish the job?

23 The digits of a positive number having three digits are in AP and their sum is 15. The number obtained by reversing the digits is 594 less than the original number. Find the number.

24 A farmer buys a used tractor of ₹12000. He pays ₹6000 cash and agrees to pay the balance in annual instalment of ₹500 plus 12% interest on the unpaid amount. How much will the tractor cost him?

25 A man deposited ₹10000 in a bank at the rate of 5% simple interest to annually. Find the amount in 15th yr, since he deposited the amount and also calculate the amount after 20 yr.

26 Insert five numbers bewteen 8 and 26 such that the resulting sequence is an AP.

27 The sum of two numbers is $\frac{13}{6}$. An even number of AM's are being inserted between them. The sum of means inserted exceeds the number of means by 1. Find the number of AM's inserted.

28 Insert four AM's between $\frac{1}{2}$ and 3 and prove that $A_1 + A_2 + A_3 + A_4 = 7$.

29 If n arithmetic means are inserted between 20 and 80 such that the ratio of first mean to the last mean is 1 : 3, then find the value of n.

30 If A is the arithmetic mean between a and b, show that $\frac{A+2a}{A-b} + \frac{A+2b}{A-a} = 4$.

31 If A_1 and A_2 are two AM's between a and b, prove that
(i) $A_1 + A_2 = a + b$ (ii) $(2A_1 - A_2)(2A_2 - A_1) = ab$

Hints & Solutions

1. **Hint** Use formula $S_n = \frac{n}{2}(2a+(n-1)d)$

Ans. (i) 576 (ii) 30 (iii) 119.5 (iv) −27.5 (v) $210\sqrt{2}$

2. **Hint** $a+d = 2$ and $a+6d = 22$

$$S_{35} = \frac{35}{2}(2a+34d)$$

Ans. 2310

3. **Hint** $S = \frac{1001}{2}(1+2001)$ **Ans.** 1002001
4. Solve as Example 10. **Ans.** (i) 36 (ii) −2
5. Solve as Example 3. **Ans.** $1, 1\frac{1}{7}, 1\frac{2}{7}, \ldots$
6. Solve as Example 6. **Ans.** 740
7. Solve as Example 4. **Ans.** 156375
8. Solve as Example 4. **Ans.** 1210
9. Solve as Example 4. **Ans.** 98450
10. Solve as Example 12. **Ans.** $n = 48$
11. **Hint** $S_n = pn + qn^2$

$$a_1 = S_1 = p + q$$
$$a_2 = S_2 - S_1 = p + 3q$$
$$\therefore a_2 - a_1 = 2q$$

Ans. Common difference $= 2q$

12. Solve as Example 8. **Ans.** 6, 13
13. **Hint** The sum of n terms of an AP,

$$S_n = \frac{n}{2}[2a+(n-1)d]$$

$$\therefore \quad \frac{\frac{n}{2}[2a_1+(n-1)d_1]}{\frac{n}{2}[2a_2+(n-1)d_2]} = \frac{7n-5}{5n+17}$$

$$\Rightarrow \quad \frac{a_1+\left(\frac{n-1}{2}\right)d_1}{a_2+\left(\frac{n-1}{2}\right)d_2} = \frac{7n-5}{5n+17}$$

For 6th term, the general term will be $a+5d$.

$$\frac{a_1+5d_1}{a_2+5d_2} = \frac{7\times11-5}{5\times11+17} = 1$$

14. **Hint** First term is a and common difference is d.

$$\therefore S_n = \frac{n}{2}[2a+(n-1)d] = qn^2$$

$$2a+(n-1)d = 2qn \quad \ldots\text{(i)}$$

$$S_m = \frac{m}{2}[2a+(m-1)d] = qm^2$$

$$2a+(m-1)d = 2qm \quad \ldots\text{(ii)}$$

From Eqs. (i) and (ii), we get

$$d = 2q$$

Put the value of d in Eq. (ii).

Ans. q^3

15. **Hint** $S_n = \frac{n}{2}[2a+(n-1)d]$, where d is the common difference and a is the first term of an AP.

$$\because S_{2n} = 3S_n \Rightarrow \frac{2n}{2}[2a+(2n-1)d] = \frac{3n}{2}[2a+(n-1)d]$$

$$\Rightarrow \quad 2a = nd + d \quad \ldots\text{(i)}$$

$$\text{Now, } \frac{S_{3n}}{S_n} = \frac{\frac{3n}{2}[2a+(3n-1)d]}{\frac{n}{2}[2a+(n-1)d]} = \left[\frac{3nd+3d+9nd-3d}{nd+d+nd+d}\right]$$

[from Eq. (i)]

Ans. 6 : 1

16. **Hint** $S_p = S_q$

$$\frac{p}{2}[2a+(p-1)d] = \frac{q}{2}[2a+(q-1)d]$$ **Ans.** $S_{p+q} = 0$

17. **Hint** $S_1 = \frac{n}{2}[2a+(n-1)d] =$ Sum of n terms ...(i)

$S_2 = \frac{2n}{2}[2a+(2n-1)d] =$ Sum of $2n$ terms ...(ii)

and $S_3 = \frac{3n}{2}[2a+(3n-1)d] =$ Sum of $3n$ terms ...(iii)

Now, solve Eqs. (i), (ii) and (iii) to get the required result.

18. **Hint** $S_p = \frac{p}{2}[2A+(p-1)d] = a$ ...(i)

$S_q = \frac{q}{2}[2A+(q-1)d] = b$ ...(ii)

and $S_r = \frac{r}{2}[2A+(r-1)d] = c$ ...(iii)

Now, solve Eqs. (i), (ii) and (iii) to get the required result.

19. **Hint** Sum of m terms of an AP $= \frac{m}{2}[2a+(m-1)d]$

Sum of n terms of an AP $= \frac{n}{2}[2a+(n-1)d]$

$$\frac{S_m}{S_n} = \frac{m^2}{n^2}$$

After solving, we get $d = 2a$

Now, the ratio of the mth and nth terms is

$$\frac{a_m}{a_n} = \frac{a+(m-1)2a}{a+(n-1)2a} = \frac{2m-1}{2n-1}$$

20. **Hint** Here, $a = 1, 2, 3, \ldots, m$

$d = 1, 3, 5, \ldots, (2m-1)$

Since, $S_n = \frac{n}{2}[2a+(n-1)d]$

$\therefore S_1 + S_2 + S_3 + \ldots + S_m$

$$= n\cdot\frac{m(m+1)}{2} + \frac{n(n-1)}{2}\cdot\frac{m}{2}[1+2m-1] \quad \left[\because S = \frac{n}{2}(a+l)\right]$$

$$= \frac{1}{2}mn(mn+1)$$

21. **Hint** We know that, sum of interior angles of a polygon of side $n =$ $(2n-4)\times 90° =$ $(n-2)\times 180°$

The sequence will be 180°, 360°, 540°, 720°, 900°, ...

We have to find the sum of interior angles of a 21 sides polygon. It means, we have to find the 19th term of the above series.[since, 180° is the sum of three angle]

Ans. 3420

22. **Hint** We have, $S = 192$, $a = 5$, $d = 2$

$$S_n = \frac{n}{2}[2a+(n-1)d] = 192 \quad \textbf{Ans. } 12 \text{ days}$$

23. **Hint** Here, $a - d + a + a + d = 15 \Rightarrow 3a = 15 \Rightarrow a = 5$

Original number $= 100(a+d) + 10a + (a-d)$

$= 111a + 99d$ ...(i)

Number after reversing the digits

$= 100(a-d) + 10a + a + d$

$= 111a - 99d$ ...(ii)

According to the question,

$111a + 99d - 594 = 111a - 99d \Rightarrow d = 3$

Ans. 852

24. Total cost of the tractor = ₹ 12000

Cash amount paid = ₹ 6000

Balance amount = ₹ 12000 − ₹ 6000 = ₹ 6000

Interest of Ist intallment = ₹ $\frac{6000\times 12\times 1}{100}$ = ₹ 720

Interest of IInd intallment = ₹ $\frac{5500\times 12\times 1}{100}$ = ₹ 660

Amount of second installment = ₹ 500 + ₹ 660 = ₹ 1160

Interest of IIIrd installment = $\frac{5000\times 12\times 1}{100}$ = ₹ 600

Amount of IIIrd installment = 500 + 600 = ₹ 1100

The sequence of installment is 1220, 1160, 1100, ...

Here, $a = 1220$, $d = -60$ and $n = 12$

$\therefore S_n = \frac{n}{2}[2a+(n-1)d]$

$S_{12} = \frac{12}{2}[2\times 1220 + (12-1)\times(-60)]$ = ₹ 10680

25. **Hint** Interest on ₹ 10000 after 1 yr

$= \frac{10000\times 5\times 1}{100}$ = ₹500

Now, interest on ₹ 10000 after 2 yr = $\frac{10000\times 5\times 2}{100}$

= ₹1000

$\therefore$ Amout after 2 yr = 10000 + 1000 = ₹11000

Hence, the amout in the account of man in first, second and third years are ₹10000, 10500, 11000, ...

It is an AP, where $a = 10000$ and $d = 500$.

Ans. T_{15} = ₹17000 and T_{20} = ₹ 19500

26. Solve as Example 23. **Ans.** {11, 14, 17, 20, 23}

27. **Hint** Let a and b be two numbers and $A_1, A_2, \ldots, A_{2n}$ be $2n$ (even numbers) AMs.

Then, $a + b = \frac{13}{6}$

and $A_1 + A_2 + \ldots + A_{2n} = 2n\left(\frac{a+b}{2}\right) = \left(\frac{13}{6}\right)n$

According to the question,

$A_1 + A_2 + \ldots + A_{2n} = 2n + 1 \Rightarrow n = 6$

Ans. 12

28. Solve as Example 23.

Ans. $1, \frac{3}{2}, \frac{4}{2}, \frac{5}{2}$

29. Solve as Example 27. **Ans.** $n = 11$

30. Since, A is the AM between a and b,

$$A = \frac{a+b}{2}$$

$$\therefore \quad \frac{A+2a}{A-b} + \frac{A+2b}{A-a} = \frac{\frac{a+b}{2}+2a}{\frac{a+b}{2}-b} + \frac{\frac{a+b}{2}+2b}{\frac{a+b}{2}-a}$$

$$= \frac{5a+b}{a-b} + \frac{5b+a}{b-a}$$

$$= \frac{(5a+b)-(5b+a)}{(a-b)}$$

$$= \frac{4a-4b}{a-b} = 4$$

31. **Hint** Arithmetic mean $A_1 = A_2 = \frac{a+b}{2}$

(i) $A_1 + A_2 = a + b$

(ii) $(2A_1 - A_2)(2A_2 - A_1)$

$$= \left[2\left(\frac{a+b}{2}\right) - \frac{a+b}{2}\right]\left[2\frac{(a+b)}{2} - \frac{a+b}{2}\right] = ab$$

Geometric Progression (GP)

A sequence of non-zero numbers is said to be a **geometric progression**, if the ratio of each term, except the first one, by its preceding term is always constant.

In other words, we can say that a sequence $a_1, a_2, \ldots, a_n$ is called geometric progression (geometric sequence), if each term is non-zero and it follows the relation

$\frac{a_{k+1}}{a_k} = r$ (constant) for all $k \in N$.

The constant ratio is called **common ratio** of the GP and it is denoted by ***r***.

In a GP, we usually denote the first term by a, the ***n*th term** by T_n or a_n.

The sequence 3, 9, 27, 81, ... is a GP because $\frac{9}{3} = \frac{27}{9} = \frac{81}{27} = \ldots 3$, which is constant with first term 3 and common ratio 3.

General Term of a GP

If a is the first term of a GP and its common ratio is r, then general term or nth term,

$$T_n = ar^{n-1}$$

or $$l = ar^{n-1}$$

where, l is the last term.

*m*th Term of a Finite GP from the End

Let a be the first term and r be the common ratio of a GP having n terms.

Then, mth term from the end is $(n - m + 1)$th term from the beginning.

$\therefore$ ***m*th term from the end** $= ar^{n-m+1-1} = ar^{n-m}$,

where, $n > m$.

Also, mth term from the end $= l\left(\frac{1}{r}\right)^{n-1}$

where, l is the last term of the finite GP.

EXAMPLE 1. For what values of k, the numbers $-\frac{2}{7}, k, -\frac{7}{2}$ are in GP?

Sol. If $-\frac{2}{7}, k, -\frac{7}{2}$ are in GP.

Then, $\frac{a_2}{a_1} = \frac{a_3}{a_2}$ $\left[\because \text{common ratio } (r) = \frac{a_2}{a_1} = \frac{a_3}{a_2} = \frac{a_4}{a_3} = \ldots\right]$

$\therefore \quad \frac{k}{-2/7} = \frac{-7/2}{k}$

$\Rightarrow \quad \frac{7}{-2}k = \frac{-7}{2} \times \frac{1}{k}$

$\Rightarrow \quad 7k \times 2k = -7 \times (-2)$

$\Rightarrow \quad 14k^2 = 14$

$\Rightarrow \quad k^2 = 1 \Rightarrow k = \pm 1$

EXAMPLE 2. Find the 12th term of the sequence $-6, 18, -54, \ldots$.

Sol. Given sequence is $-6, 18, -54, \ldots$.

Clearly, the successive ratio of the terms is same.

So, the given sequence forms a GP with first term, $a = -6$ and common ratio, $r = \frac{18}{-6} = -3$.

$T_{12} = (-1)^{12} 6 \cdot 3^{12-1} = (1) \cdot 6 \cdot 3^{11}$ $[\because T_n = ar^{n-1}]$

$= 2 \cdot 3 \cdot 3^{11} = 2 \cdot 3^{12}$

Hence, the nth term of given GP is $(-1)^n 6 \cdot 3^{n-1}$ and 12th term is $2 \cdot 3^{12}$.

EXAMPLE 3. Which term of the GP 5, 10, 20, 40, ... is 5120?

Sol. Given GP is 5, 10, 20, 40, ...

Here, $a = 5$ and $r = \frac{10}{5} = 2$

Let nth term of given GP = 5120 i.e. $T_n = 5120$

Now, $T_n = ar^{n-1} = 5120$

$\Rightarrow \quad 5(2)^{n-1} = 5120$ $[\because a = 5, r = 2]$

$\Rightarrow \quad 2^{n-1} = \frac{5120}{5} = 1024$

$\Rightarrow \quad 2^{n-1} = 1024$

$\Rightarrow \quad 2^{n-1} = 2^{10}$

On equating the powers, we get

$n - 1 = 10 \Rightarrow n = 10 + 1 = 11$

Hence, 11th term of given GP is 5120.

EXAMPLE 4. If the 4th and 9th term of a GP are 54 and 13122 respectively, then find the GP.

Sol. Let a be the first term and r be the common ratio of GP.

Given, 4th term, $T_4 = 54$

$\Rightarrow \quad ar^{4-1} = 54$

$\Rightarrow \quad ar^3 = 54$ ...(i)

and 9th term, $T_9 = 13122$

$\Rightarrow \quad ar^{9-1} = 13122$

$\Rightarrow \quad ar^8 = 13122$ ...(ii)

On dividing Eq. (ii) by Eq. (i), we get

$$\frac{ar^8}{ar^3} = \frac{13122}{54}$$

$$\Rightarrow \quad r^5 = 243$$

$$\Rightarrow \quad r^5 = (3)^5$$

$$\therefore \quad r = 3$$

On putting the value of r in Eq. (i), we get

$$a(3)^3 = 54$$

$$\Rightarrow \quad 27a = 54$$

$$\Rightarrow \quad a = \frac{54}{27} = 2$$

$\therefore$ Required GP is $a, ar, ar^2, ar^3, \ldots$ i.e. 2, 6, 18, 54, ...

EXAMPLE 5. The first term of a GP is 1. The sum of the third and fifth terms is 90. Find the common ratio of the GP.

Sol. Let r be the common ratio of the GP.

It is given that first term of GP is 1.

$\therefore$ Third term of GP, i.e. $a_3 = ar^2 = r^2$

and fifth term of GP, i.e. $a_5 = ar^4 = r^4$

Given, $\quad a_3 + a_5 = 90$

$$\therefore \quad r^2 + r^4 = 90$$

$$\Rightarrow \quad r^4 + r^2 - 90 = 0$$

$$\Rightarrow \quad r^4 + 10r^2 - 9r^2 - 90 = 0$$

$$\Rightarrow \quad (r^2 + 10)(r^2 - 9) = 0$$

$$\Rightarrow \quad r^2 = 9,\ r^2 \neq -10$$

$$\Rightarrow \quad r = \pm 3$$

Hence, the common ratio of the given GP is –3 or 3.

EXAMPLE 6. Find the 8th term from the end of the sequence 3, 6, 12, ..., 25th term.

Sol. We know that if a sequence has n terms, then mth term from end is equal to $(n - m + 1)$th term from the beginning.

Here, $a = 3$, $r = \frac{6}{3} = 2$, $m = 8$ and $n = 25$.

Now, 8th term from the end of sequence is equal to the $(25 - 8 + 1)$. i.e. 18th term from the beginning.

$$\because \quad T_n = ar^{n-1}$$

$$\therefore \quad T_{18} = ar^{18-1} = 3(2)^{18-1} \qquad [\because a = 3, r = 2]$$

$$= 3(2)^{17} = 3 \times 131072 = 393216$$

Hence, the 8th term from the end is 393216.

EXAMPLE 7. Find four numbers forming a GP in which the third term is greater than the first term by 9 and the second term is greater than 4th by 18.

Sol. Let the GP is $a, ar, ar^2, ar^3, \ldots$

Given, third term = first term +9

$$\Rightarrow \quad T_3 = a + 9$$

$$\Rightarrow \quad ar^2 = a + 9$$

$$\Rightarrow \quad ar^2 - a = 9 \qquad \ldots(i)$$

Again, second term = Fourth term +18

$$T_2 = T_4 + 18$$

$$\Rightarrow \quad ar = ar^3 + 18$$

$$\Rightarrow \quad ar - ar^3 = 18 \qquad \ldots(ii)$$

On dividing Eq. (i) by Eq. (ii), we get

$$\frac{ar^2 - a}{ar - ar^3} = \frac{9}{18}$$

$$\Rightarrow \quad \frac{a(r^2 - 1)}{ar(1 - r^2)} = \frac{1}{2}$$

$$\Rightarrow \quad \frac{-1\,(1 - r^2)}{r\,(1 - r^2)} = \frac{1}{2}$$

$$\Rightarrow \quad -\frac{1}{r} = \frac{1}{2}$$

$$\Rightarrow \quad r = -2$$

On putting $r = -2$ in Eq. (ii)

$$a(-2) - a(-2)^3 = 18$$

$$\Rightarrow \quad -2a + 8a = 18$$

$$\Rightarrow \quad 6a = 18$$

$$\Rightarrow \quad a = 3$$

$\therefore$ GP is $3, 3(-2), 3(-2)^2, 3(-2)^3, \ldots$

i.e. $\quad 3, -6, 12, -24, \ldots$

EXAMPLE 8. If the pth and qth terms of a GP are q and p respectively, then show that its $(p+q)$th term is $\left(\frac{q^p}{p^q}\right)^{\frac{1}{p-q}}$.

Sol. Let the first term and common ratio of GP be a and r, respectively.

According to the question, pth term = q

$$\Rightarrow \quad a \cdot r^{p-1} = q \qquad \ldots(i)$$

and $\quad q$th term = p

$$\Rightarrow \quad ar^{q-1} = p \qquad \ldots(ii)$$

On dividing Eq. (i) by Eq. (ii), we get

$$\frac{ar^{p-1}}{ar^{q-1}} = \frac{q}{p} \Rightarrow r^{p-1-q+1} = \frac{q}{p}$$

$$\Rightarrow \quad r^{p-q} = \frac{q}{p} \Rightarrow r = \left(\frac{q}{p}\right)^{\frac{1}{p-q}}$$

On substituting the value of r in Eq. (i), we get

$$a\left(\frac{q}{p}\right)^{\frac{p-1}{p-q}} = q \Rightarrow a = \frac{q}{\left(\frac{q}{p}\right)^{\frac{p-1}{p-q}}} = q \cdot \left(\frac{p}{q}\right)^{\frac{p-1}{p-q}}$$

$\therefore$ $(p+q)$th term, $T_{p+q} = a \cdot r^{p+q-1}$

$$= q \cdot \left(\frac{p}{q}\right)^{\frac{p-1}{p-q}} \cdot (r)^{p+q-1}$$

$$= q \cdot \left(\frac{p}{q}\right)^{\frac{p-1}{p-q}} \times \left(\frac{q}{p}\right)^{\frac{p+q-1}{p-q}}$$

$$= \frac{q^{1-\frac{p-1}{p-q}+\frac{p+q-1}{p-q}}}{p^{\frac{p+q-1}{p-q}-\frac{p-1}{p-q}}} = \frac{q^{\frac{p-q-p+1+p+q-1}{p-q}}}{p^{\frac{p+q-1-p+1}{p-q}}}$$

$$= \frac{q^{\frac{p}{p-q}}}{p^{\frac{q}{p-q}}} = \left(\frac{q^p}{p^q}\right)^{\frac{1}{p-q}}$$

EXAMPLE 9. If a, b, c are respectively the pth, qth and rth terms of a GP, show that $(q-r)\log a + (r-p)\log b + (p-q)\log c = 0$.

Sol. Let A be the first term and R the common ratio of the given GP.

Then, $a = p$th term $\Rightarrow a = AR^{p-1}$

$\Rightarrow$ $\log a = \log A + (p-1)\log R$ ...(i)

$b = q$th term $\Rightarrow b = AR^{q-1}$

$\Rightarrow$ $\log b = \log A + (q-1)\log R$ ...(ii)

$c = r$th term $\Rightarrow c = AR^{r-1}$

$\Rightarrow$ $\log c = \log A + (r-1)\log R$ ...(iii)

Now, LHS $= (q-r)\log a + (r-p)\log b + (p-q)\log c$

On substituting the values of log a, log b and log c, we get

LHS $= (q-r)\{\log A + (p-1)\log R\}$
$+ (r-p)\{\log A + (q-1)\log R\}$
$+ (p-q)\{\log A + (r-1)\log R\}$
$= \log A\{(q-r)+(r-p)+(p-q)\}$
$+ \log R\{(p-1)(q-r)+(q-1)(r-p)+(r-1)(p-q)\}$
$= (\log A)0 + \{p(q-r)+q(r-p)$
$+ r(p-q)-(q-r)-(r-p)-(p-q)\}\log R$
$= (\log A)0 + (\log R)0 = 0 =$ RHS

EXAMPLE 10. The $(m+n)$th and $(m-n)$th terms of a GP are p and q respectively. Show that the mth and nth terms are $\sqrt{pq}$ and $p\left(\frac{q}{p}\right)^{m/2n}$, respectively.

Sol. Let a be the first term and r be the common ratio. then,

$$a_{m+n} = p \text{ and } a_{m-n} = q$$

$\Rightarrow$ $ar^{m+n-1} = p$ and $ar^{m-n-1} = q$

$\Rightarrow$ $\frac{ar^{m+n-1}}{ar^{m-n-1}} = \frac{p}{q} \Rightarrow r^{2n} = \frac{p}{q}$

$\Rightarrow$ $r = \left(\frac{p}{q}\right)^{1/2n} \Rightarrow \frac{1}{r} = \left(\frac{q}{p}\right)^{1/2n}$

Now, $a_m = ar^{m-1}$

$\Rightarrow$ $a_m = ar^{(m+n-1)}\left(\frac{1}{r}\right)^n$

$\Rightarrow$ $a_m = a_{m+n}\left(\frac{1}{r}\right)^n$ $[\because a_{m+n} = ar^{m+n-1}]$

$\Rightarrow$ $a_m = p\left(\frac{q}{p}\right)^{n/2n}$ $\left[\because a_{m+n} = p \text{ and } \frac{1}{r} = \left(\frac{q}{p}\right)^{1/2n}\right]$

$\Rightarrow$ $a_m = p\left(\frac{q}{p}\right)^{1/2} = \sqrt{pq}$

and $a_n = ar^{n-1}$

$\Rightarrow$ $a_n = ar^{m+n-1}\left(\frac{1}{r}\right)^m$

$= a_{m+n}\left(\frac{1}{r}\right)^m$ $[\because a_{m+n} = ar^{m+n-1}]$

$\therefore$ $a_n = p\left(\frac{q}{p}\right)^{m/2n}$ $\left[\because a_{m+n} = p \text{ and } \frac{1}{r} = \left(\frac{q}{p}\right)^{1/2n}\right]$

EXAMPLE 11. If a and b are the roots of $x^2 - 3x + p = 0$ and c and d are roots of $x^2 - 12x + q = 0$, where a, b, c, d form a GP, prove that $(q+p):(q-p) = 17:15$.

Sol. Given, a and b are roots of $x^2 - 3x + p = 0$.

$\therefore$ Sum of roots, $a + b = -\frac{(-3)}{1} = 3$

$\left[\because \text{Sum of roots} = -\frac{\text{Coefficient of } x}{\text{Coefficient of } x^2}\right]$

$\Rightarrow$ $a + b = 3$ ...(i)

and product of roots, $ab = p$ ...(ii)

Again, given that c and d are roots of $x^2 - 12x + q = 0$

$\therefore$ Sum of roots, $c + d = -\frac{(-12)}{1} = 12$

$\Rightarrow$ $c + d = 12$ ...(iii)

and product of roots, $cd = q$ ...(iv)

$\left[\because \text{Product of roots} = \frac{\text{Constant term}}{\text{Coefficient of } x^2}\right]$

Again, it is given that a, b, c, d are in GP.

$\Rightarrow$ $b = ar,\ c = ar^2,\ d = ar^3$

On putting these values in Eqs. (i) and (iii), then dividing Eq. (i) by Eq. (iii), we get

$$\frac{a + ar}{ar^2 + ar^3} = \frac{3}{12} \Rightarrow \frac{a(1+r)}{ar^2(1+r)} = \frac{1}{4}$$

$\Rightarrow$ $\frac{1}{r^2} = \frac{1}{4}$

$\Rightarrow$ $r^2 = 4 \Rightarrow r = \pm 2$

When $r = 2$, then from Eq. (i), we get

$$a + ar = 3 \Rightarrow a + 2a = 3$$

$$\Rightarrow 3a = 3 \Rightarrow a = 1$$

So, GP is $a = 1,\ b = ar = 1 \times 2 = 2$

$$c = ar^2 = 1 \times 2^2 = 4,$$

$$d = ar^3 = 1 \times 2^3 = 8$$

From Eq. (ii), $p = ab = 1 \times 2 = 2$

From Eq. (iv), $q = cd = 4 \times 8 = 32$

Now, $\dfrac{q+p}{q-p} = \dfrac{32+2}{32-2} = \dfrac{34}{30} = \dfrac{17}{15}$

Hence, $(q+p):(q-p) = 17:15$

When $r = -2$, then from Eq. (i), $a + ar = 3$

$$\Rightarrow a - 2a = 3$$

$$\Rightarrow a = -3$$

So, GP is $a = -3,\ b = ar = (-3)(-2) = 6$

$$c = ar^2 = (-3)(-2)^2 = -12$$

$$d = ar^3 = (-3)(-2)^3 = 24$$

From Eq. (ii), $p = ab = (-3)(+6) = -18$

From Eq. (iv), $q = cd = (-12)(24) = -288$

$$\therefore \frac{q+p}{q-p} = \frac{-288-18}{-288+18}$$

$$= \frac{-306}{-270} = \frac{17}{15}$$

Hence, $(q+p):(q-p) = 17:15$

Selection of Terms in GP

Sometimes we have to select certain number of terms in GP. The convenient method of selecting terms is given below

Number of terms	Terms	Common ratio
3	$\frac{a}{r}, a, ar$	r
4	$\frac{a}{r^3}, \frac{a}{r}, ar, ar^3$	r^2
5	$\frac{a}{r^2}, \frac{a}{r}, a, ar, ar^2$	r

It is clear from the above table that

- If number of terms is odd, then the middle term is a and common difference is r.
- If number of terms is even, then the middle terms are $\frac{a}{r}$, ar and the common ratio is r^2.
- If the terms of the GP are not given, then the terms are chosen as $a, ar, ar^2, ar^3, \dots$.

EXAMPLE 12. Find three numbers in GP, whose sum is 65 and whose product is 3375.

Sol. Let the three numbers in GP be $\frac{a}{r}, a, ar$.

It is given that sum and product of these numbers are 65 and 3375 respectively.

$$\therefore \frac{a}{r} + a + ar = 65 \text{ and } \frac{a}{r} \cdot a \cdot ar = 3375$$

$$\Rightarrow a(1 + r + r^2) = 65r \text{ and } a^3 = 3375$$

$$\Rightarrow a = 15$$

Now, $15(1 + r + r^2) = 65r$

$$\Rightarrow 3(1 + r + r^2) = 13r$$

$$\Rightarrow 3r^2 - 10r + 3 = 0$$

$$\Rightarrow 3r^2 - 9r - r + 3 = 0$$

$$\Rightarrow (3r - 1)(r - 3) = 0 \Rightarrow r = \frac{1}{3}, 3$$

Putting the value of a and r in $\frac{a}{r}, a, ar$, we get

45, 15, 5 or 5, 15, 45

EXAMPLE 13. Find four numbers in GP, whose sum is 85 and product is 4096.

Sol. Let the four numbers in GP be

$$\frac{a}{r^3}, \frac{a}{r}, ar, ar^3 \quad \text{...(i)}$$

Product of four numbers = 4096 [given]

$$\Rightarrow \left(\frac{a}{r^3}\right)\left(\frac{a}{r}\right)(ar)(ar^3) = 4096$$

$$\Rightarrow a^4 = 4096$$

$$\Rightarrow a^4 = 8^4$$

On comparing the base of the power 4, we get

$$a = 8$$

and sum of four numbers = 85 [given]

$$\Rightarrow \frac{a}{r^3} + \frac{a}{r} + ar + ar^3 = 85$$

$$\Rightarrow a\left[\frac{1}{r^3} + \frac{1}{r} + r + r^3\right] = 85$$

$$\Rightarrow 8\left[r^3 + \frac{1}{r^3}\right] + 8\left[r + \frac{1}{r}\right] = 85 \quad [\because a = 8]$$

$$\Rightarrow 8\left[\left(r + \frac{1}{r}\right)^3 - 3\left(r + \frac{1}{r}\right)\right] + 8\left(r + \frac{1}{r}\right) = 85$$

$$[\because a^3 + b^3 = (a+b)^3 - 3(a+b)]$$

$$\Rightarrow 8\left(r + \frac{1}{r}\right)^3 - 16\left(r + \frac{1}{r}\right) - 85 = 0 \quad \text{...(ii)}$$

On putting $\left(r + \frac{1}{r}\right) = x$ in Eq. (ii), we get

$$8x^3 - 16x - 85 = 0$$

$\Rightarrow \quad (2x-5)(4x^2+10x+17)=0$

$\Rightarrow \quad 2x-5=0$

[$\because 4x^2+10x+17=0$ has imaginary roots]

$\Rightarrow \quad x=\frac{5}{2}$

$\Rightarrow \quad r+\frac{1}{r}=\frac{5}{2} \quad \left[\text{put } x=r+\frac{1}{r}\right]$

$\Rightarrow \quad 2r^2-5r+2=0$

$\Rightarrow \quad (r-2)(2r-1)=0$

$\Rightarrow \quad r=2 \text{ or } r=\frac{1}{2}$

On putting $a=8$ and $r=2$ or $r=\frac{1}{2}$ in Eq. (i), we obtain four numbers as

$$\frac{8}{2^3}, \frac{8}{2}, 8\times 2, 8\times 2^3 \text{ or } \frac{8}{(1/2)^3}, \frac{8}{(1/2)}, 8\times\frac{1}{2}, 8\times\left(\frac{1}{2}\right)^3$$

i.e. 1, 4, 16, 64 or 64, 16, 4, 1.

EXAMPLE 14. If a, b, c are in GP and $a^{\frac{1}{x}}=b^{\frac{1}{y}}=c^{\frac{1}{z}}$, then prove that x, y, z are in AP.

Sol. Given, $a^{\frac{1}{x}}=b^{\frac{1}{y}}=c^{\frac{1}{z}}=k$

$\therefore \quad a=k^x, b=k^y$ and $c=k^z$

Now, a, b, c are in GP.

$\therefore \quad b^2=ac$

$\Rightarrow \quad (k^y)^2=(k^x)(k^z)$

$\Rightarrow \quad k^{2y}=k^{x+z}$

$\Rightarrow \quad 2y=x+z$

$\therefore$ x, y, z are in AP.

EXAMPLE 15. If a, b, c and d are in GP, then show that $(a^2+b^2+c^2)(b^2+c^2+d^2)=(ab+bc+cd)^2$. [NCERT]

Sol. Given, a, b, c, d are in GP.

$\therefore \quad \frac{b}{a}=\frac{c}{b}=\frac{d}{c}=r$ (say)

$\Rightarrow \quad b=ar, c=br, d=cr$

$\Rightarrow \quad b=ar, c=(ar)r, d=(br)r$

$\Rightarrow \quad b=ar, c=ar^2, d=br^2$

$\Rightarrow \quad b=ar, c=ar^2, d=(ar)r^2=ar^3$ ...(i)

Now, we have to prove that

$(a^2+b^2+c^2)(b^2+c^2+d^2)=(ab+bc+cd)^2$

$$\begin{aligned}\text{LHS} &= (a^2+b^2+c^2)(b^2+c^2+d^2)\\ &= (a^2+a^2r^2+a^2r^4)(a^2r^2+a^2r^4+a^2r^6)\\ &= a^2(1+r^2+r^4)a^2r^2(1+r^2+r^4)\\ &= a^4r^2(1+r^2+r^4)^2=[a^2r(1+r^2+r^4)]^2\\ &= [a^2r+a^2r^3+a^2r^5]^2\\ &= [a\cdot ar+ar\cdot ar^2+ar^2\cdot ar^3]^2\\ &= [ab+bc+cd]^2 \quad \text{[from Eq. (i)]}\\ &= \text{RHS}\end{aligned}$$

Topic Practice 4

1 Show that the following progressions is a GP. Also, find the common ratio in each case.

(i) $4, -2, 1, -1/2, \ldots$ (ii) $a, \frac{3a^2}{4}, \frac{9a^3}{16}, \ldots$

2 For what value of x are the numbers $(x+9), (x-6)$ and 4 are is GP?

3 Find the following.

(i) 11th term of the GP 3, 6, 12, 24, ...

(ii) 10th term of the GP $12, 4, \frac{4}{3}, \frac{4}{9}, \ldots$

(iii) 17th term of the GP $2, 2\sqrt{2}, 4, 8\sqrt{2}, \ldots$

(iv) 8th term of the GP 0.3, 0.06, 0.012, ...

(v) 12th term of the GP $\frac{1}{a^3x^3}, ax, a^5x^5, \ldots$

4 Which term of the following sequences

(i) $\sqrt{3}, 3, 3\sqrt{3}, \ldots$ is 729 ?

(ii) $\frac{1}{3}, \frac{1}{9}, \frac{1}{27}, \ldots$ is $\frac{1}{19683}$?

5 Find 12th term of a GP, whose 8th term is 192 and common ratio is 2.

6 Find the 6th term from the end of the GP $8, 4, 2, \ldots, \frac{1}{1024}$.

7 Find the geometric series whose 5th and 8th terms are 80 and 640, respectively.

8 The first term of a GP is –3 and the square of the second term is equal to its 4th term. Find its 7th term.

9 The sum of first three terms of a GP is $\frac{39}{10}$ and their produt is 1. Find the common ratio and the terms.

10 The sum of three numbers in GP is 21 and the sum of their squares is 189. Find the numbers.

11 The product of first three terms of a GP is 216. If 3 is added to its second and third term, the three terms become in AP. Find the GP.

12 The sum of three numbers in GP is 35. If we subtract 2, 5, 13 from these number in that order. We obtain an arithmetic progression, find the number.

13 If a, b, c, d are in GP, prove that

(i) $(a^2-b^2), (b^2-c^2), (c^2-d^2)$, are also in GP.

(ii) $\frac{1}{a^2+b^2}, \frac{1}{b^2+c^2}, \frac{1}{c^2+d^2}$ are in GP.

(iii) $(a+b+c+d)^2=(a+b)^2+2(b+c)^2+(c+d)^2$

(iv) $(b-c)^2+(c-a)^2+(d-b)^2=(a-d)^2$

14 If a, b, c are in AP and a, x, b and b, y, c are in GP, then show that x^2, b^2, y^2 are in AP.

15 If the pth, qth and rth terms of a GP are a, b and c respectively, then prove that $a^{q-r}\, b^{r-p}\, c^{p-q}=1$.

16 If the first and nth terms of a GP are a and b respectively and P is the product of n terms, then prove that $p^2=(ab)^n$.

Hints & Solutions

1. **Hint** Use $\frac{a_{k+1}}{a_k}=r$

Ans. (i) $-\frac{1}{2}$ (ii) $\frac{3a}{4}$

2. Solve as Example 1.

Ans. 0 or 16

3. Solve as Example 2.

Ans. (i) 3072 (ii) $\frac{4}{6561}$ (iii) 512

(iv) $(0.3)(0.2)^7$ (v) $(ax)^{41}$

4. (i) **Hint** Here, $a=\sqrt{3}, r=\frac{3}{\sqrt{3}}=\sqrt{3}, T_n=729$

Now, apply the formula $T_n=ar^{n-1}$

Ans. 12

(ii) **Hint** Here, $a=\frac{1}{3}, r=\frac{1/9}{1/3}=\frac{3}{9}=\frac{1}{3}$ and $T_n=\frac{1}{19683}$

Now, apply the formula, $T_n=ar^{n-1}$.

Ans. 9

5. **Hint** Here, $T_8=192$ and $r=2$

$\because \quad T_8=ar^{8-1}=ar^7;$

$\therefore \quad a=\frac{3}{2}$

Now, $\quad T_{12}=3072$

6. Solve as Example 6.

Ans. $\frac{1}{32}$

7. Solve as Example 4. **Ans.** $5+10+20+40+\ldots$

8. **Hint** $a=-3,\ (ar)^2=ar^3 \Rightarrow a=r$

$\therefore \quad a_7=ar^6=(-3)^7=-2187$

9. **Hint** Here, $\frac{a}{r}+a+ar=\frac{39}{10}$ ...(i)

and $\left(\frac{a}{r}\right)\times(a)\times(ar)=1$

$\Rightarrow \quad a^3=1$

$\Rightarrow \quad a=1$

On putting the value of $a=1$ in Eq. (i) we get

$$\frac{1}{r}+1+r=\frac{39}{10}$$

$$\Rightarrow \quad \frac{1+r+r^2}{r}=\frac{39}{10}$$

$$\Rightarrow \quad 10r^2-29r+10=0$$

$$\Rightarrow \quad (5r-2)(2r-5)=0$$

$$\therefore \quad r=\frac{2}{5} \text{ or } r=\frac{5}{2}$$

When $a=1$ and $r=\frac{2}{5}$, then the numbers are $\frac{5}{2}, 1, \frac{2}{5}$

When $a=1$ and $r=\frac{5}{2}$, then the numbers are $\frac{2}{5}, 1, \frac{5}{2}$.

10. **Hint** $a+ar+ar^2=21 \Rightarrow a^2+(ar)^2+(ar^2)^2=189$

Ans. (3, 6, 12) or (12, 6, 3)

11. **Hint** Product = 216

$\frac{a}{r}\times a\cdot ar=216 \Rightarrow a=6$

and $\frac{a}{r},\ a+3,\ ar+3$ are in AP.

$$\Rightarrow \quad 2(a+3)=\frac{a}{r}+ar+3$$

$$\Rightarrow \quad 2(6+3)=\frac{6}{r}+6r+3$$

$$\Rightarrow \quad 2r^2-5r+2=0$$

$$\Rightarrow \quad r=2, \text{ or } \frac{1}{2}$$

Ans. (3, 6, 12) or (12, 6, 3)

12. **Hint** Here $a+ar+ar^2=35$ ...(i)

and $\quad 2(ar-5)=a-2+ar^2-13$ ...(ii)

On solving Eqs. (i) and (ii), we get

When $a=5, r=2$

and $\quad a=20, r=\frac{1}{2}$

Ans. 5, 10, 20 or 20, 10, 5.

13. (i) **Hint** $\frac{b}{a}=\frac{c}{b}=\frac{d}{c}=r$

$\Rightarrow \quad b=ar,\ c=br=ar^2,\ d=cr=ar^3$

Now, $a^2-b^2=a^2-a^2r^2=a^2(1-r^2)$

$b^2-c^2=a^2r^2-a^2r^4=a^2r^2(1-r^2)$

and $c^2-d^2=a^2r^4-a^2r^6=a^2r^4(1-r^2)$

Therefore, $\frac{b^2-c^2}{a^2-b^2}=\frac{c^2-d^2}{b^2-c^2}=r^2$

(ii) Similar as part (i).

(iii) Similar as part (i).

(iv) Similar as part (i).

14. Hint $2b=a+c,\ x^2=ab,\ y^2=bc$

Now, $x^2+y^2=b(a+c)\Rightarrow x^2+y^2=2b^2$

$\therefore\ x^2, b^2, y^2$ are in AP.

15. Hint Given, $T_p=a\Rightarrow AR^{p-1}=a$ ...(i)

$T_q=b\Rightarrow Ar^{q-1}=b$ ...(ii)

and $T_r=c\Rightarrow AR^{r-1}=c$ ...(iii)

LHS $=a^{q-r}b^{r-p}b^{p-q}$

16. Hint Let the GP be $A, AR, AR^2, AR^3\ldots$

Given, first term, $A=a$ ...(i)

and nth term,

$AR^{n-1}=b$ ...(ii)

Now, $p=$ Product of n terms

$\Rightarrow \quad p=A\times AR^1\times AR^2\times AR^3\times\ldots\times n$ terms

$\Rightarrow \quad p=A^{1+1+1+\ldots+n\text{ terms}}\times R^{1+2+3+\ldots+(n-1)}$

$\Rightarrow \quad p=A^nR^{\frac{n(n-1)}{2}}$

$\Rightarrow \quad p^2=A^nA^nR^{n(n-1)}=A^n(AR^{n-1})^n$

$\Rightarrow \quad p^2=a^nb^n$ [using Eqs. (i) and (ii)]

Sum of *n* Terms of a GP

If a and r are the first term and common ratio of a GP respectively, then sum of n terms of this GP is given by

$$S_n=\frac{a(1-r^n)}{1-r},\text{ where } r<1$$

or $$S_n=\frac{a(r^n-1)}{r-1},\text{ where } r>1\ (r\neq1)$$

Suppose a GP contains n terms with first term $=a$, common ratio $=r$ and last term $=l$.

The sum of GP

$$S_n=\frac{a-lr}{1-r},\text{ where } r<1$$

or $$S_n=\frac{lr-a}{r-1},\text{ where } r>1$$

Sum of an Infinite GP

If a is the first term and r is the common ratio of a GP such that $|r|<1$, then sum of an infinite GP is given by

$$S=\frac{a}{1-r}$$

EXAMPLE 1. Find the sum of the following sequences

(i) $\frac{1}{2},\frac{3}{2},\frac{9}{2},\ldots$ upto 10 terms.

(ii) $2,-\frac{1}{2},\frac{1}{8},\ldots,$ upto 12 terms.

Sol. (i) We have, sequence $\frac{1}{2},\frac{3}{2},\frac{9}{2},\ldots$

Clearly, the successive ratio of the terms is same. So, the above sequence forms a GP, with first term, $a=\frac{1}{2}$ and common ratio, $r=\frac{3}{2}\div\frac{1}{2}=3$.

$$\therefore \quad S_{10}=\frac{\frac{1}{2}[3^{10}-1]}{3-1}\quad\left[\because S_n=\frac{a(r^n-1)}{r-1}\text{ as } r>1\right]$$

$$=\frac{1}{2}\frac{(3^{10}-1)}{2}$$

$$=\frac{1}{4}[3^{10}-1]=14762$$

(ii) We have, sequence $2,-\frac{1}{2},\frac{1}{8},\ldots$

Clearly, the successive ratio of the terms is same. So, the above sequence forms a GP with first term, $a=2$ and common ratio, $r=-\frac{1}{2}\div2=\frac{-1}{4}$.

$$\therefore \quad S_{12}=\frac{2\left[1-\left(\frac{-1}{4}\right)^{12}\right]}{1-\left(\frac{-1}{4}\right)}\quad\left[\because S_n=\frac{a(1-r^n)}{1-r}\text{ as } r<1\right]$$

$$=\frac{2\left[1-\frac{1}{(4)^{12}}\right]}{1+\frac{1}{4}}=\frac{2\left[1-\left(\frac{1}{4}\right)^{12}\right]}{\left(\frac{5}{4}\right)}=\frac{8}{5}\left[1-\left(\frac{1}{4}\right)^{12}\right]$$

EXAMPLE 2. Find the sum of the series
$$2 + 6 + 18 + 54 + \ldots + 4374.$$

Sol. Given series is $2+6+18+54+\ldots+4374$.

Clearly, the successive ratio of the terms is same. So, the above series forms a GP with first term, $a = 2$, common ratio, $r = \frac{6}{2} = 3 > 1$ and last term, $l = 4374$.

$$\therefore \text{Required sum} = \frac{(lr-a)}{(r-1)} = \frac{(4374\times 3-2)}{(3-1)}$$
$$= \frac{13120}{2} = 6560$$

Hence, the sum of the given series is 6560.

EXAMPLE 3. How many terms of GP $3, \frac{3}{2}, \frac{3}{4}, \ldots$ are needed to give the sum $\frac{3069}{512}$?

Sol. Given, GP is $3, \frac{3}{2}, \frac{3}{4}, \ldots$

Here, $a = 3$ and $r = \frac{3}{2} \div 3 = \frac{1}{2}$

Let n be the number of terms needed.

Then, $S_n = \frac{3069}{512}$

$$\Rightarrow \frac{a(1-r^n)}{1-r} = \frac{3069}{512} \qquad [\because r<1]$$

$$\Rightarrow \frac{3\left\{1-\frac{1}{2^n}\right\}}{1-\frac{1}{2}} = \frac{3069}{512}$$

$$\Rightarrow 6\left(1-\frac{1}{2^n}\right) = \frac{3069}{512}$$

$$\Rightarrow 1-\frac{1}{2^n} = \frac{3069}{3072}$$

$$\Rightarrow \frac{1}{2^n} = 1-\frac{3069}{3072} = \frac{3072-3069}{3072}$$

$$\Rightarrow \frac{1}{2^n} = \frac{3}{3072} = \frac{1}{1024}$$

$$\Rightarrow 2^n = 1024$$

$$\Rightarrow 2^n = 2^{10}$$

On comparing the powers from both sides, we get
$$n = 10$$

Hence, 10 terms are needed to give the sum $\frac{3069}{512}$.

EXAMPLE 4. Find the sum to n terms of the sequence given by $a_n = 2^n + 3n, n \in N$.

Sol. Let S_n denotes the sum to n terms of the given sequence.

Then, $S_n = a_1 + a_2 + a_3 + \ldots + a_n$

$$\Rightarrow S_n = (2^1 + 3\times 1) + (2^2 + 3\times 2) + (2^3 + 3\times 3) + \ldots + (2^n + 3\times n)$$

$$\Rightarrow S_n = (2^1 + 2^2 + 2^3 + \ldots + 2^n) + (3\times 1 + 3\times 2 + 3\times 3 + \ldots + 3\times n)$$
$$= (2^1 + 2^2 + 2^3 + \ldots + 2^n) + 3(1+2+3+\ldots+n)$$
$$= 2\left(\frac{2^n-1}{2-1}\right) + 3\left\{\frac{n}{2}(1+n)\right\}$$
$$\left[\because 2 + 2^2 + 2^3 + 2^n \text{ is a GP and } \Sigma n = \frac{n(n+1)}{2}\right]$$
$$= 2(2^n - 1) + \frac{3n}{2}(n+1)$$

EXAMPLE 5. Find the sum of series $\frac{3}{5} + \frac{4}{5^2} + \frac{3}{5^3} + \frac{4}{5^4} + \ldots$ to $2n$ terms.

Sol. We have, $S = \frac{3}{5} + \frac{4}{5^2} + \frac{3}{5^3} + \frac{4}{5^4} + \ldots$ to $2n$ terms

$$= \left[\frac{3}{5} + \frac{3}{5^3} + \ldots + \text{to } n \text{ terms}\right] + \left[\frac{4}{5^2} + \frac{4}{5^4} + \ldots + \text{to } n \text{ terms}\right]$$

$$= \frac{\frac{3}{5}\left[1-\left(\frac{1}{5^2}\right)^n\right]}{\left[1-\left(\frac{1}{5^2}\right)\right]} + \frac{\frac{4}{5^2}\left[1-\left(\frac{1}{5^2}\right)^n\right]}{\left[1-\left(\frac{1}{5^2}\right)\right]}$$

$$\left[\because \text{sum of GP} = \frac{a(1-r^n)}{1-r}, |r|<1\right]$$

$$= \frac{\frac{3}{5}\left[1-\frac{1}{5^{2n}}\right]}{1-\frac{1}{25}} + \frac{\frac{4}{25}\left[1-\frac{1}{5^{2n}}\right]}{1-\frac{1}{25}}$$

$$= \frac{\frac{3}{5}\left[1-\frac{1}{5^{2n}}\right]}{\frac{24}{25}} + \frac{\frac{4}{25}\left[1-\frac{1}{5^{2n}}\right]}{\frac{24}{25}} = \frac{5}{8}\left[1-\frac{1}{5^{2n}}\right] + \frac{1}{6}\left[1-\frac{1}{5^{2n}}\right]$$

$$= \left[1-\frac{1}{5^{2n}}\right]\left[\frac{5}{8}+\frac{1}{6}\right] = \left[1-\frac{1}{5^{2n}}\right]\left[\frac{15+4}{24}\right] = \frac{19}{24}\left[1-\frac{1}{5^{2n}}\right]$$

EXAMPLE 6. Find the sum of the series $4 + 44 + 444 + \ldots n$ terms.

Sol. Given series is $4 + 44 + 444 + \ldots n$ terms.

On taking common 4, we get
$$S_n = 4(1 + 11 + 111 + \ldots n \text{ terms})$$

On multiplying and dividing each term of RHS by 9, we get
$$S_n = \frac{4}{9}(9 + 99 + 999 + \ldots)$$

$$\Rightarrow S_n = \frac{4}{9}[(10-1) + (100-1) + (1000-1) + \ldots n \text{ terms}]$$

$$\Rightarrow S_n = \frac{4}{9}[(10 + 100 + 1000 + \ldots n \text{ terms}) - (1 + 1 + 1 + \ldots n \text{ terms})] \quad \ldots \text{(i)}$$

For first series, $10 + 100 + 1000 + \ldots n$ terms

$$r = \frac{100}{10} = 10 > 1$$

$$\therefore\ S_n = 10(1 + 10 + 10^2 + \ldots n \text{ terms})$$

$$= 10\left(\frac{10^n - 1}{10 - 1}\right) \qquad \left[\because \text{Sum} = \frac{a(r^n - 1)}{r - 1}\right]$$

$$= \frac{10}{9}(10^n - 1)$$

Now, from Eq. (i), we get

$$S_n = \frac{4}{9}\left[\frac{10}{9}(10^n - 1) - n\right] = \frac{40}{81}(10^n - 1) - \frac{4}{9}n$$

EXAMPLE 7. Find the sum of the series $0.7 + 0.77 + 0.777 + \ldots$ to n terms.

Sol. Given series is $0.7 + 0.77 + 0.777 + \ldots$ to n terms

Let $S_n = 0.7 + 0.77 + 0.777 + \ldots$ to n terms

$$\Rightarrow S_n = 7[0.1 + 0.11 + 0.111 + 0.1111 + \ldots \text{ to } n \text{ terms}]$$

$$\Rightarrow S_n = \frac{7}{9}[0.9 + 0.99 + 0.999 + \ldots \text{ to } n \text{ terms}]$$

$$\Rightarrow S_n = \frac{7}{9}\left[\frac{9}{10} + \frac{99}{100} + \frac{999}{1000} + \ldots \text{to } n \text{ terms}\right]$$

$$\Rightarrow S_n = \frac{7}{9}\left[1 - \frac{1}{10} + 1 - \frac{1}{100} + 1 - \frac{1}{1000} + \ldots \text{to } n \text{ terms}\right]$$

$$\Rightarrow S_n = \frac{7}{9}\left[1 + 1 + \ldots \text{to } n \text{ terms} - \left(\frac{1}{10} + \frac{1}{10^2} + \frac{1}{10^3} + \ldots \text{to } n \text{ terms}\right)\right]$$

$$\Rightarrow S_n = \frac{7}{9}\left[n - \frac{1}{10}\frac{\left(1 - \frac{1}{10^n}\right)}{\left(1 - \frac{1}{10}\right)}\right] \Rightarrow S_n = \frac{7}{9}\left[n - \frac{(1 - 10^{-n})}{9}\right]$$

$$\Rightarrow S_n = \frac{7}{9}\left[\frac{9n - 1 + 10^{-n}}{9}\right] \Rightarrow S_n = \frac{7}{81}[9n - 1 + 10^{-n}]$$

EXAMPLE 8. A GP consists of an even number of terms. If the sum of all the terms is 5 times the sum of terms occupying odd places, then find its common ratio.

Sol. Let the GP is $a, ar, ar^2, ar^3, ar^4, \ldots, ar^{2n-2}, ar^{2n-1}$,

where $a, ar^2, ar^4, ar^6, \ldots$ occupy odd places and $ar, ar^3, ar^5, ar^7 \ldots$ occupy even places.

According to the question,

Sum of all terms = 5 × Sum of terms occupying odd places

i.e. $a + ar + ar^2 + \ldots + ar^{2n-1}$

$$= 5 \times (a + ar^2 + ar^4 + \ldots + ar^{2n-2})$$

$$\Rightarrow \frac{a(r^{2n} - 1)}{r - 1} = \frac{5a[(r^2)^n - 1]}{r^2 - 1} \qquad \left[\because S_n = \frac{a(r^n - 1)}{r - 1}, r > 1\right]$$

$$\Rightarrow \frac{r^{2n} - 1}{r - 1} = \frac{5(r^{2n} - 1)}{(r - 1)(r + 1)} \Rightarrow 1 = \frac{5}{r + 1}$$

$$\Rightarrow r + 1 = 5 \Rightarrow r = 4$$

EXAMPLE 9. Find the least value of n for which the sum $1 + 3 + 3^2 + \ldots$ to n terms is greater than 7000.

Sol. We have, $S_n = 1 + 3 + 3^2 + \ldots$ to n terms

Clearly, the successive ratio of the terms is same. So, the above series forms a GP, with first term, $a = 1$ and common ratio, $\frac{3}{1} = 3 > 1$.

$$\therefore\ S_n = 1 \times \left(\frac{3^n - 1}{3 - 1}\right) = \frac{3^n - 1}{2} \qquad \left[\because S_n = a\left(\frac{r^n - 1}{r - 1}\right)\right]$$

Now, $S_n > 7000$

$$\Rightarrow \frac{3^n - 1}{2} > 7000$$

$$\Rightarrow 3^n - 1 > 14000$$

$$\Rightarrow 3^n > 14001$$

$$\Rightarrow n\log 3 > \log 14001$$

$$\Rightarrow n > \frac{\log 14001}{\log 3}$$

$$\Rightarrow n > \frac{4.1461}{0.4771} = 8.69$$

Hence, the least value of n is 9.

EXAMPLE 10. The sum of the first three terms of a GP is 16 and the sum of next three terms is 128. Determine the first term, the common ratio and the sum to n terms of the GP.

Sol. Let the GP be $a, ar, ar^2, ar^3, \ldots$

According to the given condition,

Sum of first three terms $= a + ar + ar^2 = 16$ ...(i)

and sum of next three terms $= ar^3 + ar^4 + ar^5 = 128$ ...(ii)

On dividing Eq. (i) by Eq. (ii), we get

$$\frac{a + ar + ar^2}{ar^3 + ar^4 + ar^5} = \frac{16}{128}$$

$$\Rightarrow \frac{a(1 + r + r^2)}{ar^3(1 + r + r^2)} = \frac{1}{8}$$

$$\Rightarrow \left(\frac{1}{r}\right)^3 = \left(\frac{1}{2}\right)^3$$

On comparing the base of the power 3 from both sides, we get

$$\frac{1}{r} = \frac{1}{2} \Rightarrow r = 2$$

On putting $r = 2$ in Eq. (i), we get

$$a + 2a + 4a = 16$$

$$\Rightarrow 7a = 16 \Rightarrow a = \frac{16}{7}$$

Now, sum of n terms, $S_n = \dfrac{a(r^n-1)}{r-1}$ $[\because r = 2 > 1]$

$$= \frac{\frac{16}{7}(2^n-1)}{2-1} = \frac{16}{7}(2^n-1)$$

Hence, $a = \frac{16}{7}$, $r = 2$ and $S_n = \frac{16}{7}(2^n-1)$

EXAMPLE 11. If S_1, S_2 and S_3 be respectively the sum of n, $2n$ and $3n$ terms of a GP, prove that

$$S_1(S_3 - S_2) = (S_2 - S_1)^2.$$

Sol. Let a be the first term and r be the common ratio of the given GP. Then,

$$S_1(S_3 - S_2) = \frac{a(1-r^n)}{(1-r)} \cdot \left\{\frac{a(1-r^{3n})}{(1-r)} - \frac{a(1-r^{2n})}{(1-r)}\right\}$$

$$= \frac{a(1-r^n)}{(1-r)} \cdot \frac{(a - ar^{3n} - a + ar^{2n})}{(1-r)}$$

$$= \frac{a(1-r^n)}{(1-r)} \cdot \frac{ar^{2n}(1-r^n)}{(1-r)} = \frac{a^2r^{2n}(1-r^n)^2}{(1-r)^2} \quad \text{...(i)}$$

And $(S_2 - S_1)^2 = \left\{\dfrac{a(1-r^{2n})}{(1-r)} - \dfrac{a(1-r^n)}{(1-r)}\right\}^2$

$$= \frac{(a - ar^{2n} - a + ar^n)^2}{(1-r)^2}$$

$$= \frac{\{(ar^n(1-r^n)\}^2}{(1-r)^2} = \frac{a^2r^{2n}(1-r^n)^2}{(1-r)^2} \quad \text{...(ii)}$$

Hence, from Eqs. (i) and (ii), we get

$$S_1(S_3 - S_2) = (S_2 - S_1)^2$$

Hence proved.

EXAMPLE 12. Let S be the sum, P be the product and R be the sum of reciprocals of n terms in a GP. Prove that $P^2R^n = S^n$.

Sol. Let the GP is $a, ar, ar^2, ar^3 \ldots ar^{n-1}$.

Given, S = Sum of n terms

$$= a + ar + ar^2 + ar^3 + \ldots + ar^{n-1}$$

$$= \frac{a(r^n-1)}{r-1} \quad [\text{let } r > 1] \quad \text{...(i)}$$

and R = Sum of the reciprocals of n terms

$$= \frac{1}{a} + \frac{1}{ar} + \frac{1}{ar^2} + \ldots + \frac{1}{ar^{n-1}} \quad \left(\frac{1}{r} < 1\right)$$

$$= \frac{\frac{1}{a}\left[1 - \left(\frac{1}{r}\right)^n\right]}{1 - \frac{1}{r}} = \frac{1}{a}\left[\frac{1}{1} - \frac{1}{r^n}\right] \times \frac{1}{\frac{r-1}{r}}$$

$$= \frac{1}{a}\left[\frac{r^n-1}{r^n}\right] \times \frac{r}{r-1} \Rightarrow R = \frac{(r^n-1)r}{ar^n(r-1)} \quad \text{...(ii)}$$

and P = Product of n terms

$$= a \times ar \times ar^2 \times ar^3 \times \ldots \times ar^{n-1}$$

$$= a^{1+1+1+\ldots+n \text{ terms}} r^{1+2+3+\ldots+(n-1)\text{terms}}$$

$$= a^n r^{\frac{n(n-1)}{2}} \quad \left[\because \Sigma n = \frac{n(n+1)}{2}\right]$$

$$\Rightarrow \quad P^2 = a^{2n} r^{n(n-1)} \quad \text{...(iii)}$$

Now, we have to prove $P^2R^n = S^n$

or $P^2 = \dfrac{S^n}{R^n}$ or $P^2 = \left(\dfrac{S}{R}\right)^n$

$$\text{RHS} = \left(\frac{S}{R}\right)^n = \left[\frac{a(r^n-1)}{r-1} \times \frac{ar^n(r-1)}{(r^n-1)r}\right]^n$$

[using Eqs. (i) and (ii)]

$$= [a^2r^nr^{-1}]^n = (a^2r^{n-1})^n = [a^{2n}r^{n(n-1)}]$$

$$= P^2 = \text{LHS} \quad [\text{from Eq. (iii)}]$$

Hence proved.

EXAMPLE 13. If $b = a + a^2 + a^3 + \ldots \infty$, then prove that $a = \dfrac{b}{1+b}$.

Sol. We have, $b = a + a^2 + a^3 + \ldots \infty$

Clearly, RHS is a geometric series with first term 'a' and common ratio 'a'.

$$\therefore \quad b = \frac{a}{1-a} \Rightarrow b - ab = a \Rightarrow a = \frac{b}{1+b}$$

EXAMPLE 14. Find the sum of the series $9^{1/3} \cdot 9^{1/9} \cdot 9^{1/27} \ldots \infty$.

Sol. Let $E = 9^{\frac{1}{3}} \cdot 9^{1/9} \cdot 9^{1/27} \ldots \infty = 9^{\frac{1}{3}+\frac{1}{9}+\frac{1}{27}+\ldots\infty}$ ...(i)

Again let $S_\infty = \frac{1}{3} + \frac{1}{9} + \frac{1}{27} + \ldots \infty$

Clearly, the successive ratio of the terms is same. So, the above obtained series forms a GP, with first term, $a = \frac{1}{3}$ and common ratio, $\frac{1}{9} \div \frac{1}{3} = \frac{1}{3}$.

Then, $S_\infty = \dfrac{\frac{1}{3}}{1 - \frac{1}{3}} = \dfrac{1}{2}$ $\left[\because S_\infty = \dfrac{a}{1-r}\right]$

Then, from Eq. (i), we get

$$E = 9^{\frac{1}{2}} = 3$$

EXAMPLE 15. If $|x| < 1$ and $|y| < 1$, find the sum of infinity of the following series:

$$(x + y) + (x^2 + xy + y^2) + (x^3 + x^2y + xy^2 + y^3) + \ldots$$

Sol. We have,

$$(x+y)+(x^2+xy+y^2)+(x^3+x^2y+xy^2+y^3)+\ldots\infty$$

$$=\frac{1}{x-y}\{(x^2-y^2)+(x^3-y^3)+(x^4-y^4)+\ldots \text{ to } \infty\}$$

$$\left[\because \frac{x^n-a^n}{x-a}=x^{n-1}\cdot a^0+x^{n-2}\cdot a+x^{n-3}a^2+\ldots+a^{n-1},\ n\in N\right]$$

$$=\frac{1}{x-y}\{(x^2+x^3+x^4+\ldots \text{ to } \infty)-(y^2+y^3+y^4+\ldots \text{ to } \infty)\}$$

$$=\frac{1}{x-y}\left\{\frac{x^2}{1-x}-\frac{y^2}{1-y}\right\}$$

$$=\frac{1}{x-y}\frac{\{x^2-x^2y-y^2+y^2x\}}{(1-x)(1-y)}$$

$$=\frac{1}{(x-y)}\frac{\{(x^2-y^2)-xy(x-y)\}}{(1-x)(1-y)}$$

$$=\frac{x+y-xy}{(1-x)(1-y)}$$

EXAMPLE 16. Write the rational number corresponding to the decimal expansion $0.3\overline{56}$.

Sol. Given decimal expansion is $0.3\overline{56}$.

In series form, it can be written as

$$0.3\overline{56}=0.3+0.056+0.00056+0.0000056+\ldots\infty$$

$$\Rightarrow\quad 0.3\overline{56}=0.3\times\frac{10}{10}+0.056\times\frac{10^3}{10^3}+0.00056\times\frac{10^5}{10^5}+\ldots\infty$$

$$=\frac{3}{10}+\frac{56}{10^3}+\frac{56}{10^5}+\ldots\infty$$

$$\Rightarrow\quad 0.3\overline{56}=\frac{3}{10}+\left[\frac{56}{10^3}+\frac{56}{10^5}+\ldots\infty\right]$$

Here, first term $a=\frac{56}{10^3}$

and common ratio $=\frac{56}{10^5}\div\frac{56}{10^3}=\frac{1}{10^2}<1$

$$\therefore\quad 0.3\overline{56}=\frac{3}{10}+\frac{\frac{56}{10^3}}{1-\frac{1}{10^2}}\qquad\left[\because S_\infty=\frac{a}{1-r},\text{ if } r<1\right]$$

$$=\frac{3}{10}+\frac{56}{10^3}\times\frac{10^2}{99}=\frac{3}{10}+\frac{56}{990}$$

$$\therefore\quad 0.3\overline{56}=\frac{353}{990}$$

EXAMPLE 17. The sum of an infinite GP is 57 and the sum of their cubes is 9747. Find the GP.

Sol. Let a be the first term and r be the common ratio of an infinite GP.

Given, sum $=57\Rightarrow\frac{a}{1-r}=57$ ...(i)

and sum of the cubes $=9747$

$$\Rightarrow\quad a^3+a^3r^3+a^3r^6+\ldots=9747$$

$$\Rightarrow\quad \frac{a^3}{1-r^3}=9747 \qquad \text{...(ii)}$$

On dividing the cube of Eq. (i) by Eq. (ii), we get

$$\frac{a^3}{(1-r)^3}\cdot\frac{(1-r^3)}{a^3}=\frac{(57)^3}{9747}$$

$$\Rightarrow\quad \frac{1-r^3}{(1-r)^3}=19\Rightarrow\frac{1+r+r^2}{(1-r)^2}=19$$

$$[\because a^3-b^3=(a-b)(a^2+b^2+ab)]$$

$$\Rightarrow\quad 1+r+r^2=19(1+r^2-2r)$$

$$[\because (a-b)^2=a^2+b^2-2ab]$$

$$\Rightarrow\quad 18r^2-39r+18=0$$

$$\Rightarrow\quad (3r-2)(6r-9)=0$$

$$\Rightarrow\quad r=2/3 \text{ or } r=3/2$$

$$\Rightarrow\quad r=2/3$$

$[\because r\neq 3/2$, because $-1<r<1$ for an infinite GP$]$

On putting $r=2/3$ in Eq. (i), we get

$$\frac{a}{1-(2/3)}=57$$

$$\Rightarrow\quad 3a=57\Rightarrow a=19$$

Hence, the required GP is $19, 19\times\frac{2}{3}, 19\times\left(\frac{2}{3}\right)^2, \ldots$

i.e. 19, 38/3, 76/9, ...

Applications of GP

Sometimes we can solve the some real life problems by using the concept of GP.

Some of them are given below.

EXAMPLE 18. At the end of each year the value of a certain machine has depreciated by 20% of its value at the beginning of that year. If its initial value was ₹ 1250, then find the value at the end of 5 yr.

Sol. Given, depreciation in value of machine = 20%

After each year the value of the machine is 80% (100 – 20)% of its value of the previous year, so at the end of 5 yr, the machine will depreciate as many times as 5.

Hence, we have to find the 6th terms of the G P whose first term a_1 is 1250 and common ratio r is 0.8.

Hence, value at the end 5 yrs $=t_6=a_1r^5$

$$=1250\,(0.8)^5$$

$$=409.6$$

EXAMPLE 19. The lengths of three unequal edges of a rectangular solid block are in GP. If the volume of the block is 216 cm^3 and the total surface area is 252 cm^2, then find the length of its edges.

Sol. Let the length, breadth and height of rectangular solid block is $\frac{a}{r}$, a and ar, respectively.

$$\therefore \quad \text{Volume} = \frac{a}{r} \times a \times ar = 216 \text{ cm}^3$$

$$\Rightarrow \quad a^3 = 216$$

$$\Rightarrow \quad a^3 = 6^3$$

$$\therefore \quad a = 6$$

$$\text{Surface area} = 2\left(\frac{a^2}{r} + a^2 r + a^2\right) = 252$$

$$\Rightarrow \quad 2a^2\left(\frac{1}{r} + r + 1\right) = 252$$

$$\Rightarrow \quad 2 \times 36\left(\frac{1 + r^2 + r}{r}\right) = 252$$

$$\Rightarrow \quad \frac{1 + r^2 + r}{r} = \frac{252}{2 \times 36}$$

$$\Rightarrow \quad 1 + r^2 + r = \frac{126}{36} r$$

$$\Rightarrow \quad 1 + r^2 + r = \frac{21}{6} r$$

$$\Rightarrow \quad 6 + 6r^2 + 6r = 21r$$

$$\Rightarrow \quad 6r^2 - 15r + 6 = 0$$

$$\Rightarrow \quad 2r^2 - 5r + 2 = 0$$

$$\Rightarrow \quad (2r - 1)(r - 2) = 0$$

$$\Rightarrow \quad r = \frac{1}{2} \text{ or } 2$$

For $r = \frac{1}{2}$,

$$\text{Length} = \frac{a}{r} = \frac{6 \times 2}{1} = 12, \text{ breadth} = a = 6$$

and height $= ar = 6 \times \frac{1}{2} = 3$

For $r = 2$, Length $= \frac{a}{r} = \frac{6}{2} = 3$, breadth $= a = 6$

and height $= ar = 6 \times 2 = 12$

EXAMPLE 20. The side of a given square is 10 cm. The mid-points of its sides are joined to form a new square. Again, the mid-point of the sides of this new square are joined to form another square. This process is continued indefinitely. Find the sum of the area and the sum of the perimeteres of the squares.

Sol. Let $ABCD$ be the given square with each side equal to 10 cm. Let E, F, G, H be the mid-points of the sides AB, BC, CD and DA respectively.

Let P, Q, R, S be the mid-point of the sides EF, FG, GH and HE respectively.

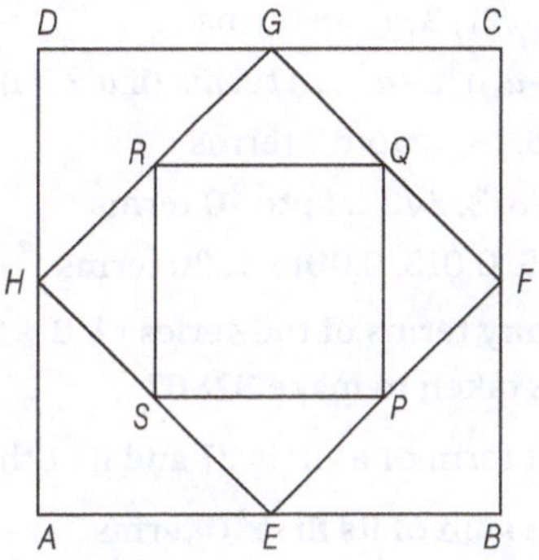

$$\therefore \quad BE = BF = 5 \text{ cm}$$

$$\Rightarrow \quad EF = \sqrt{BE^2 + BF^2} = \sqrt{50} = 5\sqrt{2} \text{ cm}$$

$$FQ = FP = \frac{1}{2} EF$$

$$= \frac{5\sqrt{2}}{2} = \frac{5}{\sqrt{2}} \text{ cm}$$

$$\Rightarrow \quad PQ = \sqrt{FP^2 + FQ^2}$$

$$= \sqrt{\frac{25}{2} + \frac{25}{2}}$$

$$= \sqrt{25} = 5 \text{ cm}$$

Thus, the sides of the squares are 10 cm, $5\sqrt{2}$ cm, 5 cm, ...

(i) Sum of the areas of squares formed

$$= \{(10)^2 + (5\sqrt{2})^2 + 5^2 + \ldots \infty\}$$

$$= (100 + 50 + 25 + \ldots \infty) \qquad \left[\because \text{ it is infinite GP with } a = 100 \text{ and } r = \frac{1}{2}\right]$$

$$= \frac{100}{\left(1 - \frac{1}{2}\right)} = 200 \text{ cm}^2$$

(ii) Sum of perimeters of the given squares

$$= (40 + 20\sqrt{2} + 20 + \ldots)$$

$$= \frac{40}{\left(1 - \frac{1}{\sqrt{2}}\right)}$$

$$= \frac{40\sqrt{2}}{(\sqrt{2} - 1)} \times \frac{(\sqrt{2} + 1)}{(\sqrt{2} + 1)}$$

$$= (80 + 40\sqrt{2}) \text{ cm}$$

Topic Practice 5

1 Find the sum of following geometric progressions. (Each part carries 1 mark)

(i) $\sqrt{7}, \sqrt{21}, 3\sqrt{7}, \ldots n$ terms

(ii) $1, -a, a^2, -a^3, \ldots n$ terms (if $a \neq -1$)

(iii) 2, 6, 18, ... upto 7 terms

(iv) $1, \sqrt{3}, 3, 3\sqrt{3}$ ... upto 10 terms

(v) 0.15, 0.015, 0.0015, ... 20 terms

2 How many terms of the series $1 + 3 + 3^2 + 3^3 + \ldots$ must be taken to make 3280?

3 The first term of a GP is 27 and its 8th term is $\frac{1}{81}$. Find the sum of its first 10 terms.

4 The 2nd and 5th terms of a GP are $\frac{-1}{2}$ and $\frac{1}{16}$, respectively. Find the sum of the GP upto 8 terms.

5 Given a GP with $a = 729$ and 7th term 64, determine S_7.

6 Find the sum of the series $3+6+12+\ldots+1536$.

7 The common ratio of finite GP is 3 and its last term is 486. If the sum of those term is 728, then find the first term.

8 Show that the ratio of the sum of the first n terms of a GP to the sum of terms from $(n+1)$th to $(2n)$th term is $\frac{1}{r^n}$.

9 The sum of the some terms of a GP is 315 whose first term and the common ratio are 5 and 2, respectively. Find the last term and the number of terms.

10 Find the sum of the following series.

(i) $5 + 55 + 555 + \ldots$ upto n terms.

(ii) $0.3 + 0.33 + 0.333 + \ldots$ upto n terms.

11 Find the sum to infinity of the following GP.

(i) $6, 1.2, 0.24, \ldots \infty$

(ii) $10, -9, 8.1, \ldots \infty$

12 The common ratio of a GP is $-\frac{4}{5}$ and the sum to infinity is $\frac{80}{9}$. Find the first term.

13 The sum of an infinite geometric series is 15 and the sum of the squares of these terms is 45. Find the series.

14 Represent the following as rational numbers $0.\overline{15}$.

15 If $x = a + \frac{a}{r} + \frac{a}{r^2} + \ldots \infty$, $y = b - \frac{b}{r} + \frac{b}{r^2} - \ldots \infty$ and $z = c + \frac{c}{r^2} + \frac{c}{r^4} + \ldots \infty$, then prove that $\frac{xy}{z} = \frac{ab}{c}$.

16 Prove that $2^{\frac{1}{2}} \cdot 4^{\frac{1}{8}} \cdot 8^{\frac{1}{24}} \cdot 16^{\frac{1}{64}} \ldots \infty = 2$.

17 If S denotes the sum of an infinite GP and S_1 denotes the sum of the squares of its terms, then prove that the first term and common ratio are respectively

$$\frac{2SS_1}{S^2 + S_1} \text{ and } \frac{S^2 - S_1}{S^2 + S_1}.$$

18 If f is a function satisfying $f(x + y) = f(x) \cdot (y)$ for all $x, y \in N$ such that $f(1) = 3$ and $\sum_{x=1}^{n} f(x) = 120$, find the value of n.

19 If $x = \sum_{n=0}^{\infty} \cos^{2n}\theta$, $y = \sum_{n=0}^{\infty} \sin^{2n}\phi$,

$z = \sum_{n=0}^{\infty} \cos^{2n}\theta \sin^{2n}\phi$, where $0 < \theta, \phi < \pi/2$, then prove that $xz + yz - z = xy$.

20 Find the natural number a for which

$\sum_{k=1}^{n} f(a + k) = 16(2^n - 1)$, where the function

f satisfies $f(x + y) = f(x) \cdot f(y)$ for all natural numbers x, y and further $f(1) = 2$.

21 The inventor of the chessboard suggested a reward of one grain of wheat for the first square; 2 grains for the second; 4 grains for the third and so on, doubling the number of grains for subsequent squares. How many grains would have to be given to the inventor? (Note that there are 64 squares in the chessboard.)

22 A man writes a letter to four of his friends. He asks each one of them to copy the letter and mail to four different persons with the instruction that they move the chain similarly. Assuming that the chain is not broken and it costs ₹2 to mail one letter, find the amount spent on postage when 8th set of letters is mailed.

23 One side of an equilateral triangle is 18 cm. The mid-points of its sides are joined to form another triangle whose mid-points, in term, are joined to form further another triangle and so on up to infinity. Find the sum of

(i) perimeters of all the triangles.

(ii) areas of all the triangles.

Hints & Solutions

1. (i) **Hint** Here, $a = \sqrt{7}, r = \frac{\sqrt{21}}{\sqrt{7}} = \frac{\sqrt{7 \times 3}}{\sqrt{7}} = \sqrt{3} > 1$

$$\Rightarrow \quad S_n = \frac{\sqrt{7}[(\sqrt{3})^n - 1]}{\sqrt{3} - 1} = \frac{\sqrt{7}}{2}(\sqrt{3}+1)(3^{n/2} - 1)$$

(ii) **Hint** Here, $A = 1, R = -\frac{a}{1} = -a < 1$

$$S_n = \frac{1\{1-(-a)^n\}}{1-(-a)} = \frac{1-(-a)^n}{1+a}$$

(iii) Solve as part (i). **Ans.** 2186

(iv) Solve as part (i). **Ans.** $121(\sqrt{3}+1)$

(v) Solve as part (i). **Ans.** $\frac{1}{6}[1-(0.1)^{20}]$

2. Hint Here, $a = 1, r = \frac{3}{1} = 3$;

$$\therefore \quad \frac{1 \cdot (3^n - 1)}{3-1} = 3280 \quad \textbf{Ans. } n = 8$$

3. Hint $\frac{1}{81} = 27(r)^{8-1} \Rightarrow r = \frac{1}{3}$ **Ans.** $\frac{81}{2}\left(1 - \frac{1}{3^{10}}\right)$

4. Hint $a_2 = -\frac{1}{2}, \ a_5 = \frac{1}{16}$

$$\because \ a_2 = ar^{n-1} = ar = -\frac{1}{2}, \ a_5 = ar^4 = \frac{1}{16} \quad \textbf{Ans. } \frac{85}{128}$$

5. Hint $ar^{7-1} = 64 \Rightarrow r^6 = \left(\frac{2}{3}\right)^6 \Rightarrow r = \frac{2}{3}$

$$\therefore \quad S_7 = \frac{729\left[1-\left(\frac{2}{3}\right)^7\right]}{1-\frac{2}{3}} = 2059$$

6. Solve as Example 2. **Ans.** 3069

7. Hint $r = 3, \ l = 486, \ S = 728$

$$S = \left(\frac{lr-a}{r-1}\right) \Rightarrow 728 = \left(\frac{486 \times 3 - a}{3-1}\right) \Rightarrow a = 2$$

8. Hint Let the GP is $\underbrace{ar, ar^2, ar^3, ar^4, ar^5, \ldots, ar^{n-1}}_{n \text{ terms}}$,

$$\underbrace{ar^n, ar^{n+1}, \ldots, ar^{2n-1}}_{n \text{ terms}}$$

Now, required ratio $= \dfrac{\frac{a(r^n - 1)}{r-1}}{\frac{ar^n(r^n-1)}{r-1}} = \dfrac{1}{r^n}$

9. Hint Given, $a = 5, r = 2$ and $S_n = 315$

Therefore, $315 = \frac{5(2^n - 1)}{2-1} \Rightarrow n = 6$

Ans. $T_6 = 160$

10. (i) Solve as Example 6. **Ans.** $\frac{50}{81}(10^n - 1) - \frac{5n}{9}$

(ii) Solve as Example 7. **Ans.** $\frac{1}{3}n - \frac{1}{27}(1 - 10^{-n})$

11. (i) **Hint** Here, $a = 6$ and $r = \frac{T_2}{T_1} = \frac{1.2}{6} = 0.2$

Since, $|0.2| = 0.2 < 1$ **Ans.** $S_\infty = 7.5$

(ii) **Hint** Here, $a = 10$ and $r = \frac{T_2}{T_1} = \frac{-9}{10} = -0.9$

Since, $|-0.9| = 0.9 < 1$ **Ans.** $S_\infty = \frac{100}{19}$

12. Hint We have, $r = -\frac{4}{5}$ and $S = \frac{80}{9}$.

$$\therefore \quad \frac{80}{9} = \frac{a}{1-\left(\frac{-4}{5}\right)}$$

Ans. $a = 16$

13. Hint Sum $= 15 \Rightarrow \frac{a}{1-r} = 15$

Sum of the squares $= 45$

$$\Rightarrow \quad (a^2 + a^2r^2 + a^2r^4 + \ldots \infty) = 45$$

$$\Rightarrow \quad \frac{a^2}{1-r^2} = 45, \ \frac{a^2}{(1-r)^2} \times \frac{1-r^2}{a^2} = \frac{(15)^2}{45}$$

Ans. $5 + \frac{10}{3} + \frac{20}{9} + \frac{40}{27} + \ldots \infty.$

14. Hint $0.1\overline{5} = 0.15555\ldots$

$$= 0.1 + 0.05 + 0.005 + 0.0005 + \ldots \infty]$$

$$= 0.1 + \left[\frac{5}{100} + \frac{5}{1000} + \frac{5}{10000} + \ldots \infty\right]$$

$$= 0.1 + \frac{\left(\frac{5}{100}\right)}{1 - \frac{1}{10}} \quad \textbf{Ans. } \frac{7}{45}$$

15. Hint Clearly, x, y and z are the sums of infinite geometric progression.

$$\therefore \quad x = \frac{a}{1-\frac{1}{r}} = \frac{ar}{r-1}, \ y = \frac{b}{1-\left(-\frac{1}{r}\right)} = \frac{br}{1+r}$$

and $\quad z = \dfrac{c}{1-\frac{1}{r^2}} = \dfrac{cr^2}{r^2-1}$

Now, $\quad xy = \left(\frac{ar}{r-1}\right)\left(\frac{br}{r+1}\right) = \frac{abr^2}{r^2-1}$

$$\Rightarrow \quad \frac{xy}{z} = \left\{\left(\frac{abr^2}{r^2-1}\right) \div \frac{cr^2}{(r^2-1)}\right\} = \frac{ab}{c}$$

16. Hint $2^{1/2}\cdot 4^{1/8}\cdot 8^{1/24}\cdot 16^{1/64}\ldots\infty$

$$= 2^{\frac{1}{2}}\cdot 2^{\frac{1}{4}}\cdot 2^{\frac{3}{24}}\cdot 2^{\frac{1}{16}}\ldots = 2^{\frac{1}{2}+\frac{1}{4}+\frac{1}{8}+\frac{1}{16}+\ldots\infty}$$

17. Hint $S=\dfrac{a}{1-r},\ S_1=\dfrac{a^2}{1-r^2}$

$$\Rightarrow \frac{S}{S_1}=\frac{1+r}{a} \Rightarrow r=\frac{Sa-S_1}{S_1}$$

$$\therefore \quad S=\frac{a}{1-\dfrac{Sa-S_1}{S_1}}$$

$$\Rightarrow \quad S=\frac{S_1 a}{2S_1-Sa}$$

$$\Rightarrow \quad a=\frac{2S_1}{S^2-S_1} \text{ and } r=\frac{S^2-S_1}{S^2+S_1}$$

18. Hint Given, $f(x+y)=f(x)\cdot f(y)$ ...(i)

Putting $x=y=1$ in Eq. (i), we get

$$f(1+1)=f(1)f(1)$$

$$\Rightarrow \quad f(2)=3\times 3=9 \quad [\because f(1)=3]$$

Putting $x=2,\ y=1$ in Eq. (i), we get

$$f(2+1)=f(2)f(1)$$

$$\Rightarrow \quad f(3)=9\times 3=27 \quad [\because f(2)=9,\ f(1)=3]$$

Putting $x=3,\ y=1$ in Eq. (i), we get

$$f(3+1)=f(3)f(1)$$

$$\Rightarrow \quad f(4)=27\times 3=81 \quad [\because f(3)=27]$$

Now, $\sum_{x=1}^{n} f(x)=120$

$$\Rightarrow f(1)+f(2)+f(3)+\ldots+f(n)=120$$

$$\Rightarrow \quad 3+9+27+\ldots n \text{ terms}=120$$

$$=\frac{3(3^n-1)}{3-1}=120$$

$$\left[\text{here, } a=3,\ r=\frac{9}{3}=3\right]$$

$$\Rightarrow \quad 3(3^n-1)=120\times 2$$

$$\Rightarrow \quad 3(3^n-1)=240$$

$$\Rightarrow \quad 3^n-1=\frac{240}{3}$$

$$\Rightarrow \quad 3^n-1=80$$

$$\Rightarrow \quad 3^n=80+1$$

On comparing the power of 3 from both sides, we get

$$3^n=81$$

$$\Rightarrow \quad 3^n=3^4$$

$$\Rightarrow \quad n=4$$

19. Hint We have,

$$x=\sum_{n=0}^{\infty}\cos^{2n}\theta=1+\cos^2\theta+\cos^4\theta+\ldots\infty$$

$$\Rightarrow \quad x=\frac{1}{1-\cos^2\theta} \Rightarrow \sin^2\theta=\frac{1}{x}$$

$$y=\sum_{n=0}^{\infty}\sin^{2n}\phi=1+\sin^2\phi+\sin^4\phi+\ldots\infty$$

$$\Rightarrow \quad y=\frac{1}{1-\sin^2\phi} \Rightarrow \cos^2\phi=\frac{1}{y}$$

ad $\quad z=\sum_{n=0}^{\infty}\cos^{2n}\theta\sin^{2n}\phi$

$$=1+\cos^2\theta\sin^2\phi+\cos^4\theta\sin^4\phi+\ldots\infty$$

$$\Rightarrow \quad z=\frac{1}{1-\cos^2\theta\sin^2\phi}$$

$$\Rightarrow \quad z=\frac{1}{1-(1-\sin^2\theta)(1-\cos^2\phi)}$$

$$\Rightarrow \quad z=\frac{1}{1-\left(1-\dfrac{1}{x}\right)\left(1-\dfrac{1}{y}\right)}$$

$$\Rightarrow \quad z=\frac{1}{\dfrac{1}{x}+\dfrac{1}{y}-\dfrac{1}{xy}}$$

$$\Rightarrow \quad z=\frac{xy}{x+y-1} \Rightarrow xz+yz-z=xy$$

Hence proved.

20. Hint Given, $f(x+y)=f(x)\cdot f(y)$ and $f(1)=2$

Therefore, $f(2)=f(1+1)=f(1)\cdot f(1)=2^2$

$$f(3)=f(1+2)=f(1)\cdot f(2)=2^3$$

$$f(4)=f(1+3)=f(1)\cdot f(3)=2^4 \text{ and so on.}$$

Continuing the process, we obtain

$$f(k)=2^k \text{ and } f(a)=2^a$$

Hence, $\sum_{k=1}^{n} f(a+k)=\sum_{k=1}^{n} f(a)\cdot f(k)=f(a)\sum_{k=1}^{n} f(k)$

$$=2^a(2^1+2^2+2^3+\ldots+2^n)$$

$$=2^a\left\{\frac{2\cdot(2^n-1)}{2-1}\right\}$$

$$=2^{a+1}(2^n-1) \quad \text{...(i)}$$

But we are given, $\sum_{k=1}^{n} f(a+k)=16(2^n-1)$ ...(ii)

From Eqs. (i) and (ii), we get

$$2^{a+1}(2^n-1)=16(2^n-1)$$

$$\Rightarrow \quad 2^{a+1}=2^4$$

$$\Rightarrow \quad a+1=4 \Rightarrow a=3$$

21. Hint Required number of grains

$$=1+2+2^2+\ldots \text{ to 64 terms}$$

$$=1+(2+2^2+2^3+\ldots+2^{63})$$

$$=\left\{1+\frac{2(2^{63}-1)}{(2-1)}\right\}$$

Ans. $(2^{64}-1)$

22. **Hint** Successive number of letters are 4, 16, 64, … .
This is a GP with $a = 4$ and $r = 4$.
Number of letters in the 8th set $= 4 \times 4^{(8-1)}$
$$= 4^8 = 65536$$
Ans. Cost of postage = ₹ (65536 × 2) = ₹ 131072

23. (i) **Hint** Sum of the perimeters of all the triangles is given by
$$S_p = 54 + 27 + 13.5 + \ldots \infty = \frac{54}{1 - \frac{1}{2}} = 54 \times 2$$
Ans. 108 cm

(ii) **Hint** We know that the area of the triangle formed by joining the mid-points of the sides one-fourth of the given triangle.
$$\therefore \text{Area of equilateral } \Delta ABC = \frac{\sqrt{3}}{4} \times (18)^2 = 81\sqrt{3}\text{cm}$$
$$\text{Area of } \Delta DEF = \frac{1}{4} \times \text{Area of } \Delta ABC = \frac{1}{4} \times 81\sqrt{3} = \frac{81}{4}\sqrt{3} \text{ cm}$$
$$\text{and area of } \Delta GHI = \frac{1}{4} \times \text{Area of } \Delta DEF = \frac{1}{4} \times \frac{81}{4}\sqrt{3} = \frac{81}{16}\sqrt{3} \text{ cm}$$
∴ Sum of the areas of all the triangles is
$$S_a = 81\sqrt{3} + \frac{81}{4}\sqrt{3} + \frac{81}{16}\sqrt{3} + \ldots \infty$$
Clearly, it is geometric series whose
$$a = 81\sqrt{3} \text{ and } r = \frac{1}{4}$$
$$\therefore \quad S_a = \frac{a}{1-r} = \frac{81\sqrt{3}}{1 - \frac{1}{4}} = 81\sqrt{3} \times \frac{4}{3}$$ **Ans.** $108\sqrt{3}$ cm²

Geometric Mean and Its Relation with Arithmetic Mean

Geometric Mean (GM)

Let a and b be two positive numbers. If we insert a single number G between them, so that a, G, b is a GP, then G is called **geometric mean**. Thus, a, G, b are in GP.
$$\therefore \quad \frac{G}{a} = \frac{b}{G} \Rightarrow G^2 = ab \Rightarrow G = \sqrt{ab}$$

Inserting n GM's between Two Positive Numbers

Let a and b be two positive numbers and $G_1, G_2, G_3, \ldots, G_n$ be the n GM's between a and b.
Then, $a, G_1, G_2, G_3, \ldots, G_n, b$ are in GP with common ratio r and number of terms are $n+2$.
Here, b is $(n+2)$th term.
$$\text{i.e.} \quad b = T_{n+2} = ar^{n+1} \Rightarrow r = \left(\frac{b}{a}\right)^{\frac{1}{n+1}}$$
Thus, the n geometric means are given below
$$G_1 = ar = a\left(\frac{b}{a}\right)^{\frac{1}{n+1}}$$
$$G_2 = ar^2 = a\left(\frac{b}{a}\right)^{\frac{2}{n+1}}$$
....

....
$$G_n = ar^n = a\left(\frac{b}{a}\right)^{\frac{n}{n+1}}$$

EXAMPLE 1. Find a geometric mean of 4 and 16.

Sol. Geometric mean between 4 and 16 $= \sqrt{4 \times 16} = \sqrt{64} = 8$

EXAMPLE 2. Insert two numbers between 3 and 81, so that resulting sequence is GP.

Sol. Let the two numbers are a and b, then 3, a, b, 81 are in GP.
$$\because \quad n\text{th term, } T_n = Ar^{n-1}$$
$$\therefore \quad T_4 = 81 = 3r^{4-1}$$
$$\Rightarrow \quad r^3 = \frac{81}{3}$$
$$\Rightarrow \quad r^3 = 27$$
$$\Rightarrow \quad r^3 = 3^3$$
On comparing the base of power 3 from both sides, we get
$$r = 3$$
Hence, $a = Ar = 3 \times 3 = 9$,
$b = Ar^2 = 3 \times 3^2 = 27$.

EXAMPLE 3. Insert 4 GM's between 3 and 96.

Sol. Let G_1, G_2, G_3 and G_4 be the required GM's. Then, 3, G_1, G_2, G_3, G_4, 96 are in GP.
Let r be the common ratio. Here, 96 is the 6th term.
$$\therefore \quad 96 = ar^{6-1} = 3r^5$$
$$\Rightarrow \quad 32 = r^5 \Rightarrow (2)^5 = r^5 \Rightarrow r = 2$$
$$\therefore \quad G_1 = ar = 3 \cdot 2 = 6$$
$$G_2 = ar^2 = 3 \cdot 2^2 = 12$$
$$G_3 = ar^3 = 3 \cdot 2^3 = 24$$
$$\text{and} \quad G_4 = ar^4 = 3 \cdot 2^4 = 48$$

EXAMPLE 4. Prove that the product of n GMs between any two positive numbers is equal to nth power of the GM between them.

Sol. Let $G_1, G_2, \dots, G_n$ be the n GMs between positive numbers a and b. Then, $a, G_1, G_2, G_3, \dots, G_n, b$ are in GP. Let r be the common ratio of this GP and b is $(n+2)$ th term.

Now, $\quad b = T_{n+2} = ar^{n+1}$

$\Rightarrow \quad r = \left(\dfrac{b}{a}\right)^{\frac{1}{n+1}}$

Product of n GMs between a and b

$= G_1, G_2, \dots, G_n = ar \cdot ar^2, \dots, ar^n$

$= a^n\, r^{1+2+\dots+n} = a^n \cdot r^{\frac{n}{2}[2A+(n-1)D]}$

$= a^n \cdot r^{\frac{n(n+1)}{2}} = a^n \left[\left(\dfrac{b}{a}\right)^{\frac{1}{n+1}}\right]^{\frac{n(n+1)}{2}}$ $\quad \left[\because r = \left(\dfrac{b}{a}\right)^{1/n+1}\right]$

$= a^n \left(\dfrac{b}{a}\right)^{\frac{n}{2}} = a^{n-\frac{n}{2}} \cdot b^{\frac{n}{2}} = a^{\frac{n}{2}} \cdot b^{\frac{n}{2}} = (\sqrt{ab})^n$

Hence, product of n GMs between a and b is equal to the nth power of the GM between a and b.

Relation between AM and GM

Let A and G be the AM and GM of two positive real numbers a and b, respectively.

Then, $\quad A = \dfrac{a+b}{2}$ and $G = \sqrt{ab}$

Now, $\quad A - G = \dfrac{a+b}{2} - \sqrt{ab} = \dfrac{a+b-2\sqrt{ab}}{2}$

$= \dfrac{(\sqrt{a}-\sqrt{b})^2}{2} \geq 0$

$\therefore \quad A \geq G$

EXAMPLE 5. Find two positive numbers whose difference is 12 and whose AM exceeds the GM by 2.

Sol. Let the two numbers be a and b such that $a > b$.

Given, $\quad a - b = 12 \quad$ ...(i)

and $\quad$ AM − GM = 2

$\Rightarrow \quad \dfrac{a+b}{2} - \sqrt{ab} = 2 \quad \left[\because \text{AM} = \dfrac{a+b}{2} \text{ and GM} = \sqrt{ab}\right]$

$\Rightarrow \quad a + b - 2\sqrt{ab} = 4$

$\Rightarrow \quad (\sqrt{a}-\sqrt{b})^2 = 4$

$\Rightarrow \quad \sqrt{a} - \sqrt{b} = 2 \quad$ ...(ii)

Now, $\quad a - b = 12$

$\Rightarrow (\sqrt{a}+\sqrt{b})(\sqrt{a}-\sqrt{b}) = 12$

$[\because x^2 - y^2 = (x-y)(x+y)]$

$\Rightarrow \quad (\sqrt{a}+\sqrt{b}) \times (2) = 12 \quad$ [using Eq. (ii)]

$\Rightarrow \quad \sqrt{a}+\sqrt{b} = 6 \quad$ ...(iii)

On adding Eqs. (ii) and (iii), we get

$2\sqrt{a} = 8$

$\Rightarrow \quad \sqrt{a} = 4$

$\Rightarrow \quad a = (4)^2$

$\Rightarrow \quad a = 16$

Then, from Eq. (i), we get

$16 - b = 12$

$\Rightarrow \quad b = 16 - 12 = 4$

Hence, required numbers are 16 and 4.

EXAMPLE 6. The sum of two numbers is 6 times their geometric mean, show that the numbers are in the ratio $(3+2\sqrt{2}):(3-2\sqrt{2})$.

Sol. Let the numbers are a and b.

According to the question,

$a + b = 6\sqrt{ab} \Rightarrow \dfrac{a+b}{2\sqrt{ab}} = \dfrac{3}{1}$

Now, applying componendo and dividendo, we get

$\dfrac{a+b+2\sqrt{ab}}{a+b-2\sqrt{ab}} = \dfrac{3+1}{3-1}$

$\Rightarrow \quad \dfrac{(\sqrt{a})^2+(\sqrt{b})^2+2\sqrt{ab}}{(\sqrt{a})^2+(\sqrt{b})^2-2\sqrt{ab}} = \dfrac{4}{2}$

$\Rightarrow \quad \dfrac{(\sqrt{a}+\sqrt{b})^2}{(\sqrt{a}-\sqrt{b})^2} = \dfrac{2}{1}$

$\Rightarrow \quad \dfrac{\sqrt{a}+\sqrt{b}}{\sqrt{a}-\sqrt{b}} = \dfrac{\sqrt{2}}{1}$

Again, applying componendo and dividendo, we get

$\dfrac{\sqrt{a}+\sqrt{b}+\sqrt{a}-\sqrt{b}}{\sqrt{a}+\sqrt{b}-(\sqrt{a}-\sqrt{b})} = \dfrac{\sqrt{2}+1}{\sqrt{2}-1}$

$\Rightarrow \quad \dfrac{2\sqrt{a}}{2\sqrt{b}} = \dfrac{\sqrt{2}+1}{\sqrt{2}-1} \Rightarrow \dfrac{\sqrt{a}}{\sqrt{b}} = \dfrac{\sqrt{2}+1}{\sqrt{2}-1}$

Now, on squaring both sides, we get

$\dfrac{a}{b} = \dfrac{(\sqrt{2}+1)^2}{(\sqrt{2}-1)^2}$

$\Rightarrow \quad \dfrac{a}{b} = \dfrac{2+1+2\sqrt{2}}{2+1-2\sqrt{2}} \quad \left[\because (a+b)^2 = a^2+b^2+2ab \text{ and } (a-b)^2 = a^2+b^2-2ab\right]$

$\Rightarrow \quad \dfrac{a}{b} = \dfrac{3+2\sqrt{2}}{3-2\sqrt{2}}$

$\therefore \quad a:b = (3+2\sqrt{2}):(3-2\sqrt{2})$

EXAMPLE 7.

(i) If a, b, c, d are four distinct positive quantities in AP, then show that $bc > ad$.

(ii) If a, b, c, d are four distinct positive quantities in GP then show that $a + d > b + c$.

Sol. (i) Given a, b, c, d are in AP and we know that AM > GM, then for the first three terms.

$$b > \sqrt{ac} \qquad \left[\text{here, } \frac{a+c}{2} = b\right]$$

On squaring both sides, we get

$$b^2 > ac \qquad \text{...(i)}$$

Similarly, for the last three terms

$$c > \sqrt{bd} \qquad \left[\text{here, } \frac{b+d}{2} = c\right]$$

$$\Rightarrow \quad c^2 > bd \qquad \text{...(ii)}$$

On multiplying Eqs. (i) and (ii), we get

$$b^2c^2 > (ac)(bd) \Rightarrow bc > ad$$

(ii) Given, a, b, c, d are in GP and we know that AM > GM then for the first three terms

$$\frac{a+c}{2} > b \qquad [\because \sqrt{ac} = b]$$

$$\Rightarrow \quad a + c > 2b \qquad \text{...(iii)}$$

Similarly, for the last three terms

$$\frac{b+d}{2} > c \qquad [\because \sqrt{bd} = c]$$

$$\Rightarrow \quad b + d > 2c \qquad \text{...(iv)}$$

On adding Eqs. (iii) and (iv), we get

$$(a + c) + (b + d) > 2b + 2c \Rightarrow a + d > b + c$$

EXAMPLE 8. If A and G be AM and GM respectively, between two positive numbers, then prove that the numbers are $A \pm \sqrt{(A+G)(A-G)}$.

Sol. Let the numbers be α and β.

Given, sum of the roots,

$$\frac{\alpha+\beta}{2} = A \qquad \text{[arithmetic mean]}$$

$$\Rightarrow \quad \alpha + \beta = 2A$$

and product of the roots,

$$\sqrt{\alpha\beta} = G \qquad \text{[geometric mean]}$$

$$\Rightarrow \quad \alpha\beta = G^2$$

Now, quadratic equation having roots α and β is

$$x^2 - (\alpha + \beta)x + \alpha\beta = 0$$

$$\Rightarrow \quad x^2 - 2A\,x + G^2 = 0$$

$$\Rightarrow \quad x = \frac{2A \pm \sqrt{4A^2 - 4 \times 1 \times G^2}}{2 \times 1} \qquad \left[\because x = \frac{-b \pm \sqrt{b^2 - 4ac}}{2a}\right]$$

$$= \frac{2A \pm 2\sqrt{A^2 - G^2}}{2}$$

$$= A \pm \sqrt{(A+G)(A-G)} \qquad [\because a^2 - b^2 = (a+b)(a-b)]$$

Hence proved.

Problems Based on AP and GP

Sometimes, in given problem we have some terms in AP or in GP and we have to show that other given terms will be in GP or in AP. To solve these types of problems we use the following conditions and then simplify

(i) a, b, c are in AP iff $b = \dfrac{a+c}{2}$

(ii) a, b, c are in GP iff $b^2 = ac$

EXAMPLE 9. Three numbers whose sum is 15 are in A.P. If 1, 4, 19 be added to them respectively, then they are in GP. Find the numbers.

Sol. Let the three numbers be $a - d, a, a + d$.

Then, sum $= 15 \Rightarrow (a - d) + a + (a + d) = 15 \Rightarrow a = 5$.

So, the numbers are $5 - d, 5, 5 + d$.

Adding 1, 4, 19, respectively to these numbers, we get

$$6 - d, 9, 24 + d$$

These numbers are in GP.

$$\therefore \quad 9^2 = (6 - d)(24 + d)$$

$$\Rightarrow \quad 81 = 144 + 6d - 24d - d^2$$

$$\Rightarrow \quad d^2 + 18d - 63 = 0$$

$$\Rightarrow \quad (d + 21)(d - 3) = 0$$

$$\Rightarrow \quad d = -21 \text{ or } d = 3.$$

When $d = -21$ then numbers are $5 + (21), 5, 5 + (-21)$ i.e., 26, 5, -16 and when $d = 3$, then numbers are $5 - 3, 5, 5 + 3$ i.e., 2, 5, 8.

Hence, the numbers are 26, 5, -16 or 2, 5, 8.

EXAMPLE 10. If pth, qth, rth terms of an AP and GP are both a, b and c, respectively, then show that $a^{b-c} \cdot b^{c-a} \cdot c^{a-b} = 1$

Sol. Let A and d be the first term and common difference of AP and x, R be the first term and common ratio of GP, respectively.

According to the given condition,

$$A + (p - 1)d = a \qquad \text{...(i)}$$

$$A + (q - 1)d = b \qquad \text{...(ii)}$$

$$A + (r - 1)d = c \qquad \text{...(iii)}$$

and

$$a = xR^{p-1} \qquad \text{...(iv)}$$

$$b = xR^{q-1} \qquad \text{...(v)}$$

$$c = xR^{r-1} \qquad \text{...(vi)}$$

On subtracting Eq. (ii) from Eq. (i), we get

$$d(p-1-q+1)=a-b$$

$\Rightarrow$ $a-b=d(p-q)$ ...(vii)

On subtracting Eq. (iii) from Eq. (ii), we get

$$d(q-1-r+1)=b-c$$

$\Rightarrow$ $b-c=d(q-r)$ ...(viii)

On subtracting Eq. (i) from Eq. (iii), we get

$$d(r-1-p+1)=c-a$$

$\Rightarrow$ $c-a=d(r-p)$ ...(ix)

Now, we have to prove $a^{b-c}\,b^{c-a}\,c^{a-b}=1$

$$\text{LHS}=a^{b-c}\,b^{c-a}\,c^{a-b}$$

Using Eqs. (iv), (v), (vi) and (vii), (viii), (ix), we get

$$\text{LHS}=(xR^{p-1})^{d(q-r)}\,(xR^{q-1})^{d(r-p)}\,(xR^{r-1})^{d(p-q)}$$

$$=x^{d(q-r)+d(r-p)+d(p-q)}\,R^{(p-1)\,d(q-r)+(q-1)\,d\,(r-p)+(r-1)d(p-q)}$$

$$=x^{d(q-r+r-p+p-q)}\,R^{d(pq-pr-q+r+qr-pq-r+p+rp-rq-p+q)}$$

$=x^0\,R^0=1=\text{RHS}$ **Hence proved.**

Topic Practice 6

1 Find the GM between the following numbers.

(i) 1 and $\frac{9}{16}$ (ii) a^3b and ab^3.

2 Insert three GMs between 1 and 256.

3 Insert three numbers between $\frac{1}{3}$ and 432, so that the resulting sequence is a GP.

4 Insert four numbers between 6 and 192, so that the resulting sequence is an GP.

5 Find two numbers whose arithmetic mean is 34 and the geometric mean is 16.

6 Find the minimum value of $4^x+4^{1-x}, x\in R$.

7 If the AM of two positive numbers a and $b\,(a>b)$ is twice their geometric mean. Prove that $a:b(2+\sqrt{3}):(2-\sqrt{3})$.

8 If x, y, z are distinct positive integers, then prove that $(x+y)(y+z)(z+x)>8xyz$.

9 The sum of the three numbers in GP is 56. If we substract the 1, 7, 21, from these numbers in that order, we obtain an arithmetic progression (AP). Find the numbers.

10 If $x, 2y$ and $3z$ are in AP, where the distinct numbers x, y, z are in GP, then find the common ratio of the GP.

11 If A is the arithmetic mean and G_1, G_2 be two geometric means between any two numbers, then prove that $\frac{G_1^2}{G_2}+\frac{G_2^2}{G_1}=2A$.

12 If reciprocals of $\frac{x+y}{2}, y, \frac{y+z}{2}$ are in AP. Show that x, y, z in GP.

13 If a, b and c are positive numbers, then prove that $a^2+b^2+c^2$ is greater than $ab+bc+ca$.

14 If a, b, c are in AP and b, c, d are in GP and $\frac{1}{c}, \frac{1}{d}, \frac{1}{e}$ are in AP, then prove that a, c, e are in GP.

15 Find the value of n so that $\frac{a^{n+1}+b^{n+1}}{a^n+b^n}$ may be the geometric mean between a and b.

16 If arithmetic mean and geometric mean between two numbers is 5 and 4 respectively, then find the two numbers.

Hints & Solutions

1. **Hint** Use the formula, $G^2=ab$

Ans. (i) $\frac{3}{4}$ (ii) a^2b^2

2. **Hint** Let 1, G_1, G_2, G_3, 256 are in GP.

$\therefore$ $T_5=256$

$\Rightarrow$ $1(r)^{5-1}=256 \Rightarrow r=\pm 4$

If $r=4$, then $G_1=1\times(4)^1=4$; $G_2=1(4)^2=16$;

$$G_2=1(4)^3=64$$

and if $r=-4$,

then $G_1=1(-4)=-4$; $G_2=1(-4)^2=16$;

$$G_3=-(-4)^3=-64$$

Ans. 4, 16, 64 or $-$4, 16, $-$64 are the three GMs.

3. Solve as Example 2. **Ans.** (2, 12, 72) or ($-$2, 12, $-$72)

4. Solve as Example 3. **Ans.** 12, 24, 48, 96

5. **Hint** Let the two numbers be a and b such that $a>b$.

Then, $\frac{a+b}{2}=34$ and $\sqrt{ab}=16$

Now, $(a-b)^2 = (a+b)^2 - 4ab$

$\Rightarrow \quad a - b = 60$

Ans. 64 and 4

6. **Hint** We know that AM $\geq$ GM

$$\therefore \quad \frac{4^x + \frac{4}{4^x}}{2} \geq \sqrt{4^x \times \frac{4}{4^x}}$$

$$\Rightarrow \quad 4^x + \frac{4}{4^x} \geq 2\sqrt{4} \Rightarrow 4^x + \frac{4}{4^x} \geq 4$$

Hence, the minimum value of given expression is 4.

7. Solve as Example 6.

8. **Hint** Since, AM > GM

$$\frac{x+y}{2} > \sqrt{xy}, \frac{y+z}{2} > \sqrt{yz} \text{ and } \frac{z+x}{2} > \sqrt{zx}$$

On multiplying the above inequalities, we get

$$\frac{x+y}{2} \cdot \frac{y+z}{2} \cdot \frac{y+z}{2} > \sqrt{(xy)(yz)(zx)}$$

or $(x+y)(y+z)(z+x) > 8xyz$

9. **Hint** Given, $a + ar + ar^2 = 56$ ...(i)

Again, $a-1$, $ar-7$, ar^2-21 are in AP.

$\Rightarrow \quad 2(ar-7) = (a-1) + (ar^2 - 21)$

$\Rightarrow \quad a + ar^2 - 2ar = 8$ ...(ii)

On dividing Eq. (i) by Eq. (ii), we get

$$\frac{a + ar + ar^2}{a + ar^2 - 2ar} = \frac{56}{8} \Rightarrow 6r^2 - 15r + 6 = 0$$

$$\Rightarrow \quad r = 2, \frac{1}{2}$$

If $r = 2$, then from Eq. (i), we get

$$a + 2a + 4a = 56 \Rightarrow a = 8$$

If $r = \frac{1}{2}$, then from Eq. (i), we get

$$\frac{a}{1} + \frac{a}{2} + \frac{a}{4} = 56 \Rightarrow a = 32$$

Ans. Required numbers are 8, 16, 32 or 32, 16, 8.

10. **Hint** Since, x, $2y$ and $3z$ are in AP.

$\therefore \quad 4y = x + 3z$ ...(i)

and x, y, z are in GP.

$\therefore \quad y = rx$ and $z = xr^2$

On putting the value of y and z in Eq. (i), we get

$$4xr = x + 3xr^2 \Rightarrow 3r^2 - 4r + 1 = 0$$

Ans. $r = \frac{1}{3}$ $\quad [\because r = 1 \text{ is not possible}]$

11. **Hint** $A = \frac{a+b}{2}$ and $G_1 = ar$, $G_2 = ar^2$

where, $r = \left(\frac{b}{a}\right)^{\frac{1}{2+1}} = \left(\frac{b}{a}\right)^{1/3}$ ...(i)

$$\therefore \quad \frac{G_1^2}{G_2} + \frac{G_2^2}{G_1} = \frac{a^2r^2}{ar^2} + \frac{a^2r^4}{ar} = 2A$$

12. **Hint** $\frac{2}{y} = \frac{2}{x+y} + \frac{2}{y+z}$

$$\Rightarrow \quad \frac{1}{y} = \frac{x + 2y + z}{xy + xz + y^2 + yz}$$

$$\Rightarrow \quad xy + xz + y^2 + yz = xy + 2y^2 + yz \Rightarrow y^2 = xz$$

13. **Hint** AM $\geq$ GM

$$a^2 + b^2 > 2ab,\ b^2 + c^2 > 2bc,\ c^2 + a^2 > 2ac$$

$$\Rightarrow \quad 2(a^2 + b^2 + c^2) > 2(ab + bc + ca)$$

$$\Rightarrow \quad a^2 + b^2 + c^2 > ab + bc + ca$$

14. **Hint** a, b, c are in AP $\Rightarrow a + c = 2b$ ...(i)

and b, c, d are in GP.

$\Rightarrow \quad c^2 = bd$ ...(ii)

Similarly, $\frac{1}{c}, \frac{1}{d}, \frac{1}{e}$ are in AP.

$\Rightarrow \quad \frac{2}{d} = \frac{1}{c} + \frac{1}{e} \Rightarrow d = \frac{2ce}{c+e}$ ...(iii)

On putting the values of b and d from Eq. (i) and (iii), in Eq. (ii), we get

$$c^2 = \left(\frac{a+c}{2}\right) \times \left(\frac{2ce}{c+e}\right) \Rightarrow c^2 = ae$$

Therefore, a, c, e are in GP.

15. **Hint** Given, $\frac{a^{n+1} + b^{n+1}}{a^n + b^n} = \frac{a^{\frac{1}{2}} b^{\frac{1}{2}}}{1}$

$$\Rightarrow \quad a^{n+1} + b^{n+1} = a^{n+\frac{1}{2}} b^{\frac{1}{2}} + a^{\frac{1}{2}} b^{n+\frac{1}{2}}$$

$$\Rightarrow \quad (a^{n+1} - a^{n+\frac{1}{2}} b^{\frac{1}{2}}) + (b^{n+1} - a^{\frac{1}{2}} b^{n+\frac{1}{2}}) = 0$$

$$\Rightarrow \quad (a^{n+\frac{1}{2}} - b^{n+\frac{1}{2}})(a^{\frac{1}{2}} - b^{\frac{1}{2}}) = 0$$

$$\Rightarrow \quad a^{n+\frac{1}{2}} - b^{n+\frac{1}{2}} = 0 \quad [\because a^{\frac{1}{2}} - b^{\frac{1}{2}} \neq 0]$$

$$\therefore \quad a^{n+\frac{1}{2}} = b^{n+\frac{1}{2}}$$

$$\Rightarrow \quad \left(\frac{a}{b}\right)^{n+\frac{1}{2}} = 1 = \left(\frac{a}{b}\right)^0$$

$$\Rightarrow \quad n + \frac{1}{2} = 0 \Rightarrow n = -\frac{1}{2}$$

16. **Hint** Given, arithmetic mean, $A = 5$

and geometric mean, $G = 4$

Let the two numbers be a and b.

Then, $a = A + \sqrt{A^2 - G^2}$ and $b = A - \sqrt{A^2 - G^2}$

$\therefore \quad a = 5 + \sqrt{5^2 - 4^2}$ and $b = 5 - \sqrt{5^2 - 4^2}$

$\Rightarrow a = 5 + \sqrt{25 - 16}$ and $b = 5 - \sqrt{25 - 16}$

$\Rightarrow a = 5 + \sqrt{9}$ and $b = 5 - \sqrt{9}$

$\Rightarrow a = 5 + 3$ and $b = 5 - 3$

$\Rightarrow a = 8$ and $b = 2$

Hence, the required numbers are 2 and 8.

Exam Pattern Exercise

Part A - Objective Type Questions

Multiple Choice Type Questions

1 The sum of three consecutive terms of an AP is 15, and their product is 105, then the common difference is

(a) ±1 (b) ±2 (c) ±3 (d) ±4

2 40 is which term of the sequence 72, 70, 68 ....

(a) 18th (b) 17th (c) 15th (d) 10th

3 If *a*, *b*, *c* be in AP, and *p* is the AM between *a* and *b* and *q* is the AM between *b* and *c*, then the value of *b* is

(a) $\frac{p-q}{2}$ (b) $\frac{q-p}{2}$ (c) $\frac{p+a}{2}$ (d) $\frac{pq}{2}$

4 The numbers of integers between 100 and 1000 that are divisible by 7 is

(a) 229 (b) 128 (c) 113 (d) 129

5 The sum of first three terms of a GP is $\frac{13}{12}$ and their product is −1, then the common ratio of the GP is

(a) $\frac{-4}{3}$ or $\frac{-3}{4}$ (b) $\frac{3}{4}$ or $\frac{4}{3}$

(c) $\frac{1}{4}$ or $\frac{-1}{4}$ (d) $\frac{5}{3}$ or $\frac{-3}{5}$

6 The product 32, $(32)^{1/6}$, $(32)^{1/36}$, ... upto ∞ is equal to

(a) 64 (b) 16 (c) 32 (d) 0

7 8th term from the end of the sequence $12, 4, \frac{4}{3}, \frac{4}{9}, \ldots$, 20th term is

(a) $12\times\left(\frac{1}{3}\right)^{13}$ (b) $12\times\left(\frac{1}{3}\right)^{12}$

(c) $3\times\left(\frac{1}{12}\right)^{12}$ (d) 0

8 A man starts repaying a loan as first instalment of ₹100. If he increases the instalment by ₹5 every month, then the amount he will pay in the 30th instalment is

(a) ₹ 241 (b) ₹ 250 (c) ₹ 245 (d) ₹ 265

9 A person has 2 parents, 4 grandparents, 8 great grandparents and so on. Then, the number of ancestors during the ten generations preceding his own is

(a) 1084 (b) 2046

(c) 2250 (d) 1024

10 The length of three unequal edges of a rectangular solid block are in GP. The volume of the Hock is 216 cm^3 and the total surface area is 252 cm^2. The length of the longest edges is

(a) 6 cm (b) 14 cm (c) 10 cm (d) 12 cm

Assertion-Reason Based Questions

Directions (Q. Nos. 11-13) *In the questions given below are two statements labelled as Assertion (A) and Reason (R). In the context of the two statements, which one of the following is correct?*

(a) Both A and R are correct; R is the correct explanation of A

(b) Both A and R are correct; R is not the correct explanation of A

(c) A is correct; R is incorrect

(d) R is correct; A is incorrect

11 **Assertion (A)** 1, 2, 4, 8, ... is a GP 4, 8, 16, 32, ... is a GP and 1 + 4, 2 + 8, 4 + 16, 8 + 32, ... is also a GP.

Reason (R) Let general term of a GP with common ratio *r* be T_{k+1} and general term of another GP with common ratio *r* be T_{k+1}, then the series whose general term $T_{k+1} = T_{k+1} + T_{k+1}$ is also a GP with common ratio *r*.

12 **Assertion (A)** The minimum value of $4^{\sin^2 x} + 4^{\cos^2 x}$ is 2.

Reason (R) AM ≥ GM

13 **Assertion (A)** The 9th term from the end of the sequence 3, 4, 5, ... 20th term is 14.

Reason (R) Let *a* be the first term and *d* be the common difference of AP. Then nth term is $a_n = a + (n-1)d$.

Part-B Descriptive Questions

Very Short Answer Type Questions

14 Find the sum of the sequence.
16, 11, 6, ..., 23rd term

15 Find 4 geometric means between 3 and 96.

16 Find the minimum value of $2^x + 2^{1-x}, x \in R$.

Short Answer Type Questions

17 What is the *r*th term of an AP sum of whose first *n* terms is $2n + 3n^2$?

18 In an AP, if Kth term is $5K+1$. Find, the sum of first n terms.

19 In a GP, the 3rd term is 24 and the 6th term is 192. Find, the 10th term.

20 What is the common ratio of four numbers of a GP in which the third term is greater than the first term by 9 and the second term is greater than 4th by 18.

Long Answer Type Questions

21 What is the sum of first n terms of the series $0.6+0.66+0.666 \,........ + n$?

22 If in an AP, first term is 2 and the sum of first five terms is one-fourth of the next five terms, find the 20th terms.

23 A man accepts a position with an initial salary of ₹ 5200 per month. It is understood that he will receive an automatic increase of ₹ 320 in the very next month and each month thereafter.

(i) Find his salary for the tenth month.

(ii) What is his total earning during the first year?

24 If a, b, c are in GP, then prove that

$$\frac{a^2+ab+b^2}{bc+ca+ab}=\frac{b+a}{c+b}$$

Case Study Based Questions

25 A company produces 500 computers in the third year and 600 computers in the seventh year. Assuming that the production increases uniformly by a constant number every year.

Based on the above information, answer the following questions.

(i) Find the value of the fixed number by which production is increasing every year.

(ii) Find the production in first year.

(iii) Find the number of computers produced in 21st year.

Or

Find the difference in number of computers produced in 10th year and 8th year.

26 A sequence whose terms increases or decreases by a fixed number, is called an Arithmetic Progression (AP). In other words, we can say that, a sequence is called an arithmetic progression if the difference of a term and the previous term is always same i.e. $a_{n+1}-a_n=$ constant for all n. This constant or same difference is called the common difference of an AP and it is denoted by d.

In an AP, we usually denote the first term by a, common difference by d and the nth term by a_n or T_n defined as $T_n=a_n=a+(n-1)d$.

Also, $l=a+(n-1)d$, where l is the last term of the sequence. The sum of n terms, S_n of this AP is given by $S_n=\frac{n}{2}[2a+(n-1)d]$.

Also, if l be the last term, then the sum of n terms of this AP is $S_n=\frac{n}{2}(a+l)$.

Based on the above information, answer the following questions.

(i) If nth term of an AP is given by $a_n=2n^2+1$, then find its 10th term.

(ii) If the sum of n terms of an AP is given by $S_n=3n+2n^2$, then find the common difference of the AP.

(iii) If 9 times the 9th term of an AP is equal to 13 times the 13th term, then find the 22nd term of the AP.

Or Let S_n denote the sum of the first n terms of an AP, if $S_{2n}=3S_n$, then find $S_{3n}:S_n$.

Hints & Solutions

1. (b)	*2.* (b)	*3.* (c)	*4.* (d)
5. (a)	*6.* (a)	*7.* (b)	*8.* (c)
9. (b)	*10.* (d)	*11.* (a)	*12.* (d)
13. (b)			

14. **Hint** $S_n=\frac{n}{2}[2a+(n-1)d]$

$$S_{23}=\frac{23}{2}[2\times16+(22)\times(-5)]$$

$$=\frac{23}{2}[32-110]=\frac{23}{2}[-78]=-897$$

15. **Hint** $G_1=6,\ G_2=12,\ G_3=24,\ G_5=48$

16. **Hint** $\frac{2^x+2^{1-x}}{2}\geq\sqrt{2^x\cdot2^{1-x}}$

$$2^x+2^{(1-x)}\geq2\sqrt{2}$$

$$2^x+2^{1-x}\geq2\sqrt{2}$$

17. Hint $S_n = 2n + 3n^2$

$$T_n = S_n - S_{n-1}$$
$$= (2n+3n^2) - [2(n-1) + 3(n-1)^2]$$
$$= (2n+3n^2) - [2n - 2 + 3(n^2+1-2n)]$$
$$= (2n+3n^2) - (2n - 2 + 3n^2 + 3 - 6n)$$
$$= 2n + 3n^2 - 2n + 2 - 3n^2 - 3 + 6n = 6n - 1$$

$\therefore$ rth term $T_r = 6r - 1$

18. Hint Putting $K = 1, 2$, we get

$$T_1 = 5\times 1 + 1 = 6$$

and $T_2 = 5 \times 2 + 1 = 11$

$\Rightarrow$ $a = 6,\ d = 11 - 6 = 5$

Now, $S_n = \frac{n}{2}[2a + (n-1)d] = \frac{n}{2}[2\times 6 + (n-1)5]$

$$= \frac{n}{2}[12 + 5n - 5] = \frac{n}{2}[5n+7]$$

19. Hint Here, $a_3 = ar^2 = 24$ ...(i)

and $a_6 = ar^5 = 192$ ...(ii)

Dividing Eq. (ii) by Eq. (i), we get

$$r^3 = \frac{192}{24} \Rightarrow r^3 = 8 \Rightarrow r = 2$$

Substituting $r = 2$ in Eq. (i), we get

$$a = 6$$

Hence, $a_{10} = 6(2)^9 = 3072$

20. Hint T_3 = Ist term + 9

$$T_3 = a + 9,\ T_2 = ar^3 + 18$$
$$\frac{a(r^2-1)}{ar(1-r^2)} = \frac{1}{2}$$
$$-\frac{1}{r}\frac{(1-r^2)}{(1-r^2)} = \frac{1}{2}$$
$$-\frac{1}{r} = \frac{1}{2}$$
$$r = -2$$

21. Hint

$S = 0.6 + 0.66 + 0.666 + \dots$ upto n terms

$S = 6(01 + 0.11 + 0.111 + \dots$ upto n terms)

$$= \frac{6}{9}(0.9 + 0.99 + 0.999 + \dots \text{ upto } n \text{ terms})$$
$$= \frac{2}{3}\left[\frac{9}{10} + \frac{99}{100} + \frac{999}{1000} + \dots \text{ upto } n \text{ terms}\right]$$
$$= \frac{2}{3}\left[\left(1-\frac{1}{10}\right) + \left(1-\frac{1}{100}\right) + \left(1-\frac{1}{1000}\right) + \dots \text{ upto } n \text{ terms}\right]$$
$$= \frac{2}{3}\left[(1+1+1+\dots \text{ upto } n \text{ terms}) - \left(\frac{1}{10} + \frac{1}{100} + \frac{1}{1000} + \dots \text{ upto } n \text{ terms}\right)\right]$$
$$= \frac{2}{3}\left[n - \frac{\frac{1}{10}\left\{1-\left(\frac{1}{10}\right)^n\right\}}{1-\frac{1}{10}}\right] = \frac{2}{3}\left[n - \frac{\frac{1}{10}\left\{1-\left(\frac{1}{10}\right)^n\right\}}{\frac{9}{10}}\right]$$
$$= \frac{2}{3}\left[n - \frac{1}{9}\left\{1-\left(\frac{1}{10}\right)^n\right\}\right]$$

22. Hint Let the AP is $a, a+d, a+2d, a+3d, \dots$

Now, given $a = 2$

According to the given condition,

Sum of first five terms = $\frac{1}{4}$ (Sum of next five terms)

$$a + (a+d) + (a+2d) + (a+3d) + a + 4d$$
$$= \frac{1}{4}[a + 5d + a + 6d + a + 7d + a + 8d + a + 9d]$$

$\Rightarrow$ $5a + 10d = \frac{1}{4}[5a + 35d]$

$\Rightarrow$ $4[5a + 10d] = 5a + 35d$

$\Rightarrow$ $20a + 40d = 5a + 35d$

$\Rightarrow$ $20a - 5a = 35d - 40d$

$\Rightarrow$ $15a = -5d$

$\Rightarrow$ $15 \times 2 = -5d$ $[\because a = 2]$

$\Rightarrow$ $30 = -5d \Rightarrow d = \frac{-30}{5} = -6$

Now, $T_n = a + (n-1)d$

$\Rightarrow$ $T_{20} = 2 + (20-1)(-6) = 2 + 19(-6)$

$$= 2 - 19\times 6 = 2 - 114 = -112$$

23. Hint Since, the man get a fixed increment of ₹ 320 each month.

Therefore, this forms an AP whose First term = 5200 and Common difference $(d) = 320$

(i) Salary for tenth month i.e. for $n = 10$,

$$a_{10} = a + (n-1)d$$

$\Rightarrow$ $a_{10} = 5200 + (10-1)\times 320$

$\Rightarrow$ $a_{10} = 5200 + 9 \times 320$

$\therefore$ $a_{10} = 5200 + 2880$

$\therefore$ $a_{10} = 8080$

(ii) Total earning during the first year.

In a year, there are 12 month i.e. $n = 12$,

$$S_{12} = \frac{12}{2}[2\times 5200 + (12-1)320]$$
$$= 6[10400 + 11 \times 320]$$
$$= 6[10400 + 3520] = 6 \times 13920 = 83520$$

24. Hint Put the value of a, b, c assuming $b = ar,\ c = ar^2$ in given expression of LHS and RHS.

25. (i) 25 (ii) 450 (iii) 950 *Or* 50

26. (i) Given sequence is not an AP.

(ii) 4

(iii) 0 or 6

CHAPTER 11

Permutations and Combinations

In this Chapter...

- Fundamental Principles of Counting
- Factorial Notation
- Permutations
- Restricted Permutations
- Combinations
- Practical Problems on Combinations

The study of permutation and combination is concerned with determining the number of different ways of arranging and selecting objects, out of a given number of objects.

In this chapter, we shall learn about some basic counting techniques which will be useful in determining the number of different ways of arranging and selecting objects, without actually listing them.

Fundamental Principles of Counting

There are two fundamental principles of counting which are the base of permutations and combinations.

Fundamental Principle of Multiplication (FPM)

If an event can occur in m different ways, another event can occur in n different ways, then the total number of occurrence of the events in the given order is $m \times n$.

e.g. In a school, there are 200 boys and 150 girls. The teacher wants to select a boy and a girl to represent the school in inter school competition.

Here, the teacher can select a boy in 200 ways and a girl in 150 ways. So, by principle of multiplication, the teacher can select a boy and a girl in $200 \times 150 = 30000$ ways.

If there are n events, say $E_1, E_2, \dots, E_n$ such that E_1 can occur in m_1 ways, E_2 can occur in m_2 ways, E_3 can occur in m_3 ways and so on, then the total number of ways in which all the events can occur in the stated order is $m_1 \times m_2 \times m_3 \times \dots \times m_n$.

EXAMPLE 1. A room has 7 doors. In how many ways can a man enter the room through one door and come out through a different door?

Sol. Here, we need to perform two operations :

(i) Selecting a door to enter.

(ii) Selecting a door to come out.

Clearly, the man can enter the room through anyone of the seven doors.

So, there are seven ways of entering into the room. Note that the man can come out through anyone of the remaining six doors. So, he can come out through a different door in 6 ways.

Hence, by fundamental principle of multiplication, required number of ways $= 7 \times 6 = 42$

EXAMPLE 2. In a monthly test, the teacher decides that there will be three questions, one from each of the Exercises 7, 8 and 9 of textbook. If there are 11 questions in Exercise 7, 15 in Exercise 8 and 10 in Exercise 9, then in how many ways can three questions be selected?

Sol. Clearly, from Exercise 7, one question can be selected in 11 ways.

From Exercise 8, one question can be selected in 15 ways.

and from Exercise 9, one question can be selected in 10 ways.

Since, each operation is performed after performing the previous operation, so we use fundamental principle of multiplication.

∴ Number of ways of selecting three questions

$$= 11 \times 15 \times 10 = 1650$$

EXAMPLE 3. In how many ways can 6 letters be posted in 5 letter boxes?

Sol. Let L_1, L_2, L_3, L_4, L_5 and L_6 be six letters. Since, each letter can be posted in anyone of the five letter boxes.

So, L_1 can be posted in 5 ways. Similarly, each of L_2, L_3, L_4, L_5 and L_6 can be posted in 5 ways.

Hence, the total number of ways in which all the six letters can be posted is $5 \times 5 \times 5 \times 5 \times 5 \times 5 = 5^6$

$$= 15625 \text{ ways}$$

EXAMPLE 4. In an examination, there are three multiple choice questions and each question has 4 choices. Find the number of ways in which a student can fail to get all answer correct.

Sol. Since, each question can be answered in 4 ways.

So, the total number of ways answering 3 questions is $4 \times 4 \times 4 = 64$.

Out of these possible ways, only one way will be correct and hence the number of ways in which a student can fail to get all correct answer is $64 - 1 = 63$.

EXAMPLE 5. How many three-letter words can be formed using a, b, c, d, e, if

(i) repetition is not allowed?

(ii) repetition is allowed?

Sol. (i) It is clear that, the total number of three-letter words is equal to the number of ways of filling three places.

First place can be filled in 5 ways.

Now, four letters are left. So, the second place can be filled in 4 ways.

Since, the repetition of letters is not allowed, so the third place can be filled from any one of the remaining 3 letters in 3 ways.

Hence, by fundamental principal of counting, total number of words $= 5 \times 4 \times 3 = 60$

(ii) Since, in this case repetition of letters is allowed, so each of the three place can be filled in 5 ways. Hence, by fundamental principal of counting, total number of words $= 5 \times 5 \times 5 = 125$

EXAMPLE 6. The flag of a newly formed forum is in the form of three blocks □□□, each to be coloured differently. If there are six different colours on the whole to choose from, then how many such designs are possible?

Sol. Here, we have six colours to colour three blocks.

So, first block can be coloured in 6 ways.

Since, each block should be coloured differently, so second block can be coloured by anyone of the remaining 5 colours.

Thus, second block can be coloured in 5 ways.

Similarly, third block can be coloured in 4 ways.

Since, each block is coloured after colouring the previous block.

∴ By FPM, required number of designs $= 6 \times 5 \times 4$

$$= 120$$

EXAMPLE 7. How many 3-digit numbers can be formed from the digits 1, 2, 3, 4 and 5, assuming

(i) repetition of digits allowed? **[NCERT]**

(ii) repetition of digits not allowed?

Sol. (i) There are 5 digits *viz.* 1, 2, 3, 4 and 5.

Since, every digit can be repeated any number of times and we have to form 3-digit numbers.

So, hundred's place can be fill in 5 ways, ten's place can be fill in 5 ways and unit's place can be fill in 5 ways.

Hundred's place	Ten's place	Unit's place
↓	↓	↓
5 ways	5 ways	5 ways

Thus, by the fundamental principle of multiplication, the number of ways in which the 3-digit number can be formed $= 5 \times 5 \times 5 = 125$ ways.

Hence, the number of 3-digit numbers is 125.

(ii) When repetition of digits is not allowed.

Hundred's place can be fill in 5 ways.

Ten's place can be fill in 4 ways.

Unit's place can be fill in 3 ways.

Hundred's place	Ten's place	Unit's place
↓	↓	↓
5 ways	4 ways	3 ways

According to FPM, total number of ways

$$= 5 \times 4 \times 3 = 60 \text{ ways}$$

Hence, number of 3-digit numbers is 60.

EXAMPLE 8. In a certain city, all telephone numbers have six digits, the first two digits always being 41 or 42 or 46 or 62 or 64. How many telephone numbers have all six digits distinct?

Sol. Suppose first two digit is 41. Then, we are left with 8 digits, namely 0, 2, 3, 5, 6, 7, 8, 9 which can be used in constructing the telephone numbers.

Clearly, third digit can be selected in 8 ways.

Fourth digit can be selected in $8 - 1 = 7$ ways.

Fifth digit can be selected in 6 ways.

and sixth digit can be selected in 5 ways.

Now, according to fundamental principle of multiplication, number of telephone starting with 41

$$= 8 \times 7 \times 6 \times 5$$
$$= 1680$$

Similarly, if the telephone number start with 42 or 46 or 62 or 64, the remaining 4 digits can be selected in 1680 ways.

Hence, the total number of required telephone numbers

$$= 1680 \times 5$$
$$= 8400$$

EXAMPLE 9. Find the number of positive integers greater than 6000 and less than 7000 which are divisible by 5, provided that no digit is to be repeated.

Sol. We know a number will be divisible by 5, if either 0 or 5 is at unit place.

$\therefore$ Number of ways to fill the unit's place = 2

Also note that, for number to be greater than 6000 and less than 7000, digit 6 should be fixed at thousand's place.

$\therefore$ Number of ways to fill the thousand's place = 1

Now, we are left with 8 digits. So, hundred's place can be filled in 8 ways and ten's place can be filled in 7 ways.

Thousand's place	Hundred's place	Ten's place	Unit's place
6			0 or 5
↓	↓	↓	↓
1 way	8 ways	7 ways	2 ways

$\therefore$ Total number of numbers $= 1 \times 8 \times 7 \times 2 = 112$

EXAMPLE 10. How many 4-digit numbers are there, when a digit may be repeated any number of times?

Sol. The thousand's place of a 4-digit number cannot be 0. So, thousand's place can be filled with any digit from 1 to 9. Thus, thousand's place can be filled in 9 ways.

Since, repetition of digits is allowed, therefore each of the remaining 3 places can be filled in 10 ways by using the digits from 0 to 9.

Hence, by the fundamental principal of multiplication, the required number of numbers $= 9 \times 10 \times 10 \times 10$

$$= 9000$$

EXAMPLE 11. Find the number of 4 letter words, with or without meaning which can be formed out of the letters of the word POSE, when

(i) the repetition of the letters is not allowed.

(ii) the repetition of the letters is allowed.

Sol. (i) When the repetition of the letters is not allowed. In this case, the total number of words is the same as the number of ways of filling 4 places □□□□ by 4 different letters chosen from P, O, S, E.

The first place can be filled by any of the 4 letters.

Thus, there are 4 ways of filling first place. Since, the repetition of letters is not allowed, so the second place can be filled by any of the remaining 3 letters in 3 different ways.

Following it, the third place can be filled by any of the two remaining letters in 2 different ways. And, the fourth place can be filled by the remaining one letter in 1 way.

So, by the fundamental principle of multiplication, the required number of 4 letter words

$$= 4 \times 3 \times 2 \times 1 = 24$$

Hence, the required number of words = 24

(ii) When the repetition of the letters is allowed:

In this case, each of the four different places can be filled in succession in 4 different ways.

So, the required number of 4 letter words

$$= 4 \times 4 \times 4 \times 4 = 4^4 = 256$$

EXAMPLE 12. A code word is to consist of two distinct English alphabets followed by two distinct numbers between 1 and 9. e.g. CA23 is a code word.

(i) How many such code words are there?

(ii) How many of them end with an even integer?

Sol. (i) There are in all 26 English alphabets, we have to choose 2 distinct alphabets.

1st alphabet can be selected in 26 ways.

2nd alphabet can be selected in 25 ways.

Again, out of 9 digits (1 to 9),

1st number can be selected in 9 ways.

2nd number can be selected in 8 ways.

Thus, by the fundamental principle of multiplication, the number of distinct codes $= 26 \times 25 \times 9 \times 8$

$$= 46800$$

(ii) As above, two distinct alphabets can be selected in 26×25 ways.

We have, in all 1, 2, 3, 4, 5, 6, 7, 8 and 9 digits, unit place can be filled up in 4 ways (by 2, 4, 6, 8). Ten's place can be filled up in 8 ways.

[since, one of the digits is already used]

Thus, the number of such codes $= 26 \times 25 \times 8 \times 4$

$$= 20800$$

EXAMPLE 13. In how many ways can 3 prizes be distributed among 4 boys, when

(i) no boy gets more than one prize?

(ii) a boy may get any number of prizes?

(iii) no boy gets all the prizes?

Sol. (i) The first prize can be given in 4 ways. The 2nd prize can be given in 3 ways because the boy who got the first prize cannot receive the prize.

The 3rd prize can be given to anyone of the remaining 2 boys in 2 ways.

$\therefore$ Total number of ways in which all the prizes can be given $= 4 \times 3 \times 2 = 24$

(ii) The first prize can be given in 4 ways.

The 2nd prize can also be given in 4 ways, because it may be obtained by the boy who has already received a prize.

Similarly, 3rd prize can be given in 4 ways.

Hence, the number of ways in which all the prizes can be given $= 4 \times 4 \times 4 = 4^3 = 64$

(iii) If anyone of the 4 boys may get all the prizes, then, the number of ways in which all the 3 prizes given to a boy $= 4$

So, the number of ways in which no boy get all the prizes $= 64 - 4 = 60$

Fundamental Principle of Addition (FPA)

If there are two events such that they can be performed independently in m and n ways respectively, then either of the two events can occur in $(m + n)$ ways.

e.g. In a school, there are 200 boys and 150 girls. The teacher wants to select either a boy or a girl to represent the school in inter school competition.

Here, the teacher can select a boy in 200 ways and a girl in 150 ways.

So, by fundamental principle of addition, the teacher can select a boy or a girl in $(200 + 150) = 350$ ways

Note The above principle can be extended to any finite number of operation.

EXAMPLE 14. In how many ways, two books of different languages can be selected from 10 Hindi, 5 English and 7 Sanskrit books?

Sol. Clearly, a book of Hindi and a book of English can be selected in $10 \times 5 = 50$ ways

A book of English and a book of Sanskrit can be selected in $5 \times 7 = 35$ ways

A book of Hindi and a book of Sanskrit can be selected in $10 \times 7 = 70$ ways

Now, by fundamental principle of addition, two books of different languages can be selected in $50 + 35 + 70 = 155$ ways

EXAMPLE 15. By using the digits 0, 1, 2, 3, 4 and 5 (repetition not allowed) numbers are formed by using any number of digits. Find the total number of non-zero numbers that can be formed.

Sol. Required number of numbers

= Number of 1-digit numbers + Number of 2-digit numbers + ... + Number of 6-digit numbers

$= 5 + 5 \times 5 + 5 \times 5 \times 4 + 5 \times 5 \times 4 \times 3 + 5 \times 5 \times 4 \times 3 \times 2 + 5 \times 5 \times 4 \times 3 \times 2 \times 1$

$= 5 + 25 + 100 + 300 + 600 + 600 = 1630$

EXAMPLE 16. Find the number of different signals that can be generated by arranging atleast 2 flags in order (one below the other) on a vertical staff, if five different flags are available. [NCERT]

Sol. Here, we have to find number of different signals that can be generated by arranging atleast 2 flags in order. So, a signal can consist of either 2 flags, 3 flags, 4 flags or 5 flags. If a signal consist of 2 flags, then two vacant places are available.

$\therefore$ Number of ways of filling first vacant place = 5 and number of ways of filling second vacant place = 4

Thus, total number of signals consisting 2 flags $= 5 \times 4 = 20$

Now, if a signal consist of 3 flags, then three vacant places are available.

$\therefore$ Number of ways of filling first vacant place = 5, number of ways of filling second vacant place = 4 and number of ways of filling third vacant place = 3

Thus, total number of signals consisting 3 flags $= 5 \times 4 \times 3 = 60$

Similarly, total number of signals consisting 4 flags $= 5 \times 4 \times 3 \times 2 = 120$

and total number of signals consisting 5 flags $= 5 \times 4 \times 3 \times 2 \times 1 = 120$

Since, different signals can be generated by arranging either 2 flags or 3 flags or 4 flags or 5 flags.

$\therefore$ Total number of signals $= 20 + 60 + 120 + 120 = 320$

EXAMPLE 17. How many numbers are there between 100 and 1000 which have exactly one of their digits as 7?

Sol. We have to find numbers between 100 and 1000 i.e. 3-digit numbers which have exactly one of their digits as 7.

Now, consider the following cases:

Case I When 7 is at unit's place.

In this case, ten's and hundred's place can be filled by the digits 0, 1, 2, 3, 4, 5, 6, 8 and 9.

Clearly, the number of ways to fill ten's place = 9 [by anyone of the digits 0, 1, 2, 3, 4, 5, 6, 8, 9]

and the number of ways to fill the hundred's place = 8 [$\because$ hundred's place cannot be filled by zero]

$\therefore$ Number of such numbers $= 1 \times 9 \times 8 = 72$

Case II When 7 is at ten's place.

In this case, unit's and hundred's place can be filled by the digits 0, 1, 2, 3, 4, 5, 6, 8 and 9.

Clearly, the number of ways to fill unit's place = 9

[by anyone of digits 0, 1, 2, 3, 4, 5, 6, 8, 9]

and the number of ways to fill hundred's place = 8

[∵ hundred's place cannot be filled by zero]

∴ Number of such numbers $= 9 \times 1 \times 8 = 72$

Case III When 7 is at hundred's place.

In this case, unit's and ten's place can be filled by the digits 0, 1, 2, 3, 4, 5, 6, 8 and 9.

Clearly, the number of ways to fill unit's place = 9

[by anyone of the digits 0, 1, 2, 3, 4, 5, 6, 8, 9]

and the number of ways to fill the tens place = 9

[by anyone of the digits 0, 1, 2, 3, 4, 5, 6, 8, 9]

∴ Number of such numbers $= 1 \times 9 \times 9$

$= 81$

Hence, the total number of required numbers

$= 72 + 72 + 81$

$= 225$

Topic Practice 1

1 A telegraph has 5 arms and each arm is capable of 4 distinct positions, including the position of rest, then find the total number of signals that can be made.

2 A sequence is a ternary sequence, if it contains digits 0, 1 and 2, then find the total number of ternary sequences of length 9 which either begin with 210 or end with 210.

3 Pratiksha wants to go abroad by ship and to return by airline. She has a choice of 6 different ships to go and 4 airlines to return. In how many ways can she perform her journey?

4 How many AP's with 10 terms are there whose first terms is in the set {1, 2, 3} and whose common difference is in the set {1, 2, 3, 4, 5}?

5 How many words (with or without meaning) of three distinct letters of the English alphabets are there?

6 How many 2-digit even numbers can be formed from the digits 1, 2, 3, 4 and 5, if the digits can be repeated? [NCERT]

7 In how many ways can this diagram be coloured subject to the following two conditions.

(i) Each of the smaller triangle is to be painted with one of three colours : red, black, green.

(ii) No two adjacent regions have the same colour. [NCERT Exemplar]

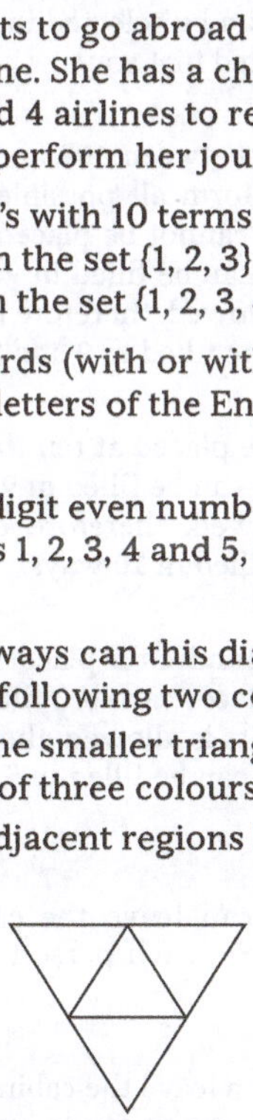

8 A team consists of 6 boys and 4 girls and other has 5 boys and 3 girls. How many single matches can be arranged between the two teams when a boy plays against a boy and a girl plays against a girl?

9 A gentleman has 6 friends to invite. In how many ways can he send invitation cards to them, if he has three servants to carry the cards?

10 Given 5 flags of different colours. How many different signals can be generated, if each signal requires the use of 2 flags, one below the other? [NCERT]

11 How many numbers are there between 100 and 1000 in which all the digits are distinct?

12 How many 5-digit numbers are there, when a digit may be repeated any number of times?

13 How many 3-digit numbers more than 600 can be formed by using the digits 2, 3, 4, 6 and 7?

14 Five persons entered in the lift cabin on the ground floor of 8-floor house. Suppose each of them can leave the cabin independently at any floor beginning with the first. Find the total number of ways in which each of the five persons can leave the cabin

(i) at anyone of the 7 floors.

(ii) at different floors.

15 Each of the six squares in the strip, shown in figure, is to be coloured with anyone of 10 different colours so that no two adjacent squares have the same colour. Find the number of ways of colouring the strip.

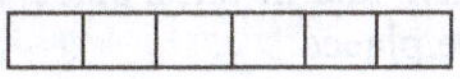

16 How many natural numbers less than 1000 can be formed with the digits 1, 2, 3, 4 and 5, if repetition of digits is allowed?

17 How many five-digit telephone numbers can be constructed using the digits 0 to 9, if each number starts with 67 and no digit appears more than once?

18 There are 3 candidates for Classical language, 5 for Mathematics and 4 for Natural Science scholarship.
(i) In how many ways, can these scholarships be awarded?
(ii) In how many ways, one of these scholarships be awarded?

19 How many numbers greater than 1000, but not greater than 4000 can be formed with the digits 0, 1, 2, 3, 4, if
(i) repetition of digits is allowed?
(ii) repetition of digits is not allowed?

Hints & Solutions

1. **Hint** Since, each arm can be kept in 4 positions and a signal is possible when all the 5 arms are simultaneously placed in positions.
$\therefore$ Total number of ways placing the arms $= 4^5$
But, this includes one inadmissible case, when all the arms are in the position of rest and then no signal can be made.
Hence, the required number of signals $= 4^5 - 1$
Ans. 1023

2. **Hint** Since, each digit in a ternary sequence of length 9 can be filled in 3 ways.
Therefore, the number of nine-digit ternary sequence beginning with 210 is 3^6.
and number of nine-digit ternary sequence ending with 210 is also 3^6.
The number of ternary sequence of 9 digits which begin and end with 210 is 3^3.
$\therefore$ Required number of such numbers $= 3^6 + 3^6 - 3^3$
Ans. 1431

3. **Hint** Number of ways to go by ship = 6
and number of ways to return by airline = 4
$\therefore$ Number of ways, she can perform her journey $= 6 \times 4 = 24$
Ans. 24

4. **Hint** There are 3 ways to choose the first term and corresponding to each such way, there are 5 ways of selecting the common difference.
Ans. 15

5. **Hint** There are 26 letters of English alphabets and we have to fill three places by distinct letters of English alphabets. Then, number of words $= 26 \times 25 \times 24 = 15600$
Ans. 15600

6. **Hint** In unit's place, only one even number (2, 4) can be placed in 2 ways and in ten's place, anyone of the given number can be placed.
Ans. 10

7. **Hint**
(i) There are 4 smaller triangles and each triangle can be painted by anyone of the three given colours.
(ii) The given condition can be satisfied only when we paint the central triangle with any one of the three colours and remaining 3 triangles with anyone of the remaining two colours.
Ans. (i) 81 (ii) 24

8. **Hint** A boy can be selected from the first team in 6 ways, and from the second in 5 ways, so, number of single matches between the boys of two teams $= 6 \times 5 = 30$
Similarly, the number of single matches between the girls of two teams $= 4 \times 3 = 12$
Ans. 42

9. **Hint** Since, the gentleman has 3 servants, so number of ways of sending the invitation card to the first friend = 3
Similarly, for each of the remaining friends, there are 3 ways each. Total number of ways $= 3^6$
Ans. 729

10. **Hint** First flag can be selected in 5 ways and the second flag can be selected in 4 ways.
Ans. 20

11. **Hint** A number between 100 and 1000 has three digits. So, we need to form all possible 3-digit numbers with distinct digits. 0 cannot be placed at hundred's place, so hundred's place can be filled in 9 ways. Since, repetition of digits is not allowed, therefore the remaining ten's and unit's place can be filled in 9 and 8 ways, respectively.
Ans. 648

12. **Hint** 0 cannot be placed at ten thousand's place. So, ten thousand's place can be filled in 9 ways. Since, repetition of digits is allowed, therefore each of the remaining 4 places can be filled in 10 ways.
Ans. 90000

13. **Hint** Digit at hundred's place will be either 6 or 7. So, hundred's place can be filled in 2 ways. Since, repetition of digits is allowed, therefore each of the ten's and one's places can be filled in 5 ways.
Ans. 50

14. **Hint**
(i) Each person can leave the cabin at anyone of the seven floors. So, each person can leave the cabin in 7 ways.
Ans. 7^5
(ii) First person can leave the cabin at anyone of the seven floors. Second person can leave the cabin at anyone of the remaining 6 floors. Similarly, we can calculate for others. **Ans.** 2520

15. **Hint** First square can be coloured in 10 ways (by using anyone of the given colour). Second square can be coloured in 9 ways (by using anyone of the remaining 9 colours). Third square can be coloured in 9 ways (by using anyone of the given colours except the colour used in second square).
Similarly, other squares can be coloured.
Ans. 590490
16. **Hint** Required numbers will be of 1 digit, 2 digits or 3 digits. **Ans.** 155
17. **Hint** It is given that 5-digit telephone number always start with 67.
First two digits among 5-digit telephone numbers are fixed and rest 3 digits are variable 6, 7, _, _, _.
The 10 digits are from 0 to 9.
Ans. 336
18. **Hint** Number of ways of awarding scholarship for Classical language = 3
Number of ways of awarding scholarship for Mathematics = 5
Number of ways of awarding scholarship for Natural Science = 4
Ans. (i) 60 (ii) 12
19. **Hint** Thousand's place can be filled either by 1 or 2 or 3, i.e. thousand's place can be filled in 3 ways.
Ans. (i) 375 (ii) 72

Factorial Notation

Let n be a positive integer. Then, the continued product of first n natural numbers is called the '**n factorial**' and it is denoted by $n!$ or $\underline{|n}$.

Thus, $n! = n(n-1)(n-2)(n-3)\ldots\ldots 3\cdot 2\cdot 1$.

When n is negative or a fraction, $n!$ is not defined.

Zero Factorial

It does not make any sense to define 0! as product of the integers from 1 to 0. So, we define $0! = 1$. Factorial of proper fractions or negative integers are not defined. $n!$ is defined only for whole numbers, i.e. for non-negative integers.

EXAMPLE 1. Compute $\frac{8!}{4!}$. Is $\frac{8!}{4!} = 2!$?

Sol. We have, $\frac{8!}{4!} = \frac{8\times 7\times 6\times 5\times 4!}{4!}$ $[\because n! = n(n-1)(n-2)\ldots 3\cdot 2\cdot 1]$

$= 8\times 7\times 6\times 5$

$= 1680$

Also, $2! = 2\times 1 = 2 \neq 1680$

$\therefore \frac{8!}{4!} \neq 2!$

EXAMPLE 2. Evaluate $\frac{n!}{(n-r)!}$ when $r = 3$.

Sol. We have, $\frac{n!}{(n-r)!} = \frac{n!}{(n-3)!}$ $[\because r = 3, \text{ given}]$

$= \frac{n(n-1)(n-2)(n-3)!}{(n-3)!}$ $[\because n! = n(n-1)(n-2)(n-3)!]$

$= n(n-1)(n-2)$

EXAMPLE 3. Convert product into factorials.

(i) $6\cdot 7\cdot 8\cdot 9\cdot 10$ (ii) $2\cdot 4\cdot 6\cdot 8\cdot 10$

Sol. (i) We have, $6\cdot 7\cdot 8\cdot 9\cdot 10 = \frac{(1\cdot 2\cdot 3\cdot 4\cdot 5)\cdot 6\cdot 7\cdot 8\cdot 9\cdot 10}{(1\cdot 2\cdot 3\cdot 4\cdot 5)}$

[multiplying numerator and denominator by $1\cdot 2\cdot 3\cdot 4\cdot 5$]

$= \frac{10!}{5!}$

(ii) We have, $2\cdot 4\cdot 6\cdot 8\cdot 10$

$= (2\times 1)\cdot(2\times 2)\cdot(2\times 3)\cdot(2\times 4)\cdot(2\times 5)$

$= 2^5\cdot(1\cdot 2\cdot 3\cdot 4\cdot 5) = 2^5\cdot 5!$

EXAMPLE 4. Compute $\frac{(12!)-(10!)}{9!}$.

Sol. We have, $\frac{(12!)-(10!)}{9!} = \frac{12\times 11\times 10! - 10!}{9!}$

$= \frac{10!(132-1)}{9!}$

$= \frac{10\times 9!\times 131}{9!} = 1310$

EXAMPLE 5. Find the LCM of 6!, 7! and 8!.

Sol. We have, $7! = 7\times 6!$ and $8! = 8\times 7\times 6!$

$\therefore$ LCM of 6!, 7! and 8! = LCM $(6!, 7\times 6!, 8\times 7\times 6!)$

$= 6!\times 7\times 8$

$= 8\times 7\times 6! = 8!$

EXAMPLE 6. If $\frac{1}{7!} + \frac{1}{9!} = \frac{x}{10!}$, then find x.

Sol. We have, $\frac{1}{7!} + \frac{1}{9!} = \frac{x}{10!}$

$\Rightarrow \frac{1}{7!} + \frac{1}{9\times 8\times 7!} = \frac{x}{10\times 9\times 8\times 7!}$

$$\Rightarrow \quad \frac{1}{7!}\left(1+\frac{1}{72}\right)=\frac{1}{7!}\left(\frac{x}{10\times 9\times 8}\right)$$

$$\Rightarrow \quad \frac{73}{72}=\frac{x}{10\times 9\times 8}$$

$$\therefore \quad x=\frac{73}{72}\times 10\times 9\times 8=730$$

EXAMPLE 7. If $(n+3)!=56\times(n+1)!$, then find n.

Sol. We have, $(n+3)!=56\times(n+1)!$

$\Rightarrow (n+3)(n+2)(n+1)!=56\times(n+1)!$

$\Rightarrow (n+3)(n+2)=56$

$\Rightarrow n^2+5n+6-56=0$

$\Rightarrow n^2+5n-50=0$

$\Rightarrow n^2+10n-5n-50=0$

$\Rightarrow n(n+10)-5(n+10)=0$

$\Rightarrow (n+10)(n-5)=0$

$\Rightarrow n=5$ [$\because n$ can't be -10]

EXAMPLE 8. Prove that $\frac{(2n)!}{n!}=\{1\cdot 3\cdot 5\cdot\ldots\cdot(2n-1)\}2^n$.

Sol. LHS $=\frac{(2n)!}{n!}$

$$=\frac{1\cdot 2\cdot 3\cdot 4\cdot 5\cdot\ldots\cdot(2n-2)(2n-1)(2n)}{n!}$$

$$=\frac{\{1\cdot 3\cdot 5\cdot\ldots\cdot(2n-1)\}\{2\cdot 4\cdot 6\cdot\ldots\cdot(2n-2)(2n)\}}{n!}$$

$$=\frac{\{1\cdot 3\cdot 5\cdot\ldots\cdot(2n-1)\}\cdot 2^n\{1\cdot 2\cdot 3\cdot\ldots\cdot(n-1)n\}}{n!}$$

$$=\frac{\{1\cdot 3\cdot 5\cdot\ldots\cdot(2n-1)\}\cdot 2^n\cdot n!}{n!}$$

[$\because 1\cdot 2\cdot 3\cdot\ldots\cdot(n-1)\,n=n!$]

$=\{1\cdot 3\cdot 5\cdot\ldots\cdot(2n-1)\}2^n=$ RHS **Hence proved.**

EXAMPLE 9. If $\frac{n!}{2!(n-2)!}$ and $\frac{n!}{4!(n-4)!}$ are in the ratio 2 : 1, then find the value of n.

Sol. We have, $\frac{n!}{2!(n-2)!}:\frac{n!}{4!(n-4)!}=2:1$

$$\Rightarrow \quad \frac{n!}{2!(n-2)!}\times\frac{4!(n-4)!}{n!}=\frac{2}{1}$$

$$\Rightarrow \quad \frac{4!(n-4)!}{2!(n-2)!}=2$$

$$\Rightarrow \quad \frac{4\times 3\times 2!\times(n-4)!}{2!\times(n-2)(n-3)(n-4)!}=2$$

$$\Rightarrow \quad \frac{12}{(n-2)(n-3)}=2$$

$\Rightarrow 12=2(n-2)(n-3)$

$\Rightarrow 12=2(n^2-5n+6)$

$\Rightarrow 6=n^2-5n+6$

$\Rightarrow n^2-5n=0$

$\Rightarrow n(n-5)=0$

$\Rightarrow n=0$ or 5

When $n=0$, then $(n-2)!$ and $(n-4)!$ are not defined, so rejecting $n=0$.

$\therefore n=5$

EXAMPLE 10. Prove that $(n!)^2\le(n!)\times n^n<(2n)!$ for all $n\in N$.

Sol. We have, $(n!)^2=(n!)\times(n!)=n!\times(1\times 2\times 3\times\ldots\times n)$

$\le(n!)\times n^n$ [$\because r\le n$ for each $r=1,2,3,\ldots n$]

$\therefore \quad (n!)^2\le(n!)\times n^n$ ...(i)

Again, we have

$(2n!)=(1\times 2\times 3\times\ldots\times n)\times(n+1)\times(n+2)\times\ldots\times 2n$

$>(n!)\times n^n$ [$\because (n+r)>n$ for each $r=1,2,\ldots n$]

Thus, $(n!)\times n^n<(2n)!$ ...(ii)

From Eqs. (i) and (ii), we have

$(n!)^2\le(n!)\times n^n<(2n)!$ **Hence proved.**

EXAMPLE 11. What is the largest integer n such that 33! is divisible by 2^n?

Sol. Clearly, $33!=1\times 2\times 3\times\ldots\times 30\times 31\times 32\times 33$

$=[2\cdot 4\cdot 6\cdot 8\cdot\ldots\cdot 30\cdot 32](1\cdot 3\cdot 5\cdot 7\cdot 9\cdot\ldots\cdot 31\cdot 33)$

$=[2^1\cdot 2^2\cdot(2\times 3)\cdot 2^3\cdot(2\times 5)\cdot(2^2\times 3)\cdot(2\times 7)\cdot 2^4$

$(2\times 9)\cdot(2^2\times 5)\cdot(2\times 11)\cdot(2^3\times 3)\cdot(2\times 13)$

$(2^2\times 7)\cdot(2\times 15)\cdot 2^5]\cdot(1\cdot 3\cdot 5\cdot\ldots\cdot 31\cdot 33)$

$=[2^{1+2+1+3+1+2+1+4+1+2+1+3+1+2+1+5}$

$\cdot(3\cdot 5\cdot 3\cdot 7\cdot 9\cdot 5\cdot 11\cdot 3\cdot 13\cdot 7\cdot 15)](1\cdot 3\cdot 5\ldots 31\cdot 33)$

$=2^{31}[3\cdot 5\cdot 3\cdot 7\cdot 9\cdot 5\cdot 11\cdot 3\cdot 13\cdot 7\cdot 15](1\cdot 3\cdot 5\ldots 31\cdot 33)$

Thus, 33! is divisible by 2^{31}.

Hence, the maximum power of 2 in 33! is 31.

Topic Practice 2

1 Find the value of $1\cdot1!+2\cdot2!+3\cdot3!+\ldots+n\cdot n!$.

2 If $(n+1)!=12\times(n-1)!$, then find the value of n.

3 Evaluate the following.
(i) $4!-3!$
(ii) $2\times6!-3\times5!$

4 Evaluate : $\dfrac{20!}{18!(20-18)!}$.

5 If $\dfrac{1}{9!}+\dfrac{1}{10!}=\dfrac{x}{11!}$, then find x.

6 If $\dfrac{1}{8!}+\dfrac{1}{9!}=\dfrac{x}{10!}$, then find x.

7 Prove that $n(n-1)(n-2)\ldots(n-r+1)=\dfrac{n!}{(n-r)!}$.

8 Convert the following products into factorials, $(n+1)(n+2)(n+3)\ldots(2n)$.

9 Prove that $(n!)\cdot(n+2)=[n!+(n+1)!]$.

10 Which of the following are true or false?
(i) $(2+3)!=2!+3!$
(ii) $(2\times3)!=(2!)\times(3!)$

11 Find n, if $(n+2)!=2550\times n!$.

12 Prove that $\dfrac{n!}{(n-r)!r!}+\dfrac{n!}{(n-r+1)!(r-1)!}=\dfrac{(n+1)!}{r!(n-r+1)!}$.

13 Prove that $\dfrac{(2n+1)!}{n!}=2^n[1\cdot3\cdot5\ldots(2n-1)(2n+1)]$.

14 If $\dfrac{(2n)!}{3!(2n-3)!}$ and $\dfrac{n!}{2!(n-2)!}$ are in the ratio 44 : 3, then find n.

15 Prove that 35! is divisible by 2^{12}. What is the largest integer n such that 35! is divisible by 2^n?

Hints & Solutions

1. **Hint** $1\cdot1!+2\cdot2!+3\cdot3!+\ldots+n\cdot n!$

$$=\sum_{r=1}^{n}r(r!)=\sum_{r=1}^{n}[(r+1)r!-r!]$$
$$=(2!-1!)+(3!-2!)+\ldots+[(n+1)!-n!]$$
$$=(n+1)!-1!$$

Ans. $(n+1)!-1$

2. **Hint** $(n+1)!=12(n-1)!$

$\Rightarrow\ (n+1)(n)(n-1)!=12(n-1)!$

$\Rightarrow\ n^2+n=12$

$\Rightarrow\ n^2+n-12=0 \Rightarrow (n+4)(n-3)=0$

Ans. $n=3$

3. **Hint** (i) $4!-3!=4\times3!-3!=(4-1)\times3!$

(ii) $2\times6!-3\times5!=2\times6\times5!-3\times5!=(12-3)\times5!$

Ans. (i) 18 (ii) 1080

4. **Hint** $\dfrac{20!}{18!(20-18)!}=\dfrac{20\times19\times18!}{18!\times2!}$ **Ans.** 190

5. **Hint** $\dfrac{1}{9!}+\dfrac{1}{10!}=\dfrac{x}{11!}$

$\Rightarrow\ \dfrac{1}{9!}+\dfrac{1}{10\times9!}=\dfrac{x}{11\times10\times9!}$

$\Rightarrow\ 1+\dfrac{1}{10}=\dfrac{x}{110}\Rightarrow\dfrac{11}{10}=\dfrac{x}{110}$ **Ans.** $x=121$

6. Solve as Example 6.

Ans. $x=100$

7. **Hint** In LHS, multiply numerator and denominator by $(n-r)!$.

8. **Hint** Multiply numerator and denominator by $n!$.

Ans. $\dfrac{(2n)!}{n!}$

9. **Hint** Consider RHS and write it as $n!+(n+1)\,n!$.

10. (i) **Hint** $(2+3)!=2!+3!$

LHS $=(2+3)!=5!$

RHS $=2!+3!=2\times1+3\times2\times1=8$

LHS $\neq$ RHS **Ans.** False

(ii) Solve as part (i). **Ans.** False

11. Solve as Example 7.

Ans. $n=49$

12. **Hint** LHS can be written as

$$\frac{n!}{(n-r)!r(r-1)!}+\frac{n!}{(n-r+1)(n-r)!(r-1)!}$$
$$=\frac{n!}{(n-r)!(r-1)!}\left[\frac{1}{r}+\frac{1}{n-r+1}\right]$$
$$\left[\begin{array}{ll}\because (n-r+1)(n-r)!=(n-r+1)! \\ \text{and} \quad (n+1)n!=(n+1)!\end{array}\right]$$

13. Solve as Example 8.

14. Solve as Example 9.

Ans. $n=6$

15. Solve as Example 11.

Ans. $n=32$

Permutation

A **permutation** is an arrangement of objects in a definite order. Arrangement can be made by taking some or all objects at a time.

e.g. If there are three objects say A, B and C, then the permutations of these three objects taking two at a time are AB, BA, AC, CA BC, CB and the permutations of these three objects taking all at a time are ABC, ACB, BAC, BCA, CAB, CBA.

Here, in each case, number of permutations is 6.

Note that the order of arrangement is important. Because when the order is changed, then different permutation is obtained.

Permutations, when all the Objects are Distinct

When all given objects are distinct, then we can find the number of permutations with the help of following theorem.

Theorem 1

The number of permutations of n different objects taken r at a time, where $0 < r \leq n$ and the objects do not repeat, is $n(n-1)(n-2)\ldots(n-r+1)$, which is denoted by ${}^nP_r$ or $P(n, r)$.

i.e. $$P(n, r) = {}^nP_r = \frac{n!}{(n-r)!}, 0 \leq r \leq n$$

- When $r = 0$, then ${}^nP_0 = 0! = \frac{n!}{(n-0)!} = \frac{n!}{n!} = 1$
- When $r = n$, then ${}^nP_n = \frac{n!}{(n-n)!} = \frac{n!}{0!} = n!$ [$\because$ $0! = 1$]
- Number of permutations of n different things taken all at a time $= n!$

Let us look at different types of problems based on above concepts.

Problems Based on the Formula of $P(n, r)$

EXAMPLE 1. Find the values of the following.

(i) ${}^6P_4$ (ii) $P(15, 2)$

Sol. We know that ${}^nP_r = P(n, r) = \frac{n!}{(n-r)!}$

(i) $${}^6P_4 = \frac{6!}{(6-4)!} = \frac{6!}{2!} = \frac{6 \times 5 \times 4 \times 3 \times 2!}{2!}$$
$$= 6 \times 5 \times 4 \times 3$$
$$= 360$$

(ii) $$P(15, 2) = {}^{15}P_2 = \frac{15!}{(15-2)!} = \frac{15!}{13!} = \frac{15 \times 14 \times 13!}{13!}$$
$$= 15 \times 14 = 210$$

EXAMPLE 2. If $P(n, 5) = 20P(n, 3)$, then find n.

Sol. We have, $P(n, 5) = 20P(n, 3)$

$$\Rightarrow \frac{n!}{(n-5)!} = 20 \times \frac{n!}{(n-3)!}$$
$$\Rightarrow (n-3)! = 20 \times (n-5)!$$
$$\Rightarrow (n-3)(n-4)(n-5)! = 20 \times (n-5)!$$
$$\Rightarrow (n-3)(n-4) = 20 = 5 \times 4$$
$$\Rightarrow (n-3)(n-4) = (8-3)(8-4)$$

On comparing, we get
$$n = 8$$

EXAMPLE 3. If $P(9, r) = 3024$, then find r.

Sol. We have, $P(9, r) = 3024 \Rightarrow {}^9P_r = 3024$

$$\Rightarrow \frac{9!}{(9-r)!} = 3024 \Rightarrow \frac{9!}{(9-r)!} = 9 \times 336$$
$$\Rightarrow \frac{9!}{(9-r)!} = 9 \times 8 \times 7 \times 6$$
$$\Rightarrow \frac{9!}{(9-r)!} = \frac{9 \times 8 \times 7 \times 6 \times 5!}{5!}$$

[multiplying numerator and denominator by 5!]

$$\Rightarrow \frac{9!}{(9-r)!} = \frac{9!}{5!} \Rightarrow (9-r)! = 5!$$

On comparing, we get
$$9 - r = 5$$
$$\Rightarrow r = 4$$

EXAMPLE 4. If ${}^9P_5 + 5 \cdot {}^9P_4 = {}^{10}P_r$, then find r.

Sol. We have, ${}^9P_5 + 5 \cdot {}^9P_4 = {}^{10}P_r$

$$\Rightarrow \frac{9!}{(9-5)!} + 5 \cdot \frac{9!}{(9-4)!} = \frac{10!}{(10-r)!}$$
$$\Rightarrow \frac{9!}{4!} + 5 \cdot \frac{9!}{5!} = \frac{10!}{(10-r)!}$$
$$\Rightarrow \frac{9!}{4!} + 5 \cdot \frac{9!}{5 \times 4!} = \frac{10 \times 9!}{(10-r)!}$$
$$\Rightarrow \frac{1}{4!} + \frac{1}{4!} = \frac{10}{(10-r)!} \Rightarrow \frac{2}{4!} = \frac{10}{(10-r)!}$$

[dividing both sides by 9!]

$$\Rightarrow (10-r)! = 5 \times 4! = 5! \Rightarrow (10-r)! = 5!$$

On comparing, we get
$$10 - r = 5 \Rightarrow r = 5$$

EXAMPLE 5. Find the value of r, if ${}^5P_r = 2 \times {}^6P_{r-1}$.

Sol. Given, ${}^5P_r = 2 \times {}^6P_{r-1}$

$$\therefore \quad \frac{5!}{(5-r)!} = 2 \times \frac{6!}{(6-r+1)!} \quad \left[\because {}^nP_r = \frac{n!}{(n-r)!}\right]$$

$$\Rightarrow \quad \frac{5!}{(5-r)!} = 2 \times \frac{6 \times 5!}{(7-r)!}$$

$$\Rightarrow \quad \frac{1}{(5-r)!} = \frac{12}{(7-r)(6-r)(5-r)!}$$

$$\Rightarrow \quad \frac{1}{1} = \frac{12}{(7-r)(6-r)}$$

$$\Rightarrow \quad (7-r)(6-r) = 12$$

$$\Rightarrow \quad 42 - 7r - 6r + r^2 = 12$$

$$\Rightarrow \quad r^2 - 13r + 30 = 0$$

$$\Rightarrow \quad r^2 - 10r - 3r + 30 = 0$$

$$\Rightarrow \quad r(r-10) - 3(r-10) = 0$$

$$\Rightarrow \quad (r-3)(r-10) = 0 \Rightarrow r = 3, 10$$

$$\therefore \quad r = 3$$

[$\because$ for $r = 10$, ${}^5P_r$ and ${}^6P_{r-1}$ are invalid]

EXAMPLE 6. If $P(2n-1, n) : P(2n+1, n-1) = 22 : 7$, then find n.

Sol. We have, ${}^{2n-1}P_n : {}^{2n+1}P_{n-1} = 22 : 7$

$$\therefore \quad \frac{\dfrac{(2n-1)!}{(2n-1-n)!}}{\dfrac{(2n+1)!}{(2n+1-n+1)!}} = \frac{22}{7}$$

$$\Rightarrow \quad \frac{(2n-1)!}{(n-1)!} \times \frac{(n+2)!}{(2n+1)!} = \frac{22}{7}$$

$$\Rightarrow \quad \frac{(2n-1)!}{(n-1)!} \times \frac{(n+2)(n+1)n(n-1)!}{(2n+1)(2n)(2n-1)!} = \frac{22}{7}$$

$$\Rightarrow \quad \frac{(n+2)(n+1)n}{(2n+1)(2n)} = \frac{22}{7}$$

$$\Rightarrow \quad \frac{(n+1)(n+2)}{2(2n+1)} = \frac{22}{7}$$

$$\Rightarrow \quad 7(n^2 + 3n + 2) = 44(2n+1)$$

$$\Rightarrow \quad 7n^2 + 21n + 14 = 88n + 44$$

$$\Rightarrow \quad 7n^2 - 67n - 30 = 0$$

$$\Rightarrow \quad 7n^2 - 70n + 3n - 30 = 0$$

$$\Rightarrow \quad 7n(n-10) + 3(n-10) = 0$$

$$\Rightarrow \quad (n-10)(7n+3) = 0$$

$$\Rightarrow \quad n = 10 \text{ or } n = \frac{-3}{7}$$

$$\therefore \quad n = 10$$

[$\because n$ can't be negative]

EXAMPLE 7 Prove that

$$P(n, r) = P(n-1, r) + r \cdot P(n-1, r-1).$$

Sol. Consider RHS $= P(n-1, r) + r \cdot P(n-1, r-1)$

$$= \frac{(n-1)!}{(n-1-r)!} + r \cdot \frac{(n-1)!}{(n-1-r+1)!}$$

$$= \frac{(n-1)!}{(n-r-1)!} + r \cdot \frac{(n-1)!}{(n-r)!}$$

$$= \frac{(n-1)!}{(n-r-1)!} + \frac{r \cdot (n-1)!}{(n-r)(n-r-1)!}$$

$$= \frac{(n-1)!}{(n-r-1)!}\left[1 + \frac{r}{n-r}\right]$$

$$= \frac{(n-1)!}{(n-r-1)!}\left[\frac{n-r+r}{(n-r)}\right]$$

$$= \frac{n(n-1)!}{(n-r)(n-r-1)!}$$

$$= \frac{n!}{(n-r)!}$$

$$= P(n, r)$$

$= \text{LHS}$ **Hence proved.**

EXAMPLE 8. If $r < s \le n$, then prove that ${}^nP_s$ is divisible by ${}^nP_r$.

Sol. We have,

$${}^nP_s = n(n-1)(n-2)\ldots(n-r+1)(n-r)\ldots(n-s+1)$$

$$= \{n(n-1)(n-2)\ldots(n-r+1)\} \times \{(n-r)(n-r-1)\ldots(n-s+1)\}$$

$$= {}^nP_r \times \{(n-r)(n-r-1)\ldots(n-s+1)\}$$

which is divisible by ${}^nP_r$.

Hence, ${}^nP_s$ is divisible by ${}^nP_r$.

Simple Applications on Permutation

Here, we will discuss some simple practical problems, where the formula for ${}^nP_r$ and its meaning can be applied.

EXAMPLE 9. In how many ways two different rings can be worn in four fingers with atmost one in each finger?

Sol. Clearly, required number of ways is same as number of permutations (or arrangements) of 4 different things taken 2 at a time.

So, required number of ways $= {}^4P_2$

$$= \frac{4!}{2!}$$

$$= \frac{4 \times 3 \times 2!}{2!}$$

$$= 12$$

EXAMPLE 10. In how many ways can 6 persons occupy 4 vacants seats?

Sol. Required number of ways is same as number of permutations of 6 different things taken 4 at a time.

Hence, required number of ways

$$= {}^6P_4 = \frac{6!}{(6-4)!} = \frac{6!}{2!}$$

$$= 6 \times 5 \times 4 \times 3 = 360$$

EXAMPLE 11. How many 4-letter words, with or without meaning, can be formed out of the letters of the word 'LOGARITHMS', if repetition of letters is not allowed?

Sol. There are 10 letters in the word 'LOGARITHMS'.

So, the number of 4-letter word

= Number of arrangements of 10 letters, taken 4 at a time

$$= {}^{10}P_4 = 5040$$

EXAMPLE 12. How many 3-digit numbers can be formed by using the digits 1 to 9, if no digit is repeated?

Sol. Required number of 3-digit numbers is same as number of permutations of 9 different things taken 3 at a time.

Hence, total number of 3-digit numbers $= {}^9P_3$

$$= \frac{9!}{(9-3)!} = \frac{9!}{6!} = \frac{9 \times 8 \times 7 \times 6!}{6!} = 504$$

EXAMPLE 13. From a committee of 8 persons, in how many ways can we choose a chairman and a vice-chairman assuming one person cannot hold more than one position? **[NCERT]**

Sol. Since, a person cannot hold more than one position, therefore required number of ways is same as number of permutations of 8 different things taken 2 at a time.

Hence, required number of ways $= {}^8P_2$

$$= \frac{8!}{(8-2)!} = \frac{8!}{6!} = \frac{8 \times 7 \times 6!}{6!} = 56$$

EXAMPLE 14. How many words, with or without meaning can be made from the letters of the word 'MONDAY,' assuming that no letter is repeated, if

(i) 4 letters are used at a time?

(ii) all letters are used at a time? **[NCERT]**

Sol. Here, the word 'MONDAY' contains 6 distinct letters.

(i) Required number of words = Number of permutations of 6 different things taken 4 at a time

$$= {}^6P_4 = \frac{6!}{2!} = \frac{6 \times 5 \times 4 \times 3 \times 2!}{2!} = 360$$

(ii) Required number of words = Number of permutations of 6 different things taken all at a time

$$= {}^6P_6 = 6! = 720$$

EXAMPLE 15 How many different signals can be made by using any number of flags from 6 flags of different colours? **[NCERT Exemplar]**

Sol. Clearly, the signals can be made by using one or two or three or four or five or six flags.

Now, number of signals when one flag is used at a time $= {}^6P_1$

Number of signals when two flags are used at a time $= {}^6P_2$

Similarly, number of signals when three, four, five, six flags are used at a time are ${}^6P_3$, ${}^6P_4$, ${}^6P_5$, ${}^6P_6$, respectively.

Hence, by fundamental principle of addition, total number of signals formed from 6 flags of different colours $= {}^6P_1 + {}^6P_2 + {}^6P_3 + {}^6P_4 + {}^6P_5 + {}^6P_6$

$$= \frac{6!}{(6-1)!} + \frac{6!}{(6-2)!} + \frac{6!}{(6-3)!} + \frac{6!}{(6-4)!} + \frac{6!}{(6-5)!} + \frac{6!}{(6-6)!}$$

$$= \frac{6!}{5!} + \frac{6!}{4!} + \frac{6!}{3!} + \frac{6!}{2!} + \frac{6!}{1!} + \frac{6!}{0!}$$

$$= 6 + 6 \times 5 + 6 \times 5 \times 4 + 6 \times 5 \times 4 \times 3 + 6 \times 5 \times 4 \times 3 \times 2 + 6!$$

$$= 6 + 30 + 120 + 360 + 720 + 720 = 1956$$

EXAMPLE 16. Three men have 4 coats, 5 waistcoats and 6 caps. In how many ways, can they wear them?

Sol. Here, all the 4 coats are distinct, all 5 waistcoats are distinct and all 6 caps are also distinct.

So, the number of ways in which three men can wear 4 coats will be equal to the number of arrangements of 4 different things taken 3 at a time.

∴ Number of ways in which three men can wear 4 coats

$$= {}^4P_3 = \frac{4!}{(4-3)!}$$

$$= 4 \times 3 \times 2 = 24$$

Similarly, number of ways in which three men can wear 5 waistcoats

$$= {}^5P_3 = \frac{5!}{(5-3)!} = \frac{5 \times 4 \times 3 \times 2!}{2!} = 5 \times 4 \times 3 = 60$$

and number of ways in which three men can wear 6 caps

$$= {}^6P_3 = \frac{6!}{(6-3)!} = \frac{6 \times 5 \times 4 \times 3!}{3!} = 6 \times 5 \times 4 = 120$$

Since, all three men wear coat, waistcoat and cap, so by the fundamental principal of multiplication,

Required number of ways $= {}^4P_3 \times {}^5P_3 \times {}^6P_3$

$$= 24 \times 60 \times 120 = 172800$$

EXAMPLE 17. How many four-digit numbers are there with distinct digits?

Sol. The total number of arrangements of ten digits 0, 1, 2, 3, 4, 5, 6, 7, 8, 9 taking 4 at a time is ${}^{10}P_4$. But, these arrangements also include those numbers which have 0 at thousand's place. That type of numbers are not four-digit numbers. When 0 is fixed at thousand's place, we have to arrange remaining 9 digits by taking 3 at a time. The number of such arrangements is ${}^9P_3$.

So, the total number of numbers having 0 at thousand's place $= {}^9P_3$

Hence, total numbers of four-digit numbers

$= {}^{10}P_4 - {}^9P_3$

$= 5040 - 504$

$= 4536$

Permutations with Repetitions

When repetition of objects is allowed, then number of permutations can be obtained with the help of following theorem.

Theorem 2

The number of permutations of n different objects taken r at a time, when each may be repeated any number of times in each arrangement, is n^r (permutations with repetitions).

- The number of permutations of n different objects, all at a time, when each may be repeated any number of times in each arrangement, is n^n.

EXAMPLE 18. In how many ways, 3 prizes can be given to 7 boys when each boy is eligible for any of the prizes?

Sol. Here, three prizes can be given to the same boy but two boys cannot get the same prize. Thus, boys can be repeated. So, here we have $n = 7$ and $r = 3$

Hence, required number of ways $= 7^3 = 343$

EXAMPLE 19. How many 4-digit numbers can be formed with the digits 1, 2, 3, 4, 5, 6 when a digit may be repeated any number of times in any arrangement?

Sol. Required number of numbers is same as number of permutation of 6 different things taken 4 at a time, when a digit may be repeated any number of times.

Hence, required number of numbers $= 6^4 = 1296$

EXAMPLE 20. Find the number of 5-digit telephone numbers having atleast one of their digits repeated. **[NCERT Exemplar]**

Sol. Using the digits 0, 1, 2, ..., 9, the number of 5-digit telephone numbers which can be formed is 10^5 (since, repetition is allowed).

The number of 5-digit telephone numbers, which have none of the digits repeated $= {}^{10}P_5 = \frac{10!}{5!} = 30240$

Hence, the required number of telephone numbers having atleast one of their digits repeated

$= 10^5 - {}^{10}P_5 = 100000 - 30240 = 69760$

Permutations when all the Objects are not Distinct Objects

When all the objects are not distinct i.e. some objects are of same kind, then we can find the number of permutations with the help of following theorems (without proof).

Theorem 3

The number of permutations of n objects, where p objects are of the same kind or identical and other are distinct, is given by $\frac{n!}{p!}$.

EXAMPLE 21. How many permutations of the letters of the words 'INDIA' are there?

Sol. Here, we have 5 letters, two of which are of the same kind and others are different.

$\therefore$ Required number of permutations (or arrangements)

$$= \frac{5!}{2!} = 5 \times 4 \times 3 = 60$$

Theorem 4

The number of permutations of n objects, where p_1 objects are of one kind, p_2 are of second kind, ... p_k are of kth kind and the rest if any, are of different kind is $\frac{n!}{p_1!\,p_2!\ldots p_k!}$.

EXAMPLE 22. Find the number of permutations of the letters of the word 'INDEPENDENCE'.

Sol. Here, we have 12 letters of which 3 are N's, 4 are E's, 2 are D's and rest are different.

$\therefore$ Required number of permutations $= \frac{12!}{3!4!2!}$

[here, $n = 12$, $p_1 = 3$, $p_2 = 4$ and $p_3 = 2$]

$$= \frac{12 \times 11 \times 10 \times 9 \times 8 \times 7 \times 6 \times 5 \times 4!}{6 \times 2 \times 4!}$$

$$= 11 \times 10 \times 9 \times 8 \times 7 \times 6 \times 5$$

$$= 1663200$$

EXAMPLE 23. In how many ways, 5 flags in which 3 are red, 1 is white and 1 is blue, be arranged on a staff, one below the other, if flags of one colour are not distinguishable?

Sol. Since, out of 5 flags, 3 are of the same kind (red) and others are different.

$\therefore$ Required number of ways

$$= \frac{5!}{3!1!1!} = 5 \times 4 = 20$$

Topic Practice 3

1 Evaluate
(i) ${}^{75}P_2$ (ii) ${}^{8}P_8$.

2 If ${}^nP_4 = 360$, then find the value of n.

3 If ${}^nP_4 : {}^nP_5 = 1:2$, find n.

4 If ${}^{10}P_r = 5040$, then find the value of r.

5 Find the value of n such that
$P(n, 5) = 42\,P(n, 3)$, $n > 4$.

6 Find r, if $5 \cdot {}^4P_r = 6 \cdot {}^5P_{r-1}$.

7 If ${}^{n-1}P_3 : {}^{n+1}P_3 = 5:12$, then find n.

8 If ${}^{2n+1}P_{n-1} : {}^{2n-1}P_n = 3:5$, then find n.

9 If ${}^{22}P_{r+1} : {}^{20}P_{r+2} = 11:52$, then find r.

10 Prove that following.
(i) ${}^nP_n = 2 \cdot {}^nP_{n-2}$
(ii) ${}^nP_n = {}^nP_{n-1}$
(iii) ${}^nP_r = n \cdot {}^{n-1}P_{r-1}$

11 Find the number of permutations of n different things taken r at a time, when repetition is allowed.

12 In a class of 10 students, there are 3 girls A, B, C. Find the number of different ways they can be arranged in a row such that no two of three girls are consecutive.

13 Find the total number of 9-digit numbers which have all different digits. **[NCERT Exemplar]**

14 How many numbers lying between 100 and 1000 can be formed with the digits 1, 2, 3, 4 and 5, if the repetition of digits is not allowed?

15 How many 3-digit numbers are there with distinct digits with each digit odd?

16 There are 6 items in column A and 6 items in column B. A student is asked to match each item in column A with an item in column B. How many possible, correct or incorrect answers are there to this question?

17 Find the number of 4-digit numbers that can be formed with the digits 2, 3, 4, 7 and using each digit only once.

18 In how many ways can 18 people line up at a ticket window of a cinema hall?

19 How many words, with or without meaning can be formed using all the letters of the word EQUATION, using each letter exactly once? **[NCERT]**

20 Find the number of different 4-letter words, with or without meaning that can be formed from the letters of the word 'NUMBER'.

21 How many different signals can be made by 5 flags from 8 flags of different colours?

22 From a committee of 12 persons, in how many ways can we choose a chairman and a vice-chairman assuming one person cannot hold more than one position?

23 Sunil wants to arrange 3 Economics, 2 History and 4 Language books on a shelf. If the books of the same subject are different. Determine the number of all possible arrangements.

24 Eight students are contesting the election for the presidentship of the student's union. In how many ways can their names be listed on the ballot papers?

25 Find the number of 4-digit numbers that can be formed using the digits 1, 2, 3, 4, 5, if no digit is repeated? How many of these will be even?

26 In how many ways can 4 red, 3 yellow and 2 green discs be arranged in a row if the discs of the same colour are indistinguishable?

27 If x denotes the number of permutations of $(n+2)$ things taken all at a time, y denotes the number of permutations of n things taken 12 at a time and z denotes the number of permutations of $n-12$ things taken all at a time such that $x = 132yz$, then find the value of n.

28 Ten different letters of English alphabet are given. Words with five letters are formed from these given letters. Find the number of words which have atleast one letter repeated.

Hints & Solutions

1. Solve as Example 1 (i).
   Ans. (i) 5550 (ii) 40320

2. **Hint** Write the given equation as
   $$n(n-1)(n-2)(n-3) = 6 \times 5 \times 4 \times 3$$
   $$= 6(6-1)(6-2)(6-3)$$
   and then compare it. **Ans.** $n = 6$

3. Solve as Example 2. **Ans.** $n = 6$

4. Solve as Example 3. **Ans.** $r = 4$

5. Solve as Example 2. **Ans.** $n = 10$

6. Solve as Example 5. **Ans.** $r = 3$

7. Solve as Example 6. **Ans.** $n = 8$

8. Solve as Example 6. **Ans.** $n = 4$

9. Solve as Example 6. **Ans.** $r = 7$

10. **Hint** Consider RHS and use the formula ${}^nP_r = \frac{n!}{(n-r)!}$ to simplify RHS.

11. The number of permutations = The number of ways of filling r vacant places by n different things
    $= \square \; \square \text{------} \square$ (r places)
    ∴ Number of permutations
    $$= n \times n \times \ldots \times n \,(r \text{ times}) = n^r$$

12. **Hint** $X\,B_1\,X\,B_2\,X\,B_3\,X\,B_4\,X\,B_5\,X\,B_6\,X\,B_7\,X$
    First, we arrange 7 boys in 7! ways.
    Now for girls, we have eight places and 3 girls need to be arranged. This can be done in ${}^8P_3$ ways.
    Total ways $= 7! \times {}^8P_3$
    Ans. $7! \times 336$

13. **Hint** The total number of 9-digit numbers, having all digits different $= 9 \times {}^9P_8$
    Ans. $9 \times 9!$

14. **Hint** Required numbers are 3-digit numbers formed with the given digits. Solve as Example 12.
    Ans. 60

15. **Hint** Required numbers are 3-digit numbers formed with the digits 1, 3, 5, 7 and 9.
    Ans. 60

16. **Hint** First item of column A can match to any item in column B in 6 ways.
    Second item of column A can match to the remaining items in column B in 5 ways.
    Total number of ways $= 6 \times 5 \times 4 \times 3 \times 2 \times 1$
    Ans. 6! ways

17. **Hint** Required number of numbers is same as number of permutations of 4 distinct objects taken all at a time.
    Ans. 24

18. Required number of ways is same as number of permutations of 18 different things taken all at a time.
    Ans. 18!

19. **Hint** There are 8 distinct letters in a given word. So, total number of that words can be formed is 8!.
    Ans. 40320

20. There are 6 distinct letters in the given word. So, number of different 4-letter words that can be formed is ${}^6P_4$.
    Ans. 360

21. **Hint** Required number of signals is same as number of permutations of 8 different things taken 5 at a time.
    Ans. 6720

22. Solve as Example 13. **Ans.** 132

23. **Hint** Number of possible arrangements is same as number of permutations of 9 different things taking all at a time.
    Ans. 362880

24. **Hint** Required number of ways is same as number of permutations of 8 different things taken all at a time.
    Ans. 40320

25. **Hint** Required number of numbers is same as number of permutations of 5 different things taken only 4 at a time.
    ∴ Number of required 4-digit numbers $= {}^5P_4 = 120$
    Number ending with either 2 or 4 digits $= \frac{120}{5} \times 2 = 48$
    ∴ Number of even numbers = 48
    [∵ There are equal chances of that the last digit be 1, 2, 3, 4 and 5]

26. Solve as Example 23.
    Ans. 1260

27. **Hint** We have, $(n+2)! = 132\, {}^nP_{12}(n-12)!$
    On solving, we get $n = 10$, which is not satisfied by ${}^nP_{12}$.
    Hence, no value of n exists.

28. Solve as Example 20. **Ans.** 69760

Restricted Permutation

Here, we shall discuss permutations of objects under certain conditions.

Some Important Results

- If particular things out of n different things are taken together, then we count these r particular thing as one thing and remaining $(n-r)$ things as separate thing.
  Then, total number of things $= (n-r)+1 = n-r+1$
  Since, these are different things, therefore number of permutations of these things $= (n-r+1)!$.
  But, r particular things can also be arranged among themselves in $r!$ ways.
  $\therefore$ Required number of permutations $= (n-r+1)!r!$
  If r particular things are identical, then required number of permutations $= (n-r+1)!$
- The number of permutations of n different objects taken r at a time, when a particular object is taken in each arrangement, is $r \cdot {}^{n-1}P_{r-1}$.
- The number of permutations of n objects taken r at a time, when a particular object is never taken in each arrangement, is ${}^{n-1}P_r$.
- The number of permutations of n different objects taken r at a time in which two specific objects always occur together, is $2!(r-1) \cdot {}^{n-2}P_{r-2}$.

Restricted Permutations when all the Objects are distinct

EXAMPLE 1. Find the number of different words that can be formed from the letters of the word 'TRIANGLE', so that

(i) all vowels occur together.

(ii) all vowels do not occur together.

Sol. There are 8 distinct letters in the word TRIANGLE, out of which 3 are vowels, namely A, E, I and 5 are consonants, namely T, R, N, G, L.

(i) Since, the vowels have to occur together, so let us assume them as a single object (AEI).

[A E I] T, R, N, G, L

Now, this single object together with 5 remaining letters will be counted as 6 objects and these can be arrange in ${}^6P_6 = 6!$ ways.

Corresponding to each of these permutations, we have

$$3! = 6$$

permutations of the three vowels A, E and I taken all at a time.

Hence, by fundamental principle of multiplication, the required number of words $= 6! \times 3! = 4320$

(ii) Clearly, required number of words

= Number of all possible arrangements of 8 letters taken all at a time

– Number of permutation in which the vowels are always together

$$= {}^8P_8 - 6! \times 3! = 8! - 6! \times 3!$$

$$= 8 \times 7 \times 6! - 6! \times 3!$$

$$= 6!(56-6) = 720 \times 50 = 36000$$

EXAMPLE 2. In how many ways can 5 children be arranged in a line such that

(i) two particular children of them are always together?

(ii) two particular children of them are never together?

[NCERT Exemplar]

Sol. (i) Let us take 2 particular children together as one.

Now, the remaining 4 (particular childrens and other three childrens) can be arranged in $4! = 24$ ways

Again, two particular children taken together can be arranged in $2! = 2$ ways

Hence, there are $24 \times 2 = 48$ ways of arrangement.

(ii) Clearly, required number of arrangements = Number of permutation of 5 children taken all at a time – Number of permutations of children in which two particular children are together

$$= 5! - 4! \times 2 = 5 \times 4! - 4! \times 2$$

$$= 4!(5-2) = 24 \times 3 = 72.$$

Hence, the required number of arrangements = 72

EXAMPLE 3. How many words with or without meaning, can be formed using all the letters of the word EQUATION at a time so that the vowels and consonants occur together? **[NCERT]**

Sol. There are 8 distinct letters in the word EQUATION, out of which 5 are vowels, namely A, E, I, O, U and 3 are consonants namely Q, T, N.

Now, let us take all vowels together as one object and all consonants together as another object.

(A, E, I, O, U) (Q, T, N)

Clearly, these objects can be arranged in $2! = 2$ ways

Again, all vowels taken together can be arranged in $5! = 120$ ways and all consonants taken together can be arranged in $3! = 6$ ways

Hence, by fundamental principle of multiplication required number of words $= 2 \times 5! \times 3!$

$$= 2 \times 120 \times 6 = 1440$$

EXAMPLE 4. In how many ways, can 8 Indians, 4 Americans and 4 Englishmen be seated in a row so that all persons of the same nationality sit together?

Sol. Let us take persons of same nationality as one unit. Then, there are 3 units which can be arranged in $3! = 6$ ways

Now, in each of arrangements, 8 Indians can be arranged among themselves in 8! ways, 4 Americans can be arranged among themselves in 4! ways and 4 Englishmen can be arranged among themselves in 4! ways.

Hence, by fundamental principle of multiplication, required number of ways

$$= 3! \times 8! \times 4! \times 4!$$

EXAMPLE 5. All the letters of the word 'EAMCOT' are arranged in different possible ways. Find the number of such arrangements in which no two vowels are adjacent to each other. **[NCERT Exemplar]**

Sol. There are 3 consonants and 3 vowels.

Since, no two vowels can occur together, therefore the possible choices for vowels are the places marked as '×'.

$$\times M \times C \times T \times$$

Clearly, the vowels can be arranged in ${}^4P_3$ ways and the consonants can be arranged in 3! ways. Hence, by fundamental principle of multiplication, required number of ways $= {}^4P_3 \times 3! = \frac{4!}{1!} \times 3! = 24 \times 6 = 144$

EXAMPLE 6. It is required to seat 5 men and 4 women in a row so that the women occupy the even places. How many such arrangements are possible? **[NCERT]**

Sol. There are 9 seats, out of which 4 are at even places and rest are at odd places.

Thus, there are 4 even places.

Clearly, 4 women can be placed in 4 even places in 4! ways. In rest of the five places, five men can be placed in 5! ways.

Hence, the required number of ways $= 4! \times 5! = 2880$

EXAMPLE 7. The letters of the word 'TUESDAY' are arranged in a line, each arrangement ending with letter S. How many different arrangements are possible? How many of them start with letter D?

Sol. Here, the given word contains 7 letters. Since, all words must end with S, so we fix S at last place. Now, remaining 6 letters can be arranged in $P(6, 6) = 6!$ ways

∴ Total number of words = 6!

$$= 6 \times 5 \times 4 \times 3 \times 2 \times 1 = 720$$

If the words begin with D and end with S, we fix D at the first place and S at the last place. Now, remaining 5 letters can be arranged in $P(5, 5) = 5!$

$$= 5 \times 4 \times 3 \times 2 \times 1$$
$$= 120 \text{ ways}$$

∴ Required number of words = 120

EXAMPLE 8. Find the number of ways in which 5 boys and 5 girls be seated in a row, so that

(i) no two girls sit together.

(ii) boys and girls sit alternatively. **[NCERT Exemplar]**

Sol. We have 5 boys and 5 girls.

(i) Since, no two girls sit together, therefore the possible choices for girls are the places marked as '×'.

$$\times B_1 \times B_2 \times B_3 \times B_4 \times B_5 \times$$

Clearly, the girls can be arranged in ${}^6P_5$ ways and the boys can be arranged in 5! ways.

Hence, by fundamental principle of multiplication, required number of ways $= {}^6P_5 \times 5!$

$$= \frac{6!}{(6-5)!} \times 5! = 6! \times 5! = 86400$$

(ii) Let us first seat the 5 girls (or 5 boys). This can be done in 5! ways.

Now, for each such arrangement, the 5 boys can be seated only at the cross marked places as shown below:

(I) $\times G_1 \times G_2 \times G_3 \times G_4 \times G_5$

(II) $G_1 \times G_2 \times G_3 \times G_4 \times G_5 \times$

In Case I, 5 boys can be seated in ${}^5P_5 = 5!$ ways

Thus, number of ways of seating $= 5! \times 5! = (5!)^2$

Similarly, in Case II, number of ways of seating $= (5!)^2$

Hence, the required number of ways $= (5!)^2 + (5!)^2$

$$= 2 \cdot (5!)^2 = 28800$$

EXAMPLE 9. The principal wants to arrange 5 students on the platform such that the boy SALIM occupies the second position and such that the girl SITA is always adjacent to the girl RITA. How many such arrangements are possible?

Sol. Since, SALIM occupies the second position and the two girls RITA and SITA are always adjacent to each other. So, none of these two girls can occupy the first seat. Thus, first seat can be occupied by any one of the remaining two students in 2 ways. Second seat can be occupied by SALIM in only one way

Now, in the remaining three seats SITA and RITA can be seated in the following four ways

	I	II	III	IV	V
1.	X	SALIM	SITA	RITA	X
2.	X	SALIM	RITA	SITA	X
3.	X	SALIM	X	SITA	RITA
4.	X	SALIM	X	RITA	SITA

Now, only one seat is left which can be occupied by the 5th student in one way

Hence, the total number of required type of arrangements $= 2 \times 4 \times 1 = 8$

EXAMPLE 10. A code word is to consist of two distinct English alphabets followed by two distinct numbers from 1 to 9. For example, CA23 is a code word. How many such code words are there? How many of them end with an even integer?

Sol. **Case I** There are 26 English alphabets. So, in the code word first two places can be filled in ${}^{26}P_2$ ways. In last two places, we have to use two distinct numbers from 1 to 9. So, last two places can be filled in ${}^{9}P_2$ ways.

Hence, the total number of code words

$$= {}^{26}P_2 \times {}^{9}P_2$$
$$= 650 \times 72 = 46800$$

Case II Number of code words ending with an even integer.

In this case, the code word can have any of the numbers 2, 4, 6, 8 at the extreme right position. So, the extreme right position can be filled in 4 ways. Now, next left position can be filled with any one of the remaining 8 digits in 8 ways and the two extreme left position can be filled by two English alphabets in ${}^{26}P_2$ ways.

Hence, the total number of code words which end with an even integer $= 4 \times 8 \times {}^{26}P_2$

$$= 4 \times 8 \times 650$$
$$= 20800$$

Finding the Number of Numbers having Distinct Digits which are Formed Under Certain Conditions

EXAMPLE 11. How many numbers between 400 and 1000 can be made with the digits 2, 3, 4, 5, 6 and 0, when repetition of digits is not allowed?

Sol. Given digits are, 2, 3, 4, 5, 6 and 0.

Any number between 400 and 1000 will be of three digits.

Since, the number should be greater than 400.

Therefore, hundred's place can be filled up by anyone of the digits 4, 5 and 6 in 3 ways.

$\therefore \quad k = 3$

Now, remaining two places can be filled up by the remaining five digits in ${}^{5}P_2$ ways.

Hence, required numbers $= 3 \times {}^{5}P_2 = 3 \times \dfrac{5!}{3!} = 60$

EXAMPLE 12. Determine the number of natural numbers smaller than 10^4, in the decimal notation of which all the digits are distinct.

Sol. The required natural numbers consist of 4-digit, 3-digit, 2-digit and 1-digit numbers.

Clearly, total number of 4-digit natural numbers

$$= 9 \times {}^{9}P_3$$

[$\because$ in thousand place, 0 does not exist]

Total number of 3-digit natural numbers $= 9 \times {}^{9}P_2$

Total number of 2-digit natural numbers $= 9 \times {}^{9}P_1$

and total number of 1-digit natural numbers $= 9$

Hence, the required number of natural numbers

$$= 9 \times {}^{9}P_3 + 9 \times {}^{9}P_2 + 9 \times {}^{9}P_1 + 9$$
$$= 9({}^{9}P_3 + {}^{9}P_2 + {}^{9}P_1 + 1)$$
$$= 9\left(\frac{9!}{6!} + \frac{9!}{7!} + \frac{9!}{8!} + 1\right)$$
$$= 9(9 \times 8 \times 7 + 9 \times 8 + 9 + 1)$$
$$= 9(504 + 72 + 10) = 9 \times 586 = 5274$$

EXAMPLE 13. How many different 4-digit numbers can be formed from the digits 2, 3, 4 and 6, if each digit is used only once in a number? Further, how many of these numbers

(i) end at 4? (ii) end at 3? (iii) end at 3 or 4?

Sol. The number of 4-digit numbers formed by the digits 2, 3, 4 and 6

$$= P(4, 4) = \frac{4!}{(4-4)!} = \frac{4!}{0!} \quad \left[\because {}^{n}P_r = \frac{n!}{(n-r)!}\right]$$
$$= \frac{4!}{1} = 4 \times 3 \times 2 \times 1 = 24 \quad [\because 0! = 1]$$

(i) In this case, '4' is fixed at the unit's place. Therefore, remaining 3 digits are 2, 3 and 6. Hence, the required number of 4-digit numbers $= P(3, 3)$

$$= \frac{3!}{(3-3)!} \quad \left[\because {}^{n}P_r = \frac{n!}{(n-r)!}\right]$$
$$= \frac{3!}{0!} = 3 \times 2 \times 1 = 6 \quad \text{...(i)}$$

(ii) In this case, '3' is fixed at unit's place. Therefore, remaining 3 digits are 2, 4 and 6. Hence, the required number of 4-digit numbers $= P(3, 3)$

$$= \frac{3!}{0!} = 6 \quad \text{...(ii)}$$

(iii) The number of 4-digit numbers ending with either 3 or 4

$$= 6 + 6 = 12 \quad \text{[from Eqs. (i) and (ii)]}$$

Restricted Permutations When all the Objects are not distinct

EXAMPLE 14. In how many different ways, the letters of the word 'ALGEBRA' can be arranged in a row, if

(i) the two A's are together?

(ii) the two A's are not together?

Sol. There are 7 letters in the word ALGEBRA. In these letters, 'A' occurs twice and rest all are different.

(i) Since, two A's are always together, so let us consider two A's as one letter.

AA, L, G, E, B, R

Now, we have 6 letters, which can be arranged in $^6P_6 = 6!$ ways

Hence, required number of ways $= 6! = 720$

[$\because$ two A's can be arranged among themselves in one way only]

(ii) Required number of ways = Number of all possible arrangements of the letters of the word ALGEBRA – Number of arrangements in which two A's are together

$$= \frac{7!}{2!} - 6! = 6!\left(\frac{7}{2} - 1\right) = 720 \times \frac{5}{2} = 360 \times 5 = 1800$$

EXAMPLE 15. Find the number of different words that can be formed from the letters of the word 'INTERMEDIATE' such that two vowels never come together. **[NCERT Exemplar]**

Sol. There are 12 letters in the word INTERMEDIATE.

In these letters, I occurs twice, T occurs twice, E occurs thrice and rest all are distinct. Also the word INTERMEDIATE contains 6 vowels I, I, E, E, E and A.

Since, two vowels never come together, therefore possible choices for vowels are the places marked with '×'.

× N× T× R× M× D× T×

Clearly, number of ways of arranging vowels

$$= {}^7P_6 \times \frac{1}{3!} \times \frac{1}{2!}$$

[$\because$ E occurs three times and I occurs two times]

and number of ways of arranging 6 consonants of which two are alike $= \frac{6!}{2!}$

Hence, the required number of words

$$= {}^7P_6 \times \frac{1}{3!} \times \frac{1}{2!} \times \frac{6!}{2!}$$

$$= \frac{7! \times 6!}{3! \times 2! \times 2!}$$

$$= 151200$$

EXAMPLE 16. How many different words can be formed by using all the letters of the word 'ALLAHABAD'? In how many of them, vowels occupy the even position?

Sol. There are 9 letters in the word ALLAHABAD. In these letters, A occurs 4 times, L occurs twice and rest all are different.

$\therefore$ Total number of words $= \frac{9!}{4!\,2!} = 7560$

Now, consider the case, where vowels occupy the even position.

Since, the word ALLAHABAD contains 4 vowels, A, A, A and A, and there are 4 even places, therefore 4 vowels can be arranged in 4 even places.

This can be done in $^4P_4 \times \frac{1}{4!} = 4! \times \frac{1}{4!} = 1$ way

Now, we are left with 5 places and 5 letters, which can be arranged in $^5P_5 \times \frac{1}{2!} = \frac{5!}{2!}$ ways

[$\because$ out of 5 letters, 2 are alike]

Hence, the number of words in which vowels occupy the even position $= \frac{5!}{2!} = 60$

EXAMPLE 17. How many numbers can be formed with the digits 1, 2, 3, 4, 3, 2 and 1, so that odd digits always occupy the odd places?

Sol. The given digits are 1, 2, 3, 4, 3, 2, 1. Out of these, 1, 3, 3, 1 are odd digits.

Since, there are 4 odd places, therefore odd digits can occupy the odd places in $^4P_4 \times \frac{1}{2!} \times \frac{1}{2!} = \frac{4!}{2!\,2!} = 6$ ways

Now, we are left with 3 places in which remaining 3 digits (2, 2 and 4) can be arranged in $^3P_3 \times \frac{1}{2!} = \frac{3!}{2!}$

$= 3$ ways

Hence, the required number of numbers $= 6 \times 3 = 18$

EXAMPLE 18. In how many ways can the letters of the word 'PERMUTATIONS' be arranged, if

(i) words start with P and end with S?

(ii) vowels are all together? **[NCERT]**

Sol. There are 12 letters in the word PERMUTATIONS.

In this letter, T occurs twice and rest all are different. Also, the word PERMUTATIONS contains all the five vowels, namely, A, E, I, O and U.

(i) Since, the words start with P and end with S, so let us fix P at first place and S at last place.

P	I	II	III	IV	V	VI	VII	VIII	IX	X	S

Now, we are left with 10 letters (E, R, M, U, T, A, T, I, O, N) which can be arranged in $\frac{10!}{2!}$ ways.

[$\because$ T occurs twice]

Hence, the required number of ways $= \frac{10!}{2!} = 1814400$

(ii) Since, the vowels are together, so let us take all vowels together and consider it as one letter.

[A E I O U], P, R, M, T, T, N, S

Now, we have 8 letters, which can be arranged in $\frac{8!}{2!}$ ways.

Corresponding to each such arrangement, all the five vowels can be arranged among themselves in $^5P_5$ $= 5!$ ways

Hence, the required number of ways $= \frac{8!}{2!} \times 5!$

$= 2419200$

Topic Practice 4

1 Find the number of 5-digit telephone numbers having atleast one of their digits repeated.

2 Find the sum of all the numbers that can be formed with the digits 2, 3, 4, 5 taken all at a time.

3 How many number lying between 999 and 10000 can be formed with the help of the digits 0, 2, 3, 6, 7, 8, when the digits are not be repeated?

4 In how many ways can the letters of the word 'GOLDEN' be arranged so that N and E are always together?

5 In how many ways can the letters of the word 'PENCIL' be arranged so that N is always next to E?

6 Find the number of different words that can be formed with the letters of the word 'ENGLISH' so that the word begin with E and end with I?

7 How many 3-digit even numbers can be made using the digits 1, 2, 3, 4, 5, 6, 7, if no digits is repeated?

8 In how many ways 3 Mathematics books, 4 History books, 3 Chemistry books and 2 Biology books can be arranged on a shelf so that all books of the same subjects are together? **[NCERT Exemplar]**

9 In how many ways can 5 girls and 3 boys be seated in a row so that no two boys are together? **[NCERT]**

10 Find the number of ways in which the letters of the word 'MACHINE' can be arranged so that the vowels occupy the odd places.

11 How many words can be formed out of the letters of the word 'ORIENTAL' so that the vowels always occupy the odd places?

12 How many different words can be formed with the letters of the word 'SUNDAY'? How many of these begin with *N*? How many begin *N* and end in *Y*?

13 How many 4-digit numbers are there with no digit repeated? **[NCERT]**

14 In how many ways can 7 plus (+) signs and 5 minus (–) signs be arranged in a row so that no two minus signs are together?

15 How many four-digit numbers divisible by 4 can be made with the digits 1, 2, 3, 4, 5, if the repetition of digits is not allowed?

16 Find the number of different 8 letters arrangements that can be made from the letters of the word 'DAUGHTER' so that

(i) all vowels occur together.

(ii) all vowels do not occur together.

17 In how many ways can 10 examination papers be arranged so that the best and the worst papers are never together?

18 How many numbers lying between 100 and 1000 can be formed with the digits 0, 1, 2, 3, 4, 5, if the repetition of the digits is not allowed? **[NCERT]**

19 Three married couples are to be seated in a row having six seats in a cinema halls. If spouses are to be seated next to each other, then in how many ways can they be seated? Also, find the number of ways of their seating, if all the ladies sit together. **[NCERT Exemplar]**

20 Find the number of ways in which 5 boys and 5 girls be seated in a row, so that

(i) all the girls sit together.

(ii) all the girls and all the boys sit together.

(iii) all the girls never sit together.

21 In how many ways can the letters of the word 'MATHEMATICS' be arranged so that vowels are always together?

22 In how many of the distinct permutations of the letters in 'MISSISSIPPI' do the four I's not come together?

23 How many different words can be formed with the letters of the word 'HARYANA'? How many of these

(i) have H and N together?

(ii) begin with H and end with N?

(iii) have three vowels together?

24 How many numbers greater than 1000000 can be formed by using the digits 2, 3, 0, 3, 4, 2, 3?

Hints & Solutions

1. **Hint** If all the digits repeated, then number of 5-digit telephone numbers can be formed in 10^5 ways and if no digit repeated, then 5-digit telephone numbers can be formed in ${}^{10}P_5$ ways.

   $\therefore$ Required number of ways $= 10^5 - {}^{10}P_5$

   Ans. 69760

2. **Hint** Total number of numbers formed with the digits 2, 3, 4, 5 taken all at a time = Number of arrangements of 4 digits, taken all at a time $= {}^4P_4 = 24$

   Consider the digits in the unit's places in all these numbers. Each of the digit 2, 3, 4, 5 occurs in $3!(=6)$ times in the unit's place.

   So, total for the digits in the unit's place in all the numbers $= (2+3+4+5)\times 3! = 84$

   Since, each of the digits 2, 3, 4, 5 occurs 3! times in any one of the remaining places.

   So, the sum of the digits in the ten's, hundred's, thousand's places in all the numbers

   $$= (2+3+4+5)\times 3! = 84$$

   $\therefore$ Sum of all the numbers $= 84\,(10^0 + 10^1 + 10^2 + 10^3)$

   Ans. 93324

3. **Hint** The number of 4-digit numbers formed by digits 0, 2, 3, 6, 7, 8 is ${}^6P_4 = 360$

   But here those numbers are also involved which begin from 0. So, we take those numbers as three-digit numbers. Taking initial digit 0, the number of ways to fill remaining 3 places from five digits 2, 3, 6, 7, 8 are ${}^5P_3 = 60$

   So, the required number $= 360 - 60$

   Ans. 300

4. **Hint** Let us take E and N together and consider it as one letter. Further, solve as Example 2 (i).

   Ans. 240

5. **Hint** Here, we consider E and N together as one unit.

   $\therefore$ Required number of ways $= 5! = 120$

   Ans. 120

6. Solve as Example 18 (i). **Ans.** 120

7. **Hint** For even numbers, even number should be placed on unit place (2, 4, 6)

   $\therefore$ 3-digit distinct even number of ways $= 6\times 5\times 3$.

   Ans. 90

8. Solve as Example 4. **Ans.** 41472

9. Solve as Example 8 (i). **Ans.** 14400

10. **Hint** Firstly, fix the odd position of vowels (A, I, E) 1, 2, 3, 4, 5, 6, 7 i.e. ${}^4P_3$ ways and constants at 4 places can be arranged in $4!$ ways. **Ans.** 576

11. Solve as Question 10. **Ans.** 576

12. Solve as Example 18. (i). **Ans.** 720, 120, 24

13. Solve as Example 13. **Ans.** 4536

14. Solve as Example 8. **Ans.** 56

15. **Hint** Since a number is divisible by 4, if the number formed by the last two digits is divisible by 4. Then, the digits at unit's and ten's place can be arranged as follows:

TH	H	T	O
X	X	1	2
X	X	2	4
X	X	3	2
X	X	5	2

   Ans. 24

16. Solve as Example 1. **Ans.** (i) 4320 (ii) 36000

17. **Hint** Required number of ways = Number of all possible arrangement of 10 papers – Number of arrangement of paper in which best and worst occur together. **Ans.** $8\times 9!$

18. Solve as Example 11. **Ans.** 100

19. **Hint** Consider each married couple as one unit, then the three units can be arranged in $3! = 6$ ways

   Again, each couple can be arranged in $2! = 2$ ways

   If the ladies sit together, then consider all ladies together as one unit. Now, this single unit together with 3 remaining mens will be counted as 4 objects. **Ans.** 48; 144

20. (i) **Hint** Take all the girls together as one unit. **Ans.** $6!\times 5!$

   (ii) **Hint** Take all the girls together as one unit and all the boys together as another unit. **Ans.** $2!\times 5!\times 5!$

   (iii) **Hint** Required number of ways = Number of all possible arrangements of 5 boys and 5 girls – Number of arrangement in which all girls sit together

   Ans. $10! - 5!\times 6!$

21. Solve as Example 18 (ii). **Ans.** 120960

22. **Hint** Solve as Example 14 (ii). Firstly, find the number of permutations in which four I's come together.

   Required number of ways = Number of permutation of letters of the word MISSISSIPPI – Number of permutation in which four I's come together. **Ans.** 33810

23. Solve as Example 18.

   Ans. 840; (i) 240 (ii) 20 (iii) 120

24. **Hint** Since, 1000000 is a 7-digit number and the number of digits to be used is also 7. Therefore, the number to be counted will be 7-digit only.

   Now, let us arrange the given seven digits. This can be done in $\frac{7!}{2!\,3!} = 420$ ways. But these arrangements will include those also where 0 is at the million's place.

   So, keeping 0 fixed at million's place, the remaining 6 digits can be arranged in $\frac{6!}{2!\,3!} = 60$ ways.

   Hence, required number of numbers $= 420 - 60$

   Ans. 360

Combinations

The word **combination** means selection. Each of the different selection, which is made by taking some or all of a number of different objects at a time, irrespective of their arrangements is called a combination.

e.g. The different combinations formed from three letters *A*, *B*, *C* taking two at a time are *AB*, *AC*, *BC*.

In a combination, only selection is made and the order in which the objects are arranged is immaterial, while in a permutation, not only the selection is formed but also an arrangement in a definite order is considered.

Meaning of ^nC_r

The number of combinations of *n* distinct objects taken *r* at a time is given by $^nC_r = \dfrac{n!}{r!(n-r)!}$.

In particular,

(i) When $r = 0$, then $^nC_0 = 1$

(ii) When $r = n$, then $^nC_n = 1$

EXAMPLE 1. Evaluate the following.

(i) $^{14}C_3$ (ii) $^{100}C_{99}$ (iii) $^{35}C_{35}$ (iv) $^{30}C_0$

Sol. (i) $^{14}C_3 = \dfrac{14!}{3!(14-3)!}$ $\left[\because {}^nC_r = \dfrac{n!}{r!(n-r)!}\right]$

$$= \frac{14!}{3!\times 11!} = \frac{14\times 13\times 12\times 11!}{(3\times 2\times 1)\times 11!}$$

$$= \frac{14\times 13\times 12}{6} = 14\times 13\times 2 = 364$$

(ii) $^{100}C_{99} = \dfrac{100!}{99!(100-99)!}$

$$= \frac{100!}{99!\times 1!} = \frac{100\times 99!}{99!\times 1} = 100$$

(iii) $^{35}C_{35} = 1$ $[\because {}^nC_n = 1]$

(iv) $^{30}C_0 = 1$ $[\because {}^nC_0 = 1]$

EXAMPLE 2. If $^nP_r = 840$ and $^nC_r = 35$, then find *r*. **[NCERT Exemplar]**

Sol. We know that $^nP_r = r!\times {}^nC_r$

$\therefore$ $840 = r!\times 35$

$\Rightarrow$ $r! = \dfrac{840}{35}$

$\Rightarrow$ $r! = 24 = 4!$

$\Rightarrow$ $r = 4$

EXAMPLE 3 If the ratio $^{2n}C_3 : {}^nC_3$ is equal to 11 : 1, then find the value of *n*. **[NCERT]**

Sol. We have, $^{2n}C_3 : {}^nC_3 = 11:1$

$$\Rightarrow \frac{^{2n}C_3}{^nC_3} = \frac{11}{1}$$

$$\Rightarrow \frac{\dfrac{2n(2n-1)(2n-2)}{3\cdot 2\cdot 1}}{\dfrac{n(n-1)(n-2)}{3\cdot 2\cdot 1}} = \frac{11}{1}$$

$$\Rightarrow \frac{2n(2n-1)2(n-1)}{3\cdot 2\cdot 1}\times\frac{3\cdot 2\cdot 1}{n(n-1)(n-2)} = \frac{11}{1}$$

$$\Rightarrow \frac{4(2n-1)}{n-2} = \frac{11}{1}$$

$$\Rightarrow 8n-4 = 11n-22$$

$$\Rightarrow 18 = 3n$$

$$\Rightarrow n = 6$$

Hence, the value of *n* is 6.

EXAMPLE 4. If $^{n+2}C_8 : {}^{n-2}P_4 = 57:16$, then find the value of *n*.

Sol. We have, $^{n+2}C_8 : {}^{n-2}P_4 = 57:16$

$$\Rightarrow \frac{^{n+2}C_8}{^{n-2}P_4} = \frac{57}{16}$$

$$\Rightarrow \frac{\dfrac{(n+2)!}{8!(n+2-8)!}}{\dfrac{(n-2)!}{(n-2-4)!}} = \frac{57}{16}$$

$$\Rightarrow \frac{(n+2)!}{8!(n-6)!}\times\frac{(n-6)!}{(n-2)!} = \frac{57}{16}$$

$$\Rightarrow \frac{(n+2)(n+1)n(n-1)(n-2)!}{8!}\times\frac{1}{(n-2)!} = \frac{57}{16}$$

$$\Rightarrow (n+2)(n+1)n(n-1) = \frac{57}{16}\times 8!$$

$$= \frac{19\times 3}{16}\times 8\times 7\times 6\times 5\times 4\times 3\times 2\times 1$$

$$\Rightarrow (n-1)n(n+1)(n+2) = 19\times 3\times 7\times 6\times 5\times 4\times 3$$

$$\Rightarrow (n-1)n(n+1)(n+2) = 19\times(3\times 7)\times(6\times 3)\times(5\times 4)$$

$$\Rightarrow (n-1)n(n+1)(n+2) = 18\times 19\times 20\times 21$$

On comparing both sides, we get

$$n-1 = 18$$

$$\Rightarrow n = 19$$

EXAMPLE 5. Prove that $r \cdot {}^nC_r = n \cdot {}^{n-1}C_{r-1}$.

Sol. $\text{LHS} = r \cdot {}^nC_r = r \cdot \frac{n!}{r!(n-r)!}$ $\quad \left[\because {}^nC_r = \frac{n!}{r!(n-r)!}\right]$

$$= \frac{r \cdot n!}{r(r-1)!(n-r)!} \quad [\because r! = r(r-1)!]$$

$$= \frac{n!}{(r-1)!(n-r)!} \quad \text{...(i)}$$

$$\text{RHS} = n \cdot {}^{n-1}C_{r-1} = n \cdot \frac{(n-1)!}{(r-1)!\{(n-1)-(r-1)\}!}$$

$$= \frac{n \cdot (n-1)!}{(r-1)!(n-r)!} = \frac{n!}{(r-1)!(n-r)!} \quad [\because n(n-1)! = n!] \text{ ...(ii)}$$

From Eqs. (i) and (ii), we get

LHS = RHS

$\Rightarrow \quad r \cdot {}^nC_r = n \cdot {}^{n-1}C_{r-1}$ **Hence proved.**

EXAMPLE 6 Prove that ${}^{2n}C_n = \frac{2^n\{1 \cdot 3 \cdot 5 \ldots (2n-1)\}}{n!}$.

Sol. We have, ${}^{2n}C_n = \frac{2n!}{(2n-n)!\,n!} = \frac{(2n)!}{n!\,n!}$

$$= \frac{(2n)(2n-1)(2n-2)\ldots 5 \cdot 4 \cdot 3 \cdot 2 \cdot 1}{n!\,n!}$$

$$= \frac{\{1 \cdot 3 \cdot 5 \ldots (2n-1)\}\{2 \cdot 4 \cdot 6 \ldots 2n\}}{n!n!}$$

$$= \frac{\{1 \cdot 3 \cdot 5 \ldots (2n-1)\} \times 2^n\{1 \cdot 2 \cdot 3 \ldots n\}}{n!n!}$$

$$= \frac{\{1 \cdot 3 \cdot 5 \ldots (2n-1)\} \times 2^n \times n!\}}{n!n!}$$

$$= \frac{2^n\{1 \cdot 3 \cdot 5 \ldots (2n-1)\}}{n!}$$ **Hence proved.**

EXAMPLE 7. If ${}^{n-1}C_r : {}^nC_r : {}^{n+1}C_r = 6:9:13$, then find the values of n and r.

Sol. We have, $\frac{{}^{n-1}C_r}{{}^nC_r} = \frac{6}{9}$

$$\Rightarrow \frac{\frac{(n-1)!}{r!(n-1-r)!}}{\frac{n!}{r!(n-r)!}} = \frac{2}{3}$$

$$\Rightarrow \frac{(n-1)!}{(n-(r+1))!} \times \frac{(n-r)!}{n!} = \frac{2}{3}$$

$$\Rightarrow \frac{(n-1)!}{(n-(r+1))!} \times \frac{(n-r)(n-(r+1))!}{n(n-1)!} = \frac{2}{3}$$

$$\Rightarrow \frac{n-r}{n} = \frac{2}{3}$$

$$\Rightarrow 3n - 3r = 2n \Rightarrow n - 3r = 0 \quad \text{...(i)}$$

Also, we have $\frac{{}^nC_r}{{}^{n+1}C_r} = \frac{9}{13}$

$$\Rightarrow \frac{n!}{r!(n-r)!} \times \frac{r!(n+1-r)!}{(n+1)!} = \frac{9}{13}$$

$$\Rightarrow \frac{n!}{(n-r)!} \times \frac{(n-(r-1))!}{(n+1)n!} = \frac{9}{13}$$

$$\Rightarrow \frac{(n-(r-1))(n-r)!}{(n-r)!(n+1)} = \frac{9}{13}$$

$$\Rightarrow \frac{n-r+1}{n+1} = \frac{9}{13}$$

$$\Rightarrow 13n - 13r + 13 = 9n + 9$$

$$\Rightarrow 4n - 13r = -4 \quad \text{...(ii)}$$

On solving Eqs. (i) and (ii), we get

$n = 12$ and $r = 4$

EXAMPLE 8. Prove that the product of r consecutive positive integers is divisible by $r!$.

Sol. Let the r consecutive positive integers be $(n+1), (n+2), (n+3)\ldots(n+r)$. Then,

$$\text{Product} = (n+1)(n+2)(n+3)\ldots(n+r)$$

$$= \frac{n!(n+1)(n+2)(n+3)\ldots(n+r)}{n!}$$

$$= \frac{1 \cdot 2 \cdot 3 \ldots n(n+1)(n+2)\ldots(n+r)}{n!}$$

$$= \frac{(n+r)!}{n!} = \frac{(n+r)!}{r!\{(n+r)-r\}!}(r!) = ({}^{n+r}C_r)\,r!$$

which is divisible by $r!$. **Hence proved.**

Some Important Theorems

Theorem 1 ${}^nP_r = {}^nC_r \cdot r!,\ 0 < r \leq n$

Proof The number of combinations of n distinct objects taken r at a time is ${}^nC_r$. In these combinations, r things can be arranged among themselves in $r!$ ways. So, we have $r!$ permutations.

Therefore, the total number of permutations of n different things taken r at a time is ${}^nC_r \times r!$, which is equal to ${}^nP_r$.

$\therefore \quad {}^nP_r = r! \times {}^nC_r, 0 < r \leq n$ **Hence proved.**

Theorem 2 ${}^nC_r = {}^nC_{n-r},\ 0 \leq r \leq n$

Theorem 3 ${}^nC_r + {}^nC_{r-1} = {}^{n+1}C_r$

Proof $\text{LHS} = {}^nC_r + {}^nC_{r-1} = \frac{n!}{r!(n-r)!} + \frac{n!}{(r-1)!(n-r+1)!}$

$$= \frac{n!(n-r+1)}{r!(n-r+1)(n-r)!} + \frac{n!\,r}{r(r-1)!(n-r+1)!}$$

$$= \frac{n!(n-r+1)}{r!(n-r+1)!} + \frac{n!\,r}{r!(n-r+1)!} = n!\left[\frac{n-r+1+r}{r!(n-r+1)!}\right]$$

$$= \frac{(n+1)\,n!}{r!(n+1-r)!} = \frac{(n+1)!}{r!(n+1-r)!} = {}^{n+1}C_r = \text{RHS}$$

Hence proved.

Theorem 4

If ${}^nC_x = {}^nC_y$, then either $x = y$ or $x + y = n$.

Theorem 5

If n is an even natural number, then the greatest of the values ${}^nC_0, {}^nC_1, {}^nC_2, \dots {}^nC_n$ is ${}^nC_{n/2}$.

If n is an odd natural number, then the greatest of the values ${}^nC_0, {}^nC_1, {}^nC_2, \dots {}^nC_n$ is ${}^nC_{\frac{n-1}{2}} = {}^nC_{\frac{n+1}{2}}$.

EXAMPLE 9. Evaluate ${}^{13}C_6 + {}^{13}C_5$.

Sol. We have, ${}^{13}C_6 + {}^{13}C_5 = {}^{14}C_6$ $\quad [\because {}^nC_r + {}^nC_{r-1} = {}^{n+1}C_r]$

$$= \frac{14!}{6!(14-6)!} \quad \left[\because {}^nC_r = \frac{n!}{r!(n-r)!}\right]$$

$$= \frac{14!}{6! \times 8!} = \frac{14 \times 13 \times 12 \times 11 \times 10 \times 9 \times 8!}{6 \times 5 \times 4 \times 3 \times 2 \times 1 \times 8!}$$

$$= 7 \times 13 \times 11 \times 3$$

$$= 3003$$

EXAMPLE 10. Evaluate $\sum_{r=1}^{5} {}^5C_r$.

Sol. Consider, $\sum_{r=1}^{5} {}^5C_r = {}^5C_1 + {}^5C_2 + {}^5C_3 + {}^5C_4 + {}^5C_5$

$$= {}^5C_1 + {}^5C_2 + {}^5C_2 + {}^5C_1 + {}^5C_0 \quad [\because {}^nC_r = {}^nC_{n-r}]$$

$$= 5 + 2 \times {}^5C_2 + 5 + 1 \quad [\because {}^nC_1 = n \text{ and } {}^nC_0 = 1]$$

$$= 11 + 2 \times \frac{5 \times 4}{2 \times 1}$$

$$= 11 + 20 = 31$$

EXAMPLE 11. If ${}^nC_{10} = {}^nC_{12}$, then find the value of ${}^{23}C_n$.

Sol. We know that ${}^nC_x = {}^nC_y$

$\Rightarrow$ $x + y = n$ or $x = y$

Here $x \neq y$, so $x + y = n$

$\Rightarrow$ $n = 10 + 12 = 22$

Now, ${}^{23}C_n = {}^{23}C_{22} = {}^{23}C_{23-22} = {}^{23}C_1 = 23$

EXAMPLE 12. If ${}^{16}C_r = {}^{16}C_{r+2}$, then find ${}^rC_4$.

Sol. We know that ${}^nC_x = {}^nC_y$

$\Rightarrow$ $x = y$ or $x + y = n$

$\therefore$ $r + (r+2) = 16$ $\quad [\because r \neq r+2]$

$\Rightarrow$ $2r + 2 = 16$

$\Rightarrow$ $2r = 14$

$\Rightarrow$ $r = 7$

Hence, ${}^7C_4 = {}^7C_3 = \frac{7 \times 6 \times 5}{3 \times 2 \times 1} = 35$

EXAMPLE 13. If ${}^8C_r - {}^7C_3 = {}^7C_2$, then find r.

Sol. We have,

$${}^8C_r - {}^7C_3 = {}^7C_2$$

$\Rightarrow$ ${}^8C_r = {}^7C_3 + {}^7C_2$

$\Rightarrow$ ${}^8C_r = {}^8C_3$ $\quad [\because {}^nC_r + {}^nC_{r-1} = {}^{n+1}C_r]$

$\Rightarrow$ $r = 3$ or $r + 3 = 8$

$[\because {}^nC_x = {}^nC_y \Rightarrow x = y \text{ or } x + y = n]$

$\Rightarrow$ $r = 3$ or $r = 5$

EXAMPLE 14. Evaluate ${}^nC_r + 2 \cdot {}^nC_{r-1} + {}^nC_{r-2}$.

Sol. Consider, ${}^nC_r + 2 \cdot {}^nC_{r-1} + {}^nC_{r-2}$

$$= {}^nC_r + {}^nC_{r-1} + {}^nC_{r-1} + {}^nC_{r-2}$$

$$= ({}^nC_r + {}^nC_{r-1}) + ({}^nC_{r-1} + {}^nC_{r-2})$$

$$= {}^{n+1}C_r + {}^{n+1}C_{r-1} = {}^{n+2}C_r$$

$[\because {}^nC_r + {}^nC_{r-1} = {}^{n+1}C_r]$

EXAMPLE 15. Find the value of the expression

$${}^{47}C_4 + \sum_{j=1}^{5} {}^{52-j}C_3.$$

Sol. We have, ${}^{47}C_4 + \sum_{j=1}^{5} {}^{52-j}C_3$

$$= {}^{47}C_4 + {}^{52-1}C_3 + {}^{52-2}C_3 + {}^{52-3}C_3 + {}^{52-4}C_3 + {}^{52-5}C_3$$

$$= {}^{47}C_4 + {}^{51}C_3 + {}^{50}C_3 + {}^{49}C_3 + {}^{48}C_3 + {}^{47}C_3$$

$$= ({}^{47}C_3 + {}^{47}C_4) + {}^{48}C_3 + {}^{49}C_3 + {}^{50}C_3 + {}^{51}C_3$$

$$= {}^{48}C_4 + {}^{48}C_3 + {}^{49}C_3 + {}^{50}C_3 + {}^{51}C_3$$

$[\because {}^nC_{r-1} + {}^nC_r = {}^{n+1}C_r]$

$$= {}^{49}C_4 + {}^{49}C_3 + {}^{50}C_3 + {}^{51}C_3$$

$$= {}^{50}C_4 + {}^{50}C_3 + {}^{51}C_3$$

$$= {}^{51}C_4 + {}^{51}C_3 = {}^{52}C_4$$

$$= \frac{52 \times 51 \times 50 \times 49}{4 \times 3 \times 2 \times 1}$$

$$= 13 \times 17 \times 25 \times 49$$

$$= 270725$$

EXAMPLE 16. A person wishes to make up as many different parties as he can out of his 20 friends such that each party consists of the same number of persons. How many friends should he invite?

Sol. Let he invites r friends at a time, then the total number of parties is ${}^{20}C_r$.

Since, we have to find the maximum value of ${}^{20}C_r$ which is for $r = 10$ because ${}^nC_r$ is maximum for $r = \frac{n}{2}$, when n is even.

Hence, he should invite 10 friends at a time in order to form the maximum number of parties.

Topic Practice 5

1. Evaluate the following.
   (i) ${}^{10}C_8$ (ii) ${}^{50}C_{50}$
2. If ${}^nP_r = 720$ and ${}^nC_r = 120$, then find r.
3. If $n = {}^mC_2$, then find the value of ${}^nC_2$.
4. Find the number of ways a team of 2 players can be formed out of a group of 3 lawn tennis players X, Y, Z.
5. Verify that $2 \times {}^7C_4 = {}^8C_4$.
6. Evaluate ${}^{31}C_{26} - {}^{30}C_{26}$.
7. Determine n, if ${}^{2n}C_3 : {}^nC_3 = 12:1$. **[NCERT]**
8. If ${}^{28}C_{2r} : {}^{24}C_{2r-4} = 225 : 11$, then find r.
9. Prove that
   ${}^{4n}C_{2n} : {}^{2n}C_n = [1 \cdot 3 \cdot 5 \dots (4n-1)] : [1 \cdot 3 \cdot 5 \dots (2n-1)]^2$.
10. If ${}^nC_{r-1} = 36$, ${}^nC_r = 84$, ${}^nC_{r+1} = 126$, then find ${}^rC_2$. **[NCERT Exemplar]**
11. If ${}^nC_{12} = {}^nC_8$, then find the value of n.
12. Find the value of ${}^{15}C_8 + {}^{15}C_9 - {}^{15}C_6 - {}^{15}C_7$.
13. If ${}^nC_9 = {}^nC_8$, then find ${}^nC_{17}$.
14. If ${}^{24}C_x = {}^{24}C_{2x+3}$, then find x.
15. Evaluate ${}^{10}C_4 + {}^{10}C_5$.
16. Prove that ${}^nC_r \times {}^rC_s = {}^nC_s \times {}^{n-s}C_{r-s}$
17. Evaluate ${}^{20}C_5 + \sum_{r=2}^{5} {}^{25-r}C_4$.
18. Prove that the product of $2n$ consecutive negative integers is divisible by $(2n)!$.
19. A person wishes to make up as many different parties as he can out of his 36 friends, such that each party consists of the same number of persons. How many friends should he invite?

Hints & Solutions

1. Solve as Example 1.
   Ans. (i) 45 (ii) 1
2. Solve as Example 2.
   Ans. $r = 3$
3. **Hint** $n = {}^mC_2 = \dfrac{m(m-1)}{2}$

   $$\therefore \quad {}^nC_2 = \frac{n(n-1)}{2}$$
   $$= \frac{m(m-1)}{4}\left\{\frac{m(m-1)}{2} - 1\right\}$$
   $$= 3\left\{\frac{1}{24}(m+1)\,m\,(m-1)(m-2)\right\}$$

   Ans. $3 \times {}^{m+1}C_4$
4. **Hint** There are only 3 possible ways in which the team could be constructed.
   These are XY, YZ and ZX.
5. Evaluate LHS and RHS separately and verify the result.
6. **Hint** ${}^{31}C_{26} - {}^{30}C_{26} = {}^{31}C_5 - {}^{30}C_4$

   $$= \left(\frac{31 \times 30 \times 29 \times 28 \times 27}{5 \times 4 \times 3 \times 2 \times 1}\right) - \left(\frac{30 \times 29 \times 28 \times 27}{4 \times 3 \times 2 \times 1}\right)$$

   Ans. 142506
7. Solve as Example 3. **Ans.** 5
8. **Hint** Use ${}^nC_r = \dfrac{n!}{r!(n-r)!}$ and simplify. **Ans.** 7
9. Solve as Example 7.
10. **Hint** $\dfrac{{}^nC_{r-1}}{{}^nC_r} = \dfrac{36}{84}$ and $\dfrac{{}^nC_r}{{}^nC_{r+1}} = \dfrac{84}{126}$, we get

    $$r = 3$$
    $$\therefore \quad {}^rC_2 = {}^3C_2 = 3$$

    Ans. 3
11. **Hint** ${}^nC_{12} = {}^nC_8 \Rightarrow {}^nC_{n-12} = {}^nC_8$ $\quad [\because {}^nC_r = {}^nC_{n-r}]$
    Ans. 20
12. **Hint** ${}^{15}C_8 + {}^{15}C_9 - {}^{15}C_6 - {}^{15}C_7$

    $= {}^{15}C_{15-8} + {}^{15}C_{15-9} - {}^{15}C_6 - {}^{15}C_7$ $\quad [\because {}^nC_r = {}^nC_{n-r}]$

    $= {}^{15}C_7 + {}^{15}C_6 - {}^{15}C_6 - {}^{15}C_7$ **Ans.** 0
13. Solve as Example 11. **Ans.** 1
14. Solve as Example 11. **Ans.** 7
15. Solve as Example 9. **Ans.** 462
16. **Hint** Simplify LHS and RHS separately and get the result.
17. Solve as Example 15. **Ans.** 42504
18. **Hint** Let $-r, -r-1, -r-2, \dots (-r-2n+1)$ be $2n$ consecutive negative integers.
19. Solve as Example 16. **Ans.** 10 friends

Practical Problems on Combinations

In this topic, we will discuss some practical problems, where the formula for ${}^nC_r$ and its meaning can be applied.

TYPE I

Simply Based on the Formula of ${}^nC_r$

EXAMPLE 1. In how many ways, can 5 sportsmen be selected from a group of 10?

Sol. Required number of ways $= {}^{10}C_5$

$$= \frac{10 \times 9 \times 8 \times 7 \times 6}{5 \times 4 \times 3 \times 2 \times 1}$$
$$= 2 \times 3 \times 7 \times 6 = 252$$

EXAMPLE 2. If there are 15 persons in a party and if each two of them shake hands with each other. How many hand-shakes happen in the party?

Sol. The total number of hand-shakes is same as the number of ways of selecting 2 persons among 15 persons $= {}^{15}C_2$

$$= \frac{15 \times 14}{2 \times 1} = 15 \times 7 = 105$$

EXAMPLE 3. Everybody in a room shakes hands with everybody else. The total number of hand-shakes is 66. Find the total number of persons in the room. **[NCERT Exemplar]**

Sol. Let total number of persons be n.

Since, total number of hand-shakes = 66

$\therefore \quad {}^nC_2 = 66$

$\Rightarrow \quad \dfrac{n(n-1)}{2} = 66$

$\Rightarrow \quad n^2 - n - 132 = 0 \Rightarrow (n-12)(n+11) = 0$

$\therefore \quad n = 12 \qquad [\because n \text{ cannot be negative}]$

TYPE II

Finding Number of Combinations when Some Particular Things are Included or Excluded

EXAMPLE 4. In how many ways, can a cricket team of 11 players be selected out of 16 players,

(i) if two particular players are always be included?

(ii) if two particular players are always be excluded?

Sol. (i) Since, two particular players are always included, so we have to select 9 players out of 14 players. This can be done in ${}^{14}C_9$ ways.

Hence, required number of ways $= {}^{14}C_9 = {}^{14}C_5$

$[\because {}^nC_r = {}^nC_{n-r}]$

$$= \frac{14 \times 13 \times 12 \times 11 \times 10}{5 \times 4 \times 3 \times 2 \times 1}$$
$$= 14 \times 13 \times 11 = 2002$$

(ii) Since, two particular players are always excluded, so we have to select 11 players out of 14 players. This can be done in ${}^{14}C_{11}$ ways.

Hence, required number of ways $= {}^{14}C_{11} = {}^{14}C_3$

$[\because {}^nC_r = {}^nC_{n-r}]$

$$= \frac{14 \times 13 \times 12}{3 \times 2 \times 1}$$
$$= 14 \times 13 \times 2$$
$$= 364$$

EXAMPLE 5. From a class of 25 students, 10 are to be chosen for an excursion party. There are 3 students who decide that either all of them will join or none of them will join. In how many ways can the excursion party be chosen? **[NCERT]**

Sol. Here, we have to choose 10 students out of a class of 25 students, such that the given condition satisfied.

Let us make the following cases and find the number of possible choices in each case.

***Case* I When 3 particular students join the party**

In this case, we have to choose 7 students out of 22 students. This can be done in ${}^{22}C_7$ ways.

***Case* II When 3 particular students do not join the party** In this case, we have to choose 10 students out of 22 students. This can be done in ${}^{22}C_{10}$ ways.

Hence, the total number of ways in which excursion party can be chosen $= {}^{22}C_7 + {}^{22}C_{10}$

EXAMPLE 6. We wish to select 6 persons from 8 but if the person A is chosen, then B must be chosen. In how many ways, can the selection be made?

Sol. Let us make the following cases and find the number of possible selection in each case.

***Case* I When *A* is chosen**

In this case B must be chosen also. So, we have to choose 4 persons out of 6 persons. This can be done in

$${}^6C_4 = {}^6C_2 = \frac{6 \times 5}{2 \times 1} = 15 \text{ ways}$$

***Case* II When *A* is not chosen**

In this case, we have to choose 6 persons out of 7 persons. This can be done in ${}^7C_6 = {}^7C_1 = 7$ ways

Hence, the total number of ways of selecting 6 persons $= 15 + 7 = 22$

TYPE III

Finding Number of Combination when Given Number of Things are to be Selected from Different Groups of Things

EXAMPLE 7. In how many ways, can a team of 3 boys and 3 girls be selected from 5 boys and 4 girls? **[NCERT]**

Sol. There are 5 boys and 4 girls. We have to select 3 boys out of 5 boys and 3 girls out of 4 girls.

Clearly, 3 boys out of 5 boys can be selected in ${}^5C_3$ ways, and 3 girls out of 4 girls can be selected in ${}^4C_3$ ways.

Hence, by fundamental principle of multiplication, number of ways of selecting 3 boys and 3 girls

$$= {}^5C_3 \times {}^4C_3$$

$$= {}^5C_2 \times {}^4C_1 \qquad [\because {}^nC_r = {}^nC_{n-r}]$$

$$= \frac{5\times 4}{2\times 1}\times 4 \qquad [\because {}^nC_1 = n]$$

$$= 10 \times 4 = 40$$

EXAMPLE 8. In an examination, Yamini has to select 4 questions from each part. There are 6, 7 and 8 questions in part I, part II and part III, respectively. What is the number of possible combinations in which she can choose the questions?

Sol.

Name of parts and number of questions in the parts	Number of questions selected by Yamini
Part I = 6	4
Part II = 7	4
Part III = 8	4

Clearly, total number of ways of selection

= Number of ways of selecting 4 questions from 6 questions × Number of ways of selecting 4 questions from 7 questions × Number of ways of selecting 4 questions from 8 questions

$$= {}^6C_4 \times {}^7C_4 \times {}^8C_4 \qquad [\because {}^nC_r = {}^nC_{n-r}]$$

$$= {}^6C_2 \times {}^7C_3 \times {}^8C_4$$

$$= \frac{6\times 5}{2\times 1}\times\frac{7\times 6\times 5}{3\times 2\times 1}\times\frac{8\times 7\times 6\times 5}{4\times 3\times 2\times 1}$$

$$= 15 \times 35 \times 70 = 36750 \text{ ways}$$

Hence, the total number of possible combinations in which she can choose the questions is 36750 ways.

EXAMPLE 9. Find the number of ways of selecting 9 balls from 6 red balls, 5 white balls and 5 blue balls, if each selection consists of 3 balls of each colour. **[NCERT]**

Sol. The required number of ways

= Number of ways of selecting 3 balls from 6 red balls × Number of ways of selecting 3 balls from 5 white balls × Number of ways of selecting 3 balls from 5 blue balls

$$= {}^6C_3 \times {}^5C_3 \times {}^5C_3 = {}^6C_3 \times {}^5C_2 \times {}^5C_2$$

$$= \frac{6\times 5\times 4}{3\times 2\times 1}\times\frac{5\times 4}{2\times 1}\times\frac{5\times 4}{2\times 1}$$

$$= 20 \times 10 \times 10 = 2000$$

Hence, the number of ways of selecting 3 balls of each colour is 2000.

EXAMPLE 10. There are 10 professors and 20 students out of whom a committee of 2 professors and 3 students is to be formed. Find the number of ways in which this can be done. Further find in how many of these committees

(i) a particular professors is included?

(ii) a particular student is included?

(iii) a particular student is excluded?

Sol. Clearly, for forming a committee of 2 professors and 3 students, we have to select 2 professors out of 10 professors and 3 students out of 20 students.

This can be done in ${}^{10}C_2 \times {}^{20}C_3$ ways.

Thus, required number of ways

$$= \frac{10\times 9}{2\times 1}\times\frac{20\times 19\times 18}{3\times 2\times 1} = 45\times 60\times 19 = 51300$$

(i) When a particular professor is included, then we have to select 1 professor out of 9 professors and 3 students out of 20 students.

This can be done in ${}^9C_1 \times {}^{20}C_3$ ways.

Thus, required number of ways

$$= 9\times\frac{20\times 19\times 18}{3\times 2\times 1} = 9\times 60\times 19 = 10260$$

(ii) When a particular students is included, then we have to select 2 professors out of 10 professors and 2 students out of 19 students.

This can be done in ${}^{10}C_2 \times {}^{19}C_2$.

Thus, required number of ways

$$= \frac{10\times 9}{2\times 1}\times\frac{19\times 18}{2\times 1} = 45\times 171 = 7695$$

(iii) When a particular student is excluded, then we have to select 2 professors out of 10 professors and 3 students out of 19 students. This can be done in ${}^{10}C_2 \times {}^{19}C_3$ ways.

Thus, required number of ways

$$= \frac{10\times 9}{2\times 1}\times\frac{19\times 18\times 17}{3\times 2\times 1} = 45\times 969 = 43605$$

EXAMPLE 11. A bag contains six white marbles and five red marbles. Find the number of ways in which four marbles can be drawn from the bag, if

(i) they can be of any colour.

(ii) two must be white and two red.

(iii) they must all be of the same colour.

[NCERT Exemplar]

Sol. Total number of marbles = 6 white + 5 red = 11 marbles

(i) Since, the 4 marbles can be of any colour, therefore we have to select 4 marbles out of 11 marbles.

This can be done in $^{11}C_4$ ways.

Hence, required number of ways = 330 ways

(ii) Since out of four marbles two are white and two are red, therefore we have to select 2 white marbles out of 6 white marbles and 2 red marbles out of 5 red marbles.

This can be done in $^6C_2 \times {}^5C_2$ ways.

Hence, required number of ways $= 15 \times 10 = 150$

(iii) Since, all the 4 marbles must be of same colour, therefore we have to select 4 marbles of white colour or red colour.

Clearly, number of ways of selecting 4 white marbles out of 6 white marbles $= {}^6C_4 = {}^6C_2 = 15$

and number of ways of selecting 4 red marbles out of 5 red marbles $= {}^5C_4 = {}^5C_1 = 5$

Hence, required number of ways = 15 + 5 = 20 ways

TYPE IV

Finding Number of Combinations when Selection of Things Involves Given Conditions

EXAMPLE 12. A committee of 7 members has to be formed from 9 boys and 4 girls. In how many ways, can this be done when the committee consists of

(i) exactly 3 girls? (ii) atleast 3 girls?

(iii) atmost 3 girls? [NCERT]

Sol. There are 9 boys and 4 girls. We have to form a committee of 7 members.

(i) Since, the committee has exactly 3 girls. Therefore, we have to choose 3 girls out of 4 girls and the rest 4 members out of 9 boys.

This can be done in $^4C_3 \times {}^9C_4$ ways.

Hence, the number of ways of forming a committee

$$= {}^4C_3 \times {}^9C_4$$

$$= {}^4C_1 \times \frac{9 \times 8 \times 7 \times 6}{4 \times 3 \times 2 \times 1}$$

$$= 4 \times 9 \times 7 \times 2 = 504 \text{ ways}$$

(ii) Since the committee has at least 3 girls. Therefore, we can form the committee in the following ways

(a) Selecting 3 girls and 4 boys

(b) Selecting 4 girls and 3 boys

Hence, the number of ways of forming a committee

$$= {}^4C_3 \times {}^9C_4 + {}^4C_4 \times {}^9C_3$$

$$= 504 + 1 \times \frac{9 \times 8 \times 7}{3 \times 2 \times 1}$$

$$= 504 + 84 = 588 \text{ ways}$$

(iii) Since, the committee has atmost 3 girls, therefore we can form committee in the following ways.

(a) Selecting 7 boys and no girl

(b) Selecting 6 boys and 1 girl

(c) Selecting 5 boys and 2 girls

(d) Selecting 4 boys and 3 girls

Hence, the number of ways of forming a committee

$$= {}^9C_7 \times {}^4C_0 + {}^9C_6 \times {}^4C_1 + {}^9C_5 \times {}^4C_2 + {}^9C_4 \times {}^4C_3$$

$$= {}^9C_2 + {}^9C_3 \times 4 + {}^9C_4 \times {}^4C_2 + {}^9C_4 \times {}^4C_1$$

$$[\because {}^nC_r = {}^nC_{n-r}, {}^nC_1 = n \text{ and } {}^nC_0 = 1]$$

$$= 36 + 84 \times 4 + 126 \times 6 + 126 \times 4$$

$$= 36 + 336 + 756 + 504 = 1632$$

EXAMPLE 13. A committee of 10 is to be formed from 8 gentlemen and 9 ladies. In how many ways this can be done, if atleast five ladies have to be included in a committee? In how many of these committees

(i) the ladies are in majority?

(ii) the gentlemen are in majority?

Sol. There are 9 ladies and 8 gentlemen. We have to form a committee of 10, consisting of atleast 5 ladies.

This can be formed by selecting

(a) 5 ladies and 5 gentlemen

(b) 6 ladies and 4 gentlemen

(c) 7 ladies and 3 gentlemen

(d) 8 ladies and 2 gentlemen

(e) 9 ladies and 1 gentleman

Now, the number of ways of forming a committee

$$= {}^9C_5 \times {}^8C_5 + {}^9C_6 \times {}^8C_4 + {}^9C_7 \times {}^8C_3 + {}^9C_8 \times {}^8C_2 + {}^9C_9 \times {}^8C_1$$

$$= {}^9C_4 \times {}^8C_3 + {}^9C_3 \times {}^8C_4 + {}^9C_2 \times {}^8C_3 + {}^9C_1 \times {}^8C_2 + {}^9C_0 \times {}^8C_1 \quad [\because {}^nC_r = {}^nC_{n-r}]$$

$$= \frac{9 \times 8 \times 7 \times 6}{4 \times 3 \times 2 \times 1} \times \frac{8 \times 7 \times 6}{3 \times 2 \times 1} + \frac{9 \times 8 \times 7}{3 \times 2 \times 1} \times \frac{8 \times 7 \times 6 \times 5}{4 \times 3 \times 2 \times 1} + \frac{9 \times 8}{2 \times 1} \times \frac{8 \times 7 \times 6}{3 \times 2 \times 1} + 9 \times \frac{8 \times 7}{2 \times 1} + 1 \times 8$$

$$= 126 \times 56 + 84 \times 70 + 36 \times 56 + 9 \times 28 + 8$$

$$= 7056 + 5880 + 2016 + 252 + 8 = 15212$$

(i) Clearly, ladies are in majority in (b), (c), (d) and (e) cases as discussed above.

$\therefore$ Number of committees in which ladies are in majority $= 15212 - {}^9C_5 \times {}^8C_5$

$$= 15212 - 7056 = 8156$$

(ii) Clearly, gentlemen are not in majority in the cases discussed above.

Thus, there is no committee in which gentlemen are in majority. Hence, number of such committee = 0

EXAMPLE 14. Determine the number of 5 cards combinations out of a deck of 52 cards, if atleast one of the 5 cards has to be a king.

Sol. Selection of 5 cards can be done in the following ways

Case	I	II	III	IV
King	1	2	3	4
Other cards	4	3	2	1

The number of combinations in case I, II, III and IV are respectively,

$^4C_1 \times {}^{48}C_4;\ {}^4C_2 \times {}^{48}C_3;\ {}^4C_3 \times {}^{48}C_2$ and ${}^4C_4 \times {}^{48}C_1$

Hence, the required number of combinations

$$= {}^4C_1 \times {}^{48}C_4 + {}^4C_2 \times {}^{48}C_3 + {}^4C_3 \times {}^{48}C_2 + {}^4C_4 \times {}^{48}C_1$$

$$= 4 \times \frac{48 \times 47 \times 46 \times 45}{4 \times 3 \times 2 \times 1} + \frac{4 \times 3}{2 \times 1} \times \frac{48 \times 47 \times 46}{3 \times 2 \times 1} + 4 \times \frac{48 \times 47}{2 \times 1} + 1 \times 48$$

$$= 8 \times 47 \times 46 \times 45 + 48 \times 47 \times 46 + 2 \times 48 \times 47 + 48$$

$$= 778320 + 103776 + 4512 + 48 = 886656$$

EXAMPLE 15. A sports team of 11 students is to be constituted, choosing atleast 5 from class XI and atleast 5 from class XII. If there are 20 students in each of these classes, then how many ways can the team be constituted? **[NCERT Exemplar]**

Sol. To constitute a sports team, there are two cases

***Case* I** Choosing 5 students from class XI and 6 students from class XII.

$\therefore$ In this case, number of ways $= {}^{20}C_5 \times {}^{20}C_6$

***Case* II** Choosing 6 students from class XI and 5 students from class XII.

In this case, number of ways $= {}^{20}C_6 \times {}^{20}C_5$

$\therefore$ Required number of ways $= ({}^{20}C_5 \times {}^{20}C_6) + ({}^{20}C_6 \times {}^{20}C_5)$

$$= 2({}^{20}C_5 \times {}^{20}C_6)$$

Hence, the total number of ways of constituting a sports team of 11 students is $2({}^{20}C_5 \times {}^{20}C_6)$ ways.

EXAMPLE 16. In an examination, a question paper consists of 12 questions divided into two parts I and II containing 5 and 7 questions, respectively. A students is required to attempt 8 questions in all, selecting atleast 3 from each part. In how many ways, can a student select the questions? **[NCERT]**

Sol. Student may select 8 questions, according to the following scheme.

	I (5 Questions)	II (7 Questions)
(i)	3	5
(ii)	4	4
(iii)	5	3

Now, the required number of ways

$$= {}^5C_3 \times {}^7C_5 + {}^5C_4 \times {}^7C_4 + {}^5C_5 \times {}^7C_3$$

$$= {}^5C_2 \times {}^7C_2 + {}^5C_1 \times {}^7C_3 + {}^5C_0 \times {}^7C_3$$

$$= 10 \times 21 + 5 \times 35 + 1 \times 35 = 210 + 175 + 35 = 420$$

Hence, the total number of ways of selecting the questions by the student is 420 ways.

EXAMPLE 17. A man has 7 friends. In how many ways, can he invite one or more of them to party?

Sol. A man may invite one of them, two of them, three of them, ... or all of them and this can be done in ${}^7C_1, {}^7C_2, {}^7C_3, \dots, {}^7C_7$ ways, respectively.

$\therefore$ Total number of ways

$$= {}^7C_1 + {}^7C_2 + {}^7C_3 + {}^7C_4 + {}^7C_5 + {}^7C_6 + {}^7C_7$$

$$= 7 + 21 + 35 + 35 + 21 + 7 + 1 = 127$$

TYPE V

Problems Based on Geometry

EXAMPLE 18. How many chords can be drawn through 21 points on a circle? **[NCERT]**

Sol. Clearly, number of chords that can be drawn from 21 points $= {}^{21}C_2 = \frac{21 \times 20}{2 \times 1} = 210$

Hence, the total number of chords that can be drawn through 21 points on a circle is 210.

EXAMPLE 19. If 20 lines are drawn in a plane such that no two of them are parallel and no three are concurrent, in how many points will they intersect each other?

Sol. There are 20 lines in a plane. Since, it is given that no two lines are parallel, therefore all lines are intersecting lines. Also, as no three lines are concurrent, i.e. no three lines intersect at a point, therefore only pair of lines intersect at a point.

We know that a pair of lines intersect at a unique point. Therefore, corresponding to every pair of lines, we have a unique point of intersection.

Thus, number of points of intersection = Number of pair of lines $= {}^{20}C_2 = \frac{20 \times 19}{2 \times 1} = 190$

EXAMPLE 20. If a polygon has 44 diagonals, then find the number of its sides. **[NCERT Exemplar]**

Sol. Let n be the number of sides of a polygon.

Then, number of vertices of polygon $= n$

Now, number of diagonals $= {}^nC_2 - n = 44$

[$\because$ diagonal will be formed by joining any two non-adjacent vertices of the polygon, therefore total number of diagonals is ${}^nC_2 - n$]

$$\Rightarrow \frac{n(n-1)}{2} - n = 44 \Rightarrow n^2 - 3n - 88 = 0$$

$$\Rightarrow n = -8 \text{ or } 11 \Rightarrow n = 11 \quad [\because n \text{ cannot be negative}]$$

EXAMPLE 21. Find the number of parallelograms that can be formed from a set of four parallel lines intersecting another set of three parallel lines. **[NCERT Exemplar]**

Sol. Clearly, a parallelogram is formed by choosing two parallel lines from the set of 4 parallel lines and two parallel lines from the set of 3 parallel lines.

$\therefore$ Total number of parallelogram formed

= Number of ways of selecting two lines from set I

$\times$ Number of ways of selecting two lines from set II

$= {}^4C_2 \times {}^3C_2$

$= 6 \times 3 = 18$

EXAMPLE 22. Out of 18 points in a plane, no three are in the same line except five points which are collinear. Find the number of lines that can be formed by joining these points in pairs. **[NCERT Exemplar]**

Sol. There are 18 points in a plane, out of which five are collinear.

Note that, required number of lines

= (Number of lines formed by joining 18 points, taken 2 at a time) − (Number of lines formed by joining 5 collinear points, taken 2 at a time) +1 (line formed by collinear points) $= {}^{18}C_2 - {}^5C_2 + 1$

$= 153 - 10 + 1$

$= 144$

EXAMPLE 23. Find the number of triangles that are formed by choosing the vertices from a set of 12 points, seven of which lie on the same line. **[NCERT Exemplar]**

Sol. We know that a triangle will be formed by taking three non-collinear points at a time.

$\therefore$ Required number of triangles $= {}^{12}C_3 - {}^7C_3$

$$= \frac{12\times11\times10}{3\times2\times1} - \frac{7\times6\times5}{3\times2}$$

$= 220 - 35$

$= 185$

Hence, the total number of such triangles is 185.

EXAMPLE 24. The straight lines l_1, l_2 and l_3 are parallel and lie in the same plane. A total number of m points are taken on l_1; n points on l_2; k points on l_3. Find the maximum number of triangles formed with vertices at these points. **[NCERT Exemplar]**

Sol. Total number of points $= m + n + k$

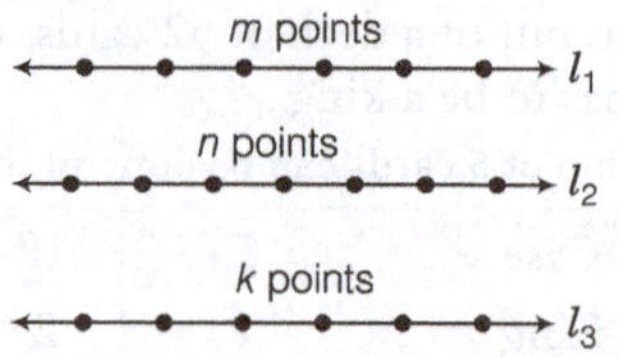

This can give ${}^{m+n+k}C_3$ number of triangles. But m points on l_1, taking 3 at a time, gives ${}^mC_3$ combinations which produce no triangle.

Similarly, ${}^nC_3$ and ${}^kC_3$ number of triangles are not formed.

$\therefore$ Required number of triangles

$= {}^{m+n+k}C_3 - {}^mC_3 - {}^nC_3 - {}^kC_3$

TYPE VI

Practical Problems Involving Both Permutations and Combinations

EXAMPLE 25. The English alphabets has 5 vowels and 21 consonants. How many words with 2 different vowels and 2 different consonants can be formed from the alphabets?

Sol. Here, we have 5 vowels and 21 consonants. We have to select 2 vowels out of 5 vowels and 2 consonants out of 21 consonants. Also, we have to arrange these 4 letters which can be done in 4! ways.

$\therefore$ Required number of words $= {}^5C_2 \times {}^{21}C_2 \times 4!$

$$= \frac{5\times4}{2} \times \frac{21\times20}{2} \times 24$$

$= 10 \times 210 \times 24 = 50400$

Hence, the total number of words having 2 consonants and 2 vowels is 50400.

EXAMPLE 26. How many words with or without meaning, each of 2 vowels and 3 consonants can be formed from the letters of the word 'DAUGHTER'? **[NCERT]**

Sol. There are 8 letters in the word 'DAUGHTER' including 3 vowels and 5 consonants. We have to select 2 vowels out of 3 vowels and 3 consonants out of 5 consonants.

$\therefore$ Number of ways of selection

$= {}^3C_2 \times {}^5C_3 = 3 \times 10 = 30$

Since, each word containing 5 letters can be arranged among themselves in 5! ways.

So, total number of words $= 5! \times 30 = 120 \times 30 = 3600$

Topic Practice 6

1 From a class of 32 students, 4 are to be chosen for a competition. In how many ways can this be done?

2 If there are 10 persons in a party and each two of them shake hands with each other, then how many hand-shakes happen in the party?

3 Find the number of ways in which a mixed double game can be arranged from amongst 9 married couples, if no husband and wife play in the same game.

4 Eighteen guests have to be seated, half on each side of a long table. Four particular guests desire to sit on one particular side and three others on the other side. Find the number of ways in which the seating arrangement can be made.

5 A committee of 3 persons is to be constituted from a group of 2 men and 3 women. In how many ways can this be done?

6 In a football championship, 153 matches were played. Every two teams played one match with each other. Find the number of teams, participating in the championship. **[NCERT Exemplar]**

7 Find the number of ways in which a team of eleven players can be selected from 22 players, if two particular players are always including and four are always excluding. **[NCERT Exemplar]**

8 Out of 6 gentlemen and 4 ladies, a committee of 5 is to be formed. In how many ways, can this be done so as to include atleast one lady in each committee?

9 A committee of 5 is to be formed out of 6 gents and 4 ladies. In how many ways this can be done, when

(i) atleast two ladies are included?

(ii) atmost two ladies are included?

10 A committee of 8 is to be formed from 7 gentleman and 8 ladies. In how many ways is atleast 4 ladies have to be included in a committee?

11 Find the number of ways in which 2 black and 3 red balls can be selected from a bag containing 5 black and 6 red balls.

12 A question paper has two parts, Part *A* and Part *B*, each containing 10 questions. If the student has to choose 8 from Part *A* and 5 from Part *B*, then in how many ways can he choose the questions?

13 A boy has 3 library tickets and 8 books of his interest in the library. Of these 8, he does not want to borrow Mathematics Part II, unless Mathematics Part I is also borrowed. In how many ways can he choose the three books to be borrowed? **[NCERT Exemplar]**

14 In how many ways can a cricket team be selected from a group of 25 players containing 10 batsmen, 8 bowlers, 5 all-rounders and 2 wicket keepers, assuming that the team of 11 players requires 5 batsmen, 3 all-rounders, 2 bowlers and 1 wicket keeper?

15 For the post of 5 teachers, there are 23 applicants, 2 posts are reserved for SC candidates and there are 7 SC candidates among the applicants. In how many ways can the selection be made?

16 A box contains two white, three black and four red balls. In how many ways can three balls be drawn from the box, if atleast one black ball is to be included in the draw. **[NCERT Exemplar]**

17 In how many ways can a student choose a programme of 5 courses, if 9 courses are available and 2 specific courses are compulsory for every student?

18 In an examination, a student has to answer 4 questions out of 5 questions, questions 1 and 2 are however compulsory. Find the number of ways in which the student can make the choice. **[NCERT Exemplar]**

19 Determine the number of 5 cards combination out of a deck of 52 cards, if there is exactly one ace in each combination.

20 Find the number of ways in which we can choose a committee from 4 men and 6 women, so that the committee includes atleast 2 men and exactly twice as many women as men. **[NCERT Exemplar]**

21 A candidate is required to answer 7 questions out of 12 questions, which are divided into two groups each containing 6 questions. He is not permitted to attempt more than 5 questions from either group. Find the number of different ways of doing questions. **[NCERT Exemplar]**

22 A man has 8 friends. In how many ways, can be invite one or more them to party?

23 What is the number of ways of choosing 4 cards from a pack of 52 playing cards?

In how many of these

(i) four cards are of the same suit?

(ii) four cards belong to four different suits?

(iii) are face cards?

(iv) two are red and two are black cards?

(v) cards are of the same colour? [NCERT]

24 In a polygon no three diagonals are concurrent. If the total number of points of intersection of diagonals interior to the polygon is 70, then find the number of diagonals of polygon.

25 Let T_n denote the number of triangles which can be formed using the vertices of a regular polygon of n sides. If $T_{n+1} - T_n = 21$, then find the value of n.

26 Find the number of chords that can be drawn through 16 points on a circle.

27 If m parallel lines in plane are intersected by a family of n parallel lines, then find the number of parallelograms formed.

28 A polygon has 65 diagonals, then find the number of its sides.

29 Find the number of triangles, that are formed by choosing the vertices from a set of 10 points, 6 of which lie on the same line.

30 There are 10 points in a plane, no three of which are in the same straight line, excepting 4 points, which are collinear.

(i) Find the number of straight lines obtained from the pairs of these points.

(ii) Find the number of triangles that can be formed with the vertices as these points.

31 Find the total number of words formed by 2 vowels and 3 consonants taken from 4 vowels and 5 consonants. **[NCERT Exemplar]**

32 In how many ways can 21 identical books on English and 19 identical books on Hindi be placed in a row on a self so that two books on Hindi may not be together?

33 How many words each of 3 vowels and 2 consonants can be formed from the letters of the word 'INVOLUTE'? [NCERT]

Hints & Solutions

1. Solve as Example 1. **Ans.** 35960
2. Solve as Example 3. **Ans.** 45
3. **Hint** Out of 9 men, two men can be chosen in ${}^9C_2$ ways.
   Since, no husband and wife are to play in the same game, so we have to select two women from the remaining 7 women.
   The number of ways to select two women out of 7 $= {}^7C_2$
   Thus, the number of ways of arranging the game ${}^9C_2 \times {}^7C_2 \times 2!$ **Ans.** 1512
4. **Hint** Since, four particular guests want to sit on a particular side A (say) and three others on the other side B (say).
   So, we are left with 11 guests. Out of which we choose 5 for side A in ${}^{11}C_5$ ways and the remaining 6 for side B in ${}^6C_6$ ways.
   Hence, the number of selections for the two sides is ${}^{11}C_5 \times {}^6C_6$.
   Now, 9 persons on each side of the table can be arranged among themselves in 9! ways.
   Hence, the total number of arrangements $= {}^{11}C_5 \times {}^6C_6 \times 9! \times 9!$
   Ans. $\frac{11!}{6!5!} \times 9! \times 9!$
5. **Hint** Required number of ways $= {}^5C_3$ **Ans.** 10
6. **Hint** Let the number of teams participating in championship be n.
   Since, it is given that every two teams played one match with each other.
   $\therefore$ Total number of matches played $= {}^nC_2$
   According to the question, ${}^nC_2 = 153$ **Ans.** $n = 18$
7. **Hint** We have to select 9 players out of 16 players. **Ans.** 11440
8. Solve as Example 13. **Ans.** 246
9. Solve as Example 12. **Ans.** (i) 186 (ii) 186
10. Solve as Example 13. **Ans.** 5055
11. **Hint** Out of 5 black balls, 2 black balls can be selected in ${}^5C_2$ ways.
    Out of 6 red balls, 3 red balls can be selected in ${}^6C_3$ ways.
    FPC, total number of ways $= {}^5C_2 \times {}^6C_3$ **Ans.** 200 ways
12. Solve as Example 8. **Ans.** 11340
13. **Hint** Let us make the following cases and find the number of possible choices in each case.
    Case I Boy borrows Mathematics Part II
    In this case, boy borrows Mathematics Part I also.
    So, number of possible choices are ${}^6C_1$.
    Case II Boy does not borrow Mathematics Part II.
    In this case, possible choices are ${}^7C_3$. **Ans.** 41

14. **Hint** Required number of ways $= {}^{10}C_5 \times {}^5C_3 \times {}^8C_2 \times {}^2C_1$

Ans. 141120

15. **Hint** Here, we have to select 2 out of 7 SC candidates and 3 out of 16 others. **Ans.** 11760

16. **Hint** Selection of three balls, consisting of atleast one black ball can be done in following ways

(i) Selecting 1 black ball and 2 non-black balls

(ii) Selecting 2 black balls and 1 non-black ball

(iii) Selecting 3 black balls and 0 non-black ball

Required number of ways

$$= {}^3C_1 \times {}^6C_2 + {}^3C_2 \times {}^6C_1 + {}^3C_3$$

Ans. 64

17. **Hint** Since, 2 specific courses are compulsory, therefore we have to select 3 courses out of rest 7 courses i.e. ${}^7C_3$ ways. **Ans.** 35

18. **Hint** Since, questions 1 and 2 are compulsory, so student has to select two questions out of rest three questions.

Ans. 3

19. Solve as Example 14. **Ans.** 778320

20. **Hint** Committee can be choose in following ways

(i) Selecting 2 men and 4 women

(ii) Selecting 3 men and 6 women **Ans.** 94

21. **Hint** Total number of ways of attempting 7 questions out of 12 questions = Number of ways of

(Attempting 2 from group I and 5 from group II)
+ (Attempting 3 from group I and 4 from group II)
+ (Attempting 4 from group I and 3 from group II)
+ (Attempting 5 from group I and 2 from group II)

Solve as Example 16. **Ans.** 780

22. Solve as Example 17. **Ans.** 255

23. **Hint** Number of ways of choosing 4 cards $= {}^{52}C_4$

(i) There are 4 suits and each suit has 13 cards. So, from each suit, 4 cards can be choosen in ${}^{13}C_4$ ways separately.

$\therefore$ Required number of ways

$$= {}^{13}C_4 + {}^{13}C_4 + {}^{13}C_4 + {}^{13}C_4$$

Ans. 2860

(ii) We have to select one card from each suit.

Required number of ways $= {}^{13}C_1 \times {}^{13}C_1 \times {}^{13}C_1 \times {}^{13}C_1$

Ans. 13^4

(iii) There are 12 face cards and we have to select 4 cards out of these.

Required number of ways $= {}^{12}C_4$. **Ans.** 495

(iv) There are 26 red cards and 26 black cards.

$\therefore$ Required number of ways $= {}^{26}C_2 \times {}^{26}C_2$

Ans. 105625

(v) Required number of ways $= {}^{26}C_4 + {}^{26}C_4$

Ans. 29900

24. **Hint** Let there be n-sides of the polygon. Then, number of vertices is also n.

We know that in a convex polygon every group of four vertices determines two diagonals and hence, one point of intersection.

$\therefore \quad {}^nC_4 = 70 \Rightarrow n(n-1)(n-2)(n-3) = 70 \times 24$

$\Rightarrow \quad n = 8$

$\therefore$ Number of diagonals $= {}^nC_2 - n = {}^8C_2 - 8$

Ans. 20

25. **Hint** We have,

$$T_n = {}^nC_3$$

$\therefore \quad T_{n+1} - T_n = 21$

$\Rightarrow \quad {}^{n+1}C_3 - {}^nC_3 = 21$

$\Rightarrow \quad {}^nC_2 + {}^nC_3 - {}^nC_3 = 21 \quad [\because {}^nC_r + {}^nC_{r-1} = {}^{n+1}C_r]$

$\Rightarrow \quad {}^nC_2 = 21$

Ans. 7

26. Solve as Example 18. **Ans.** 120

27. Solve as Example 21. **Ans.** $\dfrac{mn(m-1)(n-1)}{4}$

28. Solve as Example 20. **Ans.** $n = 13$

29. Solve as Example 23. **Ans.** 100

30. (i) Solve as Example 22. **Ans.** 40

(ii) Solve as Example 23. **Ans.** 116

31. Solve as Example 25. **Ans.** 7200

32. **Hint** We must first arrange all books in English in a row. Since, all English books are identical, so they can be arranged in a row in only one way as shown below

$$\times E \times E \times E \times E \times \ldots\ldots\ldots \times E \times E$$

Ans. 1540

33. Solve as Example 26.

Ans. 2880

Exam Pattern Exercise

Part A - Objective Type Questions

Multiple Choice Type Questions

1 Suppose you have a suitcase with a number lock. The number lock has 4 wheels each labelled with 10 digits from 0 to 9. The lock can be opened, if 4 specific digits are arranged in a particular sequence with no repetition. Some how, you have forgotten this specific sequence of digits. You remember only the first digit which is 7. In order to open the lock, how many sequences of 3 digits you may have to check with?

(a) 720 (b) 504

(c) 500 (d) None of these

2 The sum of the digits in unit place of all the numbers formed with the help of 3, 4, 5 and 6 taken all at a time is [NCERT Exemplar]

(a) 432 (b) 108

(c) 36 (d) 18

3 If $\frac{(2n)!}{3!\,(2n-3)!}$ and $\frac{n!}{2!\,(n-2)!}$ are in the ratio 44 : 3, then n is equal to

(a) 1 (b) 2 (c) 4 (d) 6

4 Mohan has 3 pants and 2 shirts. The number of different pairs of a pant and shirt he can wear are

(a) 5 (b) 6

(c) 7 (d) None of these

5 The number of ways in which 3 prize can be distributed to 4 childrens, so that no child gets all the three prizes, are

(a) 64 (b) 62

(c) 60 (d) None of these

6 The number of natural numbers smaller than 10^4, in the decimal notation of which all the digits are distinct is

(a) 5274 (b) 5275 (c) 5276 (d) 5277

7 The number of ways in which three girls and nine boys can be seated in two vans, each having numbered seats 3 in the front and 4 at the back, such that 3 girls always sit together in a back row on adjacent seats, is

(a) ${}^{11}P_9 \times 4! \times 3$ (b) ${}^{11}P_9 \times 4 \times 3!$

(c) ${}^{14}P_{12} \times 4! \times 3$ (d) ${}^{14}P_{12} \times 4 \times 3!$

8 The number of combinations of 4 different objects A, B, C, D taken 2 at a time is

(a) 4 (b) 6 (c) 7 (d) 8

9 Person wishes to make up as many different parties as he can out of his 20 friends such that each party consists of the same number of persons. The number of friends he should invite are ...A... . Here, A refers to

(a) 8 (b) 9

(c) 10 (d) None of these

10 A five-digit number divisible by 3 is to be formed using the numbers 0, 1, 2, 3, 4 and 5, without repetition. The total number of ways this can be done, is [NCERT Exemplar]

(a) 216 (b) 240

(c) 600 (d) 3125

Assertion-Reason Based Questions

Directions (Q. Nos. 11-14) *In the questions given below are two statements labelled as Assertion (A) and Reason (R). In the context of the two statements, which one of the following is correct?*

(a) Both A and R are correct; R is the correct explanation of A

(b) Both A and R are correct; R is not the correct explanation of A

(c) A is correct; R is incorrect

(d) R is correct; A is incorrect

11 **Assertion (A)** If $P(n, 5) = 20\, P(n, 4)$, then value of n is 24.

Reason (R) $P(n, r) = {}^nP_r = \frac{n!}{(n-r)!}, 0 \le r \le n.$

12 **Assertion (A)** If ${}^{n-1}C_r : {}^nC_r : {}^{n+1}C_r = 6 : 9 : 13$, then values of n and r are 12 and 4 respectively.

Reason (R) ${}^nC_r = \frac{n!}{r!\,(n-r)!}$.

13 **Assertion (A)** If a polygon has 54 diagonals, then the number of its sides is 13.

Reason (R) When diagonals are formed by joining any two non-adjacent vertices of a polygon. Then, the total number of diagonals is ${}^nC_2 - n$.

14 **Assertion (A)** If the letters W, I, F, E are arranged in a row in all possible ways and the words (with or without meaning) so formed are written as in a dictionary, then the word WIFE occurs in the 24th position.

Reason (R) The number of ways of arranging four distinct objects taken all at a time is $C(4, 4)$.

Part B - Descriptive Questions

Very Short Answer Type Questions

15 Prove that $\frac{1}{9!}+\frac{1}{10!}+\frac{1}{11!}=\frac{122}{11!}$.

16 Evaluate $\frac{n!}{(n-r)!}$, when $n=9$ and $r=5$.

17 Evaluate the following.
(i) ${}^5P_2$ (ii) ${}^{10}P_4$ (iii) ${}^6P_6$

18 If $P(n,4)=12\cdot P(n,2)$, then find n.

19 If $P(11,r)=P(12,r-1)$, then find r.

20 Find the value of n such that
$P(n,4):P(n-1,4)=5:3, n>4$

21 If ${}^{56}P_{r+6}:{}^{54}P_{r+3}=30800:1$, then find r.

22 If ${}^nC_{12}={}^nC_5$, find the value of n.

23 If ${}^nC_8={}^nC_6$, then find ${}^nC_2$.

24 If ${}^{18}C_x={}^{18}C_{x+2}$, then find x.

Short Answer Type Questions

25 Find n, if $(n+1)!=12\times(n-1)!$.

26 Find the value of n, if $\frac{n!}{(n-2)!}=930, n\geq 2$.

27 If ${}^{15}C_r:{}^{15}C_{r-1}=11:5$, then find r.

28 If ${}^{2n}C_3:{}^nC_2=44:3$, then find n.

29 In a cinema hall, there are three entrance doors and two exit doors. In how many ways can a person enter the hall and then come out?

30 25 buses are running between Delhi and Noida. In how many ways, can a person go from Delhi to Noida and return by a different bus?

31 There are 6 multiple choice questions in an examination. How many sequences of answers are possible, if the first three questions have 4 choices each and remaining three have 3 each?

32 In how many ways, can 50 voters vote for the 4 candidates contesting the election for the post of secretary of their association?

33 How many numbers are there between 100 and 1000 such that every digit is either 2 or 9?

34 How many 3 letter words can be made using the letters of the word 'ORIENTAL'?

35 Find how many arrangements can be made with the letters of the word 'MATHEMATICS'?

36 How many words can be formed using the letter A thrice, the letter B twice and the letter C thrice?

37 From a group of 15 cricket players, a team of 11 players is to be chosen. In how many ways can this be done?

38 In how many ways a committee of 3 men and 2 women can be chosen from 7 men and 5 women?

39 A flag is in the form of three blocks, each to be coloured differently. If there are 8 different colours to choose from, then how many flags are possible?

40 How many 4 letters code can be formed using the first 10 letters of the English alphabets, if no letters can be repeated? [NCERT]

41 How many 3-digit numbers can be formed using the digits 0, 2, 3, 6, 8, when the digits may be repeated any number of times?

42 A coin is tossed 6 times and the outcomes are recorded. How many possible outcomes are there?

43 Find the number of ways in which 8 distinct toys can be distributed among 5 children.

44 In how many ways can three jobs I, II and III be assigned to three persons A, B and C, if one person is assigned only one job and all are capable of doing each job?

45 From among the 35 teachers in a school, one principal and one vice-principal are to be appointed. In how many ways can this be done?

Long Answer Type Questions

46 18 mice were placed in two experimental groups and one control group, with all group equally large. In how many ways, can the mice be placed into three groups? [NCERT Exemplar]

47 There are 6 English, 4 Sanskrit and 5 Hindi books. In how many ways can they be arranged on a shelf so as to keep all the books of the same language together?

48 In how many ways can the letters of the word 'ARRANGE' be arranged so that the two R's are never together?

49 If the different permutations of the word 'EXAMINATION' are listed as in a dictionary, then how many words are there in the list before the first word starting with E? [NCERT]

50 Out of 5 men and 2 women, a committee of 3 is to be formed. In how many ways can it be formed, if atleast one women is to be included?

51 There are 12 points in a plane of which 5 points are collinear. Find the number of lines obtained by joining these points in pairs.

52 Find the number of combinations, when some or all of n objects are taken at a time. [NCERT Exemplar]

53 How many automobile licence plates can be made, if each plate contains two different letters followed by three different digits? [NCERT Exemplar]

54 How many odd numbers less than 1000 can be formed by using the digits 0, 2, 5, 7 when the repetition of digits is allowed?

55 In how many ways can 10 books be arranged on a shelf, so that a particular pair of books shall be
(i) always together (ii) never together.

56 In how many ways can 6 balls of different colours, namely white, black, blue, red, green and yellow be arranged in a row in such a way that the white and black balls are never together?

57 How many numbers divisible by 5 and lying between 3000 and 4000 can be formed by using the digits 3, 4, 5, 6, 7, 8, when no digit is repeated in any such number?

58 How many different numbers, greater than 50000 can be formed by using the digits 0, 1, 1, 5, 9?

59 The letters of the word 'SURITI' are written in all possible orders and these words are written out as in a dictionary. Find the rank of the word 'SURITI'.

60 How many different selections of 4 books can be made from 10 different books, if
(i) there is no restriction?
(ii) two particular books are always selected?
(iii) two particular books are never selected?

61 A group consists of 4 girls and 7 boys. In how many ways, a team of 5 members be selected, if the team has
(i) no girl?
(ii) atleast one boy and one girl?
(iii) atleast 3 girls? [NCERT]

62 There are 4 routes between Delhi and Patna. In how many different ways can a man go from Delhi to Patna and return, if for returning
(i) any of the routes is taken?
(ii) the same route is taken?
(iii) the same route is not taken?

63 Find the number of arrangements of the letters of the word 'INDEPENDENCE'. In how many of these arrangements
(i) do the words start with P?
(ii) do all the vowels always occur together?
(iii) do all the vowels never occur together?
(iv) do the words begin with I and end in P? [NCERT]

64 Using the digits 1, 2, 3, 4, 5, 6, 7 a number of 4 different digits is formed. Find how many numbers are formed? Further, find how many of these are
(i) exactly divisible by 2?
(ii) exactly divisible by 25?
(iii) exactly divisible by 4? [NCERT Exemplar]

Case Study Based Questions

65 Mr. Arvind Shukla a mathematics teacher of class XI. He writes a word INDEPENDENCE on the white board. He asks some questions which are based on the arrangements of the letters of the above word.
Then, answer the following questions.
(i) Find the number of permutations of n objects, where p objects are of the one kind, p_2 are of second kind, ... p_k are of kth kind and the rest, if any are of different kind.
(ii) Find the number of arrangements of the letters of the word starting with P.
(iii) Find the number of arrangements of the letter of word, when all the vowels never occur together.

Or

Find the number of arrangements of the letter of word when word begins with I and ends in P.

66 Mr. Ankit Triwedi a mathematics teacher of class XI write two things about Mohan and Sohan, which are below in figure.

	Mohan	Sohan
Age	${}^nP_r$	${}^nP_{r+1}$
Height (in feet)	${}^nC_r$	${}^nC_{r-1}$

Now, answer the following question which are based on above data.
(i) If the age of mohan and Sohan are equal, then find the value of $(n-r)$.
(ii) Which of the following formula is used to find ${}^nP_r$?
(iii) Find the age of Mohan.
Or Find the height of Sohan.

Hints & Solutions

1. (b) 2. (b) 3. (d) 4. (b)
5. (c) 6. (a) 7. (b) 8. (b)
9. (c) 10. (a) 11. (a) 12. (a)
13. (d) 14. (c)

15. **Hint** LHS $= \frac{1}{9!} + \frac{1}{10!} + \frac{1}{11!}$

$= \frac{11 \times 10}{11!} + \frac{11}{11!} + \frac{1}{11!}$

$= \frac{122}{11!} = \text{RHS}$

Hence proved.

16. 15120

17. (i) **Hint** (i) $^5P_2 = \frac{5!}{3!} = 20$ (ii) 5040 (iii) 720

18. **Hint** $^nP_4 = 12 \cdot {^nP_2} \Rightarrow \frac{n!}{(n-4)!} = 12 \times \frac{n!}{(n-2)!}$

$\Rightarrow \quad 1 = 12 \times \frac{1}{(n-2)(n-3)}$

$\Rightarrow \quad (n-2)(n-3) = 12$

$\Rightarrow \quad (n-2)(n-3) = 4 \times 3 \Rightarrow n = 6$

19. $r = 9$ 20. $n = 10$ 21. $r = 41$

22. **Hint** $^nC_{12} = {^nC_5}$

$\Rightarrow {^nC_{n-12}} = {^nC_5}$

$\Rightarrow n - 12 = 5$

$\Rightarrow n = 17$

23. **Hint** $^nC_8 = {^nC_6} \Rightarrow {^nC_{n-8}} = {^nC_6}$

$\Rightarrow \quad n - 8 = 6 \Rightarrow n = 14$ **Ans.** 91

24. 8

25. **Hint** $(n+1)! = 12 \times (n-1)!$

$\Rightarrow \quad (n+1)\,n = 12$

$\Rightarrow \quad n^2 + n - 12 = 0 \Rightarrow (n+4)(n-3) = 0$

$\therefore \quad n = 3$ $[\because n$ cannot be negative$]$

26. 31

27. **Hint** $\frac{^{15}C_r}{^{15}C_{r-1}} = \frac{11}{5}$

$\Rightarrow \frac{15!}{(15-r)!\,r!} \times \frac{(15-r+1)! \times (r-1)!}{15!} = \frac{11}{5}$

$\Rightarrow \quad \frac{(16-r)}{r} = \frac{11}{5}$

$\Rightarrow \quad 80 - 5r = 11r \Rightarrow r = 5$

28. 6 29. 6 30. 600

31. **Hint** Total number of sequences of answers are possible $= 4 \times 4 \times 4 \times 3 \times 3 \times 3$

32. **Hint** Each person gives a vote for any of the four persons. **Ans.** 4^{50}

33. **Hint** Only three-digit numbers exist between 100 and 1000. But each digit only any of two numbers 2 or 9 that can be placed.

$\therefore$ Total number of ways $= 2 \times 2 \times 2 = 8$

34. **Hint** All letters in a given word are distinct.

The number of ways in which 3-letter words can be formed from 8 letters $= {^8P_3} = 336$

35. **Hint** The letters in the word 'MATHEMATICS' are (MM, AA, TT, H, E, I, C, S).

$\therefore$ Total arrangements $= \frac{11!}{2!\,2!\,2!}$ **Ans.** 4989600

36. **Hint** Total number of words $= \frac{8!}{3!\,2!\,3!} = 560$

37. $^{15}C_{11}$ 38. $^7C_3 \times {^5C_2}$

39. $^8P_3$ 40. $^{10}P_4$

41. **Hint** 0 does not come in hundred's place, so only 4 numbers are possible in hundred's place. Since, the digits are repeated, so in remaining two digits, 5 numbers are possible in each place.

$\therefore$ Total number of ways $= 4 \times 5 \times 5 = 100$

42. $6 \times 6 = 36$

43. **Hint** Each toy can be ditributed to any of the children. **Ans.** 5^8

44. **Hint** Three different jobs can be assigned to three different persons $= {^3P_3} = 3!$

45. **Hint** $^{35}P_2$ **Ans.** 595

46. **Hint** Number of mice $= 18$

Number of groups $= 3$

The number of mice in each group can be $= 6$ mice

Ans. $\frac{18!}{(6!)^3}$

47. **Hint** There are three different types of books. They can be arranged in 3! ways.

$\therefore$ Required number of ways $= 3! \times 6! \times 4! \times 5!$

48. **Hint** Required number of ways = Total number of arrangements – When two R's together, the total arrangements $= \frac{7!}{2!\,2!} - \frac{6!}{2!}$

49. **Hint** The letters of given word are A, A, E, I, I, M, N, N, O, T, X i.e. words starting with A are formed with the letters 2I's, 2N's, A, E, X, M, T, O (total 10 letters). Hence, the number of words formed by these letters

$= \frac{10!}{2!\,2!} = \frac{10 \times 9 \times 8 \times 7 \times 6 \times 5 \times 4 \times 3 \times 2 \times 1}{2 \times 1 \times 2 \times 1} = 907200$

50. ${}^2C_1 \times {}^5C_2 + {}^2C_2 \times {}^5C_1$

51. ${}^{12}C_2 - {}^5C_2 + 1$

52. ${}^nC_1 + {}^nC_2 + ... + {}^nC_n$
$= {}^nC_0 + {}^nC_1 + {}^nC_2 + ... + {}^nC_n - {}^nC_0 = 2^n - 1$

53. **Hint** In automobile licence plates, two different letters can be arranged in ${}^{26}P_2$ ways and next three different digits can be arranged in ${}^{10}P_3$ ways.

$\therefore$ Total number of ways $= {}^{26}P_2 \times {}^{10}P_3$

$= 26 \times 25 \times 10 \times 9 \times 8 = 468000$

54. **Hint** For odd number, first place should be odd number and rest of places may any of the number.
Also, less than 1000 means, number should be one digit, two digits and three digits odd numbers.
Number of one digit odd numbers = 2
Number of two digits odd numbers = 6
Number of three digits odd numbers = 24
Ans. 32

55. (i) $2! \times 9!$
(ii) $10! - 2! \times 9!$

56. **Hint** Total number of ways = Arrangement of 6 differnt colours – Arrangement of different balls when white and black are together $= 6! - 2! \times 5!$

57. **Hint** In thousands place, digit should be 3 and in units place, digit should be 5.
For middle of the two digits, the arrangement of two digits from 4 digits is ${}^4P_2$ ways. **Ans.** 12

58. **Hint** In thousands place, only number (5 or 9) can be placed.

$\therefore$ Total number of ways $= {}^2C_1 \times \frac{4!}{2!}$

59. **Hint** The letters in a word SURITI are {I, I, R, S, T, U}.
When words start with I, then number of arrangements $= 5!$
When words start with R, then number of arrangements $= \frac{5!}{2!}$
When words start with SI, then number of arrangement $= 4!$
When words start with SR, then number of arrangements $= \frac{4!}{2!}$
When words start with ST, then number of arrangements $= \frac{4!}{2!}$
When words start with SUI, then number of arrangements $= 3!$
When words start with SURI, the number of arrangements $= 2!$

$\therefore$ Required rank $= 5! + \frac{5!}{2} + 4! + \frac{4!}{2!} + \frac{4!}{2} + 3! + 2!$
$= 120 + 60 + 24 + 12 + 12 + 6 + 2 = 236$

60. (i) Number of different selections $= {}^{10}C_4$
(ii) Number of different selections $= {}^{10-2}C_{4-2} = {}^8C_2$
(iii) Number of different selections $= {}^8C_4$

61. (i) Number of ways $= {}^7C_5$
(ii) Number of ways $= {}^7C_1 \times {}^4C_4 + {}^7C_2 \times {}^4C_3 + {}^7C_3 \times {}^4C_2 + {}^7C_4 \times {}^4C_1$
(iii) Number of ways $= {}^4C_3 \times {}^7C_2 + {}^4C_4 \times {}^7C_1$

62. (i) Total number of different routes $= 4 \times 4$
(ii) Total number of different routes = 4
(iii) Total number of different routes $= 4 \times 3$

63. **Hint** The letters in the word INDEPENDENCE are (I, N, N, N, D, D, E, E, E, E, P, C).

$\therefore$ Total number of arrangements $= \frac{12!}{3! \times 2! \times 4!}$

(i) Total number of words starting with P $= \frac{11!}{3! \times 2! \times 4!}$

(ii) Total number of words, when all the vowels occur together $= \frac{8! \times 5!}{3! \times 2! \times 4!}$
[consider all vowels as one unit]

(iii) Total number of ways
= Total arrangements – Number of arrangements when vowels occur together
$= \frac{12!}{3! \times 2! \times 4!} - \frac{8! \times 5!}{3! \times 2! \times 4!}$

(iv) Total number of words $= \frac{10!}{3! \times 2! \times 4!}$

64. **Hint** Number of numbers form four different digits formed $= {}^7C_4$
(i) Even number should be in unit's place and on remaining three places, any different number can be placed.
$\therefore$ Total number of ways $= {}^6P_4 \times {}^3C_1$
(ii) Any four-digit number is divisible by 25, if number formed by last two digits is divisible by 25 i.e. 25, 75.
$\therefore$ Total number of ways $= {}^5P_2 \times {}^2C_1$
(iii) Any number is divisible by 4, if number formed by last two digits is divisible by 4 i.e. last digits can be 12, 16, 24, 32, 36, 52, 56, 54, 72, 76.
$\therefore$ Total number of ways $= {}^5P_2 \times {}^{10}C_1$

65. (i) $\frac{n!}{P_1! P_2! ... P_k!}$ (ii) 138600 (iii) 1646400 or 12600

66. (i) 1 (ii) $\frac{n!}{(n-r)!}$ (iii) 6 yr or 3 feet

CHAPTER 12

Logical Reasoning

In this Chapter...

- Coding-Decoding
- Odd Man Out or Odd One Out
- Blood Relation
- Syllogism

Coding-Decoding

Coding

The process of converting a meaningful word into a meaningless word/letter according to a special rule is called coding. Coding is a method of encrypting a word or number.

Decoding

It means in tracing out the actual meaning of a coded letter/word/sentence.

Generally, coding is done on the basis of the letters of English alphabet and their corresponding positions.

To solve the questions based on coding-decoding, first of all it is necessary to remember the positions of all alphabetical letters, both in forward and backward order. Several ways for remembering these positions easily are discussed here.

Positions of letter are of two types

Forward Order Position (Left to Right)

English Letter	A	B	C	D	E	F	G	H	I	J	K	L	M
Forward Position	1	2	3	4	5	6	7	8	9	10	11	12	13
English Letter	N	O	P	Q	R	S	T	U	V	W	X	Y	Z
Forward Position	14	15	16	17	18	19	20	21	22	23	24	25	26

Backward Order Position (Right to Left)

English Letter	Z	Y	X	W	V	U	T	S	R	Q	P	O	N
Backward Order	1	2	3	4	5	6	7	8	9	10	11	12	13
English Letter	M	L	K	J	I	H	G	F	E	D	C	B	A
Backward Order	14	15	16	17	18	19	20	21	22	23	24	25	26

Note Backward order position of any letter
= 27 – Forward order position of that letter

∴ Backward order position of A
= 27 – Forward order position of A = 27 – 1 = 26

Trick to Learn Position/Rank of the Alphabets

Forward order positions of letters can be remembered in the following ways

A to D First four letters A to D's, rank is 1 to 4 (Easy to learn). No trick is required to learn them.

E For this you have to learn one word "EJOTY".

E	J	O	T	Y
5	10	15	20	25

Learning this word helps you to learn the position of 5 letters which are the multiple of 5.

F For this you have to learn another word "CFILORUX".

C	F	I	L	O	R	U	X
3	6	9	12	15	18	21	24

Learning this word helps you to learn the position of 8 letters which are the multiple of 3.

Opposite Letters

These are called opposite letters as the forward order corresponding position of an opposite letter is as same as the backward order corresponding position of its opposite letter.

Alphabet Starting to End	A	B	C	D	E	F	G	H	I	J	K	L	M
	1	2	3	4	5	6	7	8	9	10	11	12	13
	26	25	24	23	22	21	20	19	18	17	16	15	14
	↕	↕	↕	↕	↕	↕	↕	↕	↕	↕	↕	↕	↕
Alphabet Starting to End	Z	Y	X	W	V	U	T	S	R	Q	P	O	N
	26	25	24	23	22	21	20	19	18	17	16	15	14
	1	2	3	4	5	6	7	8	9	10	11	12	13

A and Z is a pair of opposite letters. Now, it is clear from the above presentation that two letters are called opposite to each other, if sum of their corresponding positions is equal to 27.

Note Opposite position of any letter

= 27 – Corresponding position of that letter

∴ Opposite position of A

= 27 – Corresponding position of A

= 27 – 1 = 26 = Z

Type 01 - Letter Coding

In this type of questions, the letters of a certain word are arranged in different orders which can be a reverse order or a fragmented order in which first-half of the word follows some other rule and second part of the word follows some other rule for coding.

1. Coding Based on Rearrangement of Letters

In this type of coding, the letters of the original word are rearranged in a particular manner to obtain the code. *Such coding can be of following types*

(a) When all the letters of a word are written in reverse order

EXAMPLE 1. In a certain code, if MAHESH is written as HSEHAM, then how will MANEGER written in that code?

Sol. As,

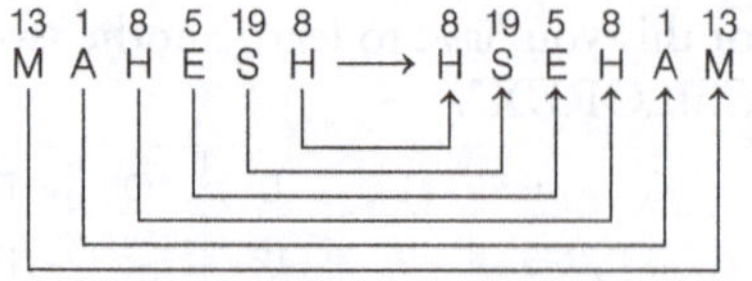

Similarly,

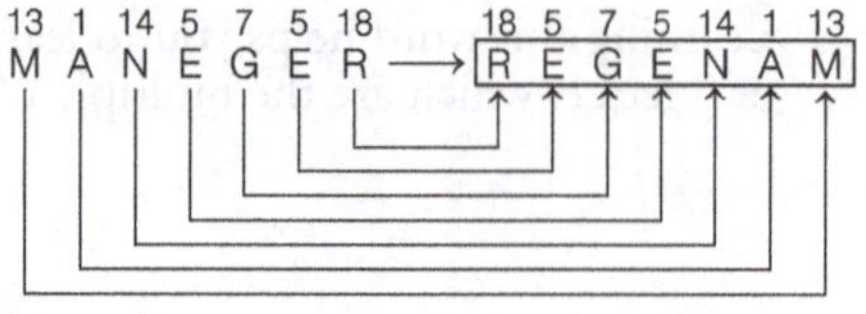

∴ MANEGER ⇒ REGENAM

(b) When letters of the word are divided into two parts and then both the parts are written in reverse order or the first part is written in reverse order at the place of second part and second part is written in reverse order at place of first part.

EXAMPLE 2. If in a certain code language 'THREAT' is written as 'RHTTAE', then how will 'PEARLY' be written in that code?

Sol. As, T H R E A T ⟶ R H T T A E
1 2 3 4 5 6   3 2 1 6 5 4

Similarly, P E A R L Y ⟶ A E P Y L R
1 2 3 4 5 6   3 2 1 6 5 4

∴ PEARLY ⇒ AEPYLR

EXAMPLE 3. If in a certain code language 'MIGHT' is written as 'GHMTI', then how will 'EARTH' be written in that code?

Sol. As, M I G H T ⟶ G H M T I
1 2 3 4 5   3 4 1 5 2

Similarly, E A R T H ⟶ R T E H A
1 2 3 4 5   3 4 1 5 2

∴ EARTH ⇒ RTEHA

2. Coding Based on Replacement of Letters

In this type of coding, the letters of the words are replaced by other letters following a certain pattern to obtain the code.

Such coding can be of following types

A. Forward Sequence Coding

Under this pattern of coding, every letter of a letter group/word is coded in increasing order of English alphabet.

Let us consider the coding of ABCD which can be done in following ways

(i)

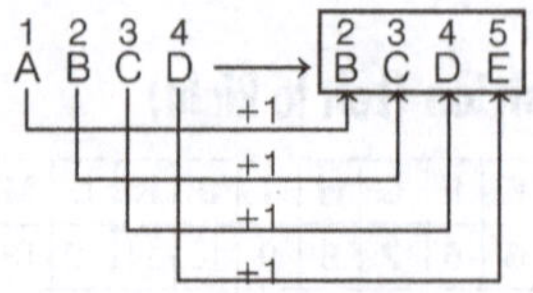

(ii)

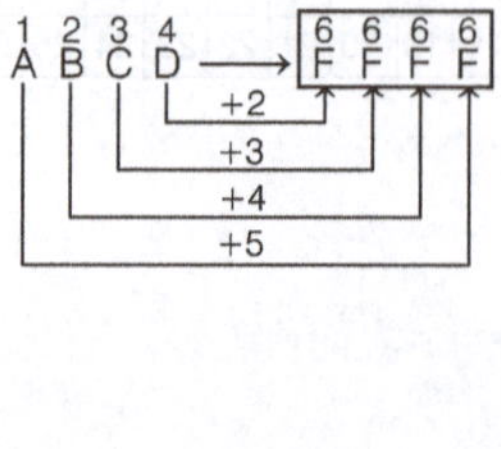

EXAMPLE 4. If RATIONAL is CLETZYLW, then EXPERIENCE is

Sol. As,

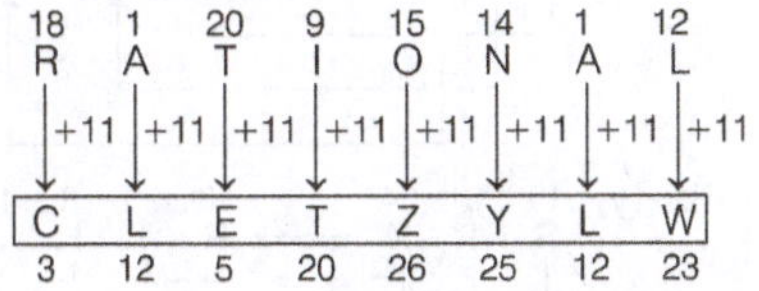

Similarly,

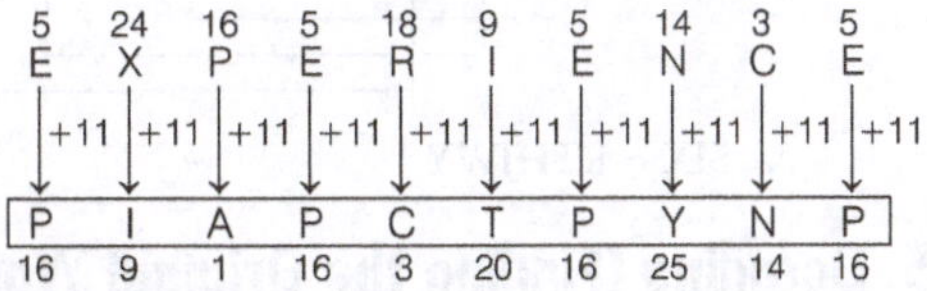

∴ EXPERIENCE ⇒ PIAPCTPYNP

B. Backward Sequence Coding

Under this pattern of coding, every letter of a letter group/word is coded in decreasing order of English alphabetical series.

Let us consider the coding of ABCD which can be done in following ways

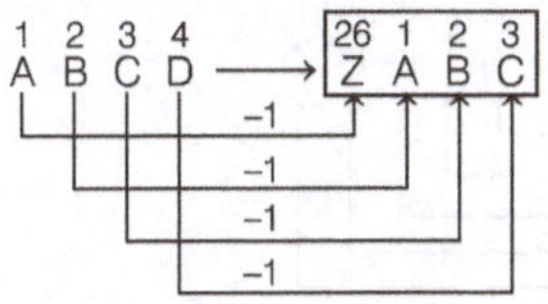

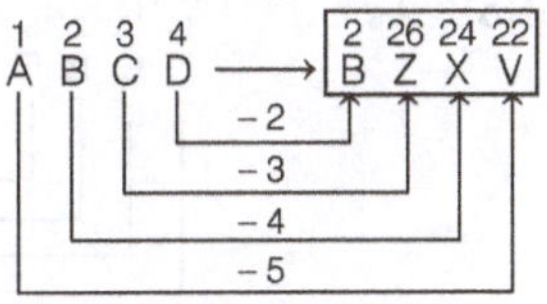

EXAMPLE 5. If in a certain code language 'FRESH' is written as 'EQDRG', then how will 'BLEND' be written in that code?

Sol. As,

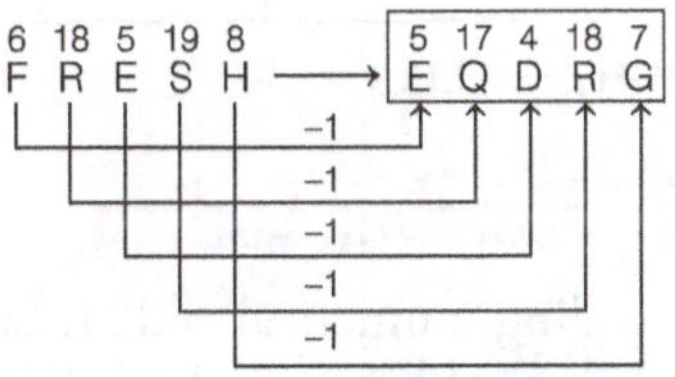

Similarly,

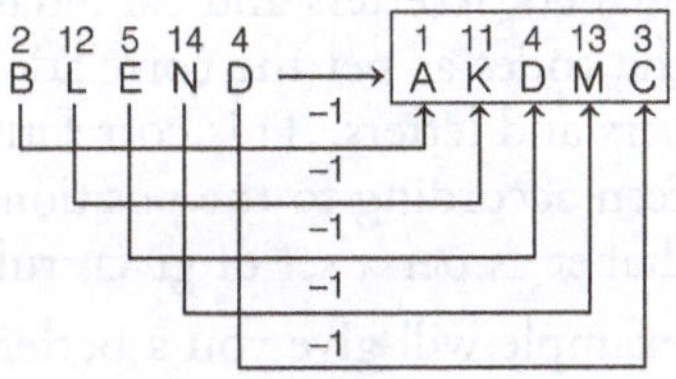

∴ BLEND = AKDMC

C. Mixed Sequence Coding (Forward and Backward)

Under this pattern, forward and backward sequence coding takes place simultaneously.

Let us consider the coding of ABCD which can be done in following ways

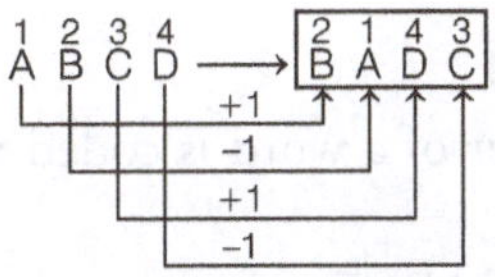

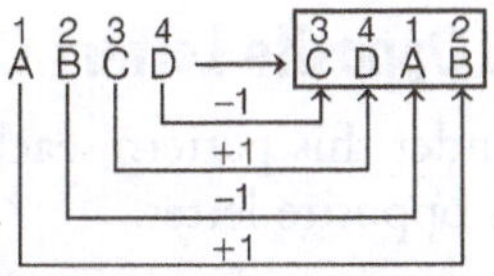

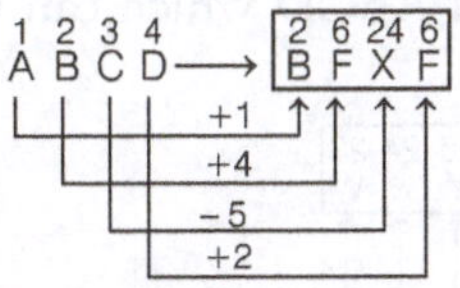

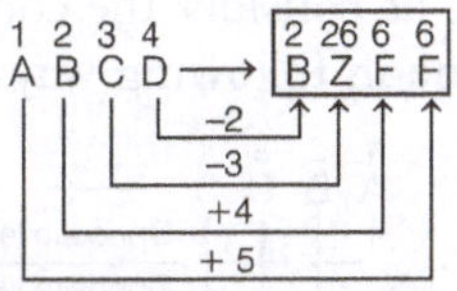

EXAMPLE 6. In a certain code language "NIGHT" is written as "ODDGM" and "DARK" is written as "GOYC". How is "GREEN" written in that code language?

Sol. As,

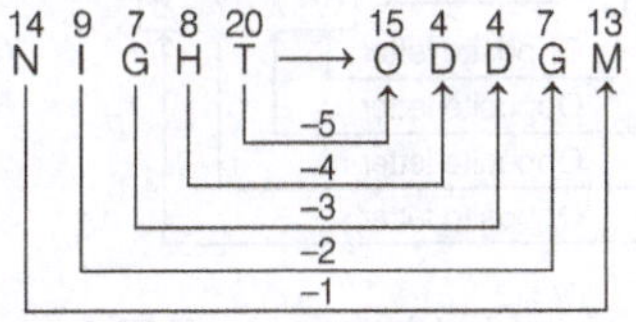

and

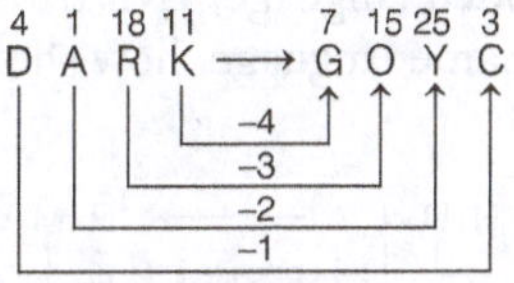

Similarly,

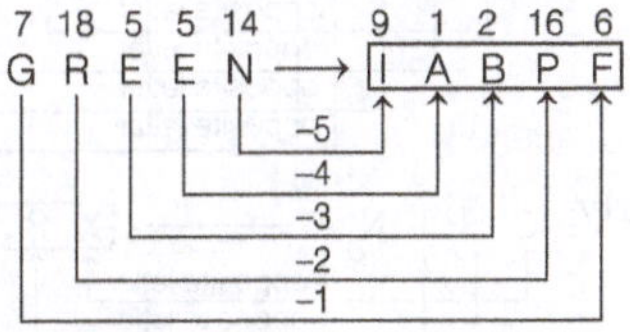

∴ GREEN = IABPF

D. Direct Letter Coding

In this type of coding, some letters groups/words are assigned some codes which do not follow any particular rule but are direct codes for a particular letter of the letter group/ words. These direct codes are then used to form the codes of an another given word.

Example given below will give a better idea about such type of questions.

EXAMPLE 7. In a certain code language, 'GRASP' is written as INOPQ and BROWN is written as RNSTU. How will SPARROW be written as in that code language?

Sol. As,

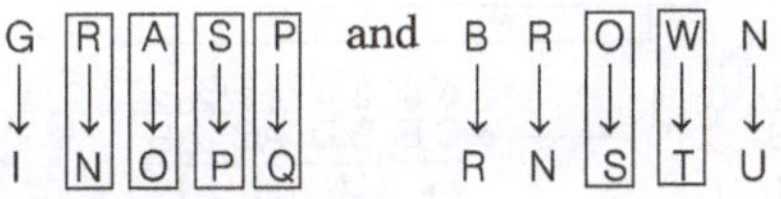

Therefore,

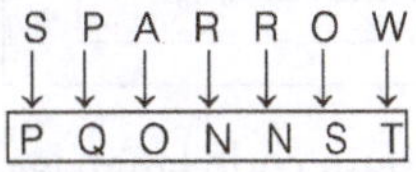

∴ SPARROW = PQONNST

3. Opposite Letters Coding

Under this pattern, each letter of a word is coded with its opposite letter.

Let us consider the coding of ABCD which can be done in following ways

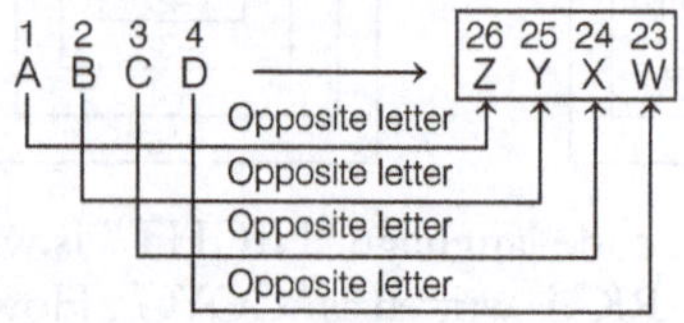

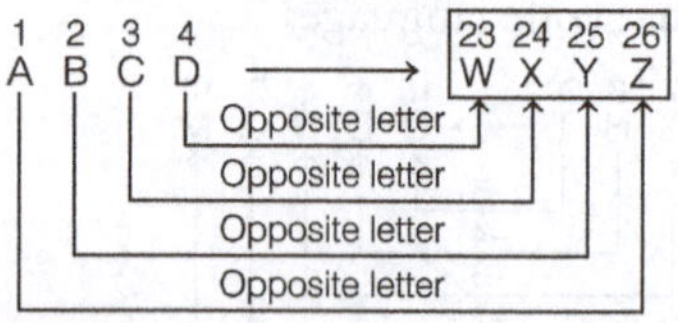

EXAMPLE 8. In a coded language, INDIA is written as RMWRZ. In the same language, how should CHINA be written?

Sol. (b) As,

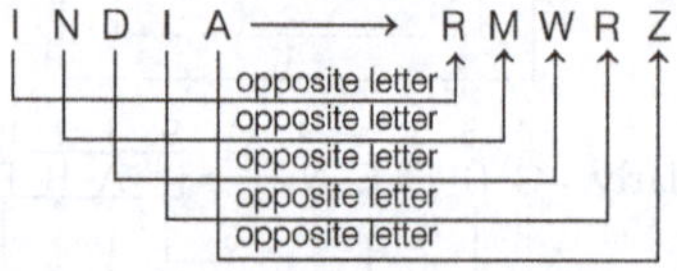

Similarly,

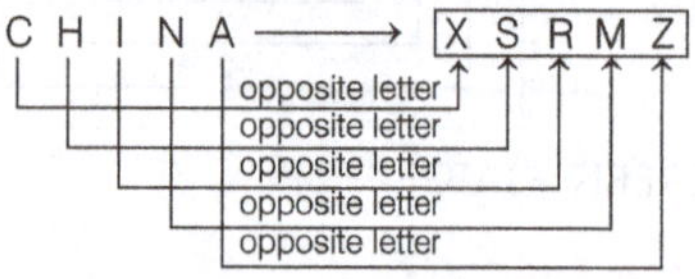

∴ CHINA = XSRMZ

4. Coding of Letters by Their Left and Right Letters of English Alphabet

Under this pattern each letter of a letter group/word is coded by its left and right letters of English alphabet.

Let us consider the coding of ABCD

(i)

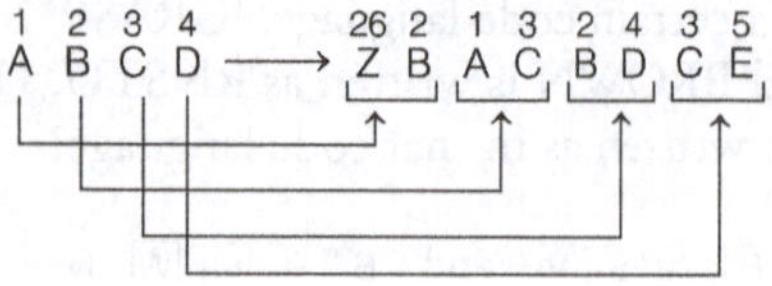

(ii)

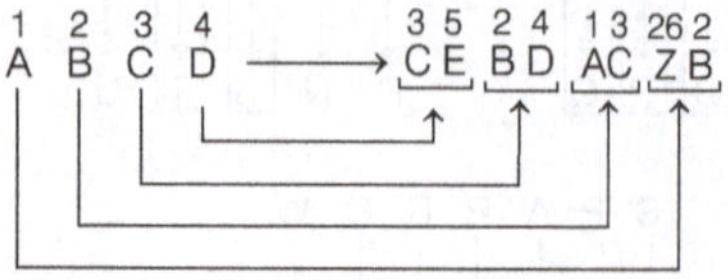

EXAMPLE 9. If in a certain code language 'BAT' is written as 'ACZBSU', then how will 'SIX' be written in that code?

Sol. Here, each letter is coded by its left and right letters.

As,

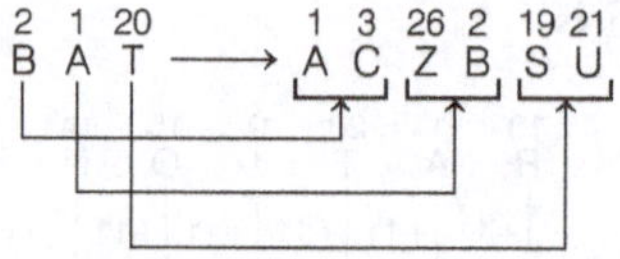

Similarly,

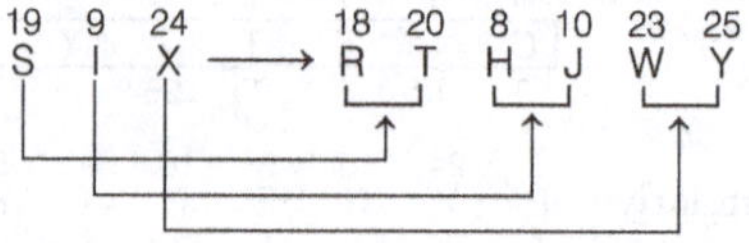

∴ SIX = RTHJWY

5. Decoding (Finding the Original Word of a code)

In this type of questions the code of a word or letters group is given. The candidates are also given a coded word/letters group and they have to find out the original word/letters group of that code.

EXAMPLE 10. In a certain code language NOBEL is written as QIEQO, then in the same code language which word would be written as YLJKS?

Sol. As,

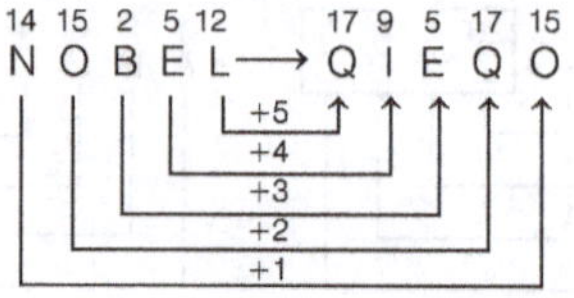

Similarly,

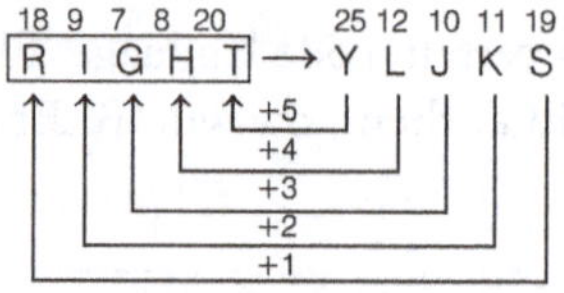

∴ RIGHT ⇒ YLJKS

Type 02 - Number Coding

In number coding, numerical code is assigned to the word or alphabetical letters and candidates are required to analyse the codes as per the correlation between these numbers and letters. This correlation is based on certain pattern according to the position of letters in English alphabet as per a set of given rules.

Following example will give you a better idea about the type of question asked.

EXAMPLE 11. If 'MYSTICAL' is coded as '1325192093112' in a code language, how would 'DUMBBELL' be coded in the same language?

Sol. As,

M	Y	S	T	I	C	A	L	
↓	↓	↓	↓	↓	↓	↓	↓	
13	25	19	20	9	3	1	12	Positional values

Similarly,

D	U	M	B	B	E	L	L
↓	↓	↓	↓	↓	↓	↓	↓
4	21	13	2	2	5	12	12

Positional values

∴ DUMBBELL ⇒ 421132251212

EXAMPLE 12. In a certain code language, 'ROK' is written as '44' and 'MIG' is written as '29'. What will be the code for 'TAL' in that code language?

Sol. Here, the positional values of letters are added to obtain the code.

As, $\overset{18}{R}\overset{15}{O}\overset{11}{K} = 18+15+11 = 44$

and $\overset{13}{M}\overset{9}{I}\overset{7}{G} = 13+9+7 = 29$

Similarly, $\overset{20}{T}\overset{1}{A}\overset{12}{L} = 20+1+12 = 33$

EXAMPLE 13. If 'PKROK' is coded as '72962' and 'KRRPK' as '29972', then how can 'NJMLZ' be coded?

Sol. As,

16	11	18	15	11
P	K	R	O	K
1+6 ↓	1+1 ↓	1+8 ↓	1+5 ↓	1+1 ↓
7	2	9	6	2

and

11	18	18	16	11
K	R	R	P	K
1+1 ↓	1+8 ↓	1+8 ↓	1+6 ↓	1+1 ↓
2	9	9	7	2

P is coded as 7, K as 2, R as 9 and O as 6 that means code of NJMLZ does not have either 7, 2, 9 or 6.

Hence, required code will be 51438.

Type 03 - Symbol Coding Based on Similarity

In symbol coding, various symbols are assigned to the letters of a word and based upon their correlation or similarity, the candidates are required to determine the rules or pattern which is being followed.

Under this pattern each letter of a letter group/word is coded on the basis of the similarity of two or more given codes.

Following example will give you a better idea about the type of questions asked.

EXAMPLE 14. In a certain code language, SHOUT is written as *$59# and HATES is written as $4#6*. How will HOUSE be coded in the same code language?

Sol. As,

S	H	O	U	T
↓	↓	↓	↓	↓
*	$	5	9	#

H	A	T	E	S
↓	↓	↓	↓	↓
$	4	#	6	*

Similarly,

H	O	U	S	E
↓	↓	↓	↓	↓
$	5	9	*	6

∴ HOUSE ⇒ $5 9*6

Type 04 - Fictitious Language Coding

In this type of questions, some messages are provided in the code language and some codes are assigned to each word of the messages.

The candidates are required to decipher the code of each word by finding the common code for two words and this process is followed to decipher the code for each word thereafter and hence the entire message is decoded.

In some cases, there is no common word/number in the message given. In those cases, the words/numbers are coded separately. You have to identify the correct pattern of coding and find the code for the word or message given in the question.

Following examples will give you a better idea about the type of questions asked.

EXAMPLE 15. In a certain code language 'he is great' is written as 'ka pa ra' and 'is Ram hungry' is written as 'na sa ka'. Find the code for 'is'.

Sol. he (is) great ⟶ (ka) pa ra

(is) Ram hungry ⟶ na sa (ka)

Clearly, code for 'is' = ka

In the above example, code for 'he' = pa or ra

code for 'great' = pa or ra

code for 'Ram' = na or sa

code for 'hungry' = na or sa

Note In place of fictious language, words can also be coded with digits (1, 2, 3, ...), letters (A, B, C, ...) or symbols (ϕ, %, +, ⇒, ...).

Topic Practice 1

1 If in a certain code, 'GIGANTIC' is written as 'GIGTANCI'. How 'MIRACLES' be written in that language?

2 If in a certain code, 'EXPLAINING' is written as 'PXEALNIGNI'. How will 'PRODUCED' be written in that language?

3 If in a certain code language 'SYSTEM' is written as 'SYSMET', 'NEARER' is written as 'AENRER', then how will 'FRACTION' be written in that language?

4 If 'MEAT' is written as 'TEAM', then 'BALE' is written as ....

5 In a certain coded language, if 'LITMUS' is written as 'SMIUTL' and 'INDIGO' is written as 'OINGDI', then how is the word 'JAGGER', would be written in that language?

6 If 'GERMANY' is written as '7, 5, 18, 13, 1, 14, 25', how can 'FRANCE' be written in that code?

7 In a certain code language if '41095' is 'READY' and '840327' is 'FRAILS', then '83145 419' is ....

8 If 7 is coded as 'CBRT343', then '9' is coded as ....

9 If each letter of the English alphabet is assigned an odd numerical value in increasing order, such as A = 1, B = 3 and so on, then what will be the code of HONEY?

10 If 'HELLO' is coded as 15 | 12 | 12 | 5 | 8, then 'WHERE' is coded as ....

11 If in a certain code language 'RAT' is written as '★Δ %', 'CAT' is written as '# Δ %' and 'FAT' is written as '$ Δ %', then how will 'CAR' be written in that language?

12 In a certain code language, 'Sue Re Nik' means 'She is brave', 'Pi Sor Re Nik' means 'She is always smiling' and 'Sor Re Zhi' means 'Is always cheerful'. What is the code used for the word' smiling'?

13 In a certain code language, '786' means 'study very hard' '958' means 'hard work pays and '645' means 'study and work'. Which of the following is the code for 'very'?

Hints & Solutions

1.

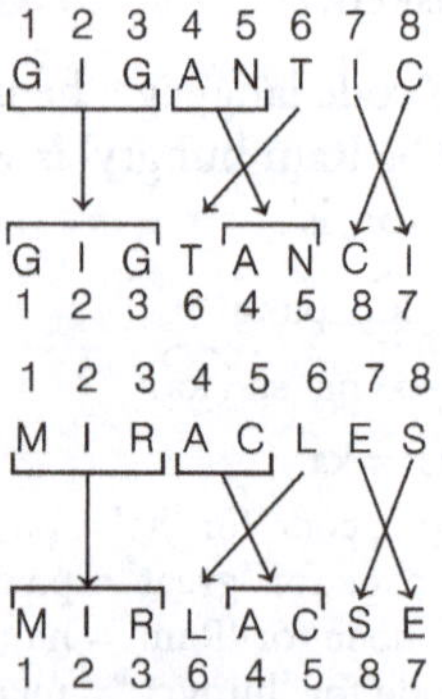

∴ MIRACLES ⇒ MIRLACSE

2. As, E X P L A I N I N G → P X E A L N I G N I
1 2 3 4 5 6 7 8 9 10 → 3 2 1 5 4 7 6 10 9 8

Similarly, P R O D U C E D → O R P U D D E C
1 2 3 4 5 6 7 8 → 3 2 1 5 4 8 7 6

∴ PRODUCED ⇒ ORPUDDEC

Here, the first three and the last letters are reversed as pairs and the rest of the letters are reversed in pair of two letters.

3.

S Y S T E M → S Y S M E T
1 2 3 4 5 6 → 3 2 1 6 5 4

N E A R E R → A E N R E R
1 2 3 4 5 6 → 3 2 1 6 5 4

F R A C T I O N → C A R F N O I T
1 2 3 4 5 6 7 8 → 4 3 2 1 8 7 6 5

∴ FRACTION ⇒ CARFNOIT

Here, the first half and second half of letter are within the reverse order.

4.

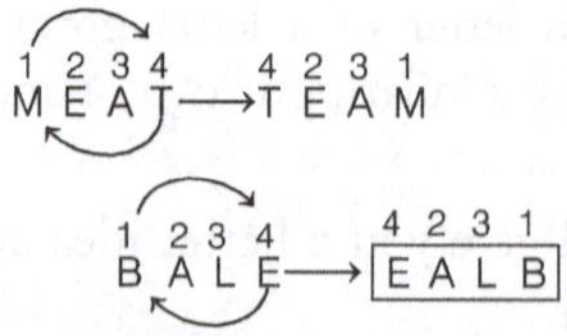

∴ BALE ⇒ EALB

5. As,

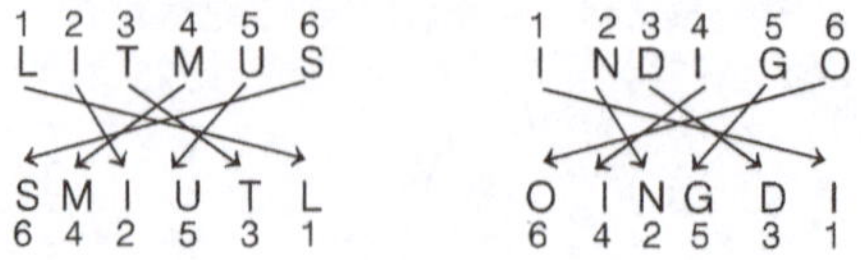

Similarly,

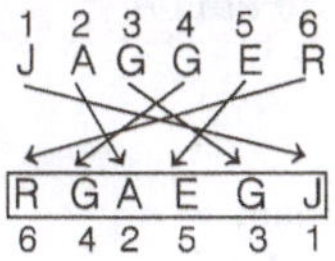

∴ JAGGER ⇒ RGAEGJ

6. Letters are coded with their corresponding positions in alphabetical series.

As,

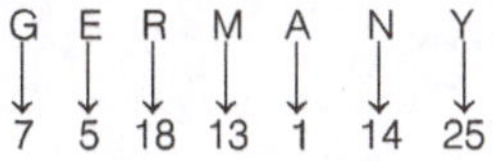

Similarly,

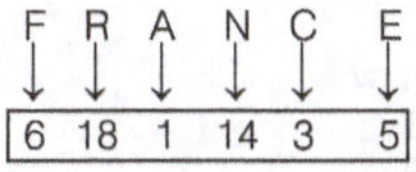

∴ FRANCE ⇒ 6, 18, 1, 14, 3, 5

7. As,

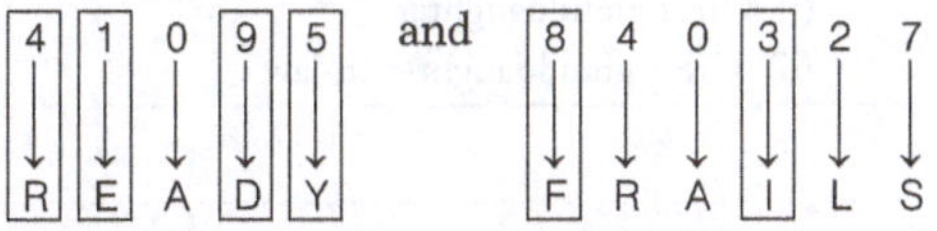

Similarly,

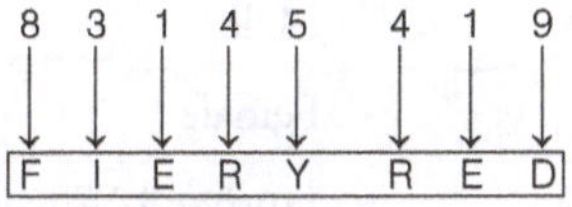

∴ 83145 419 ⇒ FIERY RED

8. 7 is coded as CBRT 343.

343 is the cube of 7 i.e. ($7^3 = 343$).

Similarly, 9 is coded as CBRT 729.

729 is the cube of 9 i.e. ($9^3 = 729$).

9. A = 1, B = 3, C = 5, D = 7, E = 9, F = 11, G = 13, H = 15, I = 17, J = 19, K = 21, L = 23, M = 25, N = 27, O = 29, P = 31, Q = 33, R = 35, S = 37, T = 39, U = 41, V = 43, W = 45, X = 47, Y = 49, Z = 51

∴ HONEY = 1 5 2 9 2 7 9 4 9

10.

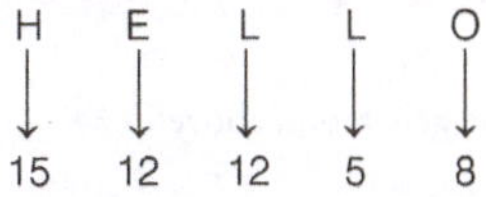

'H' has 8th position in the alphabetical order and 'O' has 15th position as in the alphabetical order. Both the positions of numeric form are interchanged as shown in the above figure. Similarly, 'L' has 12th position which is interchanged with 'E's position i.e. '5' and so on in the same way.

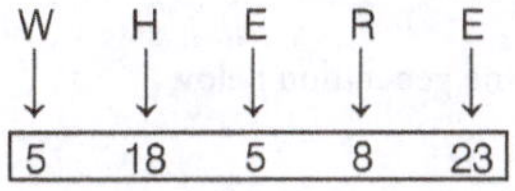

∴ WHERE ⇒ 5/18/5/8/23

11.

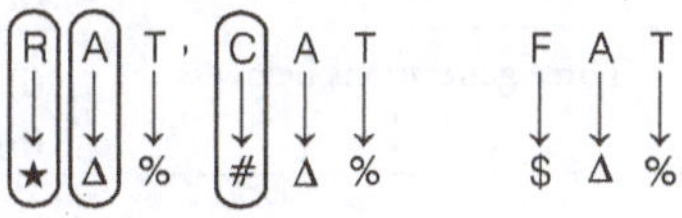

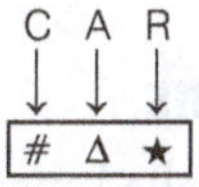

∴ CAR ⇒ # Δ ★

12.

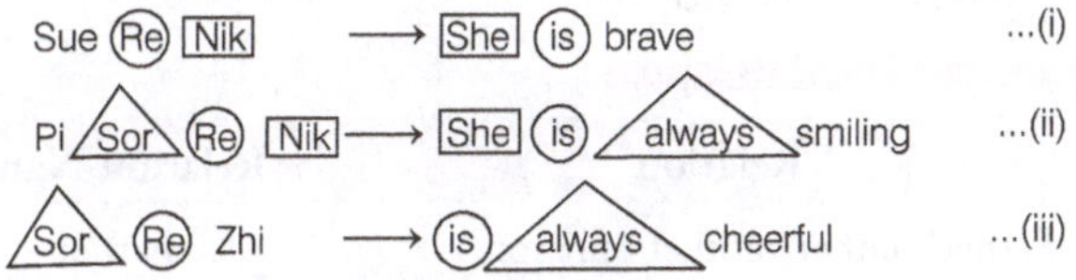

From Eqs. (i), (ii) and (iii), code for smiling is Pi.

13.

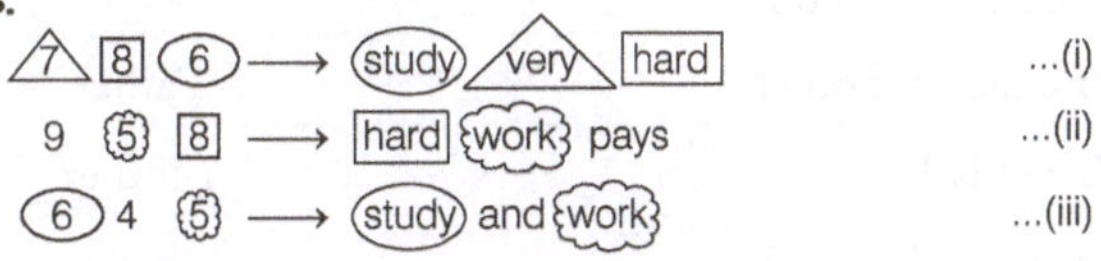

Here, from Eq. (i), very ⟶ 7

Blood Relations

Blood relation between two individuals is defined as a relation between them by the virtue of their birth rather than by their marriage or any other reasons. (i.e. seven generations of the family) which is generally three generation above and three generation below the current generation.

Different relationships between the family members of different generations

Generation	Male	Female
Three generations above ↑↑↑	(i) Great grandfather (ii) Maternal great grandfather (iii) Great grandfather-in-law	(i) Great grandmother (ii) Maternal great grandmother (iii) Great grandmother-in-law
Two generations above ↑↑	(i) Grandfather (ii) Maternal grandfather (iii) Grandfather- in- law	(i) Grandmother (ii) Maternal grandmother (iii) Grandmother-in-law

Generation	Male	Female
One generation above ↑	(i) Father (ii) Uncle (iii) Maternal uncle (iv) Father-in-law	(i) Mother (ii) Aunt (iii) Maternal aunt (iv) Mother-in- law
Current generation (self) →	(i) Husband (ii) Brother (iii) Cousin (iv) Brother-in-law	(i) Wife (ii) Sister (iii) Cousin (iv) Sister-in-law
One generation below ↓	(i) Son (ii) Nephew (iii) Son-in-law	(i) Daughter (ii) Niece (iii) Daughter-in-law
Two generations below ↓↓	(i) Grandson (ii) Grandson-in-law	(i) Granddaughter (ii) Granddaughter-in-law
Three generations below ↓↓↓	(i) Great grandson (ii) Great grandson-in-law	(i) Great granddaughter (ii) Great granddaughter-in-law

Maternal and Paternal Relations

The relation on mother's side is called maternal, e.g. maternal uncle or aunt. The relation on father's side is called paternal e.g. Paternal uncle or aunt.

Important Blood Relations

Relation	Relation Name
✦ Father's father/mother only son	Father
✦ Only daughter-in-law of father's father/father's mother	Mother
✦ Husband of mother	Father
✦ Wife of father	Mother
✦ Son of brother or sister or brother-in-law or sister-in-law	Nephew
✦ Daughter of brother or sister or brother-in-law or sister-in-law	Niece
✦ Grandson of father/mother or mother-in-law or father-in-law	Son/Nephew
✦ Granddaughter of father/mother or mother-in-law or father-in-law	Daughter/Niece
✦ Husband of daughter	Son-in-law
✦ Wife of brother/brother-in-law	Sister-in-law

Family Diagram

In the questions related to Blood Relations, the diagram formed by representing the various relations with the help of symbols, is called family tree.

S.No.	Symbols	Meaning
1.	$\oplus$	Male
2.	$\ominus$	Female
3.	$\oplus \leftrightarrow \ominus$	Husband-Wife (Married couple)
4.	$\oplus — \oplus$	Brother-Brother
5.	$\ominus — \ominus$	Sister-Sister
6.	$\oplus — \ominus$	Brother-Sister
7.	$\oplus$ $\vert$ $\oplus$	Father-Son
8.	$\oplus$ $\vert$ $\ominus$	Father-Daughter
9.	$\ominus$ $\vert$ $\oplus$	Mother-Son
10.	$\ominus$ $\vert$ $\ominus$	Mother-Daughter

Type 01 - Blood Relation Based on Conversation

In such questions, a person gives information to another person either about a particular person in a photograph or a person present in front of him.

Using this information, a candidate is required to establish a relationship between a given person and the person in the photograph/the person about whom the information is provided.

EXAMPLE 1. Amit said to Mohan, "That boy in red shirt is younger of the two brothers of the daughter of my father's wife". How is the boy in red shirt related to Amit. Who is a boy?

Sol. Let us draw the family diagram,

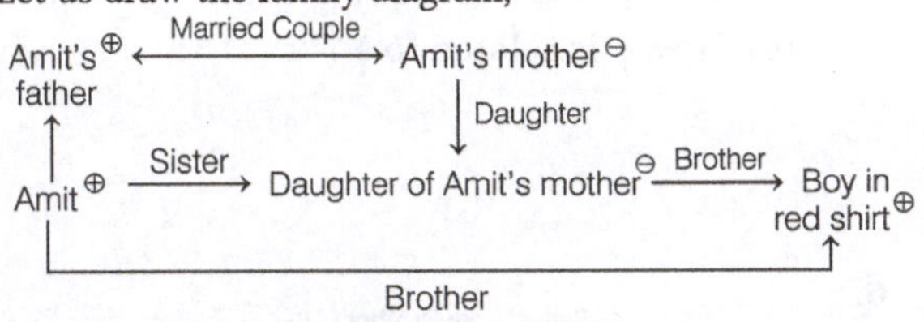

Now, it is clear that the boy in red shirt is the brother of Amit.

EXAMPLE 2. Gopal said, pointing to Govind, "His father is my father's only son". How is Gopal related to Govind?

Sol. Let us draw the family diagram,

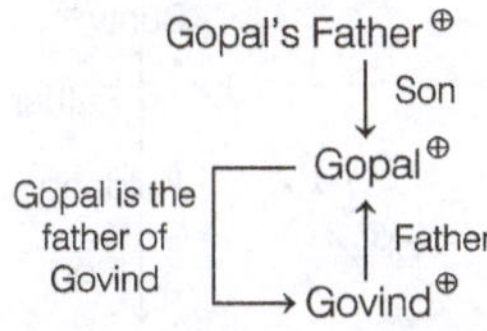

Clearly, the only son of Gopal's father is Gopal himself. This means Gopal is the father of Govind.

EXAMPLE 3. Introducing Kavi, Veena said, "She is sister of my husband's wife's son." How is Veena related to Kavi?

Sol. Let us draw the family diagram,

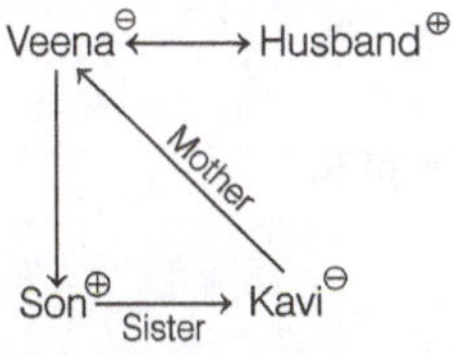

Now, it is clear that Veena is the mother of Kavi.

Type 02 - Blood Relation Based on Puzzle

In such questions, more than one information in the form of some puzzle is given and based on the informations, a candidate is required to deduce the relation between the two individuals.

EXAMPLE 4. If A is B's sister, C is B's mother, D is C's father and E is D's mother, then how is A related to D?

Sol. Let us draw the family diagram,

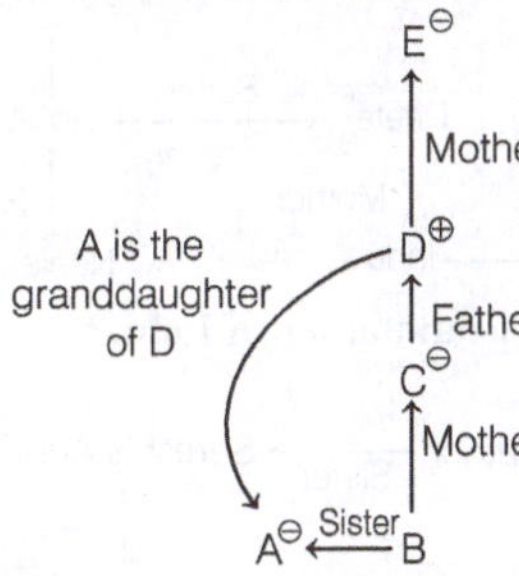

Now, it is clear that A is the granddaughter of D.

EXAMPLE 5. Rajesh is the brother of Ankit. Shano is the sister of Shubham. Ankit is the son of Shano. How is Rajesh related to Shano?

Sol. Let us draw the family diagram,

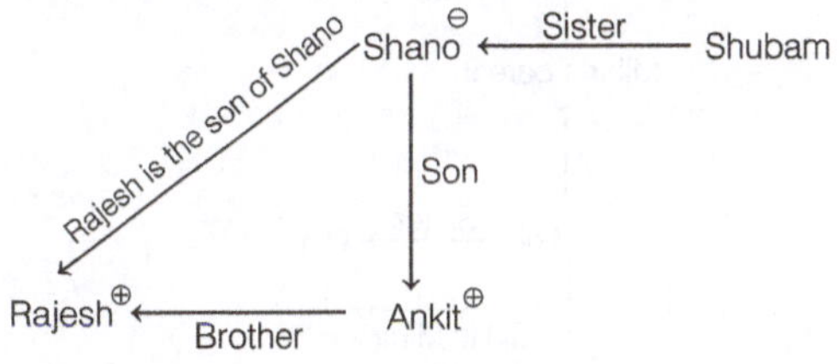

Now , it is clear that Rajesh is the son of Shano.

Topic Practice 2

1 Neelam, who is Rohit's daughter, says to Indu, Your mother Reeta is the younger sister of my father, who is third child of Sohanji". How is Sohanji related to Indu?

2 Pointing towards a woman, Suresh said, "She is the daughter of my father's sister". How is the woman related to Suresh?

3 Pointing towards a girl, Mihir said, "She is the only daughter of only child of my grandfather". How is the girl related to Mihir?

4 Pointing to a woman in the photograph, Rajesh said, "The only daughter of her grandfather is my wife". How is Rajesh related to that woman?

5 Introducing a man, a woman said, "His wife is the only daughter of my mother." How is the woman related with the man?

6 A is brother of B. C is sister of A. D is brother of E. E is daughter of B. Who is uncle of D?

7 Deepak has a brother named Aditya. Deepak is the son of Kuldeep. Bunty is Kuldeep's father. How is Aditya related to Bunty?

8 A is brother of B. B is sister of T. T is mother of P. If R is the maternal grandfather of P, how is T related to R?

9 A, Q, Y and Z are different persons. Z is the father of Q. A is the daughter of Y and Y is the son of Z. If P is the son of Y and B is the brother of P, then find who is the sister of B?

10 Read the information given below and answer the questions.

All the given members belong to the same the family.

J is the brother of L. J is the only son of R. W is the father-in-law of L. D is the maternal grandfather of P, who is a male. Q is the only son of W. W is the grandfather of N and C is the daughter of N.

(i) How L is related to C?

(ii) How P is related to N?

Hints & Solutions

1.

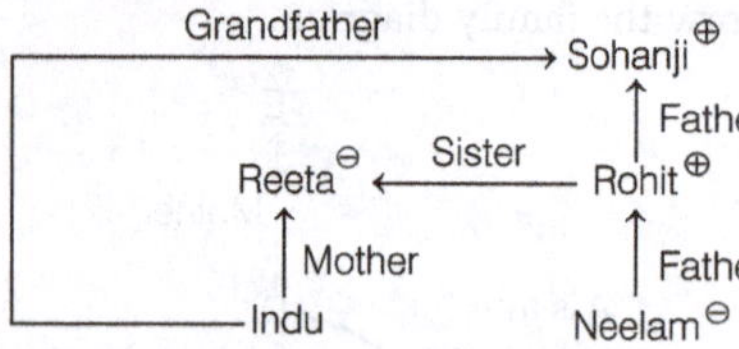

Sohanji is the grandfather of Indu.

2.

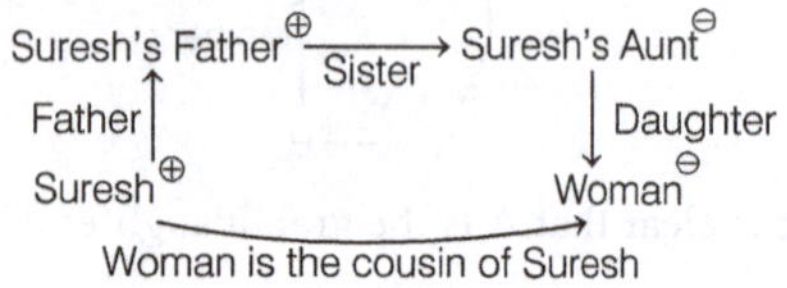

Woman is the cousin of Suresh.

3.

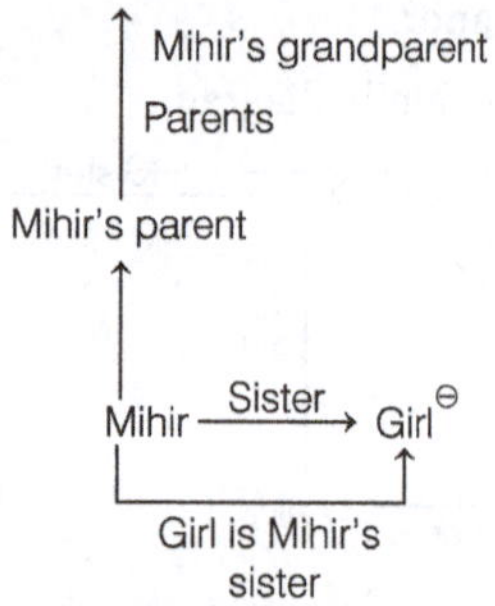

Girl is Mihir's sister.

4.

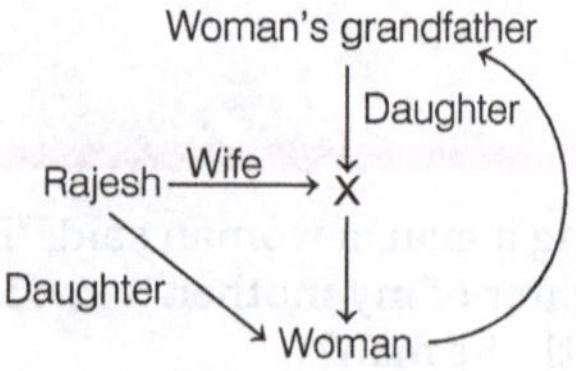

Rajesh is father of that woman.

5.

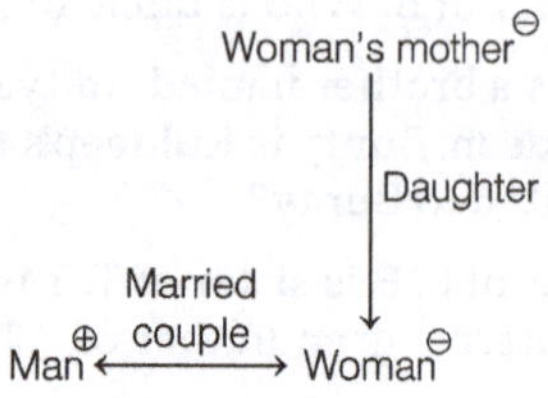

Woman is the wife of that man.

6.

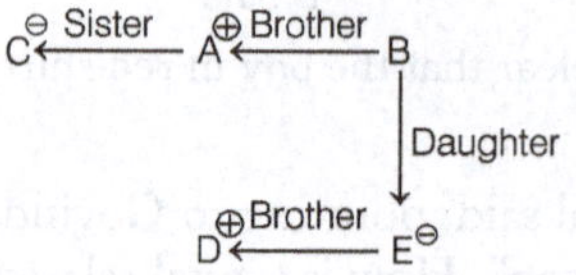

A is the uncle of D.

7.

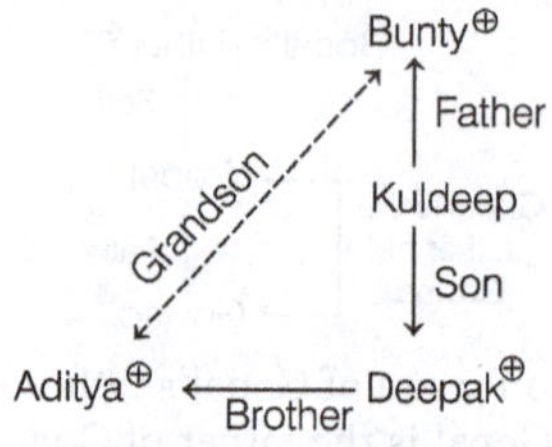

Aditya is the grandson of Bunty.

8.

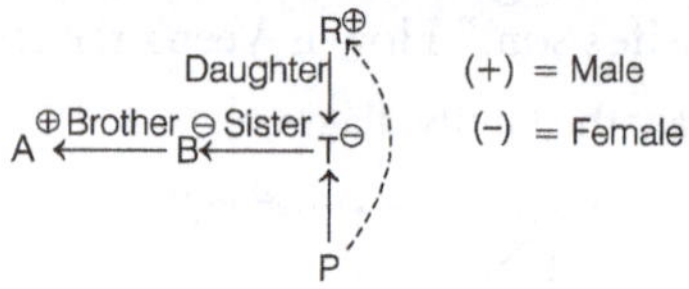

T is the daughter of R.

9.

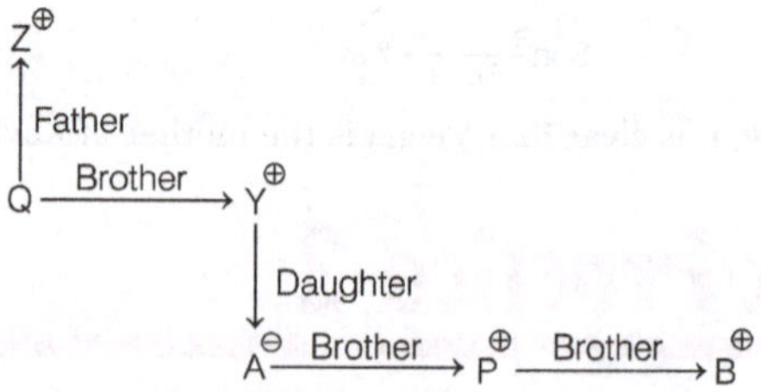

A is the sister of B.

10.

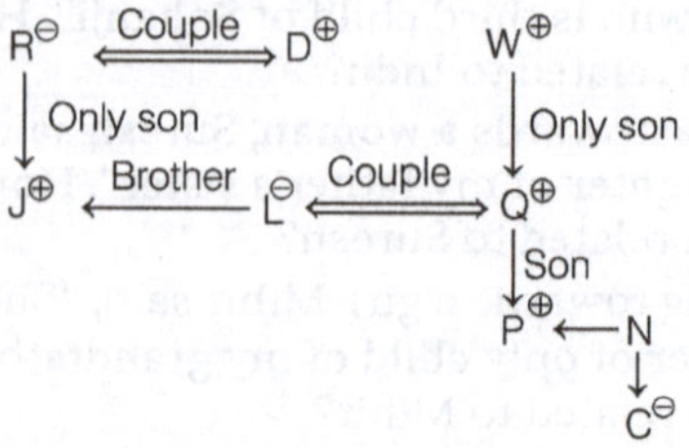

(i) L is grandmother of C.

(ii) P is brother of N.

Odd Man Out or Odd One Out

In odd man out problems all the terms given in the problem except one follow a certain pattern. The term which does not follow the pattern is called odd term or odd man

Types of Problems Based on Odd Man Out

(i) Alphabet problems (ii) Words problems
(iii) Numbers problems

Find odd man out in the following examples

EXAMPLE 1. B, C, D, E, F, G and H

Sol. Out of given 7 letters of english alphabet, E is odd man,because all other alphabets are consonants.

EXAMPLE 2. A, E, D, H and G

Sol. Out of given 5 letters, H is odd man, because H is the only mirror image letter.

EXAMPLE 3. WU, DB, OL, RP, KI and NL

Sol. Out of given 6 pairs of alphabets, OL is odd man, because in all other pairs of alphabets gap is 2.

EXAMPLE 4. Apple, potato, orange, mango and cherry.

Sol. Out of given 5 words, potato is odd man, because except potato all other are fruits.

EXAMPLE 5. January, May, July, August and November

Sol. Out of given 5 months, November is odd man because all except November are months having 31 days.

EXAMPLE 6. Red, yellow, blue and green.

Sol. Out of given 4 colours, green is odd man, because all other are primary colours.

EXAMPLE 7. 1, 4, 9, 16, 25, 48 and 49

Sol. Out of given 7 numbers, 48 is odd man, because except 48 all others are perfect squares.

EXAMPLE 8. 13, 23, 33, 43 and 53

Sol. Out of given 5 numbers, 33 is odd man, because except 33 all are prime.

EXAMPLE 9. 8, 27, 64, 125 and 343

Sol. Out of given 5 numbers, 64 is odd man, because except 64, all are cubes of prime numbers.

Topic Practice 3

Find odd man out in each of the following questions.

1 A, B, C and D
2 P, Q, R, S, T and U
3 AE, GK, LP, QU and VY
4 ABC, BCD, CDE and DEF
5 Violet, blue, green, white and yellow
6 Include-exclude, import-export, admit-deny, scared-afraid
7 Square, Triangle, Rectangle, Circle and Cuboid
8 Banana, Mango, Cashew, Apple and Guava
9 Cabbage, Papaya, Gourd, Cucumber and Brinjal
10 121, 253, 286, 372, 473 and 594
11 3, 5, 11, 14, 17 and 21
12 10, 25, 45, 54, 60 and 75
13 6, 9, 15, 21, 24, 28 and 30

Hints & Solutions

1. A is vowel. **Ans.** A is odd man
2. U is vowel. **Ans.** U is odd man
3. Gap in pair of alphabets in 4. **Ans.** VY is odd man
4. No vowel in BCD. **Ans.** BCD is odd man
5. Except white all are colours of rainbow.
   Ans. White is odd man
6. Both the words in scared afraid have the same meaning.
   Ans. Scared afraid is odd man.
7. All except cuboid are 2D plane figures.
   Ans. Cuboid is odd man
8. All except cashew are fruits.
   Ans. Cashew is odd man
9. All except papaya are vegetables.
   Ans. Papaya is odd man
10. Except 372 in all other numbers the sum of ones and hundreds digit is tens digit. **Ans.** 372 is odd man
11. 14 is even number. **Ans.** 14 is odd man
12. 54 is not a multiple of 5. **Ans.** 54 is odd man
13. 28 is not a multiple of 3. **Ans.** 28 is odd men

Syllogism

The word syllogism is derived from the Greek word 'Syllogismos' which means 'Conclusion, inference or deduction'. These deductions are based on propositions (premise).

'Syllogism' checks basic aptitude and ability of a candidate to derive inferences from given statements using step by step methods of solving problems.

Proposition

A **proposition** or **premise** is grammatical sentence comprising of four components

- Quantifier
- Subject
- Copula
- Predicate

Let us consider the following sentences,

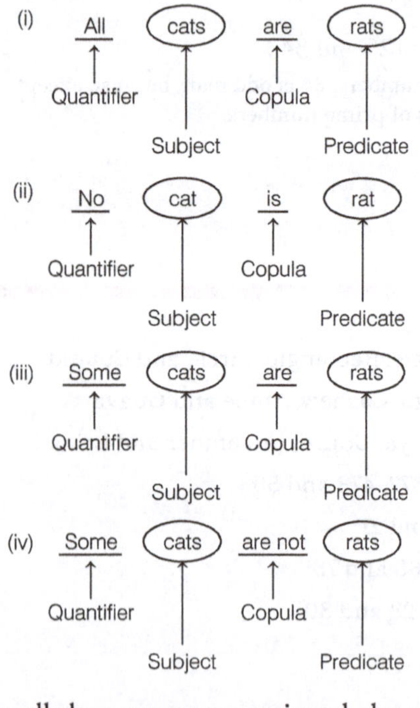

In all the sentences mentioned above, a relation is established between **subject** and **predicate** with the help of **quantifier** and **copula**.

Components of Proposition

- **Quantifier** The words 'All', 'No' and 'Some' are called quantifiers as they specify a quantity.

  Keep in mind that 'All' and 'No' are universal quantifiers because they refer to each and every object of a certain set.

  'Some' is a particular quantifier as it refers to atleast one existing object in a certain set.
- **Subject (S)** A subject is that part of a proposition about which something is said.
- **Copula (C)** It is that part of a proposition that denotes the relation between subject and predicate.
- **Predicate (P)** It is that part of a proposition which is affirmed detail about that subject.

Important Terms Used in Syllogism

To find a logical deduction from two statements there should be three terms present. Those three terms are

1. **Major term** It is the predicate of the conclusion and is denoted by 'P' (for predicate).
2. **Minor term** It is the subject of the conclusion and is denoted by 'S' (for subject).
3. **Middle term** It is the term common to both the statements and is denoted by 'M' (for middle).

   The middle term should not appear in the conclusion.

e.g. **Statements**

All ships are buses.

All cars are ships.

Conclusion All cars are buses.

Here, 'buses' is the predicate of the conclusion. Therefore, it is major term, P. 'Cars' is the subject of the conclusion. Therefore, it is the minor term, S. 'Ships' is the term common to both the statements. Therefore, it is the middle term, M.

Major and Minor Statements

The 'major statement' is that in which the middle term is the subject and the 'minor statement' is that in which the middle term is the predicate.

e.g. **Statements**

All dogs are cats.

All cats are white.

Here, the middle term 'cats' is the subject of second statement.

So, it is the major statement and the middle term, 'cats' is the predicate of first statement. So, it is the minor statement.

Types of Categorical Proposition

Propositions have been classified on the basis of quality and quantity. Quality denotes whether the proposition is affirmative or negative in nature. Quantity denotes whether the proposition is universal or particular.

Types of proposition can be understood by the following diagram

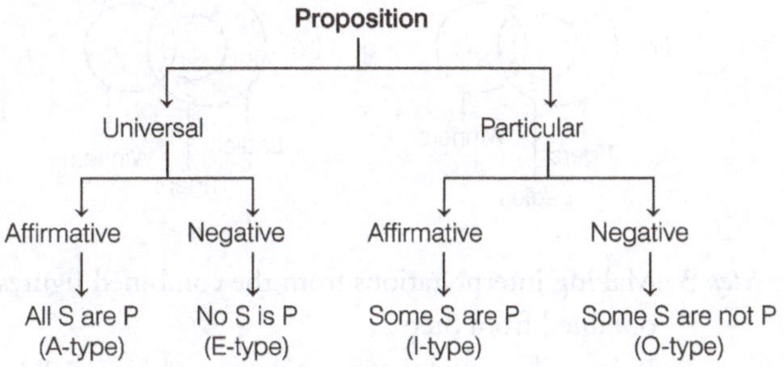

From the above diagram, following things are very much clear

(i) **Universal propositions**

Either (a) completely include the subject (A-type)

or (b) completely exclude the subject (E-type)

(ii) **Particular propositions**

Either (a) partly include the subject (I-type)

or (b) partly exclude the subject (O-type)

Now, we can summarize the four standard types of propositions (premises) as below

Type	Proposition	Quantity	Quality
A	All A are B	Universal	Affirmative
E	No A is B	Universal	Negative
I	Some A are B	Particular	Affirmative
O	Some A are not B	Particular	Negative

To draw valid inferences from the statements, the candidate is required to have a clear understanding of A, E, I, O relationships.

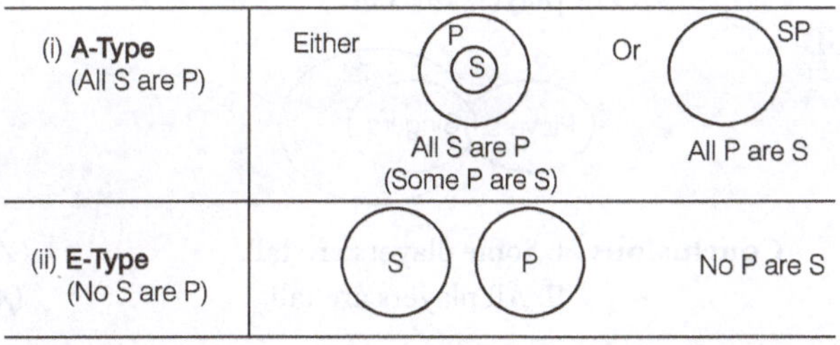

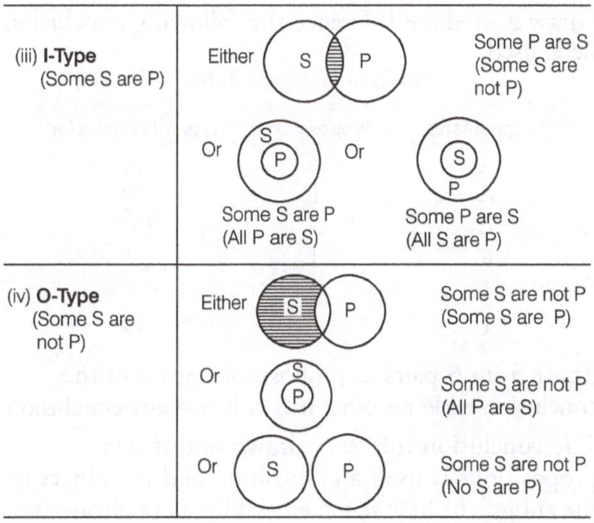

Inference

Inference is a logical conclusion derived from premises or statements known or assumed to be true.

Types of Inferences

Inferences drawn from statements can be of two types

1. **Immediate Inference** When an inference is drawn from a single statement, then that inference is known as an immediate inference.

   e.g. **Statement** All books are pages.

   Conclusion Some pages are books.

   In the above example, a conclusion is drawn from a single statement and does not require the second statement to be referred, hence the inference is called an immediate inference.

2. **Mediate Inference** In mediate inference, conclusion is drawn from two given statements.

   e.g. **Statements** All dogs are cats.
   All cats are black.

   Conclusion All dogs are black.

   In the above example, conclusion is drawn from the two statements or in other words, both the statements are required to draw the conclusion. Hence, the above conclusion is known as mediate inference.

Method to Draw Mediate Inferences

Mediate inference can be drawn only if,

- there are two statements/propositions.
- there is a common term in the given two statements.
- the common term is predicate of the first statement and subject of the second statement.

To draw a Mediate Inference the following conclusion table is used,

Mediate Inference Table

Proposition I	Proposition II	Type of conclusion
A	A	A
A	E	E
E	A	O^R
E	I	O^R
I	A	I
I	E	O

- Apart from 6 pairs of propositions given in the conclusion table no other pair will give any conclusion.
- The conclusion/inference drawn out of two propositions is itself a proposition and its subject is the subject of first statement while its predicate is predicate of the second statement. The common term gets disappeared.
- O^R means, the conclusion is of O-type but is in reverse order. In this case, the subject of the inference/conclusion is the predicate of the second statement and the predicate of the inference or conclusion is the subject of the first statement.
- The mediate inference table gives correct inference/conclusion if and only if the two statements are in proper alignment.

Method To Solve Problems Through Venn Diagram

There are following steps to solve problems through Venn diagram.

Step 1 Drawing standard representation for each statement separately.

Point to be noted that standard representation means a representation which is most common and usually sufficient way to denote the statement.

Let us consider the following pair of statements

Statements I. Some tigers are winners.

II. Some winners are ladies.

Standard representation for Statement I

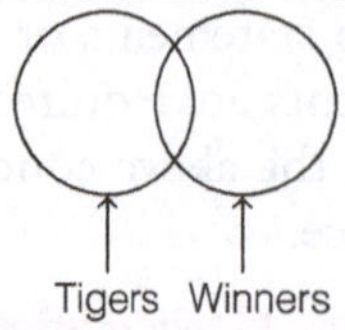

Standard representation for Statement II

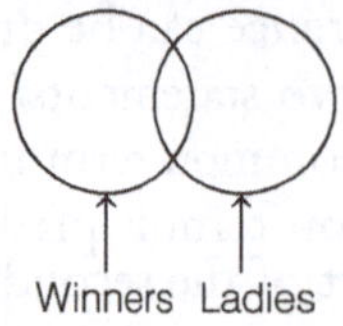

Step 2 Combining the representations (drawn in Step 1) in all possible ways. Let us see

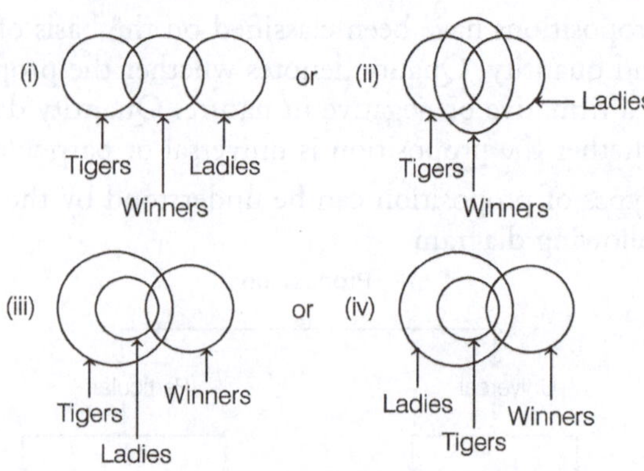

Step 3 Making interpretations from the combined figures obtained from Step 2.

Point to be noted that any given conclusion will be true if and only if it is supported by all the combined figures and no combined figure contradicts it.

Let us consider over two conclusions

X. Some winners are tigers.

Y. Some tigers are ladies.

- **Conclusion** X (Some winners are tigers) is a valid conclusion as it is supported by all the combined figures (i), (ii), (iii) and (iv) represented in Step 2.
- **Conclusion** Y (Some tigers are ladies) is an invalid conclusion at it is rejected by figure (i) represented in Step 2.

Two Statements and Two Conclusions

In this type of questions, two statements and two conclusions are given. The candidate is required to check the validity of the given conclusions on the basis of the given statements.

EXAMPLE 1. Statements Some players are singers.

All singers are tall.

Conclusions I. Some players are tall.

II. All players are tall.

Sol.

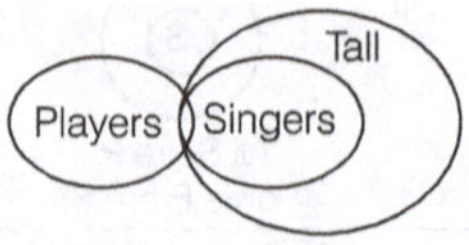

Conclusions I. Some players are tall. (✓)

II. All players are tall. (✗)

EXAMPLE 2. **Statements** All stones are water.
Some water are clean.

Conclusions I. Some water are stones.
II. All clean are water.

Sol. According to the given statements,

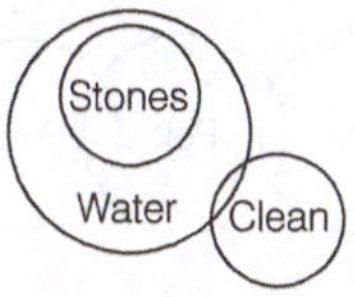

Conclusions I. Some water are stones. (✓)
II. All clean are water. (✗)

EXAMPLE 3. **Statements** All tables are books.
All pens are books.

Conclusions I. Some tables are pens.
II. Some books are pens.

Sol. According to the given statements,

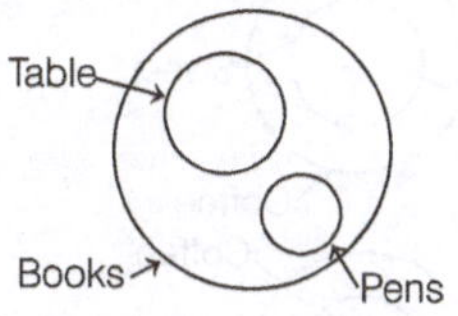

Conclusions I. All tables are books. ✗
II. All pens are books. ✓

Only Conclusion II is true.

EXAMPLE 4. **Statements** Some books are cars.
Some cars are dogs.

Conclusions I. Some dogs are cars.
II. Some cars are books.

Sol. According to the statements,

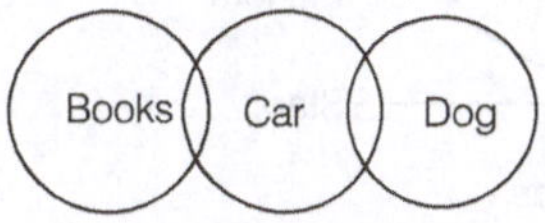

Conclusions I. Some dogs are cars. ✓
II. Some cars are books. ✓

EXAMPLE 5. **Statements** Only a few books are reading.
All readings are general.

Conclusions I. All books are general.
II. Some general are reading.

Sol. According to the given statements,

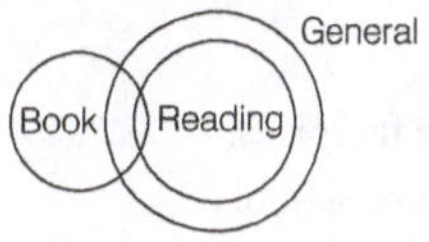

Conclusions I. All books are general. ✗
II. Some general are reading. ✓

Hence, only Conclusion II follows.

Topic Practice 4

1 **Statements** All stars are planets.
All planets are galaxies.
Conclusions
I. All galaxies are planets.
II. All stars are galaxies.

2 **Statements** Some schools are factories.
All factories are shops.
Conclusions
I. All shops are factories.
II. Some shops are schools.

3 **Statements** All pens are ink.
No ink is an eraser.
Conclusions
I. No pen is an eraser.
II. Some erasers are pens.

4 **Statements** All DSLR are lenses.
Some camera are DSLR.
Conclusions
I. All camera is lenses.
II. Some lenses are camera.

5 **Statements**
Some books are pen.
Some pens are pencil.
Conclusions
I. No book is pencil.
II. All pencils are books.

6 **Statements** No toffee is coffee.
No sweet is toffee.
Conclusions
I. No coffee is sweet.
II. All sweets are coffee.

7 **Statements** Only a few strong is tough.
Only a few tough is dark.
Conclusions
I. Some strong is not dark.
II. No tough is strong.

Hints & Solutions

1.

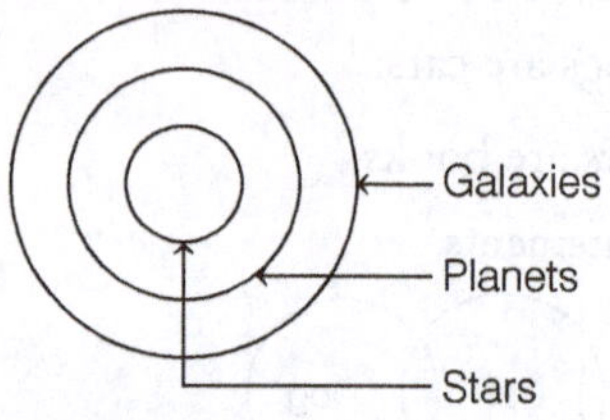

Conclusions

I. All galaxies are planets. (✗)

II. All stars are galaxies. (✓)

2.

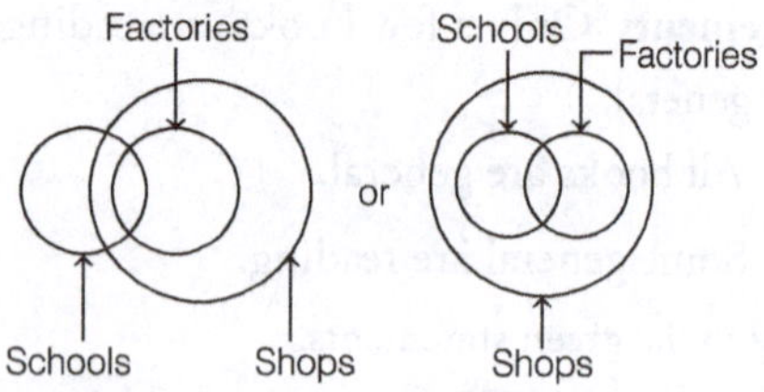

Conclusions

I. All shops are factories. (✗)

II. Some shops are schools. (✓)

3.

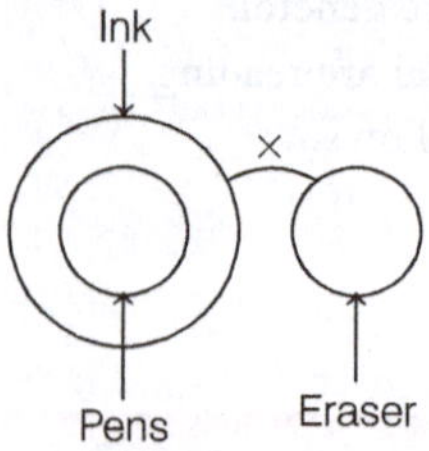

Conclusions

I. No pen is an eraser. (✓)

II. Some erasers are pens. (✗)

4.

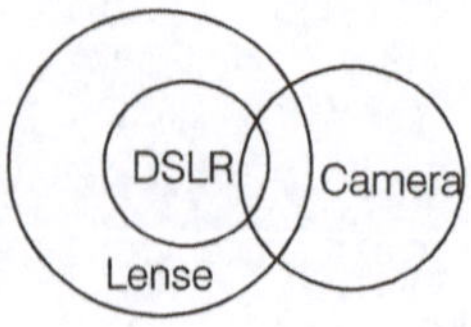

Conclusions

I. All camera is lenses. (✗)

II. Some lenses are camera. (✓)

5. According to the statements,

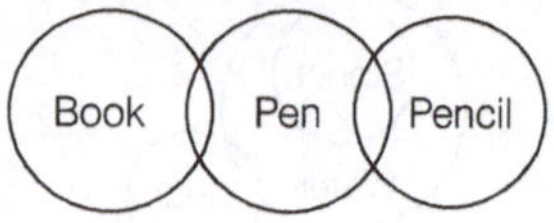

Conclusions

I. No book is pencil. (✗)

II. All pencils are book. (✗)

6.

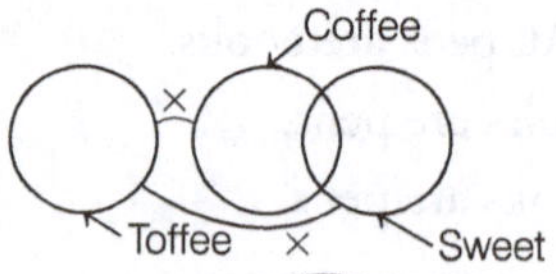

or

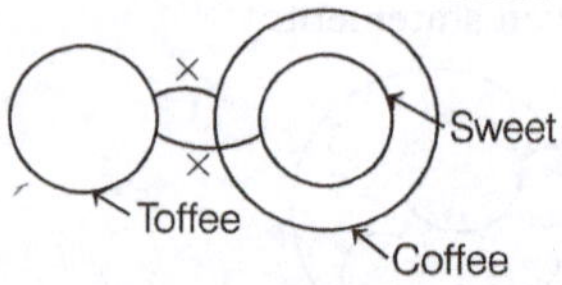

or

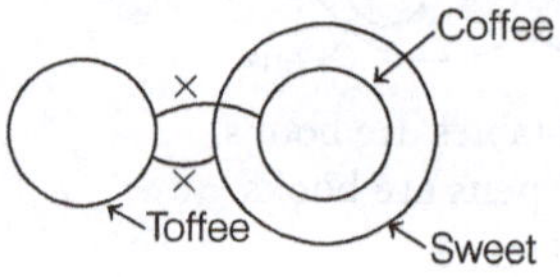

or

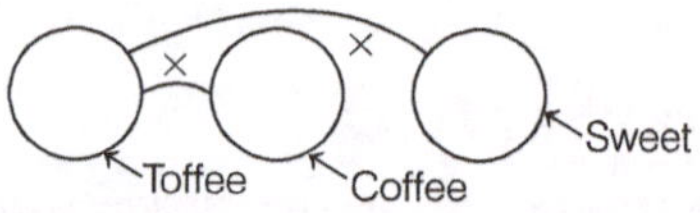

Conclusions

I. No coffee is sweet. (✗)

II. All sweets are coffee. (✗)

7. As per question,

Conclusions

I. Some strong is not dark. (✗)

II. No tough is strong. (✗)

Exam Pattern Exercise

Part A - Objective Type Questions

Multiple Choice Type Questions

1 If CHAIR is coded as FKDLU, then RAID is coded as
(a) UDLG (b) ULKG (c) UDGL (d) ULGD

2 If TEMPLE is coded as VHQNIA how would you code CHURCH?
(a) EKYWI (b) EKYQWD
(c) EKYPZD (d) EKYDPD

3 If 'SWAMINATHAN' is coded as 'NAHTANIMAWS' in a certain code language, then how would you code 'SIRNAME' in that language?
(a) EMAMSIR (b) EMARNIS
(c) EMNARIS (d) EMANRIS

4 Mathew told his friend Sham, pointing to a photograph, "Her father is the only son of my mother." The photograph is of whom?
(a) Mathew's niece (b) Mathew's mother
(c) Mathew's daughter (d) Mathew's sister

5 Pointing to a man in a photograph, a man said to a woman, "His mother is the only daughter of your father." The woman related to the man in the photograph is
(a) Wife (b) Mother (c) Daughter (d) Sister

6 Amit said, "This girl is the wife of the grandson of my mother." How is Amit related to the girl?
(a) Husband (b) Father
(c) Father-in-law (d) Mother-in-law

7 The odd one out in the following letters.
(a) NOP (b) RTU (c) JKL (d) EFG

8 **Statements**
(i) Some players are singers.
(ii) All singers are tall.
Find the conclusion which follows the given statements.
(a) Some players are tall.
(b) All players are tall.
(c) All singers are players.
(d) All tall are singers.

9 **Statements**
(i) All rats are cows. (ii) No cow is white.
Find the conclusion which follows the given statements.
(a) No cows is rat. (b) Some cows are white.
(c) No white is cow. (d) All cows are rats

10 **Statements**
(i) Some stones are bricks.
(ii) Some bricks are trees.
Find the conclusion which follows the given statements.
(a) Some stones are trees.
(b) Some stones are not trees.
(c) Some trees is bricks.
(d) All bricks are trees.

Assertion-Reason Based Questions

Directions (Q. Nos. 11-13) *In the questions given below are two statements labelled as Assertion (A) and Reason (R). In the context of the two statements, which one of the following is correct?*
(a) Both A and R are correct; R is the correct explanation of A
(b) Both A and R are correct; R is not the correct explanation of A
(c) A is correct; R is incorrect
(d) R is correct; A is incorrect

11 **Assertion (A)** In a certain code FINGER is written as DGLECP. Then, KIDNEY is written as IGBLCW.
Reason (R) If CRUDE is written as BSTED, then MOIST will be coded as LPHTS.

12 **Assertion (A)** Introducing Asha to guests. Bhaskar said, "Her father is the only son of my father." Asha is Bhaskar's daughter.
Reason (R) If B says that his mother is the only daughter of A's mother, then A is father of B.

13 **Assertion (A) Statements**
(i) Some doors are mangoes.
(ii) All mangoes are bananas.
Conclusion Some bananas are mangoes.
Reason (R) Statement No parrot is crow.
Conclusion No crow is parrot.

Part B - Descriptive Questions

Very Short Answer Type Questions

Directions (Q. Nos. 14-16) *In the following, find out odd one out.*

14 Father, Mother, Friend, Sister, Brother.
15 LNMO, SUTV, EUFV, CRDT, GWHX
16 16, 29, 27, 25, 51

Short Answer Type Questions

17 Answer the following questions.
(i) If STOVE is coded as EVOTS and CANDLE is coded as ELDNAC, then REPORT is coded as?
(ii) In a certain code, 'REFRIGERATOR' is coded as 'ROTAREGIRFER'. Which words would be coded as 'NOITINUMMA'?

(iii) If 'VEHEMENT' is written as 'VEHETNEM', then how 'MOURNFUL' be written in that code language?

18 **Statements** Some cats are rats. All bats are tables. All rats are bats.

Conclusion

I. Some cats are bats. II. All bats are rats.
III. All tables are cats. IV. All bats are cats.

Decide which of the given conclusions logically follows from the given statements.

Long Answer Type Questions

19 Find odd man out in each of the following

(i) BDF, GIK, LMN, OQS and TVX
(ii) Venus, Jupiter, Mercury, Pluto, Moon and Neptune
(iii) City, Town, District, Village and Towel
(iv) 15, 25, 45, 55, 65, 72, 75 and 85
(v) 7, 26, 63, 124, 217, 342 and 511

20 Read the information given below and answer the questions that follow.

A family of Ravi, Rekha, Gaurav, Saurabh, Payal. Mohit, Monika, Swasti and Shaurya consists of 3 generations. Ravi is husband of Rekha and has 2 sons and one daughter Payal. Mohit is Rekha's son-in-law. Saurabh is Payal's brother and Monika's brother-in-law. Gaurav has two children.

(i) How is Gaurav related to Mohit?
(ii) How is Saurabh related to Ravi?
(iii) How is Ravi related to Shaurya?
(iv) How is Mohit related to Payal?
(v) How is Mohit related to Swasti?

21 Read the information given below and answer the questions that follow.

In a family there are 6 persons A, B, C, D, E and F. They are Entrepreneur, Lawyer, Teacher, Manager, Doctor and Engineer. The doctor is the grandfather of F, who is an Entrepreneur.

The Engineer D is married to A. C the Manager is married to Lawyer.

B is the mother of E and F. There are two married couples in the family.

(i) What is the profession of B?
(ii) What is the profession of E?

Case Study Based Questions

22 In a family, there are seven members, A, B, C, D, E, F and G. A and B are married couple. A being the male member. D is the only son of C, who is the brother of A. E is the cousin sister of D. G is the daughter in law of F, whose husband has died.

Based on the above information, answer the following questions

(i) How E is related to B?
(a) E is daughter of B
(b) E is granddaughter of B
(c) E is mother of B
(d) E is mother in law of B

(ii) How G is related to C?
(a) G is sister of C (b) G is husband of C
(c) G is wife of C (d) G is mother of C

(iii) How A is related to F?
(a) A is father of F (b) A is son of F
(c) A is grandson of F (d) A is brother of F

(iv) How D is related to A?
(a) D is son of A (b) D is daughter of A
(c) D is father of A (d) D is a nephew of A

(v) How F is related to D?
(a) F is grandmother of D (b) F is father of D
(c) F is daughter of D (d) F is son of D

Hints & Solutions

1. (a) 2. (c) 3. (d) 4. (c)
5. (b) 6. (c) 7. (b) 8. (a)
9. (c) 10. (c) 11. (b) 12. (c)
13. (b)

14. Friend
All other are blood relations.

15. CRDT
In all other group, first and third letters and second and fourth letters are in alphabetical sequence.

16. 29
All other are not prime numbers.

17. (i) TROPER (ii) AMMUNITION (iii) MOURLUFN

18. Conclusion I follows.

19. (i) LMN (ii) Moon (iii) Towel (iv) 72 (v) 217

20. (i) Gaurav is Mohit's brother-in-law.
(ii) Saurabh is Ravi's son.
(iii) Ravi is grandfather of Shaurya.
(iv) Mohit is husband of Payal.
(v) Mohit is Swasti's uncle.

21. (i) B is a Lawyer.
(ii) E is a teacher.

22. (i) (a) (ii) (c) (iii) (b)
(iv) (d) (v) (a)

CHAPTER 13

Functions

In this Chapter...

- Functions, Domain and Range of Real Function
- Some Standard Real Functions and Their Graphs
- Composition of Functions
- Algebra of Real Functions

Functions, Domain and Range of Real Function

A special type of relation is called **function**. The word 'function' is derived from a Latin word meaning **'operation'**.

Function as a Relation

A relation f from a non-empty set A to a non-empty set B is said to be a function, if every element of set A has one and only one image in set B.

In other words, we can say that a function f is a relation from a non-empty set A to a non-empty set B such that the domain of f is A and no two distinct ordered pairs in f have the same first element.

If f is a function from a set A to a set B, then we write

$$f : A \to B \text{ or } A \xrightarrow{f} B$$

and it is read as f is a function from A to B or f maps A to B.

If $(a, b) \in f$, then we can also write it as $f(a) = b$. Here, b is called the **image** of a under f and a is called the **pre-image** of b under f.

e.g.

(i) Let $A = \{2, 3, 4\}$, $B = \{3, 4, 5\}$ and f_1, f_2 and f_3 be three subsets of

$A \times B$ defined as $f_1 = \{(2, 3), (3, 4), (4, 5)\}$,

$f_2 = \{(2, 3), (2, 4), (3, 4), (4, 5)\}$

and $f_3 = \{(2, 4), (3, 5)\}$

Then, f_1 is a function from A to B, since every element of A has one and only one image in set B. f_2 is not a function from A to B, since $2 \in A$ has two images 3 and 4 in B. Also, f_3 is not a function from A to B, since $4 \in A$ has no image in B.

(ii) In the form of arrow diagram

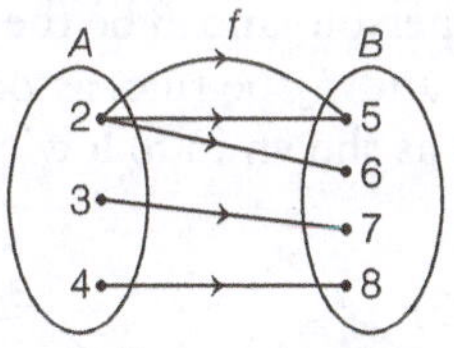

(a) f is not a function

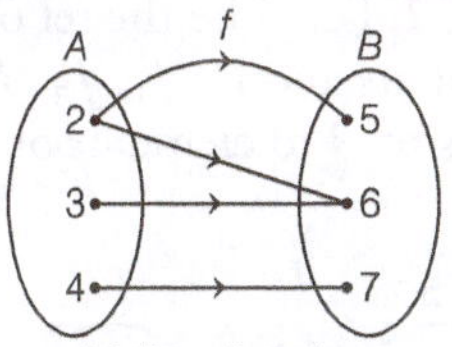

(b) f is a function

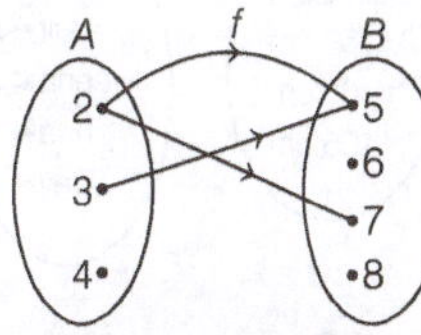

(c) f is not a function

EXAMPLE 1. Which of the following relations are functions?

(i) $\{(3, 3), (4, 2), (5, 1), (6, 0), (7, 7)\}$

(ii) $\{(2,0), (4, 8), (2, 1), (3, 6)\}$

Sol. (i) $\{(3, 3), (4, 2), (5, 1), (6, 0), (7, 7)\}$

It is a function, because first element of each ordered pair is different.

(ii) $\{(2, 0), (4, 8), (2, 1), (3, 6)\}$

It is not a function, because first elements of $(2, 0)$ and $(2, 1)$ are same.

Function as a Correspondence

A function f from a non-empty set A to a non-empty set B is a **rule or method or correspondence** which associates elements of set A to elements of set B such that

(i) All elements of set A are associated to elements in set B.

(ii) An element of set A is associated with one and only one element of set B.

In other words, a **function 'f' from a non-empty set A to a non-empty set B, associate each element of set A to an unique element of set B.**

Characteristics of a Function $f: A \to B$

- For each element $x \in A$, there is unique element $y \in B$.
- The element $y \in B$ is called the **image** of x under the function f. Also, y is called the **value of function f at x** i.e. $f(x) = y$.
- $f: A \to B$ is not a function if there is an element in A which has more than one image in B. But more than one element of A may be associated to the same element of B.
- $f: A \to B$ is not a function, if an element in A does not have an image in B.

EXAMPLE 2. Let A be the set of persons and B be the set of their heights and let f_1, f_2, f_3 and f_4 be rules associating elements of A to elements of B as shown in following figures.

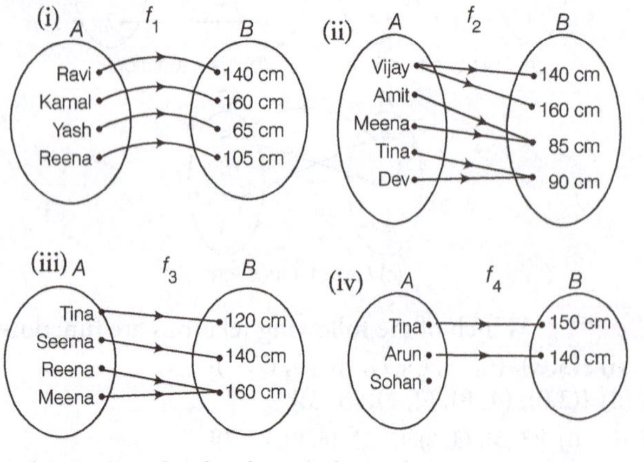

Check whether f_1, f_2, f_3 and f_4 are functions or not and why?

Sol. In f_1 [arrow diagram (i)], we observe that each element of A is associated with exactly one element of B, Therefore, f_1 is a function from A to B.

In f_2 [arrow diagram (ii)], we observe that Vijay is associated with 140 cm and 160 cm. Any person can have only one unique height, so the height of Vijay cannot be 140 cm and 160 cm together.

Hence, $f_2 : A \to B$ is not a function.

In f_3 [arrow diagram (iii)], we observe that Reena and Meena are associated with 160 cm. It is possible that because the height of two persons may be equal.

Hence, f_3 is a function from A to B.

In f_4 [arrow diagram (iv)], we observe that Sohan (an element of A) is not associated to any element of B. But, according to the definition of a function, all the elements of A should be associated with elements of B.

Hence, f_4 is not a function from A to B.

Independent and Dependent Variables

Independent variable is a variable that serves as input to the function, while the output i.e. dependent variable depends on the independent variable.

e.g. If y is a function of $f(x)$, then x is independent variable and y is dependent variable.

Domain, Codomain and Range of a Function

If f is a function from A to B, i.e. each element of A corresponds to one and only one element of B, whereas every element in B need not be the image of some x in A. Then the set A is called the **domain** of function f and the set B is called the **codomain** of f.

The subset of B containing the images of elements of A under f is called the **range** of f. Thus, if a function f is expressed as the set of ordered pairs, then the domain of f is the **set of first elements** of all ordered pairs of f and the range of f is **the set of second elements** of all ordered pairs of f i.e.

$$\textbf{Domain of } f = \{a : (a, b) \in f\}$$

$$\textbf{Range of } f = \{b : (a, b) \in f\}$$

EXAMPLE 3. Which of the following relations are functions? Give reasons. If it is a function, determine its domain and range.

(i) $\{(2, 1), (5, 1), (8, 1), (11, 1), (14, 1), (17, 1)\}$

(ii) $\{(2, 1), (4, 2), (6, 3), (8, 4), (10, 5), (12, 6), (14, 7)\}$

(iii) $\{(1, 3), (1, 5), (2, 5)\}$

Sol. Here,

(i) {(2, 1), (5, 1), (8, 1), (11, 1), (14, 1), (17, 1)}

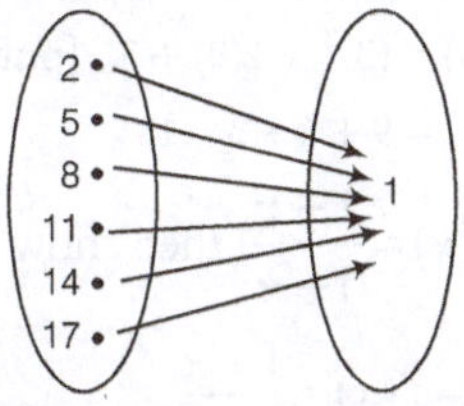

It is clear from arrow diagram that

(a) it is a function, as each element have an unique image.

(b) its domain is {2, 5, 8, 11, 14, 17}.

(c) its range is {1}.

(ii) {(2, 1), (4, 2), (6, 3), (8, 4), (10, 5), (12, 6), (14, 7)}.

It is clear from arrow diagram that

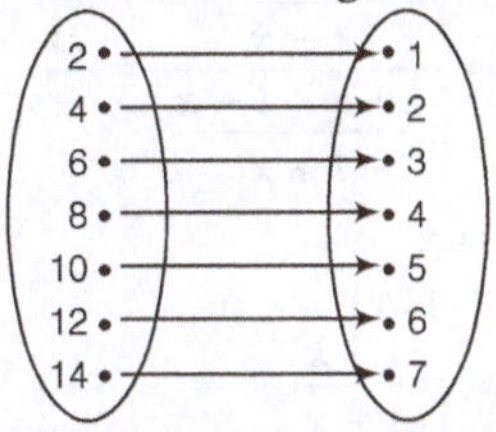

(a) it is a function, as each element have an unique image.

(b) its domain is {2, 4, 6, 8, 10, 12, 14}.

(c) its range is {1, 2, 3, 4, 5, 6, 7}.

(iii) {(1, 3), (1, 5), (2, 5)}

It is clear from the arrow diagram that

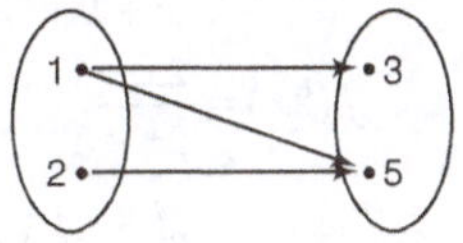

It is not a function because 1 has two images 3 and 5.

EXAMPLE 4. Let $A = \{-2, -1, 0, 1, 2\}$ and $f : A \to Z$ be given by $f(x) = x^2 - 2x - 3$. Find

(i) the range of f

(ii) pre-images of 6, -3 and 5

Sol. (i) We have, $f(x) = x^2 - 2x - 3$

$\therefore \quad f(-2) = (-2)^2 - 2(-2) - 3 = 5$

$f(-1) = (-1)^2 - 2(-1) - 3 = 0$

$f(0) = -3$

$f(1) = 1^2 - 2 \times 1 - 3 = -4$

and $\quad f(2) = 2^2 - 2 \times 2 - 3 = -3.$

So, range $(f) = \{f(-2), f(-1), f(0), f(1), f(2)\}$

$= \{0, 5, -3, -4\}$

(ii) Let x be a pre-image of 6, then

$f(x) = 6 \Rightarrow x^2 - 2x - 3 = 6$

$\Rightarrow x^2 - 2x - 9 = 0 \Rightarrow x = 1 \pm \sqrt{10}$

Since, $x = 1 \pm \sqrt{10} \notin A$.

So, there is no pre-image of 6.

Let x be a pre-image of -3.

Then, $\quad f(x) = -3$

$\Rightarrow \quad x^2 - 2x - 3 = -3$

$\Rightarrow \quad x^2 - 2x = 0$

$\Rightarrow \quad x = 0, 2$

Clearly, $0, 2 \in A$.

So, 0 and 2 are pre-images of -3.

Let x be a pre-image of 5.

Then, $\quad f(x) = 5$

$\Rightarrow \quad x^2 - 2x - 3 = 5$

$\Rightarrow \quad x^2 - 2x - 8 = 0$

$\Rightarrow \quad (x - 4)(x + 2) = 0$

$\Rightarrow \quad x = 4, -2$

Since, $-2 \in A$ but $4 \notin A$.

So, -2 is a pre-image of 5.

Equal Functions

Two functions f and g are said to be equal iff

(i) domain of f = domain of g

(ii) codomain of f = codomain of g

(iii) $f(x) = g(x)$ for every x belonging to their common domain and then we write $f = g$.

e.g. Let $A = \{1, 2\}$, $B = \{3, 6\}$ and $f : A \to B$ is given by $f(x) = x^2 + 2$ and $g : A \to B$ given by $g(x) = 3x$.

Here, we observe that f and g have the same domain and codomain.

Also, $\quad f(1) = 3 = g(1)$ and $f(2) = 6 = g(2)$

Hence, $\quad f = g$

EXAMPLE 5. Let $A = \left\{-2, \frac{1}{2}\right\}$ and $B = \left\{7, \frac{-1}{2}\right\}$, $f : A \to B$ defined by $f(x) = 2x^2 - 1$ and $g : A \to B$ defined by $g(x) = 1 - 3x$. Find whether $f = g$ or not.

Sol. We observe that f and g both have same domain and codomain. Also, we have

$$f(-2) = 7 = g(-2) \text{ and } f\left(\frac{1}{2}\right) = \frac{-1}{2} = g\left(\frac{1}{2}\right)$$

Hence, $f = g$

EXAMPLE 6. $f : R - \{3\} \to R$ be defined by $f(x) = \dfrac{x^2 - 9}{x - 3}$ and $g : R \to R$ be defined by $g(x) = x + 3$. Find whether $f = g$ or not.

Sol. Here, $f(x) = \dfrac{x^2 - 9}{x - 3} = \dfrac{(x-3)(x+3)}{x-3} = (x+3)$

and $g(x) = x + 3 \Rightarrow f(x) = g(x) = x + 3$

But $f(x) \neq g(x)$ as domain of $f(x)$ is $R - \{3\}$ and domain of $g(x)$ is R.

$\Rightarrow$ Domain of $f(x) \neq$ Domain of $g(x)$ $\Rightarrow$ $f \neq g$

EXAMPLE 7. Find the values of x for which the functions $f(x) = 3x^2 - 1$ and $g(x) = 3 + x$ are equal.

Sol. Given, $f(x) = 3x^2 - 1$ and $g(x) = 3 + x$

Let $f(x) = g(x)$

Then, $3x^2 - 1 = 3 + x$

$\Rightarrow 3x^2 - x - 4 = 0$

$\Rightarrow 3x^2 - 4x + 3x - 4 = 0$

$\Rightarrow x(3x - 4) + 1(3x - 4) = 0$

$\Rightarrow (3x - 4)(x + 1) = 0$

$\Rightarrow x = -1, \dfrac{4}{3}$

Real Functions

A function which has either R (set of real numbers) or one of its subsets as its range is called a **real valued function** and if its domain is also either R or a subset of R i.e. range and domain both are either R or a subset of R, then function is called **real function.**

For real functions, generally domain and codomain both are infinite subsets of R. Therefore, a real function is generally described by some general formula.

e.g. Let f be a function define by $f(x) = 2x + 1$ from N to N. Then,

x	1	2	3	4	5	...
$f(x) = 2x + 1$	$f(1) = 3$	$f(2) = 5$	$f(3) = 7$	$f(4) = 9$	$f(5) = 11$	...

Thus, range = $\{3, 5, 7, 9, 11, \dots\} \subseteq R$, codomain = N and domain = $N \subseteq R$.

Value of a Real Function

If any function x is defined from $f : A \to B$, then the value of function at any point a of A will be $f(a)$.

A function does not exist if its domain is empty set.

EXAMPLE 8. If $f(x) = x^2 + 2x + 3$, then find $f(1)$, $f(2)$ and $f(3)$.

Sol. We have, $f(x) = x^2 + 2x + 3$ ...(i)

$f(1) = (1)^2 + 2(1) + 3$ [putting $x = 1$ in Eq. (i)]

$= 1 + 2 + 3 = 6$

$f(2) = (2)^2 + 2(2) + 3$ [putting $x = 2$ in Eq. (i)]

$= 4 + 4 + 3 = 11$

$f(3) = (3)^2 + 2(3) + 3$ [putting $x = 3$ in Eq. (i)]

$= 9 + 6 + 3 = 18$

EXAMPLE 9. If $y = f(x) = \dfrac{1-x}{1+x}$, then show that $x = f(y)$.

Sol. We have, $y = f(x) = \dfrac{1-x}{1+x}$ ...(i)

Then, $f(y) = \dfrac{1-y}{1+y} = \dfrac{1 - \left(\dfrac{1-x}{1+x}\right)}{1 + \left(\dfrac{1-x}{1+x}\right)}$ [from Eq. (i)]

$= \dfrac{\dfrac{1 + x - (1 - x)}{1 + x}}{\dfrac{1 + x + 1 - x}{1 + x}} = \dfrac{2x}{2}$

$\Rightarrow f(y) = x$

$\therefore x = f(y)$

when $y = f(x) = \dfrac{1-x}{1+x}$

Example 10. If f is a real function defined by $f(x) = \dfrac{x-1}{x+1}$, then prove that $f(2x) = \dfrac{3f(x)+1}{f(x)+3}$.

Sol. Given, $f(x) = \dfrac{x-1}{x+1}$ ...(i)

$\Rightarrow f(2x) = \dfrac{2x-1}{2x+1}$ ...(ii)

Now, consider $\dfrac{3f(x)+1}{f(x)+3} = \dfrac{3\left(\dfrac{x-1}{x+1}\right)+1}{\dfrac{x-1}{x+1}+3}$ [from Eq. (i)]

$= \dfrac{\dfrac{3(x-1)+(x+1)}{(x+1)}}{\dfrac{(x-1)+3(x+1)}{(x+1)}}$

$= \dfrac{3x - 3 + x + 1}{x - 1 + 3x + 3} = \dfrac{4x-2}{4x+2}$

$= \dfrac{2(2x-1)}{2(2x+1)} = \dfrac{2x-1}{2x+1}$ ...(iii)

From Eqs. (ii) and (iii), we get

$f(2x) = \dfrac{3f(x)+1}{f(x)+3}$ **Hence proved.**

EXAMPLE 11. Given $A = \{-1, 0, 2, 5, 6, 11\}$, $B = \{-2, -1, 0, 18, 28, 108\}$ and $f(x) = x^2 - x - 2$. Is $f(A) = B$? Find $f(A)$.

Sol. Given, $f(x) = x^2 - x - 2,$

$A = \{-1, 0, 2, 5, 6, 11\}$

and $B = \{-2, -1, 0, 18, 28, 108\}$

Clearly, $f(-1) = (-1)^2 - (-1) - 2 = 0$

$f(0) = (0)^2 - 0 - 2 = -2$

$f(2) = (2)^2 - 2 - 2 = 0$

$f(5) = (5)^2 - 5 - 2 = 18$

$f(6) = (6)^2 - 6 - 2 = 28$

and $f(11) = (11)^2 - 11 - 2 = 108$

Now, $f(A) = \{f(x) : x \in A\} = \{0, -2, 18, 28, 108\}$

Here, we see that $-1 \in B$ but $-1 \notin f(A)$

$\therefore \quad f(A) \neq B$

EXAMPLE 12. $f = \{(1, 1), (2, 3), (0, -1), (-1, -3)\}$ be a function describe by the formula $f(x) = ax + b$ for some integers a, b. Determine a, b.

Sol. Given, $f = \{(1, 1), (2, 3), (0, -1), (-1, -3)\}$

Here, $f(1) = 1, f(2) = 3, f(0) = -1, f(-1) = -3$

It is given that $f(x) = ax + b$

$\therefore \quad f(1) = 1$ and $f(2) = 3$

$\Rightarrow \quad a + b = 1$ and $2a + b = 3$

On solving both equations, we get

$a = 2, b = -1$

Thus, $f(x) = 2x - 1$

This also satisfy $f(0) = -1$ and $f(-1) = -3$

Hence, $a = 2, b = -1$

Domain of Real Functions

As we know that real functions are generally described by providing the general formula for finding the images of elements of its domain.

In such cases, the domain of the real function $f(x)$ is the set of all those real numbers for which the expression for $f(x)$ or the formula for $f(x)$ assumes real values only.

In other words, we can say that the domain of $f(x)$ is the set of all those real numbers for which $f(x)$ is meaningful.

Working Rule for Finding the Domain of Real Functions

The domain of a real function depends on the nature of function. e.g. Polynomial function is always define for all real numbers, so its domain is R. Depending upon function, we may use the following steps to determine their domain.

For Rational Functions

I. First put the denominator equal to zero and find the values of variable.

II. The value of variable obtained in step I are the values at which rational function is not defined. Then, omit the set of these values from R to get required domain.

EXAMPLE 13. Find the domain of real function

$$f(x) = \frac{x^2 + 3x + 5}{x^2 - 5x + 4}$$

Sol. Here, denominator $= x^2 - 5x + 4$

On putting it equal to zero, we get

$x^2 - 5x + 4 = 0$

$\Rightarrow \quad x^2 - 4x - x + 4 = 0$

$\Rightarrow \quad x(x - 4) - 1(x - 4) = 0$

$\Rightarrow \quad (x - 4)(x - 1) = 0$

$\Rightarrow \quad x = 4$ or $x = 1$

Clearly, at $x = 1$ and $x = 4$ denominator becomes zero and thus given function will not be define for these value.

So, required domain of given function $= R - \{1, 4\}$

For Square Root Function

We know that expression under the square root should not be negative. So, for finding the domain of square root function, put the expression without root greater than equal to zero and then find the value of variable for which it is positive.

EXAMPLE 14. Find the domain of each of the following function

(i) $\dfrac{1}{\sqrt{x-2}}$ (ii) $\sqrt{4 - x^2}$

Sol. (i) Let $f(x) = \dfrac{1}{\sqrt{x-2}}$

$f(x)$ assumes real values if $x - 2 > 0$

[here, we take only greater than sign, because it is in rational form and so denominator should not be equal to zero]

$\Rightarrow \quad x > 2 \Rightarrow x \in (2, \infty)$

Hence, domain of f is $(2, \infty)$.

(ii) Given, $f(x) = \sqrt{4 - x^2}$

Clearly, $f(x)$ assumes real values, if $4 - x^2 \geq 0$

$\Rightarrow \quad -(x^2 - 4) \geq 0 \Rightarrow x^2 - 4 \leq 0$

[multiplying by -1 on both sides]

$\Rightarrow \quad (x - 2)(x + 2) \leq 0$

$[\because a^2 - b^2 = (a - b)(a + b)]$

$\Rightarrow \quad x \in [-2, 2]$

Hence, domain of $f = [-2, 2]$

EXAMPLE 15. Find the domain of $f(x)=\frac{1}{\sqrt{x+|x|}}$.

Sol. We have, $f(x)=\frac{1}{\sqrt{x+|x|}}$

We know that, $|x|=\begin{cases}x, & \text{if } x\ge 0\\ -x, & \text{if } x<0\end{cases}$

$\therefore \quad x+|x|=\begin{cases}x+x, & \text{if } x\ge 0\\ x-x, & \text{if } x<0\end{cases}$

$\Rightarrow \quad x+|x|=\begin{cases}2x, & \text{if } x\ge 0\\ 0, & \text{if } x<0\end{cases}$ ...(i)

Here, the function $f(x)=\frac{1}{\sqrt{x+|x|}}$ assumes real values, if $x+|x|>0$

$\Rightarrow \quad 2x>0 \Rightarrow x>0$ [using Eq. (i)]

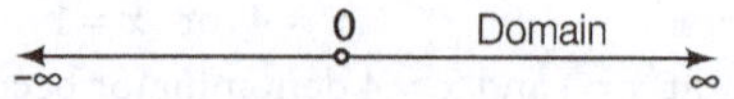

$\therefore \quad x\in(0,\infty)$

Hence, domain of $f=(0,\infty)$.

Range of Real Functions

The range of a real function f of a real variable x is the set of all real values taken by $f(x)$ at points of its domain.

Working Rule for Finding Range of Real Functions

Let $y=f(x)$ be a real function, then for finding the range we may use the following steps

I. Find the domain of the function $y=f(x)$.

II. Transform the equation $y=f(x)$ as $x=g(y)$. i.e. convert x in terms of y.

III. Find the values of y from $x=g(y)$ such that the values of x are real and lying in the domain of f.

IV. The set of values of y obtained in Step III will be the range of function f.

EXAMPLE 16. Find the range of $f(x)=\frac{x-2}{3-x}$.

Sol. Given, $f(x)=\frac{x-2}{3-x}=y$ (say)

Here, denominator $=3-x$

Put denominator $=0$, we get

$3-x=0 \Rightarrow x=3$

$\therefore$ Domain of $y=f(x)$ is $R-\{3\}$.

Now, consider $y=\frac{x-2}{3-x}$

$\Rightarrow \quad y(3-x)=(x-2)$

$\Rightarrow \quad 3y-xy=x-2$

$\Rightarrow \quad x+xy=3y+2$

$\Rightarrow \quad x(1+y)=3y+2$

$\Rightarrow \quad x=\frac{3y+2}{1+y}$

It will define, if $1+y\ne 0 \Rightarrow y\ne -1$.

So, $x=g(y)$ takes real values, if $y\in R-\{-1\}$.

Also, $\frac{3y+2}{1+y}\ne 3$ for all $y\in R-\{-1\}$

$\left[\because \text{ if } \frac{3y+2}{1+y}=3, \text{ then } 3y+2=3+3y \Rightarrow 2=3, \text{ which is absurd}\right]$

$\Rightarrow \quad x=\frac{3y+2}{1+y}\ne 3$ for all $y\in R-\{-1\}$

Thus, $x=\frac{3y+2}{1+y}\in$ Domain (f), $\forall\ y\in R-\{1\}$

Hence, the range of $f(x)$ is $R-\{-1\}$.

EXAMPLE 17. Find the domian and range of

$$f(x)=\left\{\left(x,\frac{1}{1-x^2}\right): x\in R,\ x\ne\pm 1\right\}.$$

Sol. Given, $f(x)=\left\{\left(x,\frac{1}{1-x^2}\right): x\in R,\ x\ne\pm 1\right\}$

Clearly, $f(x)=\frac{1}{1-x^2}$ is not defined, when $(1-x^2)=0$

i.e. when $x=\pm 1$.

$\therefore$ Domain of $f(x)=R-\{-1,1\}$

Further, let $y=\frac{1}{1-x^2}$

$\Rightarrow \quad (1-x^2)=\frac{1}{y} \Rightarrow x^2=1-\frac{1}{y}$

$\Rightarrow \quad x=\pm\sqrt{\left(1-\frac{1}{y}\right)}=\pm\sqrt{\frac{y-1}{y}}$

Clearly, x is define, if $\frac{y-1}{y}\ge 0$ and $y\ne 0$

$\Rightarrow \quad (y-1)\,y\ge 0$ and $y\ne 0$

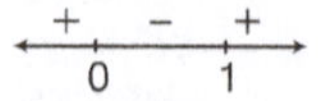

$\Rightarrow \quad -\infty<y<0$ or $1\le y<\infty$

Also, $\sqrt{\frac{y-1}{y}}\ne 1$ for all $y\in(-\infty,0)\cup[1,\infty)$

$\Rightarrow \quad x=\pm\sqrt{\frac{y-1}{y}}\ne\pm 1$ for all $y\in(-\infty,0)\cup[1,\infty)$

$\left[\because \text{ if } \sqrt{\frac{y-1}{y}}=1, \text{ then } y-1=y \Rightarrow -1=0, \text{ which is absurd}\right]$

Thus, $x=\pm\sqrt{\frac{y-1}{y}}\in$ domain (f), $\forall\ y\in(-\infty,0)\cup[1,\infty)$

Hence, range $(f)=(-\infty,0)\cup[1,\infty)$.

EXAMPLE 18. Find the domain and range of the function $f(x)=\left\{\left(x, \frac{x^2-1}{x-1}\right): x \in R, x \neq 1\right\}$.

Sol. Let $f(x)=\left\{\left(x, \frac{x^2-1}{x-1}\right): x \in R, x \neq 1\right\}$

Clearly, f is not defined, when $x=1$

So, f is defined for all real values of x, except at $x=1$.

$\therefore$ Domain $(f)=R-\{1\}$

Let $y=\frac{x^2-1}{x-1}$

$=\frac{(x-1)(x+1)}{(x-1)}=x+1$ [as $x \neq 1$]

$\Rightarrow x=y-1$

Clearly, x is not defined, when $y=2$ as $x \neq 1$.

Range $(f)=R-\{2\}$

EXAMPLE 19. Let $f: R \rightarrow R$ be such that $f(x)=2^x$. Determine

(i) range of f

(ii) whether $f(x+y)=f(x) \cdot f(y)$ holds.

(iii) $\{x: f(x)=1\}$

Sol. (i) Given, $f(x)=2^x$, which is well-defined for all $x \in R$.

$\therefore$ Domain $(f)=R$

Now, let $y=f(x)=2^x$

Taking log with base 2 on both sides, we get

$\log_2 y=\log_2 2^x$

$\Rightarrow \log_2 y=x \log_2 2=x$ [$\because \log_a a=1$]

$\Rightarrow x=\log_2 y$, which is define for all $y>0$.

Hence, the range of f is set of all positive real numbers.

(ii) We have, $f(x+y)=2^{x+y}=2^x \cdot 2^y=f(x) \cdot f(y)$

$\therefore f(x+y)=f(x) \cdot f(y)$ holds for all $x, y \in R$.

(iii) $\because f(x)=1 \Rightarrow 2^x=1 \Rightarrow x=0$

$\therefore \{x: f(x)=1\}=\{0\}$

EXAMPLE 20. Find the domain and the range of the function $f(x)=\sqrt{16-x^2}$.

Sol. Given, $f(x)=\sqrt{16-x^2}$

Domain of f We observe that $f(x)$ is defined for all x satisfying $16-x^2 \geq 0$

$\Rightarrow x^2-16 \leq 0$

$\Rightarrow (x-4)(x+4) \leq 0$ [$\because a^2-b^2=(a-b)(a+b)$]

$\Rightarrow -4 \leq x \leq 4 \Rightarrow x \in[-4,4]$

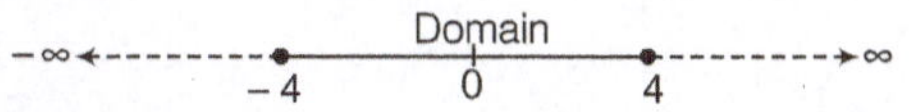

Range of f Let $y=f(x)$. Then,

$y=\sqrt{16-x^2}$

$\Rightarrow y^2=16-x^2$

$\Rightarrow x^2=16-y^2$

$\Rightarrow x=\pm\sqrt{16-y^2}$

Clearly, x will take real values, if

$16-y^2 \geq 0 \Rightarrow y^2-16 \leq 0$

$\Rightarrow (y-4)(y+4) \leq 0 \Rightarrow -4 \leq y \leq 4$

$\Rightarrow y \in[-4,4]$

Also, $y=\sqrt{16-x^2} \geq 0$ for all $x \in[-4,4]$

$\therefore y \in[0,4]$ for $x \in[-4,4]$

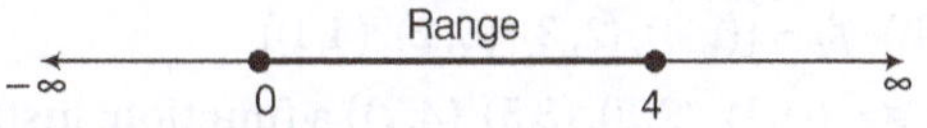

Hence, range of f [0, 4].

EXAMPLE 21. Find the domain and range of the function $f(x)=\frac{1}{\sqrt{x-5}}$

Sol. We have, $f(x)=\frac{1}{\sqrt{x-5}}$

Domain of f

Clearly, $f(x)$ takes real values, if

$x-5>0 \Rightarrow x>5 \Rightarrow x \in(5, \infty)$

Domain of $f=(5, \infty)$

Range of f

For $x>5$, we have $x-5>0$

$\Rightarrow \sqrt{x-5}>0$

$\Rightarrow \frac{1}{\sqrt{x-5}}>0 \Rightarrow f(x)>0$

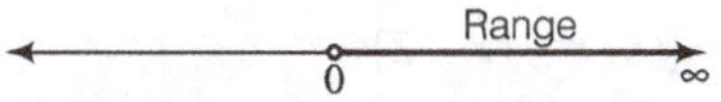

Thus, $f(x)$ takes all real values greater than zero.

Hence, range of $f=(0, \infty)$.

EXAMPLE 22. Find the domain and range of the real valued function $f(x)$ given by $f(x)=\frac{4-x}{x-4}$.

Sol. Given, $f(x)=\frac{4-x}{x-4}$

Domain of f Here, we see that $f(x)$ is defined for all x except $=4$

$\therefore$ Domain $(f)=R-\{4\}$

$\because f(x)=\frac{4-x}{x-4}=\frac{-(x-4)}{x-4}=-1$

$\therefore$ Range $(f)=\{-1\}$

EXAMPLE 23. Find the domain and range of the function $f(x)=1-|x-2|$.

Sol. Given function is $f(x)=1-|x-2|$.

We know that, $|x|$ is defined for $x \in (-\infty, \infty)$.

$\therefore$ Domain of $|x-2|$ is $(-\infty, \infty)$.

Hence, domain of $f(x)=1-|x-2|$ is $(-\infty, \infty)$.

Also we know that, range of $|x|$ is $[0, \infty)$.

$\therefore$ Range of $|x-2|$ is $[0, \infty)$.

$\therefore \quad 0 \le |x-2| < \infty$

$\Rightarrow \quad -\infty < -|x-2| \le 0$

$\Rightarrow \quad -\infty + 1 < 1-|x-2| \le 1$

$\Rightarrow \quad -\infty < f(x) \le 1$

$\therefore$ Range of $f(x)$ is $(-\infty, 1]$.

Topic Practice 1

1 Which of the relations are functions?
(i) $f_1 = \{(2,1),(3,1),(4,1),(3,2),(4,2),(4,3)\}$
(ii) $f_2 = \{(1,4),(2,3),(3,2),(4,1)\}$

2 Is $g=\{(1,1),(2,3),(3,5),(4,7)\}$ a function, justify? If this is described by the relation, $g(x)=\alpha x+\beta$, then what values should be assigned to α and β?

3 Let f be a relation on the set N of natural numbers defined by $f=\{(n, 3n): n \in N\}$. Is f a function from N to N. If so, find the range of f.

4 Let $f: R \to R$ be given by $f(x)=x^2+3$. Find $\{x: f(x)=28\}$.

5 In question 4, find the pre-images of 39 and 2 under f.

6 If $A=\{1,2,3,4\}$, $B=\{1,2,\ldots,10\}$ and $f: A \to B$ is a function defined by $f(x)=2x+1$, $x \in A$, then find the range of f.

7 Express the function $f: X \to R$ given by $f(x)=x^3+1$ as set of ordered pairs, where $X=\{-1,0,3,9,7\}$.

8 Let $f: Z \to Z$, $g: Z \to Z$ be functions defined by
$f=\{(x,x^2): x \in Z\}$
$g=\{(x,|x|^2): x \in Z\}$, show that $f=g$

9 Let f be defined by $f(x)=(x-4)$ and g be defined by $g(x)=\begin{cases} \dfrac{x^2-16}{x+4}, & x \ne -4 \\ \lambda, & x=-4 \end{cases}$

Find λ such that $f(x)=g(x)$ for all x.

10 If $f: R \to R$ be defined as follows
$$f(x)=\begin{cases} 1, & x \in Q \\ -1, & x \notin Q \end{cases}$$
Find (i) $f\left(\frac{1}{2}\right)$, $f(\pi)$ (ii) pre-image of 1 and -1.

11 If $f(x)=3x^4-5x^2+9$, find $f(x-1)$.

12 If $f(x)=x^2$, find $\dfrac{f(1.1)-f(1)}{(1.1)-1}$.

13 If the function t which maps temperature in degree Celcius into temperature in degree Fahrenheit is defined by $t(C)=\dfrac{9C}{5}+32$, then find
(i) $t(0)$
(ii) $t(28)$
(iii) $t(-10)$
(iv) the value of C, when $t(C)=212$

14 Find the domain of the function
$$f(x)=\frac{x}{x^2+3x+2}.$$

15 If $f(x)=x+\dfrac{1}{x}$, then prove that
$$[f(x)]^3=f(x^3)+3f\left(\frac{1}{x}\right).$$

16 Let f and g be real functions defined by $f(x)=2x+1$ and $g(x)=4x-7$.
(i) For what real numbers x, $f(x)=g(x)$?
(ii) For what real numbers x, $f(x)<g(x)$?

17 Find the domain of $\sqrt{a^2-x^2}$, $(a>0)$.

18 A function $f: R \to R$ is defined by $f(x)=x^2$. Determine
(i) Range of f (ii) $\{x: f(x)=4\}$

19 Find the range of the following function.
$$f(x)=\frac{x}{1+x^2}$$

20 Let $f=\left\{\left(x, \dfrac{x^2}{1+x^2}\right): x \in R\right\}$ be a functions R to R determine the range of R.

Hints & Solutions

1. (i) It is not a function because the elements 3 and 4 of ordered pairs have more than one images.

   (ii) It is a function bacause first element of each ordered pair has one and only one image.

2. **Hint** We have, $g = \{(1, 1), (2, 3), (3, 5), (4, 7)\}$

   Since, every element has unique image under g.

   So, g is a function.

   Now, $g(x) = \alpha x + \beta$

   When $x = 1$, then $g(1) = \alpha(1) + \beta$ ...(i)

   $\Rightarrow 1 = \alpha + \beta$

   When $x = 2$, then $g(2) = \alpha(2) + \beta$

   $\Rightarrow 3 = 2\alpha + \beta$ ...(ii)

   On solving Eqs. (i) and (ii), we get

   $\alpha = 2, \beta = -1$

3. **Hint** Since, for each $n \in N$, there exist a unique $3n \in N$ such $(n, 3n) \in f$. Therefore, f is a function from N to N

   Now, range $(f) = \{3n : n \in N\}$

4. **Hint** Given, $f(x) = x^2 + 3$ and $f(x) = 28$

   $\therefore \quad x^2 + 3 = 28 \Rightarrow x^2 = 28 - 3$

   $\Rightarrow \quad x^2 = 25 \Rightarrow x = \pm 5$

   $\Rightarrow \quad x \in \{-5, 5\}$

5. **Hint** Let x be the pre-image of 39.

   $\Rightarrow f(x) = 39$

   $\Rightarrow x^2 + 3 = 39$

   $\Rightarrow x^2 = 36 \Rightarrow x = \pm 6$

   Again, let pre-image of 2 be x.

   $\Rightarrow f(x) = 2$

   $\Rightarrow x^2 + 3 = 2$

   $\Rightarrow x^2 = -1$ [which is not possible]

   $\therefore$ 2 does not have any pre-image.

6. **Hint** Given, $f(x) = 2x + 1$

   $\therefore \quad f(1) = 2 \times 1 + 1 = 2 + 1 = 3 \in B$

   $\Rightarrow \quad f(2) = 2 \times 2 + 1 = 4 + 1 = 5 \in B$

   $\Rightarrow \quad f(3) = 2 \times 3 + 1 = 6 + 1 = 7 \in B$

   $\Rightarrow \quad f(4) = 2 \times 4 + 1 = 8 + 1 = 9 \in B$

   $\therefore$ Range $f = \{3, 5, 7, 9\}$

7. $f = \{(-1, 0), (0, 1), (3, 28), (9, 730), (7, 344)\}$

8. **Hint** Here, domain (f) = domain (g)

   codomain f = codomain g

   Now, $f(x) = x^2$ and $g(x) = |x|^2 = x^2$ $[\because |x|^2 = x^2]$

   $\Rightarrow f(x) = g(x), \forall x \in Z$

9. **Hint** Given, $f(x) = g(x), \forall x \in R$

   $\Rightarrow f(-4) = g(-4)$

   $\Rightarrow -4 - 4 = \lambda \Rightarrow \lambda = -8$

10. (i) **Hint** The value of the function for every rational number is 1 and for every irrational number is -1.

    $\therefore \quad f\left(\frac{1}{2}\right) = 1 \quad \left[\because \frac{1}{2} \in Q\right]$

    and $\quad f(\pi) = -1 \quad [\because \pi \notin Q]$

    (ii) **Hint** $\because f(x) = 1 \ \forall \ x \in Q$

    $\therefore$ pre-image of 1 are rational numbers

    $\because \quad f(x) = -1 \ \forall \ x \notin Q$

    $\therefore$ Pre-image of -1 are all real number except rational number i.e. $R - Q$ = Set of irrational numbers

11. **Hint** $\quad f(x) = 3x^4 - 5x^2 + 9$

    $\therefore \quad f(x-1) = 3(x-1)^4 - 5(x-1)^2 + 9$

    $= 3x^4 - 12x^3 + 13x^2 - 2x + 7$

12. **Hint** We have, $f(x) = x^2$

    $$\therefore \frac{f(1.1) - f(1)}{(1.1) - 1} = \frac{(1.1)^2 - 1^2}{(1.1) - 1} = \frac{(1.1 + 1)(1.1 - 1)}{(1.1 - 1)} = 2.1$$

13. **Hint**

    (i) On putting $C = 0$ in Eq. (i), we get

    $$t(0) = \frac{9 \times 0}{5} + 32 = 0 + 32 = 32$$

    (ii) On putting $C = 28$ in Eq. (i), we get

    $$t(28) = \frac{9 \times 28}{5} + 32 = \frac{252}{5} + \frac{32}{1} = \frac{252 + 160}{5} = \frac{412}{5}$$

    (iii) On putting $C = -10$ in Eq. (i), we get

    $$t(-10) = \frac{9 \times (-10)}{5} + 32$$

    $$= -18 + 32 = 14$$

    (iv) Now, on putting $t(C) = 212$ in Eq. (i), we get

    $$212 = \frac{9C}{5} + 32$$

    $$\Rightarrow \quad C = \frac{5 \times 180}{9}$$

    $$\Rightarrow \quad C = 5 \times 20 = 100$$

14. **Hint** $f(x) = \dfrac{x}{x^2 + 3x + 2} = \dfrac{x}{(x+1)(x+2)}$

    Clearly, $f(x)$ is not defined at $x = -1, -2$.

    $\therefore$ Domain $(f) = R - \{-1, -2\}$.

15. **Hint** $\because \quad f(x) = x + \dfrac{1}{x}$

    $$\Rightarrow \quad f(x^3) = x^3 + \frac{1}{x^3}$$

    Now, $$[f(x)]^3 = \left(x + \frac{1}{x}\right)^3 = x^3 + \frac{1}{x^3} + 3\left(x + \frac{1}{x}\right)$$

    $[\because (a+b)^3 = a^3 + b^3 + 3ab(a+b)]$

    $$= f(x^3) + 3f(x)$$

    $$= f(x^3) + 3f\left(\frac{1}{x}\right) \quad \left[\because f(x) = f\left(\frac{1}{x}\right)\right]$$

16. Hint We have, $f(x) = 2x + 1$ and $g(x) = 4x - 7$

(i) $\because$ $f(x) = g(x)$

$\therefore$ $2x + 1 = 4x - 7 \Rightarrow 2x = 8 \Rightarrow x = 4$

(ii) $\because$ $f(x) < g(x)$

$\therefore$ $2x + 1 < 4x - 7$

$\Rightarrow$ $-2x + 1 < -7$

$\Rightarrow$ $-2x < -8 \Rightarrow x > 4$

17. Hint Let $f(x) = \sqrt{a^2 - x^2}$

For $f(x)$ to be defined $a^2 - x^2 \geq 0$

$\Rightarrow$ $x^2 \leq a^2 \Rightarrow x \in [-a, a]$

18. (i) **Hint** $f(x) = x^2$, clearly $\forall\, x \in R$, $f(x) = x^2 \geq 0$

$\therefore$ Range $= [0, \infty)$

(ii) **Hint** $f(x) = 4$

$\Rightarrow$ $x^2 = 4 \Rightarrow x = \pm 2 \Rightarrow x \in \{-2, 2\}$

19. Hint Let $y = f(x) = \dfrac{x}{1 + x^2} \Rightarrow yx^2 - x + y = 0$

$\Rightarrow$ $x = \dfrac{1 \pm \sqrt{1 - 4y^2}}{2y}$

Clearly, x will assume real values, if

$1 - 4y^2 \geq 0$ and $y \neq 0$

$\Rightarrow$ $y^2 - \dfrac{1}{4} \leq 0$ and $y \neq 0$

$\Rightarrow$ $-\dfrac{1}{2} \leq y \leq \dfrac{1}{2}$ and $y \neq 0$

$\Rightarrow$ $y \in \left[\dfrac{-1}{2}, \dfrac{1}{2}\right] - \{0\}$

Also, $y = 0$ for $x = 0$

Hence, range $(f) = \left[-\dfrac{1}{2}, \dfrac{1}{2}\right]$

20. $f(x)$ is defined for all $x \in R$.

As $x^2 + 1 \neq 0$ for any $x \in R$.

Now, let $y = f(x) = \dfrac{x^2}{x^2 + 1}$

$\Rightarrow$ $x^2 = \dfrac{y}{1 - y} \Rightarrow x = \pm \sqrt{\dfrac{y}{1 - y}}$

Clearly, x will be real, if $\dfrac{y}{1 - y} \geq 0$ and $y \neq 1$

$\Rightarrow$ $\dfrac{y}{y - 1} \leq 0$ and $y \neq 1$

$\Rightarrow$ $0 \leq y < 1$

$\therefore$ Range $(f) = [0, 1)$.

Some Standard Real Functions and Their Graphs

Here, we shall study some important real functions, which are frequently used in the study of calculus.

The set of all x-coordinates will constitute the domain of the function and the values of y-coordinates will constitute the range of the function.

Identity Function

The real function $f : R \rightarrow R$ defined by $f(x) = x$, $\forall\, x \in R$ is called an **identity function.** Its domain is R and range is also R.

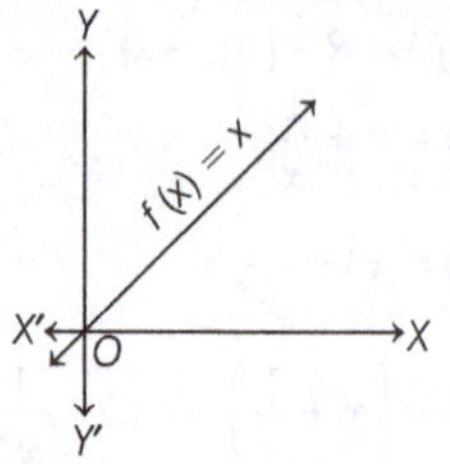

It may be observed that

- Graph of identity function is a straight line.
- It passes through origin.

Constant Function

A function $f : R \rightarrow R$ is said to be a **constant function**, if there exists a **real number** k, such that

$f(x) = k$, $\forall\, x \in R$

Here, domain of $f = R$ and its range $= \{k\}$

e.g. $f(x) = 5$, $\forall\, x \in R$ (symbol '$\forall$' means for all)

Here, $f(x)$ is a constant function whose

domain $= \{x : x \in R\}$ and range $= \{5\}$

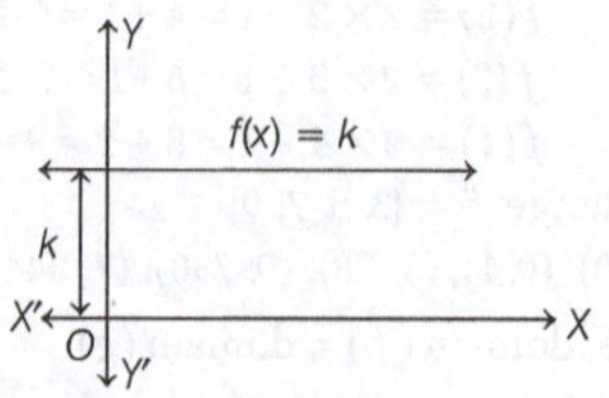

It may be observed that

- The graph of a constant function is a line parallel to X-axis.
- If $k > 0$, then the line will be above X-axis.
- If $k = 0$, then graph coincides with the X-axis.
- If $k < 0$, then the line will be below X-axis.

EXAMPLE 1. Draw the graph of each the following function.

(i) $f(x)=5$ (ii) $f(x)=-5$

(iii) $f(x)=0$

Sol. (i) Given, $f(x)=5, \forall\, x \in R$

Clearly, domain of f is R and range of f is {5}.

Now, we prepare a table for different value of x as shown below

x	−3	−2	−1	0	1	2	3
$f(x)$	5	5	5	5	5	5	5

Locate the points (−3, 5), (−2, 5), (−1, 5), (0, 5), (1, 5), (2, 5) and (3, 5) on the graph paper and joint them, we obtained the required graph as shown below.

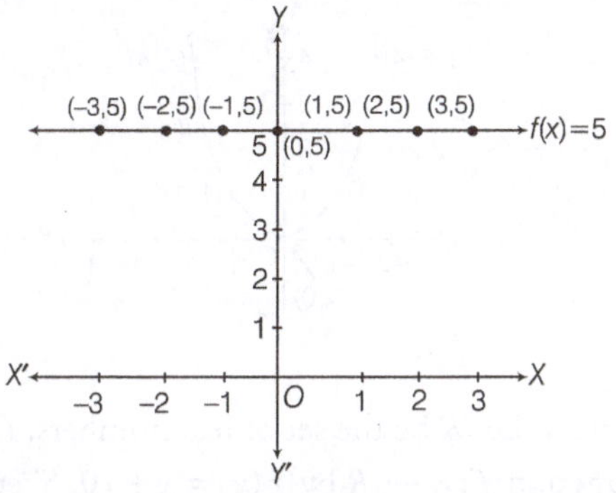

Clearly the graph of $f(x)=5$ represents a straight line parallel to X-axis and at a distance of 5 unit above the X-axis and symmetric with respect to Y-axis.

(ii) Given, $f(x)=-5$

Clearly, domain of $f(x)$ is R.

Range of $f(x)$ is {−5}.

Now, we prepare a table for different values of x as shown below.

x	−3	−2	−1	0	1	2	3
$f(x)$	−5	−5	−5	−5	−5	−5	−5

Locate the points (−3, −5), (−2, −5), (−1, −5), (0, −5), (1, −5), (2, −5), (3, −5) on the graph paper and join them we obtained the graph of the function as shown below.

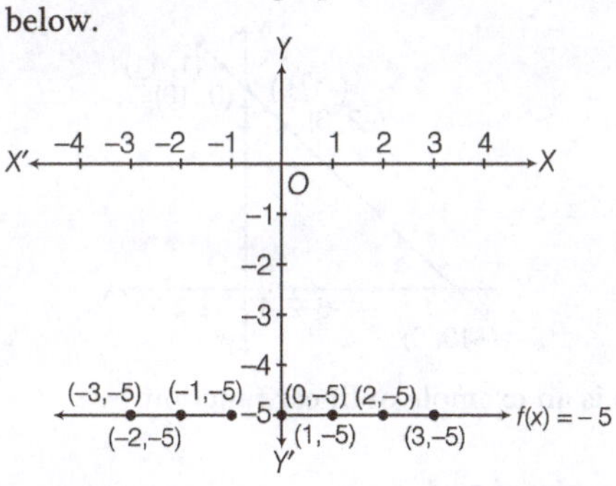

Clearly, the graph of $f(x)=-5$ represent a straight line parallel to X-axis and at a distance of 5 unit below the X-axis and symmetric with respect to Y-axis.

(iii) Given, $f(x)=0$

Clearly, domain of f is R and range of f is {0}.

We have the following table for different value of x.

x	−2	−1	0	1	2
$f(x)$	0	0	0	0	0

Now, locate the point (−2, 0), (−1, 0), (0, 0), (1, 0), (2, 0) on the graph paper, we get the required graph of the function.

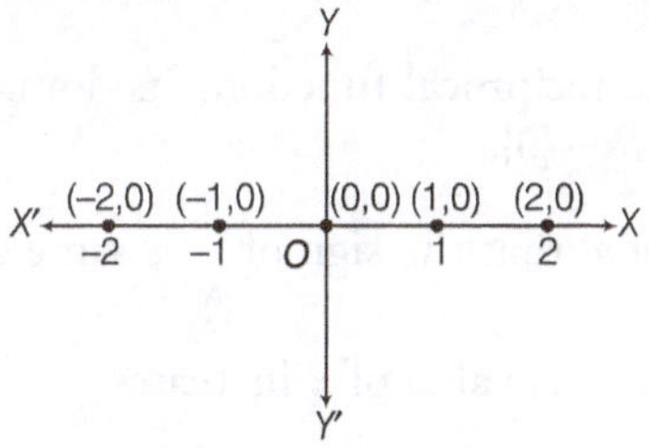

Clearly, the graph of $f(x)=0$ represent X-axis and symmetric with respect to Y-axis.

Square Root Function

The square root of a function is defined as $f(x)=\sqrt{x}$, whose domain is $[0, \infty)$ and range is R^+ i.e. $[0, \infty)$.

We observe that the values of $f(x)=\sqrt{x}$ increases as value of x increases.

So, its graph is given below

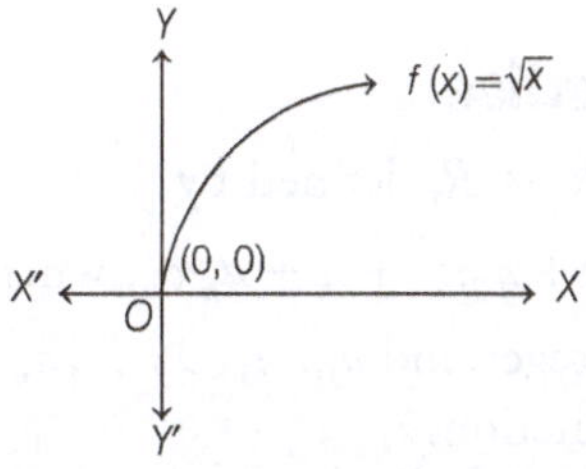

It may be observe that it is passing through origin.

EXAMPLE 2. Find the domain and range of the function $f(x)=\sqrt{x^2-x-20}$.

Sol. The expression $\sqrt{x^2-x-20}$ will be define if and only if

$$x^2-x-20 \geq 0$$

$$\Rightarrow \quad (x-5)(x+4) \geq 0$$

$$\Rightarrow \quad x \in (-\infty, -4] \cup [5, \infty)$$

$\therefore$ Domain $(f)=(-\infty, -4] \cup [5, \infty)$

We know that

$$0 \le \sqrt{x}$$

and $\quad f(5) = \sqrt{5^2 - 5 - 20} = 0$

and $x^2 - x - 20$ tends from 0 to ∞ as x tends from 5 to ∞.

$\therefore\ 0 \le \sqrt{x^2 - x - 20}\ \forall\ x \in$ Domain (f).

$\therefore$ Range $(f) = [0, \infty)$

Reciprocal Function

The function $f : R - \{0\} \to R$ defined by $f(x) = \dfrac{1}{x}$ is called the reciprocal function. Its domain as well as range is $R - \{0\}$.

We observe that the sign of $\dfrac{1}{x}$ is same as that of x and $\dfrac{1}{x}$ decreases as value of x increases.

So, its graph is given below

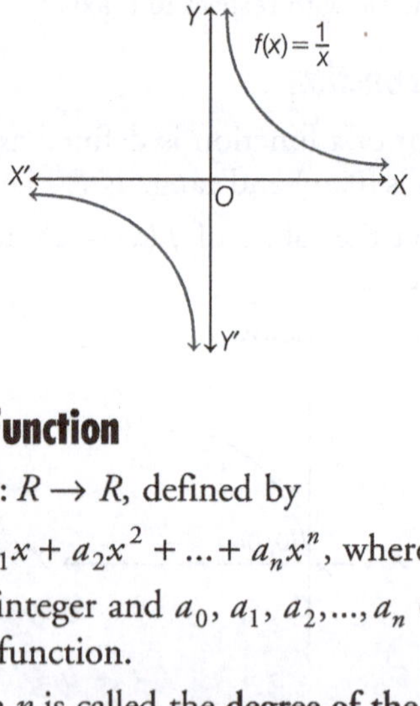

Polynomial Function

A function $f : R \to R$, defined by

$f(x) = a_0 + a_1x + a_2x^2 + \ldots + a_nx^n$, where n is a non-negative integer and $a_0, a_1, a_2, \ldots, a_n \in R$, is called a polynomial function.

If $a_n \ne 0$, then n is called the **degree of the polynomial.**

The domain of a polynomial function is R and range depends on the polynomial representing the function.

e.g. (i) $f(x) = x^3 - x^2 + 9$ is polynomial function in x.

(ii) $h(x) = x^5 + \sqrt{3}x$ is polynomial function in x.

(iii) $g(x) = x^{\frac{3}{2}} + 3x$ is not a polynomial function.

Since, power $\dfrac{3}{2}$ is not a non-negative integer.

EXAMPLE 3. Let R be the set of real numbers. Define the real function $f : R \to R$ be $f(x) = x^2$. Sketch the graph of this function.

Sol. We have, $f(x) = x^2, \forall x \in R$

Here, domain of $f = R$ and range of $f = \{x : x \in R, x \ge 0\}$

For different values of x from domain f, the corresponding value of $f(x)$ are given below

x	-2	-1	0	1	2
$f(x) = x^2$	4	1	0	1	4

Plot the points $(-2, 4), (-1, 1), (0, 0), (1, 1), (2, 4)$ on a graph paper and join them to get parabolic curve which is shown below

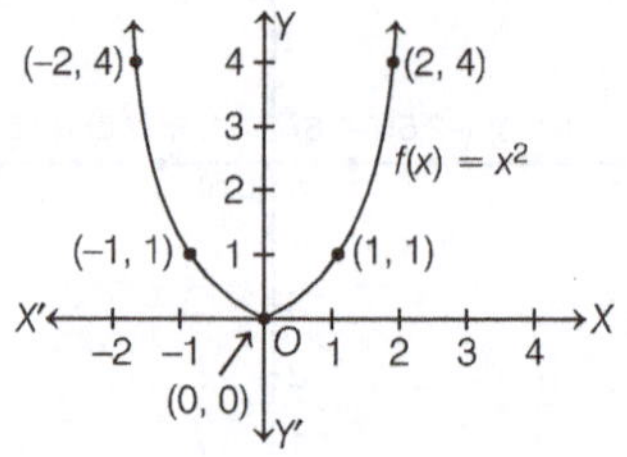

EXAMPLE 4. Let R be the set of real numbers. Define the real function $f : R \to R$ by $f(x) = x + 10$. Sketch the graph of this function.

Sol. Given, $f : R \to R$ define by $f(x) = x + 10$.

Here, at $x = 0, \quad f(0) = 10$

at $x = 1, \quad f(1) = 11$

at $x = 2, f(2) = 12$

$\ldots \quad \ldots$

at $x = 10, \ f(10) = 20$ and so on

Also, at $x = -1, f(-1) = 9$

at $x = -2, \quad f(-2) = 8$

at $x = -10, f(-10) = 0$ and so on

On plotting the points $(0, 10), (1, 11), (10, 20), (-1, 9), (-2, 8)$ and $(-10, 0)$ on graph paper, we get the following graph

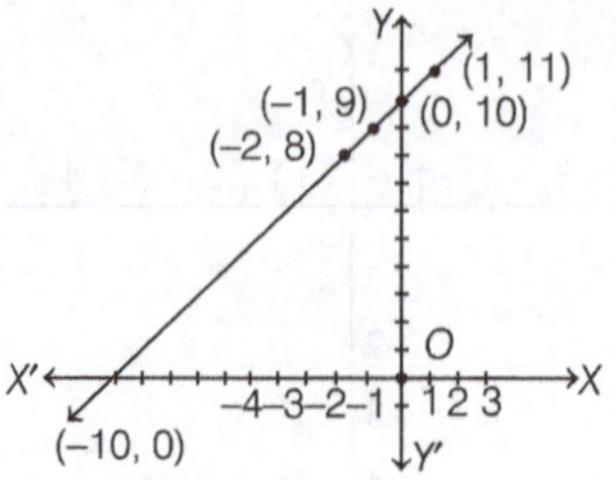

This is an example of linear function.

Rational Function

A function of the form $f(x) = \frac{P(x)}{Q(x)}$, where $P(x)$ and $Q(x)$ are polynomial functions of x defined in a domain and $Q(x) \neq 0$, is called a rational function.

The domain of a rational function is $R - \{x : Q(x) = 0\}$ and range depends on the expression representing the function.

Thus, $f(x) = \left(\frac{x^2+4}{x^3-6x+4}\right)$ is called a rational function, where $x^3 - 6x + 4 \neq 0$. Its domain is $R - \{x : x^3 - 6x + 4 = 0\}$.

Modulus Function or Absolute Value Function

The function $f : R \to R$ defined by

$$f(x) = |x| = \begin{cases} x, & \text{if } x \geq 0 \\ -x, & \text{if } x < 0 \end{cases}$$

is called the modulus function. It is also called **absolute value function**. Its domain is R and its range is $[0, \infty)$.

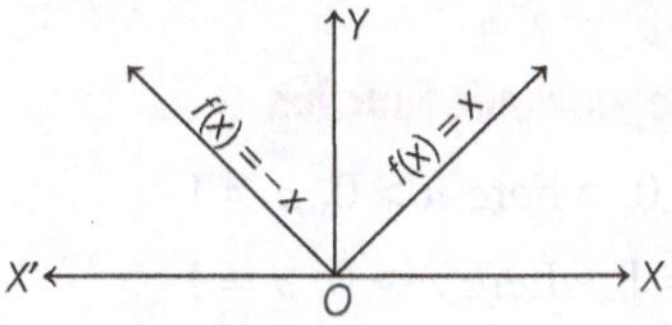

It may be observed that

- The graph is symmetrical with respect to Y-axis.
- Graph does not lies below the X-axis.
- It passes through the origin.
- In the first quadrant, it coincides with the graph of the identity function.

EXAMPLE 5. The function f is defined by

$$f(x) = \begin{cases} 1-x, & x < 0 \\ 1, & x = 0 \\ x+1, & x > 0 \end{cases}$$

Draw the graph of $f(x)$. **[NCERT]**

Sol. Here, $f(x) = 1 - x,\ x < 0$, this gives

$f(-4) = 1 - (-4) = 5;\ f(-3) = 1 - (-3) = 4$

$f(-2) = 1 - (-2) = 3;\ f(-1) = 1 - (-1) = 2$

and $f(x) = x + 1,\ x > 0;\ f(1) = 2, f(2) = 3, f(3) = 4;$

$f(4) = 5$ and so on.

Now, the graph of f is as shown in following figure.

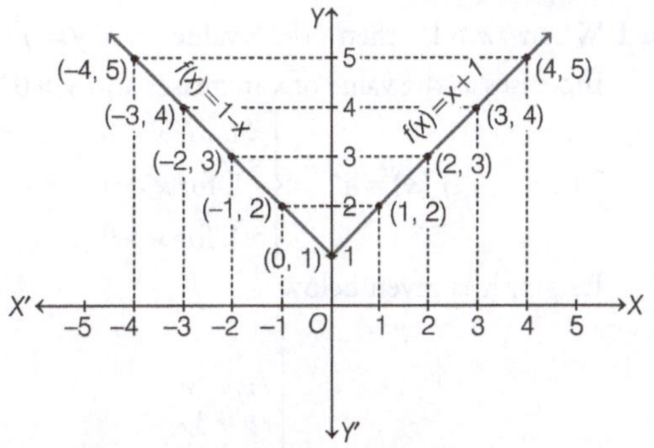

EXAMPLE 6. Draw the graph of the function $f : R \to R$ such that $f(x) = |x - 2|$.

Sol. Clearly, $y = |x - 2| = \begin{cases} x - 2, & \text{if } x - 2 \geq 0 \\ -(x - 2), & \text{if } x - 2 < 0 \end{cases}$

$$= \begin{cases} x - 2, & \text{if } x \geq 2 \\ 2 - x, & \text{if } x < 2 \end{cases}$$

We know that, a linear equation in x and y represents a line. For drawing a line, we need only two points.

For $y = x - 2$

x	2	4
y	0	2

So, plot the points $P(2, 0)$, $Q(4, 2)$ and join PQ to get the graph of $y = x - 2$.

For $y = 2 - x$

x	1	0
y	1	2

Plot the points $R(1, 1)$, $S(0, 2)$ and join RS to get the graph of $y = 2 - x$.

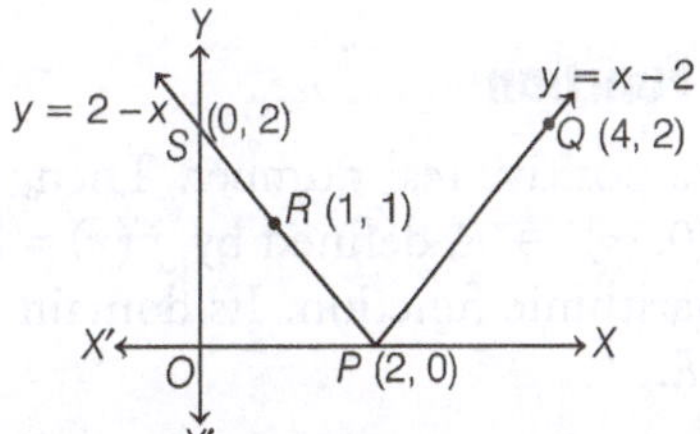

Exponential Function

Let $a(\neq 1)$ be a positive real number.

Then, the function $f : R \to R$, defined by $f(x) = a^x$, is called the exponential function.

Its domain is R and range is $(0, \infty)$ as it attains only positive values.

As, $a > 0$ and $a \neq 1$.

So, following cases aries

Case I When $a > 1$, then the value of $y = f(x) = a^x$ increases as the value of x increases and $y > 0 \; \forall x \in R$.

Thus, $$f(x) = a^x = \begin{cases} < 1, & \text{for } x < 0 \\ 1, & \text{for } x = 0 \\ > 1, & \text{for } x > 0 \end{cases}$$

Its graph is given below

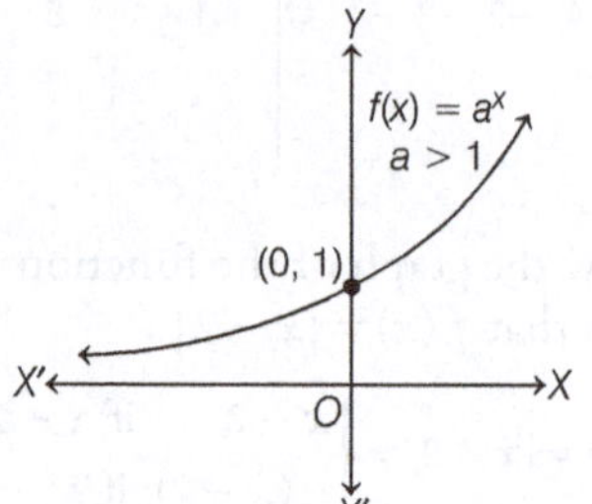

Case II When $0 < a < 1$, then the value of $y = f(x) = a^x$ decreases as the value of x increases and $y > 0$ for all $x \in R$.

Thus, $$f(x) = a^x = \begin{cases} > 1, & \text{for } x < 0 \\ 1, & \text{for } x = 0 \\ < 1, & \text{for } x > 0 \end{cases}$$

Its graph is given below

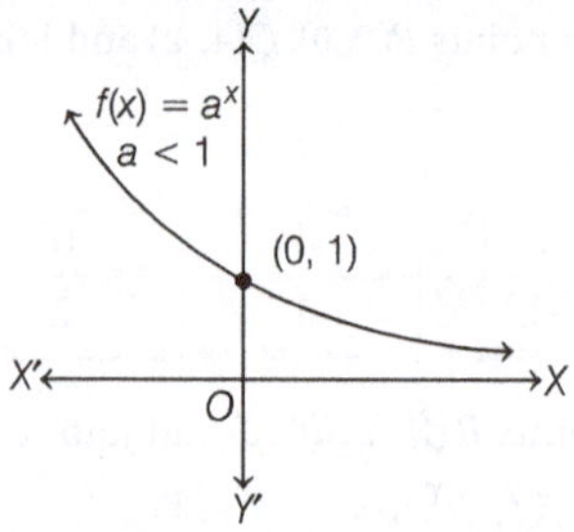

Logarithmic Function

Let $a (\neq 1)$ be a positive real number. Then, the function $f : (0, \infty) \to R$, defined by $f(x) = \log_a x$, is called the logarithmic function. Its domain is $(0, \infty)$ and range is R.

As, $a > 0$ and $a \neq 1$.

So, following cases aries

Case I When $a > 1$, then value of y increases as value of x increases.

So, $$y = \log_a x = \begin{cases} < 0, & \text{for } x < 1 \\ 0, & \text{for } x = 1 \\ > 0, & \text{for } x > 1 \end{cases}$$

Its graph is given below

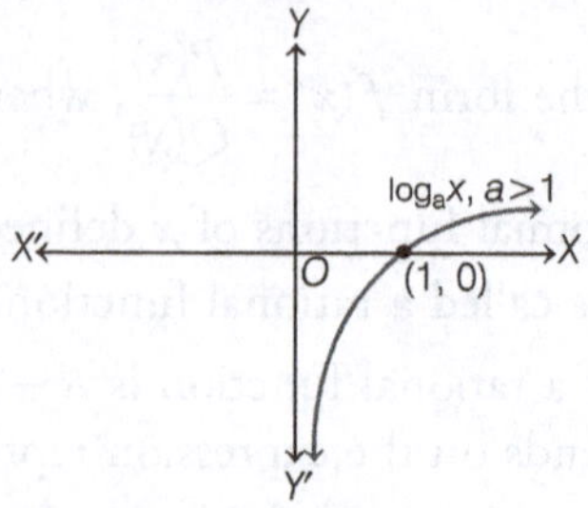

Case II When $0 < a < 1$, then value of y decreases as value of x increases.

So, $$y = \log_a x = \begin{cases} > 0, & \text{for } 0 < x < 1 \\ 0, & \text{for } x = 1 \\ < 0, & \text{for } x > 1 \end{cases}$$

Its graph is given below

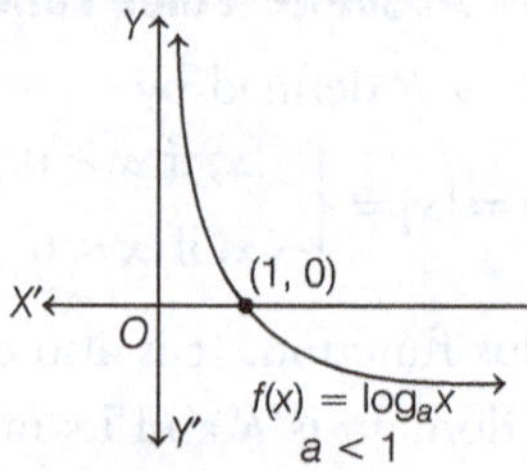

Properties of Logarithmic Function

(i) $\log_a 1 = 0$, where $a > 0$, $a \neq 1$

(ii) $\log_a a = 1$, where $a > 0$, $a \neq 1$

(iii) $\log_a (xy) = \log_a (x) + \log_a (y)$, where $a > 0$, $a \neq 1$ and $x, y > 0$

(iv) $\log_a (x / y) = \log_a (x) - \log_a (y)$, where $a > 0$, $a \neq 1$ and $x, y > 0$

(v) $\log_a x^m = m \log_a x$, where $a > 0$, $a \neq 1$ and $x > 0$

(vi) $\log_{a^n} x^m = \dfrac{m}{n} \log_a (x)$, where $a > 0$, $a \neq 1$, $n \neq 0$ and $x > 0$

(vii) $\log_a x = \dfrac{\log_b x}{\log_b a}$, where $a > 0$, $b > 0$, $b \neq 1$, $a \neq 1$ and $x > 0$

(viii) $a^{\log_a x} = x$, where $a > 0$, $a \neq 1$ and $x > 0$

When the base is e, the function $f(x) = \log_e x$ is called natural logarithmic function. It is also can be written as $f(x) = \ln x$.

Topic Practice 2

Directions (Q. Nos 1-9) Draw the graph of the following functions. Find its domain and range.

1 $f(x)=x-1$

2 $f(x)=\dfrac{1}{x^2}$

3 $f(x)=4-2x$

4 $f(x)=x^3$

5 $f(x)=|x-2|$

6 $f(x)=2$

7 $f(x)=-2$

8 $f(x)=|x-3|$

9 $f(x)=\begin{cases} x^2, & x\ge 0 \\ x, & x<0 \end{cases}$

10 Let $f: R \to R$ defined by $f(x)=1-x^2$ for all $x \in R^+$. Find its domain and range. Also, draw its graph.

11 Draw the graph of $f(x)=\dfrac{1}{2}x^3$. Also, find it domain and range.

12 Find the solution set for the following equation

$$|3x+4|=10$$

13 Find the domain of the following functions.

(i) $\dfrac{2x+3}{x^2+2x+4}$ (ii) $\dfrac{1}{\log(25-x^2)}$

14 Find the domain and range of the function $f(x)=3^{x+2}+4$.

Hints & Solutions

1.

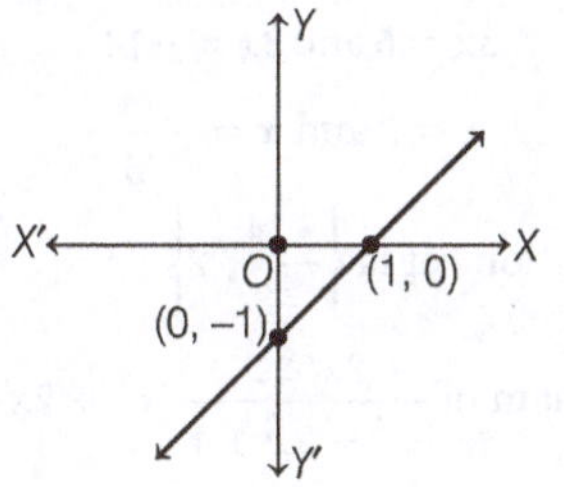

Domain $(f)=R$;
Range $(f)=R$

2.

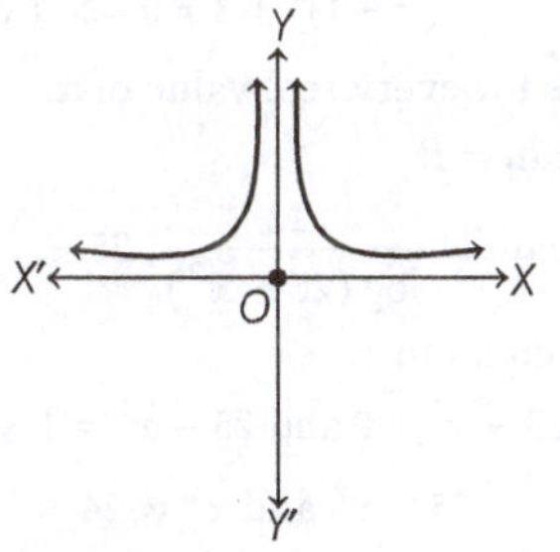

Domain $(f)=R-\{0\}$;
Range $(f)=(0,\infty)$

3.

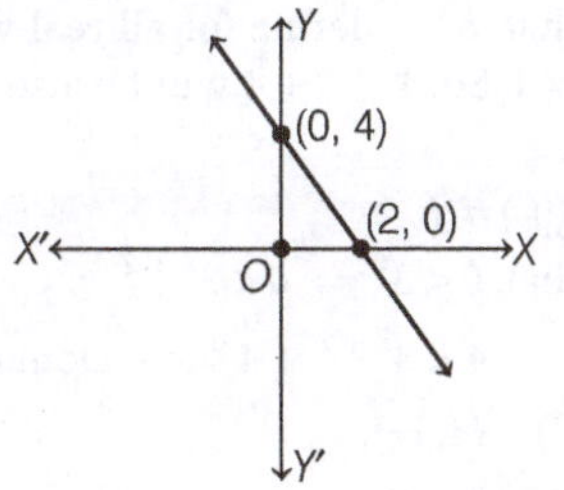

Domain $(f)=R$;
Range $(f)=R$

4.

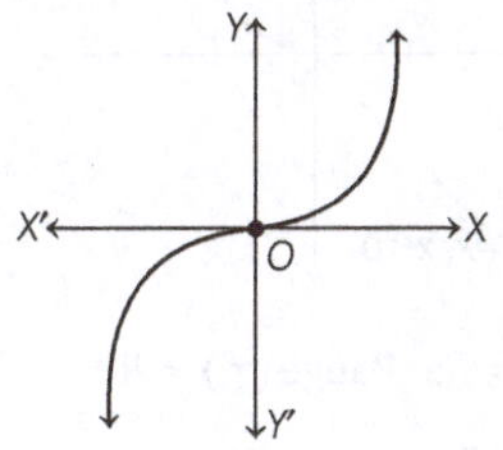

Domain $(f)=R$; Range $(f)=R$

5.

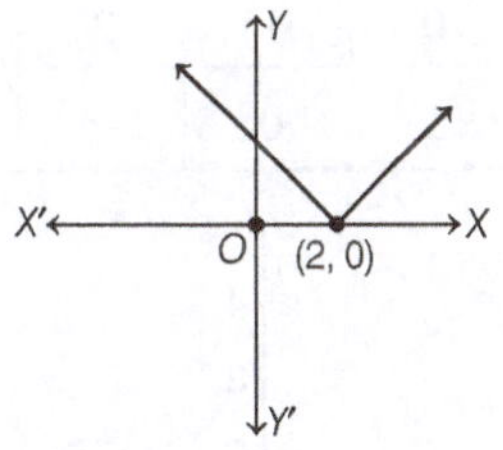

Domain $(f)=R$; Range $(f)=[0,\infty)$

6.

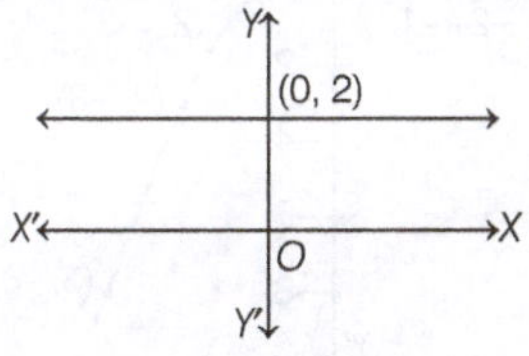

Domain $(f)=R$; Range $(f)=\{2\}$

7.

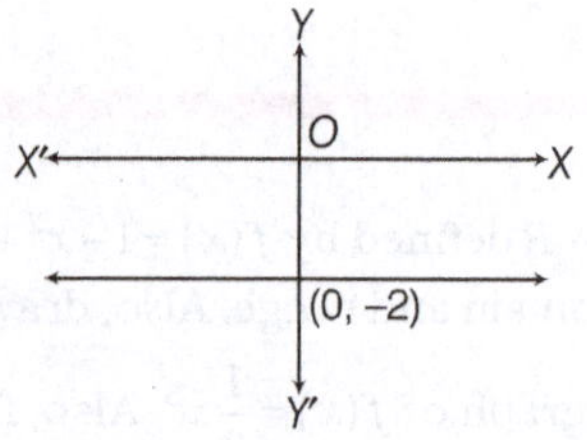

Domain $(f) = R$; Range $(f) = \{-2\}$

8.

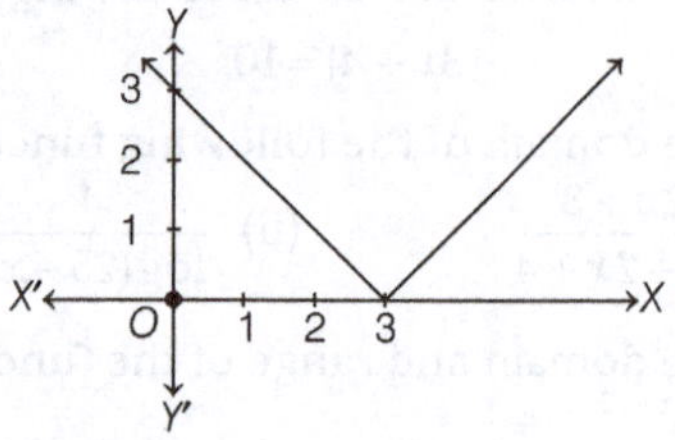

Domain $(f) = R$; Range $(f) = [0, \infty)$

9.

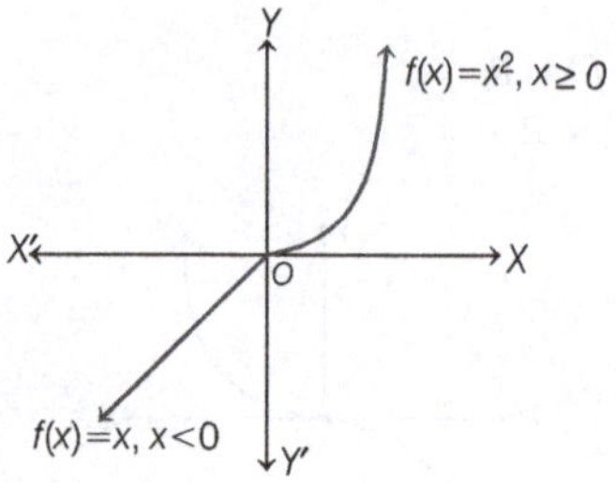

Domain $(f) = R$; Range $(f) = R$

10. $f(x) = 1 - x^2 \ \forall x \in R^+$

Domain of $f = (0, \infty)$ and Range of $f = (-\infty, 1)$

x	0	1	2	3
$f(x)$	1	0	–3	–8

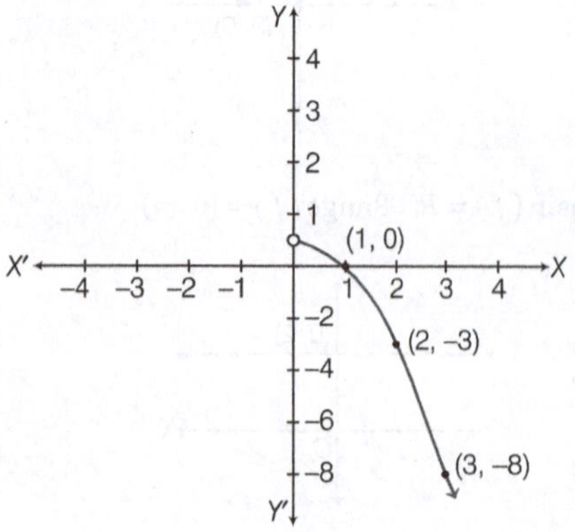

11. $f(x) = \frac{1}{2}x^3 \ \forall x \in R$

x	–2	0	2
$f(x)$	–4	0	4

Doamin of $f = (-\infty, \infty)$; Range of $f = (-\infty, \infty)$

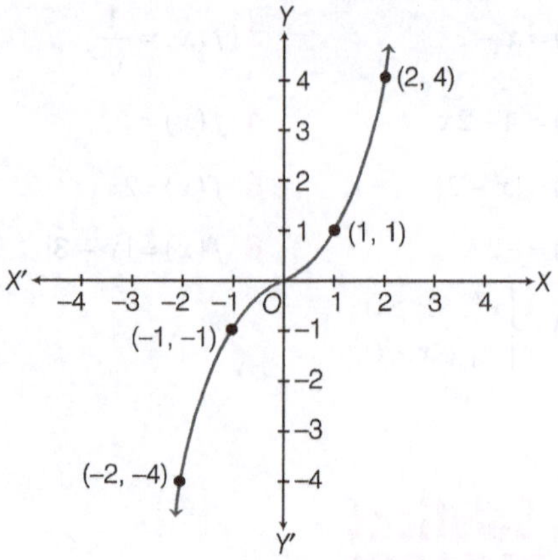

12. Given, $|3x + 4| = 10 \Rightarrow 3x + 4 = \pm 10$

$\Rightarrow \quad 3x = 6$ and $3x = -14$

$\Rightarrow \quad x = 2$ and $x = -\frac{14}{3}$

Hence, solution set is $\left\{-\frac{14}{3}, 2\right\}$

13. (i) For domain of $\frac{2x+3}{x^2+2x+4}$, $x^2 + 2x + 4$ must be non-zero.

$\Rightarrow \quad x^2 + 2x + 4 \neq 0$

$\Rightarrow \quad (x+1)^2 + 3 \neq 0 \Rightarrow (x+1)^2 \neq -3$

It is true for every real value of x.

$\therefore$ Domain $= R$

(ii) For domain of $\frac{1}{\log(25 - x^2)}$, $25 - x^2$ must be positive but not equal to 1.

$\Rightarrow \quad 25 - x^2 > 0$ and $25 - x^2 \neq 1$

$\Rightarrow \quad 25 > x^2$ and $x^2 \neq 24$

$\Rightarrow \quad -5 < x < 5$ and $x = \pm\sqrt{24}$

$\therefore$ Domain $(-5, 5) - \{\pm\sqrt{24}\}$

14. We know that, a^x is define for all real values of x, where $a > 0$ and $a \neq 1$. So, $3^{x+2} + 4$ will be also define for all real values of x.

$\therefore$ Domain $(f) = R$

We know that, $0 < 3^x \Rightarrow 0 < 3^{x+2}$

$\Rightarrow \quad 4 < 3^{x+2} + 4 \ \forall x \in$ Domain (f)

$\therefore$ Range $(f) = (4, \infty)$.

Composition of Functions

Let $f : A \to B$ and $g : B \to C$ be any two functions. Then, the composition of f and g, denoted by gof is defined as function $gof: A \to C$ given by

$$gof(x) = g(f(x)), \forall x \in A.$$

Clearly, domain (gof) = domain (f).

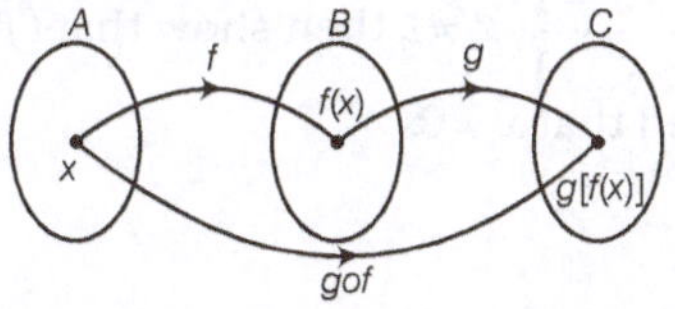

It is clear from the definition that gof is defined only, if for each $x \in A$, $f(x)$ is an element of domain of g, so that we can take its g-image. Thus, gof exists, iff the range of f is a subset of domain of g.

Similarly, fog exists, iff range of g is a subset of domain of f.

e.g. If $f(x) = 3x+5$ and $g(x) = x^2$, then

$$fog(3) = f[g(3)]$$
$$= f(3^2) = f(9)$$
$$= 3 \times 9 + 5 = 32$$

Note (i) $gof(x) = g\{f(x)\}$, i.e. first 'f' rule is applied, then 'g' rule is applied.

(ii) $fog(x) = f\{g(x)\}$, i.e. first 'g' rule is applied, then 'f' rule is applied.

(iii) Generally, the composition of functions is not commutative, i.e. $fog \neq gof$.

(iv) If $f : R \to R$ and $g : R \to R$ are real functions, then both fog and gof exists.

(v) It may happen that gof may exist and fog may not exist.

EXAMPLE 1. Let $f : \{1, 3, 4\} \to \{1, 2, 5\}$ and $g : \{1, 2, 5\} \to \{1, 3\}$, given by $f = \{(1, 2), (3, 5), (4, 1)\}$ and $g = \{(1, 3), (2, 3), (5, 1)\}$. Write down gof.

Sol. Given, $f : \{1, 3, 4\} \to \{1, 2, 5\}$ and $g : \{1, 2, 5\} \to \{1, 3\}$

Also, $f(1) = 2, f(3) = 5, f(4) = 1$

and $g(1) = 3, g(2) = 3, g(5) = 1$

Now, $gof(1) = g\{f(1)\} = g(2) = 3$

$gof(3) = g\{f(3)\} = g(5) = 1$

and $gof(4) = g\{f(4)\} = g(1) = 3$

$\therefore \quad gof = \{(1, 3), (3, 1), (4, 3)\}$

EXAMPLE 2. Find gof and fog, if $f : R \to R$ and $g : R \to R$ are given by $f(x) = x^2$ and $g(x) = 2x + 1$.

Sol. Here, range of f is a subset of domain of g and range of g is a subset of domain of f, so fog and gof both exist.

$$gof(x) = g\{f(x)\} = g(x^2) = 2x^2 + 1$$

and $$fog(x) = f\{g(x)\} = f(2x+1) = (2x+1)^2$$

EXAMPLE 3. Show that, if $f : R - \left\{\frac{7}{5}\right\} \to R - \left\{\frac{3}{5}\right\}$ is defined by $f(x) = \frac{3x+4}{5x-7}$ and $g : R - \left\{\frac{3}{5}\right\} \to R - \left\{\frac{7}{5}\right\}$ is defined by $g(x) = \frac{7x+4}{5x-3}$, then $fog = I_A$ and $gof = I_B$, where $A = R - \left\{\frac{3}{5}\right\}$, $B = R - \left\{\frac{7}{5}\right\}$; $I_A(x) = x, \forall x \in A$ and $I_B(x) = x, \forall x \in B$ are identity functions on sets A and B, respectively.

Sol. Given, $f : B \to A$ defined by $f(x) = \frac{3x+4}{5x-7}$

and $g : A \to B$ defined by $g(x) = \frac{7x+4}{5x-3}$

where, $A = R - \left\{\frac{3}{5}\right\}$ and $B = R - \left\{\frac{7}{5}\right\}$.

Now, $gof(x) = g(f(x)) = g\left(\frac{3x+4}{5x-7}\right) = \dfrac{7\left(\frac{3x+4}{5x-7}\right)+4}{5\left(\frac{3x+4}{5x-7}\right)-3}$

$$= \frac{21x + 28 + 20x - 28}{15x + 20 - 15x + 21} = \frac{41x}{41} = x$$

Similarly, $fog(x) = f(g(x)) = f\left(\frac{7x+4}{5x-3}\right)$

$$= \dfrac{3\left(\frac{7x+4}{5x-3}\right)+4}{5\left(\frac{7x+4}{5x-3}\right)-7}$$

$$= \frac{21x + 12 + 20x - 12}{35x + 20 - 35x + 21}$$

$$= \frac{41x}{41} = x$$

Thus, $gof(x) = x = I_B(x), \forall x \in B$

and $fog(x) = x = I_A(x), \forall x \in A$

Topic Practice 3

1 If $f(x)=x+7$ and $g(x)=x-7$, $x \in R$ then find $fog(6)$.

2 Let $f: R \to R$ be defined by $f(x)=2x-3$ and $g: R \to R$ be defined by $g(x)=\frac{x+3}{2}$, show that $fog = I_R$.

3 If $f: R \to R$ is given by $f(x)=(3-x^3)^{1/3}$, then find $(fof)x$.

4 If the function $f: R \to R$ is given by $f(x)=x^2+2$ and $g: R \to R$ is given by $g(x)=\frac{x}{x-1}$; $x \neq 1$, then find fog and gof and hence find $fog(2)$ and $gof(-3)$.

5 If $f(x)=\frac{x^2-1}{x^2+1}$, $x \neq 1$, then show that $(fof)(x)=\frac{-2x^2}{1+x^4}$ provided that $x \neq 0$.

Hints & Solutions

1. **Hint** $fog(6)=f(g(6))=f(6-7)=f(-1)$

2. **Hint** $(fog)x=f(g(x))=f\left(\frac{x+3}{2}\right)$

3. **Hint** $(fof)x=f(f(x))=f\{(3-x^3)^{1/3}\}$

4. **Hint** $(fog)(x)=f(g(x))=f\left(\frac{x}{x-1}\right)$

$(gof)(x)=g(f(x))=g(x^2+2)$

5. **Hint** $(fof)(x)=f(f(x))=f\left(\frac{x^2-1}{x^2+1}\right)$

Algebra of Real Functions

Let $f: D_1 \to R$ and $g: D_2 \to R$ be two real functions with domain D_1 and D_2, respectively. Then, algebraic operations such as addition, subtraction, multiplication, division and scalar multiplication on two real functions are given below

(i) **Addition of two real functions** The sum function $(f+g)$ is defined by

$$(f+g)(x)=f(x)+g(x),\ \forall\, x \in D_1 \cap D_2$$

The domain of $(f+g)$ is $D_1 \cap D_2$.

(ii) **Subtraction of two real functions** The difference function $(f-g)$ is defined by

$$(f-g)(x)=f(x)-g(x),\ \forall\, x \in D_1 \cap D_2$$

The domain of $(f-g)$ is $D_1 \cap D_2$.

(iii) **Multiplication of two real functions** The product function (fg) is defined by

$$(fg)(x)=f(x)\cdot g(x),\ \forall\, x \in D_1 \cap D_2$$

The domain of (fg) is $D_1 \cap D_2$.

(iv) **Quotient of two real functions** The quotient function is defined by

$$\frac{f}{g}(x)=\frac{f(x)}{g(x)},\ \forall\, x \in D_1 \cap D_2 - \{x : g(x)=0\}$$

The domain of $\left(\frac{f}{g}\right)$ is $D_1 \cap D_2 - \{x : g(x)=0\}$.

(v) **Multiplication of a real function by a scalar** The scalar multiplication function cf is defined by

$$(cf)(x)=c\cdot f(x),\ \forall\, x \in D_1$$

where, c is a scalar (real number).

The domain of cf is D_1.

EXAMPLE 1. If two functions are defined as $f(x)=\frac{1}{(x-2)}$, $x \neq 2$ and $g(x)=(x-2)^2$, then find

(i) $f+g$ (ii) $f-g$ (iii) fg (iv) $\frac{f}{g}$

Sol. Given functions are

$$f(x)=\frac{1}{x-2},\ x \neq 2 \text{ and } g(x)=(x-2)^2$$

(i) $(f+g)(x)=f(x)+g(x)=\frac{1}{x-2}+(x-2)^2,\ x \neq 2$

$$=\frac{1+(x-2)^3}{x-2},\ x \neq 2$$

(ii) $(f-g)(x) = f(x) - g(x) = \dfrac{1}{(x-2)} - (x-2)^2,\ x \neq 2$

$= \dfrac{1-(x-2)^3}{(x-2)},\ x \neq 2$

(iii) $(fg)(x) = f(x)\cdot g(x) = \dfrac{1}{(x-2)} \times (x-2)^2,\ x \neq 2$

$= (x-2)$

(iv) $\left(\dfrac{f}{g}\right)(x) = \dfrac{f(x)}{g(x)} = \dfrac{\left(\dfrac{1}{x-2}\right)}{(x-2)^2},\ x \neq 2$

$= \dfrac{1}{(x-2)^3},\ x \neq 2$

EXAMPLE 2. Find the sum and difference of the identity function and the modulus function.

Sol. We know that,

$f: R \to R$ defined by $f(x) = x$ is the identity function.

$g: R \to R$ defined by $g(x) = |x|$ is the modulus function.

$\therefore$ Sum, $(f+g): R \to R$ defined by

$(f+g)(x) = f(x) + g(x) = x + |x|$

$$= \begin{cases} x + x, & \text{if } x \geq 0 \\ x - x, & \text{if } x < 0 \end{cases} = \begin{cases} 2x, & \text{if } x \geq 0 \\ 0, & \text{if } x < 0 \end{cases}$$

Difference, $(f-g): R \to R$ defined by

$(f-g)(x) = f(x) - g(x) = x - |x|$

$$= \begin{cases} x - x, & \text{if } x \geq 0 \\ x - (-x), & \text{if } x < 0 \end{cases} = \begin{cases} 0, & \text{if } x \geq 0 \\ 2x, & \text{if } x < 0 \end{cases}$$

EXAMPLE 3. Find the quotient of the identity function by the modulus function.

Sol. Let f and g denote respectively the identity function and the modulus function. Then,

$f: R \to R$ is defined as $f(x) = x$

and $g: R \to R$ is defined as $g(x) = |x|$.

Clearly, f and g have the same domain.

Also, $g(x) = 0 \Rightarrow |x| = 0 \Rightarrow x = 0$.

Therefore, the quotient of f by g i.e. $\dfrac{f}{g}$ is a function from $R - \{0\} \to R$ and it is defined as

$$\left(\frac{f}{g}\right)(x) = \frac{f(x)}{g(x)} = \frac{x}{|x|} = \begin{cases} \dfrac{x}{x} = 1, & x > 0 \\ \dfrac{x}{-x} = -1, & x < 0 \end{cases}$$

EXAMPLE 4. Find the product of the identity function and the reciprocal function.

Sol. Let f and g denote respectively the identity function and the reciprocal function.

Then, $f: R \to R$ is defined as $f(x) = x$ for all $x \in R$ and $g: R - \{0\} \to R$ and is defined as $g(x) = \dfrac{1}{x}$ for all $x \in R - \{0\}$

We have,

domain $(f) \cap$ domain $(g) = R \cap R - \{0\} = R - \{0\}$

Therefore, the product fg is a function from $R - \{0\}$ to R and is defined as

$(fg)(x) = f(x)g(x) = x \times \dfrac{1}{x} = 1$ for all $x \in R - \{0\}$

EXAMPLE 5. Let λ be a non-zero number and $f: R \to R$ be a function defined by $f(x) = \dfrac{x}{\lambda}\ \forall\, x \in R$. Find

(i) λf (ii) $\lambda^2 f$ (iii) $\left(\dfrac{1}{\lambda}\right) f$

Sol. Clearly, $\lambda f, \lambda^2 f$ and $\left(\dfrac{1}{\lambda}\right) f$ are functions from R to itself

(i) $(\lambda f)(x) = \lambda \cdot f(x) = \lambda \times \dfrac{x}{\lambda} = x, \forall\, x \in R$

(ii) $(\lambda^2 f)(x) = \lambda^2 \cdot f(x) = \lambda^2 \times \dfrac{x}{\lambda} = \lambda x, \forall\, x \in R$

(iii) $\left(\dfrac{1}{\lambda} f\right)(x) = \dfrac{1}{\lambda} \cdot f(x) = \dfrac{1}{\lambda} \times \dfrac{x}{\lambda} = \dfrac{x}{\lambda^2}, \forall\, x \in R$

EXAMPLE 6. Let f be the exponential function and g be the logarithmic function. Find

(i) $(f+g)(1)$ (ii) $(f \cdot g)(1)$

(iii) $(3f)(1)$ (iv) $(5g)(1)$

Sol. We have, $f: R \to R$ given by $f(x) = e^x$

and $g: R \to R$ given by $g(x) = \log_e x$

(i) Since, domain $(f) \cap$ domain $(g) = R \cap R^+ = R^+$

$\therefore f + g: R^+ \to R$ is defined as

$(f+g)(x) = f(x) + g(x) = e^x + \log_e x\ \forall\, x \in R^+$

Clearly, $1 \in R^+$

$\therefore\ (f+g)(1) = f(1) + g(1) = e^1 + \log_e 1 = e + 0 = e$

$[\because \log 1 = 0]$

(ii) $f.g: R^+ \to R$ and is defined as

$(f.g)(x) = f(x)\, g(x) = e^x \log_e x$

$(f.g)(1) = f(1)\, g(1) = e^1 \log_e 1 = 0$

(iii) $(3f)(x) = 3\cdot(f(x)) = 3e^x$;

$(3f)(1) = 3 \cdot e^1 = 3e$

(iv) $(5g)(x) = 5(g(x)) = 5\log_e x$;

$(5g)(1) = 5\log_e 1 = 0$

EXAMPLE 7. Let f and g be two real functions defined by $f(x) = \dfrac{1}{x+4}$ and $g(x) = (x+4)^3$.

Find the following

(i) $f+g$ (ii) $f-g$ (iii) fg (iv) $\dfrac{f}{g}$

Sol. We have, $f(x)=\dfrac{1}{x+4}$ is defined for all $x \neq -4$.

So, domain $(f)=R-\{-4\}$

Clearly, $g(x)=(x+4)^3$ is defined for all $x \in R$.

So, domain $(g)=R$

$\therefore$ Domain $(f) \cap$ Domain $(g)=R-\{-4\}$

(i) $f+g: R-\{-4\} \to R$ is given by

$$(f+g)(x)=f(x)+g(x)=\frac{1}{x+4}+(x+4)^3$$
$$=\frac{(x+4)^4+1}{x+4}$$

(ii) $f-g: R-\{-4\} \to R$ is defined as

$$(f-g)(x)=f(x)-g(x)=\frac{1}{x+4}-(x+4)^3$$
$$=\frac{1-(x+4)^4}{(x+4)}$$

(iii) $fg: R-\{-4\} \to R$ is given by

$$(fg)(x)=f(x)g(x)$$
$$=\frac{1}{x+4}\times(x+4)^3$$
$$=(x+4)^2$$

(iv) $g(x)=0 \Rightarrow (x+4)^3=0 \Rightarrow x=-4$

$\therefore$ Domain $\left(\dfrac{f}{g}\right)$

$$= \text{Domain }(f) \cap \text{Domain }(g)-\{x: g(x)=0\}$$
$$=R-\{-4\}$$

Thus, $\dfrac{f}{g}: R-\{-4\} \to R$ is given by $\left(\dfrac{f}{g}\right)x$

$$=\frac{f(x)}{g(x)}=\frac{1}{(x+4)^4}$$

Topic Practice 4

1 Let f and g be real functions defined by $f(x)=\sqrt{x+2}$ and $g(x)=\sqrt{4-x^2}$, then find each of the following functions

(i) $f+g$ (ii) $f-g$

(iii) $f \cdot g$ (iv) $\dfrac{f}{g}$

(v) $\dfrac{g}{f}$ (vi) $2f-\sqrt{5}g$

(vii) f^2+7f (viii) $\dfrac{5}{g}$

2 Let $f(x)=x^2$ and $g(x)=2x+1$ be two real functions. Find

(i) $f+g$

(ii) $f-g$

(iii) $f \cdot g$

(iv) $\dfrac{f}{g}$

3 Let $f: R \to R$ and $g: R \to R$ defined by $f(x)=x+1$, $g(x)=2x-3$. Find $f+g$, $f-g$, and $\dfrac{f}{g}$.

4 If f and g be two real function defined by $f(x)=\sqrt{x+1}$ and $g(x)=\sqrt{9-x^2}$.

Then, describe each of the following functions.

(i) $f+g$ (ii) $g-f$

(iii) $f \cdot g$ (iv) $\dfrac{f}{g}$

5 Let $f:[2,\infty) \to R$ and $g:[-2,\infty) \to R$ be two real functions defined by $f(x)=\sqrt{x-2}$ and $g(x)=\sqrt{x+2}$. Find $f+g$ and $f-g$.

6 If $f(x)=x^3-\dfrac{1}{x^3}$, then find $f(x)+f\left(\dfrac{1}{x}\right)$.

7 If $f(x)=\log\left(\dfrac{1+x}{1-x}\right)$ and $g(x)=\dfrac{(3x+x^3)}{1+3x^2}$, then find $f[g(x)]$.

8 If $x \neq 1$ and $f(x)=\dfrac{x+1}{x-1}$ is a real function, then find $f(f(f(2)))$.

9 If $f(x)=\dfrac{4^x}{4^x+2}$, then find

$$f\left(\frac{1}{97}\right)+f\left(\frac{2}{97}\right)+\ldots+f\left(\frac{96}{97}\right).$$

10 What are the sum and difference of identity function and the reciprocal function?

11 If f, g, h are real functions defined by $f(x)=\sqrt{x+1}$, $g(x)=\dfrac{1}{x}$ and $h(x)=2x^2-3$, then find the values of $(2f+g-h)(1)$ and $(2f+g-h)(0)$.

Hints & Solutions

1. **Hint** $f(x)=\sqrt{x+2},\ g(x)=\sqrt{4-x^2}$

$f(x)$ is defined for $x+2\geq 0 \Rightarrow x\geq -2$

$\therefore$ Domain $(f)=[-2,\infty)$

$g(x)$ is defined for $4-x^2 \geq 0$

$\Rightarrow x^2-4\leq 0 \Rightarrow (x-2)(x+2)\leq 0$

$\Rightarrow x\in[-2,2]$

Domain $(g)=[-2,2]$

Domain $(f)\cap$ domain $(g)=[-2,2]$

Ans. (i) $(\sqrt{x+2})[1+\sqrt{2-x}]$ (ii) $\sqrt{x+2}\ [1-\sqrt{2-x}]$

(iii) $(x+2)\sqrt{2-x}$ (iv) $1/\sqrt{2-x}$

2. **Hint** $f+g=(x+1)^2,\ f-g=x^2-2x-1,$

Ans. $f\cdot g=2x^3+x^2,\ \dfrac{f}{g}=\dfrac{x^2}{2x+1}$

3. **Hint** $f+g=3x-2,\ f-g=-x+4$

$\dfrac{f}{g}:R-\left\{\dfrac{3}{2}\right\}\to R,\ \dfrac{f}{g}=\dfrac{x+1}{2x-3}$

4. Domain $(f)\cap$ Domain $(g)=[-1,3]$

(i) $(f+g)(x)=\sqrt{x+1}+\sqrt{9-x^2}$

(ii) $(g-f)(x)=\sqrt{9-x^2}-\sqrt{x+1}$

(iii) $(fg)(x)=\sqrt{9+9x-x^2-x^3}$

(iv) $\left(\dfrac{f}{g}\right)(x)=\sqrt{\dfrac{x+1}{9-x^2}}$

(v) $\left(\dfrac{g}{f}\right)(x)=\sqrt{\dfrac{9-x^2}{x+1}},\ x\neq -1$

(vi) $(2f-\sqrt{5}g)(x)=2\sqrt{x+1}-\sqrt{45-5x^2}$

(vii) $(f^2+7f)(x)=x+1+7\sqrt{x+1}$

(viii) $\left(\dfrac{5}{g}\right)(x)=\dfrac{5}{\sqrt{9-x^2}},\ x\neq -3, 3$

5. **Hint** Domain $(f)=[2,\infty)=D_1$ [say]

Domain $g=[-2,\infty)=D_2$ [say]

$D_1\cap D_2=[2,\infty)$

Ans. $(\sqrt{x-2}+\sqrt{x+2})$ and $(\sqrt{x-2}-\sqrt{x+2})$

6. **Hint** $f(x)=x^3-\dfrac{1}{x^3}$

$f\left(\dfrac{1}{x}\right)=\dfrac{1}{x^3}-x^3$

$\therefore\ f(x)+f\left(\dfrac{1}{x}\right)=x^3-\dfrac{1}{x^3}+\dfrac{1}{x^3}-x^3$

Ans. 0

7. **Hint** Given, $f(x)=\log\left(\dfrac{1+x}{1-x}\right)$ and $g(x)=\dfrac{(3x+x^3)}{1+3x^2}$

Now, $f[g(x)]=\log\left(\dfrac{1+g(x)}{1-g(x)}\right)=\log\left(\dfrac{1+3x^2+3x+x^3}{1+3x^2-3x-x^3}\right)$

$=\log\left(\dfrac{1+x}{1-x}\right)^3=3\log\left(\dfrac{1+x}{1-x}\right)$ **Ans.** $3[f(x)]$

8. **Hint** We have, $f(x)=\dfrac{x+1}{x-1}$

$\therefore\ f(f(x))=\dfrac{f(x)+1}{f(x)-1}=\dfrac{\dfrac{x+1}{x-1}+1}{\dfrac{x+1}{x-1}-1}$

$=\dfrac{x+1+x-1}{x+1-x+1}=\dfrac{2x}{2}=x$

$\therefore\ f(f(f(x)))=f(x)=\dfrac{x+1}{x-1}$

$\Rightarrow\ f(f(f(2)))=\dfrac{2+1}{2-1}$ **Ans.** 3

9. **Hint** We have, $f(x)=\dfrac{4^x}{4^x+2}$

$\therefore\ f(1-x)+f(x)=\dfrac{4^{1-x}}{4^{1-x}+2}+\dfrac{4^x}{4^x+2}$

$=\dfrac{4}{4+2\cdot 4^x}+\dfrac{4^x}{4^x+2}$

$=\dfrac{2}{2+4^x}+\dfrac{4^x}{4^x+2}=\dfrac{2+4^x}{2+4^x}=1$

Now, putting $x=\dfrac{1}{97},\dfrac{2}{97},\dfrac{3}{97},\ldots,\dfrac{48}{97}$ and adding, we get

$$\left(f\left(\frac{1}{97}\right)+f\left(\frac{96}{97}\right)\right)+\left(f\left(\frac{2}{97}\right)+f\left(\frac{95}{97}\right)\right)+\ldots+\left(f\left(\frac{48}{97}\right)+f\left(\frac{49}{97}\right)\right)$$

$=1+1+\ldots+1$ (48 times)

$\Rightarrow f\left(\dfrac{1}{97}\right)+f\left(\dfrac{2}{97}\right)+\ldots+f\left(\dfrac{96}{97}\right)$ **Ans.** 48

10. **Hint** Let $f(x)=x,\ g(x)=\dfrac{1}{x}$; Domain $(f)=R=D_1$

Domain $(g)=R-\{0\}=D_2$

$D_1\cap D_2=R-\{0\}$

Ans. Sum $=x+\dfrac{1}{x}$ and difference $=x-\dfrac{1}{x}$

11. We have, $f(x)=\sqrt{x+1},\ g(x)=\dfrac{1}{x}$

and $h(x)=2x^2-3$

Now, $(2f+g-h)(1)=2\sqrt{2}+1-2+3=2\sqrt{2}+2$

$(2f+g-h)(0)$ does not exist because 0 does not lie in the domain $x\in[-1,\infty]-\{0\}$.

Exam Pattern Exercise

Part A - Objective Type Questions

Multiple Choice Type Questions

1 Which one of the following relations is a function from {1, 2, 3, 4} to {1, 2, 3, 4, 5}?

(a) {(1, 2), (2, 3), (3, 3), (1, 1)}
(b) {(2, 4), (4, 2), (3, 2)}
(c) {(1, 2), (2, 3), (3, 4)}
(d) {(1, 5), (2, 4), (3, 3), (4, 5)}

2 The range of real function $f(x)=\frac{1}{x}-\frac{1}{x-1}$ is

(a) $R-\{0,1\}$ (b) $R-[0,1]$
(c) $R-[0,4)$ (d) $R-[0,4]$

3 The domain of real function $f(x)=\frac{1}{\sqrt{x^2+5x+6}}$ is

(a) $R-(-3,-2)$ (b) $R-[-3,-2]$
(c) $R-(2,3)$ (d) $R-[2,3]$

4 The solution set of the equation $|x^2-x-12|=12.25$ is

(a) $\{-4.45, 0.5, 5.45\}$
(b) $\{4.45, -0.5, 5.45\}$
(c) $\{4.45, -0.5, -5.45\}$
(d) $\{-4.45, 0.5, -5.45\}$

5 Which one of the following statement is incorrect?

(a) The graph of the constant function is symmetric about the *Y*-axis.
(b) The graph about the function $f(x)=x^2+2$ is symmetric about the *Y*-axis.
(c) The graph of the function $f(x)=e^{|x|}$ is symmetric about the *Y*-axis.
(d) The graph of the identity function is symmetric about the *Y*-axis.

6 If $f(x)=\frac{1+x}{1-x}$, then $(fof)(x)$ is equal to

(a) $\frac{1}{x}$ (b) $-\frac{1}{x}$ (c) $\frac{1}{x^2}$ (d) $-\frac{1}{x^2}$

7 Let $f: R \to R$ be such that $f(x)=2^x$. Then, consider the following statements

I. Range of $f=(0,\infty)$
II. $\{x: f(x)=1\}=\{0\}$
III. $f(x+y)=f(x)\cdot f(y)$

Which of the above statements is/are correct?

(a) Only I (b) I and II
(c) II and III (d) All of these

8 The graph of the function defined by

$$f(x)=\begin{cases}1-x, & x<0\\ 1, & x=0\\ 1+x, & x>0\end{cases}$$ is

(a)

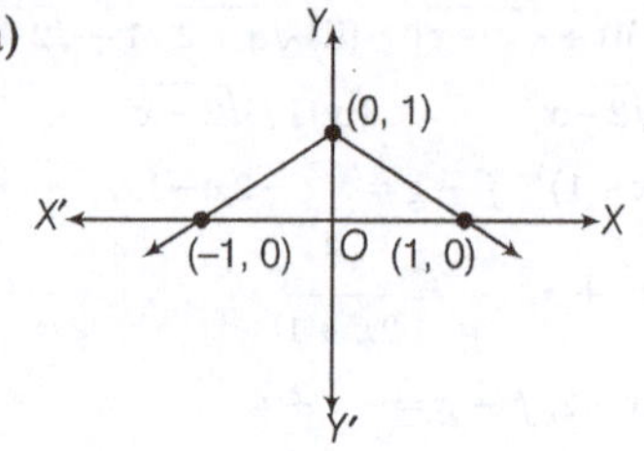

(b)

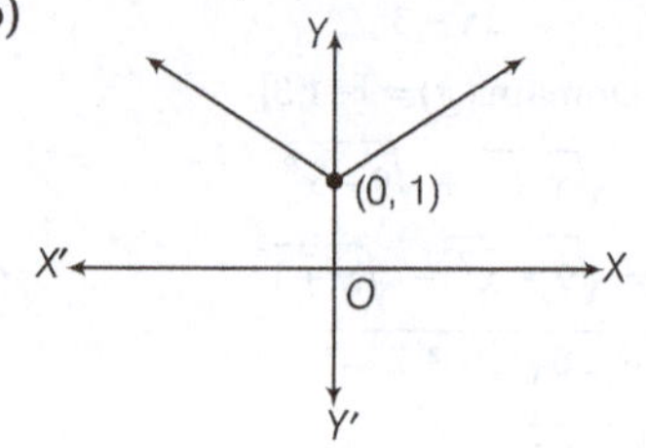

(c)

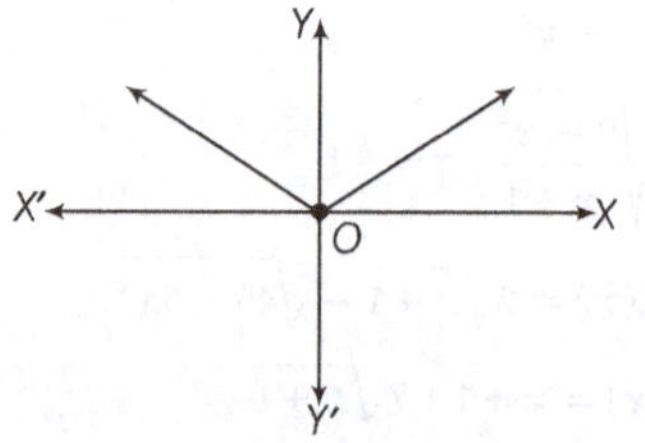

(d)

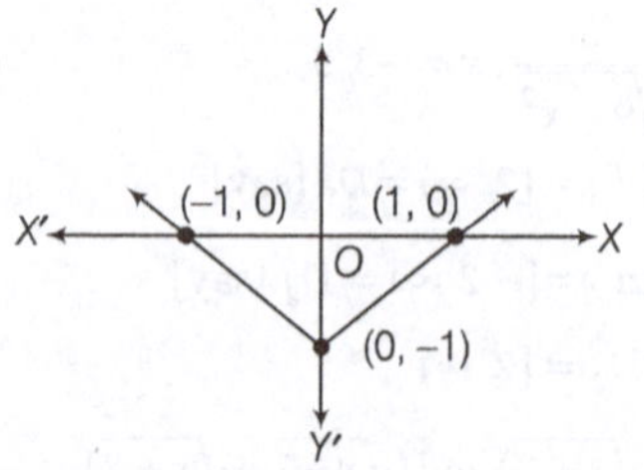

9 Let $f: R\to R$ be defined by $f(x)=3x^2-5$ and $g: R\to R$ by $g(x)=\frac{x}{x^2+1}$. Then, gof is

(a) $\frac{3x^2-5}{9x^4-30x^2+26}$ (b) $\frac{3x^2-5}{9x^4-6x^2+26}$
(c) $\frac{3x^2}{x^4+2x^2-4}$ (d) $\frac{3x^2}{9x^4+30x^2-2}$

10 If $f(x) = \cos(\log x)$, then

$f(x)\,f(y) - \frac{1}{2}\left[f\left(\frac{x}{y}\right) + f(xy)\right]$ has the value

(a) -1 (b) $\frac{1}{2}$

(c) -2 (d) 0

Assertion-Reason Based Questions

Directions (Q. Nos. 12-15) *In the questions given below are two statements labelled as Assertion (A) and Reason (R). In the context of the two statements, which one of the following is correct?*

(a) Both A and R are correct; R is the correct explanation of A

(b) Both A and R are correct; R is not the correct explanation of A

(c) A is correct; R is incorrect

(d) R is correct; A is incorrect

11 **Assertion (A)** The relation $\{(1, 2), (2, 4), (3, 6), (4, 8)\}$ is a function from $\{1, 2, 3, 4\}$ to $\{2, 4, 6, 8, 10\}$.

Reason (R) A relation from a non-empty set A to a non-empty set B if and only if each element of set A is associates with one and only one element of set B.

12 **Assertion (A)** If $f: R - \{4\} \to R$ be defined by $f(x) = \frac{x^2 - 16}{x - 4}$ and $g: R \to R$ be defined by $g(x) = x + 4$, then $f = g$.

Reason (R) Two functions f and g are said to be equal iff

(i) domain of f = domain of g

(ii) Codomain of f = Codomain of g

and (iii) $f(x) = g(x)$ for every x belonging to their common domain.

13 **Assertion (A)** The value of the expression $\log_9(2187)$ is $\frac{7}{2}$.

Reason (R) $\log_{a^n}(x^m) = \frac{m}{n}\log_a x$ and $\log_a a = 1$, where $a > 0$, $a \neq 1$, $n \neq 0$ and $x > 0$.

14 **Assertion (A)** If f and g are two real functions, then *fog* and *gof* may or may not be equal.

Reason (R) If $f: A \to B$ and $g: B \to C$, then domain of (gof) = domain (f).

Part B - Descriptive Questions

Very Short Answer Type Questions

15 Which of the following are functions, if $X = \{a, b, c, d\}$ and $Y = \{1, 2, 3, 4, 5\}$?

(i) $f_1 = \{(a,1), (b,1), (c,3), (d,4)\}$

(ii) $f_2 = \{(a,1), (b,2), (c,4), (a,2), (d,5)\}$

16 If $A = \{9, 10, 11, 12, 13\}$ and $f: A \to N$ be defined by $f(n)$ = the highest prime factor of n, then find the range of f.

17 Find the range of the function $f(x) = x$, x is a real number.

18 If $f(x) = 8x^3$ and $g(x) = x^{1/3}$, then find $fog\,(x)$.

Short Answer Type Questions

19 If a function $f: R \to R$ be defined by

$$f(x) = \begin{cases} 3x - 2, & x < 0 \\ 1, & x = 0 \\ 4x + 1, & x > 0 \end{cases}$$

Find $f(1)$, $f(-1)$, $f(0)$, $f(2)$.

20 If $f(x) = x^2$, find $\frac{f(2.1) - f(1)}{2.1 - 1}$.

21 If $X = \{1, 2, 3, 4, 5\}$, $Y = \{1, 2, 5, 6, 7, 9, 10, 11, 12, 13, 14\}$ and $f: X \to Y$ be defined by $f(x) = 2x + 3$, then find the domain and range of f.

22 Find *gof* and *fog*, if $f: R \to R$ and $g: R \to R$ are given by $f(x) = \cos x$ and $g(x) = 3x^2$, then show that $gof \neq fog$.

23 If $f(x) = x^3 - \frac{1}{x^3}$, show that $f(x) + f\left(\frac{1}{x}\right) = 0$.

Long Answer Type Questions

24 Is $g = \{(2, 3), (4, 5), (6, 7)\}$ a function? If this is described by the formula $g(x) = \alpha x + 2\beta$, then what values would be assigned to α and β?

25 Find the domain of the function $f(x) = \frac{x}{\log(x^2 + 2x - 8)}$.

26 Find the domain and range of the following real functions.

(i) $f(x) = -|2x|$ (ii) $f(x) = \sqrt{9 - x^2}$

27 (i) Find the domain and range of the function
$$f(x)=\frac{x^2-9}{x-3}.$$
(ii) Find the domain of the function
$$f(x)=\frac{x^2+3x+5}{x^2+x-6}.$$
(iii) Find the domain of $f(x)=\sqrt{4-x}+\frac{1}{\sqrt{x^2-1}}$.

Or

Find the domain of $f(x)=\frac{1}{\sqrt{x^2-|x|}}$.

28 If $f(x)=\begin{cases}1+x\,, & -1\le x<0\\ x^2-1, & 0<x<2\\ 2x\,, & 2\le x\end{cases}$, then find

$f(3), f(-2), f(0), f\left(\frac{1}{2}\right), f(2-h)$ and $f(-1+h)$,

where $h>0$ is very small.

29 Find the solution set of the following equation
$$|x^2+x-6|=6.25$$

30 Find domain and range of the real function $f(x)$ defined by $f(x)=\begin{cases}1-x, & x<0\\ 1, & x=0\\ x-1, & x>0\end{cases}$ and draw its graph.

Case Study Based Questions

31 Aman a student of class XI was preparing the topic domain of real functions for his upcoming test.

Domain of Real Functions

As we know that real functions are generally described by providing the general formula for finding the images of elements of its domain. In such cases, the domain of the real function $f(x)$ is the set of all those real numbers for which the expression for $f(x)$ or the formula for $f(x)$ assumes real values only.

In other words, we can say that the domain of $f(x)$ is the set of all those real numbers for which $f(x)$ is meaningful.

On the basis of above information answer the following questions.

(i) Find the domain of $f(x)=-|x|$.

(ii) Find the domain of $f(x)=\sqrt{9-x^2}$.

32 Let $f:A\to B$ and $g:B\to C$ be two real functions, then composition of f and g denoted by gof is the function $gof:A\to C$ defined by
$$(gof)(x)=g(f(x)),\ \forall x\in A$$

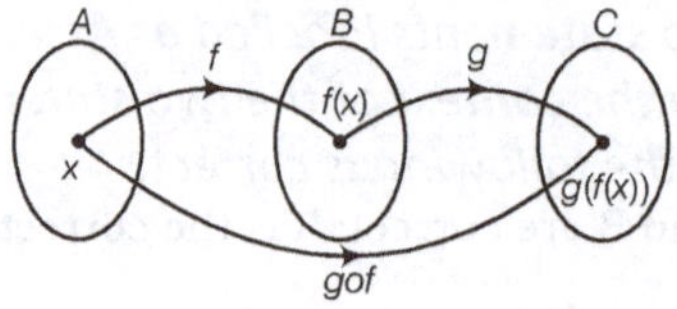

For gof to exist, Range of $f\subset$ Domain of g.
Also, Domain of gof = Domain of f
The function f and g are given by
$f=\{(2,4),(5,3),(8,9)\}$ and $g=\{(4,8),(9,5),(3,2)\}$
Based on the above information, answer the following questions.

(i) Find domain of f.

(ii) Find range of g

(iii) Find gof as a set of ordered pairs.

Or

Find fog as a set of ordered pairs.

33 Hanuman Pareek and Pawan Saini are two students of class XIth in a school. The ages of both students is represented by f and g are real functions defined by $f(x)=\sqrt{x+4}$ and $g(x)=\sqrt{16-x^2}$. Then, answer the some questions which are based on above ages.

(i) Find the sum of both ages i.e. $(f+g)$.

(ii) Find the product of both ages i.e. (fg).

(iii) Find the different of both ages i.e. $(f-g)$.

Or

Find the $\left(\frac{f}{g}\right)$.

Hints & Solutions

1. (d) 2. (c) 3. (b) 4. (a)
5. (d) 6. (b) 7. (d) 8. (b)
9. (a) 10. (d) 11. (a) 12. (d)
13. (a) 14. (b)

15. (i) f_1 is a function.

(ii) $\because f(a) = 1$ and $f(a) = 2$, f_2 is not a function.

16. {3, 5, 11, 13}

17. Range = R

18. $8x$

19. $f(1) = 5,\ f(-1) = -5,\ f(0) = 1,\ f(2) = 9$

20. 3.1

21. Domain = {1, 2, 3, 4, 5} and Range = {5, 7, 9, 11, 13}

22. $gof(x) = 3(\cos x)^2,\ fog(x) = \cos(3x^2)$

24. g is a function, $\alpha = 1, \beta = \dfrac{1}{2}$

25. Domain $= ((-\infty, -4) \cup (2, \infty)) - \{-1 \pm \sqrt{10}\}$

26. (i) Domain = R Range = $(-\infty, 0]$
(ii) Domain = $[-3, 3]$ Range = $[0, 3]$

27. (i) Domain = $R - \{3\}$, Range = $R - \{6\}$
(ii) Domain = $R - \{-3, 2\}$

28. $f(3) = 6,\ f(-2) =$ Not defined,

$f(0) =$ Not defined,

$f\left(\dfrac{1}{2}\right) = \dfrac{-3}{4};\ f(2-h) = h^2 - 4h + 3,\ f(-1+h) = h$

29. $\left\{-\dfrac{1}{2} \pm \dfrac{5\sqrt{2}}{2}, -\dfrac{1}{2}\right\}$

30. Domain = R Range = $(-1, \infty)$

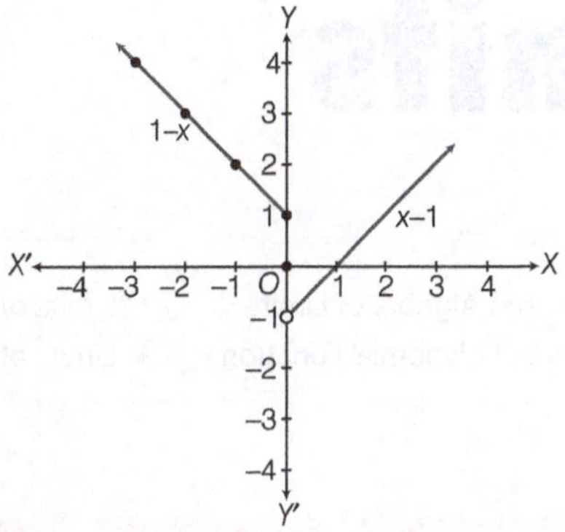

31. (i) R
(ii) $[-3, 3]$
(iii) $(-\infty, -1) \cup [1, 4]$
Or $(-\infty, -1) \cup (1, \infty)$

32. (i) {2,5, 8}
(ii) {8, 5, 2}
(iii) {(2, 8), (5, 2), (8, 5)}
Or {(4, 9), (9, 3), (3, 4)}

33. (i) $\sqrt{x+4} + \sqrt{16 - x^2}$
(ii) $(x+4)\sqrt{4-x}$
(iii) $\sqrt{x+4} - \sqrt{16 - x^2}$
Or $\dfrac{1}{\sqrt{4-x}}$

CHAPTER 14

Limits

In this Chapter...

- Limits and Algebra of Limits
- Limits of Polynomial Function
- Limits of Rational Functions
- Limits of Exponential Functions and Logarithmic Functions

Limits and Algebra of Limits

If $f(x)$ approaches to a real number l, when x approaches to a (through lesser or greater values to a) i.e. if $f(x) \to l$ when $x \to a$, then l is called limit of the function $f(x)$.

In symbolic form, it can be written as $\lim_{x \to a} f(x) = l$

Left Hand Limit and Right Hand Limit

There are two ways through which x can approach to a, either from left side (from values lower than a) or from right side (from values higher than a). Therefore, two types of limit exists; **left hand limit** and **right hand limit.**

Left hand limit can be written as $\lim_{x \to a^-} f(x)$ is the expected value of f at $x = a$, when we have the values of f near x to the left of a.

Similarly, right hand limit can be written as $\lim_{x \to a^+} f(x)$ is the expected value of f at $x = a$, when we have the values of f near x to the right of a.

Existence of Limit

If the left hand limit and right hand limit both exist (i.e. finite and unique) and coincide (i.e. same), then we say that limit exists and their common value is called the limit of $f(x)$ at $x = a$.

i.e. if $\lim_{x \to a^-} f(x) = \lim_{x \to a^+} f(x) = l$, then $\lim_{x \to a} f(x) = l$

Method to Solve the Left Hand and Right Hand Limits of a Function

With the help of following steps, we can find the left hand and right hand limits of a function easily

I. For left hand limit, write the given function as $\lim_{x \to a^-} f(x)$ and for right hand limit, write the given function as $\lim_{x \to a^+} f(x)$.

II. For left hand limit, put $x = a - h$ and change the limit $x \to a^-$ by $h \to 0$.

Then, limit obtained from step I is $\lim_{h \to 0} f(a-h)$.

Similarly, for right hand limit, put $x = a + h$ and change the limit $x \to a^+$ by $h \to 0$. Then, limit obtained from step I is $\lim_{h \to 0} f(a+h)$.

III. Now, simplify the result obtained in step II i.e. $\lim_{h \to 0} f(a-h)$ or $\lim_{h \to 0} f(a+h)$.

EXAMPLE 1. Suppose the function is defined by

$$f(x) = \begin{cases} x^2, & x \neq 2 \\ 0, & x = 2 \end{cases}.$$

(i) Find the left hand limit of $f(x)$ at $x = 2$.

(ii) Find the right hand limit of $f(x)$ at $x = 2$.

Sol. (i) Given, $f(x) = \begin{cases} x^2, & x \neq 2 \\ 0, & x = 2 \end{cases}$

$\therefore$ Left hand limit at $x = 2$ is

$$\lim_{x \to 2^-} f(x) = \lim_{x \to 2^-} x^2 \quad \text{...(i)}$$

On putting $x = 2 - h$ and changing the limit $x \to 2^-$ by $h \to 0$ in Eq. (i), we get

$$\lim_{x\to 2^-} f(x) = \lim_{h\to 0} (2-h)^2 = (2-0)^2 = 4$$

(ii) Right hand limit at $x = 2$ is

$$\lim_{x\to 2^+} f(x) = \lim_{x\to 2^+} x^2 \quad \text{...(ii)}$$

On putting $x = 2 + h$ and changing the limit $x \to 2^+$ by $h \to 0$ in Eq. (ii), we get

$$\lim_{x\to 2^+} f(x) = \lim_{h\to 0} (2+h)^2 = (2+0)^2 = 4$$

EXAMPLE 2. Find the left hand limit and right hand limit of the greatest integer function $f(x) = [x] =$ greatest integer less than or equal to x at $x = k$, where k is an integer. Also, show that $\lim_{x\to k} f(x)$ does not exist.

Sol. We have, $f(x) = [x]$

LHL of f at $x = k$,

$$f(x) = \lim_{x\to k^-} f(x)$$

$$= \lim_{h\to 0} f(k-h)$$

[putting $x = k - h$ and when $x \to k^-$, then $h \to 0$]

$$= \lim_{h\to 0} [k-h] = \lim_{h\to 0} (k-1)$$

$[\because k-1 < k-h < k \Rightarrow [k-h] = k-1]$

$$= k-1$$

RHL of f at $x = k$,

$$f(x) = \lim_{x\to k^+} f(x)$$

$$= \lim_{h\to 0} f(k+h)$$

[putting $x = k + h$ and when $x \to k^+$, then $h \to 0$]

$$= \lim_{h\to 0} [k+h]$$

$$= \lim_{h\to 0} k$$

$[\because k < k+h < k+1 \Rightarrow [k+h] = k]$

$$= k$$

Here, LHL $\neq$ RHL

$\therefore \lim_{x\to k} f(x)$ does not exist.

Algebra of Limits

Sometimes two or more functions involving algebraic operations such as addition, subtraction, multiplication and division are given, then to find the limit of these functions involving algebraic operations, we use the following theorem.

Let f and g be two real functions with common domain D, such that $\lim_{x\to a} f(x)$ and $\lim_{x\to a} g(x)$ exists.

Then,

- Limit of sum of two functions is sum of the limits of the functions.
  i.e. $\lim_{x\to a} (f+g)(x) = \lim_{x\to a} f(x) + \lim_{x\to a} g(x)$
- Limit of difference of two functions is difference of the limits of the function.
  i.e. $\lim_{x\to a} (f-g)(x) = \lim_{x\to a} f(x) - \lim_{x\to a} g(x)$
- Limit of product of a constant and one function is the product of that constant and limit of a function.
  i.e. $\lim_{x\to a} [c \cdot f(x)] = c \lim_{x\to a} f(x)$, where c is a constant.
- Limit of product of two functions is product of the limits of the function.
  i.e. $\lim_{x\to a} [f(x) \cdot g(x)] = \lim_{x\to a} f(x) \cdot \lim_{x\to a} g(x)$
- Limit of quotient of two functions is quotient of the limits of the functions.
  i.e. $\lim_{x\to a} \dfrac{f(x)}{g(x)} = \dfrac{\lim_{x\to a} f(x)}{\lim_{x\to a} g(x)}$, where $\lim_{x\to a} g(x) \neq 0$
- $\lim_{x\to a} |f(x)| = |\lim_{x\to a} f(x)|$
- $\lim_{x\to a} \{f(x)\}^{g(x)} = \{\lim_{x\to a} f(x)\}^{\lim_{x\to a} g(x)}$
- If $f(x) \leq g(x)$ for all x in the domain of definition, then for some a, $\lim_{x\to a} f(x) \leq \lim_{x\to a} g(x)$
- (Sandwich Theorem) If $f(x) \leq g(x) \leq h(x)$ for all x is the common domain of definition. For some real number a, if $\lim_{x\to a} f(x) = l = \lim_{x\to a} h(x)$,
  Then, $\lim_{x\to a} g(x) = l$
- If $\lim_{x\to a} f(x) = \infty$, then $\lim_{x\to a} \dfrac{1}{f(x)} = 0$
- $\lim_{x\to a} \dfrac{1}{f(x)} = \dfrac{1}{\lim_{x\to a} f(x)}$, where $\lim_{x\to a} f(x) \neq 0$
- $\lim_{x\to a} (f(x))^n = \left(\lim_{x\to a} f(x)\right)^n$

Indeterminate Forms

Consider the limit $\lim_{x\to a} \dfrac{f(x)}{g(x)} = \dfrac{\lim_{x\to a} f(x)}{\lim_{x\to a} g(x)}$,

where $\lim_{x\to a} g(x) \neq 0$.

Now, if $\lim_{x \to a} f(x) = \lim_{x \to a} g(x) = 0$, then $\lim_{x \to a} \frac{f(x)}{g(x)}$ is said to assume indeterminate form $\left(\frac{0}{0}\right)$.

Sometimes $\left(\frac{0}{0}\right)$ is referred to as undetermined form or illusory form.

Some other indeterminate forms are $\frac{\infty}{\infty}$, $0 \times \infty$, $\infty - \infty$, 0^0, ∞^0 and 1^∞. Among all these $\frac{0}{0}$ form is the fundamental one because all the remaining forms can be reduced to this forms.

$\Rightarrow$ The limits can be divided into two categories :

(i) Algebraic limits (ii) Non-algebraic limits

The limits that involve trigonometric, inverse trigonometric, exponential and logarithmic function are called non-algebraic limits otherwise algebraic limits.

EXAMPLE 3. Let us consider two functions $f(x) = x^2 + 4$ and $g(x) = x - 3$ such that $f(x)$ and $g(x)$ exist at $x = 5$. Find the limit of the following functions at $x = 5$.

(i) $f(x) + g(x)$ (ii) $f(x) - g(x)$

(iii) $f(x) \times g(x)$ (iv) $\frac{f(x)}{g(x)}$

Sol. Given functions are $f(x) = x^2 + 4$ and $g(x) = x - 3$

Clearly, $\lim_{x \to 5} f(x) = \lim_{x \to 5} x^2 + 4$

$= (5)^2 + 4 = 25 + 4 = 29$ ...(i)

and $\lim_{x \to 5} g(x) = \lim_{x \to 5} (x - 3)$

$= (5 - 3) = 2$ ...(ii)

(i) $\lim_{x \to 5} [f(x) + g(x)] = \lim_{x \to 5} f(x) + \lim_{x \to 5} g(x)$

$= 29 + 2$ [from Eqs. (i) and (ii)]

$= 31$

(ii) $\lim_{x \to 5} [f(x) - g(x)] = \lim_{x \to 5} f(x) - \lim_{x \to 5} g(x)$

$= 29 - 2$

$= 27$ [from Eqs. (i) and (ii)]

(iii) $\lim_{x \to 5} [f(x) \times g(x)] = \lim_{x \to 5} f(x) \times \lim_{x \to 5} g(x)$

$= 29 \times 2$

$= 58$ [from Eqs. (i) and (ii)]

(iv) $\lim_{x \to 5} \frac{f(x)}{g(x)} = \frac{\lim_{x \to 5} f(x)}{\lim_{x \to 5} g(x)}$ [from Eqs. (i) and (ii)]

$= \frac{29}{2} = 14.5$

Limits of Polynomial Function

A function f is said to be a **polynomial function** of degree n, if $f(x) = a_0 + a_1 x + a_2 x^2 + \ldots + a_n x^n$, where a_i's are real numbers and $a_n \neq 0$ and n is non-negative integer.

Limit of a polynomial function $f(x)$

$$= \lim_{x \to a} f(x) = \lim_{x \to a} [a_0 + a_1 x + a_2 x^2 + \ldots + a_n x^n]$$

$$= \lim_{x \to a} a_0 + \lim_{x \to a} a_1 x + \lim_{x \to a} a_2 x^2 + \ldots + \lim_{x \to a} a_n x^n$$

$$= a_0 + a_1 \lim_{x \to a} x + a_2 \lim_{x \to a} x^2 + \ldots + a_n \lim_{x \to a} x^n$$

$$= a_0 + a_1 a + a_2 a^2 + \ldots + a_n a^n = f(a)$$

EXAMPLE 4. Evaluate the limits

$\lim_{x \to 3} (4x^3 - 2x^2 - x + 1)$.

Sol. $\lim_{x \to 3} (4x^3 - 2x^2 - x + 1)$

$= 4 \lim_{x \to 3} x^3 - 2 \lim_{x \to 3} x^2 - \lim_{x \to 3} x + \lim_{x \to 3} 1$

$= 4(3)^3 - 2(3)^2 - 3 + 1$

$= 108 - 18 - 2 = 88$

EXAMPLE 5. Evaluate the left hand and right hand limits of the following function at $x = 2$.

$$f(x) = \begin{cases} 2x + 3, \text{ if } x \le 2 \\ x + 5, \text{ if } x > 2 \end{cases}$$

Does $\lim_{x \to 2} f(x)$ exist?

Sol. Given, $f(x) = \begin{cases} 2x + 3, \text{ if } x \le 2 \\ x + 5, \text{ if } x > 2 \end{cases}$

LHL $= \lim_{x \to 2^-} f(x) = \lim_{x \to 2^-} 2x + 3$

[$\because f(x) = 2x + 3$, if $x \le 2$]

$= \lim_{h \to 0} [2(2 - h) + 3] = 2(2 - 0) + 3$

[putting $x = 2 - h$ and when $x \to 2^-$, then $h \to 0$]

$= 4 + 3 = 7$

and RHL $= \lim_{x \to 2^+} f(x)$

$= \lim_{x \to 2^+} (x + 5)$ [$\because f(x) = x + 5$, if $x > 2$]

$= \lim_{h \to 0} (2 + h + 5)$

$= 2 + 0 + 5 = 7$

[putting $x = 2 + h$ and $x \to 2^+$, then $h \to 0$]

$\because$ LHL of $f(at\ x = 2)$ = RHL of $f(at\ x = 2)$

$\therefore \lim_{x \to 2} f(x)$ exists and it is equal to 7.

EXAMPLE 6. Evaluate the left hand and right hand limits of the function defined by

$$f(x)=\begin{cases}1+x^2, \text{ if } 0\le x\le 1\\ 2-x^2, \text{ if } x>1\end{cases} \text{ at } x=1.$$

Also, show that $\lim_{x\to 1} f(x)$ does not exist.

Sol. We have, $f(x)=\begin{cases}1+x^2, \text{ if } 0\le x\le 1\\ 2-x^2, \text{ if } x>1\end{cases}$

At $x=1$, LHL $= \lim_{x\to 1^-} f(x) = \lim_{x\to 1^-}(1+x^2)$

$[\because f(x)=1+x^2, \text{ if } 0\le x\le 1]$

$= \lim_{h\to 0}[1+(1-h)^2] = 1+(1-0)^2 = 2$

[putting $x=1-h$ and when $x\to 1^-$, then $h\to 0$]

RHL $= \lim_{x\to 1^+} f(x) = \lim_{x\to 1^+}(2-x^2)$

$[\because f(x)=2-x^2, \text{ if } x>1]$

$= \lim_{h\to 0}[2-(1+h)^2]$

[putting $x=1+h$ and when $x\to 1^+$, then $h\to 0$]

$= 2-1=1$

Since, LHL $\neq$ RHL

Therefore, $\lim_{x\to 1} f(x)$ does not exist.

EXAMPLE 7. Suppose the function is defined by

$$f(x)=\begin{cases}\dfrac{|x-3|}{x-3}, & x\neq 3\\ 0, & x=3\end{cases}.$$

(i) Find the left hand limit of $f(x)$ at $x=3$.

(ii) Find the right hand limit of $f(x)$ at $x=3$.

Sol. (i) Given, $f(x)=\begin{cases}\dfrac{|x-3|}{x-3}, & x\neq 3\\ 0, & x=3\end{cases}$

$\therefore$ Left hand limit at $x=3$ is

$$\lim_{x\to 3^-} f(x) = \lim_{x\to 3^-}\frac{|x-3|}{x-3} \quad \text{...(i)}$$

On putting $x=3-h$ and changing the limit $x\to 3^-$ by $h\to 0$ in Eq. (i), we get

$$\lim_{x\to 3^-} f(x) = \lim_{x\to 3^-}\frac{|x-3|}{x-3} = \lim_{h\to 0}\frac{|-h|}{-h}$$

$$\Rightarrow \lim_{x\to 3^-} f(x) = \lim_{h\to 0}\frac{h}{(-h)} \quad [\because |x|=x]$$

$$=-1$$

(ii) Right hand limit at $x=3$ is

$$\lim_{x\to 3^+} f(x) = \lim_{x\to 3^+}\frac{|x-3|}{x-3} \quad \text{...(ii)}$$

On putting $x=3+h$ and changing the limit $x\to 3^+$ by $h\to 0$ in Eq. (ii), we get

$$\lim_{x\to 3^+} f(x) = \lim_{x\to 3^+}\frac{|x-3|}{x-3} = \lim_{h\to 0}\frac{|h|}{h}$$

$$\Rightarrow \lim_{x\to 3^+} f(x) = \lim_{h\to 0}\frac{|h|}{h} = \lim_{h\to 0}\frac{h}{h} = 1 \quad [\because |x|=x]$$

Alternate Method

Given, $f(x)=\begin{cases}\dfrac{|x-3|}{x-3}, & x\neq 3\\ 0, & x=3\end{cases}$

$$=\begin{cases}\dfrac{-(x-3)}{(x-3)}, & \text{if } x<3\\ \dfrac{x-3}{x-3}, & \text{if } x>3\\ 0, & \text{if } x=3\end{cases} = \begin{cases}-1, & \text{if } x<3\\ 1, & \text{if } x>3\\ 0, & \text{if } x=3\end{cases}$$

(i) LHL $= \lim_{x\to 3^-} f(x) = \lim_{x\to 3^-}(-1)$ $[\because f(x)=-1, \text{ for } x<3]$

$=-1$

(ii) RHL $= \lim_{x\to 3^+} f(x) = \lim_{x\to 3^+}(1)$ $[\because f(x)=1, \text{ for } x>3]$

$=1$

EXAMPLE 8. For what integers m and n does $\lim_{x\to 0} f(x)$ and $\lim_{x\to 1} f(x)$ exist, if

$$f(x)=\begin{cases}mx^2+n, & x<0\\ nx+m, & 0\le x\le 1\\ nx^2+m, & x>1\end{cases}$$

Sol. Given, $f(x)=\begin{cases}mx^2+n, & x<0\\ nx+m, & 0\le x\le 1\\ nx^2+m, & x>1\end{cases}$

Limit at x = 0

LHL $= \lim_{x\to 0^-} f(x) = \lim_{x\to 0^-} mx^2+n$

$= \lim_{h\to 0} m(0-h)^2+n$

[putting $x=0-h$ and as $x\to 0^-$, then $h\to 0$]

$=n$

RHL $= \lim_{x\to 0^+} f(x) = \lim_{x\to 0^+} nx+m$

$= \lim_{h\to 0} n(0+h)+m = m$

[putting $x=0+h$ and as $x\to 0^+$, then $h\to 0$]

Now, for $\lim_{x\to 0} f(x)$ to be exists.

LHL = RHL $\Rightarrow$ $n=m$

Hence, $\lim_{x\to 0} f(x)$ exist when $m=n$

Limit at $x=1$

Here, LHL $= \lim_{x \to 1^-} f(x) = \lim_{x \to 1^-} (nx+m)$

$= \lim_{h \to 0} [n(1-h)+m]$

[putting $x = 1-h$ and as $x \to 1^-$, then $h \to 0$]

$= n+m$

RHL $= \lim_{x \to 1^+} f(x) = \lim_{x \to 1^+} (nx^2+m)$

$= \lim_{h \to 0} n(1+h)^2 + m$

[putting $x = 1+h$ and as $x \to 1^+$, then $h \to 0$]

$= n+m$

Now, for $\lim_{x \to 1} f(x)$ to be exists,

$\lim_{x \to 1^+} f(x) = \lim_{x \to 1^-} f(x)$

$\Rightarrow$ $n+m = n+m$, which is true for all $n, m \in Z$.

Hence, $\lim_{x \to 1} f(x)$ exists for all $n, m \in Z$.

EXAMPLE 9. If $f(x) = \begin{cases} |x|+1, & x<0 \\ 0, & x=0 \\ |x|-1, & x>0 \end{cases}$, for what value(s) of a does $\lim_{x \to a} f(x)$ exist?

Sol. We have, $f(x) = \begin{cases} -x+1, & x<0 \\ 0, & x=0 \\ x-1, & x>0 \end{cases}$ $\left[\because |x| = \begin{cases} x, \text{ if } x \ge 0 \\ -x, \text{ if } x<0 \end{cases}\right]$

***Case* I When $a = 0$**

In this case, LHL $= \lim_{h \to 0^-} f(x) = \lim_{h \to 0} f(0-h)$

$= \lim_{h \to 0} -(0-h)+1$

[$\because$ For $x<0$, $f(x) = -x+1$]

$= \lim_{h \to 0} (h+1) = \lim_{h \to 0} h + \lim_{h \to 0} 1$

$= 0+1 = 1$

and RHL $= \lim_{x \to 0^+} f(x)$

$= \lim_{h \to 0} f(0+h)$

$= \lim_{h \to 0} (0+h) - 1 = -1$

[$\because$ For $x>0$, $f(x) = x-1$]

$\because$ LHL $\neq$ RHL

$\therefore$ For $a=0$, $\lim_{x \to a} f(x)$ does not exists.

***Case* II When $a < 0$**

In this case, $\lim_{x \to a} f(x) = \lim_{x \to a} (-x+1)$

[$\because$ For $x<0$, $f(x) = -x+1$]

$= -a+1$,

which is a fixed real number.

$\therefore$ For $a<0$, $\lim_{x \to a} f(x)$ exists.

***Case* III When $a > 0$**

In this case, $\lim_{x \to a} f(x) = \lim_{x \to a} (x-1)$

[$\because$ For $x>0$, $f(x) = x-1$]

$= a-1$, which is a fixed real number.

$\therefore$ For $a>0$, $\lim_{x \to a} f(x)$ exists.

Hence, from case I, II and III, we conclude that $\lim_{x \to a} f(x)$ exists for all $a \neq 0$.

Topic Practice 1

1 Find

(i) $\lim_{x \to 2^-} (x^2-x+1)$ (ii) $\lim_{x \to 2^+} \frac{x-3}{x^2+4}$

(iii) $\lim_{x \to 0^+} \frac{2}{x^{1/5}}$ (iv) $\lim_{x \to -8^+} \frac{2x}{x-8}$

(v) $\lim_{x \to 1^+} \frac{x^3+x-1}{x+1}$

2 Evaluate LHL and RHL of the $\lim_{x \to 0} \frac{|x|}{x}$.

3 Find the limits.

(i) $\lim_{x \to 1} [x^2-x-1]$ (ii) $\lim_{x \to 3} [x^2(x+1)]$

(iii) $\lim_{x \to -1} (1+x+x^2+\ldots+x^9)$

4 Evaluate $\lim_{x \to 1} [x-1]$, where [$\cdot$] is greatest integer function.

5 Evaluate the left hand and right hand limits of the following functions at $x=1$.

$$f(x) = \begin{cases} 5x-4, & \text{if } 0<x \le 1 \\ 4x^2-3x, & \text{if } 1<x<2 \end{cases}$$

Does $\lim_{x \to 1} f(x)$ exist?

6 Let $f(x) = \begin{cases} 2x+3, & \text{if } x \le 0 \\ 3(x+1), & \text{if } x>0 \end{cases}$, then evaluate

(i) $\lim_{x \to 0} f(x)$

(ii) $\lim_{x \to 1} f(x)$

7 Evaluate $\lim_{x \to 0} f(x)$, where $f(x) = \begin{cases} \frac{x}{|x|}, & x \neq 0 \\ 0, & x=0 \end{cases}$.

8 If $f(x)=\begin{cases}\dfrac{x-|x|}{x}, & \text{if } x\neq 0\\ 2, & \text{if } x=0\end{cases}$, then show that $\lim_{x\to 0} f(x)$ does not exist.

9 Show that $\lim_{x\to 4}\dfrac{|x-4|}{x-4}$ does not exist.

10 If $f(x)=\begin{cases}x+2, & x\le -1\\ cx^2, & x>-1\end{cases}$, then find c when $\lim_{x\to -1} f(x)$ exists.

11 Let $f(x)$ be a function defined by

$$f(x)=\begin{cases}6x-6, & \text{if } x\le 3\\ 2x-k, & \text{if } x>3\end{cases}$$

Find the value of k, if $\lim_{x\to 3} f(x)$ exists.

12 Suppose $f(x)=\begin{cases}a+bx, & x<1\\ 4, & x=1\\ b-ax, & x>1\end{cases}$, and if $\lim_{x\to 1} f(x)=f(1)$, then what are the possible values of a and b?

Hints & Solutions

1. (i) **Hint** $\lim_{x\to 2^-}(x^2-x+1)=\lim_{h\to 0}\{(2-h)^2-(2-h)+1\}$ **Ans.** 3

   (ii) Solve as part (i). **Ans.** $\dfrac{-1}{8}$

   (iii) Solve as part (i). **Ans.** ∞

   (iv) Solve as part (i). **Ans.** 1

   (v) Solve as part (i). **Ans.** $\dfrac{1}{2}$

2. **Hint** LHL $=\lim_{x\to 0^-}\dfrac{|x|}{x}=\dfrac{-x}{x}$ and RHL $=\lim_{x\to 0^+}\dfrac{|x|}{x}=\dfrac{x}{x}$

   Ans. LHL $=-1$ and RHL $=1$

3. (i) **Hint** $\lim_{x\to 1}[x^2-x-1]=[1^2-1-1]=-1$

   (ii) Solve as part (i). **Ans.** 36

   (iii) Solve as part (i). **Ans.** 0

4. **Hint** LHL $=\lim_{x\to 1^-}[x-1]=\lim_{h\to 0}[1-h-1]=\lim_{h\to 0}[-h]=-1$

   and RHL $=\lim_{x\to 1^+}[x-1]=\lim_{h\to 0}[1+h-1]=\lim_{h\to 0}[h]=0$

   Ans. Does not exist

5. **Hint** LHL $=\lim_{x\to 1^-}(5x-4)=\lim_{h\to 0}[5(1-h)-4]=1$

   and RHL $=\lim_{x\to 1^+}f(x)=\lim_{x\to 1^+}(4x^2-3x)$

   $=\lim_{h\to 0}[4(1+h)^2-3(1+h)]=1$

   Ans. $\lim_{x\to 1}f(x)$ exists and it is equal to 1.

6. (i) **Hint** LHL $=\lim_{x\to 0^-}(2x+3)=\lim_{h\to 0}[2(0-h)+3]=3$

   RHL $=\lim_{x\to 0^+}3(x+1)=\lim_{h\to 0}[3(0+h+1)]=3$ **Ans.** 3

   (ii) **Hint** $\lim_{x\to 1}f(x)=\lim_{x\to 1}3(x+1)$ **Ans.** 6

7. **Hint** LHL $=\lim_{x\to 0^-}f(x)=\lim_{h\to 0}f(0-h)$

   $=\lim_{h\to 0}\dfrac{(0-h)}{|0-h|}=\lim_{h\to 0}\dfrac{(0-h)}{-(0-h)}=-1$

   RHL $=\lim_{x\to 0^+}f(x)=\lim_{h\to 0}f(0+h)$

   $=\lim_{h\to 0}\dfrac{0+h}{|0+h|}=\lim_{h\to 0}\dfrac{0+h}{(0+h)}=1$

   Ans. At $x=0$, limit does not exist.

8. **Hint** LHL $=\lim_{x\to 0^-}f(x)$

   $=\lim_{x\to 0^-}\dfrac{x-|x|}{x}=\lim_{h\to 0}\dfrac{(0-h)-|0-h|}{(0-h)}$

   $=\lim_{h\to 0}\dfrac{-h-h}{-h}=2$

   and RHL $=\lim_{x\to 0^+}f(x)=\lim_{x\to 0^+}\dfrac{x-|x|}{x}$

   $=\lim_{h\to 0}\dfrac{(0+h)-|0+h|}{0+h}=0$

   Ans. $\lim_{x\to 0}f(x)$ does not exist.

9. **Hint** Given, $\lim_{x\to 4}\dfrac{|x-4|}{x-4}$

   LHL $=\lim_{x\to 4^-}\dfrac{-(x-4)}{x-4}=-1$ $\quad [\because |x-4|=-(x-4),\ x<4]$

   RHL $=\lim_{x\to 4^+}\dfrac{(x-4)}{x-4}=1$ $\quad [\because |x-4|=(x-4),\ x>4]$

10. **Hint** LHL $=\lim_{x\to -1^-}(x+2)=\lim_{h\to 0}(-1-h+2)=1$

    RHL $=\lim_{x\to -1^+}f(x)=\lim_{x\to -1^+}cx^2=\lim_{h\to 0}c(-1+h)^2$

    Ans. $c=1$

11. **Hint** We have, $f(x)=\begin{cases}6x-6, & \text{if } x\le 3\\ 2x-k, & \text{if } x>3\end{cases}$

    $\therefore$ LHL $=\lim_{x\to 3^-}f(x)=\lim_{x\to 3^-}(6x-6)$

    $=\lim_{h\to 0}[6(3-h)-6]=12$

    and RHL $=\lim_{x\to 3^+}f(x)=\lim_{x\to 3^+}(2x-k)$

    $=\lim_{h\to 0}[2(3+h)-k]=6-k$ **Ans.** $k=-6$

12. **Hint** LHL $=\lim_{x\to 1^-}(a+bx)=\lim_{h\to 0}[a+b(1-h)]=a+b$

    RHL $=\lim_{x\to 1^+}(b-ax)=\lim_{h\to 0}[b-a(1+h)]=b-a$

    $\because$ LHL $=$ RHL $=f(1)\Rightarrow a+b=b-a=4$

    Ans. $a=0$, $b=4$

Limits of Rational Functions

A function f is said to be a rational function, if $f(x) = \frac{g(x)}{h(x)}$, where $g(x)$ and $h(x)$ are polynomial functions such that $h(x) \neq 0$.

Then, $\lim_{x \to a} f(x) = \lim_{x \to a} \frac{g(x)}{h(x)} = \frac{\lim_{x \to a} g(x)}{\lim_{x \to a} h(x)} = \frac{g(a)}{h(a)}$

However, if $h(a) = 0$, then there are two cases arise,
(i) $g(a) \neq 0$ (ii) $g(a) = 0$.

In the first case, we say that the limit does not exist.

In the second case, we can find limit.

Limit of a rational function can be find with the help of following methods

Direct Substitution Method

In this method, we substitute the point, to which the variable tends to in the given limit. If it give us a real number, then the number so obtained is the limit of the function and if it does not give us a real number, then use other methods.

EXAMPLE 1. Find the limits of the following.

(i) $\lim_{x\to 2} \frac{x^2-4}{x+3}$ (ii) $\lim_{x\to -1} \frac{(x-1)^2+3x^2}{(x^4+1)^2}$

(iii) $\lim_{x\to 0} \frac{\sqrt{2+x}+\sqrt{2-x}}{2+x}$

Sol. (i) $\lim_{x\to 2} \frac{x^2-4}{x+3} = \frac{4-4}{2+3} = \frac{0}{5} = 0$ [here, $h(a) \neq 0$]

(ii) $\lim_{x\to -1} \frac{(x-1)^2+3x^2}{(x^4+1)^2} = \frac{(-1-1)^2+3(-1)^2}{((-1)^4+1)^2} = \frac{(-2)^2+3(1)}{(1+1)^2}$

$= \frac{4+3}{2^2} = \frac{7}{4}$

(iii) $\lim_{x\to 0} \frac{\sqrt{2+x}+\sqrt{2-x}}{2+x} = \frac{\sqrt{2+0}+\sqrt{2-0}}{2+0}$

$= \frac{\sqrt{2}+\sqrt{2}}{2} = \frac{2\sqrt{2}}{2} = \sqrt{2}$

EXAMPLE 2. Evaluate $\lim_{x \to 1} \frac{x-4}{3-\sqrt{13-x}}$.

Sol. $\lim_{x \to 1} \frac{x-4}{3-\sqrt{13-x}} = \frac{-3}{3-\sqrt{12}} = \frac{-3}{3-2\sqrt{3}} = \frac{-3(3+2\sqrt{3})}{(3-2\sqrt{3})(3+2\sqrt{3})}$

$= \frac{-3(3+2\sqrt{3})}{9-12} = \frac{-3(3+2\sqrt{3})}{-3} = 3+2\sqrt{3}$

Factorisation Method

Let $\lim_{x \to a} \frac{f(x)}{g(x)}$ reduces to the form $\frac{0}{0}$. When we substitute $x = a$, then we factorise $f(x)$ and $g(x)$ and then cancel out the common factor to evaluate the limit.

Useful Results

- $a^2 - b^2 = (a-b)(a+b)$
- $a^3 - b^3 = (a-b)(a^2+b^2+ab)$
- $a^3 + b^3 = (a+b)(a^2+b^2-ab)$
- $a^4 - b^4 = (a^2-b^2)(a^2+b^2) = (a-b)(a+b)(a^2+b^2)$
- If $f(a) = 0$, then $x - a$ is a factor of $f(x)$

EXAMPLE 3. Evaluate $L = \lim_{x \to 2} \frac{x^3-8}{(x-2)}$.

Sol. We have, $L = \lim_{x\to 2} \frac{x^3-8}{x-2}$.

Let $f(x) = x^3 - 8$ and $g(x) = x - 2$

Here, $\lim_{x\to 2} f(x) = \lim_{x\to 2} x^3 - 8 = 2^3 - 8 = 0$

and $\lim_{x\to 2} g(x) = \lim_{x\to 2} x - 2 = 2 - 2 = 0$

Thus, we get $\frac{0}{0}$ form.

Now, factorise $f(x)$ and $g(x)$ such that $(x-2)$ is a common factor.

Here, $f(x) = x^3 - 8 = (x^3 - 2^3)$

$= (x-2)(x^2+4+2x)$ and $g(x) = x - 2$

$\therefore \quad L = \lim_{x \to 2} \frac{(x-2)(x^2+4+2x)}{(x-2)}$

On cancelling the common factor $(x-2)$, we get

$L = \lim_{x \to 2} (x^2+4+2x)$

$= (2)^2 + 4 + 2(2) = 4 + 4 + 4 = 12$

Hence, $\lim_{x\to 2} \frac{x^3-8}{x-2} = 12$

EXAMPLE 4. Evaluate $\lim_{x \to 2} \left[\frac{x^2-4}{x^3-4x^2+4x}\right]$.

Sol. On putting $x = 2$, we get the form $\frac{0}{0}$.

So, let us first factorise it.

Consider, $\lim_{x \to 2} \frac{x^2 - 4}{x^3 - 4x^2 + 4x} = \lim_{x \to 2} \frac{(x+2)(x-2)}{x(x-2)^2}$

$= \lim_{x \to 2} \frac{(x+2)}{x(x-2)} = \frac{2+2}{2(2-2)} = \frac{4}{0}$

which is not defined.

$\therefore \lim_{x \to 2} \left[\frac{x^2 - 4}{x^3 - 4x^2 + 4x} \right]$ does not exist.

EXAMPLE 5. Evaluate $\lim_{x \to \sqrt{3}} \frac{x^2 - 3}{x^2 + 3\sqrt{3}\,x - 12}$.

Sol. $\lim_{x \to \sqrt{3}} \frac{x^2 - 3}{x^2 + 3\sqrt{3}\,x - 12} = \lim_{x \to \sqrt{3}} \frac{(x - \sqrt{3})(x + \sqrt{3})}{x^2 + 4\sqrt{3}x - \sqrt{3}x - 12}$

$= \lim_{x \to \sqrt{3}} \frac{(x - \sqrt{3})(x + \sqrt{3})}{(x + 4\sqrt{3})(x - \sqrt{3})}$

$= \lim_{x \to \sqrt{3}} \frac{(x + \sqrt{3})}{(x + 4\sqrt{3})}$

$= \frac{\sqrt{3} + \sqrt{3}}{\sqrt{3} + 4\sqrt{3}}$

$= \frac{2\sqrt{3}}{5\sqrt{3}} = \frac{2}{5}$

EXAMPLE 6. Evaluate $\lim_{x \to 1} \left(\frac{2}{1 - x^2} + \frac{1}{x - 1} \right)$.

Sol. We have,

$\lim_{x \to 1} \left(\frac{2}{1 - x^2} + \frac{1}{x - 1} \right) = \lim_{x \to 1} \left(\frac{2}{1 - x^2} - \frac{1}{1 - x} \right)$ $[\infty - \infty \text{ form}]$

$= \lim_{x \to 1} \frac{2 - (1 + x)}{1 - x^2}$ $\left[\frac{0}{0} \text{ form} \right]$

$= \lim_{x \to 1} \frac{1 - x}{1 - x^2} = \lim_{x \to 1} \frac{1}{1 + x} = \frac{1}{2}.$

EXAMPLE 7. Evaluate $\lim_{x \to 1} \left[\frac{x - 2}{x^2 - x} - \frac{1}{x^3 - 3x^2 + 2x} \right]$.

Sol. Here, $\left[\frac{x - 2}{x^2 - x} - \frac{1}{x^3 - 3x^2 + 2x} \right]$

$= \left[\frac{x - 2}{x(x - 1)} - \frac{1}{x(x^2 - 3x + 2)} \right]$

$= \left[\frac{x - 2}{x(x - 1)} - \frac{1}{x(x - 1)(x - 2)} \right]$

$= \frac{(x - 2)^2 - 1}{x(x - 1)(x - 2)} = \left[\frac{x^2 - 4x + 4 - 1}{x(x - 1)(x - 2)} \right]$

$= \left[\frac{x^2 - 4x + 3}{x(x - 1)(x - 2)} \right] = \frac{(x - 3)(x - 1)}{x(x - 1)(x - 2)}$

$\therefore \lim_{x \to 1} \left[\frac{x^2 - 2}{x^2 - x} - \frac{1}{x^3 - 3x^2 + 2x} \right]$

$= \lim_{x \to 1} \frac{(x - 3)(x - 1)}{x(x - 1)(x - 2)}$

$= \lim_{x \to 1} \frac{x - 3}{x(x - 2)} = \frac{1 - 3}{1(1 - 2)} = \frac{-2}{-1} = 2$

EXAMPLE 8. Prove that $\lim_{x \to 2} \frac{3^x + 3^{3-x} - 12}{3^{3-x} - 3^{x/2}} = -\frac{4}{3}$.

Sol. We have, $\lim_{x \to 2} \frac{3^x + 3^{3-x} - 12}{3^{3-x} - 3^{x/2}} = \lim_{x \to 2} \frac{(3^x)^2 - 12(3^x) + 27}{3^3 - (3^{x/2})^3}$

$= \lim_{x \to 2} \frac{(3^x - 3)(3^x - 9)}{(3 - 3^{x/2})(9 + 3 \times 3^{x/2} + 3^x)}$

$[\because a^3 - b^3 = (a - b)(a^2 + ab + b^2)]$

$= -\lim_{x \to 2} \frac{(3^x - 3)(3^{x/2} - 3)(3^{x/2} + 3)}{(3^{x/2} - 3)(3^x + 3 \times 3^{x/2} + 9)}$

$= -\lim_{x \to 2} \frac{(3^x - 3)(3^{x/2} + 3)}{(3^x + 3 \times 3^{x/2} + 9)}$

$= -\frac{(9 - 3)(3 + 3)}{(9 + 9 + 9)} = -\frac{6 \times 6}{27} = -\frac{4}{3}$ **Hence proved.**

Rationalisation Method

If we get $\frac{0}{0}$ form and numerator or denominator or both have radical sign, then we rationalise the numerator or denominator or both by multiplying their conjugate to remove $\frac{0}{0}$ form and then find limit by direct substitution method.

EXAMPLE 9. Evaluate $\lim_{x \to 0} \frac{\sqrt{2 + x} - \sqrt{2}}{x}$.

Sol. When $x = 0$, then the expression $\frac{\sqrt{2 + x} - \sqrt{2}}{x}$ becomes of the form $\frac{0}{0}$.

So, we will rationalising the numerator by multiplying and dividing its conjugate i.e. $\sqrt{2 + x} + \sqrt{2}$.

$\therefore \lim_{x \to 0} \frac{\sqrt{2 + x} - \sqrt{2}}{x} = \lim_{x \to 0} \frac{(\sqrt{2 + x} - \sqrt{2})(\sqrt{2 + x} + \sqrt{2})}{x(\sqrt{2 + x} + \sqrt{2})}$

$= \lim_{x \to 0} \frac{2 + x - 2}{x(\sqrt{2 + x} + \sqrt{2})}$

$= \lim_{x \to 0} \frac{1}{\sqrt{2 + x} + \sqrt{2}} = \frac{1}{2\sqrt{2}}$

[using direct substitution method]

EXAMPLE 10. Evaluate $\lim_{x \to a} \frac{\sqrt{a+2x}-\sqrt{3x}}{\sqrt{3a+x}-2\sqrt{x}}$.

Sol. We have, $\lim_{x \to a} \frac{\sqrt{a+2x}-\sqrt{3x}}{\sqrt{3a+x}-2\sqrt{x}}$

$$= \lim_{x \to a} \frac{\sqrt{a+2x}-\sqrt{3x}}{\sqrt{3a+x}-2\sqrt{x}} \times \frac{\sqrt{a+2x}+\sqrt{3x}}{\sqrt{a+2x}+\sqrt{3x}}$$

[multiplying numerator and denominator by $\sqrt{a+2x}+\sqrt{3x}$]

$$= \lim_{x \to a} \frac{a+2x-3x}{(\sqrt{3a+x}-2\sqrt{x})(\sqrt{a+2x}+\sqrt{3x})}$$

$[\because (A-B)(A+B) = A^2 - B^2]$

$$= \lim_{x \to a} \frac{(a-x)(\sqrt{3a+x}+2\sqrt{x})}{(\sqrt{a+2x}+\sqrt{3x})(\sqrt{3a+x}-2\sqrt{x})(\sqrt{3a+x}+2\sqrt{x})}$$

[multiplying numerator and denominator by $\sqrt{3a+x}+2\sqrt{x}$]

$$= \lim_{x \to a} \frac{(a-x)[\sqrt{3a+x}+2\sqrt{x}]}{(\sqrt{a+2x}+\sqrt{3x})(3a+x-4x)}$$

$$= \lim_{x \to a} \frac{(a-x)(\sqrt{3a+x}+2\sqrt{x})}{(\sqrt{a+2x}+\sqrt{3x})(3a-3x)}$$

$$= \frac{\sqrt{3a+a}+2\sqrt{a}}{3(\sqrt{a+2a}+\sqrt{3a})}$$

$$= \frac{4\sqrt{a}}{3 \times 2\sqrt{3}\sqrt{a}} = \frac{2}{3\sqrt{3}} = \frac{2\sqrt{3}}{9}$$

EXAMPLE 11. Evaluate $\lim_{x \to 1} \frac{(2x-3)(\sqrt{x}-1)}{2x^2+x-3}$.

Sol. When $x = 1$, the expression $\frac{(2x-3)(\sqrt{x}-1)}{2x^2+x-3}$ becomes of the form $\frac{0}{0}$.

So, rationalising $(\sqrt{x}-1)$ in the numerator. by multiplying and dividing its conjugate i.e. $\sqrt{x}+1$.

We have, $\lim_{x \to 1} \frac{(2x-3)(\sqrt{x}-1)}{2x^2+x-3}$

$$= \lim_{x \to 1} \frac{(2x-3)(\sqrt{x}-1)(\sqrt{x}+1)}{(\sqrt{x}+1)(2x^2+x-3)}$$

$$= \lim_{x \to 1} \frac{(2x-3)(x-1)}{(\sqrt{x}+1)(2x^2+x-3)} \quad \left[\frac{0}{0}\text{ form}\right]$$

$$= \lim_{x \to 1} \frac{(2x-3)(x-1)}{(\sqrt{x}+1)(2x+3)(x-1)}$$

$$= \lim_{x \to 1} \frac{2x-3}{(\sqrt{x}+1)(2x+3)} = -\frac{1}{10}$$

By Using Some Standard Limits

Theorem Let n be any positive integer.

Then, $\lim_{x \to a} \frac{x^n - a^n}{x - a} = n\,a^{n-1}$

The expression in the above theorem for the limit is true even if n is any rational number and a is positive.

- $\lim_{x \to a} \alpha = \alpha$, where $\alpha \in R$
- $\lim_{x \to a} x^n = a^n \ \forall\ n \in N$
- $\lim_{x \to a} f(x) = f(a)$, where $f(x)$ is a polynomial in x.
- $\lim_{x \to a} |x| = |a|$

EXAMPLE 12. Evaluate $\lim_{x \to 2} \frac{x^{10}-1024}{x-2}$.

Sol. When $x = 2$, the expression $\frac{x^{10}-1024}{x-2}$ becomes of the form $\frac{0}{0}$.

Now, $\lim_{x \to 2} \frac{x^{10}-1024}{x-2} = \lim_{x \to 2} \frac{x^{10}-2^{10}}{x-2}$

$$= 10(2^{10-1}) = 5120$$

EXAMPLE 13. Evaluate $\lim_{x \to 2} \frac{x-2}{\sqrt[3]{x}-\sqrt[3]{2}}$.

Sol. $\lim_{x \to 2} \frac{x-2}{x^{1/3}-2^{1/3}} = \frac{1}{\lim_{x \to 2} \frac{x^{1/3}-2^{1/3}}{x-2}}$

$$= \frac{1}{\frac{1}{3}(2^{1/3-1})} = \frac{1}{\frac{1}{3} \times (2^{-2/3})} = 3(2^{2/3})$$

EXAMPLE 14. Find all the possible values of a, if

$$\lim_{x \to a} \frac{x^9 - a^9}{x - a} = \lim_{x \to 5} (4 + x).$$

Sol. We have, $\lim_{x \to a} \frac{x^9 - a^9}{x - a} = \lim_{x \to 5} (4 + x)$ ...(i)

Now, $\lim_{x \to a} \frac{x^9 - a^9}{x - a} = 9(a)^{9-1} = 9a^8$

$\left[\because \lim_{x \to a} \frac{x^n - a^n}{x - a} = na^{n-1}\right]$

and $\lim_{x \to 5} (4 + x) = 4 + 5 = 9$

From Eq. (i), $9a^8 = 9$

$\Rightarrow a^8 = 1 \Rightarrow a = \pm 1$

EXAMPLE 15. Evaluate $\lim\limits_{x \to 2} \dfrac{x^5 - 32}{x^3 - 8}$.

Sol. $\lim\limits_{x \to 2} \dfrac{x^5 - 32}{x^3 - 8} = \lim\limits_{x \to 2} \dfrac{x^5 - 2^5}{x^3 - 2^3}$ $\quad [\because 2^5 = 32 \text{ and } 2^3 = 8]$

$$= \lim_{x \to 2} \frac{\dfrac{x^5 - 2^5}{x - 2}}{\dfrac{x^3 - 2^3}{x - 2}}$$

[dividing numerator and denominator by $(x - 2)$]

$$= \lim_{x \to 2} \frac{x^5 - 2^5}{x - 2} \div \lim_{x \to 2} \frac{x^3 - 2^3}{x - 2}$$

$$\left[\because \lim_{x \to a} \frac{f(x)}{g(x)} = \lim_{x \to a} f(x) \div \lim_{x \to a} g(x)\right]$$

$$= 5 \times 2^{5-1} \div 3 \times 2^{3-1}$$

$$\left[\because \lim_{x \to a} \frac{x^n - a^n}{x - a} = na^{n-1}\right]$$

$$= 5 \times 2^4 \div 3 \times 2^2 = \frac{5 \times 2^4}{3 \times 2^2}$$

$$= \frac{5}{3} \times 2^2 = \frac{5}{3} \times 4 = \frac{20}{3}$$

EXAMPLE 16. If $\lim\limits_{x \to 1} \dfrac{x^4 - 1}{x - 1} = \lim\limits_{x \to k} \dfrac{x^3 - k^3}{x^2 - k^2}$, then find the value of k.

Sol. Given, $\lim\limits_{x \to 1} \dfrac{x^4 - 1}{x - 1} = \lim\limits_{x \to k} \dfrac{x^3 - k^3}{x^2 - k^2}$

$$\Rightarrow 4(1)^{4-1} = \lim_{x \to k} \frac{\dfrac{x^3 - k^3}{x - k}}{\dfrac{x^2 - k^2}{x - k}} \quad \left[\because \lim_{x \to a} \frac{x^n - a^n}{x - a} = na^{n-1}\right]$$

$$\Rightarrow 4 = \frac{\lim\limits_{x \to k} \dfrac{x^3 - k^3}{x - k}}{\lim\limits_{x \to k} \dfrac{x^2 - k^2}{x - k}} \quad \left[\because \lim_{x \to a} \frac{f(x)}{g(x)} = \frac{\lim\limits_{x \to a} f(x)}{\lim\limits_{x \to a} g(x)}\right]$$

$$\Rightarrow 4 = \frac{3k^2}{2k} \Rightarrow 4 = \frac{3}{2}k,$$

$$\therefore k = \frac{4 \times 2}{3} = \frac{8}{3}$$

EXAMPLE 17. Evaluate $\lim\limits_{x \to 1} \dfrac{x^7 - 2x^5 + 1}{x^3 - 3x^2 + 2}$.

Sol. $\lim\limits_{x \to 1} \dfrac{x^7 - 2x^5 + 1}{x^3 - 3x^2 + 2}$ $\quad \left[\dfrac{0}{0} \text{ from}\right]$

$$= \lim_{x \to 1} \frac{x^7 - x^5 - x^5 + 1}{x^3 - x^2 - 2x^2 + 2} = \lim_{x \to 1} \frac{x^5(x^2 - 1) - 1(x^5 - 1)}{x^2(x - 1) - 2(x^2 - 1)}$$

[dividing numerator and denominator by $(x - 1)$]

$$= \lim_{x \to 1} \frac{\dfrac{x^5(x^2 - 1)}{(x - 1)} - \dfrac{1(x^5 - 1)}{(x - 1)}}{\dfrac{x^2(x - 1)}{(x - 1)} - \dfrac{2(x^2 - 1)}{(x - 1)}}$$

$$= \frac{\lim\limits_{x \to 1} x^5(x + 1) - \lim\limits_{x \to 1} \left(\dfrac{x^5 - 1}{x - 1}\right)}{\lim\limits_{x \to 1} x^2 - 2 \lim\limits_{x \to 1} (x + 1)}$$

$$= \frac{1 \times 2 - 5 \times (1)^4}{1 - 2 \times 2} = \frac{2 - 5}{1 - 4} = \frac{-3}{-3} = 1$$

EXAMPLE 18. Find the limit $\lim\limits_{x \to 0} \dfrac{\sqrt{1 + x} - 1}{x}$.

Sol. Put $y = 1 + x$, then $y \to 1$ as $x \to 0$

$$\therefore \lim_{x \to 0} \frac{\sqrt{1 + x} - 1}{x} = \lim_{y \to 1} \frac{\sqrt{y} - 1}{y - 1} \quad [\because x + 1 = y \Rightarrow x = y - 1]$$

$$= \lim_{y \to 1} \frac{y^{\frac{1}{2}} - 1^{\frac{1}{2}}}{y - 1} = \frac{1}{2}(1)^{\frac{1}{2} - 1}$$

$$\left[\because \lim_{x \to a} \frac{x^n - a^n}{x - a} = na^{n-1}\right]$$

$$= \frac{1}{2}$$

EXAMPLE 19. Evaluate $\lim\limits_{x \to a} \dfrac{(x + 2)^{3/2} - (a + 2)^{3/2}}{x - a}$.

Sol. Let $x + 2 = y$, then $y \to a + 2$ as $x \to a$

$$\therefore \lim_{x \to a} \frac{(x + 2)^{3/2} - (a + 2)^{3/2}}{x - a}$$

$$= \lim_{y \to (a + 2)} \frac{y^{3/2} - (a + 2)^{3/2}}{y - (a + 2)} \quad [\because x + 2 = y \Rightarrow x = y - 2]$$

$$= \frac{3}{2}(a + 2)^{\frac{3}{2} - 1} = \frac{3}{2}(a + 2)^{1/2} \quad \left[\because \lim_{x \to a} \frac{x^n - a^n}{x - a} = na^{n-1}\right]$$

EXAMPLE 20. Evaluate $\lim\limits_{x \to 0} \dfrac{(1 + x)^6 - 1}{(1 + x)^2 - 1}$.

Sol. Put $1 + x = y$, then $y \to 1$ as $x \to 0$

$$\therefore \lim_{x \to 0} \frac{(1 + x)^6 - 1}{(1 + x)^2 - 1} = \lim_{y \to 1} \frac{y^6 - 1}{y^2 - 1} = \lim_{y \to 1} \left(\frac{\dfrac{y^6 - 1}{y - 1}}{\dfrac{y^2 - 1}{y - 1}}\right)$$

[dividing numerator and denominator by $y - 1$]

$$= \lim_{y \to 1} \frac{y^6 - 1}{y - 1} \div \lim_{y \to 1} \frac{y^2 - 1}{y - 1}$$

$$= \frac{6(1)^{6-1}}{2(1)^{2-1}} = \frac{6}{2} = 3 \quad \left[\because \lim_{x \to a} \frac{x^n - a^n}{x - a} = na^{n-1}\right]$$

EXAMPLE 21. Evaluate $\lim_{x \to 2} \frac{(2x+4)^{1/3} - 2}{x-2}$.

Sol. Put $2x + 4 = y$, then $y \to 8$ as $x \to 2$

$$\therefore \lim_{x \to 2} \frac{(2x+4)^{1/3} - 2}{x-2} = \lim_{y \to 8} \frac{y^{1/3} - 2}{\frac{y-4}{2} - 2} \quad \left[\because 2x+4 = y \Rightarrow x = \frac{y-4}{2}\right]$$

$$= 2 \lim_{y \to 8} \frac{y^{1/3} - (8)^{1/3}}{y - 4 - 4} \quad [\because 2 = (8)^{1/3}]$$

$$= 2 \lim_{y \to 8} \frac{y^{1/3} - 8^{1/3}}{y - 8}$$

$$= 2 \cdot \frac{1}{3} (8)^{\frac{1}{3} - 1} \quad \left[\because \lim_{x \to a} \frac{x^n - a^n}{x - a} = na^{n-1}\right]$$

$$= 2 \cdot \frac{1}{3} (2^3)^{-\frac{2}{3}}$$

$$= \frac{2}{3} \cdot (2)^{-2} = \frac{2}{3} \times \frac{1}{4} = \frac{1}{6}$$

Method of Evaluation of Algebraic Limit at Infinity

$\lim_{x \to \infty} \frac{f(x)}{g(x)}$ reduces to the form $\frac{\infty}{\infty}$, when we substitute $x = \infty$.

Method to determine the limit at infinity are as follows

I. Write down the given expression in the form of a rational function, i.e. $\frac{f(x)}{g(x)}$, if it is not so.

II. If n is the highest degree of x in both numerator and denominator, then divide each term in numerator and denominator by x^n.

III. Use the results

$$\lim_{x \to \infty} \frac{k}{x^n} = 0 \text{ and } \lim_{x \to \infty} k = k, \text{ when } n > 0.$$

EXAMPLE 22. Evaluate $\lim_{x \to \infty} \frac{ax^2 + bx + c}{dx^2 + ex + f}$.

Sol. We have, $\lim_{x \to \infty} \frac{ax^2 + bx + c}{dx^2 + ex + f} = \lim_{x \to \infty} \frac{a + \frac{b}{x} + \frac{c}{x^2}}{d + \frac{e}{x} + \frac{f}{x^2}}$

[$\because$ dividing numerator and denominator by x^2]

$$= \frac{a+0+0}{d+0+0} = \frac{a}{d}$$

EXAMPLE 23. Evaluate $\lim_{x \to \infty} \frac{5x^3 - 6}{\sqrt{9 + 4x^6}}$.

Sol. We have, $\lim_{x \to \infty} \frac{5x^3 - 6}{\sqrt{9 + 4x^6}}$

$$= \lim_{x \to \infty} \frac{5 - \frac{6}{x^3}}{\sqrt{\frac{9}{x^6} + 4}}$$

[$\because$ dividing numerator and denominator by x^3]

$$= \frac{5-0}{\sqrt{0+4}} = \frac{5}{2}$$

EXAMPLE 24. Evaluate $\lim_{x \to \infty} (\sqrt{x^2 + 7x} - x)$.

Sol. We have, $\lim_{x \to \infty} (\sqrt{x^2 + 7x} - x)$

$$= \lim_{x \to \infty} (\sqrt{x^2 + 7x} - x) \times \frac{(\sqrt{x^2 + 7x} + x)}{(\sqrt{x^2 + 7x} + x)}$$

$$= \lim_{x \to \infty} \frac{x^2 + 7x - x^2}{\sqrt{x^2 + 7x} + x}$$

$$= \lim_{x \to \infty} \frac{7x}{\sqrt{x^2 + 7x} + x}$$

$$= \lim_{x \to \infty} \frac{7}{\sqrt{1 + \frac{7}{x}} + 1}$$

[$\because$ dividing numerator and denominator by x]

$$= \frac{7}{\sqrt{1+0} + 1} = \frac{7}{2}$$

EXAMPLE 25. Evaluate $\lim_{n \to \infty} \frac{n^2}{1 + 2 + 3 + \ldots + n}$.

Sol. We have, $\lim_{n \to \infty} \frac{n^2}{1 + 2 + 3 + \ldots + n}$

$$= \lim_{n \to \infty} \frac{n^2}{\left(\frac{n(n+1)}{2}\right)} \quad \left[\because 1 + 2 + 3 + \ldots + n = \frac{n(n+1)}{2}\right]$$

$$= \lim_{n \to \infty} \frac{2n}{n+1}$$

$$= \lim_{n \to \infty} \frac{2}{1 + \frac{1}{n}}$$

[$\because$ dividing numerator and denominator by n]

$$= \frac{2}{1+0} = 2$$

Topic Practice 2

1 Evaluate the following limits.

(i) $\lim_{x\to 0}\dfrac{ax+b}{cx+1}$ (ii) $\lim_{x\to 2}\dfrac{x^2-4}{x+3}$

(iii) $\lim_{x\to 3}\dfrac{\sqrt{2x+3}}{x+3}$ (iv) $\lim_{x\to -1}\dfrac{x^{10}+x^5+1}{x-1}$

(v) $\lim_{x\to 1}\dfrac{ax^2+bx+c}{cx^2+bx+a}, a+b+c\neq 0$

2 Evaluate the following limits.

(i) $\lim_{x\to 2}\dfrac{x^2-4}{x-2}$ (ii) $\lim_{x\to -2}\dfrac{\frac{1}{x}+\frac{1}{2}}{x+2}$

(iii) $\lim_{x\to 2}\dfrac{x^2-3x+2}{x^2+x-6}$ (iv) $\lim_{x\to 5}\dfrac{x^2-9x+20}{x^2-6x+5}$

(v) $\lim_{x\to 1}\dfrac{x^3-1}{x-1}$ (vi) $\lim_{x\to\sqrt{2}}\dfrac{x^4-4}{x^2+3\sqrt{2}x-8}$

(vii) $\lim_{x\to 3}\dfrac{x^4-81}{2x^2-5x-3}$ (viii) $\lim_{x\to 2}\dfrac{3x^2-x-10}{x^2-4}$

(ix) $\lim_{x\to 2}\dfrac{x^3-7x^2+14x-8}{x^2+2x-8}$

(x) $\lim_{x\to 2}\left[\dfrac{1}{x-2}-\dfrac{2(2x-3)}{x^3-3x^2+2x}\right]$

(xi) $\lim_{x\to 1}\left(\dfrac{x^4-3x^2+2}{x^3-5x^2+3x+1}\right)$

3 Evaluate the following limits.

(i) $\lim_{x\to 0}\dfrac{\sqrt{a+x}-\sqrt{a}}{x\sqrt{a^2+ax}}$ (ii) $\lim_{x\to 0}\dfrac{\sqrt{1+x^3}-\sqrt{1-x^3}}{x^2}$

(iii) $\lim_{x\to 1}\dfrac{(\sqrt{3+x}-\sqrt{5-x})}{x^2-1}$

(iv) $\lim_{x\to 0}\dfrac{(\sqrt{1+x+x^2}-\sqrt{x+1})}{2x^2}$

(v) $\lim_{x\to 0}\left(\dfrac{\sqrt{1+x^2}-\sqrt{1+x}}{\sqrt{1+x^3}-\sqrt{1+x}}\right)$

4 Evaluate the following limits.

(i) $\lim_{x\to b}\dfrac{x^{5/2}-b^{5/2}}{x-b}$ (ii) $\lim_{x\to 3}\dfrac{x^4-81}{x-3}$

(iii) $\lim_{x\to b}\dfrac{\sqrt{x}-\sqrt{b}}{x-b}$ (iv) $\lim_{h\to 0}\dfrac{\sqrt{x+h}-\sqrt{x}}{h}$

(v) $\lim_{x\to -1}\dfrac{x^3+1}{x^5+1}$ (vi) $\lim_{x\to 1}\dfrac{x^{15}-1}{x^{10}-1}$

(vii) $\lim_{x\to 0}\dfrac{(1+x)^n-1}{x}$ (viii) $\lim_{x\to 1}\dfrac{x^m-1}{x^n-1}$

(ix) $\lim_{x\to b}\dfrac{(x+3)^{5/2}-(b+3)^{5/2}}{x-b}$

5 Find n, $\lim_{x\to 2}\dfrac{x^n-2^n}{x-2}=80, n\in N$.

6 If $\lim_{x\to b}\dfrac{x^3-b^3}{x-b}=\lim_{x\to 1}\dfrac{x^4-1}{x-1}$, find all possible values of b.

7 If $\lim_{x\to a}\dfrac{x^8-a^8}{x-a}=\lim_{x\to 4}(4+x)$, find all possible value of a.

8 Evaluate the following.

(i) $\lim_{x\to\infty}\dfrac{3x^3-4x^2+6x-1}{2x^3+x^2-5x+7}$ (ii) $\lim_{x\to\infty}\dfrac{5x-6}{\sqrt{4x^2+9}}$

(iii) $\lim_{x\to\infty}(\sqrt{x^2+cx}-x)$ (iv) $\lim_{n\to\infty}\dfrac{1^3+2^3+\ldots+n^3}{(n-1)^4}$

Hints & Solutions

1. Do same as Example 1.

Ans. (i) b (ii) 0 (iii) $\frac{1}{2}$ (iv) $-\frac{1}{2}$ (v) 1

2. (i) **Hint** $\lim_{x\to 2}\dfrac{x^2-4}{x-2}=\lim_{x\to 2}\dfrac{(x-2)(x+2)}{(x-2)}=\lim_{x\to 2}(x+2)$

Ans. 4

(ii) **Hint** $\lim_{x\to -2}\dfrac{\frac{1}{x}+\frac{1}{2}}{x+2}=\lim_{x\to -2}\dfrac{(2+x)}{2x(x+2)}$ **Ans.** $-\frac{1}{4}$

(iii) **Hint** $\lim_{x\to 2}\dfrac{x^2-3x+2}{x^2+x-6}=\lim_{x\to 2}\dfrac{(x-2)(x-1)}{(x-2)(x+3)}$ **Ans.** $\frac{1}{5}$

(iv) **Hint** Given limit $=\lim_{x\to 5}\dfrac{(x-4)(x-5)}{(x-1)(x-5)}$ **Ans.** $\frac{1}{4}$

(v) **Hint** $\lim_{x\to 1}\dfrac{x^3-1}{x-1}=\lim_{x\to 1}\dfrac{(x-1)(x^2+x+1)}{(x-1)}$ **Ans.** 3

(vi) **Hint** $\lim_{x\to\sqrt{2}}\dfrac{x^4-4}{x^2+3\sqrt{2}x-8}$

$=\lim_{x\to\sqrt{2}}\dfrac{(x+\sqrt{2})(x-\sqrt{2})(x^2+2)}{(x-\sqrt{2})(x+4\sqrt{2})}$

Ans. $\frac{8}{5}$

(vii) **Hint** $\lim_{x\to 3}\frac{x^4-81}{2x^2-5x-3}=\lim_{x\to 3}\frac{(x-3)(x+3)(x^2+9)}{(x-3)(2x+1)}$

Ans. $\frac{108}{7}$

(viii) **Hint** $\lim_{x\to 2}\frac{3x^2-x-10}{x^2-4}=\lim_{x\to 2}\frac{(x-2)(3x+5)}{(x-2)(x+2)}$ **Ans.** $\frac{11}{4}$

(ix) **Hint** Given limit $=\lim_{x\to 2}\frac{(x-1)(x-2)(x-4)}{(x-2)(x+4)}$ **Ans.** $-\frac{1}{3}$

(x) **Hint** Given limit $=\lim_{x\to 2}\left[\frac{1}{x-2}-\frac{2(2x-3)}{x(x-1)(x-2)}\right]$

$=\lim_{x\to 2}\left[\frac{x^2-5x+6}{x(x-1)(x-2)}\right]=\lim_{x\to 2}\left[\frac{(x-2)(x-3)}{x(x-1)(x-2)}\right]$ **Ans.** $\frac{-1}{2}$

(xi) **Hint** Given limit $=\lim_{x\to 1}\frac{(x-1)(x+1)(x^2-2)}{(x-1)(x^2-4x-1)}$ **Ans.** $\frac{1}{2}$

3. (i) **Hint** Given limit $=\lim_{x\to 0}\frac{\sqrt{a+x}-\sqrt{a}}{x\sqrt{a^2+ax}}\times\frac{\sqrt{a+x}+\sqrt{a}}{\sqrt{a+x}+\sqrt{a}}$

$=\lim_{x\to 0}\frac{x}{x(\sqrt{a^2+ax})(\sqrt{a+x}+\sqrt{a})}$ **Ans.** $\frac{1}{2a\sqrt{a}}$

(ii) **Hint** Given limit

$=\lim_{x\to 0}\frac{\sqrt{1+x^3}-\sqrt{1-x^3}}{x^2}\cdot\frac{\sqrt{1+x^3}+\sqrt{1-x^3}}{\sqrt{1+x^3}+\sqrt{1-x^3}}$

$=\lim_{x\to 0}\frac{(1+x^3)-(1-x^3)}{x^2(\sqrt{1+x^3}+\sqrt{1-x^3})}$

$=\lim_{x\to 0}\frac{2x^3}{x^2(\sqrt{1+x^3}+\sqrt{1-x^3})}$ **Ans.** 0

(iii) **Hint** Given limit

$=\lim_{x\to 1}\frac{(\sqrt{3+x}-\sqrt{5-x})}{(x-1)(x+1)}\times\frac{(\sqrt{3+x}+\sqrt{5-x})}{(\sqrt{3+x}+\sqrt{5-x})}$

$=\lim_{x\to 1}\frac{2x-2}{(x-1)(x+1)(\sqrt{3+x}+\sqrt{5-x})}$ **Ans.** $\frac{1}{4}$

(iv) **Hint** Multiplying numerator and denominator by $\sqrt{1+x+x^2}+\sqrt{x+1}$ **Ans.** $\frac{1}{4}$

(v) **Hint** Given limit

$=\lim_{x\to 0}\left\{\frac{\sqrt{1+x^2}-\sqrt{1+x}}{(\sqrt{1+x^3}-\sqrt{1+x})}\times\frac{(\sqrt{1+x^3}+\sqrt{1+x})}{(\sqrt{1+x^3}+\sqrt{1+x})}\times\frac{(\sqrt{1+x^2}+\sqrt{1+x})}{(\sqrt{1+x^2}+\sqrt{1+x})}\right.$

$=\lim_{x\to 0}\frac{\{(1+x^2)-(1+x)\}\times(\sqrt{1+x^3}+\sqrt{1+x})}{\{(1+x^3)-(1+x)\}\times(\sqrt{1+x^2}+\sqrt{1+x})}$

$=\lim_{x\to 0}\frac{x(x-1)(\sqrt{1+x^3}+\sqrt{1+x})}{x(x-1)(x+1)(\sqrt{1+x^2}+\sqrt{1+x})}$ **Ans.** 1

4. (i) **Hint** $\lim_{x\to b}\frac{x^{5/2}-b^{5/2}}{x-b}=\frac{5}{2}(b)^{5/2-1}$ **Ans.** $\frac{5}{2}b^{3/2}$

(ii) **Hint** $\lim_{x\to 3}\frac{x^4-81}{x-3}=\lim_{x\to 3}\frac{x^4-3^4}{x-3}=4(3)^{4-1}$

Ans. 108

(iii) **Hint** $\lim_{x\to b}\frac{\sqrt{x}-\sqrt{b}}{x-b}=\lim_{x\to 0}\frac{(x)^{1/2}-(b)^{1/2}}{x-b}$

$=\frac{1}{2}(b)^{1/2-1}$ **Ans.** $\frac{1}{2\sqrt{b}}$

(iv) **Hint** Put $x+h=y$, then $y\to x$ as $h\to 0$.

Now, $\lim_{h\to 0}\frac{(x+h)^{1/2}-(x)^{1/2}}{h}$

$=\lim_{y\to x}\frac{y^{1/2}-(x)^{1/2}}{y-x}=\frac{1}{2}x^{\frac{1}{2}-1}$ **Ans.** $\frac{1}{2\sqrt{x}}$

(v) **Hint** $\lim_{x\to -1}\frac{x^3+1}{x^5+1}=\lim_{x\to -1}\frac{\frac{x^3+1}{(x+1)}}{\frac{x^5+1}{x+1}}$

$=\lim_{x\to -1}\frac{x^3+1}{x+1}\div\lim_{x\to -1}\frac{x^5+1}{x+1}$

$=\lim_{x\to -1}\frac{x^3-(-1)^3}{x-(-1)}\div\lim_{x\to -1}\frac{x^5-(-1)^5}{x-(-1)}$ **Ans.** $\frac{3}{5}$

(vi) **Hint** $\lim_{x\to 1}\frac{x^{15}-1}{x^{10}-1}=\lim_{x\to 1}\frac{\frac{x^{15}-1}{x-1}}{\frac{x^{10}-1}{x-1}}$

$=\lim_{x\to 1}\frac{x^{15}-1}{x-1}\div\lim_{x\to 1}\frac{x^{10}-1}{x-1}$

$=\lim_{x\to 1}\frac{x^{15}-1^{15}}{x-1}\div\lim_{x\to 1}\frac{x^{10}-1^{10}}{x-1}$ **Ans.** $\frac{3}{2}$

(vii) **Hint** Put $1+x=y$, then $y\to 1$ as $x\to 0$.

Now, $\lim_{x\to 0}\frac{(1+x)^n-1}{x}=\lim_{y\to 1}\frac{y^n-1}{y-1}=\lim_{y\to 1}\frac{y^n-1^n}{y-1}$ **Ans.** n

(viii) **Hint** Given limit $=\lim_{x\to 1}\frac{\frac{x^m-1}{x-1}}{\frac{x^n-1}{x-1}}=\frac{\lim_{x\to 1}\frac{x^m-1^m}{x-1}}{\lim_{x\to 1}\frac{x^n-1^n}{x-1}}$ **Ans.** $\frac{m}{n}$

(ix) **Hint** Given, limit $=\lim_{y\to(b+3)}\frac{y^{5/2}-(b+3)^{5/2}}{y-(b+3)}$,

where $y=x+3$ **Ans.** $\frac{5}{2}(b+3)^{3/2}$

5. **Hint** $\lim_{x\to 2} \frac{x^n - 2^n}{x-2} = 80$

$\Rightarrow \quad n(2)^{n-1} = 80$

$\Rightarrow \quad n \cdot 2^{n-1} = 5 \times 2^{5-1}$ **Ans.** 5

6. **Hint** $3b^{3-1} = 4(1)^{4-1}$ **Ans.** $b = \pm\frac{2}{\sqrt{3}}$

7. Do same as Q. 6. **Ans.** 1

8. (i) Do same as Example 22. **Ans.** $\frac{3}{2}$

(ii) Do same as Example 23. **Ans.** $\frac{5}{2}$

(iii) Do same as Example 24. **Ans.** $\frac{c}{2}$

(iv) Do same as Example 25. **Ans.** $\frac{1}{4}$

Limits of Exponential Functions and Logarithmic Functions

Some Useful Expansions

- $(1+x)^n = 1 + nx + \frac{n(n-1)}{2!}x^2 + \frac{n(n-1)(n-2)}{3!}x^3 + \ldots.$
- $\log_e(1+x) = x - \frac{x^2}{2} + \frac{x^3}{3} - \frac{x^4}{4} + \frac{x^5}{5} \ldots\ldots$
- $\log_e(1-x) = -x - \frac{x^2}{2} - \frac{x^3}{3} - \frac{x^4}{4} - \frac{x^5}{5} \ldots\ldots$
- $e^x = 1 + x + \frac{x^2}{2!} + \frac{x^3}{3!} + \frac{x^4}{4!} + \ldots$
- $e^{-x} = 1 - x + \frac{x^2}{2!} - \frac{x^3}{3!} + \frac{x^4}{4!} \ldots$
- $a^x = 1 + x(\log_e a) + \frac{x^2}{2!}(\log_e a)^2 + \ldots$

Limits of Exponential Functions

A function of the form of $f(x) = e^x$ is called exponential function. *The graph of the function is given below*

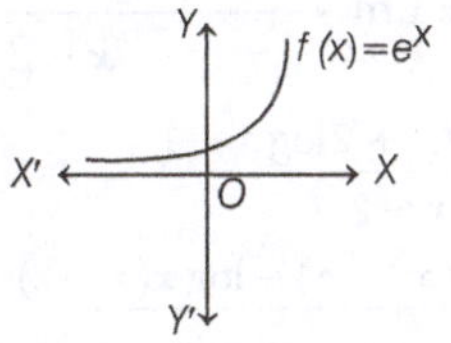

(i) Domain of $f(x) = (-\infty, \infty)$

(ii) Range of $f(x) = (0, \infty)$

To find the limit of a function involving exponential function, we use the following theorem

Theorem $\lim_{x\to 0} \frac{e^x - 1}{x} = 1$

Method to find the limit of Exponential Functions

If given function has exponential term, then we convert the given theorem in the form of $\frac{e^x - 1}{x}$ and then use the theorem $\lim_{x\to 0} \frac{e^x - 1}{x} = 1$

EXAMPLE 1. Find the value of $\lim_{x\to 0} \frac{e^{3x} - 1}{x}$.

Sol. $\lim_{x\to 0} \frac{e^{3x} - 1}{x} = \lim_{x\to 0} \frac{e^{3x} - 1}{x} \times \frac{3}{3}$

[multiplying numerator and denominator by 3]

$= 3 \lim_{x\to 0} \frac{e^{3x} - 1}{3x}$ ...(i)

Let $h = 3x$.

Then, $x \to 0 \Rightarrow h \to 0$

Now, from Eq. (i), we get

$\lim_{x\to 0} \frac{e^{3x} - 1}{x} = 3 \lim_{h\to 0} \frac{e^h - 1}{h} = 3(1) \quad \left[\because \lim_{\theta\to 0} \frac{e^\theta - 1}{\theta} = 1\right]$

$= 3$

EXAMPLE 2. Evaluate $\lim_{x\to 0} \frac{e^x + e^{-x} - 2}{x^2}$.

Sol. $\lim_{x\to 0} \frac{e^x + e^{-x} - 2}{x^2} = \lim_{x\to 0} \frac{e^{2x} + 1 - 2e^x}{x^2 e^x}$

$= \lim_{x\to 0} \left(\frac{e^x - 1}{x}\right)^2 \times e^{-x}$

$= \lim_{x\to 0} \left(\frac{e^x - 1}{x}\right)^2 \times \lim_{x\to 0} e^{-x}$

$= (1)^2 \times e^0 = 1$

EXAMPLE 3. Evaluate $\lim_{x \to 3} \frac{e^x - e^3}{x - 3}$.

Sol. We have, $\lim_{x \to 3} \frac{e^x - e^3}{x - 3}$

On putting $h = x - 3$, we get

$$\lim_{x \to 3} \frac{e^x - e^3}{x - 3} = \lim_{h \to 0} \frac{e^{h+3} - e^3}{h} \quad [\because x \to 3 \Rightarrow h \to 0]$$

$$= \lim_{h \to 0} \frac{e^h e^3 - e^3}{h}$$

$$= e^3 \lim_{h \to 0} \frac{e^h - 1}{h} \quad \left[\because \lim_{\theta \to 0} \frac{e^\theta - 1}{\theta} = 1\right]$$

$$= e^3 \times 1$$

$$= e^3$$

Limits of Logarithmic Functions

The logarithmic function expressed as $\log_e R^+ \to R$ and given by $\log_e x = y$ iff $e^y = x$.

The graph of the function is given below

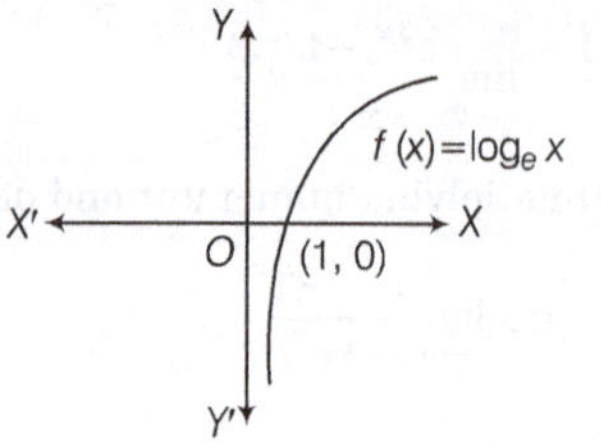

(i) **Domain of $f(x) = (0, \infty)$ or R^+**

(ii) **Range of $f(x) = (-\infty, \infty)$ or R**

To find the limit of functions involving logarithmic function, we use the following theorem

Theorem $\lim_{x \to 0} \frac{\log_e(1+x)}{x} = 1$ and $\lim_{x \to 0} \frac{\log_e(1-x)}{-x} = 1$

Corollary

I. $\lim_{x \to 0} \frac{\log_e(1-x)}{-x} = 1$ II. $\lim_{x \to 0} \frac{a^x - 1}{x} = \log a$

Method to Find the Limit of Logarithmic Function

If given function involves logarithmic function, then we convert the given function in the form of $\frac{\log_e(1+x)}{x}$ and then use the theorem $\lim_{x \to 0} \frac{\log_e(1+x)}{x} = 1$.

EXAMPLE 4. Evaluate $\lim_{x \to 0} \frac{\log_e(1+2x)}{x}$.

Sol. We have, $\lim_{x \to 0} \frac{\log_e(1+2x)}{x} \times \frac{2}{2}$

[multiplying numerator and denominator by 2]

$$= 2 \lim_{x \to 0} \frac{\log_e(1+2x)}{2x}$$

On putting $h = 2x$, we get

$$\lim_{x \to 0} \frac{\log_e(1+2x)}{x} = 2 \lim_{h \to 0} \frac{\log_e(1+h)}{h} \quad [\because x \to 0 \Rightarrow h \to 0]$$

$$= 2(1) \quad \left[\because \lim_{x \to 0} \frac{\log_e(1+x)}{x} = 1\right]$$

$$= 2$$

EXAMPLE 5. Evaluate $\lim_{x \to 0} \frac{\sqrt{1+x} - 1}{\log(1+x)}$.

Sol. $\lim_{x \to 0} \frac{\sqrt{1+x} - 1}{\log(1+x)}$

On multiplying numerator and denominator by $\sqrt{1+x} + 1$, we get

$$\lim_{x \to 0} \frac{\sqrt{1+x} - 1}{\log(1+x)} \times \frac{\sqrt{1+x} + 1}{(\sqrt{1+x} + 1)}$$

$$= \lim_{x \to 0} \frac{1 + x - 1}{(\sqrt{1+x} + 1)\log(1+x)}$$

$$= \lim_{x \to 0} \frac{x}{(\sqrt{1+x} + 1)\log(1+x)}$$

$$= \frac{1}{(\sqrt{1+0} + 1)} \lim_{x \to 0} \frac{1}{\frac{\log(1+x)}{x}}$$

$$= \frac{1}{1+1} \times 1 = \frac{1}{2}$$

EXAMPLE 6. Evaluate $\lim_{x \to 2} \frac{x^2 - x\log x + 2\log x - 4}{x - 2}$.

Sol. $\lim_{x \to 2} \frac{x^2 - x\log x + 2\log x - 4}{x - 2}$

$$= \lim_{x \to 2} \frac{(x^2 - 4) - \log x(x - 2)}{x - 2}$$

$$= \lim_{x \to 2} \frac{(x + 2)(x - 2) - \log x\,(x - 2)}{(x - 2)}$$

$$= \lim_{x \to 2} \frac{(x - 2)[x + 2 - \log x]}{(x - 2)}$$

$$= \lim_{x \to 2} [x + 2 - \log x]$$

$$= 2 + 2 - \log 2$$

$$= 4 - \log 2$$

EXAMPLE 7. Evaluate $\lim\limits_{x \to e} \dfrac{\log x - 1}{x - e}$.

Sol. We have, $\lim\limits_{x \to e} \dfrac{\log x - 1}{x - e}$

$$= \lim_{x \to e} \frac{\log x - \log e}{e\left(\dfrac{x}{e} - 1\right)} \qquad [\because \log e = 1]$$

$$= \lim_{x \to e} \frac{\log \dfrac{x}{e}}{e\left(\dfrac{x}{e} - 1\right)} \qquad \left[\because \log m - \log n = \log \frac{m}{n}\right]$$

On putting $x = h + e$, we get

$$\lim_{x \to e} \frac{\log x - 1}{x - e} = \frac{1}{e} \lim_{h \to 0} \frac{\log\left(\dfrac{h+e}{e}\right)}{\left(\dfrac{h+e}{e} - 1\right)} \qquad [\because x \to e \Rightarrow h \to 0]$$

$$= \frac{1}{e} \lim_{h \to 0} \frac{\log\left(1 + \dfrac{h}{e}\right)}{\left(\dfrac{h}{e}\right)} \qquad \text{...(i)}$$

Again, putting $y = \dfrac{h}{e}$ in Eq. (i), we get

$$\lim_{x \to e} \frac{\log x - 1}{x - e} = \frac{1}{e} \lim_{y \to 0} \frac{\log(1 + y)}{y} \qquad [\because h \to 0 \Rightarrow y \to 0]$$

$$= \frac{1}{e} \times 1 = \frac{1}{e}$$

EXAMPLE 8. Evaluate $\lim\limits_{x \to 0} \dfrac{\log(6 + x) - \log(6 - x)}{x}$.

Sol. $\lim\limits_{x \to 0} \dfrac{\log(6 + x) - \log(6 - x)}{x}$

$$= \lim_{x \to 0} \frac{\log 6\left(1 + \dfrac{x}{6}\right) - \log 6\left(1 - \dfrac{x}{6}\right)}{x}$$

$$= \lim_{x \to 0} \frac{\left[\log 6 + \log\left(1 + \dfrac{x}{6}\right)\right] - \left[\log 6 + \log\left(1 - \dfrac{x}{6}\right)\right]}{x}$$

$$= \lim_{x \to 0} \left[\frac{\log\left(1 + \dfrac{x}{6}\right)}{x} - \frac{\log\left(1 - \dfrac{x}{6}\right)}{x}\right]$$

$$= \lim_{x \to 0} \frac{1}{6} \frac{\log\left(1 + \dfrac{x}{6}\right)}{\dfrac{x}{6}} + \lim_{x \to 0} \frac{1}{6} \frac{\log\left(1 - \dfrac{x}{6}\right)}{-\dfrac{x}{6}}$$

$$\left[\because \lim_{x \to 0} \frac{\log(1 + x)}{x} = \lim_{x \to 0} \frac{\log(1 - x)}{-x} = 1\right]$$

$$= \frac{1}{6} \times 1 + \frac{1}{6} \times 1$$

$$= \frac{1}{6} + \frac{1}{6} = \frac{2}{6} = \frac{1}{3}$$

EXAMPLE 9. Evaluate $\lim\limits_{x \to 0} \left(\dfrac{3^{2x} - 1}{2^{3x} - 1}\right)$.

Sol. $$\lim_{x \to 0} \left(\frac{3^{2x} - 1}{2^{3x} - 1}\right) = \lim_{x \to 0} \frac{\left\{\left(\dfrac{3^{2x} - 1}{2x}\right) \cdot 2x\right\}}{\left\{\left(\dfrac{2^{3x} - 1}{3x}\right) \cdot 3x\right\}}$$

$$= \frac{2}{3} \cdot \frac{\lim\limits_{2x \to 0} \left(\dfrac{3^{2x} - 1}{2x}\right)}{\lim\limits_{3x \to 0} \left(\dfrac{2^{3x} - 1}{3x}\right)}$$

$$= \frac{2}{3} \cdot \frac{\log 3}{\log 2} \qquad \left[\because \lim_{x \to 0} \left(\frac{a^x - 1}{x}\right) = \log a\right]$$

$$= \frac{2 \log 3}{3 \log 2} = \frac{\log(3^2)}{\log(2^3)}$$

$$= \frac{\log 9}{\log 8}$$

EXAMPLE 10. Evaluate $\lim\limits_{x \to 0} \dfrac{2^x - 1}{\sqrt{1 + x} - 1}$.

Sol. $$\lim_{x \to 0} \frac{2^x - 1}{\sqrt{1 + x} - 1} = \lim_{x \to 0} \frac{2^x - 1}{\sqrt{1 + x} - 1} \times \frac{(\sqrt{1 + x} + 1)}{(\sqrt{1 + x} + 1)}$$

$$= \lim_{x \to 0} \frac{2^x - 1}{x} \times \{\sqrt{1 + x} + 1\}$$

$$= \lim_{x \to 0} \frac{2^x - 1}{x} \times \lim_{x \to 0} (\sqrt{1 + x} + 1)$$

$$= (\log 2) 2$$

$$= 2 \log 2$$

Topic Practice 3

Evaluate the following.

1 $\lim_{x\to 0} \frac{e^{bx}-1}{x}$

2 $\lim_{x\to 0} \left(\frac{3^x-1}{x}\right)$

3 $\lim_{x\to 0} \frac{\log(1+5x)}{x}$

4 $\lim_{x\to 0} \frac{\log(1+cx)}{x}$

5 $\lim_{x\to 0} \frac{a^x-b^x}{x}$

6 $\lim_{x\to 0} \left(\frac{e^{2+x}-e^2}{x}\right)$

7 $\lim_{x\to 4} \left(\frac{e^x-e^4}{x-4}\right)$

8 $\lim_{x\to 5} \frac{e^x-e^5}{x-5}$

9 $\lim_{x\to 0} \frac{e^x-e^{-x}}{x}$

10 $\lim_{x\to 0} \frac{a^x-a^{-x}}{x}$

11 $\lim_{x\to 0} \left(\frac{e^x-x-1}{x}\right)$

12 $\lim_{x\to 0} \frac{e^{3x}-e^{2x}}{x}$

13 $\lim_{x\to 0} \frac{3^{2+x}-9}{x}$

14 $\lim_{x\to 1} \frac{x-1}{\log_e x}$

15 $\lim_{x\to 5} \frac{\log x-\log 5}{x-5}$

16 $\lim_{x\to 0} \left(\frac{3^{2x}-2^{3x}}{x}\right)$

Hints & Solutions

1. b

2. $\log 3$

3. Given limit $= \lim_{x\to 0} \frac{5\log(1+5x)}{5x}$ **Ans.** 5

4. c

5. Given limit $= \lim_{x\to 0} \frac{b^x\left[\left(\frac{a}{b}\right)^x-1\right]}{x}$ **Ans.** $b^x \log\left(\frac{a}{b}\right)$

6. Given limit $= \lim_{x\to 0} \frac{e^2(e^x-1)}{x}$ **Ans.** e^2

7. Given limit $= \lim_{x\to 4} e^4\left(\frac{e^{x-4}-1}{x-4}\right)$

   Ans. e^4

8. Put $x-5=h$ and as $x\to 5$, then $h\to 0$.

   $\therefore$ We have,

   $$\lim_{h\to 0} \frac{e^{h+5}-e^5}{h} = \lim_{h\to 0} \frac{e^h e^5-e^5}{h}$$

   $$= e^5 \lim_{h\to 0} \frac{e^h-1}{h}$$ **Ans.** e^5

9. $L = \lim_{x\to 0} \frac{e^{2x}-1}{xe^x} = \lim_{x\to 0} \frac{e^{2x}-1}{2x} \times \lim_{x\to 0} \frac{2}{e^x}$ **Ans.** 2

10. $\lim_{x\to 0} \frac{a^{-x}(a^{2x}-1)}{2x} \times 2 = a^0 \log a^2$ **Ans.** $2\log a$

11. $\lim_{x\to 0} \left(\frac{e^x-x-1}{x}\right) = \lim_{x\to 0} \left(\frac{e^x-1}{x}\right) - \lim_{x\to 0} \frac{x}{x}$

    Ans. 0

12. $\lim_{x\to 0} \frac{e^{3x}-1}{x} - \left(\lim_{x\to 0} \frac{e^{2x}-1}{x}\right)$

    $$= \lim_{x\to 0} \frac{e^{3x}-1}{3x} \times 3 - \left(\lim_{x\to 0} \frac{e^{2x}-1}{2x}\right) 2$$

    Ans. 1

13. $\lim_{x\to 0} \frac{3^{2+x}-9}{x} = \lim_{x\to 0} \frac{3^2(3^x-1)}{x}$

    Ans. $9\log 3$

14. $\lim_{h\to 0} \frac{1+h-1}{\log_e(1+h)} = \lim_{h\to 0} \frac{h}{\log_e(1+h)}$

    $$= \frac{1}{\lim_{h\to 0} \frac{\log(1+h)}{h}}$$ **Ans.** 1

15. Put $x-5=h$ and as $x\to 5$, then $h\to 0$

    $$\therefore \lim_{h\to 0} \frac{\log(h+5)-\log 5}{h} = \lim_{h\to 0} \frac{\log\left(1+\frac{h}{5}\right)}{\frac{h}{5}\times 5}$$

    Ans. $\frac{1}{5}$

16. $\lim_{x\to 0} \left\{\frac{(3^{2x}-1)-(2^{3x}-1)}{x}\right\}$

    $$= 2\cdot \lim_{2x\to 0} \left(\frac{3^{2x}-1}{2x}\right) - 3\cdot \lim_{3x\to 0} \left(\frac{2^{3x}-1}{3x}\right)$$

    Ans. $\log\left(\frac{9}{8}\right)$

Exam Pattern Exercise

Part A - Objective Type Questions

Multiple Choice Type Questions

1 If $f(x) = \begin{cases} x^2 - 1, & x \le 1 \\ -x^2 - 1, & x > 1 \end{cases}$ then

(a) LHL $\ne$ RHL, at $x = 1$
(b) LHL = RHL = -2, at $x = 1$
(c) LHL = RHL = -1, at $x = 1$
(d) None of the above

2 $\lim_{x \to 0} \frac{\sqrt{2+x} - \sqrt{2}}{x}$ is equal to

(a) $\frac{1}{2}$ (b) $\frac{1}{\sqrt{2}}$ (c) $\frac{1}{2\sqrt{2}}$ (d) $\sqrt{2}$

3 $\lim_{x \to 1} \frac{(\sqrt{x} - 1)(2x - 3)}{2x^2 + x - 3}$ is equal to

(a) $\frac{1}{10}$ (b) $\frac{-1}{10}$
(c) 1 (d) None of these

4 $\lim_{x \to 0} e^x$ is equal to

(a) -1 (b) 0 (c) 1 (d) 5

5 $\lim_{x \to 0} \frac{3^x - 2^x}{x}$ is equal to

(a) $\log \frac{3}{2}$ (b) $\log \frac{2}{3}$ (c) $\log \frac{1}{2}$ (d) $\log \frac{1}{3}$

6 $\lim_{n \to \infty} \frac{1 + 2 + 3 + \ldots + n}{n^2}, n \in N$ is equal to [NCERT Exemplar]

(a) 0 (b) 1 (c) $\frac{1}{2}$ (d) $\frac{1}{4}$

7 $\lim_{x \to \infty} \frac{x!}{(x+1)! - x!}$ is equal to

(a) 0 (b) -1 (c) 1 (d) 2

8 If $\lim_{x \to a} \frac{x^4 - a^4}{x - a} = 32$, then a is equal to

(a) 2 (b) 4
(c) -2 (d) None of these

9 $\lim_{x \to 1} \frac{\log x}{x - 1}$ is equal to

(a) ∞ (b) 0 (c) -1 (d) 1

10 $\lim_{x \to 0} \frac{\log(2 + x) - \log 2}{x}$ is equal to

(a) $\frac{1}{2}$ (b) 0
(c) $-\frac{1}{2}$ (d) None of these

Assertion-Reason Based Questions

Directions (Q. Nos. 11-13) *In the questions given below are two statements labelled as Assertion (A) and Reason (R). In the context of the two statements, which one of the following is correct?*

(a) Both A and R are correct; R is the correct explanation of A
(b) Both A and R are correct; R is not the correct explanation of A
(c) A is correct; R is incorrect
(d) R is correct; A is incorrect

11 **Assertion (A)** The value of $\lim_{x \to 2^+} \frac{x^2 - 1}{2x + 4}$ is $\frac{3}{8}$.

Reason (R) $\lim_{x \to a^+} f(x) = \lim_{h \to 0} f(a + h)$.

12 **Assertion (A)** $\lim_{x \to 0} \frac{5^{2+x} - 25}{x}$ is equal to $25 \log 2$.

Reason (R) $\lim_{x \to 0} \frac{a^x - 1}{x}$ is equal to $\log a$.

13 **Assertion (A)** $\lim_{x \to 1} \frac{ax^2 + bx + c}{bx^2 + cx + a}$ is equal to 1, when $a + b + c \ne 0$.

Reason (R) $\lim_{x \to -2} \frac{\frac{1}{x} + \frac{1}{2}}{x + 2}$ is equal to $-\frac{1}{4}$.

Part B - Descriptive Questions

Very Short Answer Type Questions

14 Evaluate $\lim_{x \to 1} \frac{x^2 + 3x + 2}{x^2 + 1}$

15 Evaluate $\lim_{x \to 4} \frac{x^3 - 2x^2 - 9x + 4}{x^2 - 2x - 8}$

16 Find the positive integer x so that
$\lim_{x \to 3} \frac{x^n - 3^n}{x - 3} = 108$

17 Evaluate $\lim_{x \to 0} \frac{5^x - 1}{\sqrt{1 + x} - 1}$

18 Evaluate $\lim_{x \to 0} \frac{e^{4x} - 1}{x}$

Short Answer Type Questions

19 Evaluate $\lim\limits_{x\to\sqrt{2}} \dfrac{x^4-4}{x^2+3\sqrt{2}x-8}$

20 Evaluate $\lim\limits_{x\to a} \dfrac{\sqrt{a+2x}-\sqrt{3x}}{\sqrt{3a+x}-2\sqrt{x}}, a\neq 0$

21 Evaluate $\lim\limits_{x\to 1} \dfrac{x^n+x^{n-1}+x^{n-2}+\ldots+x^2+x-n}{x-1}$

22 Evaluate $\lim\limits_{x\to 1} \dfrac{x^4-\sqrt{x}}{\sqrt{x}-1}$

23 Evaluate $\lim\limits_{x\to 0} \dfrac{\log(5+x)-\log(5-x)}{x}$

Long Answer Type Questions

24 Evaluate $\lim\limits_{x\to 1/2} \left(\dfrac{8x-3}{2x-1}-\dfrac{4x^2+1}{4x^2-1}\right)$

25 Evaluate $\lim\limits_{x\to\sqrt{2}} \dfrac{x^9-3x^8+x^6-9x^4-4x^2-16x+84}{x^5-3x^4-4x+12}$.

26 Evaluate $\lim\limits_{x\to 2} \dfrac{x^2-4}{\sqrt{3x-2}-\sqrt{x+2}}$

27 Evaluate $\lim\limits_{x\to\sqrt{10}} \dfrac{\sqrt{7-2x}-(\sqrt{5}-\sqrt{2})}{x^2-10}$

28 Evaluate $\lim\limits_{x\to\sqrt{6}} \dfrac{\sqrt{5+2x}-(\sqrt{3}+\sqrt{2})}{x^2-6}$

Case Study Based Questions

29 Suraj was learning limit of the logarithmic function from his tutor Rajesh. His tutor told that the logarithmic function expressed as $\log_e R^+ \to R$ and given by $\log_e x = y$ iff $e^y = x$. The graph of the function is given below

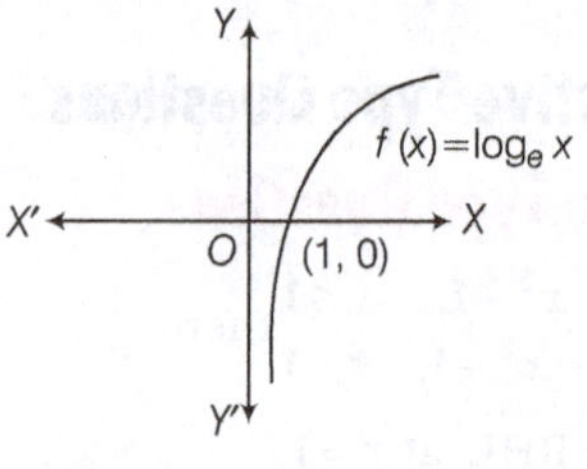

(i) Domain of $f(x)=(0,\infty)$

(ii) Range of $f(x)=(-\infty,\infty)$

To find the limit of functions involving logarithmic function, we use the following theorem.

Theorem $\lim\limits_{x\to 0} \dfrac{\log_e(1+x)}{x}=1$

On the basis of above information answer the following question

(i) Evaluate $\lim\limits_{x\to 0} \dfrac{\log_e(1+8x)}{x}$.

(ii) Evaluate $\lim\limits_{x\to 0} \dfrac{\log_e(1+6x)-5x^2}{x}$.

(iii) Evaluate $\lim\limits_{x\to 0} \dfrac{\sqrt{3+x}-3}{\log_e(1+x)}$.

Or

Evaluate $\lim\limits_{x\to 0} \dfrac{\log(8+x)-\log(8-x)}{x}$.

Hints & Solutions

1. (a)	*2.* (c)	*3.* (b)	*4.* (c)
5. (a)	*6.* (c)	*7.* (a)	*8.* (a)
9. (d)	*10.* (a)	*11.* (a)	*12.* (d)
13. (b)			

14. 3

15. **Hint** $\lim\limits_{x\to 4} \dfrac{x^3-2x^2-9x+4}{x^2-2x-8}$

$$= \lim_{x\to 4} \frac{(x-4)(x^2+2x-1)}{(x-4)(x+2)} = \lim_{x\to 4} \frac{x^2+2x-1}{x+2} \quad \textbf{Ans. } \frac{23}{6}$$

16. **Hint** $\lim\limits_{x\to 3} \dfrac{x^n-3^n}{x-3} = 108 \Rightarrow n\,3^{n-1}=108$ **Ans.** $n=4$

17. **Hint** $\lim\limits_{x\to 0} \dfrac{5^x-1}{\sqrt{1+x}-1} = \lim\limits_{x\to 0} \dfrac{(5^x-1)(\sqrt{1+x}+1)}{(\sqrt{1+x}-1)(\sqrt{1+x}+1)}$

$$= \lim_{x\to 0} \frac{(5^x-1)(\sqrt{1+x}+1)}{1+x-1}$$

$$= \lim_{x\to 0} \frac{(5^x-1)}{x} \times \lim_{x\to 0} (\sqrt{1+x}+1) \quad \textbf{Ans. } 2\log 5$$

18. **Hint** $\lim\limits_{x\to 0} \dfrac{e^{4x}-1}{x}$ put $4x=y$ as $x\to 0, y\to 0$

$$= \lim_{y\to 0} \frac{e^y-1}{\frac{y}{4}} = 4\lim_{y\to 0} \frac{e^y-1}{y} \quad \textbf{Ans. } 4$$

19. **Hint** $\lim\limits_{x\to\sqrt{2}} \dfrac{x^4-4}{x^2+3\sqrt{2}x-8} = \lim\limits_{x\to\sqrt{2}} \dfrac{(x^4-2^2)}{(x-\sqrt{2})(x+4\sqrt{2})}$

$$= \lim_{x\to\sqrt{2}} \frac{(x^2+2)(x^2-2)}{(x-\sqrt{2})(x+4\sqrt{2})}$$

$$= \lim_{x\to\sqrt{2}} \frac{(x+\sqrt{2})(x-\sqrt{2})(x^2+2)}{(x-\sqrt{2})(x+4\sqrt{2})}$$

$$= \lim_{x\to\sqrt{2}} \frac{(x+\sqrt{2})(x^2+2)}{x+4\sqrt{2}} \quad \textbf{Ans. } \frac{8}{5}$$

20. **Hint** $\lim_{x \to a} \dfrac{\sqrt{a+2x}-\sqrt{3x}}{\sqrt{3a+x}-2\sqrt{x}}$

$$= \lim_{x \to a} \left(\frac{\sqrt{a+2x}-\sqrt{3x}}{\sqrt{3a+x}-2\sqrt{x}} \times \frac{(\sqrt{a+2x}+\sqrt{3x})}{(\sqrt{3a+x}+2\sqrt{x})} \times \frac{(\sqrt{3a+x}+2\sqrt{x})}{(\sqrt{a+2x}+\sqrt{3x})} \right)$$

$$= \lim_{x \to a} \left(\frac{(a+2x-3x)}{(3a+x-4x)} \frac{\sqrt{3a+x}+2\sqrt{x}}{\sqrt{a+2x}+\sqrt{3x}} \right)$$

$$= \lim_{x \to a} \frac{1}{3} \left(\frac{\sqrt{3a+x}+2\sqrt{x}}{\sqrt{a+2x}+\sqrt{3x}} \right) \quad \textbf{Ans. } \frac{2}{3\sqrt{3}}$$

21. **Hint** $\lim_{x \to 1} \dfrac{x^n + x^{n-1} + x^{n-2} + \ldots + x^2 + x - n}{x-1}$

$$= \lim_{x \to 1} \left[\frac{x^n - 1 + x^{n-1} - 1 + \ldots + x^2 - 1 + x - 1}{x-1} \right]$$

$$= \lim_{x \to 1} \left[\frac{x^n - 1^n}{x-1} + \frac{x^{n-1} - 1^{n-1}}{x-1} + \ldots + \frac{x^2 - 1^2}{x-1} + \frac{x-1}{x-1} \right]$$

$$= \lim_{x \to 1} \frac{x^n - 1^n}{x-1} + \lim_{x \to 1} \frac{x^{n-1} - 1^{n-1}}{x-1} + \ldots + \lim_{x \to 1} \frac{x^2 - 1^2}{x-1} + \lim_{x \to 1} 1$$

$$= n + n - 1 + n - 2 + \ldots + 2 + 1 \quad \textbf{Ans. } \frac{n(n+1)}{2}$$

22. **Hint** $\lim_{x \to 1} \dfrac{x^4 - \sqrt{x}}{\sqrt{x}-1}$

$$= \lim_{x \to 1} \frac{(\sqrt{x}-1)(x^{7/2} + x^3 + x^{5/2} + x^2 + x^{3/2} + x + \sqrt{x})}{(\sqrt{x}-1)}$$

$$= \lim_{x \to 1} (x^{7/2} + x^3 + x^{5/2} + x^2 + x^{3/2} + x + x^{1/2}) \quad \textbf{Ans. } 7$$

23. **Hint** $\lim_{x \to 0} \dfrac{\log(5+x) - \log(5-x)}{x}$

$$= \lim_{x \to 0} \frac{\log 5\left(1 + \frac{x}{5}\right) - \log 5\left(1 - \frac{x}{5}\right)}{x}$$

$$= \lim_{x \to 0} \left[\frac{\log 5 + \log\left(1 + \frac{x}{5}\right) - \log 5 - \log\left(1 - \frac{x}{5}\right)}{x} \right]$$

$$= \lim_{x \to 0} \left[\frac{\log\left(1 + \frac{x}{5}\right) - \log\left(1 - \frac{x}{5}\right)}{x} \right]$$

$$= \lim_{x \to 0} \frac{\log\left(1 + \frac{x}{5}\right)}{x} + \lim_{x \to 0} \frac{\log\left(1 - \frac{x}{5}\right)}{-x} \quad \textbf{Ans. } \frac{2}{5}$$

24. **Hint** $\lim_{x \to \frac{1}{2}} \left(\dfrac{8x-3}{2x-1} - \dfrac{4x^2+1}{4x^2-1} \right)$

$$= \lim_{x \to \frac{1}{2}} \left[\frac{16x^2 + 8x - 6x - 3 - 4x^2 - 1}{(2x-1)(2x+1)} \right]$$

$$= \lim_{x \to \frac{1}{2}} \left[\frac{12x^2 + 2x - 4}{(2x-1)(2x+1)} \right]$$

$$= \lim_{x \to \frac{1}{2}} \left[\frac{2(2x-1)(3x+2)}{(2x-1)(2x+1)} \right] \quad \textbf{Ans. } \frac{7}{2}$$

25. **Hint** $\lim_{x \to \sqrt{2}} \dfrac{x^9 - 3x^8 + x^6 - 9x^4 - 4x^2 - 16x + 84}{x^5 - 3x^4 - 4x + 12}$

$$= \lim_{x \to \sqrt{2}} \frac{(x-3)(x^2-2)(x^2+2)(x^4+x+7)}{(x-3)(x^2-2)(x^2+2)}$$

$$= \lim_{x \to \sqrt{2}} x^4 + x + 7 \quad \textbf{Ans. } \sqrt{2} + 11$$

26. **Hint** $\lim_{x \to 2} \dfrac{x^2 - 4}{\sqrt{3x-2} - \sqrt{x+2}}$

$$= \lim_{x \to 2} \frac{(x^2-4)(\sqrt{3x-2} + \sqrt{x+2})}{(\sqrt{3x-2} - \sqrt{x+2})(\sqrt{3x-2} + \sqrt{x+2})}$$

$$= \lim_{x \to 2} \frac{(x^2-4)(\sqrt{3x-2} + \sqrt{x+2})}{3x - 2 - x - 2}$$

$$= \lim_{x \to 2} \frac{(x-2)(x+2)(\sqrt{3x-2} + \sqrt{x+2})}{2x-4}$$

$$= \lim_{x \to 2} \frac{1}{2}(x+2)(\sqrt{3x-2} + \sqrt{x+2}) \quad \textbf{Ans. } 8$$

27. **Hint** $\lim_{x \to \sqrt{10}} \dfrac{\sqrt{7-2x} - (\sqrt{5} - \sqrt{2})}{x^2 - 10}$

$$= \lim_{x \to \sqrt{10}} \frac{(\sqrt{7-2x} - (\sqrt{5} - \sqrt{2}))(\sqrt{7-2x} + \sqrt{5} - \sqrt{2})}{(x+\sqrt{10})(x-\sqrt{10})(\sqrt{7-2x} + \sqrt{5} - \sqrt{2})}$$

$$= \lim_{x \to \sqrt{10}} \frac{7 - 2x - (5 + 2 - 2\sqrt{10})}{(x+\sqrt{10})(x-\sqrt{10})(\sqrt{7-2x} + \sqrt{5} - \sqrt{2})}$$

$$= \lim_{x \to \sqrt{10}} \frac{-2x + 2\sqrt{10}}{(x+\sqrt{10})(x-\sqrt{10})(\sqrt{7-2x} + \sqrt{5} - \sqrt{2})}$$

$$= \lim_{x \to \sqrt{10}} \frac{-2}{(x+\sqrt{10})(\sqrt{7-2x} + \sqrt{5} - \sqrt{2})}$$

Ans. $\dfrac{-(\sqrt{5} + \sqrt{2})}{6\sqrt{10}}$

28. $\dfrac{\sqrt{3} - \sqrt{2}}{2\sqrt{6}}$

29. (i) 8 (ii) 6 (iii) $\dfrac{1}{2\sqrt{3}}$ *Or* $\dfrac{1}{4}$

CHAPTER 15

Continuity

In this Chapter...

- Continuity of a Function at a Point
- Algebra of Continuous Functions

Continuity of a Function at a Point

A function $f(x)$ is said to be continuous at a point $x = a$, if the value of function at $x = a$ is equal to the limit of the function at $x = a$.

i.e. $f(x)$ is continuous at $x = a$

if $\quad (\text{LHL})_{x=a} = (\text{RHL})_{x=a} = f(a)$

A function $f(x)$ is said to be left continuous or continuous from the left at $x = a$

if $\quad (\text{LHL})_{x=a} = f(a)$ i.e. $\lim\limits_{x \to a^-} f(x) = f(a)$

A function $f(x)$ is said to be right continuous or continuous from the right at $x = a$

if $\quad (\text{RHL})_{x=a} = f(a)$ i.e. $\lim\limits_{x \to a^+} f(x) = f(a)$

A function $f(x)$ is said to be **discontinuous** at $x = a$, if it is not continuous at $x = a$, i.e.

- $f(x)$ is not defined at $x = a$
- $\lim\limits_{x \to a} f(a)$ does not exist.
- Left hand limit and right hand limit are not equal.
- $\lim\limits_{x \to a} f(x) \neq f(a)$

When $\lim\limits_{x \to a} f(x)$ exists but either $f(a)$ does not exist or $\lim\limits_{x \to a} f(x) \neq f(a)$

we say that f has a **removable discontinuity** otherwise f has **non-removable discontinuity**.

EXAMPLE 1. Examine the continuity of the following functions at given points.

(i) $f(x) = x^2$ at $x = -2$ (ii) $f(x) = 2x^2 - 1$ at $x = 3$

(iii) $f(x) = |x - 5|$ at $x = 5$ **[NCERT]**

Sol. (i) Given, $f(x) = x^2$

At point $x = -2$, $f(-2) = (-2)^2 = 4$

Now, $\lim\limits_{x \to -2} f(x) = \lim\limits_{x \to -2} x^2$

$= (-2)^2 = 4$

Here, $f(-2) = \lim\limits_{x \to -2} f(x)$

Hence, $f(x)$ is continuous at $x = -2$.

(ii) Given, $f(x) = 2x^2 - 1$

At point $x = 3$, $f(3) = 2(3)^2 - 1 = 2(9) - 1 = 17$

Now, $\lim\limits_{x \to 3} f(x) = \lim\limits_{x \to 3} (2x^2 - 1)$

$= 2(3)^2 - 1 = 17$

Here, $f(3) = \lim\limits_{x \to 3} f(x)$

Hence, $f(x)$ is continuous at $x = 3$.

(iii) Given, $f(x) = |x - 5| = \begin{cases} x - 5, & \text{if } x \geq 5 \\ 5 - x, & \text{if } x < 5 \end{cases}$

At point $x = 5$, $f(5) = |5 - 5| = 0$

Now, LHL $= \lim\limits_{x \to 5^-} f(x) = \lim\limits_{x \to 5^-} (5 - x)$

$= \lim\limits_{h \to 0} [5 - (5 - h)] = \lim\limits_{h \to 0} h = 0$

[put $x = 5 - h$; when $x \to 5^-$, then $h \to 0$]

and RHL $= \lim\limits_{x \to 5^+} f(x) = \lim\limits_{x \to 5^+} (x - 5)$

$= \lim\limits_{h \to 0} [(5 + h) - 5] = \lim\limits_{h \to 0} h = 0$

[put $x = 5 + h$; when $x \to 5^+$, then $h \to 0$]

Thus, LHL = RHL = $f(5) = 0$

Hence, $f(x)$ is continuous at $x = 5$.

EXAMPLE 2. Discuss the continuity of the function $f(x)$ at $x=0$, if $f(x)=\begin{cases}2x-1, & x<0\\ 2x+1, & x\ge 0\end{cases}$.

Sol. We have, $f(x)=\begin{cases}2x-1, & x<0\\ 2x+1, & x\ge 0\end{cases}$

At $x=0$, $\lim\limits_{x\to 0^-} f(x)=\lim\limits_{x\to 0}(2x-1)=2(0)-1=-1$

$\lim\limits_{x\to 0^+} f(x)=\lim\limits_{x\to 0}(2x+1)=2(0)+1=1$

Here, $\lim\limits_{x\to 0^-}\ne\lim\limits_{x\to 0^+}$

Hence, $f(x)$ is not continuous at $x=0$.

EXAMPLE 3. Discuss the continuity of the function

$$f(x)=\begin{cases}\dfrac{x^2-x-6}{x+2}, & \text{if } x\ne -2\\ -5, & \text{if } x=-2\end{cases} \text{ at } x=-2.$$

Sol. We have, $f(x)=\begin{cases}\dfrac{x^2-x-6}{x+2}, & \text{if } x\ne -2\\ -5, & \text{if } x=-2\end{cases}$

At $x=-2$, $\lim\limits_{x\to -2} f(x)=\lim\limits_{x\to -2}\dfrac{x^2-x-6}{x+2}$ ...(i)

Now, factorising the numerator, we get

$$\lim_{x\to -2} f(x)=\lim_{x\to -2}\frac{(x-3)(x+2)}{(x+2)}$$

$$=\lim_{x\to -2}(x-3)$$

$$=-2-3=-5$$

Also, at $x=-2$, $f(x)=-5$ i.e. $f(-2)=-5$

Thus, $\lim\limits_{x\to -2} f(x)=f(-2)$

Hence, $f(x)$ is continuous at $x=-2$.

EXAMPLE 4. Discuss the continuity of the function

$$f(x)=\begin{cases}\dfrac{|x|}{x}, & \text{if } x\ne 0\\ 0, & \text{if } x=0\end{cases} \text{ at } x=0.$$

Sol. We have, $f(x)=\begin{cases}\dfrac{|x|}{x}, & \text{if } x\ne 0\\ 0, & \text{if } x=0\end{cases}$

At $x=0$, LHL $=\lim\limits_{x\to 0^-} f(x)$

$$=\lim_{x\to 0^-}\frac{|x|}{x}=\lim_{h\to 0}\frac{|0-h|}{0-h}$$

[put $x=0-h$; when $x\to 0^-$, then $h\to 0$]

$$=\lim_{h\to 0}\frac{h}{-h} \quad [\because |0-h|=|-h|=h]$$

$$=\lim_{h\to 0}(-1)=-1$$

and RHL $=\lim\limits_{x\to 0^+} f(x)=\lim\limits_{x\to 0^+}\dfrac{|x|}{x}$

$$=\lim_{h\to 0}\frac{|0+h|}{0+h}$$

[put $x=0+h$; when $x\to 0^+$, then $h\to 0$]

$$=\lim_{h\to 0}\frac{h}{h} \quad [\because |0+h|=|h|=h]$$

$$=\lim_{h\to 0}(1)=1$$

Thus, LHL $\ne$ RHL.

Hence, $f(x)$ is not continuous at $x=0$.

EXAMPLE 5. Discuss the continuity of the function $f(x)$ at $x=1/2$, when $f(x)$ is defined as follows.

$$f(x)=\begin{cases}1/2+x, & \text{if } 0\le x<1/2\\ 1, & \text{if } x=1/2\\ 3/2+x, & \text{if } 1/2<x\le 1\end{cases}.$$

Sol. The given function is $f(x)=\begin{cases}\dfrac{1}{2}+x, & \text{if } 0\le x<\dfrac{1}{2}\\ 1, & \text{if } x=\dfrac{1}{2}\\ \dfrac{3}{2}+x, & \text{if } \dfrac{1}{2}<x\le 1\end{cases}$

We have to check continuity of $f(x)$ at $x=\dfrac{1}{2}$.

Now, LHL $=\lim\limits_{x\to \frac{1}{2}^-} f(x)=\lim\limits_{x\to \frac{1}{2}^-}\left(\dfrac{1}{2}+x\right)$

$$=\lim_{h\to 0}\left(\frac{1}{2}+\frac{1}{2}-h\right)$$

$$\left[\text{put } x=\frac{1}{2}-h;\text{ when } x\to\frac{1^-}{2},\ h\to 0\right]$$

$$=\lim_{h\to 0}(1-h)=1 \quad [\text{put } h=0]$$

RHL $=\lim\limits_{x\to \frac{1}{2}^+} f(x)=\lim\limits_{x\to \frac{1}{2}^+}\left(\dfrac{3}{2}+x\right)=\lim\limits_{h\to 0}\left(\dfrac{3}{2}+\dfrac{1}{2}+h\right)$

$$\left[\text{put } x=\frac{1}{2}+h;\text{ when } x\to\frac{1^+}{2},\ h\to 0\right]$$

$$=\lim_{h\to 0}(2+h)=2 \quad [\text{put } h=0]$$

We know that a function $f(x)$ is said to be continuous at point $x=a$, if LHL $=$ RHL $=f(a)$.

Here, LHL $\ne$ RHL

Hence, $f(x)$ is discontinuous at $x=\dfrac{1}{2}$.

EXAMPLE 6. Show that the function

$$f(x)=\begin{cases}\dfrac{e^{1/x}-1}{e^{1/x}+1}, & \text{when } x\ne 0\\ 0, & \text{when } x=0\end{cases} \text{ is discontinuous at } x=0.$$

Sol. We have, $\begin{cases} \dfrac{e^{1/x}-1}{e^{1/x}+1}, & \text{when } x \neq 0 \\ 0, & \text{when } x = 0 \end{cases}$

At $x = 0$, $f(0) = 0$

$$\text{LHL} = \lim_{x \to 0^-} f(x) = \lim_{x \to 0^-} \frac{(e^{1/x}-1)}{(e^{1/x}+1)}$$

$$= \lim_{h \to 0} \frac{e^{\frac{1}{0-h}}-1}{e^{\frac{1}{0-h}}+1} = \lim_{h \to 0} \frac{e^{-1/h}-1}{e^{-1/h}+1}$$

[put $x = 0 - h$; when $x \to 0^-$, then $h \to 0$]

$$= \lim_{h \to 0} \frac{\frac{1}{e^{1/h}}-1}{\frac{1}{e^{1/h}}+1} = \frac{0-1}{0+1} = -1 \quad \left[\because \lim_{h \to 0} \frac{1}{e^{1/h}} = 0\right]$$

and $\text{RHL} = \lim_{x \to 0^+} f(x) = \lim_{x \to 0^+} \dfrac{e^{1/x}-1}{e^{1/x}+1}$

$$= \lim_{h \to 0} \frac{e^{\frac{1}{(0+h)}}-1}{e^{\frac{1}{(0+h)}}+1}$$

[put $x = 0 + h$; when $x \to 0^+$, then $h \to 0$]

$$= \lim_{h \to 0} \frac{e^{1/h}-1}{e^{1/h}+1}$$

On dividing numerator and denominator by $e^{1/h}$, we get

$$\text{RHL} = \lim_{h \to 0} \frac{\left(1-\frac{1}{e^{1/h}}\right)}{\left(1+\frac{1}{e^{1/h}}\right)} = \frac{1-0}{1+0} = 1 \quad \left[\because \lim_{h \to 0} \frac{1}{e^{1/h}} = 0\right]$$

Here, LHL $\neq$ RHL

Hence, $f(x)$ is not continuous at $x = 0$.

Continuity of a Function in its Domain

A function $f(x)$ is said to be continuous in its domain, if it is continuous at every point in its domain.

(i) A function $f(x)$ is said to be continuous in open interval (a, b), if it is continuous for every value of x in the interval (a, b).

(ii) A function $f(x)$ is said to be continuous in closed interval $[a, b]$, if

(a) it is continuous for every value of x in the open interval (a, b).

(b) $f(x)$ is continuous at $x = a$ from right, i.e. $\lim_{x \to a^+} f(x) = f(a)$.

(c) $f(x)$ is continuous at $x = b$ from left, i.e. $\lim_{x \to b^-} f(x) = f(b)$.

EXAMPLE 7. Discuss the continuity of the function f given by $f(x) = x^3 + x^2 - 1$ in the set of real number.

Sol. Given, $f(x) = x^3 + x^2 - 1$.

Here, $f(x)$ is always defined in R.

Let c be any real number, i.e. $c \in R$.

Then, at $x = c$, $f(c) = c^3 + c^2 - 1$

and $\lim_{x \to c} f(x) = \lim_{x \to c} (x^3 + x^2 - 1)$

$$= c^3 + c^2 - 1$$

Thus, $f(c) = \lim_{x \to c} f(x)$

So, $f(x)$ is continuous at every real number.

Hence, f is continuous for every real values of x.

EXAMPLE 8. Discuss the continuity of the function f in the set of real number, where f is defined by

$$f(x) = \begin{cases} -2, & \text{if } x \leq -1 \\ 2x, & \text{if } -1 < x \leq 1. \\ 2, & \text{if } x > 1 \end{cases}$$

Sol. We have, $f(x) = \begin{cases} -2, & \text{if } x \leq -1 \\ 2x, & \text{if } -1 < x \leq 1. \\ 2, & \text{if } x > 1 \end{cases}$

At $x = -1$, $f(-1) = -2$

$\text{LHL} = \lim_{x \to -1^-} f(x) = \lim_{x \to -1^-} (-2) = -2$

$\text{RHL} = \lim_{x \to -1^+} f(x) = \lim_{x \to -1^+} 2x = \lim_{h \to 0} 2(-1+h)$

[put $x = -1 + h$; when $x \to -1^+$, then $h \to 0$]

$= \lim_{h \to 0} (-2 + 2h)$

$= -2$

Thus, $f(-1) = \text{LHL} = \text{RHL}$

$\therefore$ $f(x)$ is continuous at $x = -1$.

At $x = 1$, $f(1) = 2$

$\text{LHL} = \lim_{x \to 1^-} f(x) = \lim_{x \to 1^-} 2x = \lim_{h \to 0} 2(1-h)$

[put $x = 1 - h$; when $x \to 1^-$, then $h \to 0$]

$= \lim_{h \to 0} (2 - 2h) = 2$

$\text{RHL} = \lim_{x \to 1^+} f(x) = \lim_{x \to 1^+} 2 = 2$

Thus, $f(1) = \text{LHL} = \text{RHL}$

So, $f(x)$ is continuous at $x = 1$.

Clearly $f(x)$ is continuous at all real numbers with 1 and -1.

Hence, $f(x)$ is continuous for every value of x.

Algebra of Continuous Functions

We know that continuity of a function at a point is entirely dictated by the limit of the function at that point, so algebra of continuous function is similar to algebra of limits, as given below

Theorem 1

Let f and g be two real functions continuous at a real number c, then

(i) $(f+g)$ is continuous at $x=c$.

(ii) $(f-g)$ is continuous at $x=c$.

(iii) f g is continuous at $x=c$.

(iv) $\frac{f}{g}$ is continuous at $x=c$, provided that $g(c)\neq 0$.

(v) αf is continuous at $x=c$, where α is any real number.

(vi) $\frac{1}{f}$ is continuous at $x=c$, provided that $f(c)\neq 0$

Theorem 2

Suppose f and g are real valued functions such that (fog) is defined at c. If g is continuous at c and if f is continuous at $g(c)$, then (fog) is continuous at c.

Other Important Results

There are some functions which are always continuous in their respective domain. e.g.

(i) Every constant function is continuous.

(ii) Every identity function is continuous.

(iii) Every rational function is continuous.

(iv) Every polynomial function is continuous.

(v) Modulus function $f(x)=|x|$ is continuous.

(vi) All trigonometric functions are continuous.

The exponential function a^x, $a>0$ is everywhere continuous. The logarithmic function is continuous in its domain.

EXAMPLE 9. Examine that $e^{|x|}$ is a continuous function.

Sol. Let $g(x)=|x|$ and $h(x)=e^x$

Then, $hog(x)=h[g(x)]=h(|x|)=e^{|x|}=f(x)$

Since, $g(x)$ and $h(x)$ are both continuous function for all $x\in R$, so composition of $g(x)$ and $h(x)$ is also a continuous function for all $x\in R$.

Hence, $f(x)=e^{|x|}$ is a continuous function.

Problems Based on Finding Unknown Constant in Continuous Function

EXAMPLE 10. Find the value of a, so that

$$f(x)=\begin{cases} ax+5, & \text{if } x\le 2 \\ x-1, & \text{if } x>2 \end{cases} \text{ is continuous at } x=2.$$

Sol. Given, $f(x)=\begin{cases} ax+5, & \text{if } x\le 2 \\ x-1, & \text{if } x>2 \end{cases}$

and at $x=2$, $f(x)$ is continuous.

$\therefore \quad x=c=2$

Here, a is an unknown constant.

At $x=2$, $f(2)=a(2)+5=2a+5$

$$\text{LHL}=\lim_{x\to 2^-} f(x)=\lim_{x\to 2^-}(ax+5)$$

$$=\lim_{h\to 0}[a(2-h)+5]=\lim_{h\to 0}(2a-ah+5)=2a+5$$

$$\text{RHL}=\lim_{x\to 2^+} f(x)=\lim_{x\to 2^+}(x-1)$$

$$=\lim_{h\to 0}[(2+h)-1]=\lim_{h\to 0}(1+h)=1$$

Since, $f(x)$ is continuous at $x=2$.

At $x=2$, LHL = RHL = $f(2)$

$\Rightarrow \quad 2a+5=1=2a+5$

$\therefore \quad 2a+5=1 \Rightarrow 2a=-4 \Rightarrow a=-2$

Hence, the required value of a is -2 for which $f(x)$ is continuous at $x=2$.

EXAMPLE 11. Find the relationship between a and b so that the function f defined by

$$f(x)=\begin{cases} ax+1, & \text{if } x\le 3 \\ bx+3, & \text{if } x>3 \end{cases} \text{ is continuous at } x=3.$$

Sol. Given, $f(x)=\begin{cases} ax+1, & \text{if } x\le 3 \\ bx+3, & \text{if } x>3 \end{cases}$

and $f(x)$ is continuous at $x=3$.

Here, a and b are two unknowns.

Now, at $x=3$, $f(3)=a(3)+1=3a+1$

$$\text{LHL}=\lim_{x\to 3^-} f(x)=\lim_{x\to 3^-}(ax+1)=\lim_{h\to 0}\{a(3-h)+1\}$$

[put $x=3-h$; when $x\to 3^-$ then $h\to 0$]

$$=\lim_{h\to 0}(3a-ah+1)=3a+1$$

$$\text{and RHL}=\lim_{x\to 3^+} f(x)=\lim_{x\to 3^+}\{bx+3\}=\lim_{h\to 0}\{b(3+h)+3\}$$

[put $x=3+h$; when $x\to 3^+$, then $h\to 0$]

$$=\lim_{h\to 0}\{3b+bh+3\}=3b+3$$

Since, $f(x)$ is continuous at $x=3$.

At $x=3$, $f(3)=$ LHL = RHL.

i.e. $\quad 3a+1=3a+1=3b+3$

$\Rightarrow \quad 3a+1=3b+3 \Rightarrow 3a=3b+3-1$

$\Rightarrow \quad a=\frac{(3b+2)}{3} \Rightarrow a=b+\frac{2}{3}$

which is the required relation between a and b.

EXAMPLE 12. Find the values of a and b such that the function defined by $f(x)=\begin{cases}5, \text{ if } x\le 2\\ ax+b, \text{ if } 2<x<10\\ 21, \text{ if } x\ge 10\end{cases}$ is continuous function.

Sol. Here, $f(x)=\begin{cases}5, & \text{if } x\le 2\\ ax+b, & \text{if } 2<x<10\\ 21, & \text{if } x\ge 10\end{cases}$

At $x=2$, LHL $=\lim_{x\to 2^-} f(x)=\lim_{x\to 2^-}(5)=5$

and RHL $=\lim_{x\to 2^+} f(x)=\lim_{x\to 2^+}(ax+b)$

$\therefore$ RHL $=\lim_{h\to 0}[a(2+h)+b]$

[put $x=2+h$; when $x\to 2^+$, then $h\to 0$]

$=\lim_{h\to 0}(2a+ah+b)=2a+b$

Also, $f(2)=5$

Since, $f(x)$ is continuous at $x=2$.

$\therefore$ LHL = RHL = $f(2) \Rightarrow 2a+b=5$ ...(i)

Now, at $x=10$, LHL $=\lim_{x\to 10^-} f(x)=\lim_{x\to 10^-}(ax+b)$

$\therefore$ LHL $=\lim_{h\to 0}[a(10-h)+b]=\lim_{h\to 0}(10a-ah+b)$

[put $x=10-h$; when $x\to 10^-$, then $h\to 0$]

$=10a+b$

and RHL $=\lim_{x\to 10^+} f(x)=\lim_{x\to 10^+}(21)=21$

Also, $f(10)=21$.

Since, $f(x)$ is continuous at $x=10$.

$\therefore$ LHL = RHL = $f(10) \Rightarrow 10a+b=21$ ...(ii)

On subtracting Eq. (i) from Eq. (ii), we get

$8a=16 \Rightarrow a=2$

On putting $a=2$ in Eq. (i), we get

$2\times 2+b=5 \Rightarrow b=1$

Hence, the values of a and b are 2 and 1, respectively.

Problems Based on Finding Points of Discontinuity of a Function

EXAMPLE 13. Find the point of the function f defined by $f(x)=\begin{cases}x+2, \text{ if } x\le 1\\ x-2, \text{ if } x>1\end{cases}$.

Sol. Given, $f(x)=\begin{cases}x+2, \text{ if } x\le 1\\ x-2, \text{ if } x>1\end{cases}$

When $x<1$, we have $f(x)=x+2$, which is a polynomial function, so it is continuous at each point for $x<1$.

Also, when $x>1$, we have $f(x)=x-2$, which is a polynomial function, so it is continuous at each point for $x>1$.

Now, we have to check the continuity at $x=1$.

LHL $=\lim_{x\to 1^-} f(x)=\lim_{x\to 1^-}(x+2)=\lim_{h\to 0}(1-h+2)=3$

[put $x=1-h$; when $x\to 1^-$, then $h\to 0$]

and RHL $=\lim_{x\to 1^+} f(x)=\lim_{x\to 1^+}(x-2)$

$=\lim_{h\to 0}(1+h-2)=-1$

[put $x=1+h$; when $x\to 1^+$, then $h\to 0$]

$\because$ LHL $\ne$ RHL at $x=1$.

So, $f(x)$ is not continuous at $x=1$.

Hence, $x=1$ is the only point of discontinuity of f.

EXAMPLE 14. Find all points of discontinuity of f, where f is defined by $f(x)=\begin{cases}|x|+3, & \text{if } x\le -3\\ -2x, & \text{if } -3<x<3\\ 6x+2, & \text{if } x\ge 3\end{cases}$.

Sol. Given, $f(x)=\begin{cases}|x|+3, & \text{if } x\le -3\\ -2x, & \text{if } -3<x<3\\ 6x+2, & \text{if } x\ge 3\end{cases}$

Here, we have to check the continuity only at points $x=-3$ and $x=3$.

[$\because$ functions defined in each interval is a polynomial, so it is continuous in each interval]

At $x=-3$,

LHL $=\lim_{x\to -3^-} f(x)=\lim_{x\to -3^-}\{|x|+3\}$

$=\lim_{h\to 0}\{|-3-h|+3\}$

[put $x=-3-h$; when $x\to -3^-$, then $h\to 0$]

$=\lim_{h\to 0}(3+h+3)=\lim_{h\to 0}(6+h)=6$

RHL $=\lim_{x\to -3^+} f(x)=\lim_{x\to -3^+}(-2x)=\lim_{h\to 0}-2(-3+h)$

[put $x=-3+h$; when $x\to -3^+$, then $h\to 0$]

$=\lim_{h\to 0}(6-2h)=6$ and $f(-3)=|-3|+3=6$

Thus, $f(-3)=$ LHL = RHL.

So, $f(x)$ is continuous at $x=-3$.

At $x=3$,

LHL $=\lim_{x\to 3^-} f(x)=\lim_{x\to 3^-}(-2x)=\lim_{h\to 0}-2(3-h)$

[put $x=3-h$; when $x\to 3^-$, then $h\to 0$]

$=\lim_{h\to 0}(-6+2h)=-6$

RHL $=\lim_{x\to 3^+} f(x)=\lim_{x\to 3^+}(6x+2)=\lim_{h\to 0}\{6(3+h)+2\}$

[put $x=3+h$; when $x\to 3^+$, then $h\to 0$]

$=\lim_{h\to 0}(18+6h+2)=20$

Thus, LHL $\ne$ RHL.

So, $f(x)$ is not continuous at $x=3$.

Hence, point of discontinuity is $x=3$.

Exam Pattern Exercise

Part A - Objective Type Questions

Multiple Choice Type Questions

1 If $f(x)=\begin{cases} mx+1, & \text{if } x \le \frac{\pi}{2} \\ \sin x+n, & \text{if } x > \frac{\pi}{2} \end{cases}$ is continuous at $x=\frac{\pi}{2}$, then

(a) $m=1, n=0$ (b) $m=\frac{n\pi}{2}+1$
(c) $n=\frac{m\pi}{2}$ (d) $m=n=\frac{\pi}{2}$

2 If $f(x)=\begin{cases} \frac{x^2-4}{x-4}, & x \ne 2 \\ 2x+k, & x=2 \end{cases}$ is continuous at $x=2$, then the value of k is

(a) 1 (b) -1 (c) 0 (d) 2

3 The function $f(x)=[x]$ is continuous at

(a) 2 (b) 1.4 (c) 0 (d) 1

4 The set of discontinuity of $f(x)=\frac{1}{x-[x]}$ is

(a) Z (b) Q
(c) R (d) None of these

5 The function $f(x)=\frac{4-x^2}{4x-x^3}$

(a) discontinuous at only one point
(b) discontinuous exactly at two points
(c) discontinuous exactly at three points
(d) None of the above

6 The function $f(x)=\begin{cases} \frac{|x^2-x|}{x^2-x}, & x \ne 0,1 \\ 1, & x=0 \\ -1, & x=1 \end{cases}$ then $f(x)$ is

(a) continuous at $x=0$ (b) discontinuous at $x=0$
(c) continuous at $x=1$ (d) None of these

7 The function $f(x)=\begin{cases} \frac{x-4}{|x-4|}+a, & x<4 \\ a+b, & x=4 \\ \frac{x-4}{|x-4|}+b & x>4 \end{cases}$

is continuous at $x=4$, when

(a) $a=0, b=0$ (b) $a=1, b=1$
(c) $a=-1, b=1$ (d) $a=1, b=-1$

8 Let $f(x)=\begin{cases} \frac{x^4-5x^2+4}{|(x-2)|}, & x \ne 2 \\ 7, & x=2 \end{cases}$ Then, $f(x)$ is continuous on the set

(a) R (b) $R-\{2\}$
(c) $R-\{1\}$ (d) None of these

9 The value of a for which the function

$f(x)=\begin{cases} 3x-2, & 0<x\le 1 \\ 2x^2+5ax, & 1<x<2 \end{cases}$ is continuous at every point of its domain, is

(a) 0 (b) 1 (c) 5 (d) $-\frac{1}{5}$

10 If $f(x)=3x$ and $g(x)=\frac{x^2}{5}+9$, then which of the following can be a discontinuous function?

(a) $f(x)+g(x)$ (b) $f(x)-g(x)$
(c) $f(x)\,g(x)$ (d) $\frac{g(x)}{f(x)}$

Assertion-Reason Based Questions

Directions (Q. Nos. 11-13) *In the questions given below are two statements labelled as Assertion (A) and Reason (R). In the context of the two statements, which one of the following is correct?*

(a) Both A and R are correct; R is the correct explanation of A
(b) Both A and R are correct; R is not the correct explanation of A
(c) A is correct; R is incorrect
(d) R is correct; A is incorrect

11 Consider the function $f(x)=\begin{cases} \frac{kx}{|x|}, & \text{if } x<0 \\ 3, & \text{if } x \ge 0 \end{cases}$ which is continuous at $x=0$.

Assertion (A) The value of k is -3.

Reason (R) $|x|=\begin{cases} -x, & \text{if } x<0 \\ x, & \text{if } x \ge 0 \end{cases}$

12 Consider the function $f(x)=\begin{cases} \frac{x^2+3x-10}{x-2}, & \text{if } x \ne 2 \\ k, & \text{if } x=2 \end{cases}$

which is continuous at $x=2$.

Assertion (A) The value of k is 7.

Reason (R) $f(x)$ is continuous at $x=a$, if $\lim_{x \to a} f(x)=f(a)$

13 **Assertion (A)** $f(x)=\begin{cases} x+1, & \text{if } x\le 1 \\ 3-x^2, & \text{if } x>1 \end{cases}$ is continuous at $x=1$.

Reason (R) A function $f(x)$ at $x=a$ is continuous then $\lim_{x\to a^-} f(x)=\lim_{x\to a^+} f(x)=f(a)$.

Part B - Descriptive Questions

Very Short Answer Type Questions

14 Examine the continuity of the following functions at the given point.

(i) $f(x)=5x-3$ at $x=-3$

(ii) $f(x)=x^2+5$ at $x=-1$

(iii) $f(x)=x^3+2x^2-1$ at $x=1$

(iv) $f(x)=|x-2|$ at $x=2$

Directions (Q.Nos. 15-19) *Discuss the continuity of the following function at the indicated point(s).*

15 $f(x)=\begin{cases} 4x+3, \text{ if } x\ne 4 \\ 3x+7, \text{ if } x=4 \end{cases}$.

16 $f(x)=\begin{cases} \dfrac{x^2-49}{x-7}, & \text{if } x\ne 7 \\ 14, & \text{if } x=7 \end{cases}$.

17 $f(x)=\begin{cases} x^3-2x^2+x+2, & \text{if } x\ne 1 \\ 2, & \text{if } x=1 \end{cases}$.

18 $f(x)=\begin{cases} \dfrac{x}{|x|}, & \text{if } x\ne 0 \\ 1, & \text{if } x=0 \end{cases}$.

19 $f(x)=\begin{cases} 1, & \text{if } x\le -1 \\ -2x-1, & -1<x<0 \\ -1, & x\ge 0 \end{cases}$.

20 The function $f(x)=\begin{cases} \dfrac{x^2-2x-3}{x+1}, & x\ne -1 \\ \lambda, & x=-1 \end{cases}$ is continuous at $x=-1$, then find the value of λ.

21 Determine the value of constant 'k', so that function $f(x)=\begin{cases} \dfrac{kx}{|x|}, & x<0 \\ 3, & x\ge 0 \end{cases}$ is continuous at $x=0$.

22 If $f(x)=\begin{cases} \dfrac{x^2-16}{x-4}, & x\ne 4 \\ k, & x=4 \end{cases}$ is continuous at $x=4$, then find the value of k.

23 If $f(x)=\begin{cases} 5x-4, & 0<x\le 1 \\ 4x^2+3bx, & 1<x<2 \end{cases}$ is continuous at $x=1$, then find the value of b.

24 If $f(x)=\begin{cases} \dfrac{x^2+3x-10}{x-2}, & x\ne 2 \\ k, & x=2 \end{cases}$ is continuous at $x=2$, then find the value of k.

Short Answer Type Questions

25 Show that the function $f(x)=\begin{cases} \dfrac{e^{1/x}}{1+e^{1/x}}, & \text{if } x\ne 0 \\ 0, & \text{if } x=0 \end{cases}$ is discontinuous at $x=0$.

26 Show that the function $f(x)=2x-|x|$ is continuous at $x=0$.

27 Given, $f(x)=\dfrac{1}{x-1}$. Find the point(s) of discontinuity of composite function $y=f\{f(x)\}$.

Directions (Q.Nos. 28-31) *Determine the value of constant involved in the definition such that the following functions are continuous at the indicated point.*

28 $f(x)=\begin{cases} \dfrac{(x+3)^2-36}{x-3}, & x\ne 3 \\ k, & x=3 \end{cases}$, at $x=3$.

29 $f(x)=\begin{cases} \dfrac{\sqrt{1+kx}-\sqrt{1-kx}}{x}, & \text{if } -1\le x<0 \\ \dfrac{2x+1}{x-1}, & \text{if } 0\le x<1 \end{cases}$ at $x=0$.

30 $f(x)=\begin{cases} \dfrac{2^{x+2}-16}{4^x-16}, & \text{if } x\ne 2 \\ k, & \text{if } x=2 \end{cases}$ at $x=2$.

31 $f(x)=\begin{cases} \lambda(x^2-2x), & \text{if } x\le 0 \\ 4x+1, & \text{if } x>0 \end{cases}$ at $x=0$ and $x=1$.

32 If the function $f(x)$ defined by

$$f(x)=\begin{cases} \dfrac{\log(1+ax)-\log(1-bx)}{x}, & x\ne 0 \\ k, & x=0 \end{cases}$$ is continuous at $x=0$, then find the value of k.

33 If the function $f(x)=\begin{cases} 3ax+b, & x>1 \\ 11, & x=1 \\ 5ax-2b, & x<1 \end{cases}$ is continuous at $x=1$, then find the values of a and b.

34 The function $f(x)=\begin{cases} \dfrac{x^2}{a}, & 0\le x<1 \\ a, & 1\le x<\sqrt{2} \\ \dfrac{2b^2-4b}{x^2}, & \sqrt{2}\le x<\infty \end{cases}$ is continuous on $[0,\infty)$. Find the most suitable values of a and b.

35 Examine the continuity of the function

$$f(x)=\begin{cases}\dfrac{x}{2|x|}, & x\neq 0\\ \dfrac{1}{2}, & x=0\end{cases} \text{ at } x=0$$

36 Find the point of discontinuity of the function

$$f(x)=\begin{cases}x^{10}-1, & x\le 1\\ x^2, & x>1\end{cases}$$

Long Answer Type Questions

Directions (Q.Nos. 37-39) *Determine the values of a and b for which the functions f(x) is continuous.*

37 $f(x)=\begin{cases}2, \text{ if } x\le 3\\ ax+b, \text{ if } 3<x<5\\ 9, \text{ if } x\ge 5\end{cases}$.

38 $f(x)=\begin{cases}x+2, \text{ if } x\le 2\\ ax+b, \text{ if } 2<x<5\\ 3x-2, \text{ if } x\ge 5\end{cases}$.

39 $f(x)=\begin{cases}\dfrac{x-4}{|x-4|}+a, \text{ if } x<4\\ a+b, \text{ if } x=4\\ \dfrac{x-4}{|x-4|}+b, \text{ if } x>4\end{cases}$ at $x=4$.

40 If $f(x)=\begin{cases}\dfrac{|x-4|}{4-x}, & x\neq 4\\ 0, & x=4\end{cases}$, show that $f(x)$ is continuous everywhere except at $x=4$.

41 Find the value of k is the function

$$f(x)=\begin{cases}2x-1, & x<2\\ k, & x=2\\ x+1, & x>2\end{cases}$$ is continuous at $x=2$.

42 Discuss the continuity of the function

$$f(x)=\begin{cases}x+1, & x\ge 1\\ x^2+1, & x<1\end{cases} \text{ at } x=1$$

43 Is the function f defined by $f(x)=\begin{cases}x, \text{ if } x\le 1\\ 5, \text{ if } x>1\end{cases}$ continuous at $x=0$, at $x=1$ and at $x=2$?

Directions (Q.Nos. 44-47) *Find the points of discontinuity of the following functions.*

44 $f(x)=\begin{cases}x^3-3, \text{ if } x\le 2\\ x^2+1, \text{ if } x>2\end{cases}$.

45 $f(x)=\begin{cases}\dfrac{1}{2}-x, \text{ if } 0\le x<\dfrac{1}{2}\\ 1, \text{ if } x=\dfrac{1}{2}\\ \dfrac{3}{2}-x, \text{ if } \dfrac{1}{2}<x\le 1\end{cases}$.

46 $f(x)=\begin{cases}2x+3, \text{ if } -3\le x<-2\\ x+1, \text{ if } -2\le x<0\\ x+2, \text{ if } 0\le x\le 1\end{cases}$.

47 $f(x)=|x|-|x+1|$.

48 Prove that function $f(x)=\begin{cases}\dfrac{x}{|x|}+2x^2, & x\neq 0\\ k, & x=0\end{cases}$ remains discontinuous at $x=0$, regardless of the choice of k.

Case Study Based Questions

49 A function $f(x)$ is said to be continuous at a point $x=a$, if the value of function at $x=a$ is equal to the limit of the function at $x=a$

i.e. $f(x)$ is continuous at $x=a$ if

$(\text{LHL})_{x=a}=(\text{RHL})_{x=a}=f(a)$ or $\lim_{x\to a} f(x)=f(a)$

If $f(x)$ is not continuous at a, we say $f(x)$ is discontinuous at a, and a is called a point of discontinuity of $f(x)$.

On the basis of above information answer the following questions.

(i) Find the point of discontinuity of the function $f(x)=\begin{cases}2x+3, & x\le 2\\ 2x-3, & x>2\end{cases}$.

(ii) Find all the points of discontinuity of the function of defined by $f(x)=\begin{cases}3, & 0\le x\le 1\\ 4, & 1<x<3\\ 5, & 3\le x\le 10\end{cases}$.

(iii) If $f(x)=\begin{cases}\dfrac{\sqrt{1+kx}-\sqrt{1-kx}}{x}, & -1\le x<0\\ 2x^2+3x-2, & 0\le x\le 1\end{cases}$ is continuous at $x=0$, then find the value of k.

Or

If $f(x)=\begin{cases}ax+3, & x\le 2\\ a^2x-1, & x>2\end{cases}$, then find the values of a for which f is continuous for all x.

50 Every polynomial function, constant functions are continuous everywhere. Also, for a function to be continuous at $x = a$, $\lim_{x \to a} f(x) = f(a)$.
On the basis of above information, answer the following questions.

(i) Examine the continuity of of the function $f(x) = \begin{cases} 3x, & \text{for } x \le 0 \\ 0, & \text{for } x > 0 \end{cases}$, then at $x = 0$

(ii) Show that $f(x) = |x - 2|, x \in R$ is continuous at $x = 2$.

(iii) If $f(x) = \begin{cases} kx + 3, & x < 1 \\ x + 2, & x \ge 1 \end{cases}$ is continuous at $x = 1$, then find the value of k.

Or

Find the value of k, if the function $f(x)$ defined by $f(x) = \begin{cases} \dfrac{x^2 - 25}{x - 5}, & x \ne 5 \\ k, & x = 5 \end{cases}$ is continuous at $x = 5$.

Hints & Solutions

1. (c)	2. (c)	3. (b)	4. (a)
5. (c)	6. (b)	7. (d)	8. (b)
9. (d)	10. (d)	11. (a)	12. (a)
13. (a)			

14. (i) Given, $f(x) = 5x - 3$
At $x = -3$,

$$\lim_{x \to -3} f(x) = \lim_{x \to -3} (5x - 3)$$
$$= 5(-3) - 3 = -15 - 3 = -18$$

and $f(-3) = 5(-3) - 3 = -15 - 3 = -18$

$$\therefore \lim_{x \to -3} f(x) = f(-3).$$

Hence, $f(x)$ is continuous at $x = -3$.

(ii) Solve as Example 1(ii). **Ans.** Yes

(iii) Solve as Example 1(ii). **Ans.** Yes

(iv) Solve as Example 1(iii). **Ans.** Yes

15. Continuous at $x = 4$.

16. Continuous at $x = 7$.

17. Continuous at $x = 1$.

18. Discontinuous at $x = 0$.

19. Everywhere continuous.

20. $\lambda = -4$

21. $k = -3$

22. 8

23. $b = -1$

24. $k = 7$

26. **Hint** The given function is $f(x) = 2x - |x|$.

$$\therefore f(x) = \begin{cases} 2x - x, & \text{if } x \ge 0 \\ 2x - (-x), & \text{if } x < 0 \end{cases}$$

$$\left[\because |x| = \begin{cases} x, & \text{if } x \ge 0 \\ -x, & \text{if } x < 0 \end{cases}\right]$$

i.e. $f(x) = \begin{cases} x, & \text{if } x \ge 0 \\ 3x, & \text{if } x < 0 \end{cases}$

27. **Hint** We have, $f(x) = \dfrac{1}{x - 1}$

$$y = f\{f(x)\} = \frac{1}{f(x) - 1} = \frac{1}{\frac{1}{x - 1} - 1} = \frac{x - 1}{1 - x + 1} = \frac{x - 1}{2 - x}$$

At $x = 2$, $f\{f(x)\}$ is not defined. **Ans.** 2

28. $k = 12$

29. $k = -1$

30. **Hint** $\lim_{x \to 2} f(x) = \lim_{x \to 2} \dfrac{2^{x+2} - 16}{4^x - 16} = \lim_{x \to 2} \dfrac{4(2^x - 4)}{(2^x)^2 - 4^2}$

$$= \lim_{x \to 2} \frac{4(2^x - 4)}{(2^x + 4)(2^x - 4)} = \lim_{x \to 2} \frac{4}{2^x + 4} = \frac{1}{2}$$

Ans. $k = \dfrac{1}{2}$

31. Here, $f(x) = \begin{cases} \lambda(x^2 - 2x), & \text{if } x \le 0 \\ 4x + 1, & \text{if } x > 0 \end{cases}$

At $x = 0$, LHL $= \lim_{x \to 0^-} f(x) = \lim_{x \to 0^-} \lambda(x^2 - 2x)$

$$\therefore \text{LHL} = \lim_{h \to 0} \lambda[(0 - h)^2 - 2(0 - h)]$$
$$= \lim_{h \to 0} [\lambda(h^2 + 2h)] = 0$$

[put $x = 0 - h$; when $x \to 0^-$, then $h \to 0$]

$$\text{RHL} = \lim_{x\to 0^+} f(x) = \lim_{x\to 0^+}(4x+1)$$

$$\therefore\ \text{RHL} = \lim_{h\to 0}[4(0+h)+1] = \lim_{h\to 0}[4h+1] = 0+1=1$$

[put $x = 0+h$; when $x\to 0^+$, then $h\to 0$]

$\therefore$ LHL $\neq$ RHL

Thus, $f(x)$ is not continuous at $x=0$ for any value of λ.

At $x=1$,

$$\text{LHL} = \lim_{x\to 1^-} f(x) = \lim_{x\to 1^-}(4x+1)$$

$$\therefore\ \text{LHL} = \lim_{h\to 0}[4(1-h)+1] = \lim_{h\to 0}[5-4h] = 5-0=5$$

[put $x = 1-h$; when $x\to 1^-$, then $h\to 0$]

$$\text{RHL} = \lim_{x\to 1^+} f(x) = \lim_{x\to 1^+}(4x+1)$$

$$\therefore \lim_{h\to 0}[4(1+h)+1] = \lim_{h\to 0}(5+4h) = 5+0=5$$

[put $x = 1+h$; when $x\to 1$, then $h\to 0$]

Also, $f(1) = 4\times 1+1 = 5$ [$\because f(x) = 4x+1$]

Thus, $f(x)$ is continuous at $x=1$ for all values of λ.

32. Hint Given, $f(x) = \begin{cases} \dfrac{\log(1+ax)-\log(1-bx)}{x}, & x\neq 0 \\ k, & x=0 \end{cases}$

is continuous at $x=0$,

$\therefore$ $f(0)=k$

$$\text{Now, } \lim_{x\to 0} f(x) = \lim_{x\to 0}\frac{\log(1+ax)-\log(1-bx)}{x}$$

$$= \lim_{x\to 0}\frac{\log(1+ax)}{x} + \lim_{x\to 0}\frac{\log(1-bx)}{-x}$$

$$= a+b$$

Ans. $a+b$

33. Hint Given, $f(x) = \begin{cases} 3ax+b, & x>1 \\ 11, & x=1 \\ 5ax-2b, & x<1 \end{cases}$

is continuos at $x=1$.

$\therefore$ $f(1)=11$ ...(i)

$$\text{Now, LHL} = \lim_{x\to 1^-} f(x) = \lim_{x\to 1^-}(5ax-2b)$$

$$= \lim_{h\to 0} 5a(1-h)-2b = 5a-2b \quad \text{...(ii)}$$

$$\text{RHL} = \lim_{x\to 1^+} f(x) = \lim_{h\to 0} f(1+h)$$

$$= \lim_{h\to 0} 3a(1+h)+b = 3a+b \quad \text{...(iii)}$$

Since, $f(1) = \text{LHL} = \text{RHL}$

$\therefore$ $5a-2b=11$ ...(iv)

and $3a+b=11$ ...(v)

Ans. $a=3, b=2$

34. Hint Given, $f(x) = \begin{cases} \dfrac{x^2}{a}, & 0\le x<1 \\ a, & 1\le x<\sqrt{2} \\ \dfrac{2b^2-4b}{x^2}, & \sqrt{2}\le x<\infty \end{cases}$

is continuous on $[0,\infty)$.

$$\lim_{x\to 1^{-1}} f(x) = \lim_{h\to 0} f(1-h) = \lim_{h\to 0}\frac{(1-h)^2}{a} = \frac{1}{a}$$

and $\lim_{x\to 1^+} f(x) = a$

$$\because \lim_{x\to 1^-} f(x) = \lim_{x\to 1^+} f(x) \Rightarrow \frac{1}{a} = a \Rightarrow a^2 = 1$$

$$a = \pm 1$$

$$\text{Now, } \lim_{x\to\sqrt{2}^-} f(x) = \pm a$$

$$\lim_{x\to\sqrt{2}^+} f(x) = \lim_{x\to\sqrt{2}^+}\frac{2b^2-4b}{x^2} = b^2-2b$$

$$\because \lim_{x\to\sqrt{2}^-} f(x) = \lim_{x\to\sqrt{2}^+} f(x)$$

$$b^2-2b = \pm 1$$

Ans. $a=-1, b=1$, or $a=1, b=\pm\sqrt{2}$

35. Hint $f(x) = \begin{cases} \dfrac{x}{2|x|}, & x\neq 0 \\ \dfrac{1}{2}, & x=0 \end{cases}$

$$\text{LHL} = \lim_{x\to 0^-} f(x) = \lim_{h\to 0} f(0-h)$$

$$= \frac{0-h}{2|0-h|} = -\frac{1}{2}$$

$$\text{and RHL} = \lim_{x\to 0^+} f(x) = \lim_{h\to 0} f(0+h)$$

$$= \frac{0+h}{2|0+h|} = \frac{1}{2}$$

$\because$ LHL $\neq$ RHL

Ans. $f(x)$ is discontinuous at $x=0$.

36. Hint When $x<1$, we have $f(x) = x^{10}-1$

Clearly, $f(x)$ is polynomial function for $x<1$.

So, $f(x)$ is continuous for all $x<1$.

When $x>1$, we have $f(x) = x^2$, clearly $f(x)$ is polynomial function for $x>1$. So, $f(x)$ is continuous for all $x>1$.

Let us now consider the point $x=1$ at $x=1$

$$\lim_{x\to 1^-} f(x) = \lim_{h\to 0} f(1-h) = (1-h)^{10}-1 = 0$$

$$\text{and } \lim_{x\to 1^+} f(x) = \lim_{h\to 0} f(0+h) = (1+h)^2 = 1$$

Ans. $f(x)$ is discontinuous at $x=1$.

37. $a = 7/2, b = -17/2$

38. $a = 3$ and $b = -2$

39. **Hint** $f(x) = \begin{cases} a-1, & x<4 \\ a+b, & x=4 \\ b+1, & x>4 \end{cases}$

$\because f(x)$ is continuous at $x = 4$.

$\therefore \ a-1 = a+b = b+1$

Ans. $a = 1, b = -1$

40. **Hint** When $x<4$, we have $f(x)=1$, which being a constant function, is continuous at each point $x<4$. Also, when $x>4$, we have $f(x) = -1$, which being a constant function, is continuous at each point $x > 4$.

Now, at $x = 4$

We have, $\lim_{x\to 4^-} f(x) = \lim_{x\to 4^-} 1 = 1$,

$\lim_{x\to 4^+} f(x) = \lim_{x\to 4^+} -1 = -1$

and $f(4) = 0$

$\therefore \quad \lim_{x\to 4^-} f(x) \neq \lim_{x\to 4^+} f(x)$

So, $f(x)$ is not continuous at $x = 4$.

41. **Hint** Given, $f(x) = \begin{cases} 2x-1, & x<2 \\ k, & x=2 \\ x+1, & x>2 \end{cases}$ is continuous at $x = 2$

$\therefore \quad f(2) = k$

Now, $\lim_{x\to 2^-} f(x) = \lim_{h\to 0} f(2-h) = \lim_{h\to 0} 2(2-h)-1 = 3$

and $\lim_{x\to 2^+} f(x) = \lim_{h\to 0} f(2+h) = \lim_{h\to 0} 2+h+1 = 3$

Since, $f(x)$ is continuous at $x = 2$

$\therefore f(2) = \lim_{x\to 2^-} f(x) = \lim_{x\to 2^+} f(x)$

Ans. $k = 3$

42. **Hint** We have, $f(x) = \begin{cases} x+1, & x\geq 1 \\ x^2+1, & x<1 \end{cases}$

When, $x = 1$, we have $f(x) = 1+1 = 2$

Now, $\lim_{x\to 1^-} f(x) = \lim_{h\to 0} f(1-h)$

$= \lim_{h\to 0} (1-h)+1 = 2$

and $\lim_{x\to 2^+} f(x) = \lim_{h\to 0} f(1+h) = \lim_{h\to 0} (1+h)^2 + 1 = 2$

Ans. $f(x)$ is continuous $x = 1$.

43. **Hint** For $x = 0$; $f(x) = x$, which is continuous and at $x = 1$, LHL $= 1$ and RHL $= 5$, hence discontinuous and at $x = 2$; $f(x) = 5$, which is continuous.

Ans. At $x = 0$, $f(x)$ is continuous; at $x = 1$, $f(x)$ is not continuous and at $x = 2$, $f(x)$ is continuous

44. No point

45. $x = \frac{1}{2}$

46. $x = 0$

47. **Hint** Let $g(x) = |x|$ and $h(x) = |x+1|$

Now, $g(x) = |x|$ is the absolute valued function, so it is a continuous function for all $x \in R$.

$h(x) = |x+1|$ is the absolute valued function, so it is a continuous function for all $x \in R$.

Since, $g(x)$ and $h(x)$ are both continuous functions for all $x \in R$, so difference of two continuous function is a continuous function for all $x \in R$, thus $f(x) = |x| - |x+1|$ is a continuous function at all points.

Hence, there is no point at which $f(x)$ is discontinuous.

48. **Hint** $f(x) = \begin{cases} \frac{x}{-x} + 2x^2, & x<0 \\ \frac{x}{x} + 2x^2, & x>0 \\ k, & x=0 \end{cases}$

$\Rightarrow \quad f(x) = \begin{cases} 2x^2-1, & x<0 \\ 2x^2+1, & x>0 \\ k & x=0 \end{cases}$

LHL at $x = 0$

$\lim_{x\to 0^-} f(x) = \lim_{h\to 0} f(0-h) = \lim_{h\to 0} f(-h)$

$\Rightarrow \lim_{h\to 0} 2(-h)^2 - 1 = \lim_{h\to 0} 2h^2 - 1 = -1$

RHL at $x = 0$

$\lim_{h\to 0} 2(h)^2 + 1 = \lim_{h\to 0} 2h^2 + 1 = 1$

$\because \quad \lim_{x\to 0^-} f(x) \neq \lim_{x\to 0^+} f(x)$

Hence, $f(x)$ is discontinuous at $x = 0$ regardless the choice of k.

49. (i) 2 (ii) 1, 3 (iii) -2 *Or* -1 and 2

50. (i) $f(x)$ is continuous at $x = 0$

(iii) $k = 0$ *Or* $k = 10$

CHAPTER 16

Differentiation

In this Chapter...

- Derivative of a Function and First Principal of Derivative
- Fundamental Rules for Differentiation
- Exponential Function and Logarithmic Differentiation
- Differentiation of Parametric Functions
- Differentiation of a Function w.r.t. Another Function and Differentiation of Infinite Series

Derivative of a Function and First Principle of Derivative

Derivative of a Function

Suppose f is a real valued function and a is a point in its domain. Then, derivative of f at a is defined by $\lim_{h \to 0} \frac{f(a+h) - f(a)}{h}$ provided this limit exists.

The derivative of $f(x)$ at a is denoted by $f'(a)$ or $\left[\frac{df(x)}{dx}\right]_{x=a}$

EXAMPLE 1. Find the derivative of $f(x) = 4x + 5$ at $x = 3$.

Sol. Given, $f(x) = 4x + 5$

We know that the derivative of a function f at $x = a$,

$$f'(a) = \lim_{h \to 0} \frac{f(a+h) - f(a)}{h}$$

$$\therefore \quad f'(3) = \lim_{h \to 0} \frac{f(3+h) - f(3)}{h}$$

$$= \lim_{h \to 0} \frac{4(3+h) + 5 - (4 \times 3 + 5)}{h}$$

$$= \lim_{h \to 0} \frac{12 + 4h + 5 - 17}{h} = \lim_{h \to 0} \frac{4h}{h} = 4$$

EXAMPLE 2. Find the derivative of the function $f(x) = 2x^2 + 3x - 5$ at $x = -1$. Also, prove that $f'(0) + 3f'(-1) = 0$.

Sol. Clearly, $f'(-1) = \lim_{h \to 0} \frac{f(-1+h) - f(-1)}{h}$

$$\left[\because f'(a) = \lim_{h \to 0} \frac{f(a+h) - f(a)}{h}\right]$$

$$= \lim_{h \to 0} \frac{[2(-1+h)^2 + 3(-1+h) - 5] - [2(-1)^2 + 3(-1) - 5]}{h}$$

$$= \lim_{h \to 0} \frac{[2(1 + h^2 - 2h) - 3 + 3h - 5] - [2 - 3 - 5]}{h}$$

$$= \lim_{h \to 0} \frac{2h^2 - h}{h} = \lim_{h \to 0} (2h - 1) = 2(0) - 1 = -1$$

and $f'(0) = \lim_{h \to 0} \frac{f(0+h) - f(0)}{h}$

$$\left[\because f'(a) = \lim_{h \to 0} \frac{f(a+h) - f(a)}{h}\right]$$

$$= \lim_{h \to 0} \frac{[2(0+h)^2 + 3(0+h) - 5] - [2(0)^2 + 3(0) - 5]}{h}$$

$$= \lim_{h \to 0} \frac{2h^2 + 3h}{h} = \lim_{h \to 0} (2h + 3) = 2(0) + 3 = 3$$

Now, $f'(0) + 3f'(-1) = 3 - 3 = 0$ **Hence proved.**

First Principle of Derivative

Suppose f is a real valued function, the function defined by $\lim_{h \to 0} \frac{f(x+h) - f(x)}{h}$, wherever the limit exists, is defined to be the derivative of f at x and is denoted by $f'(x)$. This definition of derivative is called the first principle of derivative.

Thus, $f'(x) = \lim_{h \to 0} \frac{f(x+h) - f(x)}{h}$

Sometimes $f'(x)$ is denoted by $\frac{d}{dx}[f(x)]$ or if $y = f(x)$, then it is denoted by $\frac{dy}{dx}$ and referred to as derivative of $f(x)$ or y with respect to x. It is also denoted by $D[f(x)]$.

Derivative of f at $x = a$ is also given by substituting $x = a$ in $f'(x)$ and it is denoted by

$$\left.\frac{d}{dx}f(x)\right|_a \quad \text{or} \quad \left.\frac{df}{dx}\right|_a \quad \text{or} \quad \left(\frac{df}{dx}\right)_{x=a}.$$

Note If $y = f(x)$, then $\frac{dy}{dx} = \lim_{h\to 0}\frac{f(x+h)-f(x)}{h}$ is known as the instantaneous rate of change of y w.r.t. x or it is denoted as $\frac{\Delta y}{\Delta x} = \lim_{\Delta x\to 0}\frac{f(x+\Delta x)-f(x)}{\Delta x}$.

EXAMPLE 3. Find the derivative of $f(x) = \frac{1}{x}$ from first principle.

Sol. We have, $f(x) = \frac{1}{x}$

By using first principle,

$$f'(x) = \lim_{h\to 0}\frac{f(x+h)-f(x)}{h}$$

$$\therefore \quad f'(x) = \lim_{h\to 0}\frac{\frac{1}{x+h}-\frac{1}{x}}{h} \qquad \left[\begin{array}{l}\because \quad f(x) = \frac{1}{x}\\ \therefore f(x+h) = \frac{1}{x+h}\end{array}\right]$$

$$= \lim_{h\to 0}\frac{1}{h}\left[\frac{x-(x+h)}{x(x+h)}\right]$$

$$= \lim_{h\to 0}\frac{1}{h}\left[\frac{-h}{x(x+h)}\right] = \lim_{h\to 0}\left[\frac{-1}{x(x+h)}\right] = \frac{-1}{x^2}$$

EXAMPLE 4. Find the derivative of $f(x) = ax + b$, where a and b are non-zero constants, by first principle.

Sol. We have, $f(x) = ax + b$

By definition of first principle, we have

$$f'(x) = \lim_{h\to 0}\frac{f(x+h)-f(x)}{h}$$

$$= \lim_{h\to 0}\frac{a(x+h)+b-(ax+b)}{h} = \lim_{h\to 0}\frac{ah}{h} = a$$

EXAMPLE 5. Find the derivative of $f(x) = x^n$, where n is positive integer, by first principle.

Sol. By definition of first principle, we have

$$f'(x) = \lim_{h\to 0}\frac{f(x+h)-f(x)}{h} = \lim_{h\to 0}\frac{(x+h)^n - x^n}{h} \quad \text{...(i)}$$

By binomial theorem, we have

$$(x+h)^n = {}^nC_0x^n + {}^nC_1x^{n-1}h + {}^nC_2x^{n-2}h^2 + \dots + {}^nC_nh^n$$

$$\Rightarrow (x+h)^n = x^n + nhx^{n-1} + \frac{n(n-1)}{2}h^2x^{n-2} + \dots + h^n$$

$$\Rightarrow (x+h)^n - x^n = nhx^{n-1} + \frac{n(n-1)}{2}h^2x^{n-2} + \dots + h^n$$

On putting this value in Eq. (i), we get

$$f'(x) = \lim_{h\to 0}\frac{nhx^{n-1} + \frac{n(n-1)}{2}h^2x^{n-2} + \dots + h^n}{h}$$

$$= \lim_{h\to 0}\frac{h\left[nx^{n-1} + \frac{n(n-1)}{2}hx^{n-2} + \dots + h^{n-1}\right]}{h}$$

$$= \lim_{h\to 0}\left[nx^{n-1} + \frac{n(n-1)}{2}hx^{n-2} + \dots + h^{n-1}\right] = nx^{n-1}$$

Hence, $f'(x)$ or $\frac{d}{dx}f(x) = nx^{n-1}$

EXAMPLE 6. Find the derivative of $(x-1)(x-2)$ from first principle.

Sol. Let $f(x) = (x-1)(x-2) = x^2 - 3x + 2$

By first principle of derivative, we have

$$f'(x) = \lim_{h\to 0}\frac{f(x+h)-f(x)}{h}$$

$$= \lim_{h\to 0}\frac{[(x+h)^2 - 3(x+h) + 2] - [x^2 - 3x + 2]}{h}$$

$$= \lim_{h\to 0}\frac{[x^2 + h^2 + 2xh - 3x - 3h + 2] - [x^2 - 3x + 2]}{h}$$

$$= \lim_{h\to 0}\frac{2hx + h^2 - 3h}{h} = \lim_{h\to 0}\frac{h(2x+h-3)}{h} = 2x - 3$$

EXAMPLE 7. Find the derivative of $\left(\frac{x+1}{x-1}\right)$ from the first principle.

Sol. Let $f(x) = \frac{x+1}{x-1}$

By first principle of derivative, we have

$$f'(x) = \lim_{h\to 0}\frac{f(x+h)-f(x)}{h}$$

$$= \lim_{h\to 0}\frac{\left[\frac{(x+h)+1}{(x+h)-1} - \frac{x+1}{x-1}\right]}{h}$$

$$= \lim_{h\to 0}\frac{(x+h+1)(x-1) - (x+1)(x+h-1)}{h(x+h-1)(x-1)}$$

$$= \lim_{h\to 0}\frac{(x^2 - x + xh - h + x - 1) - (x^2 + xh - x + x + h - 1)}{h(x+h-1)(x-1)}$$

$$= \lim_{h\to 0}\frac{-2h}{h(x+h-1)(x-1)}$$

$$= \lim_{h\to 0}\frac{-2}{(x+h-1)(x-1)} = \frac{-2}{(x-1)^2}$$

EXAMPLE 8. Find the derivative of $\sqrt{ax+b}$ from first principle.

Sol. We have, $f(x)=\sqrt{ax+b}$

By using first principle,

$$f'(x)=\lim_{h\to 0}\frac{f(x+h)-f(x)}{h}$$

$$=\lim_{h\to 0}\frac{\sqrt{a(x+h)+b}-\sqrt{ax+b}}{h}$$

$$=\lim_{h\to 0}\frac{\sqrt{(ax+b)+ah}-\sqrt{ax+b}}{h}\times\frac{\sqrt{(ax+b)+ah}+\sqrt{ax+b}}{\sqrt{(ax+b)+ah}+\sqrt{ax+b}}$$

$$=\lim_{h\to 0}\frac{(ax+b)+ah-(ax+b)}{h(\sqrt{ax+b+ah}+\sqrt{ax+b})}$$

$$=\lim_{h\to 0}\frac{ah}{h(\sqrt{ax+b+ah}+\sqrt{ax+b})}$$

$$=\lim_{h\to 0}\frac{a}{(\sqrt{(ax+b)+ah}+\sqrt{ax+b})}$$

$$=\frac{a}{\sqrt{ax+b}+\sqrt{ax+b}}$$

$$=\frac{a}{2\sqrt{ax+b}}$$

Topic Practice 1

1. Find the derivative of $f(x)=3$ at $x=0$ and at $x=3$.
2. Find the derivative of x^2-2 at $x=10$ from first principle.
3. By using first principle, find the derivative of $99x$ at $x=100$.

Directions (Q. Nos. 4-9) Find the derivative of the following functions from first principle.

4. x^3-27
5. $\frac{1}{x^3}$
6. $\sqrt{4-x}$
7. $x^{2/3}$
8. $(x^2+1)(x-5)$
9. $\frac{ax+b}{cx+d}$

Hints & Solutions

1. **Hint** $f'(0)=\lim_{h\to 0}\frac{f(0+h)-f(0)}{h}=\lim_{h\to 0}\frac{3-3}{h}=0$

Similarly, $f'(3)=\lim_{h\to 0}\frac{f(3+h)-f(3)}{h}=\lim_{h\to 0}\frac{3-3}{h}=0$

2. **Hint** $f'(10)=\lim_{h\to 0}\frac{[(10+h)^2-2]-[(10)^2-2]}{h}$

Ans. 20

3. **Hint** $f'(x)=\lim_{h\to 0}\frac{99(x+h)-99x}{h}$ **Ans.** 99

4. **Hint** $f'(x)=\lim_{h\to 0}\frac{[(x+h)^3-27]-(x^3-27)}{h}$ $[\because f(x)=x^3-27]$

$$=\lim_{h\to 0}\frac{(x+h)^3-x^3}{h}=\lim_{h\to 0}\frac{h^3+3xh(x+h)}{h}$$

$$=\lim_{h\to 0}\frac{h[h^2+3x(x+h)]}{h}$$ **Ans.** $3x^2$

5. **Hint** $f'(x)=\lim_{h\to 0}\frac{\frac{1}{(x+h)^3}-\frac{1}{x^3}}{h}=\lim_{h\to 0}\frac{x^3-(x+h)^3}{(x+h)^3x^3h}$

$$=\lim_{h\to 0}\frac{x^3-[x^3+h^3+3xh(x+h)]}{(x+h)^3x^3h}$$

$$=\lim_{h\to 0}\frac{-h[h^2+3x(x+h)]}{(x+h)^3x^3h}$$

Ans. $\frac{-3}{x^4}$

6. Solve as Example 8. **Ans.** $\frac{-1}{2\sqrt{4-x}}$

7. **Hint** $f'(x)=\lim_{h\to 0}\left[\frac{(x+h)^{2/3}-x^{2/3}}{h}\right]$

$$=\lim_{(x+h)\to x}\left[\frac{(x+h)^{2/3}-x^{2/3}}{(x+h)-x}\right]$$ **Ans.** $\frac{2}{3}x^{-1/3}$

8. **Hint** $f'(x)=\lim_{h\to 0}\frac{((x+h)^2+1)(x+h-5)-(x^2+1)(x-5)}{h}$

Ans. $3x^2-10x+1$

9. Solve as Example 7. **Ans.** $\frac{ad-bc}{(cx+d)^2}$

Fundamental Rules for Differentiation

The process of finding derivative of a function is called **differentiation.** The derivative of a function is also called the **differential coefficient** of the function.

Derivatives of some standard functions are given below

(i) $\frac{d}{dx}(\text{constant}) = 0$

(ii) $\frac{d}{dx}(x^n) = nx^{n-1}$ (Power formula)

(iii) $\frac{d}{dx}(ax+b)^n = n(ax+b)^{n-1} \times a$

(iv) $\frac{d}{dx}(e^x) = e^x$

(v) $\frac{d}{dx}(a^x) = a^x \log_e a, a > 0$

(vi) $\frac{d}{dx}(\log_e x) = \frac{1}{x}, x > 0$

(vii) $\frac{d}{dx}(\log_a x) = \frac{1}{x \log_e a}, a > 0, a \neq 1$

Algebra of Derivatives

(i) $\frac{d}{dx}[cf(x)] = c\frac{d}{dx} f(x); c \in R$

(ii) **Sum and Difference Rule** Let $y = f(x) \pm g(x)$.

Then, its derivative is written as

$$\frac{dy}{dx} = \frac{d}{dx} f(x) \pm \frac{d}{dx} g(x).$$

(iii) **Product Rule** Let $y = f(x)\, g(x)$.

Then, its derivative is written as

$$\frac{dy}{dx} = \left[\frac{d}{dx} f(x)\right] g(x) + \left[\frac{d}{dx} g(x)\right] f(x).$$

Let $y = f(x)\, g(x)\, h(x)$.

Then, its derivative is written as

$$\frac{dy}{dx} = \frac{d}{dx}[f(x)\, g(x)\, h(x)]$$
$$= f(x)\, g(x) \frac{d}{dx}[h(x)] + f(x)\, h(x) \frac{d}{dx}[g(x)] + g(x)h(x)\frac{d}{dx}[f(x)]$$

(iv) **Quotient Rule** Let $y = \frac{f(x)}{g(x)}; g(x) \neq 0.$

Then, its derivative is written as

$$\frac{dy}{dx} = \frac{g(x) \times \frac{d}{dx}[f(x)] - f(x) \times \frac{d}{dx}[g(x)]}{[g(x)]^2}.$$

EXAMPLE 1. Find the derivative of $x^4 + 3x^{5/3} + 10x + 7$.

Sol. Let $y = x^4 + 3x^{5/3} + 10x + 7$

On differentiating both sides, w.r.t. x, we get

$$\frac{dy}{dx} = \frac{d}{dx}(x^4 + 3x^{5/3} + 10x + 7)$$
$$= \frac{d}{dx}(x^4) + \frac{d}{dx}(3x^{5/3}) + \frac{d}{dx}(10x) + \frac{d}{dx}(7)$$

[using sum and difference rule]

$$= 4x^{4-1} + 3\left(\frac{5}{3}\right)x^{\frac{5}{3}-1} + 10x^{1-1} + 0$$

$\left[\because \frac{d}{dx}x^n = nx^{n-1}; \frac{d}{dx}(cx^n) = cnx^{n-1} \text{ and } \frac{d}{dx}(\text{constant}) = 0\right]$

$$= 4x^3 + 5x^{2/3} + 10$$

EXAMPLE 2. Find the differential coefficient of $(7x^5 + 9)(px^{7/2} + q)$.

Sol. Let $y = (7x^5 + 9)(px^{7/2} + q)$

On differentiating both sides w.r.t. x, we get

$$\frac{dy}{dx} = (7x^5 + 9)\frac{d}{dx}(px^{7/2} + q) + (px^{7/2} + q)\frac{d}{dx}(7x^5 + 9)$$

[using Product rule]

$$= (7x^5 + 9)\left(p \cdot \frac{7}{2} x^{\frac{7}{2}-1} + 0\right) + (px^{7/2} + q)(7 \cdot 5x^{5-1} + 0)$$
$$= \frac{7p}{2} x^{5/2}(7x^5 + 9) + 35x^4(px^{7/2} + q)$$

EXAMPLE 3. If $y = \frac{x}{x+5}$, then prove that $x\frac{dy}{dx} = y(1-y)$.

Sol. We have, $y = \frac{x}{x+5}$ ...(i)

On differentiating both sides of Eq. (i) w.r.t. x, we get

$$\frac{dy}{dx} = \frac{d}{dx}\left(\frac{x}{x+5}\right) = \frac{(x+5)\frac{d}{dx}x - x\frac{d}{dx}(x+5)}{(x+5)^2}$$

$\left[\because \frac{d}{dx}\left(\frac{u}{v}\right) = \frac{v\frac{du}{dx} - u\frac{dv}{dx}}{v^2}\right]$

$$= \frac{(x+5)(1) - x(1+0)}{(x+5)^2} = \frac{x+5-x}{(x+5)^2}$$

$$\Rightarrow \frac{dy}{dx} = \frac{5}{(x+5)^2}$$

Now, $\text{LHS} = x\frac{dy}{dx} = \frac{5x}{(x+5)^2}$ ...(ii)

and $\text{RHS} = y(1-y) = \frac{x}{x+5}\left(1 - \frac{x}{x+5}\right)$

$$= \frac{x}{x+5}\left(\frac{x+5-x}{x+5}\right) = \frac{5x}{(x+5)^2} \quad \text{...(iii)}$$

From Eqs. (ii) and (iii), we get

$$x\frac{dy}{dx} = y(1-y)$$ **Hence proved.**

EXAMPLE 4. Find the derivative of $f(x) = 1 + x + x^2 + x^3 + \ldots + x^{50}$ at $x = 1$. [NCERT]

Sol. Given, $f(x) = 1 + x + x^2 + x^3 + \ldots + x^{50}$

On differentiating both sides w.r.t. x, we get

$$f'(x) = 0 + 1 + 2x + 3x^2 + \ldots + 50x^{49}$$

At $x = 1$, $f'(1) = 1 + 2(1) + 3(1)^2 + \ldots + 50(1)^{49}$

$$= 1 + 2 + 3 + \ldots + 50$$

$$= \frac{(50)(51)}{2} = 1275 \quad \left[\because \Sigma n = \frac{n(n+1)}{2}\right]$$

Derivatives of Composite Functions

Derivative of a composite function can be found out by chain rule.

Chain Rule

Chain rule is applied when the given function is the function of function, i.e. a function is in the form of $fog(x)$ or $f[g(x)]$.

Let $y = f(u)$ and $u = f(x)$, then by using chain rule, we may write

$$\frac{dy}{dx} = \frac{dy}{du} \cdot \frac{du}{dx}, \text{ when } \frac{dy}{du} \text{ and } \frac{du}{dx} \text{ both exist.}$$

Extension of Chain Rule

Extension of chain rule is applied when the given function (say y) is a composite of three functions.

e.g. If $y = f(u)$, $u = g(v)$ and $v = h(x)$, then

$$\frac{dy}{dx} = \frac{dy}{du} \cdot \frac{du}{dv} \cdot \frac{dv}{dx} = f'(u) \cdot g'(v) \cdot h'(x)$$

i.e. $\frac{d}{dx}[f(g(h(x)))] = f'[g(h(x)]. g'(h(x)) \cdot h'(x)$.

Derivative of Absolute Value Function

$$\frac{d}{dx}(|x|) = \frac{x}{|x|}, x \neq 0$$

EXAMPLE 5. Differentiate $\sqrt{2x-3}$, $x > \frac{3}{2}$ w.r.t. x.

Sol. Let $y = \sqrt{2x-3} = (2x-3)^{1/2}$

On differentiating both sides w.r.t. x, we get

$$\frac{dy}{dx} = \frac{d}{dx}(2x-3)^{1/2} = \frac{1}{2}(2x-3)^{1/2-1}\frac{d}{dx}(2x-3)$$

[using chain rule]

$$\frac{1}{2}(2x-3)^{-1/2}(2) = \frac{1}{\sqrt{2x-3}}$$

EXAMPLE 6. Differentiate $(3x^2 - 5x + 1)^7$, w.r.t. x.

Sol. Let $y = (3x^2 - 5x + 1)^7$

On differentiating both sides w.r.t. x, we get

$$\frac{dy}{dx} = \frac{d}{dx}(3x^2 - 5x + 1)^7$$

$$= 7(3x^2 - 5x + 1)^{7-1}\frac{d}{dx}(3x^2 - 5x + 1)$$

[using chain rule]

$$= 7(3x^2 - 5x + 1)^6(6x - 5)$$

EXAMPLE 7. If $y = (x + \sqrt{x^2 - 1})^m$, prove that

$$(x^2 - 1)\left(\frac{dy}{dx}\right)^2 = m^2y^2.$$

Sol. Given $y = (x + \sqrt{x^2 - 1})^m$

On differentiating both sides, w.r.t. x, we get

$$\frac{dy}{dx} = \frac{d}{dx}(x + \sqrt{x^2 - 1})^m$$

$$= m(x + \sqrt{x^2 - 1})^{m-1}\frac{d}{dx}(x + \sqrt{x^2 - 1})$$

[using chain rule]

$$\Rightarrow \frac{dy}{dx} = m(x + \sqrt{x^2 - 1})^{m-1}\left[1 + \frac{1}{2}(x^2 - 1)^{-1/2} . 2x\right]$$

$$\Rightarrow \frac{dy}{dx} = m(x + \sqrt{x^2 - 1})^{m-1}\left(1 + \frac{x}{\sqrt{x^2 - 1}}\right)$$

$$= m(x + \sqrt{x^2 - 1})^{m-1}\frac{(\sqrt{x^2 - 1} + x)}{\sqrt{x^2 - 1}}$$

$$\Rightarrow \frac{dy}{dx} = \frac{m(x + \sqrt{x^2 - 1})^m}{\sqrt{x^2 - 1}} = \frac{my}{\sqrt{x^2 - 1}}$$

On squaring both sides, we get

$$\left(\frac{dy}{dx}\right)^2 = \frac{m^2y^2}{(x^2 - 1)}$$

$$\Rightarrow (x^2 - 1)\left(\frac{dy}{dx}\right)^2 = m^2y^2$$

EXAMPLE 8. Differentiate $e^{e^{e^x}}$ w.r.t. x.

Sol. Let $y = e^{e^x}$

On differentiating both sides w.r.t. x, we get

$$\frac{dy}{dx} = \frac{d}{dx}(e^{e^x}) = e^{e^x}\frac{d}{dx}(e^x) \quad \text{[using chain rule]}$$

$$= e^{e^x} . e^x$$

EXAMPLE 9. Differentiate $\log_7(\log_7 x)$ w.r.t. x.

Sol. Let $y = \log_7(\log_7 x)$

On differentiating both sides w.r.t. x,we get

$$\frac{dy}{dx} = \frac{d}{dx}\log_7(\log_7 x)$$

$$= \frac{1}{(\log_7 x)\log_e 7}\frac{d}{dx}(\log_7 x) \quad \text{[using chain rule]}$$

$$= \frac{1}{(\log_7 x)(\log_e 7)} \cdot \frac{1}{x(\log_e 7)} = \frac{1}{x(\log_7 x)(\log_e 7)^2}$$

EXAMPLE 10. Differentiate $|x^3 - 2x + 1|$ w.r.t. x.

Sol. Let $y = |x^3 - 2x + 1|$

On differentiating both sides w.r.t. x, we get

$$\frac{dy}{dx} = \frac{x^3 - 2x + 1}{|x^3 - 2x + 1|}\frac{d}{dx}(x^3 - 2x + 1) \left[\because \frac{d}{dx}|x| = \frac{x}{|x|}\right]$$

$$= \frac{(3x^2 - 2)(x^3 - 2x + 1)}{|x^3 - 2x + 1|}, x \neq 1$$

Derivatives of Implicit Functions

A function of the form $f(x, y) = 0$, where it is not possible to express y directly as a function of x in the form of $y = \phi(x)$, is said to be an **implicit function** of x and y.

e.g. $x^2 + y^2 = xy$, $e^{x+y} = \log(xy)$, etc.

Following steps are used to find $\frac{dy}{dx}$ of implicit functions.

I. Write the given equation in x and y and then differentiate both sides of the given equation w.r.t. x.

II. Take all terms involving $\frac{dy}{dx}$ on LHS and transfer the remaining terms on RHS to get equation in the form of $\frac{dy}{dx} f(x, y) = g(x, y)$.

III. Now, $\frac{dy}{dx} = \frac{g(x, y)}{f(x, y)}$.

EXAMPLE 11. If $x^3 + y^3 = 3axy$, then find $\frac{dy}{dx}$.

Sol. Given, $x^3 + y^3 = 3axy$

On differentiating both sides w.r.t. x, we get

$$3x^2 + 3y^2\frac{dy}{dx} = 3a\frac{d}{dx}(xy)$$

$$\Rightarrow 3x^2 + 3y^2\frac{dy}{dx} = 3a\left(1 \cdot y + x\frac{dy}{dx}\right)$$

[by product rule of derivative]

$$\Rightarrow 3x^2 + 3y^2\frac{dy}{dx} = 3ay + 3ax\frac{dy}{dx}$$

$$\Rightarrow 3y^2\frac{dy}{dx} - 3ax\frac{dy}{dx} = 3ay - 3x^2$$

[taking terms involving dy/dx in LHS]

$$\Rightarrow 3(y^2 - ax)\frac{dy}{dx} = 3(ay - x^2)$$

$$\Rightarrow (y^2 - ax)\frac{dy}{dx} = ay - x^2 \Rightarrow \frac{dy}{dx} = \frac{ay - x^2}{y^2 - ax}$$

EXAMPLE 12. If $x + y = t + \frac{1}{t}$ and $x^3 + y^3 = t^3 + \frac{1}{t^3}$, then prove that $\frac{dy}{dx} = -\frac{1}{x^2}$.

Sol. Given, $(x + y) = t + \frac{1}{t}$

On cubing both sides, we get

$$(x + y)^3 = \left(t + \frac{1}{t}\right)^3$$

$$\Rightarrow x^3 + y^3 + 3xy(x + y) = t^3 + \frac{1}{t^3} + 3\left(t + \frac{1}{t}\right)$$

$[\because (a + b)^3 = a^3 + b^3 + 3ab(a + b)]$

$$\Rightarrow x^3 + y^3 + 3xy(x + y) = x^3 + y^3 + 3(x + y)$$

$\left[\because x^3 + y^3 = t^3 + \frac{1}{t^3} \text{ and } (x + y) = t + \frac{1}{t}\right]$

$$\Rightarrow 3xy(x + y) = 3(x + y)$$

$$\Rightarrow xy = 1 \quad \text{...(i)}$$

On differentiating both sides w.r.t. x, we get

$$x \cdot \frac{dy}{dx} + y \cdot \frac{d}{dx}(x) = \frac{d}{dx} \cdot 1$$

[product rule of derivative]

$$\Rightarrow x \cdot \frac{dy}{dx} + y = 0$$

$$\Rightarrow x\frac{dy}{dx} = -y$$

$$\Rightarrow x\frac{dy}{dx} = -\frac{1}{x} \quad \text{[from Eq. (i)]}$$

$$\Rightarrow \frac{dy}{dx} = -\frac{1}{x^2}$$

Hence proved.

EXAMPLE 13. If $x^{2/3} + y^{2/3} = a^{2/3}$, then find $\frac{dy}{dx}$.

Sol. Given, $x^{2/3} + y^{2/3} = a^{2/3}$

On differentiating both sides w.r.t. x, we get

$$\frac{2}{3}x^{-1/3} + \frac{2}{3}y^{-1/3}\frac{dy}{dx} = 0$$

$$\Rightarrow \frac{2}{3}y^{-1/3}\frac{dy}{dx} = -\frac{2}{3}x^{-1/3}$$

$$\Rightarrow \frac{dy}{dx} = -\frac{x^{-1/3}}{y^{-1/3}} = \frac{-y^{1/3}}{x^{1/3}} = -\sqrt[3]{\frac{y}{x}}$$

EXAMPLE 14. If $xy^2 = 1$, prove that $2\frac{dy}{dx} + y^3 = 0$

Sol. Given, $xy^2 = 1 \Rightarrow x = \frac{1}{y^2} = y^{-2}$

On differentiating both sides w.r.t. y, we get

$$\frac{dx}{dy} = -2y^{-2-1} = -2y^{-3} = -\frac{2}{y^3}$$

$$\Rightarrow \frac{dy}{dx} = -\frac{y^3}{2}$$

$$\Rightarrow 2\frac{dy}{dx} + y^3 = 0$$

Topic Practice 2

1 Differentiate the following functions with respect to x.

(i) $x^{20} + 30$ (ii) $7x^6 + \frac{5}{4}x^8$

(iii) $-3x^{-5} + \frac{1}{\sqrt{x}}$ (iv) $(ax^2 + b)(px^{5/3} + q)$

(v) $\frac{1}{ax + b}$ (vi) $\frac{x + 3}{x^2 + 1}$

2 Differentiate $(3x^2 - 9x + 5)^9$, w.r.t. x.

3 Differentiate $\sqrt{3x + 2} + \frac{1}{\sqrt{2x^2 + 4}}$, w.r.t. x.

4 Differentiate $\frac{\sqrt{x^2 + 1} - x}{\sqrt{x^2 + 1} + x}$ w.r.t. x.

5 If $y = \left[x + \sqrt{x^2 + a^2}\right]^n$, then prove that $\frac{dy}{dx} = \frac{ny}{\sqrt{x^2 + a^2}}$.

Directions (Q.Nos. 6-11) Find the derivatives of the following functions.

6 $xy = a^2$ 7 $x^2 + y^2 - 4xy = 5$

8 $x^3 + x^2y + xy^2 + y^3 = 81$ 9 $(x^2 + y^2)^2 = xy$

10 $4x + 3y = \log(4x - 3y)$ 11 $e^{x-y} = \log\left(\frac{x}{y}\right)$

12 If $ax^2 + 2hxy + by^2 + 2gx + 2fy + c = 0$, then show that $\frac{dy}{dx} \cdot \frac{dx}{dy} = 1$.

13 If $x\sqrt{1 + y} + y\sqrt{1 + x} = 0$ for $-1 < x, y < 1$, then prove that $\frac{dy}{dx} = \frac{-1}{(x + 1)^2}$.

Hints & Solutions

1. (i) Solve as Example 1. **Ans.** $20x^{19}$

(ii) Solve as Example 1. **Ans.** $42x^5 + 10x^7$

(iii) Solve as Example 1. **Ans.** $15x^{-6} - \frac{1}{2}x^{-3/2}$

(iv) Solve as Example 2.

Ans. $(ax^2 + b)\left(\frac{5p}{3}x^{2/3}\right) + (2ax)(px^{5/3} + q)$

(v) **Hint** Use quotient rule. **Ans.** $\frac{-a}{(ax + b)^2}$

(vi) **Hint** Use quotient rule. **Ans.** $\frac{1 - 6x - x^2}{(x^2 + 1)^2}$

2. Hint Let $y = (3x^2 - 9x + 5)^9$

$$\therefore \frac{dy}{dx} = 9(3x^2 - 9x + 5)^{9-1}\frac{d}{dx}(3x^2 - 9x + 5)$$ [using chain rule]

Ans. $27(2x - 3)(3x^2 - 9x + 5)^8$

3. Hint Let $y = (3x + 2)^{1/2} + (2x^2 + 4)^{-1/2}$

$$\therefore \frac{dy}{dx} = \frac{1}{2}(3x + 2)^{\left(\frac{1}{2}-1\right)}\frac{d}{dx}(3x + 2) - \frac{1}{2}(2x^2 + 4)^{\frac{-1}{2}-1}\frac{d}{dx}(2x^2 + 4)$$ [using chain rule]

Ans. $\frac{3}{2\sqrt{3x + 2}} - \frac{2x}{(2x^2 + 4)^{3/2}}, x > -\frac{2}{3}$

4. Hint Let $y = \frac{\sqrt{x^2 + 1} - x}{\sqrt{x^2 + 1} + x} = \frac{\sqrt{x^2 + 1} - x}{\sqrt{x^2 + 1} + x} \times \frac{\sqrt{x^2 + 1} - x}{\sqrt{x^2 + 1} - x}$

Ans. $2\left[2x - \frac{2x^2 + 1}{\sqrt{x^2 + 1}}\right]$

5. Solve as Example 7.

6. Solve as Example 11. **Ans.** $-y/x$

7. Solve as Example 11. **Ans.** $\dfrac{2y-x}{y-2x}$

8. **Hint** We have, $x^3 + x^2y + xy^2 + y^3 = 81$

On differentiating both sides w.r.t. x, we get

$$3x^2 + x^2\frac{dy}{dx} + y\cdot 2x + x\cdot 2y\frac{dy}{dx} + y^2\cdot 1 + 3y^2\frac{dy}{dx} = 0$$

$$\Rightarrow x^2\frac{dy}{dx} + 2xy\frac{dy}{dx} + 3y^2\frac{dy}{dx} = -3x^2 - 2xy - y^2$$

$$\Rightarrow \frac{dy}{dx}(x^2 + 2xy + 3y^2) = -3x^2 - 2xy - y^2$$

$$\frac{dy}{dx} = \frac{-(3x^2 + 2xy + y^2)}{x^2 + 2xy + 3y^2}$$

9. Solve as Example 11. **Ans.** $\dfrac{y - 4x^3 - 4xy^2}{4yx^2 + 4y^3 - x}$

10. **Hint** Differentiate both sides w.r.t. x, we get

$$4 + \frac{3dy}{dx} = \frac{1}{4x-3y}\left(4 - 3\frac{dy}{dx}\right)$$

Ans. $\dfrac{dy}{dx} = \dfrac{4 - 16x + 12y}{3 + 12x - 9y}$

11. **Hint** $e^{x-y} = \log(x/y)$

$\Rightarrow e^x \cdot e^{-y} = \log x - \log y$

Now, differentiating both sides w.r.t. x.

Ans. $\dfrac{dy}{dx} = \left[\dfrac{e^{x-y} - 1/x}{e^{x-y} - 1/y}\right]$

12. **Hint** We have,

$$ax^2 + 2hxy + by^2 + 2gx + 2fy + c = 0 \quad \text{...(i)}$$

On differentiating both sides w.r.t. x, we get

$$\frac{d}{dx}(ax^2) + \frac{d}{dx}(2hxy) + \frac{d}{dx}(by^2) + \frac{d}{dx}(2gx) + \frac{d}{dx}(2fy) + \frac{d}{dx}(c) = 0$$

$$\Rightarrow 2ax + 2h\left(x\cdot\frac{dy}{dx} + y\cdot 1\right) + b\cdot 2y\frac{dy}{dx} + 2g + 2f\frac{dy}{dx} + 0 = 0$$

$$\Rightarrow \frac{dy}{dx}[2hx + 2by + 2f] = -2ax - 2hy - 2g$$

$$\Rightarrow \frac{dy}{dx} = \frac{-2(ax + hy + g)}{2(hx + by + f)} = \frac{-(ax + hy + g)}{(hx + by + f)} \quad \text{...(ii)}$$

Now, differentiating both sides of Eq. (i) w.r.t. y, we get

$$\frac{d}{dy}(ax^2) + \frac{d}{dy}(2hxy) + \frac{d}{dy}(by^2) + \frac{d}{dy}(2gx) + \frac{d}{dy}(2fy) + \frac{d}{dy}(c) = 0$$

$$\Rightarrow a\cdot 2x\cdot\frac{dx}{dy} + 2h\cdot\left(x\cdot 1 + y\cdot\frac{d}{dy}x\right) + b\cdot 2y + 2g\cdot\frac{dx}{dy} + 2f + 0 = 0$$

$$\Rightarrow \frac{dx}{dy}[2ax + 2hy + 2g] = -2hx - 2by - 2f$$

$$\Rightarrow \frac{dx}{dy} = \frac{-2(hx + by + f)}{2(ax + hy + g)} = \frac{-(hx + by + f)}{(ax + hy + g)} \quad \text{...(iii)}$$

$$\therefore \frac{dy}{dx}\cdot\frac{dx}{dy} = \frac{-(ax + hy + g)}{(hx + by + f)}\cdot\frac{-(hx + by + f)}{(ax + hy + g)}$$

[using Eqs. (ii) and (iii)]

$= 1 =$ RHS **Hence proved.**

13. **Hint** We have, $x\sqrt{1+y} + y\sqrt{1+x} = 0$

$\Rightarrow x\sqrt{1+y} = -y\sqrt{1+x}$

On squaring both sides, we get

$$x^2(1+y) = y^2(1+x)$$

$$\Rightarrow x^2 - y^2 + x^2y - y^2x = 0$$

$$\Rightarrow (x+y)(x-y) + xy(x-y) = 0$$

$$\Rightarrow (x-y)(x+y+xy) = 0$$

But $x \neq y$

$\therefore x + y + xy = 0$

$\Rightarrow y(1+x) = -x$

$\Rightarrow y = \dfrac{-x-1+1}{1+x}$

$\Rightarrow y = -1 + \dfrac{1}{1+x}$

On differentiating both sides w.r.t. x, we get

$$\frac{dy}{dx} = \frac{-1}{(1+x)^2}$$

Hence proved.

Exponential Function and Logarithmic Differentiation

Exponential Function

The function defined as $y = f(x) = b^x$ with positive base $b > 0$, $b \neq 1$ is called the exponential function.

- If the base of an exponential function is e, i.e. $b = e$, then it is called **natural exponential** function.
- If the base of an exponential function is 10, i.e. $b = 10$, then it is called the **common exponential function.**

Logarithmic Function

If b is any number such that $b > 0$ and $b \neq 1$ and $x > 0$, then

$$y = \log_b x \text{ is equivalent to } b^y = x.$$

We usually read as 'log base b of x'.

Basic properties of logarithms are given below:

(i) $\log_a (mn) = \log_a m + \log_a n$, $m > 0, n > 0, a > 0, a \neq 1$

(ii) $\log_a x = \log_a e \log_e x$, $a > 0, a \neq 1, x > 0$

(iii) $\log_a \frac{m}{n} = \log_a m - \log_a n$, $m > 0, n > 0$, $a > 0, a \neq 1$

(iv) $\log_a m^n = n \log_a m$, $m > 0, a > 0$, $a \neq 1$

(v) $e^{\log_e x} = x$, $x > 0$

(vi) $\log_a x = \frac{\log x}{\log a}$, $a > 0, a \neq 1, x > 0$

(vii) $\log_n m = \frac{1}{\log_m n}$, $m, n > 0$ and $m, n \neq 1$

(viii) $\log_{10} 10 = 1, \log_e e = 1$ and $\log_a 1 = 0$, $a > 0, a \neq 1$

Important Theorems

Theorem 1 The derivative of e^x w.r.t. x is e^x

i.e. $\frac{d}{dx}(e^x) = e^x$.

Theorem 2 The derivative of $\log x$ w.r.t. x is $\frac{1}{x}$

i.e. $\frac{d}{dx}(\log x) = \frac{1}{x}$.

- $\frac{d}{dx}(a^x) = a^x \log a$, $a > 0$, $a \neq 1$
- $\frac{d}{dx}(\log_a x) = \frac{1}{x \log a}$, $x > 0$, $a > 0$, $a \neq 1$
- $\frac{d}{dx}(\log|x|) = \frac{1}{x}$, $x \neq 0$
- $\frac{d}{dx}(\log_a |x|) = \frac{1}{x \log a}$, $x \neq 0$, $a > 0$, $a \neq 1$

EXAMPLE 1. Differentiate e^{x^3} w.r.t. x.

Sol. Let $y = e^{x^3}$

On differentiating both sides w.r.t. x, we get

$$\frac{dy}{dx} = \frac{d}{dx} e^{x^3} \frac{d}{dx}(x^3) \quad \text{[by chain rule]}$$

$$= e^{x^3} \cdot 3x^2 = 3x^2 e^{x^3}$$

Logarithmic Differentiation

When the given function is in the form $[f(x)]^{g(x)}$, where $f(x)$ and $g(x)$ are functions of x.

Then, we take logarithm both sides and use properties of logarithm to simplify it and then differentiate it. This process is known as **logarithmic differentiation.**

Let $\quad y = [f(x)]^{g(x)}$

Taking logarithm (to base e), we get

$$\log y = g(x) \log (f(x))$$

Using chain rule, we get

$$\frac{dy}{dx} = [f(x)]^{g(x)} \left[\frac{g(x)}{f(x)} f'(x) + g'(x) \log f(x) \right]$$

Here, functions should always be positive otherwise their logarithms are not defined.

EXAMPLE 2. Differentiate each of the following functions w.r.t. x.

(i) a^x, where a is a positive constant (ii) $x^{\frac{1}{x}}$

Sol. (i) Let $y = a^x$.

Taking log on both sides, we get

$$\log y = \log a^x \Rightarrow \log y = x \log a$$

On differentiating both sides w.r.t. x, we get

$$\frac{1}{y}\frac{dy}{dx} = \log a \Rightarrow \frac{dy}{dx} = y \log a$$

Thus, $\frac{d}{dx}(a^x) = a^x \log a$.

(ii) Let $y = x^{\frac{1}{x}}$

Taking log on both sides, we get

$$\log y = \log x^{\frac{1}{x}} \Rightarrow \log y = \frac{1}{x}\log x = \frac{\log x}{x}$$

On differentiating both sides w.r.t. x, we get

$$\frac{1}{y}\frac{dy}{dx} = \frac{x\frac{d}{dx}(\log x) - \log x\frac{d}{dx}(x)}{x^2}$$

$$\Rightarrow \quad \frac{1}{y}\frac{dy}{dx} = \frac{x\cdot\frac{1}{x} - \log x\cdot 1}{x^2} \Rightarrow \frac{dy}{dx} = \frac{y(1-\log x)}{x^2}$$

Thus, $\frac{d}{dx}x^{\frac{1}{x}} = \frac{x^{\frac{1}{x}}(1-\log x)}{x^2}$

EXAMPLE 3. Differentiate $\sqrt{\frac{(x-3)(x^2+4)}{3x^2+4x+5}}$ w.r.t. x.

Sol. Let given function be

$$y = \sqrt{\frac{(x-3)(x^2+4)}{3x^2+4x+5}}$$

$$\Rightarrow \quad y = \left\{\frac{(x-3)(x^2+4)}{3x^2+4x+5}\right\}^{1/2}$$

Taking log on both sides, we get

$$\log y = \log\left\{\frac{(x-3)(x^2+4)}{3x^2+4x+5}\right\}^{1/2}$$

$$= \frac{1}{2}\log\left\{\frac{(x-3)(x^2+4)}{3x^2+4x+5}\right\} \quad [\because \log m^n = n\log m]$$

$$= \frac{1}{2}[\log(x-3)(x^2+4) - \log(3x^2+4x+5)]$$

$[\because \log(m/n) = \log m - \log n]$

$$= \frac{1}{2}[\log(x-3) + \log(x^2+4) - \log(3x^2+4x+5)] \quad \text{...(i)}$$

$[\because \log mn = \log m + \log n]$

On differentiating both sides of Eq. (i) w.r.t. x, we get

$$\frac{1}{y}\frac{dy}{dx} = \frac{1}{2}\left[\frac{1}{(x-3)}\frac{d}{dx}(x-3) + \frac{1}{(x^2+4)}\frac{d}{dx}(x^2+4) - \frac{1}{(3x^2+4x+5)}\frac{d}{dx}(3x^2+4x+5)\right]$$

[by chain rule]

$$= \frac{1}{2}\left[\frac{1}{x-3} + \frac{2x}{x^2+4} - \frac{6x+4}{3x^2+4x+5}\right]$$

$$\Rightarrow \quad \frac{dy}{dx} = \frac{y}{2}\left[\frac{1}{x-3} + \frac{2x}{x^2+4} - \frac{6x+4}{3x^2+4x+5}\right]$$

$$= \frac{1}{2}\sqrt{\frac{(x-3)(x^2+4)}{3x^2+4x+5}}\left[\frac{1}{x-3} + \frac{2x}{x^2+4} - \frac{6x+4}{3x^2+4x+5}\right]$$

EXAMPLE 4. If $y = x^{x^x}$, then find $\frac{dy}{dx}$.

Sol. Given, $y = x^{x^x}$ ...(i)

Taking log on both sides, we get

$$\log y = \log x^{x^x} \quad \text{...(ii)}$$

$$\Rightarrow \quad \log y = x^x \log x \quad [\because \log m^n = n\log m]$$

Again, taking log on both sides, we get

$$\log\log y = \log(x^x \log x)$$

$$\Rightarrow \quad \log\log y = \log x^x + \log\log x$$

$[\because \log(mn) = \log m + \log n]$

$$\Rightarrow \quad \log\log y = x\log x + \log\log x$$

On differentiating both sides w.r.t. x, we get

$$\frac{1}{\log y}\cdot\frac{d}{dx}(\log y) = \left[x\frac{d}{dx}(\log x) + \log x\frac{d}{dx}(x)\right] + \left[\frac{1}{\log x}\cdot\frac{d}{dx}(\log x)\right]$$

[by product rule and chain rule]

$$\Rightarrow \quad \frac{1}{\log y}\cdot\frac{1}{y}\cdot\frac{dy}{dx} = \left[x\cdot\frac{1}{x} + \log x\cdot 1\right] + \left[\frac{1}{\log x}\cdot\frac{1}{x}\right]$$

$$\Rightarrow \quad \frac{1}{y\log y}\cdot\frac{dy}{dx} = 1 + \log x + \frac{1}{x\log x}$$

$$\Rightarrow \quad \frac{dy}{dx} = y\log y\left[1 + \log x + \frac{1}{x\log x}\right]$$

$$= x^{x^x}\log x^{x^x}\left[1 + \log x + \frac{1}{x\log x}\right]$$

[from Eqs. (i) and (ii)]

EXAMPLE 5. Differentiate $(\log x)^x + x^{\log x}$ w.r.t. x.

Sol. Let $y = (\log x)^x + x^{\log x}$

$$y = e^{x\log(\log x)} + e^{\log x\log x}$$

On differentiating both sides w.r.t. x, we get

$$\frac{dy}{dx} = \frac{d}{dx}[e^{x\log(\log x)} + e^{\log(x\log x)}]$$

$$\frac{dy}{dx} = e^{x\log(\log x)} \times \frac{d}{dx}\{x\log(\log x)\} + (x\log x)\times\frac{d}{dx}(\log x)^2$$

$$\Rightarrow \frac{dy}{dx} = (\log x)^x \left\{\log(\log x) \times \frac{d}{dx}(x) + x \times \frac{d}{dx}\{\log(\log x)\}\right\} + x^{\log x}\left\{2(\log x)\frac{d}{dx}(\log x)\right\}$$

$$\Rightarrow \frac{dy}{dx} = (\log x)^x \left\{\log(\log x) + x \times \frac{1}{\log x} \times \frac{1}{x}\right\} + x^{\log x}\left\{2(\log x)\frac{1}{x}\right\}$$

$$\Rightarrow \frac{dy}{dx} = (\log x)^x \left\{\log(\log x) + \frac{1}{\log x}\right\} + x^{\log x}\left\{\frac{2\log x}{x}\right\}$$

EXAMPLE 6. If $x^y = e^{x-y}$, then show that $\frac{dy}{dx} = \frac{\log x}{(1+\log x)^2}$.

Sol. Given, $x^y = e^{x-y}$

Taking log both sides, we get

$$\log x^y = \log e^{x-y}$$

$$\Rightarrow \quad y\log x = x - y \Rightarrow y\log x + y = x$$

$$\Rightarrow \quad y(1+\log x) = x \Rightarrow y = \frac{x}{1+\log x}$$

On differentiating both sides w.r.t. x, we get

$$\frac{dy}{dx} = \frac{(1+\log x)\times 1 - x\left(0 + \frac{1}{x}\right)}{(1+\log x)^2}$$

$$= \frac{\log x}{(1+\log x)^2}$$

EXAMPLE 7. If $y = \frac{\sqrt{1-x^2}\,(2x-3)^{1/2}}{(x^2+2)^{2/3}}$, then find $\frac{dy}{dx}$.

Sol. Given, $y = \frac{\sqrt{1-x^2}\,(2x-3)^{1/2}}{(x^2+2)^{2/3}}$

Now, taking log of both sides, we get

$$\log y = \log\left[\frac{\sqrt{1-x^2}\,(2x-3)^{1/2}}{(x^2+2)^{2/3}}\right]$$

$$\log y = \frac{1}{2}\log(1-x^2) + \frac{1}{2}\log(2x-3) - \frac{2}{3}\log(x^2+2)$$

On differentiating both sides w.r.t. x, we get

$$\frac{1}{y}\frac{dy}{dx} = \frac{1}{2(1-x^2)}(-2x) + \frac{1}{2(2x-3)} \times 2 - \frac{2}{3} \times \frac{1}{x^2+2} \times 2x$$

$$\therefore \quad \frac{dy}{dx} = y\left\{-\frac{x}{1-x^2} + \frac{1}{2x-3} - \frac{4x}{3(x^2+2)}\right\}$$

$$\Rightarrow \frac{dy}{dx} = \frac{\sqrt{1-x^2}\,(2x-3)^{1/2}}{(x^2+2)^{2/3}}\left\{-\frac{x}{1-x^2} + \frac{1}{2x-3} - \frac{4x}{3(x^2+2)}\right\}$$

EXAMPLE 8. Differentiate $\frac{\sqrt{x}\,(x+4)^{3/2}}{(4x-3)^{4/3}}$ w.r.t. x.

Sol. Let $y = \frac{\sqrt{x}\,(x+4)^{3/2}}{(4x-3)^{4/3}}$

Now, taking log of both sides, we get

$$\log y = \log\left[\frac{\sqrt{x}\,(x+4)^{3/2}}{(4x-3)^{4/3}}\right]$$

$$\log y = \frac{1}{2}\log x + \frac{3}{2}\log(x+4) - \frac{4}{3}\log(4x-3)$$

On differentiating both sides w.r.t. x, we get

$$\frac{1}{y}\frac{dy}{dx} = \frac{1}{2x} + \frac{3}{2}\frac{1}{(x+4)}\frac{d}{dx}(x+4) - \frac{4}{3} \times \frac{1}{(4x-3)}\frac{d}{dx}(4x-3)$$

$$\Rightarrow \quad \frac{dy}{dx} = y\left\{\frac{1}{2x} + \frac{3}{2(x+4)} - \frac{4}{3(4x-3)} \times 4\right\}$$

$$\Rightarrow \quad \frac{dy}{dx} = \frac{\sqrt{x}(x+4)^{3/2}}{(4x-3)^{4/3}}\left\{\frac{1}{2x} + \frac{3}{2(x+4)} - \frac{16}{3(4x-3)}\right\}$$

EXAMPLE 9. If $x^p y^q = (x+y)^{p+q}$, then $\frac{dy}{dx} = \frac{y}{x}$.

Sol. We have, $x^p y^q = (x+y)^{p+q}$

Taking log on both sides, we get

$$\log x^p + \log y^q = \log (x+y)^{p+q}$$

$$\Rightarrow p\log x + q\log y = (p+q)\log(x+y)$$

On differentiating both sides w.r.t. x, we get

$$p\frac{1}{x} + q\frac{1}{y}\cdot\frac{dy}{dx} = (p+q)\frac{1}{(x+y)}\cdot\frac{d}{dx}(x+y)$$

$$\Rightarrow \quad \frac{p}{x} + \frac{q}{y}\cdot\frac{dy}{dx} = \left(\frac{p+q}{x+y}\right)\left[1 + \frac{dy}{dx}\right]$$

$$\Rightarrow \quad \frac{p}{x} + \frac{q}{y}\frac{dy}{dx} = \frac{p+q}{x+y} + \left(\frac{p+q}{x+y}\right)\frac{dy}{dx}$$

$$\Rightarrow \quad \frac{q}{y}\frac{dy}{dx} - \left(\frac{p+q}{x+y}\right)\frac{dy}{dx} = \frac{p+q}{x+y} - \frac{p}{x}$$

$$\Rightarrow \quad \frac{dy}{dx}\left[\frac{qx+qy-py-qy}{y(x+y)}\right] = \frac{px+qx-px-py}{(x+y)x}$$

$$\Rightarrow \quad \frac{dy}{dx}\left[\frac{qx-py}{y(x+y)}\right] = \frac{(qx-py)}{x(x+y)}$$

$$\Rightarrow \quad \frac{dy}{dx} = \frac{(qx-py)}{(x+y)x}\cdot\frac{y(x+y)}{(qx-py)}$$

$$\Rightarrow \quad \frac{dy}{dx} = \frac{y}{x}$$

Hence proved.

EXAMPLE 10. Differentiate $x^y + y^x = a^b$ w.r.t. x.

Sol. Given, $x^y + y^x = a^b$ ...(i)

Let $x^y = v$ and $y^x = u$ ...(ii)

On putting these values in Eq. (i), we get

$$v + u = a^b$$

On differentiating both sides w.r.t. x, we get

$$\frac{dv}{dx} + \frac{du}{dx} = 0 \quad \text{...(iii)}$$

Now, $x^y = v$ [from Eq. (ii)]

Taking log on both sides, we get

$$\log x^y = \log v \Rightarrow y \log x = \log v$$

On differentiating both sides w.r.t. x, we get

$$y \cdot \frac{1}{x} + \log x \cdot \frac{dy}{dx} = \frac{1}{v}\frac{dv}{dx}$$

$$\Rightarrow v\left(\frac{y}{x} + \log x \cdot \frac{dy}{dx}\right) = \frac{dv}{dx}$$

$$\Rightarrow \frac{dv}{dx} = x^y\left(\frac{y}{x} + \log x \cdot \frac{dy}{dx}\right) \quad \text{...(iv)}$$

[from Eq. (ii)]

and $y^x = u$ [from Eq. (ii)]

Taking log on both sides, we get

$$\log y^x = \log u$$

$$\Rightarrow x \log y = \log u$$

On differentiating both sides w.r.t. x, we get

$$x \cdot \frac{1}{y}\frac{dy}{dx} + 1 \cdot \log y = \frac{1}{u}\frac{du}{dx}$$

$$\Rightarrow \frac{x}{y}\frac{dy}{dx} + \log y = \frac{1}{u}\frac{du}{dx}$$

$$\Rightarrow u\left[\frac{x}{y}\frac{dy}{dx} + \log y\right] = \frac{du}{dx}$$

$$\Rightarrow y^x\left[\frac{x}{y}\frac{dy}{dx} + \log y\right] = \frac{du}{dx} \quad \text{[from Eq. (ii)] ...(v)}$$

On putting the values of $\frac{dv}{dx}$ and $\frac{du}{dx}$ from Eqs. (iv) and (v) respectively in Eq. (iii), we get

$$x^y\left(\frac{y}{x} + \log x \cdot \frac{dy}{dx}\right) + y^x\left(\frac{x}{y}\frac{dy}{dx} + \log y\right) = 0$$

$$\Rightarrow x^y \frac{y}{x} + x^y \log x \cdot \frac{dy}{dx} + y^x \cdot \frac{x}{y}\frac{dy}{dx} + y^x \log y = 0$$

$$\Rightarrow x^y \log x \cdot \frac{dy}{dx} + y^x \frac{x}{y}\frac{dy}{dx} = -x^y \frac{y}{x} - y^x \log y$$

$$\Rightarrow \frac{dy}{dx}\left[x^y \log x + y^x \cdot \frac{x}{y}\right] = -x^y \cdot \frac{y}{x} - y^x \log y$$

$$\therefore \frac{dy}{dx} = \frac{-x^{y-1} \cdot y - y^x \log y}{x^y \log x + y^{x-1} \cdot x}$$

Topic Practice 3

1 Differentiate the following function with respect to x.

(i) e^{-x} (ii) e^{4x}

(iii) e^{ax^2+b} (iv) $e^{\sqrt{3x}}$

(v) $\log\left(x + \frac{1}{x}\right)$ (vi) $\log\left(x + \sqrt{1+x^2}\right)$

(vii) $\frac{\log x}{x}$ (viii) $\log(\log x), x > 1$

(ix) $\log[\log(\log x^5)]$

2 Differentiate each of the following functions with respect to x.

(i) x^x (ii) $\left(\frac{1}{x}\right)^x$ (iii) $x^{\sqrt{x}}$

Directions (Q.Nos. 3-5) *Differentiate the following function w.r.t. x.*

3 $y^x = x^y$

4 $y = (x+3)^2 (x+4)^3 (x+5)^4$.

5 $y = (\log x)^x + x^{\log x}$.

6 If $\frac{x}{x-y} = \log\left(\frac{a}{x-y}\right)$, then $\frac{dy}{dx} = 2 - \frac{x}{y}$.

7 If $(x-y)\cdot e^{\frac{x}{x-y}} = a$, then $y\frac{dy}{dx} + x = 2y$.

8 If $e^x + e^y = e^{x+y}$, then $\frac{dy}{dx} + \frac{e^x(e^y-1)}{e^y(e^x-1)} = 0$.

Or

If $e^x + e^y = e^{x+y}$, then $\frac{dy}{dx} + e^{y-x} = 0$.

9 If $y = \frac{ax^2}{(x-a)(x-b)(x-c)} + \frac{bx}{(x-b)(x-c)} + \frac{c}{(x-c)} + 1$, then $\frac{y'}{y} = \frac{1}{x}\left[\frac{a}{a-x} + \frac{b}{b-x} + \frac{c}{c-x}\right]$.

10 Find the derivative of the function given by $f(x) = (1+x)(1+x^2)(1+x^4)(1+x^8)$ and hence find $f'(1)$.

Hints & Solutions

1. (i) Solve as Example 1. **Ans.** $-e^{-x}$

(ii) Solve as Example 1. **Ans.** $4e^{4x}$

(iii) Solve as Example 1. **Ans.** $2ax\, e^{ax^2+b}$

(iv) Solve as Example 1. **Ans.** $\dfrac{3e^{\sqrt{3x}}}{2\sqrt{3x}}$

(v) Let $y = \log\left(x + \dfrac{1}{x}\right)$

On differentiating both sides w.r.t. x, we get

$$\frac{dy}{dx} = \frac{1}{\left(x+\frac{1}{x}\right)} \cdot \frac{d}{dx}\left(x + \frac{1}{x}\right)$$

$$= \frac{1}{\left(x+\frac{1}{x}\right)}\left(1 - \frac{1}{x^2}\right) = \frac{x}{(x^2+1)} \cdot \frac{(x^2-1)}{x^2} = \frac{x^2-1}{x(x^2+1)}$$

(vi) Solve as part (v). **Ans.** $\dfrac{1}{\sqrt{1+x^2}}$

(vii) We have, $y = \dfrac{\log x}{x}$

On differentiating both sides w.r.t. x, we get

$$\frac{dy}{dx} = \frac{\left(x\frac{d}{dx}(\log x) - \log x \frac{d}{dx}(x)\right)}{x^2}$$

[by quotient rule of derivative]

$$= \frac{\left(x \times \frac{1}{x} - \log x\right)}{x^2} = \frac{1 - \log x}{x^2}$$

(viii) Solve as part (v). **Ans.** $\dfrac{1}{x \log x}$

(ix) Let $y = \log[\log(\log x^5)]$

On differentiating both sides, we get

$$\frac{dy}{dx} = \frac{1}{\log(\log x^5)} \times \frac{1}{\log x^5} \times \frac{1}{x^5} \times 5x^4$$

$$\Rightarrow \quad \frac{dy}{dx} = \frac{5}{x\,(\log(\log x^5)) \cdot \log x^5}$$

2. (i) Solve as Example 2. (ii). **Ans.** $x^x(1 + \log x)$

(ii) Solve as Example 2. (ii). **Ans.** $-\left(\dfrac{1}{x}\right)^x (1 + \log x)$

(iii) Solve as Example 2. (ii). **Ans.** $x^{\sqrt{x}}\left(\dfrac{2 + \log x}{2\sqrt{x}}\right)$

3. Solve as Example 4. **Ans.** $\dfrac{dy}{dx} = \dfrac{y}{x}\left[\dfrac{y - x\log y}{x - y\log x}\right]$

4. **Hint** Taking log on both sides and then differentiate it.
Ans. $(x+3)(x+4)^2(x+5)^3\,[9x^2 + 70x + 133]$

5. **Hint** Let $y = (\log x)^x + x^{\log x}$ and $u = (\log x)^x$ and $v = x^{\log x}$.

Then, $y = u + v$.

On differentiating both sides w.r.t. x, we get

$$\frac{dy}{dx} = \frac{du}{dx} + \frac{dv}{dx} \quad \text{...(i)}$$

Now, $u = (\log x)^x$

Taking log on both sides, we get

$$\log u = \log(\log x)^x \Rightarrow \log u = x \log(\log x)$$

On differentiating both sides w.r.t. x, we get

$$\frac{1}{u}\cdot\frac{du}{dx} = x\frac{d}{dx}\log(\log x) + \log(\log x)\frac{d}{dx}(x)$$

[by chain rule]

$$\Rightarrow \quad \frac{1}{u}\cdot\frac{du}{dx} = \frac{x}{\log x} \times \frac{1}{x} + \log(\log x)$$

$$\Rightarrow \quad \frac{du}{dx} = u\left[\frac{1}{\log x} + \log(\log x)\right]$$

$$\Rightarrow \quad \frac{du}{dx} = (\log x)^x\left[\frac{1}{\log x} + \log(\log x)\right]$$

Again, $v = x^{\log x}$

Taking log on both sides, we get

$$\log v = \log x^{\log x}$$

$$\Rightarrow \quad \log v = (\log x)(\log x)$$

$$\Rightarrow \quad \log v = (\log x)^2$$

On differentiating both sides w.r.t. x, we get

$$\frac{1}{v}\cdot\frac{dv}{dx} = 2\log x \frac{d}{dx}(\log x) = 2\log x \times \frac{1}{x}$$

$$\Rightarrow \quad \frac{dv}{dx} = v\left[\frac{2\log x}{x}\right] \Rightarrow \frac{dv}{dx} = x^{\log x}\left[\frac{2\log x}{x}\right]$$

Now, putting the values of $\dfrac{du}{dx}$ and $\dfrac{dv}{dx}$ in Eq. (i), we get

$$\frac{dy}{dx} = (\log x)^x\left[\frac{1}{\log x} + \log(\log x)\right] + x^{\log x}\left[\frac{2\log x}{x}\right]$$

$$\frac{dy}{dx} = (\log x)^{x-1}[1 + \log x \log(\log x)] + 2x^{\log x - 1} \cdot \log x$$

6. **Hint** $x = (x - y)[\log a - \log(x - y)]$

Then, differentiate w.r.t. y on both side and simplify.

7. Given, $(x - y)\cdot e^{\frac{x}{x-y}} = a$

Taking log on both sides, we get

$$\log(x-y) + \log e^{\frac{x}{x-y}} = \log a$$

$$\Rightarrow \quad \log(x-y) + \frac{x}{x-y} = \log a \quad \text{... (i)}$$

$$\Rightarrow \quad (x-y)\log(x-y) + x = (x-y)\log a$$

On differentiating both sides w.r.t. y, we get

$$\left(\frac{dx}{dy} - 1\right)\log(x-y) + (x-y) \times \frac{1}{x-y} \times \left(\frac{dx}{dy} - 1\right) + \frac{dx}{dy}$$

$$= \left(\frac{dx}{dy} - 1\right)\log a$$

$$\Rightarrow \left(\frac{dx}{dy}-1\right)\log(x-y)+2\frac{dx}{dy}-1=\left(\frac{dx}{dy}-1\right)\left[\log(x-y)+\frac{x}{x-y}\right]\text{ [from Eq. (i)]}$$

$$\Rightarrow 2\frac{dx}{dy}-1=\left(\frac{dx}{dy}-1\right)\left(\frac{x}{x-y}\right)$$

$$\Rightarrow \frac{dx}{dy}\left(2-\frac{x}{x-y}\right)=-\frac{x}{x-y}+1$$

$$\Rightarrow \frac{dx}{dy}\left(\frac{x-2y}{x-y}\right)=-\frac{y}{x-y}\Rightarrow\frac{dx}{dy}(x-2y)=-y$$

$$\Rightarrow \frac{ydy}{dx}+x=2y$$

Hence proved.

8. **Hint** We have, $e^x+e^y=e^{x+y}$.

On differentiating both sides w.r.t. x, we get

$$e^x+e^y\frac{dy}{dx}=e^{x+y}\frac{d}{dx}(x+y)$$

[by chain rule of derivative]

$$\Rightarrow e^x+e^y\frac{dy}{dx}=e^{x+y}\left[1+\frac{dy}{dx}\right]$$

$$\Rightarrow e^x+e^y\frac{dy}{dx}=e^{x+y}+e^{x+y}\frac{dy}{dx}$$

$$\Rightarrow e^y\frac{dy}{dx}-e^{x+y}\frac{dy}{dx}=e^{x+y}-e^x$$

$$\Rightarrow -e^y\frac{dy}{dx}(e^x-1)=e^x(e^y-1)$$

$$\Rightarrow \frac{dy}{dx}=\frac{-e^x(e^y-1)}{e^y(e^x-1)}\Rightarrow\frac{dy}{dx}+\frac{e^x(e^y-1)}{e^y(e^x-1)}=0$$

Or $$\frac{dy}{dx}=\frac{-e^{x+y}+e^x}{e^{x+y}-e^y}=\frac{-e^x-e^y+e^x}{e^x+e^y-e^y}\quad\text{[given]}$$

$$\Rightarrow \frac{dy}{dx}=\frac{-e^y}{e^x}=-e^{y-x}\Rightarrow\frac{dy}{dx}+e^{y-x}=0$$

Hence proved.

9. **Hint** We have,

$$y=\frac{ax^2}{(x-a)(x-b)(x-c)}+\frac{bx}{(x-b)(x-c)}+\frac{c}{(x-c)}+1$$

$$=\frac{ax^2}{(x-a)(x-b)(x-c)}+\frac{bx}{(x-b)(x-c)}+\frac{c+x-c}{x-c}$$

$$=\frac{ax^2}{(x-a)(x-b)(x-c)}+\frac{bx}{(x-b)(x-c)}+\frac{x}{x-c}$$

$$=\frac{ax^2}{(x-a)(x-b)(x-c)}+\frac{bx+x(x-b)}{(x-b)(x-c)}$$

$$=\frac{ax^2}{(x-a)(x-b)(x-c)}+\frac{bx+x^2-xb}{(x-b)(x-c)}$$

$$=\frac{ax^2}{(x-a)(x-b)(x-c)}+\frac{x^2}{(x-b)(x-c)}$$

$$=\frac{ax^2+x^2(x-a)}{(x-a)(x-b)(x-c)}=\frac{ax^2+x^3-ax^2}{(x-a)(x-b)(x-c)}$$

$$\Rightarrow y=\frac{x^3}{(x-a)(x-b)(x-c)}$$

Taking log on both sides, we get

$$\log y=\log x^3-[\log(x-a)+\log(x-b)+\log(x-c)]$$

$$\Rightarrow \log y=3\log x-\log(x-a)-\log(x-b)-\log(x-c)$$

On differentiating both sides w.r.t. x, we get

$$\frac{1}{y}\cdot\frac{dy}{dx}=3\times\frac{1}{x}-\frac{1}{x-a}-\frac{1}{x-b}-\frac{1}{x-c}$$

$$\Rightarrow \frac{y'}{y}=\frac{3}{x}-\frac{1}{x-a}-\frac{1}{x-b}-\frac{1}{x-c}$$

$$=\frac{1}{x}+\frac{1}{x}+\frac{1}{x}-\frac{1}{x-a}-\frac{1}{x-b}-\frac{1}{x-c}$$

$$=\left[\frac{1}{x}-\frac{1}{x-a}\right]+\left[\frac{1}{x}-\frac{1}{x-b}\right]+\left[\frac{1}{x}-\frac{1}{x-c}\right]$$

$$=\left[\frac{x-a-x}{x(x-a)}\right]+\left[\frac{x-b-x}{x(x-b)}\right]+\left[\frac{x-c-x}{x(x-c)}\right]$$

$$=-\frac{a}{x(x-a)}-\frac{b}{x(x-b)}-\frac{c}{x(x-c)}$$

$$\Rightarrow \frac{y'}{y}=\frac{1}{x}\left[\frac{a}{(a-x)}+\frac{b}{(b-x)}+\frac{c}{c-x}\right]$$

Hence proved.

10. **Hint** Given, $f(x)=(1+x)(1+x^2)(1+x^4)(1+x^8)$

Taking log on both sides, we get

$$\log\{f(x)\}=\log\{(1+x)(1+x^2)(1+x^4)(1+x^8)\}$$

$$\Rightarrow \log\{f(x)\}=\log(1+x)+\log(1+x^2)+\log(1+x^4)+\log(1+x^8)$$

On differentiating both sides w.r.t. x, we get

$$\frac{d}{dx}\log\{f(x)\}=\frac{d}{dx}\log(1+x)+\frac{d}{dx}\log(1+x^2)+\frac{d}{dx}\log(1+x^4)+\frac{d}{dx}\log(1+x^8)$$

$$\frac{1}{f(x)}f'(x)=\frac{1}{1+x}(0+1)+\frac{1}{1+x^2}(0+2x)+\frac{1}{1+x^4}(0+4x^3)+\frac{1}{1+x^8}(0+8x^7)$$

$$\Rightarrow f'(x)=f(x)\left\{\frac{1}{1+x}+\frac{2x}{1+x^2}+\frac{4x^3}{1+x^4}+\frac{8x^7}{1+x^8}\right\}$$

$$=(1+x)(1+x^2)(1+x^4)(1+x^8)\left\{\frac{1}{1+x}+\frac{2x}{1+x^2}+\frac{4x^3}{1+x^4}+\frac{8x^7}{1+x^8}\right\}$$

$$\therefore f'(1)=(1+1)(1+1)(1+1)(1+1)\left\{\frac{1}{1+1}+\frac{2}{1+1}+\frac{4}{1+1}+\frac{8}{1+1}\right\}$$

$$=2^4\left\{\frac{1}{2}+1+2+4\right\}=16\left(\frac{15}{2}\right)=120$$

Differentiation of Parametric Functions

Sometimes, x and y are given as functions of some other variable, say $x = f(t)$, $y = g(t)$ are two functions and t is a variable. In such case, x and y are called **parametric functions** and t is called the **parameter**.

Let $x = f(t)$ and $y = g(t)$, where t is a parameter, then

$$\frac{dy}{dx} = \frac{\left(\frac{dy}{dt}\right)}{\left(\frac{dx}{dt}\right)}, \text{ whenever } \frac{dx}{dt} \neq 0$$

$\frac{dy}{dx}$ is expressed in terms of parameter only without directly involving the main variables x and y.

EXAMPLE 1. If $x = a\left(t + \frac{1}{t}\right)$ and $y = a\left(t - \frac{1}{t}\right)$, prove that $\frac{dy}{dx} = \frac{x}{y}$.

Sol. We have, $x = a\left(t + \frac{1}{t}\right)$ and $y = a\left(t - \frac{1}{t}\right)$

On differentiating w.r.t. t, we get

$$\frac{dx}{dt} = a\left(1 - \frac{1}{t^2}\right) = a\left(\frac{t^2 - 1}{t^2}\right) \text{ and } \frac{dy}{dt} = a\left(1 + \frac{1}{t^2}\right) = a\left(\frac{t^2 + 1}{t^2}\right)$$

$$\therefore \quad \frac{dy}{dx} = \frac{(dy/dt)}{(dx/dt)} = \frac{a(t^2+1)/t^2}{a(t^2-1)/t^2} = \frac{t^2+1}{t^2-1} \quad \text{...(i)}$$

Now, consider $\frac{x}{y} = \frac{a\left(\frac{t^2+1}{t}\right)}{a\left(\frac{t^2-1}{t}\right)} = \frac{t^2+1}{t^2-1}$ ...(ii)

From Eqs. (i) and (ii), we get $\frac{dy}{dx} = \frac{x}{y}$ **Hence proved.**

EXAMPLE 2. If $x = a\left(\frac{1+t^2}{1-t^2}\right)$ and $y = \frac{2t}{1-t^2}$, then prove that $\frac{dy}{dx} = \frac{1+t^2}{2at}$.

Sol. Given, $x = a\left(\frac{1+t^2}{1-t^2}\right)$ and $y = \left(\frac{2t}{1-t^2}\right)$

On differentiating w.r.t. t, we get

$$\frac{dx}{dt} = a\left[\frac{(1-t^2)2t - (1+t^2)(-2t)}{(1-t^2)^2}\right] = \frac{4at}{(1-t^2)^2}$$

and $$\frac{dy}{dt} = \left[\frac{(1-t^2)\times 2 - 2t(-2t)}{(1-t^2)^2}\right] = \frac{2(1+t^2)}{(1-t^2)^2}$$

Now, $$\frac{dy}{dx} = \frac{(dy/dt)}{(dx/dt)} = \frac{2(1+t^2)}{(1-t^2)^2} \times \frac{(1-t^2)^2}{4at} = \frac{1+t^2}{2at}$$

Topic Practice 4

Directions (Q. Nos. 1-5) Find $\frac{dy}{dx}$.

1. $x = at^2$ and $y = 2at$
2. $x = \frac{e^t + e^{-t}}{2}$ and $y = \frac{e^t - e^{-t}}{2}$
3. $x = \frac{1-t^2}{1+t^2}$ and $y = \frac{2t}{1+t^2}$
4. $x = e^{\theta}\left(\theta + \frac{1}{\theta}\right)$ and $y = e^{-\theta}\left(\theta - \frac{1}{\theta}\right)$
5. $x = \left(t + \frac{1}{t}\right)^a$ and $y = a^{t + \frac{1}{t}}$

Hints & Solutions

1. **Hint** $\frac{dx}{dx} = 2at$, $\frac{dy}{dt} = 2a$ **Ans.** $\frac{1}{t}$

2. **Hint** $\frac{dx}{dt} = \frac{e^t - e^{-t}}{2}$, $\frac{dy}{dt} = \frac{e^t + e^{-t}}{2}$ **Ans.** $\frac{x}{y}$

3. **Hint** Solve as Example 2. **Ans.** $\frac{t^2 - 1}{2t}$

4. **Hint** $\frac{dx}{d\theta} = e^{\theta}\left(1 - \frac{1}{\theta^2}\right) + \left(\theta + \frac{1}{\theta}\right)e^{\theta}$

$\frac{dy}{d\theta} = e^{-\theta}\left(1 + \frac{1}{\theta^2}\right) + \left(\theta - \frac{1}{\theta}\right)(-e^{-\theta})$

Ans. $e^{-2\theta}\left(\frac{-\theta^3 + \theta^2 + \theta + 1}{\theta^3 + \theta^2 + \theta - 1}\right)$

5. **Hint** $\frac{dx}{dt} = a\left(t + \frac{1}{t}\right)^{a-1}\left(1 - \frac{1}{t^2}\right)$

and $\frac{dy}{dt} = a^{t+\frac{1}{t}} \log a\left(1 - \frac{1}{t^2}\right)$ **Ans.** $\frac{a^{t+\frac{1}{t}} \log a}{a\left(t + \frac{1}{t}\right)^{a-1}}$

Differentiation of a Function w.r.t. Another Function and Differentiation of Infinite Series

Differentiation of a Function w.r.t. Another Function

Suppose it is required to differentiate a function $f(x)$ with respect to another function $g(x)$.

Let $y = f(x)$ and $z = g(x)$.

Here, both functions are different but both are in same variable x. Then, to find the derivative of $f(x)$ with respect to $g(x)$ or derivative of $g(x)$ with respect to $f(x)$,

i.e. to find $\frac{dy}{dz}$ or $\frac{dz}{dy}$.

First differentiate both functions $f(x)$ and $g(x)$ with respect to x separately and then put these values in the following formulae

$$\frac{dy}{dz} = \frac{dy/dx}{dz/dx} \text{ or } \frac{dz}{dy} = \frac{dz/dx}{dy/dx}$$

EXAMPLE 1. Differentiate x^6 w.r.t. $\frac{1}{\sqrt{x}}$.

Sol. Let $f(x) = x^6$ and $g(x) = \frac{1}{\sqrt{x}} = x^{-1/2}$

$$\Rightarrow \frac{df}{dx} = 6x^5 \text{ and } \frac{dg}{dx} = -\frac{1}{2} x^{-\frac{1}{2}-1} = -\frac{1}{2} x^{-\frac{3}{2}}$$

$$\because \frac{df}{dg} = \frac{df/dx}{dg/dx} = \frac{6x^5}{-\frac{1}{2}x^{-\frac{3}{2}}} = -12\, x^{5+\frac{3}{2}} = -12\, x^{\frac{13}{2}}$$

EXAMPLE 2. Find the derivative of $x^{\log x}$ w.r.t. $\log x$.

Sol. Let $y = x^{\log x}$

Taking log on both sides, we get

$$\log y = \log x \cdot \log x = (\log x)^2$$

On differentiating both sides w.r.t. x, we get

$$\frac{1}{y}\frac{dy}{dx} = 2 \log x \frac{d}{dx}(\log x)$$

$$\frac{1}{y}\frac{dy}{dx} = 2 \log x\left(\frac{1}{x}\right) \Rightarrow \frac{dy}{dx} = y\left(\frac{2 \log x}{x}\right)$$

$$\Rightarrow \frac{dy}{dx} = x^{\log x}\left(\frac{2 \log x}{x}\right) = x^{\log x - 1}(2 \log x)$$

Again, let $z = \log x$

On differentiating both sides w.r.t. x, we get

$$\frac{dz}{dx} = \frac{1}{x}$$

Now, $$\frac{dy}{dz} = \frac{\frac{dy}{dx}}{\frac{dz}{dx}} = \frac{x^{\log x - 1}(2 \log x)}{\frac{1}{x}} = x^{\log x}(2 \log x)$$

Differentiation of Infinite Series

When the value of y is given as an infinite series, then the process to find the derivative of such infinite series is called **differentiation of infinite series.** In such cases, we use the fact that, if one term is deleted from an infinite series, it remains unaffected, so we can replace all terms except first term by y. Thus, we convert it into a finite series or function. Then, we differentiate it to find the required value.

EXAMPLE 3. If $y = x^{x^{x^{x^{x\ldots}}}}$, then $\frac{dy}{dx}$ is equal to

Sol. We have, $y = x^{x^{x^{x^{x\ldots}}}}$ Then, $y = x^y$

[we know that, by deleting a single term from an infinite series, it remains unaffected.]

$$\Rightarrow y = e^{y \log x} \quad [\because e^{\log_e x} = x]$$

$$\Rightarrow \frac{dy}{dx} = e^{y \log x} \frac{d}{dx}(y \log x)$$

$$\Rightarrow \frac{dy}{dx} = x^y\left(\frac{dy}{dx}\log x + \frac{y}{x}\right)$$

$$\Rightarrow \frac{dy}{dx} = y\left(\frac{dy}{dx}\log x + \frac{y}{x}\right) \quad [\because y = x^y]$$

$$\Rightarrow \frac{dy}{dx} = \frac{y^2}{x(1 - y \log x)}$$

EXAMPLE 4. If $y = \sqrt{\log x + \sqrt{\log x + \sqrt{\log x + \ldots + \infty}}}$, then find $\frac{dy}{dx}$.

Sol. We have, $y = \sqrt{\log x + \sqrt{\log x + \sqrt{\log x + \ldots + \infty}}}$

Then, $y = \sqrt{\log x + y}$

$$\Rightarrow y^2 = \log x + y \quad \text{[squaring both sides]}$$

On differentiating both sides w.r.t. x, we get

$$2y \cdot \frac{dy}{dx} = \frac{1}{x} + \frac{dy}{dx} \Rightarrow 2y\frac{dy}{dx} - \frac{dy}{dx} = \frac{1}{x}$$

$$\Rightarrow \frac{dy}{dx}(2y - 1) = \frac{1}{x} \Rightarrow \frac{dy}{dx} = \frac{1}{x(2y-1)}$$

Topic Practice 5

1 Differentiate x^4 w.r.t. x^3.

2 Differentiate x^x w.r.t. $x \log x$.

3 Differentiate $\log(1+x^2)$ w.r.t. e^{x^3}.

4 Differentiate $(\log x)^x$ w.r.t. $\log x$.

5 If $y = \sqrt{x + \sqrt{x + \sqrt{x + \dots \text{ to } \infty}}}$, then prove that $\frac{dy}{dx} = \frac{1}{2y-1}$.

6 If $y = e^{x + e^{x + e^{x + e^{x + \dots + \infty}}}}$, then prove that $\frac{dy}{dx} = \frac{y}{1-y}$.

7 If $y = x + \cfrac{1}{x + \cfrac{1}{x + \cfrac{1}{x + \dots + \infty}}}$, then prove that $\frac{dy}{dx} = \frac{y}{2y - x}$.

8 If $y = a^{x^{a^{x^{\dots \infty}}}}$, then prove that $\frac{dy}{dx} = \frac{y^2 (\log y)}{x[1 - y(\log x)(\log y)]}$.

Hints & Solutions

1. Solve as Example 1. **Ans.** $\frac{4}{3}x$

2. Solve as Example 2. **Ans.** x^x

3. Solve as Example 2. **Ans.** $\frac{2e^{-x^3}}{3x(1+x^2)}$

4. Solve as Example 2.
Ans. $x(\log x)^{x-1}\{1 + \log x \cdot \log(\log x)\}$

5. **Hint** $y = \sqrt{x + y}$

$$\Rightarrow \quad y^2 = x + y \Rightarrow 2y\frac{dy}{dx} = 1 + \frac{dy}{dx}$$

6. We have, $y = e^{x + e^{x + e^{x + \dots \infty}}}$.

Then, $y = e^{x + y}$

Taking log on both sides, we get

$$\log y = \log e^{(x+y)}$$

$$\Rightarrow \quad \log y = (x+y) \log e$$

$$\Rightarrow \quad \log y = (x+y) \qquad [\because \log e = 1]$$

On differentiating both sides w.r.t. x, we get

$$\frac{1}{y}\frac{dy}{dx} = 1 + \frac{dy}{dx}$$

$$\Rightarrow \quad \frac{1}{y}\frac{dy}{dx} - \frac{dy}{dx} = 1 \Rightarrow \frac{dy}{dx}\left(\frac{1}{y} - 1\right) = 1$$

$$\Rightarrow \quad \frac{dy}{dx}\left(\frac{1-y}{y}\right) = 1 \Rightarrow \frac{dy}{dx} = \frac{y}{1-y}$$

7. We have, $y = x + \cfrac{1}{x + \cfrac{1}{x + \cfrac{1}{x + \dots + \infty}}}$

$$\therefore \quad y = x + \frac{1}{y}$$

$$\Rightarrow \quad y = \frac{xy + 1}{y}$$

$$\Rightarrow \quad y^2 = xy + 1$$

On differentiating both sides w.r.t. x, we get

$$2y\frac{dy}{dx} = x\frac{dy}{dx} + y \cdot 1 + 0$$

[by product rule of derivative]

$$\Rightarrow \quad 2y\frac{dy}{dx} - x\frac{dy}{dx} = y$$

$$\Rightarrow \quad (2y - x)\frac{dy}{dx} = y$$

$$\Rightarrow \quad \frac{dy}{dx} = \frac{y}{2y - x}$$

8. **Hint** $y = a^{x^y} \Rightarrow \log y = x^y \log a$

$$\Rightarrow \quad \log\log y = \log x^y + \log\log a$$

Now, find $\frac{dy}{dx}$ by differentiating the above expression.

Exam Pattern Exercise

Part A - Objective Type Questions

Multiple Choice Type Questions

1 If $y = \frac{(3x+1)(2\sqrt{x}-1)}{\sqrt{x}}$, then $\frac{dy}{dx}$ at $x = 1$ is

(a) 5 (b) -5 (c) 6 (d) $\frac{11}{2}$

2 If $y = \sqrt{x} + \frac{1}{\sqrt{x}}$, then $\frac{dy}{dx}$ at $x = 1$ is

(a) 1 (b) $\frac{1}{2}$ (c) $\frac{1}{\sqrt{2}}$ (d) 0

3 If $y = \frac{1 + \frac{1}{x^2}}{1 - \frac{1}{x^2}}$, then $\frac{dy}{dx}$ is

(a) $-\frac{4x}{(x^2-1)^2}$ (b) $\frac{-4x}{x^2-1}$

(c) $\frac{1-x^2}{4x}$ (d) $\frac{4x}{x^2-1}$

4 If $y = \frac{x^{100}}{100} + \frac{x^{99}}{99} + \dots + \frac{x^2}{2} + x + 1$, then $\frac{dy}{dx}$ at $x = 1$ is

(a) 100 (b) 50 (c) 101 (d) 55

5 For the curve $\sqrt{x} + \sqrt{y} = 1$, $\frac{dy}{dx}$ at the point $\left(\frac{1}{4}, \frac{1}{4}\right)$ is

(a) 1 (b) -1 (c) 0 (d) 2

6 If $f(x) = \log(3x+2)$ and $f'(x) = \frac{\lambda}{3x+2}$, then λ is a polynomial of degree

(a) 0 (b) 1 (c) 2 (d) 3

7 If $xy = 4$, then $x\left(\frac{dy}{dx} + y^2\right)$ is equal to

(a) y (b) $2y$
(c) $3y$ (d) $4y$

8 If $y = \sqrt{x^2 + x + 1}$, then $y\frac{dy}{dx}$ is equal to

(a) $2x + 1$ (b) $\frac{1}{2}(2x+1)$

(c) $\frac{1}{4}(2x+1)$ (d) None of these

9 If $f(x) = \frac{e^x + e^{-x}}{e^x - e^{-x}}$ and $f'(x) = \frac{k}{(e^x - e^{-x})^2}$, then k is equal to

(a) 2 (b) 4
(c) -2 (d) -4

10 If $y = \frac{1}{(x^2+3)^2}$, then $\frac{dy}{dx}$ is equal to

(a) $\frac{4x}{(x^2+3)^3}$

(b) $\frac{-4x}{(x^2+3)^3}$

(c) $\frac{2x}{(x^2+3)^3}$

(d) $\frac{-2x}{(x^2+3)^3}$

Assertion-Reason Based Questions

Directions (Q. Nos. 11-13) *In the questions given below are two statements labelled as Assertion (A) and Reason (R). In the context of the two statements, which one of the following is correct?*

(a) Both A and R are correct; R is the correct explanation of A
(b) Both A and R are correct; R is not the correct explanation of A
(c) A is correct; R is incorrect
(d) R is correct; A is incorrect

11 **Assertion (A)** For the function $f(x) = \frac{x^{100}}{100} + \frac{x^{99}}{99} + \dots + \frac{x^2}{2} + x + 1$, $f'(1) = 100f'(0)$.

Reason (R) $\frac{d}{x}(x^n) = n \cdot x^{n-1}$

12 **Assertion (A)** Derivative of $f(x) = x|x|$ is $2|x|$.

Reason (R) For function u and v, $(uv)' = uv' + vu'$.

13 **Assertion (A)** Derivative of $f(x) = 3$ is zero.

Reason (R) Diffrentiation of a constant function is zero.

Part B - Descriptive Questions

Very Short Answer Type Questions

14 If $y = \frac{x-4}{2\sqrt{x}}$, the find $\frac{dy}{dx}$ at $x = 1$.

15 Differentiate $\left(\sqrt{x} + \frac{1}{\sqrt{x}}\right)^2$ w.r.t. x.

16 If $x^2 + y^2 = t - \frac{1}{t}$ and $x^4 + y^4 = t^2 + \frac{1}{t^2}$, then find $\frac{dy}{dx}$.

17 Differentiate $e^{\sqrt{x}}$ w.r.t. x.

Short Answer Type Questions

18 Find the derivative of e^x, using first principle.

19 Differentiate $x^2 \log_2 x + x^2 2^x$ w.r.t. x.

20 Differentiate $x^3 e^x + (x^2+1)(x-1)$ w.r.t. x.

21 If $y = 1 + \frac{x}{1!} + \frac{x^2}{2!} + \frac{x^3}{3!} + \dots$, show that $\frac{dy}{dx} = y$.

22 If $y = (x-1)\log(x-1) - (x+1)\log(x+1)$, prove that $\frac{dy}{dx} = \log\left(\frac{x-1}{1+x}\right)$.

23 Differentiate $(x^x)^x$ w.r.t. x.

Long Answer Type Questions

24 Differentiate $\frac{2x+3}{3x+2}$ w.r.t. x from first principle.

25 If $y = \frac{\sqrt{a^2+x^2} + \sqrt{a^2-x^2}}{\sqrt{a^2+x^2} - \sqrt{a^2-x^2}}$, then show that $\frac{dy}{dx} = -\frac{2a^2}{x^3}\left\{1 + \frac{a^2}{\sqrt{a^4-x^4}}\right\}$.

26 If $\log(\sqrt{1+x^2} - x) = y\sqrt{1+x^2}$, then show that $(1+x^2)\frac{dy}{dx} + xy + 1 = 0$.

27 Find $\frac{dy}{dx}$, if $y^x + x^y + x^x = a^b$.

28 Differentiate $x^{x^{x^2}}$ w.r.t. x.

Case Study Based Questions

29. $\frac{d}{dx}$ is an operator such that when it is applied on $y = f(x)$, gives us $\frac{d}{dx}[f(x)] = \frac{dy}{dx}$. The operator $\frac{d}{dx}$ is called the differential operator.

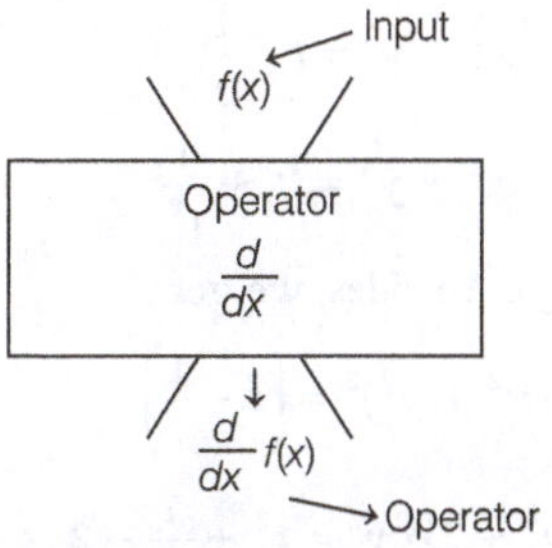

On the basis of above information, answer the following questions.

(i) Find the derivative of $e^{\sqrt{x}}$.

(ii) Find the derivative of $x^2 e^x$.

(iii) Find the derivative of $\frac{x}{x+1}$.

Or

Find the derivative of $\log(x^2 + 3x + 1)$.

30 Let u and v are two functions of x, then

I. $\frac{d}{dx}(u \pm v) = \frac{du}{dx} \mp \frac{dv}{dx}$

II. $\frac{d}{dx}(u \cdot v) = u\frac{dv}{dx} + v\frac{du}{dx}$

III. $\frac{d}{dx}\left(\frac{u}{v}\right) = \frac{v\frac{du}{dx} - u\frac{dv}{dx}}{v^2}$

Now, on the basis of above information, answer the following questions.

(i) Find the value of $\frac{d}{dx}[x^{-4}(3 - 4x^{-5})]$.

(ii) Find the derivative of $\frac{x^2}{3} + \frac{3}{x^2}$.

(iii) Find the value of $\frac{d}{dx}\left(\frac{3x+4}{5x^2-7x+9}\right)$.

Or

Find the value of $\frac{d}{dx}\left(\frac{x^n - a^n}{x-a}\right)$.

Hints & Solutions

1. (a)	2. (d)	3. (a)	4. (a)
5. (b)	6. (d)	7. (c)	8. (b)
9. (d)	10. (b)	11. (a)	12. (a)
13. (a)			

14. **Hint** We have, $y = \frac{x-4}{2\sqrt{x}} \Rightarrow y = \frac{\sqrt{x}}{2} - \frac{2}{\sqrt{x}}$

On differentiating w.r.t. x, we get

$$\frac{dy}{dx} = \frac{1}{4\sqrt{x}} + \frac{1}{(x)^{3/2}}$$

$$\therefore \quad \left.\frac{dy}{dx}\right]_{x=1} = \frac{1}{4} + 1 = 5/4 \quad \textbf{Ans. } \frac{5}{4}$$

15. **Hint** Let $y = \left(\sqrt{x} + \frac{1}{\sqrt{x}}\right)^2$

$$\Rightarrow \quad y = x + \frac{1}{x} + 2$$

On differentiating w.r.t. x, we get

$$\frac{dy}{dx} = 1 - \frac{1}{x^2}$$

16. Hint Given, $x^2 + y^2 = t - \frac{1}{t}$ ...(i)

and $x^4 + y^4 = t^2 + \frac{1}{t^2}$ ...(ii)

On squaring both sides, we get

$$(x^2 + y^2)^2 = \left(t - \frac{1}{t}\right)^2$$

$$\Rightarrow \quad x^4 + y^4 + 2x^2y^2 = t^2 + \frac{1}{t^2} - 2$$

$$\Rightarrow \quad 2x^2y^2 = -2 \quad \text{[using Eq. (ii)]}$$

$$\Rightarrow \quad y^2 = -\frac{1}{x^2}$$ **Ans.** $\frac{1}{x^3y}$

17. Hint Let $y = e^{\sqrt{x}}$

On differentiating w.r.t. x, we get

$$\frac{dy}{dx} = e^{\sqrt{x}} \cdot \frac{d}{dx}(\sqrt{x}) = \frac{1}{2\sqrt{x}} e^{\sqrt{x}}$$

Ans. $\frac{1}{2\sqrt{x}} e^{\sqrt{x}}$

18. Hint By using first principle of derivative, we have

$$f'(x) = \lim_{h \to 0} \frac{f(x+h) - f(x)}{h}$$

$$= \lim_{h \to 0} \frac{e^{x+h} - e^x}{h} = \lim_{h \to 0} \frac{e^x(e^h - 1)}{h}$$

$$= e^x \lim_{h \to 0} \frac{\left[\left(1 + \frac{h}{1!} + \frac{h^2}{2!} + \ldots \infty\right) - 1\right]}{h}$$

Ans. e^x

19. Hint Let $y = x^2 \log_2 x + x^2 2^x$

On differentiating both sides w.r.t. x, we get

$$\frac{dy}{dx} = \frac{d}{ax}(x^2 \log_2 x) + \frac{d}{dx}(x^2 2^x)$$

$$= x^2 \frac{d}{dx}(\log_2 x) + \log_2 x \frac{d}{dx}(x^2) + \frac{d}{dx}(x^2) \cdot 2^x + x^2 \frac{d}{dx}(2^x)$$

$$= x^2 \frac{1}{x \log 2} + 2x \log_2 x + 2x 2^x + x^2 2^x \log 2$$

$$= \frac{x}{\log 2} + 2x \log_2 x + 2^x(2x + x^2 \log 2)$$

Ans. $\frac{x}{\log 2} + 2x \log_2 x + x 2^x(2 + x \log 2)$

20. Hint Let $y = x^3 e^x + (x^2 + 1)(x - 1)$

On differentiating both sides w.r.t. x, we get

$$\frac{dy}{dx} = e^x \frac{d}{dx} x^3 + x^3 \frac{d}{dx} e^x + (x^2 + 1)\frac{d}{dx}(x - 1) + (x - 1)\frac{d}{dx}(x^2 + 1)$$

$$= 3x^2 e^x + x^3 e^x + x^2 + 1 + (x - 1)2x$$

$$= (3x^2 + x^3) e^x + 3x^2 - 2x + 1$$

Ans. $(3x^2 + x^3) e^x + 3x^2 - 2x + 1$

21. Hint We have,

$$y = 1 + \frac{x}{1!} + \frac{x^2}{2!} + \frac{x^3}{3!} + \ldots \quad \text{...(i)}$$

On differentiating both sides w.r.t. x, we get

$$\frac{dy}{dx} = 0 + \frac{1}{1!} + \frac{2x}{2!} + \frac{3x^2}{3!} + \ldots$$

$$= 1 + x + \frac{x^2}{2!} + \frac{x^3}{3!} + \ldots$$

$$\frac{dy}{dx} = y \quad \text{[using Eq. (i)]}$$

22. Hint Given, $y = (x - 1)\log(x - 1) - (x + 1)\log(x + 1)$

On differentiating both sides w.r.t. x, we get

$$\frac{dy}{dx} = \frac{d}{dx}(x-1)\log(x-1) + (x-1)\frac{d}{dx}\log(x-1) - (x+1)\frac{d}{dx}\log(x+1) - \log(x+1)\frac{d}{dx}(x+1)$$

$$= \log(x - 1) + \frac{x-1}{x-1} - \frac{x+1}{x+1} - \log(x + 1)$$

$$\therefore \quad \frac{dy}{dx} = \log\left(\frac{x-1}{x+1}\right)$$ **Hence proved.**

23. Hint Let $y = (x^x)^x = x^{x^2}$

Taking log both sides, we get

$$\log y = \log(x^{x^2}) = x^2 \log x$$

On differentiating both sides w.r.t. x, we get

$$\frac{1}{y}\frac{dy}{dx} = x^2 \frac{1}{x} + 2x \log x$$

$$\frac{dy}{dx} = y[x + 2x \log x]$$

Ans. $x^{x^2}(x + 2x \log x)$

24. Hint Let $f(x) = \frac{2x + 3}{3x + 2}$

By first principle of derivative, we have

$$f'(x) = \lim_{h \to 0} \frac{f(x+h) - f(x)}{h}$$

$$= \lim_{h \to 0} \frac{\left[\frac{2(x+h) + 3}{3(x+h) + 2} - \frac{2x + 3}{3x + 2}\right]}{h}$$

$$= \lim_{h \to 0} \left[\frac{(3x + 2)(2x + 2h + 3) - (2x + 3)(3x + 3h + 2)}{h(3x + 3h + 2)(3x + 2)}\right]$$

Ans. $-\frac{5}{(3x + 2)^2}$

25. **Hint** We have,

$$y = \frac{\sqrt{a^2 + x^2} + \sqrt{a^2 - x^2}}{\sqrt{a^2 + x^2} - \sqrt{a^2 - x^2}}$$

$$= \frac{(\sqrt{a^2 + x^2} + \sqrt{a^2 - x^2})(\sqrt{a^2 + x^2} + \sqrt{a^2 - x^2})}{(\sqrt{a^2 + x^2})^2 - (\sqrt{a^2 - x^2})^2}$$

$$= \frac{a^2 + x^2 + a^2 - x^2 + 2\sqrt{a^4 - x^4}}{2x^2}$$

$$y = \frac{a^2 + \sqrt{a^4 - x^4}}{x^2}$$

On differentiating both sides w.r.t. x, we get

$$\frac{dy}{dx} = \frac{(x^2)\frac{d}{dx}(a^2 + \sqrt{a^4 - x^4}) - (a^2 + \sqrt{a^4 - x^4})2x}{(x^2)^2}$$

$$= \frac{\frac{x^2(-4x^3)}{2\sqrt{a^4 - x^4}} - 2x(a^2 + \sqrt{a^4 - x^4})}{x^4}$$

$$= \frac{-2x^5}{x^4\sqrt{a^4 - x^4}} - \frac{2}{x^3}(a^2 + \sqrt{a^4 - x^4})$$

$$\therefore \frac{dy}{dx} = \frac{-2a^2}{x^3}\left[1 + \frac{a^2}{\sqrt{a^2 - x^4}}\right]$$ **Hence proved.**

26. **Hint** We have, $\log(\sqrt{1 + x^2} - x) = y\sqrt{1 + x^2}$

On differentiating both sides w.r.t. x, we get

$$\frac{1}{\sqrt{1 + x^2} - x}\frac{d}{dx}(\sqrt{1 + x^2} - x) = \frac{y \times x}{\sqrt{1 + x^2}} + \frac{dy}{dx}\cdot\sqrt{1 + x^2}$$

$$\Rightarrow \frac{1}{\sqrt{1 + x^2} - x} \times \left(\frac{x}{\sqrt{1 + x^2}} - 1\right) = \frac{xy}{\sqrt{1 + x^2}} + \frac{dy}{dx}\sqrt{1 + x^2}$$

$$\Rightarrow \quad -1 = xy + (1 + x^2)\frac{dy}{dx}$$

$$\therefore (1 + x^2)\frac{dy}{dx} + xy + 1 = 0$$ **Hence proved.**

27. **Hint** Let $y^x = u$ ...(i)

$x^y = v$ ...(ii)

and $x^x = w$ ...(iii)

So, $u + v + w = a^b$

On differentiating both sides w.r.t. x, we get

$$\frac{du}{dx} + \frac{dv}{dx} + \frac{dw}{dx} = 0 \quad \text{...(iv)}$$

Now, from Eq. (i), we get

$$y^x = u$$

Taking log both sides, we get

$$x \log y = \log u$$

On differentiating both sides w.r.t. x, we get

$$\frac{x}{y}\frac{dy}{dx} + \log y = \frac{1}{u}\frac{du}{dx}$$

$$\Rightarrow \quad \frac{du}{dx} = y^x\left[\frac{x}{y}\frac{dy}{dx} + \log y\right] \quad \text{...(v)}$$

Similarly from Eq. (i), we get

$$v = x^y$$

$$\Rightarrow \quad \log v = y \log x$$

$$\Rightarrow \quad \frac{1}{v}\frac{dv}{dx} = \frac{y}{x} + \log x\frac{dy}{dx}$$

$$\Rightarrow \quad \frac{dv}{dx} = x^y\left[\frac{y}{x} + \log x\frac{dy}{dx}\right] \quad \text{...(vi)}$$

and $w = x^x$

$$\log w = x \log x$$

$$\Rightarrow \quad \frac{1}{w}\frac{dw}{dx} = 1 + \log x$$

$$\Rightarrow \quad \frac{dw}{dx} = x^x(1 + \log x) \quad \text{...(vii)}$$

From Eqs. (v), (vi) and (vii) put in Eq. (iv), we get

$$y^x\left(\frac{x}{y}\frac{dy}{dx} + \log y\right) + x^y\left(y/x + \log x\frac{dy}{dx}\right) + x^x(1 + \log x) = 0$$

$$\therefore \quad \frac{dy}{dx} = \frac{-[y^x \log y + yx^{y-1} + x^x(1 + \log x)]}{xy^{x-1} + x^y \log x}$$

28. **Hint** Let $y = x^{x^{x^2}}$

Taking log both sides, we get

$$\log y = x^{x^2} \log x$$

Again, taking log both sides

$$\log(\log y) = \log x^{x^2} + \log(\log x)$$

$$= x^2 \log x + \log(\log x)$$

On differentiating both sides w.r.t. x, we get

$$\frac{1}{\log y}\frac{1}{y}\frac{dy}{dx} = \frac{x^2}{x} + 2x\log x + \frac{1}{x\log x}$$

$$\therefore \quad \frac{dy}{dx} = y\log y\left[x + 2x\log x + \frac{1}{x\log x}\right]$$

Ans. $x^{x^{x^2}}\log(x^{x^{x^2}})\left[x + 2x\log x + \frac{1}{x\log x}\right]$

29. (i) $\frac{e^{\sqrt{x}}}{2\sqrt{x}}$

(ii) $e^x(2x + x^2)$

(iii) $\frac{1}{(x + 1)^2}$ *Or* $\frac{2x + 3}{(x^2 + 3x + 1)}$

30. (i) $-12x^{-5}(1 - 3x^{-5})$

(ii) $\frac{2x}{3} - \frac{6}{x^3}$

(iii) $\frac{55 - 40x - 15x^2}{(5x^2 - 7x + 9)^2}$ *Or* $\frac{(n - 1)x^n - nax^{n-1} + a^n}{(x - a)^2}, x \neq a$

CHAPTER 17

Probability

In this Chapter...

- Experiment and Sample Space
- Event and Algebra of Events
- Addition Rule of Probability
- Conditional Probability
- Multiplication Theorem on Probability and Independent Events

In earlier classes, we have study the statistical and classical approach of probability. But both the theories have some serious difficulties and limitations. To overcome these difficulties, modern probability theory has been developed axiomatically. To understand this approach, we must know about some basic terms, *viz.* experiment, random experiment, sample space, events, etc.

Experiment and Sample Space

Experiment

An operation which can produce some well-defined outcomes, is known as experiment. There are two types of experiments

(i) **Deterministic Experiments** An experiment which gives the same result every time, when it is repeated under identical conditions, is called deterministic experiments. e.g. sum of angles of any triangle is always 180°.

(ii) **Random or probabilistic Experiments** The experiment which do not give the same result, when repeated under identical conditions are called random experiments. Here, the result obtained is one of the several possible outcomes of the experiment. e.g. when a fair coin is tossed it may turn up a head or a tail, but we are not sure which one of these results will be actually obtained. Such experiments are called random experiments.

An experiment is called random experiment, if it satisfies the following two conditions.

- It has more than one possible outcomes.
- It is not possible to predict the outcomes in advance.

Outcomes and Sample Space

A possible result of a random experiment is called its outcome and the set of all possible outcomes in a random experiment is called a sample space and it is generally denoted by S

i.e. **Sample space (S) = {All possible outcomes}**

Each element of a sample space is called a **sample point** or an **event point.**

e.g.

(i) On tossing a fair coin, there are two possible outcomes, namely head (H) and tail (T).

$\therefore$ The sample space S is $\{H, T\}$ i.e. $S = \{H, T\}$.

(ii) When we throw a die, then possible outcomes of this experiment are 1, 2, 3, 4, 5 or 6.

$\therefore$ The sample space S is $\{1, 2, 3, 4, 5, 6\}$

i.e. $S = \{1, 2, 3, 4, 5, 6\}$

Common Terms Related to Probability Problems

(i) **Coin** A coin has two sides, head and tail. If an experiment consists of more than one coin, then coins are considered as distinct.

- Sample space of one coin = $\{H, T\}$
- Sample space of two coins $= \{(H, T), (T, H), (H, H), (T, T)\}$
- Sample space of three coins $= \{(H,H,H), (H, H, T), (H,T,H), (T, H,H), (H,T,T), (T, H, T), (T,T,H), (T, T,T)\}$

(ii) **Die** A die has six faces marked with numbers 1, 2, 3, 4, 5 and 6. (or dots 1, 2, 3, 4, 5 and 6). If an experiment consists of more than one die, then all dice are considered as distinct.

- Sample space of a die = $\{1, 2, 3, 4, 5, 6\}$
- Sample space of two dice

$$= \left\{\begin{matrix} (1,1), (1,2), (1,3), (1,4), (1,5), (1,6), \\ (2,1), (2,2), (2,3), (2,4), (2,5), (2,6), \\ (3,1), (3,2), (3,3), (3,4), (3,5), (3,6), \\ (4,1), (4,2), (4,3), (4,4), (4,5), (4,6), \\ (5,1), (5,2), (5,3), (5,4), (5,5), (5,6), \\ (6,1), (6,2), (6,3), (6,4), (6,5), (6,6) \end{matrix}\right\}$$

(iii) **Playing Cards** A pack of playing cards has 52 cards. There are 4 suits (spade, heart, diamond and club), each having 13 cards in pack. These are of two colours, **red** (heart and diamond) and **black** (spade and club), each having 26 cards.

In 13 cards of each suit, there are 3 face cards namely **king, queen and jack**, so there are total 12 face cards. Also, there are 16 honour cards, 4 of each suit namely **ace, king, queen and jack.**

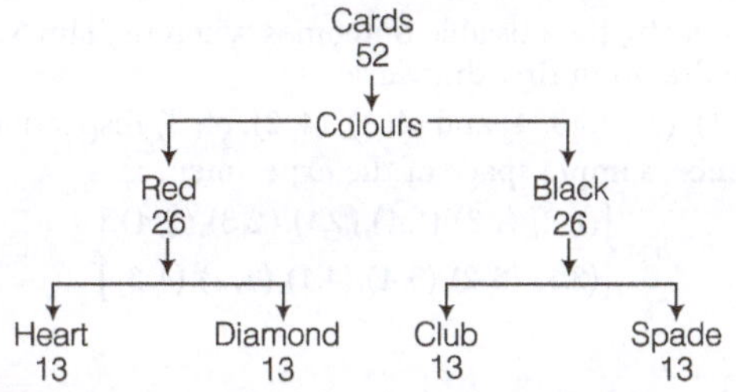

EXAMPLE 1. A bag contains 4 identical red balls and 3 identical black balls. The experiment consists of drawing one ball, then putting it into the bag and again drawing a ball. What are the possible outcomes of the experiment?

Sol. Let R denotes a red ball and B denotes a black ball. Then, possible outcomes of the experiment are RR, RB, BR and BB.

EXAMPLE 2. An experiment consists of recording boy-girl composition of families with 2 children.

(i) What is the sample space, if we are interested in knowing whether it is a boy or girl in the order of their births?

(ii) What is the sample space, if we are interested in the number of girls in the family?

Sol. Let B denotes a boy and G denotes a girl.

Then,

(i) Required sample space = $\{BB, BG, GB, GG\}$

(ii) There can be no girl, 1 girl or 2 girls.

$\therefore$ Required sample space = $\{0, 1, 2\}$

EXAMPLE 3. 2 boys and 2 girls are in room X and 1 boy and 3 girls are in room Y. Specify the sample space for the experiment in which a room is selected and then a person.

Sol. Let the boys and girls in room X be denoted by B_1, B_2, G_1, G_2 and those in room Y be denoted by b_1, g_1, g_2, g_3. A room out of the two can be selected in two ways; either the room X is selected or the room Y is selected. Corresponding to either case, there are four ways of selecting a person.

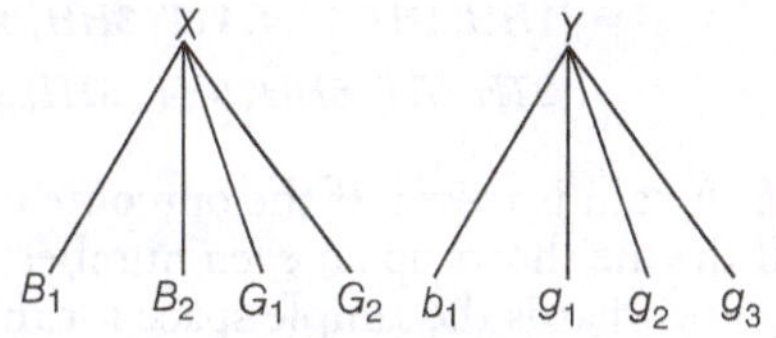

$$\therefore \quad S = \{(X, B_1), (X, B_2), (X, G_1), (X, G_2), (Y, b_1), (Y, g_1), (Y, g_2), (Y, g_3)\}$$

EXAMPLE 4. Suppose 3 bulbs are selected at random from a lot. Each bulb is tested and classified as defective (D) or non-defective (N). Write the sample space for this experiment.

Sol. Given, defective bulb denoted by D and non-defective bulb denoted by N.

There are $2^3 = 8$ possible outcomes.

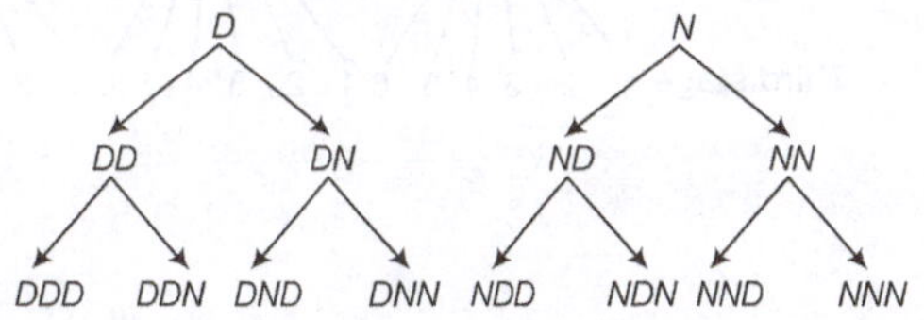

Hence, the required sample space

$= \{DDD, DDN, DND, DNN, NDD, NDN, NND, NNN\}$

EXAMPLE 5. An experiment consists of rolling a die and then tossing a coin once, if the number on the die is even. If the number on the die is odd, then coin is tossed twice. Write the sample space for this experiment.

Sol. It is a two stage experiment. When a die is rolled, then it may show up any one of the six numbers 1, 2, 3, 4, 5, 6.

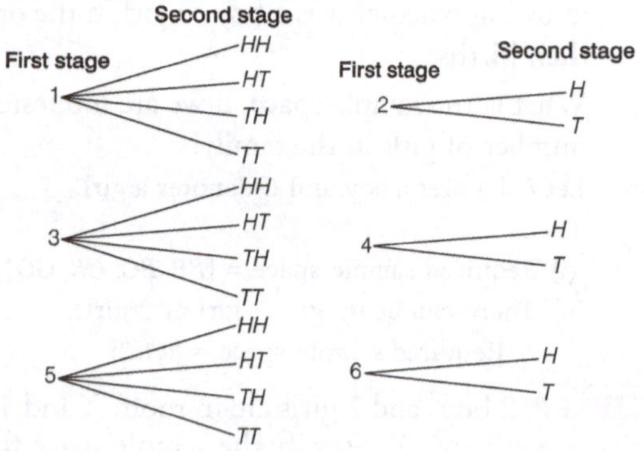

When the die shows up an odd number, a coin is tossed twice and hence, corresponding to each of 1, 3 and 5, there are four possibilities.

When the die shows up an even number, a coin is tossed once and hence, corresponding to each of 2, 4 and 6, there are only two possibilities.

Hence, the sample space is

$$S = \begin{Bmatrix} 2H, 2T, 4H, 4T, 6H, 6T, \\ 1HH, 1HT, 1TH, 1TT, 3HH, 3HT, \\ 3TH, 3TT, 5HH, 5HT, 5TH, 5TT \end{Bmatrix}$$

EXAMPLE 6. A coin is tossed. If the outcome is head, a die is thrown. If the die shows up an even number, the die is thrown again, what is the sample space for this experiment?

Sol. In tossing of a coin, if we get a tail, experiment is completed and if we get a head, the stage experiment has three stages.

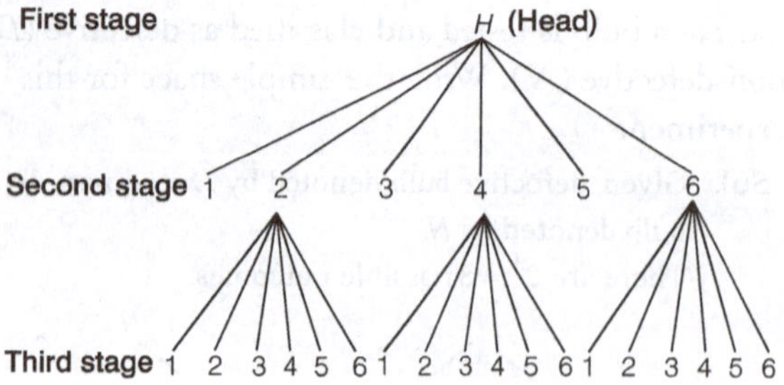

Hence, the sample space

$$S = \begin{Bmatrix} T, (H, 1), (H, 3), (H, 5), (H, 2, 1), (H, 2, 2), \\ (H, 2, 3), (H, 2, 4), (H, 2, 5), (H, 2, 6), \\ (H, 4, 1), (H, 4, 2), (H, 4, 3), (H, 4, 4), \\ (H, 4, 5), (H, 4, 6), (H, 6, 1), (H, 6, 2), \\ (H, 6, 3), (H, 6, 4), (H, 6, 5), (H, 6, 6) \end{Bmatrix}.$$

EXAMPLE 7. From a group of 2 men and 3 women, two persons are selected. Describe the sample space of this experiment.

Sol. Let 2 men be represented by M_1 and M_2 and 3 women be represented by W_1, W_2 and W_3.

Thus, sample space,

$$S = \{M_1M_2, M_1W_1, M_1W_2, M_1W_3, M_2W_1, M_2W_2, M_2W_3, W_1W_2, W_1W_3, W_2W_3\}.$$

EXAMPLE 8. A die is thrown repeatedly until a six comes up. What is the sample space for this experiment?

Sol. In this experiment, 6 may comes up in 1st throw or in the 2nd throw or in the 3rd throw and so on, till 6 is obtained.

Hence, the desired sample space is

$$S = \begin{Bmatrix} 6, (1,6), (2,6), (3,6), (4,6), (5,6), (1,1,6), \\ (1, 2, 6), (1, 3, 6), \ldots, (1, 5, 6), (2, 1, 6), \ldots, \\ (2, 5, 6), \ldots, (5, 1, 6), (5, 2, 6), \ldots, (5, 5, 6), \ldots \end{Bmatrix}.$$

EXAMPLE 9. The numbers 1, 2, 3 and 4 are written separately on the four slips of paper, the slips are put in a box and mixed thoroughly. A person draw two slips from the box, one after the other, without replacement. Describe the sample space for the experiment.

Sol. Here, slips are drawn one after the other, without replacement. So, if the slip 1 is drawn in first draw, then the slip drawn in second draw may be the numbers 2, 3 and 4. Thus, in this case, possible outcomes are (1, 2), (1, 3) and (1, 4). If the slip 2 is drawn in first draw, then the slip drawn in second draw may be the numbers 1, 3 and 4. Thus, in this case, possible outcomes are (2, 1), (2, 3) and (2, 4).

Similarly, the possible outcomes when the slip 3 and 4 are drawn in first draw are

(3, 1), (3, 2), (3, 4) and (4, 1), (4, 2), (4, 3) respectively.

Hence, sample space of the experiment is

$$S = \begin{Bmatrix} (1, 2), (1, 3), (1, 4), (2, 1), (2, 3), (2, 4), \\ (3, 1), (3, 2), (3, 4), (4, 1), (4, 2), (4, 3) \end{Bmatrix}$$

Topic Practice 1

1 A coin is tossed and then a die is rolled only in case a head is shown on the coin. Describe the sample space.

2 A coin is tossed. If it shows head, we throw a die. If it shows a tail, we toss another coin. Describe the sample space.

3 A coin is tossed. If it shows tail, we draw a ball from a box which contains 2 red and 3 black balls. If it shows head, we throw a die. Find the sample space for this experiment.

4 A coin is tossed twice. If the second throw results in a tail, a die is thrown. Describe the sample space for this experiment.

5 A coin is tossed repeatedly until a head comes up. Describe the sample space.

6 Two coloured dice Black (B) and Pink (P) are placed in a bag. One die is drawn at random from the bag and its colour and the number appearing on its top face is noted. Describe the sample space for this experiment.

7 1 boy and 2 girls are in a room X and 3 boys and 1 girl are in room Y. Write the sample space for the experiment in which a room is selected and then a person.

8 From a group of 2 boys and 2 girls, we select two persons to form a committee. What will be the sample space for this experiment?

9 A box contains 1 red and 3 black balls. Two balls are drawn at random in succession without replacement. Write the sample space for this experiment.

10 Suppose 3 bulbs are selected at random from a lot. Among them two are defective (D) and one is non-defective (N). Write the sample space for this experiment.

11 The numbers 4, 5, 6 and 7 are written separately on the form slips of the paper. The slips are put in a box and mixed thoroughly. A person draw two slips from the box, one after the other without replacement. Describe the sample space for the experiment.

12 One ticket is drawn at random from a box containing 30 tickets numbered 1 to 30. Represent the sample space and also write the sample space of drawing a ticket containing number which is a multiple of 4.

Hints & Solutions

1. **Hint** When head is shown on the coin, then possible outcomes are $(H, 1), (H, 2), (H, 3), \ldots, (H, 6)$
   Ans. $\{T, (H, 1), (H, 2), (H, 3), (H, 4), (H, 5), (H, 6)\}$

2. **Hint** First stage

   Second stage

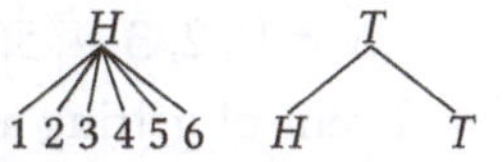

   Ans. $\{(H, 1), (H, 2), (H, 3), (H, 4), (H, 5), (H, 6), (T, T), (T, H)\}$

3. **Hint** Let the balls in the box be represented by R_1, R_2 and B_1, B_2, B_3.
   Ans. $\{(H, 1), (H, 2), (H, 3), (H, 4), (H, 5), (H, 6), (T, R_1), (T, R_2), (T, B_1), (T, B_2), (T, B_3)\}$

4. $\{HH, TH, (HT, 1), (HT, 2), (HT, 3), (HT, 4), (HT, 5), (HT, 6), (TT, 1), (TT, 2), (TT, 3), (TT, 4), (TT, 5), (TT, 6)\}$

5. Solve as Example 8.
   Ans. $\{H, TH, TTH, TTTH, TTTTH, \ldots\}$

6. **Hint** If a die of black colour is selected, the possible outcomes are $(B, 1) (B, 2) (B, 3) (B, 4) (B, 5) (B, 6)$ similarly, for die of pink colour.
   $\{(B, 1), (B, 2), (B, 3), (B, 4), (B, 5), (B, 6), (P, 1), (P, 2), (P, 3), (P, 4), (P, 5), (P, 6)\}$

7. Solve as Example 3.
   Ans. $\{(x, B_1), (x, G_1), (x, G_2), (y, b_1), (y, b_2), (y, b_3), (y, g_1)\}$

8. Solve as Example 7.
   Ans. $\{(B_1, B_2), (B_1, G_1), (B_1, G_2), (B_2, G_1), (B_2, G_2), (G_1, G_2)\}$

9. **Hint** Let us represent the red ball by R and 3 black balls by B , B , B .
   Ans. $\{(R, B_1), (R, B_2), (R, B_3), (B_1, R), (B_1, B_2), (B_1, B_3), (B_2, R), (B_2, B_1), (B_2, B_3), (B_3, R), (B_3, B_1), (B_3, B_2)\}$

10. Solve as Example 4.
    Ans. $\{(D, D, N), (D, N, D), (N, D, D)\}$

11. Solve as Example 9.
    Ans. $\{(4, 5), (4, 6), (4, 7), (5, 4), (5, 6), (5, 7), (6, 4), (6, 5), (6, 7), (7, 4), (7, 5), (7, 6)\}$

12. **Hint** Let S be the sample space of containing the number on ticket from 1 to 30. And E be the event of getting a number which is a multiple of 4.
    Ans. $S = \{1, 2, \ldots, 30\}$
    and $E = \{4, 8, 12, 16, 20, 24, 28\}$.

Event and Algebra of Events

Event

Any subset E of a sample space S is called an event.

e.g. On throwing a die, we have the sample space

$$S = \{1, 2, 3, 4, 5, 6\}$$

Then, $E = \{2, 3, 4\}$ is an event. $[\because E \subseteq S]$

We can define as many events as there are subsets of a sample space.

Thus, number of events of a sample space $S = n(P(S))$, where $P(S)$ is the power set of S.

EXAMPLE 1. List all events associated with the random experiment of tossing of two coins.

Sol. On tossing of two coins, we have the sample space

$$S = \{HH, HT, TH, TT\}$$

Here, $n(P(S)) = 2^4 = 16$

So, there are 16 events, which are defined as follows.

[if a set have n elements, then its power set have 2^n elements]

$\{\phi, \{HH\}, \{HT\}, \{TH\}, \{TT\}, \{HH, HT\}, \{HH, TH\}, \{HH, TT\}, \{HT, TH\}, \{HT, TT\}, \{TH, TT\}, \{HH, HT, TH\}, \{HH, HT, TT\}, \{HH, TH, TT\}, \{HT, TH, TT\}, \{HH, HT, TH, TT\}\}$

EXAMPLE 2. An ordinary deck of cards contains 52 cards divided into four suits. The red suits are diamonds and hearts and black suits are clubs and spades. The cards Jack (J), Queen (Q), King (K) are called face cards. Suppose we pick one card from the deck at random.

(i) What is the sample space of the experiment?

(ii) Describe the event that the chosen card is a black face card.

Sol. We have the following flowchart.

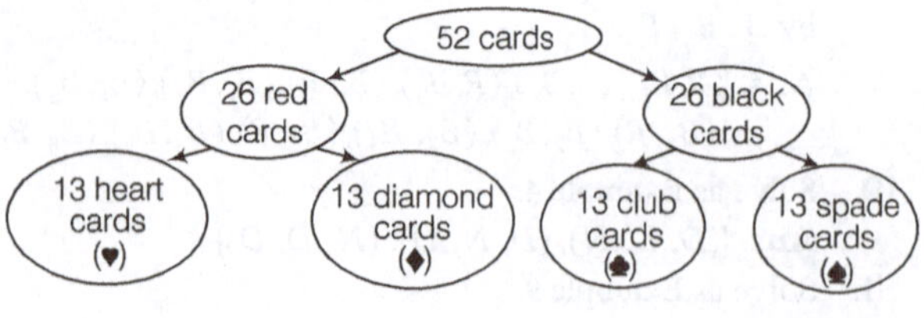

(i) Since, a card is drawn at random, therefore the outcomes in the sample space S are all 52 cards in the deck.

(ii) Let E be the event that the chosen card is a black face card. Then, the outcomes in E are Jack, Queen, King of spade and club cards.

Symbolically, $E = \{J♣, Q♣, K♣, J♠, Q♠, K♠\}$

Occurrence of an Event

An event associated with a random experiment is said to occur, if any one of the elementary events associated to it is an outcome of the experiment.

e.g. Suppose a die is thrown and let A be an event of getting an odd number.

Then, $A = \{1, 3, 5\}$

Now, if the outcome of experiment is 3, then we can say that event A has occurred.

Suppose, in another trial, outcome is 4, then we can say that event A has not occurred.

Types of Events

Events can be classified into various types on the basis of their elements.

Sure (or Certain) Event

The whole sample space S is also a subset of S, so it represents an event. Since, every outcome of an experiment carried out a member of S, therefore the event represented by S is called a sure or a certain event.

e.g.

(i) Sun rises in the East, is a sure event.

(ii) On tossing a coin, either head or tail will occur, is a sure event.

(iii) On throwing a die, we have sample space

$$S = \{1, 2, 3, 4, 5, 6\}$$

Let E = Event of getting a number less than 7

Then, $E = \{1, 2, 3, 4, 5, 6\}$

So, E is a sure event.

Impossible Event

The empty set ϕ is also a subset of the sample space (S), so it represents an event. Since, there is no element in the empty set, therefore it can not occur.

That's why event ϕ is called an impossible event.

e.g. On throwing a die, we have the sample space

$$S = \{1, 2, 3, 4, 5, 6\}$$

Let E = Event of getting a number less than 1

Then, $E = \phi$

So, E is called an impossible event.

EXAMPLE 3. Identify that following events as sure/impossible events.

(i) Event of getting a number multiple of 7 in a single toss of a die.

(ii) Event of getting five kings in a pack of cards.

(iii) Event of drawing a club queen in a pack of cards.

Sol. (i) We know that in a single toss of a die only 1 to 6 number exist.

So, multiple of 7 does not exist. Hence, it is an impossible event.

(ii) We know that in a pack of cards only four kings exist. So five kings does not exist. Hence, it is an impossible event.

(iii) We know that in a pack of cards club queen exist. Hence, it is a sure events.

Simple Event

If an event has only one sample point, then it is called a simple or elementary event or indecomposible event.

e.g. Let a die is thrown, then sample space

$$S = \{1, 2, 3, 4, 5, 6\}$$

Again, let A = Event of getting 4 = $\{4\}$

B = Event of getting 1 = $\{1\}$

Here, A and B are simple events.

Compound Event

If an event has more than one sample point, then it is called a compound event or decomposible event.

e.g. On rolling a die, we have sample space

$$S = \{1, 2, 3, 4, 5, 6\}$$

Then, the events

E : Getting an even number

F : Getting an odd number

G : Getting a multiple of 3

are all compound events. The subsets of S associated with these events are

$$E = \{2, 4, 6\},$$
$$F = \{1, 3, 5\}$$
and $$G = \{3, 6\}$$

Each of the above subsets contain more than one sample point, therefore they are all compound events.

EXAMPLE 4. Two dice are rolled. Let A, B, C be the events of getting a sum of 2, a sum of 3 and a sum of 4 respectively.

(i) Which events are elementary events?

(ii) Which events are compound events?

Sol. On throwing of two dice, we get the sample space

$$S = \begin{Bmatrix} (1,1),(1,2),(1,3),(1,4),(1,5),(1,6), \\ (2,1),(2,2),(2,3),(2,4),(2,5),(2,6), \\ (3,1),(3,2),(3,3),(3,4),(3,5),(3,6), \\ (4,1),(4,2),(4,3),(4,4),(4,5),(4,6), \\ (5,1),(5,2),(5,3),(5,4),(5,5),(5,6), \\ (6,1),(6,2),(6,3),(6,4),(6,5),(6,6) \end{Bmatrix}$$

Now, as A is the event of getting a sum of 2.

$\therefore \quad A = \{(1,1)\}$

Similarly, $B = \{(1,2),(2,1)\}$ and $C = \{(1,3),(3,1),(2,2)\}$

(i) Since, A consists a single sample point, therefore it is an elementary or simple event.

(ii) Since, both B and C contain more than one sample points, therefore each of them is compound event.

Equally Likely Events

The given events are said to be equally likely, if none of them is expected to occur in preference to the other. e.g. In throwing an unbiased die, all the six faces are equally likely to come.

Algebra of Events

We know that how to combine two or more sets by using the operations on sets union ($\cup$), intersection ($\cap$)and difference ($-$). Like-wise, we can combine two or more events using the analogous set notations.

Let A and B be two events associated with a sample space S, then

1. Complementary Event (Event 'not A')

For every event E, there corresponds another event E' called the complementary event of E, which consist of those outcomes that do not correspond to the occurrence of E. E' is also called the event 'not E'.

2. The Event 'A or B'

The event 'A or B' is same as the event '$A \cup B$' and it contains all those elements which are either in event A or in event B or in both.

Thus, A or $B = A \cup B = \{\omega : \omega \in A$ or $\omega \in B$

3. The Event 'A and B'

The event 'A and B' is same as the event '$A \cap B$' and it contains all those elements which are common to both A and B.

Thus, A and $B = A \cap B = \{\omega : \omega \in A$ and $\omega \in B\}$

4. The Event 'A but not B'

The event 'A but not B' is same as the event $A - B = A \cap B'$ and it contains all those elements which are in A but not in B.

Thus, A but not $B = A - B = \omega : \omega \in A$ and $\omega \notin B\}$

In the following table, we give verbal description of some events and their equivalent set alongwith the Venn Diagram.

	Events	Verbal Description	Equivalent Set	Venn Diagram
(i)	Neither A nor B	It is the intersection of sets $\overline{A}$ and $\overline{B}$, which contains the common elements of $\overline{A}$ and $\overline{B}$.	$\overline{A} \cap \overline{B}$ or $U-(A\cup B)$	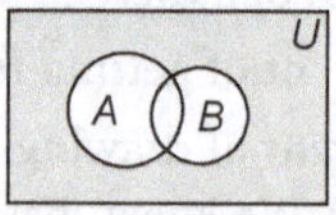
(ii)	Exactly one of A and B	It is the union of one event and complement of other events. or It is the difference of union and intersection of both events.	$(A\cap \overline{B})\cup(\overline{A}\cap B)$ or $(A\cup B)-(A\cap B)$	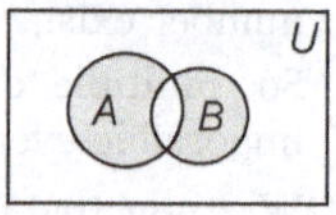
(iii)	Atleast one of A, B or C	It is a union of all three sets, which contains either A or B or C etc.	$A\cup B\cup C$	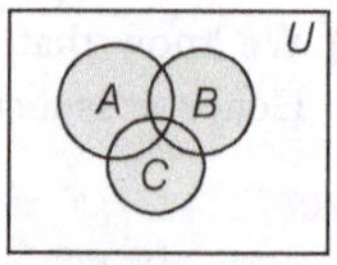
(iv)	All three of A, B and C	It is an intersection of all three sets, which contains common elements of A, B and C.	$A\cap B\cap C$	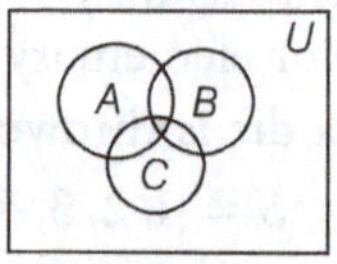
(v)	Exactly two of A, B and C	It is the union of three conditions, where in each condition we take intersection of any two events and complement of remaining third event.	$(A\cap B\cap \overline{C})$ $\cup(A\cap \overline{B}\cap C)$ $\cup(\overline{A}\cap B\cap C)$	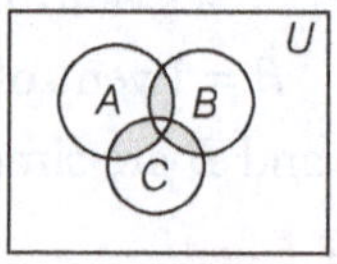

EXAMPLE 5. Two dice are thrown once. The events A, B, E are as follows

A: Getting an even number on first die.

B: Getting an odd number on first die.

E: Getting the sum of numbers on the dice ≥ 10.

Describe the events

(i) A' (ii) B' (iii) E'

Sol. On throwing of two dice, we have sample space

$$S=\left\{\begin{matrix}(1,1),(1,2),(1,3),(1,4),(1,5),(1,6),\\(2,1),(2,2),(2,3),(2,4),(2,5),(2,6),\\(3,1),(3,2),(3,3),(3,4),(3,5),(3,6),\\(4,1),(4,2),(4,3),(4,4),(4,5),(4,6),\\(5,1),(5,2),(5,3),(5,4),(5,5),(5,6),\\(6,1),(6,2),(6,3),(6,4),(6,5),(6,6)\end{matrix}\right\}$$

(i) A: Getting an even number on first die.

Then, A': Getting an odd number on first die.

$$=\left\{\begin{matrix}(1,1),(1,2),(1,3),(1,4),(1,5),(1,6),\\(3,1),(3,2),(3,3),(3,4),(3,5),(3,6),\\(5,1),(5,2),(5,3),(5,4),(5,5),(5,6)\end{matrix}\right\}$$

(ii) B: Getting an odd number on first die.

Then, B': Getting an even number on first die.

$$=\left\{\begin{matrix}(2,1),(2,2),(2,3),(2,4),(2,5),(2,6),\\(4,1),(4,2),(4,3),(4,4),(4,5),(4,6),\\(6,1),(6,2),(6,3),(6,4),(6,5),(6,6)\end{matrix}\right\}$$

(iii) E: Getting the sum of the numbers on the dice ≥ 10.

Then, E': Getting the sum of the numbers on the dice <10.

$$=\left\{\begin{matrix}(1,1),(1,2),(1,3),(1,4),(1,5),(1,6),(2,1),(2,2),\\(2,3),(2,4),(2,5),(2,6),(3,1),(3,2),(3,3),\\(3,4),(3,5),(3,6),(4,1),(4,2),(4,3),(4,4),(4,5),\\(5,1),(5,2),(5,3),(5,4),(6,1),(6,2),(6,3)\end{matrix}\right\}$$

EXAMPLE 6. Consider the experiment of rolling a die. If A be the event 'getting a prime number' and B be the event 'getting an odd number'. Write the sets representing the events

(i) A or B (ii) A and B

(iii) A but not B (iv) 'not A'

Sol. Here, $S=\{1,2,3,4,5,6\}$, $A=\{2,3,5\}$ and $B=\{1,3,5\}$.

Clearly,

(i) 'A or B' $=A\cup B=\{1,2,3,5\}$

(ii) 'A and B' $=A\cap B=\{3,5\}$

(iii) 'A but not B' $=A-B=\{2\}$

(iv) 'not A' $=A'=\{1,4,6\}$

EXAMPLE 7. A die is thrown. Describe the following events

(i) A : a number less than 7.

(ii) B : a number greater than 7.

(iii) C : a multiple of 3.

(iv) D : a number less than 4.

(v) E : an even number greater than 4.

(vi) F : a number not less than 3.

Also, find $A \cup B, A \cap B, B \cup C, E \cap F, D \cap E, A-C, D-E, F'$ and $E \cap F'$.

Sol. When a die is thrown, then sample space

$S = \{1, 2, 3, 4, 5, 6\}$

(i) A : a number less than 7 = $\{1, 2, 3, 4, 5, 6\}$

(ii) B : a number greater than 7 = $\{\} = \phi$

(iii) C : a multiple of 3 = $\{3, 6\}$

(iv) D : a number less than 4 = $\{1, 2, 3\}$

(v) E : an even number greater than 4 = $\{6\}$

(vi) F : a number not less than 3 = $\{3, 4, 5, 6\}$

Now, $A \cup B$ = The elements which are in A or B or both

$= \{1, 2, 3, 4, 5, 6\} \cup \phi$

$= \{1, 2, 3, 4, 5, 6\}$

$A \cap B$ = The elements which are common in both A and B

$= \{1, 2, 3, 4, 5, 6\} \cap \phi = \phi$

$B \cup C$ = The elements which are in B or C or both

$= \{\} \cup \{3, 6\} = \{3, 6\}$

$E \cap F$ = The elements which are common in both E and F

$= \{6\} \cap \{3, 4, 5, 6\} = \{6\}$

$D \cap E$ = The elements which are common in both D and E

$= \{1, 2, 3\} \cap \{6\} = \phi$

$A - C$ = The elements which are in A but not in C

$= \{1, 2, 3, 4, 5, 6\} - \{3, 6\} = \{1, 2, 4, 5\}$

$D - E$ = The elements which are in D but not in E

$= \{1, 2, 3\} - \{6\} = \{1, 2, 3\}$

F' = The elements which are not in F

$= (S - F) = \{1, 2, 3, 4, 5, 6\} - \{3, 4, 5, 6\} = \{1, 2\}$

and $E \cap F' = E \cap (S - F)$

$= E \cap (\{1, 2, 3, 4, 5, 6\} - \{3, 4, 5, 6\})$

$= \{6\} \cap \{1, 2\} = \phi$

Mutually Exclusive Events

Two events are said to be mutually exclusive, if the occurrence of any one of them excludes the occurrence of other event i.e. if they cannot occur simultaneously.

Thus, two events E_1 and E_2 are said to be mutually exclusive, if $E_1 \cap E_2 = \phi$

e.g. In throwing a die, we have sample space

$$S = \{1, 2, 3, 4, 5, 6\}$$

Let E_1 = Event of getting even numbers = $\{2, 4, 6\}$

E_2 = Event of getting odd numbers = $\{1, 3, 5\}$

Here, $E_1 \cap E_2 = \phi$

So, E_1 and E_2 are mutually exclusive events.

In general, events $E_1, E_2, \ldots, E_n$ are said to be mutually exclusive, if they are pair-wise disjoint i.e. if $E_i \cap E_j = \phi$ for all $i \neq j$.

The simple events of a sample space are always mutually exclusive.

EXAMPLE 8. An experiment involves rolling a pair of dice and recording the numbers that comes up. Describe the following events.

A : the sum is greater than 8.

B : 2 occurs on either die.

C : the sum is atleast 7 and multiple of 3.

Which pairs of these events are mutually exclusive?

Sol. There are 36 elements in the sample space

$$S = \{(x, y) : x, y = 1, 2, 3, 4, 5, 6\}$$

Given, A = Events of getting the sum greater than 8 i.e. events of getting the sum 9, 10, 11 and 12.

$\therefore \quad A = \{(6,3), (3,6), (4,5), (5,4), (6,4), (4,6), (5,5), (6,5), (5,6), (6,6)\}$

B = Event of getting 2 on either die.

$\therefore \quad B = \{(2,1), (2,2), (2,3), (2,4), (2,5), (2,6), (1,2), (3,2), (4,2), (5,2), (6,2)\}$

and C = Event of getting the sum atleast 7 and a multiple of 3 i.e. event of getting the sum 9 and 12.

$= \{(4,5), (5,4), (6,3), (3,6), (6,6)\}$

Here, $A \cap B = \phi$, $B \cap C = \phi$ and $A \cap C \neq \phi$

Thus, we can say that, the pairs A and B; B and C are mutually exclusive events.

EXAMPLE 9. Three coins are tossed once. Let A denotes the event "three heads show", B denotes the event "two heads and one tail show", C denotes the event "three tails show" and D denotes the event "a head shows on the first coin". Which pair of events are **[NCERT]**

(i) mutually exclusive events.

(ii) simple events.

(iii) compound events.

Sol. When three coins are tossed, then the sample space is

$S = \{HHH, HHT, HTH, THH, HTT, THT, TTH, TTT\}$

Given, A = event of getting three heads

$\therefore$ $A = \{HHH\}$

B = Event of getting two heads and one tail

$\therefore$ $B = \{HHT, HTH, THH\}$

C = Event of getting three tails

$\therefore$ $C = \{TTT\}$

and D = Event of getting a head on first coin

$\therefore$ $D = \{HHH, HTT, HHT, HTH\}$

(i) Clearly, $A \cap B = \phi$, $A \cap C = \phi$, $A \cap D = \{HHH\}$, $B \cap C = \phi$, $B \cap D = \{HHT, HTH\}$ and $C \cap D = \phi$

$\therefore$ We can say, A and B; A and C; B and C; C and D are mutually exclusive events.

(ii) A and C are simple events, since both have only one sample point.

(iii) B and D are compound event, since they have more than one sample point.

Exhaustive Events

For a random experiment, a set of events is said to be exhaustive, if one of them necessarily occurs whenever the experiment is performed.

Let $E_1, E_2, E_3, \ldots, E_n$ be n subsets of a sample space S. Then, events $E_1, E_2, E_3, \ldots, E_n$ are called exhaustive events, if $E_1 \cup E_2 \cup E_3 \cup \ldots \cup E_n = S$

e.g. Consider the experiment of throwing a die.

We have, $S = \{1, 2, 3, 4, 5, 6\}$

Let us define the following events

E_1 : a number less than 4 appears

E_2 : a number greater than 2 but less than 5 appears.

E_3 : a number greater than 4 appears.

Then, $E_1 = \{1,2,3\}$, $E_2 = \{3,4\}$, $E_3 = \{5,6\}$.

We observe that

$$E_1 \cup E_2 \cup E_3 = \{1, 2, 3\} \cup \{3, 4\} \cup \{5, 6\} = S$$

Thus, the events E_1, E_2 and E_3 are exhaustive events.

If $E_i \cap E_j = \phi$ for $i \neq j$ i.e. events E_i and E_j are pairwise disjoint and $\bigcup_{i=1}^{n} E_i = S$, then events $E_1, E_2, \ldots, E_n$ are called mutually exclusive and exhaustive events.

Mutually Exclusive and Exhaustive Events

Let S be the sample space associated with a random experiment, then the events $E_1, E_2, \ldots, E_n$ of S are called mutually exclusive and exhaustive if $E_1 \cup E_2 \cup \ldots \cup E_n = S$ and $E_i \cap E_j = \phi$ for all $i \neq j$

e.g. Let A = {getting odd number in throwing a die}

B = {getting even number in throwing a die}

then A, B are mutually exclusive and exhaustive events.

Exhaustive Number of Cases

The total number of possible outcomes fo an experiment constitutes exhaustive number of cases.

e.g. When a coin thrown, the exhaustive number of cases is 2 as we may get either heads or tails.

Favourable Number of Cases

The number of cases favourable to an event is called the favourable number of cases.

e.g. If the experiment is simultaneous throw of two die, the number of cases favourable to the event 'getting atleast one six' is parallel as the cases (1, 6), (2, 6), (3, 6), (4, 6), (5, 6), (6, 1), (6, 2), (6, 3), (6, 4), (6, 5), (6, 6) are favourable to it.

EXAMPLE 10. A coin is tossed three times, consider the following events?

A : No head appears.

B : Exactly one head appears.

and C : Atleast two heads appears.

Do they form a set of mutually exclusive and exhaustive events?

Sol. When a coin is tossed three times, then the sample space is

$S = \{HHH, HHT, HTH, THH, THT, TTH, HTT, TTT\}$

Given, A = Event of getting no head

$\therefore$ $A = \{TTT\}$

B = Event of getting exactly one head

$\therefore$ $B = \{TTH, HTT, THT\}$

and C = Event of getting atleast two heads

$\therefore$ $C = \{HHT, HTH, THH, HHH\}$

Clearly, $A \cap B = \phi$, $A \cap C = \phi$ and $B \cap C = \phi$

So, we can say that A, B and C are mutually exclusive events. [$\because$ A, B and C are pair-wise disjoint]

Also, $A \cup B \cup C = \{TTT, TTH, HTT, THT, HHT, HTH, THH, HHH\} = S$

$\therefore$ A, B and C are exhaustive events.

Hence, A, B and C form a set of mutually exclusive and exhaustive events.

Odds of an Event

If an event E occurs in m ways and not occur in n ways, then we say that

(i) odds in favour of event $E = \frac{m}{n}$ or $m : n$

and corresponding probability $= \frac{m}{m+n}$

(ii) odds against the event $E = \frac{n}{m}$ or $n : m$

and corresponding probability $= \frac{n}{m+n}$

If E is any event, then probability of event 'not E'

i.e. $P(\text{not } E) = 1 - P(E)$

EXAMPLE 11. The odds in favour of an event are 2:4. Find the probability of the occurrence of this event.

Sol. We know that if odds in favour of an event are m:n, then probability of occurrence of this event is $\frac{m}{m+n}$

$\therefore$ Required probability $= \frac{2}{2+4}$

$= \frac{2}{6} = \frac{1}{3}$

Topic Practice 2

1 A coin is tossed. Find the total number of elementary events and also the total number of events associated with the random experiment.

2 Two dice are rolled. Let E_1, E_2 and E_3 be the events of getting a sum of 4, 5 and 6 respectively.
(i) Which events are elementary events?
(ii) Which events are compound events?

3 Consider the experiment of rolling a die. Let A be the event 'getting a prime number' and B be the event 'getting an even number'. Write the sets representing events
(i) A and B. (ii) A or B.
(iii) A but not B. (iv) not A.

4 An experiment involves tossing of two coins and recording them in the following events
A : No tail, B : exactly one tail, C : atleast one tail.
Write the sets representing events
(i) A and C.
(ii) A not B.

5 A die is tossed. Let E denotes the event of getting a number multiple of 2 and F denotes the event of getting a number less than 7. Simplify the following events
(i) $E \cup F$ (ii) $F - E$
(iii) E' (iv) $E \cap F$

6 Two dice are thrown. The events A, B and C are as follows:
A : getting an even number on the first die.
B : getting an odd number on the first die.
C : getting the sum of the numbers on the dice ≤ 5.
Describe the events
(i) A' (ii) not B
(iii) A or B (iv) A and B
(v) A but not C (vi) B or C
(vii) B and C (viii) $A \cap B' \cap C'$

7 A coin is tossed two times, consider the following events.
E_1 : No head appears.
E_2 : Exactly one head appears.
and E_3 : Atleast one head appears.
Do, they form a set of mutually exclusive and exhaustive events?

8 Two dice are rolled, A is the event that the sum of the numbers shown on the two dice is 5 and B is the event that atleast one of the dice shown up a 3. Are the two events A and B
(i) mutually exclusive? (ii) exhaustive?

9 Three coins are tossed once. Let A denotes the event "three tails show", B denotes the event "one tail and two head show", C denotes the event "tail on the first coin".
Which pair of events are
(i) mutually exclusive? (ii) simple events?
(iii) compound events?

10 Two dice are thrown and the sum of the numbers which come up on the dice is noted. Let us consider the following events associated with this experiment.
A : 'the sum is even'.
B : 'the sum is a multiple of 3'.
C : 'the sum is less than 4'.
D : 'the sum is greater than 11'.
Which pairs of these events are mutually exclusive?

Hints & Solutions

1. Solve as Example 1.
Ans. 2, 4
2. **Hint** $E_1 = \{(1, 3), (2, 2), (3, 1)\}$
$E_2 = \{(1, 4), (2, 3), (3, 2), (4, 1)\}$
$E_3 = \{(1, 5), (2, 4), (3, 3), (5, 1), (4, 2)\}$
Now, solve as Example 4.
Ans. (i) No event (ii) E_1, E_2 and E_3
3. **Hint** $A = \{2,3,5\}$ and $B = \{2, 4, 6\}$
Now, solve as Example 6.
Ans. (i) {2} (ii) {2, 3, 4, 5, 6} (iii) {3, 5} (iv) {1,4,6}
4. **Hint** $A = \{(H, H)\}, B = \{(H, T), (T, H)\}$
and $C = \{(H, T), (T, H), (T, T)\}$
Now, solve as Example 6.
Ans. (i) A and $C = A \cap C = \phi$
(ii) A not $B = A - B = \{(H, H)\}$
5. **Hint** $E = \{2, 4, 6\}$ and $F = \{1, 2, 3, 4, 5, 6\}$
Now, solve as Example 7.
Ans. (i) {1, 2, 3, 4, 5, 6} (ii) {1, 3, 5}
(iii) {1, 3, 5} (iv) {2, 4, 6}
6. **Hint** $A = \left\{\begin{matrix}(2,1),(2,2),\ldots,(2,6),\\(4,1),(4,2),\ldots,(4,6),\\(6,1),(6,2),\ldots,(6,6)\end{matrix}\right\}$,
$B = \left\{\begin{matrix}(1,1),(1,2),\ldots,(1,6),\\(3,1),(3,2),\ldots,(3,6),\\(5,1),(5,2),\ldots,(5,6)\end{matrix}\right\}$
and $C = \{(1,1),(1,2),(2,1),(1,3),(3,1),(2,2),(2,3),(3,2),(1,4),(4,1)\}$
Ans. (i) $A' = \left\{\begin{matrix}(1,1),(1,2),\ldots,(1,6),\\(3,1),(3,2),\ldots,(3,6),\\(5,1),(5,2),\ldots,(5,6)\end{matrix}\right\} = B$
(ii) $B' = \{(2,1),(2,2),(2,3),(2,4),(2,5),(2,6),(4,1),(4,2),(4,3),(4,4),(4,5),(4,6),(6,1),(6,2),(6,3),(6,4),(6,5),(6,6)\} = A$
(iii) $A \cup B = \{(1,1),(1,2),(1,3),(1,4),(1,5),(1,6),(3,1),(3,2),(3,3),(3,4),(3,5),(3,6),(5,1),(5,2),(5,3),(5,4),(5,5),(5,6),(2,1),(2,2),(2,3),(2,4),(2,5),(2,6),(4,1),(4,2),(4,3),(4,4),(4,5),(4,6),(6,1),(6,2),(6,3),(6,4),(6,5),(6,6)\} = S$
(iv) $A \cap B = \phi$
(v) $A - C = \{(2,4),(2,5),(2,6),(4,2),(4,3),(4,4),(4,5),(4,6),(6,1),(6,2),(6,3),(6,4),(6,5),(6,6)\}$
(vi) $B \cup C = \{(1,1),(1,2),(1,3),(1,4),(1,5),(1,6),(2,1),(2,2),(2,3),(3,1),(3,2),(3,3),(3,4),(3,5),(3,6),(4,1),(5,1),(5,2),(5,3),(5,4),(5,5),(5,6)\}$
(vii) $B \cap C = \{(1,1),(1,2),(1,3),(1,4),(3,1),(3,2)\}$
(viii) $A \cap B' \cap C' = \{(2,4),(2,5),(2,6),(4,2),(4,3),(4,4),(4,5),(4,6),(6,1),(6,2),(6,3),(6,4),(6,5),(6,6)\}$
7. **Hint** $E_1 = \{(T, T)\}$, $E_2 = \{(H, T), (T, H)\}$
and $E_3 = \{(H, T), (T, H), (H, H)\}$
Here, $E_1 \cap E_2 = \phi$, $E_1 \cap E_3 = \phi$ and $E_2 \cap E_3 \neq \phi$
Also, $E_1 \cup E_2 \cup E_3 = \{(H, T), (T, H), (T, T), (H, H)\} = S$
Ans. E_1, E_2 and E_3 are not mutually exclusive but they are exhaustive events.
8. (i) **Hint** $A = \{(1, 4), (4, 1), (3, 2), (2, 3)\}$
and $B = \{(3, 1), (3, 2), (3, 3), (3, 4), (3, 5), (3, 6), (1, 3), (2, 3), (4, 3), (5, 3), (6, 3)\}$
$\therefore A \cap B = \{(3, 2), (2, 3)\} \neq \phi$ **Ans.** No
(ii) **Hint** $A \cup B \neq S$ **Ans.** No
9. Solve as Example 9.
Ans. (i) A and B, B and C (ii) A (iii) B and C.
10. Solve as Example 8. **Ans.** C and D

Addition Rule of Probability

If A and B are two events associated with a random experiment, then

$$P(A \cup B) = P(A) + P(B) - P(A \cap B)$$

i.e. $P(A \text{ or } B) = P(A) + P(B) - P(A \text{ and } B)$

It is known as addition law of probability for two events.

Also, when events A and B are mutually exclusive, then

$$P(A \cup B) = P(A) + P(B)$$

when events A and B are mutually exclusive and exhaustive, then $P(A \cup B) = P(A) + P(B) = 1$

Probability of the Event A or B or C

If A, B and C are three events associated with a random experiment, then

$$P(A \cup B \cup C) = P(A) + P(B) + P(C) - P(A \cap B) - P(B \cap C) - P(C \cap A) + P(A \cap B \cap C)$$

If A, B and C are mutually exclusive events,

i.e. $A \cap B = \phi$, $B \cap C = \phi$,

$A \cap C = \phi$, $A \cap B \cap C = \phi$.

Then, $P(A \cup B \cup C) = P(A) + P(B) + P(C)$

Probability of Complementary Event

Let E be any event and $\overline{E}$ (or E') be its complementary event.

Then, $\quad P(\overline{E}) = 1 - P(E)$

The odds in favour of occurrence of the event E are defined by $P(E) : P(\overline{E})$ and the odds against the occurrence of event E are defined by $P(\overline{E}) : P(E)$.

Important Results

1. For any two events A and B, $A \subseteq B$
   $\Rightarrow P(A) \le P(B)$
2. For any two events A and B,
   (i) $P(A - B) = P(A) - P(A \cap B)$
   or $P(A \cap \overline{B}) = P(A) - P(A \cap B)$
   (ii) $P(B - A) = P(B) - P(A \cap B)$
   or $P(B \cap \overline{A}) = P(B) - P(A \cap B)$
   (iii) $P(\overline{A} \cap \overline{B}) = P(\overline{A \cup B})$
3. $P(A \cap B) \le P(A)$ and $P(A \cap B) \le P(B)$
   [if these conditions hold true, then events are said to be consistently defined]
4. $P(A \cap \overline{B}) \cup (\overline{A} \cap B) = P(A) + P(B) - 2P(A \cap B)$
5. $P(A \cup B) = P(A) + P(B - A) = P(B) + P(A - B)$
6. $P(A \cup B) = P(A - B) + P(B - A) + P(A \cap B)$
7. $P(A) + P(B) = P(A - B) + P(B - A) + 2P(A \cap B)$
8. $P(A \cap B) \le P(A) \le P(A \cup B) \le P(A) + P(B)$
9. $P(A) + P(B) - 2P(A \cup B) = P(A \cup B) - P(A \cap B)$

Note $P(A \cap \overline{B})$ or $P(A - B)$ is called probability of occurence of A only $P(\overline{A} \cap B)$ or $P(B - A)$ is called probability of occurence of B only $P((A \cap \overline{B}) \cup (\overline{A} \cap B))$ is called probability of occurence of exactly one of two events A and B.

Problems Based on Addition Rule of Probability

TYPE I

PROBLEMS DIRECTLY BASED ON FORMULA

EXAMPLE 1. If A and B are two events such that

$$P(A) = \frac{1}{4}, P(B) = \frac{1}{2} \text{ and } P(A \cap B) = \frac{1}{8}.$$

Then, find P (not A and not B).

Sol. P (not A and not B) $= P(\overline{A} \cap \overline{B})$

$$= P(\overline{A \cup B}) = 1 - P(A \cup B)$$
$$= 1 - [P(A) + P(B) - P(A \cap B)]$$
$$= 1 - \left[\frac{1}{4} + \frac{1}{2} - \frac{1}{8}\right]$$
$$= 1 - \left[\frac{2 + 4 - 1}{8}\right] = 1 - \frac{5}{8} = \frac{3}{8}$$

EXAMPLE 2. The accompanying Venn diagram shows three events A, B and C and also the probabilities of the various intersections [for instance $P(A \cap B) = 0.07$]. Determine

(i) $P(A)$ (ii) $P(B \cap \overline{C})$
(iii) $P(A \cup B)$ (iv) $P(A \cap \overline{B})$
(v) $P(B \cap C)$
(vi) Probability of exactly one of the three event occurs.

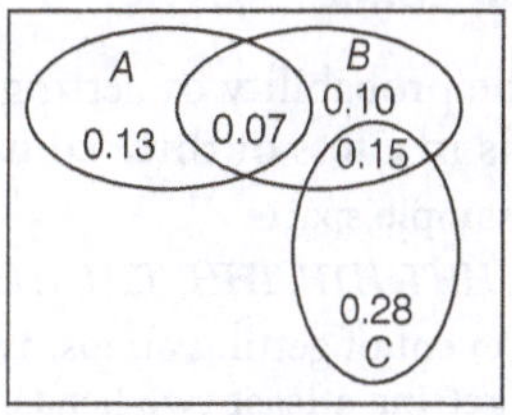

Sol. (i) $P(A) = 0.13 + 0.07 = 0.20$

(ii) $P(B \cap \overline{C}) = P(B) - P(B \cap C)$
$= (0.07 + 0.10 + 0.15) - (0.15) = 0.17$

(iii) $P(A \cup B) = P(A) + P(B) - P(A \cap B)$
$= 0.20 + (0.07 + 0.10 + 0.15) - 0.07$
$= 0.20 + 0.25 = 0.45$

(iv) $P(A \cap \overline{B}) = P(A) - P(A \cap B) = 0.20 - 0.07 = 0.13$

(v) $P(B \cap C) = 0.15$

(vi) P (exactly one of the three events occurs)
$= P(A \text{ only}) + P(B \text{ only}) + P(C \text{ only})$
$= 0.13 + 0.10 + 0.28 = 0.51$

EXAMPLE 3. A and B are two events that $P(A) = 0.54$, $P(B) = 0.69$ and $P(A \cap B) = 0.35$. Find

(i) $P(A \cup B)$ (ii) $P(A' \cap B')$
(iii) $P(A \cap B')$ (iv) $P(B \cap A')$

Sol. We have, $P(A) = 0.54$, $P(B) = 0.69$ and $P(A \cap B) = 0.35$

(i) $P(A \cup B) = P(A) + P(B) - P(A \cap B)$
$= 0.54 + 0.69 - 0.35$
$= 0.88$

(ii) $P(A' \cap B') = P((A \cup B)') = 1 - P(A \cup B)$
$[\because P(E') = 1 - P(E)]$
$= 1 - 0.88 = 0.12$

(iii) $P(A \cap B') = P(A) - P(A \cap B) = 0.54 - 0.35 = 0.19$

(iv) $P(B \cap A') = P(B) - P(A \cap B) = 0.69 - 0.35 = 0.34$

EXAMPLE 4. Check whether the following probabilities $P(A)$ and $P(B)$ are consistently defined

(i) $P(A) = 0.5$, $P(B) = 0.7$, $P(A \cap B) = 0.6$
(ii) $P(A) = 0.5$, $P(B) = 0.4$, $P(A \cup B) = 0.8$

Sol. (i) We have, $P(A)=0.5$, $P(B)=0.7$ and $P(A\cap B)=0.6$.
We know that, $A\cap B\subseteq A$ and $A\cap B\subseteq B$
$\therefore\ P(A\cap B\le P(A)$ and $P(A\cap B)\le P(B)$
But for the given probabilities $P(\ \ \cap B)\not\le P(A)$.
So, given probabilities are not consistently defined.

(ii) We have, $P(A)=0.5$, $P(B)=0.4$ and $P(A\cup B)=0.8$
Clearly, $P(A\cap B)=P(A)+P(B)-P(A\cup B)$
$=0.5+0.4-0.8=0.1$
Here, $P(A\cap B)\le P(A)$
and $P(A\cap B)\le P(B)$.
So, given probabilities are consistently defined.

TYPE II
PROBLEMS BASED ON COINS

EXAMPLE 5. Find the probability of getting atmost two tails or atleast two heads in a toss of three coins.

Sol. Clearly, the sample space
$S=\{HHH, HHT, HTH, THH, TTH, THT, HTT, TTT$
Let A be the event of getting atmost two tails and B be the event of getting atleast two heads.
Then, $A=\{HHH, HHT, HTH, THH, TTH, THT, HTT\}$
and $B=\{HHT, HTH, THH, HHH\}$

$$P(A)=\frac{7}{8};\ P(B)=\frac{4}{8}\text{ and }P(A\cap B)=\frac{4}{8}$$

Now, required probability $=P(A\cup B)$

$$=P(A)+P(B)-P(A\cap B)=\frac{7}{8}+\frac{4}{8}-\frac{4}{8}=\frac{7}{8}$$

TYPE III
PROBLEMS BASED ON DICE

EXAMPLE 6. A coin is tossed and a die is thrown. Find the probability that the outcome will be a head or a number greater than 4.

Sol. When a coin and a die are thrown, then sample space is
$S=\{H1, H2, H3, H4, H5, H6, T1, T2, T3, T4, T5, T6\}$
$\therefore\ n(S)=12$
Let A : Event of getting a head.
$\Rightarrow\ A=\{H1, H2, H3, H4, H5, H6\}$
$\therefore\ n(A)=6$

Then, $P(A)=\frac{n(A)}{n(S)}=\frac{6}{12}$

B : Event of getting a number greater than 4.
$\Rightarrow\ B=\{H5, H6, T5, T6\}$
$\therefore\ n(B)=4$

Then, $P(B)=\frac{n(B)}{n(S)}=\frac{4}{12}$

Also, $A\cap B=$ Event of getting a head and a number greater than 4
$=\{H5, H6\}$
$\therefore\ n(A\cap B)=2$

Then, $P(A\cap B)=\frac{2}{12}$

Now, required probability,

$$P(A\cup B)=P(A)+P(B)-P(A\cap B)$$
$$=\frac{6}{12}+\frac{4}{12}-\frac{2}{12}=\frac{8}{12}=\frac{2}{3}$$

EXAMPLE 7. Two dice are tossed together. Find the probability of getting a doublet or a total of 6.

Sol. Let S be the sample space. Then, $n(S)=36$.
Also, let A be the event of getting a doublet and B be the event of getting a total of 6.
Then, $A=\{(1,1),(2,2),(3,3),(4,4),(5,5),(6,6)\}$
and $B=\{(1,5),(5,1),(2,4),(4,2),(3,3)\}$
$\Rightarrow\ n(A)=6,\ n(B)=5$ and $n(A\cap B)=1$

Then, $P(A)=\frac{6}{36};\ P(B)=\frac{5}{36}$ and $P(A\cap B)=\frac{1}{36}$

Now, required probability $=P(A\cup B)$

$$=P(A)+P(B)-P(A\cap B)$$
$$=\frac{6}{36}+\frac{5}{36}-\frac{1}{36}=\frac{10}{36}=\frac{5}{18}$$

TYPE IV
PROBLEMS BASED ON PLAYING CARDS

EXAMPLE 8. A card is drawn at random from a well-shuffled pack of 52 cards. Find the probability that it is either a king or a spade.

Sol. Let S be the sample space associated with the given random experiment, then $n(S)=52$.
Also, let A be the event that the drawn card is a king and B be the event that the drawn card is a spade.
Then, $n(A)=4,\ n(B)=13$ and $n(A\cap B)=1$
[$\because A\cap B$ denotes the event that the drawn card is a king of spade.]

$\therefore\ P(A)=\frac{4}{52},\ P(B)=\frac{13}{52}$ and $P(A\cap B)=\frac{1}{52}$

Now, required probability $=P(A\cup B)$

$$=P(A)+P(B)-P(A\cap B)$$
$$=\frac{4}{52}+\frac{13}{52}-\frac{1}{52}$$
$$=\frac{16}{52}=\frac{4}{13}$$

EXAMPLE 9. A card is drawn from a deck of 52 cards. Find the probability of getting a king or a heart or a red card.

Sol. Let S be the sample space.
Then, $n(S)=52$
Let A, B and C be the events of getting a king, a heart and a red card, respectively.
Then, $n(A)=4,\ n(B)=13,\ n(C)=26$

$$\therefore \quad P(A) = \frac{n(A)}{n(S)} = \frac{4}{52} = \frac{1}{13}$$

$$P(B) = \frac{n(B)}{n(S)} = \frac{13}{52} = \frac{1}{4}$$

$$P(C) = \frac{n(C)}{n(S)} = \frac{26}{52} = \frac{1}{2}$$

Clearly, $(A \cap B)$ is the event of getting a king among hearts.
$(B \cap C)$ is the event of getting a heart among red cards.
$(A \cap C)$ is the event of getting a king among red cards.
$(A \cap B \cap C)$ is the event of getting a king among heart and the red cards.

$\Rightarrow \quad n(A \cap B) = 1, n(B \cap C) = 13, n(A \cap C) = 2$

and $\quad n(A \cap B \cap C) = 1$

$$\therefore \quad P(A \cap B) = \frac{n(A \cap B)}{n(S)} = \frac{1}{52},$$

$$P(B \cap C) = \frac{n(B \cap C)}{n(S)} = \frac{13}{52} = \frac{1}{4}$$

$$P(A \cap C) = \frac{n(A \cap C)}{n(S)} = \frac{2}{52} = \frac{1}{26}$$

and $\quad P(A \cap B \cap C) = \dfrac{n(A \cap B \cap C)}{n(S)} = \dfrac{1}{52}$

Now, P (getting a king or heart or red card)

$$= P(A \text{ or } B \text{ or } C) = P(A \cup B \cup C)$$

$$= P(A) + P(B) + P(C) - P(A \cap B) - P(A \cap C) - P(B \cap C) + P(A \cap B \cap C)$$

$$= \frac{1}{13} + \frac{1}{4} + \frac{1}{2} - \frac{1}{52} - \frac{1}{26} - \frac{1}{4} + \frac{1}{52} = \frac{28}{52} = \frac{7}{13}$$

TYPE V

PROBLEMS BASED ON PERMUTATION OR ARRANGEMENTS

EXAMPLE 10. If the letters of the word ALGORITHM are arranged at random in a row, what is the probability the letters GOR must remain together as a unit?

Sol. There are 9 letters in the word 'ALGORITHM'.

These 9 letters can be arranged in a row in 9! ways.

$\therefore$ Total number of possible outcomes = 9!

Now, if the letters GOR remain together, then we have 7 letters (considering GOR as 1 letter i.e. ALITHMGOR) which can be arranged in 7!.

Number of favourable outcomes = 7!

Hence, required probability $= \dfrac{7!}{9!} = \dfrac{1}{9 \times 8} = \dfrac{1}{72}$

TYPE VI

PROBLEMS BASED ON COMBINATIONS

When two or more things are selected, then to find the total outcomes or outcomes favourable to an event, we use the combination. Number of combinations out of n things taken r at a time is denoted by ^nC_r and it is defined as

$$^nC_r = \frac{n!}{r!(n-r)!}.$$

EXAMPLE 11. Find the probability that, when a hand of 7 cards is drawn from a well-shuffled deck of 52 cards, it contains

(i) all kings. (ii) 3 kings. (iii) atleast 3 kings.

Sol. Let S be the sample space associated with the given random experiment. Then, $n(S) = {}^{52}C_7$

(i) Let A be the event that it contains all kings.

Then, $n(A) = {}^4C_4 \times {}^{48}C_3$

$$\Rightarrow \quad n(A) = \frac{^{48}C_3}{^{52}C_7} = \frac{\dfrac{48 \times 47 \times 46}{3 \times 2 \times 1}}{\dfrac{52 \times 51 \times 50 \times 49 \times 48 \times 47 \times 46}{7 \times 6 \times 5 \times 4 \times 3 \times 2 \times 1}}$$

$$= \frac{1}{7735} \qquad [\because {}^4C_4 = 1]$$

(ii) Let B be the event that it contains 3 kings.

Then, $n(B) = {}^4C_3 \times {}^{48}C_4$

$$\Rightarrow P(B) = \frac{4 \times {}^{48}C_4}{^{52}C_7} = \frac{\dfrac{48 \times 47 \times 46 \times 45}{4 \times 3 \times 2 \times 1}}{\dfrac{52 \times 51 \times 50 \times 49 \times 48 \times 47 \times 46}{7 \times 6 \times 5 \times 4 \times 3 \times 2 \times 1}}$$

$$= \frac{9}{1547} \qquad [\because {}^4C_3 = {}^4C_1 = 4]$$

(iii) Let C be the event that it contains atleast 3 kings.

Then, $\quad P(C) = P(A \cup B)$

$$= P(A) + P(B)$$

[$\because$ A and B are mutually exclusive]

$$= \frac{1}{7735} + \frac{9}{1547} = \frac{46}{7735}$$

EXAMPLE 12. An urn contains 7 white, 5 black and 3 red balls. Two balls are drawn at random. Find the probability that

(i) both the balls are red.

(ii) one ball is red, other is black.

(iii) one ball is white.

Sol. Number of white balls = 7; Number of black balls = 5

Number of red balls = 3

Total number of balls = 7 + 5 + 3 = 15

Total number of ways of drawing 2 balls out of 15 balls $= {}^{15}C_2$

$\Rightarrow$ Total number of possible outcomes $= {}^{15}C_2$

(i) If both balls are red, then number of favourable outcomes = ${}^3C_2$

Hence, P (drawing both balls are red) $= \dfrac{{}^3C_2}{{}^{15}C_2}$

$$= \frac{3}{\frac{15 \times 14}{2 \times 1}} = \frac{1}{35}$$

(ii) If one ball is red and other is black, then number of favourable outcomes $= {}^3C_1 \times {}^5C_1 = 3 \times 5 = 15$

Hence, P (drawing one red ball and one black ball)

$$= \frac{{}^3C_1 \times {}^5C_1}{{}^{15}C_2} = \frac{15}{\frac{15 \times 14}{2 \times 1}} = \frac{1}{7}$$

(iii) If one ball is white, then other ball can be red or black.

So, number of favourable outcomes $= {}^7C_1 \times {}^8C_1$

$$= 7 \times 8 = 56$$

Hence, P (drawing one white ball) $= \dfrac{56}{{}^{15}C_2}$

$$= \frac{56}{\frac{15 \times 14}{2 \times 1}} = \frac{8}{15}$$

TYPE VII

PROBLEMS BASED ON SELECTING NUMBERS

EXAMPLE 13. An integer is chosen at random from first two hundred natural numbers. What is the probability that the integer chosen is divisible by 6 or 8?

Sol. Let S be the sample space associated with the given random experiment.

Then, $n(S) = 200$

Now, let A be the event that the chosen number is divisible by 6 and B be the event that the chosen number is divisible by 8.

Then, $A = \{6, 12, 18, \ldots, 198\}$ and $B = \{8, 16, 24, \ldots, 192\}$

$\Rightarrow$ $n(A) = 33$ and $n(B) = 24$

[to find $n(A)$ and $n(B)$, divide 198 by 6 and 192 by 8]

Also, $A \cap B =$ 8, 72, ..., 192

[$\because A \cap B$ denotes the event that the chosen number is divisible by LCM (6,8)]

Now, $P(A) = \dfrac{33}{200}$; $P(B) = \dfrac{24}{200}$ and $P(A \cap B) = \dfrac{8}{200}$

$\therefore$ P (chosen integer is divisible by 6 or 8)

$$= P(A \cup B) = P(A) + P(B) - P(A \cap B)$$

$$= \frac{33}{200} + \frac{24}{200} - \frac{8}{200} = \frac{49}{200}$$

EXAMPLE 14. Tickets numbered 1 to 20 are mixed up together and then a ticket is drawn at random. What is the probability that the ticket has a number which is a multiple of 3 or 7?

Sol. Let S be the sample space associated with the given random experiment. Then, $n(S) = 20$.

Now, let A be the event of getting a ticket bearing number which is a multiple of 3 and B be the event of getting a ticket bearing a number which is a multiple of 7.

Then, $A = \{3, 6, 9, 12, 15, 18\}$ and $B = \{7, 14\}$

$\Rightarrow$ $n(A) = 6$, $n(B) = 2$ and $n(A \cap B) = 0$

$\therefore$ $P(A) = \dfrac{6}{20}$ and $P(B) = \dfrac{2}{20}$

Now, required probability $= P(A \cup B) = P(A) + P(B)$

[$\because A$ and B are mutually exclusive events]

$$= \frac{6}{20} + \frac{2}{20} = \frac{8}{20} = \frac{2}{5}$$

TYPE VIII

PROBLEMS BASED ON SELECTING THINGS FROM A BAG/BOX CONTAINING DIFFERENT TYPES OF THINGS

EXAMPLE 15. A box contains 6 red, 4 white and 5 black balls. A person draws 4 balls from the box at random. Find the probability that among the balls drawn, there is atleast one ball of each colour.

Sol. Given, total number of red balls = 6

Total number of white balls = 4

and total number of black balls = 5

$\therefore$ Total number of balls = 15

Let S be the sample space associated with the random experiment.

Then, $n(S) = {}^{15}C_4 = 1365$

Here, atleast one ball of each colour can be drawn in one of the following ways :

(i) 1 red, 1 white and 2 black balls

(ii) 2 red, 1 white and 1 black balls

(iii) 1 red, 2 white and 1 black balls

Now, let A be the event of getting 1 red, 1 white and 2 black balls; B be the event of getting 2 red, 1 white and 1 black balls and C be the event of getting 1 red, 2 white and 1 black balls.

Then, $n(A) = {}^6C_1 \times {}^4C_1 \times {}^5C_2 = 6 \times 4 \times 10 = 240$

$n(B) = {}^6C_2 \times {}^4C_1 \times {}^5C_1 = 15 \times 4 \times 5 = 300$

and $n(C) = {}^6C_1 \times {}^4C_2 \times {}^5C_1 = 6 \times 6 \times 5 = 180$

$\therefore$ $P(A) = \dfrac{240}{1365}$; $P(B) = \dfrac{300}{1365}$ and $P(C) = \dfrac{180}{1365}$

Now, required probability

$$= P(A \cup B \cup C) = P(A) + P(B) + P(C)$$

[$\because A$, B and C are mutually exclusive events]

$$= \frac{240}{1365} + \frac{300}{1365} + \frac{180}{1365} = \frac{720}{1365} = \frac{48}{91}$$

TYPE IX

MISCELLANEOUS PROBLEMS

EXAMPLE 16. Probability that Ram passed in Mathematics is $\frac{2}{3}$ and the probability that he passed in English is $\frac{4}{9}$. If the probability of passing in both subjects is $\frac{1}{4}$, then what is the probability that Ram will pass in atleast one of these subjects?

Sol. Let M be the event that Ram passed in Mathematics, E be the event that Ram passed in English and $M \cap E$ be the event that Ram passed in both subjects

Now, P (Ram pass in atleast one subject)

$$= P(M \cup E)$$
$$= P(M) + P(E) - P(M \cap E)$$
$$= \frac{2}{3} + \frac{4}{9} - \frac{1}{4}$$
$$= \frac{24 + 16 - 9}{36} = \frac{31}{36}$$

EXAMPLE 17. Probability that a truck stopped at a roadblock will have faulty brakes or badly worn tires are 0.23 and 0.24, respectively. Also, the probability is 0.38 that a truck stopped at the roadblock will have faulty brakes and/or badly working tires. What is the probability that a truck stopped at this roadblock will have faulty breaks as well as badly worn tires?

Sol. Let B be the event that a truck stopped at the roadblock will have faulty breaks and T be the event that it will have badly worn tires. Then, we have

$$P(B) = 0.23,\ P(T) = 0.24 \text{ and } P(B \cup T) = 0.38$$

Now, consider, $P(B \cup T) = P(B) + P(T) - P(B \cap T)$

$\Rightarrow \quad 0.38 = 0.23 + 0.24 - P(B \cap T)$

$\Rightarrow \quad P(B \cap T) = 0.23 + 0.24 - 0.38 = 0.09$

Hence, the probability that a truck stopped at the roadblock will have faulty breaks as well as badly worn tires is 0.09.

EXAMPLE 18. The probability that a student will pass the final examination in both English and Hindi is 0.5 and the probability of passing neither is 0.1. If the probability of passing the English examination is 0.75, then what is the probability of passing the Hindi examination?

Sol. Let events H and E denote the students that, passing Hindi and English examination, respectively.

Given, probability of passing both examinations

$$= P(H \cap E) = 0.5$$

and probability of passing neither examinations

$$= P(H' \cap E') = P(H \cup E)' = 0.1$$

Then, $P(H \cup E) = 1 - P(H \cup E)' = 1 - 0.1 = 0.9$

Also, it is given, that probability of passing English examination, $P(E) = 0.75$

Now, consider $P(H \cup E) = P(H) + P(E) - P(H \cap E)$

$\Rightarrow \quad 0.9 = P(H) + 0.75 - 0.5$

$\Rightarrow \quad 0.9 = P(H) + 0.25$

$\Rightarrow \quad P(H) = 0.9 - 0.25 = 0.65$

Hence, probability of passing Hindi examination is 0.65.

EXAMPLE 19. Four candidates A, B, C, D have applied for the assignment to coach a school cricket team. If A is twice as likely to be selected as B, and B and C are given about the same chance of being selected, while C is twice as likely to be selected as D, what are the probabilities that

(i) C will be selected? (ii) A will not be selected?

Sol. Let E_1, E_2, E_3 and E_4 denote respectively the events that the person A, B, C and D is selected.

Also, let the probability of D selected be p, i.e. $P(E\ ) = p$.

Then, according to given condition we have

$$P(E_1) = 2P(E_2) \text{ and } P(E_2) = P(E_3) = 2P(E_4)$$

$\Rightarrow \quad P(E\ ) = 2 \times 2p,\ P(E\ ) = 2p$ and $P(E\ ) = 2p$

$\Rightarrow \quad P(E\ ) = 4p,\ P(E\ ) = 2p$ and $P(E\ ) = 2p$

Since, E_1, E_2, E_3 and E_4 are mutually exclusive and exhaustive events, therefore we have

$$P(E\ ) + P(E\ ) + P(E\ ) + P(E\ ) = 1$$

$\Rightarrow \quad 4p + 2p + 2p + p = 1$

$\Rightarrow \quad 9p = 1 \Rightarrow p = \frac{1}{9}$

(i) $P(C \text{ selected}) = P(E\ ) = 2p = \frac{2}{9}$

(ii) Now, $P(A \text{ selected}) = P(E\ ) = 4p = \frac{4}{9}$

$\therefore \quad P(A \text{ is not selected}) = 1 - P\ (A \text{ selected}) = 1 - \frac{4}{9} = \frac{5}{9}$

Topic Practice 3

1 If $\frac{2}{11}$ is the probability of an event A, then what is the probability of the event 'not A' ?

2 If A and B are two events such that $P(A)=\frac{1}{4}$, $P(B)=\frac{1}{2}$ and P (A and B) $=\frac{1}{8}$. Then, find P (A or B).

3 Given, $P(A)=\frac{3}{5}$ and $P(B)=\frac{1}{5}$. Find $P(A \quad B)$, if A and B are mutually exclusive events.

4 A and B are two events, such that $P(A)=0.42$, $P(B)=0.48$ and $P(A$ and $B)=0.16$. Determine

(i) P(not A) (ii) P(not B) (iii) P(A or B)

5 If E and F are events such that $P(E)=\frac{1}{4}$, $P(F)=\frac{1}{2}$ and P(E and F) $=\frac{1}{8}$, then find

(i) P(E or F) (ii) P (not E and not F)

6 If A and B are mutually exclusive events, such that $P(A)=0.28$ and $P(B)=0.38$, then find

(i) $P(A \cup B)$ (ii) $P(A \cap B)$
(iii) $P(A \cap B')$ (iv) $P(A' \cap B')$

7 Check whether the following probabilities $P(A)=0.3$, $P(B)=0.65$ and $P(A \cup B)=7$ are consistently defined.

8 The probabilities of happening of two events A and B are 0.25 and 0.50, respectively. If the probablity of happening of A and B together is 0.14, then find the probability that neither A nor B occurs.

9 The probability of an event A occurring is 0.5 and that of B is 0.3. If A and B are mutually exclusive events, then find the probability that neither A nor B occurs.

10 A and B are mutually exclusive events of an experiment. If P (not A) $=0.65$, $P(A \cup B)=0.65$ and $P(B)=p$, then find the value of p.

11 The probabilities of three events shown in the Venn diagram is shown below

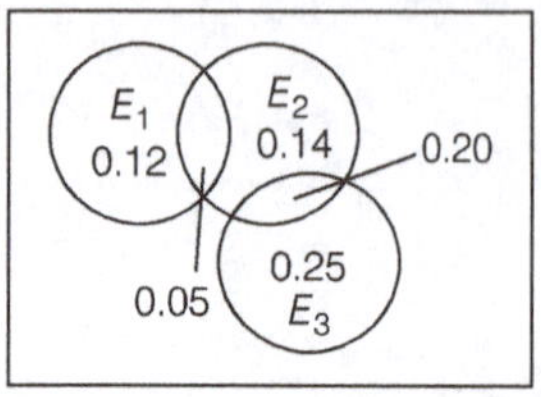

Determine

(i) $P(E_2)$ (ii) $P(E_2 \cap \overline{E}_3)$
(iii) $P(E_1 \cup E_2)$ (iv) $P(E_1 \cap \overline{E}_2)$

12 If A and B are mutually exclusive events, such that $P(A)=0.35$ and $P(B)=0.45$, then find

(i) $P(A')$ (ii) $P(B')$
(iii) $P(A \cup B)$ (iv) $P(A \cap B)$
(v) $P(A \cap B')$ (vi) $P(A' \cap B')$

13 A coin is tossed and a die is thrown. Find the probability that the outcomes will be a tail or a number greater than 3.

14 Two unbiased dice are thrown. Find the probability that neither a doublet nor a total of 10 will appear.

15 Two dice are thrown. Find

(i) odds in favour of getting the sum 5.
(ii) the odd against getting the sum 6.

16 A die has two faces each with number '1', three faces each with number '2' and one faces with number '3'. If die is rolled once, determine

(i) $P(2)$ (ii) P(1 or 3) (iii) P(not 3).

17 From a well-shuffled pack of 52 cards, a card is drawn at random. Find the probability that it is either a heart or a queen.

18 Find the probability that, when a hand of 5 cards is drawn from a well-shuffled deck of 52 cards, it contains

(i) all queens.
(ii) 3 queens.
(iii) atleast 3 queens.

19 A card is drawn from a well-shuffled deck of 52 cards. Find

(i) the odds in favour of getting a face card.
(ii) the odds against getting a spade.

20 One number is chosen from numbers 1 to 200. Find the probability that it is divisible by 4 or 6.

21 Tickets numbered 1 to 30 are mixed up together and then a ticket is drawn at random. What is the probability that the ticket has a number which is a multiple of 2 or 5?

22 A box contains 4 red, 5 white and 6 black balls. A person draws 4 balls from the box at random. Find the probability of selecting atleast one ball of each colour.

23 A bag contains 5 white and 7 black balls and a man draw 4 balls at random. What are the odds against these being all black?

24. In an entrance test that is graded on the basis of two examinations, the probability of a randomly chosen student passing the first examination is 0.8 and the probability of passing the second examination is 0.7. The probability of passing atleast one of them is 0.95. What is the probability of passing both?

25 In any school examination, probability that Mohan passed in Chemistry is $\frac{1}{3}$ and the probability that he passed in Physics is $\frac{2}{5}$. If the probability of passing in both subjects is $\frac{1}{6}$, then what is the probability that Mohan will pass in atleast one of these subjects?

Hints & Solutions

1. **Hint** $P(\text{not } A) = P(\overline{A}) = 1 - P(A)$ **Ans.** $\frac{9}{11}$

2. **Hint** $P(A \text{ or } B) = P(A) + P(B) - P(A \cap B)$ **Ans.** $\frac{5}{8}$

3. **Hint** $P(A \cup B) = P(A) + P(B)$ **Ans.** $\frac{4}{5}$

4. (i) **Hint** $P(\text{not } A) = 1 - P(A)$ **Ans.** 0.58
   (ii) **Hint** $P(\text{not } B) = 1 - P(B)$ **Ans.** 0.52
   (iii) **Hint** $P(A \text{ or } B) = P(A) + P(B) - P(A \cap B)$ **Ans.** 0.74

5. (i) **Hint** $P(E \text{ or } F) = P(E) + P(F) - P(E \text{ and } F)$ **Ans.** $\frac{5}{8}$
   (ii) **Hint** $P(\overline{E} \cap \overline{F}) = P(\overline{E \cup F}) = 1 - P(E \cup F)$ **Ans.** $\frac{3}{8}$

6. (i) **Hint** $P(A \cup B) = P(A) + P(B)$ **Ans.** 0.66
   (ii) **Hint** $P(A \cap B) = 0$ **Ans.** 0
   (iii) **Hint** $P(A \cap B') = P(A) - P(A \cap B)$ **Ans.** 0.28
   (iv) **Hint** $P(A' \cap B') = P(A \cup B)' = 1 - P(A \cup B)$
   Ans. 0.34

7. Solve as Example 4 part (ii). **Ans.** Yes.

8. **Hint** $P(A \cup B) = 0.25 + 0.50 - 0.14 = 0.61$
   $\therefore P(\text{neither } A \text{ nor } B) = P(\overline{A} \cap \overline{B})] = 1 - P(A \cup B)$
   Ans. 0.39

9. **Hint** $P(\overline{A} \cap \overline{B}) = P(\overline{A \cup B}) = 1 - P(A \cup B)$
   $= 1 - [P(A) + P(B)]$ **Ans.** 0.2

10. **Hint** Use $P(A \cup B) = P(A) + P(B)$, for mutually exclusive events. **Ans.** 0.3

11. Solve as Example 2.
    Ans. (i) 0.39 (ii) 0.19 (iii) 0.31 (iv) 0.12

12. **Hint** We have, A and B are mutually exclusive events.
    Also, it is given that $P(A) = 0.35$ and $P(B) = 0.45$
    (i) $P(A') = 1 - P(A) = 1 - 0.35 = 0.65$
    (ii) $P(B') = 1 - P(B) = 1 - 0.45 = 0.55$
    (iii) $P(A \cup B) = P(A) + P(B) = 0.35 + 0.45 = 0.8$
    [$\because$ A and B are mutually exclusive]
    (iv) $P(A \cap B) = 0$
    [$\because$ A and B are mutually exclusive, therefore $A \cap B = \phi$]
    (v) $P(A \cap B') = P(A) - P(A \cap B)$
    $= P(A) - 0 = P(A) = 0.35$
    (vi) $P(A' \cap B') = P((A \cup B)') = 1 - P(A \cup B)$
    $= 1 - 0.8 = 0.2$

13. Solve as Example 6. **Ans.** $\frac{3}{4}$

14. Solve as Example 7.
    Hint P (getting neither a doublet nor a total of 10)
    $= 1 - P$ (getting a doublet or a total of 10) **Ans.** $\frac{7}{9}$

15. **Hint** Let S be the sample space associated with the given random experiment. Then, $n(S) = 36$.
    (i) Let E be the event of getting the sum 5. Then,
    $$E = \{(1,4), (4,1), (2,3), (3,2)\}$$
    $\Rightarrow \quad n(E) = 4$
    $$\therefore \quad P(E) = \frac{n(E)}{n(S)} = \frac{4}{36} = \frac{1}{9} \Rightarrow P(\overline{E}) = 1 - \frac{1}{9} = \frac{8}{9}$$
    Hence, odds in favour of getting the sum 5 $= \frac{P(E)}{P(\overline{E})}$
    Ans. 1:8
    (ii) Let F be the event of getting the sum 6. Then,
    $$F = \{(1,5), (5,1), (2,4), (4,2), (3,3)\} \Rightarrow n(F) = 5$$
    $$\therefore \quad P(F) = \frac{n(F)}{n(S)} = \frac{5}{36} \Rightarrow P(\overline{F}) = 1 - \frac{5}{36} = \frac{31}{36}$$
    Hence, odds against getting the sum 6 $= \frac{P(\overline{F})}{P(F)}$
    Ans. 31:5

16. (i) **Hint** Number of faces with number '2' = 3
    $\therefore \quad P(2) = \frac{3}{6} = \frac{1}{2}$
    (ii) **Hint** $P(1 \text{ or } 3) = (P \text{ not } 2) = 1 - P(2) = 1 - \frac{1}{2} = \frac{1}{2}$
    (iii) **Hint** Number of faces with number '3' = 1
    $\therefore \quad P(3) = \frac{1}{6}$
    $\Rightarrow P(\text{not } 3) = 1 - P(3) = 1 - \frac{1}{6} = \frac{5}{6}$

17. Solve as Example 8. **Ans.** $\frac{4}{13}$

18. Solve as Example 10.

Ans. (i) $\frac{1}{54145}$ (ii) $\frac{94}{54145}$ (iii) $\frac{19}{10829}$

19. **Hint** Let S be the sample space associated with the given random experiment. Then, $n(S)=52$.

(i) Let E be the event of getting of face card.

Then, $n(E)=12$

$$\therefore \quad P(E)=\frac{n(E)}{n(S)}=\frac{12}{52}=\frac{3}{13}$$

$$\Rightarrow \quad P(\bar{E})=1-P(E)=1-\frac{3}{13}=\frac{10}{13}$$

Hence, odds in favour of getting a face card

$$=\frac{P(E)}{P(\bar{E})}=\frac{\frac{3}{13}}{\frac{10}{13}}=\frac{3}{10}=3:10$$

(ii) Let F be the event of getting a spade.

Then $n(F)=13$.

$$\therefore \quad P(F)=\frac{n(F)}{n(S)}=\frac{13}{52}=\frac{1}{4}$$

$$\Rightarrow P(\bar{F})=1-P(F)=1-\frac{1}{4}=\frac{3}{4}$$

Hence, odds against of getting a spade

$$=\frac{P(\bar{F})}{P F}=\frac{\frac{3}{4}}{\frac{1}{4}}=\frac{3}{1}=3:1$$

20. Solve as Example 13. **Ans.** $\frac{67}{200}$

21. Solve as Example 14. **Ans.** $\frac{3}{5}$

22. **Hint** Let A = event that 1 red, 1 white and 2 black balls are drawn, B = event that 1 red, 2 white and 1 black balls are drawn and C = event that 2 red, 1 white and 1 black balls are drawn.

Here A, B and C are mutually exclusive events.

Hence, required probability

$$=P(A\cup B\cup C)=P(A)+P(B)+P(C)$$

Ans. $\frac{48}{91}$

23. **Hint** Given, total number of white balls = 5

and total number of black balls = 7

$\therefore$ Total number of balls = 12

Let S be the sample space associated with the given experiment.

Then, $n(S)={}^{12}C_4$.

Now, let E be the event of getting black balls only.

Then, $n(E)={}^{7}C_4$

$$\Rightarrow \quad P(E)=\frac{{}^{7}C_4}{{}^{12}C_4}=\frac{7\times 6\times 5\times 4}{12\times 11\times 10\times 9}=\frac{7}{99}$$

$$\Rightarrow \quad P(\bar{E})=1-P(E)=1-\frac{7}{99}=\frac{92}{99}$$

Hence, odds against getting black balls

$$=\frac{P(\bar{E})}{P(E)}=\frac{\frac{92}{99}}{\frac{7}{99}}=\frac{92}{7}=92:7$$

24. **Hint** Let E and F denote the events that, students passing the first and second examination, respectively.

Then, $P(E)=0.8$, $P(F)=0.7$ and $P(E\cup F)=0.95$

Ans. 0.55

25. Solve as Example 16. **Ans.** $\frac{17}{30}$

Conditional Probability

If A and B are two events associated with the same sample space of a random experiment, then conditional probability of the event A given that B has occurred i.e. $P(A/B)$ is given by

$$P\left(\frac{A}{B}\right)=\frac{P(A\cap B)}{P(B)}, \text{ provided } P(B)\neq 0$$

Probability of occurrence of event B, when A has already occurred i.e. $P(B/A)$ is given by

$$P\left(\frac{B}{A}\right)=\frac{P(B\cap A)}{P(A)}, \text{ provided } P(A)\neq 0$$

Properties of Conditional Probability

Let A and B be the events of a sample space S of an experiment.

Then,

(i) $0\leq P(A/B)\leq 1$

(ii) $P(S/A)=P(A/A)=1$

(iii) If A and B are any two events of a sample space S and C is an event of S, such that $P(C)\neq 0$, then

$P\{(A\cup B)/C\}=P(A/C)+P(B/C)-P\{(A\cap B)/C\}$

In particular, if A and B are disjoint events, then

$$P\left(\frac{A\cup B}{C}\right)=P\left(\frac{A}{C}\right)+P\left(\frac{B}{C}\right)$$

(iv) $P(A'/B)=1-P(A/B)$, where A' is complement of A.

Note If A and B are mutually exclusive events, then $P(A/B)=0$.

Method to Solve Problem Based on Conditional Probability

To solve problems based on conditional probability, we use the following steps

I. Firstly, write the sample space for given experiment and then assume the given events as A, B, which are associated with sample space.

II. Find the probability of that event A or B, which is already occurred and find $P(A \cap B)$.

III. Find the required conditional probability by using suitable formula

$$P\left(\frac{A}{B}\right) = \frac{P(A \cap B)}{P(B)} \quad \text{or} \quad P\left(\frac{B}{A}\right) = \frac{P(A \cap B)}{P(A)}$$

Note If elementary events of the sample space are not equally likely, then probabilities $P(A \cap B)$ and $P(A)$ or $P(B)$ being calculated accordingly.

EXAMPLE 1. If $P(A) = \frac{6}{11}$, $P(B) = \frac{5}{11}$ and $P(A \cup B) = \frac{7}{11}$, then find

(i) $P(A \cap B)$ (ii) $P(A/B)$ (iii) $P(B/A)$.

Sol. Given, $P(A) = \frac{6}{11}$, $P(B) = \frac{5}{11}$ and $P(A \cup B) = \frac{7}{11}$

(i) $P(A \cup B) = P(A) + P(B) - P(A \cap B)$

$$\Rightarrow \frac{7}{11} = \frac{6}{11} + \frac{5}{11} - P(A \cap B)$$

$$\Rightarrow P(A \cap B) = \frac{6}{11} + \frac{5}{11} - \frac{7}{11}$$

$$\therefore P(A \cap B) = \frac{4}{11}$$

(ii) $P\left(\frac{A}{B}\right) = \frac{P(A \cap B)}{P(B)}$

$$= \frac{4/11}{5/11} = \frac{4}{5} \qquad \left[\because P(A \cap B) = \frac{4}{11}\right]$$

(iii) $P\left(\frac{B}{A}\right) = \frac{P(A \cap B)}{P(A)} = \frac{4/11}{6/11} = \frac{4}{6} = \frac{2}{3}$

EXAMPLE 2. Two dice are thrown. Find the probability of getting an even number on first die, if the outcomes on the two dice always exhibits a sum of 8.

Sol. Here, two dice are thrown. So, sample space is

$$S = \left\{\begin{matrix} (1,1),(1,2),(1,3),(1,4),(1,5),(1,6), \\ (2,1),(2,2),(2,3),(2,4),(2,5),(2,6), \\ (3,1),(3,2),(3,3),(3,4),(3,5),(3,6), \\ (4,1),(4,2),(4,3),(4,4),(4,5),(4,6), \\ (5,1),(5,2),(5,3),(5,4),(5,5),(5,6), \\ (6,1),(6,2),(6,3),(6,4),(6,5),(6,6) \end{matrix}\right\}$$

$\therefore \quad n(S) = 36$

Let A = Event of getting an even number on first die

i.e. $$A = \left\{\begin{matrix} (2,1),(2,2),(2,3),(2,4),(2,5),(2,6), \\ (4,1),(4,2),(4,3),(4,4),(4,5),(4,6), \\ (6,1),(6,2),(6,3),(6,4),(6,5),(6,6) \end{matrix}\right\}$$

$\therefore \quad n(A) = 18$

and B = Event of getting a sum of 8

$= \{(2, 6), (3, 5), (4, 4), (5, 3), (6, 2)\}$

$\therefore \quad n(B) = 5$

Here, $(A \cap B) = \{(2, 6), (4, 4), (6, 2)\}$

$\therefore \quad n(A \cap B) = 3$

Now, $P(A \cap B) = \frac{n(A \cap B)}{n(S)} = \frac{3}{36}$ and $P(B) = \frac{n(B)}{n(S)} = \frac{5}{36}$

Since, we have to find the conditional probability of getting an even number on first die, when the dice always exhibits a sum of B.

$$\therefore \text{Required probability} = P\left(\frac{A}{B}\right) = \frac{P(A \cap B)}{P(B)} = \frac{3/36}{5/36} = \frac{3}{5}$$

EXAMPLE 3. Given that, the two numbers appearing on throwing two dice are different. Find the probability of the events

(i) the sum of numbers on the dice is 4.

(ii) the sum of numbers on the dice is not 4.

Sol. Here, two dice are thrown, so number of outcomes in the sample space, $S = 6 \times 6 = 36$ (equally likely sample events) i.e. $n(S) = 36$.

Let E be the event of getting sum of the numbers on the dice is 4 and F be the event that numbers appearing on the two dice are different.

Then, $E = \{(1, 3), (2, 2), (3, 1)\} \Rightarrow n(E) = 3$

and $$F = \left\{\begin{matrix} (1, 2), (1, 3), (1, 4), (1, 5), (1, 6), \\ (2, 1), (2, 3), (2, 4), (2, 5), (2, 6), \\ (3, 1), (3, 2), (3, 4), (3, 5), (3, 6), \\ (4, 1), (4, 2), (4, 3), (4, 5), (4, 6), \\ (5, 1), (5, 2), (5, 3), (5, 4), (5, 6), \\ (6, 1), (6, 2), (6, 3), (6, 4), (6, 5) \end{matrix}\right\}$$

$\Rightarrow n(F) = 30$

Here, $E \cap F = \{(1, 3), (3, 1)\} = 2$

$$\therefore \quad P(F) = \frac{\text{Number of favourable outcomes}}{\text{Total number of outcomes}} = \frac{30}{36} = \frac{5}{6}$$

and $P(E \cap F) = \frac{2}{36} = \frac{1}{18}$

(i) The probability that the sum of numbers on the dice showing different number is 4,

$$P\left(\frac{E}{F}\right) = \frac{P(E \cap F)}{P(F)} = \frac{1/18}{5/6} = \frac{1}{15}$$

(ii) The probability that the sum of numbers on the dice showing different numbers is not 4,

$$P\left(\frac{E'}{F}\right)=1-P\left(\frac{E}{F}\right)=1-\frac{1}{15}=\frac{14}{15}$$

EXAMPLE 4. Consider the experiment of tossing a coin. If the coin shows head, toss it again but if it shows tail, then throw a die. Find the conditional probability of the event that 'the die shows a number greater than 4' given that there is atleast one tail.

Sol. The outcomes of the experiment can be represented in the following tree diagram.

The sample space S of the experiment is given as

$S=\{(H, H), (H, T), (T, 1), (T, 2), (T, 3), (T, 4), (T, 5), (T, 6)\}$

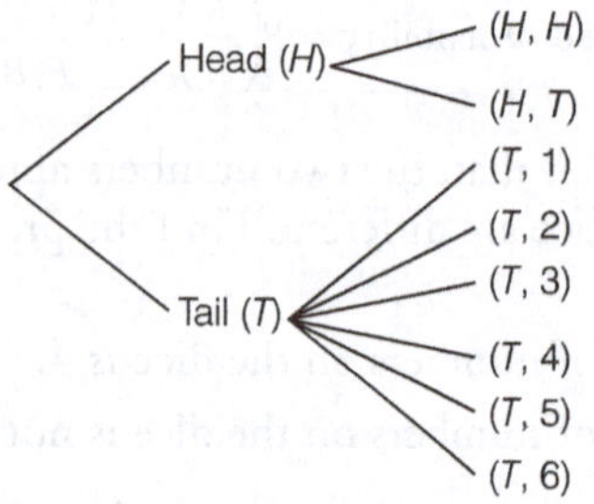

The probabilities of these elementary events are

$$P\{(H, H)\}=\frac{1}{2}\times\frac{1}{2}=\frac{1}{4},$$

$$P\{(H, T)\}=\frac{1}{2}\times\frac{1}{2}=\frac{1}{4},$$

$$P\{(T, 1)\}=\frac{1}{2}\times\frac{1}{6}=\frac{1}{12},$$

$$P\{(T, 2)\}=\frac{1}{2}\times\frac{1}{6}=\frac{1}{12},$$

$$P\{(T, 3)\}=\frac{1}{2}\times\frac{1}{6}=\frac{1}{12},$$

$$P\{(T, 4)\}=\frac{1}{2}\times\frac{1}{6}=\frac{1}{12},$$

$$P\{(T, 5)\}=\frac{1}{2}\times\frac{1}{6}=\frac{1}{12}$$

and $P\{(T, 6)\}=\frac{1}{2}\times\frac{1}{6}=\frac{1}{12}$

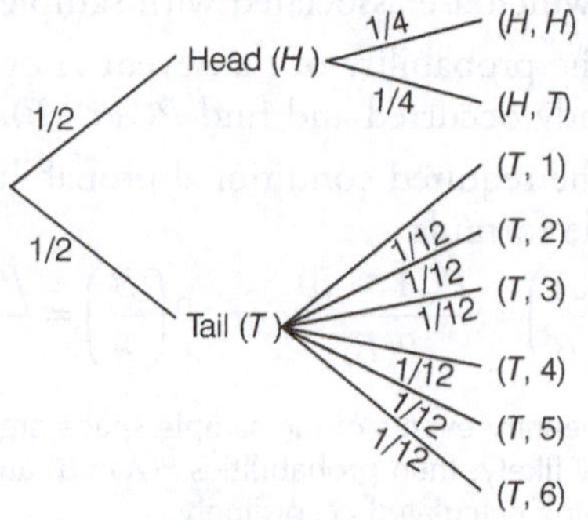

Consider the following events

A = The die shows a number greater than 4

and B = There is atleast one tail.

We have, $A=\{(T, 5), (T, 6)\}$,

$B=\{(H, T), (T, 1), (T, 2), (T, 3), (T, 4), (T, 5), (T, 6)\}$

and $A\cap B=\{(T, 5), (T, 6)\}$

$\therefore\quad P(B)=P\{(H, T)\}+P\{(T, 1)\}+P\{(T, 2)\}+P\{(T, 3)\}+P\{(T, 4)\}+P\{(T, 5)\}+P\{(T, 6)\}$

$$\Rightarrow P(B)=\frac{1}{4}+\frac{1}{12}+\frac{1}{12}+\frac{1}{12}+\frac{1}{12}+\frac{1}{12}+\frac{1}{12}=\frac{3}{4}$$

and $P(A\cap B)=P\{(T, 5)\}+P\{(T, 6)\}=\frac{1}{12}+\frac{1}{12}=\frac{1}{6}$

$\therefore$ Required probability $=P\left(\frac{A}{B}\right)=\frac{P(A\cap B)}{P(B)}$

$$=\frac{1/6}{3/4}=\frac{4}{18}=\frac{2}{9}$$

Topic Practice 4

1 Evaluate $P(A\cup B)$, if $2P(A)=P(B)=\frac{5}{13}$ and $P\left(\frac{A}{B}\right)=\frac{2}{5}$.

2 Three events A, B and C have probabilities $\frac{2}{5}, \frac{1}{3}$ and $\frac{1}{2}$, respectively. If $P(A\cap C)=\frac{1}{5}$ and $P(B\cap C)=\frac{1}{4}$, then find the values of $P(C/B)$ and $P(A'\cap C')$.

3 A black and a red die are rolled together. Find the conditional probability of obtaining the sum 8, given that the red die resulted in a number less than 4.

4 Given that E and F are events such that $P(E)=0.6$, $P(F)=0.3$ and $P(E\cap F)=0.2$. Find $P\left(\frac{E}{F}\right)$ and $P\left(\frac{F}{E}\right)$.

5 If $P(A)=0.8$, $P(B)=0.5$ and $P\left(\frac{B}{A}\right)=0.4$, then find the value of $P(A\cup B)$.

6 If $P(B)=\frac{3}{5}, P(A/B)=\frac{1}{2}$ and $P(A\cup B)=\frac{4}{5}$, then find $P(A\cup B)' + P(A'\cup B)$.

7 If $P(A)=\frac{2}{5}, P(B)=\frac{3}{10}$ and $P(A\cap B)=\frac{1}{5}$, then find $P(A'/B')\cdot P(B'/A')$.

8 A and B are two events such that $P(A)\neq 0$.
Find $P\left(\frac{B}{A}\right)$, if
(i) A is a subset of B. (ii) $A\cap B=\phi$.

9 A couple has two children. Find the probability that both children are males, if it is known that atleast one of the children is male.

10 Two coins are tossed once, if E : tail appears on one coin and F : one coin shows head, then find $P\left(\frac{E}{F}\right)$.

11 A die is thrown three times. Events A and B are defined as below
A : 4 on the third throw
B : 6 on the first and 5 on the second throw.
Find the probability of A, given that B has already occurred.

12 A die is thrown twice and the sum of the numbers appearing is observed to be 8. What is the conditional probability that the number 5 has appeared atleast once?

13 A black and a red die are rolled. Find the conditional probability of obtaining a sum greater than 9, given that the black die resulted in a 5.

14 Consider the experiment of throwing a die, if a multiple of 3 comes up, then throw the die again and if any other numbers comes, then toss a coin. Find the conditional probability of the event 'the coin shows a tail', given that 'atleast one die shows 3'?

Hints & Solutions

1. **Hint** Given, $2P(A)=P(B)=\frac{5}{13}$ and $P\left(\frac{A}{B}\right)=\frac{2}{5}$

$$\Rightarrow \quad P(A)=\frac{5}{26}, P(B)=\frac{5}{13} \text{ and } P\left(\frac{A}{B}\right)=\frac{2}{5}$$

Now, $P\left(\frac{A}{B}\right)=\frac{P(A\cap B)}{P(B)} \Rightarrow \frac{2}{5}=\frac{P(A\cap B)}{\frac{5}{13}}$

$$\Rightarrow P(A\cap B)=\frac{2}{5}\times\frac{5}{13}=\frac{2}{13}$$

Ans. $\frac{11}{26}$

2. **Hint** Given, $P(A)=\frac{2}{5}, P(B)=\frac{1}{3}, P(C)=\frac{1}{2}$,
$P(A\cap C)=\frac{1}{5}$ and $P(B\cap C)=\frac{1}{4}$

$$\therefore \quad P\left(\frac{C}{B}\right)=\frac{P(B\cap C)}{P(B)}$$

and $P(A'\cap C')=1-P(A\cup C)$

Ans. $\frac{3}{4}, \frac{3}{10}$

3. Let us denote the numbers on black die by $B_1, B_2, \ldots, B_6$ and the numbers on red die by $R_1, R_2, \ldots, R_6$.
Then, we get the following sample space.

$$S=\begin{Bmatrix}(B_1,R_1),(B_1,R_2),\ldots,(B_1,R_6),(B_2,R_1),(B_2,R_2),\ldots,\\ (B_2,R_6),\ \ldots,\ (B_6,R_1),(B_6,R_2),\ldots,(B_6,R_6)\end{Bmatrix}$$

Clearly, $n(S)=36$
Now, let A be the event that sum of number obtained on the die is 8 and B be the event that red die shows a number less than 4.
Then, $A=\{(B_2,R_6),(B_6,R_2),(B_3,R_5),(B_5,R_3),(B_4,R_4)\}$ and

$$B=\begin{Bmatrix}(B_1,R_1),(B_1,R_2),(B_1,R_3),(B_2,R_1),(B_2,R_2),(B_2,R_3)\\ ,\ldots,(B_6,R_1),(B_6,R_2),(B_6,R_3)\end{Bmatrix}$$

$$\Rightarrow A\cap B=\{(B_6,R_2),(B_5,R_3)\}$$

Now, required probability,

$$P\left(\frac{A}{B}\right)=\frac{P(A\cap B)}{P(B)}=\frac{\frac{2}{36}}{\frac{18}{36}}=\frac{2}{18}=\frac{1}{9}$$

4. Solve as Example 1. **Ans.** $\frac{2}{3}$ and $\frac{1}{3}$

5. **Hint** $P(A\cap B)=P(A)\times P(B/A)$
and $P(A\cup B)=P(A)+P(B)-P(A\cap B)$
Ans. 0.98

6. Here, $P(B)=\frac{3}{5}, P(A/B)=\frac{1}{2}$ and $P(A\cup B)=\frac{4}{5}$

Since, $P(A/B)=\frac{P(A\cap B)}{P(B)}$

$$\Rightarrow \quad P(A\cap B)=P(A/B)\cdot P(B)=\frac{1}{2}\times\frac{3}{5}=\frac{3}{10}$$

Also, $P(A \cup B) = P(A) + P(B) - P(A \cap B)$

$\Rightarrow \quad P(A) = \frac{4}{5} - \frac{3}{5} + \frac{3}{10} = \frac{1}{2}$

$\therefore \quad P(A \cup B)' = 1 - P(A \cup B) = 1 - \frac{4}{5} = \frac{1}{5}$

and $P(A' \cup B) = 1 - P(A - B) = 1 - P(A \cap B')$

$= 1 - P(A) \cdot P(B') = 1 - \frac{1}{2} \cdot \frac{2}{5} = \frac{4}{5}$

$\Rightarrow \quad P(A \cup B)' + P(A' \cup B) = \frac{1}{5} + \frac{4}{5} = \frac{5}{5} = 1$

7. **Hint** $P\left(\frac{A'}{B'}\right) \times P\left(\frac{B'}{A'}\right) = \frac{[1 - P(A \cup B)]^2}{[1 - P(B)][1 - P(A)]}$

Ans. $\frac{25}{42}$

8. **Hint** $P(A \cap B) = P(A)$ **Ans.** (i) 1 (ii) 0

9. **Hint** A = Both children are male and B = Atleast one children is male

$\therefore \quad P(A) = \frac{1}{4}, P(B) = \frac{3}{4}, P(A \cap B) = \frac{1}{4}$

Now, $P\left(\frac{A}{B}\right) = \frac{P(A \cap B)}{P(B)}$ **Ans.** $\frac{1}{3}$

10. **Hint** $P(E) = \frac{2}{4}, P(F) = \frac{2}{4}, P(E \cap F) = \frac{2}{4}$

Now, $P\left(\frac{E}{F}\right) = \frac{P(E \cap F)}{P(F)}$ **Ans.** 1

11. **Hint** $P(B) = \frac{6}{216}, P(A \cap B) = \frac{1}{216}$

Now, $P\left(\frac{A}{B}\right) = \frac{P(A \cap B)}{P(B)}$ **Ans.** $\frac{1}{6}$

12. **Hint** Let E : Sum of numbers is 8 and F : Number 5 appear atleast once

Then, $P(E) = \frac{5}{36}$, $P(F) = \frac{11}{36}$ and $P(E \cap F) = \frac{2}{36}$

Required probability $= P\left(\frac{F}{E}\right)$ **Ans.** $\frac{2}{5}$

13. **Hint** A = Sum greater than 9 and B = Black die resulted 5

$\therefore \quad P(A) = \frac{6}{36}, P(B) = \frac{6}{36}, P(A \cap B) = \frac{2}{36}$,

Now, $P\left(\frac{A}{B}\right) = \frac{P(A \cap B)}{P(B)}$ **Ans.** $\frac{1}{3}$

14. Solve as Example 4. **Ans.** 0

Multiplication Theorem on Probability and Independent Events

Multiplication Theorem

Let A and B be two events associated with a random experiment, then

$$P(A \cap B) = \begin{cases} P(A) \cdot P(B/A), \text{ where } P(A) \neq 0 \\ P(B) \cdot P(A/B), \text{ where } P(B) \neq 0 \end{cases}$$

Here, $A \cap B$ denotes the simultaneous occurrence of the events A and B. The event $A \cap B$ is also written as AB.

The above result is known as the multiplication rule of probability.

EXAMPLE 1. Find the probability of drawing a diamond card in each of the two consecutive draws from a well-shuffled pack of cards, if the card drawn is not replaced after the first draw.

Sol. Let A be the event of drawing a diamond card in the first draw and B be the event of drawing a diamond card in the second draw.

Then, $\quad P(A) = \frac{13}{52} = \frac{1}{4}$

After drawing a diamond card in first draw, 51 cards are left out of which 12 cards are diamond cards.

$\therefore \quad P(B/A)$ = Probability of drawing a diamond card in second draw when a diamond card has already been drawn in first draw

$\Rightarrow \quad P\left(\frac{B}{A}\right) = \frac{12}{51} = \frac{4}{17}$

Now, required probability $= P(A \cap B)$

$= P(A) \cdot P\left(\frac{B}{A}\right)$

$= \frac{1}{4} \times \frac{4}{17} = \frac{1}{17}$

EXAMPLE 2. A bag contains 19 tickets, numbered from 1 to 19. A ticket is drawn and then another ticket is drawn without replacement. Find the probability that both tickets will show even numbers.

Sol. Let A be the event of drawing an even numbered ticket in first draw and B be the event of drawing an even numbered ticket in the second draw. Then,

Required probability $= P(A \cap B) = P(A) \cdot P(B/A)$ ...(i)

Since, there are 19 tickets numbered 1 to 19 in the bag, out of which 9 are even numbered *viz.* 2, 4, 6, 8, 10, 12, 14, 16 and 18.

Therefore, $\quad P(A) = \frac{9}{19}$

Since, the ticket drawn in the first draw is not replaced, therefore second ticket drawn is from the remaining 18 tickets, out of which 8 are even numbered.

$\therefore \quad P\left(\frac{B}{A}\right) = \frac{8}{18} = \frac{4}{9}$

Hence, required probability $= P(A \cap B)$

$= P(A) \cdot P(B/A)$ [from Eq. (i)]

$= \frac{9}{19} \times \frac{4}{9} = \frac{4}{19}$

Multiplication Rule for More than Two Events

Let E, F, G and H be four events of sample space S. Then,

(i) $P(E \cap F \cap G) = P(E) \cdot P\left(\frac{F}{E}\right) \cdot P\left(\frac{G}{E \cap F}\right)$

(ii) $P(E \cap F \cap G \cap H)$

$= P(E) \cdot P\left(\frac{F}{E}\right) \cdot P\left(\frac{G}{E \cap F}\right) \cdot P\left(\frac{H}{E \cap F \cap G}\right)$

EXAMPLE 3. Three cards are drawn successively without replacement from a pack of 52 well-shuffled cards. What is the probability that first two cards are king and the third card drawn is an ace?

Sol. There are 52 cards in a pack.

$\therefore \quad n(S) = 52$

Let A = Event that the card drawn is king

and B = Event that the card drawn is an ace

Now, $P(A) = 4/52$

$P\left(\frac{A}{A}\right)$ = Probability of drawing second king when one king has already been drawn $= \frac{3}{51}$

[$\because$ remaining cards are $(52 - 1) = 51$]

$P(B/AA)$ = Probability of drawing third card to be an ace when two kings have already been drawn $= \frac{4}{50}$

Now, probability of getting first two cards are king and third card is an ace $= P(A \cap A \cap B)$

$= P(A) \cdot P\left(\frac{A}{A}\right) \cdot P\left(\frac{B}{AA}\right)$ [by multiplication theorem]

$= \frac{4}{52} \times \frac{3}{51} \times \frac{4}{50} = \frac{2}{5525}$

EXAMPLE 4. A bag contains 5 white, 7 red and 8 black balls. If four balls are drawn one by one without replacement, then find the probability of getting all white balls.

Sol. Let A, B, C and D denote events of getting a white ball in first, second, third and fourth draw, respectively.

Then, required probability $= P(A \cap B \cap C \cap D)$

$= P(A)\, P(B/A)\, P(C/A \cap B)\, P(D/A \cap B \cap C)$ ...(i)

Now, $P(A)$ = Probability of drawing a white ball in first draw

$= \frac{5}{20} = \frac{1}{4}$

When a white ball is drawn in the first draw, there are 19 balls left in the bag, out of which 4 are white.

$\therefore \quad P(B/A) = \frac{4}{19}$

Since, the ball drawn is not replaced, therefore after drawing a white ball in second draw, there are 18 balls left in the bag, out of which 3 are white.

$\therefore \quad P(C/A \cap B) = \frac{3}{18} = \frac{1}{6}$

After drawing a white ball in third draw, there are 17 balls left in the bag, out of which 2 are white.

$\therefore \quad P(D/A \cap B \cap C) = \frac{2}{17}$

Hence, required probability $= P(A \cap B \cap C \cap D)$

$= P(A) \cdot P(B/A)\, P(C/A \cap B)\, P(D/A \cap B \cap C)$

$= \frac{1}{4} \times \frac{4}{19} \times \frac{1}{6} \times \frac{2}{17} = \frac{1}{969}$

Independent Events

Two events A and B are said to be independent, if the occurrence or non-occurrence of one event does not affect the occurrence or non-occurrence of another event. Two events E and F are said to be independent, if

$$P\left(\frac{F}{E}\right) = P(F), \text{ provided } P(E) \neq 0$$

and $$P\left(\frac{E}{F}\right) = P(E), \text{ provided } P(F) \neq 0.$$

In other words, let E and F be two events associated with the same random experiment, then E and F are said to be independent, if $P(E \cap F) = P(E) \cdot P(F)$.

Properties of Independent Events

If A and B are independent events, then

(i) A and B' are also independent events.

(ii) A' and B are also independent events.

(iii) A' and B' are also independent events.

EXAMPLE 5. An unbiased die is thrown twice. Let the event A be 'odd number on the first throw' and B be the event 'odd number on the second throw'. Check the independence of the events A and B.

Sol. On throwing a die twice, we get 36 elementary events of the experiment which are to be considered to be equally likely. Odd numbers are 1, 3 and 5.

$P(A) = P$ (odd number on the first throw) $= \dfrac{18}{36} = \dfrac{1}{2}$

[∵ possible outcomes (1, 1), (1, 2), (1, 3), (1, 4), (1, 5), (1, 6), (3, 1), (3, 2), (3, 3), (3, 4), (3, 5), (3, 6), (5, 1), (5, 2), (5, 3), (5, 4), (5, 5) and (5, 6) i.e. 18 outcomes]

Similarly, $P(B) = P$ (odd number on the second throw)

$= \dfrac{18}{36} = \dfrac{1}{2}$

Also, $P(A \cap B) = P$(odd number on both throws)

$= \dfrac{9}{36} = \dfrac{1}{4}$

[∵ events are (1, 1), (1, 3), (1, 5), (3, 1), (3, 3), (3, 5), (5, 1), (5, 3) and (5, 5) i.e. 9 outcomes]

Now, $P(A) \cdot P(B) = \dfrac{1}{2} \times \dfrac{1}{2} = \dfrac{1}{4}$

Thus, $P(A \cap B) = P(A) \cdot P(B)$

Hence, A and B are independent events.

EXAMPLE 6. Two dice are thrown, find the probability of getting an odd number on the first die and a multiple of 3 on the other die. Also, show that both events are not dependent.

Sol. Let A be the event of getting an odd number on the first die and B be the event of getting a multiple of 3 on the second die.

On throwing two dice, total outcomes = 36

Outcomes favourable to $A \cap B$, i.e. an odd number on first die and a multiple of 3 on the other die are

{(1, 3), (1, 6), (3, 3), (3, 6), (5, 3), (5, 6)}

∴ $n(A \cap B) = 6$

Then, required probability, $P(A \cap B) = \dfrac{6}{36} = \dfrac{1}{6}$

Now, A = {(1, 1), (1, 2), (1, 3), (1, 4), (1, 5), (1, 6), (3, 1), (3, 2), (3, 3), (3, 4), (3, 5), (3, 6), (5, 1), (5, 2), (5, 3), (5, 4), (5, 5), (5, 6)}

and B = {(1, 3), (1, 6), (2, 3), (2, 6), (3, 3), (3, 6), (4, 3), (4, 6), (5, 3), (5, 6), (6, 3), (6, 6)}

So, $n(A) = 18$, $n(B) = 12$

$\therefore\ P(A) = \dfrac{n(A)}{n(S)} = \dfrac{18}{36} = \dfrac{1}{2}$ and $P(B) = \dfrac{12}{36} = \dfrac{1}{3}$

Here, $P(A) \cdot P(B) = \dfrac{1}{2} \times \dfrac{1}{3} = \dfrac{1}{6} \neq P(A \cap B)$

Hence, A and B are not dependent events.

Note If A and B are two dependent events, then we cannot apply $P(A \cap B) = P(A) \cdot P(B)$.

EXAMPLE 7. If each element of a second order determinant is either zero or one. What is the probability that the values of the determinants is positive? Assume that the individual entries of the determinant are chosen independently, each value being assumed with probability 1/2.

Sol. A second order determinant has four entries which may be 0 or 1.

Total number of determinants = $2^4 = 16$

The only positive determinants are

$$\begin{vmatrix} 1 & 0 \\ 0 & 1 \end{vmatrix}, \begin{vmatrix} 1 & 0 \\ 1 & 1 \end{vmatrix} \text{ and } \begin{vmatrix} 1 & 1 \\ 0 & 1 \end{vmatrix}.$$

Since, each entry of the above determinant can be selected with probability 1/2.

Therefore, required probability $= 3\left(\dfrac{1}{2} \times \dfrac{1}{2} \times \dfrac{1}{2} \times \dfrac{1}{2}\right) = \dfrac{3}{16}$

EXAMPLE 8. A and B throw a pair of dice alternately. A wins the game, if he gets a total of 7 and B wins the game, if he gets a total of 10. If A starts the game, then find the probability that B wins.

Sol. Here, $n(S) = 6 \times 6 = 36$

Let A = Event of getting a sum of 7 in pair of dice = {(1, 6), (2, 5), (3, 4), (6, 1), (5, 2), (4, 3)}

$\Rightarrow n(A) = 6$

and B = Event of getting a sum of 10 in pair of dice = {(4, 6), (5, 5), (6, 4)}

$\Rightarrow n(B) = 3$

$\therefore\ P(A) = \dfrac{n(A)}{n(S)} = \dfrac{6}{36} = \dfrac{1}{6}$ and $P(B) = \dfrac{n(B)}{n(S)} = \dfrac{3}{36} = \dfrac{1}{12}$

$\Rightarrow P(\bar{A}) = 1 - \dfrac{1}{6} = \dfrac{5}{6}$ and $P(\bar{B}) = 1 - \dfrac{1}{12} = \dfrac{11}{12}$

Now, the probability that if A start the game, then B wins

$$P(B \text{ wins}) = P(\bar{A} \cap B) + P(\bar{A} \cap \bar{B} \cap \bar{A} \cap B) + P(\bar{A} \cap \bar{B} \cap \bar{A} \cap \bar{B} \cap \bar{A} \cap B) + \dots$$

$$= P(\bar{A})\,P(B) + P(\bar{A})P(\bar{B})P(\bar{A})P(B) + P(\bar{A})P(\bar{B})P(\bar{A})P(\bar{B})P(\bar{A})\,P(B) + \dots$$

[∵ events are independent]

$$= \frac{5}{6} \times \frac{1}{12} + \frac{5}{6} \times \frac{11}{12} \times \frac{5}{6} \times \frac{1}{12} + \frac{5}{6} \times \frac{11}{12} \times \frac{5}{6} \times \frac{11}{12} \times \frac{5}{6} \times \frac{1}{12} + \dots$$

$$= \frac{5}{72} + \frac{5}{72} \times \frac{55}{72} + \frac{5}{72} \times \left(\frac{55}{72}\right)^2 + \dots$$

$$= \frac{5}{72}\left[1 + \frac{55}{72} + \left(\frac{55}{72}\right)^2 + \dots\right] = \frac{5}{72}\left(\frac{1}{1 - \frac{55}{72}}\right)$$

$\left[\because \text{ sum of infinite GP series is } \dfrac{a}{1-r}\right]$

$$= \frac{5}{72}\left(\frac{1}{17/72}\right) = \frac{5}{17}$$

Topic Practice 5

1 Events A and B are such that $P(A)=\frac{1}{2}$, $P(B)=\frac{7}{12}$ and P (not A or not B) $=\frac{1}{4}$. State whether A and B are independent.

2 A die is tossed thrice. Find the probability of getting an even number atleast once.

3 Two cards are drawn at random and without replacement from a pack of 52 playing cards. Find the probability that both the cards are black.

4 An urn contains 10 black and 5 white balls. Two balls are drawn from the urn one after the other without replacement. What is the probability that both drawn balls are black?

5 A fair coin and an unbiased die are tossed. Let A be the event 'head appears on the coin' and B be the event '3 on the die'. Check whether A and B are independent events or not.

6 Prove that if E and F are independent events, then the events E and F' are also independent.

7 A die, whose faces are marked 1, 2, 3 in red and 4, 5, 6 in green, is tossed. Let A be the event "number obtained is even" and B be the event "number obtained is red". Find if A and B are independent events.

8 A die marked 1, 2, 3 in red and 4, 5, 6 in green is tossed. Let A be the event, 'number is odd' and B be the event, 'number is green'. Are A and B independent?

9 If A and B are independent events, then prove that
(i) $P(A)=P(A\cap B)+P(A\cap \bar{B})$.
(ii) $P(A\cup B)=P(A\cap B)+P(A\cap \bar{B})+P(\bar{A}\cap B)$.

10 Given two independent events A and B such that $P(A)=0.3$ and $P(B)=0.6$. Find
(i) $P(A$ and not $B)$ (ii) $P(A$ or $B)$.

11 If A and B are two independent events, then prove that the probability of occurrence of atleast one of A and B is given by $1-P(A')\cdot P(B')$.

12 If A and B are two events such that $P(A)=\frac{1}{4}$, $P(B)=\frac{1}{2}$ and $P(A\cap B)=\frac{1}{8}$, then find P (not A and not B).

13 One card is drawn at random from a well-shuffled deck of 52 cards. Events E and F are defined below
E: the card drawn is a spade
F: the card drawn is an ace
Check whether the events are dependent or independent.

14 Two balls are drawn at random with replacement from a box containing 10 black and 8 red balls. Find the probability that
(i) both balls are red.
(ii) first ball is black and second ball is red.

Hints & Solutions

1. Given, P (not A or not B) $=\frac{1}{4}$

$\Rightarrow \quad P(A' \text{ or } B')=\frac{1}{4}$

$\Rightarrow \quad P(A'\cup B')=\frac{1}{4} \Rightarrow P[(A\cap B)']=\frac{1}{4}$
$[\because P(A'\cup B')=P(A\cap B)']$

$\Rightarrow \quad P(A\cap B)=1-\frac{1}{4}=\frac{3}{4}$

Also, $P(A)\cdot P(B)=\frac{1}{2}\times\frac{7}{12}=\frac{7}{24}\neq\frac{3}{4}$
$\left[\because P(A)=\frac{1}{2}, P(B)=\frac{7}{12}, \text{given}\right]$

$\Rightarrow \quad P(A)\cdot P(B)\neq P(A\cap B)$

Hence, A and B are not independent events.

2. P(getting even number on a die) $=\frac{3}{6}=\frac{1}{2}$

$\therefore$ Required probability
$=1-$ Probability of getting an even number in none of the throw
$=1-\frac{1}{2}\times\frac{1}{2}\times\frac{1}{2}=\frac{7}{8}$

3. There are 26 black cards in a pack of 52 cards.

Required probability $=P(E \text{ and } F)=P(E)\cdot P\left(\frac{F}{E}\right)$

where, E : First card drawn is black and F : Second card drawn is black.

$$P(E)=\frac{\text{Number of favourable outcomes}}{\text{Total number of outcomes}}$$
$$=\frac{26}{52}=\frac{1}{2}$$

$P\left(\frac{F}{E}\right) = \frac{25}{51}$ [after drawing 1 black card, there will be 25 black cards left]

$\therefore$ Required probability,

$$P(E \cap F) = P(E) \cdot P\left(\frac{F}{E}\right) = \frac{1}{2} \times \frac{25}{51} = \frac{25}{102}$$

4. Hint $P(BB) = \frac{10}{15} \times \frac{9}{14}$ $\left[\textbf{Ans. } \frac{3}{7}\right]$

5. If a fair coin and an unbiased die are tossed, then the sample space S is given by

$$S = \begin{Bmatrix} (H,1), (H,2), (H,3), (H,4), (H,5), (H,6), \\ (T,1), (T,2), (T,3), (T,4), (T,5), (T,6) \end{Bmatrix}$$

$\Rightarrow n(S) = 12$

Also, A : Head appears on the coin

and B : 3 appears on die.

$\Rightarrow A =$ Event having head on coin

$= \{(H,1), (H,2), (H,3), (H,4), (H,5), (H,6)\}$

$B =$ Event having 3 on die

$= \{(H,3), (T,3)\}$; $A \cap B = \{(H,3)\}$

$\therefore n(A) = 6, n(B) = 2, n(A \cap B) = 1$

Hence, $P(A) = \frac{n(A)}{n(S)} = \frac{6}{12} = \frac{1}{2}$,

$$P(B) = \frac{n(B)}{n(S)} = \frac{2}{12} = \frac{1}{6}$$

and $P(A \cap B) = \frac{n(A \cap B)}{n(S)} = \frac{1}{12}$

Now, $P(A) \times P(B) = \frac{1}{2} \times \frac{1}{6} = \frac{1}{12} = P(A \cap B)$

Hence, A and B are independent events.

6. Given, E and F are independent events, therefore

$\Rightarrow P(E \cap F) = P(E)P(F)$ ...(i)

Now, we have

$P(E \cap F') + P(E \cap F) = P(E)$

$\Rightarrow P(E \cap F') = P(E) - P(E \cap F)$

$\Rightarrow P(E \cap F') = P(E) - P(E)P(F)$ [using Eq. (i)]

$\Rightarrow P(E \cap F') = P(E)[1 - P(F)]$

$\Rightarrow P(E \cap F') = P(E)P(F')$

$\therefore E$ and F' are also independent events.

Hence proved.

7. When a die is thrown, then sample space is

$S = \{1, 2, 3, 4, 5, 6\}$

$\Rightarrow n(S) = 6$

Also, A : Number is even and B : Number is red.

$\therefore A = \{2, 4, 6\}$ and $B = \{1, 2, 3\}$ and $A \cap B = \{2\}$

$\Rightarrow n(A) = 3, n(B) = 3$ and $n(A \cap B) = 1$

Now, $P(A) = \frac{n(A)}{n(S)} = \frac{3}{6} = \frac{1}{2}$, $P(B) = \frac{n(B)}{n(S)} = \frac{3}{6} = \frac{1}{2}$

and $P(A \cap B) = \frac{n(A \cap B)}{n(S)} = \frac{1}{6}$

Now, $P(A) \times P(B) = \frac{1}{2} \times \frac{1}{2} = \frac{1}{4} \neq \frac{1}{6} = P(A \cap B)$

$\therefore P(A \cap B) \neq P(A) \times P(B)$

Thus, A and B are not independent events.

8. When a die is thrown, then sample space,

$S = \{1, 2, 3, 4, 5, 6\} \Rightarrow n(S) = 6$

Also, A : Number is odd and B : Number is green

$\therefore A = \{1, 3, 5\}$, $B = \{4, 5, 6\}$ and $A \cap B = \{5\}$

$\Rightarrow n(A) = 3, n(B) = 3, n(A \cap B) = 1$

Now, $P(A) = \frac{n(A)}{n(S)} = \frac{3}{6} = \frac{1}{2}$, $P(B) = \frac{n(B)}{n(S)} = \frac{3}{6} = \frac{1}{2}$,

$P(A \cap B) = \frac{n(A \cap B)}{n(S)} = \frac{1}{6}$

and $P(A) \times P(B) = \frac{1}{2} \times \frac{1}{2} = \frac{1}{4} \neq \frac{1}{6} = P(A \cap B)$

$\therefore P(A \cap B) \neq P(A) \times P(B)$

Thus, A and B are not independent events.

9. (i) **Hint** RHS $= P(A \cap B) + P(A \cap \overline{B})$

$= P(A) \cdot P(B) + P(A) \cdot P(\overline{B})$

$= P(A)[P(B) + P(B)]$

$= P(A)[P(B) + 1 - P(B)]$

$= P(A) =$ LHS

(ii) Similar as part (i).

10. Hint (i) $P(A \text{ and not } B) = P(A) - P(A \cap B)$

$= 0.3 - (0.3)(0.6)$

[$\because A$ and B are independent events]

(ii) $P(A \text{ or } B) = P(A) + P(B) - P(A \cap B)$

$= 0.3 + 0.6 - 0.18$

[**Ans.** (i) 0.12 (ii) 0.72]

11. Required probability $= P(A \cup B)$

$= P(A) + P(B) - P(A) \cdot P(B) = P(A)[1 - P(B)] + 1 - P(B')$

$= P(A)P(B') - P(B') + 1$

$= 1 - P(B')[1 - P(A)] = 1 - P(A')P(B')$ **Hence proved.**

12. Hint $P(\text{not } A \text{ and not } B) = P(A') \times P(B')$

[$\because A$ and B are independent events]

$= [1 - P(A)][1 - P(B)] = \left(1 - \frac{1}{4}\right)\left(1 - \frac{1}{2}\right)$ $\left[\textbf{Ans. } \frac{3}{8}\right]$

13. Hint $P(E) = \frac{1}{4}, P(F) = \frac{1}{13}, P(E \cap F) = \frac{1}{52}$

Now, $P(E \cap F) = P(E) \times P(F)$

[**Ans.** E and F are independent events]

14. Hint (i) $P(RR) = \frac{8}{18} \times \frac{8}{18}$

(ii) $P(BR) = \frac{10}{18} \times \frac{8}{18}$ $\left[\textbf{Ans. } \text{(i) } \frac{16}{81} \text{ (ii) } \frac{20}{81}\right]$

Exam Pattern Exercise

Part A - Objective Type Questions

Multiple Choice Type Questions

1 A bag contains one white and one red ball. A ball is drawn from the bag. If the ball drawn is red, it is replaced in the bag and again a ball is drawn. Otherwise a coin is tossed, then which of the following is true?

I. Total number of outcomes is 14.

II. Sample space $S = \{(R, W), (R, R), (W, H), (W, T)\}$.

(a) Only I is true
(b) Only II is true
(c) Both I and II are true
(d) Both I and II are false

2 A die is rolled. Let E be the event "die shows 4" and F be the event "die shows even number". Then, E and F are

(a) mutually exclusive
(b) exhaustive
(c) mutually exclusive and exhaustive
(d) None of the above

3 Let A and B be two events. If $P(A) = 0.2$, $P(B) = 0.4$, $P(A \cup B) = 0.6$, then $P(A/B)$ is equal to

(a) 0.8 (b) 0.5 (c) 0.3 (d) 0

4 If three mutually independent events are A, B and C, then

(a) $P(A \cap B) = P(A) \cdot P(B)$; $P(A \cap C) = P(A) \cdot P(C)$
(b) $P(B \cap C) = P(B) \cdot P(C)$
(c) $P(A \cap B \cap C) = P(A) \cdot P(B) \cdot P(C)$
(d) All of the above

5 If A and B are two independent events with $P(A) = \frac{3}{5}$ and $P(B) = \frac{4}{9}$, then $P(A' \cap B')$ equals to

(a) $\frac{4}{15}$ (b) $\frac{8}{45}$ (c) $\frac{1}{3}$ (d) $\frac{2}{9}$

6 A and B are two independent events. The probability that both A and B occur is $\frac{1}{6}$ and the probability that neither of them occur is $\frac{1}{3}$. Then, the probability of the two events are

(a) $\frac{1}{5}, \frac{1}{6}$ (b) $\frac{1}{3}, \frac{1}{2}$ (c) $\frac{1}{4}, \frac{1}{5}$ (d) $\frac{1}{3}, \frac{1}{4}$

7 The probabilities of a specific problem being solved independently by A and B are $\frac{1}{3}$ and $\frac{1}{4}$ respectively. If both try to solve the problem independently, then exactly one of them solves the problems.

(a) $\frac{6}{11}$ (b) $\frac{5}{12}$ (c) $\frac{4}{9}$ (d) $\frac{6}{13}$

8 A and B are two events such that $P(A) = \frac{1}{2}$, $P(B) = \frac{1}{3}$ and $P(A \cap B) = \frac{1}{4}$, then $P\left(\frac{A'}{B'}\right)$ is

(a) $\frac{4}{9}$ (b) $\frac{5}{11}$ (c) $\frac{5}{8}$ (d) $\frac{4}{7}$

9 The probability that an automobile will be stolen and found within one week is 0.0006. The probability that an automobile will be stolen is 0.0015. The probability that a stolen automobile will be found in one week is

(a) $\frac{2}{5}$ (b) $\frac{3}{5}$ (c) $\frac{1}{5}$ (d) $\frac{4}{5}$

Assertion-Reason Based Questions

Directions (Q. Nos. 10-12) *In the questions given below are two statements labelled as Assertion (A) and Reason (R). In the context of the two statements, which one of the following is correct?*

(a) Both A and R are correct; R is the correct explanation of A
(b) Both A and R are correct; R is not the correct explanation of A
(c) A is correct; R is incorrect
(d) R is correct; A is incorrect

10 **Assertion (A)** An unbiased die is tossed twice. The probability of getting a 4, 5 or 6 on the first toss and a 1, 2, 3 or 4 on the second is $\frac{1}{3}$.

Reason (R) A and B appear for an interview for two vacancies in the same post. The probability of A's selection is $\frac{1}{6}$ and that of B's is selection is $\frac{1}{4}$, then probability that at least one of them is selected is $\frac{3}{8}$.

11 **Assertion (A)** A coin is tossed and a die is thrown, the probability that the outcome will be a head or a number greater than 4, or both is $\frac{3}{4}$.

Reason (R) Two cards are drawn without replacement from a well shuffled pack of 52 cards the probability that one is a spade and other is a queen of red colour is $\frac{1}{51}$.

12 **Assertion (A)** A speaks truth in 60% and B in 50% of the cases. The probability that they contradict each other while narrating the some incident is $\frac{1}{2}$.

Reason (R) If A and B are independent event such that $P(B)=\frac{2}{7}$, $P(A\cup B)=0.8$, then $P(A)=0.65$.

Part-B Descriptive Questions

Very Short Answer Type Questions

13 In each of the following experiments, specify appropriate sample space.
(i) A boy has a 1 rupee coin, a 2 rupee coin and a 5 rupee coin in his pocket. He takes out two coins out of his pocket, one after the other.
(ii) A person is noting down the number of accidents along a busy highway during a year.

14 A bag contains 9 red and 12 white balls. One ball is drawn at random. Find the probability that the ball drawn is red.

15 If $P(A)=\frac{3}{10}$, $P(B)=\frac{2}{5}$ and $P(A\cup B)=\frac{3}{5}$, then find $P(B/A)+P(A/B)$.

16 If $P(A)=0.4$, $P(B)=0.8$ and $P(B/A)=0.6$, then find $P(A\cup B)$.

17 A die is tossed thrice. Find the probability of getting an odd number atleast once.

Short Answer Type Questions

18 A bag contains 6 disces of which 4 are red, 3 are blue and 2 are yellow. The discs are similar in shape and size. A disc is drawn at random from the bag. Calculate the probability that it will be
(i) red (ii) yellow
(iii) blue (iv) not blue
(v) either red or blue.

19 In a single throw of three dice, find the probability of getting a total of 17 or 18.

20 If A and B are two events such that $P(A)=\frac{1}{2}$, $P(B)=\frac{1}{3}$ and $P\left(\frac{A}{B}\right)=\frac{1}{4}$, then find $P(A'\cap B')$.

21 Three persons A, B and C fire at a target in turn, starting with A. Their probability of hitting the target are 0.4, 0.3 and 0.2, respectively. Find the probability that exactly two of them hit the target.

Long Answer Type Questions

22 On her vacations, Veena visits four cities (A, B, C and D) in a random order. What is the probability that she visits
(i) A before B?
(ii) A before B and B before C?
(iii) A first and B last?
(iv) A either first or second?
(v) A just before B?

23 Four candidates A, B, C, D have applied for the assignment to coach a school cricket team. If A is twice as likely to be selected as B, and B and C are given about the same chance of being selected, while C is twice as likely to be selected as D, then what are the probabilities that
(i) C will be selected? (ii) A will not be selected?

24 Out of 100 students, two sections of 40 and 60 are formed. If you and your friend are among the 100 students, then what is the probability that
(i) you both enter the same section?
(ii) you both enter the different sections?

Case Study Based Questions

25 Two friends are playing with two dice. They throw them simultaneously and note the results on both dice.

On the basis of above information, answer the following questions.

(i) Probability (an even number as the sum) =
(a) $\frac{1}{3}$ (b) $\frac{1}{2}$ (c) $\frac{1}{4}$ (d) $\frac{1}{6}$

(ii) Probability (a total of at least 10) =
(a) $\frac{1}{3}$ (b) $\frac{1}{2}$ (c) $\frac{1}{4}$ (d) $\frac{1}{6}$

(iii) Probability (same number on both dice) =
(a) $\frac{1}{3}$ (b) $\frac{1}{2}$ (c) $\frac{1}{4}$ (d) $\frac{1}{6}$

(iv) Probability (a multiple of 3 as the sum) =
(a) $\frac{1}{3}$ (b) $\frac{1}{2}$ (c) $\frac{1}{4}$ (d) $\frac{1}{6}$

(v) Probability (the sum as a prime number) =
(a) $\frac{1}{3}$ (b) $\frac{3}{5}$ (c) $\frac{5}{12}$ (d) $\frac{1}{2}$

Hints & Solutions

1. (b) 2. (d) 3. (d) 4. (d)
5. (d) 6. (b) 7. (b) 8. (c)
9. (a) 10. (b) 11. (d) 12. (c)

13. (i) {QH, QR, HQ, HR, RH, RQ} where Q denotes a 1 rupee coin, H denotes a 2 rupee coin and R denotes a 5 rupees coin.
(ii) (0, 1, 2, 3 ....)

14. $\frac{3}{7}$ 15. $\frac{7}{12}$ 16. 0.96 17. $\frac{7}{8}$

18. (i) $\frac{4}{9}$ (ii) $\frac{2}{9}$ (iii) $\frac{1}{3}$ (iv) $\frac{2}{3}$ (v) $\frac{7}{9}$

19. **Hint** Total number of sample space = 216
Let A : Sample space to get a sum of 17
$= \{(6, 6, 5), (5, 6, 6), (6, 5, 6)\}$
and B : Sample space to get a sum of 18 = $\{(6, 6, 6)\}$
$P(A) = \frac{3}{216}$, $P(B) = \frac{1}{216}$ **Ans.** $\frac{1}{54}$

20. $\frac{1}{4}$

21. **Hint** $P(A) = 0.4$, $P(B) = 0.3$, $P(C) = 0.2$
$P(\overline{A}) = 0.6$, $P(\overline{B}) = 0.7$, $P(\overline{C}) = 0.8$
Required probability
$= P(\overline{A})P(B)P(C) + P(A)P(\overline{B})P(C) + P(A)P(B)P(\overline{C})$
Ans. 0.188

22. **Hint** $n(S) = 24$
(i) P (she visits A before B) $= P(E_1) = \frac{n(E_1)}{n(S)} = \frac{12}{24}$
Ans. $\frac{1}{2}$
(ii) $n(E_2) = 2$, $P(E_2) = \frac{n(E_2)}{n(S)} = \frac{4}{24}$ **Ans.** $\frac{1}{6}$
(iii) $n(E_3) = 2$
$P(E_3) = \frac{n(E_3)}{n(S)} = \frac{2}{24}$ **Ans.** $\frac{1}{12}$
(iv) $n(E_4) = 12$
$P(E_4) = \frac{n(E_4)}{n(S)} = \frac{12}{24}$ **Ans.** $\frac{1}{2}$
(v) $n(E_5) = 6$, $P(E_5) = \frac{n(E_s)}{n(S)} = \frac{6}{24}$ **Ans.** $\frac{1}{4}$

23. $P(E_1) + P(E_2) + P(E_3) + P(E_4) = 1$
$\Rightarrow \quad 4p + 2p + 2p + p = 1$
$\Rightarrow \quad 9p = 1$
$\Rightarrow \quad p = \frac{1}{9}$
(i) $P(C \text{ selected}) = P(E_3) = 2p$ **Ans.** $\frac{2}{9}$
(ii) Now, $P(A \text{ selected}) = P(E_1) = 4p$ **Ans.** $\frac{4}{9}$
$\therefore P(A \text{ is not selected}) = 1 - P(A \text{ selected})$
$= 1 - \frac{4}{9}$ **Ans.** $\frac{5}{9}$

24. **Hint** Let there be two sections A and B of 40 and 60 students, respectively.
(i) Let both students enter the section A.
So, 38 students are to selected out of 98, since two particular students are already in section A.
$\therefore$ Number of ways of selecting 38 students out of 98 = ${}^{98}C_{38}$ ways
Number of exhaustive cases of selecting 40 students out of 100 = ${}^{100}C_{40}$ ways
Ans. $\frac{17}{33}$
(ii) The probability that they enter different sections
$= 1 - P$ (that two particular students enter either section A or B)
$= 1 - \frac{17}{33}$ **Ans.** $\frac{16}{33}$

25. (i) (b), (ii) (d), (iii) (d), (iv) (a), (v) (c)

CHAPTER 18

Descriptive Statistics

In this Chapter...

- Measure of dispersion
- Variance and Standard Deviation
- Percentile Rank and Correlation

Measure of Dispersion

Due to variability in data, the measures of central tendency (mean, median or mode) are not sufficient to give complete information about given data as they provide us a rough idea about the point where data are centered. So, we need other measures to have better idea, measure of dispersion is the single number that describes variability.

It is the measure of spreading (scatter) of the data about some central tendency.

The dispersion or scatter in a data is measured on the basis of the observations and the types of measure of central tendency used.

There are following measures of dispersion

1. Range
2. Mean deviation
3. Quartile deviation
4. Standard deviation

Range

Range is the difference of maximum and minimum values of data.

Range = Maximum value − Minimum value

Mean Deviation

Mean deviation is defined as the arithmetic mean of the absolute deviations of all the values taken from a central value or a fixed number 'a'. The mean deviation from 'a' is denoted as MD (a).

Thus, mean deviation from 'a',

$$\text{MD}(a) = \frac{\textbf{[Sum of absolute values of deviations from } a\textbf{]}}{\textbf{Number of observations}}$$

Mean Deviation for Ungrouped Data

Let $x_1, x_2, \ldots, x_n$ be n observations. Then, mean deviation about mean or median can be determined by following steps:

I. Find the mean or median of given observations using the suitable formula.

II. Find the deviation of each observation x_i from $\bar{x}$ (mean) or M (median) and then take their absolute values

i.e. $|x_i - \bar{x}|$ or $|x_i - M|$

III. Find the sum of absolute values of deviations obtained in Step II

i.e. $\sum_{i=1}^{n} |x_i - \bar{x}|$ or $\sum_{i=1}^{n} |x_i - M|$

IV. Now, find mean deviation about mean or median using the formula

$$\frac{\sum_{i=1}^{n} |x_i - \bar{x}|}{n} \text{ or } \frac{\sum_{i=1}^{n} |x_i - M|}{n},$$

where n is the number of observations.

EXAMPLE 1. Find the mean deviation about the mean for the following data. [NCERT]

38, 70, 48, 40, 42, 55, 63, 46, 54, 44

Sol. Given, observations are

38, 70, 48, 40, 42, 55, 63, 46, 54 and 44

Here, number of observations, $n = 10$

$\therefore$ Mean,

$$\bar{x} = \frac{(38 + 70 + 48 + 40 + 42 + 55 + 63 + 46 + 54 + 44)}{10}$$

$$= \frac{500}{10} = 50$$

Let us make the table for deviation and absolute deviation

x_i	$x_i - \bar{x}$	$\lvert x_i - \bar{x}\rvert$
38	$38 - 50 = -12$	12
70	$70 - 50 = 20$	20
48	$48 - 50 = -2$	2
40	$40 - 50 = -10$	10
42	$42 - 50 = -8$	8
55	$55 - 50 = 5$	5
63	$63 - 50 = 13$	13
46	$46 - 50 = -4$	4
54	$54 - 50 = 4$	4
44	$44 - 50 = -6$	6
Total		$\sum_{i=1}^{10} \lvert x_i - \bar{x}\rvert = 84$

Now, $\text{MD} = \dfrac{\sum_{i=1}^{10} |x_i - \bar{x}|}{10}$

$$= \frac{84}{10} = 8.4$$

EXAMPLE 2. Find the mean deviation about the median for the data 34, 66, 30, 38, 44, 50, 40, 60, 42, 51.

Sol. The given data can be arranged in ascending order as 30, 34, 38, 40, 42, 44, 50, 51, 60, 66. Here, total number of observations are 10. i.e. $n = 10$, which is even.

$\therefore$ Median

$$M = \frac{\left(\frac{n}{2}\right)\text{th observation} + \left(\frac{n}{2}+1\right)\text{th observation}}{2}$$

$$= \frac{\left(\frac{10}{2}\right)\text{th observation} + \left(\frac{10}{2}+1\right)\text{th observation}}{2}$$

$$= \frac{(5\text{th observation} + 6\text{th observation})}{2}$$

$$= \frac{42+44}{2} = \frac{86}{2} = 43$$

Let us make the table for absolute deviation

x_i	$\lvert x_i - M\rvert$
30	$\lvert 30 - 43\rvert = 13$
34	$\lvert 34 - 43\rvert = 9$
38	$\lvert 38 - 43\rvert = 5$
40	$\lvert 40 - 43\rvert = 3$
42	$\lvert 42 - 43\rvert = 1$
44	$\lvert 44 - 43\rvert = 1$
50	$\lvert 50 - 43\rvert = 7$
51	$\lvert 51 - 43\rvert = 8$
60	$\lvert 60 - 43\rvert = 17$
66	$\lvert 66 - 43\rvert = 23$
Total	$\sum_{i=1}^{10} \lvert x_i - M\rvert = 87$

Now, mean deviation about median,

$$\text{MD} = \frac{\sum_{i=1}^{10} |x_i - M|}{10} = \frac{87}{10} = 8.7$$

EXAMPLE 3. The mean of 6, 8, 5, 7, a and 4 is 7. Find the mean deviation about median of these observation.

Sol. Here, number of observations, $n = 6$

By the given condition, $\dfrac{6 + 8 + 5 + 7 + a + 4}{6} = 7$

$\Rightarrow \quad 30 + a = 6 \times 7 \Rightarrow a = 42 - 30 = 12$

Now, on arranging the observations in ascending order, we have 4, 5, 6, 7, 8, 12.

Now, median

$$M = \frac{\left(\frac{6}{2}\right)\text{th observation} + \left(\frac{6}{2}+1\right)\text{th observation}}{2}$$

$$= \frac{3\text{rd observation} + 4\text{th observation}}{2} = \frac{6+7}{2} = \frac{13}{2} = 6.5$$

Let us make the table for deviation and absolute deviation.

x_i	$x_i - M$	$\lvert x_i - M\rvert$
4	-2.5	2.5
5	-1.5	1.5
6	-0.5	0.5
7	0.5	0.5
8	1.5	1.5
12	5.5	5.5
Total		$\sum_{i=1}^{6} \lvert x_i - M\rvert = 12$

$\therefore$ Mean deviation about median $= \dfrac{\sum_{i=1}^{6} |x_i - M|}{6} = \dfrac{12}{6} = 2$

EXAMPLE 4. Calculate the mean deviation about the mean of the set of first n natural numbers when n is an odd number.

Sol. Consider first n natural number when n is odd i.e. 1, 2, 3, 4, ..., n (odd).

Clearly, mean $(\bar{x}) = \dfrac{1+2+3+...+n}{n}$

$$= \frac{n(n+1)}{2n} = \frac{n+1}{2}$$

$$\left[\because \text{sum of first } N \text{ natural numbers} = \frac{N(N+1)}{2}\right]$$

Now, $$\text{MD} = \frac{\left|1-\frac{n+1}{2}\right| + \left|2-\frac{n+1}{2}\right| + \left|3-\frac{n+1}{2}\right| + ... + \left|n-\frac{n+1}{2}\right|}{n}$$

$$\left[\because \text{MD} = \frac{\sum_{i=1}^{n}|x_i - \bar{x}|}{n}\right]$$

$$= \frac{\left|1-\frac{n+1}{2}\right| + \left|2-\frac{n+1}{2}\right| + ... + \left|\frac{n-1}{2}-\frac{n+1}{2}\right| + \left|\frac{n+1}{2}-\frac{n+1}{2}\right| + \left|\frac{n+3}{2}-\frac{n+1}{2}\right| + ... + \left|\frac{2n-2}{2}-\frac{n+1}{2}\right| + \left|n-\frac{n+1}{2}\right|}{n}$$

$$= \frac{\left|\frac{1-n}{2}\right| + \left|\frac{3-n}{2}\right| + ... + |-1| + 0 + |1| + |2| + ... + \left|\frac{n-3}{2}\right| + \left|\frac{n-1}{2}\right|}{n}$$

$$= \frac{2}{n}\left[\underbrace{1+2+...+\frac{n-3}{2}+\frac{n-1}{2}}_{\left(\frac{n-1}{2}\right)\text{ terms}}\right] = \frac{2}{n}\left[\frac{\left(\frac{n-1}{2}\right)\left(\frac{n-1}{2}+1\right)}{2}\right]$$

$$\left[\because \text{sum of first } N \text{ natural numbers} = \frac{N(N+1)}{2}\right]$$

$$= \frac{2}{n}\cdot\frac{1}{2}\left[\left(\frac{n-1}{2}\right)\left(\frac{n+1}{2}\right)\right] = \frac{1}{n}\left(\frac{n^2-1}{4}\right) = \frac{n^2-1}{4n}$$

EXAMPLE 5. Calculate the mean deviation about the mean of the set of first n natural numbers when n is an even number.

Sol. Consider first n natural number when n is even i.e. 1, 2, 3, 4, ..., n (even).

Clearly, mean $(\bar{x}) = \dfrac{1+2+3+...+n}{n} = \dfrac{n(n+1)}{2n} = \dfrac{n+1}{2}$

Now, $$\text{MD} = \frac{1}{n}\left[\left|1-\frac{n+1}{2}\right| + \left|2-\frac{n+1}{2}\right| + \left|3-\frac{n+1}{2}\right| + ... + \left|\frac{n-2}{2}-\frac{n+1}{2}\right| + \left|\frac{n}{2}-\frac{n+1}{2}\right| + \left|\frac{n+2}{2}-\frac{n+1}{2}\right| + ... + \left|n-\frac{n+1}{2}\right|\right]$$

$$= \frac{1}{n}\left[\left|\frac{1-n}{2}\right| + \left|\frac{3-n}{2}\right| + \left|\frac{5-n}{2}\right| + ... + \left|\frac{-3}{2}\right| + \left|\frac{1}{2}\right| + ... + \left|\frac{n-1}{2}\right|\right]$$

$$= \frac{2}{n}\left[\underbrace{\frac{1}{2}+\frac{3}{2}+...+\frac{n-1}{2}}_{\left(\frac{n}{2}\right)\text{ terms}}\right] = \frac{1}{n}\cdot\left(\frac{n}{2}\right)^2$$

$$[\because \text{sum of first } N \text{ odd natural numbers} = N^2]$$

$$= \frac{1}{n}\cdot\frac{n^2}{4} = \frac{n}{4}$$

Mean Deviation for Grouped Data

(a) For Discrete Frequency Distribution

Let the given data have n distinct values $x_1, x_2, ..., x_n$ and their corresponding frequencies are $f_1, f_2, ..., f_n$, respectively.

Then, this data can be represented in the tabular form, as

x_i	x_1	x_2	x_3	...	x_n
f_i	f_1	f_2	f_3	...	f_n

and is called discrete frequency distribution.

Here, mean deviation about mean or median is given by $\dfrac{\sum_{i=1}^{n} f_i\,|x_i - A|}{N}$, where $N = \sum_{i=1}^{n} f_i$ = total frequency and A = mean or median.

Method to find the Mean Deviation about Mean

For finding the mean deviation about mean, we use the following steps:

I. Find the mean of given observations using the formula $\bar{x} = \dfrac{\Sigma f_i x_i}{\Sigma f_i}$.

II. Find the deviation of each observation x_i from $\bar{x}$ and take their absolute values i.e. $|x_i - \bar{x}|$ and then find $f_i|x_i - \bar{x}|$.

III. Find the sum of absolute values of deviations obtained in Step II i.e. $\Sigma f_i\,|x_i - \bar{x}|$.

IV. Now, find the mean deviation about mean by using the formula, $\dfrac{\Sigma f_i\,|x_i - \bar{x}|}{\Sigma f_i}$,

EXAMPLE 6. Find the mean deviation about the mean for the following data.

x_i	2	5	6	8	10	12
f_i	2	8	10	7	8	5

Sol. Let us make the following table from the given data.

x_i	f_i	f_ix_i	$\lvert x_i - \bar{x}\rvert$	$f_i\lvert x_i - \bar{x}\rvert$
2	2	4	5.5	11
5	8	40	2.5	20
6	10	60	1.5	15
8	7	56	0.5	3.5
10	8	80	2.5	20
12	5	60	4.5	22.5
Total	40	300		92

Here, $N = \Sigma f_i = 40, \Sigma f_ix_i = 300$

Now, mean $(\bar{x}) = \frac{1}{N}\Sigma f_ix_i = \frac{1}{40} \times 300 = 7.5$

$\therefore$ Mean deviation about the mean,

$\text{MD}(\bar{x}) = \frac{1}{N}\Sigma f_i\lvert x_i - \bar{x}\rvert = \frac{1}{40} \times 92 = 2.3$

Hence, the mean deviation about mean is 2.3.

Method to find the Mean Deviation about Median

For finding the mean deviation about median, we use the following steps:

I. Arrange the given data either in ascending order or descending order.

II. Make a cumulative frequency table.

III. Find the median by using the formula,

- If $\Sigma f_i = N$ is even, then

$$\text{Median} = \frac{\text{Value of}\left(\frac{N}{2}\right)\text{th observation} + \text{Value of}\left(\frac{N}{2}+1\right)\text{th observation}}{2}$$

- If $\Sigma f_i = N$ is odd, then

$$\text{Median} = \text{Value of}\left(\frac{N+1}{2}\right)\text{th observation}$$

IV. Find the absolute values of deviations of observations x_i from M.

V. Find the product of frequency with absolute deviations i.e. $f_i\lvert x_i - M\rvert$.

VI. Find the mean deviation from median by using the formula, $\text{MD} = \frac{\sum f_i\lvert x_i - M\rvert}{\Sigma f_i}$.

EXAMPLE 7. Find the mean deviation from the median of the following frequency distribution.

Age (in years)	10	12	15	18	21	23
Frequency	3	5	4	10	8	4

Sol. The given observations are already in ascending order. Now, let us make the cumulative frequency table.

Age (x_i)	Frequency (f_i)	cf
10	3	3
12	5	8
15	4	12
18	10	22
21	8	30
23	4	34
Total	$N = 34$	

Here, $\Sigma f_i = N = 34$, which is even.

$$\therefore \text{Median} = \frac{\text{Value of}\left(\frac{34}{2}\right)\text{th observation} + \text{Value of}\left(\frac{34}{2}+1\right)\text{th observation}}{2}$$

$$= \frac{\text{Value of 17th observation} + \text{Value of 18th observation}}{2}$$

$$= \frac{18+18}{2} = 18$$

[$\because$ both of these observation lies in the cumulative frequency 22 and its corresponding observation is 18.]

Now, let us make the following table from the given data.

$\lvert x_i - 18\rvert$	8	6	3	0	3	5	**Total**
$f_i\lvert x_i - 18\rvert$	24	30	12	0	24	20	110

$$= \frac{\Sigma f_i\lvert x_i - M\rvert}{\Sigma f_i}$$

$$= \frac{110}{34} = 3.24 \text{ yr}$$

EXAMPLE 8. Find the mean deviation from the median for the following data. [NCERT]

x_i	15	21	27	30	35
f_i	3	5	6	7	8

Sol. The given observations are already in ascending order. Now, let us make the following table from the given data.

x_i	f_i	cf	$\lvert x_i - M\rvert$	$f_i\lvert x_i - M\rvert$
15	3	3	15	45
21	5	8	9	45
27	6	14	3	18
30	7	21	0	0
35	8	29	5	40
Total	29	32		148

Here, $N = \Sigma f_i = 29$, which is odd.

So, the median $= \left(\dfrac{N+1}{2}\right)$th observation

i.e. $\dfrac{29+1}{2} = 15$th observation, which is equal to 30.

[$\because$ 15th observation lie in the cumulative frequency 21 and its corresponding observation is 30]

Thus, the median $(M) = 30$.

Hence, the mean deviation from the median

$$= \frac{\Sigma f_i \lvert x_i - 30\rvert}{\Sigma f_i} = \frac{148}{29} = 5.1$$

(b) For Continuous Frequency Distribution

A continuous frequency distribution is a series in which the data is classified into different class intervals without gaps alongwith their respective frequencies.

Mean Deviation about Mean

For calculating mean deviation from mean of a continuous frequency distribution, the procedure is same as for a discrete frequency distribution. The only difference is that here we have to obtain the mid-points of the various classes and take the deviations of these mid-points from the mean.

EXAMPLE 9. Find the mean deviation about the mean for the following data.

Marks obtained	10-20	20-30	30-40	40-50	50-60	60-70	70-80
Number of students	2	3	8	14	8	3	2

Sol. Let us make the following table from the given data.

Marks obtained	Number of students (f_i)	Mid-points (x_i)	$f_i x_i$	$\lvert x_i - \bar{x}\rvert$	$f_i\lvert x_i - \bar{x}\rvert$
10-20	2	15	30	30	60
20-30	3	25	75	20	60
30-40	8	35	280	10	80
40-50	14	45	630	0	0
50-60	8	55	440	10	80
60-70	3	65	195	20	60
70-80	2	75	150	30	60
Total	40		1800		400

Here, $N = \sum_{i=1}^{7} f_i = 40$ and $\sum_{i=1}^{7} f_i x_i = 1800$

Therefore, mean $(\bar{x}) = \dfrac{1}{N}\sum_{i=1}^{7} f_i x_i = \dfrac{1800}{40} = 45$

Now, mean deviation,

$$\text{MD}(\bar{x}) = \frac{1}{N}\sum_{i=1}^{7} f_i\lvert x_i - \bar{x}\rvert \quad \left[\because \sum_{i=1}^{7} f_i\lvert x_i - \bar{x}\rvert = 400\right]$$

$$= \frac{1}{40}\times 400$$

$$= 10$$

Hence, the mean deviation about mean is 10.

Mean Deviation about Median

For calculating mean deviation from median of a continuous frequency distribution, the procedure is same as about mean. The only difference is that, here we replace mean by median and median is calculated by the following formula,

$$M = l + \frac{\dfrac{N}{2} - cf}{f} \times h$$

l, f, h and cf are respectively the lower limit, the frequency, the width of median class and cumulative frequency of class just preceding the median class.

EXAMPLE 10. Find the mean deviation about the median of the following frequency distribution.

Class	0-6	6-12	12-18	18-24	24-30
Frequency	8	10	12	9	5

Sol. Let us make the following table from the given data.

Class	Mid-value (x_i)	Frequency (f_i)	Cumulative frequency (cf)	$\lvert x_i - 14\rvert$	$f_i\lvert x_i - 14\rvert$
0-6	3	8	8	11	88
6-12	9	10	18	5	50
12-18	15	12	30	1	12
18-24	21	9	39	7	63
24-30	27	5	44	13	65
Total		$N = \Sigma f_i = 44$			$\Sigma f_i\lvert x_i - 14\rvert = 278$

Here, $N = 44$, so $\dfrac{N}{2} = 22$ and the cumulative frequency just greater than $\dfrac{N}{2}$ is 30.

Therefore, 12-18 is the median class.

Now, median $= l + \dfrac{\frac{N}{2} - cf}{f} \times h$

where, $l = 12$, $f = 12$, $cf = 18$ and $h = 6$

$\therefore$ Median $= 12 + \dfrac{22-18}{12} \times 6 = 12 + \dfrac{4 \times 6}{12} = 14$

Mean deviation about median $= \dfrac{1}{N} \Sigma f_i |x_i - 14|$

$= \dfrac{278}{44} = 6.318$

EXAMPLE 11. Calculate the mean deviation about median for the following data. **[NCERT]**

Class	0-10	10-20	20-30	30-40	40-50	50-60
Frequency	6	7	15	16	4	2

Sol. Let us make the following table from the given data.

Class	Mid-point (x_i)	f_i	cf	$\lvert x_i - M\rvert$	$f_i \lvert x_i - M\rvert$
0-10	5	6	6	23	138
10-20	15	7	13	13	91
20-30	25	15	28	3	45
30-40	35	16	44	7	112
40-50	45	4	48	17	68
50-60	55	2	50	27	54
Total		50			508

Here, $\dfrac{N}{2} = \dfrac{50}{2} = 25$,

which lies in the cumulative frequency 28 .

Therefore, 20-30 is the median class.

So, we have, $l = 20$, $cf = 13$, $f = 15$, $h = 10$ and $N = 50$

Now, median, $M = l + \dfrac{\frac{N}{2} - cf}{f} \times h$

$= 20 + \dfrac{25-13}{15} \times 10$

$= 20 + 8 = 28$

Hence, the mean deviation about median is given by

$$\text{MD}(M) = \frac{1}{N} \sum_{i=1}^{6} f_i |x_i - M|$$

$$= \frac{1}{50} \times 508 = 10.16$$

Hence, the mean deviation about median is 10.16.

EXAMPLE 12. Calculate the mean deviation about median for the age distribution of 100 persons given below. **[NCERT]**

Age	16-20	21-25	26-30	31-35	36-40	41-45	46-50	51-55
Number	5	6	12	14	26	12	16	9

Sol. Let us make the following table from the given data.

Class	Mid-value (x_i)	f_i	cf	$\lvert x_i - M\rvert$	$f_i \lvert x_i - M\rvert$
15.5-20.5	18	5	5	$\lvert 18-38\rvert = 20$	100
20.5-25.5	23	6	11	$\lvert 23-38\rvert = 15$	90
25.5-30.5	28	12	23	$\lvert 28-38\rvert = 10$	120
30.5-35.5	33	14	37	$\lvert 33-38\rvert = 5$	70
35.5-40.5	38	26	63	$\lvert 38-38\rvert = 0$	0
40.5-45.5	43	12	75	$\lvert 43-38\rvert = 5$	60
45.5-50.5	48	16	91	$\lvert 48-38\rvert = 10$	160
50.5-55.5	53	9	100	$\lvert 53-38\rvert = 15$	135
Total		$N = 100$			735

Here, $\dfrac{N}{2} = 50$

So, the median class is 35.5-40.5.

$\therefore$ $l = 35.5$, $cf = 37$, $f = 26$ and $h = 5$

Now, median $(M) = l + \dfrac{\frac{N}{2} - cf}{f} \times h = 35.5 + \dfrac{50-37}{26} \times 5$

$= 35.5 + \dfrac{13}{26} \times 5 = 35.5 + 2.5 = 38$

and mean deviation about the median

$= \dfrac{\Sigma f_i |x_i - M|}{\Sigma f_i} = \dfrac{735}{100} = 7.35$

Hence, the mean deviation about median is 7.35.

Shortcut Method for Calculating the Mean Deviation about Mean

Sometimes, the data is too large and then the calculation by the previous method is tedious. So, we apply the step deviation method.

In this method, we take an assumed mean, which is in the middle or just close to it, in the data. The process of taking step deviation is to change of scale on the number line as shown in the figure given below

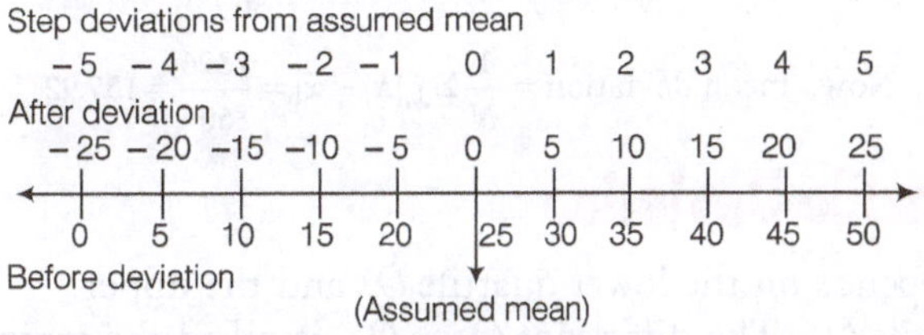

For step deviation method, we denote the new variable by u_i and it is defined as $u_i = \dfrac{x_i - a}{h}$

where, a is the assumed mean and h is the common factor or length of the class interval.

The mean $\bar{x}$ by step deviation method is given by

$$\bar{x} = a + \frac{\sum_{i=1}^{n} f_i u_i}{N} \times h$$

EXAMPLE 13. Find the mean deviation from the mean of the following data by shortcut or step deviation method.

Class	Frequency
0-100	4
100-200	8
200-300	9
300-400	10
400-500	7
500-600	5
600-700	4
700-800	3

Sol. Let us make the following table for step deviation and product of frequency with absolute deviation.

Class	Mid-points (x_i)	Frequency (f_i)	$u_i = \frac{x_i - 450}{100}$ $(a = 450, n = 100)$	$f_i u_i$	$\lvert x_i - \bar{x}\rvert = \lvert x_i - 358\rvert$	$f_i \lvert x_i - \bar{x}\rvert$
0-100	50	4	−4	−16	308	1232
100-200	150	8	−3	−24	208	1664
200-300	250	9	−2	−18	108	972
300-400	350	10	−1	−10	8	80
400-500	450	7	0	0	92	644
500-600	550	5	1	5	192	960
600-700	650	4	2	8	292	1168
700-800	750	3	3	9	392	1176
Total		$N = \Sigma f_i = 50$		−46		7896

Here, $a = 450$, $\Sigma f u_i = -46$ and $h = 100$

$$\therefore \quad \bar{x} = a + h\left(\frac{1}{N}\Sigma f u_i\right) = 450 + 100 \times \left(-\frac{46}{50}\right) = 358$$

$$\text{Now, mean deviation} = \frac{1}{N}\Sigma f_i \lvert x_i - \bar{x}\rvert = \frac{7896}{50} = 157.92$$

Quartile Deviation

It depends on the lower quartile Q_1 and the upper quartile Q_3. The difference $Q_3 - Q_1$ is called the **inter quartile range.** The difference $Q_3 - Q_1$ divided by 2 is called the quartile deviation or semi-inter quartile range.

$$\text{Quartile deviation} = \frac{Q_3 - Q_1}{2}$$

EXAMPLE 14. Find the quartile deviation for the following data.

12, 5, 7, 3, 1, 13, 17, 5, 19, 13, 1

Sol. Arrange the data in ascending order

1, 1, 3, 5, 5, 7, 12, 13, 13, 17, 19

Here, $N = 11$

$$Q_1 = \text{Size of} \left(\frac{N+1}{4}\right) \text{th observation}$$

$$= \text{Size of 3rd deviation}$$

$$= 3$$

$$Q_3 = \text{Size of } 3\left(\frac{N+1}{4}\right) \text{th observation}$$

$$= \text{Size of 9th observation}$$

$$= 13$$

$$\therefore \text{Quartile deviation} = \frac{Q_3 - Q_1}{2} = \frac{13 - 3}{2} = 5$$

EXAMPLE 15. Calculate the quartile deviation for the following distribution.

Class interval	Frequency
0-10	5
10-20	3
20-30	4
30-40	3
40-50	3
50-60	4
60-70	7
70-80	9
80-90	7
90-100	8

Sol.

Class interval	Frequency	Cumulative Frequency
0-10	5	5
10-20	3	5 + 3 = 8
20-30	4	8 + 4 = 12
30-40	3	12 + 3 = 15
40-50	3	15 + 3 = 18
50-60	4	18 + 4 = 22
60-70	7	22 + 7 = 29
70-80	9	29 + 9 = 38
80-90	7	38 + 7 = 45
90-100	8	45 + 8 = 53

Here, $N = 53$

We know that

$$Q_r = l_1 + \frac{r\left(\frac{N}{4}\right) - c}{f}(l_2 - l_1)$$

$$r = 1, \frac{N}{4} = \frac{53}{4} = 13.25$$

Here, Q_1 lies in the interval 30-40.

Quartile class = 30 − 40

$$\therefore \quad Q_1 = 30 + \frac{(13.5 - 12)}{3} \times (40 - 30)$$

$$= 30 + \frac{1.25}{3} \times 10$$

$$= 30 + \frac{12.5}{3} = 30 + 4.167 = 34.167$$

$$r = 3, \frac{3N}{4} = 3 \times 13.25 = 39.75$$

$\therefore$ Q_3 lies in the interval 80-90.

Quartile class = 80-90

$$\therefore \quad Q_3 = 80 + \frac{39.75 - 38}{7} \times (90 - 80)$$

$$= 80 + \frac{1.75}{7} \times 10 = 80 + \frac{17.5}{7} = 80 + 2.5 = 82.5$$

$\therefore$ The quartile deviation $= \frac{Q_3 - Q_1}{2}$

$$= \frac{82.5 - 34.167}{2}$$

$$= \frac{48.333}{2} = 24.1665$$

Topic Practice 1

1 Find the mean deviation from the mean for the following data
6, 5, 5.25, 5.5, 4.75, 4.5, 6.25, 7.75, 9.

2 The scores of a batsman in 10 innings are 48, 80, 58, 44, 52, 65, 73, 56, 64, 54. Find the mean deviation from the median.

3 Find the mean deviation from the mean for the following data.

x_i	10	30	50	70	90
f_i	4	24	28	16	8

4 Find the mean deviation about the median for the following data.

x_i	3	6	9	12	13	15	21	22
f_i	3	4	5	2	4	5	4	3

5 Find the mean deviation from the median for the following data. [NCERT]

x_i	15	21	27	30	35
f_i	3	5	6	7	8

6 Calculate the mean deviation from the mean of the following distribution.

Marks	0-10	10-20	20-30	30-40	40-50
Number of students	5	8	15	16	6

7 Find the mean deviation from the mean for the following data. [NCERT]

Class	0-10	10-20	20-30	30-40	40-50	50-60
Frequency	6	8	14	16	4	2

8 Calculate the mean deviation from the median for the following data.

Wages per day	20-30	30-40	40-50	50-60	60-70
Number of workers	3	8	12	9	8

9 Find the mean deviation from the mean for the following data by shortcut method.

Class	Frequency
10-20	8
20-30	10
30-40	15
40-50	25
50-60	20
60-70	18
70-80	9
80-90	5

10 If $\bar{x}$ is the mean and $(\bar{x})$ is mean deviation from mean, then find the number of observations lying between $\bar{x}$ − $(\bar{x})$ and $\bar{x}$ + $(\bar{x})$. Use the following data 22, 24, 30, 27, 29, 31, 25, 28, 41, 42.

11 Calculate quartile deviation for the following data: 30, 18, 23, 15, 11, 29, 37, 42, 10, 21.

12 Calculate quartile deviation form the following figures.

Size	0-5	5-10	10-15	15-20	20-25	25-30
Frequency	6	18	30	46	60	40

Hints & Solutions

1. Solve as Example 1. **Ans.** 1.1
2. Solve as Example 2. **Ans.** 8.6
3. Solve as Example 6. **Ans.** 16
4. Solve as Example 8. **Ans.** 4.97
5. 5.1
6. Solve as Example 9. **Ans.** 9.44
7. Solve as Example 9. **Ans.** 10.24
8. Solve as Example 12. **Ans.** 47.5
9. Solve as Example 13. **Ans.** 14.95
10. **Hint** On arranging the given data in ascending order, we have 22, 24, 25, 27, 28, 29, 30, 31, 41, 42.

$$\text{Now, mean } (\bar{x}) = \frac{22+24+25+27+28+29+30+31+41+42}{10}$$

$$= \frac{299}{10} = 29.9$$

and mean deviation from the mean, $MD(\bar{x}) = \frac{\sum_{i=1}^{n}|x_i - \bar{x}|}{n}$

$$= \frac{\left[\begin{array}{l}|22-29.9| + |24-29.9| + |25-29.9| + |27-29.9| \\ + |28-29.9| + |29-29.9| + |30-29.9| \\ + |31-29.9| + |41-29.9| + |42-29.9|\end{array}\right]}{10}$$

$$= \frac{7.9+5.9+4.9+2.9+1.9+0.9+0.1+1.1+11.1+12.1}{10}$$

$$= \frac{48.8}{10} = 4.88 = 4.9 \text{ (approx)}$$

$\therefore \quad \bar{x} - MD(\bar{x}) = 29.9 - 4.9 = 25$

and $\quad \bar{x} + MD(\bar{x}) = 29.9 + 4.9 = 34.8$

On examining the arranged data, we find that observations between 25 and 34.8 are 27, 28, 29, 30, 31. Hence, there are 5 observations lying between $\bar{x} - MD(\bar{x})$ and $\bar{x} + MD(\bar{x})$.

11. Given data in ascending order 10, 11, 15, 18, 21, 23, 29, 30, 37, 42.

Here, $N = 10$

$\therefore Q_1 = \text{Value of}\left(\frac{n+1}{4}\right)\text{th observation}$

$= 2.75\text{th observation}$

$= 11 + 0.75(15 - 11) = 14$

$Q_3 = \text{Value of } 3\left(\frac{n+1}{4}\right)\text{th observation}$

$= 8.25\text{th observation}$

$= 30 + 0.25(37 - 30) = 31.75$

$\therefore \text{Quartile deviation} = \frac{Q_3 - Q_1}{2} = \frac{31.75 - 14}{2}$

$= 8.875$

12. Solve as Example 15. **Ans.** 4.915

Variance and Standard Deviation

Variance

Mean of the squares of the deviations from the mean is called the variance, it is denoted by σ^2.

Standard Deviation

The positive square root of variance is called standard deviation and it is denoted by σ.

Variance and Standard Deviation of Ungrouped Data

Variance of n observations $x_1, x_2, x_3, \ldots x_n$ is given by

$$\sigma^2 = \frac{\sum_{i=1}^{n}(x_i - \bar{x})^2}{n} \text{ or } \frac{\sum_{i=1}^{n} x_i^2}{n} - \left(\frac{\sum_{i=1}^{n} x_i}{n}\right)^2$$

We know that standard deviation $= \sqrt{\text{Variance}}$

$$\therefore \quad \sigma = \sqrt{\frac{\sum_{i=1}^{n}(x_i - \bar{x})^2}{n}} \text{ or } \sqrt{\frac{\sum_{i=1}^{n} x_i^2}{n} - \left(\frac{\sum_{i=1}^{n} x_i}{n}\right)^2}$$

$$\text{or} \quad \frac{1}{n}\sqrt{n\sum_{i=1}^{n} x_i^2 - \left(\sum_{i=1}^{n} x_i\right)^2}$$

Method to Find Variance and Standard Deviation

To find the standard deviation or variance when deviations are taken from actual mean, we use the following steps

I. Calculate the mean $\bar{x}$ of the given observation $x_1, x_2, \ldots, x_n$.

II. Take the deviations of the observations from their mean i.e. find $x_i - \bar{x}; i = 1, 2, \ldots, n$.

III. Square the deviations obtained in Step II and then find the sum i.e. $\sum_{i=1}^{n}(x_i - \bar{x})^2$.

IV. Find the variance and standard deviation by using the formula, variance, $\sigma^2 = \dfrac{\sum_{i=1}^{n}(x_i - \bar{x})^2}{n}$

and standard deviation $= \sqrt{\sigma^2} = \sigma$

EXAMPLE 1. Find the mean, variance and standard deviation for the following data, 6, 7, 10, 12, 13, 4, 8, 12.

Sol. Given, observations are 6, 7, 10, 12, 13, 4, 8, 12.

Number of observations = 8

$$\therefore \text{Mean}(\bar{x}) = \frac{6+7+10+12+13+4+8+12}{8}$$

$$= \frac{72}{8} = 9$$

Now, let us make the following table for deviation.

x_i	$x_i - \bar{x}$	$(x_i - \bar{x})^2$
6	$6-9=-3$	9
7	$7-9=-2$	4
10	$10-9=1$	1
12	$12-9=3$	9
13	$13-9=4$	16
4	$4-9=-5$	25
8	$8-9=-1$	1
12	$12-9=3$	9
Total		74

$\therefore$ Sum of squares of deviations, $\sum_{i=1}^{8}(x_i - \bar{x})^2 = 74$

Hence, variance, $\sigma^2 = \dfrac{\sum_{i=1}^{8}(x_i - \bar{x})^2}{n} = \dfrac{74}{8} = 9.25$

and standard deviation $= \sqrt{\sigma^2} = \sqrt{9.25} = 3.04$

EXAMPLE 2. Find the standard deviation and the variance of first n natural numbers.

Sol. The first n natural numbers are 1, 2, 3, …, n.

$$\because \text{Standard deviation, SD} = \sqrt{\frac{\sum_{i=1}^{n} x_i^2}{n} - \left(\frac{\sum_{i=1}^{n} x_i}{n}\right)^2}$$

$$\therefore \text{SD} = \sqrt{\frac{n(n+1)(2n+1)}{6n} - \left(\frac{n(n+1)}{2n}\right)^2}$$

$$\left[\because \sum_{i=1}^{n} x_i^2 = \frac{n(n+1)(2n+1)}{6} \text{ and } \sum_{i=1}^{n} x_i = \frac{n(n+1)}{2}\right]$$

$$= \sqrt{(n+1)\left(\frac{2n+1}{6} - \frac{n+1}{4}\right)}$$

$$= \sqrt{(n+1)\left(\frac{4n+2-3n-3}{12}\right)}$$

$$= \sqrt{\frac{(n+1)(n-1)}{12}}$$

$$= \sqrt{\frac{n^2-1}{12}}$$

$$\therefore \text{Variance} = (\text{SD})^2 = \frac{n^2-1}{12}$$

Variance and Standard Deviation of a Discrete Frequency Distribution

Let the discrete frequency distribution be

$x : x_1, x_2, x_3, \ldots, x_n$ and $f : f_1, f_2, f_3, \ldots, f_n$.

Then, by

Direct Method

$$\text{Variance } (\sigma^2) = \frac{1}{N}\sum_{i=1}^{n} f_i(x_i - \bar{x})^2$$

or $$\sigma^2 = \frac{1}{N}\Sigma f_i x_i^2 - \left(\frac{\Sigma f_i x_i}{N}\right)^2$$

and standard deviation,

$$\sigma = \sqrt{\frac{1}{N}\sum_{i=1}^{n} f_i(x_i - \bar{x})^2}$$

or $$\sigma = \frac{1}{N}\sqrt{N\Sigma f_i x_i^2 - (\Sigma f_i x_i)^2}$$

where, $N = \sum_{i=1}^{n} f_i$

Shortcut Method

$$\text{Variance, } \sigma^2 = \frac{1}{N}\sum_{i=1}^{n} f_i d_i^2 - \left(\frac{\Sigma f_i d_i}{N}\right)^2$$

and standard deviation,

$$\sigma = \sqrt{\frac{1}{N}\sum_{i=1}^{n} f_i d_i^2 - \left(\frac{\Sigma f_i d_i}{N}\right)^2}$$

where, $d_i = x_i - a$, deviation from assumed mean and a = assumed mean

EXAMPLE 3. Find the variance and standard deviation of the following data. [NCERT]

x_i	4	8	11	17	20	24	32
f_i	3	5	9	5	4	3	1

Sol. Let us make the following table from the given data.

x_i	f_i	$f_i x_i$	$x_i - \bar{x} = x_i - 14$	$(x_i - \bar{x})^2$	$f_i(x_i - \bar{x})^2$
4	3	12	−10	100	300
8	5	40	−6	36	180
11	9	99	−3	9	81
17	5	85	3	9	45
20	4	80	6	36	144
24	3	72	10	100	300
32	1	32	18	324	324
Total	30	420			1374

Here, we have, $N = \Sigma f_i = 30, \Sigma f_i x_i = 420$

$$\therefore \quad \bar{x} = \frac{\sum_{i=1}^{7} f_i x_i}{N} = \frac{420}{30} = 14$$

Hence, variance $(\sigma^2) = \frac{1}{N} \sum_{i=1}^{7} f_i (x_i - \bar{x})^2$

$$\left[\because \sigma^2 = \frac{1}{N}\left\{\sum_{i=1}^{n} f_i(x_i - \bar{x})^2\right\}\right]$$

$$= \frac{1}{30} \times 1374 = 45.8$$

and standard deviation, $\sigma = \sqrt{\sigma^2} = \sqrt{45.8} = 6.77$

Alternate Method

Let us make the following table from the given data.

x_i	f_i	$f_i x_i$	x_i^2	$f_i x_i^2$
4	3	12	16	48
8	5	40	64	320
11	9	99	121	1089
17	5	85	289	1445
20	4	80	400	1600
24	3	72	576	1728
32	1	32	1024	1024
Total	30	420		7254

Here, $N = \sum_{i=1}^{7} f_i = 30, \sum_{i=1}^{7} f_i x_i = 420$ and $\sum_{i=1}^{7} f_i x_i^2 = 7254$

$$\therefore \text{ Variance, } \sigma^2 = \frac{1}{N}\sum_{i=1}^{7} f_i x_i^2 - \left(\frac{\sum_{i=1}^{7} f_i x_i}{N}\right)^2$$

$$= \frac{1}{30} \times 7254 - \left(\frac{420}{30}\right)^2 = \frac{7254}{30} - 196$$

$$= 241.8 - 196 = 45.8$$

and standard deviation, $\sigma = \sqrt{45.8} = 6.77$

EXAMPLE 4. Find the variance and standard deviation for the following distribution using shortcut method. **[NCERT]**

x_i	60	61	62	63	64	65	66	67	68
f_i	2	1	12	29	25	12	10	4	5

Sol. Let the assumed mean be $a = 64$

Now, let as make a table from the given data.

x_i	f_i	$d_i = x_i - 64$	$f_i d_i$	d_i^2	$f_i d_i^2$
60	2	$60 - 64 = -4$	−8	16	32
61	1	$61 - 64 = -3$	−3	9	9
62	12	$62 - 64 = -2$	−24	4	48
63	29	$63 - 64 = -1$	−29	1	29
64	25	$64 - 64 = 0$	0	0	0
65	12	$65 - 64 = 1$	12	1	12
66	10	$66 - 64 = 2$	20	4	40
67	4	$67 - 64 = 3$	12	9	36
68	5	$68 - 64 = 4$	20	16	80
Total	100		0	60	286

Here, $N = \Sigma f_i = 100, \Sigma f_i d_i = 0$ and $\Sigma f_i d_i^2 = 286$

Now, variance, $(\sigma^2) = \left[\frac{1}{N}\Sigma f_i d_i^2 - \left(\frac{1}{N}\Sigma f_i d_i\right)^2\right]$

$$= \frac{1}{100} \times 286 - \left(\frac{1}{100} \times 0\right)^2 = 2.86$$

and standard deviation, $\sigma = \sqrt{2.86} = 1.69$

Variance and Standard Deviation of a Continuous Frequency Distribution

Direct Method

In this method, we first replace each class by its mid-point, then this method becomes similar to the discrete frequency distribution. If there is a frequency distribution of n classes and each class defined by its mid-point x_i with corresponding frequency f_i, then variance and standard deviation are respectively,

$$\sigma^2 = \frac{1}{N}\sum_{i=1}^{n} f_i (x_i - \bar{x})^2 \text{ and } \sigma = \sqrt{\frac{1}{N}\sum_{i=1}^{n} f_i (x_i - \bar{x})^2}$$

or $\quad \sigma^2 = \frac{1}{N^2}[N \Sigma f_i x_i^2 - (\Sigma f_i x_i)^2]$

and $\quad \sigma = \frac{1}{N}\sqrt{N \Sigma f_i x_i^2 - (\Sigma f_i x_i)^2}$

EXAMPLE 5. Calculate the variance and standard deviation for the following distribution.

Class	30-40	40-50	50-60	60-70	70-80	80-90	90-100
Frequency	3	7	12	15	8	3	2

Sol. Let us construct the following table.

Class	Frequency (f_i)	Mid-point (x_i)	$f_i x_i$	$(x_i-\bar{x})^2$	$f_i(x_i-\bar{x})^2$
30-40	3	35	105	729	2187
40-50	7	45	315	289	2023
50-60	12	55	660	49	588
60-70	15	65	975	9	135
70-80	8	75	600	169	1352
80-90	3	85	255	529	1587
90-100	2	95	190	1089	2178
Total	50		3100		10050

Here, $N = 50$ and $\Sigma f_i x_i = 3100$

$\therefore$ Mean, $\bar{x} = \frac{1}{N}\Sigma f_i x_i = \frac{3100}{50} = 62$

Now, variance, $\sigma^2 = \frac{1}{N}\Sigma f_i(x_i - \bar{x})^2 = \frac{1}{50}\times 10050 = 201$

and standard deviation, $\sigma = \sqrt{201} = 14.18$

Shortcut Method Or Step-Deviation Method

Sometimes the values of mid-points x_i of different classes in a continuous distribution are large and so the calculation of mean and variance becomes tedious and time consuming. For this, we use the **step deviation method** to find mean and variance.

$$\text{Variance, } \sigma^2 = h^2\left[\frac{1}{N}\sum_{i=1}^{n} f_i u_i^2 - \left(\frac{\sum_{i=1}^{n} f_i u_i}{N}\right)^2\right]$$

and standard deviation,

$$\sigma = h\sqrt{\frac{1}{N}\sum_{i=1}^{n} f_i u_i^2 - \left(\frac{\sum_{i=1}^{n} f_i u_i}{N}\right)^2}$$

where, $u_i = \frac{x_i - a}{h}$, a = assumed mean

and h = width of class interval

Method to find Variance and Standard Deviation by Shortcut Method

To find variance and standard deviation, use the following steps

I. Select an assumed mean, say a and then calculate $u_i = \frac{x_i - a}{h}$, where h = width of class interval or common factor.

II. Multiply the frequency of each class with the corresponding u_i and obtain $\Sigma f_i u_i$.

III. Square the values of u_i and multiply them with the corresponding frequencies and obtain $\Sigma f_i u_i^2$.

IV. Substitute the values of $\Sigma f_i u_i$, $\Sigma f_i u_i^2$ and $\Sigma f_i = N$ in the formula,

$$\text{Variance } (\sigma^2) = h^2\left[\frac{1}{N}\Sigma f_i u_i^2 - \left(\frac{1}{N}\Sigma f_i u_i\right)^2\right]$$

and standard deviation $= \sqrt{\sigma^2}$ to get the required values.

EXAMPLE 6. The diameter of circles (in mm) drawn in a design are given below.

Diameter (in mm)	33-36	37-40	41-44	45-48	49-52
Number of circles	15	17	21	22	25

Calculate the standard deviation and mean diameter of circles. **[NCERT]**

Sol. Let us first make the data continuous by making classes as 32.5-36.5, 36.5-40.5, 40.5-44.5, 44.5-48.5, 48.5-52.5.

Let assumed mean is 42.5 and $h = 4$

Then, $u_i = \frac{x_i - a}{h} = \frac{x_i - 42.5}{4}$

Now, let us make the following table from the given data.

Class interval	Mid-value (x_i)	f_i	$u_i = \frac{x_i - 42.5}{4}$	$f_i u_i$	u_i^2	$f_i u_i^2$
32.5-36.5	34.5	15	−2	−30	4	60
36.5-40.5	38.5	17	−1	−17	1	17
40.5-44.5	42.5	21	0	0	0	0
44.5-48.5	46.5	22	1	22	1	22
48.5-52.5	50.5	25	2	50	4	100
Total		100		25		199

Now, mean $(\bar{x}) = a + \frac{\Sigma f_i u_i}{\Sigma f_i} \times h = 42.5 + 4 \times \frac{25}{100}$

[using step deviation method]

$= 42.5 + 1 = 43.5$

Standard deviation, $\sigma = \sqrt{h^2\left[\frac{1}{N}\Sigma f_i u_i^2 - \left(\frac{1}{N}\Sigma f_i u_i\right)^2\right]}$

[by shortcut method]

$= \sqrt{(4)^2\left[\frac{1}{100}\times 199 - \left(\frac{1}{100}\times 25\right)^2\right]}$

$= \sqrt{16\left(1.99 - \frac{1}{16}\right)} = \sqrt{16\left(\frac{31.84 - 1}{16}\right)}$

$= \sqrt{30.84} = 5.55$

Hence, the standard deviation and mean diameter of circles are 5.55 and 43.5.

EXAMPLE 7. Calculate the mean and standard deviation of the following cumulative data.

Wages (in ₹)	0-15	15-30	30-45	45-60	60-75	75-90	90-105	105-120
Number of workers	12	30	65	107	157	202	222	230

Sol. We are given the cumulative frequency distribution. So, first we will prepare the frequency distribution as given below

Class interval	cf	Mid-value (x_i)	f_i	$u_i = \frac{x_i - 67.5}{15}$	f_iu_i	$f_iu_i^2$
0-15	12	7.5	12	− 4	− 48	192
15-30	30	22.5	18	− 3	− 54	162
30-45	65	37.5	35	− 2	− 70	140
45-60	107	52.5	42	− 1	− 42	42
60-75	157	67.5	50	0	0	0
75-90	202	82.5	45	1	45	45
90-105	222	97.5	20	2	40	80
105-120	230	112.5	8	3	24	72
Total			230		− 105	733

Here, $a = 67.5, h = 15, N = \Sigma f_i = 230,$

$\Sigma f_iu_i = -105$ and $\Sigma f_iu_i^2 = 733$

Now, mean $= a + h\left(\frac{1}{N}\Sigma f_iu_i\right) = 67.5 + 15\left(\frac{-105}{230}\right)$

$= 67.5 - 6.85 = 60.65$

Standard deviation,

$$\sigma = \sqrt{h^2\left[\frac{1}{N}\Sigma f_iu_i^2 - \left(\frac{1}{N}\Sigma f_iu_i\right)^2\right]}$$

$$= \sqrt{225\left[\frac{733}{230} - \left(-\frac{105}{230}\right)^2\right]} = \sqrt{225\,[3.187 - (0.46)^2]}$$

$$= \sqrt{225\,(3.1870 - 0.2116)} = \sqrt{669.465} = 25.87$$

EXAMPLE 8. If each of the observation $x_1, x_2, \ldots, x_n$ is increased by a, where a is a negative or positive number, then show that the variance remains unchanged. **[NCERT]**

Sol. Let $\bar{x}$ be the mean of $x_1, x_2, \ldots, x_n$.

Then, the variance is given by $\sigma_1^2 = \frac{1}{n}\sum_{i=1}^{n}(x_i - \bar{x})^2$ ...(i)

If a is added to each observation, then the new observation will be $y_i = x_i + a$ ...(ii)

Let the mean of the new observation be $\bar{y}$. Then,

$$\bar{y} = \frac{1}{n}\sum_{i=1}^{n} y_i = \frac{1}{n}\sum_{i=1}^{n}(x_i + a) = \frac{1}{n}\left[\sum_{i=1}^{n} x_i + \sum_{i=1}^{n} a\right]$$

$$= \frac{1}{n}\left[\sum_{i=1}^{n} x_i + na\right] = \bar{x} + a \text{ i.e. } \bar{y} = \bar{x} + a \quad ...(iii)$$

Now, new variance, σ_2^2 is given by

$$\sigma_2^2 = \frac{1}{n}\sum_{i=1}^{n}(y_i - \bar{y})^2 = \frac{1}{n}\sum_{i=1}^{n}(x_i + a - \bar{x} - a)^2$$

[using Eqs. (ii) and (iii)]

$$= \frac{1}{n}\sum_{i=1}^{n}(x_i - \bar{x})^2 = \sigma_1^2$$

Hence, the variance remains unchanged.

EXAMPLE 9. Given $\bar{x}$ is the mean and σ^2 is variance of n observations $x_1, x_2, \ldots, x_n$. Prove that the mean and variance of the observations $ax_1, ax_2, ax_3, \ldots, ax_n$ are $a\bar{x}$ and $a^2\sigma^2$, respectively, $(a \neq 0)$. **[NCERT]**

Sol. Mean of $ax_1, ax_2, \ldots, ax_n = \frac{ax_1 + ax_2 + \ldots + ax_n}{n}$

$$= a\left(\frac{x_1 + x_2 + x_3 + \ldots + x_n}{n}\right)$$

$$= a\bar{x} \quad \left[\because \bar{x} = \frac{x_1 + x_2 + \ldots + x_n}{n}\right]$$

Variance of $ax_1, ax_2, \ldots, ax_n$

$$= \frac{\Sigma(ax_i - a\bar{x})^2}{n}$$

$$= \frac{(ax_1 - a\bar{x})^2 + (ax_2 - a\bar{x})^2 + \ldots + (ax_n - a\bar{x})^2}{n}$$

$$= \frac{a^2[(x_1 - \bar{x})^2 + (x_2 - \bar{x})^2 + \ldots + (x_n - \bar{x})^2]}{n}$$

$$= a^2\frac{\Sigma(x_i - \bar{x})^2}{n} = a^2\sigma^2 \quad \left[\because \sigma^2 = \frac{\Sigma(x_i - \bar{x})^2}{n}\right]$$

Hence proved.

EXAMPLE 10. The mean and variance of 7 observations are 8 and 16, respectively. If five of them are 2, 4, 10, 12, 14. Find the remaining two observations. **[NCERT]**

Sol. Let the remaining two observations be a and b.

Given, $\bar{x} = 8$ and $\sigma^2 = 16$

$$\because \frac{\text{Sum of all observations}}{\text{Number of observations}} = 8$$

$$\Rightarrow \frac{2 + 4 + 10 + 12 + 14 + a + b}{7} = 8$$

$$\Rightarrow 42 + a + b = 56 \Rightarrow a + b = 14 \quad ...(i)$$

Again, $\sigma^2 = \frac{\Sigma x_i^2}{n} - \left(\frac{\Sigma x_i}{n}\right)^2 \Rightarrow \sigma^2 = \frac{\Sigma x_i^2}{n} - (\bar{x})^2$

$$\Rightarrow 16 = \frac{4 + 16 + 100 + 144 + 196 + a^2 + b^2}{n} - (8)^2$$

$$\Rightarrow 16 + 64 = \frac{460 + a^2 + b^2}{7}$$

$$\Rightarrow 7 \times (80) = 460 + a^2 + b^2 \Rightarrow a^2 + b^2 = 560 - 460$$

$$\Rightarrow a^2 + b^2 = 100 \quad ...(ii)$$

Now, from Eq. (i), putting $b = 14 - a$ in Eq. (ii),

$$a^2 + (14 - a)^2 = 100$$

$$\Rightarrow \quad a^2 + 196 + a^2 - 28a = 100$$

$$\Rightarrow \quad 2a^2 - 28a + 196 - 100 = 0$$

$$\Rightarrow \quad 2a^2 - 28a + 96 = 0$$

$$\Rightarrow \quad a^2 - 14a + 48 = 0$$

$$\Rightarrow \quad a^2 - 8a - 6a + 48 = 0$$

$$\Rightarrow \quad a(a-8) - 6(a-8) = 0$$

$$\Rightarrow \quad (a-6)(a-8) = 0$$

$$\Rightarrow \quad a = 6 \text{ or } 8$$

From Eq. (i), $b = 8$ or 6

Hence, the observations are 6, 8.

EXAMPLE 11. For a group of 200 candidates, the mean and standard deviation were found to be 40 and 15, respectively. Later on it was found that the score 43 was misread as 34. Find the correct mean and correct standard deviation.

Sol. We have, $n = 200$, $\bar{x} = 40$, $\sigma = 15$

$$\therefore \bar{x} = \frac{1}{n}\sum x_i \Rightarrow \sum x_i = n\bar{x} = 200 \times 40 = 8000$$

Now, corrected $\sum x_i$ = Incorrect $\sum x_i$

− (Sum of incorrect values)

+ (Sum of correct values)

$$= 8000 - 34 + 43 = 8009$$

$$\therefore \quad \text{Corrected mean} = \frac{\text{Corrected} \sum x_i}{n} = \frac{8009}{200} = 40.045$$

Again, $\sigma = 15 \Rightarrow \sigma^2 = 15^2$

$$\Rightarrow \quad \frac{1}{200}\sum x_i^2 - \left(\frac{\sum x_i}{200}\right)^2 = 225$$

$$\Rightarrow \quad \frac{\sum x_i^2}{200} - \left(\frac{8000}{200}\right)^2 = 225$$

$$\Rightarrow \quad \frac{\sum x_i^2}{200} - 1600 = 225$$

$$\Rightarrow \quad \frac{\sum x_i^2}{200} = 1825$$

$$\Rightarrow \quad \sum x_i^2 = 1825 \times 200 = 365000$$

$$\Rightarrow \quad \text{Incorrect} \sum x_i^2 = 365000$$

$\therefore$ Corrected $\sum x_i^2$ = (Incorrect $\sum x_i^2$)

− (Sum of squares of incorrect values)

+ (Sum of squares of correct values)

$$\Rightarrow \text{Corrected} \sum x_i^2 = 365000 - (34)^2 + (43)^2$$

$$= 365693$$

$$\text{So, corrected } \sigma = \sqrt{\frac{1}{n}\text{correct}\sum x_i^2 - \left(\frac{\text{Corrected}\sum x_i}{n}\right)^2}$$

$$= \sqrt{\frac{365693}{200} - \left(\frac{8009}{200}\right)^2}$$

$$= \sqrt{1828.465 - 1603.602} = 14.995$$

Topic Practice 2

1 The marks obtained by 7 students are 8, 9, 11, 13, 14, 15, 21. Find the mean, variance and standard deviation of these marks.

2 Find the standard deviation of first 10 natural numbers.

3 The mean of 100 observations is 50 and their standard deviation is 5. Find the sum of squares of all the observations. [NCERT Exemplar]

4 The following relates to a sample of size 60, $\Sigma x^2 = 18000$ and $\Sigma x = 960$, find the variance.

5 Find the standard deviation and variance of the following data.

x_i	140	145	150	155	160	165	170	175
f_i	4	6	15	30	36	24	8	2

6 Find the mean, variance and standard deviation for the following.

x_i	4	8	11	17	20	24	32
f_i	3	5	9	5	4	3	1

[NCERT]

7 Calculate the mean and variance for the following data.

Class	Frequency
0-30	2
30-60	3
60-90	5
90-120	10
120-150	3
150-180	5
180-210	2

8 Calculate the mean, variance and standard deviation for the following distribution.

Class	0-5	5-10	10-15	15-20	20-25	25-30	30-35	35-40	40-45
Frequency	20	24	32	28	20	11	26	15	24

9 The mean and variance of 15 observations are 3.8 and 4, respectively. If each observation is increased by 11, then find the mean and variance of the resulting observation.

10 The mean and standard deviation of 6 observations are 8 and 4 respectively. If each observation is multiplied by 3, then find the new mean and new standard deviation of the resulting observations.

11 The mean and standard deviation of 20 observations are found to be 10 and 2, respectively. On rechecking, it was found that an observation 8 was incorrect. Calculate the correct mean and standard deviation in each of the following cases:

(i) If wrong item is omitted.
(ii) If it is replaced by 12.

12 The frequency distribution

x_i	A	$2A$	$3A$	$4A$	$5A$	$6A$
f_i	2	1	1	1	1	1

where, A is a positive integer, has a variance of 160. Determine the value of A.

13 The runs of two players for 10 innings each are as follows.

A	58	59	60	54	65	66	52	75	69	52
B	94	26	92	65	96	78	14	34	98	13

Who may be regarded as more consistent player?

14 The mean and variance of eight observations are 9 and 9.25, respectively. If six of the observations are 6, 7, 10, 12, 12 and 13, then find the remaining two observations. **[NCERT]**

Hints & Solutions

1. Solve as Example 1.
   Ans. Variance = 16.29, Standard deviation = 4.04, Mean = 13
2. Solve as Example 2. **Ans.** 2.87
3. **Hint** Given, $\bar{x} = 50$, $n = 100$ and $\sigma = 5$

We know that $\sigma^2 = \dfrac{\Sigma x_i^2}{n} - (\bar{x})^2$

$\Rightarrow \quad \dfrac{\Sigma x_i^2}{n} = \sigma^2 + (\bar{x})^2$

$\Rightarrow \quad \Sigma x_i^2 = n[\sigma^2 + (\bar{x})^2] = 100\,[5^2 + (50)^2]$

$= 100\,(25 + 2500) = 252500$

Hence, the sum of squares of all the observations is 252500.

4. **Hint** Use, $\sigma^2 = \dfrac{\Sigma x_i^2}{n} - \left(\dfrac{\Sigma x_i}{n}\right)^2$ **Ans.** 44
5. Solve as Example 3.
   Ans. Variance = 52.7136,
   Standard deviation = 7.26 (approx)
6. Solve as Example 3. **Ans.** 14, 45.80, 6.77
7. Solve as Example 5.
   Ans. Mean = 107, Variance = 2276
8. Solve as Example 5. **Ans.** 21.5, 164.75, 12.835
9. Solve as Example 8. **Ans.** 14.8, 4
10. Solve as Example 9. **Ans.** 24, 36
11. Solve as Example 11. **Ans.** (i) 10.1, 2.02 (ii) 10.2, 1.98
12. **Hint** Let us make the following table from the given data.

x_i	f_i	$f_i x_i$	$(x_i - \bar{x})^2 = \left(x_i - \frac{22}{7}A\right)^2$	$(x_i - \bar{x})^2 f_i$
A	2	$2A$	$(225/49)A^2$	$(450/49)A^2$
$2A$	1	$2A$	$(64/49)A^2$	$(64/49)A^2$
$3A$	1	$3A$	$(1/49)A^2$	$(1/49)A^2$
$4A$	1	$4A$	$(36/49)A^2$	$(36/49)A^2$
$5A$	1	$5A$	$(169/49)A^2$	$(169/49)A^2$
$6A$	1	$6A$	$(400/49)A^2$	$(400/49)A^2$
	$N = \Sigma f_i = 7$	$\Sigma f_i x_i = 22A$		$\Sigma f_i(x_i - \bar{x})^2 = \frac{1120}{49}A^2$

Hence, $N = \Sigma f_i = 7$ and $\Sigma f_i x_i = 22A$

$\therefore \quad \bar{x} = \dfrac{\sum_{i=1}^{6} f_i x_i}{N} = \dfrac{22A}{7}$

Now, variance $= \dfrac{1}{N}\sum_{i=1}^{6} f_i (x_i - \bar{x})^2$

$\Rightarrow \quad 160 = \dfrac{1}{7}\left(\dfrac{1120}{49}\right)A^2$ [$\because$ variance = 60, given]

Ans. $A = 7$

13. Hint Let us make the table from the given data.

Player *A*			Player *B*		
x_i	$x_i - 61$	$(x_i - 61)^2$	y_i	$y_i - 61$	$(y_i - 61)^2$
58	−3	9	94	33	1089
59	−2	4	26	−35	1225
60	−1	1	92	31	961
54	−7	49	65	4	16
65	4	16	96	35	1225
66	5	25	78	17	289
52	−9	81	14	−47	2209
75	14	196	34	−27	729
69	8	64	98	37	1369
52	−9	81	13	−48	2304
$\Sigma x_i = 610$		$\Sigma (x_i - 61)^2 = 526$	$\Sigma y_i = 610$		$\Sigma (y_i - 61)^2 = 11416$

For Player *A* Mean $= \dfrac{\Sigma x_i}{n} = \dfrac{610}{10} = 61$

$$SD = \sqrt{\frac{\Sigma (x_i - 61)^2}{N}} = \sqrt{\frac{526}{10}} = 7.25$$

For Player *B* Mean $= \dfrac{\Sigma y_i}{n} = \dfrac{610}{10} = 61$

$$SD = \sqrt{\frac{\Sigma (y_i - 61)^2}{N}} = \sqrt{\frac{11416}{10}} = 33.79$$

Since, SD for player *A* is 7.25 < SD for player *B* is 33.79.

Hence, player *A* is more consistent player.

14. Hint Let the remaining two observations be *a* and *b*.

Given, $\bar{x} = 9$ and $\sigma^2 = 9.25 \quad \because \bar{x} = 9$

$$\Rightarrow \frac{\text{Sum of all observations}}{\text{Number of observations}} = 9$$

$$\Rightarrow \text{Sum of all observations} = 9 \times 8$$

$$\Rightarrow 6 + 7 + 10 + 12 + 12 + 13 + a + b = 72$$

$$\Rightarrow a + b = 12 \quad \text{...(i)}$$

Again, $\sigma^2 = \dfrac{\Sigma x_i^2}{n} - \left(\dfrac{\Sigma x_i}{n}\right)^2 \Rightarrow \sigma^2 = \dfrac{\Sigma x_i^2}{n} - (\bar{x})^2$

$$\Rightarrow 9.25 = \frac{36 + 49 + 100 + 144 + 144 + 169 + a^2 + b^2}{8} - (9)^2$$

$$\Rightarrow a^2 + b^2 = 80 \quad \text{...(ii)}$$

Now, from Eq. (i), put $b = (12 - a)$ in Eq. (ii), we get

$$a^2 + (12 - a)^2 = 80 \Rightarrow a = 4 \text{ or } a = 8$$

On putting $a = 4$ or $a = 8$ in Eq. (i), we get $b = 8$ or $b = 4$

Hence, the two observations are 4 and 8.

Percentile Rank and Correlation

Percentile

Percentile rank is used to compare a specific score to other score in a group of scores. In statistics percentile rank refers to the percentage of scores that are equal to or less than a given score like percentage, it is fall on a continuum from 0 to 100. It is denoted by P_R, P_R of 60 marks is 70, means that 70% of total students who appeared in exam had scored 60 marks or less than 60 marks.

Percentile Rank for Ungrouped Data

Let $x_1, x_2, x_3, \ldots x_n$ be *n* observations. Here, firstly arrange these observations in ascending order. Then, for calculating the percentile rank of observation x_i, we use the formula

$$P_R = \frac{L + 0.5 \times E}{n} \times 100,$$

where L = number of observations (scores) less than x_i

E = number of observations (scores) equal to x_i

n = total number of observations (scores)

EXAMPLE 1. The test score of 10 students are given below 15, 35, 43, 75, 54, 76, 76, 62, 92, 84.

Find the percentile rank of score 76.

Sol. Marks in ascending order

15, 35, 43, 54, 62, 75, 76, 76, 84, 92

Here, $n = 10$

For score 76, $L = 6$ and $E = 2$

$$\therefore \text{Percentile Rank } P_R = \frac{L + 0.5 \times E}{n} \times 100$$

$$= \frac{6 + 0.5 \times 2}{10} \times 100$$

$$= \frac{6 + 1.0}{10} \times 100 = 7 \times 10 = 70$$

Correlation

Correlation studies and measures the direction and intensities of relationship between two variables in which change in the value of one variable, are associated with changes in the value of the other variable. e.g. As the summer heat rises, ice-cream sales become more brisk. Thus, the temperature is related to sale of ice-creams.

Types of Correlation

(i) **Positive Correlation** When two related variables move together in the same direction, it is said to be positive correlation.

(ii) **Negative Correlation** When two variables move in the opposite direction, it is said to be negative correlation.

Scatter Diagram

It is a technique for visually examining the form of relationship, without calculating any numerical value. To construct a scatter diagram, x variable is taken on X-axis and y variable is taken on Y-axis. The cluster of points, plotted is referred to as a scatter diagram.

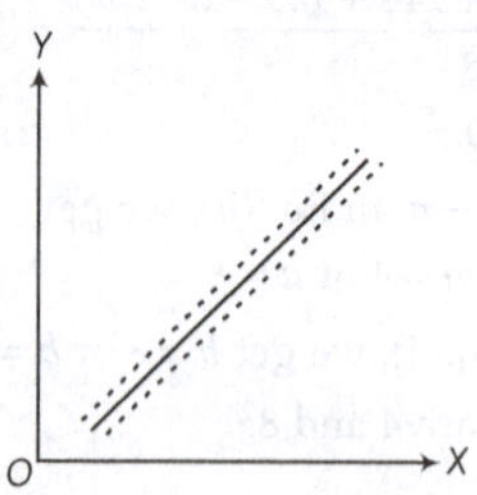

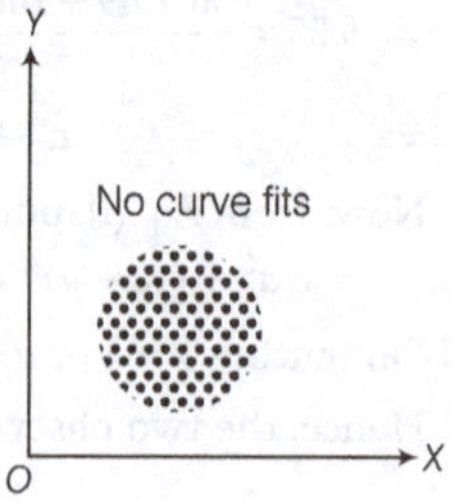

Covariance of *X* and *Y*

The mean of the product of deviation $(x_i - \bar{x})$ and $(y_i - \bar{y})$ is called covariance of X and Y. It is denoted by the symbol Cov (X, Y).

i.e. $$\text{Cov}(X, Y) = \frac{\Sigma(x - \bar{x})(y - \bar{y})}{n}$$

$$= \frac{1}{n}\left[\Sigma xy - \frac{1}{n}\Sigma x \Sigma y\right],$$

where n is a number of order pair.

Properties of Correlation Coefficient

(i) Correlation coefficient r has no unit and it is a pure number. It means unit of measurement is not a part of r.

(ii) A negative value of r indicates an inverse relation.

(iii) If r is positive, the two variables move in the same direction.

(iv) The value of the correlation coefficient lies from minus one to plus one i.e. $-1 \le r \le 1$. If the value of r lies outside this range, it indicates that there is some error in calculation.

(v) If $r = 0$, then the two variables are not correlated (uncorrelated) and there is no linear relation between them.

(vi) If $r = 1$ or $r = -1$, then the correlation is perfect.

(vii) A high value of r i.e. $+1$ or -1 indicates strong linear relationship.

(viii) A low value of r indicates a weak linear relationship.

(ix) The value of r is unaffected by the change of origin and change of scale.

(x) Correlation is said to be of high degree, if $\frac{3}{4} \le |r| \le 1$, of moderate degree, if $\frac{1}{4} \le |r| \le \frac{3}{4}$ and of low degree, if $0 \le |r| < \frac{1}{4}$.

Spearman's Rank Correlation

This method is used when it is difficult to measure numerical values to a quality e.g. Honesty, beauty, intelligence etc. The **Edward Spearman's coefficient** of rank correlation is given by

(i) **When ranks are not repeated**

$$R = 1 - \frac{6\Sigma d^2}{n(n^2 - 1)},$$

where, d = Difference between ranks of corresponding x and y.

n = Number of pairs of values (x, y).

(ii) **When ranks are repeated** If n ranks are repeated $m_1, m_2, \ldots, m_n$ times, then rank correlation is given by

$$R = 1 - 6\,\frac{\left[\Sigma d^2 + \frac{1}{12}(m_1^3 - m_1) + \frac{1}{12}(m_2^3 - m_2) + \cdots + \frac{1}{12}(m_n^3 - m_n)\right]}{n(n^2 - 1)}$$

EXAMPLE 2. Calculated Spearman's rank correlation coefficient between the advertisement cost and sales from the following data.

Advertisement cost (in ₹ thousand)	39	65	62	90	82	75	25	98	36	78
Sales (in ₹ lakh)	47	53	58	86	62	68	60	91	51	84

Sol. To make a rank correlation table which in given below

Adventise ment cost	Sales (in lakh)	R_1	R_2	$d = R_1 - R_2$	d^2
39	47	8	10	− 2	4
65	53	6	8	− 2	4
62	58	7	7	0	0
90	86	2	2	0	0
82	62	3	5	−2	4
75	68	5	4	1	1
25	60	10	6	4	16
98	91	1	1	0	0
36	51	9	9	0	0
78	84	4	3	1	1
Total					$\Sigma d^2 = 30$

We know that Spearman's rank correlation coefficient,

$$R = 1 - \frac{6\,\Sigma d^2}{n(n^2-1)}$$

$$= 1 - \frac{6 \times 30}{10[(10)^2 - 1)]} \quad [n = 10]$$

$$= 1 - \frac{6 \times 30}{10 \times 99} = 1 - \frac{180}{990} = 1 - 0.181 = 0.819$$

EXAMPLE 3. Ten candidates received percentage marks in two subjects as follows

Candidate	A	B	C	D	E	F	G	H	I	J
Mathematics marks	80	88	76	74	68	65	40	43	40	80
Statistics marks	72	84	90	66	54	50	54	38	30	43

Calculate Spearman's rank correlation coefficient and interpret your result.

Note Coefficient of correlation is independent of change of origin and scale.

Sol. Let x = Marks in Mathematics

y = Marks is Statistics

R_1 = Rank in Mathematics

R_2 = Rank in Statistics

To make a rank correlation table which is given below

Candidate	x	y	R_1	R_2	$d = R_1 - R_2$	d^2
A	80	72	2.5	3	− 0.5	0.25
B	88	84	1	2	−1	1
C	76	90	4	1	3	9
D	74	66	5	4	1	1
E	68	54	6	5.5	0.5	0.25
F	65	50	7	7	0	0
G	40	54	8.5	5.5	3	9
H	43	38	8	9	−1	1
I	40	30	8.5	10	− 1.5	2.25
J	80	43	2.5	8	− 5.5	30.25
Total						$\Sigma d^2 = 54$

We know that

Spearman's rank correlation coefficient

$$R = 1 - \frac{6\left[\Sigma d^2 + \frac{1}{12}(m_1^3 - m_1) + \frac{1}{12}(m_2^3 - m_2) + \frac{1}{12}(m_3^3 - m_3)\right]}{n(n^2-1)}$$

$$= 1 - \frac{6\left[54 + \frac{1}{12}(2^3 - 2) + \frac{1}{12}(2^3 - 2) + \frac{1}{12}(2^3 - 2)\right]}{10(10^2 - 1)}$$

$$= 1 - \frac{6\left(54 + \frac{1}{12} \times 6 + \frac{1}{12} \times 6 + \frac{1}{12} \times 6\right)}{10(100 - 1)}$$

$$= \frac{1 - 6\left(54 + \frac{1}{2} + \frac{1}{2} + \frac{1}{2}\right)}{10 \times 99}$$

$$= 1 - \frac{6\left(54 + \frac{3}{2}\right)}{10 \times 99}$$

$$= 1 - \frac{6 \times (54 + 1.5)}{990}$$

$$= 1 - \frac{6 \times 55.5}{990} = 1 - \frac{333}{990}$$

$$= \frac{990 - 333}{990} = \frac{657}{990} = 0.66 \text{ (approx.)}$$

Hence, increases in marks in Statistics shows increases in marks in Mathematics.

Topic Practice 3

1 An examination of 8 applicants for a clerical post was taken by a firm. The marks obtained by the applicants in the reasoning and aptitude tests are given below

Applicant	*A*	*B*	*C*	*D*	*E*	*F*	*G*	*H*
Reasoning test	20	28	15	60	40	80	20	12
Aptitude test	30	50	40	20	10	60	30	30

Calculate the Spearman's coefficient of rank correlation from the data given above.

2 Internal and external assessments were conducted on a group of 10 students who were studying in a postgraduate class in a college. The following marks were obtained in the assessments

Roll number of students	1	2	3	4	5	6	7	8	9	10
Internal assessment	45	62	67	32	12	38	47	68	42	85
External assessment	39	48	65	32	20	35	45	77	30	62

Find the Spearman's Rank correlation coefficient and comment on the result.

3 The Mathematical Aptitude Score (MAS) of ten computer programmers with Job Programmers Rating (JPR) is given below, calculate Spearman's rank correlation coefficient whether these who have aptitude for Maths are likely to be better programmers.

Person	*A*	*B*	*C*	*D*	*E*	*F*	*G*	*H*	*I*	*J*
MAS	2	5	0	4	3	1	6	8	7	9
JPR	8	16	8	9	5	4	3	17	8	12

4 The test scores of 10 students are given below:
13, 52, 42, 22, 44, 105, 45, 88, 88, 76
Find the percentile rank of score 88.

5 From the following information of wages of 30 workers in a factory calculate 40th percentile.

S. No.	Wages (₹)	S. No.	Wages (₹)
1	330	16	240
2	320	17	330
3	550	18	420
4	470	19	380
5	210	20	450
6	500	21	260
7	270	22	330
8	120	23	440
9	680	24	480
10	490	25	520
11	400	26	300
12	170	27	580
13	440	28	370
14	480	29	380
15	620	30	350

Hints & Solutions

1. Solve as Example 3. **Ans.** 0.0238
2. To make a rank correlation table which is given below

Internal assessment	External assessment	R_1	R_2	$d = R_1 - R_2$	d^2
45	39	6	6	0	0
62	48	4	4	0	0
67	65	3	2	1	1
32	32	9	8	1	1
12	20	10	10	0	0
38	35	8	7	1	1
47	45	5	5	0	0
68	77	2	1	1	1
42	30	7	9	−2	4
85	62	1	3	−2	4
Total					$\Sigma d^2 = 12$

Here, $n = 10$

We know that Spearman's rank correlation coefficient,

$$R = 1 - \frac{6\Sigma d^2}{n(n^2-1)} [\because n = 10] = 1 - \frac{6 \times 12}{10(100-1)} = 1 - \frac{6 \times 12}{10 \times 99}$$

$$= 1 - \frac{72}{990} = \frac{990 - 72}{990} = \frac{918}{990} = 0.927 = 0.93$$

3. Here, MAS = Mathematical Aptitude Score,
JPR = Job Programmers Rating.
To make a rank correlation table which is given below

Person	MAS	JPR	R_1	R_2	$d = R_1 - R_2$	d^2
A	2	8	8	6	2	4
B	5	16	5	2	3	9
C	0	8	10	6	4	16
D	4	9	6	4	2	4
E	3	5	7	8	−1	1
F	1	4	9	9	0	0
G	6	3	4	10	− 6	36
H	8	17	2	1	1	1
I	7	8	3	6	− 3	9
J	9	12	1	3	− 2	4
Total						$\Sigma d^2 = 84$

We know that, Spearman's correlation coefficient,

$$R = 1 - \frac{6\left[\Sigma d^2 + \frac{1}{12}(m^3 - m)\right]}{n(n^2-1)} = 1 - \frac{6\left[84 + \frac{1}{12}(3^3 - 3)\right]}{10\,[(10)^2 - 1]}$$

[$\because n = 10$ (total number of person)]

$$= 1 - \frac{6\left(84 + \frac{24}{12}\right)}{10(100-1)} = 1 - \frac{6(84+2)}{10 \times 99}$$

$$= 1 - \frac{6(86)}{990} = \frac{990 - 516}{990}$$

$$= \frac{474}{990} = 0.478787 \approx 0.479$$

4. Arrange the given marks in ascending order 13, 22, 42, 44, 45, 52, 76, 88, 88, 105.
Here, $n = 10$. For score 88, $L = 7$ and $E = 2$

$$\therefore \; P_R = \frac{L + 0.5 \times E}{n} \times 100$$

$$= \frac{7 + 0.5 \times 2}{10} = \frac{8}{10} \times 100 = P_R = 80$$

5. Arranging the wages in ascending order we obtain the following table:

S. No.	Wages (₹)	S. No.	Wages (₹)
1	120	16	400
2	170	17	420
3	210	18	440
4	240	19	440
5	260	20	450
6	270	21	470
7	300	22	480
8	320	23	480
9	330	24	490
10	330	25	500
11	330	26	520
12	350	27	550
13	370	28	580
14	380	29	620
15	380	30	680

$n = 30$

$$\therefore \; P_{40} = \text{Value of } \left[40\left(\frac{30+1}{100}\right)\right]^{\text{th}} \text{observation}$$

$$= \text{Value of } 12.4\text{th observation}$$

$$\Rightarrow P_{40} = \text{Value of 12th observation} + \frac{4}{10}(\text{Value of 13th observation} - \text{Value of 12th observation})$$

$$\Rightarrow P_{40} = 350 + \frac{4}{10}(370 - 350) = 350 + \frac{4}{10} \times 20 = 358$$

Hence, 40th percentile is ₹ 358.

Exam Pattern Exercise

Part A - Objective Type Questions

Multiple Choice Type Questions

1 The first four central moments of a distribution are 0, 2.5, 0.7 and 18.75. Then, distribution is
(a) Laptokurtic (b) Mesokurtic
(c) Platykurtic (d) None of these

2 The coefficient of correlation between X and Y, when $\text{cov}(X, Y) - 16.5$, $\text{var}(X) = 2.89$ and $\text{var}(Y) = 100$, is
(a) – 0.97 (b) 0.46 (c) 1.20 (d) – 0.56

3 The covariance between x and y when $\Sigma x = 50$, $\Sigma y = -30$, $\Sigma xy = 115$ and $n = 10$, is
(a) 37.6 (b) 32.8 (c) 24.4 (d) 26.5

4 The test scores of 10 students are given below: 13, 52, 42, 22, 44, 105, 45, 88, 88, 76, then percentile rank of score 88 is
(a) 85 (b) 75 (c) 80 (d) 73

5 If $\Sigma x_i = 55$, $\Sigma y_i = 74$, $\Sigma x_i y_i = 411$ and $n = 10$, then $\text{cov}(x, y)$ is
(a) 0.5 (b) 0.7 (c) 0.6 (d) 0.4

6 If $\Sigma(x_i - 2) = 10$, $\Sigma(y_i - 5) = 20$, $\Sigma x_i y_i = 148$ and $n = 5$, then $\text{cov}(x, y)$ is
(a) – 6.4 (b) – 6.0 (c) 7.2 (d) 7.5

Assertion-Reason Based Questions

Directions (Q. Nos. 11-15) *In the questions given below are two statements labelled as Assertion (A) and Reason (R). In the context of the two statements, which one of the following is correct?*
(a) Both A and R are correct; R is the correct explanation of A
(b) Both A and R are correct; R is not the correct explanation of A
(c) A is correct; R is incorrect
(d) R is correct; A is incorrect

7 **Assertion (A)** If $y_i = -2x_i + 3$ and $\sigma_x = 4$, then $\sigma_y = 8$.
Reason (R) If $y_i = ax_i + b$, then $\sigma_y = |a| \sigma_x$.

8 **Assertion (A)** The variance of first 10 natural number is $\frac{33}{4}$.
Reason (R) The variance of first n natural number is $\frac{n^2 - 1}{12}$.

9 **Assertion (A)** The test scores of 10 students are given below 15, 62, 48, 25, 46, 108, 50, 93, 93, 85, then the percentile rank of score 93 is 80.
Reason (R) $\text{cov}(x, y) = \frac{1}{n}\left(\Sigma xy - \frac{1}{n} \Sigma x \, \Sigma y\right)$

10 **Assertion (A)** The quartile deviation for the following data 12, 5, 7, 3, 1, 13, 17, 5, 19, 13, 1 is 5.
Reason (R) Quartile deviation is an absolute measure of spread or dispersion based on the quartiles.

Part B - Descriptive Questions

Short Answer Type Questions

11 Calculate mean deviation (from median) for the following data.

Marks	0-10	10-20	20-30	30-40	40-50
Number of students	5	8	15	16	6

12 Find the mean and standard deviation of the following frequency distribution.

x_i	6	10	14	18	24	28	30
f_i	2	4	7	12	8	4	3

13 Find the variance and standard deviation for the following distribution.

x_i	4.5	14.5	24.5	34.5	44.5	54.5	64.5
f_i	1	5	12	22	17	9	4

14 Find the first four central moments for the following set of observations:

4, 6, 7, 10, 13

Long Answer Type Questions

15 An original frequency table with mean 11 and variance 9.9 was lost but the following table derived from it was found. Construct the original table.

Value of deviation (u)	−2	−1	0	1	2
Frequency (f)	1	6	7	4	2

16 The scores of a screening test conducted by a company for the post of manager are given below

48, 37, 35, 46, 39, 55, 89, 67, 55, 46

Find the percentile rank of score 55.

17 Compute 27th percentile from the following frequency distribution.

x	0	2	3	4	5	6	7	8	9
f	1	9	26	59	72	52	29	7	1

18 A psychologist selected a random sample of 22 students. He grouped them in 11 pairs, so that the students in each pair have nearly equal scores in an intelligence test. In each pair, one student was taught by method *A* and the other method *B* and examined after the course.

The marks obtained by them after the course as follows

Pairs	1	2	3	4	5	6	7	8	9	10	11
Method *A*	24	29	19	14	30	19	27	30	20	28	11
Method *B*	37	35	16	26	23	27	19	20	16	11	21

Calculate Spearman's rank correlation.

Case Study Based Questions

19 The marks of students of Class XI in Maths test (out of 20) are given below:

Marks (x_i)	5	7	9	11	13	15	17
Number of students (f_i)	2	4	6	8	10	12	8

On the basis of above information, answer the following questions.

(i) Total number of students in the class is

(a) 20 (b) 30 (c) 40 (d) 50

(ii) Cumulative frequency corresponding to mark 11 is

(a) 10 (b) 20 (c) 22 (d) 28

(iii) Median (M) of given data is

(a) 11 (b) 13 (c) 15 (d) None of these

(iv) The value of $\sum_{i=1}^{n} f_i |x_i - M|$ is

(a) 116 (b) 126 (c) 136 (d) 146

(v) The value of mean deviation from median of given data is

(a) 2.72 (b) 2.70 (c) 2.68 (d) 2.66

20 Let x_i and y_i be two data such that $y_i = ax_i + b$. If $\bar{x}$, $\bar{y}$ are mean and σ_x, σ_y are standard deviation of the given data x_i and y_i respectively. Then, we have $\bar{y} = a\bar{x} + b$ and $\sigma_y = |a| \sigma_x$.

On the basis of above information, answer the following question.

(i) If $y_i = 4x_i - 3$ and $\bar{x}$ is 10, then $\bar{y}$ is

(a) 40 (b) 7 (c) 37 (d) 43

(ii) If $y_i = \dfrac{ax_i + b}{c}$, then σ_y is

(a) $\dfrac{a\sigma_x + b}{c}$ (b) $\dfrac{a}{c}\sigma_x$

(c) $\left|\dfrac{a}{c}\right|\sigma_x$ (d) None of these

(iii) If $y_i = x_i + 10$, then

(a) $\sigma_y = \sigma_x + 10$ (b) $\sigma_y = \sigma_x$

(c) $\sigma_y = \sigma_x - 10$ (d) None of these

(iv) If $x_i = 3y_i + 2$, then

(a) $\bar{y} = \bar{x}$ (b) $\bar{y} = 3\bar{x} + 2$

(c) $\bar{y} = \bar{x} - 2$ (d) None of these

(v) If $y_i = ax_i + b$, then

(a) $\text{var}(Y) = a^2 \text{var}(X)$ (b) $\text{var}(X) = a^2 \text{var}(Y)$

(c) $\text{var}(Y) = \text{var}(X) + b$ (d) None of these

21 Consider the following data

Variable	5	15	25	35	45
Frequency	10	20	40	20	10

On the basis of above information answer the following questions.

(i) Lower quartile Q_1 is

(a) 30 (b) 15 (c) 26 (d) 22

(ii) Median is

(a) 32 (b) 30 (c) 25 (d) 20

(iii) Upper quartile Q_3 is

(a) 35 (b) 40 (c) 29 (d) 42

Hints & Solutions

1. (b) 2. (a) 3. (d) 4. (c)
5. (d) 6. (a) 7. (a) 8. (a)
9. (c) 10. (a)

11. **Hint** Let us make the following table from the given data.

Marks (Class -interval)	Number of students (f_i)	cf	x_i	$\lvert x_i - M\rvert = \lvert x_i - 28\rvert$	$f_i\lvert x_i - 28\rvert$
0-10	5	5	5	23	115
10-20	8	13	15	13	104
20-30	15	28	25	3	45
30-40	16	44	35	7	112
40-50	6	50	45	17	102
	$N = \Sigma f_i = 50$				$\Sigma f_i\lvert x_i - 28\rvert = 478$

Here, $N = 50$, so $\frac{N}{2} = 25$, $cf = 13$, $l = 20$, $f = 15$ and $h = 10$

Now, median $(M) = \dfrac{l + \left(\frac{N}{2} - cf\right)}{f} \times h = 20 + \dfrac{25-13}{15} \times 10$

$= 28$

$\therefore$ Mean deviation about median $= \frac{1}{N}(\Sigma f_i \lvert x_i - M\rvert)$

$= \frac{478}{50} = 9.56$

12. **Hint** Let us make the following table from the given data.

x_i	f_i	$f_i x_i$	$(x_i - \bar{x}) = (x_i - 19)$	$(x_i - \bar{x})^2$	$f_i(x_i - \bar{x})^2$
6	2	12	−13	169	338
10	4	40	−9	81	324
14	7	98	−5	25	175
18	12	216	−1	1	12
24	8	192	5	25	200
28	4	112	9	81	324
30	3	90	11	121	363
	$\Sigma f_i = 40$	$\Sigma f_i x_i = 760$			$\Sigma f_i(x_i - \bar{x})^2 = 1736$

$\therefore \quad \bar{x} = \dfrac{\Sigma f_i x_i}{N} = \dfrac{760}{40} = 19$

and standard deviation $= \sqrt{\frac{1}{N}[\Sigma f_i(x_i - \bar{x})^2]} = \sqrt{\frac{1736}{40}}$

$= \sqrt{43.4} = 6.59$

Ans. 196.59

13. Variance = 13.259 and standard deviation = 175.8

14. $\mu_1 = 0, \mu_2 = 10, \mu_3 = 12, \mu_4 = 182.8$

15. **Hint** Let us make the table from the given data.

u	f	u^2	fu	fu^2
−2	1	4	−2	4
−1	6	1	−6	6
0	7	0	0	0
1	4	1	4	4
2	2	4	4	8
Total	$\Sigma f = 20$		$\Sigma fu = 0$	$\Sigma fu^2 = 22$

We know that $\bar{x} = a + h\dfrac{\Sigma fu}{\Sigma f} \Rightarrow 11 = a + h \times \dfrac{0}{20}$

$\Rightarrow \quad a = 11$

Also, variance, $\sigma^2 = h^2\left[\dfrac{\Sigma fu^2}{\Sigma f} - \left(\dfrac{\Sigma fu}{\Sigma f}\right)^2\right]$

$\Rightarrow \quad (9.9) = h^2\left[\dfrac{22}{20}\right] \Rightarrow h = 3$

Mid value, $\quad u = \dfrac{x - a}{h} \Rightarrow x = a + uh$

$\therefore$ Different values of x for different values of u, we have

$11 - 2 \times 3, 11 - 1 \times 3, 11 - 0 \times 3, 11 + 1 \times 3, 11 + 2 \times 3$

i.e. 5, 8, 11, 14, 17.

Thus, the original frequency table is as follows

Class	5	8	11	14	17
Frequency	1	6	7	4	2

16. Solve as Example 1 of Topic 3. **Ans.** 70

17. First we prepare the cumulative frequency distribution as given below:

x	f	cf
0	1	1
1	9	10
2	26	36
3	59	95
4	72	167
5	52	219
6	29	248
7	7	255
8	1	256
	$N = \Sigma f = 256$	

Here, $\quad N = 256 \Rightarrow \dfrac{27N}{100} = \dfrac{27 \times 256}{100} = 69.12$

The cumulative frequency just greater than 69.12 is 95 and the corresponding value of x is 3.

Hence, $P_{27} = 3$.

18. To make a rank correlation table which is given below.

Pairs	By Method A	By Method B	R_1 = Rank from method A	R_2 = Rank for method B	$d = R_1 - R_2$	d^2
1	24	37	6	1	5	25
2	29	35	3	2	1	1
3	19	16	8.5	9.5	−1	1
4	14	26	10	4	6	36
5	30	23	1.5	5	− 3.5	12.25
6	19	27	8.5	3	5.5	30.25
7	27	19	5	8	− 3	9
8	30	20	1.5	7	− 5.5	30.25
9	20	16	7	9.5	− 2.5	6.25
10	28	11	4	11	− 7	49
11	11	21	11	6	5	25
Total						$\Sigma d^2 = 225$

Now, by using method A, the rank of 30 = $\frac{1+2}{2} = 1.5$

and 19 = $\frac{8+9}{2} = 8.5$

But by using method B, the rank of 16 = $\frac{9+10}{2} = 9.5$

Correction for rank

$$= \frac{1}{12}(m_1^3 - m_1) + \frac{1}{12}(m_2^3 - m_2) + \frac{1}{12}(m_3^3 - m_3)$$

$$= \frac{1}{12}(2^3 - 2) + \frac{1}{12}(2^3 - 2) + \frac{1}{12}(2^3 - 2)$$

$$= \frac{1}{12}(8-2) + \frac{1}{12}(8-2) + \frac{1}{12}(8-2)$$

$$= \frac{1}{12} \times 6 + \frac{1}{12} \times 6 + \frac{1}{12} \times 6 = \frac{1}{2} + \frac{1}{2} + \frac{1}{2} = \frac{3}{2} = 1.5$$

$\therefore$ Spearman's rank correlation,

$$R = 1 - \frac{6[(\Sigma d^2) + 1.5]}{n^3 - n}$$

$$= 1 - \frac{6(225 + 1.5)}{(11)^3 - 11} \qquad [\because \Sigma d^2 = 225]$$

$\because n = 11$, so the total number of pairs

$$= 1 - \frac{6 \times 226.5}{1331 - 11} = 1 - \frac{1359}{1320}$$

$$= \frac{1320 - 1359}{1320} = \frac{-39}{1320}$$

$$= -0.0296$$

19. **Hint** We construct following table.

Marks (x_i)	Number of students (f_i)	cf	$\lvert x_i - M \rvert$	$f_i(x_i - M)$
5	2	2	8	16
7	4	6	6	24
9	6	12	4	24
11	8	20	2	16
13	10	30	0	0
15	12	42	2	24
17	8	50	4	32
	50			136

$$\text{MD}(M) = \frac{\Sigma f_i(x_i - M)}{\Sigma f_i} = \frac{136}{50} = 2.72$$

Ans. (i) (d), (ii) (b), (iii) (b), (iv) (c), (v) (a)

20. (i) (c), (ii) (c), (iii) (b), (iv) (d), (v) (a)

21. We construct following table.

Variable (X)	Frequency (f)	Cumulative frequency (cf)
5	10	10
15	20	30
25	40	70
35	20	90
45	10	100
	$N = 100$	

Here, $N = 100$

$$\therefore \quad \frac{N}{4} = \frac{100}{4} = 25$$

The cumulative frequency just greater than $\frac{N}{4}$ i.e. 25 is 30 and the corresponding value of X is 15.

$\therefore$ Lower quartile $= Q_1 = 15$

Cumulative frequency just greater than $\frac{N}{2}$ i.e 50 is 70 and the corresponding value of X is 25.

$\therefore$ Median = 25

The cumulative frequency just greater than $\frac{3N}{4}$ i.e. $\frac{3 \times 100}{4} = 75$ is 90 and the corresponding value of variable X is 35.

$\therefore$ Upper quartile, $Q_3 = 35$

Ans. (i) (b), (ii) (c), (iii) (a)

CHAPTER 19

Interest and Annuity

In this Chapter...

- Interest
- Annuities

Interest

When a person borrows some amount of money from another person or organisation (bank), then the person borrowing money (borrower) pays some extra money during repayment that extra money during repayment is called **interest**.

e.g. If A takes ₹ 50 from B and after using ₹ 50, A returns ₹ 55 to B, then A pays (55 − 50) i.e. ₹ 5 as interest.

In borrowing and lending money, there are following terms which are commonly used.

- **Principal** (P) Principal is the money borrowed or deposited for a certain time.
- **Amount** (A) The sum of principal and interest is called amount.

  Amount = Principal + Simple Interest
- **Rate of Interest** (r) It is the rate at which the interest charged on principal. It is always specified is percentage terms.
- **Time** (t) The period, for which the money is borrowed or deposited, is called time.

Simple Interest (SI)

If the interest is calculated on the original principal for any period of time, then it is called simple interest.

$$\text{Simple Interest} = \frac{\text{Principal} \times \text{Rate} \times \text{Time}}{100} = \frac{P \times r \times t}{100}$$

We can also write as

$$P = \frac{100 \times A}{100 + rt} \quad \text{and} \quad \text{SI} = \frac{A \times r \times t}{100 + rt}$$

where, SI = Simple Interest, P = Principal,
r = Rate of interest, t = Time and A = Amount

EXAMPLE 1. Find the unknown value for the following parts.

(i) Principal value = ₹ 8000,
Rate of interest = 10% per annum,
Time = 4 yr,
Simple interest = ?

(ii) Principal value = ₹ 1000,
Rate of interest = 5% per annum,
Simple interest = ₹ 300,
Time = ?

(iii) Simple interest = ₹ 420,
Rate of interest = 6% per annum,
Time = 6 months,
Principal value = ?

(iv) Principal value = ₹ 10000,
Simple interest = ₹ 1200,
Time = 219 days,
Rate of interest = ?

(v) Principal value = ₹ 8000,
Rate of interest = 10% per annum,
Time = 146 days,
Simple interest = ?,
Amount = ?

Sol. (i) We have, $P =$ ₹ 8000, $r = 10\%$ and $t = 4$ yr

$$\therefore \text{SI} = \frac{P \times r \times t}{100} = \frac{8000 \times 10 \times 4}{100} = ₹\ 3200$$

(ii) We have, $P =$ ₹ 1000, $r = 5\%$ and SI = ₹ 300

$$\therefore \quad t = \frac{\text{SI} \times 100}{P \times r} = \frac{300 \times 100}{1000 \times 5} = 6 \text{ yr}$$

(iii) We have, SI = ₹ 420, $r = 6\%$

and $t = 6$ months $= \frac{6}{12}$ yr $= 0.5$ yr

$$\therefore \quad P = \frac{\text{SI} \times 100}{r \times t} = \frac{420 \times 100}{6 \times 0.5} = ₹\ 14000$$

(iv) We have, $P = 10000$, SI = 1200 and $t = 219$ days

$$\therefore \quad r = \frac{\text{SI} \times 100}{P \times t} = \frac{1200 \times 100}{10000 \times 219} \times 365 = 20\%$$

Rate = 20% per annum

(v) We have, $P =$ ₹ 8000, $r = 10\%$ and $t = 146$ days

$$\therefore \quad \text{SI} = \frac{P \times r \times t}{100} = \frac{8000 \times 10 \times 146}{100 \times 365} = 320$$

$$A = P + \text{SI} = 8000 + 320 = ₹\ 8320$$

EXAMPLE 2. A sum at simple interest of 15% per annum amounts to ₹ 4550 in 5 yr. Find the sum.

Sol. Let sum = ₹ P, $r = 15\%$ and $t = 5$ yr

Then, $$\text{SI} = \frac{P \times r \times t}{100} = \frac{P \times 15 \times 5}{100} = \frac{3P}{4}$$

$$\therefore \quad \text{Amount} = ₹\left(P + \frac{3P}{4}\right) = ₹\ \frac{7P}{4}$$

According to question,

$$\frac{7P}{4} = 4550$$

$$\Rightarrow \quad P = \frac{4 \times 4550}{7} = ₹\ 2600$$

EXAMPLE 3. Divide ₹ 15500 into two parts such that if one part be lent out at 15% per annum and the other at 24% per annum, the total income is ₹ 3000.

Sol. Let one part be ₹ x.

Then, the other part is ₹ $(15500 - x)$.

For the first part, we have

$$P = x, r = \frac{15}{100} \text{ and } t = 1 \text{ yr}$$

$$\therefore \quad I_1 = \text{SI} = P \times r \times t = \frac{x \times 15 \times 1}{100} = \frac{3x}{20}$$

For the second part, we have

$$P = (15500 - x), r = \frac{24}{100} = \frac{6}{25} \text{ and } t = 1 \text{ yr}$$

$$\therefore \quad I_2 = \text{SI} = P \times r \times t = \frac{(15500 - x) \times 6 \times 1}{25} = \frac{1}{25}(93000 - 6x)$$

It is given that total annual interest is ₹ 3000.

$$\therefore \quad I_1 + I_2 = 3000$$

$$\Rightarrow \quad \frac{3x}{20} + \frac{93000 - 6x}{25} = 3000$$

$$\Rightarrow \quad 15x + 372000 - 24x = 300000$$

$$\Rightarrow \quad 9x = 72000$$

$$\Rightarrow \quad x = 8000$$

Hence, two part are ₹ 8000 and ₹(15500 − 8000) = ₹ 7500

EXAMPLE 4. Find the sum, which amounts to ₹ 364.80 in 8 yr at 3.5% simple interest per annum.

Sol. Given, $t = 8$ yr, $r = 3.5\%$ and $S =$ ₹ 364.80

Let principal be ₹P.

Since, $$S = P\left(1 + \frac{rt}{100}\right)$$

$$\Rightarrow \quad 364.80 = P\left(1 + \frac{3.5 \times 8}{100}\right)$$

$$\Rightarrow \quad \frac{36480}{100} = P\frac{(128)}{100} \Rightarrow P = \frac{36480}{128} = ₹\ 285$$

EXAMPLE 5. At what rate percent per annum simple interest will a sum of money triple itself in 25 yr?

Sol. Let the principal be ₹ P.

$\therefore$ Amount in 25 yr = ₹ $3P$

Rate of interest per annum = $r\%$

Time = 25 yr

$$A = P + P \times r \times t$$

$$\therefore \quad 3P = P[1 + r(25)] \Rightarrow 3 = 1 + 25r \Rightarrow r = \frac{2}{25}$$

$$\therefore \text{ Rate of interest} = \left(\frac{2}{25} \times 100\right)\% = 8\%$$

EXAMPLE 6. In how many years will a sum of money double itself at 18.75% per annum simple interest?

Sol. Let the principle be ₹ P and suppose it take t yr to get double at 18.75% per annum simple interest.

Then, Principle = P, Amount = $2P$, $r = \frac{18.75}{100} = \frac{1875}{10000}$

Amount = Principle + Simple interest

$$2P = P + Prt \Rightarrow P = Prt$$

$$\Rightarrow \quad t = \frac{1}{r} = \frac{10000}{1875} = \frac{16}{3} = 5\frac{1}{3}$$

$\therefore$ Amount will be double itself in 5 yr and 4 months.

EXAMPLE 7. The simple interest on a certain sum for 4 yr at 9% per annum is ₹ 216 less than simple interest on the same sum for 3 yr at 18% per annum. Find sum.

Sol. Let the sum of money be ₹ x

When $P = x, r = \frac{9}{100}, t = 4$

$$(\text{SI})_1 = x \times \frac{9}{100} \times 4 = \frac{36x}{100}$$

When $P = x, r = \frac{18}{100}, t = 3$

$$(\text{SI})_2 = x \times \frac{18}{100} \times 3 = \frac{54}{100}x$$

It is given that

$$(\text{SI})_2 - (\text{SI})_1 = 216$$

$$\therefore \quad \frac{54x}{100} - \frac{36x}{100} = 216$$

$$\Rightarrow \quad (54 - 36)x = 216 \times 100$$

$$\Rightarrow \quad 18x = 216 \times 100$$

$$\Rightarrow \quad x = \frac{216 \times 100}{18} = 1200$$

∴ Sum = ₹ 1200

EXAMPLE 8. A sum of money invested at 20% per annum simple interest amounts to ₹ 650 in $1\frac{1}{2}$ yr. What will it amount to in 2 yr at 12% per annum simple interest?

Sol. Let P be the sum of money.

We have, Principal = P, $r = 20\%$, $t = \frac{3}{2}$ yr and $A =$ ₹ 650

$$\therefore \quad A = P(1 + rt) = P\left(1 + \frac{20 \times 3}{100 \times 2}\right)$$

$$\Rightarrow \quad 650 = P\left(1 + \frac{3}{10}\right) = \frac{13P}{10}$$

$$\Rightarrow \quad P = \left(\frac{10 \times 650}{13}\right) = ₹\ 500$$

This sum of money is invested for 2 yr at 12% per annum. Let S be the amount after 2 yr.

Then, $A = P(1 + rt)$

$$= 500\left(1 + \frac{12}{100} \times 2\right) = 500\left(1 + \frac{6}{25}\right)$$

$$= 500 \times \frac{31}{25} = 620$$

Hence, amount after 2 yr is ₹ 620.

Compound Interest

Compound interest is the interest calculated both on the principal and the interest earned previously. It is denoted by CI.

Compound interest = Amount − Principal

Basic Formulae Related to Compound Interest

Let principal = P, rate = r% per annum and time = n yr

(i) If interest is compounded annually, then

$$\text{Amount} = P\left(1 + \frac{r}{100}\right)^n$$

Compound interest = Amount − Principal

$$\text{Compound interest} = P\left[\left(1 + \frac{r}{100}\right)^n - 1\right]$$

(ii) If interest is compounded half-yearly, then

$$r = \frac{r}{2} \text{ and } n = 2n$$

$$\text{Amount} = P\left(1 + \frac{r}{2 \times 100}\right)^{2n}$$

(iii) If interest is compounded quarterly, then

$$r = \frac{r}{4} \text{ and } n = 4n$$

$$\text{Amount} = P\left(1 + \frac{r}{4 \times 100}\right)^{4n}$$

(iv) If interest in compounded annually but time is in fraction (suppose, time = $n\frac{a}{b}$ yr), then

$$\text{Amount} = P\left(1 + \frac{r}{100}\right)^n \times \left(1 + \frac{(a/b)r}{100}\right)$$

(v) If rates of interest are r_1%, r_2% and r_3% for 1st, 2nd and 3rd yr respectively, then

$$\text{Amount} = P\left(1 + \frac{r_1}{100}\right)\left(1 + \frac{r_2}{100}\right)\left(1 + \frac{r_3}{100}\right)$$

Effective Rate of Interest

Effective interest rate is the true interest rate that a company or an individual earns or pay over a given period of time as a result of compounding.

$$\text{Effective rate of interest } (r_e) = \left(1 + \frac{r}{m}\right)^m - 1$$

where, r = nominal rate of interest

and m = conversion period in a year

EXAMPLE 9. Find the compound amount and compound interest of ₹ 10000 invested for 5 yr at 6% compounded

(i) annually

(ii) half-yearly

Sol. (i) When interest is compound annually, we have

$$P = ₹10000,\ n = 5,\ r = 6\% = \frac{6}{100}$$

$$\therefore \text{ Amount} = P\left(1 + \frac{r}{100}\right)^n = 10000\left(1 + \frac{6}{100}\right)^5$$

$$= 10000(1.06)^5 = 10000 \times 1.3382 = 13382$$

Hence, amount = ₹ 13382

and compound interest = Amount − Principal

= ₹ (13382 − 10000)

= ₹ 3382

(ii) When compound interest is half-yearly.

$$P = ₹10000,\ n = 2 \times 5 = 10,\ r = \frac{6}{2}\% = 3\% = \frac{3}{100}$$

$$\therefore A = P\left(1 + \frac{r}{200}\right)^{2n} = 10000\left(1 + \frac{3}{100}\right)^{10}$$

$$= 10000(1.03)^{10} = 10000 \times 1.3439 = ₹\ 13439$$

Hence, amount = ₹ 13439

and compound interest = Amount − Principal

= ₹ (13439 − 10000)

= ₹ 3439

EXAMPLE 10. Find the compound interest on ₹ 12000 at 20% per annum for 9 months compounded quarterly.

Sol. Given that, $P = ₹\,12000$,

$$n = 9 \text{ months} = \frac{3}{4} \text{ yr}$$

and $r = 20\%$ per annum

$$\therefore \quad \text{Amount} = P\left(1 + \frac{r}{4 \times 100}\right)^{4n}$$

$$= 12000\left(1 + \frac{20}{400}\right)^{3/4 \times 4}$$

$$= 12000\left(1 + \frac{5}{100}\right)^3$$

$$= 12000 \times \frac{21}{20} \times \frac{21}{20} \times \frac{21}{20}$$

$$= ₹\ 13891.5$$

$$\therefore \quad CI = ₹\ (13891.5 - 12000)$$

$$= ₹\ 1891.5$$

EXAMPLE 11. What sum of money will amount for ₹ 3704.40 in 3 yr at 5% compound interest?

Sol. Here, $A = ₹\ 3704.40,\ r = 5\%,\ n = 3$

$$\therefore \quad A = P\left(1 + \frac{r}{100}\right)^n$$

$$\Rightarrow \quad 3704.40 = P\left(1 + \frac{5}{100}\right)^3$$

$$\Rightarrow \quad 3704.40 = P(1.05)^3$$

$$\Rightarrow \quad P = \frac{3704.40}{(1.05)^3} = 3200$$

∴ Principal = ₹ 3200

EXAMPLE 12. On what sum will the compound interest for 2 yr at 4% per annum be ₹ 5712?

Sol. Here, compound interest = ₹ 5712, $r = 4\%,\ n = 2$

$$\therefore \quad CI = P\left(1 + \frac{r}{100}\right)^n - P$$

$$\Rightarrow \quad 5712 = P\left(1 + \frac{4}{100}\right)^2 - P$$

$$\Rightarrow \quad 5712 = P\left(1 + \frac{1}{25}\right)^2 - P$$

$$\Rightarrow \quad 5712 = P\left(\frac{26}{25}\right)^2 - P$$

$$\Rightarrow \quad 5712 = P\left(\frac{676 - 625}{625}\right) = \frac{51}{625}P$$

$$\Rightarrow \quad P = \frac{5712 \times 625}{51} = 70000$$

Hence, principal = ₹ 70000

EXAMPLE 13. Anurag invested ₹ 6000 in a company at compound interest compounded semi-annually. He receives ₹7986 after $1\frac{1}{2}$ yr from the company. Find the rate of interest per annum.

Sol. Here, $P = ₹6000,\ A = ₹\ 7986,\ n = \frac{3}{2} \times 2 = 3,\ r = \frac{r}{2}$

$$\therefore \quad 7986 = 6000\left(1 + \frac{r}{200}\right)^3$$

$$\Rightarrow \quad \left(1 + \frac{r}{200}\right)^3 = \frac{7986}{6000} = \frac{1331}{1000}$$

$$\Rightarrow \quad 1 + \frac{r}{200} = \left(\frac{1331}{1000}\right)^{1/3} = \frac{11}{10}$$

$$\Rightarrow \quad \frac{r}{200} = \frac{11}{10} - 1 = \frac{1}{10}$$

$$\Rightarrow \quad r = \frac{200}{10} = 20 \Rightarrow r = 20$$

Hence, rate of interest = 20%

EXAMPLE 14. A sum of ₹ 25000 invested at 8% per annum compounded semi-annual amounts to ₹ 28121.60. Compute the time period of investment.

Sol. Here $P = ₹\ 25000,\ A = ₹\ 28121.60,\ r = \frac{8}{2}\% = 4\%,\ t = 2n$

$$\therefore \quad A = P\left(1 + \frac{r}{200}\right)^{2n}$$

$$\Rightarrow \quad 28121.60 = 25000\left(1+\frac{4}{100}\right)^{2n}$$

$$\Rightarrow \quad \frac{2812160}{25000\times 100} = \left(\frac{26}{25}\right)^{2n}$$

$$\Rightarrow \quad \frac{17576}{15625} = \left(\frac{26}{25}\right)^{2n}$$

$$\Rightarrow \quad \left(\frac{26}{25}\right)^{3} = \left(\frac{26}{25}\right)^{2n}$$

$$\Rightarrow \quad 2n = 3 \Rightarrow n = \frac{3}{2}$$

$\therefore$ Time period of investment $= 1\frac{1}{2}$ yr

EXAMPLE 15. A sum of money double itself at compound interest in 15 yr. In how many years it will be becomes 8 times?

Sol. Let Principle $= P$, Amount $= 2P$, Time $= n = 15$

$$\therefore \quad A = P\left(1+\frac{r}{100}\right)^{n}$$

$$\Rightarrow \quad 2P = P\left(1+\frac{r}{100}\right)^{15}$$

$$\Rightarrow \quad 2 = \left(1+\frac{r}{100}\right)^{15}$$

Let money becomes 8 time in n yr.

Then, $$A = P\left(1+\frac{r}{100}\right)^{n}$$

$$\Rightarrow \quad 8P = P\left(1+\frac{r}{100}\right)^{n}$$

$$\Rightarrow \quad 8 = \left(1+\frac{r}{100}\right)^{n}$$

$$\Rightarrow \quad 2^3 = \left(1+\frac{r}{100}\right)^{n}$$

$$\Rightarrow \quad \left(\left(1+\frac{r}{100}\right)^{15}\right)^{3} = \left(1+\frac{r}{100}\right)^{n}$$

$$\Rightarrow \quad \left(1+\frac{r}{100}\right)^{45} = \left(1+\frac{r}{100}\right)^{n} \Rightarrow n = 45$$

Hence, the money will becomes 8 times in 45 yr.

EXAMPLE 16. Money invested in a mutual fund double in 4 yr. What is the rate of interest?

Sol. Let P be the initial amount and r% be the annual rate of interest.

Then, $$2P = P\left(1+\frac{r}{100}\right)^{4}$$

$$\Rightarrow \quad \left(1+\frac{r}{100}\right)^{4} = 2$$

Taking log on both sides, we get

$$4\log\left(1+\frac{r}{100}\right) = \log 2$$

$$\Rightarrow \quad \log\left(1+\frac{r}{100}\right) = \frac{0.3010}{4}$$

$$\Rightarrow \quad \log\left(1+\frac{r}{100}\right) = 0.0752$$

$$\Rightarrow \quad \left(1+\frac{r}{100}\right) = \text{antilog}\,(0.0752) = 1.187$$

$$\Rightarrow \quad \frac{r}{100} = 1.187 - 1$$

$$\Rightarrow \quad \frac{r}{100} = 0.187$$

$$\Rightarrow \quad r = 18.7\%$$

EXAMPLE 17. Find the amount to which ₹ 10000 will accumulate at the effective rate of 4% for 8 yr, 6% for 6 yr and 10% for 4 yr. [given, $(1.04)^8 = 1.3685$, $(1.06)^6 = 1.4185$ and $(1.10)^4 = 1.4641$]

Sol. Let S be the required sum.

Since, the effective rate is the actual rate compounded annually.

Here, $P = 10000$, $r_1 = 4\%$, $r_2 = 6\%$, $r_3 = 10\%$,

$n_1 = 8$, $n_2 = 6$ and $n_3 = 4$

$$\therefore \quad S = 10000\left(1+\frac{4}{100}\right)^{8}\left(1+\frac{6}{100}\right)^{6}\left(1+\frac{10}{100}\right)^{4}$$

$$= 10000(1+0.04)^8(1+0.06)^6(1+0.10)^4$$

$$= 10000\,(1.04)^8\,(1.06)^6(1.10)^4$$

$$= 10000(1.3685)(1.4185)(1.4641)$$

$$= ₹\ 28421.36$$

EXAMPLE 18. If the nominal rate 5.5% compounded monthly, find the corresponding effective rate. [given, $(1.0045833)^{12} = 1.05640$]

Sol. Given, nominal rate, $r = 5.5\%$

Number of conversions in a year, $p = 12$

Let r_e be the effective rate of interest.

Then, $$r_e = \left(1+\frac{r}{100p}\right)^{12} - 1$$

$$= \left(1+\frac{5.5}{100\times 12}\right)^{12} - 1$$

$$= (1+0.0045833)^{12} - 1$$

$$= (1.0045833)^{12} - 1 = 1.05640 - 1 = 0.05640$$

$\therefore$ Effective rate of interest $= (0.05640\times 100)\% = 5.64\%$

Topic Practice 1

1 Solve the following.

(i) Principal value = ₹ 9000,
Rate of interest = 7% per annum,
Time = 4 yr,
Simple interest = ?
Amount = ?

(ii) Principal value = ₹ 1100,
Rate of interest = 5% per annum,
Simple interest = ₹ 440,
Time = ?

(iii) Amount = ₹ 1350,
Simple interest = ₹250,
Time = 3 yr,
Principal value = ?
Rate of interest = ?

2 In a certain time, a sum becomes 4 times at the rate of 5% per annum. At what rate of simple interest, the same sum becomes 8 times in the same duration?

3 In 4 yr, ₹ 6000 amounts to ₹ 8000. In what time at the same rate, will ₹ 525 amount to ₹ 700?

4 Aman and Ajay borrowed ₹ 2500 and ₹ 3000, respectively at the same rate of simple interest for $2\frac{1}{2}$ yr. If Ajay paid ₹ 175 more interest than Aman. Find the rate of interest per annum.

5 A sum of money invested at a certain rate of simple interest, double itself in 10 yr. In how much time will it become three times of itself at the same rate?

6 Divide ₹ 20000 into two parts such that if one part be lent out at 18% per annum and the other at 12% per annum the total income is ₹ 3000.

7 Vishal deposited ₹ 80000 in a bank. After 2 yr, he withdrawl ₹ 30000 and at the end of 4 yr, he received an amount of ₹ 68000. Find the rate of simple interest.

8 What will be ratio of simple interest earned by certain amount at the same rate of interest for 12 yr and for 18 yr?

9 Raju lent ₹ 4000 to Sagar for 2 yr and ₹ 1000 to Manoj for 4 yr at SI and received from both ₹ 600 as collective interest. Find the rate of interest.

10 ₹ 800 amounts to ₹ 920 in 3 yr at simple interest. If the interest is increased by 3% it what would be amount?

11 A man invested $\frac{1}{3}$rd of the sum at 7%, $\frac{1}{4}$th at 8% and remaining at 10% for one year. If the annual interest is ₹ 408, then find the investment.

12 Find the compound interest on ₹ 8000 at 5% per annum for 2 yr.

13 A sum amounts to ₹ 1352 in 2 yr at 4% compound interest. Find the sum.

14 In what time will ₹ 64000 amount to ₹ 68921 at 5% per annum compounded semi-annually?

15 What amount will be received on a sum of ₹ 1750 in $2\frac{1}{2}$ yr. If the interest is compounded at the rate of 8% per annum?

16 A sum of ₹ 400 amounts to ₹ 441 in 2 yr. What will be the amount, if the rate of interest is increased by 5%?

17 At what rate percent compounded annually, a certain sum amounts to 27 times of itself in 3 yr?

18 A sum amounts to ₹ 2916 in 2 yr and ₹ 3149.28 in 3 yr at compound interest. Find the sum.

19 How much will ₹ 25000 amounts to in 2 yr at compound interest, if the rates for the successive years are 4% and 5%, respectively?

20 A sum of money lent at compound interest for 2 yr at 20% per annum would fetch ₹ 964 more, if the interest was payable half-yearly than if it was payable annually, what is the sum?

21 A sum of money triples itself at compound interest in 15 yr. In how many years will it becomes 9 times?

22 Simple interest on a sum at $12\frac{1}{2}$% per annum for 2 yr is ₹ 256. What is the compound interest on the same sum at the same rate and for the same time period?

23 If the difference between the compound interest and simple interest on a certain sum for 2 yr at 8% per annum is ₹ 32, then find the sum.

24 The simple interest on a certain sum for 2 yr is ₹ 5000 and compound interest is ₹ 5500 compounded annually. Find the sum and rate of interest.

25 How many years will it take for money to double at the effective rate of 6%?

26 Find the amount to which ₹ 12000 will accumulate at the effective rate of 3% for 10 yr, 4% for 4 yr and 5% for 2 yr. [given, $(1.03)^{10} = 1.3439, (1.04)^4 = 1.1698$ and $(1.05)^2 = 1.1025$]

27 Which gives better yield, 7.8% compounded semi-annually or 8% effective? [given, $(1.039)^2 = 1.0795$]

28 Find the declared rate of return compounded semi-annually which is equivalent to 8.16%, effective rate of return.

Hints & Solutions

1. Solve as Example 1.

Ans. (i) SI = ₹ 2520, Amount = ₹ 11520

(ii) Time = 8 yr

(iii) Principal = ₹ 1100, Rate of interest = 7.57% per annum

2. Solve as Example 5. **Ans.** $11\frac{2}{3}\%$

3. **Hint** Here, $P =$ ₹ 6000, $S =$ ₹ 8000 and $t = 4$ yr

$\therefore\ S = P\left(1+\frac{rt}{100}\right) \Rightarrow 8000 = 6000\left(1+\frac{4r}{100}\right) \Rightarrow r = \frac{25}{3}\%$

Now, again

Here, $P =$ ₹ 525, $S =$ ₹ 700 and $r = \frac{25}{3}\%$

$\Rightarrow\ S = P\left(1+\frac{rt}{100}\right) \Rightarrow 700 = 525\left(1+\frac{25t}{300}\right)$

$\Rightarrow\ t = \frac{175 \times 12}{525} = 4$ yr

4. **Hint** Let the rate of interest be $r\%$.

Let I_1 and I_2 be the interest paid by Aman and Ajay, respectively.

Then, $I_1 = 2500 \times r \times \frac{5}{2}$ and $I_2 = 3000 \times r \times \frac{5}{2}$

Given, $I_2 - I_1 = 175$

$\therefore\ 3000 \times r \times \frac{5}{2} - 2500 \times r \times \frac{5}{2} = 175$

$\Rightarrow \frac{5r}{2}(3000 - 2500) = 175 \Rightarrow r = \frac{175 \times 2}{5 \times 500} = \frac{175}{1250} = \frac{14}{100}$

Hence, rate of interest is $\left(\frac{14}{100} \times 100\right)\% = 14\%$

5. **Hint** Let the principal = ₹P, Rate of interest = $r\%$, $t = 10$ yr and $A = 2P$

$\therefore\ A = P(1 + rt) \Rightarrow 2P = P\left(1+\frac{10r}{100}\right) \Rightarrow r = 10\%$

Same amount will be tripled at 10%.

Here, $P = P$, $A = 3P$, $r = 10\%$ and $t = ?$

$\therefore\ 3P = P\left(1+\frac{10t}{100}\right) \Rightarrow 3 = 1 + \frac{t}{10} \Rightarrow t = 20$

$\therefore$ The sum will become three times in 20 yr.

6. Solve as Example 3. **Ans.** ₹ 10000 each

7. Let r be the interest, since ₹ 80000 were in the bank for 2 yr and the balance ₹ (80000 − 30000) = ₹ 50000 were in the bank for 4 yr.

Total interest = Interest on 80000 for 2 yr + Interest on 50000 for 4 yr

$= \frac{80000 \times r \times 2}{100} + \frac{50000 \times r \times 4}{100} = 36000r$

Also, interest earned = ₹ (30000 + 68000 − 80000) = ₹ 18000

$\therefore\ r = \frac{18000}{36000} = \frac{1}{20} = 5\%$ per annum

8. Let the principal be ₹ P and rate of interest = $r\%$

$I_1 = \frac{P \times r \times 12}{100} = \frac{12Pr}{100}$ and $I_2 = \frac{P \times r \times 18}{100} = \frac{18Pr}{100}$

$\frac{I_1}{I_2} = \frac{\frac{12Pr}{100}}{\frac{18Pr}{100}} = \frac{2}{3}$

$\therefore$ Hence, ratio is 2 : 3.

9. **Hint** $\frac{4000 \times r \times 2}{100} + \frac{1000 \times r \times 4}{100} = 600$ **Ans.** $r = 5\%$

10. Here, $P =$ ₹800, $S =$ ₹ 920 and $t = 3$ yr

Simple interest = $S - P = 920 - 800 =$ ₹120

$I = P \times r \times t \Rightarrow 120 = 800 \times r \times 3 \Rightarrow r = \frac{120}{800 \times 3} = 0.05$

Rate of interest = $(0.05 \times 100)\% = 5\%$

Now, rate of interest increased by 3%.

$\therefore r = 8\%$

$I = 800 \times \frac{8}{100} \times 3 =$ ₹ 192

$\therefore S = P + I =$ ₹$(800 + 192) =$ ₹ 992

11. Let the investment be ₹ P.

$\therefore$ Total interest in one year is ₹ 408.

$\therefore$ 7% of ₹ $\frac{P}{3}$ + 8% ₹ $\frac{P}{4}$ + 10% of ₹ $\left(P - \left(\frac{P}{3} + \frac{P}{4}\right)\right) = 408$

$\Rightarrow\ \frac{7P}{300} + \frac{8P}{400} + \frac{50P}{1200} = 408$

$\Rightarrow\ 28P + 24P + 50P = 408 \times 1200$

$\Rightarrow\ 102P = 408 \times 1200$

$\Rightarrow\ P = \frac{408 \times 1200}{102} = 4 \times 1200 =$ ₹4800

12. Solve as Example 9 (i). **Ans.** ₹ 820

13. Solve as Example 11. **Ans.** ₹ 1250

14. Solve as Example 13. **Ans.** $1\frac{1}{2}$ yr

15. We have, $P = ₹\ 1750, r = 8\%$ and $n = 2$

$$\therefore\ A = 1750\left(1+\frac{8}{100}\right)^2 = 1750\left(\frac{27}{25}\right)^2 = 1750 \times \frac{27 \times 27}{25 \times 25}$$

$= 2041.20$

Now, $P = 2041.20$ after 2 yr

$$r = 8\%, t = \frac{6}{12} = \frac{1}{2}\text{ yr}$$

$$\text{SI} = \frac{2041.20 \times 8 \times 1}{100 \times 2} = 81.648$$

Amount after $2\frac{1}{2}$ yr $= 2041.20 + 81.648 = ₹\ 2122.85$

16. Here, $A = ₹\ 441, P = ₹\ 400$ and $n = 2$

$$\therefore\ A = P\left(1+\frac{r}{100}\right)^n \Rightarrow 441 = 400\left(1+\frac{r}{100}\right)^2$$

$$\Rightarrow \left(1+\frac{r}{100}\right)^2 = \frac{441}{400} \Rightarrow 1+\frac{r}{100} = \sqrt{\frac{441}{400}} = \frac{21}{20}$$

$$\Rightarrow \frac{r}{100} = \frac{21}{20} - 1 = \frac{1}{20} \Rightarrow r = 5\%$$

Now, new rate is $(5 + 5)\% = 10\%$

$$\therefore\ A = 400\left(1+\frac{10}{100}\right)^2 = 400\left(\frac{11}{10}\right)^2 = 400 \times \frac{121}{100} = ₹\ 484$$

17. Let sum $= ₹\ P, n = 3$ and $A = 27P$

$$\therefore\ A = P\left(1+\frac{r}{100}\right)^n \Rightarrow 27P = P\left(1+\frac{r}{100}\right)^3$$

$$\Rightarrow \left(1+\frac{r}{100}\right)^3 = 27 \Rightarrow 1+\frac{r}{100} = 3 \Rightarrow \frac{r}{100} = 2 \Rightarrow r = 200$$

Hence, rate of interest is 200%.

18. We have, $A = 2916, n = 2, r = r$ and $P = P$

$$\therefore\ 2916 = P\left(1+\frac{r}{100}\right)^2 \quad \text{...(i)}$$

Again, we have $A = 3149.28, n = 3, r = r, P = P$

$$\therefore\ 3149.28 = P\left(1+\frac{r}{100}\right)^3 \quad \text{...(ii)}$$

On dividing Eqs. (i) and (ii), we get

$$1+\frac{r}{100} = 1.08$$

On putting the value of $1+\frac{r}{100} = 1.08$ in Eq. (i), we get

$$P = \frac{2916}{(1.08)^2} = 2500$$

$\therefore$ Principal $= ₹\ 2500$

19. **Hint** $A = P\left(1+\frac{r_1}{100}\right)\left(1+\frac{r_2}{100}\right) = 25000\left(1+\frac{4}{100}\right)\left(1+\frac{5}{100}\right)$

Ans. ₹ 27300

20. Let the principal be ₹ P.

Then, compound interest when compounded half-yearly.

$$\therefore\ \text{CI} = P\left[\left(1+\frac{20}{200}\right)^4 - 1\right] = ₹\ \frac{4641P}{10000}$$

Compound interest when compounded annually.

$$\text{CI} = P\left[\left(1+\frac{20}{100}\right)^2 - 1\right] = ₹\ \frac{11P}{25}$$

According to the question, $\frac{4641P}{10000} - \frac{11P}{25} = 964$

Ans. Principal $= ₹\ 40000$

21. Solve as Example 15. **Ans.** 30 yr

22. **Hint** Let Principal $= ₹\ P$, SI $= ₹\ 256$, $r = \frac{25}{2}\%$ and $t = 2$ yr

$$\therefore\ P = \frac{\text{SI}}{rt} = \frac{256 \times 100}{\frac{25}{2} \times 2} = ₹\ 1024$$

Principal $= ₹\ 1024$, $r = \frac{25}{2}\%$ and $n = 2$

$$\text{CI} = P\left[\left(1+\frac{r}{100}\right)^2 - 1\right] = 1024\left[\left(1+\frac{25}{200}\right)^2 - 1\right] = ₹\ 272$$

$\therefore$ Compound interest $= ₹\ 272$

23. **Hint** Here, CI – SI $= ₹\ 32$, $r = 8\%$ and $n = 2$ yr

$$\text{CI} - \text{SI} = P\left(1+\frac{r}{100}\right)^2 - P - \frac{P \times r \times t}{100}$$

$$\Rightarrow 32 = P\left[\left(1+\frac{8}{100}\right)^2 - 1 - \frac{8 \times 2}{100}\right] = ₹\ 5000$$

24. **Hint** Let the sum $= ₹\ P$ and rate of interest $= r\%$

Given, SI $= ₹\ 5000$ and $t = 2$ yr

$$\therefore\ \text{SI} = \frac{P \times r \times t}{100} \Rightarrow 5000 = \frac{Pr \times 2}{100}$$

$$\Rightarrow Pr = 250000 \Rightarrow P = \frac{250000}{r}$$

Also, given CI $= 5500$ and $n = 2$

$$\therefore\ \text{CI} = P\left[\left(1+\frac{r}{100}\right)^2 - 1\right]$$

$$\Rightarrow 5500 = P\left(1+\frac{r^2}{10000}+\frac{2r}{100}-1\right) \Rightarrow 5500 = P\left(\frac{r^2+200r}{10000}\right)$$

$$\Rightarrow 5500 = \frac{250000}{r}\left(\frac{r^2+200r}{10000}\right) \quad \left[\because P = \frac{250000}{r}\right]$$

$$\Rightarrow r = \frac{500}{25} = 20\% \Rightarrow P = \frac{250000}{r} = \frac{250000}{20} = 12500$$

$\therefore$ Rate of interest $= 20\%$ per annum

Sum of money $= ₹\ 12500$

25. **Hint** $2P = P\left(1+\frac{6}{100}\right)^n \Rightarrow 2 = (1.06)^n$

$$\Rightarrow \log 2 = n \log 1.06 \Rightarrow n = \frac{\log 2}{\log 1.06} = \frac{0.3010}{0.0253} = 11.89$$

Ans. 11.89 yr (approx)

26. **Hint** $A = P\left(1+\frac{r}{100}\right)^n$

Ans. ₹ 16126.80, ₹ 14037.60, ₹ 13230

27. Solve as Example 18. **Ans.** 8% effective

28. Solve as Example 18. **Ans.** 8%

Annuities

An **annuity** is a sequence of equal payments made at equal intervals of time with compound interest on these payments.

There are some related terms to annuities given below

- **Payment Period** The time period between successive payments is called payment period or payment interval. It may be weekly, monthly, quarterly, annually etc., or any fixed period of time.
- **Duration of the Annuity** The time from the beginning of the first interval to the end of the last interval is called the term or duration of the annuity.
- **Periodic Payment** The size of each payment of an annuity is called the periodic payment of the annuity. The person who receives the payment is called annuitant.
- **Instalment** The payment of each single annuity is called an instalment.

Types of Annuities

Annuities are of three types

(i) **Certain annuities** the number of payments is fixed i.e. the payments begin and end on fixed dates.

(ii) A **contingent annuity** is one where the term depends upon some event whose occurrence is not fixed.

(iii) A **perpetual annuity** or **perpetuity** is an annuity whose term does not end i.e. it extends till infinity.

Annuities are further classified in three categories on the basis of payment dates

(i) **Ordinary Annuity or Immediate Annuity** An ordinary annuity or immediate annuity is an annuity, where payments are made at the end of each payment period i.e. first payment is made at the end of the first payment interval and so on.

(ii) **Annuity Due** An annuity due is an annuity, where payments are made at the beginning of each period.

(iii) **Deferred Annuity** If the payments start after a specified number of periods, we get a deferred annuity.

In deferred annuity a first payment is postponed for a certain number of payment periods.

Future Value (A)

The amount or future value of an annuity is the total amount due at the end of the term of the annuity.

The future value of an annuity is

Case I In case of annuity due

$$A = \frac{R}{i}(1+i)\,[(1+i)^n - 1]$$

Case II In case of immediate annuity

$$A = \frac{R}{i}[(1+i)^n - 1]$$

[for deferred annuity use same formula]

where, A = Future value, R = Monthly instalment, i = Interest rate, n = Time

EXAMPLE 1. Find the amount of an ordinary annuity of ₹ 600 payable at the end of each year for 8 yr at 8% per year compounded annually. [given, $(1.08)^8 = 1.8509$]

Sol. Given, $R = ₹\ 600$, $n = 8$ yr and $i = \frac{8}{100} = 0.08$

We know that, $A = R\left[\frac{(1+i)^n - 1}{i}\right]$

$$\Rightarrow \quad A = 600\left[\frac{(1+0.08)^8 - 1}{0.08}\right] = 600\left[\frac{(1.08)^8 - 1}{0.08}\right]$$

$$= \frac{600}{0.08}(1.8509 - 1) = \frac{600}{0.08} \times 0.8509$$

$= ₹\ 6381.98$

EXAMPLE 2. Find the amount of an ordinary annuity of payment of ₹ 500 is made at the end of every quarter for 10 yr at the rate of 8% per year compounded quarterly. [Use $(1.02)^{40} = 2.2080$]

Sol. Given, $R = 500$,

n = Number of payment periods

= Number of years × Number of payment per year

$= 10 \times 4 = 40$

$i = \text{interest} = \frac{8}{400} = 0.02$

We know that, $A = R\left[\frac{(1+i)^n - 1}{i}\right]$

$$\because \quad A = 500\left(\frac{(1.02)^{40} - 1}{0.02}\right) = 500\left(\frac{2.2080 - 1}{0.02}\right)$$

$= 500 \times 60.4 = 30200$

Hence, amount of the given annuity = ₹ 30200

EXAMPLE 3. A man wants to have ₹ 16000 in his account after 10 yr. He deposits, annual payments in account that pays 6% rate of interest compounded annually. How much should he deposited each year? [given, $(1.06)^{10} = 1.7908$]

Sol. Given, $A = ₹\ 16000, n = 10$ and $i = \frac{6}{100} = 0.06$

We know that, $A = R\left[\frac{(1+i)^n - 1}{i}\right]$

$$\Rightarrow \quad 16000 = R\left[\frac{(1+0.06)^{10} - 1}{i}\right]$$

$$\Rightarrow \quad 16000 \times 0.06 = R\{(1.06)^{10} - 1\}$$

$$\Rightarrow \quad R = \frac{16000 \times 0.06}{(1.06)^{10} - 1}$$

$$= \frac{960}{(1.7908 - 1)}$$

$$= \frac{960}{0.7908}$$

$$= ₹\ 1213.9605$$

EXAMPLE 4. A bank pays 8% interest, compounded quarterly, what equal deposits have to be made at the end of each quarter for 3 yr, if you want to have ₹ 1600 at the end of 3 yr. [use $(1.02)^{12} = 1.2682$]

Sol. Let equal deposit = ₹ R

n = Number of periods = Number of equal deposits $= 3 \times 4 = 12$

i = Interest per period $= \frac{8}{100 \times 4} = 0.02$

Future value of annuity = ₹ 1600

$$\Rightarrow \quad A = R\left\{\frac{(1+i)^n - 1}{i}\right\}$$

$$\Rightarrow \quad 1600 = R\left\{\frac{(1+0.02)^{12} - 1}{0.02}\right\}$$

$$\Rightarrow \quad R = \frac{1600 \times 0.02}{(1.02)^{12} - 1}$$

$$= \frac{1600 \times 0.02}{0.2682}$$

$$= \frac{32}{0.2682}$$

$$= 119.313$$

Present Value

If money is worth i per period, then the present value of amount R due n periods.

Hence, that principal which, invested now at the rate i per period will amount to R in n period.

The present value P of an amount R due n period.

Hence, at the rate i per period is given by $P = R(1+i)^{-n}$.

Present value of an annuity = Amount $\times (1+i)^{-n}$

Present Value in Different Cases

Case I In case of an **ordinary annuity**, the present value (P) is

$$P = \frac{R}{i}[1 - (1+i)^{-n}]$$

where, R = Monthly instalment, i = Interest rate, n = Time

Case II In case of an **annuity due** the present value (P) is

$$P = \frac{R}{i}(1+i)[1 - (1+i)^{-n}]$$

where, R = Monthly instalment, i = Interest rate, n = Time

The present value (P) for **perpetual annuity** is

$$P = \frac{a}{i}$$

where, a = Monthly instalment, i = Interest rate

EXAMPLE 5. Find the present value of ₹ 30000 due 10 yr hence when interest 8% compound annually.

Sol. We have, $R = ₹\ 30000, i = \frac{8}{100} = 0.08$ and $n = 10$

$$\therefore \quad P = R(1+i)^{-n}$$

$$\Rightarrow \quad P = 30000(1+0.08)^{-10}$$

$$\Rightarrow \quad P = 30000(0.4631) \qquad [\because (1.08)^{-10} = 0.4631]$$

$$\Rightarrow \quad P = 13893$$

Hence, present value = ₹ 13893

EXAMPLE 6. Find the present value of ₹ 60000 due 20 yr, when interest of 5% is compounded semi-annually. [given, $(1.025)^{-40} = 0.3724$]

Sol. Here, $R = ₹\ 60000, r = \frac{5}{2}\%$ (semi-annually)

and $n = 20 \times 2 = 40$

$$\therefore \quad P = A(1+r)^{-n} = 60000\left(1 + \frac{5}{200}\right)^{-40}$$

$$= 60000(1.025)^{-40}$$

$$= 60000 \times 0.3724$$

$$= 22344$$

$\therefore$ Present value = ₹ 22344

EXAMPLE 7. What equal payments mode at the begining of each year for 20 yr will pay for the shop priced at ₹ 500000, if money is worth 8% per annum compounded annually.

Sol. Given, the value of shop (Present value) $(A) = 500000$

$$\text{Rate } (i) = \frac{8}{100} = 0.08$$

$$n = 20$$

For annuity due present value

$$P = R\left[(1+i)\left(\frac{1-(1+i)}{i}\right)^{-n}\right]$$

$$\Rightarrow \quad 500000 = R\left[(1+0.08)\left(\frac{1-(1+0.08)}{0.08}\right)^{-10}\right]$$

$$\Rightarrow \quad 500000 = R(1.08)\left[\frac{1-0.4631}{0.08}\right]$$

$$\Rightarrow \quad R = \frac{500000 \times 0.08}{(1.08)\times(0.5369)}$$

$$= \frac{40000}{0.5798}$$

$$= 68989.3066$$

EXAMPLE 8. Find the present value of a sequence of annual payments of ₹ 10000 each, the first being made at the end of 5th yr and the last being made at the end of 12th yr, if money is worth 6%.

Sol. We have a defferred annuity of 8 terms, i.e. $n = 8$ and defferred for 4 terms i.e. $m = 4$

$$R = ₹\ 10000 \text{ and } i = \frac{6}{100} = 0.06$$

Now, we know that

$$P = \frac{R}{i}\left[\frac{1}{(1+i)^m} - \frac{1}{(1+i)^{m+n}}\right]$$

$$= \frac{10000}{0.06}\left[\frac{1}{(1+0.06)^4} - \frac{1}{(1+0.06)^{4+8}}\right]$$

$$= \frac{10000}{0.06}[(1.06)^{-4} - (1.06)^{-12}] \quad \text{...(i)}$$

Let $x = (1.06)^{-4}$ and $y = (1.06)^{-12}$

Now, $\log x = -4\log(1.06)$

$\Rightarrow \log x = -4 \times 0.0253$

$\Rightarrow \log x = -0.1012$

$\Rightarrow x = \text{antilog}(-0.1012)$

$\Rightarrow x = 0.7921$

Find, $\log y = -12\log(1.06)$

$\Rightarrow \log y = -12 \times 0.0253$

$\Rightarrow \log y = -0.3036$

$\Rightarrow y = \text{antilog}(-0.3036)$

$\Rightarrow y = 0.4971$

Now, putting value of x and y in Eq. (i), we get

$$P = \frac{10000}{0.06}[0.7921 - 0.4971]$$

$$= \frac{10000}{0.06} \times 0.295$$

$$= ₹\ 49166.67$$

EXAMPLE 9. A project requires an initial investment of ₹ 250000 and is expected to generate the following net cash inflows year-1 : ₹ 98000, year-2 : ₹ 120000, year-3 : ₹ 150000. Compute the net present value of the investment, if the discount rate is 12%. [given, $(1.12)^{-2} = 0.7973$, $(1.12)^{-3} = 0.7119$]

Sol. Given, present value of cash out flow = 250000

Cash inflow = 98000 (for Ist year)

= 120000 (for IInd year)

= 150000 (for IIIrd year)

$$\text{Rate } (i) = \frac{12}{100} = 0.12$$

So, the present value of cash inflow of Ist year

$$= \frac{98000}{1.12} = ₹\ 87500$$

and the present value of cash inflow of IInd year

$$= \frac{120000}{(1.12)^2}$$

$$= 120000 \times 0.7973$$

$$= ₹\ 95676$$

The present value of cash inflow for IIIrd year

$$= \frac{150000}{(1.12)^3}$$

$$= 150000 \times 0.7119$$

$$= ₹\ 106785$$

∴ Net present value = (Sum of present value of all cash inflow) − Present value of cash outflow

Sum of present value of all cash inflows

$$= (87500 + 95676 + 106785)$$

$$= ₹\ 289961$$

Net present value = 289961 − 250000 = ₹ 39961

Hence, net present value of instalment = ₹ 39961

Topic Practice 2

1 Find the amount of regular annuity of ₹ 6000 payable at the end of each year for 11 yr at 8% per annum compounded annually. [given, $(1.08)^{11} = 2.3316$]

2 Rohan deposited in a bank ₹ 12000 at the end of each year for 8 yr. If compound interest at 12% per annum is reckoned, what would be the sum standing to his credit at the end of period? [given, $(1.12)^{8} = 2.4759$]

3 Find the amount of an annuity consisting of payments of ₹ 500 made at the end of every 3 months for 4 yr at the rate of 6% compounded quarterly. [given, $(1.015)^{16} = 1.2689$]

4 A man wants to have ₹ 15000 in his account after 10 yr. He deposits, annual payments in account that pays 4% rate of interest compounded annually. How much should he deposited each year? [given, $(1.04)^{10} = 1.479$]

5 If a bank pays 6% interest per annum compounded half-yearly. Then, find the equal amount should be deposited at the end of each half-year for $2\frac{1}{2}$ yr to get an amount of ₹ 3000 at the end of 30 months. [given, $(1.03)^{5} = 1.159$]

6 Find the least number of years for which an annuity of ₹ 1500 per annum must run in order that its amount just exceeds ₹ 30000 at 9% compounded annually.

7 An annuity consists of 24 quarterly instalments of ₹ 800 each, the first being made at the end of 4 yr. Find the amount of this annuity, if money is worth 10% per annum compounded quarterly. [given, $(1.025)^{24} = 1.8087$]

8 A machine costs ₹ 98000 and its effective life is estimated to 12 yr. If the scrap value is ₹ 3000 only, what should be retained out of profits at the end of each year to accumulate at compound interest at 5% per annum for depreciation, so that a new machine can be purchased at the same price after 12 yr. [given, $\log 1.05 = 0.0212$ and $\log 1.797 = 0.2544$]

9 Find the present value of ₹ 30000 due 20 yr, hence when the interest is 6% compounded annually. [given, $(1.06)^{-20} = 0.3118$]

10 Find the present value of ₹ 40000 due 20 yr at the rate of 8% compounded semi-annually. [given, $(1.04)^{-40} = 0.2082$]

11 How much money should Sanjiv deposit with the bank, so that he receives ₹ 25000 after 4 yr and another ₹ 50000 after 6 yr from the date of deposit, if the rate of interest is 8% per annum. [given, $(1.08)^{-4} = 0.7350$ and $(1.08)^{-6} = 0.6302$]

12 Find the present value of a regular annuity of ₹ 2000 payable for 5 yr at 10% per annum compounded annually. [given, $(1.10)^{-5} = 0.6209$]

13 Find the present value of a regular annuity of ₹ 1000 payable for 3 yr at 12% per annum compounded annually.

Hints & Solutions

1. Solve as Example 1. **Ans.** ₹ 99870
2. Solve as Example 1. **Ans.** ₹ 147590
3. Solve as Example 2. **Ans.** ₹ 8963.33
4. Solve as Example 3. **Ans.** ₹ 1252.60
5. Solve as Example 4. **Ans.** ₹ 566.03
6. Here, $A = ₹\ 30000$, $R = 1500$ and $i = \frac{9}{100} = 0.09$

$$\therefore \quad A = R\left(\frac{(1+i)^n - 1}{i}\right)$$

$$\Rightarrow \quad 30000 = 1500\frac{((1.09)^n - 1)}{0.09}$$

$$\Rightarrow \quad (1.09)^n - 1 = \frac{30000 \times 0.09}{1500} = 1.8$$

$$\Rightarrow \quad (1.09)^n = 1 + 1.8 = 2.8$$

Taking log on both sides, we get

$$n\log(1.09) = \log 2.8$$

$$\Rightarrow \quad n = \frac{\log 2.8}{\log 1.09} = \frac{0.4771}{0.0374} = 12.75$$

∴ Minimum years = 12 yr

7. Solve as Example 2. **Ans.** ₹ 25878.40
8. **Hint** Given,

Total cost of machine = ₹ 98000

Amount realised from scrap = ₹ 3000

∴ Remaining amount = ₹ (98000 – 3000) = ₹ 95000

$n = 12$ and $i = \frac{5}{100} = 0.05$

$$\therefore \quad A = R\left\{\frac{(1+i)^n - 1}{i}\right\}$$

$\Rightarrow \quad 95000 = R\left\{\frac{(1+0.05)^{12}-1}{0.05}\right\}$

$\Rightarrow \quad 95000 = R\left\{\frac{(1.05)^{12}-1}{0.05}\right\}$

Let $\quad x = (1.05)^{12}$

$\Rightarrow \quad \log x = 12\log 1.05 = 12 \times 0.0212 = 0.2544$

$\Rightarrow \quad x = 1.797$

$\Rightarrow \quad 95000 = R\left(\frac{1.797-1}{0.05}\right)$

$\Rightarrow \quad R = \frac{95000 \times 0.05}{0.797} \Rightarrow R = 5959.84$

Thus, ₹ 5959.84 should be retain out.

9. Solve as Example 5. **Ans.** ₹ 9354

10. **Hint** Given, $S =$ ₹ 40000,

$r = 8\%$ compounded semi-annually

$\therefore \quad r = \frac{8}{2}\% = 0.04$

$\Rightarrow \quad n = 20 \times 2 = 40$

$\therefore \quad P = S(1+r)^{-n}$

$= 40000(1+0.04)^{-40} = 40000(1.04)^{-40}$

$= 40000 \times 0.2082 = 8328$

Hence, present value are ₹ 8328.

11. **Hint** Let P_1 be the present value of $A_1 = 25000$ due after 4 yr and P_2 be the present value of $A_2 = 50000$ due after 6 yr.

Then, $P_1 = A_1(1+r)^{-4}$ and $P_2 = A_2(1+r)^{-6}$

$\Rightarrow \quad P_1 = 25000(1+0.08)^{-4}$ and $P_2 = 50000(1+0.08)^{-6}$

$\Rightarrow \quad P_1 = 25000(1.08)^{-4}$ and $P_2 = 50000(1.08)^{-6}$

$\Rightarrow \quad P_1 = 25000(0.7350)$ and $P_2 = 50000(0.6302)$

$\Rightarrow \quad P_1 = 18375$ and $P_2 = 31510$

$\therefore \quad P_1 + P_2 = 18375 + 31525 = 49885$

Hence, Sanjiv should deposit ₹ 49885.

12. **Hint** Given, $R =$ ₹ 2000, $i = \frac{10}{100} = 0.10$ and $n = 5$ yr

We know that

$$P = R\left[\frac{1-(1+i)^{-n}}{i}\right]$$

$$= 2000\left[\frac{1-(1+0.10)^{-5}}{0.10}\right]$$

$$= \frac{2000}{0.10}[1-(1.10)^{-5}]$$

$$= 20000(1-0.6209)$$

$$= 20000 \times 0.3791 = ₹\ 7582$$

13. **Hint** We have, $R =$ ₹ 1000, $i = \frac{12}{100} = 0.12$ and $n = 3$

Since, $\quad P = R\left[\frac{(1-(1+i)^{-n}}{i}\right]$

$$= \frac{1000}{0.12}[1-(1+0.12)^{-3}] = \frac{1000}{0.12}(1-(1.12)^{-3})$$

Let $\quad x = (1.12)^{-3}$

$\Rightarrow \quad \log x = -3\log 1.12$

$= -3 \times 0.0492 = -0.1476$

$\Rightarrow \quad x = \text{antilog}(-0.1476)$

$= 0.7119$

$\therefore \quad P = \frac{1000}{0.12}(1-0.7119) = \frac{1000}{0.12} \times 0.2881$

$= ₹\ 2400.83$

$\therefore$ Hence, present value of the annuity is ₹ 2400.83.

Exam Pattern Exercise

Part A - Objective Type Questions

Multiple Choice Type Questions

1 If the simple interest on a sum of money for 2 yr at 6% per annum is ₹ 120, then the compound interest on the same sum at the same rate for the same time is

(a) ₹ 123.50 (b) ₹ 123.60
(c) ₹ 123.80 (d) ₹ 123.90

2 The compound interest on ₹ 50000 at 5% per annum is ₹ 5125. The time period is

(a) $1\frac{1}{2}$ yr (b) 2 yr
(c) $2\frac{1}{2}$ yr (d) 3 yr

3 The compound interest for 2 yr at 5% per annum be ₹ 246, then the sum will be

(a) ₹ 2400 (b) ₹ 2000
(c) ₹ 2500 (d) ₹ 2450

4 A sum of ₹ 25000 invested at 8% per annum compounded semi-annually amount to ₹ 28121.60. Then, the time period of investment is

(a) 2 yr (b) $2\frac{1}{2}$ yr (c) $1\frac{1}{2}$ yr (d) 3 yr

5 The difference between simple interest and compound interest on ₹ 15000 for one year at 8% per annum calculated half-yearly is

(a) ₹ 620 (b) ₹ 622 (c) ₹ 624 (d) ₹ 626

6 The effective rate of return, which is equivalent to a declared rate of 10% compounded semi-annually is

(a) 10.20% (b) 10.10%
(c) 10.15% (d) 10.25%

7 The declared rate of return compounded semi-annually which is equivalent to 12.36%, effective rate of return is

(a) 11% (b) 12%
(c) 12.25% (d) 12.20%

8 The amount of money today which is equal to series of payment is future is

(a) nominal value of annuity
(b) sinking value of annuity
(c) present value of annuity
(d) future value of annuity

9 The amount of a regular annuity of ₹ 1000 payable at the end of each year for 3 yr at 10% per annum compounded annually is

(a) ₹ 3310
(b) ₹ 3300
(c) ₹ 3410
(d) ₹ 3515

10 The present value of ₹ 15000 due 15 yr, hence when the interest of 8% is compounded semi-annually is [given, $(1.04)^{-30} = 0.3083$]

(a) ₹ 4000 (b) ₹ 5000
(c) ₹ 4625 (d) ₹ 4825

Assertion-Reason Based Questions

Directions (Q. Nos. 11-13) *In the questions given below are two statements labelled as Assertion (A) and Reason (R). In the context of the two statements, which one of the following is correct?*

(a) Both A and R are correct; R is the correct explanation of A
(b) Both A and R are correct; R is not the correct explanation of A
(c) A is correct; R is incorrect
(d) R is correct; A is incorrect

11 **Assertion (A)** The compound amount of ₹ 20000 invested for 2 yr at 6% compound annually is ₹ 22472.

Reason (R) The compound interest of ₹ P invested to n years at r% compounded annually is $P\left[\left(1+\frac{r}{100}\right)^n - 1\right]$

12 **Assertion (A)** The effective rate that is equivalent to a nominal rate of 8% compounded semi-annually is 8.25%.

Reason (R) Effective rate of interest $= \left(1+\frac{r}{m}\right)^m - 1$.

13 **Assertion (A)** The amount of an ordinary annuity of ₹ 2000 payable at the end of each year of 2 yr at 10% per annum compounded annually is ₹ 4200.

Reason (R) The amount of an ordinary annuity of ₹ R period for n periods at the rate of i per period is given by $A = R\left[\frac{(1+i)^n}{i} - 1\right]$.

Part B - Descriptive Questions

Very Short Answer Type Questions

14 Ashwani invested ₹ 6000 in a company at compound interest compounded semi-annually. He receives ₹ 7986 after $1\frac{1}{2}$ yr from the company. Find the rate of interest per annum.

15 The difference between compound and simple interest on an amount of ₹ 10000 for 2 yr is ₹ 64. Find the rate of interest per annum.

16 Find the amount and the compound interest on ₹ 2000 in 2 yr, if the rate is 4% for the first year and 3% for the second year.

17. The simple interest on a certain sum for 2 yr is ₹ 1200 and compound interest is ₹ 1290. Find the sum and rate of interest.

18 If a person wants to accumulate ₹ 42000 by making equal payments at the end of each quarter for the next 5 yr, what will be the size of these investments, if money is worth 6% converted quarterly? [given, $(1.015)^{20} = 1.343$]

Short Answer Type Questions

19 Find the sum of money lent out at simple interest amounts to ₹ 2200 in one year and to ₹ 2800 in 4 yr.

20 Divide ₹ 43500 in two parts, so that the simple interest on the first, when deposited for one year at 9% per annum and that on the second, when deposited for two years at 10% per annum in a bank are the same.

21 On a certain sum of money, the difference between the compound interest for a year, payable half-yearly, and the simple interest for a year is ₹ 180. Find the sum lent out, if the rate of interest in both the cases is 10%.

22 Find the amount of an ordinary annuity of ₹ 1500 at the end of each year for 3 yr at 10% per year compounded annually.

23 Veena is allotted a LIG flat for which she has to make an immediate payment of ₹ 300000 and 12 semi-annual instalments of ₹ 10000 each, the first being paid at the end of 4 yr. Find the cash price of the flat, if money is worth 16% per annum computed semi-annually.

Long Answer Type Questions

24 In what time will ₹ 10800 amount to ₹ 18000 at 5% compounded quarterly.
[given, $\log(1.0125) = 0.0053$]

25 A sum of money is deposited in a bank at compound interest compounded semi-annually. The amount at the end of 4 yr is ₹ 10948.55 and the amount became ₹ 14983.85 at the end of 8 yr. Find the money deposited and the rate of interest.

26 A sum invested under compound interest double itself in 10 yr. In how many years will it becomes 8 times of the initial sum.

27 How much should a company set aside at the end of each year, if it has to buy a machine expected to cost ₹ 100000 at the end of 4 yr and the rate of interest is 5% per annum compounded annually?

28 The price of a tape recorder is ₹ 1561. A person purchases it by paying ₹ 300 in cash and the balance is to be paid with due interest in 3 half-yearly equal instalments. If the dealer charges interest at the rate of 10% per annum compounded half-yearly, then find the value of each instalment.

Case Study Based Questions

29 The effective rate of return is the rate of interest on an investment when compounding occurs more than once.

The formula for the effective rate of return is

$$\text{Effective rate of return } (r_e) = \left(1 + \frac{r}{m}\right)^m - 1$$

Where, r = annual rate of return

m = number of compounding in a year

Based on above information, answer the following questions.

(i) Find the effective rate of return, which is equivalent to declared rate of 6% compounded semi-annually.

(ii) The declared rate of return compounded semi-annually which is equivalent to 10.25%, then find effective rate of return.

(iii) Find the amount will ₹ 12000 accumulate in 12 yr, if invested at an effective rate of 5%. [given, $(1.05)^{12} = 1.7958$]

Or

How many years will it take for money to double at the effective rate of 8%? [given, $\log(1.08) = 0.0334$]

30 A project requires an initial investment of ₹ 250000 and is expected to generate the following net cash inflows year-1 : ₹ 98000, year-2 : ₹ 120000 and year-3 : ₹ 150000. The discount rate is 12% per annum.

Based on the above information, answer the following questions.

(i) Find the present value of cash inflow expected to generate at the end of year-1.

(ii) Find the present value of cash inflow expected to generate at the end of second year. [given, $(1.12)^{-2} = 0.7973$]

(iii) Find the present value of cash inflow expected to generate at end of third year. [given, $(1.12)^{-3} = 0.7119$]

Or

Find the difference between the net present value and the present value of cash outflow.

Hints & Solutions

1. (b)	2. (b)	3. (a)	4. (c)
5. (c)	6. (d)	7. (b)	8. (c)
9. (a)	10. (c)	11. (a)	12. (d)
13. (c)			
14. 20%	15. 8%	16. ₹ 142.40	

17. Rate = 15%, Principal value = ₹ 4000

18. **Hint** Given, $A = ₹\,42000$, $i = \dfrac{6}{4 \times 100} = 0.015$

and $n = 5 \times 4 = 20$

We know that,

$$A = R\left\{\frac{(1+i)^n - 1}{i}\right\}$$

$$\Rightarrow \quad 42000 = R\left\{\frac{(1+0.015)^{20} - 1}{0.015}\right\}$$

$$\Rightarrow \quad 42000 = R\left\{\frac{(1.015)^{20} - 1}{0.015}\right\}$$

$$\Rightarrow \quad 42000 = R\left\{\frac{1.343 - 1}{0.015}\right\}$$

$$\Rightarrow \quad R = \frac{42000 \times 0.015}{0.343}$$

$$= ₹\,1834.59$$

19. **Hint** Let the sum be ₹ P and rate of interest is r %.

Let S_1 and S_2 be the amount in one and 4 yr, respectively.

$\therefore \quad S_1 = P(1 + r)$ and $S_2 = P(1 + 4r)$

$$\Rightarrow \quad 2200 = P(1 + r) \quad \text{...(i)}$$

$$\text{and} \quad 2800 = P(1 + 4r) \quad \text{...(ii)}$$

On dividing Eq. (ii) by Eq. (i), we get

$$\frac{2800}{2200} = \frac{P(1+4r)}{P(1+r)} = \frac{1+4r}{1+r}$$

$$\Rightarrow \quad \frac{14}{11} = \frac{1+4r}{1+r}$$

$$\Rightarrow \quad 14 + 14r = 11 + 44r$$

$$\Rightarrow \quad r = \frac{1}{10}$$

Putting the value of r in Eq. (i), we get

$$2200 = P\left(1 + \frac{1}{10}\right) \Rightarrow 2200 = P\left(\frac{11}{10}\right)$$

$$\Rightarrow \quad P = \frac{2200 \times 10}{11} = 2000$$

Hence, sum of money is ₹ 2000.

20. **Hint** Let the first part be ₹ x, then the second part be ₹ $(43500 - x)$.

For the first part, we have

$$P = x,\ r = \frac{9}{100} \text{ and } t = 1 \text{ yr}$$

$$\therefore \quad I_1 = P \times r \times t = \frac{x \times 9 \times 1}{100} = \frac{9x}{100}$$

For the second part, we have

$$P = ₹(43500 - x),\ r = \frac{10}{100} \text{ and } t = 2 \text{ yr}$$

$$\therefore \quad I_2 = \frac{(43500 - x) \times 10 \times 2}{100} = \frac{20}{100}(43500 - x)$$

Given, $I_1 = I_2$

$$\therefore \quad \frac{9x}{100} = \frac{20}{100}(43500 - x)$$

$$\Rightarrow \quad 9x = 20 \times 43500 - 20x$$

$$\Rightarrow \quad 29x = 20 \times 43500$$

$$\Rightarrow \quad x = \frac{20 \times 43500}{29} \Rightarrow x = 30000$$

Hence, the required parts are ₹ 30000 and ₹ 13500, respectively.

21. ₹ 72000

22. **Hint** Given, $R = ₹\,1500$, $n = 3$ and $i = \dfrac{10}{100} = 0.1$

$$\therefore \quad A = R\left\{\frac{(1+i)^n - 1}{i}\right\}$$

$$\Rightarrow \quad A = 1500\left\{\frac{(1+0.1)^3 - 1}{0.1}\right\}$$

$$= 1500\left\{\frac{(1.1)^3 - 1}{0.1}\right\}$$

$$= 1500\left(\frac{1.331-1}{0.1}\right)$$

$$= 1500 \times \left(\frac{0.331}{0.1}\right) = ₹\ 4965$$

23. **Hint** We have, $R = ₹\ 10000$, $i = \frac{16}{2 \times 100} = \frac{16}{200} = 0.08$,

$n = 12$ and deferment period is $3\frac{1}{2}$ yr i.e. $m = 7$ terms.

Now, present value of annuity

$$P = 10000\,(9.6036 - 5.2064)$$
$$= 43972$$
$$\Rightarrow \quad P = ₹\ 43972$$

$\therefore$ Cash price of flat = Down payment + Present value of annuity

$$= ₹(300000 + 43972) = ₹\ 343972$$

24. **Hint** Let the required time be t yr.

It is given that

$P = ₹\ 10800$, $A = ₹\ 18000$, $n = 4t$ and $r = \frac{5}{400} = 0.0125$

We know that, $A = P(1 + r)^n$

$$\therefore \quad 18000 = 10800(1 + 0.0125)^{4t}$$

$$\Rightarrow \quad \frac{18000}{10800} = (1.0125)^{4t} \Rightarrow \frac{5}{3} = (1.0125)^{4t}$$

Taking log on both sides, we get

$$\log 5 - \log 3 = 4t \log(1.0125)$$

$$\Rightarrow \quad 0.6990 - 0.4771 = 4t\,(0.0053)$$

$$\Rightarrow \quad 4t = \frac{0.2219}{0.0053} = 41.86$$

$$\Rightarrow \quad t = \frac{41.86}{4} = 10.46$$

Hence, required time is 10.46 yr.

25. $r = 8\%$, $P = ₹\ 8000$

26. **Hint** Let the sum be ₹ P.

It is given that sum becomes double in 10 yr.

$$\therefore \quad A = 2P \text{ and } n = 10$$

$$\Rightarrow \quad A = P(1 + r)^n \Rightarrow 2P = P(1 + r)^{10}$$

$$\Rightarrow \quad 2 = (1 + r)^{10} \quad \text{...(i)}$$

Let money becomes 8 times of itself in n yr.

Then, $\quad A = P(1 + r)^n$

$$\Rightarrow \quad 8P = P(1 + r)^n \Rightarrow 8 = (1 + r)^n$$

$$\Rightarrow \quad 2^3 = (1 + r)^n \quad \text{...(ii)}$$

From Eqs. (i) and (ii), we get

$$[(1 + r)^{10}]^3 = (1 + r)^n$$

$$\Rightarrow \quad (1 + r)^{30} = (1 + r)^n \Rightarrow n = 30$$

Hence, the money will becomes 8 times in 30 yr.

27. **Hint** According to the question,

The total amount (P) is ₹ 100000.

The rate of interest, $i = 5\%$ per annum $= \frac{5}{100}$ per annum

Since, the amount to be paid in 4 yr.

$$\therefore \quad n = 4$$

Let the amount R to be paid by company at the end of each year,

We know that,

$$P = \frac{R}{i}[(1 + i)^n - 1]$$

$$\Rightarrow \quad 100000 = \frac{R}{\frac{5}{100}}\left[\left(1 + \frac{5}{100}\right)^4 - 1\right]$$

$$\Rightarrow \quad 100000 = \frac{R}{\frac{5}{100}}\left[\left(1 + \frac{1}{20}\right)^4 - 1\right]$$

$$\Rightarrow \quad 100000 = \frac{R}{\frac{1}{20}}\left[\left(\frac{21}{20}\right)^4 - 1\right]$$

$$\Rightarrow \quad 100000 = \frac{R}{0.05}[(1.05)^4 - 1]$$

$$\Rightarrow \quad 100000 = \frac{R}{0.05}(1.2155 - 1)$$

$$\Rightarrow \quad 100000 = \frac{R}{0.05} \times 0.2155$$

$$\therefore \quad R = \frac{100000 \times 0.05}{0.2155}$$

$$= \frac{5000}{2155} \times 10000$$

$$= \frac{50000000}{2155} = 23201.85$$

Hence, the company have to paid ₹ 23201.85 at the end of each year.

28. **Hint** According to the question,

The total price of a tape recorder is ₹ 1561.

Cash down payment at the time of purchase is ₹ 300.

Balance to be paid in instalment (P) = ₹(1561 − 300)

= ₹ 1261

The total number of instalment (n) = 3 (half-yearly)

The rate of interest, $i = \frac{10}{2 \times 100}$

= 5% per annum half-yearly

Let the value of each instalment is R.

We know that,

$$P = \frac{R}{i}[1 - (1 + i)^{-n}] \quad \text{...(i)}$$

Now, we put the values of P, i and n in Eq. (i), we get

$$1261 = \frac{R}{\frac{5}{100}}\left[1-\left(1+\frac{5}{100}\right)^{-3}\right]$$

$$\Rightarrow \quad 1261 = \frac{R}{0.05}[1-(1.05)^{-3}] \quad \ldots(ii)$$

Let $\quad x = (1.05)^{-3} \quad \ldots(iii)$

Taking log on both sides Eq. (iii), we get

$$\log x = -3\log(1.05) = -3\log(1.05)$$
$$= -3\times 0.0212 = -0.0636$$

Taking antilog of -0.0636, we get

Antilog $-0.0636 = 0.8638$

Now, put the value of $(1.05)^{-3} = 0.8638$ in Eq. (ii), we get

$$1261 = \frac{R}{0.05}(1-0.8638)$$

$$\Rightarrow \quad 1261 = \frac{R}{0.05}\times 0.1362$$

$$\therefore \quad R = \frac{1261\times 0.05}{0.1362}$$
$$= \frac{63.05}{0.1362} = \frac{630500}{1362}$$
$$= 462.92 \text{ (approx.)}$$

Hence, the value of each instalment is ₹ 462.92.

29. **Hint** (i) Here, $r = 6\%$ and $m = 2$

$$r_e = \left(1+\frac{r}{m}\right)^m - 1$$

$$\Rightarrow \quad r_e = \left(1+\frac{6}{200}\right)^2 - 1$$

$$\Rightarrow \quad r_e = (1.03)^2 - 1 = 1.0609 - 1 = 0.0609$$

∴ Effective rate $= (0.0609 \times 100)\% = 6.09\%$

(ii) Here, $r_e = 10.25\% = 0.1025$ and $m = 2$

$$\therefore \quad r_e = \left(1+\frac{r}{m}\right)^m - 1$$

$$\Rightarrow \quad 0.1025 = \left(1+\frac{r}{2}\right)^2 - 1$$

$$\Rightarrow \left(1+\frac{r}{2}\right)^2 = 1.1025$$

$$\Rightarrow \quad 1+\frac{r}{2} = 1.05 \Rightarrow \frac{r}{2} = 0.05 \Rightarrow r = 0.10$$

∴ Declared rate $= (0.10 \times 100)\% = 10\%$

(iii) Here, $P =$ ₹ 12000, $r = 5\%$ and $n = 12$ yr

$$\therefore \quad A = P(1+r)^n$$
$$= 12000(1+0.05)^{12}$$
$$= 12000(1.05)^{12} = 12000(1.7958) = 21550$$

∴ Amount = ₹ 21550

Or

Let principal = ₹ P, Amount = $2P$

and $r = 8\% = 0.08$

$$\therefore \quad A = P(1+r)^n$$

$$\Rightarrow \quad 2P = P(1+0.08)^n \Rightarrow 2 = (1.08)^n$$

Taking log on both sides, we get

$$\log 2 = n \log 1.08$$

$$\Rightarrow \quad n = \frac{\log 2}{\log 1.08} = \frac{0.3010}{0.0334} = 9.01 \text{ yr}$$

∴ Time = 9 yr

30. **Hint** We have, present value of cash outflow = ₹ 250000

and $i = \frac{12}{100} = 0.12$

(i) Cash inflows of year-1 = ₹ 98000

Present value of cash inflow of year-1

$$= \frac{98000}{(1+i)} = \frac{98000}{(1+0.12)} = \frac{98000}{1.12}$$
$$= ₹\ 87500$$

(ii) Cash inflows of year-2 = ₹ 12000

Present value of cash inflow of year-2

$$= ₹\ \frac{120000}{(1+i)^2} = \frac{120000}{(1+0.12)^2}$$
$$= 120000 \times (1.12)^{-2}$$
$$= 120000 \times 0.7973$$
$$= ₹\ 95676$$

(iii) Cash inflows of year-3 = ₹ 15000

Present value of cash inflow of year-3

$$= ₹\ \frac{150000}{(1+i)^3} = \frac{150000}{(1+0.12)^3}$$
$$= 150000 \times (1.12)^{-3}$$
$$= 150000 \times 0.7119 = ₹\ 106785$$

Or

Sum of present values of all cash inflows

$$= ₹\ (87500 + 95676 + 106785) = ₹\ 289961$$

∴ The difference between the net present value and the present value of cash outflow

$$= ₹\ (289961 - 250000) = ₹\ 39961$$

CHAPTER 20

Taxation

In this Chapter...

- Goods and Services Tax
- Income Tax

Taxation is an important component of modern economies. It is the process by which governments collect money from individuals and businesses in the form of **taxes**, to fund public services, infrastructure and other essential functions.

The **primary purpose** of taxation is to generate funds for government expenditures.

Taxes can also be designed to **reduce income inequality** by transferring wealth from higher-income individuals to those with lower incomes.

Classification of Taxes

1. Direct Tax

This tax is imposed directly on individuals or entities. The burden of this tax cannot be shifted to another person or entity.

e.g. Income tax, corporate tax, property tax, etc.

2. Indirect Tax

This tax is imposed on goods and services rather than on individuals or entities directly. The burden of this tax can be shifted to the final consumer.

e.g. Value Added Tax (VAT), excise duty, custom duty, sales tax, etc.

From the year 2017, **Goods and Services Tax** (GST) has replaced many Central level and State level indirect taxes like excise duty, custom duty, service tax, central sales tax, Value Added Tax (VAT), entertainment tax, etc.

Difference between Direct and Indirect Taxes

Basis	Direct Tax	Indirect Tax
Imposition	It is imposed directly on individuals or entities.	It is imposed on goods and services.
Incidence	The impact and incidence of direct tax falls directly on the taxpayers, affecting their income, profits or wealth.	The burden of indirect tax is initially borne by the producer or seller of goods and services, but it can be passed on to the consumer through higher prices.
Nature	Often designed to be progressive in nature i.e. the tax rate increases as the taxpayer's income or wealth increases. This is aimed at distributing the tax burden more equitably based on the ability to pay.	Generally proportional in nature, as the rate of tax remain fixed as per a definite slab but the amount of tax increases with the increase in production.
Example	Income tax, corporate tax, etc.	GST, custom duty, etc

Goods and Services Tax

Goods and Services Tax (GST) is a comprehensive indirect tax levied on the supply of goods and services at each stage of the production and distribution chain. It is a destination-based tax i.e. it is collected at the point of consumption rather than at the point of origin.

Goods and Services Tax (GST) was introduced in India to simplify the complex indirect tax structure prevailing in the country. It marked a significant shift from the previous multi-layered taxation system to a unified, destination-based tax. The introduction of GST in India took place on July 1, 2017.

Key Terms related to GST

1. **Dealer/Trader** A trader is the person who is engaged in the supply of goods or services for consideration and undertakes transactions in the course of furtherance of business.
2. **Intrastate sales** It refers to the supply of goods or services within the boundaries of a Same/single State.
3. **Interstate sales** It refers to the supply of goods or services from one State to another State.
4. **Input and Output GST** Input GST refers to the GST paid by a business on its purchases of goods or services. Output GST, on the other hand, is the GST that a business collects from customers on the sales of goods or services.

GST Structure

1. **Dual Model** GST in India operates on a dual model, comprising Central GST (CGST) and State GST (SGST). The central government levies and collects CGST, and the State government levies and collects SGST. These both taxes are levied on intrastate sales.
2. **Integrated GST (IGST)** For interstate transactions, IGST is applicable. It is levied and collected by the central government. It is also levied on import of goods and services into India and on export of goods and services outside India.

Categories of GST in India

There are five tax slabs under GST

Tax Rate	Items
0%	Essential items including unpacked food like eggs, milk etc.
5%	Common use items like sugar, tea etc.
12%	Frozen meat products, butter, cheese, ghee, dry fruits in packaged form, animal fat, sausages and ayurvedic medicines.
18%	Biscuits, flavoured refined sugar, pasta, cornflakes, pastries and cakes, preserved vegetables, jams, sauces, soups, ice-cream, instant food mixes, mineral water, tissues, envelopes and tampons.
28%	Luxury and sin (tobacco) goods

Objectives and Advantages of GST

1. **Simplified Tax Structure** To simplify the complex and multi-layered tax structure prevailing before GST.
2. **One Nation, One Tax** To establish a common and uniform tax regime across the country, eliminating multiple State-level taxes.
3. **Cascading Tax Elimination** To remove the cascading effect of taxes (tax on tax) by providing input tax credit, ensuring that tax is levied only on the value addition at each stage of the supply chain.
4. **Uniform Compliance** To establish a common compliance framework, making it easier for businesses to comply with tax regulations and reducing the compliance burden.
5. **Reduced Tax Evasion** With improved tracking and transparency, GST helps in reducing tax evasion, as all transactions are recorded and reported electronically.

Rules for States under GST

1. **Levy and Collection of State GST (SGST)** State governments are responsible for levying and collecting State Goods and Services Tax (SGST) on intrastate supplies of goods and services.

2. **State GST Act** Each State has its own State GST Act, which outlines the rules and regulations related to the levy and collection of SGST within the State.
3. **Composition Scheme** State governments have the authority to prescribe the rules for the composition scheme for taxpayers with a turnover below a specified limit.
4. **SGST Rate** The State governments, in consultation with the GST council, have the flexibility to decide the rate of SGST within the prescribed slabs.
5. **Administration and Assessment** State tax authorities are responsible for the administration and assessment of SGST. They handle tasks such as registration of taxpayers, filing of returns, and conducting audits within their respective States.
6. **Input Tax Credit (ITC)** State governments play a crucial role in ensuring the proper implementation of the Input Tax Credit (ITC) mechanism.
7. **Anti-Profiteering Measures** State governments, along with the central government, monitor and enforce anti-profiteering measures to ensure that the benefits of GST rate reductions or input tax credits are passed on to consumers.
8. **Compensation Cess** In certain cases, State governments may receive compensation from the central government for any revenue loss incurred due to the implementation of GST.

Rules under Central Goods and Services Tax (CGST)

1. **Levy and Collection** CGST is levied by the Central government on the supply of goods and services within a State or Union Territory. The CGST Act specifies the rates of CGST applicable to different categories of goods and services.
2. **GST Registration** The rules under CGST govern the registration process for taxpayers liable to pay CGST. Taxpayers meeting the prescribed turnover threshold are required to register under CGST and obtain a unique Goods and Services Tax Identification Number (GSTIN).
3. **Input Tax Credit (ITC)** CGST rules detail the mechanism for claiming input tax credit on taxes paid on inputs, input services and capital goods used in the course of business. Taxpayers can offset their CGST liability with the ITC available on eligible inputs.
4. **Filing of Returns** CGST rules prescribe the procedures for filing various GST returns, including GSTR-1 (for outward supplies), GSTR-3B (monthly summary return) and annual return (GSTR-9), Taxpayers are required to file returns electronically through the GST portal within the specified due dates.
5. **Payment of Taxes** CGST rules specify the timelines and modes of payment for remitting CGST liability. Taxpayers are required to deposit the CGST amount due electronically through the GST portal using authorised banking channels.
6. **Refunds** CGST rules outline the procedures for claiming refunds of excess tax paid, input tax credit accumulated on account of inverted tax structure, exports and other specified situations. Taxpayers can file refund applications electronically and receive refunds through the prescribed process.
7. **Assessment and Audit** The CGST Act empowers tax authorities to conduct assessments, audits and investigations to ensure compliance with GST laws. CGST rules provide guidelines for conducting audits, issuing audit reports and taking appropriate enforcement actions.
8. **Anti-Profiteering Measures** CGST rules include provisions for implementing anti-profiteering measures to ensure that the benefits of GST rate reductions and input tax credits are passed on to consumers by businesses. The National Anti-Profiteering Authority (NAA) oversees anti-profiteering investigations and enforcement actions.

Calculation of GST

Step 1 Check the GST rate applicable for the goods or services you are selling or purchasing.

Step 2 Determine the transaction value of the goods or services on which GST is to be calculated.

Step 3 Calculate the GST amount by multiplying the transaction value with the applicable GST rate.

Step 4 Determine the gross amount payable by adding the GST amount to the transaction value.

EXAMPLE 1. An article is marked at ₹18000. A dealer sells it to a consumer at 10% profit. If the rate of GST is 12%, find

(i) the selling price (excluding tax) of the article.

(ii) the amount of tax (under GST) paid by the consumer.

(iii) the total amount paid by the consumer.

Sol. (i) Marked price of the article = ₹18000

When sold at 10% profit

$$\text{Profit} = \left(\frac{10}{100}\right) \times 18000 = ₹1800$$

Thus, the selling price (excluding tax)

= ₹18000 + ₹1800 = ₹19800

(ii) The rate of GST is 12%

Thus, the amount of tax (GST) paid by the consumer would be

$$= \left(\frac{12}{100}\right) \times ₹19800$$

= ₹2376

(iii) The total amount paid by the consumer

= Selling price + GST

= ₹19800 + ₹2376

= ₹22176

EXAMPLE 2. A shopkeeper buy goods worth ₹5000 and sells these at a profit of 20% to a consumer in the same State. If GST is charged at 5%, find

(i) the selling price (excluding tax) of the goods.

(ii) CGST paid by the consumer.

(iii) SGST paid by the consumer.

(iv) the total amount paid by the consumer.

Sol. (i) Actual price of the goods = ₹5000

When sold at a profit of 20%

$$\text{Profit} = \left(\frac{20}{100}\right) \times ₹5000 = ₹1000$$

Thus, the selling price (excluding tax) of the goods will be = Actual price + Profit

= ₹5000 + ₹1000 = ₹6000

(ii) The GST charged is 5%

CGST paid by the consumer

= 2.5% of the selling price

$$= \left(\frac{2.5}{100}\right) \times ₹6000 = ₹150$$

(iii) SGST paid by the consumer

= 2.5% of the selling price

$$= \left(\frac{2.5}{100}\right) \times ₹6000 = ₹150$$

(iv) The total amount paid by the consumer

= Selling price + CGST + SGST

= ₹6000 + ₹150 + ₹150 = ₹6300

EXAMPLE 3. The marked price of an article is ₹12000. A dealer in Kolkata sells the article to a consumer in the same city at a profit of 8%. If the rate of GST is 18%, then find

(i) the selling price (excluding tax) of the goods.

(ii) IGST, CGST and SGST paid by the dealer to the central and state governments.

(iii) the amount which the consumer pays for the article

Sol. (i) The marked price of the article = ₹12000

When sold at a profit of 8%.

$$\text{Profit} = \left(\frac{8}{100}\right) \times ₹12000 = ₹960$$

Thus, the selling price (excluding tax) of the article

= Marked price + Profit = ₹12000 + ₹960 = ₹12960

(ii) The rate of GST = 18%

IGST is not applicable in this case since the dealing is intra-state

CGST paid by the dealer to the central government

= 9% of the selling price

$$= \left(\frac{9}{100}\right) \times ₹12960 = ₹1166.4$$

and SGST paid by the dealer to the state government

= 9% of the selling price

$$= \left(\frac{9}{100}\right) \times ₹12960 = ₹1166.4$$

(iii) The total amount which the consumer pays for the article will be

= Selling price + CGST + SGST

= ₹12960 + ₹1166.4 + ₹1166.4 = ₹15292.8

EXAMPLE 4. A shopkeeper buys an article from a wholesaler for ₹10000 and sells it to consumer at 10% profit. If the rate of GST is 12%, then find the tax liability of the shopkeeper.

Sol. Selling price of the wholesaler = ₹10000

Now, the cost price for the shopkeeper = ₹10000

When sold at a profit of 10%

$$\text{Profit} = \left(\frac{10}{100}\right) \times ₹10000 = ₹1000$$

So, the selling of shopkeeper = Cost price + Profit

= ₹10000 + ₹1000 = ₹11000

The rate of GST = 12 %

The tax liability of shopkeeper = Profit × GST %

$$= ₹1000 \times \left(\frac{12}{100}\right) = ₹120$$

Input GST Credit

Every trader registered under GST can set off input GST (i.e. GST paid) against output GST (i.e. GST collected) in the following manner

Input GST credit	Output GST
CGST credit	First CGST, then IGST
SGST/UTGST credit	First SGST/UTGST, then IGST
IGST credit	First IGST, second CGST, then SGST/UTGST

Note CGST credit cannot be set off against SGST/UTGST and *vice-versa*.

Both centre and States allow set off of input GST against output GST. Thus, every trader is required to pay net GST (i.e. output GST – input GST) on the sale and purchase of goods and services.

EXAMPLE 5. A dealer buys an article at a discount of 30% from the wholesaler, the marked price being ₹ 6000. The dealer sells it to a consumer at a discount of 10% on the marked price. If the sales are intrastate and the rate of GST is 5%, find

(i) the amount paid by the consumer for the article.

(ii) the tax (under GST) paid by the dealer to the State government.

(iii) the amount of tax (under GST) received by the central government.

Sol. It is a case of intrastate transaction of goods and services.

$\therefore$ SGST = CGST = $\frac{1}{2}$ GST

Given,

Marked price of an article = ₹6000

Rate of GST = 5%

Rate of discount given by the wholesaler = 30%

Cost Price (CP) of an article for dealer

= Marked price – Discount

= ₹6000 – 30% of ₹6000

$= ₹6000 - \left(\frac{30}{100}\right) \times 6000$

= ₹6000 – 1800 = ₹4200

Amount of GST paid by dealer to wholesaler,

CGST = SGST = 2.5% of ₹ 4200

$= \left(\frac{2.5}{100}\right) \times 4200 = ₹105$

(i) The amount paid by the consumer for the article.

Selling Price (SP) of an article for consumer

= Marked price – Discount

= ₹6000 – (10% of ₹6000)

$= ₹6000 - \left[\left(\frac{10}{100}\right) \times 6000\right] = ₹6000 - 600 = ₹5400$

Amount of GST paid by the consumer to the dealer,

CGST = SGST = 2.5% of ₹ 5400

$= \left(\frac{2.5}{100}\right) \times 5400 = ₹135$

$\therefore$ Amount paid by consumer for article

= CP of article for consumer + CGST paid by consumer + SGST paid by consumer

= ₹5400 + ₹135 + ₹135 = ₹5670

(ii) The tax (under GST) paid by the dealer to the State government.= ₹135 – ₹105 = ₹30

(iii) The amount of tax (under GST) received by the central government.

CGST paid by wholesaler + CGST by dealer

= ₹105 + ₹30 = ₹135

EXAMPLE 6. A dealer buys an article for ₹ 5000 from a wholesaler. The dealer sells the article to a consumer at 15% profit. If the sales are intrastate and the rate of GST is 18%, find

(i) input CGST and input SGST paid by the dealer.

(ii) output CGST and output SGST collected by the dealer.

(iii) the net CGST and SGST paid by the dealer.

(iv) the total amount paid by the consumer.

Sol. Selling price of the wholesaler = ₹ 5000

$\therefore$ Cost price of the dealer = ₹5000

When sold at a profit of 15% to the consumer

Profit $= \left(\frac{15}{100}\right) \times ₹5000 = ₹750$

So, the selling price of the dealer = Cost price + Profit

= ₹5000 + ₹750

= ₹5750

(i) Rate of GST = 18%

Input CGST paid by the dealer

= 9% of selling price of wholesaler

$= \left(\frac{9}{100}\right) \times ₹5000 = ₹450$

and input SGST paid by the dealer

= 9% of selling price of wholesaler

$= \left(\frac{9}{100}\right) \times ₹5000 = ₹450$

(ii) Output CGST collected by the dealer

= 9% of selling price of the dealer

$= \left(\frac{9}{100}\right) \times ₹5750 = ₹517.5$

and output SGST collected by the dealer

$= 9\%$ of selling price of the dealer

$= \left(\frac{9}{100}\right) \times ₹5750 = ₹517.5$

(iii) Net CGST paid by the dealer

= (Output CGST – Input CGST) paid by the dealer

= ₹517.5 – ₹450

= ₹67.5

and net SGST paid by the dealer

= (Output SGST – Input SGST) paid by the dealer

= ₹517.5 – ₹450

= ₹67.5

(iv) The total amount paid by the consumer

= Selling price of the dealer + CGST + SGST

= ₹5750 + ₹517.5 + ₹517.5

= ₹6785

EXAMPLE 7. The printed price of an article is ₹ 5000. A wholesaler in Rajasthan buys an article from a manufacturer in Delhi at a discount of 12% on the printed price. The wholesaler sells an article to a retailer in Uttar Pradesh at 32% above the marked price. If the rate of GST on an article is 5%, then find

(i) the price inclusive of tax (under GST) at which the wholesaler bought an article.

(ii) the price inclusive of tax (under GST) at which the retailer bought an article.

(iii) the tax (under GST) paid by the wholesaler to the Government.

(iv) the tax (under GST) received by the Central Government.

Sol. In the given question, both the given sales from manufacturer to wholesaler and wholesaler to retailer are interstate, so IGST will be levied on these sales at 5%.

(i) Wholesaler buys an article from a manufacturer at 12% discount on the printed price.

So, the cost price of an article to the wholesaler

$= ₹\left(1 - \frac{12}{100}\right) \times 5000 = ₹\left(\frac{22}{25} \times 5000\right) = ₹\ 4400$

Amount of IGST paid by wholesaler to manufacturer

$= 5\%$ of ₹ 4400 $= ₹\left(\frac{5}{100} \times 4400\right) = ₹\ 220$

The price inclusive of tax (under GST) at which the wholesaler bought an article

= Cost of article to wholesaler + IGST paid by wholesaler

= ₹ 4400 + ₹ 220

= ₹ 4620

Thus, input IGST of the wholesaler = ₹ 220

(ii) Since, the wholesaler sells an article to a retailer at 32% above the marked price, the selling price of an article by the wholesaler

$= ₹\left(1 + \frac{32}{100}\right) \times 5000 = ₹\left(\frac{33}{25} \times 5000\right) = ₹\ 6600$

∴ Cost price (excluding tax) of an article to the retailer = ₹ 6600

Amount of IGST paid by retailer to wholesaler

$= 5\%$ of ₹ 6600 $= ₹\left(\frac{5}{100} \times 6600\right)$

= ₹ 330

The price inclusive of tax (under GST) at which the retailer bought an article

= Cost of article to retailer + IGST paid by retailer

= ₹ 6600 + ₹ 330

= ₹ 6930

(iii) Output IGST of the wholesaler = ₹ 330

Tax (under GST) paid by the wholesaler to the Central Government = Output IGST – Input IGST

= ₹ 330 – ₹ 220

= ₹ 110

(iv) Tax (under GST) received by the Central Government

= IGST received from manufacturer + IGST received from wholesaler

= ₹ 220 + ₹ 110

= ₹ 330

Note In this case, whole tax (under GST) on the sale of an article will be provided to Central Government only.

EXAMPLE 8. A shopkeeper in Delhi buys the smartphone at the printed price of ₹ 20000 from a wholesaler in Haryana. The shopkeeper sells the smartphone to a consumer in Delhi at a profit of 25% on the basic cost price. If the rate of GST is 18%, then find

(i) the price of the smartphone inclusive of tax (under GST) at which the shopkeeper bought it.

(ii) the amount of tax (under GST) paid by the shopkeeper to Government.

(iii) the amount of tax (under GST) received by Haryana Government.

(iv) the amount of tax (under GST) received by Central Government.

(v) the amount which the consumer pays for the article.

Sol. (i) As the shopkeeper buys the smartphone for ₹ 20000 from a wholesaler in Haryana, so this sale in interstate and IGST is levied at 18%.

So, IGST collected by wholesaler from shopkeeper

$= 18\%$ of ₹ 20000 $= ₹\left(\frac{18}{100} \times 20000\right)$

= ₹ 3600

∴ The price of the smartphone inclusive of tax (under GST) at which the shopkeeper bought it
= Cost price of smartphone to shopkeeper
+ GST paid by the shopkeeper
= ₹ 20000 + IGST paid by shopkeeper to wholesaler
= ₹ 20000 + ₹ 3600 = ₹ 23600

(ii) The wholesaler will pay ₹ 3600 as IGST to the Central Government.

∴ Amount of input IGST of the shopkeeper = ₹ 3600

The shopkeeper sells the smartphone to a consumer at a profit of 25% on the basic cost price, the selling price of smartphone by the shopkeeper

$$= ₹\left(1+\frac{25}{100}\right)\times 20000 = ₹\left(\frac{5}{4}\times 20000\right) = ₹\ 25000$$

As the shopkeeper sells the smartphone to a consumer in Delhi, therefore this sale is intrastate.

So, GST will comprise of CGST at 9% and SGST at 9%.

Now, amount of GST collected by shopkeeper from consumer

CGST = 9% of ₹ 25000 = ₹ 2250

SGST = 9% of ₹ 25000 = ₹ 2250

Thus, amount of output GST of the shopkeeper

CGST = ₹ SGST = ₹ 2250 each

Amount of tax (under GST) paid by the shopkeeper to Government.

First setting off ₹ 3600 input IGST against ₹ 2250 output CGST.

Then, set off the balance ₹ 1350 (₹ 3600 − ₹ 2250) input IGST against output SGST

∴ SGST paid by the shopkeeper to the State Government (Delhi)
= Output SGST − balance of input IGST
= ₹ 2250 − ₹ 1350 = ₹ 900

Thus, net tax (under GST) paid by shopkeeper to Government.

No tax is paid to the Central Government

Tax paid to Delhi Government = ₹ 900

(iii) Amount of tax (under GST) received by Haryana Government is NIL.

(iv) Amount of tax (under GST) received by the Central Government
= IGST received from wholesaler
+ CGST received from shopkeeper
= ₹ 3600 + NIL = ₹ 3600

(v) The amount which the consumer pays for the smartphone
= Cost price to consumer + GST paid by consumer
= ₹ 25000 + CGST paid by consumer
+ SGST paid by consumer
= ₹ 25000 + ₹ 2250 + ₹ 2250 = ₹ 29500

Topic Practice 1

1 What is taxation?

2 Why do governments impose taxes?

3 Who imposes taxes in a country?

4 What is the broad classification of taxes?

5 Define progressive taxation.

6 A business sells goods worth ₹ 50000 to another business located in a different state. If the GST rate applicable on these goods is 18%, how much IGST will be levied on this transaction?

7 If a taxpayer has purchased goods worth ₹ 40000, including a GST of ₹ 4000, what is the effective GST rate paid by the taxpayer on these goods?

8 A service provider earns revenue of ₹ 120000 in a month. If the GST rate applicable to the service provided is 12%, how much GST will the service provider need to remit to the government?

9 (i) A company sells goods worth INR 500000 with a GST rate of 12%. Calculate the total GST amount.

(ii) If the input GST for a business is INR 40000 and the output GST is INR 50000, then what is the net GST liability or refund?

(iii) An item is priced at INR 800 with a GST rate of 18%. Calculate the total cost including GST.

(iv) A service is billed at INR 25000 with an Integrated GST (IGST) rate of 28%. Calculate the IGST amount.

(v) A business purchases goods worth INR 120000 with a CGST rate of 9%. Calculate the CGST amount.

Hints & Solutions

1. Taxation is the process by which a government collects revenue from its citizens to fund public services and functions.
2. Governments impose taxes to generate revenue for public expenditures, regulate economic activity and address social objectives.
3. Taxes in the country are imposed by all levels of governments including central, state and local governments.
4. Taxes are broadly classified as direct tax and indirect tax.
5. Progressive taxation is a system where the tax rate increases as the taxable amount or income increases.
6. IGST = (Value of goods sold × GST rate) / 100
   = (₹ 50000 × 18) / 100 = ₹ 9000
7. Effective GST rate
   = (GST paid / Total value of goods) × 100
   = (₹ 4000 / ₹ 40000) × 100 = (1/10) × 100 = 10%
8. GST amount = (Revenue × GST rate) / 100
   = (₹ 120000 × 12) / 100 = ₹ 14400
9. (i) GST amount = (500000 × 12%) = INR 60000
   (ii) Net GST liability = Output GST − Input GST
   = 50000 − 40000
   = INR 10000 [liability]
   (iii) GST amount = (800 × 18%) = INR 144
   Total cost = 800 + 144 = INR 944
   (iv) IGST amount = (25000 × 28%) = INR 7000
   (v) CGST amount = (120000 × 9%) = INR 10800

Income Tax

Income tax is a tax imposed by a government on the income of individuals and businesses within its jurisdiction. It is one of the primary sources of revenue for governments and is used to fund public services and infrastructure.

Key Terms related to Income Tax

- **Financial Year** Financial year is the period between 1st April of current year to 31st March of the next year in India. For example, April 1, 2023 to March 31, 2024 will be considered as the financial year in India.
- **Assessment Year** It is the year in which the income earned during the financial year is assessed and taxed. It starts immediately after the end of the financial year. For example, if the financial year is April 1, 2023 to March 31, 2024, the assessment year for that financial year would be 2024-2025.
- **Assessee** It is a term commonly used in taxation to refer to a person or entity who is liable to pay tax or file a tax return.
- **Gross Income** It is the total income of an individual or business earned from different sources in a financial year.
- **Exemptions and Deductions** Exemptions refer to certain types of income that are not subject to taxation. They are typically provided to encourage specific activities or to provide relief in certain circumstances.

  Deductions are certain expenses or investments that individuals or businesses can subtract from their total income to arrive at their taxable income.

Some of these are

1. **House Rent Allowance (HRA)** The HRA is designed to help employees meet the cost of renting a home. This could be totally or partially exempted from income tax. If a person is not living in a rented house, then HRA exemption is not permissible.
2. **Standard Deduction** A standard deduction of ₹ 50000 is allowed for salaried/individual persons under the income tax exemption.
3. **Deductions under Section 80C** Section 80C of the Income Tax Act in India provides various deductions for certain investments and expenses. Here are some of the key deductions available under Section 80C
   - Life insurance premiums paid for life insurance policies.
   - Contribution made to Employee Provident Fund (EPF) account.
   - Investments made in a Public Provident Fund (PPF) account.
   - Investments made in National Savings Certificate (NSC).
   - Investments made in 5-year fixed deposits.
   - Contributions made to the Sukanya Samriddhi Yojana (SSY).
   - Investments made in Equity-Linked Savings Scheme (ELSS).
   - Investments made in Senior Citizens Savings Scheme (SCSS).
   - Tuition fees paid for the education of up to two children.

- Principal repayment of home loan
- Employee contributions to National Pension System (NPS).

4. **Deductions under Section 80D** It allows individuals to claim deductions for premiums paid for health insurance policies covering themselves, their spouse, children and parents. The deductions are available for both individuals and Hindu Undivided Families (HUFs).
5. **Interest on Home loan under Section 24** House owners having home loan can claim a deduction of up to ₹ 2 lakh for interest on home loan under this section.
6. **Deduction under 80E** It provides for the deduction of interest paid on loans taken for higher education. This deduction is available to individuals who have taken loans for themselves, their spouse or their children for higher education.
7. **Deductions under 80G** It provides deductions for donations made to certain funds and charitable institutions. This section encourages individuals and organizations to contribute to social causes by offering tax benefits. Some organizations and their deductions are given below

Prime Minister's National Relief Fund	100%
Family Welfare Relief Fund	100%
Swachh Bharat Kosh	100%
Clear Ganga Fund	100%
National Security Fund	100%
Prime Minister's Armenia Earthquake Relief Fund	100%
Chief Minister's Relief Fund	100%
Indira Gandhi Memorial Trust	50%
Jawaharlal Nehru Memorial Fund	50%
Prime Minister Drought Relief Fund	50%

8. **Deductions under Section 80TTA** It provides a deduction to individual taxpayers and Hindu Undivided Families (HUFs) in respect of interest income from savings accounts. The maximum deduction allowed is ₹ 10000.

- **Taxable Income** It is the income used to calculate the income tax in the given financial year. It is calculated by subtracting all the exemptions and deductions allowed from the gross income of individuals/institutions. Thus,

Taxable income = Gross income – Sum of all exemptions and deductions

Income Tax Slabs

Income Tax Slabs in India are announced by the finance minister every year. Income tax is calculated based upon various slabs and the tax rates. The tax slabs tend to change in every budget. There are different slabs for each category of eligible taxpayer.

New Tax Regime

The new tax regime introduced in India in the financial year 2022-23 (assessment year 2023-24) offers individuals the option to choose between the old tax regime and the new tax regime. The new tax regime comes with lower tax rates but eliminates many deductions and exemptions available in the old tax regime.

Here are the income slabs for individual taxpayers under the old and new tax regime.

For individual (resident or non-resident) less than 60 years of age anytime during the previous year:

Old Tax Regime		New Tax Regime u/s 115BAC	
Income Tax Slab	Income Tax Rate	Income Tax Slab	Income Tax Rate
Up to ₹ 250000	Nil	Up to ₹ 250000	Nil
₹ 250001 – ₹ 500000	5% above ₹ 250000	₹ 250001 – ₹ 500000	5% above ₹ 250000
₹ 500001 – ₹ 1000000	₹ 12500 + 20% above ₹ 500000	₹ 500001 – ₹ 750000	₹ 12500 + 10% above ₹ 500000
Above ₹ 1000000	₹ 112500 + 30% above ₹ 1000000	₹ 750001 – ₹ 1000000	₹ 37500 + 15% above ₹ 750000
		₹ 1000001 – ₹ 1250000	₹ 75000 + 20% above ₹ 1000000
		₹ 1250001 – ₹ 1500000	₹ 125000 + 25% above ₹ 1250000
		Above ₹ 1500000	₹ 187500 + 30% above ₹ 1500000

For individual (resident or non-resident) 60 years or more but less than 80 years of age anytime during the previous year:

Old Tax Regime		New Tax Regime u/s 115BAC	
Income Tax Slab	Income Tax Rate	Income Tax Slab	Income Tax Rate
Up to ₹ 300000	Nil	Up to 250000	Nil
₹ 300001 – ₹ 500000	5% above ₹ 300000	250001 – 500000	5% above 250000
₹ 500001 – ₹ 1000000	₹ 10000 + 20% above ₹ 500000	500001 – 750000	12500 + 10% above 500000
Above ₹ 1000000	₹ 110000 + 30% above ₹ 1000000	750001 – 1000000	37500 + 15% above 750000
		1000001 – 1250000	75000 + 20% above 1000000
		1250001 – 1500000	125000 + 25% above 1250000
		Above 1500000	187500 + 30% above 1500000

Surcharge is an additional charge levied for persons earning income above the specified limits. It is charged on the amount of income tax and calculated as per following applicable rates

10% — Taxable income above ₹ 50 lakh — up to ₹ 1 crore

15% — Taxable income above ₹ 1 crore — up to ₹ 2 crore

25% — Taxable income above ₹ 2 crore — up to ₹ 5 crore

37% — Taxable income above ₹ 5 crore

Maximum rate of surcharge on income by way of dividend or income under the provisions of Sections 111A, 112 and112A is 15%

Tax Rebate under Section 87A

Section 87A of the Income Tax Act in India provides a rebate to individual taxpayers.

- The rebate under Section 87A is available to individual taxpayers, including resident individuals and non-resident individuals, whose total income does not exceed the specified limit.
- The maximum rebate allowed under Section 87A is ₹ 12500. If the total income of an individual is equal to or less than the specified limit, the rebate is limited to the amount of income tax payable, subject to a maximum of ₹ 12500.

Health and Education Cess

- This cess is applicable in addition to the basic income tax and is levied to fund health and education initiatives in the country.
- The health and education cess rate is 4%. This rate is applied to the total income tax liability, including the surcharge but excluding the cess itself.
- The introduction of the health and education cess replaced the earlier education cess (2%) and secondary and higher education cess (1%) from the financial year 2018-19 onwards.

Note Tax rebate under Section 87A is given before calculating 4% cess.

Steps to Calculate Income Tax

1. **Identify Sources of Income**
   - Salary income
   - House property income
   - Business or profession income
   - Capital gains
   - Other sources
2. **Compute Gross Total Income (GTI) and Taxable Income**
   - Add up income from all sources mentioned above.
   - Subtract exemptions available, such as HRA (House Rent Allowance), standard deduction, exemptions on allowances, etc.
   - Deduct applicable deductions under Sections like 80C (for investments), 80D (for health insurance premiums), 80G (for donations), etc. to arrive at the total taxable income.
3. **Calculate Tax Liability**
   - Apply the applicable income tax slab rates to the total taxable income to calculate the income tax liability.
   - Consider the health and education cess at the prescribed rate.

4. **Consider Rebates and Credits**
   - Apply any rebates available under Section 87A for individuals with lower income.
   - Consider tax credits such as TDS (Tax Deducted at Source) or advance tax paid.
5. **Compute Net Tax Payable or Refundable**
   - Subtract any rebates and tax credits from the calculated tax liability.
   - The resulting amount is either the net tax payable or refundable.

EXAMPLE 9. Mr. X is a salaried individual in India. His salary details for the financial year 2022-23 are as follows

Basic salary: ₹ 500000 per annum

House Rent Allowance (HRA): ₹ 120000 per annum

Special allowance: ₹ 50000 per annum

Other income (interest from savings account): ₹ 8000 per annum

Calculate total tax liability of Mr. X as per new tax regime.

Sol. Let's calculate Mr. X's taxable income step by step

Step 1 Calculate gross salary

Gross salary = Basic salary + HRA + Special Allowance

Gross salary = ₹ 500000 + ₹ 120000 + ₹ 50000

= ₹ 670000

Step 2 Calculate total income

Total income = Gross salary + Other income

Total income = ₹ 670000 + ₹ 8000 = ₹ 678000

Step 3 Calculate taxable income

No deductions or exemptions are considered in this simplified example.

∴ Taxable income = Total income

Taxable income = ₹ 678000

Step 4 Calculate income tax

Income tax = Taxable income × Tax rate

Since, taxable income is ₹ 678000, so from the income tax slab

Income tax = ₹ 12500 + 10% of ₹ 178000

= ₹ 12500 + ₹ 17800

= ₹ 30300

Step 5 Add health and education cess

Apply the health and education cess at 4% on the income tax calculated.

Cess = Income tax × 4%

Cess = ₹ 30300 × 4% = ₹ 1212

Step 6 Calculate total tax liability

Total tax liability = Income tax + Cess

Total tax liability = ₹ 30300 + ₹ 1212

= ₹ 31512

EXAMPLE 10. In financial year 2022-23, the gross salary of Vinay (age 32 yr) was ₹ 800000 (exclusive of HRA). He deposited ₹ 9000 per month in GPF and paid ₹ 48000 as life insurance premium. He donated ₹ 15000 in Prime Minister's National Relief Fund. He took a home loan ₹ 2400000 from the State Bank of India and paid ₹ 36000 as interest on home loan and ₹ 35000 as principal of home loan. Calculate his income tax at the end of the financial year.

Sol.

Gross income	= ₹ 800000
(−) Standard deduction	= − ₹ 50000
Balance	= ₹ 750000
Deductions under Section 80G	
Prime Minister's National Relief Fund	= − ₹ 15000
Balance	= ₹ 735000
Deduction under Section 24	
Interest on Home Loan	= − ₹ 36000
Balance before Section 80 C Deduction	= ₹ 699000
Deductions under Section 80C	
Deposited in GPF ₹ (12 × 9000)	= ₹ 108000
LIC Premium	= ₹ 48000
Principal of Home Loan	= ₹ 35000
Total	= ₹ 191000

But deduction under Section 80C is allowed upto = ₹ 150000

So, Balance before Section 80C Deduction = ₹ 699000

(−) Deductions under Section 80C	= − ₹ 150000
Taxable income	= ₹ 549000

Now, taxable income is ₹ 549000, so from the income tax slab

Income tax = ₹ 12500 + 20% of ₹ 49000

= ₹ 12500 + ₹ 9800 = ₹ 22300

Since, taxable income is more than ₹ 500000, so Vinay is not eligible for tax rebate under Section 87A.

∴ Income tax	= ₹ 22300
Health and Education cess 4% on ₹ 22300	= ₹ 892
Total income tax	= ₹ 23192

EXAMPLE 11. In financial year 2021-22, Abhinav's (age 64 yr) income from salary was ₹ 900000 (exclusive of HRA) and income from interest on savings account was ₹ 20000. He deposited ₹ 10000 per month in GPF and paid ₹ 56000 as LIC premium. He donated ₹ 15000 in National Security Fund. He paid ₹ 10000 as interest on education loan for higher studies of his son. Calculate the income tax at the end of the financial year. Assuming the data given above for financial year 2022-23, calculate the income tax with new tax regime slab. Is new tax regime slab beneficial for Mr. Chawla?

Sol. Calculation of Income tax for financial year 2021-22

Income from salary	= ₹ 900000
Income from interest on savings account	= ₹ 20000
∴ Gross income	= ₹ 920000
(−) Standard deduction	= − ₹ 50000
Balance	= ₹ 870000

Deductions under Section 80G

Donation in National Security Fund (100% exemption)	= − ₹ 15000
Balance	= ₹ 855000

Deduction under Section 80TTA

Interest from savings account (₹ 20000), but deduction under Section 80TTA is allowed maximum upto ₹ 10000

∴ Less deduction under Section 80TTA	= − ₹ 10000
Balance	= ₹ 845000

Deductions under Section 80E

Interest on Education Loan	= − ₹ 10000
Balance before Section 80C Deduction	= ₹ 835000

Deduction under Section 80C

GPF = ₹ (12 × 10000)	= ₹ 120000
LIC premium	= ₹ 56000
Total	= ₹ 176000

But deduction under Section 80C is allowed maximum upto ₹ 150000.

Balance before Section 80C Deduction	= ₹ 835000
∴ (−) Deduction under Section 80C	= − ₹ 150000
Taxable income	= ₹ 685000

As Abhinav is 64 yr old, so tax upto ₹ 300000 is nil.

Further, from the income tax slab

Income tax = ₹ 10000 + 20% of 185000

= ₹ 10000 + ₹ 37000

= ₹ 47000

Since, taxable income is more than ₹ 5 lakh, so Abhinav is not eligible for tax rebate under Section 87A.

∴ Income tax	= ₹ 47000
Health and Education cess 4% on ₹ 47000	= ₹ 1880
Net income tax	= ₹ 48880

Calculation of Income tax for financial year 2022-23 with new tax regime

Gross income = ₹ 920000

From new tax regime slab,

Income tax

= ₹ 37500 + 15% of taxable income exceeding ₹ 7.5 lakh

= ₹ 37500 + 15% of ₹ 170000

= ₹ 37500 + ₹ 25500 = ₹ 63000

Health and Education cess 4% on ₹ 63000	= ₹ 2520
∴ Net income tax (63000 + 2520)	= ₹ 65520

∵ Income tax as per new regime is ₹ 16640 more than income tax as per old regime.

So, new tax regime is not beneficial for Abhinav.

Topic Practice 2

1. Calculate the income tax liability of Mr. X for the assessment year 2023-24, given his total income is ₹ 850000. Assume he is below 60 yr of age and not eligible for any deductions.
2. Mrs. Z has a total income of ₹ 500000 for the assessment year 2023-24. Calculate her tax liability.
3. Calculate the income tax payable by Mr. A for the assessment year 2023-24, given his total income consists of ₹ 300000 from salary and ₹ 50000 from interest earned on fixed deposits.
4. Mr. E has a total income of ₹ 600000 for the assessment year 2023-24. He has invested ₹ 150000 in eligible deductions under Section 80C. Calculate his tax liability after considering the deductions.
5. Answer the following parts
   (i) Mr. A has a total income of ₹ 650000 during the financial year 2022-23. Calculate his income tax liability under the new tax regime.
   (ii) Ms. B receives a salary of ₹ 900000 and HRA of ₹ 120000. If she has no other income, what is her taxable income?
   (iii) If Mr. C earns an interest income of ₹ 15000 from a savings account, what would be the taxable amount under Section 80TTA?
   (iv) Mr. D has a total income of ₹ 1080000 during the financial year 2022-23. Calculate his income tax liability under the old tax regime.
   (v) If an individual's taxable income is ₹ 300000, what is the income tax liability under the new tax regime?

Hints & Solutions

1. Tax liability = 12500 + 20% of (₹ 850000 − ₹ 500000)
   = 12500 + 70000 = 82500
2. Tax liability = 5% of (₹ 500000 − ₹ 250000)
   = 5% of ₹ 250000 = ₹ 12500

   Mrs. Z's tax liability is ₹ 12500.
3. Total income = Salary income + Interest income
   = ₹ 300000 + ₹ 50000 = ₹ 350000

   Now, tax liability = 5% of (₹ 350000 − ₹ 250000)
   = 5% of ₹ 100000
   = ₹ 5000
4. Taxable income = Total income − Deductions under Section 80C

   Taxable income = ₹ 600000 − ₹ 150000 = ₹ 450000
   Tax = 5% of (Taxable income − ₹ 250000)
   = 5% of (₹ 450000 − ₹ 250000)
   = 5% of ₹ 200000
   = ₹ 10000
5. (i) Mr. A's income tax liability under the new tax regime would be
   ₹ 27500 [(5% of ₹ 250000) + (10% of ₹ 150000)].

   (ii) Ms. B's taxable income is ₹ 1020000 (Salary of ₹ 900000 + HRA of ₹ 120000).

   (iii) The taxable amount would be ₹ 5000 (Interest income of ₹ 15000 − deduction limit of ₹ 10000).

   (iv) Income tax liability of Mr. D
   Tax slab as per old regime = ₹ 112500 + 30% of ₹ 80000
   = ₹ 112500 + ₹ 24000
   = ₹ 136500
   Add health and education cess
   = ₹ 5460 (4% of ₹ 136500)
   Total income tax liability = ₹ 136500 + ₹ 5460
   = ₹ 141960

   (v) Income tax liability = 5% of 50000 + 4% Less
   = ₹ 2500 + ₹ 100
   = ₹ 2600

Exam Pattern Exercise

Part A - Objective Type Questions

Multiple Choice Type Questions

1 What is taxation?
(a) Voluntary contribution
(b) Mandatory payment imposed by the government
(c) Charity fund
(d) Business investment

2 Which of the following is NOT a primary purpose of taxation?
(a) Revenue generation
(b) Wealth redistribution
(c) Economic stabilization
(d) Personal savings

3 Which of the following is not a type of GST in India?
(a) SGST (State Goods and Services Tax)
(b) CGST (Central Goods and Services Tax)
(c) IGST (Integrated Goods and Services Tax)
(d) RGST (Regional Goods and Services Tax)

4 What is the purpose of implementing GST?
(a) To increase the tax burden on consumers
(b) To simplify the tax structure and eliminate cascading effects
(c) To complicate tax regulations
(d) To decrease government revenue

5 Under the GST regime, which of the following taxes has been subsumed?
(a) Value Added Tax (VAT)
(b) Service Tax
(c) Central Excise Duty
(d) All of the above

6 Who administers the GST in India?
(a) Ministry of Finance
(b) Reserve Bank of India
(c) Goods and Services Tax Council
(d) Central Board of Direct Taxes

7 What is the GST rate on essential goods like food grains?
(a) 5% (b) 12%
(c) 18% (d) Exempted

8 Property tax is an example of
(a) direct tax (b) indirect tax
(c) progressive tax (d) regressive tax

9 Which type of tax is imposed on the profits of corporations?
(a) Income tax (b) Corporate tax
(c) Value-added tax (d) Excise tax

Assertion-Reason Based Questions

Directions (Q. Nos. 10-13) *In the questions given below are two statements labelled as Assertion (A) and Reason (R). In the context of the two statements, which one of the following is correct?*

(a) Both A and R are correct; R is the correct explanation of A
(b) Both A and R are correct; R is not the correct explanation of A
(c) A is correct; R is incorrect
(d) R is correct; A is incorrect

10 **Assertion** (A) The Tax Deducted at Source (TDS) system ensures the collection of taxes at the source of income itself.

Reason (R) TDS applies only to salary income and not to other sources of income.

11 **Assertion** (A) The tax slab structure for individual taxpayers is progressive in nature.

Reason (R) Progressive taxation ensures that individuals with higher incomes pay a higher percentage of their income as taxes.

12 **Assertion** (A) The Goods and Services Tax (GST) was implemented in India to streamline indirect taxation.

Reason (R) GST replaced multiple indirect taxes levied by the central and state governments, bringing uniformity and simplicity to the tax system.

13 **Assertion** (A) The composition scheme under GST is beneficial for small businesses.

Reason (R) Small businesses opting for the composition scheme are subjected to lower compliance requirements and pay tax at a fixed percentage of their turnover.

Part B - Descriptive Questions

Very Short Answer Type Questions

14 What is the primary direct tax authority in India?

15 What is the current Goods and Services Tax (GST) rate on essential items like food grains and books?

16 Under which section of the Income Tax Act can an individual claim a deduction for investments like a provident fund and life insurance premium?

17 What is the maximum income limit for an individual taxpayer to be eligible for the presumptive taxation scheme under Section 44AD of the Income Tax Act?

18 Which tax is levied on the transfer of immovable property in India?

19 What is the purpose of the PAN (Permanent Account Number) issued by the Income Tax Department?

20 Name one indirect tax that was subsumed into the Goods and Services Tax (GST) at its implementation.

21 Which tax is imposed on the income earned by a company registered in India?

22 What is the rate of long-term capital gains tax on the sale of listed equity shares in India?

23 Which authority is responsible for the administration and collection of GST in India?

Short Answer Type Questions

24 Calculate the taxable income for an individual below 60 years, given the following details

Gross income: ₹ 650000

Deductions under Section 80C: ₹ 150000

Professional tax: ₹ 2500

Standard deduction: ₹ 50000

25 A taxpayer has a long-term capital gain of ₹ 800000 from the sale of listed equity shares. Calculate the tax payable on the capital gains, considering the applicable tax rate.

26 Company XYZ has a taxable income of ₹ 1500000. Calculate the corporate tax payable by the company based on the prevailing corporate tax rate.

27 Mr. Sharma, a senior citizen, has an annual income of ₹ 420000. Calculate his income tax liability, taking into account the applicable tax slab and deductions.

28 Compute the Goods and Services Tax (GST) payable on a bill of ₹ 85000, assuming a GST rate of 18%.

29 An individual receives a gift of ₹ 500000 from a friend. Calculate the gift tax payable, considering the applicable gift tax rate.

30 A taxpayer has a total tax payable of ₹ 900000. Calculate the education cess payable at the prevailing rate.

31 A small business with an annual turnover of ₹ 120000 opts for the composition scheme. Calculate the GST payable under the composition scheme at the applicable rate.

32 Mr. Rohan (age 48 yr) works in a private company. His monthly income after deduction of allowances is ₹ 42000 and every month he contributes ₹ 3000 to GPF. He has also bought ₹ 15000 worth of NSC (National Savings Certificate) and donated ₹ 12000 to the PM's Relief Fund. Compute his income tax.

33 In a financial year, monthly salary of a person is ₹ 50000. He deposited ₹ 60000 in Prime Minister's relief fund on which income tax rebate is 100%. He denoted ₹ 20000 to a hospital on which income tax rebate is 50%. He invests ₹ 7000 per month in GPF, ₹ 15000 annually in LIC and purchases NSC for ₹ 35000. Find income tax to be paid by him in that financial year. Rates of income tax are as follows

100% rebate up to total savings of ₹ 100000.

	Taxable income	Income Tax
(i)	Upto ₹ 250000	Nil
(ii)	From ₹ 250001 to ₹ 500000	5% of amount exceeding ₹ 250000
(iii)	From ₹ 500001 to ₹ 750000	10% of amount exceeding ₹ 500000

In addition education cess: 3% of income tax.

34 Compute the income tax payable by the following individual

Mr. Mohit who is 33 yr old and has a taxable income of ₹ 1235000.

Long Answer Type Questions

35 A manufacturer sells a TV to a dealer for ₹ 18000 and the dealer sells it to a consumer at a profit of ₹ 1500. If the sales are intrastate and the rate of GST is 12%, find

(i) the amount of GST paid by the dealer to the State government.

(ii) the amount of GST received by the central government.

(iii) the amount of GST received by the State government.

(iv) the amount that the consumer pays for the TV.

36 A shopkeeper buys a camera at a discount of 20% from a wholesaler. The printed price of the camera being ₹1600. The shopkeeper sells it to a consumer at the printed price.

If the sales are intrastate and the rate of GST is 12%, find

(i) GST paid by the shopkeeper to the central government.
(ii) GST received by the central government.
(iii) GST received by the State government.
(iv) the amount at which the consumer bought the camera.

37 Mr. Sharma, an individual taxpayer in India, has the following income details for the financial year 2022-23

- Salary income: ₹ 600000
- House property income: ₹ 150000 (net annual value after deductions)
- Business income: ₹ 310000
- Other income: ₹ 100000
- Deductions under Section 80C: ₹ 150000
- Deductions under Section 10(14): ₹ 10000

Calculate Mr. Sharma's taxable income and the income tax liability for the given financial year, considering the applicable tax slabs and rates.

38 A trading company makes sales of goods amounting to INR 500000. The applicable Goods and Services Tax (GST) rate is 12%. The company also has input GST credits of INR 40000 from its purchases. Calculate the output GST, net GST liability and the amount payable or receivable by the company.

39 Mr. Rohan's gross annual income is ₹500000 for FY 2022-23. His annual savings in this year are as follows

(i) LIC premium ₹70000.
(ii) Contribution towards PF ₹12000
(iii) PPF ₹30000
(iv) NSC ₹10000

Find his taxable income and income tax for FY 2022-23.

40 A shopkeeper buy goods worth ₹ 4000 and sells these at a profit of 20% to a consumer in the same State. If GST is charged at 5%, find

(i) the selling price (excluding tax) of the goods.
(ii) CGST paid by the consumer.
(iii) SGST paid by the consumer.
(iv) the total amount paid by the consumer.

41 Mr. Z, a salaried individual in India for the financial year 2022-23, opting for the new tax regime. Details of income and investment are given below

Basic salary: ₹1000000 per annum

House Rent Allowance (HRA): ₹150000 per annum

Special allowance: ₹120000 per annum

Other income (interest from savings account): ₹15000 per annum

Deductions under Chapter VI-A: ₹50000 (consider investments in eligible)

Based on the above information, calculate income tax payable.

42 The marked price of an article is ₹ 12500. A dealer in Kolkata sells the article to a consumer in the same city at a profit of 8%. If the rate of GST is 18%, find

(i) the selling price (excluding tax) of the goods.
(ii) IGST, CGST and SGST paid by the dealer to the Central and State Governments.
(iii) the amount which the consumer pays for the article

43 Compute the income tax payable by following individuals.

(i) Mr. Kadam who is 35 years old and has a taxable income of ₹1335000.
(ii) Mr. Khan is 65 years of age and his taxable income is ₹450000.
(iii) Miss Varsha (age 26 years) has a taxable income of ₹230000.

Case Study Based Questions

44 A manufacturer who produces good *X*, buys raw material worth ₹ 7500 from the local market after paying GST at the rate of 5%. After completing production process of good *X*, he sells the finished product to the dealer of the good at profit of 40%. If the purchase and the sale both are intrastate and the rate of GST for the finished product is 12%, then find the following

(i) The input tax (under GST) paid by the manufacturer.
(ii) The output tax (under GST) collected by the manufacturer.
(iii) The tax (under GST) paid by the manufacturer to the Central and State Governments.
(iv) The amount paid by the dealer for the finished product.
(v) If the cost of raw material increase to ₹10000, what will be the input tax (under GST) paid by the manufacturer?

Hints & Solutions

1. (b) 2. (d) 3. (d) 4. (b)
5. (d) 6. (c) 7. (d) 8. (a)
9. (b) 10. (c) 11. (a) 12. (a)
13. (a) 14. Income tax department
15. 0% 16. Section 80C 17. ₹ 2 crore
18. Stamp Duty
19. Unique identification for taxpayers
20. Value Added Tax (VAT)
21. Corporate tax
22. 10%
23. Goods and Services Tax Network (GSTN).
24. Taxable income
= ₹ 447500 (₹ 650000 – ₹ 150000 – ₹ 2500 – ₹ 50000)
25. Tax payable on long-term capital gains
= ₹ 80000 (₹ 800000 × 10%)
26. Corporate tax payable
= ₹ 375000 (₹ 1500000 × 25%)
27. Given that Mr. Sharma's annual income is ₹ 420000, he falls in the second tax slab.
Therefore, we will calculate his tax liability as follows
Taxable income = ₹ 420000 – ₹ 300000 = ₹ 120000
Tax on income in the second slab (5% of ₹ 120000)
$= 0.05 \times 120000 =$ ₹ 6000
Add health and education cess = 4% of 6000 = ₹ 240
So, Mr. Sharma's total tax liability = 6000 + 240 = ₹ 6240
28. GST payable = ₹ 15300 (₹ 85000 × 18%)
29. Gift tax payable = ₹ 25000 (₹ 500000 × 5%)
30. Education cess will be 4% of tax payable
i.e. $\frac{4}{100} \times 900000 =$ ₹ 36000
31. GST payable under composition scheme
= ₹ 2400 (₹ 120000 × 2%)
32. Monthly income = ₹ 42000
Gross annual income = ₹ 42000 × 12 = ₹ 504000
Applicable deductions
Monthly GPF contribution = ₹ 3000
Annual GPF contribution = ₹ 3000 × 12 = ₹ 36000
NSC = ₹ 15000
Donation in PM's relief fund = ₹ 12000
Total applicable deductions = ₹ 36000 + 15000 + 12000
= ₹ 63000
Total taxable income
= Gross annual income – Total applicable deductions
= ₹ 504000 – ₹ 63000 = ₹ 441000
Now, the total taxable income falls in the slab of 250001 to 500000.
So, income tax = $(441000-250000) \times \frac{5}{100}$
= ₹ 9550
33. Total annual income = 12 × ₹ 50000 = ₹ 600000
Amount on which tax would be rebated on investments/donations
= 100% of Prime Minister's Relief Fund
+ 50% of Hospital Donation
= 100% of ₹ 60000 + 50% of ₹ 20000 = ₹ 70000
Total savings = Amount in GPF + Amount in LIC
+ Amount in NSC
= 12 × 7000 + 15000 + 35000 = ₹ 134000
100% Rebate on savings up to ₹ 100000.
That implies ₹ 34000 would be taxable.
Therefore, amount of salary after deduction of rebated amount
= Total salary – Rebate on investment/Donations
– Rebate on savings
= 600000 – 70000 – 100000 = ₹ 430000
Income tax = 0% × ₹ 250000 + 5%
× (₹ 430000 – ₹ 250000)
= ₹ 9000
Education cess = 3% of Income tax = 3% of ₹ 9000
= ₹ 270
Total tax = ₹ 9000 + ₹ 270 = ₹ 9270
34. We are asked to find the tax amount for Mr. Mohit who is 33 yr old and has a taxable income of ₹ 1235000. He fits into the slab of income tax rate under 60 yr old and annual income is above ₹ 1000000. We find the exceeding income by subtracting the ₹ 1000000 from the income of Mr. Mohit which is ₹ 1235000 – ₹ 1000000 = ₹ 235000
So, his tax amount is,
⇒ ₹ 112500 + 30% of income exceeding ₹ 1000000
⇒ ₹ 112500 + 30% of ₹ 235000
⇒ ₹ 112500 + ₹ 70500 = ₹ 183000
35. It is a case of intrastate transaction of goods and services.
∴ SGST = CGST = $\frac{1}{2}$ GST
Given, the manufacturer sells TV to a dealer = ₹ 18000
Amount of GST collected by the manufacturer from the dealer,
CGST = SGST = 6% of 18000 = $\left(\frac{6}{100}\right) \times 18000 =$ ₹1080
So, the manufacturer will pay ₹ 1080 as CGST and ₹ 1080 as SGST
CP of a TV for dealer = ₹18000
Profit = ₹1500
SP of a TV for dealer to customer = CP + Profit
= ₹18000 + ₹1500
= ₹19500
Amount of GST collected by the dealer from the customer,
CGST = SGST = 6% of ₹ 19500
$= \left(\frac{6}{100}\right) \times 19500 =$ ₹1170

(i) Amount of GST paid by the dealer to the State government.

$= ₹1170 - ₹1080 = ₹90$

(ii) Amount of GST received by the central government

= CGST paid by manufacturer + CGST paid by dealer

$= ₹1080 + ₹90 = ₹1170$

(iii) Amount of GST received by the State government

= SGST paid by manufacturer + SGST paid by dealer

$= ₹1080 + ₹90 = ₹1170$

(iv) Amount that the consumer pays for the TV

= CP of TV + CGST paid by customer + SGST paid by customer

$= ₹19500 + ₹1170 + ₹1170 = ₹21840$

36. It is a case of intrastate transaction of goods and services.

$\therefore$ SGST = CGST = $\frac{1}{2}$ GST

Given, printed price of a camera = ₹1600

Rate of discount = 20%

CP of camera for shopkeeper

= Printed price − Discount

= ₹1600 − 20% of ₹1600

$= ₹1600 - \left(\frac{20}{100}\right) \times 1600 = ₹1600 - ₹320 = ₹1280$

It is given that, rate of GST = 12%

Amount of GST paid by the shopkeeper to the wholesaler,

CGST = SGST = 6% of ₹1280 = $\left(\frac{6}{100}\right) \times 1280 = ₹76.80$

(i) GST paid by the shopkeeper to the central government

CGST = SGST = 6% of ₹1600 = $\left(\frac{6}{100}\right) \times 1600 = ₹96$

GST paid by the shopkeeper to the central government = ₹96 − ₹76.80 = ₹19.20

(ii) GST received by the central government.

CGST paid by wholesaler + CGST paid by shopkeeper

$= ₹76.80 + ₹19.20 = ₹96$

(iii) GST received by the State government.

SGST paid by wholesaler + SGST paid by shopkeeper

$= ₹76.80 + ₹19.20 = ₹96$

(iv) The amount at which the consumer bought the camera.

Amount paid by consumer for camera

= CP of camera + CGST paid by consumer + SGST paid by consumer

$= ₹1600 + ₹96 + ₹96 = ₹1792$

37. **Calculate Gross Total Income (GTI)**

Gross Total Income (GTI) = Salary income + House Property income + Business income + Other income

GTI = ₹ 600000 + ₹ 150000 + ₹ 310000 + ₹ 100000

GTI = ₹ 1160000

Calculate Total Deductions

Total deductions = Deductions under Section 80C + Deductions under Section 10(14)

Total deductions = ₹ 150000 + ₹ 10000 = ₹ 160000

Calculate Taxable Income

Taxable income = GTI − Total deductions

= ₹ 1160000 − ₹ 160000 = ₹ 1000000

Apply the Applicable Tax Slabs and Rates

Up to ₹ 250000: Nil

₹ 250001 to ₹ 500000: 5% on the amount exceeding ₹ 250000

₹ 500001 to ₹ 1000000: 20% on the amount exceeding ₹ 500000

Above ₹ 1000000: 30% on the amount exceeding ₹ 1000000

Tax Calculation

Nil on the first ₹ 250000

5% on the next ₹ 250000 (₹ 500000 − ₹ 250000)

20% on the next ₹ 500000 (₹ 1000000 − ₹ 500000)

So, tax liability = (0.05 × ₹ 250000) + (0.20 × ₹ 500000)

= ₹ 12500 + ₹ 100000 = ₹ 112500

38. Given, sales amount = INR 500000

GST rate = 12%

Input GST credits = INR 40000

Calculate Output GST

$$\text{Output GST} = \frac{\text{Sales amount} \times \text{GST rate}}{100}$$

$$= \frac{500000 \times 12}{100} = \frac{6000000}{100} = 60000$$

Calculate Net GST Liability

Net GST liability = Output GST − Input GST credits

= 60000 − 40000 = 20000

Determine Amount Payable or Receivable

If net GST liability is positive, it indicates an amount payable. If negative, it indicates an amount receivable.

Since, net GST liability is positive (20000), the company needs to pay this amount.

Conclusion

The output GST for the company's sales is INR 60000. After offsetting the input GST credits of INR 40000, the net GST liability is INR 20000. The company is required to pay this amount to the government.

39. Total annual income of Mr. Rohan = ₹ 500000

Annual savings

(i) LIC premium = ₹ 70000

(ii) Contribution towards PF = ₹ 12000

(iii) PPF = ₹ 30000

(iv) NSC = ₹ 10000

Total savings = ₹ 122000

Total taxable income = ₹ (500000 − 122000) = ₹ 378000

Now, income tax for FY 2022-23.

For income upto ₹ 250000 at 0% = ₹ 00.00

For income ₹ (378000 − 250000) = ₹ 128000 at 5%

= ₹ 6400

$\therefore$ Mr. Rohan will have to pay income tax ₹ 6400.

40. (i) Actual price of the goods = ₹ 4000
When sold at a profit of 20%
Profit = (20/100) × ₹ 4000 = ₹ 800
Thus, the selling price (excluding tax) of the goods will be = Actual price + profit = ₹ 4000 + ₹ 800 = ₹ 4800

(ii) The GST charged is 5%.
CGST paid by the consumer = 2.5% of the selling price
= (2.5/100) × ₹ 4800 = ₹ 120

(iii) SGST paid by the consumer
= 2.5% of the selling price
= (2.5/100) × ₹ 4800 = ₹ 120

(iv) Total amount paid by the consumer
= Selling price + CGST + SGST
= ₹ 4800 + ₹ 120 + ₹ 120 = ₹ 5040

41. **Calculate Gross Salary**
Gross salary = Basic salary + HRA + Special allowance
Gross salary = ₹ 1000000 + ₹ 150000 + ₹ 120000
= ₹ 1270000

Calculate Total Income
Total income = Gross salary + Other income
Total income = ₹ 1270000 + ₹ 15000 = ₹ 1285000

Calculate Taxable Income
Taxable income = Total income − Deductions
Taxable income = ₹ 1285000 − ₹ 50000 = ₹ 1235000

Calculate Income Tax
Income Tax = [5% × (₹ 500000 − ₹ 250000)]
+ [10% × (₹ 750000 − ₹ 500000)]
+ [15% × (₹ 1000000 − ₹ 750000)]
+ [20% × (₹ 1235000 − ₹ 1000000)]
= ₹ 122000

Add Health and Education Cess
Cess = Income tax × 4%
Cess = ₹ 122000 × 4% = ₹ 4880

Calculate Total Tax Liability
Total tax liability = Income tax + Cess
Total tax liability = ₹ 122000 + ₹ 4880 = ₹ 126880

42. (i) The marked price of the article = ₹ 12500
When sold at a profit of 8%
Profit = (8/100) × ₹ 12500 = ₹ 1000
Thus, the selling price (excluding tax) of the article
= Marked price + profit
= ₹ 12500 + ₹ 1000 = ₹ 13500

(ii) The rate of GST = 18%
IGST is not applicable in this case since the dealing is intra state.
CGST paid by the dealer to the Central Government
= 9% of the selling price
= (9/100) × ₹ 13500 = ₹ 1215
and SGST paid by the dealer to the State Government
= 9% of the selling price
= (9/100) × ₹ 13500 = ₹ 1215

(iii) The total amount which the consumer pays for the article will be
= Selling price + CGST + SGST
= ₹ 13500 + ₹ 1215 + ₹ 1215 = ₹ 15930

43. (i) Taxable income = ₹ 1335000
Income tax = ₹ 112500 + 30% of (₹ 1335000 − ₹ 1000000)
$= ₹\ 112500 + \frac{30}{100} \times 335000$
= ₹ 112500 + ₹ 100500 = ₹ 213000

(ii) Taxable income = ₹ 450000
Income tax = 5% of (₹ 450000 − ₹ 300000)
$= \frac{5}{100} \times (150000) = ₹\ 7500$

(iii) Taxable income = ₹ 230000
The tax payable is 0 as the taxable income is less than ₹ 250000.

44. (i) Cost of the raw material = ₹7500
The rate of GST = 5%
The input tax (under GST) paid by the manufacturer
$= 5\% \text{ of } ₹7500 = \left(\frac{5}{100}\right) \times ₹7500 = ₹375$
Thus, the CGST and SGST both are ₹187.50 each.

(ii) The manufacturer sells the finished product to a dealer at a profit of 40%.
$\text{Profit} = \left(\frac{40}{100}\right) \times ₹7500 = ₹3000$
Selling price = Cost price + Profit
= ₹7500 + ₹3000 = ₹10500
The output tax (under GST) collected by the manufacturer = 12% of the selling price
$= \left(\frac{12}{100}\right) \times ₹10500 = ₹1260$
Thus, both CGST and SGST = ₹630 each

(iii) The net tax (under GST) paid by the manufacturer to the Central Government (CGST)
= (input − output) CGST
= ₹630 − ₹187.50 = ₹442.5
and the net tax (under GST) paid by the manufacturer to the State Governments (SGST)
= (input − output) CGST
= ₹630 − ₹187.50 = ₹442.5

(iv) The amount paid by the dealer for the finished product = Selling price + GST = ₹ 10500 + GST
$= ₹10500 + \left(\frac{12}{100}\right) \times ₹10500$
= ₹10500 + ₹1260 = ₹11760

(v) New cost of the raw material = ₹ 10000
The rate of GST = 5%
The input tax (under GST) paid by the manufacturer
= 5% of ₹ 10000
= (5/100) × ₹ 10000 = ₹ 500
Thus, the CGST and SGST both are ₹ 250 each.

CHAPTER 21

Utility Bills

In this Chapter...

- Utility Bills
- Interpretation of Water Bills and Piped Natural Gas (PNG) Bills

Every household has to pay multiple bills every month including electricity bills, water supply bills, telephone bills, etc. These bills are referred to as **utility bills.**

Utility Bills

Utility bill is a invoice or statement that individuals or businesses receive from utility service providers for the services they use such as electricity, water, gas and sometimes other services like garbage collection or sewage.

The bill usually includes basic information such as the billing period, account number, tariff rate, issue date, due date, units utilised, surcharge, tax etc.

Customers are required to pay these bills to ensure that they continue to receive uninterrupted access to essential utilities.

Sample of Electricity Bill

See on next page 429.

Tariff Rate

Tariff rate on a utility bill refers to the charges or rates that a consumer must pay for the consumption of various utility services.

Tariff rate is determined by the appropriate government commission like Central Electricity Regulatory Commission, State Electricity Regulatory Commission, etc.

The tariff rate consists of two parts

(i) **Fixed charge**, which is not depended on consumption.

(ii) **Variable charge**, which is depended on consumption.

Tariff rates may vary for domestic and commercial consumers.

e.g. LPG bills for domestic use are charged at a different rate as compared to LPG used for commercial use.

Fixed Charge

A fixed charge in utility bills refers to a predetermined constant fee that consumers are required to pay regardless of their actual usage of the utility service.

Fixed charges remain constant/consistent for all billing periods. These charges contribute to covering the fixed costs associated with providing and maintaining the infrastructure for delivering the utility service.

e.g. Fixed charge accounts for Stearns Electric's investment in equipment like poles, wires and transformers, as well as labour to provide members with safe and reliable electric service.

Surcharge

A surcharge on a utility bill is an additional fee or charge imposed by the utility provider in addition to the basic rates of the utility.

The nature and purpose of surcharges can vary depending on the utility and the specific circumstances.

MAHAVITARAN
Maharashtra State Electricity Distribution Co. Ltd

Maharashtra State Electricity Distribution Co.Ltd.

BILL OF SUPPLY FOR THE MONTH OF Apr 2018

GSTIN: 27AAECM2933K1ZB Website : www.mahadiscom.in HSN CODE: 27160000

A' NAGAR CIRCLE :570 KARJAT (R) DIVISION : 574 BELWANDI S/DN. : 759 1

Consumer No. : 153188124462
Consumer Name : THE SUB DIV.ENGINEER, B.S.N.L. TOWER
Adress : KOLGAON
TAL.SHRIGONDA,DIST.A.NAGAR

Village : KOLGAON **Pincode :** 413701

BILL DATE	07-05-2018	17,310.00
DUE DATE	21-05-2018	
IF PAID UPTO	16-05-2018	17,160.00
IF PAID AFTER	21-05-2018	17,520.00
Last Receipt No./Date		/27-04-2018
Last Month Payment		15,130.00
Scale / Sector		Large Scale /Private Sector

Email ID :	ahsdesig@gmail.com			**Activity :**	Mobile Tower without		
Mobile No. :	0	**Meter No.:**	053-07081902	**Seasonal :**	N	**Load Shed Ind :**	
Tariff :	52 LT-II A	**Connected Load (KW):**	6.50 KW	**Urban/Rural Flag :**	R	**Express Feeder Flag :**	N
Contract Demand (KVA) :	5.00	**50% of Con. Demand(KVA) :**	2.50	**Feeder Voltage (KV) :**	11	**LIS Indicator :**	
DTC :	7591002	**PC-MR-ROUTE-SEQ :**	00-33-0001-0001	**BU :**	4759	**PC :**	00
Date of Connection :	21-02-2009	**Category :**				**GSTIN :**	
Supply at :	LT	**Elec. Duty :**	07			**PAN :**	
Prev. Highest (Mth) :		**Bill Demand (KVA) :**	0				
Security Deposit Held Rs. :	15,680.00	**Addl. S.D. Demanded Rs :**	5,900.00				
Bank Guarantee Rs. :	0.00	**S.D. Arrears Rs. :**	00.00				

BILLING HISTORY

Bill Month	Consumption (Units)	Bill Demand (KVA)	Bill Amount
Mar 2018	1,205	0	14,945.23
Feb 2018	3,213	0	41,307.92
Jan 2018	0	0	250.00
Dec 2017	1,091	0	13,243.78
Nov 2017	2,434	0	28,427.21
Oct 2017	2,054	0	23,961.00
Sep 2017	2,131	0	25,330.66
Aug 2017	1,914	0	23,978.82
Jul 2017	1,676	0	19,458.41
Jun 2017	2,826	0	37,214.01
May 2017	1,470	4	19,798.76
Apr 2017	1,479	5	16,625.27

CUSTOMER CARE Toll Free No.
1912, 1800-102-3435, 1800-233-3435

Important Message

- Consumers can pay online using Net Banking, Credit/Debit cards at https://wss.mahadiscom.in/wss/wss after registration.
- Submit / update your E-mail id and mobile number to Circle office for receiving prompt alerts through SMS.
- Submit / update your PAN and GSTIN to circle office with copies of PAN and GSTIN for verification.
- Special desk is operational for HT Consumers, please contact : htconsumer@mahadiscom.in for any clarification / query or grievance.

Here are some common surcharges that may appear on electricity bills

1. **Fuel Adjustment Surcharge** This surcharge is applied to account for fluctuations in the cost of fuel or energy sources used for electricity generation.
2. **AC Surcharge** It is a specific type of charge applied to customers who use air conditioning systems. It is typically designed to reflect the increased demand for electricity during the periods of high temperatures when air conditioners are commonly used.
3. **Peak-hour Surcharge** It is an additional charge imposed on consumers for electricity usage during periods of high demand, known as peak hours. This type of surcharge is designed to encourage consumers to shift their electricity usage to off-peak hours when demand is lower.
4. **Recovery Surcharge** It is an additional fee imposed by a utility provider to recover specific costs or expenses incurred by the utility. It is often temporary and is implemented to address a particular financial challenge or situation.

Service Charge

It is a fee or charge imposed by the utility provider for the provision of services beyond the actual consumption of the utility itself.

Many utilities have energy charge and delivery charge separately. While the former is the cost of actual electricity consumed by the consumer, the later is the fee charged for delivering electricity to the consumer. Energy charge is also known as consumption charge and delivery charge is also known as service charge.

The service charge is often a fixed or recurring fee and may be separate from charges related to the actual usage of the utility.

Interpretation of Electricity Bills

The electricity bill is determined by three elements

1. Total Units Consumed

To determine the number of units (or kilowatt-hours, kWh) consumed, one will need to look at the meter readings in the bill.

1 kWh is equivalent to running an appliance of 1000 watts (1 kW) for 1 h.

To calculate the units consumed during the billing period, subtract the previous meter reading from the current meter reading i.e.

$$\text{Units Consumed} = \text{Current Meter Reading} - \text{Previous Meter Reading}$$

2. Tariff Category of Consumer

Tariff rates are mainly divided into two categories

(i) Domestic tariff and

(ii) Commercial tariff

Domestic tariffs are designed in a way that increases with an increase in consumption. This tariff is introduced with the aim of motivating people to consume less electricity. In India, electricity tariff rates are different for different States or Union Territories.

e.g. The tariff plan of Delhi is given below

Category	> 2kW & ≤ 5 kW	> 5kW & ≤ 15 kW	> 15kW & ≤ 25 kW	> 25 kW
Fixed Charges (in kW/month)	₹ 50 per kW per month	₹ 100 per kW per month	₹ 200 per kW per month	₹ 250 per kW per month

Energy charges (₹/unit)

Category	Charges (fixed)	Energy (charges)				
Individual connections		0-200 (Units)	201-400 (Units)	401-800 (Units)	801-1200 (Units)	> 1200 (Units)
Upto 2 kW	₹ 20 per kW per month	₹ 3.00 per kWh	₹ 4.50 per kWh	₹ 6.50 per kWh	₹ 7.00 per kWh	₹ 8.00 per kWh

Note Delhi Government has announced a subsidy of 100% up to 200 units and 50% from 201-400 units subject to consumption of units up to 400.

3. Fixed Charge and Surcharge

Fixed charge is a recurring fee applied regardless of consumption, covering infrastructure and operational costs. It is part of the utility bill and depends upon the load of the connection. Every state has its fixed charges.

Surcharge is an additional fee imposed under specific conditions, such as changes in fuel costs, environmental compliance, etc. It can vary in each month and is decided by the service provider. It is imposed per unit of consumption and included in the bill.

Energy Tax or Electricity Duty

It is applied to the usage of electricity and the amount goes to the State governments. In some States, this tax is charged on the total charges while in others, it is charged on per unit consumption.

e.g. The government of Uttrakhand charges a 15% energy tax on the total tariff charges (i.e. fixed plus variable charges) from domestic consumers. On the other hand, States like UP and Delhi charge a 5% energy tax, and Himachal Pradesh charges 3% energy tax.

Also, States/UTs like Andaman and Nicobar Island, Arunachal Pradesh, Dadra and Nagar Haveli, Daman and Diu, Lakshadweep, Mizoram, Nagaland, Puducherry, Sikkim and Tripura don't charge energy tax.

Steps in the Estimation of Electricity Bill

The calculation of electricity bills involves several steps and the specific process can vary based on the tariff structure in place, whether it's a residential or commercial account and other factors. However, here's a general outline of the steps involved in calculating electricity bills as follows

- Read the meter to measure the amount of electricity consumed.
- Calculate energy consumption by subtracting the previous meter reading from the current meter reading.
- Determine the applicable tariff structure and apply the corresponding rates to the total energy consumption.
- Multiply the energy consumption by the applicable rate to calculate the energy charges.
- Check the fixed charges associated with the tariff and add them to the energy charges.
- If there is any surcharge, tax or additional fees (such as environmental fees or regulatory charges), add them to the total.
- Sum up the energy charges, fixed charges, surcharges and taxes to calculate the total bill amount i.e Total Bill Amount = Energy Charges + Fixed Charges + Surcharges + Taxes

EXAMPLE 1. Let's assume the following details for a residential consumer in Delhi:

Billing Period: January 1, 2024, to January 31, 2024

Meter Reading (Previous): 500 kWh

Meter Reading (Current): 600 kWh

Fixed Charges: ₹ 50 per month

Energy Charges (per kWh): ₹ 6 per kWh

Sol. Calculate Units Consumed

Units Consumed = Current Meter Reading − Previous Meter Reading

Units Consumed = 600 kWh − 500 kWh

= 100 kWh

Calculate Energy Charges

Energy Charges = Units Consumed × Energy Charges Rate

Energy Charges = 100 kWh × ₹ 6/kWh

= ₹ 600

Calculate Total Bill

Total Bill = Fixed Charges + Energy Charges

Total Bill = ₹ 50 + ₹ 600 = ₹ 650

EXAMPLE 2. Calculate the electricity bill of Viaan based on the following information in Delhi.

Connection : 5 kW

Units Consumed : 482

Surcharge : ₹ 0.50 per kW unit

Fixed charges : ₹ 50 per kW/month

Energy tax : 5% of tariff rates

Sol. Number of units consumed: 482, Connection load: 5 kW

Energy charges

Units	Price	Amount
0-200	₹ 3	₹ 600
201-400	₹ 4.5	₹ 900
401-482	₹ 6.5	₹ 533
	Total	₹ 2033

Fixed Charges: ₹ (50 × 5) = ₹ 250

Surcharge: ₹ (0.50 × 482) = ₹ 241

Energy Tax = 5% of (Energy charges + Fixed charges)

= 5% of (2033 + 250)

= 5% of 2283

= ₹ 114.15

Electricity bill = ₹ 2033 + ₹ 250 + ₹ 241 + ₹ 114.15

= ₹ 2638.15

Topic Practice 1

1 If a household in Delhi consumes 150 units of electricity in a month and is eligible for a subsidy of ₹ 2 per unit for the first 200 units, then calculate the total electricity bill for the month. (Energy charges = ₹ 6 per unit)

2 A commercial establishment in Delhi consumed 500 units of electricity in a month. For the first 200 units, the tariff is ₹ 5 per unit, and for the remaining units, it is ₹ 7 per unit. Calculate the total electricity bill for the month.

3 An agricultural consumer in India is eligible for a subsidy of ₹ 2 per kWh for the first 200 units of consumption. If the consumer consumes 250 units in a month and the regular energy charge is ₹ 5 per kWh, what is the total subsidy received?

4 A small business in Nagpur consumes 1500 units of electricity in a billing cycle. If the first 200 units are charged at ₹ 7 per unit and the remaining units at ₹ 9 per unit, what is the total electricity bill?

5 An apartment building in Indore has 50 flats. Each flat consumes an average of 200 units per month. If the electricity distributor imposes a fixed charge of ₹ 500 per flat and a unit charge of ₹ 6 per unit, what would be the total bill for the building in a month?

6 A monthly electricity bill has a fixed charge of ₹ 200 and a variable charge of ₹ 5 per unit. If the monthly consumption is 150 units, what is the total electricity bill?

7 The electricity tariff in Delhi for domestic consumers is ₹ 7.50 per unit. If a household consumes 150 units in a month, what will be their electricity bill?

8 If fixed monthly charge for a domestic electricity connection in UP is ₹ 250, and a household consumes 200 units in a month, what will be their total electricity bill? (Tariff rate ₹ 6.50 per unit)

9 If the electricity tariff for industrial consumers in Delhi is ₹ 5 per unit and an industrial unit consumes 5000 units in a month, calculate their electricity bill.

Hints & Solutions

1. Total units consumed = 150 units
   Subsidy per unit = ₹ 2
   Total subsidy for 150 units = 150 units × ₹ 2/unit = ₹ 300
   Total electricity bill
   = Total units consumed × Cost per unit − Subsidy
   = 150 units × ₹ 6/unit − ₹ 300 = ₹ 900 − ₹ 300 = ₹ 600
   Therefore, the total electricity bill for the month would be ₹ 600.

2. Total units consumed = 500 units
   Units in the first slab (0-200 units) = 200 units
   Units in the second slab (201-500 units) = 500 − 200 = 300 units
   Total cost for units in the first slab
   = Units in first slab × Cost per unit
   = 200 units × ₹ 5/unit = ₹ 1000
   Total cost for units in the second slab
   = Units in second slab × Cost per unit
   = 300 units × ₹ 7/unit = ₹ 2100
   Total electricity bill
   = Total cost for units in the first slab + Total cost for units in the second slab
   = ₹ 1000 + ₹ 2100
   = ₹ 3100
   Therefore, the total electricity bill for the month would be ₹ 3100.

3. Subsidy for first 200 units
   = Subsidy per unit × Number of units eligible for subsidy
   = ₹ 2/kWh × 200 kWh = ₹ 400
   Therefore, the total subsidy received for the month is ₹ 400.

4. Electricity bill = (200 units × ₹ 7 per unit) + [(1500 − 200) units × ₹ 9 per unit]
   = 1400 + (1300 × ₹ 9)
   = 1400 + 11700 = ₹ 13100

5. Total bill = (Fixed charge per flat × Number of flats) + (Unit charge per unit × Total units consumed)
   = (₹ 500 × 50) + [₹ 6 × (200 × 50)]
   = ₹ 25000 + ₹ 60000 = ₹ 85000

6. Total bill = (Fixed charges) + (Variable charges per unit × Quantity)
   = ₹ 200 + (₹ 5 × 150) = ₹ 950

7. Bill = Consumption (in units) × Tariff per unit
   = 150 units × ₹ 7.50 per unit = ₹ 1125

8. Bill = (Consumption × Tariff per unit) + Fixed monthly charge
   = (200 units × ₹ 6.50 per unit) + ₹ 250 = ₹ 1550

9. Bill = Consumption (in units) × Tariff per unit
   = 5000 units × ₹ 5 per unit = ₹ 25000

Interpretation of Water Bills and Piped Natural Gas (PNG) Bills

Interpretation of Water Bills

The components of a water bill in India can vary depending on the locality and the service provider. However, in general, water bills in India may include the following components:

1. Connection Fee or Fixed Access Charge

In order to provide the connection to a municipal water supply system, a one time fee is charged from the consumer, known as connection fee or fixed access charge. It is based on the size of the plot holding or the size of connection and ferrule or a combination of plot size and the size of the ferrule.

2. Fixed or Meter Rent Charges

Water bills include a fixed or meter rent charge, which is a flat fee for having a water meter installed at the premises. This fee may cover maintenance and administrative costs.

3. Water Tax or Service Tax

In some states, there may be additional tax imposed on water bills. This tax contributes to the overall cost of water supply and maintenance. In some states, the proceeds of water tax may be used for purposes like construction, maintenance, extension or improvement of services.

4. Water Consumption Charges

These charges are the primary component of water bill and are directly linked to the volume of water consumed. The more water a consumer uses, the higher the consumption charges. Water consumption is measured in m^3 or kilolitre (kl).

The charges are based mainly upon two components -

(i) Volume of water consumption

(ii) A set of charges other than water consumption such as water cess, license fee, maintenance charge etc.

A more common variant is to use a mix of two i.e. fixed monthly charge and charge on water consumption.

These charges are calculated on an Increasing Block Tariff (IBT) basis. An IBT structure consists of price slabs that increases as consumption rises. It is the same as we calculate in electricity bills.

Other Charge and Water Tariff

Apart from water consumption charges, a sewerage charge is also levied on every water bill.

Different types of water tariffs are used in India.

e.g. The following table shows the water tariff in Delhi

Monthly consumption (in kL)	Service charge (in ₹)	Volumetric charge per kL (in ₹)
Up to 20	₹ 146.41	₹ 5.27
20-30	₹ 219.62	₹ 26.36
>30	₹ 292.82	₹ 43.93

In addition, sewer maintenance charges 60% of the volumetric charge.

Different charges levied in water bills of different States

State	Charges
Uttar Pradesh	Water charge, Sewerage charge
Uttrakhand	Water charge, Sewerage charge
Rajasthan	Water charge, Meter rent, Development surcharge, Renewal fee, Sewerage charge
Delhi	Water charge, Service charge, Sewerage charge
Goa	Water charge, Meter rent, Sewerage charge

Sample of Water bills

See on next page 434.

Calculation of Water bills

Different states have different tariff plans for calculation of water bills.

To calculate water bill of a particular State, follow the tariff plan of that particular State and add all other charges.

EXAMPLE 1. Mr. Viaan lives in Delhi. He consumed 25 kl of water in a month. Calculate his water bill for the month.

Sol. As per the tariff plan of Delhi Jal Board, the calculation of water bill will be as follows

Service charge = ₹ 219.62

Volumetric charge = ₹ (5.27×20) + ₹ (26.36×5)

= ₹ 105.40 + ₹ 131.8 = ₹ 237.2

Sewerage charge = 60% of ₹ 237.2 = ₹ 142.32

Total water bill = Service charge + Volumetric charge + Sewerage charge

= ₹ 219.62 + ₹ 237.2 + ₹ 142.32 = ₹ 599.14

Delhi Jal Board

(Government of NCT of Delhi)
HQ: Varunalaya Phase II, Karol Bagh, New Delhi – 110005
Regular Water Bill

स्वच्छ भारत
एक कदम स्वच्छता की ओर

Name: SHRI T[redacted]
Address: [redacted]
VIHAR, Delhi

Mobile No.: [redacted]
Zone/MR Code: [redacted]
Area Code: A-1[redacted]
Old WCN: 47[redacted]
New KNO: 2[redacted]0000

Consumer Category: CAT I
Premise Detail: (No of floors-1)
Water Usage: 41-Miscellaneous
Meter No.: [redacted]
Meter Type (DJB/Pvt): PVT
Meter Size (mm): 15
Bill No.: [redacted]
Bill Cycle: ZALL(2017-05)
Bill Basis: REGULAR

Bill Date
18-JAN-2018
Bill Amount (Rs.)
5052
Bill Due Date
05-FEB-2018
Amount Payable After Due Date(Rs.)
(5% surcharge will be applicable after due date)
5305
If bill is not paid till Bill Due Date-Water connection may be disconnected

Meter No	UoM	Current Meter Read		Previous Meter Read		Current Consumption	
		Meter Reading Date	Reading / Meter Status	Meter Reading Date	Reading / Meter Status	Days	Units
[redacted]	KL	18-JAN-2018	4748 / OK	13-NOV-2017	4613 / OK	66	135

Bill Details: Current Period Charges (13-NOV-2017 to 18-JAN-2018)

Applicable Rate Period	Description	Amount(Rs.)
14-NOV-2017 to 18-JAN-2018	Total Consumption Charges	3202.59
14-NOV-2017 to 18-JAN-2018	Sewerage Charge (60 % of Water Consumption Charge)	1921.55
14-NOV-2017 to 18-JAN-2018	Service Charge - Consumption > 30 KL	644.20
14-NOV-2017 to 18-JAN-2018	Subtotal Bill Amount	5768.34
	Adjustment Details Are Listed Below	

Arrear, If any (Rs.)			-716.40
Opening Balance/Adjustment, If any (Rs.)			0
Total Consolidated Bill Amount Payable (Rs.)			5052
Late Payment Surcharge (Rs.)	252.6	**Amount with LPSC (Rs.)**	5305

Bill History

Bill Id	Bill from Date	Bill to Date	No. of Days	Amount(Rs)	Units
275220[redacted]	14-MAY-2017	13-NOV-2017	183	-716	233
275226[redacted]	17-MAR-2017	14-MAY-2017	58	-8436	25
275229[redacted]	11-SEP-2016	17-MAR-2017	187	-8436	29
275228[redacted]	07-JUL-2016	11-SEP-2016	66	864	46
275226[redacted]	20-MAY-2016	07-JUL-2016	48	4363	101

Payment History

Receipt Id	Amount(Rs)	Date
27522[redacted]	4300.00	21-JAN-2017
27527[redacted]	5000.00	15-NOV-2016
27522[redacted]	4362.26	07-JUL-2016
27522[redacted]	6919.50	06-JUN-2016
27522[redacted]	50000.00	14-MAR-2016

Important Message
Use of online booster not only increases chance of water contamination but also increases the bill.Please do not use online booster.

Delhi Jal Board

Bill Payment Counter Foil

स्वच्छ भारत
एक कदम स्वच्छता की ओर

New KNO	[redacted]	**Name**	[redacted]	**Bill No.**	[redacted]
Bill Date	18-JAN-2018	**Bill Due Date**	05-FEB-2018	**Bill Amount (Rs.)**	5052
Bill Amount with LPSC (Rs.):	5305	**Payment Date/Amount Paid(Rs.)**		**Cash/Cheque No./DD No.:**	
			Name of Bank / Branch		
Service Cycle	ZALL	**Service Route**	1	**Route Sequence**	473

EXAMPLE 2. Mr. Rohan lives in a particular State and have consumed 20 m^3 of water in a month. Calculate his water bill for the month based upon the tariff plan below

Monthly consumption (in m^3)	Water charges per m^3
Upto 15	₹ 3
15-25	₹ 8
25-50	₹ 12
> 50	₹ 20

Meter rent = ₹ 60 and Sewerage charge is 25% of water charges.

Sol. Water charge = (₹ 3 × 15) + (₹ 8 × 5)
= ₹ 45 + ₹ 40 = ₹ 85

Sewerage charge = 25% of ₹ 85 = ₹ 21.25

Meter rent = ₹ 60

Total water bill = Water charge + Sewerage charge + Meter rent
= ₹ 85 + ₹ 21.25 + ₹ 60 = ₹ 166.25

Interpretation of Piped Natural Gas (PNG) Bill

PNG bill consist of three main elements:

1. Connection Charges and Security Deposit

This is a one-time fee charged at the time of getting the new connection. The connection fee is non-refundable while the security deposit is refundable at the time of surrendering the connection.

2. Network Tariff or Minimum Charge

It is the cost of transporting the gas through the gas pipeline network. A domestic PNG connection includes laying of pipe line network up to number of appliances along with necessary fitting, meter safety valves, conversion of LPG appliance to PNG, etc. Sometimes network tariff is also included in gas charges.

3. Gas Consumption Charge

The gas consumption is measured in Standard Cubic Meter (SCM). The normal billing pattern of gas bill is bimonthly (i.e. once in two months).

This bill is calculated using the meter reading, installed in the premises of the gas user.

Gas charges also increase with the increase in consumption as in the case of electricity and water charges. Every gas company has its own tariff plans.

e.g. Domestic PNG Retail Prices
(w.e.f, 9th April, 2023)

1. In Delhi : ₹ 48.59 per SCM
2. In Noida, Gr. Noida and Ghaziabad : ₹ 48.46 per SCM
3. In Gurugram : ₹ 47.40 per SCM
4. In Rewari : ₹ 47.40 per SCM
5. In Karnal and Kaithal : ₹ 47.40 per SCM
6. In Muzaffarnagar, Meerut and Shamli : ₹ 51.97 per SCM
7. In Ajmer, Pali and Rajasmand: ₹ 54.23 per SCM
8. In Kanpur, Fatehpur & Hamirpur : ₹ 51.10 per SCM

Transportation of natural gas through pipeline will attract GST of 5% without Input Tax Credit (ITC) or 12% with full ITC.

Sample of Gas Bill

See on next page 436.

EXAMPLE 3. Mr. Vihaan lives in Noida and consumes 82 SCM gas in 2 months. Calculate his bill amount as per ₹ 48.46 per SCM.

Sol. Given consumption in two months = 82 SCM

So, Average daily consumption = $\frac{82}{60}$ SCM
= 1.37 SCM

Gas Charges = 1.37 SCM/ day × 60 days × ₹ 48.46
= ₹ 3983.41

GST = 5% of ₹ 3983.41
= ₹ 199.17

∴ Total charges = ₹ 3983.41 + ₹ 199.17
= ₹ 4182.58

INDRAPRASTHA GAS LIMITED
(A joint Venture of GAIL(India) Ltd, BPCL & Govt of NCT Delhi)
IGL Bhawan, 4, Community Center, Sector-9, R. K. Puram, New Delhi - 110022 CIN : L23201DL1998PLC097614
Find us on Social Media /IGLOnline @IGLSocial

24hr CUSTOMER CARE NOs. 1800-102-5109 1800-419-5109
IGL EMERGENCY NO 155216

BUSINESS PARTNER NO. 1000030412 ⇐ YOUR BP NO

NAME : [illegible]
ADDRESS : [illegible]
⇐ PROFILE DETAILS (ADDRESS, NAME, CONTACT NO & EMAIL

MOBILE : [redacted]
EMAIL : Please Provide Email ID

INVOICE NO.: INVOICE NO चालान संख्या :	Bill Date : 18.10.2023 बिल की तिथि :
INVOICE TYPE: Retail चालान प्रकार : खुदरा TYPE OF INVOICE	Due Date : 08.11.2023 देय तिथि :
CREDIT AMOUNT(If any) क्रेडिट राशि	₹ 0 (CREDIT OR EXCESS PAYAMENT IF ANY)
Amount Payable देय राशि	₹ 989.88 (AMOUNT TO BE PAID BEFORE DUE DATE)
After Due Date(2% LPC Applicable) देय तिथि के बाद (2% एलपीसी लागू)	₹ 1009.68
Disconnection Date : (if bill not paid within Due Date) डिस्कनेक्शन तिथि (यदि देय तिथि के भीतर ...)	23.11.2023

DISCONNECTION DATE IS BILL DUE DATE +15 DAYS FOR NON ARREAR BILL, DISCONNECTION DATE IS IMMEDIATE IF LAST BILL IS NOT PAID COMPLETELY, FOR AN ALREADY BILL/CREDIT ACCOUNT DISCONNECTION DATE WILL BE BLANK

Current Bill Details वर्तमान बिल विवरण

Bill Details - Tax Invoice / Bill of Supply
बिल विवरण

	PART A (SALE OF NATURAL GAS) भाग ए (प्राकृतिक गैस की बिक्री)	(₹)
1.1	Gas Consumption Charges गैस की खपत का शुल्क	740.48
1.2	VAT VALUE वैट	37.02
1.3	Arrears: Unpaid dues up to previous bill पिछले बिल तक बकाया राशि	
1.4	Credit Balance:- Advance/Excess paid क्रेडिट बैलेंस (जमा राशि)- अग्रिम/अतिरिक्त भुगतान	-67.30
1.5	Adjustment for Estimated Bills समायोजन	0.00
1.6	Discount/Rebate छूट	
1.7	Late Payment Charges	
	TOTAL CHARGES (PART A) कुल शुल्क	710.2

⇐ VAT AMOUNT ADDED SEPARATELY

	PART - B (CHARGES) भाग बी	(₹)
2.1	Fixed Daily Charges निर्धारित दैनिक शुल्क	
2.2	Other Charges अन्य शुल्क	256.08
2.3	Minimum Charges न्यूनतम शुल्क	
2.4	Customer Convenience Charges ग्राहक सुविधा शुल्क	20.00
2.5	SGST @ 9% स्टेट जीएसटी	1.80
2.6	CGST @ 9% सेंटर जीएसटी	1.80
2.7	Estimation Charges	
	TOTAL CHARGES (PART B) कुल शुल्क	279.68

⇐ OTHER CHARGES FOR ANY SERVICE DONE
⇐ BILL DELIVERY CHARGES

	PART - C (SECURITY DEPOSIT) भाग सी	(₹)
3.1	INSTALLATION/NORMAL SECURITY DEPOSIT PAYABLE सुरक्षा जमा देय	
3.2	CONSUMPTIOIN SECURITY DEPOSIT PAYABLE खपत सुरक्षा जमा देय	
3.3	EMI AMOUNT DUE देय ईएमआई राशि	
3.4	Current EMI No ईएमआई संख्या	
3.5	Additional Consumption SD अतिरिक्त खपत सुरक्षा जमा देय	
	TOTAL CHARGES (PART C) कुल शुल्क	0
	TOTAL PAYABLE (A+B+C) कुल देय (ए+बी+सी)	**989.88**

SECURITY OR EMI IF RAISED IN BILL WILL SHOW HERE

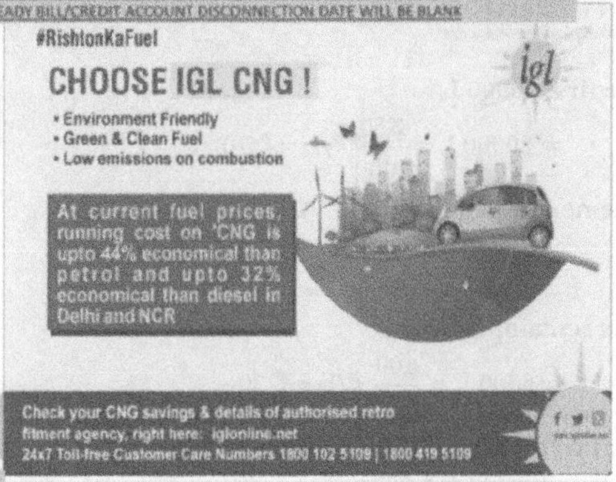

DETAILS OF CONSUMPTION CYCLE खपत चक्र का बिल विवरण

Meter No मीटर संख्या	Previous Date पिछली तारीख	Closing Date अंतिम तिथि	Previous Meter Reading पिछली मीटर रीडिंग	Closing Meter Reading वर्तमान रीडिंग	No. of days दिनों की	UNITS CONSUMED (SCM)	PRICE PER UNIT प्रति इकाई	GAS CONSUMPTION CHARGES(Exec VAT) ... शुल्क (छोड़कर)
1680381	26.08.2023	15.10.2023	1078.000	1094.000	51	16.000	46.28	740.48
				TOTAL	51	16.000		740.48

⇐ METER READING AND CONSUMPTION DETAILS WITH DATES

AVERAGE CONSMP LAST 2 CYCLES ⇓

Average Cons. in Last 2 billing cycles अंतिम २ बिलिंग चक्रों में औसत खपत	0.289 scm/day एससीएम/दिन
Price/SCM in INR (w.e.f 09.04.2023) मूल्य/एससीएम	48.59 (incl. VAT) वैट सहित

Breakup Of Price /per SCM in INR मूल्य विवरण प्रति एससीएम (₹)

Basic Cost of gas गैस की मूल लागत	Supply & Distribution cost आपूर्ति और वितरण लागत	Margin मार्जिन	VAT वैट	Total कुल
26.72	15.14	4.42	2.31	48.59

⇑ PRICE BREAKUP TABLE

> कृपया ध्यान दें की अगर द्विमासिक गैस खपत की मात्रा ४ एससीएम से कम है, आपको न्यूनतम ४ एससीएम के लिए बिल भेजा जायेगा।
> Kindly note that you will be billed for a minimum of 4 SCM, in case the bimonthly gas quantity is less than 4 SCM.
> 01.10.2017 से वस्तुओं और सेवाओं पर GST लागू है. हालाँकि GST कानून के अनुसार PNG पर वैट लागू रहेगा
> GST is applicable on Goods & Services w.e.f. 01.10.2017. However, VAT will continue to be applicable on PNG Sales as per GST law
> प्रिय ग्राहक, आपको सूचित किया जाता है कि 09.04.2023 से PNG की प्रभावी कीमतें Rs.48.59 प्रति SCM वैट सहित संशोधित की गयी है।
> Dear Customer, this is to inform you that Prices of PNG have been revised to Rs.48.59 per scm inclusive VAT w.e.f 09.04.2023
> प्रिय उपभोक्ता, अगले बिलिंग चक्र से प्रत्येक हार्ड कॉपी बिल सुविधा के लिए 20 रुपये का शुल्क लिया जाएगा
> Convenience charges of Rs. 20/- for hard copy bill facility will be charged for every invoice from next billing cycle.
> Note : Based on your past year consumption pattern ,we have revised your Consumption Security Deposit.The revised Additional Consumption Security Deposit(if any) will reflect in your next Bill
> स्मार्ट वोटर बने । अपने वोटर आईडी को आधार से लिंक करें । आज ही फॉर्म 6B ऑनलाइन भरें । अधिक जानकारी के लिए www.ceodelhi.gov.in पर जाये या हेल्पलाइन 1950 पे संपर्क करें ।

⇐ RUNNING INFO

TIN	07200216264(w.e.f 5th April 1999)
CIN :	L23201DL1998PLC097614
GSTN	07AAACI5076R1ZZ

Bill History

Billing Period	Units (scm)	Cons/day (scm)
27.04.2023-22.06.2023	18.000	0.316
23.06.2023-25.08.2023	17.000	0.266

(Authorised Signatory)
...हस्ताक्षरकर्ता

PAYMENT THORUGH CHEQUE/DD DETAIL

Please draw your cheque/DD favouring "INDRAPRASTHA GAS LIMITED A/C Business Partner No. 1000030412"
DISCLAIMER : This bill is not a document for claiming any valid address proof of the PNG customer, for submitting before any Authority Body. Anybody claimimg or accepting the said bill to be valid address proof shall be doing it at their own risk and cost.

Topic Practice 2

1 In Delhi, the water bill for residential consumers is calculated based on the following rates

For the first 20000 L : ₹ 3.50 per 1000 L

For the next 30000 L : ₹ 4.50 per 1000 L

For any consumption above 50000 L : ₹ 6.00 per 1000 L

Calculate the water bill for a household that consumes 55000 L of water in a billing cycle.

2 Do States in India follow a uniform tariff structure for water bills?

3 How is the gas connection bill calculated?

4 What are the key components of a gas connection bill in different States?

5 What metering systems are used for calculating gas consumption in different States?

Hints & Solutions

1. For the first 20000 L,

$$= 20000 \text{ L} = \frac{3.50}{1000} \text{ ₹/L} = \text{₹ } 70$$

For the next 30000 L,

$$= 30000 \text{ L} = \frac{4.50}{1000} \text{ ₹/L} = \text{₹ } 135$$

For the remaining 5000 L,

$$= 5000 \text{ L} = \frac{6.00}{1000} \text{ ₹/L} = \text{₹ } 30$$

$\therefore$ Total water bill = ₹ 70 + ₹ 135 + ₹ 30
= ₹ 235

2. No, tariff structures for water bills vary between States.
3. Calculated using the gas consumption measured in cubic meters (or cubic feet), multiplied by the unit rate specified by the gas provider.
4. Gas bills typically consist of a fixed connection charge and a variable charge. Additional charges may apply for services like pipeline maintenance or safety measures, varying across States.
5. Gas consumption is measured using gas meters that record the volume consumed. The recorded data, often in cubic meters or cubic feet, is utilized to determine the gas bill.

Exam Pattern Exercise

Part A - Objective Type Questions

Multiple Choice Type Questions

1 What is the primary factor influencing the calculation of electricity bills in India?
(a) Voltage stability
(b) Power outage frequency
(c) Consumption of electricity
(d) Distance from power plants

2 In India, what determines the tariff structure for electricity bills?
(a) Economic growth rate
(b) Government subsidies
(c) Electricity consumption slabs
(d) Political party in power

3 Which of the following is NOT a common component of an electricity bill in India?
(a) Meter rent
(b) Fuel adjustment charge
(c) Surcharge for environmental protection
(d) Maintenance fee for power lines

4 What term is used to describe the additional charge when electricity consumption exceeds a certain limit?
(a) Surcharge (b) Levy
(c) Overuse fee (d) Peak charge

5 How are water bills typically calculated in India?
(a) Fixed monthly fee
(b) Based on the number of taps in the house
(c) Consumption measured by water meters
(d) By the size of the property

6 In some Indian municipalities, what is the term used for the fixed charge that consumers pay regardless of their water consumption?
(a) Usage fee (b) Meter charge
(c) Base rate (d) Consumption fee

7 What is the primary unit of measurement for water consumption in billing?
(a) Liters (b) Gallons
(c) Cubic meters (d) Cubic feet

8 Besides water consumption, what might be included in a water bill in some States?
(a) Fixed connection charge
(b) Sewage disposal fee
(c) Water treatment surcharge
(d) All of the above

9 What is the common unit used to measure gas consumption in billing?
(a) Cubic feet (b) Liters
(c) Cubic meters (d) Gallons

10 What might be a variable charge in a gas bill?
(a) Fixed connection fee
(b) Safety surcharge
(c) Consumption-based charge
(d) Pipeline maintenance cost

11 Are gas bill calculations consistent across all states in India?
(a) Yes, completely uniform
(b) No, they vary based on State policies
(c) Uniform only for residential users
(d) Uniform only for commercial users

Assertion-Reason Based Questions

Directions (Q. Nos. 12-15) *In the questions given below are two statements labelled as Assertion (A) and Reason (R). In the context of the two statements, which one of the following is correct?*
(a) Both A and R are correct; R is the correct explanation of A
(b) Both A and R are correct; R is not the correct explanation of A
(c) A is correct; R is incorrect
(d) R is correct; A is incorrect

12 **Assertion (A)** Utility bills may vary from month to month.
Reason (R) Utility bills are influenced by factors such as consumption levels, seasonal variations, and changes in tariff rates.

13 **Assertion (A)** Utility bills include charges for services such as electricity, water and gas consumption.
Reason (R) Utility companies calculate bills based on meter readings and tariff rates applicable to different types of services.

14 **Assertion (A)** Tariff rates may vary for domestic and commercial consumers.
Reason (R) The cost of electricity production and distribution is similar in every State.

15 **Assertion (A)** Water bills in different States of India are determined solely by the quantity of water consumed by the household.
Reason (R) The cost of water treatment and distribution varies significantly among States.

Part-B Descriptive Questions

Very Short Answer Type Questions

16 If the electricity tariff rate in a particular area is ₹ 6 per unit and a household consumes 200 units of electricity in a month, what would be their total electricity bill?

17 A commercial establishment has an electricity consumption of 5000 units in a billing cycle. If the electricity tariff for commercial use is ₹ 8 per unit, what is their total electricity bill?

18 What factors influence the calculation of a water bill in India?

19 How are gas bills usually calculated in India?

20 If a gas company charges ₹ 30 per cubic meter of natural gas and a household consumes 50 cubic meters in a month, what would be their total gas bill?

Short Answer Type Questions

21 Calculate the amount of the electricity bill to be paid for the month, when 556 units of electricity is the reading of the electric meter in a month. The reading of the meter for the previous month was 423 units. Take the cost of one unit as ₹ 4.09.

22 An electric meter reads 8950 KWh at the end of the month, while at the beginning of the month, the reading was 8833 KWh. How many units of electricity are consumed? If one unit costs ₹ 4.30, find the cost of the electrical energy consumed.

23 The electricity bill of a certain establishment is partly fixed and partly varies as the number of units of electricity consumed. When in a certain month 540 units are consumed, the bill is ₹ 1800. In another month, 620 units are consumed, the bill is ₹ 2040. In yet another month, 500 units are consumed. What will be the monthly bill for 500 units?

24 Calculate the amount of electrical energy consumption for a month of 30 days in household of 220 V line with the following appliances being used

(a) five 60 W bulbs for 6 h.

(b) two 1000W heaters for 2 h.

(c) 750 W electric iron for 2 h.

(d) 100 W refrigerator for 24 h.

(e) 1100 W microwave oven for 3 h.

The cost of first 200 units is ₹ 2.40/kWh and next 200 units is ₹ 3.90/kWH respectively.

25 For an industrial connection, monthly consumption of water is 40 Kl, calculate the water bill. Tariff rates can be considered as per the table given below

Monthly Consumption (in Kilolitre)	Service charge (in ₹)	Volumetric Charge (Per Kl in ₹)
Upto 20	146.41	5.27
20-30	219.62	26.36
> 30	292.82	43.93
Plus Sewer Maintenance Charges: 60% of water volumetric charge		

26 Mr Rohit from Lucknow, consumed 78 SCM of gas in 30 days. Minimum charge is 10% of the gas charges. Calculate his PNG bill for that period. Tariff plan is given below:
Number of units (in SCM) Upto 45 per month – Price per unit (in ₹) 29.50
Above 45 per month – ₹ 42.61.

Case Study Based Questions

27 A family of four residing in Mumbai, India, is interested in estimating their utility bills for the upcoming month. They want to budget their expenses accordingly. The family consists of two adults and two children. The monthly income of the family is ₹ 75000. They live in a 2-bedroom apartment.
Electricity Bill Estimation The average monthly electricity consumption for their household appliances is 300 units. The electricity tariff in Mumbai is ₹ 7 per unit.
Water Bill Estimation The family's average water consumption is 200000 L/month. The water tariff in Mumbai is ₹ 3 per 1000 L.
Gas Bill Estimation The family uses Piped Natural Gas (PNG) for cooking. Their average monthly gas consumption is 40 m^3. The gas tariff is ₹ 25/m^3.
Based on the above information, answer the following questions

(i) What would be the estimated electricity bill for the family in Mumbai?

(ii) What is the estimated water bill for the family?

(iii) How much is the estimated gas bill for the family?

(iv) What is the total estimated amount the family should allocate for utility bills based on their budget allocation?

(v) If the water tariff is increased by ₹ 2, how much will be the new bill?

Hints & Solutions

1. (c)	2. (c)	3. (d)	4. (a)
5. (c)	6. (c)	7. (c)	8. (d)
9. (a)	10. (c)	11. (b)	12. (a)
13. (a)	14. (c)	15. (b)	

16. Total bill = Tariff rate per unit × Total units consumed
$= ₹\, 6 \times 200 = ₹\, 1200$

17. Total bill = Tariff rate per unit × Total units consumed
$= ₹\, 8 \times 5000 = ₹\, 40000$

18. Water bills in India are influenced by factors such as the volume of water consumed, the type of usage (domestic, commercial, industrial), and any fixed charges or taxes imposed by the local water authority.

19. Gas bills in India are calculated based on the volume of gas consumed, measured in units such as cubic meters or cubic feet. The consumption is multiplied by the prevailing tariff rate to determine the bill amount.

20. Total bill = Tariff rate per cubic meter × Total cubic meters consumed
$= ₹\, 30 \times 50 = ₹\, 1500$

21. Given,
Cost of a unit of electricity, Cu = ₹ 4.09/unit
Reading of the current month = 556 units
Reading of the previous month = 423 units
Number of units consumed in the month:
$E = 556 - 423 = 133$ units
Cost of electrical bill is the product of units consumed and cost per unit.
$C = E\,\text{Cu}$
$C = 133 \times 4.09 = ₹\, 543.97$

22. Final reading of the meter = 8950 kWh
Initial reading of the meter = 8833 kWh
∴ Energy consumed during the month = 8950 − 8833
= 117 kWh
Rate of 1 unit = ₹ 4.30
∴ Cost of 117 units = ₹ 4.30 × 117
= ₹ 503.10

23. Let the fixed amount be ₹ x and the cost of each unit be ₹ y.
Then, $540y + x = 1800$ ...(i)
and $620y + x = 2040$ ...(ii)
On subtracting Eq. (ii) from Eq. (i), we get
$80y = 240$
$\Rightarrow y = 3$
On putting $y = 3$ in Eq. (i), we get
$540 \times 3 + x = 1800$
$\Rightarrow x = (1800 - 1620) = 180$
∴ Fixed charges = ₹ 180, Charge per unit = ₹ 3
Total charges for consuming 500 units = ₹ (180 + 500 × 3)
= ₹ 1680

24. (a) Power consumed = 5 × 60W × 6h × 30
= 60 × 30 × 30 Wh
= 54 kWh or 54000 Wh
(b) Power consumed = 2 × 1000 W × 2 h × 30
= 120 kWh or 120000 Wh
(c) Power consumed = 750 W × 2h × 30
= 1500 × 30 Wh
= 45 kWh or 45000 Wh
(d) Power consumed = 100 × 24 × 30 Wh
= 72 kWh or 72000 Wh
(e) Power consumed = 1100 × 3 × 30 Wh
= 99 kWh or 99000 Wh
Hence, total power consumed
= 54 + 120 + 45 + 72 + 99
= 390 kWh or 390000 Wh
Hence, cost = 200 × 2.4 + 190 × 3.9 = 480 + 741
= ₹ 1221
Note 1000 Wh = 1 kWh

25. Volumetric charge for consumption upto 20 kl
= ₹ 20 × 5.27 = ₹105.4
Volumetric charge for consumption between 20-30 kl
= ₹ 10 × 26.36 = ₹ 263.6
Volumetric charge for consumption between 30-40 kl
= ₹ 10 × 43.93 = ₹ 439.3
Total volumetric charge for consumption of 40 kl
= ₹ (105.4 + 263.6 + 439.3) = ₹ 808.3
Service charge = ₹ 292.82
Sewage charge = 60% of Volumetric charge
= 808.3 × 60% = ₹484.98
Amount of water bill for the given month
= ₹(808.3 + 292.82 + 484.98) = ₹ 1586.1
Thus, amount of domestic water bill is ₹ 1586.

26. Tariff charges for the first 45 SCM units = 45 × 29.5
= 1327.5
Tariff charges for the units above 45 SCM units
= (78 − 45) × 42.61
= 33 × 42.61
= ₹ 1406.13

$\therefore$ Total charges = 1406.13 + 1327.5 = ₹ 2733.63

Minimum charges = 10% of 2733.63

= 01 × 2733.63

= ₹ 273.363

So, total PNG bill = 2733.63 + 273.363

= ₹ 3006.9

Thus, Mr. Rohit's PNG bill for the given period is ₹ 3006.9 or ₹ 3007.

27. (i) **Electricity Bill Estimation**

Total units consumed = 300 units

Tariff rate per unit = ₹ 7

Estimated electricity bill

= Total units consumed × Tariff rate per unit

= 300 × ₹ 7 = ₹ 2100

(ii) **Water Bill Estimation**

Total liters consumed = 200000 L

Tariff rate per 1000 L = ₹ 3

Estimated water bill

= (Total liters consumed / 1000) × Tariff rate per 1000 L

= (200000/1000) × ₹ 3

= ₹ 600

(iii) **Gas Bill Estimation**

Total cubic meters consumed = 40 m^3

Tariff rate per cubic meter = ₹ 25

Estimated gas bill

= Total cubic meters consumed × Tariff rate per cubic meter

= 40 × 25

= ₹ 1000

(iv) **Total Monthly Budget Estimation**

Total utility bills

= Sum of estimated electricity, water, gas bills

= 2100 + 600 + 1000 = ₹ 3700

Now, percentage of total budget allocated for utility bills

= (Total utility bills / Total monthly budget) × 100

= (3700/75000) × 100 = 4.93%

(v) **Water Bill Estimation**

Total liters consumed = 200000 L

Tariff rate per 1000 L = ₹ 5

Estimated water bill

= (Total liters consumed / 1000) × Tariff rate per 1000 L

= (200000/1000) × ₹ 5 = ₹ 1000

CHAPTER 22

Straight Lines

In this Chapter...

- Slope of a Straight Line
- Various Forms of Equation of Line
- Distance of a Point from a Line and Distance between Two Parallel Lines

In earlier classes, we initiated the study of coordinate geometry, where we studied about distance between two points, section formula, centroid of triangle, area of triangle etc. In this chapter, we will study about straight lines.

A **straight line** is a curve, such that all the points on the line segment joining any two points of it lies on it.

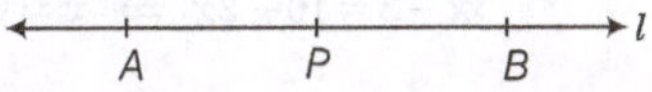

Slope of a Straight Line

Angle of Inclination of a Straight Line

An angle θ made by the line with positive X-axis in anti-clockwise direction is called angle of inclination of a line. A line in coordinate plane forms two angles with the X-axis, which are supplementary.

Thus, $\quad 0° \le \theta \le 180°$

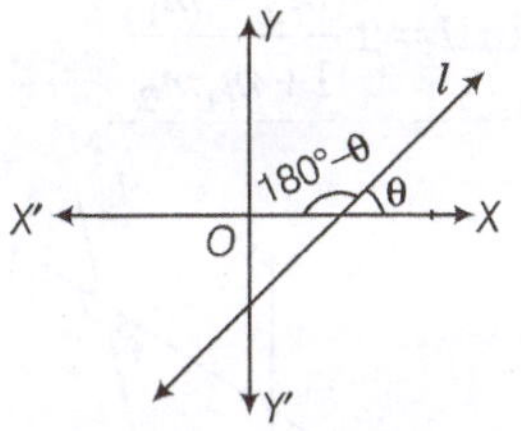

- When $\theta = 0°$, then **line is parallel to** X**-axis** (horizontal line).
- When $\theta = 90°$, then **line is perpendicular to** X**-axis** i.e. parallel to Y-axis (vertical line).

Slope or Gradient of a Line

If θ is the angle of inclination of a line l, then $\tan\theta$ is called the slope or gradient of the line l and it is denoted by m.

i.e. $\quad \boxed{m = \tan\theta}$

e.g. For figure (i), $\quad m = \tan 45° = 1$

and for figure (ii), $m = \tan 135° = -1$

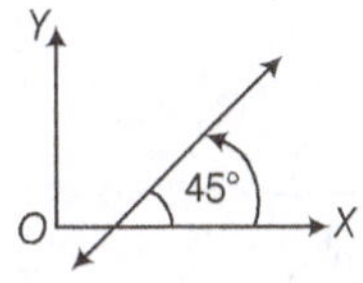

(i)

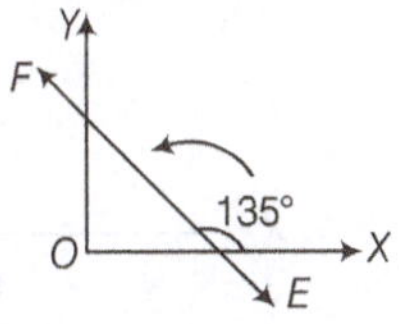

(ii)

- The slope of X-axis is, $m = \tan 0° = 0$.
- The slope of a line, when $\theta = 90°$ is not defined, i.e. the slope of Y-axis is not defined.

EXAMPLE 1. Find the slope of line, whose inclination is 60° and 150°.

Sol. Let θ be the inclination of a line, then its slope $= \tan\theta$.

At $\theta = 60°$,

$$\text{slope of a line} = \tan 60° = \sqrt{3}$$

At $\theta = 150°$,

$$\text{slope of a line} = \tan(150°) = \tan(180° - 30°)$$

$$= -\tan 30° \qquad [\because \tan(180° - \theta) = -\tan\theta]$$

$$= -\frac{1}{\sqrt{3}}$$

Slope of a Line Joining Two Points

If a line has two points (x_1, y_1) and (x_2, y_2), then the slope of line joining two points (x_1, y_1) and (x_2, y_2) is

$$m = \frac{y_2 - y_1}{x_2 - x_1}, \quad x_1 \neq x_2$$

EXAMPLE 2. Find the slope of a line joining following two points

(i) $A(1, 2)$ and $B(3, -4)$

(ii) $A(3, -2)$ and $B(7, -2)$.

Sol. We know that, slope of a line joining two points (x_1, y_1) and (x_2, y_2) is $m = \frac{y_2 - y_1}{x_2 - x_1}$

(i) Given, $A(1, 2) \equiv (x_1, y_1)$ and $B(3, -4) \equiv (x_2, y_2)$

$\therefore$ Slope of line joining points A and B is

$$m = \frac{-4-2}{3-1} = \frac{-6}{2} = -3$$

(ii) Given, $A(3, -2) \equiv (x_1, y_1)$ and $B(7, -2) \equiv (x_2, y_2)$

$\therefore$ Slope of line joining the points A and B is

$$m = \frac{-2-(-2)}{7-3} = \frac{0}{4} = 0$$

EXAMPLE 3. Find the angle between the X-axis and the line joining the points $(3, -1)$ and $(4, -2)$. **[NCERT]**

Sol. Given, $(x_1, y_1) \equiv (3, -1)$ and $(x_2, y_2) \equiv (4, -2)$

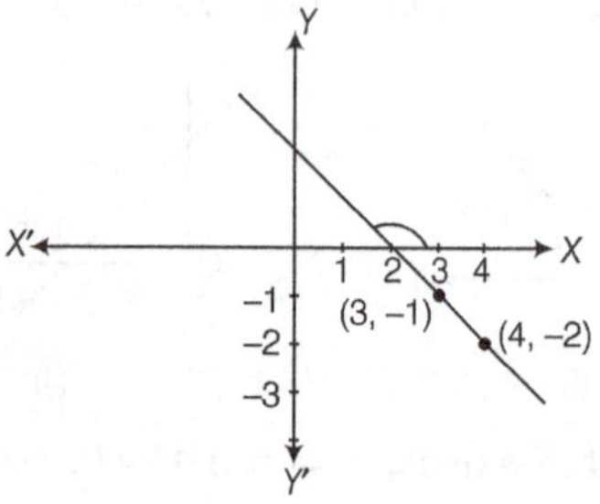

Slope of line, $m = \frac{y_2 - y_1}{x_2 - x_1} = \frac{-2+1}{4-3}$

$\Rightarrow \tan\theta = \frac{-1}{1}$

$\Rightarrow \tan\theta = -1$

$\Rightarrow \tan\theta = -\tan 45°$ $[\because 1 = \tan 45°]$

$\Rightarrow \tan\theta = \tan(180° - 45°)$

$[\because \tan(180° - \theta) = -\tan\theta]$

$\Rightarrow \tan\theta = \tan 135°$

$\Rightarrow \theta = 135°$

Hence, the required angle between X-axis and the line joining the points $(3, -1)$ and $(4, -2)$ is $135°$.

EXAMPLE 4. A ray of light coming from the point (1, 2) is reflected at a point A on the X-axis and then passes through the point (5, 3). Find the coordinates of the point A. **[NCERT Exemplar]**

Sol. Let the coordinates of point A be $(x, 0)$. From the figure, the slope of the reflected ray is given by

$$\tan\theta = \frac{3}{5-x} \quad \text{...(i)}$$

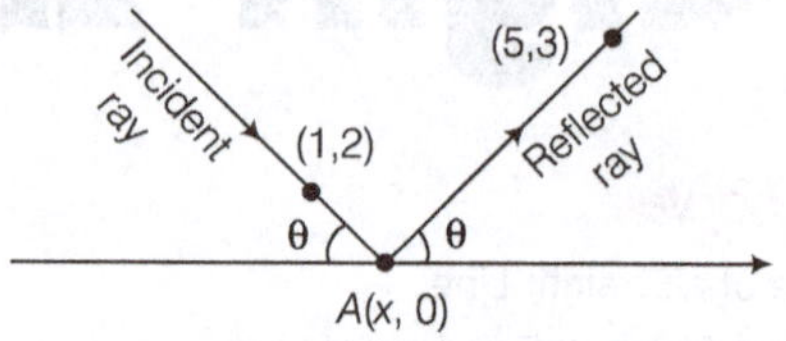

Again, the slope of the incident ray is given by

$$\tan(\pi - \theta) = \frac{-2}{x-1} \quad \left[\because m = \frac{y_2 - y_1}{x_2 - x_1}\right]$$

$$\Rightarrow -\tan\theta = \frac{-2}{x-1} \quad [\because \tan(\pi - \theta) = -\tan\theta]$$

$$\Rightarrow \tan\theta = \frac{2}{x-1} \quad \text{...(ii)}$$

From Eqs. (i) and (ii), we get

$$\frac{3}{5-x} = \frac{2}{x-1}$$

$$\Rightarrow 3x - 3 = 10 - 2x \Rightarrow x = \frac{13}{5}$$

Therefore, the required coordinates of the point A are $\left(\frac{13}{5}, 0\right)$.

Angle between Two Lines

Let l_1 and l_2 be two lines and their inclination are α_1 and α_2, respectively and their slopes are $m_1 = \tan\alpha_1$ and $m_2 = \tan\alpha_2$.

Then, angle between them is

$$\tan\theta = \pm\frac{m_2 - m_1}{1 + m_1 m_2}$$

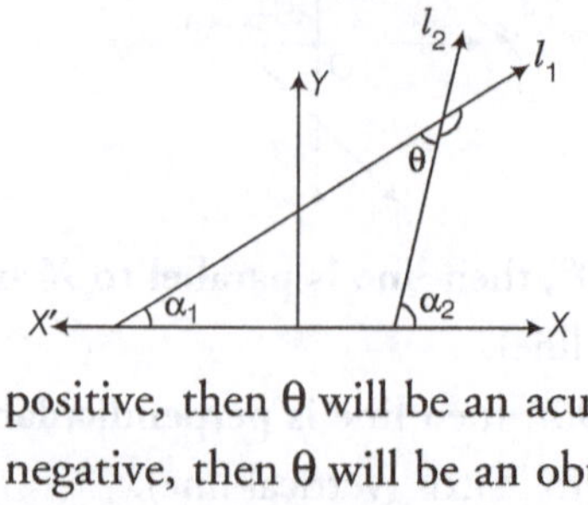

- If $\tan\theta$ is positive, then θ will be an acute angle.
- If $\tan\theta$ is negative, then θ will be an obtuse angle.

EXAMPLE 5. Find the angle between the lines joining the points (0,0), (2,3) and the points (2, – 2), (3, 5).

Sol. Let θ be the angle between the given lines.

We have,

$$m_1 = \text{Slope of the line joining } (0, 0) \text{ and } (2, 3) = \frac{3-0}{2-0} = \frac{3}{2}$$

$$m_2 = \text{Slope of the line joining } (2, -2) \text{ and } (3, 5)$$

$$= \frac{5+2}{3-2} = 7$$

Now, $\tan\theta = \pm\left(\frac{m_2 - m_1}{1 + m_1 m_2}\right) = \pm\left(\frac{7 - 3/2}{1+7(3/2)}\right)$

$$= \pm\left(\frac{11/2}{23/2}\right) = \pm\left(\frac{11}{23}\right)$$

$$\Rightarrow \quad \theta = \tan^{-1}\left(\frac{11}{23}\right) \text{ or } \pi - \tan^{-1}\left(\frac{11}{23}\right)$$

EXAMPLE 6. If the angle between two lines is $\frac{\pi}{4}$ and slope of one of the line is $\frac{1}{3}$, then find the slope of the other line.

Sol. Given, the angle between two lines is $\theta = \frac{\pi}{4}$.

Slope of a line, $m_1 = \frac{1}{3}$

Let slope of other line $= m_2$

We know that, angle between two lines is

$$\tan\theta = \left|\frac{m_2 - m_1}{1 + m_1 m_2}\right| \Rightarrow \tan\frac{\pi}{4} = \left|\frac{m_2 - \frac{1}{3}}{1 + \frac{m_2}{3}}\right|$$

$$\Rightarrow \left|\frac{3m_2 - 1}{3 + m_2}\right| = 1 \Rightarrow \frac{3m_2 - 1}{3 + m_2} = \pm 1$$

Taking (+) sign, $\frac{3m_2 - 1}{3 + m_2} = 1$

$$\Rightarrow \quad 3m_2 - 1 = 3 + m_2$$

$$\Rightarrow \quad 2m_2 = 4$$

$$\Rightarrow \quad m_2 = 2$$

Taking (–) sign, $\frac{3m_2 - 1}{3 + m_2} = -1$

$$\Rightarrow \quad 3m_2 - 1 = -3 - m_2$$

$$\Rightarrow \quad 4m_2 = -2 \Rightarrow m_2 = -\frac{1}{2}$$

$\therefore$ The slope of other line is 2 and $-\frac{1}{2}$.

EXAMPLE 7. The slope of a line is double of the slope of another line. If tangent of the angle between them is $\frac{1}{3}$, then find the slope of the lines. [NCERT]

Sol. If slope of one line is m. Then, the slope of the other line is $2m$. Let angle between these two lines be θ.

Then, $\tan\theta = \frac{1}{3}$ [given]

$$\Rightarrow \quad \left|\frac{2m - m}{1 + 2m \cdot m}\right| = \frac{1}{3} \qquad \left[\because \tan\theta = \left|\frac{m_2 - m_1}{1 + m_1 \cdot m_2}\right|\right]$$

$$\Rightarrow \quad \frac{m}{1 + 2m^2} = \pm\frac{1}{3}$$

Here, two cases arise.

***Case* I** When $\frac{m}{1 + 2m^2} = \frac{1}{3}$, then $3m = 1 + 2m^2$

$$\Rightarrow \quad 2m^2 - 3m + 1 = 0$$

$$\Rightarrow \quad 2m^2 - 2m - m + 1 = 0$$

$$\Rightarrow \quad 2m(m-1) - 1(m-1) = 0$$

$$\Rightarrow \quad (m-1)(2m-1) = 0$$

$$\Rightarrow \quad m - 1 = 0 \text{ or } 2m - 1 = 0$$

$$\Rightarrow \quad m = 1 \text{ or } m = \frac{1}{2}$$

As the slopes of the lines are m and $2m$, therefore the slopes of the lines are 1 and 2 or $\frac{1}{2}$ and 1.

***Case* II** When $\frac{m}{1 + 2m^2} = \frac{-1}{3}$, then

$$3m = -1 - 2m^2$$

$$\Rightarrow \quad 2m^2 + 3m + 1 = 0$$

$$\Rightarrow \quad 2m^2 + 2m + m + 1 = 0$$

$$\Rightarrow \quad 2m(m+1) + 1(m+1) = 0$$

$$\Rightarrow \quad (2m+1)(m+1) = 0$$

$$\Rightarrow \quad 2m + 1 = 0 \text{ or } m + 1 = 0$$

$$\Rightarrow \quad m = \frac{-1}{2} \text{ or } m = -1$$

As the slopes of the lines are m and $2m$, therefore the slopes of the lines are $\frac{-1}{2}$ and -1 or -1 and -2.

Condition of Parallelism of Two Lines

If two lines of slopes m_1 and m_2 are parallel, then the angle θ between them is 0°.

$$\therefore \quad \tan\theta = \tan 0° = 0 \qquad [\because \tan 0° = 0]$$

$$\Rightarrow \quad \frac{m_2 - m_1}{1 + m_1 m_2} = 0$$

$$\Rightarrow \quad m_2 - m_1 = 0$$

$$\Rightarrow \quad \boxed{m_1 = m_2}$$

EXAMPLE 8. What is the value of y so that the line through $(3, y)$ and (2, 7) is parallel to the line through (–1, 4) and (0, 6)?

Sol. Let $A(3, y)$, $B(2, 7)$, $C(-1, 4)$ and $D(0, 6)$ be the given points.

Then, m_1 = Slope of the line $AB = \frac{7-y}{2-3} = (y-7)$

and m_2 = Slope of the line $CD = \frac{6-4}{0-(-1)} = 2$

Since, AB and CD are parallel.

$$\therefore \quad m_1 = m_2$$
$$\Rightarrow \quad y - 7 = 2$$
$$\Rightarrow \quad y = 9$$

EXAMPLE 9. Using slopes, prove that the points $A(-2, -1)$, $B(4, 0)$, $C(3, 3)$ and $D(-3, 2)$ are the vertices of a parallelogram.

Sol. Given points are $A(-2, -1)$, $B(4, 0)$, $C(3, 3)$ and $D(-3, 2)$.

Now, Slope of $AB = \frac{0-(-1)}{4-(-2)} = \frac{1}{6}$

Slope of $DC = \frac{3-2}{3-(-3)} = \frac{1}{6}$

Slope of $BC = \frac{3-0}{3-4} = \frac{3}{-1} = -3$

and Slope of $AD = \frac{2-(-1)}{-3-(-2)} = \frac{3}{-1} = -3$

$\because$ Slope of AB = Slope of DC, therefore $AB \parallel DC$

Slope of BC = Slope of AD, therefore $BC \parallel AD$

Thus, $ABCD$ is a parallelogram. **Hence proved.**

Condition of Perpendicularity of Two Lines

If two lines of slopes m_1 and m_2 are perpendicular, then the angle θ between them is 90°.

$$\therefore \quad \tan\theta = \tan 90° = \frac{\sin 90°}{\cos 90°} = \frac{1}{0}$$

$$\Rightarrow \quad \frac{m_2 - m_1}{1 + m_1 m_2} = \frac{1}{0} \Rightarrow 1 + m_1 m_2 = 0$$

$$\therefore \quad m_1 m_2 = -1$$

Thus, two lines are perpendicular, if and only if their slopes m_1 and m_2 satisfy the following condition

$$\boxed{m_1 \cdot m_2 = -1} \quad \text{or} \quad \boxed{m_1 = -\frac{1}{m_2}}$$

EXAMPLE 10. Line through the points $(-2, 6)$ and $(4, 8)$ is perpendicular to the line through the $(8, 12)$ and $(x, 24)$. Find the value of x. **[NCERT]**

Sol. Slope of the line through the points $(-2, 6)$ and $(4, 8)$ is

$$m_1 = \frac{8-6}{4-(-2)} = \frac{2}{6} = \frac{1}{3}$$

Slope of the line through the points $(8, 12)$ and $(x, 24)$ is

$$m_2 = \frac{24-12}{x-8} = \frac{12}{x-8}$$

Since, two lines are perpendicular,

$$\therefore \quad m_1 m_2 = -1$$

$$\Rightarrow \quad \frac{1}{3} \times \frac{12}{x-8} = -1 \Rightarrow 4 = -(x-8) \Rightarrow x = 4$$

EXAMPLE 11. Without using Pythagoras theorem, show that $A(4, 4)$, $B(3, 5)$ and $C(-1, 1)$ are the vertices of a right angled triangle. **[NCERT]**

Sol. In ΔABC, we have m_1 = Slope of $AB = \frac{5-4}{3-4} = -1$

and m_2 = Slope of $BC = \frac{1-5}{(-1)-3} = \frac{4}{4} = 1$

Clearly, $m_1 m_2 = -1$

This shows that AB is perpendicular to BC.

i.e. $\angle ABC = \frac{\pi}{2}$

Hence, the given points are the vertices of a right angled triangle. **Hence proved.**

EXAMPLE 12. Prove that $A(4, 3)$, $B(6, 4)$, $C(5, 6)$ and $D(3, 5)$ are angular points of a square.

Sol. Clearly, $AB = \sqrt{(6-4)^2 + (4-3)^2} = \sqrt{5}$

$BC = \sqrt{(6-4)^2 + (5-6)^2} = \sqrt{5}$

$CD = \sqrt{(5-6)^2 + (3-5)^2} = \sqrt{5}$

and $DA = \sqrt{(5-3)^2 + (3-4)^2} = \sqrt{5}$

$\therefore \quad AB = BC = CD = DA$

Now, m_1 = Slope of $AB = \frac{4-3}{6-4} = \frac{1}{2}$

m_2 = Slope of $BC = \frac{6-4}{5-6} = -2$

and m_3 = Slope of $CD = \frac{5-6}{3-5} = \frac{1}{2}$

Clearly, $m_1 m_2 = \left(\frac{1}{2}\right)(-2) = -1$ and $m_1 = m_3$

Therefore, AB is perpendicular to BC and it is parallel to CD.

Thus, $AB = BC = CA = AD$

$AB \perp BC$ and AB is parallel to CD.

Hence, $ABCD$ is a square.

Collinearity of Three Points

If A, B and C are three points in a plane, then these points will lie on a line i.e. these points are collinear, iff

Slope of AB = Slope of AC

EXAMPLE 13. Using slope, show that the points $A(6, -1)$, $B(5, 0)$ and $C(2, 3)$ are collinear.

Sol. Given points are

$A(6, -1)$, $B(5, 0)$ and $C(2, 3)$

Now, slope of $AB = \frac{0-(-1)}{5-6} = \frac{1}{-1} = -1$

and slope of $AC = \frac{3-(-1)}{2-6}$

$= \frac{4}{-4} = -1$

$\therefore$ Slope of AB = Slope of AC

Hence, the points A, B and C are collinear.

Topic Practice 1

1 Find the slope of a line whose inclination is 90°.

2 Find the slope of a line whose inclination is

(i) 30° (ii) 135°

3 Find the inclination of a line whose slope is

(i) $\frac{1}{\sqrt{3}}$ (ii) $-\sqrt{3}$

4 Find the slope of a line which passes through the points

(i) $(0, -3)$ and $(2, 1)$ (ii) $(-2, 3)$ and $(4, -6)$

(iii) $(at_1^2, 2at_1)$ and $(at_2^2, 2at_2)$

5 If the slope of the line joining the points $A(x, 2)$ and $B(6, -8)$ is $-5/4$, find the value of x.

6 Find the slope of a line perpendicular to the line, which passes through $(0, 8)$ and $(-5, 2)$.

7 What is the value of y, so that the line through $(3, y)$ and $(2, 7)$ is parallel to the line through $(-1, 4)$ and $(0, 6)$?

8 State whether the two lines in each of the following are parallel, perpendicular or neither.

(i) Through $(5, 6)$ and $(2, 3)$; through $(9, -2)$ and $(6, -5)$.

(ii) Through $(6, 3)$ and $(1, 1)$; through $(-2, 5)$ and $(2, -5)$

(iii) Through $(3, 15)$ and $(16, 6)$; through $(-5, 3)$ and $(8, 2)$.

9 Find the angle between the lines whose slopes are

(i) $\sqrt{3}$ and $\frac{1}{\sqrt{3}}$ (ii) $(2-\sqrt{3})$ and $(2+\sqrt{3})$

10 Without using Pythagoras theorem, show that $A(12, 8)$, $B(-2, 6)$ and $C(6, 0)$ are the vertices of right angled triangle.

11 A line passes through the points $A(4, -6)$ and $B(-2, -5)$. Show that the line AB makes an obtuse angle with the X-axis.

12 Determine $\angle B$ of the triangle with vertices $A(-2, 1)$, $B(2, 3)$ and $C(-2, -4)$.

13 A quadrilateral has the vertices at the points $A(-4, 2)$, $B(2, 6)$, $C(8, 5)$ and $D(9, -7)$. Show that the mid-points of the sides of this quadrilateral are the vertices of a parallelogram.

14 If θ is the angle between the diagonals of a parallelogram $ABCD$ whose vertices are $A(0, 2)$, $B(2, -1)$, $C(4, 0)$ and $D(2, 3)$. Show that $\tan\theta = 2$.

15 Using slopes, show that the points $A(-4, -1)$, $B(-2, -4)$, $C(4, 0)$ and $D(2, 3)$ taken in order, are the vertices of a rectangle.

16 Two lines passing through the point $(2, 3)$ make an angle of 45°. If the slope of one of the lines is 2, then find the slope of the other line.

17 Find the slope of a line, which makes an angle of 30° with the positive direction of Y-axis measured anti-clockwise. **[NCERT]**

Hints & Solutions

1. **Hint** The slope of a line whose inclination is 90°, is not defined.

2. **Hint** Use the formula, $m = \tan\theta$ **Ans.** (i) $\frac{1}{\sqrt{3}}$ (ii) -1

3. (i) **Hint** $\tan\theta = \frac{1}{\sqrt{3}} = \tan 30°$ **Ans.** 30°

(ii) Solve as part (i) **Ans.** 120°

4. Solve as Example 2. **Ans.** (i) 2 (ii) $-\frac{3}{2}$ (iii) $\frac{2}{t_2+t_1}$

5. **Hint** Use formula, $m = \frac{y_2-y_1}{x_2-x_1}$ **Ans.** $x = -2$

6. **Hint** $m_1m_2 = -1$, where $m_1 = \frac{8-2}{0+5}$

Ans. $m_2 = \frac{-5}{6}$

7. **Hint** $m_1 = \dfrac{7-y}{2-3}$, $m_2 = \dfrac{6-4}{0-(-1)}$

Also, $m_1 = m_2 \Rightarrow \dfrac{7-y}{-1} = 2 \Rightarrow y = 9$

8. (i) parallel (ii) perpendicular (iii) neither

9. **Hint** Use formula $\tan\theta = \dfrac{m_1 - m_2}{1 + m_1 m_2}$

Ans. (i) 30° or 150° (ii) 60° or 120°

10. **Hint** Let $A(12, 8)$, $B(-2, 6)$ and $C(6, 0)$ are vertices of ΔABC.

Slope of $AB = \dfrac{6-8}{-2-12} = \dfrac{-2}{-14} = \dfrac{1}{7}$

Slope of $BC = \dfrac{0-6}{6+2} = \dfrac{-6}{8} = \dfrac{-3}{4}$

Slope of $AC = \dfrac{0-8}{6-12} = \dfrac{-8}{-6} = \dfrac{4}{3}$

Now, as slope of $BC \times$ slope of $AC = \dfrac{-3}{4} \times \dfrac{4}{3} = -1$,

therefore $\angle C = \dfrac{\pi}{2}$.

11. **Hint** Slope of AB is negative.

12. **Hint** Slope of line, $AB = \dfrac{3-1}{2+2} = \dfrac{2}{4} = \dfrac{1}{2} = m_1$ (say)

Slope of line, $BC = \dfrac{-4-3}{-2-2} = \dfrac{7}{4} = m_2$

$\therefore \quad \tan B = \left|\dfrac{m_2 - m_1}{1 + m_1 m_2}\right| = \left|\dfrac{\frac{7}{4} - \frac{1}{2}}{1 + \frac{1}{2}\cdot\frac{7}{4}}\right|$

Ans. $\angle B = \tan^{-1}\left(\dfrac{2}{3}\right)$

13. **Hint**

Coordinates of E = Mid-point of $A(-4, 2)$ and $B(2, 6)$

$= \left(\dfrac{-4+2}{2}, \dfrac{2+6}{2}\right) = (-1, 4)$

Coordinates of F = Mid-point of $B(2, 6)$ and $C(8, 5)$

$= \left(\dfrac{2+8}{2}, \dfrac{6+5}{2}\right) = \left(5, \dfrac{11}{2}\right)$

Coordinates of G = Mid-point of $C(8, 5)$ and $D(9, -7)$

$= \left(\dfrac{8+9}{2}, \dfrac{5-7}{2}\right) = \left(\dfrac{17}{2}, -1\right)$

Coordinates of H = Mid-point of $A(-4, 2)$ and $D(9, -7)$

$= \left(\dfrac{9-4}{2}, \dfrac{-7+2}{2}\right) = \left(\dfrac{5}{2}, \dfrac{-5}{2}\right)$

Slope of $EF = \dfrac{\frac{11}{2} - 4}{5-(-1)} = \dfrac{1}{4}$

Slope of $GH = \dfrac{-\frac{5}{2} - (-1)}{\frac{5}{2} - \frac{17}{2}} = \dfrac{1}{4}$

$\therefore$ Slope of EF = Slope of GH

$\Rightarrow \quad EF \parallel GH$

Similarly, slope of FG = slope of $EH \Rightarrow FG \parallel EH$

14. **Hint** Slope of AC, $m_1 = \dfrac{-2}{4} = -\dfrac{1}{2}$

Slope of BD, $m_2 = \dfrac{4}{0} = \tan 90°$.

Let $m_1 = \tan\alpha = -\dfrac{1}{2}$.

Then, we have $\tan\theta = \left|\dfrac{m_2 - m_1}{1 + m_1 m_2}\right| = \left|\dfrac{\tan 90° - \tan\alpha}{1 + \tan 90° \tan\alpha}\right|$

$= |\tan(90° - \alpha)|$

$= |(\cot\alpha)| = |-2| = 2$

$\Rightarrow \quad \tan\theta = 2$

15. **Hint** Slope of AB = Slope of CD

Slope of BC = Slope of DA

Also, slope of $AB \times$ slope of $BC = -1$

16. **Hint** Angle between these two lines is 45°.

$\therefore \quad 1 = \left|\dfrac{2-m}{1+2m}\right| \Rightarrow 1 = \pm\dfrac{(2-m)}{1+2m}$

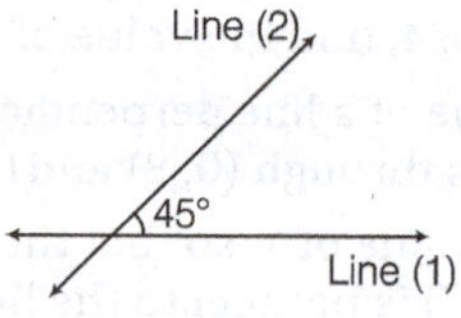

Ans. $m = \dfrac{1}{3}$ or -3

17. **Hint** Given, $\angle YPQ = 30°$

To find $\angle PAX = ?$

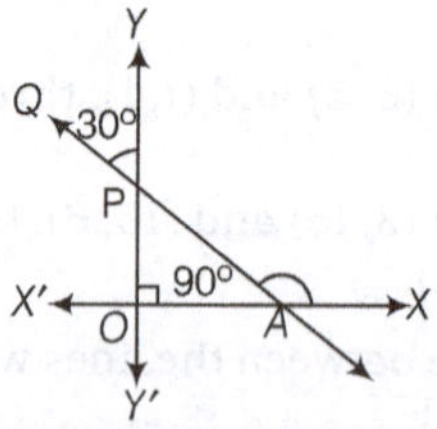

Here, $\angle YPQ = \angle OPA$ [vertically opposite angles]

$\because \quad \angle OPA + \angle POA + \angle PAO = 180°$

[$\because$ sum of all angles of a triangle is 180°]

$\therefore \quad 30° + 90° + \angle PAO = 180°$

$\Rightarrow \quad \angle PAO = 180° - 120° = 60°$

$\Rightarrow \quad \angle PAX = 180° - 60° = 120°$

[by linear pair axiom]

$\therefore$ Slope of line $AQ = m = \tan 120°$ [$\because m = \tan\theta$]

$= \tan(180° - 60°)$

[$\because \tan(180° - \theta) = -\tan\theta$]

$= -\tan 60° = -\sqrt{3}$

Various Form of Equation of Line

The equation of a straight line is the relation between x (the abscissa) and y (the ordinate) which is satisfied by the coordinates of each and every point on the line and is not satisfied by the coordinates of any point which does not lie on the line.

The various forms of the equation of a line under different conditions are given below

Equation of Axes and Lines Parallel to Them

Equation of X-axis

Every point on X-axis having y-coordinate is zero.

$\therefore$ Equation of X-axis, $y = 0$

Equation of Line Parallel to X-axis (Or Equation of Horizontal Line)

Let L be a straight line parallel to X-axis at a distance a from it, then the ordinate of every point lying on the line is either a or $-a$.

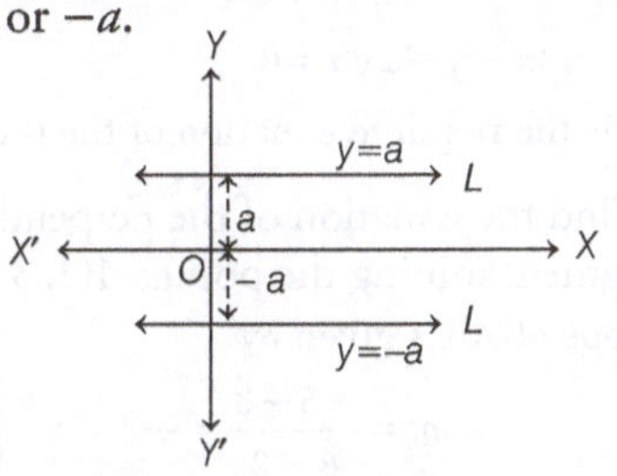

Equation of line parallel to X-axis (i.e. equation of horizontal line either above X-axis or below X-axis) is either

$$y = a \text{ or } y = -a$$

The choice of sign will depend upon the position of the line according as the line is on the positive or negative side of the Y-axis.

EXAMPLE 1. Write down the equation of a line parallel to the X-axis

(i) at a distance of 6 units above the X-axis.
(ii) at a distance of 3 units below the X-axis.

Sol. (i) The equation of a line parallel to the X-axis at a distance of 6 units above X-axis is $y = 6$.

(ii) The equation of a line parallel to the X-axis at a distance of 3 units below the X-axis is $y = -3$.

Equation of Y-axis

Every point on Y-axis having x-coordinate is zero.

$\therefore$ Equation of Y-axis, $x = 0$

Equation of Line Parallel to Y-axis (Or Equation of Vertical Line)

Let L be a straight line parallel to Y-axis at a distance b from it, then the abscissa of every point lying on the line is either b or $-b$.

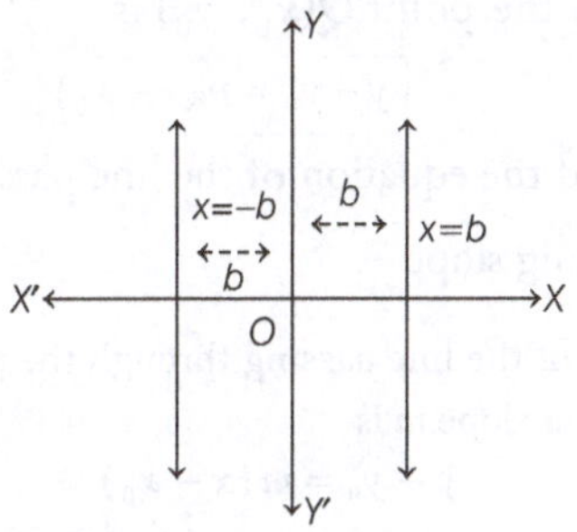

$\therefore$ Equation of line parallel to Y-axis (i.e. equation of vertical line either right of Y-axis or left of Y-axis) is either

$$x = b \text{ or } x = -b$$

Here, the choice of sign will depend upon the position of the line according as the line is on the positive or negative side of the X-axis.

EXAMPLE 2. Write down the equation of a line parallel to the Y-axis

(i) at a distance of 5 units on left hand side of the Y-axis,
(ii) at a distance of 7 units on right hand side of the Y-axis.

Sol. (i) The equation of a line parallel to the Y-axis at a distance of 5 units on its left is $x = -5$.

(ii) The equation of a line parallel to the Y-axis at a distance of 7 units on its right is $x = 7$.

EXAMPLE 3. Find the equation of the lines parallel to the axes and passing through the point $(-3, 5)$.

Sol. Clearly, the equation of a line parallel to the X-axis and passing through $(-3, 5)$ is $y = 5$.

The equation of a line parallel to the Y-axis and passing through $(-3, 5)$ is $x = -3$.

EXAMPLE 4. Find the equation of a line which is equidistant from the lines $x = -4$ and $x = 8$.

Sol. Since, the given lines are both parallel to Y-axis and the required line is equidistant from these lines.

So, it is also parallel to Y-axis and its distance from Y-axis is

$$\frac{1}{2}(-4+8) = 2 \text{ units}$$

Hence, its equation is $x = 2$.

Equation of a Line in Point-Slope Form

On the basis of number of point(s), the point slope form are of two types

Equation of a Line Passing Through a Point

The equation of the straight line having slope m and passes through the point $Q(x_0, y_0)$ is

$$\boxed{y - y_0 = m(x - x_0)}$$

EXAMPLE 5. Find the equation of the line passing through $(-4, 3)$ and having slope $\frac{1}{2}$.

Sol. Equation of the line passing through the point (x_0, y_0) and having slope m is

$$y - y_0 = m(x - x_0) \quad \text{...(i)}$$

Given, m = slope of the line $= \frac{1}{2}$ and $x_0 = -4$, $y_0 = 3$

From Eq. (i), required equation of the line is

$$y - 3 = \frac{1}{2}(x + 4)$$

$$\Rightarrow \quad 2y - 6 = x + 4 \Rightarrow x - 2y + 10 = 0$$

EXAMPLE 6. Find the equation of line intersecting the Y-axis at a distance of 2 units above the origin and making an angle of 30° with the positive direction of the X-axis. **[NCERT]**

Sol. Given, the line intersect the Y-axis at distance of 2 units above the origin.

It shows that the line passes through (0, 2).

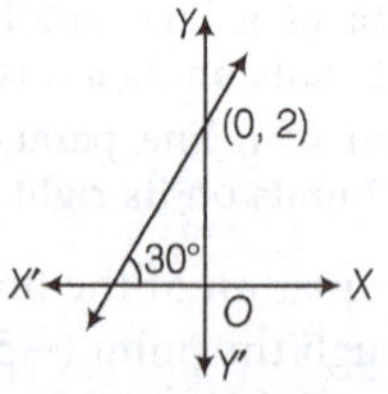

$\because$ It makes an angle 30° with the positive direction of X-axis. So, the slope of the line,

$$m = \tan 30° = \frac{1}{\sqrt{3}} \quad [\because m = \tan\theta]$$

Thus, the equation of straight line is

$$y - 2 = \frac{1}{\sqrt{3}}(x - 0) \quad [\because y - y_0 = m(x - x_0)]$$

$$\Rightarrow \quad \frac{x}{\sqrt{3}} - y + 2 = 0 \Rightarrow x - \sqrt{3}\,y + 2\sqrt{3} = 0$$

EXAMPLE 7. If the line joining two points $A(2, 0)$ and $B(3, 1)$ is rotated about A in anti-clockwise direction through an angle of 15°. Find the equation of the line in new position. **[NCERT Exemplar]**

Sol. The slope of line AB is given by

$$m = \frac{1-0}{3-2} \quad \left[\because m = \left(\frac{y_2 - y_1}{x_2 - x_1}\right)\right]$$

$$\Rightarrow \quad \tan\theta = 1 \quad [\because m = \tan\theta]$$

$$\Rightarrow \quad \tan\theta = \tan 45° \quad [\because 1 = \tan 45°]$$

$$\Rightarrow \quad \theta = 45°$$

After rotation of the line AB about A is anticlockwise direction through an angle of 15°, the slope of the line AC in new position is given by

$$m_1 = \tan(45° + 15°) = \tan 60° = \sqrt{3} \quad [\because \tan 60° = \sqrt{3}]$$

$\therefore$ The equation of the new line AC is

$$(y - y_1) = m_1(x - x_1)$$

$$\Rightarrow \quad (y - 0) = \sqrt{3}(x - 2)$$

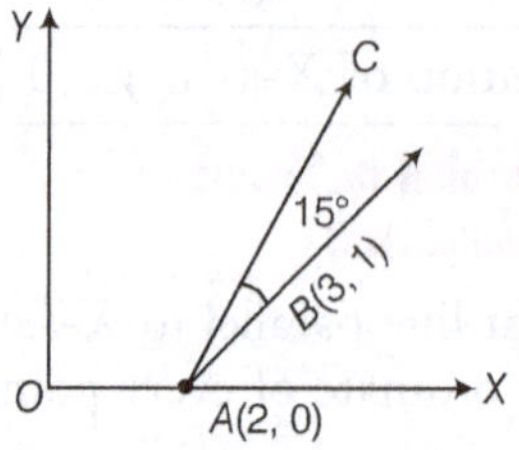

$$\Rightarrow \quad \sqrt{3}x - y - 2\sqrt{3} = 0$$

which is the required equation of the line.

EXAMPLE 8. Find the equation of the perpendicular bisector of the line segment joining the points $A(2, 3)$ and $B(6, -5)$.

Sol. The slope of AB is given by

$$m = \frac{-5-3}{6-2} = -2 \quad \left[\because m = \frac{y_2 - y_1}{x_2 - x_1}\right]$$

$\therefore$ Slope of a line perpendicular to $AB = -\frac{1}{m} = \frac{1}{2}$

Let P be the mid-point of AB.

Then, the coordinates of P are $\left(\frac{2+6}{2}, \frac{3-5}{2}\right)$

i.e. $(4, -1)$.

Thus, the required line passes through $P(4, -1)$ and has slope $\frac{1}{2}$. So, its equation is

$$y + 1 = \frac{1}{2}(x - 4) \quad [\because y - y_0 = m(x - x_0)]$$

$$\Rightarrow \quad x - 2y - 6 = 0$$

EXAMPLE 9. Two lines passing through the point (2, 3) intersect each other at an angle of 60°. If slope of one line is 2, then find the equation of the other line. **[NCERT]**

Sol. Let the slope of the other line be m.

It is given that the angle between the two lines is 60°.

$$\therefore \quad \tan 60° = \left|\frac{m-2}{1+2m}\right| \quad \left[\because \tan\theta = \left|\frac{m_2 - m_1}{1 + m_1 m_2}\right|\right]$$

$$\Rightarrow \quad \sqrt{3} = \left|\frac{m-2}{1+2m}\right|$$

$$\Rightarrow \quad \frac{m-2}{1+2m} = \pm\sqrt{3}$$

$$\Rightarrow \quad \frac{m-2}{1+2m} = \sqrt{3} \text{ or } \frac{m-2}{1+2m} = -\sqrt{3}$$

$$\Rightarrow \quad m-2 = \sqrt{3}+2\sqrt{3}m \text{ or } m-2 = -\sqrt{3}-2\sqrt{3}\,m$$

$$\Rightarrow \quad m(2\sqrt{3}-1) = -(2+\sqrt{3}) \text{ or } m(2\sqrt{3}+1) = 2-\sqrt{3}$$

$$\Rightarrow \quad m = -\left(\frac{2+\sqrt{3}}{2\sqrt{3}-1}\right) \text{ or } m = \left(\frac{2-\sqrt{3}}{2\sqrt{3}+1}\right)$$

On substituting $x_1 = 2, y_1 = 3$ and the values of m in $y - y_1 = m(x - x_1)$, we obtain that the equation of the required line is

$$y-3 = -\frac{2+\sqrt{3}}{2\sqrt{3}-1}(x-2) \text{ or } y-3 = \frac{2-\sqrt{3}}{2\sqrt{3}+1}(x-2)$$

EXAMPLE 10. A line perpendicular to the line segment joining the points (1, 0) and (2, 3) divides it in the ratio $1:n$. Find the equation of the line. **[NCERT]**

Sol. Let the given points be $A(1, 0)$ and $B(2, 3)$.

Let the line PQ divide AB in the ratio $1:n$ at R internally.

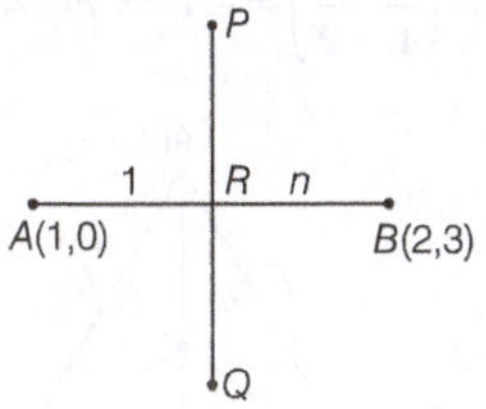

Then, coordinates of R

$$= \left(\frac{1\times x_2 + n\times x_1}{1+n}, \frac{1\times y_2 + n\times y_1}{1+n}\right)$$

[by internal division formula]

$$= \left(\frac{1\times 2 + n\times 1}{1+n}, \frac{1\times 3 + n\times 0}{1+n}\right)$$

$[\because x_1 = 1, y_1 = 0, x_2 = 2, y_2 = 3]$

$$= \left(\frac{n+2}{n+1}, \frac{3}{1+n}\right)$$

Let slope of line PQ be m.

$\because \quad PQ \perp AB$

$\therefore$ Slope of line $PQ \times$ Slope of line $AB = -1$

$[\because m_1 m_2 = -1]$

$$\Rightarrow \quad m \times \frac{y_2 - y_1}{x_2 - x_1} = -1 \Rightarrow \mu \times \frac{3-0}{2-1} = -1$$

$[\because x_1 = 1, y_1 = 0, x_2 = 2, y_2 = 3]$

$$\Rightarrow \quad m \times 3 = -1$$

$$\Rightarrow \quad m = -\frac{1}{3}$$

Now, equation of line PQ by using $y - y_0 = m(x - x_0)$ is

$$y - \frac{3}{1+n} = \frac{-1}{3}\left(x - \frac{n+2}{n+1}\right)$$

$$\left[\because R\left(\frac{n+2}{n+1}, \frac{3}{1+n}\right) = (x_0, y_0)\right]$$

$$\Rightarrow \quad \frac{3(n+1)\,y - 9}{1+n} = \frac{-x(n+1)+(n+2)}{n+1}$$

$$\Rightarrow \quad 3(n+1)\,y - 9 = -x(n+1)+(n+2)$$

$$\Rightarrow \quad x(n+1)+3(n+1)\,y = n+2+9$$

$$\Rightarrow \quad x(n+1)+3(n+1)\,y = n+11$$

which is the required equation of line.

EXAMPLE 11. If the slope of a line passing through the point A (3, 2) is $\frac{3}{4}$, then find the points on the line which are 5 units away from the point A. **[NCERT Exemplar]**

Sol. Equation of the line passing through (3, 2) having slope $\frac{3}{4}$ is given by

$$y - 2 = \frac{3}{4}(x-3) \quad [\because y - y_0 = m(x - x_0)]$$

$$\Rightarrow \quad 4y - 3x + 1 = 0 \qquad \text{...(i)}$$

Let (h, k) be the required point on the line such that distance between (h, k) and (3, 2) is 5

$$\Rightarrow \quad (h-3)^2 + (k-2)^2 = 25 \qquad \text{...(ii)}$$

[by distance formula]

Since, point (h, k) lies on the line (i)

$$4k - 3h + 1 = 0 \qquad \text{...(iii)}$$

$$\Rightarrow \quad k = \frac{3h-1}{4} \qquad \text{...(iv)}$$

On putting the value of k in Eq. (ii) and simplifying, we get

$$25h^2 - 150h - 175 = 0 \Rightarrow h^2 - 6h - 7 = 0$$

$$\Rightarrow \quad (h+1)(h-7) = 0 \Rightarrow h = -1 \text{ or } h = 7$$

On putting these values of h in Eq. (iv), we get

$$k = -1 \text{ or } k = 5$$

Therefore, the coordinates of the required points are either $(-1, -1)$ or $(7, 5)$.

EXAMPLE 12. Find the equation of line through the point (0, 2) making an angle $\frac{2\pi}{3}$ with the positive X-axis. Also, find the equation of the line parallel to it and crossing the Y-axis at a distance of 2 units below the origin. **[NCERT]**

Sol. $\because \; m = \tan\theta = \tan\frac{2\pi}{3}$

$$= \tan\left(\pi - \frac{\pi}{3}\right) = -\tan\frac{\pi}{3} \quad [\because \tan(\pi - \theta) = -\tan\theta]$$

$$\Rightarrow m = -\sqrt{3}$$

Now, the equation of line passing through the point $A(0, 2)$ and having slope $-\sqrt{3}$ is

$$y - 2 = -\sqrt{3}(x - 0) \quad [\because y - y_1 = m(x - x_1)]$$

$$\Rightarrow \quad y - 2 = -\sqrt{3}x \Rightarrow \sqrt{3}x + y - 2 = 0$$

Since, the line BD, parallel to AC, intersect below Y-axis. It means that the y-coordinate of intersection point is negative and x-coordinate is 0, Thus, intersection point is $(0, -2)$.

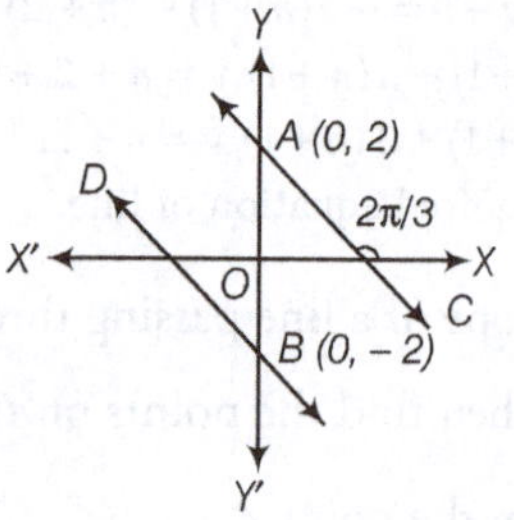

Hence, equation of line through the point $B(0, -2)$ and having slope $-\sqrt{3}$ is

$$y + 2 = -\sqrt{3}(x - 0) \quad [\because y - y_1 = m(x - x_1)]$$

$$\Rightarrow \quad \sqrt{3}x + y + 2 = 0$$

EXAMPLE 13. The mid-points of the sides of a triangle are $(2, 1), (-5, 7)$ and $(-5, -5)$. Find the equations of the sides of the triangle.

Sol. Let $D(2, 1)$, $E(-5, 7)$ and $F(-5, -5)$ be the mid-points of sides BC, CA and AB, respectively of ΔABC.

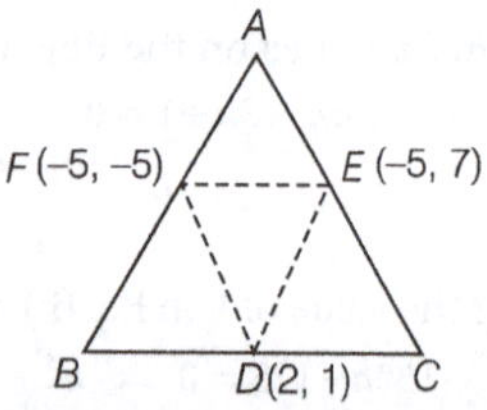

We know that the line joining the mid-points of two sides of a triangle is parallel to the third side.

$\therefore$ $DE \parallel AB$, $EF \parallel BC$ and $DF \parallel AC$

$\therefore$ Slope of AB = Slope of DE,

Slope of BC = Slope of EF and slope of AC = slope of DF

Let m_1, m_2 and m_3 be the slopes of AB, BC and CA, respectively.

Then, $m_1 = \text{Slope of } AB = \text{Slope of } DE = \dfrac{7-1}{-5-2} = \dfrac{-6}{7}$

$m_2 = \text{Slope of } BC = \text{Slope of } EF = \dfrac{7+5}{-5+5}$ (undefined)

$m_3 = \text{Slope of } CA = \text{Slope of } DF = \dfrac{1+5}{2+5} = \dfrac{6}{7}$

Since, side AB passes through $F(-5, -5)$ and has slope $m_1 = \dfrac{-6}{7}$.

So, its equation is $y + 5 = \dfrac{-6}{7}(x + 5)$

[using point slope form]

$$\Rightarrow \quad 6x + 7y + 65 = 0$$

Since, slope of side BC not defined, therefore it is parallel to Y-axis.

Also, as it is passes through $D(2, 1)$.

Therefore, its equation is $x = 2$,

Hence, equation of BC is $x = 2$.

Since, side CA passes through $E(-5, 7)$ and has slope $m_3 = \dfrac{6}{7}$.

So, its equation is $y - 7 = \dfrac{6}{7}(x + 5)$

$$\Rightarrow \quad 6x - 7y + 79 = 0$$

EXAMPLE 14. Find the equations of the altitudes of the triangle whose vertices are $A(7, -1)$, $B(-2, 8)$ and $C(1, 2)$.

Sol. Let AD, BE and CF be three altitudes of ΔABC. Let m_1, m_2 and m_3 be the slopes of AD, BE and CF, respectively.

$\because$ $AD \perp BC$

$\therefore$ Slope of AD × Slope of $BC = -1$

$$\Rightarrow \quad m_1 \times \left(\frac{2-8}{1+2}\right) = -1 \Rightarrow m_1 = \frac{1}{2}$$

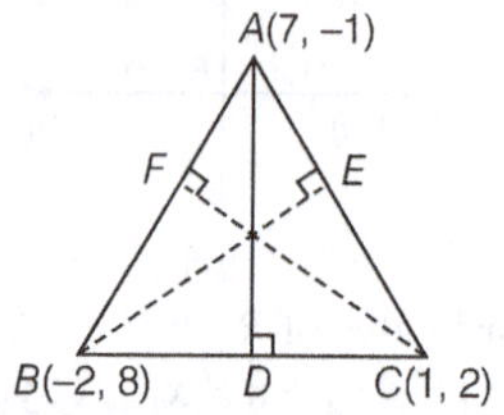

$\because$ $BE \perp AC$

$\therefore$ Slope of BE × Slope of $AC = -1$

$$\Rightarrow \quad m_2 \times \left(\frac{-1-2}{7-1}\right) = -1$$

$$\Rightarrow \quad m_2 = 2 \text{ and } CF \perp AB$$

$\therefore$ Slope of CF × Slope of $AB = -1$

$$\Rightarrow \quad m_3 \times \left(\frac{-1-8}{7+2}\right) = -1 \Rightarrow m_3 = 1$$

Since, AD passes through $A(7, -1)$ and has slope $m_1 = \dfrac{1}{2}$.

So, its equation is $y + 1 = \dfrac{1}{2}(x - 7)$

[using point slope form]

$$\Rightarrow \quad x - 2y - 9 = 0$$

Similarly, equation of BE is

$$y - 8 = 2(x + 2) \Rightarrow 2x - y + 12 = 0$$

and equation of CF is

$$y - 2 = 1(x - 1) \Rightarrow x - y + 1 = 0$$

Equation of Line Passing Through Two Points Form

The equation of a line passing through the points (x_1, y_1) and $(x_2, y_2,)$ is given by

$$y - y_1 = \frac{y_2 - y_1}{x_2 - x_1}(x - x_1)$$

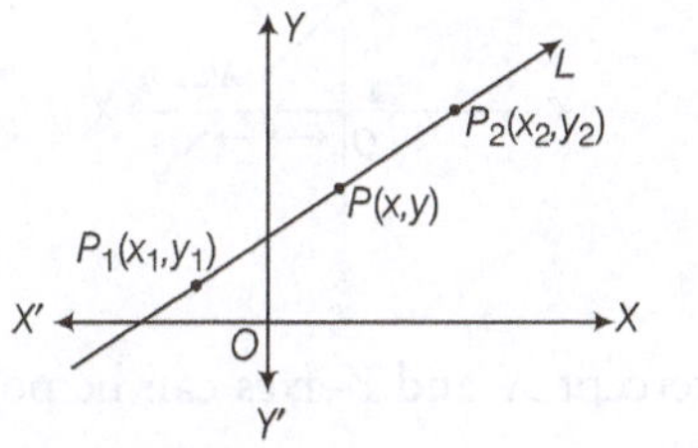

In the given point, if one point is (0, 0), then the equation of line is

$$y - y_1 = \frac{0 - y_1}{0 - x_1}(x - x_1) \text{ or } y - y_1 = \frac{y_1}{x_1}(x - x_1)$$

EXAMPLE 15. Find the equation of line passing through the points (−1, 1) and (2, − 4). **[NCERT]**

Sol. Let the given points are $A(x_1, y_1) \equiv A(-1, 1)$ and $B(x_2, y_2) \equiv B(2, -4)$, then equation of line AB is

$$y - 1 = \frac{-4 - 1}{2 + 1}(x + 1)$$

$$\left[\because y - y_1 = \frac{y_2 - y_1}{x_2 - x_1}(x - x_1)\right]$$

$$\Rightarrow \quad y - 1 = \frac{-5}{3}(x + 1)$$

$$\Rightarrow \quad 3y - 3 = -5x - 5 \Rightarrow 5x + 3y + 2 = 0$$

EXAMPLE 16. The length L (in centimetres) of a copper rod is a linear function of its celsius temperature C. In an experiment, if $L = 124.942$ when $C = 20$ and $L = 125.134$ when $C = 110$, express L in terms of C.

Sol. Given, $L = 124.942$ when $C = 20$ and $L = 125.134$ when $C = 110$

In coordinate form, (20, 124.942) and (110, 125.134) are two points. Now, the equation is given by

$$L - L_1 = \frac{L_2 - L_1}{C_2 - C_1}(C - C_1)$$

$$\left[\because y - y_1 = \frac{y_2 - y_1}{x_2 - x_1}(x - x_1)\right]$$

$$\Rightarrow \quad L - 124.942 = \frac{125.134 - 124.942}{110 - 20}(C - 20)$$

$$\Rightarrow \quad L - 124.942 = \frac{0.192}{90}(C - 20)$$

$$\Rightarrow \quad L = \frac{0.192}{90}(C - 20) + 124.942$$

EXAMPLE 17. In what ratio is the line joining the points (2, 3) and (4, 1) divides the segment joining the points (1, 2) and (4, 3)?

Sol. The equation of the line joining the points (2, 3) and (4, 1) is

$$y - 3 = \frac{1 - 3}{4 - 2}(x - 2)$$

$$\Rightarrow \quad y - 3 = -x + 2$$

$$\Rightarrow \quad x + y - 5 = 0 \quad \text{...(i)}$$

Suppose, the line joining (2, 3) and (4, 1) divides the segment joining (1, 2) and (4, 3) at point P in the ratio $\lambda : 1$.

Then, the coordinates of P are $\left(\frac{4\lambda + 1}{\lambda + 1}, \frac{3\lambda + 2}{\lambda + 1}\right)$.

Clearly, P lies on line (i).

$$\therefore \quad \frac{4\lambda + 1}{\lambda + 1} + \frac{3\lambda + 2}{\lambda + 1} - 5 = 0$$

$$\Rightarrow \quad \lambda = 1$$

Hence, the required ratio is $\lambda : 1$, i.e. $1 : 1$.

EXAMPLE 18. Find the equations of the sides of a triangle whose vertices are $A(-1, 8)$, $B(4, -2)$ and $C(-5, -3)$.

Sol. Here, we use two points form to find the equation of sides.

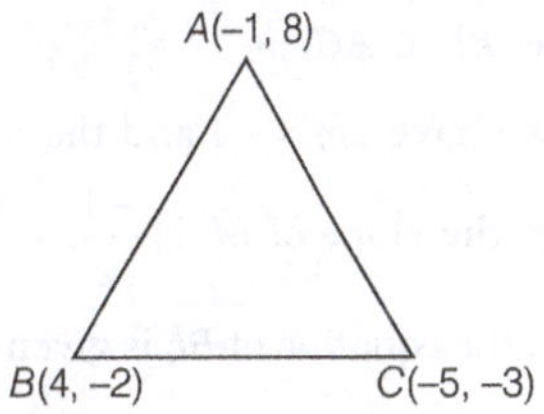

Equation of AB is $\quad y - 8 = \frac{-2 - 8}{4 + 1}(x + 1)$

$$\Rightarrow \quad 5(y - 8) + 10(x + 1) = 0$$

$$\Rightarrow \quad 10x + 5y - 30 = 0$$

$$\Rightarrow \quad 2x + y - 6 = 0 \quad \text{[dividing both sides by 5]}$$

Equation of BC is

$$y + 2 = \frac{-3 + 2}{-5 - 4}(x - 4)$$

$$\Rightarrow \quad -9(y + 2) + (x - 4) = 0$$

$$\Rightarrow \quad x - 9y - 22 = 0$$

Equation of AC is $\quad y - 8 = \frac{-3 - 8}{-5 + 1}(x + 1)$

$$\Rightarrow \quad -4(y - 8) + 11(x + 1) = 0$$

$$\Rightarrow \quad 11x - 4y + 43 = 0$$

EXAMPLE 19. If $A(2, 1)$, $B(-2, 3)$ and $C(4, 5)$ are the vertices of a ΔABC, then find the equation of

(i) the median through C.

(ii) the altitude through B.

(iii) the right bisector of side BC.

Sol. (i) Let F be the mid-point of side AB.
Then, CF is the median through C.

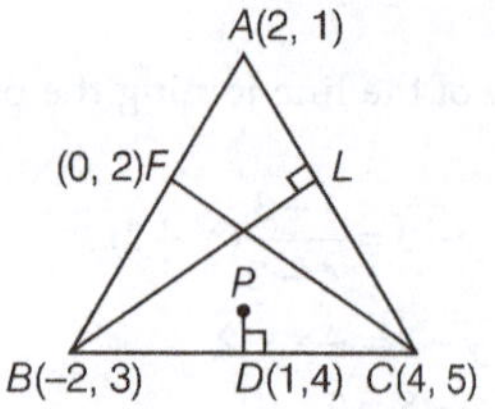

Coordinates of F are $\left(\frac{2+(-2)}{2}, \frac{1+3}{2}\right)$ i.e. $F(0, 2)$.

So, the equation of median CF is given by

$$y-5=\frac{2-5}{0-4}(x-4)$$ [using two points form]

$$\Rightarrow \quad y-5=\frac{3}{4}(x-4)$$

$$\Rightarrow \quad 4(y-5)=3(x-4) \Rightarrow 3x-4y+8=0$$

Hence, the equation of median CF is $3x-4y+8=0$.

(ii) Draw $BL \perp AC$.
Then, BL is the altitude through B.

Slope of $AC=\frac{5-1}{4-2}=2$

Let the slope BL be m.
Since, $BL \perp AC$,

So, we have $2m=-1$ and therefore, $m=\frac{-1}{2}$.

Thus, the slope of BL is $\frac{-1}{2}$.

Now, the equation of BL is given by $y-3=\frac{-1}{2}(x+2)$

[using point slope form]

$$\Rightarrow \quad 2(y-3)=-(x+2) \Rightarrow x+2y-4=0.$$

Hence, the equation of altitude BL is $x+2y-4=0$.

(iii) Let D be the mid-point of BC.

Then, the coordinates of D are $\left(\frac{-2+4}{2}, \frac{3+5}{2}\right)$

i.e. $D(1, 4)$.
Through D, draw $DP \perp BC$.

$$\text{Slope of } BC=\frac{5-3}{4+2}=\frac{2}{6}=\frac{1}{3}$$

Let the slope of PD be m.
Since, $PD \perp BC$. So, we have

$$m \times \frac{1}{3}=-1 \Rightarrow m=-3$$

Thus, the slope of PD is -3.
Now, the equation of PD is given by

$$y-4=-3(x-1)$$ [by using point slope form]

$$\Rightarrow \quad 3x+y-7=0$$

Hence, the equation of the right bisector of BC is $3x+y-7=0$.

Intercept Cut by a Line on X and Y-axes

If any line intercept the X and Y-axes at points $A(a, 0)$ and $B(0, b)$, then $OA=a$ and $OB=b$ be the intercept cut by the X and Y-axes.

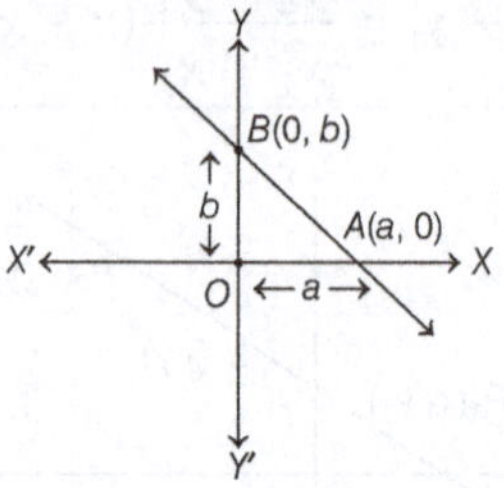

The line intercept X and Y-axes can be positive as well as negative.

Slope Intercept Form

Suppose a line L with slope m cuts the Y-axis at a distance c from the origin (distance c is called the y-intercept of the line).

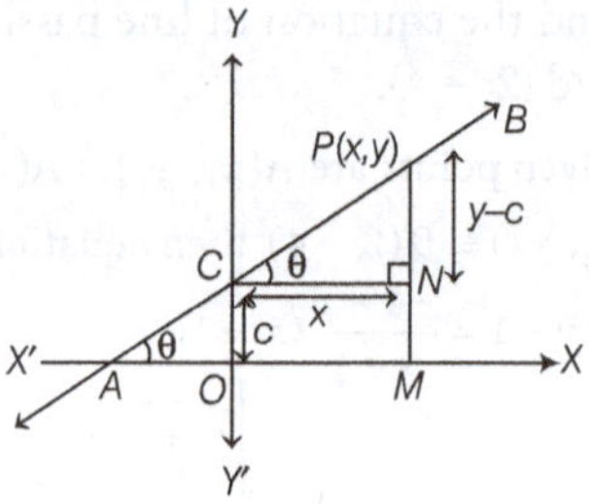

Then, equation of the line L is

$$\boxed{y=mx+c}$$

Suppose a line L with slope m cuts the X-axis at a distance d from the origin i.e. makes x-intercept, d. Then, equation of line L is

$$\boxed{y=m(x-d)}$$

EXAMPLE 20. Find the equations of the line which have slope 1/2 and cuts-off an intercept

(i) −5 on Y-axis. (ii) 4 on X-axis.

Sol. Given, $m=\text{Slope of the line}=\frac{1}{2}$

(i) Here, $c=$ Intercept of the line on Y-axis $=-5$
Hence, required equation of the line is

$$y=\frac{1}{2}x-5 \Rightarrow x-2y-10=0 \quad [\because y=mx+c]$$

(ii) Here, $d=$ Intercept of the line on X-axis $=4$.
Hence, required equation of the line is

$$y=\frac{1}{2}(x-4) \Rightarrow x-2y-4=0 \quad [\because y=m(x-d)]$$

EXAMPLE 21. Find the equation of the line intersecting the X-axis at a distance of 3 units to the left of origin with slope -2.

Sol. Given, the line intersecting the X-axis to the left of origin. It means it cuts the negative X-axis at a distance of 3 units from the origin.

$\therefore$ x-intercept of line on X-axis $(d) = -3$

Hence, required equation of the line is given by

$$y = -2(x+3) \qquad [\because y = m(x-d)]$$

$$\Rightarrow \quad y = -2x - 6$$

$$\Rightarrow \quad 2x + y + 6 = 0$$

EXAMPLE 22. Find the equation of a straight line which cuts off an intercept of length 3 on Y-axis and is parallel to the line joining the points $(3, -2)$ and $(1, 4)$.

Sol. Let m be the slope of the required line.

Since, the required line is parallel to the line joining the points $A(3, -2)$ and $B(1, 4)$.

$\therefore$ Slope of the line $AB = m = \dfrac{4-(-2)}{1-3} = -3$

We have, $c = 3$

Substituting these values in

$$y = mx + c,\ y = -3x + 3 \text{ or } 3x + y - 3 = 0.$$

Equation of Line in Intercept Form

The equation of a line which cuts-off intercepts a and b on the X-axis and Y-axis respectively, is

$$\boxed{\frac{x}{a} + \frac{y}{b} = 1}$$

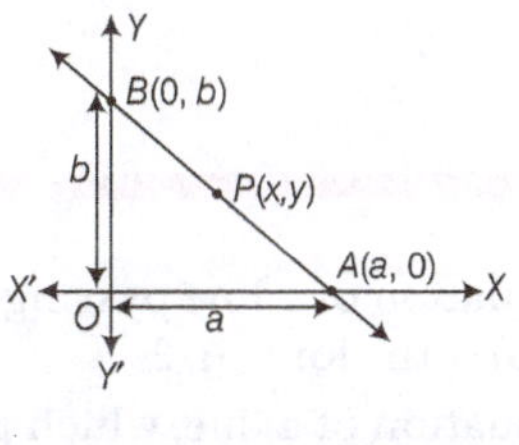

EXAMPLE 23. Find the equation of line, which intercept the X and Y-axes from -3 units and 2 units respectively.

Sol. Given, intercept cut from X-axis, $a = -3$

and intercept cut from Y-axis, $b = 2$

The equation of line in intercept form is $\dfrac{x}{a} + \dfrac{y}{b} = 1$

$$\therefore \quad \frac{x}{-3} + \frac{y}{2} = 1 \Rightarrow 2x - 3y = -6$$

$$\Rightarrow \quad 2x - 3y + 6 = 0, \text{ which is the required equation.}$$

EXAMPLE 24. Find the equation of the lines which cuts-off intercepts on the axes whose sum and product are 1 and -6, respectively.

Sol. Let a and b be the intercepts of the line on X and Y-axes, respectively.

Equation of the line will be $\dfrac{x}{a} + \dfrac{y}{b} = 1$ ...(i)

Given, sum of intercepts, $a + b = 1$ ...(ii)

and product of intercepts, $ab = -6$ ...(iii)

On putting the value of b from Eq. (ii) in Eq. (iii), we get

$$a(1-a) = -6$$

$$\Rightarrow \quad a^2 - a - 6 = 0$$

$$\Rightarrow \quad a^2 - 3a + 2a - 6 = 0$$

$$\Rightarrow \quad (a-3)(a+2) = 0 \Rightarrow a = 3 \text{ or } -2$$

From Eq. (ii), when $a = 3$, $b = -2$ and when $a = -2$, $b = 3$.

On putting the values of a and b in Eq. (i), required equation of the lines are

$$\frac{x}{3} + \frac{y}{-2} = 1 \text{ and } \frac{x}{-2} + \frac{y}{3} = 1$$

$$\Rightarrow \quad 2x - 3y - 6 = 0 \text{ and } 3x - 2y + 6 = 0$$

EXAMPLE 25. A line passes through the point $(3, -2)$. Find the locus of the middle point of the portion of the line intercepted between the axes.

Sol. Let the equation of the line be $\dfrac{x}{a} + \dfrac{y}{b} = 1$ ...(i)

It passes through $(3, -2)$.

$$\therefore \quad \frac{3}{a} - \frac{2}{b} = 1 \qquad \text{...(ii)}$$

The line (i) cuts the coordinate axes at $A(a, 0)$ and $B(0, b)$. Let $P(h, k)$ be the mid-point of the portion AB.

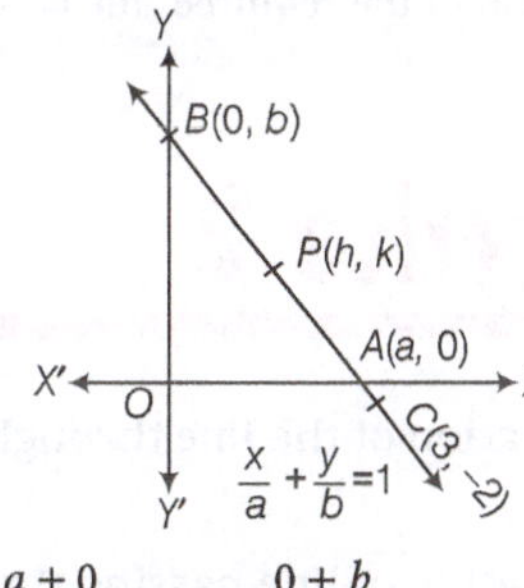

Then, $h = \dfrac{a+0}{2}$ and $k = \dfrac{0+b}{2}$

$$\Rightarrow \quad a = 2h \text{ and } b = 2k$$

On substituting the values of a and b in Eq. (ii), we get

$$\frac{3}{2h} - \frac{2}{2k} = 1$$

Hence, locus of $P(h, k)$ is $\dfrac{3}{2x} - \dfrac{1}{y} = 1$

$$\Rightarrow \quad 3y - 2x = 2xy$$

EXAMPLE 26. Find the equation of the line which passes through the point $(-4, 3)$ and the portion of the line intercepted between the axes is divided internally in the ratio $5 : 3$ by this point. **[NCERT Exemplar]**

Sol. Let the line intersects X and Y-axes respectively at $A(x, 0)$ and $B(0, y)$.

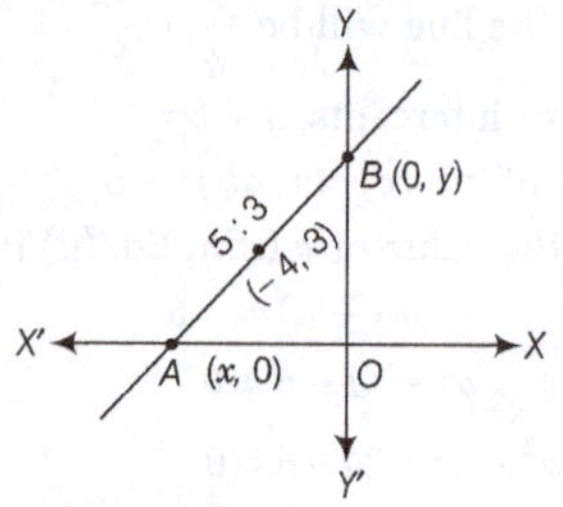

Then, $-4 = \dfrac{5 \times 0 + 3x}{5+3} \Rightarrow -4 = \dfrac{3x}{8} \Rightarrow x = \dfrac{-32}{3}$

and $3 = \dfrac{5 \times y + 3 \times 0}{5+3} \Rightarrow 3 = \dfrac{5y}{8} \Rightarrow y = \dfrac{24}{5}$

Thus, the intercept on the X and Y-axes respectively are $a = \dfrac{-32}{3}$ and $b = \dfrac{24}{5}$.

Hence, equation of required line is

$$\frac{x}{-32/3} + \frac{y}{24/5} = 1$$

$$\Rightarrow \quad \frac{-3x}{32} + \frac{5y}{24} = 1$$

$$\Rightarrow \quad -9x + 20y = 96 \Rightarrow 9x - 20y + 96 = 0$$

EXAMPLE 27. Find the equation of the line which passes through $P(1, -7)$ and meets the axes at A and B respectively so that $4AP - 3BP = 0$.

Sol. Let the equation of the required line be $\dfrac{x}{a} + \dfrac{y}{b} = 1$ ... (i)

Since, it passes through $P(1, -7)$.

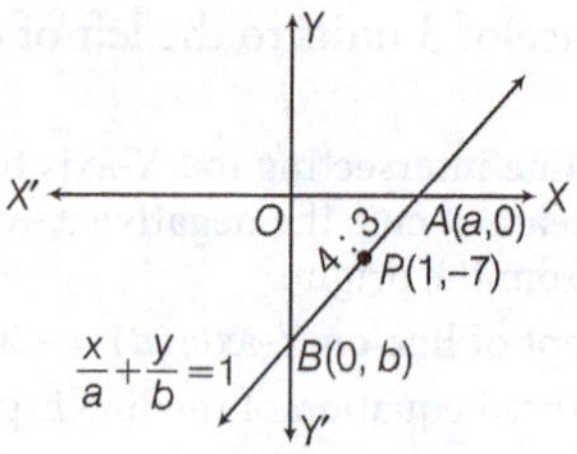

$$\therefore \quad \frac{1}{a} - \frac{7}{b} = 1 \quad \text{...(ii)}$$

It is given that the point $P(1, -7)$ divides segment AB in such a way that

$$4AP - 3BP = 0$$

$$\Rightarrow \quad \frac{AP}{BP} = \frac{3}{4}$$

$$\Rightarrow \quad AP : BP = 3 : 4$$

This means that P divides AB internally in the ratio 3 : 4. So, the coordinates of P are

$$\left(\frac{3 \times 0 + 4 \times a}{3+4}, \frac{3 \times b + 4 \times 0}{3+4} \right) = \left(\frac{4a}{7}, \frac{3b}{7} \right)$$

But, the coordinates of P are given as $(1, -7)$.

$$\therefore \quad \frac{4a}{7} = 1 \text{ and } \frac{3b}{7} = -7 \Rightarrow a = \frac{7}{4} \text{ and } b = -\frac{49}{3}$$

On substituting the values of a and b in Eq. (i), we get

$$\frac{4x}{7} - \frac{3y}{49} = 1 \text{ or } 28x - 3y = 49,$$

which is the required equation.

Topic Practice 2

1 Find the equation of the line through $(-2, 3)$ with slope -4.

2 Find the equation of line passing through $(0, 2)$ and $(3, -3)$.

3 Find the equation of a line parallel to the Y-axis at a distance of 6 units to its right.

4 Find the equation of horizontal and vertical lines passing through the point $(-5, 6)$.

5 Write the equation of a line, parallel to X-axis and 5 units below it.

6 Find the equation of a line, which is parallel to Y-axis and passes through $(-4, 3)$.

7 A line cutting off intercept -3 from the Y-axis and the tangent at angle to the X-axis is $\dfrac{3}{5}$. Find its equation.

8 Find the equation of a line passing through the point $(-4, 3)$ with slope $-1/2$.

9 Find the equation of a line, which passes through the point $(2, 3)$ and makes an angle of 30° with the positive direction of X-axis. **[NCERT Exemplar]**

10 If the line $\dfrac{x}{a} + \dfrac{y}{b} = 1$ passes through the points $(2, -3)$ and $(4, -5)$, then find (a, b).

11 Find the equation of straight line, which passes through the point $(5, 6)$ and has intercepts on the axes equal in magnitude but opposite in sign.

12 Find the equation of a line, which is equidistant from the lines $x = -2$ and $x = 6$.

13 Find the equation of line, which intersect the Y-axis at a distance of 2 units above the origin and making an angle of 60° with positive direction of X-axis. **[NCERT]**

14 A straight line moves so that the sum of the reciprocals of its intercepts made on axes is constant. Show that the line passes through a fixed point. **[NCERT Exemplar]**

15 The perpendicular from the origin to a line meets it at the point $(-2, 9)$. Find the equation of the line.

16 Find the equation of the line passing through the point (5, 2) and perpendicular to the line joining the points (2, 3) and $(3, -1)$. **[NCERT Exemplar]**

17 Find the equation of line passing through $(2, 2\sqrt{3})$ and inclined with X-axis at an angle of 75°.

18 In what ratio is the line joining the points (2, 3) and $(4, -5)$ divided by the line passing through the points (6, 8) and $(-3, -2)$.

19 The intercept cuts-off by a line from Y-axis is twice than that from X-axis and the line passes through the point (1, 2). Find the equation of the line.

20 If the coordinates of the middle point of the portion of a line intercepted between the coordinate axes is (3, 2), then find the equation of the line. **[NCERT Exemplar]**

21 A line passes through $P(1, 2)$ such that its intercept between the axes is bisected at P. Find the equation of line.

22 Find the equation of the straight line which bisects the distance between the points $A(a, b)$, $B(a', b')$ and also bisects the distance between the points $C(-a, b)$ and $D(a', -b')$.

23 Find the equation of lines passing through (1, 2) and making an angle 30° with positive Y-axis, measured clockwise.

24 $P(a, b)$ is the mid-point of a line segment between axes. Show that the equation of the line is $\frac{x}{a}+\frac{y}{b}=2$.

25 By using the concept of equation of a line, prove that the points $A(3, 0)$, $B(-2, -2)$ and $C(8, 2)$ are collinear. **[NCERT]**

26 The vertices of ΔPQR are $P(2, 1)$, $Q(-2, 3)$ and $R(4, 5)$. Find the equation of the median through the vertex Q.

27 If the intercept of a line between the coordinate axes is divided by the point $(-5, 4)$ in the ratio $1:2$, then find the equation of the line.

28 Find equation of the line passing through the point (2, 2) cutting off intercepts on the axes whose sum is 9. **[NCERT]**

29 The owner of a milk store finds that he can sell 980 L of milk each week at ₹ 14 per litre and 1220 L of milk each week at ₹ 16 per litre. Assuming a linear relationship between selling price and demand, how many litres could he sell weekly at ₹ 17 per litre.

30 Show that the perpendicular drawn from the point (4, 1) on the line segment joining (6, 5) and $(2, -1)$ divides it internally in the ratio $8:5$.

31 The hypotenuse of a right angled triangle has its ends at the points (1, 3) and $(-4, 1)$. Find the equation of the legs (perpendicular sides) of the triangle.

32 If $A(1, 4)$, $B(2, -3)$ and $C(-1, -2)$ are the vertices of a ΔABC, find the equation of

(i) the median through A.
(ii) the altitude through A.
(iii) the perpendicular bisector of BC.

33 Find the equations of the altitudes of a ΔABC, whose vertices are $A(2, -2)$, $B(1, 1)$ and $C(-1, 0)$.

34 Find the equations of the medians of a ΔABC, whose vertices are $A(2, 5)$, $B(-4, 9)$ and $C(-2, -1)$.

Hints & Solutions

1. **Hint** Use formula: $(y - y_0) = m(x - x_0)$
   Ans. $4x + y + 5 = 0$
2. **Hint** Use $(y - y_1) = \frac{y_2 - y_1}{x_2 - x_1}(x - x_1)$
   Ans. $5x + 3y - 6 = 0$
3. $x - 6 = 0$
4. Horizontal line $y - 6 = 0$ and vertical line $x + 5 = 0$
5. $y = -5$
6. $x = -4$
7. **Hint** m = Slope of line $= \tan\theta = \frac{3}{5}$. **Ans.** $5y - 3x + 15 = 0$
8. $x + 2y - 2 = 0$
9. **Hint** $m = \tan 30° = \frac{1}{\sqrt{3}}$ **Ans.** $x - \sqrt{3}y = 2 - 3\sqrt{3}$
10. **Hint** According to given condition, we have
    $$\frac{2}{a}-\frac{3}{b}=1 \text{ and } \frac{4}{a}-\frac{5}{b}=1$$
    Now, let $\frac{1}{a}=u$ and $\frac{1}{b}=v$.
    Then, we get $2u - 3v = 1$ and $4u - 5v = 1$
    Ans. $(a, b) = (-1, -1)$
11. **Hint** Let the equation of line in intercept form be
    $$\frac{x}{a}+\frac{y}{b}=1$$
    We have, $a = -b$
    Now, equation of line becomes $\frac{x}{-b}+\frac{y}{b}=1$

$\because$ It passes through (5, 6);

$\therefore \quad \frac{5}{-b} + \frac{6}{b} = 1 \Rightarrow b = 1$ **Ans.** $x - y + 1 = 0$

12. Hint Mid-point of $A(-2, 0)$ and $B(6, 0)$ is $M\left(\frac{-2+6}{2}, 0\right)$

i.e. $M(2, 0)$. **Ans.** $x = 2$

13. Hint Since, the line intersect the Y-axis above the origin. It means that the line intersects the positive Y-axis.

Here, $\quad c = 2$

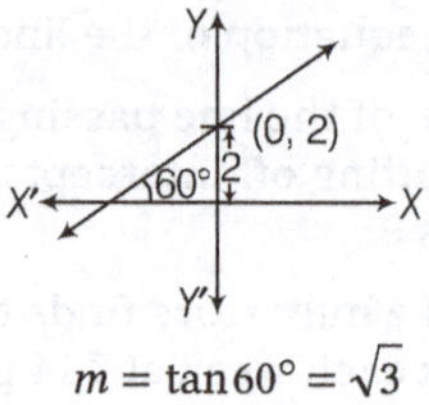

$$m = \tan 60° = \sqrt{3}$$

$$\sqrt{3}x - y + 2 = 0$$

14. Hint Given that, $\frac{1}{a} + \frac{1}{b} = \text{constant} = \frac{1}{k}$ (say)

$\because \quad \frac{1}{a} + \frac{1}{b} = \frac{1}{k} \Rightarrow \frac{k}{a} + \frac{k}{b} = 1$

So, (k, k) lies on $\frac{x}{a} + \frac{y}{b} = 1$.

15. Hint Since, $PQ \perp OR$

$\therefore$ Slope of $PQ \times$ Slope of $OR = -1$

$$m \times \left(\frac{9-0}{-2-0}\right) = -1$$

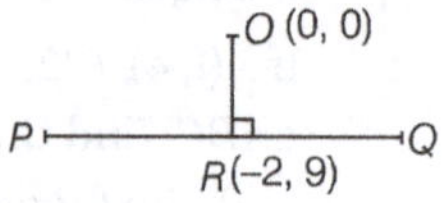

$\Rightarrow \quad m = \frac{2}{9}$

Ans. $\quad 2x - 9y + 85 = 0$

16. Hint Slope of line joining (2, 3) and (3, −1) is

$$m_1 = \frac{-1-3}{3-2} = -4$$

Slope of the line perpendicular to it is $m_2 = \frac{-1}{-4} = \frac{1}{4}$

Ans. $x - 4y + 3 = 0$

17. Hint $m = \tan 75° = \tan(45° + 30°)$;

$\therefore \quad m = 2 + \sqrt{3}$

Ans. $(2 + \sqrt{3})x - y - 4 = 0$

18. Solve as Example 17. **Ans.** 5 : 97

19. Hint Here, equation of line is of the form $\frac{x}{a} + \frac{y}{2a} = 1$. It passes through (1, 2). So, we have

$\frac{1}{a} + \frac{2}{2a} = 1 \Rightarrow a = 2$ **Ans.** $2x + y = 4$

20. Hint Let equation of line is $\frac{x}{a} + \frac{y}{b} = 1$

Since, the coordinates of the middle point are $P(3, 2)$.

$\therefore \quad 3 = \frac{0+a}{2} \Rightarrow 3 = \frac{a}{2} \Rightarrow a = 6$

Similarly, $b = 4$ **Ans.** $2x + 3y = 12$

21. Hint Let equation of line is $\frac{x}{a} + \frac{y}{b} = 1$.

Here, we have $1 = \frac{a+0}{2}$ and $2 = \frac{0+b}{2}$

Ans. $2x + y - 4 = 0$

22. Hint Let the line MN bisects the line AB at M and CD at N.

$\therefore$ Coordinates of $M = \left(\frac{a+a'}{2}, \frac{b+b'}{2}\right)$

and coordinates of $N = \left(\frac{-a+a'}{2}, \frac{b-b'}{2}\right)$

Now, equation of line MN is

$$\left(y - \frac{b+b'}{2}\right) = \left(\frac{\frac{b-b'}{2} - \frac{b+b'}{2}}{\frac{-a+a'}{2} - \frac{a+a'}{2}}\right)\left(x - \frac{a+a'}{2}\right)$$

Ans. $2b'x - 2ay + ab - a'b' = 0$

23. Hint Given that, angle with Y-axis $= 30°$

$\therefore$ Angle with X-axis $= 60°$

$\Rightarrow$ Slope of the line, $m = \tan 60° = \sqrt{3}$

Ans. $y - \sqrt{3}x - 2 + \sqrt{3} = 0$

24. Hint Let the equation of line AB be

$\frac{x}{h} + \frac{y}{k} = 1$, which intersect on X and Y-axes at $A(h, 0)$ and $B(0, k)$.

Mid-point of $AB = \left(\frac{h+0}{2}, \frac{0+k}{2}\right)$

$\because P(a, b)$ is the mid-point of AB.

$\therefore \quad \frac{h+0}{2} = a$ and $\frac{0+k}{2} = b$

25. Hint Equation of line joining the points $A(3, 0)$ and $B(-2, -2)$ is, $y - 0 = \frac{-2-0}{-2-3}(x-3)$

$\Rightarrow \quad 2x - 5y - 6 = 0 \quad$ ...(i)

On putting the point $C(8, 2)$ in Eq. (i), we get

$2 \times 8 - 5 \times 2 - 6 = 0 \Rightarrow 0 = 0$, which is true.

Thus, point C also lies on the line.

Hence, the points are collinear.

26. Hint Let QS be the median through Q. Since, the median bisects the opposite side i.e. S is the mid-point of PR.

$$S = \left(\frac{2+4}{2}, \frac{1+5}{2}\right) = (3, 3)$$

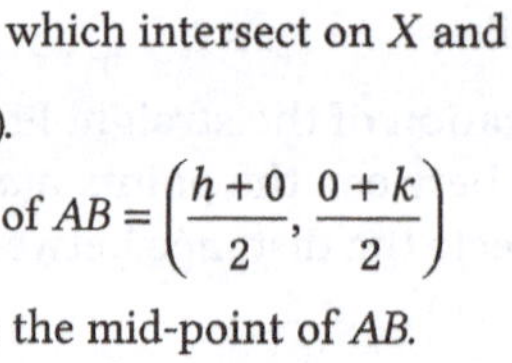

$\therefore$ Equation of line QS is $y - 3 = \frac{3-3}{3+2}(x+2)$

Ans. $y = 3$

27. **Hint** Let intercept of a line be (h, k).

The coordinates of A and B, where the line cuts the X-axis and Y-axis are $(h, 0)$ and $(0, k)$ respectively.

Then, $-5 = \dfrac{1 \times 0 + 2 \times h}{1 + 2}$

$\Rightarrow \quad h = -\dfrac{15}{2}$

and $\quad 4 = \dfrac{1 \cdot k + 0 \cdot 2}{1 + 2}$

$\Rightarrow \quad k = 12$

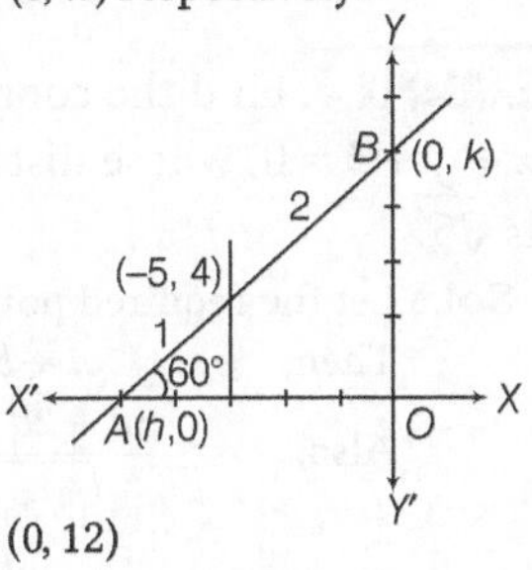

$\therefore \quad A = \left(-\dfrac{15}{2}, 0\right)$ and $B = (0, 12)$

$\Rightarrow \quad 5y = 8x + 60$ **Ans.** $8x - 5y + 60 = 0$

28. **Hint** Equation of the line in intercept form is

$$\frac{x}{a} + \frac{y}{b} = 1 \quad \text{...(i)}$$

Given, $\quad a + b = 9 \quad$ ...(ii)

and line (i) passes through the point (2, 2).

$$\therefore \quad \frac{2}{a} + \frac{2}{b} = 1 \quad \text{...(iii)}$$

$$\Rightarrow \quad \frac{2}{a} + \frac{2}{9 - a} = 1 \quad \text{[from Eq. (ii)]}$$

$$\Rightarrow \quad a^2 - 9a + 18 = 0 \Rightarrow a = 6 \text{ or } 3 \Rightarrow b = 3 \text{ or } 6$$

Hence, Eq. (i) becomes $\dfrac{x}{6} + \dfrac{y}{3} = 1$ or $\dfrac{x}{3} + \dfrac{y}{6} = 1$

Ans. $x + 2y = 6$ or $2x + y = 6$

29. **Hint** Let x denotes the rupees per litre and y denotes the quantity of milk in litre. Then, we have the following ordered pairs in the cartesian plane.

(14, 980) and (16, 1220)

Now, the equation of line joining these two points is

$$y - 980 = \frac{1220 - 980}{16 - 14}(x - 14) \Rightarrow 120x - y = 700$$

Ans. He will sell weekly 1340 L milk at the rate of ₹ 17 per litre.

30. **Hint** Let the points be A (4,1), B (6,5) and C (2, –1).

Draw $AM \perp BC$.

Slope of line $BC = \dfrac{-1-5}{2-6} = \dfrac{3}{2}$

Now, slope of line $AM \times$ slope of line $BC = -1$

Slope of line $AM \times \dfrac{3}{2} = -1 \Rightarrow$ Slope of line $AM = \dfrac{-2}{3}$

Equation of line AM is $y - 1 = \dfrac{-2}{3}(x - 4)$

$$\Rightarrow \quad 2x + 3y - 11 = 0 \quad \text{...(i)}$$

Let M divides BC in the ratio $k : 1$ internally.

Then, Coordinates of M are $\left(\dfrac{2k+6}{k+1}, \dfrac{-k+5}{k+1}\right)$.

Since, M is on line AM, therefore the coordinates of M will satisfy the Eq. (i).

$$\therefore \quad 2\left(\frac{2k+6}{k+1}\right) + 3\left(\frac{-k+5}{k+1}\right) - 11 = 0$$

Ans. 8 : 5

31. **Hint** First we plot the points $A(1, 3)$ and $B(-4, 1)$ in the XY-plane.

From the point $A(1, 3)$, we draw a line parallel to Y-axis and from the point $B(-4, 1)$, we draw a line parallel to X-axis.

The point of intersection of two lines is on C, which is right angled at C.

Clearly, the coordinate of C are (1, 1).

Now, Equation of line passing through $A(1, 3)$ and $C(1, 1)$ is

$$y - 3 = \frac{1-3}{1-1}(x - 1) \Rightarrow x = 1$$

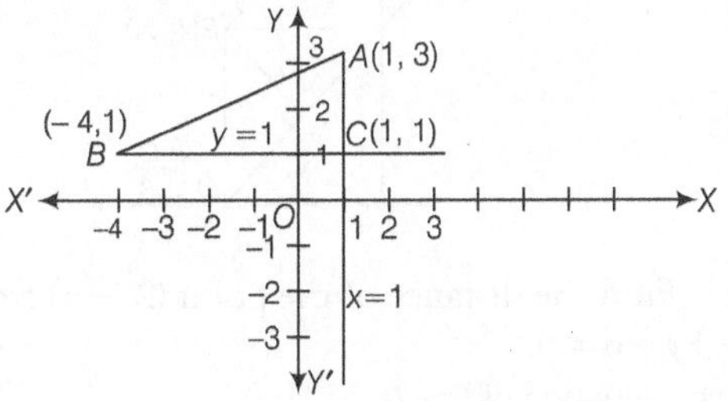

Equation of line BC is $y - 1 = \dfrac{1-1}{1+4}(x - 1) \Rightarrow y = 1$

Ans. The legs of a triangle are $x = 1$ and $y = 1$.

32. Solve as Example 19.

Ans. (i) $13x - y - 9 = 0$ (ii) $3x - y + 1 = 0$ (iii) $3x - y - 4 = 0$

33. **Hint** Slope of $BC = \dfrac{1}{2}$,

therefore slope of $AD = -2$

Equation of altitude AD,

$y + 2 = -2(x - 2)$

Similarly, we can find the others equations.

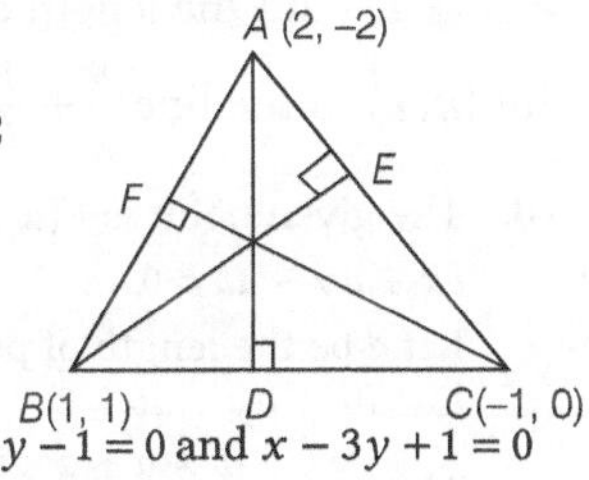

Ans. $2x + y - 2 = 0$, $3x - 2y - 1 = 0$ and $x - 3y + 1 = 0$

34. **Hint** Equation of median AD is

$$\frac{y-5}{x-2} = \frac{4-5}{-3-2}$$

Equation of median BE is

$$\frac{y-9}{x+4} = \frac{2-9}{0+4}$$

Equation of median CF is

$$\frac{y+1}{x+2} = \frac{7+1}{-1+2}$$

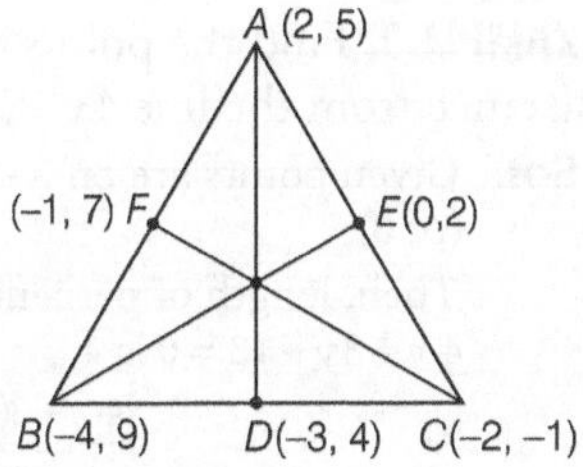

Ans. $x - 5y + 23 = 0$,

$7x + 4y - 8 = 0$

and $8x - y + 15 = 0$

Distance of a Point from a Line and Distance between Two Parallel Lines

Distance of a Point from a Line

The distance of a point from a line is the length of perpendicular drawn from the point to the line.
Let $L: Ax + By + C = 0$ be a line, whose perpendicular distance from the point $P(x_1, y_1)$ is d. Then,

$$d = \frac{|Ax_1 + By_1 + C|}{\sqrt{A^2 + B^2}}$$

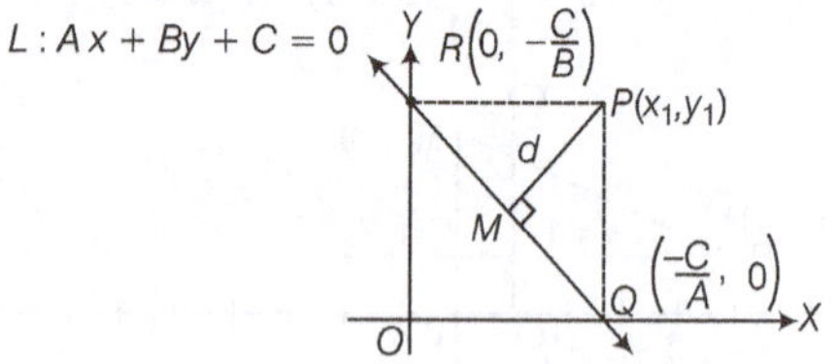

EXAMPLE 1. Find the distance of the point (2, – 3) from the line $2x - 3y + 6 = 0$.

Sol. Given equation of line is

$$2x - 3y + 6 = 0$$

∴ Required distance of the point from the line

= The perpendicular distance from point to the line

$$= \frac{|2 \times 2 - 3(-3) + 6|}{\sqrt{2^2 + (-3)^2}} = \frac{|4 + 9 + 6|}{\sqrt{4 + 9}} = \frac{19}{\sqrt{13}}$$

EXAMPLE 2. Find the length of perpendicular from the point (a, b) to the line $\frac{x}{a} + \frac{y}{b} = 1$.

Sol. The given point is $P(a, b)$ and the given line is $bx + ay - ab = 0$.
Let d be the length of perpendicular from $P(a, b)$ to the line $bx + ay - ab = 0$.

Then, $d = \frac{|b \times a + a \times b - ab|}{\sqrt{b^2 + a^2}} = \frac{|ab|}{\sqrt{a^2 + b^2}}$ units

EXAMPLE 3. Find the points on X-axis whose perpendicular distance from the line $4x + 3y = 12$ is 4.

Sol. Given points are on X-axis, so let its coordinates be $(\alpha, 0)$.
Then, length of perpendicular from $(\alpha, 0)$ to the line $4x + 3y - 12 = 0$ is 4.

$$\therefore \quad \frac{|4\alpha + 3(0) - 12|}{\sqrt{(4)^2 + (3)^2}} = 4 \Rightarrow \frac{|4\alpha - 12|}{\sqrt{16 + 9}} = 4$$

$$\Rightarrow \quad |4\alpha - 12| = 4 \times \sqrt{25} = 4 \times 5$$

$$\Rightarrow \quad \alpha - 3 = \pm 5 \Rightarrow \alpha = 8 \text{ or } -2$$

Hence, the required points are (8, 0) and (–2, 0).

EXAMPLE 4. Find the coordinates of a point on the line $x + y + 3 = 0$, whose distance from the line $x + 2y + 2 = 0$ is $\sqrt{5}$.

Sol. Let the required point be $P(a, b)$.

Then, $\quad a + b + 3 = 0 \quad$ ...(i)

Also, $\quad \frac{|a + 2b + 2|}{\sqrt{1^2 + 2^2}} = \sqrt{5} \Rightarrow |a + 2b + 2| = 5$

$\Rightarrow \quad a + 2b + 2 = 5$ or $a + 2b + 2 = -5$

$\Rightarrow \quad a + 2b = 3$ or $a + 2b = -7$

Thus, $\quad a + 2b = 3 \quad$ ...(ii)

or $\quad a + 2b = -7 \quad$ ...(iii)

On solving Eqs. (i) and (ii), we get

$a = -9$ and $b = 6$

On solving Eqs. (i) and (iii), we get

$a = 1$ and $b = -4$

Hence, the required points are (–9, 6) and (1, – 4).

EXAMPLE 5. Find the locus of a point which moves in such a way that the square of its distance from the point (3, – 2) is numerically equal to its distance from the line $5x - 12y = 13$. **[NCERT Exemplar]**

Sol. Let $P(h, k)$ be a variable point moving in such a way that the square of its distance from $A(3, -2)$ is numerically equal to its distance from the line $5x - 12y = 13$.

$$\therefore \quad (h - 3)^2 + (k + 2)^2 = \frac{|5h - 12k - 13|}{\sqrt{5^2 + (-12)^2}}$$

$$\Rightarrow \quad 13\{(h - 3)^2 + (k + 2)^2\} = \pm(5h - 12k - 13)$$

$$\Rightarrow \quad 13(h^2 + k^2) - 83h + 64k + 182 = 0$$

or $\quad 13(h^2 + k^2) - 73h + 40k + 156 = 0$

Hence, the locus of (h, k) is

$$13(x^2 + y^2) - 83x + 64y + 182 = 0$$

or $\quad 13(x^2 + y^2) - 73x + 40y + 156 = 0$

EXAMPLE 6. A variable line passes through a fixed point P. The algebraic sum of the perpendiculars drawn from the points (2, 0), (0, 2) and (1, 1) on the line is zero. Find the coordinates of the point P. **[NCERT Exemplar]**

Sol. Let slope of the line be m and the coordinates of fixed point P be (x_1, y_1).

Then, equation of line is $y - y_1 = m(x - x_1) \quad$ ...(i)

Let the given points be $A(2, 0)$, $B(0, 2)$ and $C(1, 1)$.

Now, perpendicular distance from A

$$= \frac{0 - y_1 - m(2 - x_1)}{\sqrt{1 + m^2}}$$

Perpendicular distance from $B = \frac{2 - y_1 - m(0 - x_1)}{\sqrt{1 + m^2}}$

and perpendicular distance from $C = \dfrac{1 - y_1 - m(1 - x_1)}{\sqrt{1 + m^2}}$

Now, $\dfrac{\begin{bmatrix} -y_1 - 2m + mx_1 + 2 - y_1 \\ + mx_1 + 1 - y_1 - m + mx_1 \end{bmatrix}}{\sqrt{1 + m^2}} = 0$

$\Rightarrow \quad -3y_1 - 3m + 3mx_1 + 3 = 0$

$\Rightarrow \quad -y_1 - m + mx_1 + 1 = 0$

$\Rightarrow \quad y_1 = -m + mx_1 + 1$

On substituting this value in Eq. (i), we get

$$y + m - mx_1 - 1 = mx - mx_1 \Rightarrow y - 1 = m(x - 1)$$

Thus, $\quad (x_1, y_1) = (1, 1)$

EXAMPLE 7. If p is the length of perpendicular from the origin on the line $\dfrac{x}{a} + \dfrac{y}{b} = 1$ and a^2, p^2 and b^2 are in AP, then show that $a^4 + b^4 = 0$. **[NCERT Exemplar]**

Sol. Given equation of line is $\dfrac{x}{a} + \dfrac{y}{b} = 1$ ...(i)

Perpendicular length from the origin to the line (i) is

$$p = \frac{1}{\sqrt{\frac{1}{a^2} + \frac{1}{b^2}}} = \frac{ab}{\sqrt{a^2 + b^2}} \Rightarrow p^2 = \frac{a^2b^2}{a^2 + b^2}$$

Since, a^2, p^2 and b^2 are in AP.

$\therefore \quad 2p^2 = a^2 + b^2 \Rightarrow \dfrac{2a^2b^2}{a^2 + b^2} = a^2 + b^2$

$\Rightarrow \quad 2a^2b^2 = (a^2 + b^2)^2 \Rightarrow 2a^2b^2 = a^4 + b^4 + 2a^2b^2$

$\Rightarrow \quad a^4 + b^4 = 0$ **Hence proved.**

EXAMPLE 8. Find the perpendicular distance from the origin of the line joining the points $(\cos\theta, \sin\theta)$ and $(\cos\phi, \sin\phi)$. **[NCERT]**

Sol. Let the given points be $A(\cos\theta, \sin\theta)$ and $B(\cos\phi, \sin\phi)$.

Then, equation of line AB is

$$y - \sin\theta = \frac{\sin\phi - \sin\theta}{\cos\phi - \cos\theta}(x - \cos\theta)$$

$$\left[\because y - y_1 = \frac{y_2 - y_1}{x_2 - x_1}(x - x_1)\right]$$

$$\Rightarrow y - \sin\theta = \frac{2\cos\left(\frac{\phi+\theta}{2}\right)\sin\left(\frac{\phi-\theta}{2}\right)}{-2\sin\left(\frac{\phi+\theta}{2}\right)\sin\left(\frac{\phi-\theta}{2}\right)}(x - \cos\theta)$$

$$\left[\begin{aligned} &\because \sin C - \sin D = 2\cos\left(\frac{C+D}{2}\right)\sin\left(\frac{C-D}{2}\right) \\ &\text{and } \cos C - \cos D = -2\sin\left(\frac{C+D}{2}\right)\sin\left(\frac{C-D}{2}\right) \end{aligned}\right]$$

$$\Rightarrow y\sin\left(\frac{\phi+\theta}{2}\right) - \sin\theta\sin\left(\frac{\phi+\theta}{2}\right) = -x\cos\left(\frac{\phi+\theta}{2}\right) + \cos\theta\cos\left(\frac{\theta+\phi}{2}\right)$$

$$\Rightarrow x\cos\left(\frac{\theta+\phi}{2}\right) + y\sin\left(\frac{\theta+\phi}{2}\right) - \left\{\cos\theta\cos\left(\frac{\theta+\phi}{2}\right) + \sin\theta\sin\left(\frac{\theta+\phi}{2}\right)\right\} = 0$$

$$\Rightarrow x\cos\left(\frac{\theta+\phi}{2}\right) + y\sin\left(\frac{\theta+\phi}{2}\right) - \cos\left(\theta - \frac{\theta+\phi}{2}\right) = 0$$

$$\Rightarrow x\cos\left(\frac{\theta+\phi}{2}\right) + y\sin\left(\frac{\theta+\phi}{2}\right) - \cos\left(\frac{\theta-\phi}{2}\right) = 0$$

Now, perpendicular distance from origin

$$= \frac{\left|0 + 0 - \cos\left(\frac{\theta-\phi}{2}\right)\right|}{\sqrt{\cos^2\left(\frac{\theta+\phi}{2}\right) + \sin^2\left(\frac{\theta+\phi}{2}\right)}}$$

$$\left[\because \text{distance from } (x_1, y_1) \text{ to the line } ax + by + c = 0 \text{ is } \frac{|ax_1 + by_1 + c|}{\sqrt{a^2 + b^2}}\right]$$

$$= \left|\cos\left(\frac{\theta-\phi}{2}\right)\right|$$

Distance between Two Parallel Lines

If two lines are parallel, then they have the same distance between them throughout.

Therefore, the distance between two parallel lines can be find by the following two methods

The distance between two parallel lines

$$y = mx + c_1 \quad \text{...(i)}$$

$$y = mx + c_2 \quad \text{...(ii)}$$

is given by $\boxed{d = \dfrac{|c_1 - c_2|}{\sqrt{1 + m^2}}}$

If lines are given in general form i.e. given lines are $Ax + By + C_1 = 0$ and $Ax + By + C_2 = 0$, then distance between these lines,

$$\boxed{d = \frac{|C_1 - C_2|}{\sqrt{A^2 + B^2}}}$$

EXAMPLE 9. Find the distance between following parallel lines.

(i) $3x - 4y + 9 = 0$ and $6x - 8y - 15 = 0$

(ii) $l(x + y) + h = 0$ and $l(x + y) - r = 0$ **[NCERT]**

Sol. (i) Given parallel lines are

$$3x - 4y + 9 = 0 \quad \text{...(i)}$$

and $\quad 6x - 8y - 15 = 0$

$\Rightarrow \quad 3x - 4y - \frac{15}{2} = 0 \quad$ ...(ii)

On comparing Eqs. (i) and (ii) with $Ax + By + C_1 = 0$ and $Ax + By + C_2 = 0$, we get

$$A = 3,\ B = -4,\ C_1 = 9 \text{ and } C_2 = \frac{-15}{2}$$

$$\therefore \text{ Required distance} = \frac{|C_1 - C_2|}{\sqrt{A^2 + B^2}} = \frac{\left|9 + \frac{15}{2}\right|}{\sqrt{3^2 + (-4)^2}}$$

$$= \frac{\left|\frac{18+15}{2}\right|}{\sqrt{9+16}} = \frac{33}{2\sqrt{25}}$$

$$= \frac{33}{2 \times 5} = \frac{33}{10} \text{ units}$$

Hence, the required distance is $\frac{33}{10}$ units.

(ii) Given parallel lines are

$$lx + ly + h = 0 \text{ and } lx + ly - r = 0$$

On comparing with $Ax + By + C_1 = 0$ and $Ax + By + C_2 = 0$, we get

$$A = l,\ B = l,\ C_1 = h,\ C_2 = -r$$

$$\therefore \text{Required distance} = \frac{|C_1 - C_2|}{\sqrt{A^2 + B^2}} = \left|\frac{h+r}{\sqrt{l^2 + l^2}}\right| = \left|\frac{h+r}{\sqrt{2}l}\right|$$

EXAMPLE 10. Find the equation of the line midway between the parallel lines $9x + 6y - 7 = 0$ and $3x + 2y + 6 = 0$.

Sol. Converting each of the given equations to the form $y = mx + C$, we get

$$9x + 6y - 7 = 0 \Rightarrow y = \frac{-3}{2}x + \frac{7}{6} \quad \text{...(i)}$$

and $\quad 3x + 2y + 6 = 0 \Rightarrow y = \frac{-3}{2}x - 3 \quad$ ...(ii)

Clearly, the slope of each one of the given lines is $\frac{-3}{2}$.

Let the given lines be $y = mx + C_1$ and $y = mx + C_2$.

Then, $\quad m = \frac{-3}{2},\ C_1 = \frac{7}{6}$ and $C_2 = -3$

Let L be the required line.

Then, L is parallel to each one of lines (i) and (ii) and equidistant from each one of them.

$$\therefore \quad \text{Slope of } L = \frac{-3}{2}$$

Let the equation of L be $\quad y = \frac{-3}{2}x + C \quad$ ...(iii)

Then, distance between lines (i) and (iii) must be equal to the distance between lines (ii) and (iii).

$$\therefore \quad \frac{|C_1 - C|}{\sqrt{1 + m^2}} = \frac{|C_2 - C|}{\sqrt{1 + m^2}} \Rightarrow |C_1 - C| = |C_2 - C|$$

$$\Rightarrow \quad \left|\frac{7}{6} - C\right| = |-3 - C| \Rightarrow \left|\frac{7}{6} - C\right| = |3 + C|$$

$$\Rightarrow \quad \frac{7}{6} - C = \pm(3 + C) \Rightarrow 2C = \frac{-11}{6} \Rightarrow C = \frac{-11}{12}$$

$\therefore$ Equation of L is $y = \frac{-3}{2}x - \frac{11}{12}$, i.e. $18x + 12y + 11 = 0$

Hence, the line $18x + 12y + 11 = 0$ is midway between the parallel lines $9x + 6y - 7 = 0$ and $3x + 2y + 6 = 0$.

EXAMPLE 11. Prove that the line $5x - 2y - 1 = 0$ is mid-parallel to the lines $5x - 2y - 9 = 0$ and $5x - 2y + 7 = 0$.

Sol. Clearly, the slope of each of the given lines is same equal to $\frac{5}{2}$.

Hence, the line $5x - 2y - 1 = 0$ is parallel to each of the given lines.

To prove that the line $5x - 2y - 1 = 0$ is mid-parallel to the given lines it is sufficient to show that the line $5x - 2y - 1 = 0$ is equidistant from the given lines.

Putting $y = 0$ in $5x - 2y - 1 = 0$, we get

$$x = \frac{1}{5}$$

So, the coordinates of a point on $5x - 2y - 1 = 0$ are $\left(\frac{1}{5}, 0\right)$.

The distance d_1 between the lines $5x - 2y - 1 = 0$ and $5x - 2y - 9 = 0$ is given by

$d_1 =$ Length of the perpendicular from $\left(\frac{1}{5}, 0\right)$ to $5x - 2y - 9 = 0$

$$\Rightarrow d_1 = \left|\frac{5 \times \frac{1}{5} - 2 \times 0 - 9}{\sqrt{5^2 + (-2)^2}}\right| = \frac{8}{\sqrt{29}}$$

The distance d_2 between the lines $5x - 2y - 1 = 0$ and $5x - 2y + 7 = 0$ is given by

$d_2 =$ Length of the perpendicular from $\left(\frac{1}{5}, 0\right)$ to $5x - 2y + 7 = 0$

$$\Rightarrow \quad d_2 = \left|\frac{5 \times \frac{1}{5} - 2 \times 0 + 7}{\sqrt{5^2 + (-2)^2}}\right|$$

$$= \frac{8}{\sqrt{29}}$$

Clearly, $d_1 = d_2$

Consequently the line $5x - 2y - 1 = 0$ is equidistant from the lines $5x - 2y - 9 = 0$ and $5x - 2y + 7 = 0$.

EXAMPLE 12. Find the area of a square, if two sides of a square are $x + 2y + 3 = 0$ and $x + 2y = 5$.

Sol. Given sides of a square are parallel lines.

$\therefore$ The distance between two parallel lines $x + 2y + 3 = 0$ and $x + 2y - 5 = 0$ is

$$d = \frac{|-5 - 3|}{\sqrt{1^2 + 2^2}} \quad \left[\because d = \frac{|C_1 - C_2|}{\sqrt{A^2 + B^2}}\right]$$

$$= \frac{8}{\sqrt{1+4}} = \frac{8}{\sqrt{5}}$$

$\therefore$ Length of side of a square, $a = d = \frac{8}{\sqrt{5}}$

$\therefore$ Area of a square $= a^2 = \left(\frac{8}{\sqrt{5}}\right)^2$

$$= \frac{64}{5} \text{ sq units}$$

Application of the Straight Line in Demand Curve

Demand curve, in economics, a graphic representation of the relationship between product price and the quantity of the product demanded.

On a linear demand curve, elasticity decrease as the price falls and the quantity demanded increase.

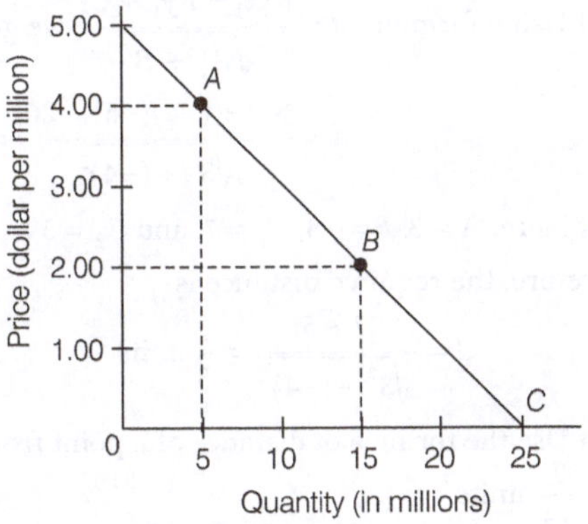

Topic Practice 3

1 Find the distance of the point $(3, -5)$ from the line $3x - 4y - 26 = 0$.

2 Find the distance between the parallel lines $3x - 4y + 7 = 0$ and $3x - 4y + 5 = 0$.

3 Find the distance of the line $12x - 5y - 7 = 0$ from the origin.

4 Find the distance of the point $P(1, -3)$ from the line $2y - 3x = 4$. **[NCERT Exemplar]**

5 Find the distance between the lines. $3x + 4y = 9$ and $6x + 8y = 15$ **[NCERT Exemplar]**

6 If p is the length of perpendicular from origin to the line whose intercept on the axes are a and b, then show that $\frac{1}{p^2} = \frac{1}{a^2} + \frac{1}{b^2}$.

7 The equation of two sides of a square are $5x - 12y - 65 = 0$ and $5x - 12y + 26 = 0$. Find the area of a square.

8 Find the values of k for which the length of perpendicular from the point $(4,1)$ on the line $3x - 4y + k = 0$ is 2 units.

9 The perpendicular distance of a line from the origin is 5 units and its slope is -1. Find the equation of the line.

10 If p and q are the lengths of perpendiculars from the origin to the lines $x\cos\theta - y\sin\theta = k\cos 2\theta$ and $x\sec\theta + y\,\text{cosec}\,\theta = k$, respectively. Prove that $p^2 + 4q^2 = k^2$.

11 Find the points on the Y-axis, whose perpendicular distance from the line $4x - 3y - 12 = 0$ is 3.

12 If sum of perpendicular distances of a variable point $P(x, y)$ from the lines $x + y - 5 = 0$ and $3x - 2y + 7 = 0$ is always 10. Show that P must moves on a line. **[NCERT]**

13 Which of the lines $2x - y + 3 = 0$ and $x - 4y - 7 = 0$, is farther from the origin?

14 Find the points on the line $x + y = 4$ which lie at a unit distance from the line $4x + 3y = 10$. **[NCERT Exemplar]**

15 Find a point which is equidistant from the lines $4x + 3y + 10 = 0$, $5x - 12y + 26 = 0$ and $7x + 24y - 50 = 0$ **[NCERT Exemplar]**

16 Find the equation of two straight lines which are parallel to $x + 7y + 2 = 0$ and at unit distance from the point $(1, -1)$.

17 Find the equation of the lines passing through the point $(1,0)$ and at a distance $\frac{\sqrt{3}}{2}$ from the origin. **[NCERT Exemplar]**

18 Find the ratio in which the line $3x + 4y + 2 = 0$ divides the distance between the lines $3x + 4y + 5 = 0$ and $3x + 4y - 5 = 0$. **[NCERT Exemplar]**

19 The points $A(2,3)$, $B(4,-1)$ and $C(-1,2)$ are the vertices of ΔABC. Find the length of perpendicular from C on AB and hence find the area of ΔABC.

20 Prove that the product of lengths of perpendicular drawn from the points $(\sqrt{a^2 - b^2}, 0)$ and $(-\sqrt{a^2 - b^2}, 0)$ to the line $\frac{x}{a}\cos\theta + \frac{y}{b}\sin\theta = 1$ is b^2.

Hints & Solutions

1. **Hint** Using formula, $d=\dfrac{|Ax_1+By_1+C|}{\sqrt{A^2+B^2}}$, we get

$$d=\frac{|3\cdot 3+(-4)(-5)-26|}{\sqrt{3^2+(-4)^2}}=\frac{3}{5}\text{ units}$$

2. **Hint** Here, $A=3$, $B=-4$, $C_1=7$, and $C_2=5$.

Therefore, the required distance is

$$d=\frac{|7-5|}{\sqrt{3^2+(-4)^2}}=\frac{2}{5}\text{ units}$$

3. **Hint** Use the formula of distance of a point from a line.

Ans. $\dfrac{7}{13}$ units

4. **Hint** Use the formula of distance of a point from a line.

Ans. $\sqrt{13}$ units

5. **Hint** Given equations can be rewritten as

$$3x+4y-9=0 \text{ and } 3x+4y-\frac{15}{2}=0$$

Since, the slope of these lines are same and hence they are parallel to each other.

Therefore, the distance between them is given by

$$d=\left|\frac{9-\frac{15}{2}}{\sqrt{3^2+4^2}}\right|$$

Ans. $\dfrac{3}{10}$ unit

6. **Hint** Equation of line in intercept form is

$$\frac{x}{a}+\frac{y}{b}=1$$

$$\Rightarrow \frac{x}{a}+\frac{y}{b}-1=0$$

Its distance from origin is $\left|\dfrac{0+0-1}{\sqrt{\frac{1}{a^2}+\frac{1}{b^2}}}\right|=p$

7. **Hint** Side of a square, $a=\dfrac{|26+65|}{\sqrt{5^2+12^2}}=\dfrac{91}{\sqrt{169}}$ units

Area of square $=a^2$

Ans. 49 sq units

8. **Hint** $\dfrac{(3\times4-4\times1+k)}{\sqrt{3^2+(-4)^2}}=\pm2$

Ans. $k=2$ or $k=-18$

9. **Hint** Let the required equation be $y=-x+c$.

$$\therefore \quad \frac{|0+0-c|}{\sqrt{1^2+1^2}}=5$$

$$\Rightarrow \quad |c|=5\sqrt{2}$$

$$\Rightarrow \quad c=5\sqrt{2} \text{ or } c=-5\sqrt{2}$$

Ans. $x+y+5\sqrt{2}=0$ or $x+y-5\sqrt{2}=0$

10. **Hint** Here, $p=\dfrac{|0\cdot\cos\theta-0\cdot(-\sin\theta)-k\cos 2\theta|}{\sqrt{\cos^2\theta+\sin^2\theta}}$

$$\Rightarrow \quad p=|k\cos 2\theta|$$

and $$q=\frac{|0\cdot\sec\theta+0\cdot\operatorname{cosec}\theta-k|}{\sqrt{\sec^2\theta+\operatorname{cosec}^2\theta}}$$

$$\therefore \quad q=\frac{|k|}{\sqrt{\frac{1}{\cos^2\theta}+\frac{1}{\sin^2\theta}}}=\frac{|k|}{\sqrt{\frac{\sin^2\theta+\cos^2\theta}{\sin^2\theta\cdot\cos^2\theta}}}$$

$$=\frac{|k|\cdot|\sin\theta\cos\theta|}{1}\times\frac{2}{2}=\frac{1}{2}|k(2\sin\theta\cos\theta)|$$

$$\Rightarrow \quad q=\frac{1}{2}|k\sin 2\theta|$$

$$\Rightarrow \quad 2q=|k\sin 2\theta|$$

$$\therefore \quad p^2+4q^2=k^2\cos^2 2\theta+k^2\sin^2 2\theta$$

11. **Hint** $\dfrac{|4(0)-3(y_1)-12|}{\sqrt{4^2+(-3)^2}}=3 \Rightarrow \dfrac{3y_1+12}{\sqrt{16+9}}=\pm3$

Ans. $(0,1)$ and $(0,-9)$

12. **Hint** $\dfrac{|x+y-5|}{\sqrt{(1)^2+(1)^2}}+\dfrac{|3x-2y+7|}{\sqrt{3^2+(-2)^2}}=10$

$$\Rightarrow \quad \sqrt{13}|x+y-5|+\sqrt{2}|3x-2y+7|-10\sqrt{26}=0$$

$$\Rightarrow x(\sqrt{13}+3\sqrt{2})+y(\sqrt{13}-2\sqrt{2})+7\sqrt{2}-5\sqrt{13}-10\sqrt{26}=0$$

[assuming $(x+y-5)$ and $(3x-2y+7)$ as positive]

Similarly, we can obtain the equation of line for any signs of $(x+y-5)$ and $(3x-2y+7)$.

Thus, point P must move on a line.

13. **Hint** $P_1=\dfrac{|0+0+3|}{\sqrt{(2)^2+(-1)^2}}=\dfrac{3}{\sqrt{5}}$

$$P_2=\frac{|0+0-7|}{\sqrt{(1)^2+(-4)^2}}=\frac{7}{\sqrt{17}}$$

Again, $$P_1=\frac{3}{\sqrt{5}}\times\frac{\sqrt{17}}{\sqrt{17}}=\sqrt{\frac{153}{85}}$$

and $$P_2=\frac{7}{\sqrt{17}}\times\frac{\sqrt{5}}{\sqrt{5}}=\sqrt{\frac{245}{85}}$$

$$\because \quad \sqrt{\frac{245}{85}}>\sqrt{\frac{153}{85}}$$

$$\Rightarrow \quad P_2>P_1$$

Ans. $x-4y-7=0$ is farther.

14. Hint Let the required point be (h, k).

Since, point (h, k) lies on the line $x+y=4$,

therefore $h+k=4$ ...(i)

Also, the distance of the point (h, k) from the line

$4x+3y=10$ is $\left|\dfrac{4h+3k-10}{\sqrt{16+9}}\right|=1$

$\Rightarrow 4h+3k-10=\pm 5$

Ans. (3,1) and (−7,11)

15. Hint Let the point (h, k) is equidistant from the given lines.

Distance from line (i) $=\dfrac{|4h+3k+10|}{\sqrt{16+9}}$

Distance from line (ii) $=\dfrac{|5h-12k+26|}{\sqrt{25+144}}$

Distance from line (iii) $=\dfrac{|7h+24k-50|}{\sqrt{7^2+24^2}}$

Since, the point (h, k) is equidistant from lines (i), (ii) and (iii).

$\therefore \dfrac{|4h+3k+10|}{\sqrt{16+9}}=\dfrac{|5h-12k+26|}{\sqrt{25+144}}=\dfrac{|7h+24k-50|}{\sqrt{49+576}}$

$\Rightarrow \dfrac{|4h+3k+10|}{5}=\dfrac{|5h-12k+26|}{13}=\dfrac{|7h+24k-50|}{25}$

Clearly, if $h=0$, $k=0$, then

$$\frac{10}{5}=\frac{26}{13}=\frac{50}{25}=2$$

Ans. (0, 0)

16. Hint Slope of required lines $=\dfrac{-1}{7}$

Now, let the equation of required lines be $y=\dfrac{-1}{7}x+c$.

Then, we have

$$\frac{\left|-1+\frac{1}{7}-c\right|}{\sqrt{1^2+\left(\frac{1}{7}\right)^2}}=1$$

$\Rightarrow \quad c=\dfrac{-6\pm 5\sqrt{2}}{7}$

Ans. $x+7y+6\pm 5\sqrt{2}=0$

17. Hint Here, $y-0=m(x-1)$

$\Rightarrow y-mx+m=0$

Since, the distance from origin is $\dfrac{\sqrt{3}}{2}$.

Then, $\dfrac{\sqrt{3}}{2}=\dfrac{|0-0+m|}{\sqrt{1+m^2}}$

Ans. $\sqrt{3}x-y-\sqrt{3}=0$ and $\sqrt{3}x+y-\sqrt{3}=0$

18. Hint $3x+4y+5=0$

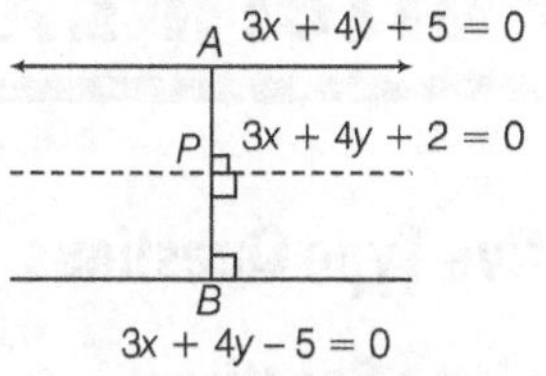

Now, distance between the lines $3x+4y+5=0$ and

$3x+4y+2=0$ is $d_1=\dfrac{|5-2|}{\sqrt{9+16}}=\dfrac{3}{5}$

and distance between the lines $3x+4y+2=0$

and $3x+4y-5=0$ is $d_2=\dfrac{|-5-2|}{\sqrt{9+16}}=\dfrac{7}{5}$ **Ans.** 3 : 7

19. Hint Equation of AB is $\dfrac{y-3}{x-2}=\dfrac{-4}{2}$

$\Rightarrow \quad 2x+y-7=0$

Now, perpendicular distance from C on AB

$$=\frac{|2\times(-1)+2-7|}{\sqrt{2^2+1^2}}$$

$$=\frac{7}{\sqrt{5}}\text{ units}$$

and $\text{ar}(\Delta ABC)=\dfrac{1}{2}\times AB\times\dfrac{7}{\sqrt{5}}$

$$=\left(\frac{1}{2}\times\sqrt{20}\times\frac{7}{\sqrt{5}}\right)\text{ sq units}$$

Ans. $\dfrac{7}{\sqrt{5}}$ units, 7 sq units

20. Hint The perpendicular distance from $(\sqrt{a^2-b^2}, 0)$ to the

given line is $p_1=\dfrac{\left|\dfrac{\cos\theta}{a}\cdot\sqrt{a^2-b^2}+0-1\right|}{\sqrt{\left(\dfrac{\cos\theta}{a}\right)^2+\left(\dfrac{\sin\theta}{b}\right)^2}}$

and the perpendicular distance from $(-\sqrt{a^2-b^2}, 0)$ to the

given line is $p_2=\dfrac{\left|\dfrac{\cos\theta}{a}(-\sqrt{a^2-b^2})-1\right|}{\sqrt{\left(\dfrac{\cos\theta}{a}\right)^2+\left(\dfrac{\sin\theta}{b}\right)^2}}$

Now, $p_1p_2=\dfrac{\left|\left(\dfrac{\sqrt{a^2-b^2}}{a}\cos\theta-1\right)\left(\dfrac{-\sqrt{a^2-b^2}}{a}\cos\theta-1\right)\right|}{\dfrac{\cos^2\theta}{a^2}+\dfrac{\sin^2\theta}{b^2}}$

$$=\frac{\left|-[a^2(1-\cos^2\theta)+b^2\cos^2\theta]\right|b^2}{a^2\sin^2\theta+b^2\cos^2\theta}$$

Exam Pattern Exercise

Part A - Objective Type Questions

Multiple Choice Type Questions

1 The distance between the points (6, – 4) and (3, 0) is

(a) 7 units (b) 25 units

(c) $\sqrt[3]{25}$ units (d) 5 units

2 The coordinates of a point which divides the line segment joining A (1, – 3) and B (– 3, 9) internally in the ratio 1 : 3, are given by

(a) (– 2, 6) (b) (0, 0)

(c) $\left(\frac{-6}{4}, \frac{18}{4}\right)$ (d) $\left(\frac{10}{4}, \frac{-30}{4}\right)$

3 Area of triangle whose vertices are (x_1, y_1), (x_2, y_2) and (x_3, y_3), is

(a) $|x_1(y_2 - y_3) + x_2(y_3 - y_1) + x_3(y_1 - y_2)|$

(b) $|x_1(y_2 - y_3) + x_2(y_1 - y_3) + x_3(y_1 - y_2)|$

(c) $\frac{1}{2}|x_1(y_2 - y_3) + x_2(y_3 - y_1) + x_3(y_1 - y_2)|$

(d) $\frac{1}{2}|x_1(y_2 - y_3) + x_2(y_1 - y_3) + x_3(y_1 - y_2)|$

4 The angle between the X-axis and the line joining the points (4, – 2) and (5, – 3) is

(a) 60° (b) 135°

(c) 90° (d) 180°

5 A line passes through (x_1, y_1) and (h, k). If slope of the line is m, then

(a) $y_1 - k = m(h - x_1)$ (b) $k - y_1 = m(h - x_1)$

(c) $h - x_1 = m(y_1 - k)$ (d) $h - x_1 = m(k - y_1)$

6 Suppose a line L make x-intercept a and y-intercept b on the axes. Then, the equation of the line L is

(a) $\frac{x}{a} + \frac{y}{b} = 1$ (b) $\frac{x}{a} - \frac{y}{b} = 1$

(c) $\frac{y}{b} - \frac{x}{a} = 1$ (d) $ax + by = 1$

7 The equation of the line which have slope –2 and cuts-off an intercept –6 on X-axis, is

(a) $2x - y + 12 = 0$ (b) $2x + y + 12 = 0$

(c) $-2x + y + 12 = 0$ (d) $2x + y - 12 = 0$

8 The equation of the line for which $p = 3$ and $\alpha = 45°$ is

(a) $x - y + 3\sqrt{2} = 0$ (b) $x + y + 3\sqrt{2} = 0$

(c) $x + y - 3\sqrt{2} = 0$ (d) $x - y - 3\sqrt{2} = 0$

9 The distance of the point (–1, 1) from the line $12(x + 6) = 5(y - 2)$ is

(a) 5 units (b) 6 units

(c) 12 units (d) 2 units

Assertion-Reason Based Questions

Directions (Q. Nos. 10-12) *In the questions given below are two statements labelled as Assertion (A) and Reason (R). In the context of the two statements, which one of the following is correct?*

(a) Both A and R are correct; R is the correct explanation of A

(b) Both A and R are correct; R is not the correct explanation of A

(c) A is correct; R is incorrect

(d) R is correct; A is incorrect

10 **Assertion (A)** If θ is the inclination of a line l, then the slope or gradient of the line l is $\tan\theta$.

Reason (R) The slope of a line whose inclination is 90°, is not defined.

11 **Assertion (A)** The equation of the line making intercepts a and b on X and Y-axis respectively is

$$\frac{X}{a} + \frac{Y}{b} = 1$$

Reason (R) The slope of the line $ax + by + c = 0$ is $\frac{b}{a}$.

12 **Assertion (A)** The equation of the straight line which passes though the point (2, – 3) and the point of the intersection of the lines $x + y + 4 = 0$ and $3x - y - 8 = 0$ is $2x - y - 7 = 0$.

Reason (R) Product of slopes of two perpendicular straight lines is –1.

Part B - Descriptive Questions

Very Short Answer Type Questions

13 Without using Pythagoras theorem, show that the points $A(1,2)$, $B(1,5)$ and $C(5,2)$ are the vertices of a right angled triangle.

14 Prove that the line joining the mid-points of the two sides of a triangle is parallel to the third side.

15 If points $(a,0)$, $(0, b)$ and (x, y) are collinear using the concept of slope. Prove that $\frac{x}{a} + \frac{y}{b} = 1$.

16 A quadrilateral has the vertices at the points $(4,1), (1,7), (-6,0)$ and $(-1,-9)$. Show that the mid-points of the sides of this quadrilateral are the vertices of a parallelogram.

17 Find the equations of the bisectors of the angles between the coordinate axes.

Short Answer Type Questions

18 Prove that the points $A(2,3)$, $B(6,7)$, $C(6,9)$ and $D(2,5)$ are the vertices of a rectangle.

19 Prove that $A(4,3)$, $B(6,4)$, $C(5,6)$ and $D(3,5)$ are the angular points of a square.

20 If $A(2,0)$, $B(0,2)$ and $C(0,7)$ are three vertices taken in order of an isosceles trapezium $ABCD$ in which $AB \| DC$. Find the coordinates of D.

21 Find the equation of a line which is perpendicular to the line joining the points (4, 2) and (3, 5) and cuts-off an intercept of length 3 on Y-axis.

22 Find the equation of a line which divides the join of (1, 0) and (3, 0) in the ratio 2 : 1 and perpendicular to it.

23 Find the equation of the right bisector of the line segment joining the points $A(1,0)$ and $B(2,3)$.

Long Answer Type Questions

24 Using the concept of slope, prove that medians of an equilateral triangle are perpendicular to the corresponding sides.

25 Find the equation of the line through the point $A(2,3)$ and making an angle of 45° with the X-axis. Also, determine the length of intercept on it between A and the line $x+y+1=0$.

26 Find the distance of the point $(2,3)$ from the line $2x-3y+9=0$ measured along a line $x-y+1=0$.

27 Find the distance of the point (2, 5) from the line $3x+y+4=0$ measured parallel to the line $3x-4y+8=0$.

28 Find the equation of the straight line passing through the origin and bisecting the portion of the line $ax+by+c=0$ intercepted between the coordinate axes.

29 Find the value of m for which the lines $mx+(2m+3)y+m+6=0$ and $(2m+1)x+(m-1)y+m-9=0$ intersect at a point on Y-axis.

Case Study Based Questions

30 Consider the ΔABC with vertices $A(1, 4)$, $B(2, -3)$ and $C(-1, -2)$ as shown in the given figure. AD is the median and AM is the altitude through A.

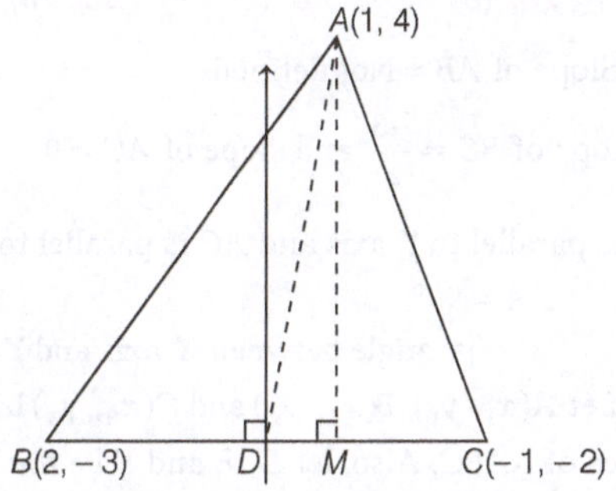

Based on the above information answer the following questions.

(i) Find the distance between A and C.

(ii) Find the slope of BC.

(iii) Find the equation of median through A.

Or

Find the equation of the altitude through A.

31 Population *vs* Year graph given below.

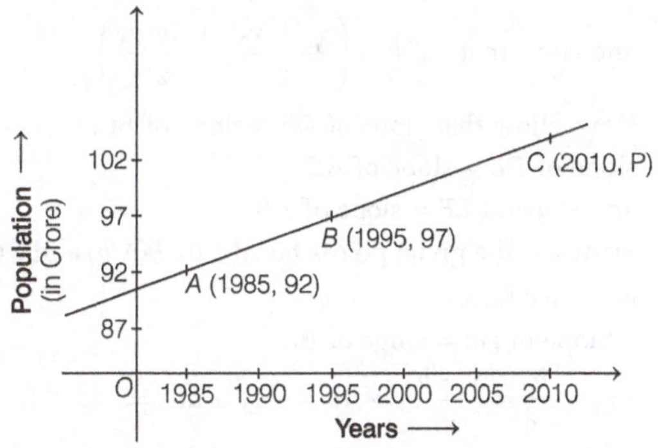

Based on the above information answer the following questions.

(i) Find the slope of line AB.

(ii) Find the equation of line AB.

(iii) Find the population (in crores) in year 2010.

Or

Find the equation of line perpendicular to line AB and passing through (1995, 97).

Hints & Solutions

1. (d) **2.** (b) **3.** (c) **4.** (b)
5. (b) **6.** (a) **7.** (b) **8.** (c)
9. (a) **10.** (b) **11.** (c) **12.** (b)

13. Hint Slope of AB = Not defined

Slope of $BC = \frac{-3}{4}$ and slope of $AC = 0$

$\because$ AB is parallel to Y-axis and AC is parallel to X-axis.

Thus $\angle A = 90^\circ$

[$\because$ angle between X-axis and Y-axis is 90°]

14. Hint Let $A(x_1, y_1)$, $B(x_2, y_2)$ and $C(x_3, y_3)$ be the vertices of ΔABC. Also, let D, E and F be the mid-points of sides AB, BC and CA, respectively.

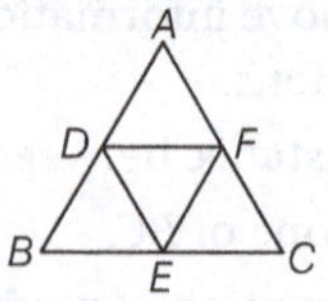

Then, coordinates of $D = \left(\frac{x_1 + x_2}{2}, \frac{y_1 + y_2}{2}\right)$,

Coordinates of $E = \left(\frac{x_2 + x_3}{2}, \frac{y_2 + y_3}{2}\right)$

and coordinate of $F = \left(\frac{x_1 + x_3}{2}, \frac{y_1 + y_3}{2}\right)$

Now, show that slope of DF = slope of BC,
slope of DE = slope of AC
and slope of EF = slope of AB

15. Hint Let the given points be $A(a, 0)$, $B(0, b)$ and $C(x, y)$.

Now, we have

Slope of AB = Slope of BC

$$\Rightarrow \frac{b}{-a} = \frac{y - b}{x} \Rightarrow xb = -ay + ab \Rightarrow ay + bx = ab$$

$$\Rightarrow \frac{x}{a} + \frac{y}{b} = 1$$

16. Hint Let $ABCD$ be the given quadrilateral.

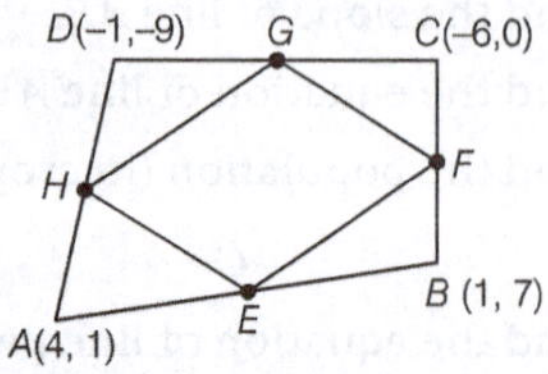

Also, let E, F, G and H be the mid-points of sides AB, BC, CD and DA, respectively.

Now, find the coordinates of E, F, G and H, and then show that slope of EF = slope of GH
and slope of FG = slope of EH.

17. Hint Bisectors of the angles between the coordinate axes, passes through origin and makes an angle of 45° or 135° with positive direction of X-axis.

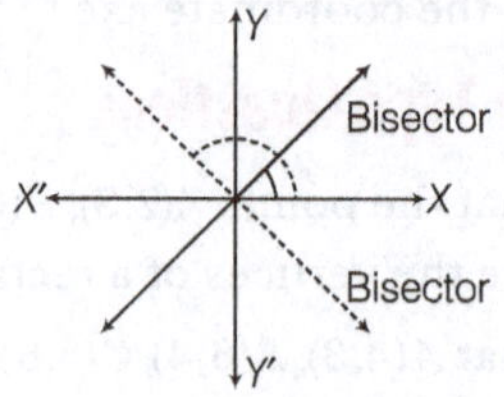

Ans. $x \pm y = 0$

18. Hint Prove that

(i) Slope of AB = Slope of DC
(ii) Slope of AD = Slope of BC
and (iii) Slope of $AB \times$ Slope of $BC = -1$.

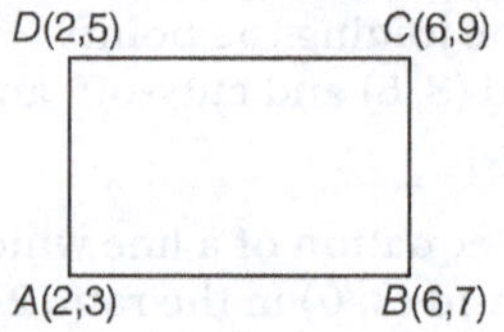

19. Hint Prove that

(i) Slope of AB = Slope of DC
(ii) Slope of AD = Slope of BC
(iii) Slope of $AC \times$ Slope of $BD = -1$
(iv) Slope of $AB \times$ Slope of $BC = -1$

20. Hint Given, $ABCD$ is an isosceles trapezium and $AB \parallel DC$.

We have, $AD = BC$ and Slope of AB = Slope of DC

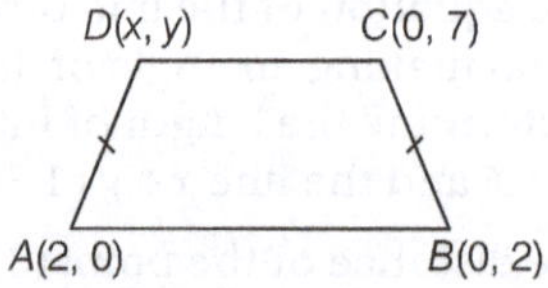

Let the coordinates of D be (x, y).

Then, we have $x^2 - 4x + y^2 = 21$ and $x + y = 7$

On solving these two equations, we get

$(x, y) = (2, 5)$ or $(7, 0)$

21. Hint Slope of line joining the points (4, 2) and (3, 5) is –3.

$\therefore$ Slope of line perpendicular to it is $\frac{1}{3}$.

$\because$ The perpendicular line cuts-off an intercept of length 3 units on Y-axis.

$\therefore$ Equation of the line is $y = \frac{1}{3}x + 3 \Rightarrow x - 3y + 9 = 0$

22. Hint Slope of perpendicular line $= \frac{-1}{\text{Slope of } AB}$

$= \frac{-1}{0}$ = Not defined

$\Rightarrow$ Perpendicular line is parallel to Y-axis.

$\because$ The coordinates of C are $\left(\frac{7}{3}, 0\right)$.

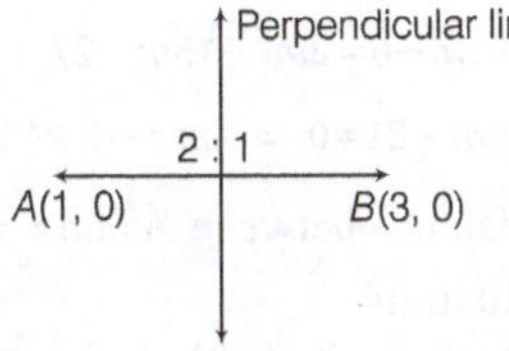

$\therefore$ Equation of the perpendicular line is $x = \frac{7}{3}$

i.e. $\quad 3x = 7$.

23. **Hint** Mid-point of $AB = \left(\frac{3}{2}, \frac{3}{2}\right)$

Slope of right bisector $= \frac{-1}{\text{Slope of } AB} = \frac{-1}{3}$

Equation of right bisector is given by

$$y - \frac{3}{2} = \frac{-1}{3}\left(x - \frac{3}{2}\right)$$

$\Rightarrow \quad x + 3y - 6 = 0$

24. **Hint** Let ABC be an equilateral triangle of side $2a$. For sake of convenience, consider BC along X-axis such that mid-point of BC be the origin. Then, the coordinates of B and C are $(-a, 0)$ and $(a, 0)$.

Let the coordinate of A be (α, β).

Since, ABC is an equilateral triangle.

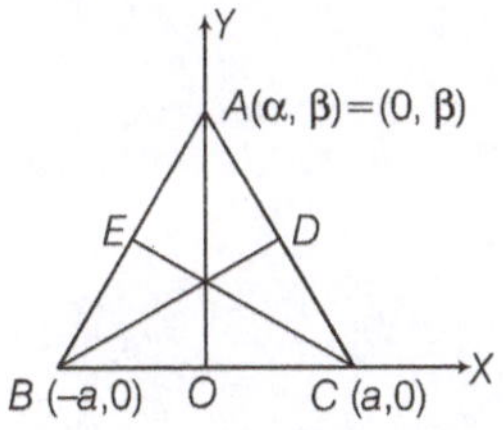

$\therefore \quad AB = AC = BC$

$\Rightarrow \quad AB = AC \Rightarrow AB^2 = AC^2 \Rightarrow \alpha = 0$

Also, $AB^2 = BC^2 \Rightarrow a^2 + \beta^2 = (2a)^2 \Rightarrow \beta^2 = 3a^2$

$\Rightarrow \quad \beta = \pm\sqrt{3}a$

Thus, the coordinates of A are $(0, \pm\sqrt{3}a)$. Consider A on positive Y-axis, i.e. consider the coordinates of A as $(0, \sqrt{3}a)$. Now, let D and E are the mid-points of sides AC and AB, respectively.

Then, coordinates of $D = \left(\frac{a}{2}, \frac{\sqrt{3}a}{2}\right)$

and coordinates of $E = \left(\frac{-a}{2}, \frac{\sqrt{3}a}{2}\right)$

Now, prove that

(ii) Slope of $BD \times$ Slope of $AC = -1$

(iii) Slope of $CE \times$ Slope of $AB = -1$

25. **Hint** Equation of line, passing through $A(2, 3)$ and making an angle of 45° with X-axis, is given by

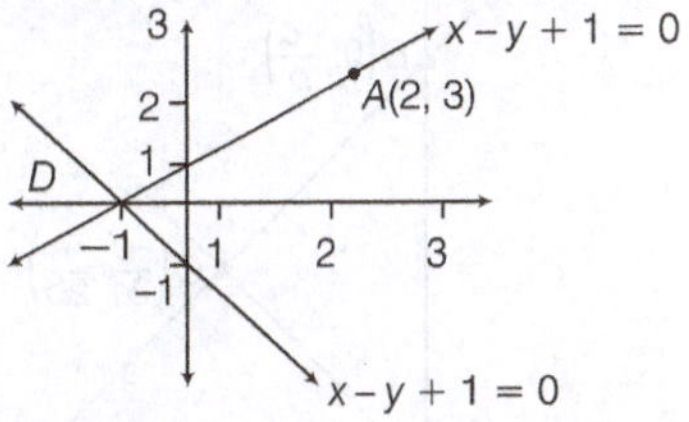

$$y - 3 = \tan 45°(x - 2) \Rightarrow x - y + 1 = 0$$

Let it intersect the line $x + y + 1$ at point D.

Then, solving these equations, we get $D(-1, 0)$

Now, length of intercept between A and the line $x + y + 1 = 0 =$ length of $AD = 3\sqrt{2}$.

26. **Hint** Let the given point be $A(2, 3)$, which lie on the line $x - y + 1 = 0$.

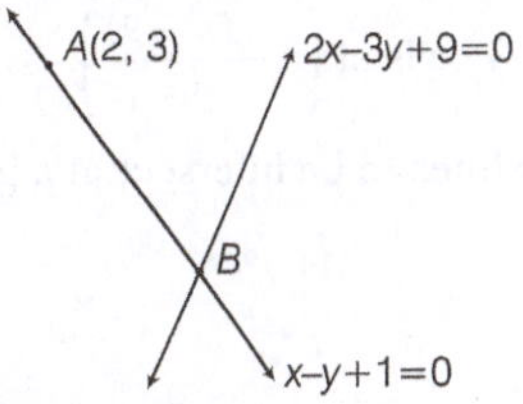

Let $x - y + 1 = 0$ intersect $2x - 3y + 9 = 0$ at point B.

Then, required distance = length of $AB = 4\sqrt{2}$ units

27. **Hint** Equation of the line parallel to $3x - 4y + 8 = 0$ is given by $3x - 4y + k = 0$

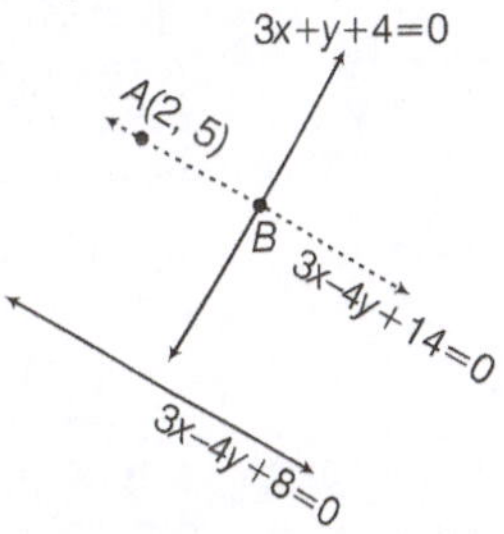

Now, required parallel line should pass through (2, 5).

We have, $3(2) - 4(5) + k = 0 \Rightarrow k = 20 - 6 = 14$

Thus, distance of the point (2, 5) from the line $3x + y + 4 = 0$ will be measured along the line

$$3x - 4y + 14 = 0.$$

Now, solving $3x + y + 4 = 0$ and $3x - 4y + 14 = 0$,

we get $\quad x = -2$ and $y = 2$

Thus, the coordinates of B are $(-2, 2)$.

Hence, required distance = length of $AB = 5$ units.

28. **Hint** Clearly, the line $ax + by + c = 0$ intersect X-axis at

$$A\left(\frac{-c}{a}, 0\right) \text{ and } B\left(0, \frac{-c}{b}\right).$$

Mid-point of AB is $C\left(\frac{-c}{2a}, \frac{-c}{2b}\right)$.

Now, the equation of line OC is given by

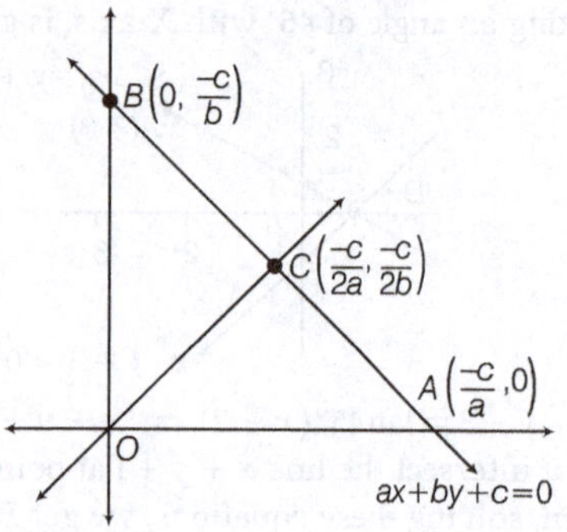

$$y-0=\frac{-c/2b}{-c/2a}(x-0) \Rightarrow ax-by=0$$

29. **Hint** Line (i) intersect Y-axis at $\left(0, \frac{-m-6}{2m+3}\right)$ and line (ii) intersect Y-axis at $\left(0, -\frac{(m-9)}{m-1}\right)$.

Now, for lines to be intersect at a point on Y-axis.

$$-\left(\frac{m+6}{2m+3}\right)=-\left(\frac{m-9}{m-1}\right) \Rightarrow \frac{m+6}{2m+3}=\frac{m-9}{m-1}$$

$$\Rightarrow m^2-m+6m-6=2m^2+3m-18m-27$$

$$\Rightarrow \quad m^2+5m-6=2m^2-15m-27$$

$$\Rightarrow m^2-20m-21=0 \Rightarrow m=-1, 21$$

30. **Hint** (i) Distance between A and $C=\sqrt{(1+1)^2+(4+2)^2}$

Ans. $\sqrt{40}$ units

(ii) Slope of $BC=\frac{-2-(-3)}{-1-2}=-\frac{1}{3}$

(iii) $13x-y-9=0$

Or

$3x-y+1=0$

31. **Hint** (i) Slope of line $AB=\frac{97-92}{1995-1985}=\frac{1}{2}$

(ii) The equation line AB, $y-97=\frac{1}{2}(x-1995)$

Ans. $x-2y=1801$

(iii) 104.5 *Or* $2x+y=4087$

CHAPTER 23

Conic Sections

In this Chapter...

- Circle
- Parabola

Circle

A **circle** is the set of all points in a plane that are equidistant from a fixed point in that plane.

In other words, a circle is the locus of a point which moves in a plane, so that it remains at a constant distance from a fixed point in a plane.

- **Centre** The fixed point C is called the centre of the circle.
- **Radius** The constant distance (CP) from the centre (C) to a point P on the circle, is called radius (r).

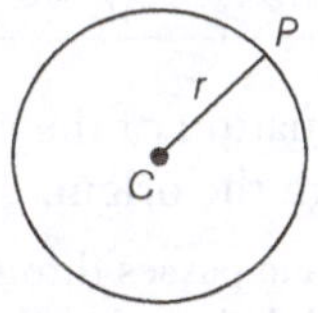

Standard Equation of a Circle

Let $C(h, k)$ be the **centre** of the circle, $P(x, y)$ be any point on the circumference of the circle and r be the radius of the circle.

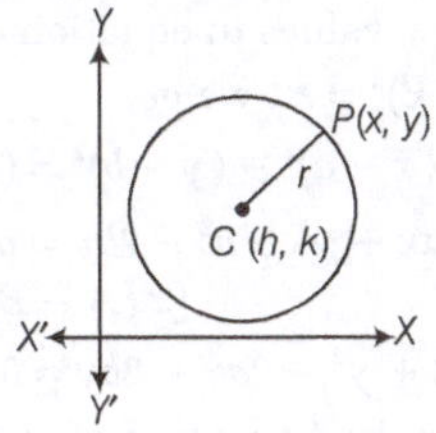

Then, equation of circle in standard form is

$$(x-h)^2+(y-k)^2=r^2$$

This equation is also known as **central form** of the equation of a circle.

If the centre of circle is at origin and radius r, then equation of circle is

$$x^2+y^2=r^2$$

EXAMPLE 1. Find the equation of the circle with

(i) centre = (2, 3) and radius = 5

(ii) centre = $(a\cos\theta, a\sin\theta)$ and radius = a

(iii) centre = $(-a, -b)$ and radius = $\sqrt{a^2-b^2}$ **[NCERT]**

(iv) centre = $\left(\frac{1}{2}, \frac{1}{4}\right)$ and radius = $\frac{1}{12}$ unit **[NCERT]**

Sol. (i) Given, centre is (2, 3).

$\therefore$ $h=2, k=3$ and radius $(r)=5$

On putting these values in equation of circle

$(x-h)^2+(y-k)^2=r^2$, we get

$$(x-2)^2+(y-3)^2=5^2$$

$\Rightarrow$ $x^2+4-4x+y^2+9-6y=25$

$[\because (A-B)^2=A^2+B^2-2AB]$

$\Rightarrow$ $x^2+y^2-4x-6y+13=25$

$\Rightarrow$ $x^2+y^2-4x-6y+13-25=0$

$\therefore$ $x^2+y^2-4x-6y-12=0$,

which is the required equation of circle.

(ii) Given, centre is $(a\cos\theta, a\sin\theta)$.

$\therefore$ $h = a\cos\theta, k = a\sin\theta$ and radius $(r) = a$

On putting these values in equation of circle $(x-h)^2+(y-k)^2=r^2$, we get

$$(x-a\cos\theta)^2+(y-a\sin\theta)^2=a^2$$

$$\Rightarrow x^2+a^2\cos^2\theta-2ax\cos\theta+y^2+a^2\sin^2\theta-2ay\sin\theta=a^2$$

$$\Rightarrow x^2+y^2-2ax\cos\theta-2ay\sin\theta+a^2(\sin^2\theta+\cos^2\theta)=a^2$$

$$\Rightarrow x^2+y^2-2a(x\cos\theta+y\sin\theta)+a^2=a^2 \quad [\because \sin^2\theta+\cos^2\theta=1]$$

$$\therefore \quad x^2+y^2-2a(x\cos\theta+y\sin\theta)=0,$$

which is the required equation of circle.

(iii) Given, centre is $(-a,-b)$.

$\therefore$ $h=-a, k=-b$ and radius $(r)=\sqrt{a^2-b^2}$

On putting these values in equation of circle $(x-h)^2+(y-k)^2=r^2$, we get

$$[x-(-a)]^2+[y-(-b)]^2=(\sqrt{a^2-b^2})^2$$

$$\Rightarrow (x+a)^2+(y+b)^2=a^2-b^2$$

$$\Rightarrow x^2+a^2+2ax+y^2+b^2+2by=a^2-b^2 \quad [\because (A+B)^2=A^2+2AB+B^2]$$

$$\Rightarrow x^2+y^2+2ax+2by+a^2+b^2=a^2-b^2$$

$$\therefore \quad x^2+y^2+2ax+2by+2b^2=0,$$

which is the required equation of circle.

(iv) Given, centre is $\left(\frac{1}{2},\frac{1}{4}\right)$.

$\therefore$ $h=\frac{1}{2}, k=\frac{1}{4}$ and radius $(r)=\frac{1}{12}$ unit

On putting these values in equation of circle $(x-h)^2+(y-k)^2=r^2$, we get

$$\left(x-\frac{1}{2}\right)^2+\left(y-\frac{1}{4}\right)^2=\left(\frac{1}{12}\right)^2$$

$$\Rightarrow x^2+\frac{1}{4}-x+y^2+\frac{1}{16}-\frac{y}{2}=\frac{1}{144}$$

$$\Rightarrow x^2+y^2-x-\frac{y}{2}+\frac{1}{4}+\frac{1}{16}-\frac{1}{144}=0$$

$$\Rightarrow x^2+y^2-x-\frac{y}{2}+\frac{11}{36}=0$$

$$\Rightarrow 36x^2+36y^2-36x-18y+11=0, \quad \text{[multiplying both sides by 36]}$$

which is the required equation of circle.

EXAMPLE 2. Find the equation of circle whose centre is (1, 2) and which passes through the point (4, 6).

Sol. Coordinates of centre of given circle is (1, 2) and it passes through the point (4, 6).

Then, radius of the circle is equal to the distance from the centre to a point on a circle.

$\therefore$ Radius of circle $=\sqrt{(1-4)^2+(2-6)^2}=\sqrt{9+16}=5$

[by distance formula, distance $=\sqrt{(x_2-x_1)^2+(y_2-y_1)^2}$]

Hence, the required equation of the circle is

$$(x-1)^2+(y-2)^2=(5)^2$$

$$\Rightarrow x^2+y^2-2x-4y-20=0$$

Equation of Circle in Special Cases

We know that, the standard equation of the circle with centre at (h,k) and radius equal to r, is

$$(x-h)^2+(y-k)^2=r^2$$

It can be change according to the different conditions, which are given below

CASE I

When the Circle Passes Through the Origin

The circle passes through origin (0,0).

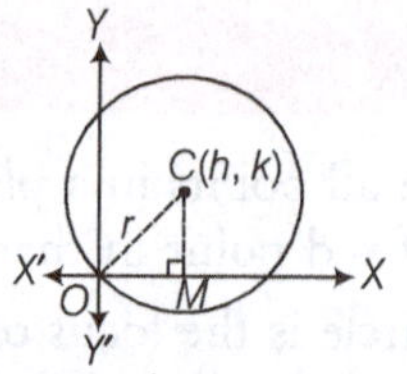

$\therefore$ Radius $= r =$ Distance between points O and C

$$=\sqrt{h^2+k^2}$$

Hence, the equation of a circle passing through the origin is

$$(x-h)^2+(y-k)^2=h^2+k^2$$

i.e. $\boxed{x^2+y^2-2hx-2ky=0}$

EXAMPLE 3. Find the equation of the circle whose centre is (a, b) and passes through the origin.

Sol. We know that, circle passes through the origin, so radius of circle will be equal to the distance between point (a, b) and origin.

$\therefore$ Radius of circle

= Distance between points (0, 0) and (a, b)

$=\sqrt{(0-a)^2+(0-b)^2}=\sqrt{a^2+b^2}$ [by distance formula]

$\because$ Centre $=(h, k)=(a, b)$

On putting these values in equation of circle $(x-h)^2+(y-k)^2=r^2$, we get

$$(x-a)^2+(y-b)^2=(\sqrt{a^2+b^2})^2$$

$$\Rightarrow x^2+a^2-2ax+y^2+b^2-2by=a^2+b^2 \quad [\because (A-B)^2=A^2-2AB+B^2]$$

$$\Rightarrow x^2+y^2-2ax-2by=0,$$

which is the required equation of circle.

CASE II

When the Centre Lies on X-axis or Y-axis

If centre lies on X-axis, then $k = 0$.

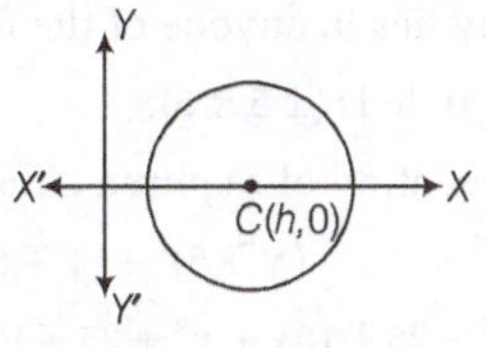

$\therefore$ Equation of circle with centre $C(h, 0)$ is

$$(x-h)^2 + y^2 = r^2$$

If centre lies on Y-axis, then $h = 0$.

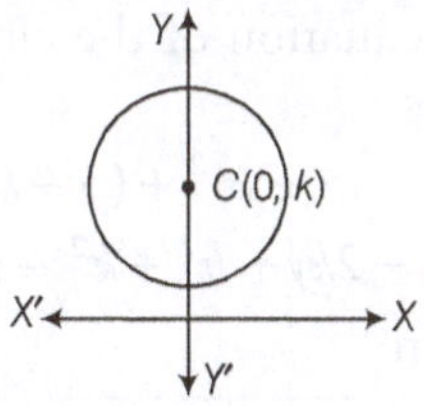

$\therefore$ Equation of circle with centre $C(0,k)$ is

$$x^2 + (y-k)^2 = r^2$$

EXAMPLE 4. If the circle passes through the point (2,3), then find the equation of the circle whose radius is 5 units and centre lies on X-axis.

Sol. Given, radius, $r = 5$ units, point lies on circle $= (2, 3)$ and centre of circle is on X-axis.

$\therefore$ Its y-coordinate will be zero.

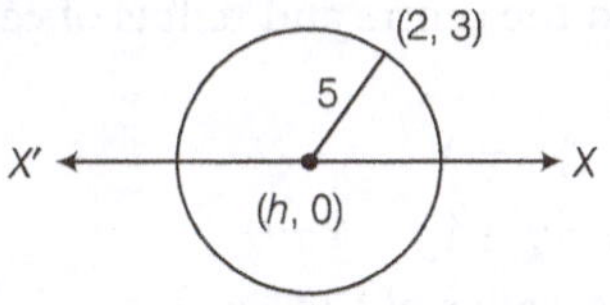

Let centre of circle $= (h, 0)$

Now, distance from the centre to a point on the circle = Radius of circle

$\therefore \sqrt{(h-2)^2 + (0-3)^2} = 5$ [by distance formula]

$\Rightarrow \sqrt{h^2 + 4 - 4h + 9} = 5$ $[\because (A-B)^2 = A^2 + B^2 - 2AB]$

$\Rightarrow h^2 + 4 - 4h + 9 = 25$ [squaring on both sides]

$\Rightarrow h^2 - 4h + 13 - 25 = 0$

$\Rightarrow h^2 - 4h - 12 = 0$

$\Rightarrow h^2 - 6h + 2h - 12 = 0$

$\Rightarrow h(h-6) + 2(h-6) = 0$

$\Rightarrow (h-6)(h+2) = 0$

$\Rightarrow h - 6 = 0$ or $h + 2 = 0$

$\Rightarrow h = 6$ or $h = -2$

So, the centre of circle is (6, 0) or (– 2, 0).

When centre $(h, k) = (6, 0)$ and radius $(r) = 5$, then the equation of circle is

$(x-6)^2 + (y-0)^2 = (5)^2$ $[\because (x-h)^2 + (y-k)^2 = r^2]$

$\Rightarrow x^2 + 36 - 12x + y^2 = 25$ $[\because (a-b)^2 = a^2 - 2ab + b^2]$

$\Rightarrow x^2 + y^2 - 12x + 11 = 0$

When centre $(h, k) = (-2, 0)$ and radius $(r) = 5$, then the equation of circle is

$(x+2)^2 + (y-0)^2 = (5)^2$ $[\because (x-h)^2 + (y-k)^2 = r^2]$

$\Rightarrow x^2 + 4 + 4x + y^2 = 25$

$\Rightarrow x^2 + y^2 + 4x + 4 - 25 = 0$

$\Rightarrow x^2 + y^2 + 4x - 21 = 0$

Hence, the equations of circle are

$x^2 + y^2 - 12x + 11 = 0$

and $x^2 + y^2 + 4x - 21 = 0$

CASE III

When Circle Touches X-axis

Since, the circle touches X-axis, so $|k| = r$. In this case, circles may lie on upper of X-axis or on the lower of X-axis.

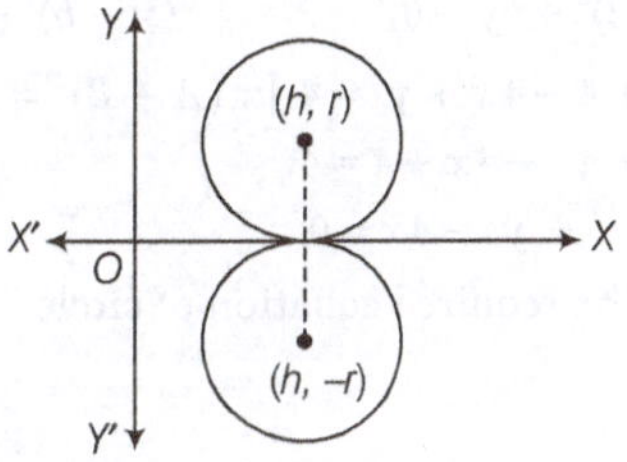

So, if r is the radius of a circle touching X-axis, then its centre is (h, r) or $(h, -r)$.

Therefore, the equations of such circles are

$$(x-h)^2 + (y \mp r)^2 = r^2$$

EXAMPLE 5. Find the equation of circle whose centre is (1, 2) and touches X-axis.

Sol. Given, centre $(h, k) = (1, 2)$ and circle touches on X-axis.

$\therefore$ Radius (r) = y-coordinate of centre = 2

So, equation of circle is

$(x-1)^2 + (y-2)^2 = 2^2$ $[\because (x-h)^2 + (y-k)^2 = r^2]$

$\Rightarrow x^2 - 2x + 1 + y^2 - 4y + 4 = 4$ $[\because (a-b)^2 = a^2 + b^2 - 2ab]$

$\Rightarrow x^2 + y^2 - 2x - 4y + 1 = 0,$

which is the required equation of circle.

CASE IV

When Circle Touches *Y*-axis

Since, the circle touches *Y*-axis, so $|h| = r$.

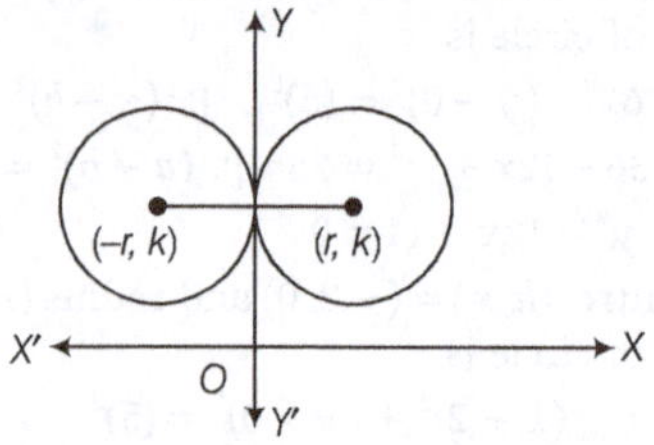

In this case, circles may lie on the right of *Y*-axis or on the left of *Y*-axis. So, if r is the radius of a circle touching *Y*-axis, then its centre is (r, k) or $(-r, k)$. Therefore, the equation of such circles are

$$\boxed{(x \mp r)^2 + (y - k)^2 = r^2}$$

EXAMPLE 6. Find the equation of circle whose centre is (2, 0) and touches *Y*-axis.

Sol. Given, centre $(h, k) = (2, 0)$ and circle touches *Y*-axis.

$\therefore$ Radius (r) = x-coordinate of centre = 2

So, the equation of circle is

$$(x-2)^2 + (y-0)^2 = 2^2 \quad [\because (x-h)^2 + (y-k)^2 = r^2]$$

$$\Rightarrow \quad x^2 + 4 - 4x + y^2 = 4 \quad [\because (A-B)^2 = A^2 + B^2 - 2AB]$$

$$\Rightarrow \quad x^2 + y^2 - 4x + 4 = 4$$

$$\therefore \quad x^2 + y^2 - 4x = 0,$$

which is the required equation of circle.

CASE V

When Circle Touches Both the Coordinate Axes

Since, the circle touches both the coordinate axes, so $|h| = |k| = r$.

In this case, circles touching both the coordinate axes may lie in any of the four quadrants. If r is the radius of such a circle, then its centre may be $(r, r), (-r, r), (-r, -r)$ and $(r, -r)$.

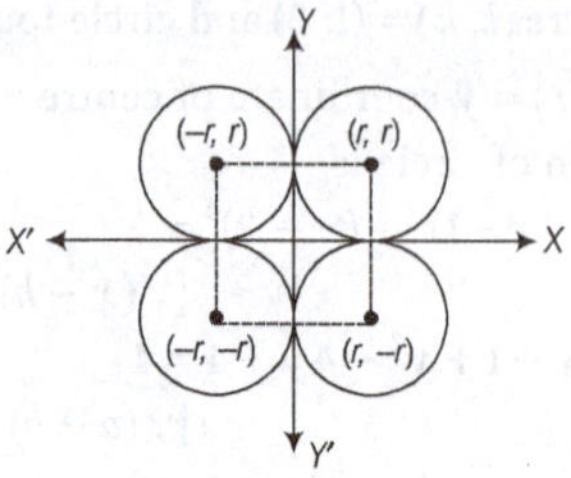

Then, the equations of such circles are

$$\boxed{(x \mp r)^2 + (y \mp r)^2 = r^2}$$

EXAMPLE 7. Find the equation of the circle which touches both the axes and whose radius is 5.

Sol. Given, radius = 5 and circle touches both the axes.

So, circle may lies in anyone of the four quadrants.

$\therefore$ Centre of circle is $(\pm 5, \pm 5)$.

Hence, the equation of required circle is

$$(x \mp 5)^2 + (y \mp 5)^2 = (5)^2$$

$$\Rightarrow \quad x^2 + 25 \mp 10x + y^2 + 25 \mp 10y = 25$$

$$\Rightarrow \quad x^2 + y^2 \mp 10x \mp 10y + 25 = 0$$

General Equation of a Circle

We know that the equation of the circle having centre (h, k) and radius r is

$$(x-h)^2 + (y-k)^2 = r^2$$

$$\Rightarrow \quad x^2 + y^2 - 2hx - 2ky + h^2 + k^2 - r^2 = 0,$$

which is of the form

$$\boxed{x^2 + y^2 + 2gx + 2fy + c = 0}$$

where, $g = -h, \quad f = -k$

and $\quad c = h^2 + k^2 - r^2$

The above equation of a circle is called the general equation of a circle with centre $(-g, -f)$ and radius, $r = \sqrt{h^2 + k^2 - c}$

or $\quad \boxed{r = \sqrt{g^2 + f^2 - c}}$

EXAMPLE 8. Find the centre and radius of each of the following circle.

(i) $x^2 + (y+2)^2 = 9$

(ii) $x^2 + y^2 + 6x - 4y + 4 = 0$

Sol. (i) Given equation of circle is

$$x^2 + (y+2)^2 = 9 \Rightarrow (x-0)^2 + \{y-(-2)\}^2 = 3^2$$

On comparing with $(x-h)^2 + (y-k)^2 = r^2$, we get

$$h = 0, k = -2 \text{ and } r = 3$$

Hence, centre of circle = $(0, -2)$ and radius = 3 units.

(ii) Given equation of circle is

$$x^2 + y^2 + 6x - 4y + 4 = 0$$

On comparing with general equation of a circle $x^2 + y^2 + 2gx + 2fy + c = 0$, we get

$$g = 3, f = -2, c = 4$$

Hence, centre of the circle $= (-g, -f)$

$$= (-3, 2)$$

and radius $= \sqrt{g^2 + f^2 - c} = \sqrt{(-3)^2 + (2)^2 - 4}$

$$= \sqrt{9} = 3 \text{ units}$$

EXAMPLE 9. Find the centre and radius of each of the following circle.

(i) $3x^2+3y^2=27$ (ii) $x^2+y^2-6x+5y-8=0$

Sol. (i) Given, circle is $3x^2+3y^2=27$.

or $x^2+y^2=9$ [dividing both sides by 3]

$\Rightarrow (x-0)^2+(y-0)^2=9$

$\Rightarrow (x-0)^2+(y-0)^2=3^2$ ...(i)

On comparing Eq. (i) with standard form of circle i.e. $(x-h)^2+(y-k)^2=r^2$, we get

Centre $(h, k)=(0, 0)$ and radius $(r)=3$

(ii) Given, equation of circle is

$x^2+y^2-6x+5y-8=0$

$\Rightarrow (x^2-6x)+(y^2+5y)=8$

$$\Rightarrow (x^2-6x+3^2)+\left[y^2+5y+\left(\frac{5}{2}\right)^2\right]=3^2+\left(\frac{5}{2}\right)^2+8$$

$$\Rightarrow (x-3)^2+\left(y+\frac{5}{2}\right)^2=\frac{93}{4} \quad ...(i)$$

On comparing Eq. (i) with standard form of circle i.e. $(x-h)^2+(y-k)^2=r^2$, we get

$$h=3, k=-\frac{5}{2} \text{ and } r=\frac{\sqrt{93}}{2}$$

EXAMPLE 10. Find the centre and radius of the circle given by the equation $2x^2+2y^2+3x+4y+\frac{9}{8}=0$.

Sol. Given, equation is $2x^2+2y^2+3x+4y+\frac{9}{8}=0$.

On dividing both sides by 2, we get

$$x^2+y^2+\frac{3}{2}x+2y+\frac{9}{16}=0 \quad ...(i)$$

From Eq. (i), we have coefficient of $x=\frac{3}{2}$

and coefficient of $y=2$

$\therefore \alpha=\frac{-1}{2}\left(\frac{3}{2}\right)=-\frac{3}{4}$

and $\beta=\frac{-1}{2}(2)=-1$

Hence, centre $=\left(-\frac{3}{4},-1\right)$

From Eq. (i), we have constant term $=\frac{9}{16}$

$$\therefore \text{Radius}=\sqrt{\left(\frac{-3}{4}\right)^2+(-1)^2-\frac{9}{16}}=\sqrt{\frac{9}{16}+1-\frac{9}{16}}=1$$

EXAMPLE 11. Find the equation of the circle passing through the point (2, 4) and having its centre at the intersection of the lines $x-y=4$ and $2x+3y+7=0$.

Sol. Given, equation of lines are $x-y=4$

and $2x+3y+7=0$

On solving these equations, we get $x=1$ and $y=-3$

Also, the point of intersection of the given lines is centre.

$\therefore$ Coordinates of centre are (1, – 3).

Now, the circle passes through the point (2, 4).

$\therefore$ Radius of circle $=\sqrt{(1-2)^2+(-3-4)^2}=\sqrt{1+49}=\sqrt{50}$

Hence, the required equation of circle whose centre is (1, – 3) and radius is $\sqrt{50}$, is

$(x-1)^2+(y+3)^2=(\sqrt{50})^2$

$\Rightarrow x^2+1-2x+y^2+9+6y=50$

$\Rightarrow x^2+y^2-2x+6y-40=0$

EXAMPLE 12. Find the equation of the circle, whose centre is (2, – 3) and passing through the intersection of the lines $3x-2y=1$ and $4x+y=27$.

Sol. Let $P(x, y)$ be the point of intersection of the lines,

$3x-2y=1$ ...(i)

and $4x+y=27$ ...(ii)

On solving Eqs. (i) and (ii), we get

$x=5$ and $y=7$

So, the coordinates of P are (5, 7).

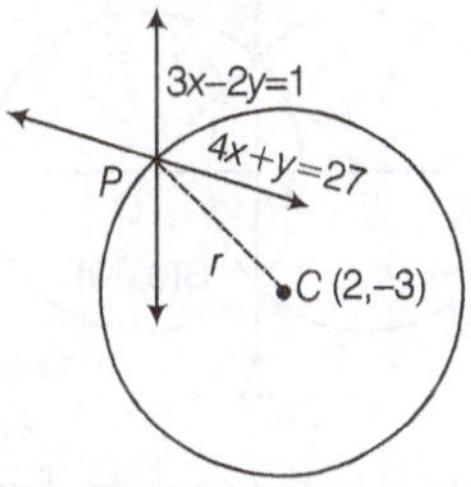

Given, coordinates of centre C are (2, – 3).

$\therefore$ CP = Radius

$\Rightarrow \sqrt{(5-2)^2+(7+3)^2}=r$

$\Rightarrow \sqrt{9+100}=r \Rightarrow r=\sqrt{109}$

Hence, the equation of required circle is

$(x-2)^2+(y+3)^2=(\sqrt{109})^2$

$\Rightarrow x^2-4x+4+y^2+6y+9=109$

$\Rightarrow x^2+y^2-4x+6y-96=0$

EXAMPLE 13. Find the equation of a circle whose diameter are $2x-3y+12=0$ and $x+4y-5=0$ and area is 154 sq units.

Sol. Given, equations of diameter of circles are

$2x-3y+12=0$ and $x+4y-5=0$

On solving these equations, we get

$x=-3$ and $y=2$

We know that centre is the point of intersection of diameter.

$\therefore$ Coordinates of centre are $(-3, 2)$.

Let r be the radius of circle.

Then, area of circle $= 154 = \pi r^2$

$$\Rightarrow \quad 154 = \frac{22}{7} \times r^2$$

$$\Rightarrow \quad r^2 = \frac{154 \times 7}{22} = 49$$

$$\therefore \quad r = 7 \quad [\because r > 0]$$

Hence, the equation of required circle is

$$(x+3)^2 + (y-2)^2 = (7)^2$$

$$\Rightarrow \quad x^2 + 6x + 9 + y^2 - 4y + 4 = 49$$

$$\Rightarrow \quad x^2 + y^2 + 6x - 4y + 13 - 49 = 0$$

$$\Rightarrow \quad x^2 + y^2 + 6x - 4y - 36 = 0$$

EXAMPLE 14. Find the equation of the circle passing through two points on Y-axis at distances 3 from the origin and having radius 5.

Sol. Let coordinates of points on Y-axis be $A \equiv (0, 3)$ and $B \equiv (0, -3)$, respectively.

Given circle passes through points A and B, therefore its centre will be on the perpendicular bisector of AB.

Clearly, two such circles are possible.

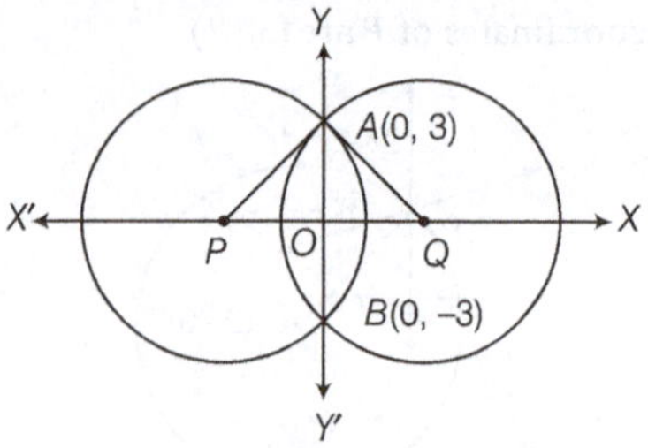

Let points P and Q be the centres of such circles.

Given, $AP = AQ = 5$, $OA = 3$

$$\Rightarrow \quad OP = OQ = \sqrt{5^2 - 3^2} = 4$$

Then, centres $P = (-4, 0)$ and $Q = (4, 0)$

Thus, centres of the required circles are $P(-4, 0)$ and $Q(4, 0)$ and their radii are 5.

$\therefore$ Equation of the required circles will be

$(x+4)^2 + y^2 = 5^2$ i.e. $x^2 + y^2 + 8x - 9 = 0$

and $(x-4)^2 + y^2 = 5^2$ i.e. $x^2 + y^2 - 8x - 9 = 0$.

EXAMPLE 15. Find the equation of the circle passing through the points $(1, -2)$ and $(4, -3)$ and whose centre lies on the line $3x + 4y = 7$.

Sol. Let points $A \equiv (1, -2)$ and $B \equiv (4, -3)$

Given line is $3x + 4y = 7$ ...(i)

Again, let L is the mid-point of AB.

$$\therefore \text{ Mid-piont } L \equiv \left(\frac{1+4}{2}, \frac{-2+(-3)}{2}\right) = \left(\frac{5}{2}, -\frac{5}{2}\right)$$

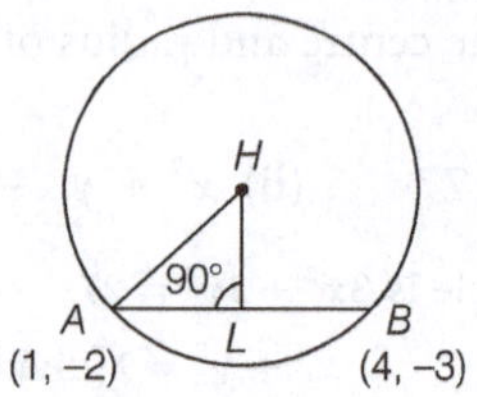

$$\text{Slope of } AB = \frac{y_1 - y_2}{x_1 - x_2} = \frac{-2+3}{1-4} = -\frac{1}{3}$$

$$\therefore \quad \text{Slope of } HL = 3 \quad [\because HL \perp AB]$$

Then, equation of HL will be $y + \frac{5}{2} = 3\left(x - \frac{5}{2}\right)$

$$\Rightarrow \quad 2y + 5 = 6x - 15$$

$$\Rightarrow \quad 6x - 2y = 20$$

$$\therefore \quad 3x - y = 10 \quad \text{...(ii)}$$

Centre H of the circle lies on lines (i) and (ii), therefore it is the point of intersection of lines (i) and (ii).

On multiplying Eq. (ii) by 4 and adding it to Eq. (i), we get

$$15x = 47 \Rightarrow x = \frac{47}{15}$$

On subtracting Eq. (ii) from Eq. (i), we get

$$5y = -3 \Rightarrow y = -\frac{3}{5}$$

$$\therefore \quad \text{Centre } H \equiv \left(\frac{47}{15}, -\frac{3}{5}\right)$$

Now, radius of the circle

$$= HA = \sqrt{\left(\frac{47}{15} - 1\right)^2 + \left(-\frac{3}{5} + 2\right)^2}$$

$$= \sqrt{\left(\frac{32}{15}\right)^2 + \left(\frac{7}{5}\right)^2} = \sqrt{\frac{32^2 + 21^2}{15^2}}$$

$$= \frac{\sqrt{1465}}{15}$$

Hence, the equation of required circle is

$$\left(x - \frac{47}{15}\right)^2 + \left(y + \frac{3}{5}\right)^2 = \frac{1465}{15^2}$$

$$\Rightarrow \quad (15x - 47)^2 + 9(5y+3)^2 = 1465$$

$$\Rightarrow \quad 225x^2 + 2209 - 1410x + 225y^2 + 81 + 270y = 1465$$

$$\Rightarrow \quad 225x^2 + 225y^2 - 1410x + 270y + 825 = 0$$

$$\Rightarrow \quad 15x^2 + 15y^2 - 94x + 18y + 55 = 0$$

EXAMPLE 16. Find the equation of a circle passing through the point $(7, 3)$ having radius 3 units and whose centre lies on the line $y = x - 1$.

Sol. Let (h, k) be the centre of circle.

$\therefore$ (h, k) lies on the line $y = x - 1$, then $k = h - 1$

Therefore, the equation of circle is

$$(x-h)^2 + [y - (h-1)]^2 = (3)^2 \quad \text{...(i)}$$

Since, the circle passes through the point (7, 3).

$\therefore \quad (7-h)^2+(3-h+1)^2=9$

$\Rightarrow \quad (7-h)^2+(4-h)^2=9$

$\Rightarrow \quad 49-14h+h^2+16-8h+h^2=9$

$\Rightarrow \quad h^2-11h+28=0$

$\Rightarrow \quad (h-7)(h-4)=0 \Rightarrow h=7$ or $h=4$

When $h=7$, then $k=7-1=6$

and when $h=4$, then $k=4-1=3$

Hence, the required equation of circles are

$$(x-7)^2+(y-6)^2=3^2$$

or $\quad (x-4)^2+(y-3)^2=3^2$

$\Rightarrow \quad x^2+y^2-14x-12y+76=0$

or $\quad x^2+y^2-8x-6y+16=0$

EXAMPLE 17. Find the equation of a circle which touches both the axes and the line $3x-4y+8=0$ and lies in third quadrant.

Sol. Let a be the radius of the circle, then $(-a,-a)$ will be centre of the circle. [$\because$ circle lies in 3rd quadrant]

Also, the line $3x-4y+8=0$ touches the circle.

Therefore, the perpendicular distance from centre to the given line is the radius of the circle.

$$\therefore \quad a=\left|\frac{3(-a)-4(-a)+8}{\sqrt{3^2+4^2}}\right| \Rightarrow a=\left|\frac{-3a+4a+8}{5}\right|$$

$\Rightarrow \quad 5a=a+8 \Rightarrow a=2$

Hence, the equation of the required circle is

$$(x+2)^2+(y+2)^2=2^2$$

$\Rightarrow \quad x^2+4x+4+y^2+4y+4=4$

$\Rightarrow \quad x^2+y^2+4x+4y+8-4=0$

$\therefore \quad x^2+y^2+4x+4y+4=0$

EXAMPLE 18. Find the equation of circle whose centre is $(3,-1)$ and which cuts off a chord of length 6 units on the line $2x-5y+18=0$.

Sol. Given, centre of circle, $O\equiv(3,-1)$.

Let OM be the perpendicular distance from O to the line $2x-5y+18=0$.

Then, $\quad OM=\left|\frac{2(3)-5(-1)+18}{\sqrt{(2)^2+(5)^2}}\right|=\left|\frac{29}{\sqrt{29}}\right|=\sqrt{29}$

In ΔOMP, $OP^2=OM^2+PM^2$ [by Pythagoras theorem]

$\Rightarrow \quad OP^2=(\sqrt{29})^2+(3)^2 \quad \left[\because PM=\frac{1}{2}PQ=\frac{1}{2}\times 6=3\right]$

$\Rightarrow \quad OP^2=29+9=38$

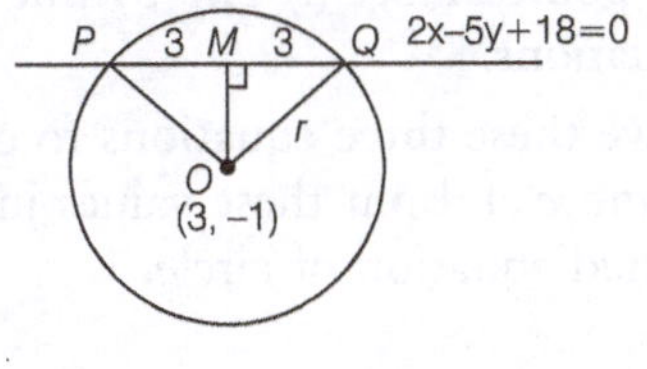

Hence, the equation of required circle is

$$(x-3)^2+(y+1)^2=38$$

$\Rightarrow \quad x^2-6x+9+y^2+2y+1=38$

$\Rightarrow \quad x^2+y^2-6x+2y+10-38=0$

$\Rightarrow \quad x^2+y^2-6x+2y-28=0$

EXAMPLE 19. A circle of radius 2 lies in the first quadrant and touches both the axes of coordinates. Find the equation of the circle with centre at (6, 5) and touching the above circle externally.

Sol. Given, $\quad AM=AL=AC=2$

and $\quad$ points $A\equiv(2,2)$, $B\equiv(6,5)$

$\therefore \quad$ Distance $AB=\sqrt{(2-6)^2+(2-5)^2}$

$=\sqrt{(4)^2+(3)^2}=5$

Then, distance $BC=AB-AC=5-2=3$

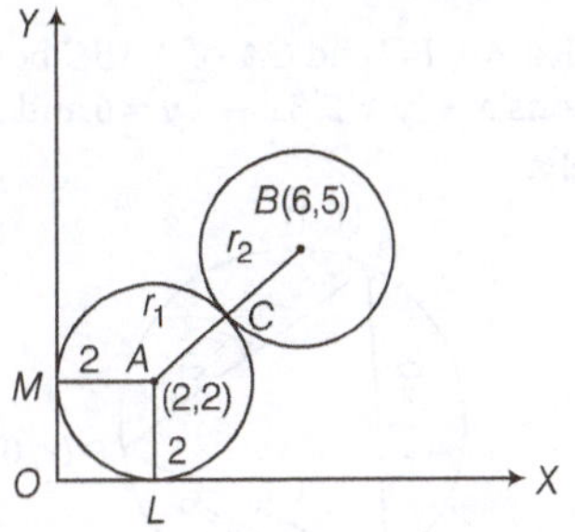

Hence, the equation of required circle whose centre is (6, 5) and radius is 3, will be

$$(x-6)^2+(y-5)^2=3^2$$

$\Rightarrow \quad x^2+y^2-12x-10y+52=0$

EXAMPLE 20. Find the equation of the image of the circle $x^2+y^2+8x-16y+64=0$ in the line mirror $x=0$.

Sol. The equation of the circle is

$$x^2+y^2+8x-16y+64=0$$

$\Rightarrow \quad (x^2+8x+16)+(y^2-16y+64)=16$

$\Rightarrow \quad (x+4)^2+(y-8)^2=4^2$

$\Rightarrow \quad (x-(-4))^2+(y-8)^2=4^2$

Clearly, its centre is at $(-4, 8)$ and radius = 4

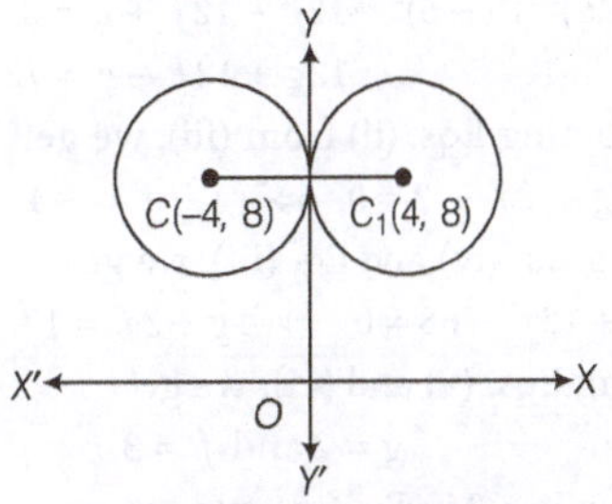

The image of this circle in the line mirror has its centre C_1 (4, 8) and radius 4. So, its equation is

$$(x-4)^2+(y-8)^2=4^2 \Rightarrow x^2+y^2-8x-16y+64=0$$

EXAMPLE 21. If the line $y = \sqrt{3}x + k$ touches the circle $x^2 + y^2 = 16$, then find the value of k.

Sol. Given, $y = \sqrt{3}x + k$ touches the circle $x^2 + y^2 = 16$.

So, length of perpendicular distance from the centre of the given circle i.e. (0, 0) on $y = \sqrt{3}x + k$ is equal to radius of circle.

$$\therefore \quad 4 = \left|\frac{0 + 0 + k}{\sqrt{1+3}}\right|$$

$$\Rightarrow \quad 4 = \left|\frac{k}{2}\right| \Rightarrow \frac{k}{2} = \pm 4 \Rightarrow k = \pm 8$$

EXAMPLE 22. Find the equation of the circle passing through the vertices of a triangle whose sides are represented by the equations $x + y = 2$, $3x - 4y = 6$ and $x - y = 0$.

Sol. Let the sides AB, BC and CA of ΔABC be represented by the equations $x + y = 2$, $3x - 4y = 6$ and $x - y = 0$, respectively.

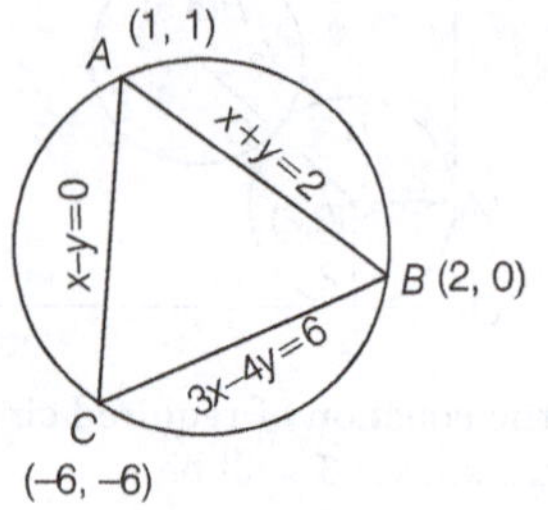

On solving $x + y = 2$ and $3x - 4y = 6$, we get $B(2, 0)$

On solving $3x - 4y = 6$ and $x - y = 0$, we get $C(-6, -6)$

On solving $x + y = 2$ and $x - y = 0$, we get $A(1, 1)$

Let the required equation of the circle be

$$x^2 + y^2 + 2gx + 2fy + c = 0 \quad \text{...(i)}$$

Since, it passes through $A(1, 1)$, $B(2, 0)$ and $C(-6, -6)$, so each of these points satisfy Eq. (i).

$$\therefore \quad 1^2 + 1^2 + 2g + 2f + c = 0$$

$$\Rightarrow \quad 2g + 2f + c = -2 \quad \text{...(ii)}$$

$$2^2 + 0^2 + 4g + c = 0$$

$$\Rightarrow \quad 4g + c + 4 = 0 \quad \text{...(iii)}$$

and $\quad (-6)^2 + (-6)^2 - 12g - 12f + c = 0$

$$\Rightarrow \quad 12g + 12f - c = 72 \quad \text{...(iv)}$$

On subtracting Eqs. (ii) from (iii), we get

$$2g - 2f + 2 = 0 \Rightarrow g - f = -1 \quad \text{...(v)}$$

On adding Eq. (iv) and Eq. (iii), we get

$$16g + 12f - 68 = 0 \Rightarrow 4g + 3f = 17 \quad \text{...(vi)}$$

On solving Eqs. (v) and (vi), we get

$$g = 2 \text{ and } f = 3$$

On putting $g = 2$ in Eq. (iii), we get

$$c = -12$$

Hence, the required equation of circle is

$$x^2 + y^2 + 4x + 6y - 12 = 0$$

EXAMPLE 23. Prove that the radius of the circles $x^2 + y^2 = 1$, $x^2 + y^2 - 2x - 6y = 6$ and $x^2 + y^2 - 4x - 12y = 9$ are in AP.

Sol. Given circles are $\quad x^2 + y^2 - 1 = 0 \quad$ ...(i)

$$x^2 + y^2 - 2x - 6y - 6 = 0 \quad \text{...(ii)}$$

and $\quad x^2 + y^2 - 4x - 12y - 9 = 0 \quad$ ...(iii)

Let r_1, r_2 and r_3 be the radii of circles (i), (ii) and (iii), respectively.

We know that the general form of the circle is

$$x^2 + y^2 + 2gx + 2fy + c = 0 \quad \text{...(iv)}$$

Now, comparing Eq. (i) with Eq. (iv), we get

$$2g = 0 \Rightarrow g = 0,\ 2f = 0$$

$$\Rightarrow \quad f = 0 \text{ and } c = -1$$

$$\therefore \quad \text{Radius } (r_1) = \sqrt{g^2 + f^2 - c} = \sqrt{0^2 - 0^2 - (-1)} = 1$$

On comparing Eq. (ii) with Eq. (iv), we get

$$2g = -2$$

$$\Rightarrow \quad g = -1, 2f = -6$$

$$\Rightarrow \quad f = -3 \text{ and } c = -6$$

$$\therefore \quad \text{Radius } (r_2) = \sqrt{g^2 + f^2 - c} = \sqrt{(-1)^2 + (-3)^2 + 6}$$

$$= \sqrt{1 + 9 + 6} = \sqrt{16} = 4$$

Again, comparing Eq. (iii) with Eq. (iv), we get

$$2g = -4$$

$$\Rightarrow \quad g = -2$$

$$2f = -12$$

$$\Rightarrow \quad f = -6 \text{ and } c = -9$$

$$\therefore \quad \text{Radius } (r_3) = \sqrt{g^2 + f^2 - c} = \sqrt{(-2)^2 + (-6)^2 - (-9)}$$

$$= \sqrt{4 + 36 + 9} = \sqrt{49} = 7$$

Now, $\quad r_2 - r_1 = 4 - 1 = 3,\ r_3 - r_2 = 7 - 4 = 3$

So, r_1, r_2 and r_3 are in arithmetic progression.

Hence proved.

The Equation of a Circle Passing through Three Non-Collinear Points

If we have to find the equation of circle passing through three non-collinear points, then for finding this equation of circle, *we use the following steps*

I. First, assume the general equation of circle.

i.e. $\quad x^2 + y^2 + 2gx + 2fy + c = 0 \quad$ ...(i)

II. Since, circle passes through three points, so each point will satisfy it.

Put each point in Eq. (i) one-by-one and get three equations.

III. Now, solve these three equations to get the values of g, f and c and put these values in Eq. (i) to get required equation of circle.

EXAMPLE 24. Find the equation of a circle passing through the points (2, – 6), (6, 4) and (– 3, 1).

Sol. Let equation of the circle passing through the given points be $x^2 + y^2 + 2gx + 2fy + c = 0$ ...(i)

Since, the circle passes through the point (2, – 6).

On, putting $x = 2, y = -6$ in Eq. (i), we get

$$4 + 36 + 4g - 12f + c = 0$$

$$\Rightarrow \quad 4g - 12f + c = -40 \quad \text{...(ii)}$$

Also, the circle passes through the point (6, 4).

On, putting $x = 6, y = 4$ in Eq. (i), we get

$$36 + 16 + 12g + 8f + c = 0$$

$$\Rightarrow \quad 12g + 8f + c = -52 \quad \text{...(iii)}$$

Also the circle passes through the point (– 3, 1).

On putting $x = -3$ and $y = 1$ in Eq. (i), we get

$$9 + 1 - 6g + 2f + c = 0$$

$$\Rightarrow \quad -6g + 2f + c = -10 \quad \text{...(iv)}$$

On subtracting Eq. (iii) from Eq. (ii), we get

$$-8g - 20f = 12 \quad \text{...(v)}$$

On subtracting Eq. (iv) from Eq. (iii), we get

$$18g + 6f = -42 \quad \text{...(vi)}$$

On solving Eqs. (v) and (vi) for g and f, we get

$$g = -\frac{32}{13}, f = \frac{5}{13}$$

On putting the values of g and f in Eq. (ii), we get

$$c = -\frac{332}{13}$$

Now, putting $g = -\frac{32}{13}$, $f = \frac{5}{13}$ and $c = -\frac{332}{13}$ in Eq. (i), we get

$$x^2 + y^2 - \frac{64}{13}x + \frac{10}{13}y - \frac{332}{13} = 0$$

$$\Rightarrow \quad 13x^2 + 13y^2 - 64x + 10y - 332 = 0,$$

which is the required equation of circle.

EXAMPLE 25. Show that the points (5, 5), (6, 4), (– 2, 4) and (7, 1) are concyclic i.e. all lie on the same circle. Find the equation, centre and radius of this circle.

Sol. Let the equation of the circle passing through the points (5, 5), (6, 4) and (7, 1) be given by

$$x^2 + y^2 + 2gx + 2fy + c = 0 \quad \text{...(i)}$$

Then, each of these points must satisfies Eq. (i).

$$\therefore \quad 25 + 25 + 10g + 10f + c = 0$$

$$\Rightarrow \quad 10g + 10f + c = -50 \quad \text{...(ii)}$$

$$36 + 16 + 12g + 8f + c = 0$$

$$\Rightarrow \quad 12g + 8f + c = -52 \quad \text{...(iii)}$$

and $\quad 49 + 1 + 14g + 2f + c = 0$

$$\Rightarrow \quad 14g + 2f + c = -50 \quad \text{...(iv)}$$

On solving Eqs. (ii), (iii) and (iv) simultaneously, we get

$$g = -2, f = -1 \text{ and } c = -20$$

On putting the values of g, f and c in Eq. (i), we get

$$x^2 + y^2 - 4x - 2y - 20 = 0$$

On putting $x = -2$ and $y = 4$ in the above circle, we get

$$4 + 16 + 8 - 8 - 20 = 0$$

This shows that the point (– 2, 4) also lies on the circle.

Hence, the points (5, 5), (6, 4), (– 2, 4) and (7, 1) are concyclic and equation of this circle is

$$x^2 + y^2 - 4x - 2y - 20 = 0$$

Its centre is $(-g, -f) = (2, 1)$

and radius $= \sqrt{g^2 + f^2 - c} = \sqrt{4 + 1 + 20} = 5$ units

Concentric Circles

Two circles having the same centre $C(h, k)$ but different radii r_1 and r_2, are called concentric circles.

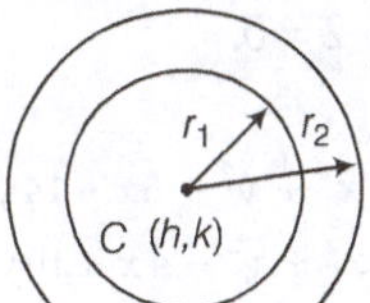

Thus, the circles $(x - h)^2 + (y - k)^2 = r_1^2$ and $(x - h)^2 + (y - k)^2 = r_2^2$, $r_1 \neq r_2$ are concentric circles.

EXAMPLE 26. Find the equation of the circle which passes through the centre of circle $x^2 + y^2 + 8x + 10y - 7 = 0$ and is concentric with the circle $2x^2 + 2y^2 - 8x - 12y - 9 = 0$.

Sol. Given, circles are $x^2 + y^2 + 8x + 10y - 7 = 0$ ...(i)

and $2x^2 + 2y^2 - 8x - 12y - 9 = 0$ ...(ii)

Centre of circle (i) is $C_1(-4, -5)$.

Equation of any circle concentric with circle (ii) is

$$2x^2 + 2y^2 - 8x - 12y + c = 0 \quad \text{...(iii)}$$

If this circle passes through (– 4, – 5), then

$$2(-4)^2 + 2(-5)^2 - 8(-4) - 12(-5) + c = 0$$

$$\Rightarrow \quad c = -174$$

On substituting the value of c in Eq. (iii), we get

$$2x^2 + 2y^2 - 8x - 12y - 174 = 0$$

Hence, the equation of required circle is

$$2x^2 + 2y^2 - 8x - 12y - 174 = 0$$

or $\quad x^2 + y^2 - 4x - 6y - 87 = 0$

Diameter Form of the Equation of a Circle

Let (x_1, y_1) and (x_2, y_2) be the end points of the diameter of a circle.

Then, equation of circle drawn on the diameter is

$$(x - x_1)(x - x_2) + (y - y_1)(y - y_2) = 0$$

EXAMPLE 27. Find the equation of the circle, whose end points of a diameter are $A(1, 5)$ and $B(-1, 3)$.

Sol. Given, end points of a diameter are $A(1,5)$ and $B(-1,3)$.

We know that, the equation of circle, the end points of one of whose diameter are (x_1, y_1) and (x_2, y_2) is given by

$$(x-x_1)(x-x_2)+(y-y_1)(y-y_2)=0$$

Hence, the required equation of circle is

$$(x-1)(x+1)+(y-5)(y-3)=0$$

$$\Rightarrow \quad x^2-1+y^2-8y+15=0$$

$$\Rightarrow \quad x^2+y^2-8y+14=0$$

EXAMPLE 28. Find the equation of the circle, if the end points of whose diameter are the centres of the circles $x^2+y^2+6x-14y-1=0$ and $x^2+y^2-4x+10y-2=0$.

Sol. Given, circles are

$$x^2+y^2+6x-14y-1=0$$

and

$$x^2+y^2-4x+10y-2=0$$

On comparing the above equation with $x^2+y^2+2gx+2fy+c=0$ one-by-one, we get the centres of given circles $(-3, 7)$ and $(2, -5)$, respectively.

Since, the points $(-3, 7)$ and $(2, -5)$ are end points of the diameter of the required circle.

Hence, the equation of circle is

$$(x+3)(x-2)+(y-7)(y+5)=0$$

$$\Rightarrow \quad x^2+y^2+x-2y-41=0$$

EXAMPLE 29. The abscissa of two points A and B are the roots of the equation $x^2+2ax-b^2=0$ and their ordinates are the roots of the equation $x^2+2px-q^2=0$. Find the equation and the radius of the circle with AB as diameter.

Sol. Given, equations are

$$x^2+2ax-b^2=0 \text{ and } x^2+2px-q^2=0.$$

Let the roots of $x^2+2ax-b^2=0$ be x_1 and x_2.

Then, $x_1+x_2=-2a$ and $x_1x_2=-b^2$

and the roots of $x^2+2px-q^2=0$ are y_1 and y_2.

Then, $y_1+y_2=-2p$ and $y_1y_2=-q^2$

Let $A\equiv(x_1, y_1)$ and $B\equiv(x_2, y_2)$

Now, equation of circle whose diameter is AB, will be

$$(x-x_1)(x-x_2)+(y-y_1)(y-y_2)=0$$

$$\Rightarrow x^2-(x_1+x_2)x+x_1x_2+y^2-(y_1+y_2)y+y_1y_2=0$$

On substituting the values of x_1+x_2, x_1x_2, y_1+y_2 and y_1y_2, we get

$$x^2+2ax-b^2+y^2+2py-q^2=0$$

$$\Rightarrow \quad x^2+y^2+2ax+2py-b^2-q^2=0$$

which is the required equation of circle.

and its radius $=\sqrt{(a)^2+(p)^2+b^2+q^2}$

$$=\sqrt{a^2+p^2+b^2+q^2}$$

Position of a Point w.r.t. Circle

Let $\quad S\equiv x^2+y^2+2gx+2fy+c=0$

or $\quad S\equiv(x-h)^2+(y-k)^2=r^2$

be the equation of the circle and $P(x_1, y_1)$ be any point in the plane of the circle, then

$$S_1\equiv x_1^2+y_1^2+2gx_1+2fy_1+c=0$$

or $\quad S_1\equiv(x_1-h)^2+(y_1-k)^2=r^2$

Case I If $S_1>0$, then the point lies *outside* the circle.

Case II If $S_1=0$, then the point lies *on* the circle.

Case III If $S_1<0$, then the point lies *inside* the circle.

EXAMPLE 30. Does the point $(-2.5, 3.5)$ lie inside, outside or on the circle $x^2+y^2=25$?

Sol. Given, equation of circle is

$$S_1\equiv x^2+y^2=25$$

or $\quad S_1\equiv x^2+y^2-25=0 \quad$ ...(i)

Now, put $x=-2.5$ and $y=3.5$ in Eq. (i), we get

$$S_1=(-2.5)^2+(3.5)^2-25$$

$$=6.25+12.25-25$$

$$=18.5-25=-6.5<0$$

Since, $S_1<0$, so the given point $(-2.5, 3.5)$ lies inside the circle.

Topic Practice 1

1 Find the equation of circle with
  (i) centre $= (-3, 2)$ and radius $= 5$
  (ii) centre $= (a, a)$ and radius $= a\sqrt{2}$
  (iii) centre $= (a, b)$ and radius $= \sqrt{a^2 + b^2}$
  (iv) centre $= \left(\frac{1}{3}, \frac{1}{4}\right)$ and radius $= 12$
  (v) centre $= (b\sin\alpha, a\cos\alpha)$ and radius $= 1$.

2 Find the equation of the circle whose centre is $(2, -5)$ and which passes through the point $(3, 2)$.

3 Find the area of the circle having centre at $(1, 2)$ and passing through $(4, 6)$.

4 Find the centre and radius of the circle of the following.
  (i) $(x + 5)^2 + (y - 3)^2 = 36$
  (ii) $x^2 + y^2 - 4x - 8y - 45 = 0$
  (iii) $x^2 + y^2 - 6x + 4y - 12 = 0$.
  (iv) $x^2 + y^2 + 8x + 10y - 8 = 0$
  (v) $x^2 + y^2 - 2x + 4y = 8$
  (vi) $x^2 + y^2 + 6x - 10y + 16 = 0$
  (vii) $x^2 + y^2 + 8x - 10y + 16 = 0$
  (viii) $x^2 + y^2 + 10x - 8y - 36 = 0$
  (ix) $3x^2 + 3y^2 + 6x - 4y - 1 = 0$

5 Find the equation of the circle whose centre is $(2, -3)$ and which passes through the intersection of the lines $3x + 2y = 11$ and $2x + 3y = 4$.

6 Find the equation of a circle concentric with the circle $2x^2 + 2y^2 + 8x + 10y - 39 = 0$ and having its area equal to 16π sq units.

7 If one end of a diameter of circle $x^2 + y^2 - 4x - 6y + 11 = 0$ is $(3, 4)$, then find the coordinate of the other end of the diameter.

8 Find the equation of the circle which touches the both axes in the first quadrant and whose radius is a.

9 Find the equation of the circle having centre $(3, -4)$ and touching the line $5x + 12y - 19 = 0$.

10 A circle of radius 5 units touches the coordinate axes in the first quadrant. If the circle makes one complete roll on X-axis along the positive direction of X-axis, then find its equation in the new position.

11 If $lx + my = 1$ touches the circle $x^2 + y^2 = a^2$, then prove that the point (l, m) lies on the circle $x^2 + y^2 = a^{-2}$.

12 Find the equation of the circle which passes through the points $(2, -2)$ and $(3, 4)$ and whose centre lies on the line $x + y = 2$.

13 Find the equation of the circle passes through the points (2, 3) and (4, 5) and the centre lies on the straight line $y - 4x + 3 = 0$.

14 Find the equation of circle which is circumscribed about the triangle whose vertices are $(-2, 3)$, $(5, 2)$ and $(6, -1)$.

15 Find the equation of the circles whose end points of one of the diameters are
  (i) $A(2, -3)$ and $(-3, 5)$
  (ii) $P(5, -3)$ and $Q(2, -4)$
  (iii) $A(p, q)$ and $B(r, s)$.

16 Find the equation of circle circumscribing the triangle whose sides are the lines $y = x + 2$, $4x - 3y = 0$ and $3x - 2y = 0$.

17 Find the equation of a circle with origin as centre and passing through the vertices of an equilateral triangle whose median of length is $3a$.

18 Show that the points $(3, -2)$, $(1, 0)$, $(-1, -2)$ and $(1, -4)$ are concyclic.

19 If $y = 2x$ is a chord of the circle $x^2 + y^2 - 10x = 0$, then find the equation of a circle with this chord as diameter.

20 Find the equation of a circle concentric with the circle $x^2 + y^2 - 6x + 12y + 15 = 0$ and has double its area.

21 Show that the points (x, y) given by $x = \frac{2at}{1+t^2}$ and $y = \frac{a(1-t^2)}{1+t^2}$ lies on a circle for all real values of t such that $-1 \le t \le 1$, where a is any given real numbers.

22 Find the equation of the circle concentric with the circle $x^2 + y^2 + 4x + 6y + 11 = 0$ and passing through the point $P(5, 4)$.

23 Does the point $(-1.5, 2.5)$ lies inside or outside or on the circle $x^2 + y^2 = 25$?

Hints & Solutions

1. (i) **Hint** Let the centre of circle be $(h, k) \equiv (-3, 2)$ and radius, $r = 5$.
On putting the values of h, k and r in the standard equation of circle i.e. $(x-h)^2+(y-k)^2=r^2$, we get
$$(x+3)^2+(y-2)^2=(5)^2$$
Ans. $x^2+y^2+6x-4y-12=0$
(ii) Solve as part (i). **Ans.** $x^2+y^2-2ax-2ay=0$
(iii) Solve as part (i). **Ans.** $x^2+y^2-2ax-2by=0$
(iv) Solve as part (i).
Ans. $144x^2+144y^2-96x-72y-20711=0$
(v) Solve as part (i).
Ans. $x^2+y^2-2bx\sin\alpha-2ay\cos\alpha+a^2\cos^2\alpha+b^2\sin^2\alpha-1=0$

2. **Hint** Let the equation of circle be $(x-2)^2+(y+5)^2=r^2$
$\Rightarrow \quad x^2+4-4x+y^2+25+10y=r^2$
$\Rightarrow \quad x^2+y^2-4x+10y+29-r^2=0$
Since, it passes through (3, 2).
$\therefore \quad 9+4-12+20+29-r^2=0$
$\Rightarrow \quad r=5\sqrt{2}$
Ans. $x^2+y^2-4x+10y-50=0$

3. **Hint** Let equation of circle having centre (1, 2) be
$$(x-1)^2+(y-2)^2=r^2$$
Since, it passes through (4, 6).
$\therefore \quad (4-1)^2+(6-2)^2=r^2$
$\Rightarrow \quad r^2=9+16=25$
$\Rightarrow \quad r=5$
Ans. 25π sq units

4. (i) **Hint** Given, $(x+5)^2+(y-3)^2=36$
On comparing the above equation with $(x-h)^2+(y-k)^2=r^2$, we get
$$h=-5, k=3 \text{ and } r=6$$
$\therefore$ Centre $(h, k) \equiv (-5, 3)$ and radius $(r)=6$
(ii) **Hint** Given, $x^2+y^2-4x-8y-45=0$
$\Rightarrow \quad (x^2-4x)+(y^2-8y)=45$
$\Rightarrow \quad (x^2-4x+4)+(y^2-8y+16)=4+16+45$
$\Rightarrow \quad (x-2)^2+(y-4)^2=(\sqrt{65})^2$
On compare the above equation with $(x-h)^2+(y-k)^2=r^2$, we get
$$h=2, k=4 \text{ and } r=\sqrt{65}$$
$\therefore \quad$ Centre $(h, k) \equiv (2, 4)$ and radius $=\sqrt{65}$
(iii) Solve as part (ii). **Ans.** Centre $\equiv (3, -2)$, radius $= 5$
(iv) Solve as part (ii). **Ans.** $(-4, -5)$, 7
(v) Solve as part (ii). **Ans.** $(1, -2)$, $\sqrt{13}$
(vi) Solve as part (ii). **Ans.** $(-3, 5)$, $3\sqrt{2}$
(vii) Solve as part (ii). **Ans.** $(-4, 5)$, 5
(viii) Solve as part (ii). **Ans.** $(-5, 4)$, $\sqrt{77}$
(ix) Solve as part (ii). **Ans.** Centre $\equiv \left(-1, \frac{2}{3}\right)$, radius $= \frac{4}{3}$

5. **Hint** Let the equation of circle be $(x-2)^2+(y+3)^2=r^2$
Intersection point is $(5, -2)$.
Ans. $x^2+y^2-4x+6y+3=0$

6. **Hint** Centre of given circle $x^2+y^2+4x+5y-\frac{39}{2}=0$ is $\left(-2, -\frac{5}{2}\right)$ and area of circle, $\pi r^2=16\pi$
$\Rightarrow \quad r^2=16$
Then, the equation of required circle is
$$(x+2)^2+\left(y+\frac{5}{2}\right)^2=16$$
Ans. $4x^2+4y^2+16x+20y-23=0$

7. **Hint** Centre of circle is mid-point of end point of diameter.
Here, centre = (2, 3)
Let the other end be (x, y).
Then, $\frac{x+3}{2}=2, \frac{y+4}{2}=3$
Ans. (1, 2)

8. **Hint** Required equation of circle is $(x-a)^2+(y-a)^2=a^2$
Ans. $x^2+y^2-2ax-2ay+a^2=0$

9. **Hint** Centre of circle = $(3, -4)$
Radius of circle = Perpendicular distance of line $5x+12y-19=0$ from $(3, -4)$.
$$=\left|\frac{5(3)+12(-4)-19}{\sqrt{25+144}}\right|$$
$$=\left|\frac{-52}{13}\right|=4$$
$\therefore$ Required equation of circle is
$$(x-3)^2+(y+4)^2=(4)^2$$
Ans. $x^2+y^2-6x+8y+9=0$

10. **Hint** Let C be the centre of the circle in its initial position and D be its centre in the new position.
Then, $C \equiv (5, 5)$ and $D = (5+10\pi, 5)$
Now, centre of the circle in the new position is $(5+10\pi, 5)$ and its radius is 5, therefore its equation will be
$$(x-5-10\pi)^2+(y-5)^2=5^2$$
$\Rightarrow \quad x^2+25+100\pi^2-10x-20\pi x+100\pi+y^2+25-10y=25$
Ans. $x^2+y^2-10(2\pi+1)x-10y+100\pi^2+100\pi+25=0$

11. **Hint** Given, $lx + my = 1$ touches the circle $x^2 + y^2 = a^2$.
Then, length of perpendicular distance from the centre of the given circle i.e. (0, 0) on $lx + my + 1 = 0$ is equal to radius.

Then, $$a = \left|\frac{0 - 0 + 1}{\sqrt{l^2 + m^2}}\right|$$

$$\Rightarrow \quad a^2 = \frac{1}{l^2 + m^2}$$

$$\Rightarrow \quad l^2 + m^2 = a^{-2}$$

12. **Hint** Let the equation of circle with centre (h, k) and radius r be
$$(x - h)^2 + (y - k)^2 = r^2 \quad \text{...(i)}$$
Since, circle passes through the points $(2, -2)$ and $(3, 4)$, so the points $(2, -2)$ and $(3, 4)$ will lie on Eq. (i).
$$\therefore \quad (2 - h)^2 + (-2 - k)^2 = r^2 \quad \text{...(ii)}$$
$$\text{and} \quad (3 - h)^2 + (4 - k)^2 = r^2 \quad \text{...(iii)}$$
Now, from Eqs. (ii) and (iii), we get
$$(2 - h)^2 + (-2 - k)^2 = (3 - h)^2 + (4 - k)^2$$
$$\Rightarrow \quad 2h + 12k = 17 \quad \text{...(iv)}$$
Also, given that centre (h, k) lies on $x + y = 2$. So, it will satisfy it.
$$\therefore \quad h + k = 2 \quad \text{...(v)}$$
On solving Eqs. (iv) and (v), we get
$$h = 0.7,\ k = 1.3$$
Now, from Eq. (ii), we get
$$r^2 = (2 - 0.7)^2 + (-2 - 1.3)^2$$
$$= 1.69 + 10.89 = 12.58$$
Now, put the values of h, k and r^2 in Eq. (i), we get the answer.
Ans. $(x - 0.7)^2 + (y - 1.3)^2 = 12.58$

13. Solve as Question 12.
Ans. $x^2 + y^2 - 4x - 10y + 25 = 0$

14. **Hint** Circle circumscribed about the triangle means the circle passes through the vertices. Let (h, k) be the centre and r be the radius of circle.
$$\text{Then,} \quad (-2 - h)^2 + (3 - k)^2 = r^2 \quad \text{...(i)}$$
$$(5 - h)^2 + (2 - k)^2 = r^2 \quad \text{...(ii)}$$
$$\text{and} \quad (6 - h)^2 + (-1 - k)^2 = r^2 \quad \text{...(iii)}$$
On solving Eqs. (i), (ii) and (iii), we get
$$h = 1,\ k = -1 \text{ and } r = 5$$
Ans. $x^2 + y^2 - 2x + 2y - 23 = 0$

15. (i) **Hint** Required equation of circle is
$$(x - 2)(x + 3) + (y + 3)(y - 5) = 0$$
Ans. $x^2 + y^2 + x - 2y - 21 = 0$

(ii) Solve as part (i). **Ans.** $x^2 + y^2 - 7x + 7y + 22 = 0$

(iii) Solve as part (i).
Ans. $(x - p)(x - r) + (y - q)(y - s) = 0$

16. Solve as Example 22.
Ans. $x^2 + y^2 - 46x + 22y = 0$

17. **Hint** Centroid of the triangle coincides with the centre of circle and the radius of circle is 2/3 of the length of median.
Ans. $x^2 + y^2 = 4a^2$

18. Solve as Example 25.

19. **Hint** The points of intersection of the given chord and the given circle are obtained by simultaneously solving $y = 2x$ and $x^2 + y^2 - 10x = 0$.
On putting $y = 2x$ in $x^2 + y^2 - 10x = 0$, we get
$$x^2 + 4x^2 - 10x = 0$$
$$\Rightarrow \quad 5x(x - 2) = 0$$
$$\Rightarrow \quad x = 0 \text{ or } x = 2$$
$$\text{Now,} \quad x = 0 \Rightarrow y = 0$$
$$\text{and} \quad x = 2,\ y = 4$$
Hence, the required equation of circle is
$$(x - 0)(x - 2) + (y - 0)(y - 4) = 0$$
$$x^2 + y^2 - 2x - 4y = 0$$

20. **Hint** Given equation of the circle is
$$x^2 + y^2 - 6x + 12y + 15 = 0$$
Centre of this circle = $(3, -6)$
Radius of this circle = $\sqrt{9 + 36 - 15} = \sqrt{30}$
The required circle is concentric to the given circle.
$\therefore$ Its centre is also coincide. So, its centre is $(3, -6)$.
Let r be the radius of the required circle.
Then, according to the question,
$$\pi r^2 = 2 \times \pi(\sqrt{30})^2$$
$$\Rightarrow \quad r^2 = 60$$
Hence, the equation of the required circle is
$$(x - 3)^2 + (y + 6)^2 = 60$$
$$\text{or} \quad x^2 + y^2 - 6x + 12y - 15 = 0$$

21. **Hint** Given, $x = \dfrac{2at}{1 + t^2}$ and $y = \dfrac{a(1 - t^2)}{1 + t^2}$
On squaring and adding, we get
$$x^2 + y^2 = \left(\frac{2at}{1 + t^2}\right)^2 + \left(\frac{a(1 - t^2)}{1 + t^2}\right)^2$$
$$= \frac{4a^2t^2}{(1 + t^2)^2} + \frac{a^2(1 - t^2)^2}{(1 + t^2)^2}$$
$$= \frac{a^2(4t^2 + 1 + t^4 - 2t^2)}{(1 + t^2)^2}$$
$$= \frac{a^2[t^4 + 1 + 2t^2]}{(1 + t^2)^2} = \frac{a^2(t^2 + 1)^2}{(t^2 + 1)^2} = a^2$$
$$\Rightarrow \quad x^2 + y^2 = a^2$$

22. **Hint** Centre of the required circle is $C(-2, -3)$.
Circle passes through the point $P(5, 4)$.
$$\therefore \quad \text{Radius} = |CP| = \sqrt{(5 + 2)^2 + (4 + 3)^2} = 7\sqrt{2}$$
Ans. $(x + 2)^2 + (y + 3)^2 = 98$

23. Solve as Example 30. **Ans.** Inside the circle.

Parabola

A **parabola** is the locus of a point which moves in a plane such that its distance from a fixed point is always equal to its distance from a fixed straight line in the same plane.

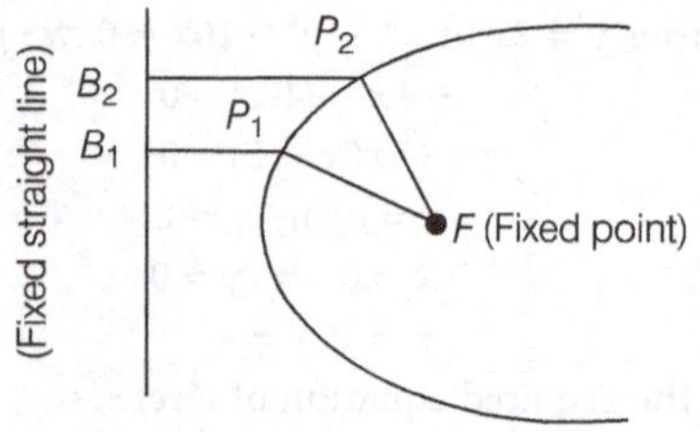

From the figure, $P_1F = P_1B_1$ and $P_2F = P_2B_2$

Here,

- The fixed line is called the **directrix** and the fixed point is called **focus** of the parabola.
- A line through the focus and perpendicular to the directix is called the **axis** of the parabola.
- Point of intersection of parabola with the axis is called the **vertex** of the parabola.

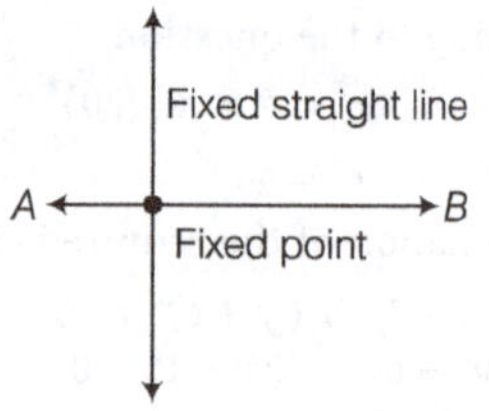

If the fixed point lies on the fixed line, then the set of points in the plane, which are equidistant from the fixed point and the fixed line is the straight line through the fixed point and perpendicular to the straight line. The straight line AB is called a degenerate case of the parabola.

Standard Equations of Parabola

If the equation of the parabola having vertex at origin and the axis of symmetry is either X-axis or Y-axis, then the equations of parabola is said to be in simplest form.

There are four standard equations of parabola which are given below.

Right Handed Parabola

If parabola opens towards right side, then it is called right handed parabola. The equation of right handed parabola is of the form $y^2 = 4ax,\ a > 0$

Some important terms related to this parabola are

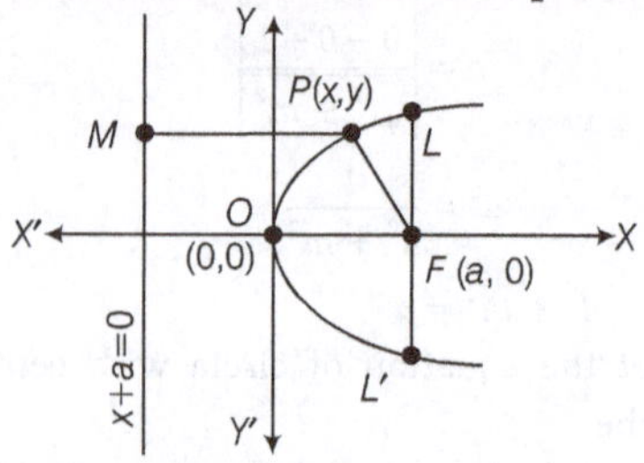

(i) Vertex is O (0, 0).

(ii) Axis is the line $y = 0$.

(iii) Focus is F $(a, 0)$.

(iv) Directrix is the line $x + a = 0$.

(v) Latusrectum of a parabola is a line segment through focus and perpendicular to the axis of the parabola, whose end points lie on the parabola i.e. $LL' = 4a$.

(vi) Coordinates of latusrectum = $(a, \pm 2a)$

(vii) Equation of latusrectum is $x = a$ or $x - a = 0$.

(viii) It is symmetrical about X-axis.

(ix) Focal distance of any point $x + a$.

Left Handed Parabola

If parabola opens towards left side, then it is called left handed parabola. The equation of the left handed parabola is of the form

$$y^2 = -4ax,\ a > 0$$

Some important terms related to this parabola are

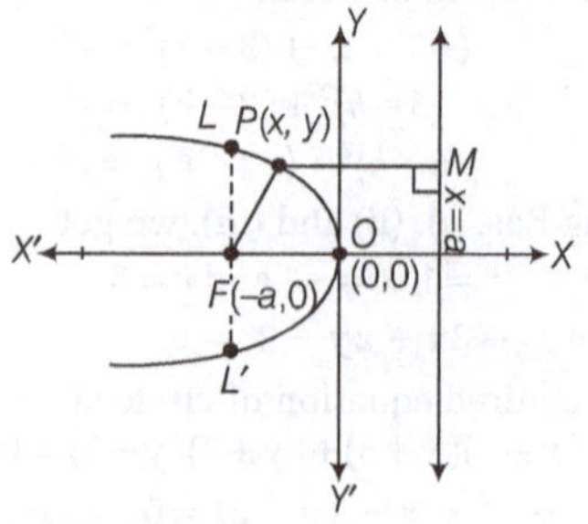

(i) Vertex is O (0, 0).

(ii) Axis is the line $y = 0$.

(iii) Focus is $F(-a, 0)$.

(iv) Directrix is the line $x - a = 0$.

(v) Length of the latusrectum is $4a$.

(vi) Coordinates of latusrectum = $(-a, \pm 2a)$

(vii) Equation of latusrectum is $x = -a$ or $x + a = 0$.

(viii) It is symmetrical about X-axis.

(ix) Focal distance of a point $P(x, y)$ is $a - x$.

Upward Parabola

If parabola opens upward, then it is called upward parabola. The equation of the upward parabola is of the form

$$x^2 = 4ay, a > 0$$

Some important terms related to this parabola are

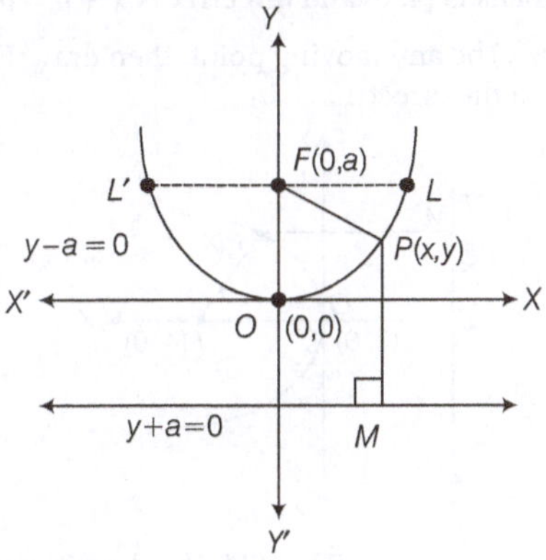

(i) Focus is $F(0, a)$.

(ii) Vertex is $O(0, 0)$.

(iii) Directrix is the line $y + a = 0$.

(iv) Axis is the line $x = 0$.

(v) Length of latusrectum is $4a$.

(vi) Coordinates of latusrectum = $(\pm 2a, a)$

(vii) Equation of latusrectum is $y = a$ or $y - a = 0$.

(viii) It is symmetrical about Y-axis.

(ix) Focal distance of a point $P(x, y)$ is $a + y$.

Downward Parabola

If parabola opens downwards, it is called downward parabola. The equation of downward parabola is of the form

$$x^2 = -4ay, a > 0$$

Some important terms related to this parabola are

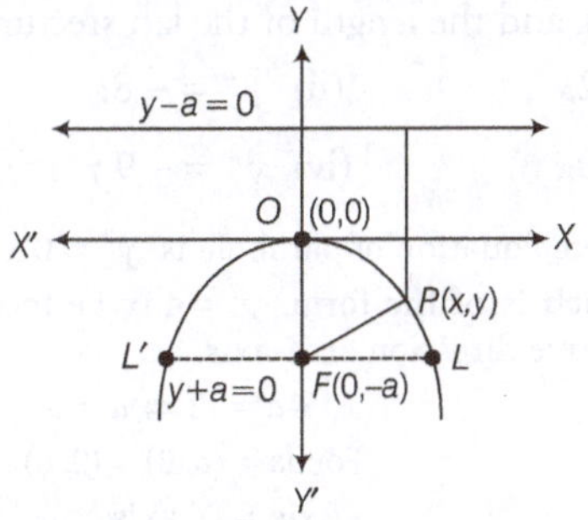

(i) Focus is $F(0, -a)$.

(ii) Vertex is $O(0, 0)$.

(iii) Directrix is the line $y - a = 0$.

(iv) Axis is the line $x = 0$.

(v) Length of latusrectum is $4a$.

(vi) Coordinates of latusrectum = $(\pm 2a, (-a))$

(vii) Equation of latusrectum is $y = -a$ or $y + a = 0$.

(viii) It is symmetrical about Y-axis.

(ix) Focal distance of a point $P(x, y)$ is $a - y$.

Table for Different Types of Parabola

Parabola	Vertex	Focus	Latusrectum	Coordinates of latusrectum	Axis	Directrix	Symmetry	Focal Distance of a Point $P(x, y)$
$y^2 = 4ax$	(0, 0)	$(a, 0)$	$4a$	$(a, \pm 2a)$	$y = 0$	$x = -a$	X-axis	$a + x$
$y^2 = -4ax$	(0, 0)	$(-a, 0)$	$4a$	$(-a, \pm 2a)$	$y = 0$	$x = a$	X-axis	$a - x$
$x^2 = 4ay$	(0, 0)	$(0, a)$	$4a$	$(\pm 2a, a)$	$x = 0$	$y = -a$	Y-axis	$a + y$
$x^2 = -4ay$	(0, 0)	$(0, -a)$	$4a$	$(\pm 2a, -a)$	$x = 0$	$y = a$	Y-axis	$a - y$

Different Types of Questions Based on Parabola

TYPE I

To Find Different Terms Related to Parabola When Standard Equation is Given

In this type of questions, equation of parabola is given and we have to find different terms related to it as coordinates of focus, axis, directrix, length of latusrectum, etc.

EXAMPLE 1. In each of the following questions, find the coordinates of the focus, axis of the parabola, the equation of the directrix and the length of the latusrectum.

(i) $y^2 = 12x$ (ii) $y^2 = -8x$

(iii) $y^2 = 10x$ (iv) $x^2 = -9y$

Sol. (i) Given, equation of parabola is $y^2 = 12x$ which is of the form, $y^2 = 4ax$ i.e focus lies on the positive direction of X-axis.

Here, $4a = 12 \Rightarrow a = 3$

$\therefore$ Focus $= (a, 0) = (3, 0)$

Axis $= X$-axis

Directrix, $x = -a \Rightarrow x = -3$

and length of latusrectum $= 4a = 4 \times 3 = 12$

(ii) Given, equation of parabola is $y^2 = -8x$ which is of the form $y^2 = -4ax$ i.e. focus lies on the negative direction of X-axis.

Here, $4a = 8 \Rightarrow a = 2$

$\therefore$ Focus $= (-a, 0) = (-2, 0)$

Axis $= X$-axis

Directrix, $x = a \Rightarrow x = 2$

and length of latusrectum $= 4a = 4 \times 2 = 8$

(iii) Given, equation of parabola is $y^2 = 10x$, which is of the form $y^2 = 4ax$ i.e. focus lies on the positive direction of X-axis.

Here, $4a = 10 \Rightarrow a = \frac{5}{2}$

$\therefore$ Focus $= (a, 0) = \left(\frac{5}{2}, 0\right)$

Axis $= X$-axis

Directrix, $x = -a \Rightarrow x = -\frac{5}{2}$

and length of latusrectum $= 4a = 4 \times \frac{5}{2} = 10$

(iv) Given, equation of parabola is $x^2 = -9y$, which is of the form $x^2 = -4ay$ i.e. focus lies on the negative direction of Y-axis.

Here, $4a = 9 \Rightarrow a = \frac{9}{4}$

$\therefore$ Focus $= (0, -a) = \left(0, -\frac{9}{4}\right)$

Axis $= Y$-axis

Directrix, $y = a \Rightarrow y = \frac{9}{4}$

and length of latusrectum $= 4a = 9$

TYPE II

To Find the Equation of Parabola in Different Cases

Case I When Focus and Directrix are given

EXAMPLE 2. Find the equation of the parabola, whose focus is the point (4, 0) and whose directrix is $x = -4$. Also, find the length of latusrectum.

Sol. Here, focus is (4, 0) and directrix is $x + 4 = 0$.

Let $P(x, y)$ be any moving point, then draw $PM \perp ZZ'$ from P to the directrix.

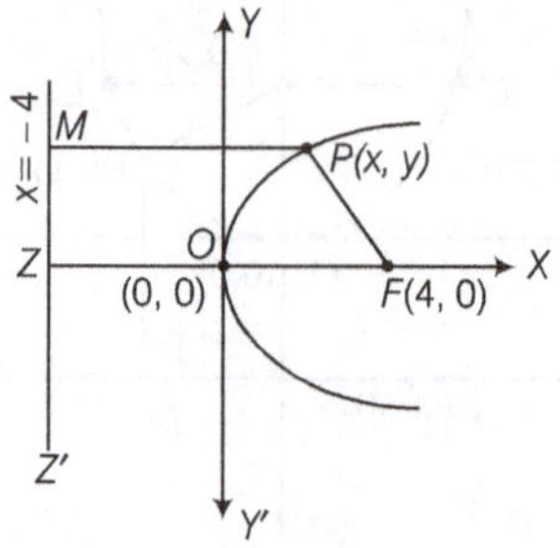

Now, $FP = PM$ [by definition of parabola]

$\Rightarrow FP^2 = PM^2$

$\Rightarrow (x-4)^2 + (y-0)^2 = \frac{(x+4)^2}{(\sqrt{1})^2}$

$\Rightarrow x^2 - 8x + 16 + y^2 = x^2 + 8x + 16 \Rightarrow y^2 = 16x$,

which is the required equation of parabola.

$\therefore$ Length of latusrectum $= 16$

EXAMPLE 3. Find the equation of parabola whose focus is (2, 3) and directrix is $x - 2y - 6 = 0$.

Sol. Let $P(x, y)$ be any point on the parabola.

Distance of $P(x, y)$ from the focus (2, 3)

$=$ Distance of $P(x, y)$ from the directrix $x - 2y - 6 = 0$

[by definition of parabola]

$PF = PM \Rightarrow PF^2 = PM^2$

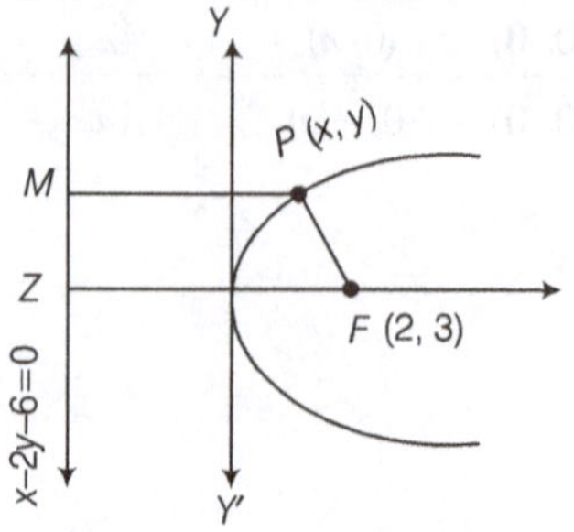

$$\Rightarrow \quad (x-2)^2+(y-3)^2=\left|\frac{x-2y-6}{\sqrt{1^2+2^2}}\right|^2$$

$$\Rightarrow \quad (x-2)^2+(y-3)^2=\frac{(x-2y-6)^2}{5}$$

$$\Rightarrow 5[(x-2)^2+(y-3)^2]=(x-2y-6)^2$$

$$\Rightarrow 5(x^2-4x+4+y^2-6y+9)$$
$$=x^2+4y^2+36-12x-4xy+24y$$

$$\Rightarrow 4x^2+y^2+4xy-8x-54y+29=0,$$

which is the required equation of parabola.

Case II When Vertex and Focus are given

EXAMPLE 4. Find out the equation of parabola, if the focus is at (–6, – 6) and the vertex is at (–2, 2).

Sol. Given, focus is at $F(-6,-6)$ and vertex is at $A(-2, 2)$.

Let $B(x_1, y_1)$ be the coordinates of the point of intersection of axis and directrix.

Then, $A(-2, 2)$ is the mid-point of line segment joining $F(-6,-6)$ and $B(x_1, y_1)$.

$$\therefore \quad -2=\frac{x_1-6}{2} \Rightarrow x_1=2$$

and $$2=\frac{y_1-6}{2} \Rightarrow y_1=10$$

So, the point $B(2, 10)$ is the point of intersection of axis and directrix.

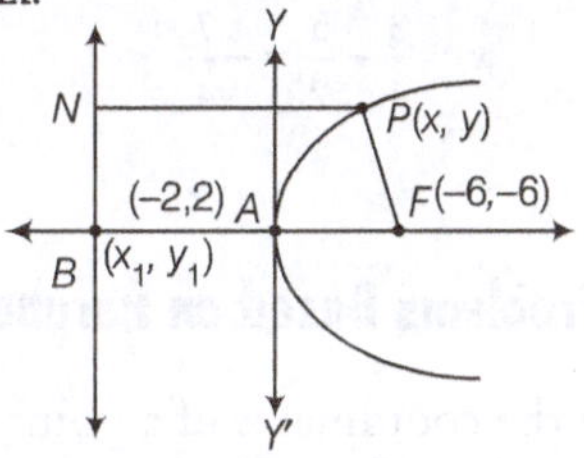

Now, slope of line segment joining vertex and focus is

$$m_1=\frac{-6-2}{-6+2}=\frac{-8}{-4}=2$$

$$\therefore \text{ Slope of directrix, } m_2=\frac{-1}{2} \quad \left[\because AF \perp NB, \text{ so } m_1m_2=-1 \Rightarrow m_2=\frac{-1}{m_1}\right]$$

Then, the equation of directrix is $y-10=\frac{-1}{2}(x-2)$

$$\Rightarrow \quad 2y-20=-x+2 \Rightarrow x+2y=22$$

Let $P(x, y)$ be any point on parabola and PN be the length of perpendicular from P on directrix and FP be the distance between focus F and point P.

So, $$FP=PN \Rightarrow (FP)^2=(PN)^2$$

$$\Rightarrow \quad (x+6)^2+(y+6)^2=\left(\frac{x+2y-22}{\sqrt{1+4}}\right)^2$$

$$\Rightarrow \quad x^2+36+12x+y^2+36+12y$$
$$=\frac{x^2+4y^2+484+4xy-44x-88y}{5}$$

$$\Rightarrow \quad 5x^2+180+60x+5y^2+60y+180$$
$$=x^2+4y^2+484+4xy-44x-88y$$

$$\Rightarrow \quad 4x^2+y^2-4xy+104x+148y-124=0,$$

which is the required equation of parabola.

EXAMPLE 5. Find the equation of parabola when the vertex is at (0, 0) and focus is at (0, – 4).

Sol. Here, the vertex is at (0, 0) and focus is at (0, –4) which lies on *Y*-axis. So, *Y*-axis is the axis of the parabola.

$\therefore$ Equation of parabola is of the form

$$x^2=-4ay \Rightarrow x^2=-4(4)y \qquad [\because a=4]$$

$$\therefore \quad x^2=-16y$$

Case III When Vertex and Directrix are given

EXAMPLE 6. Find the equation of the parabola whose vertex is at (2, 1) and the directrix is $x-y+1=0$.

Sol. Let $V(2,1)$ be the vertex and equation of directrix is

$$x-y+1=0 \qquad \text{...(i)}$$

Then, equation of line perpendicular to directrix i.e. axis is

$$x+y+\lambda=0$$

Since, this will passes through vertex (2, 1).

$$\therefore \quad 2+1+\lambda=0 \Rightarrow \lambda=-3$$

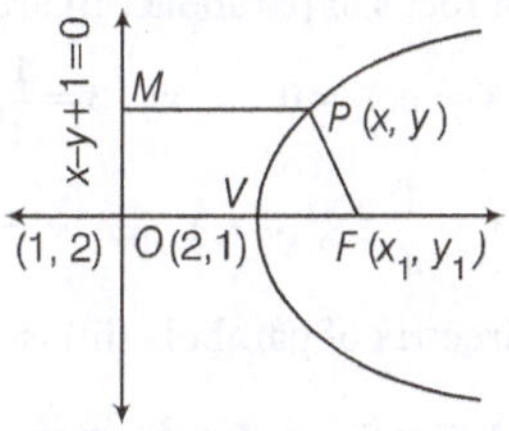

So, the equation of line perpendicular to directrix, i.e. equation of axis of parabola is

$$x+y-3=0 \qquad \text{...(ii)}$$

On solving Eqs. (i) and (ii), we get

$$x=1, y=2$$

So, the coordinates of intersection point of directrix and axis is $X(1, 2)$. Let (x_1, y_1) be the coordinates of F, then V is the mid-point of XF.

$$\therefore \quad \frac{x_1+1}{2}=2 \text{ and } \frac{y_1+2}{2}=1$$

$$\Rightarrow \quad x_1=3 \text{ and } y_1=0$$

So, the coordinates of focus are (3, 0).

Now let $P(x, y)$ be any point on the parabola.

Then by definition,

$$PF=PM \Rightarrow PF^2=PM^2$$

$$\Rightarrow \quad (x-3)^2+y^2=\frac{(x-y+1)^2}{2}$$

$$\Rightarrow 2(x^2-6x+9+y^2)=x^2+y^2+1-2xy+2x-2y$$

$$\Rightarrow \quad x^2+y^2+2xy-14x+2y+17=0,$$

which is the required equation of parabola.

TYPE III

To Find Different Terms Related to Parabola When Standard Equation is not Given

EXAMPLE 7. Find the vertex, axis, focus, directrix and length of latusrectum of parabola $y^2 - 8y - x + 19 = 0$.

Sol. Given equation is $y^2 - 8y - x + 19 = 0$

$\Rightarrow \quad y^2 - 8y + 16 = x - 19 + 16$

$\Rightarrow \quad (y-4)^2 = x - 3 \quad \text{...(i)}$

Let $\quad y - 4 = Y$ and $x - 3 = X \quad \text{...(ii)}$

Then, Eq. (i) becomes $Y^2 = X \quad \text{...(iii)}$

Now, from Eq. (iii), coordinates of vertex are

$X = 0$ and $Y = 0$

$\Rightarrow \quad x - 3 = 0$ and $y - 4 = 0$

[putting the values from Eq. (ii)]

$\Rightarrow \quad x = 3$ and $y = 4$

The equation of axis of parabola (iii) is $Y = 0$.

$\Rightarrow \quad y - 4 = 0 \Rightarrow y = 4$

On comparing Eq. (iii) with $Y^2 = 4aX$, we get

$$4a = 1 \Rightarrow a = \frac{1}{4}$$

Coordinates of focus of parabola (iii) are

$$X = a, Y = 0 \Rightarrow x - 3 = \frac{1}{4}, \; y - 4 = 0$$

$$\Rightarrow \quad x = \frac{1}{4} + 3, \; y = 4 \Rightarrow x = \frac{13}{4}, \; y = 4$$

Equation of directrix of parabola (iii) is

$$X = -a \Rightarrow x - 3 = -\frac{1}{4}$$

$$\Rightarrow \quad x = -\frac{1}{4} + 3 \Rightarrow x = \frac{11}{4}$$

Length of latusrectum $= |4a| = \left|4 \cdot \frac{1}{4}\right| = 1$

Hence, for given parabola, vertex $\equiv (3, 4)$, axis $\equiv y = 4$, focus $\equiv \left(\frac{13}{4}, 4\right)$, directrix $\equiv x = \frac{11}{4}$ and length of latusrectum $= 1$.

EXAMPLE 8. Find the vertex, focus and directrix of the parabola $4y^2 + 12x - 12y + 39 = 0$.

Sol. Given equation is $4y^2 + 12x - 12y + 39 = 0$

$$\Rightarrow \quad 4y^2 - 12y = -12x - 39$$

$$\Rightarrow \quad 4(y^2 - 3y) = -12x - 39$$

$$\Rightarrow \quad 4\left(y^2 - 3y + \frac{9}{4}\right) = -12x - 39 + 9$$

$$\Rightarrow \quad 4\left(y - \frac{3}{2}\right)^2 = -12\left(x + \frac{5}{2}\right)$$

$$\Rightarrow \quad \left(y - \frac{3}{2}\right)^2 = -3\left(x + \frac{5}{2}\right) \quad \text{...(i)}$$

Let $y - \frac{3}{2} = Y$ and $x + \frac{5}{2} = X \quad \text{...(ii)}$

Then Eq. (i) becomes $Y^2 = -3X \quad \text{...(iii)}$

Now, from Eq. (iii), coordinates of vertex are

$X = 0$ and $Y = 0$

$$\Rightarrow \quad x + \frac{5}{2} = 0 \text{ and } y - \frac{3}{2} = 0$$

$$\Rightarrow \quad x = -\frac{5}{2} \text{ and } y = \frac{3}{2}$$

On comparing Eq. (iii) with $Y^2 = 4aX$, we get

$$4a = 3 \Rightarrow a = \frac{3}{4}$$

Coordinates of focus of parabola (iii) are

$X = -a, Y = 0$

$$\Rightarrow \quad x + \frac{5}{2} = -\frac{3}{4}, \; y - 2 = 0$$

$$\Rightarrow \quad x = -\frac{13}{4}, \; y = 2$$

Equation of directrix of parabola (iii) is

$X = a$

$$\Rightarrow \quad x + \frac{5}{2} = \frac{3}{4}$$

$$\Rightarrow \quad x = \frac{3}{4} - \frac{5}{2} = -\frac{7}{4}$$

TYPE IV

Miscellaneous Problems Based on Parabola

EXAMPLE 9. Find the coordinates of a point on the parabola $y^2 = 8x$, whose focal distance is 4.

Sol. Given equation of parabola is $y^2 = 8x$.

Here, $\quad a = 2$

$\therefore \quad$ Focus $\equiv (2, 0)$

Now, focal distance $= 4$

We know that focal distance is a distance of any point $P(x, y)$ on the parabola from the focus F.

$\therefore \quad PF =$ Focal distance

$\Rightarrow \quad PF = \sqrt{(x-a)^2 + y^2} \quad$ [by distance formula]

$\Rightarrow \quad 4 = \sqrt{(x-2)^2 + 8x} \quad [\because y^2 = 8x]$

$\Rightarrow \quad 16 = x^2 - 4x + 4 + 8x$ [on squaring both sides]

$\Rightarrow \quad 16 = (x+2)^2$

$\Rightarrow \quad x + 2 = 4$

[taking positive square root on both sides]

$\Rightarrow \quad x = 2$

Now, $\quad y^2 = 8 \times 2 \Rightarrow y^2 = 16 \Rightarrow y = \pm 4$

Hence, coordinates of a point are (2, 4) and (2, – 4).

EXAMPLE 10. Find the length of the line segment joining the vertex of the parabola $y^2 = 4ax$ and a point on the parabola, where the line segment makes an angle θ to the X-axis.

Sol. Let equation of parabola be

$$y^2 = 4ax \quad \text{...(i)}$$

and its vertex is (0, 0).

Again, let any point on the parabola be $P(h, k)$.

On putting the values $x = h$ and $y = k$ in Eq. (i), we get

$$k^2 = 4ah \quad \text{...(ii)}$$

Let $OP(=l)$ be the line segment joining the vertex and point P. Also, it makes an angle θ with the X-axis.

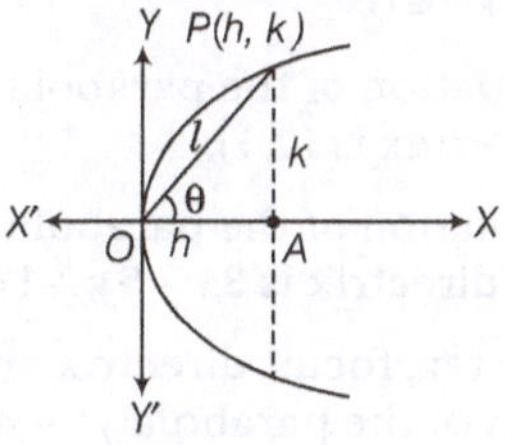

In right angled ΔOAP,

$$\sin\theta = \frac{PA}{OP} \Rightarrow \sin\theta = \frac{k}{l} \Rightarrow k = l\sin\theta$$

and $$\cos\theta = \frac{OA}{OP} \Rightarrow \cos\theta = \frac{h}{l} \Rightarrow h = l\cos\theta$$

On substituting the values of h and k in Eq. (ii), we get

$$l^2\sin^2\theta = 4al\cos\theta \Rightarrow l = \frac{4a\cos\theta}{\sin^2\theta},$$

which is the required length.

EXAMPLE 11. Prove that the line $lx + my + n = 0$ will touch the parabola $y^2 = 4ax$, if $ln = am^2$.

Sol. Given, equation of line is $lx + my + n = 0$.

$$\Rightarrow \quad y = \frac{-lx - n}{m} \quad \text{...(i)}$$

and equation of parabola is $y^2 = 4ax$ ...(ii)

From Eqs. (i) and (ii), we get

$$\left(\frac{-lx - n}{m}\right)^2 = 4ax$$

$$\Rightarrow \quad l^2x^2 + 2lxn + n^2 = 4m^2ax$$

$$\Rightarrow \quad l^2x^2 + 2lxn - 4am^2x + n^2 = 0$$

$$\Rightarrow \quad l^2x^2 + x(2ln - 4am^2) + n^2 = 0 \quad \text{...(iii)}$$

Since, the line $lx + my + n$ touches the parabola.

So, Eq. (iii) have equal roots.

i.e. Discriminant $(D) = 0 \Rightarrow B^2 - 4AC = 0$

$$\Rightarrow \quad (2ln - 4am^2)^2 - 4l^2n^2 = 0$$

$$\Rightarrow \quad 4l^2n^2 - 16lnam^2 + 16a^2m^4 - 4l^2n^2 = 0$$

$$\therefore \quad ln = am^2$$

Hence proved.

EXAMPLE 12. If the line $y = mx + 1$ is tangent to the parabola $y^2 = 4x$, then find the value of m.

Sol. Given, equation of line is $y = mx + 1$ ...(i)

and equation of parabola is $y^2 = 4x$ ...(ii)

On putting the value of y from Eq. (i) in Eq. (ii), we get

$$(mx + 1)^2 = 4x$$

$$\Rightarrow \quad m^2x^2 + 1 + 2mx - 4x = 0$$

$$\Rightarrow \quad x^2(m^2) + x(2m - 4) + 1 = 0$$

For the tangent, discriminant is zero i.e. $D = 0$.

$$\therefore \quad (2m - 4)^2 - 4m^2 \times 1 = 0 \quad [\because D = b^2 - 4ac = 0]$$

$$\Rightarrow \quad m = 1$$

EXAMPLE 13. Find the locus of the middle points of all chords of the parabola $y^2 = 4ax$ which are drawn through the vertex.

Sol. Let OA be a chord drawn through a vertex and $P(h, k)$ be its mid-points.

Let the coordinates of A be (x_1, y_1).

Then, $$\frac{x_1 + 0}{2} = h, \quad \frac{y_1 + 0}{2} = k$$

$$\Rightarrow \quad x_1 = 2h, \quad y_1 = 2k$$

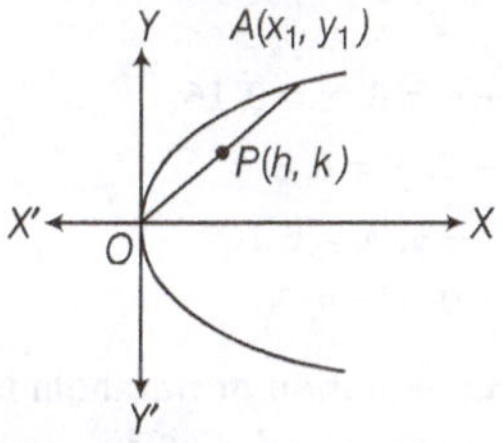

So, the coordinates of A are $(2h, 2k)$.

Since, A lies on $y^2 = 4ax$

$$\therefore \quad (2k)^2 = 4a(2h) \Rightarrow k^2 = 2ah$$

Hence, the locus of (h, k) is $y^2 = 2ax$.

Topic Practice 2

1 In each of the following questions, find the coordinates of the focus, the equation of the directrix, axis of the parabola and length of the latusrectum.

(i) $x^2 = -6y$

(ii) $x^2 = -16y$

(iii) $y^2 = 8x$

(iv) $y^2 = -16x$

(v) $x^2 = 36y$

2 Find the equation of the parabola whose focus is $(0, -3)$ and directrix is $y = 3$.

3 Find the equation of the parabola with vertex at the origin and focus at $(-2, 0)$.

4 Find the equation of the parabola with focus $(4, 0)$ and directrix is $x + 4 = 0$.

5 If the equation of the parabola is $x^2 = -8y$, then find the equation of directrix.

6 Find the equation of the parabola which is symmetric about the Y-axis and passes through the point $(2, -3)$.

7 Find the equation of the parabola with vertex at the origin, the axis along the X-axis and passing through the point $(2, 3)$.

8 The focal distance of a point on the parabola $y^2 = 12x$ is 4. Find the abscissa of this point.

9 If the parabola $y^2 = 4ax$ passes through the point $(3, 2)$, find the length of its latusrectum.

10 Find the vertex and the directrix of the parabola $y^2 - 3x - 2y + 7 = 0$.

11 Find the equation of the parabola whose focus is $(1, -1)$ and vertex is $(2, 1)$.

12 Find the equation of the parabola whose vertex is $(6, -3)$ and directrix is $3x - 5y + 1 = 0$.

13 Find the vertex, focus, directrix and length of the latusrectum of the parabola $y^2 - 4y - 2x - 8 = 0$.

14 Find the equation of the parabola whose focus is $(1, 1)$ and tangent at the vertex is $x + y = 1$.

15 Find the vertex, focus, directrix and length of latusrectum of the parabola $2y^2 + 3y - 4x - 3 = 0$.

Hints & Solutions

1. (i) $\left(0, \frac{-3}{2}\right)$, $y = \frac{3}{2}$, $x = 0$, 6

(ii) $(0, -4)$, $y - 4 = 0$, $x = 0$, 16

(iii) $(2, 0)$, $x = -2$, $y = 0$, 8

(iv) $(-4, 0)$, $x = -4$, $y = 0$, 16

(v) $(0, 9)$, $y = -9$, $x = 0$, 36

2. **Hint** Required equation of parabola is

$$x^2 + (y+3)^2 = \frac{(y-3)^2}{(\sqrt{1})^2}$$

Ans. $x^2 = -12y$

3. **Hint** Equation of parabola is $y^2 = 4ax = 4(-2)x$.

Ans. $y^2 = -8x$

4. **Hint** Equation of parabola is

$$(x-4)^2 + (y-0)^2 = \frac{(x+4)^2}{(\sqrt{1})^2}$$

Ans. $y^2 = 16x$

5. $y = 2$

6. **Hint** Parabola is symmetrical about Y-axis and passes through $(2, -3)$.

So, equation of parabola is of the form $x^2 = -4ay$.

On putting $x = 2$, $y = -3$, we get

$$4 = -4a(-3) \Rightarrow a = \frac{1}{3}$$

Ans. $3x^2 = -4y$

7. **Hint** Equation of parabola, whose axis is X-axis and passing through the point $(2, 3)$, will be of the form $y^2 = 4ax$.

On putting $x = 2$, $y = 3$, we get

$$9 = 4a(2) \Rightarrow a = \frac{9}{8}$$

Ans. $2y^2 = 9x$

8. **Hint** Given, parabola is $y^2 = 12x$.

Here, $4a = 12 \Rightarrow a = 3$

$\therefore$ Focus : $F = (3, 0)$

Let $P(x, y)$ be any point on the parabola, then $PF = 4$

$\Rightarrow (x-3)^2 + (y-0)^2 = (4)^2$

$\Rightarrow x^2 + 9 - 6x + 12x = 16$ $[\because y^2 = 12x]$

$\Rightarrow x^2 + 6x - 7 = 0$

$\Rightarrow x = 1$ $[\because x \neq -7]$

Ans. 1

9. **Hint** Parabola $y^2 = 4ax$ passes through the point (3, 2).

$\therefore \quad (2)^2 = 4a(3)$

$\Rightarrow \quad a = \frac{1}{3}$

Then, length of latusrectum $= 4a = \frac{4}{3}$

Ans. 4/3

10. **Hint** Given, parabola is $y^2 - 3x - 2y + 7 = 0$

$\Rightarrow \quad y^2 - 2y + 1 - 1 = 3x - 7$

$\Rightarrow \quad (y-1)^2 = 3(x-2)$

which is of the form $Y^2 = 4aX$, where $Y = y - 1$, $X = x - 2$

Ans. (2, 1), $4x - 5 = 0$

11. Solve as Example 4.

Ans. $4x^2 + y^2 - 4xy + 8x + 46y - 71 = 0$

12. Solve as Example 6.

Ans. $25x^2 + 9y^2 - 618x + 554y + 30xy + 4929 = 0$

13. **Hint** Given equation is

$$y^2 - 4y - 2x - 8 = 0$$

$$(y-2)^2 = 2(x+6)$$

For vertex, $y - 2 = 0 \Rightarrow y = 2$

$x + 6 = 0 \Rightarrow x = -6$

For focus, $x + 6 = \frac{1}{2}$ and $y - 2 = 0 \quad \left[\because a = \frac{1}{2}\right]$

For directrix,

$$x + 6 = -\frac{1}{2}$$

and length of latusrectum $= 4a = 4\left(\frac{1}{2}\right) = 2$

Ans. $(6, -2)$, $\left(-\frac{11}{2}, 2\right)$, $2x + 13 = 0$, 2

14. Solve as Example 6.

Ans. $x^2 + y^2 - 4x - 4y - 2xy + 4 = 0$

15. **Hint** Given, equation of parabola is $2y^2 + 3y - 4x - 3 = 0$.

$$\therefore \quad 2\left[y^2 + 2\cdot y\cdot\frac{3}{4} + \left(\frac{3}{4}\right)^2 - \left(\frac{3}{4}\right)^2\right] = 4x + 3$$

$$\Rightarrow \quad 2\left(y + \frac{3}{4}\right)^2 = 4x + 3 + \frac{9}{8}$$

$$\Rightarrow \quad \left(y + \frac{3}{4}\right)^2 = 2\left(x + \frac{33}{32}\right)$$

This is of the form $Y^2 = 4aX$, where

$$Y = y + \frac{3}{4}, X = x + \frac{33}{32}$$

Ans. $\left(\frac{-33}{32}, \frac{-3}{4}\right)$, $\left(\frac{-17}{32}, \frac{-3}{4}\right)$, $x = \frac{-49}{32}$, 2.

Exam Pattern Exercise

Part A - Objective Type Questions

Multiple Choice Type Questions

1 If two circles have same centre and different radii are called

(a) concentric circle (b) equal circle
(c) Both (a) and (b) (d) None of these

2 Find the equation of a circle whose centre is (2, – 3) and radius is 4.

(a) $x^2+y^2+4x-6y-3=0$
(b) $x^2+y^2-4x-6y-3=0$
(c) $x^2+y^2-4x+6y-3=0$
(d) $x^2+y^2-4x+6y+3=0$

3 A circle is the set of all points in a plane that are equidistant from a ...P... point in the ...Q... . Here, P and Q respectively are

(a) any, space (b) fixed, space
(c) any, plane (d) fixed, plane

4 If the equation of the circle with centre at (h, k) and radius r is $x^2+y^2=r^2$. Then, h and k respectively are

(a) (1, 1) (b) (–1, –1)
(c) (0, 0) (d) None of these

5 If the circle $x^2+y^2-kx-12y+4=0$ touches X-axis, then k is equal to

(a) 4 (b) –4
(c) Both (a) and (b) (d) None of these

6 If the line $y=\sqrt{3}x+k$ touches the circle $x^2+y^2=16$, then k is equal to

(a) ± 8 (b) ± 4 (c) ± 6 (d) ± 7

7 The vertex of the parabola $(y-2)^2=16(x-1)$ is

(a) (2, 1) (b) (1, 2) (c) (2, 2) (d) (2, 3)

8 If the vertex of the parabola $y=x^2-16x+k$ lies on X-axis, then k is equal to

(a) 63 (b) 64 (c) 58 (d) 62

9 Vertex of the parabola $9x^2-6x+36y+9=0$, is

(a) $\left(\frac{1}{3},-\frac{2}{9}\right)$ (b) $\left(-\frac{1}{3},-\frac{1}{2}\right)$
(c) $\left(-\frac{1}{3},\frac{1}{2}\right)$ (d) $\left(\frac{1}{3},\frac{1}{2}\right)$

10 The length of the latusrectum of the parabola $9x^2-6x+36y+19=0$, is

(a) 36 (b) 9 (c) 6 (d) 4

Assertion-Reason Based Questions

Directions (Q. Nos. 11-12) *In the questions given below are two statements labelled as Assertion (A) and Reason (R). In the context of the two statements, which one of the following is correct?*

(a) Both A and R are correct; R is the correct explanation of A
(b) Both A and R are correct; R is not the correct explanation of A
(c) A is correct; R is incorrect
(d) R is correct; A is incorrect

11 **Assertion (A)** If the coordinates of the end points of diameter are (– 1, 2) and (4, – 3), then the equation of circle is $x^2+y^2-3x+y-10=0$.

Reason (R) The equation of the circle drawn on the straight line joining two given points (x_1, y_1) and (x_2, y_2) as diameter is $(x-x_1)(x-x_2)+(y-y_1)(y-y_2)=0$.

12 **Assertion (A)** If the line $2x+3y+k=0$ touches the parabola $y^2=16x$, the value of k is 18.

Reason (R) If the line $lx+my+n=0$ touches the parabola $y^2=4ax$, then $ln=am^2$.

Part B - Descriptive Questions

Very Short Answer Type Questions

13 Find the equation of the circle of radius 5 units, whose centre lies on X-axis and passes through the point (2, 3).

14 If one end of a diameter of the circle $x^2+y^2-4x-6y+11=0$ is (3, 4), then find the coordinates of the other end of the diameter.

15 Find the equation of the parabola whose focus is (2, 0) and directrix is $x=-2$.

16 Find the equation of the parabola with vertex at origin, symmetric with respect to Y-axis and passing through (2, – 3).

17 Find the equation of the parabola with focus (6, 0) and directrix $x=-6$. Also, find the length of latusrectum.

Short Answer Type Questions

18 Find the centre and radius of each of the following circles.

(i) $\left(x-\frac{1}{2}\right)^2+\left(y+\frac{1}{3}\right)^2=\frac{1}{4}$

(ii) $x^2+y^2-4x+6y=5$

19 If the equations of the two diameters of a circle are $x+y=6$ and $x+2y=4$ and the radius of the circle is 10. Find the equation of the circle.

20 If two diameters of a circle lie along the lines $x-y=9$ and $x-2y=7$ and the area of the circle is 38.5 cm^2, then find the equation of the circle.

21 Find the equation of the circle concentric with the circle $x^2+y^2-4x-6y-3=0$ and which touches the Y-axis.

22 Find the coordinates of the focus and the vertex, the equation of directrix and the axis of the following

(i) $x^2=10y$ (ii) $3x^2=8y$

23 Find the coordinates of the focus and the vertex, equation of directrix and length of latusrectum of the following.

(i) $y^2=10x$ (ii) $5y^2=-16x$

24 Find the equation of the parabola with vertex at the origin, the axis along the X-axis and passing through the point (2, 3).

25 Find the equation of the parabola whose focus is (–1, 2) and directrix is $x-2y-15=0$.

26 Find the focus and directrix of the parabola $3x^2+12x+8y=0$.

Long Answer Type Questions

27 The sides of a rectangle are given by the equations $x=-2$, $x=4$, $y=-2$ and $y=5$. Find the equation of the circle drawn on the diagonal of this rectangle as its diameter.

28 Find the equation of a circle passing through the point (7, 3) having radius 3 units and whose centre lies on the line $y=x-1$.

29 In each of the following questions, find the coordinates of the focus, axis of the parabola, the equation of the directrix and the length of the latus rectum.

(i) $5y^2=-16x$ (ii) $x^2=10y$ (iii) $3x^2=8y$

30 Find the axis, vertex, directrix and length of latusrectum of the parabola $9y^2-16x-12y-57=0$.

Case Study Based Questions

31 Raj was working on the topic General Equation of a circle for his upcoming test. The equation of the circle having centre (h, k) and radius r is given by

$$(x-h)^2+(y-k^2)=r^2$$

$$\Rightarrow x^2+y^2-2hx-2ky+h^2+k^2-r^2=0,$$

which is of the form

$$x^2+y^2+2gx+2fy+c=0,$$

where $g=-h$, $f=-k$ and $c=h^2+k^2-r^2$

The above equation of a circle is called the general equation of a circle with centre $(-g,-f)$ and radius, $r=\sqrt{h^2+k^2-c}$ or $r=\sqrt{g^2+f^2-c}$

On the basis of above information, answer the following questions.

(i) Find the radius of the circle $x^2+y^2+6x-4y+4=0$.

(ii) Find the centre of the circle $x^2+y^2-6x+5y-8=0$.

(iii) Find the radius of the circle $x^2+y^2+4x+4y+4=0$.

Or

Find the centre of the circle $x^2+y^2-6x+12y+15=0$.

32 Salim made a flower-bed in his garden. Surprisingly which is in the shape of a parabola whose equation is $y^2=8x$, the flower-bed is shown as in below figure.

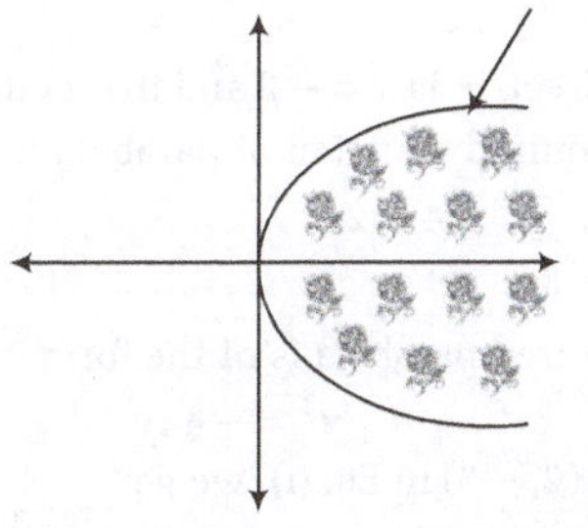

Then, answer the following questions which are based on above figure.

(i) Find the focus of given parabola.

(ii) Find axis of the parabola.

(iii) Find the equation of the directrix of the parabola.

Or

If the focal distance of a point on the parabola is 3, then find the abscissa of the point.

Hints & Solutions

1. (a) 2. (c) 3. (d) 4. (c)
5. (c) 6. (a) 7. (b) 8. (b)
9. (a) 10. (d) 11. (a) 12. (a)

13. **Hint** Let $C(k, 0)$ be the centre of the circle.

$\because$ Radius of the circle = 5 units

$\therefore$ Equation of the required circle is given by

$$(x-k)^2 + y^2 = 25 \quad \text{...(i)}$$

$\because$ Circle (i) passes through (2, 3), we get

$$(2-k)^2 + 9 = 25 \Rightarrow 2-k = \pm 4 \Rightarrow k = -2, 6$$

$\therefore$ From Eq. (i), required equation of circles are

$$(x+2)^2 + y^2 = 25 \text{ and } (x-6)^2 + y^2 = 25$$

14. **Hint** Given, equation of the circle is

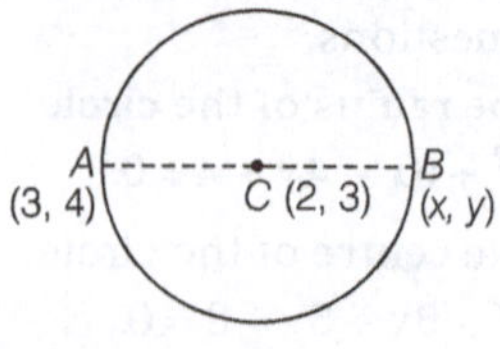

$$x^2 + y^2 - 4x - 6y + 11 = 0.$$

$\therefore$ $2g = -4$ and $2f = -6$

Since, the mid-point of AB is (2, 3).

Then, $2 = \dfrac{3+x}{2}$

$\therefore$ $x = 1$

and $3 = \dfrac{4+y}{2}$

$\Rightarrow$ $6 = 4 + y \Rightarrow y = 2$

So, the coordinates of other end of the diameter will be (1, 2).

15. **Hint** $\because$ Directrix is $x = -2$ and the focus is $(2, 0)$.

$\therefore$ i.e. Required equation of parabola is $y^2 = 4ax$

$\Rightarrow$ $y^2 = 4 \times 2x$ $\quad [\because a = 2]$

Ans. $y^2 = 8x$

16. **Hint** Required parabola is of the form

$$x^2 = -4ay \quad \text{...(i)}$$

Now, put $(2, -3)$ in Eq. (i), we get

$$4 = 12a \Rightarrow a = \frac{1}{3} \quad \text{...(ii)}$$

$\therefore$ From Eqs. (i) and (ii),

The equation of the parabola is

$$x^2 = -4\left(\frac{1}{3}\right)y \Rightarrow x^2 = -\frac{4}{3}y \Rightarrow 3x^2 = -4y$$

17. **Hint** Given, focus of the parabola $F(6, 0)$ and directrix, $x = -6$.

Now, let $P(x, y)$ be any point on the parabola and MP be the perpendicular distance from P to the directrix.

$\Rightarrow$ $FP = MP$

$$\therefore \sqrt{(x-6)^2 + (y-0)^2} = \frac{|x+6|}{1} \Rightarrow y^2 = 24x$$

Above equation is of the form $y^2 = 4ax \Rightarrow 4a = 24$

$\therefore$ Length of latusrectum $= 4a = 24$ units

18. (i) $\left(\frac{1}{2}, -\frac{1}{3}\right)$ and $\frac{1}{2}$ (ii) $(2, -3)$ and $3\sqrt{2}$

19. $x^2 + y^2 - 16x + 4y - 32 = 0$

20. $4x^2 + 4y^2 - 88x - 16y + 451 = 0$

21. **Hint** Given, $x^2 + y^2 - 4x - 6y - 3 = 0$

$\Rightarrow$ $(x^2 - 4x + 4) + (y^2 - 6y + 9) = 3 + 4 + 9$

$\Rightarrow$ $(x-2)^2 + (y-3)^2 = (4)^2$

$\therefore$ Centre of the required circle is (2, 3).

As it touches Y-axis, so its radius = x-coordinate of centre = 2.

Ans. The required circle is $(x-2)^2 + (y-3)^2 = (2)^2$

$x^2 + y^2 - 4x - 6y + 9 = 0$

22. (i) $F\left(0, \frac{5}{2}\right)$; $O(0, 0)$; $2y + 5 = 0$; $x = 0$

(ii) $F\left(0, \frac{2}{3}\right)$, $O(0, 0)$; $3y + 2 = 0$; $x = 0$

23. (i) $F\left(\frac{5}{2}, 0\right)$; $O(0, 0)$; $2x + 5 = 0$; 10 units

(ii) $F\left(-\frac{4}{5}, 0\right)$; $O(0, 0)$; $5X - 4 = 0$; $\frac{16}{5}$ units

24. $y^2 = \frac{9}{2}x$

25. $4x^2 + 4xy + y^2 + 40x - 80y - 200 = 0$

26. Focus $\equiv \left(-2, \frac{5}{6}\right)$ and directrix, $y = \frac{13}{6}$

27. **Hint** Let $A(-2, -2)$, $B(-2, 5)$, $C(4, 5)$, $D(4, -2)$

So, diagonals are AC and BD.

Find the diametrical equation of circle of any above given diagonal.

$$(x-x_1)(x-x_2) + (y-y_1)(y-y_2) = 0$$

Ans. $x^2 + y^2 - 2x - 3y - 18 = 0$

28. **Hint** Let equation of circle be

$$(x-h)^2 + (y-k)^2 = r^2$$

$\Rightarrow$ $(x-h)^2 + (y-k)^2 = (3)^2$ ...(i)

Given that, centre (h, k) lies on the line

$$y = x - 1 \text{ i.e. } k = h - 1 \quad \text{...(ii)}$$

$\therefore$ $(7-h)^2 + (3-k)^2 = (3)^2$

$\Rightarrow$ $h^2 + k^2 - 14h - 6k + 49 = 0$ ...(iii)

On putting $k = h - 1$ in Eq. (iii), we get

$$h^2 + (h-1)^2 - 14h - 6(h-1) + 49 = 0$$

$\therefore$ $h = 4, 7$

When $h=7$, then $k=7-1=6$

$\therefore$ Centre $=(7, 6)$

When $h=4$, then $k=3$

$\therefore$ Centre $=(4, 3)$

So, the required equation of circle when centre (7, 6), is

$$(x-7)^2+(y-6)^2=(3)^2$$

$$\Rightarrow \quad x^2+y^2-14x-12y+76=0$$

When centre (4, 3), then the equation of the circle is

$$(x-4)^2+(y-3)^2=9$$

$$\Rightarrow \quad x^2+y^2-8x-6y+16=0$$

29. (i) **Hint** Given, equation of parabola is $5y^2=-16x$

or $y^2=-\frac{16}{5}x$, which is of the form $y^2=-4ax$.

$\Rightarrow \quad a=\frac{4}{5}$

$\therefore \quad$ Focus $=(-a, 0)=\left(-\frac{4}{5}, 0\right)$

Axis = X-axis

Directrix, $x=a \Rightarrow x=\frac{4}{5}$

and length of latusrectum $=4a$ **Ans.** $\frac{16}{5}$ units

(ii) Given, equation of parabola is $x^2=10y$, which is of the form $x^2=4ay$.

$\Rightarrow \quad a=\frac{5}{2}$

$\therefore \quad$ Focus $=(0, a)=\left(0, \frac{5}{2}\right)$; Axis = Y-axis

Directrix, $y=-a \Rightarrow y=-\frac{5}{2}$

and length of latusrectum $=4a$ **Ans.** 10 units

(iii) **Hint** Given, equation of parabola is $3x^2=8y$

or $x^2=\frac{8}{3}y$, which is of the form $x^2=4ay$.

$\Rightarrow \quad a=\frac{2}{3}$

$\therefore \quad$ Focus $=(0, a)=\left(0, \frac{2}{3}\right)$; Axis = Y-axis

Directrix, $y=-a \Rightarrow y=-\frac{2}{3}$

and length of latusrectum $=4a$ **Ans.** $\frac{8}{3}$ units

30. Given, equation of parabola is

$$9y^2-16x-12y-57=0$$

$$\Rightarrow (3y)^2-2\times 2\times 3y+2^2=2^2+57+16x$$

$$\Rightarrow (3y-2)^2=61+16x$$

$$\Rightarrow 9\left(y-\frac{2}{3}\right)^2=16\left(x+\frac{61}{16}\right)$$

$$\Rightarrow \left(y-\frac{2}{3}\right)^2=\frac{16}{9}\left(x+\frac{61}{16}\right) \quad \text{...(i)}$$

Let $\quad Y=y-\frac{2}{3}$ and $X=x+\frac{61}{16}$ ...(ii)

$\therefore \quad Y^2-\frac{16}{9}X$ [from Eqs. (i) and ii]] ...(iii)

Now, the equation of axis of parabola (iii) is $Y=0$

$\therefore \quad y-\frac{2}{3}=0 \Rightarrow y=\frac{2}{3}$

Coordinates of vertices of parabola (iii) are $X=0$ and $Y=0$

i.e. $\quad y-\frac{2}{3}=0 \Rightarrow x=-\frac{61}{16}$ and $y=\frac{2}{3}$

On comparing Eq. (iii) with $y^2=4ax$, we get

$$4a=\frac{16}{9} \Rightarrow a=\frac{4}{9}$$

$\therefore$ Equation of directrix of parabola (iii) is $X=-a$

i.e. $\quad x+\frac{61}{16}=-\frac{4}{9} \Rightarrow x=-\frac{613}{144}$

and length of latusrectum $=|4a|=\left|4\times\frac{4}{9}\right|=\frac{16}{9}$

31. (i) 3 (ii) $\left(3, \frac{-5}{2}\right)$ (iii) 2 *Or* $(3, -6)$

32. (i) (2, 0) (ii) X-axis (iii) $(x+2)=0$ *Or* 1

SAMPLE QUESTION PAPER 1

A Highly Simulated Sample Question Paper for CBSE Class XI Examination

APPLIED MATHEMATICS (Unsolved)

Time 3 Hours **Max. Marks 80**

General Instructions

Read the following instructions very carefully and strictly follow them.

(i) This question paper contains 38 questions. All questions are compulsory.

(ii) Question paper is divided into FIVE sections - Section A, B, C, D and E.

(iii) In Section A, Question number 1 to 18 are Multiple Choice Questions (MCQs) and Question number 19 and 20 are Assertion-Reason based questions carrying 1 mark each.

(iv) In Section B, Question number 21 to 25 are Very Short Answer (VSA) type questions carrying 2 marks each.

(v) In Section C, Question number 26 to 31 are Short Answer (SA) type questions carrying 3 marks each.

(vi) In Section D, Question number 32 to 35 are Long Answer (LA) type questions carrying 5 marks each.

(vii) In Section E, Question number 36 to 38 are Case Study Based question carrying 4 marks each.

(viii) There is no overall choice. However, an internal choice has been provided in 2 questions in Section B, 2 questions in Section C, 2 questions in Section D and 3 questions in Section E.

(ix) Use of calculator is NOT allowed.

SECTION A

Multiple Choice Questions

Each question carries 1 mark

Directions (Q. Nos. 1-18) *All questions are compulsory. No Internal Choice is provided in this section.*

1. The binary equivalent of the decimal number 21 is

(a) 101011 (b) 11001
(c) 10101 (d) 11010

2. If $\log_{0.5} 64 = x$, then the value of x is

(a) -4 (b) -6
(c) 4 (d) 6

3. If $5^{3x} = 125$ and $10^y = 0.001$, then the value of $5x + y$ is

(a) 1 (b) 2 (c) 4 (d) 6

4. The angle between two hands of a clock at 8 : 30 am is

(a) 75° (b) 80°
(c) 85° (d) 45°

5. What was the day of the week on 16th July, 1776?

(a) Friday (b) Saturday
(c) Sunday (d) Tuesday

6. $\dfrac{\log_3 8}{\log_9 16 \log_4 10}$ is equal to

(a) $3\log_{10} 2$ (b) $2\log_{10} 3$
(c) $5\log_{10} 2$ (d) None of these

7. Let A and B be two sets such that $n(A) = 17$, $n(B) = 12$ and $n(A \cup B) = 21$. Then, $n(A \cap B)$ is

(a) 18 (b) 5
(c) 8 (d) 26

8. Let R be a relation of N defined by $x + 2y = 8$. The domain of R is

(a) {2, 4, 8} (b) {2, 4, 6, 8}
(c) {2, 4, 6} (d) {1, 2, 3, 4}

9. Let S_n denote the sum of first n terms of an AP. If $S_{2n} = 3S_n$, then $S_{3n} : S_n$ is equal to

(a) 4 (b) 6
(c) 8 (d) 10

10. In how many ways two different rings can be worn in four fingers with atmost one in each finger?
(a) 12 (b) 14
(c) 16 (d) 10

11. If 'VIOLET' is coded as XKQNGV, then 'YELLOW' will be coded as
(a) ZFMMPX (b) AGNNQY
(c) ANGNYQ (d) EJDFTI

12. If $x \neq 1$ and $f(x) = \frac{x+2}{x-1}$ is a real function, then $f(f(f(2)))$ is
(a) 6 (b) 3
(c) 4 (d) 2

13. If $f(x) = \frac{(3x+1)(2\sqrt{x}-1)}{\sqrt{x}}$, then $f'(1)$ is equal to
(a) 5 (b) –5
(c) 6 (d) $\frac{11}{2}$

14. 4 cards are drawn from a well-shuffled deck of 52 cards. Thus, the probability of obtaining 3 diamonds and 1 spade is
(a) $\frac{^{13}C_1 \times {}^{12}C_1}{^{52}C_1}$ (b) $\frac{^{13}C_3 \times {}^{13}C_1}{^{52}C_4}$
(c) $\frac{^{13}C_1 \times {}^{13}C_2}{^{52}C_2}$ (d) $\frac{^{13}C_3 \times {}^{13}C_2}{^{51}C_4}$

15. The coefficient of correlation is
(a) greater than the coefficient of determination.
(b) the square of the coefficient of determination
(c) the square root of the coefficient of determination
(d) equal to the coefficient of determination

16. The score of a Mathematics test of 10 students are given below
17, 28, 25, 29, 19, 26, 29, 20, 13, 30
The percentile rank of score 29 is
(a) 75 (b) 80
(c) 85 (d) 90

17. The amount of regular annuity of ₹1000 payable at the end of each year for 3 yr of at 10% per annum compounded annually is
(a) ₹ 3310 (b) ₹ 3300
(c) ₹ 3410 (d) ₹ 3515

18. If the parabola $y^2 = 4ax$ passes through the point (3, 2), then the length fo latusrectum is
(a) $\frac{2}{3}$ (b) $\frac{4}{3}$ (c) $\frac{1}{3}$ (d) 4

Assertion-Reason Based Questions

Directions *In the question number 19 and 20, a statement of Assertion (A) is followed by a statement of Reason (R). Choose the correct option.*
(a) Both (A) and (R) are true and (R) is the correct explanation of (A).
(b) Both (A) and (R) are true but (R) is not the correct explanation of (A).
(c) (A) is true but (R) is false.
(d) (A) is false but (R) is true.

19. **Assertion** (A) If $n(A) = 3$ and $B = \{1,3,5,7,6\}$, then the number of relations from A to B is 2^{20}.
Reason (R) If A and B be any two non-empty finite sets containing m and n elements, respectively, then total number of relations from set A to B is 2^{mn}.

20. **Assertion** (A) If $^{n-1}C_r : {}^nC_r : {}^{n+1}C_r = 6:9:13$, then values of n and r are 12 and 4, respectively.
Reason (R) $^nC_r = \frac{n!}{r!(n-r)!}$

SECTION B

[This section comprises of very short answer type questions (VSA) of 2 marks each]

21. (a) A and B are two sets such that $n(A-B) = 12 + x$, $n(B-A) = 2x$ and $n(A \cap B) = x$. Draw a Venn diagram to illustrate this information and if $n(A) = n(B)$, then find the value of x.

Or

(b) Is the relation R on the set Q of rational numbers defined by $R = \{(x,y): x, y \in Q, x < y^2\}$, symmetric? Justify your answer.

22. A clock gains 4 sec in 3 min and was set right at 9 : 00 am. What time will it show at 11 : 00 pm on the same day?

23. (a) Show that $f(x) = \begin{cases} \frac{|x+a|}{x-a}, & x \neq a \\ 1, & x = a \end{cases}$ is discontinuous at $x = a$.

Or

(b) Find $\frac{dy}{dx}$ when $x^2 + xy + y^2 = 100$

24. A committee of 8 persons is to be constituted from a group of 9 gents and 8 ladies. If the selection is made randomly, then find the probability that there are 5 ladies and 3 gents in the committee.

25. If the line $y = \sqrt{3}x + k$ touches the circle $x^2 + y^2 = 16$, then find the value of k.

SECTION C

[This section comprises of short answer type questions (SA) of 3 marks each]

26. (a) A and B can do piece of work in 9 days and 18 days, respectively. As they were ill, they could do 90% and 72% of their efficiency, respectively. How many days will they take to complete the work together?

Or

(b) A can complete $\frac{1}{3}$ of a work in 5 days and B can complete $\frac{2}{5}$ of the work in 10 days. In how many days both A and B together can complete the work.

27. The sum of first three terms of a GP is 16 and the sum of the next three terms is 128. Determine the first term, common ratio and the sum of n term of the GP.

28. Find $\lim_{x \to 0} f(x)$ and $\underset{x \to 1}{Lt} f(x)$, where

$$f(x)=\begin{cases} 3x+2, & x \le 0 \\ 2(x+1), & x > 0 \end{cases}$$

29. The probability of an event A occurring is $\frac{2}{3}$ and the probability of event B not occurring is $\frac{5}{7}$. If the probability of getting success in atleast one of the two events is $\frac{4}{5}$, what is the probability of success in both the events?

30. (a) Find the mean and variance of first 10 multiples of 3.

Or

(b) If in a sample of n observations, we have $\Sigma d^2 = 30$ and Spearman's rank correlation $r = \frac{9}{11}$, then find the value of n.

31. Find the value of k, so that the line $2x + ky - 9 = 0$ may be

(i) parallel to $3x - 4y + 7 = 0$

(ii) perpendicular to $3y + 2x - 1 = 0$

SECTION D

[This section comprises of long answer type questions (LA) of 5 marks each]

32. (a) At what time between 7 O' clock and 8 O' clock in the morning, will the both hands of a clock be a right angle?

Or

(b) If Republic day was celebrated in 1996 on Friday, then on which day in 2000 Independence day was celebrated?

33. (a) A sum of ₹ 3254 is borrowed from a money lender at 6% per annum compounded annually. If this amount is to be paid back in 4 equal annual instalments, then find the annual instalment.

Or

(b) An annuity consists of 20 quarterly instalments of ₹ 1200 each, the first being made at the end of 3 yr. Find the amount of this anniuty, if money is worth 8% per annum compounded quarterly.

34. Out of 100 students, two sections of 40 and 60 are formed. If you and your friend are among the 100 students, then what is the probability that

(i) you both enter the same section?

(ii) you both enter the different sections?

35. An equilateral triangle is inscribed in the parabola $y^2 = 4ax$ whose one vertex is at the vertex of the parabola, find the length of the side of the triangle.

SECTION E

[This section comprises 3 case-study/passage based questions of 4 marks each with sub parts. The first two case study questions have three sub parts (i), (ii), (iii) of marks 1, 1, 2 respectively. The third case study question has two sub parts (i), (ii) of 2 marks each]

36. Mr. Abhishek Dubey a Mathematics teacher of class XIth write a problem on black board to test preparation about the topic 'Relation and function. The problem is describe as following Let A be set of first ten natural numbers and let R be a relation on A defined by

$$(x, y) \in R \Leftrightarrow x + 2y = 14$$

i.e. $R = \{(x, y) : x \in A, y \in A \text{ and } x + 2y = 14\}$.

Then, answer the following questions which are based on above problem.

(i) Find the relation (R).

(a) {(2, 4), (4, 3), (6, 2), (8, 1)}
(b) {(2, 6), (4, 5), (6, 4), (8, 3)}
(c) {(4, 2), (3, 4), (2, 6), (1, 8)}
(d) None of the above

(ii) Find the R^{-1}.

(a) {(4, 2), (3, 4), (2, 6), (1, 8)}
(b) {(6, 2), (5, 4), (4, 6), (3, 8)}
(c) {(2, 4), (4, 3), (6, 2), (8, 1)}
(d) {(2, 6), (4, 5), (6, 4), (8, 3)}

(iii) Find Dom (R).

(a) {2, 4, 6, 8}
(b) {3, 5, 6, 8}
(c) {4, 3, 2, 1}
(d) {4, 5, 6, 8}

Or

Find Range (R).

(a) {6, 5, 4, 3} (b) {6, 3, 8, 7}
(c) {2, 4, 8, 10} (d) {5, 3, 1, 9}

37. Mr. Ankit Triwedi a Mathematics teacher of class XI write two things about Mohan and Sohan which are below in figure.

	Mohan	Sohan
Age	${}^nP_r$	${}^nP_{r+1}$
Height (in feet)	${}^nC_r$	${}^nC_{r-1}$

Now, answer the following question which are based on above data.

(i) If the age of Mohan and Sohan are equal, then find the value of $(n-r)$.

(a) 1 (b) –1
(c) –2 (d) 2

(ii) Which of the following formula is used to find ${}^nP_r$?

(a) $\frac{n!}{(n-r)!}$ (b) $\frac{(n-r)!}{n!}$
(c) $\frac{n!}{(n+r)!}$ (d) $\frac{n!}{r!(n-r)!}$

(iii) If the height of Mohan and Sohan are equal, then find the value of $(n-2r)$.

(a) 1 (b) –1
(c) 2 (d) –2

Or

Find the age of Mohan

(a) 6 yr (b) 4 yr
(c) 8 yr (d) 9 yr

38. In financial year 2019-20 Mr Narendra Kumar Mani's (age 55 yr) income from salary was ₹ 1500000 (exclusive of HRA) and income from interest on saving account was ₹ 18600. He deposited ₹ 15000 per month in GPF and paid ₹ 57000 as LIC premium. He donated ₹ 100000 in Prime Minister's National relief fund. He paid ₹ 31600 as interest on education loan for higher studies of his daughter. He also, paid ₹ 212500 as interest on home loan and ₹ 63450 as principal of home loan.

Income Tax Slab for Financial Year 2018-20
(For individual tax payers below the age of 60 yr)

Taxable Income	Income Tax
Upto ₹ 25000	NIL
₹ 250001 to ₹ 5000000	5% of taxable income exceeding ₹ 250000
₹ 500001 to ₹ 1000000	₹ 12500 + 20% of taxable income exceeding ₹ 500000
Above ₹ 1000000	₹ 112500 + 30% of taxable income exceeding ₹ 1000000

Based on the above information, answer the following questions

(i) The total amount inversted or paid by Mr. Mani under Section 80 C is

(a) ₹ 180000 (b) ₹ 237000
(c) ₹ 300450 (d) ₹ 332050

(ii) The amount donated by Mr. Mani in Prime Minister's National relief fund is deductable under section is

(a) 80E (b) 80G
(c) 80TTA (d) None of these

Or

The taxable income of Mr. Mani is

(a) ₹ 945900 (b) ₹ 977500
(c) ₹ 987500 (d) ₹ 980000

SAMPLE QUESTION PAPER 2

A Highly Simulated Sample Question Paper for CBSE Class XI Examination

APPLIED MATHEMATICS (Unsolved)

Time 3 Hours **Max. Marks 80**

General Instructions

Read the following instructions very carefully and strictly follow them.

(i) This question paper contains 38 questions. All questions are compulsory.

(ii) Question paper is divided into FIVE sections - Section A, B, C, D and E.

(iii) In Section A, Question number 1 to 18 are Multiple Choice Questions (MCQs) and Question number 19 and 20 are Assertion-Reason based questions carrying 1 mark each.

(iv) In Section B, Question number 21 to 25 are Very Short Answer (VSA) type questions carrying 2 marks each.

(v) In Section C, Question number 26 to 31 are Short Answer (SA) type questions carrying 3 marks each.

(vi) In Section D, Question number 32 to 35 are Long Answer (LA) type questions carrying 5 marks each.

(vii) In Section E, Question number 36 to 38 are Case Study Based question carrying 4 marks each.

(viii) There is no overall choice. However, an internal choice has been provided in 2 questions in Section B, 2 questions in Section C, 2 questions in Section D and 3 questions in Section E.

(ix) Use of calculator is NOT allowed.

SECTION A

Multiple Choice Questions

Each question carries 1 mark

Directions (Q. Nos. 1-18) *All question are compulsory. No Internal Choice is provided in this section.*

1. The value of $2 + \log_{10}(0.01)$ is

(a) 4 (b) 3

(c) 1 (d) 0

2. If each observation of the data is decreased by 7, then their mean

(a) remains the same.

(b) become 7 times the original mean.

(c) is decreased by 7.

(d) is increased by 7.

3. A watch gains 5 min in an hour and was set right at 7 am. What time will it show at 6 pm on the same day?

(a) 7 pm (b) 6 : 55 pm

(c) 5 : 55 pm (d) 7 : 05 pm

4. If the ratio of the diameters of the two spheres is 4 : 7, then the ratio of their surface area is

(a) 7 : 4 (b) 4 : 7

(c) 64 : 343 (d) 16 : 49

5. For any two sets $A \cup B = A$ iff

(a) $B \subseteq A$ (b) $A \subseteq B$

(c) $A \neq B$ (d) $A = B$

6. If R is the relation on the set $A = \{1,2,3\}$ given by $R = \{(1,1),(1,2),(2,1)\}$, then R is

(a) reflexive (b) symmetric

(c) transitive (d) None of these

7. How many two-digit numbers are divisible by 4?

(a) 21 (b) 22

(c) 24 (d) 25

8. If the letters of the word 'RACHIT' are arranged in all possible ways as listed in the dictionary, then the rank of the word 'RACHIT' is

(a) 480 (b) 481

(c) 482 (d) 483

9. A woman introduces a man as the son of the brother of her mother. How is that man related to the woman?

(a) Son (b) Uncle
(c) Nephew (d) Cousin

10. The domain of the function f defined by $f(x)=\frac{x^2+2x+1}{x^2-x-6}$ is

(a) $R-[3,-2]$ (b) $R-\{-3,2\}$
(c) $R-\{3,-2\}$ (d) $R-(-3,2)$

11. $\lim_{x\to 3}\frac{e^x-e^3}{x-3}$ is equal to

(a) e^3 (b) e^x
(c) 4 (d) 5

12. If A and B are mutually exclusive events, then

(a) $P(B)\le P(\overline{A})$ (b) $P(B)\ge P(\overline{A})$
(c) $P(B)=P(\overline{A})$ (d) None of these

13. If $P(A)=0.4, P(B)=0.8$ and $P(B/A)=0.6$, then $P(A\cup B)$ is equal to

(a) 0.24 (b) 0.96
(c) 0.3 (d) 0.48

14. Mode of the data 15, 14, 19, 20, 14, 15, 16, 14, 15, 18, 14, 19, 15, 17, 15 is

(a) 14 (b) 15
(c) 16 (d) 17

15. The coefficient of correlation is independent of

(a) change of scale but not of origin
(b) change of origin but not of scale
(c) change of origin and scale both
(d) neither change of origin nor of scale

16. Section 80TTA refers to the deduction of

(a) interest on home loan
(b) interest on education loan
(c) interest on saving account
(d) interest on fixed deposit

17. The equation of two diameters of a circle are $x-y=5$ and $2x+y=4$ and the radius of the circle is 5, then the equation of the circle is

(a) $x^2+y^2-6x+4y-12=0$
(b) $x^2+y^2+6x-4y-12=0$
(c) $x^2+y^2+6x+4y+12=0$
(d) $x^2+y^2-6x+4y+12=0$

18. Which of following represent the left hand parabola?

(a) $y^2=-4ax, a>0$ (b) $y^2=4ax, a>0$
(c) $x^2=4ay, a>0$ (d) $x^2=-4ay, a>0$

Assertion-Reason Based Questions

Directions *In the question number 19 and 20, a statement of Assertion (A) is followed by a statement of Reason (R). Choose the correct option.*

(a) Both (A) and (R) are true and (R) is the correct explanation of (A).
(b) Both (A) and (R) are true but (R) is not the correct explanation of (A).
(c) (A) is true but (R) is false.
(d) (A) is false but (R) is true.

19. **Assertion** (A) The angle traced by hour hand in 15 min is $7\frac{1}{2}^{\circ}$.

Reason (R) Hour hand traces an angle of 6° in one minute.

20. **Assertion** (A) Mode of the given data 3,5,1,2,4,6,0,2,2,3 is 2

Reason (R) Mode of an ungrouped data is the observation which has minimum frequency.

SECTION B

[This section comprises of very short answer type questions (VSA) of 2 marks each]

21. (a) If one man or two women or three boys can finish a work in 88 days, then how many days will one man, one women and one boy together take to finish the same work?

Or

(b) Two trains 110 m and 90 m long are running in opposite directions at 40 km/h and 50 km/h. In what time will they cross each other completely from the moment they meet?

22. From the adjoining Venn diagram, determine the following sets

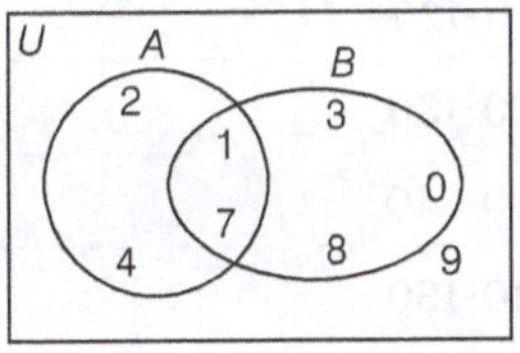

(i) $A\cup B$ (ii) $A-B$

23. (a) Find the number of permutations of the letters of the word HYDERABAD.

Or

(b) A tea party is arranged for 18 people along two sides of a long table with 9 chairs on each side. Four men wish to sit on one particular side and three on the other side. In how many ways can they be seated?

24. How much will ₹ 35000 amount to in 2 yr, at compound interest, if the rates for the successive years are 4% and 5% per year?

25. Find the equation of the circle when the end points of a diameter are $A(-2,3)$ and $B(3,-5)$.

SECTION C

[This section comprises of short answer type questions (SA) of 3 marks each]

26. (a) Let Z be the set of all integers and R be a relation on Z defined as $R=\{(a,b):a,b \in z$ and $(a-b)$ is divisible by $2\}$. Prove that R is an equivalence relation.

Or

(b) If the first and the nth terms of a GP are a and b respectively and if P is the product of first n terms, prove that $p^2=(ab)^n$.

27. Find the domain and the range of the function f defined by $f(x)=\dfrac{x+3}{|x+3|}$.

28. (a) Find the points on the curve $y=x^3$ at which the slope of the tangent is equal to the y-coordinate of the point.

Or

(b) Find the point at which the tangent to the curve $y=\sqrt{4x-3}-1$ has its slope $\dfrac{2}{3}$.

29. The weights (in kg) of 50 wrestlers are recorded in the following table

Weight (in kg)	Number of wrestlers
100-110	4
110-120	14
120-130	21
130-140	8
140-150	3

Find the mean weight of wrestlers by using short cut method.

30. Find the amount of regular annuity of ₹ 5000 payable at the end of each year of 3 yr at 10% per annum compounded annually.

31. If the coordinates of two points A and B are (1, 2) and (3, 8) respectively, then find a point P such that $|PA|=|PB|$ and area of $\Delta PAB=10$.

SECTION D

[This section comprises of long answer type questions (LA) of 5 marks each]

32. (a) In a survey of 200 students of a school, it was found that 120 study Mathematics, 90 study Physics and 70 study Chemistry, 40 study Mathematices and Physics, 30 study Physics and Chemistry, 50 study Chemistry and Mathematics and 20 none of these subjects. Find the number of students who study all the three subjects.

Or

(b) Let $A=\{8,11,12,15,18,23\}$ and f is a function from $A \rightarrow N$, such that $f(x)=$ highest prime factor of x, find f and its range and also find the domain of the function f defined by $f(x)=\dfrac{x^2+2x+1}{x^2-8x+12}$

33. (a) The population of two states A and B are 8.25×10^7 and 1.11×10^8 respectively. If the rate of growth in these states be 2.7% and 2.6% respectively. In how many years the population of two states will be equal?

Or

(b) Find the area of a quadrilateral $ABCD$ in which $AB=143$ cm, $BC=154$ cm, $CD=60$ cm, $AD=125$ cm and diagonal $AC=165$ cm.

34. Calculated Spearman's rank correlation coefficient between the advertisement cost and sales from the following data.

Advertisement cost (in ₹ thousand)	39	65	62	90	82	75	25	98	36	78
Sales (in ₹ lakh)	47	53	58	86	62	68	60	91	51	84

35. Prove that the radius of the circles $x^2+y^2=1, x^2+y^2-2x-6y=6$ and $x^2+y^2-4x-12y=9$ are in AP.

SECTION E

[This section comprises 3 case-study/passage based questions of 4 marks each with sub parts. The first two case study questions have three sub parts (i), (ii), (iii) of marks 1, 1, 2 respectively. The third case study question has two sub parts (i), (ii) of 2 marks each]

36. In a certain city all telephone numbers have seven digits. City is divided into 6 zones. Each zone is allotted a specific non-zero digit which is to be used as first digit of all telephone numbers of that zone.

Based on the above information, answer the following questions

(i) How many different telephone numbers are there in each zone, if the digit on first place is not used again?

(a) 9^6 (b) 10^6

(c) ${}^{10}P_6$ (d) ${}^{9}P_6$

(ii) How many different telephone numbers are there in the city, if there is not restriction?

(a) 6×9^6 (b) 6×10^6

(c) $6\times {}^{10}P_6$ (d) $6\times {}^{9}P_6$

(iii) How many different telephone numbers are there in each zone with all digits distinct?

(a) 9^6 (b) 10^6

(c) ${}^{10}P_6$ (d) ${}^{9}P_6$

Or

How many different telephone numbers are there in each zone, if repetition of digits is allowed?

(a) 9^6 (b) 10^6

(c) ${}^{10}P_6$ (d) ${}^{9}P_6$

37. The reliability of a Covid-19 test is specified as follows

Of people having Covid-19, 90% of the test detect the disease but 10% go undetected. Of people free of Covid-19, 99% of the test are judged Covid-19 negative but 1% are diagnosed as showing Covid-19 positive .

From a large population of which only 0.1% have Covid-19, one person is selected at random, given the Covid-19 test and Pathologist reports him/her as Covid-19 positive.

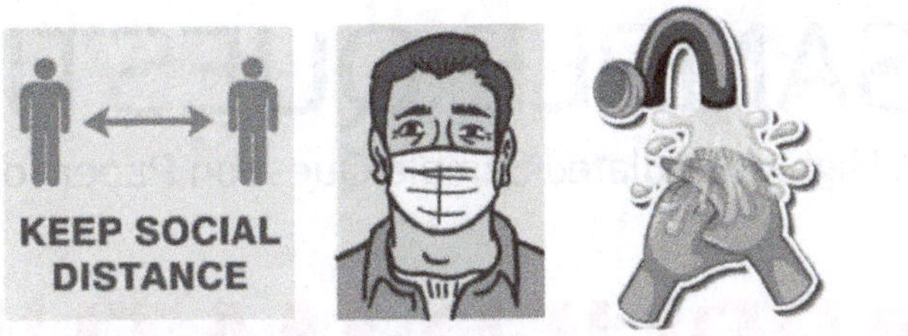

Keep Social distancing   Wearing Mask   Regular Washing of Hands

Based on the above information, answer the following question

(i) What is the probability of the person to be tested as Covid-19 positive given that he is actually having Covid-19

(a) 0.001 (b) 0.1 (c) 0.8 (d) 0.9

(ii) What is the probability of the person to be tested as Covid-19 positive given that he is not actually having Covid-19?

(a) 0.01 (b) 0.99 (c) 0.1 (d) 0.001

(iii) What is the probability that the person is actually not having Covid-19?

(a) 0.998 (b) 0.999 (c) 0.001 (d) 0.111

Or

What is the probability that the person is actually having Covid-19?

(a) 0.998 (b) 0.999 (c) 0.001 (d) 0.111

38. Study the following information carefully to answer the given questions.

Seven boxes S, P, L, Q, R, M and I are places one above the other in any particular order. Box number 1 is at the bottom and box number 7 is at the top. Three boxes are placed between I and M. M is placed on the place just above S, which did not place on an odd numbered place. P is neither placed on odd number place nor on topmost place. I did not place on bottom place. Two boxes are placed between R and S. Q is placed neither on the bottom nor onthe fourth place. Box M is not placed on top place.

(i) Which box is placed on just above M?

(ii) How many boxes are there between L and P?

(iii) Which of the above pairs of boxes is placed on bottom must and the topmost place, respectively?

Or

Which of the above box is placed on the topmost place?

SAMPLE QUESTION PAPER 3

A Highly Simulated Sample Question Paper for CBSE Class XI Examination

APPLIED MATHEMATICS (Unsolved)

Time 3 Hours **Max. Marks 80**

General Instructions

Read the following instructions very carefully and strictly follow them.

(i) This question paper contains 38 questions. All questions are compulsory.
(ii) Question paper is divided into FIVE sections - Section A, B, C, D and E.
(iii) In Section A, Question number 1 to 18 are Multiple Choice Questions (MCQs) and Question number 19 and 20 are Assertion-Reason based questions carrying 1 mark each.
(iv) In Section B, Question number 21 to 25 are Very Short Answer (VSA) type questions carrying 2 marks each.
(v) In Section C, Question number 26 to 31 are Short Answer (SA) type questions carrying 3 marks each.
(vi) In Section D, Question number 32 to 35 are Long Answer (LA) type questions carrying 5 marks each.
(vii) In Section E, Question number 36 to 38 are Case Study Based question carrying 4 marks each.
(viii) There is no overall choice. However, an internal choice has been provided in 2 questions in Section B, 2 questions in Section C, 2 questions in Section D and 3 questions in Section E.
(ix) Use of calculator is NOT allowed.

SECTION A

Multiple Choice Questions

Each question carries 1 mark

Directions (Q. Nos. 1-18) *All questions are compulsory. No Internal Choice is provided in this section.*

1. Two dice are tossed together. Find the probability of getting a doublet or a total of 6.

(a) $\frac{3}{18}$ (b) $\frac{4}{18}$ (c) $\frac{5}{18}$ (d) $\frac{7}{18}$

2. For the equation of parabola $x^2 = +9y$, find the equation of the directrix.

(a) $y = \frac{9}{4}$ (b) $x = \frac{9}{4}$

(c) $y = -\frac{9}{4}$ (d) $x = -\frac{9}{4}$

3. Let $f(x) = \begin{cases} \frac{k}{2}x^2, & \text{if } x \le 1 \\ 4, & \text{if } x > 1 \end{cases}$. Find k if $f(x)$ continuous at $x = 1$.

(a) 4 (b) 8 (c) 2 (d) 6

4. Find the derivative of $f(x) = 1 + x + x^2 + x^3 + \ldots + x^{50}$ at $x = 1$.

(a) 1075 (b) 1275 (c) 400 (d) 1250

5. The effective rate of return which is equivalent to a declared rate of 10% compounded semi-annually is

(a) 10.20% (b) 10.10% (c) 12.25% (d) 10.25%

6. If $A = \{3, 5, 7, 9, 11\}$, $B = \{7, 9, 11, 13\}$ and $C = \{11, 13, 15\}$, then find $(A \cap B) \cap C$.

(a) {7, 9} (b) {7, 9, 11}
(c) {11} (d) {7, 9, 11, 13, 15}

7. Find the values of x for which the functions $f(x) = 3x^2 - 1$ and $g(x) = 3 + x$ are equal.

(a) $-1, \frac{4}{3}$ (b) $\frac{4}{3}, -2$ (c) $-\frac{3}{4}, 1$ (d) 0, 1

8. Everybody in a room shakes hands with everybody else. The total number of hand-shakes is 66. Find the total number of persons in the room.

(a) −11 (b) 12 (c) 10 (d) 11

9. If the mth term of an AP be $\frac{1}{n}$ and its nth term be $\frac{1}{m}$, then its mnth term is

(a) mn (b) 1 (c) $\frac{1}{mn}$ (d) -1

10. Find the ratio in which the line $3x+4y+2=0$ divides the distance between the lines $3x+4y+5=0$ and $3x+4y-5=0$.

(a) 7:3 (b) 3:5 (c) 7:5 (d) 3:7

11. If the line $y=\sqrt{3}x+k$ touches the circle $x^2+y^2=16$, then find the values of k.

(a) ± 8 (b) -8 (c) ± 4 (d) $+4$

12. Coefficient of variation of two distributions are 50 and 60 and their arithmetic means are 30 and 25 respectively. Find the difference of their standard deviation.

(a) 15 (b) 0 (c) -1 (d) 20

13. The product of $\sqrt[3]{3}$, $\sqrt[3]{4}$ and $\sqrt[12]{243}$ is equal to

(a) 3 (b) 9 (c) $\sqrt{3}$ (d) $(3)^{3/2}$

14. The value of the decimal number 15.8675 to binary number is

(a) $(1111.1011)_2$ (b) $(111.100)_2$
(c) $(1010.011)_2$ (d) $(11.0111)_2$

15. If $2\log x+3\log y-2=0$, then the value of $x^2y^3+\log(1)$ is

(a) log(100) (b) 108 (c) 101 (d) 100

16. What sum will amount to ₹ 5500 at 5% per annum compounded yearly for 15 yr?

(a) 2640.5 (b) 2645.5 (c) 2646.6 (d) 2745.5

17. A car starts running with the initial speed of 30 km/h with its speed increasing every hour by 5 km/h. How many hours will it take to cover a distance of 380 km?

(a) 7 (b) 6 (c) 8 (d) 10

18. Which angle will be traced by the hands of a clock at 12 : 55?

(a) $87\frac{1}{2}^\circ$ (b) $67\frac{1}{2}^\circ$ (c) $57\frac{1}{2}^\circ$ (d) $27\frac{1}{2}^\circ$

Assertion-Reason Based Questions

Directions *In the question number 19 and 20, a statement of Assertion (A) is followed by a statement of Reason (R). Choose the correct option.*

(a) Both (A) and (R) are true and (R) is the correct explanation of (A).
(b) Both (A) and (R) are true but (R) is not the correct explanation of (A).
(c) (A) is true but (R) is false.
(d) (A) is false but (R) is true.

19. **Assertion** (A) $\frac{7x^4y^3}{42x^3y^5}=\frac{x}{6y^2}$

Reason (R) Division Law states that if a is any non-zero real number and m, n are rational numbers, then $\frac{a^m}{a^n}=a^{m-n}$.

20. **Assertion** (A) A can complete $\frac{1}{5}$ of a piece of work in 12 h and B an complete $\frac{1}{6}$ of the same work in 15 h. Both working together can complete the work in 32 h.

Reason (R) Time required to do a certain work is the ratio of work to be done and one day's work.

SECTION B

[This section comprises of very short answer type questions (VSA) of 2 marks each]

21. (a) If x is a positive real number and the exponents are rational numbers, show that

$$\frac{x^{a(b-c)}}{x^{b(a-c)}}\div\left(\frac{x^b}{x^a}\right)^c=1$$

Or (b) If $9^{x+2}=720+9^x$, then find the value of $\left(\frac{9}{4}x\right)^{\frac{2}{x}}$.

22. A telegraph has 5 arms and each arm is capable of 4 distinct positions, including the position of rest. What is the total number of signals that can be made?

23. Find four numbers forming a geometric progression in which the third term is greater than the first terms by 9, and second term is greater than the 4th by 18.

24. Two finite sets have m and n elements. The total number of subsets of the first set is 992 more than the total number of subsets of the second set. Find the values of m and n.

25. (a) Find the correlation coefficient between X and Y when $\Sigma x=125$, $\Sigma y=100$, $\Sigma x^2=650$, $\Sigma y^2=464$, $\Sigma xy=508$ and $n=25$.

Or (b) For a certain frequency distribution mean is 190, median is 185 and standard deviation is 30 calculate the Karl Pearson's coefficient of skewness of the distribution.

SECTION C

[This section comprises of short answer type questions (SA) of 3 marks each]

26. (a) Find the derivatives of the following functions

(i) $\log(x+\sqrt{x^2-a^2})$ (ii) $\log\left(\frac{\sqrt{x+1}+\sqrt{x-1}}{\sqrt{x+1}-\sqrt{x-1}}\right)$

Or (b) (i) If $e^x+e^y=e^{x+y}$, then prove $\frac{dy}{dx}=-\frac{e^x(e^y-1)}{e^y(e^x-1)}$.

(ii) If $e^x+e^y=e^{x+y}$, then prove $\frac{dy}{dx}=-e^{y-x}$.

27. The following table gives information regarding weekly income of labourers working at a dam site:

Income (in ₹)	600-700	700-800	800-900	900-1000	1000-1100	1100-1200	1200-1300
Number of labourers	40	68	86	120	90	40	26

Estimate
(i) median (ii) lower quartile
(iii) upper quartile.

28. Mr. Pandey lives in Lucknow, Uttar Pradesh. The reading of electric meter of his house is found to be 5475 units. If the previous month's reading was 3904 units and connection load is 4 kW, calculate his electricity bill for that month.

Tariff plan is given below.

Energy charges

Number of units	0-150	151-300	301-500	> 500
Price per unit (in ₹)	₹ 5.5	₹ 6	₹ 6.5	₹ 7

Fixed charges ₹ 110 per kW/month
Energy tax is 5% of tariff rates
Surcharge is ₹ 0.26 per unit

29. (a) Find the value of n, so that $\frac{a^{n+1}+b^{n+1}}{a^n+b^n}$ may be the geometric mean between a and b.

Or (b) If the AM and GM between two numbers are in the ratio $m:n$, then prove that the numbers are in the ratio $m+\sqrt{m^2-n^2}:m-\sqrt{m^2-n^2}$.

30. In an examination, a question paper consists of 15 questions divided into two parts I and II, containing 8 and 7 questions. A student is required to attempt 8 questions in all, selecting atleast 3 from each part. In how many ways can a student select the questions.

31. (i) Find the domain of the function
$$f(x)=\frac{1}{\log(1-x)}+\sqrt{x+3}.$$

(ii) Find the domain of the function
$$f(x)=\sqrt{4-x}+\frac{1}{\sqrt{x^2-1}}.$$

SECTION D

[This section comprises of long answer type questions (LA) of 5 marks each]

32. A project requires an initial investment of ₹ 250000 and is expected to generate the following net cash inflows year-1 : ₹ 98000, year-2 : ₹ 120000, year-3 : ₹ 150000. Compute the net present value of the investment, if the discount rate is 12%.

33. (a) If A and B are independent events, then prove that

(i) $P(A)=P(A\cap B)+P(A\cap \bar{B})$.

(ii) $P(A\cup B)=P(A\cap B)+P(A\cap \bar{B})+P(\bar{A}+B)$.

Or (b) An electronic assembly consists of two subsystems A and B. Past testing procedures data show that probabilities of failure are P (A fails) = 0.2, P (B fails alone) = 0.15, P (A and B fail) = 0.15.

Evaluate (i) P (A fails | B has failed)
(ii) P (A fails alone).

34. Manufacturer A sells a washing machine to a dealer B for ₹ 12500. The dealer B sells it to a consumer at a profit of ₹ 1500. If the sales are intra-state and the rate of GST is 12%, find

(i) the amount of tax (under GST) paid by the dealer B to the Central Government.

(ii) the amount of tax (under GST) received by the State Government.

(iii) the amount that the consumer pays for the machine.

35. (a) Show that the points (7, 5), (6, −2), (−1, −1) and (0, 6) are concyclic. Also, find the radius and the centre of the circle on which they lie.

Or

(b) Find the coordinates of focus, the equation of axis, the equation of the directrix and the length of the latusrectum of the following parabola equations.

(i) $3y^2=8x$ (ii) $5x^2=-12y$ (iii) $y^2=24x$

SECTION E

[This section comprises 3 case-study/passage based questions of 4 marks each with sub parts. The first two case study questions have three sub parts (i), (ii), (iii) of marks 1, 1, 2 respectively. The third case study question has two sub parts (i), (ii) of 2 marks each]

36. In financial year 2019-20 Mr Narendra Kumar Mani's (age 55 yr) income from salary was ₹ 150000 (exclusive of HRA) and income from interest on saving account was ₹ 18600. He deposited ₹ 15000 per month in GPF and paid ₹ 57000 as LIC premium. He donated ₹ 100000 in Prime Minister's National relief fund. He paid ₹ 31600 as interest on education loan for higher studies of his daughter. He also paid ₹ 212500 as interest on home loan and ₹ 63450 as principal of home loan.

Income Tax Slab for Financial Year 2019-20 (For individual tax payers below the age of 60 yr)

Taxable Income	Income Tax
Upto ₹ 250000	NIL
₹ 250001 to ₹ 5000000	5% of taxable income exceeding ₹ 250000
₹ 500001 to ₹ 1000000	₹ 12500 + 20% of taxable income exceeding ₹ 500000
Above ₹ 1000000	₹ 112500 + 30% of taxable income exceeding ₹ 1000000

Based on the above information, answer the following questions

(i) The total amount invested or paid by Mr. Mani under Section 80C is

(a) ₹ 180000 (b) ₹ 237000
(c) ₹ 300450 (d) ₹ 332050

(ii) The amount donated by Mr Mani in Prime Minister's National relief fund is deductable under section is

(a) 80 E (b) 80 G
(c) 80 TTA (d) None of these

(iii) The taxable income of Mr Mani is

(a) ₹ 945900 (b) ₹ 977500
(c) ₹ 987500 (d) ₹ 980000

Or Income tax paid by Mr Mani for FY 2019-20 is

(a) ₹ 101680 (b) ₹ 105747
(c) ₹ 106845 (d) ₹ 110756

37. Let $f: R \to [0, \infty)$ be a function defined as $f(x) = |x|$ and $g(x) = f(x+1) + f(x-1)$, $\forall x \in R$.

Based on the above information, answer the following questions:

(i) The value of $g(x)$ is

(a) $g(x) = \begin{cases} -2x, & x < -1 \\ 2, & -1 \le x < 1 \\ 2x, & x \ge 1 \end{cases}$

(b) $g(x) = \begin{cases} -2x+1, & x < -1 \\ -2x, & -1 \le x < 1 \\ 2x-1, & x \ge 1 \end{cases}$

(c) $g(x) = \begin{cases} 2x, & x < -1 \\ -2, & -1 \le x < 1 \\ -2x, & x \ge 1 \end{cases}$

(d) $g(x) = \begin{cases} 2x-1, & x < -1 \\ -2x, & -1 \le x < 1 \\ -2x+1, & x \ge 1 \end{cases}$

(ii) If $\lim_{x \to -1} g(x) = a$, then the value of a is

(a) 0 (b) – 2
(c) 2 (d) does not exist

(iii) The value of $\lim_{x \to 1^+} g(x)$ is

(a) 0 (b) 2
(c) – 2 (d) does not exist

Or The points of discontinuity of the function $g(x)$ are

(a) $\{-1, 1\}$
(b) $\{-1, 0, 1\}$
(c) $\{0\}$
(d) no points of discontinuity

38. A clock has two hands, the longer hand is called the minute hand and the shorter hand is called hour hand. The minute hand trace an angle of 6° in one minute and hour hand trace an angle of $\left(\frac{1}{2}\right)^\circ$ in one minute.

Based on the above information, answer the following questions.

(i) How much angular distance will be covered by the minute hand of a correct clock in a period of 2 hr 20 min?

(ii) What is the angle traced by hour hand in 30 minute?

(iii) What will be the angle between the two hands of a clock, when the time is 8 : 50?

Or

At half past 5 in the evening, find the smaller angle between the hour hand minute hands of a clock.

Answers

Sample Paper 1

1. (c) 2. (b) 3. (b) 4. (a)
5. (d) 6. (a) 7. (c) 8. (c)
9. (b) 10. (a) 11. (b) 12. (c)
13. (a) 14. (b) 15. (c) 16. (b)
17. (a) 18. (b) 19. (d) 20. (a)

21. (a)

Or (b) No

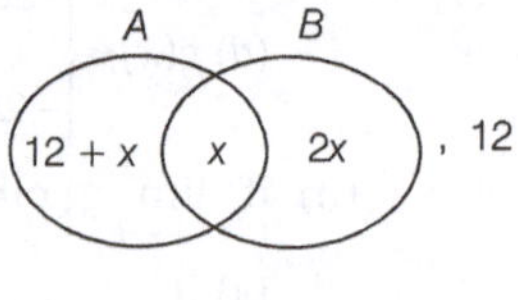

22. 11 : 18 : 40 pm

23. (a) Do Yourself Or

(b) $-\frac{2x+y}{x+2y}$

24. $\frac{2352}{12155}$ 25. 8, –8

26. (a) $7\frac{1}{7}$ days Or (b) $9\frac{3}{8}$ days

27. $\frac{16}{7}(2^n-1)$ 28. 2, 4 29. $\frac{14}{45}$

30. 16.5, 74.25 Or 10

31. (i) $\frac{-8}{3}$ (ii) $\frac{-4}{3}$

32. (a) $21\frac{9}{11}$ min post 7, $54\frac{6}{11}$ min post 7 Or

(b) Tuesday

33. ₹ 1017 Or ₹ 29160 34. (i) $\frac{17}{33}$ (ii) $\frac{16}{33}$ 35. $8\sqrt{3}a$

36. (i) (a), (ii) (b), (iii) (a) Or (a)

37. (i) (a), (ii) (a), (iii) (b) Or (a)

38. (i) (c), (ii) (b) Or (b)

Sample Paper 2

1. (d) 2. (c) 3. (b) 4. (d)
5. (a) 6. (b) 7. (b) 8. (b)
9. (d) 10. (c) 11. (a) 12. (a)
13. (b) 14. (b) 15. (c) 16. (c)
17. (a) 18. (a) 19. (c) 20. (c)

21. (a) 48 days Or (b) 8 sec

22. (i) {0,1,2,3,4,7,8} (ii) {2,4}

23. (a) 90720 Or (b) $66\times(9!)^2$

24. ₹ 38220

25. $x^2+y^2-x+2y-21=0$

26. Do yourself

27. $D_f = R-\{-3\}$, $R_f = \{-1,1\}$

28. (0,0), (3, 27) Or (3, 2)

29. 123.4 kg 30. ₹ 16550

31. Either (–1,6) or (5,4)

32. 20 Students

Or $f = \{(8, 2), (11, 11), (12, 3), (15, 5), (18, 3), (23, 23)\}$

Range = {2,3,5,11,23}, Domain = $R-\{2,6\}$

33. 322 yr Or 13.336 cm^2 34. 0.819

36. (i) (a), (ii) (b), (iii) (d) Or (b)

37. (i) (d), (ii) (a), (iii) (b) Or (c)

38. (i) Box *P* is placed just above *M*.

(ii) There are two boxes, *M* and *S* between *L* and *P*.

(iii) *L* is placed at the bottom most place and *I* is placed at the top most place.

Or

Box *I* is placed at topmost place.

Sample Paper 3

1. (c) 2. (c) 3. (b) 4. (d)
5. (d) 6. (c) 7. (a) 8. (b)
9. (b) 10. (d) 11. (a) 12. (b)
13. (a) 14. (a) 15. (d) 16. (b)
17. (c) 18. (c) 19. (a) 20. (d)

21. (a) Or (b) $\frac{81}{16}$ 22. 1023

23. 3, – 6, 12, – 24 24. $m=10$ and $n=5$

25. 0.2 Or 0.5

26. (i) $\frac{1}{\sqrt{x^2-a^2}}$ (ii) $\frac{1}{\sqrt{x^2-1}}$

27. (i) ₹ 934.17 (ii) ₹ 811 (iii) ₹ 1042.78

28. ₹ 6802.96 29. $n=-\frac{1}{2}$

30. 2828

31. (i) $[-3, 0)\cup(0, 1)$ (ii) $(-\infty, -1)\cup(1, 4]$

32. ₹ 39961

33. $\frac{448}{475}$ Or (i) 0.5 (ii) 0.05

34. (i) ₹ 90 (ii) ₹ 840 (iii) ₹ 15680

35. Centre = (3, 2) and $r = 5$

Or (i) $\left(\frac{2}{3}, 0\right)$, *X*-axis, $3x+2=0$, $\frac{8}{3}$

(ii) $\left(0, -\frac{3}{5}\right)$, *Y*-axis, $5y-3=0$, $\frac{12}{5}$

(iii) (6, 0), *X*-axis, $x+6=0$, 24

36. (i) (c), (ii) (b), (iii) (a) Or (b)

37. (i) (a), (ii) (c), (iii) (b) Or (d)

38. (i) 840° (ii) 15° (iii) 35° Or 15°

LOGARITHMS

N	0	1	2	3	4	5	6	7	8	9	Mean Differences								
											1	2	3	4	5	6	7	8	9
10	0000	0043	0086	0128	0170	0212	0253	0294	0334	0374	5 4	9 8	13 12	17 16	21 20	26 24	30 28	34 32	38 36
11	0414	0453	0492	0531	0569	0607	0645	0682	0719	0755	4 4	8 7	12 11	16 15	20 18	23 22	27 26	31 29	35 33
12	0792	0828	0864	0899	0934	0969	1004	1038	1072	1106	3 3	7 7	11 10	14 14	18 17	21 20	25 24	28 27	32 31
13	1139	1173	1206	1239	1271	1303	1335	1367	1399	1430	3 3	6 7	10 10	13 13	16 16	19 19	23 22	26 25	29 29
14	1461	1492	1523	1553	1584	1614	1644	1673	1703	1732	3 3	6 6	9 9	12 12	15 14	19 17	22 20	25 23	28 26
15	1761	1790	1818	1847	1875	1903	1931	1959	1987	2014	3 3	6 6	9 8	11 11	14 14	17 17	20 19	23 22	26 25
16	2041	2068	2095	2122	2148	2175	2201	2227	2253	2279	3 3	6 5	8 8	11 10	14 13	16 16	19 18	22 21	24 23
17	2304	2330	2355	2380	2405	2430	2455	2480	2504	2529	3 3	5 5	8 8	10 10	13 12	15 15	18 17	20 20	23 22
18	2553	2577	2601	2625	2648	2672	2695	2718	2742	2765	2 2	5 4	7 7	9 9	12 11	14 14	17 16	19 18	21 21
19	2788	2810	2833	2856	2878	2900	2923	2945	2967	2989	2 2	4 4	7 6	9 8	11 11	13 13	16 15	18 17	20 19
20	3010	3032	3054	3075	3096	3118	3139	3160	3181	3201	2	4	6	8	11	13	15	17	19
21	3222	3243	3263	3284	3304	3324	3345	3365	3385	3404	2	4	6	8	10	12	14	16	18
22	3424	3444	3464	3483	3502	3522	3541	3560	3579	3598	2	4	6	8	10	12	14	15	17
23	3617	3636	3655	3674	3692	3711	3729	3747	3766	3784	2	4	6	7	9	11	13	15	17
24	3802	3820	3838	3856	3874	3892	3909	3927	3945	3962	2	4	5	7	9	11	12	14	16
25	3979	3997	4014	4031	4048	4065	4082	4099	4116	4133	2	3	5	7	9	10	12	14	15
26	4150	4166	4183	4200	4216	4232	4249	4265	4281	4298	2	3	5	7	8	10	11	13	15
27	4314	4330	4346	4362	4378	4393	4409	4425	4440	4456	2	3	5	6	8	9	11	13	14
28	4472	4487	4502	4518	4533	4548	4564	4579	4594	4609	2	3	5	6	8	9	11	12	14
29	4624	4639	4654	4669	4683	4698	4713	4728	4742	4757	1	3	4	6	7	9	10	12	13
30	4771	4786	4800	4814	4829	4843	4857	4871	4886	4900	1	3	4	6	7	9	10	11	13
31	4914	4928	4942	4955	4969	4983	4997	5011	5024	5038	1	3	4	6	7	8	10	11	12
32	5051	5065	5079	5092	5105	5119	5132	5145	5159	5172	1	3	4	5	7	8	9	11	12
33	5185	5198	5211	5224	5237	5250	5263	5276	5289	5302	1	3	4	5	6	8	9	10	12
34	5315	5328	5340	5353	5366	5378	5391	5403	5416	5428	1	3	4	5	6	8	9	10	11
35	5441	5453	5465	5478	5490	5502	5514	5527	5539	5551	1	2	4	5	6	7	9	10	11
36	5563	5575	5587	5599	5611	5623	5635	5647	5658	5670	1	2	4	5	6	7	8	10	11
37	5682	5694	5705	5717	5729	5740	5752	5763	5775	5786	1	2	3	5	6	7	8	9	10
38	5798	5809	5821	5832	5843	5855	5866	5877	5888	5899	1	2	3	5	6	7	8	9	10
39	5911	5922	5933	5944	5955	5966	5977	5988	5999	6010	1	2	3	4	5	7	8	9	10
40	6021	6031	6042	6053	6064	6075	6085	6096	6107	6117	1	2	3	4	5	6	8	9	10
41	6128	6138	6149	6160	6170	6180	6191	6201	6212	6222	1	2	3	4	5	6	7	8	9
42	6232	6243	6253	6263	6274	6284	6294	6304	6314	6325	1	2	3	4	5	6	7	8	9
43	6335	6345	6355	6365	6375	6385	6395	6405	6415	6425	1	2	3	4	5	6	7	8	9
44	6435	6444	6454	6464	6474	6484	6493	6503	6513	6522	1	2	3	4	5	6	7	8	9
45	6532	6542	6551	6561	6571	6580	6590	6599	6609	6618	1	2	3	4	5	6	7	8	9
46	6628	6637	6646	6656	6665	6675	6684	6693	6702	6712	1	2	3	4	5	6	7	7	8
47	6721	6730	6739	6749	6758	6767	6776	6785	6794	6803	1	2	3	4	5	5	6	7	8
48	6812	6821	6830	6839	6848	6857	6866	6875	6884	6893	1	2	3	4	4	5	6	7	8
49	6902	6911	6920	6928	6937	6946	6955	6964	6972	6981	1	2	3	4	4	5	6	7	8
50	6990	6998	7007	7016	7024	7033	7042	7050	7059	7067	1	2	3	3	4	5	6	7	8
51	7076	7084	7093	7101	7110	7118	7126	7135	7143	7152	1	2	3	3	4	5	6	7	8
52	7160	7168	7177	7185	7193	7202	7210	7218	7226	7235	1	2	2	3	4	5	6	7	7
53	7243	7251	7259	7267	7275	7284	7292	7300	7308	7316	1	2	2	3	4	5	6	6	7
54	7324	7332	7340	7348	7356	7364	7372	7380	7388	7396	1	2	2	3	4	5	6	6	7
55	7404	7412	7419	7427	7435	7443	7451	7459	7466	7474	1	2	2	3	4	5	5	6	7
56	7482	7490	7497	7505	7513	7520	7528	7536	7543	7551	1	2	2	3	4	5	5	6	7
57	7559	7566	7574	7582	7589	7597	7604	7612	7619	7627	1	2	2	3	4	5	5	6	7
58	7634	7642	7649	7657	7664	7672	7679	7686	7694	7701	1	2	2	3	4	4	5	6	7
59	7709	7716	7723	7731	7738	7745	7752	7760	7767	7774	1	1	2	3	4	4	5	6	7
60	7782	7789	7796	7803	7810	7818	7825	7832	7839	7846	1	1	2	3	4	4	5	6	6
61	7853	7860	7868	7875	7882	7889	7896	7903	7910	7917	1	1	2	3	4	4	5	6	6
62	7924	7931	7938	7945	7952	7959	7966	7973	7980	7987	1	1	2	3	3	4	5	6	6
63	7993	8000	8007	8014	8021	8028	8035	8041	8048	8055	1	1	2	3	3	4	5	5	6
64	8062	8069	8075	8082	8089	8096	8102	8109	8116	8122	1	1	2	3	3	4	5	5	6
65	8129	8136	8142	8149	8156	8162	8169	8176	8182	8189	1	1	2	3	3	4	5	5	6
66	8195	8202	8209	8215	8222	8228	8235	8241	8248	8254	1	1	2	3	3	4	5	5	6
67	8261	8267	8274	8280	8287	8293	8299	8306	8312	8319	1	1	2	3	3	4	5	5	6
68	8325	8331	8338	8344	8351	8357	8363	8370	8376	8382	1	1	2	3	3	4	4	5	6
69	8388	8395	8401	8407	8414	8420	8426	8432	8439	8445	1	1	2	2	3	4	4	5	6
70	8451	8457	8463	8470	8476	8482	8488	8494	8500	8506	1	1	2	2	3	4	4	5	6
71	8513	8519	8525	8531	8537	8543	8549	8555	8561	8567	1	1	2	2	3	4	4	5	5
72	8573	8579	8585	8591	8597	8603	8609	8615	8621	8627	1	1	2	2	3	4	4	5	5
73	8633	8639	8645	8651	8657	8663	8669	8675	8681	8686	1	1	2	2	3	4	4	5	5
74	8692	8698	8704	8710	8716	8722	8727	8733	8739	8745	1	1	2	2	3	4	4	5	5
75	8751	8756	8762	8768	8774	8779	8785	8791	8797	8802	1	1	2	2	3	3	4	5	5
76	8808	8814	8820	8825	8831	8837	8842	8848	8854	8859	1	1	2	2	3	3	4	5	5
77	8865	8871	8876	8882	8887	8893	8899	8904	8910	8915	1	1	2	2	3	3	4	4	5
78	8921	8927	8932	8938	8943	8949	8954	8960	8965	8971	1	1	2	2	3	3	4	4	5
79	8976	8982	8987	8993	8998	9004	9009	9015	9020	9025	1	1	2	2	3	3	4	4	5
80	9031	9036	9042	9047	9053	9058	9063	9069	9074	9079	1	1	2	2	3	3	4	4	5
81	9085	9090	9096	9101	9106	9112	9117	9122	9128	9133	1	1	2	2	3	3	4	4	5
82	9138	9143	9149	9154	9159	9165	9170	9175	9180	9186	1	1	2	2	3	3	4	4	5
83	9191	9196	9201	9206	9212	9217	9222	9227	9232	9238	1	1	2	2	3	3	4	4	5
84	9243	9248	9253	9258	9263	9269	9274	9279	9284	9289	1	1	2	2	3	3	4	4	5
85	9294	9299	9304	9309	9315	9320	9325	9330	9335	9340	1	1	2	2	3	3	4	4	5
86	9345	9350	9355	9360	9365	9370	9375	9380	9385	9390	1	1	2	2	3	3	4	4	5
87	9395	9400	9405	9410	9415	9420	9425	9430	9435	9440	0	1	1	2	2	3	3	4	4
88	9445	9450	9455	9460	9465	9469	9474	9479	9484	9489	0	1	1	2	2	3	3	4	4
89	9494	9499	9504	9509	9513	9518	9523	9528	9533	9538	0	1	1	2	2	3	3	4	4
90	9542	9547	9552	9557	9562	9566	9571	9576	9581	9586	0	1	1	2	2	3	3	4	4
91	9590	9595	9600	9605	9609	9614	9619	9624	9628	9633	0	1	1	2	2	3	3	4	4
92	9638	9643	9647	9652	9657	9661	9666	9671	9675	9680	0	1	1	2	2	3	3	4	4
93	9685	9689	9694	9699	9703	9708	9713	9717	9722	9727	0	1	1	2	2	3	3	4	4
94	9731	9736	9741	9745	9750	9754	9759	9763	9788	9773	0	1	1	2	2	3	3	4	4
95	9777	9782	9786	9791	9795	9800	9805	9809	9814	9818	0	1	1	2	2	3	3	4	4
96	9823	9827	9832	9836	9841	9845	9850	9854	9859	9863	0	1	1	2	2	3	3	4	4
97	9868	9872	9877	9881	9886	9890	9894	9899	9903	9908	0	1	1	2	2	3	3	4	4
98	9912	9917	9921	9926	9930	9934	9939	9943	9948	9952	0	1	1	2	2	3	3	4	4
99	9956	9961	9965	9969	9974	9978	9983	9987	9991	9996	0	1	1	2	2	3	3	3	4

ANTILOGARITHMS

	0	1	2	3	4	5	6	7	8	9	Mean Differences								
											1	2	3	4	5	6	7	8	9
.00	1000	1002	1005	1007	1009	1012	1014	1016	1019	1021	0	0	1	1	1	1	2	2	2
.01	1023	1026	1028	1030	1033	1035	1038	1040	1042	1045	0	0	1	1	1	1	2	2	2
.02	1047	1050	1052	1054	1057	1059	1062	1064	1067	1069	0	0	1	1	1	1	2	2	2
.03	1072	1074	1076	1079	1081	1084	1086	1089	1091	1094	0	0	1	1	1	1	2	2	2
.04	1096	1099	1102	1104	1107	1109	1112	1114	1117	1119	0	1	1	1	1	2	2	2	2
.05	1122	1125	1127	1130	1132	1135	1138	1140	1143	1146	0	1	1	1	1	2	2	2	2
.06	1148	1151	1153	1156	1159	1161	1164	1167	1169	1172	0	1	1	1	1	2	2	2	2
.07	1175	1178	1180	1183	1186	1189	1191	1194	1197	1199	0	1	1	1	1	2	2	2	2
.08	1202	1205	1208	1211	1213	1216	1219	1222	1225	1227	0	1	1	1	1	2	2	2	3
.09	1230	1233	1236	1239	1242	1245	1247	1250	1253	1256	0	1	1	1	1	2	2	2	3
.10	1259	1262	1265	1268	1271	1274	1276	1279	1282	1285	0	1	1	1	1	2	2	2	3
.11	1288	1291	1294	1297	1300	1303	1306	1309	1312	1315	0	1	1	1	2	2	2	2	3
.12	1318	1321	1324	1327	1330	1334	1337	1340	1343	1346	0	1	1	1	2	2	2	2	3
.13	1349	1352	1355	1358	1361	1365	1368	1371	1374	1377	0	1	1	1	2	2	2	3	3
.14	1380	1384	1387	1390	1393	1396	1400	1403	1406	1409	0	1	1	1	2	2	2	3	3
.15	1413	1416	1419	1422	1426	1429	1432	1435	1439	1442	0	1	1	1	2	2	2	3	3
.16	1445	1449	1452	1455	1459	1462	1466	1469	1472	1476	0	1	1	1	2	2	2	3	3
.17	1479	1483	1486	1489	1493	1496	1500	1503	1507	1510	0	1	1	1	2	2	2	3	3
.18	1514	1517	1521	1524	1528	1531	1535	1538	1542	1545	0	1	1	1	2	2	2	3	3
.19	1549	1552	1556	1560	1563	1567	1570	1574	1578	1581	0	1	1	1	2	2	3	3	3
.20	1585	1589	1592	1596	1600	1603	1607	1611	1614	1618	0	1	1	1	2	2	3	3	3
.21	1622	1626	1629	1633	1637	1641	1644	1648	1652	1656	0	1	1	2	2	2	3	3	3
.22	1660	1663	1667	1671	1675	1679	1683	1687	1690	1694	0	1	1	2	2	2	3	3	3
.23	1698	1702	1706	1710	1714	1718	1722	1726	1730	1734	0	1	1	2	2	2	3	3	4
.24	1738	1742	1746	1750	1754	1758	1762	1766	1770	1774	0	1	1	2	2	2	3	3	4
.25	1778	1782	1786	1791	1795	1799	1803	1807	1811	1816	0	1	1	2	2	2	3	3	4
.26	1820	1824	1828	1832	1837	1841	1845	1849	1854	1858	0	1	1	2	2	3	3	3	4
.27	1862	1866	1871	1875	1879	1884	1888	1892	1897	1901	0	1	1	2	2	3	3	3	4
.28	1905	1910	1914	1919	1923	1928	1932	1936	1941	1945	0	1	1	2	2	3	3	4	4
.29	1950	1954	1959	1963	1968	1972	1977	1982	1986	1991	0	1	1	2	2	3	3	4	4
.30	1995	2000	2004	2009	2014	2018	2023	2028	2032	2037	0	1	1	2	2	3	3	4	4
.31	2042	2046	2051	2056	2061	2065	2070	2075	2080	2084	0	1	1	2	2	3	3	4	4
.32	2089	2094	2099	2104	2109	2113	2118	2123	2128	2133	0	1	1	2	2	3	3	4	4
.33	2138	2143	2148	2153	2158	2163	2168	2173	2178	2183	0	1	1	2	2	3	3	4	4
.34	2188	2193	2198	2203	2208	2213	2218	2223	2228	2234	1	1	2	2	3	3	4	4	5
.35	2239	2244	2249	2254	2259	2265	2270	2275	2280	2286	1	1	2	2	3	3	4	4	5
.36	2291	2296	2301	2307	2312	2317	2323	2328	2333	2339	1	1	2	2	3	3	4	4	5
.37	2344	2350	2355	2360	2366	2371	2377	2382	2388	2393	1	1	2	2	3	3	4	4	5
.38	2399	2404	2410	2415	2421	2427	2432	2438	2443	2449	1	1	2	2	3	3	4	4	5
.39	2455	2460	2466	2472	2477	2483	2489	2495	2500	2506	1	1	2	2	3	3	4	5	5
.40	2512	2518	2523	2529	2535	2541	2547	2553	2559	2564	1	1	2	2	3	4	4	5	5
.41	2570	2576	2582	2588	2594	2600	2696	2612	2618	2624	1	1	2	2	3	4	4	5	5
.42	2630	2636	2642	2649	2655	2661	2667	2673	2679	2685	1	1	2	2	3	4	4	5	6
.43	2692	2698	2704	2710	2716	2723	2729	2735	2742	2748	1	1	2	3	3	4	4	5	6
.44	2754	2761	2767	2773	2780	2786	2793	2799	2805	2812	1	1	2	3	3	4	4	5	6
.45	2818	2825	2831	2838	2844	2851	2858	2864	2871	2877	1	1	2	3	3	4	5	5	6
.46	2884	2891	2897	2904	2911	2917	2924	2931	2938	2944	1	1	2	3	3	4	5	5	6
.47	2951	2958	2965	2972	2979	2985	2992	2999	3006	3013	1	1	2	3	3	4	5	5	6
.48	3020	3027	3034	3041	3048	3055	3062	3069	3076	3083	1	1	2	3	4	4	5	6	6
.49	3090	3097	3105	3112	3119	3126	3133	3141	3148	3155	1	1	2	3	4	4	5	6	6
.50	3162	3170	3177	3184	3192	3199	3206	3214	3221	3228	1	1	2	3	4	4	5	6	7
.51	3236	3243	3251	3258	3266	3273	3281	3289	3296	3304	1	2	2	3	4	5	5	6	7
.52	3311	3319	3327	3334	3342	3350	3357	3365	3373	3381	1	2	2	3	4	5	5	6	7
.53	3388	3396	3404	3412	3420	3428	3436	3443	3451	3459	1	2	2	3	4	5	6	6	7
.54	3467	3475	3483	3491	3499	3508	3516	3524	3532	3540	1	2	2	3	4	5	6	6	7
.55	3548	3556	3565	3573	3581	3589	3597	3606	3614	3622	1	2	2	3	4	5	6	7	7
.56	3631	3639	3648	3656	3664	3673	3681	3690	3698	3707	1	2	3	3	4	5	6	7	8
.57	3715	3724	3733	3741	3750	3758	3767	3776	3784	3793	1	2	3	3	4	5	6	7	8
.58	3802	3811	3819	3828	3837	3846	3855	3864	3873	3882	1	2	3	4	4	5	6	7	8
.59	3890	3899	3908	3917	3926	3936	3945	3954	3963	3972	1	2	3	4	5	5	6	7	8
.60	3981	3990	3999	4009	4018	4027	4036	4046	4055	4064	1	2	3	4	5	6	6	7	8
.61	4074	4083	4093	4102	4111	4121	4130	4140	4150	4159	1	2	3	4	5	6	7	8	9
.62	4169	4178	4188	4198	4207	4217	4227	4236	4256	4256	1	2	3	4	5	6	7	8	9
.63	4266	4276	4285	4295	4305	4315	4325	4335	4345	4355	1	2	3	4	5	6	7	8	9
.64	4365	4375	4385	4395	4406	4416	4426	4436	4446	4457	1	2	3	4	5	6	7	8	9
.65	4467	4477	4487	4498	4508	4519	4529	4539	4550	4560	1	2	3	4	5	6	7	8	9
.66	4571	4581	4592	4603	4613	4624	4634	4645	4656	4667	1	2	3	4	5	6	7	9	10
.67	4677	4688	4699	4710	4721	4732	4742	4753	4764	4775	1	2	3	4	5	7	8	9	10
.68	4786	4797	4808	4819	4831	4842	4853	4864	4875	4887	1	2	3	4	6	7	8	9	10
.69	4898	4909	4920	4932	4943	4955	4966	4977	4989	5000	1	2	3	5	6	7	8	9	10
.70	5012	5023	5035	5047	5058	5070	5082	5093	5105	5117	1	2	4	5	6	7	8	9	11
.71	5129	5140	5152	5164	5176	5188	5200	5212	5224	5236	1	2	4	5	6	7	8	10	11
.72	5248	5260	5272	5284	5297	5309	5321	5333	5346	5358	1	2	4	5	6	7	9	10	11
.73	5370	5383	5395	5408	5420	5433	5445	5458	5470	5483	1	3	4	5	6	8	9	10	11
.74	5495	5508	5521	5534	5546	5559	5572	5585	5598	5610	1	3	4	5	6	8	9	10	12
.75	5623	5636	5649	5662	5675	5689	5702	5715	5728	5741	1	3	4	5	7	8	9	10	12
.76	5754	5768	5781	5794	5808	5821	5834	5848	5861	5875	1	3	4	5	7	8	9	11	12
.77	5888	5902	5916	5929	5943	5957	5970	5984	5998	6012	1	3	4	5	7	8	10	11	12
.78	6026	6039	6053	6067	6081	6095	6109	6124	6138	6152	1	3	4	6	7	8	10	11	13
.79	6166	6180	6194	6209	6223	7237	6252	6266	6281	6295	1	3	4	6	7	9	10	11	13
.80	6310	6324	6339	6353	6368	6383	6497	6412	6427	6442	1	3	4	6	7	9	10	12	13
.81	6457	6471	6486	6501	6516	6531	6546	6561	6577	6592	2	3	5	6	8	9	11	12	14
.82	6607	6622	6637	6653	6668	6683	6699	6714	6730	6745	2	3	5	6	8	9	11	12	14
.83	6761	6776	6792	6808	6823	6839	6855	6871	6887	6902	2	3	5	6	8	9	11	13	14
.84	6918	6934	6950	6966	6982	6998	7015	7031	7047	7063	2	3	5	6	8	10	11	13	15
.85	7079	7096	7112	7129	7145	7161	7178	7194	7211	7228	2	3	5	7	8	10	12	13	15
.86	7244	7261	7278	7295	7311	7328	7345	7362	7379	7396	2	3	5	7	8	10	12	13	15
.87	7413	7430	7447	7464	7482	7499	7516	7534	7551	7568	2	3	5	7	9	10	12	14	16
.88	7586	7603	7621	7638	7656	7674	7691	7709	7727	7745	2	4	5	7	9	11	12	14	16
.89	7762	7780	7798	7816	7834	7852	7870	7889	7907	7925	2	4	5	7	9	11	13	14	16
.90	7943	7962	7980	7998	8017	8035	8054	8072	8091	8110	2	4	6	7	9	11	13	15	17
.91	8128	8147	8166	8185	8204	8222	8241	8260	8279	8299	2	4	6	8	9	11	13	15	17
.92	8318	8337	8356	8375	8395	8414	8433	8453	8472	8492	2	4	6	8	10	12	14	15	17
.93	8511	8531	8551	8570	8590	8610	8630	8650	8670	8690	2	4	6	8	10	12	14	16	18
.94	8710	8730	8750	8770	8790	8810	8831	8851	8872	8892	2	4	6	8	10	12	14	16	18
.95	8913	8933	8954	8974	8995	9016	9036	9057	9078	9099	2	4	6	8	10	12	15	17	19
.96	9120	9141	9162	9183	9204	9226	9247	9268	9290	9311	2	4	6	8	11	13	15	17	19
.97	9333	9354	9376	9397	9419	9441	9462	9484	9506	9528	2	4	7	9	11	13	15	17	20
.98	9550	9572	9594	9616	9638	9661	9683	9705	9727	9750	2	4	7	9	11	13	16	18	20
.99	9772	9795	9817	9840	9863	9886	9908	9931	9954	9977	2	5	7	9	11	14	16	18	20

NATURAL SINES

	0′	6′	12′	18′	14′	30′	36′	42′	48′	54′	Mean Differences				
	0°.0	0°.1	0°.2	0°.3	0°.4	0°.5	0°.6	0°.7	0°.8	0°.9	1′	2′	3′	4′	5′
0	.0000	0017	0035	0052	0070	0087	0105	0122	0140	0157	3	6	9	12	15
1	.0175	0192	0209	0227	0244	0262	0279	0297	0314	0332	3	6	9	12	15
2	.0349	0366	0384	0401	0419	0436	0454	0471	0488	0506	3	6	9	12	15
3	.0523	0541	0558	0576	0593	0610	0628	0645	0663	0680	3	6	9	12	15
4	.0698	0715	0732	0750	0767	0785	0802	0819	0837	0854	3	6	9	12	15
5	.0872	0889	0906	0924	0941	0958	0976	0993	1011	1028	3	6	9	12	14
6	.1045	1063	1080	1097	1115	1132	1149	1167	1184	1201	3	6	9	12	14
7	.1219	1236	1253	1271	1288	1305	1323	1340	1357	1374	3	6	9	12	14
8	.1392	1409	1426	1444	1461	1478	1495	1513	1530	1547	3	6	9	12	14
9	.1564	1582	1599	1616	1633	1650	1668	1685	1702	1719	3	6	9	12	14
10	.1736	1654	1771	1788	1805	1822	1840	1857	1874	1891	3	6	9	12	14
11	.1908	1925	1942	1959	1977	1994	2011	2028	2045	2062	3	6	9	11	14
12	.2079	2096	2113	2130	2147	2164	2181	2198	2215	2232	3	6	9	11	14
13	.2250	2267	2284	2300	2317	2334	2351	2368	2385	2402	3	6	8	11	14
14	.2419	2436	2453	2470	2487	2504	2521	2538	2554	2571	3	6	8	11	14
15	.2588	2605	2622	2639	2656	2672	2689	2706	2723	2749	3	6	8	11	14
16	.2756	2773	2790	2807	2823	2840	2857	2874	2890	2907	3	6	8	11	14
17	.2924	2940	2957	2974	2990	3007	3024	3040	3057	3074	3	6	8	11	14
18	.3090	3107	3123	3140	3156	3173	3190	3206	3223	3239	3	6	8	11	14
19	.3256	3272	3289	3305	3322	3338	3355	3371	3387	3404	3	5	8	11	14
20	.3420	3437	3453	3469	3486	3502	3518	3535	3551	4567	3	5	8	11	14
21	.3584	3600	3616	3633	3649	3665	3681	3697	3714	3730	3	5	8	11	14
22	.3746	3762	3778	3795	3811	3827	3843	3859	3875	3891	3	5	8	11	14
23	.3907	3923	3939	3955	3971	3987	4003	4019	4035	4051	3	5	8	11	14
24	.4067	4083	4099	4115	4131	4147	4163	4179	4195	4210	3	5	8	11	13
25	.4226	4242	4258	4274	4289	4305	4321	4337	4352	4368	3	5	8	11	13
26	.4384	4399	4415	4431	4446	4462	4478	4493	4509	4524	3	5	8	10	13
27	.4540	4555	4571	4586	4602	4617	4633	4648	4664	4679	3	5	8	10	13
28	.4695	4710	4726	4741	4756	4772	4787	4802	4818	4833	3	5	8	10	13
29	.4848	4863	4879	4894	4909	4924	4939	4955	4970	4985	3	5	8	10	13
30	.5000	5015	5030	5045	5060	5075	5090	5105	5120	5135	3	5	8	10	13
31	.5150	5165	5180	5195	5210	5225	5240	5255	5270	5284	2	5	7	10	12
32	.5299	5314	5329	5344	5358	5373	5388	5402	5417	5432	2	5	7	10	12
33	.5446	5461	5476	5490	5505	5519	5534	5548	5563	5577	2	5	7	10	12
34	.5592	5606	5621	5635	5650	5664	5678	5693	5707	5721	2	5	7	10	12
35	.5736	5750	5764	5779	5793	5807	5821	5835	5850	5864	2	5	7	10	12
36	.5878	5892	5906	5920	5934	5948	5962	5976	5990	6004	2	5	7	9	12
37	.6018	6032	6046	6060	6074	6088	6101	6115	6129	6143	2	5	7	9	11
38	.6157	6170	6184	6198	6211	6225	6239	6252	6266	6280	2	5	7	9	11
39	.6293	6307	6320	6334	6347	6361	6374	6388	6401	6414	2	4	7	9	11
40	.6428	6441	6455	6468	6481	6494	6508	6521	6534	6547	2	4	7	9	11
41	.6561	6574	6587	6600	6613	6626	6639	6652	6665	6678	2	4	7	9	11
42	.6691	6704	6717	6730	6743	6756	6769	6782	6794	6807	2	4	6	9	11
43	.6820	6833	6845	6858	6871	6884	6896	6909	6921	6934	2	4	6	8	11
44	.6947	6959	6972	6984	6997	7009	7022	7034	7046	7059	2	4	6	8	10
45	.7071	7083	7096	7108	7120	7133	7145	7157	7169	7181	2	4	6	8	10
46	.7193	7206	7218	7230	7242	7254	7266	7278	7290	7302	2	4	6	8	10
47	.7314	7325	7337	7349	7361	7373	7385	7396	7408	7420	2	4	6	8	10
48	.7431	7443	7455	7466	7478	7490	7501	7513	7524	7536	2	4	6	8	10
49	.7547	7558	7570	7581	7593	7694	7615	6727	7638	7649	2	4	6	8	9
50	.7660	7672	7683	7694	7705	7716	7727	7738	7749	7760	2	4	6	7	9
51	.7771	7782	7793	7804	7815	7826	7837	7848	7859	7869	2	4	5	7	9
52	.7880	7891	7902	7912	7923	7934	7944	7955	7965	7976	2	4	5	7	9
53	.7986	7997	8007	8018	8028	8039	8049	8059	8070	8080	2	3	5	7	9
54	.8090	8100	8111	8121	8131	8141	8151	8161	8171	8181	2	3	5	7	8
55	.8192	8202	8211	8221	8231	8241	8251	8261	8271	8281	2	3	5	7	8
56	.8290	8300	8310	8320	8329	8339	8348	8358	8368	8377	2	3	5	6	8
57	.8387	8396	8406	8415	8425	8434	8443	8453	8462	8471	2	3	5	6	8
58	.8480	8490	8499	8508	8517	8526	8536	8545	8554	8563	2	3	5	6	8
59	.8572	8581	8590	8599	8607	8616	8625	8634	8643	8652	1	3	4	6	7
60	.8660	8669	8678	8686	8695	8704	8712	8721	8729	8738	1	3	4	6	7
61	.8746	8755	8763	8771	8780	8788	8796	8805	8813	8821	1	3	4	6	7
62	.8829	8838	8846	8854	8862	8870	8878	8886	8894	8902	1	3	4	5	7
63	.8910	8918	8926	8934	8942	8949	8957	8965	8973	8980	1	3	4	5	6
64	.8988	8996	9003	9011	9018	9026	9033	9041	9048	9056	1	3	4	5	6
65	.9063	9070	9078	9085	9092	9100	9107	9114	9121	9128	1	2	4	5	6
66	.9135	9143	9150	9157	9164	9171	9178	9184	9191	9198	1	2	3	5	6
67	.9205	9212	9219	9225	9232	9239	9245	9252	9259	9265	1	2	3	4	6
68	.9272	9278	9285	9291	9298	9304	9311	9317	9323	9330	1	2	3	4	5
69	.9336	9342	9348	9354	9361	9367	9373	9379	9385	9391	1	2	3	4	5
70	.9397	9403	9409	9415	9421	9426	9432	9438	9444	9449	1	2	3	4	5
71	.9455	9461	9466	9472	9478	9483	9489	9494	9500	9505	1	2	3	4	5
72	.9511	9516	9521	9527	9532	9537	9542	9548	9553	9558	1	2	3	4	5
73	.9563	9568	9573	9578	9583	9588	9593	9558	9603	9608	1	2	3	3	4
74	.9613	9617	9622	9627	9632	9636	9641	9646	9650	9655	1	2	2	3	4
75	.9659	9664	9668	9673	9677	9681	9686	9690	9694	9699	1	1	2	3	4
76	.9703	9707	9711	9715	9720	9724	9728	9732	9736	9740	1	1	2	3	3
77	.9744	9748	9751	9755	9759	9763	9768	9770	9774	9778	1	1	2	2	3
78	.9781	9785	9789	9792	9696	9799	9803	9806	9810	9813	1	1	2	2	3
79	.9816	9820	9823	9826	9829	9833	9836	9839	9842	9845	1	1	2	2	3
80	.9848	9851	9854	9857	9860	9863	9866	9869	9871	9874	0	1	1	2	2
81	.9877	9880	9882	9885	9888	9890	9893	9895	9898	9900	0	1	1	2	2
82	.9903	9905	9907	9910	9912	9914	9917	9919	9921	9923	0	1	1	2	2
83	.9925	9928	9930	9932	9934	9936	9938	9940	9942	9943	0	1	1	1	2
84	.9945	9947	9949	9951	9952	9954	9956	9957	9959	9960	0	1	1	1	2
85	.9962	9963	9965	9966	9968	9969	9971	9972	9973	9974	0	0	1	1	1
86	.9976	9977	9978	9979	9980	9981	9982	9983	9984	9985	0	0	1	1	1
87	.9986	9987	9988	9989	9990	9990	9991	9992	9993	9993	0	0	0	1	1
88	.9994	9995	9995	9996	9996	9997	9997	9997	9998	9998	0	0	0	0	0
89	.9998	9999	9999	9999	9999	1.000	1.000	1.000	1.000	1.000	0	0	0	0	0
90	1.000														

NATURAL COSINES

Degrees	0′	6′	12′	18′	24′	30′	36′	42′	48′	54′	Mean Differences				
	0°.0	0°.1	0°.2	0°.3	0°.4	0°.5	0°.6	0°.7	0°.8	0°.9	1′	2′	3′	4′	5′
0	1.000	1.000	1.000	1.000	1.000	1.000	.9999	.9999	.9999	.9999	0	0	0	0	0
1	.9998	9998	9998	9997	9997	9997	9996	9996	9995	9995	0	0	0	0	0
2	.9994	9993	9993	9992	9991	9990	9990	9989	9988	9987	0	0	0	1	1
3	.9986	9985	9984	9983	9982	9981	9980	9979	9978	9977	0	0	1	1	1
4	.9976	9974	9973	9972	9971	9969	9968	9966	9965	9963	0	0	1	1	1
5	.9962	9960	9959	9957	9956	9954	9952	9951	9949	9947	0	1	1	1	2
6	.9945	9943	9942	9940	9938	9936	9934	9932	9930	9928	0	1	1	1	2
7	.9925	9923	9921	9919	9917	9914	9912	9910	9907	9905	0	1	1	2	2
8	.9903	9900	9898	9895	9893	9890	9888	9885	9882	9880	0	1	1	2	2
9	.9877	9874	9871	9869	9866	9863	9860	9857	9854	9851	0	1	1	2	2
10	.9848	9845	9842	9839	9836	9833	9829	9826	9823	9820	1	1	2	2	3
11	.9816	9813	9810	9806	9803	9799	9796	9792	9789	9785	1	1	2	2	3
12	.9781	9778	9774	9770	9767	9763	9759	9755	9751	9748	1	1	2	3	3
13	.9744	9740	9736	9732	9728	9724	9720	9715	9711	9707	1	1	2	3	3
14	.9703	9699	9694	9690	9686	9681	9677	9613	9668	9664	1	1	2	3	3
15	.9659	9655	9650	9646	9641	9636	9632	9627	9622	9617	1	2	2	3	4
16	.9613	9608	9603	9598	9593	9588	9583	9578	9573	9568	1	2	2	3	4
17	.9563	9558	9553	9548	9542	9537	9532	9527	9521	9516	1	2	3	3	4
18	.9511	9505	9500	9494	9489	9483	9478	9472	9466	9461	1	2	3	4	5
19	.9455	9449	9444	9438	9432	9426	9421	9415	9409	9403	1	2	3	4	5
20	.9397	9391	9385	9379	9373	9367	9361	9354	9348	9342	1	2	3	4	5
21	.9336	9330	9323	9317	9311	9304	9298	9291	9285	9278	1	2	3	4	5
22	.9272	9265	9259	9252	9245	9239	9232	9225	9219	9212	1	2	3	4	5
23	.9205	9198	9191	9184	9178	9171	9164	9197	9150	9143	1	2	3	4	6
24	.9135	9128	9121	9114	9107	9100	9092	9085	9078	9070	1	2	4	5	6
25	.9063	9056	9048	9041	9033	9026	9018	9011	9003	8996	1	3	4	5	6
26	.8988	8980	8973	8965	8957	8949	8942	8934	8926	8918	1	3	4	5	6
27	.8910	8902	8894	8886	8878	8870	8862	8854	8846	8838	1	3	4	5	7
28	.8829	8821	8813	8805	8796	8788	8780	8771	8763	8755	1	3	4	6	7
29	.8746	8738	8729	8721	8712	8704	8695	8695	8678	8669	1	3	4	6	7
30	.8660	8652	8643	8634	8625	8616	8607	8599	8590	8581	1	3	4	6	7
31	.8572	8563	8554	8545	8536	8526	8517	8508	8499	8490	2	3	5	6	8
32	.8480	8471	8462	8453	8443	8434	8425	8415	8406	8396	2	3	5	6	8
33	.8387	8377	8368	8358	8348	8339	8329	8320	8310	8300	2	3	5	6	8
34	.8290	8281	8271	8261	8251	8241	8231	8221	8211	8202	2	3	5	7	8
35	.8192	8181	8171	8161	8151	8141	8131	8121	8111	8100	2	3	5	7	8
36	.8090	8080	8070	8059	8049	8039	8028	8018	8007	7997	2	3	5	7	9
37	.7986	7976	7965	7955	7944	7934	7923	7912	7902	7891	2	4	5	7	9
38	.7880	7859	7869	7848	7837	7826	7815	7804	7793	7782	2	4	5	7	9
39	.7771	7760	7749	7738	7727	7716	7705	7694	7683	7672	2	4	5	7	9
40	.7660	7649	7638	7627	7615	7604	7593	7581	7570	7559	2	4	6	7	9
41	.7547	7536	7524	7513	7501	7490	7478	7466	7455	7443	2	4	6	8	10
42	.7431	7420	7408	7396	7385	7373	7361	7339	7337	7325	2	4	6	8	10
43	.7314	7302	7290	7278	7366	7254	7242	7230	7218	7206	2	4	6	8	10
44	.7193	7181	7169	7157	7145	7133	7120	7108	7096	7083	2	4	6	8	10
45	.7071	7059	7046	7034	7022	7009	6997	6984	6972	6959	2	4	6	8	10
46	.6947	6934	6921	6909	6896	6884	6871	6858	6845	6833	2	4	6	8	10
47	.6820	6807	6794	6782	6769	6756	6743	6730	6717	6704	2	4	6	8	11
48	.6691	6678	6665	6652	6639	6626	6613	6600	6587	6574	2	4	7	9	11
49	.6561	6547	6534	6521	6508	6494	6481	6468	6455	6441	2	4	7	9	11
50	.6428	6414	6401	6388	6374	6361	6347	6334	6320	6307	2	4	7	9	11
51	.6293	6280	6266	6252	6239	6225	6211	6198	6184	6170	2	5	7	9	11
52	.6157	6143	6129	6115	6101	6088	6074	6060	6046	6032	2	5	7	9	12
53	.6018	6004	5990	5976	5962	5948	5934	5920	5906	5892	2	5	7	9	12
54	.5878	5864	5850	5835	5821	5807	5793	5779	5764	5750	2	5	7	9	12
55	.5737	5721	5707	5693	5678	5664	5650	5635	5621	5606	2	5	7	10	12
56	.5592	5577	5563	5548	5534	5519	5505	5490	5476	5461	2	5	7	10	12
57	.5446	5432	5417	5402	5388	5373	5358	5344	5329	5314	2	5	7	10	12
58	.5299	5284	5270	5255	5240	5225	5210	5195	5180	5165	2	5	7	10	12
59	.5150	5135	5120	5105	5090	5075	5060	5045	5030	5015	3	5	8	10	13
60	.5000	4985	4970	4955	4939	4924	4909	4894	4879	4863	3	5	8	10	13
61	.4848	4833	4818	4802	4787	4772	4756	4741	4726	4710	3	5	8	10	13
62	.4695	4679	4664	4648	4633	4617	4602	4586	4571	4555	3	5	8	10	13
63	.4540	4524	4509	4493	4478	4462	4446	4431	4415	4399	3	5	8	10	13
64	.4384	4368	4352	4337	4321	4305	4289	4274	4258	4242	3	5	8	10	13
65	.4226	4210	4195	4179	4163	4147	4131	4115	4099	4083	3	5	8	11	13
66	.4067	4051	4035	4019	4003	3987	3971	3955	3939	3923	3	5	8	11	14
67	.3907	3891	3875	3859	3843	3827	3811	3795	3778	3762	3	5	8	11	14
68	.3746	3730	3714	3697	3681	3665	3649	3633	3616	3600	3	5	8	11	14
69	.3584	3567	3551	3535	3518	3502	3486	3469	3453	3437	3	5	8	11	14
70	.3420	3404	3387	3371	3355	3338	3322	3305	3289	3272	3	5	8	11	14
71	.3256	3239	3223	3206	3190	3173	3156	3140	3123	3107	3	6	8	11	14
72	.3090	3074	3057	3040	3024	3007	2990	2974	2957	2940	3	6	8	11	14
73	.2924	2907	2890	2874	2857	2840	2823	2807	2870	2773	3	6	8	11	14
74	.2756	2740	2723	2706	2689	2672	2656	2639	2622	2605	3	6	8	11	14
75	.2588	2571	2554	2538	2521	2504	2487	2470	2453	2436	3	6	8	11	14
76	.2419	2402	2385	2368	2351	2334	2317	2300	2284	2267	3	6	8	11	14
77	.2250	2233	2215	2198	2181	2164	2147	2130	2113	2096	3	6	8	11	14
78	.2079	2062	2045	2028	2011	1994	1977	1959	1942	1925	3	6	9	11	14
79	.1908	1891	1874	1857	1840	1822	1805	1788	1771	1754	3	6	9	11	14
80	.1736	1719	1702	1685	1668	1650	1633	1616	1599	1582	3	6	9	12	14
81	.1564	1547	1530	1513	1495	1478	1461	1444	1426	1409	3	6	9	12	14
82	.1392	1374	1357	1340	1323	1305	1288	1271	1253	1236	3	6	9	12	14
83	.1219	1201	1184	1167	1149	1132	1115	1097	1080	1063	3	6	9	12	14
84	.1045	1028	1011	0993	0976	0958	0941	0924	0906	0889	3	6	9	12	14
85	.0872	0854	0837	0819	0802	0785	0767	0750	0732	0715	3	6	9	12	14
86	.0698	0680	0663	0645	0623	0610	0593	0576	0558	0541	3	6	9	12	15
87	.0523	0506	0488	0471	0454	0436	0419	0401	0384	0366	3	6	9	12	15
88	.0349	0332	0314	0297	0279	0262	0244	0227	0209	0192	3	6	9	12	15
89	.0175	0157	0140	0122	0105	0087	0070	0052	0035	0017	3	6	9	12	15
90	.0000														